SMITHSONIAN INSTITUTION
BUREAU OF AMERICAN ETHNOLOGY
BULLETIN 30

HANDBOOK

OF

AMERICAN INDIANS

NORTH OF MEXICO

EDITED BY

FREDERICK WEBB HODGE

VOLUME II H to M

WASHINGTON
GOVERNMENT PRINTING OFFICE
(Fourth impression, September, 1912)

Handbook of North American Indian
North of Mexico

Volume 1 ISBN 9781582187396
Volume 2 ISBN 9781582187402
Volume 3 ISBN 9781582187440
Volume 4 ISBN 9781582187426

Volumes 1-4
ISBN 9781582187433

Library of Congress Control Number: 2018953449

Republished 2018 by
Digital Scanning Inc.
Scituate Ma 02066

VOLUME II　H to M

ANCIENT CLIFF-DWELLING, MESA VERDE, COLORADO

Haaialikyauae (*Haai'alik·auaē,* 'the shamans'). A gens of the Hahuamis, a Kwakiutl tribe.—Boas in Rep. Nat. Mus., 331, 1895.

Haailakyemae ('the shamans'). A gens of the Kwakiutl proper, found among the Komoyue and Matilpe subdivisions.
Haai'lak·Emaē.—Boas in Rep. Nat. Mus., 330, 1895. Ḳaaílakyemaē—Boas, 6th Rep. N. W. Tribes Can., 54, 1890. **Haialikyā'ūaē.**—Boas in Petermanns Mitt., pt. 5, 131, 1887. **Lâqsē.**—Boas in 6th Rep. N. W. Tribes Can., 54, 1890. **Lâ'xsē.**—Boas in Rep. Nat. Mus., 330, 1895 (sig. 'going through').

Haanatlenok ('the archers'). A gens of the Komoyue, a subdivision of the Kwakiutl.
Hā'anaLēnôx.—Boas in Nat. Mus. Rep., 330, 1895. Hā'anatlēnoq.—Boas, 6th Rep. N. W. Tribes Can., 54, 1890. **Hā'na***tl***inō.**—Boas in Petermanns Mitt., pt. 5, 131, 1887.

Haanka Ullah (*Hankha aiola,* 'wild goose there cries'). A former Choctaw town situated on a long flat-topped ridge between Petickfa cr. and Blackwater cr., Kemper co., Miss. It received its name from a pond of water about 7 acres in extent which was much frequented by wild fowl.—Romans, Florida, 310, 1775; Halbert in Miss. Hist. Soc. Publ., vi, 420, 1902.

Haaskouan. See *Grangula.*

Haatze (Queres: 'earth'). A prehistoric pueblo of the Cochiti near the foot of the Sierra San Miguel, above Cochiti pueblo, N. Mex. It is claimed to have been occupied after the abandonment of the Potrero de las Vacas.—Bandelier in Arch. Inst. Papers, iv, 157, 1892.
Haatse.—Hewett in Am. Anthrop., vi, 638, 1904. Ha-a-tze.—Bandelier in Arch. Inst. Papers, iv, 157, 1892.—Ibid., pl. 1, fig. 13. Rät-je Kama Tse-shu-ma.—Lummis in Scribner's Mag., 98, 1893. Rä-tya.—Lummis in Scribner's Mag., 98, 1893. Rä-tye Ka-ma Tze-shuma.—Bandelier, op. cit., 159 (='the old houses at the rabbit,' in allusion to the rabbit-like outline of the neighboring crest). San Miguel.—Lummis, op. cit.

Habachaca. A clan of the Chulufichi phratry of the ancient Timucua of Florida.—Pareja (*ca.* 1614) quoted by Gatschet in Am. Philos. Soc. Proc., xvii, 492, 1878.

Habamouk. See *Hobomok, Hobomoko.*

Habitations. The habitations of the Indians of northern America may be classed as community houses (using the term "community" in the sense of comprising more than one family) and single, or family, dwellings. "The house architecture of the northern tribes is of little importance, in itself considered; but as an outcome of their social condition and for comparison with that of the southern village Indians, is highly important" (Mor-

DWELLINGS, PUEBLO OF HANO, ARIZONA

gan). The typical community houses, as those of the Iroquois tribes, were 50 to 100 ft long by 16 to 18 ft wide, with frame of poles and with sides and triangular roof covered with bark, usually of the elm; the interior was divided into compartments and a smoke hole was left in the roof. A Mahican house, similar in form, 14 by 60 ft, had the sides and roof made of rushes and chestnut bark, with an opening along the top of the roof from end to end. The Mandan circular community house was usually about 40 ft in diameter; it was supported by two series of posts and cross-beams, and the wide roof and sloping sides were covered with willow or brush matting and earth. The fireplace was in the center. Morgan thinks that the oblong, round-roof houses of the Virginia and North Carolina tribes, seen and described by Capt. John Smith and drawn by John White, were of the community order. That some of them housed a number of families is distinctly stated. Morgan includes also in the community class the circular, dome-shaped earth lodges of Sacramento valley and the L-form, tent-shaped, thatched lodges of the higher areas of California; but the leading examples of community houses are the large, sometimes massive, many-celled clusters of stone or adobe in New Mexico and Arizona known as *pueblos* (q. v.). These dwellings vary in form, some of those built in prehistoric times being semicircular, others oblong, around or inclosing a court or plaza. These buildings were constructed usually in terrace form, the lower having a one-story tier of apartments, the next two stories, and so on to the uppermost tier, which sometimes constituted a seventh story. The masonry consisted usually of small, flat stones laid in adobe mortar and chinked with spalls; but sometimes large balls of adobe were used as building stones, or a double row of wattling was erected and filled in with grout, solidly tamped. By the latter method, known as *pisé* construction, walls 5 to 7 ft thick were sometimes built (see *Adobe, Casa Grande*). The outer walls of the lowest story were pierced only by small openings, access to the interior being gained by means of ladders, which could be drawn up, if necessary, and of a hatchway in the roof. It is possible that some of the elaborate structures of Mexico were developed from such hive-like buildings as those of the typical pueblos, the cells increasing in size toward the S., as suggested by Bandelier. Chimneys appear to have been unknown in North America until after contact of the natives with Europeans, the hatchway in the roof serving the double purpose of entrance and flue.

Other forms, some community and others not, are the following: Among the Eskimo, the *karmak*, or winter residence, for which a pit of the required diameter is dug 5 or 6 ft deep, with a frame of wood or whalebone constructed within 2 or 3 ft above the surface of the ground and covered with a dome-shaped roof of poles or whale ribs, turfed and earthed over.

Entrance is gained by an underground passageway. The temporary hunting lodge of the Labrador Eskimo was sometimes constructed entirely of the ribs and vertebræ of the whale. Another form of Eskimo dwelling is the hemispherical snow house, or *iglu*, built of blocks of snow laid in spiral courses. The Kaniagmiut build large permanent houses, called *barabara* by the Russians, which accommodate 3 or 4 families;

ESKIMO HOUSE, EAST CAPE, SIBERIA. (NELSON)

lies; these are constructed by digging a square pit 2 ft deep, the sides of which are lined with planks that are carried to the required height above the surface and roofed with boards, poles, or whale ribs, thickly covered with grass; in the roof is a smoke hole, and on the eastern side a door. The Tlingit, Haida, and some other tribes build substantial rectangular houses with sides and ends formed of planks and with the fronts elaborately carved and painted with symbolic figures. Directly in front of the house a totem pole is placed, and near by a memorial pole is erected.

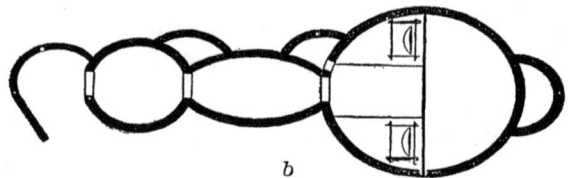

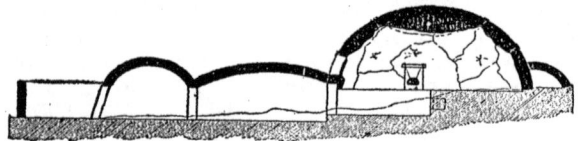

SNOW HOUSE OF CENTRAL ESKIMO. *a*, FRONT VIEW; *b*, GROUND PLAN; *c*, SECTION. (BOAS)

These houses are sometimes 40 by 100 ft in the Nootka and Salish region, and are occupied by a number of families. Formerly some of the Haida houses are said to have been built on platforms supported by posts; some of these seen by such early navigators as Vancouver were 25 or 30 ft above ground, access being had by notched logs serving as ladders. Among the N. W. inland tribes, as the Nez Percés, the dwelling was a frame of poles covered with rush matting or with buffalo or elk skins. The houses of the California tribes, some of which are above noted, were rectangular or circular; of the latter, some were conical, others dome-shaped. There was

HAIDA HOUSE WITH TOTEM POLE.   (NIBLACK)

also formerly in use in various parts of California, and to some extent on the interior plateaus, a semisubterranean earth-covered lodge known among the Maidu as *kŭm*.

The most primitive abodes were those of the Paiute and the Cocopa, consisting simply of brush shelters for summer,

HOUSE OF NORTHERN CALIFORNIA INDIANS; KLAMATH RIVER.
(POWERS)

and for winter of a framework of poles bent together at the top and covered with brush, bark, and earth. Somewhat similar structures are erected by the Pueblos as farm shelters, and more elaborate houses of the same general type are built by the Apache of Arizona. As

APACHE HOUSE OF BRUSH AND CANVAS

indicated by archeological researches, the circular wigwam, with sides of bark or mats, built over a shallow excavation in the soil, and with earth thrown against the base, appears to have been the usual form of dwelling in the Ohio valley and the immediate valley of the Mississippi in pre-

historic and early historic times. Another kind of dwelling, in use in Arkansas before the discovery, was a rectangular structure with two rooms in front and one in the rear; the walls were of upright posts thickly plastered with clay on a sort of wattle.

HOUSE CONSTRUCTION, MOUND BUILDERS.   PLASTERED
WATTLE WORK.   (THOMAS)

With the exception of the Pueblo structures, buildings of stone or adobe were unknown until recent times.

The dwellings of some of the tribes of the plains, as the Sioux, Arapaho, Comanche, and Kiowa, were generally portable skin tents or tipis, but those of the Omaha,

VILLAGE OF TIPIS; PLAINS INDIANS

Osage, and some others were more substantial (see *Earth lodge, Grass lodge*). The dwellings of the Omaha, according to Miss Fletcher, "are built by setting carefully selected and prepared posts together in a circle, and binding them firmly with willows, then backing them with dried

NAVAHO HOGAN (EARTH LODGE)

grass, and covering the entire structure with closely packed sods. The roof is made in the same manner, having an additional support of an inner circle of posts, with crotchets to hold the cross logs which act as beams to the dome-shaped roof. A circular opening in the center serves as a chimney and also to give light to the interior of the dwelling; a sort of

PALMETTO HOUSE; LOUISIANA INDIANS

sail is rigged and fastened outside of this opening to guide the smoke and prevent it from annoying the occupants of the lodge. The entrance passage-way, which usu-ally faces east-ward, is from 6 to 10 ft long and is built in the same manner as the lodge." An important type is the Wichita grass hut, circu-lar, dome-shaped with conical top. The frame is built somewhat

CHIPPEWA BARK HOUSE; MINNESOTA. (GILFILLAN)

in panels formed by ribs and crossbars; these are covered with grass tied on shin-gle fashion. These grass lodges vary in di-ameter from 40 to 50 ft. The early Florida houses, according to Le Moyne's illustra-tions published by De Bry, were either cir-cular with dome-like roof, or oblong with rounded roof like those of Secotan in North Carolina, as shown in John White's fig-ures. The frame was of poles; the sides and roof were covered with bark, or the latter was sometimes thatched. The Chip-pewa usually constructed a conical or hem-ispherical framework of poles, covered with bark. Formerly caves and rock shelters were used in some sections as abodes, and in the Pueblo region houses were formerly constructed in natural recesses or shelters in the cliffs, whence the designation cliff-dwellings. Similar habitations are still in use to some extent by the Tarahumare of Chihuahua, Mexico. Cavate houses with several rooms were also hewn in the sides of soft volcanic cliffs; so numerous are these in Verde valley, Ari-zona, and the Jemez plateau, New Mex-ico, that for miles the cliff face is honey-combed with them. As a rule the women were the builders of the houses where wood was the structural material, but the men assisted with the heavier work. In the Southern states it was a common custom to erect mounds as foundations for

council houses, for the chief's dwelling, or for structures designed for other official uses.

The erection of houses, especially those of a permanent character, was usually attended with great ceremony, particu-larly when the time for dedication came. The construction of the Navaho hogán, for example, was done in accordance with fixed rules, as was the cutting and sewing of the tipi among the Plains tribes, while the new houses erected during the year were usually dedicated with ceremony and feasting. Although the better types of houses were symmetrical and well pro-portioned, their builders had not learned the use of the square or the plumb-line; the unit of measure was also appar-ently unknown, and even in the best types of ancient Pueblo masonry the joints of the stonework were not "broken."

The Indian names for some of their struc-tures, as tipi, wigwam, wicki-up, hogan, and iglu, have come into use to a greater or less extent by English-speak-ing people. See Adobe, Archeology, Archi-tecture, Cliff-dwellings, Earth lodge, Forti-fication and Defense, Grass lodge, Hogan, Kiva, Mounds, Pueblos, Tipi.

SECOTAN, A TOWN OF THE CAROLINA COAST. (HARIOT)

Consult Boas in Proc. Nat. Mus., XI, 1889; Hrdlicka in Am. Anthrop., V, 385, 1903; VI, 51, 1904; VII, 480, 1905; VIII, 39, 1906; De Bry, Brevis Narratio, 1591; Hariot, Virginia, repr. 1874. Dixon in Bull. Am. Mus. Nat. Hist., XVII, pt. 3, 1905; Catlin, Manners and Customs N. A. Inds., 1841; Goddard, Life and Culture of the Hupa, 1903; Bandelier in various Papers of the Archæol. Inst. America; Morgan, Houses and House-life of the American Aborigines, Cont. N. A. Ethnol., IV, 1881; Willoughby in Am. Anthrop., VIII, No. 1, 1906; Holm, Descr. New Sweden, 1834; Schoolcraft, Ind. Tribes, I–VI, 1851–57; Dellenbaugh, North Americans of Yesterday, 1901; Matthews, Navaho Legends, 1897; also, the various reports of the B. A. E.: Boas, Murdoch, Nelson, and Turner for the Eskimo; Dorsey for the Omaha; C. and V. Mindeleff for the Navaho and Pueblos; Fewkes for the Pueblos; Hoffman for the Menominee and Chippewa, etc.   (C. T.)

Hacanac. Mentioned by the Gentleman of Elvas in 1557 (Hakluyt Soc. Publ., IX, 132, 1851) as a province of which Moscoso was informed in 1542; apparently on the N. E. Texan border. Unidentified.

Hachaath. An extinct Nootka tribe which formerly lived on or N. of Barclay sd., Vancouver id.

A-y-charts.—Jewitt, Narr., 120, 1849. Aytch-arts.—Ibid., 37. Hacā′ath.—Boas, 6th Rep. N. W. Tribes Can., 32, 1890. Hatcā′ath.—Ibid., 31.

Hachepiriinu ('young dogs'). A former Arikara band under chief Chinanitu, The Brother.

Ha-ĉe′-pi-ri-i-nu′.—Hayden, Ethnog. and Philol. Mo. Val., 357, 1862. Young Dogs.—Culbertson in Smithson. Rep. 1850, 143, 1851.

Hachimuk. A former Aleut village on Agattu id., Alaska, one of the Near id. group of the Aleutians, now uninhabited.

Hachos (prob. Span.: a fagot or bundle of straw or grass covered with resin). Mentioned as a wild tribe of New Mexico in the 18th century.—Villa-Señor, Theatro Am., pt. 2, 412, 1748.

Hackensack (*Ackkinkas-hacky*, 'the stream that unites with another in low level ground.'—Heckewelder). A former division of the Unami Delawares, occupying the territory designated by the Indians Ackkinkashacky, embracing the valleys of Hackensack and Passaic rs. in N. New Jersey. Their principal village was Gamoenapa, usually known as Communipaw. They took a prominent part in the events of 1643–44, but subsequently appear as mediators through their chief Oritany (Oratamy, Oratam, etc.), who enjoyed, to a ripe old age, the confidence of his people and the surrounding chieftaincies, as well as that of the whites. The lands of the tribe embraced Jersey City, Hoboken, a part of Staten island, Weehawken, Newark, Passaic, etc. Their

number was estimated at 1,000 in 1643, of which 300 were warriors, probably an exaggeration (Ruttenber).   (J. M.   C. T.)

Achkingkesacky.—Doc. of 1663 in N. Y. Doc. Col. Hist., XIII, 276, 1881. Achkinkehacky.—Treaty of 1645, ibid., 18. Achkinkes hacky.—Doc. of 1643, ibid., 14. Ackinckesaky.—Doc. of 1663, ibid., 280. Hacansacky.—Doc. of 1662, ibid., XIV, 512, 1883. Haccinsack.—Doc. ca. 1643, ibid., I, 198, 1856. Hachinghsack.—Deed of 1657, ibid., XIV, 394, 1883. Hachkinkeshaky.—Doc. of 1655, ibid., XIII, 55, 1881. Hackensack.—Treaty of 1673, ibid., 476. Hackinckesaky.—Stuyvesant (1663), ibid., 323. Hackinghesaky.—Doc. of 1662, ibid., 218. Hackinghsack.—Deed of 1657, ibid., XIV, 393, 1883. Hackinghsackin.—Doc. of 1660, ibid., 182. Hackinghsakij.—Doc. of 1663, ibid., XIII, 305, 1881. Hackingkesacky.—Doc. of 1663, ibid., 294. Hackingkescaky.—Doc. of 1663, ibid., 289. Hackingsack.—Report of 1644, ibid., I, 150, 1856. Hackinkasacky.—Treaty of 1660, ibid., XIII, 148, 1881. Hackinkesackinghs.—Doc. of 1660, ibid., 183. Hackinkesacky.—Doc. of 1663, ibid., 294. Hackinkesaky.—Doc. ca. 1643, ibid., I, 199, 1856. Hackinsagh.—Doc. of 1673, ibid., II, 606, 1858. Hackquinsack.—Doc. of 1650, ibid., I, 411, 1856. Hacquinsack.—Ibid.

Haddo. See *Huddoh.*—

Hadley Indians. A small body or band, possibly Nipmuc, which, at the time of King Philip's war in 1675, occupied a small fort about a mile above Hatfield, on the W. side of Connecticut r., in Hampshire co., Mass. They abandoned their village to join Philip's forces and thereafter ceased to be known under the name above given.   (J. M.)

Hadsapoke's Band (from the name of its chief, "Horse-stopper"). A Paviotso band formerly at Gold canyon, Carson r., W. Nev., said to number 110 in 1859.

Had-sa-poke's band.—Dodge in Ind. Aff. Rep. 1859, 373, 1860.

Hadtuitazhi ('touches no green corn husks'). A former subgens of the Hanga gens of the Omaha.

Ha-ʒu-it′aji.—Dorsey in 15th Rep. B. A. E., 227, 1897.

Haena. A former Haida town on the E. end of Maude id., Skidegate inlet, Queen Charlotte ids., Brit. Col. It is said to have been occupied in very early times by the Djahui-skwahladagai, and in recent years it was reoccupied by the west coast Haida, who desired to be nearer the traders, but after a comparatively short occupancy the people moved to Skidegate about 1880. There are said to have been 13 houses, which would indicate a population of about 150.   (J. R. S.)

Khīna Hāadē.—Harrison in Proc. and Trans. Roy. Soc. Can., sec. II, 125, 1895 (Khīna = Haena). New Gold Harbour Village.—Dawson, Queen Charlotte Ids., 168B, 1880. Xa′ina.—Swanton, Cont. Haida, 279, 1905.

Haeser. A former tribe near the lower Rio Grande, living with the Gueiquesales, Manos Prietas, Bocores, Pinanaca, Escaba, Cacastes, Cocobipta, Cocomaque, Codame, Contotores, Colorados, Babiamares, and Taimamares. Probably Coahuiltecan.

Siaexer.—Fernando del Bosque (1675) in Nat. Geog. Mag., XIV, 340, 1903. Xaeser.—Ibid., 344.

Hagi (*Xā′gî*, said to mean 'striped'). A Haida town on or near the largest of the

Bolkus ids., Queen Charlotte ids., Brit. Col. It derived its name from a reef which, in local mythology, was the first land to appear above the waters of the flood, bearing the ancestress of all the Raven people upon it. The town was occupied by a Ninstints division of the same name.—Swanton, Cont. Haida, 277, 1905.

Hagi-lanas (*Xági-lä′nas*, 'people of striped (?) town'). A subdivision of the Haida, belonging to the Raven clan and occupying the town of Hagi, on Hagi id., Queen Charlotte ids., Brit. Col. From the circumstance attending their supposed origin (see *Hagi*) the family claimed to be the oldest on the islands, but it is now represented by only two or three individuals. There were two subdivisions, the Huldanggats and the Keda-lanas.—Swanton, Cont. Haida, 268, 1905.

Haglli. A Yuman tribe or division which in 1604–05 occupied 5 rancherias on the lower Rio Colorado, between the Cohuanas (Yuma) and the Halliguamayas, of which latter (identifiable with the Quigyuma) they apparently formed a part.

Haclli.—Bandelier in Arch. Inst. Papers, III, 110, 1890. Haglli.—Zarate-Salmeron (*ca.* 1629), Rel., in Land of Sunshine, 106, Jan. 1900. Tlaglii.—Bancroft, Ariz. and N. Mex., 156, 1889.

Hagonchenda. A former Iroquois town, probably belonging to the people of Tequenondahi, and situated in 1535 not far from the junction of Jacques Cartier r. with the St Lawrence. The chief of this town gave a small girl to Cartier on his second voyage, and placed Cartier on his guard against the machinations of the chiefs of the peoples dwelling around Stadacona and elsewhere on the St Lawrence. For this reason Cartier, in his third voyage, in 1540, gave this chief 2 small boys to learn the language, and also a "cloake of Paris red, which cloake was set with yealow and white buttons of Tinne, and small belles." See Cartier, Bref Récit, 67, 1863.   (J. N. B. H.)

Hagwilget (Tsimshian: 'well dressed'). The chief village of the Hwotsotenne, on Bulkley r., 3 m. s. E. of Hazelton, Brit. Col.; pop. 500 in 1870, 161 in 1904.

Achwlget.—Horetzky, Canada on Pac., 103, 1874. Ahwilgate.—Dawson in Rep. Geol. Surv. Can., 1879–80, 20B, 1881. Hagulget.—Scott in Ind. Aff. Rep. 1869, 563, 1870. Hagwilget.—Can. Ind. Aff. 1904, pt. 2, 73, 1905. Ha-gwíl′-kĕt.—Henshaw, MS. note, B. A. E., 1887. Tschah.—Morice in Trans. Roy. Soc. Can., map, 1892. Tsitsk.—Can. Ind. Aff., 212, 1902 (Kitksun form).

Hahamatses ('old mats'). A subdivision or sept of the Lekwiltok, a Kwakiutl tribe. They received their name because they were slaves of the Wiwekae sept. Recently they have taken the name of Walitsum, 'the great ones.' Pop. 53 in 1901, 43 in 1904.

Chāchamātses.—Boas in Petermanns Mitt., pt. 5, 131, 1887. H′ah′amatses.—Boas in Bull. Am. Geog. Soc., 230, 1887. Kahk-ah-mah-tsis.—Can. Ind. Aff., 119, 1880. Kakamatsis.—Brit. Col. map, 1872. Qā′-

qamātses.—Boas, 6th Rep. N. W. Tribes Can., 55, 1890. Wā′-lit-sum.—Dawson in Trans. Roy. Soc. Can., V, sec. II, 65, 1887. Wau-lit-sah-mosk.—Sproat in Can. Ind. Aff., 149, 1879. Waw-lit-sum.—Can. Ind. Aff., 189, 1884. Xā′xamatsEs.—Boas in Rep. Nat. Mus., 331, 1895.

Hahamogna. A former Gabrieleño rancheria in Los Angeles co., Cal., at a locality later called Rancho Verdugos.—Ried (1852) quoted by Taylor in Cal. Farmer, June 8, 1860.

Hahas. A former Chumashan village at the principal port of Santa Cruz id., Cal., probably at Prisoners' harbor.—Henshaw, Buenaventura MS. vocab., B. A. E., 1884.

Hahatonwanna ('small village at the falls'). A former Sioux village or division at the Falls of St Anthony, Minn.; mentioned doubtfully by Dorsey (1880). Given by Lewis and Clark in 1804 as a subdivision of the Yankton of the north, of which Mahpeondotak was chief. The name may refer to an incorporated Chippewa band.

Hahatouadeba.—Jefferys, Am. Atlas, map 5, 1776. Hah-har-tones.—Orig. Jour. Lewis and Clark, VI, 99, 1905. Har-har-tones.—Lewis and Clark, Discov., 34, 1806. Horheton.—De l'Isle (1701), map in Neill, Hist. Minn., 164, 1858. Horhetton.—Jefferys, Am. Atlas, map 5, 1776. Morheton.—La Tour, Am. Sept., map, 1779 (misprint).

Hahekolatl (*Hä′hĕqolaL*, descendants of Hakolatl'). A subdivision of the Lalauitlela, a gens of the Tlatlasikoala (q. v.), a Kwakiutl tribe.—Boas in Rep. Nat. Mus., 332, 1895.

Hahuamis. A Kwakiutl tribe living on Wakeman sd., Brit. Col.; pop. 63 in 1901, the last time they were officially reported. They are divided into three gentes: Gyeksem, Gyigyilkam, and Haaialikyauae.—Boas in Rep. Nat. Mus., 331, 1895.

Ah-knaw-ah-mish.—Can. Ind. Aff., 189, 1884. Ah-know-ah-mish.—Ibid., 314, 1892. Ah-wha-mish.—Ibid., 364, 1897. A-kwā′-amish.—Dawson in Trans. Roy. Soc. Can. for 1887, sec. II, 65. A-qua-mish.—Kane, Wand. in N. Am., app., 1859. Chachuā′mis.—Boas in Petermanns Mitt., pt. 5, 130, 1887. Ecquamish.—Brit. Col. map, 1872. H′ah′uámis.—Boas in Bull. Am. Geog. Soc., 228, 1887. Haquā′mis.—Boas, 6th Rep. N. W. Tribes Can., 55, 1890. Haxuā′mîs.—Boas in Rep. Nat. Mus. 331, 1895.

Haida (*Xa′ida*, 'people'). The native and popular name for the Indians of the Queen Charlotte ids., Brit. Col., and the s. end of Prince of Wales id., Alaska, comprising the Skittagetan family (q. v.). By the natives themselves the term may be applied generally to any human being or specifically to one speaking the Haida language. Some authors have improperly restricted the application of the term to the Queen Charlotte islanders, calling the Alaskan Haida, Kaigani (q. v.). Several English variants of this word owe their origin to the fact that a suffix usually accompanies it in the native language, making it Hä′dē in one dialect and Haidaga′i in the other.

On the ground of physical characteristics the Haida, Tlingit, and Tsimshian peoples should be grouped together. Language and social organization indicate still closer affinities between the Haida and Tlingit.

According to their own traditions the oldest Haida towns stood on the E. shore, at Naikun and on the broken coast of

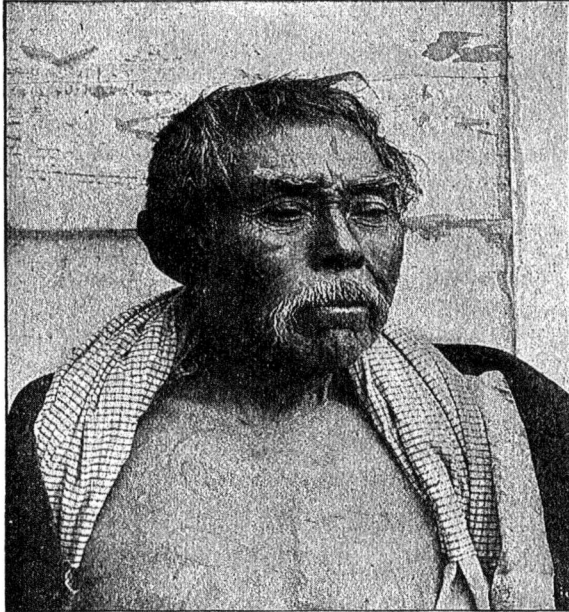

HAIDA MAN.　(AM. MUS. NAT. HIST.)

Moresby id. Later a portion of the people moved to the w. coast, and between 150 and 200 years ago a still larger section, the Kaigani, drove the Tlingit from part of Prince of Wales id. and settled there. Although it is not impossible that the Queen Charlotte ids. were visited by Spaniards during the 17th century, the first certain account of their discovery is that by Ensign Juan Perez, in the corvette *Santiago*, in 1774. He named the N. point of the islands Cabo de Santa Margarita. Bodega and Maurelle visited them the year after. In 1786 La Perouse coasted the shores of the islands, and the following year Capt. Dixon spent more than a month around them, and the islands are named from his vessel, the *Queen Charlotte*. After that time scores of vessels from England and New England resorted to the coast, principally to trade for furs, in which business the earlier voyagers reaped golden harvests. The most important expeditions, as those of which there is some record, were by Capt. Douglas, Capt. Jos. Ingraham of Boston, Capt. Etienne Marchand in the French ship *Solide*, and Capt. Geo. Vancouver (Dawson, Queen Charlotte Ids., 1880).

The advent of whites was, as usual, disastrous to the natives. They were soon stripped of their valuable furs, and, through smallpox and general immorality,

they have been reduced in the last 60 years to one-tenth of their former strength. A station of the Hudson's Bay Company was long established at Masset, but is now no longer remunerative. At Skidegate there are works for the extraction of dogfish oil, which furnish employment to the people during much of the year; but in summer all the Indians from this place and Masset go to the mainland to work in salmon canneries. The Masset people also make many canoes of immense cedars to sell to other coast tribes. The Kaigani still occupy 3 towns, but the population of 2 of them, Kasaan and Klinkwan, is inconsiderable. Neighboring salmon canneries give them work all summer.

Mission stations are maintained by the Methodists at Skidegate, by the Church of England at Masset, and by the Presbyterians at Howkan, Alaska. Nearly all of the people are nominally Christians.

The Haida, Tlingit, and Tsimshian seem to show greater adaptability to civilization and to display less religious conservatism than many of the tribes farther s. They are generally regarded as superior to them by the white settlers, and they certainly showed themselves such in war and in the arts. Of all peoples of the N. W. coast the Haida were the best carvers, painters, and canoe and house builders, and they still earn considerable money by selling carved objects of wood and slate to traders and

HAIDA WOMAN.　(AM. MUS. NAT. HIST.)

tourists. Standing in the tribe depended more on the possession of property than on ability in war, so that considerable interchange of goods took place and the people became sharp traders. The morals of the people were, however, very loose.

Canoes were to the people of this coast what the horse became to the Plains Indians. They were hollowed out of single logs of cedar, and were sometimes very large. Houses were built of huge cedar beams and planks which were worked out with adzes and wedges made anciently of stone, and put together at great feasts called by the whites by the jargon word "potlatch" (q. v.). Each house ordinarily had a single carved pole in the middle of the gable end presented to the beach (see *Architecture*). Often the end posts in front were also carved and the whole house front painted. The dead were placed in mortuary houses, in boxes on carved poles, or sometimes in caves. Shamans were placed after death in small houses built on prominent points along shore. Among the beliefs of the Haida reincarnation held a prominent place.

An estimate of the Haida population made, according to Dawson, by John Work, between 1836 and 1841, gives a total of 8,328, embracing 1,735 Kaigani and 6,593 Queen Charlotte islanders. Dawson estimated the number of people on the Queen Charlotte ids. in 1880 as between 1,700 and 2,000. An estimate made for the Canadian Department of Indian Affairs in 1888 (Ann. Rep., 317) gives 2,500, but the figures were evidently exaggerated, for when a census of Masset, Skidegate, and Gold Harbor was taken the year after (Ann. Rep., 272) it gave only 637. This, however, left out of consideration the people of New Kloo. In 1894 (Ann. Rep., 280), when these were first added to the list, the entire Haida population was found to be 639. The figures for the year following were 593, but from that time showed an increase and stood at 734 in 1902. In 1904, however, they had suffered a sharp decline to 587. Petroff in 1880–81 reported 788 Kaigani, but this figure may be somewhat too high, since Dall about the same time estimated their number at 300. According to the census of 1890 there were 391, and they are now (1905) estimated at 300. The entire Haida population would thus seem to be about 900.

The Alaskan Haida are called Kaigani. By the Queen Charlotte islanders they are designated Kets-hade (*Q!ĕts xā′dĕ*), which probably means 'people of the strait.' The people of Masset inlet and the N. end of Queen Charlotte ids. generally are called by their southern kinsmen Gao-haidagai (*Gao xa′-ida-ga-i*), 'inlet people,' and those living around the southern point of the group are called Gunghet-haidagai (*Gᴀ′ n̄xet-xā′-idᴀga-i*), from the name of one of the most southerly capes in their territory. All of these latter finally settled in the town afterward known to whites as Ninstints, and hence came to be called Ninstints people.

The entire stock is divided into two "sides" or clans—Raven (Hoya) and Eagle (Got)—each of which is subdivided and resubdivided into numerous smaller local groups, as given below. (The braces indicate that the families grouped thereunder were related. Theoretically each clan was descended from one woman.)

RAVEN

Aokeawai.
    a. Hlingwainaas-hadai.
    b. Taolnaas-hadai.
Daiyuahl-lanas (or) Kasta-kegawai.
Djahui-skwahladagai.
Hlgaiu-lanas.
    a. Hlgagilda-kegawai.
Kogangas.
Skwahladas.
    a. Nasto-kegawai.
Hagi-lanas.
    a. Huldanggats.
    b. Keda-lanas.
Hlgahetgu-lanas.
    a. Kilstlaidjat-taking-galung.
    b. Sels.
Stasaos-kegawai.
    a. Gunghet-kegawai.
Kadusgo-kegawai.
Yaku-lanas.
    a. Aoyaku-lnagai.
    b. (Alaskan branch.)
        1. Kaadnaas-hadai.
        2. Yehlnaas-hadai.
        3. Skistlainai-hadai.
        4. Nakeduts-hadai.
Naikun-kegawai.
    a. Huados.
Kuna-lanas.
    a. Hlielungkun-lnagai.
    b. Saguikun-lnagai.
    c. Teeskun-lnagai.
    d. Yagunkun-lnagai.
Stlenga-lanas.
    a. Aostlan-lnagai.
    b. Dostlan-lnagai.
        1. Kaiihl-lanas.
    c. Teesstlan-lnagai.
    d. Yagunstlan-lnagai.
Kagials-kegawai.
    a. Kils-haidagai.
    b. Kogahl-lanas.
Tadji-lanas. There were two great divisions of this name, the southern one with a subdivision called—
    a. Kaidju-kegawai.
Kas-lanas.
Kianusili.
Sagangusili.
Skidaokao.
Koetas.
    a. Hlkaonedis.
    b. Huadjinaas-hadai.
    c. Nakalas-hadai.
    d. Neden-hadai.
    e. Chats-hadai.

EAGLE

Djahui-gitinai.
Gitins of Skidegate.
 a. Nayuuns-haidagai.
 b. Nasagas-haidagai.
 c. Lgalaiguahl-lanas.
 d. Gitingidjats.
Hlgahet-gitinai.
 a. Djahuihlgahet-kegawai.
 b. Yaku-gitinai.
 c. Hlgahet-kegawai.
 d. Kahlgui-hlgahet-gitinai.
 e. Gweundus.
Sagui-gitunai.
 a. Kialdagwuns.
Djiguaahl-lanas.
 a. Tlduldjitamae.
Kaiahl-lanas.
 a. Stasaos-lanas.
Kona-kegawai.
 a. Dagangasels.
 b. Sus-haidagai.
Stawas-haidagai.
 a. Heda-haidagai.
 b. Kahligua-haidagai.
 c. Sa-haidagai.
Do-gitunai.
Gituns (of Masset).
 a. Mamun-gitunai.
  1. Ao-gitunai.
 b. Undlskadjins-gitunai.
 c. Tees-gitunai.
 d. Sadjugahl-lanas.
Djus-hade.
Sagua-lanas.
 a. Dotuskustl.
Chets-gitunai.
Tohlka-gitunai.
Widja-gitunai.
Gunghet-kegawai.
Saki-kegawai.
Skidai-lanas.
Stagi-lanas.
Lana-chaadus.
Salendas.
 a. Hlimulnaas-hadai.
 b. Nahawas-hadai.
Stustas.
 a. Kawas.
 b. Kangguatl-lanas.
 c. Hlielung-keawai.
 d. Hlielung-stustai.
 e. Nekun-stustai.
 f. Chawagis-stustae.
 g. Yadus.
  1. Ildjunai-hadai.
  2. Naalgus-hadai.
  3. Nakons-hadai.
  4. Otkialnaas-hadai.
  5. Otnaas-hadai.
Chaahl-lanas.
 a. Lanagukunhlin-hadai.
 b. Hotagastlas-hadai.
 c. Skahene-hadai.
 d. Stulnaas-hadai.
Taahl-lanas (clan uncertain).

The principal towns known to have been occupied by large bodies of people in comparatively recent times, although not always contemporaneously, are the following, the Kaigani towns being marked with an asterisk: Chaahl (on Moresby id.), Cumshewa, Dadens, Gahlinskun, Haena, Hlielung, Howkan, *Kaisun, Kasaan, *Kayung, Kiusta, Klinkwan,* Kloo, Kung, Kweundlas,* Masset, Naikun, Ninstints, Skedans, Skidegate, Sukkwan,* Tigun, Yaku, and Yan. Of these only Howkan, Kasaan, Kayung, Klinkwan, Masset, and Skidegate are now inhabited.

In addition there was formerly an immense number of small towns hardly distinguishable from camps, places that had been occupied as towns at some former time, and mythic or semimythic towns. The following is a partial list of these: Aiodjus, Atana, Atanus, Chaahl (on North id.), Chatchini, Chets, Chuga, Chukeu, Dadjingits, Dahua, Daiyu, Djigogiga, Djigua, Djihuagits, Edjao, Gachigundae, Gado (2 towns), Gaedi, Gaesigusket, Gaiagunkun, Gaodjaos, Gasins, Gatgainans, Gitinkalana, Guhlga, Gulhlgildjing, Gwaeskun, Hagi, Heudao, Hlagi, Hlakeguns, Hlgadun, Hlgaedlin, Hlgahet, Hlgai, Hlgaiha, Hlgaiu, Hlgihla-ala, Hlgadun, Hlkia, Hluln, Hotao, Hotdjihoas, Hoya-gundla, Huados, Kadadjans, Kadusgo, Kae, Kaidju, Kaidjudal, Kaigani,* Kasta, Katana, Kesa, Ket, Kil, Koagaogit, Koga, Kogalskun, Kostunhana, Kundji (2 towns), Kungga, Kungielung, Kunhalas, Kunkia, Kuulana, Lanadagunga, Lanagahlkehoda, Lanahawa (2 towns), Lanahilduns, Lanas-lnagai (3 towns), Lanaungsuls, Nagus, Sahldungkun, Sakaedigialas, Sgilgi, Sindaskun, Sindatahla, Singa, Skae, Skaito, Skaos, Skena, Skudus, Stlindagwai, Stunhlai, Sulustins, Ta, Te, Tlgunghung, Tlhingus, Tohlka, Widja, Yagun, Yaogus, Yastling, Yatza, Youahnoe(?)　　　　(J. R. S.)

Haida.—Dawson, Queen Charlotte Ids., 103B, 1880. **Haidah.**—Scouler in Jour. Roy. Geog. Soc., XI, 184, 221, 1841. **Hai-dai.**—Kane, Wand. in N. Am., app., 1859 (after Work, 1836–41). **Hydahs.**—Taylor in Cal. Farmer, July 19, 1862. **Hyder.**—Simmons in Ind. Aff. Rep., 190, 1860. **Tlaidas.**—Morgan, Anc. Soc., 176, 1877.

Haiglar. The principal chief of the Catawba about the middle of the 18th century, commonly known to the English colonists as King Haiglar. It is probable that he became chief in 1748, as it is stated in Gov. Glenn's letter of May 21, 1751, to the Albany Conference (N. Y. Doc. Col. Hist., VI, 722, 1855), that the Catawba king had died a year and a half before that time. This must refer to Haiglar's predecessor. Haiglar, though disposed to peace, offered his services to the governor of South Carolina when war with the Cherokee broke out in 1759. He joined Col. Grant's forces and took an active part in the severe battle of

Etchoe (Itseyi), assisting materially in gaining the victory for the whites. He is described as a man of sterling character, just in his dealings and true to his word, acting the part of a father to his people, by whom he was greatly beloved. Seeing that strong drink was injuring them, he sent a written petition to Chief Justice Henley, May 26, 1756, requesting him to put a stop to the sale of spirituous liquors to the members of his tribe. In 1762 the Shawnee waylaid, killed, and scalped him while he was returning from the Waxaw attended by a single servant. Col. Samuel Scott, who was a chief in 1840, and signed the treaty of Mar. 13 in that year with South Carolina, was Haiglar's grandson. (c. t.)

Haim. A body of Salish of Kamloops agency, Brit. Col., numbering 26 in 1885.
Ha-im.—Can. Ind. Aff. 1885, 196, 1886.

Haimaaksto (*Hai'mäaxstō*). A subdivision of the Tsentsenkaio, a clan of the Walaskwakiutl.—Boas in Rep. Nat. Mus., 332, 1895.

Hainai. A tribe of the Caddo confederacy, otherwise known as Inie, or Ioni. After the Spanish occupancy their village was situated 3 leagues w. of the mission of Nacogdoches, in E. Texas; it contained 80 warriors, the same number assigned to the Hainai by Sibley in 1805, who perhaps obtained his information from the same sources. Sibley places their village 20 m. from Natchitoches, La. In manners, customs, and social organization the Hainai do not appear to have differed from the other tribes of the Caddo confederacy (q. v.), whose subsequent fate they have shared. By Sibley and others they are called "Tachies or Texas" (see *Texas*), as if that term applied to them particularly. The "great nation called Ayano, or Cannohatinno," according to the narrative of the La Salle expedition in 1687, were not the Hainai, as has been sometimes supposed, or any tribe at all, properly speaking. *Ayano*, or *hayano*, is merely the Caddo word for 'people,' while Kano-hatino (q. v.) is the Caddo equivalent for 'Red river,' presumably the same stream now so called. The Indians simply informed the explorer that many people lived on Red r., a statement which the French, in their ignorance of the language, construed to contain the definite name and synonym of a powerful tribe. (j. r. s. j. m.)
Aenay.—Linarès (1716) in Margry, Déc., VI, 217, 1886. Agerones.—Davis, Span. Conq. N. Mex., 82, note, 1869. Ahinai.—MS. Census of 1790 in Tex. State Archives. Ainais.—Carver, Trav., map, 1778. Anais.—Soc. Geog. Mex., 504, 1869. Annay.—Linarès (1716) in Margry, Déc., VI, 218, 1886. Ayanais.—Domenech, Deserts N. Am., I, 440, 1860. Ayenai.—Gatschet, Creek Migr. Leg., I, 43, 1884. Ayenis.—Alcedo, Dic.Geog., I, 190, 1786. Ayennis.—Charlevoix, New France, IV, 80, note, 1870. Aynais.—Mota-Padilla, Hist. de la Conquista, 384, 1742. Aynays.—Rivera, Diario y Derrotero, leg.

2140, 1736. Aynics.—Burnet (1847) in Schoolcraft, Ind. Tribes, I, 239, 1851. Ayonai.—Talon quoted by Gatschet, Karankawa Inds., 27, 1891. Hainais.—Whipple, Explor. for R. R. to Pac., III, pt. 3, 76, 1856. Hini.—Morse, Rep. to Sec. War, 373, 1822. Inay.—La Harpe (1716) in Margry, Déc., VI, 193, 1886. Ini.—Latham in Trans. Philol. Soc. Lond., 101, 1856. Inics.—Keane in Stanford, Compend., 504, 1878. Inies.—Sibley (1805), Hist. Sketches, 67, 1806. Innies.—Pénicaut (1701) in French, Hist. Coll. La., I, 73, note, 1869. Iondes.—Foote, Tex., I, 299, 1841. Ionees.—Ind. Aff. Rep., 899, 1846. I-on-i.—Sen. Ex. Confid. Doc. 13, 29th Cong., 2d sess., I, 1846. Ionias.—Ind. Aff. Rep. 1871, 191, 1872. Ionies.—Ind. Aff. Rep., 894, 1846. Ironeyes.—Edward, Hist. Tex., 92, 1836. Ironies.—Foote, Tex., I, 299, 1841. Jonies.—Parker, Tex., 213, 1856. Youays.—La Harpe (1716) in French, Hist. Coll. La., III, 47, 1851.

Haines Mission. A missionary post among the Chilcat at Deshu (q. v.), in Portage cove, near the head of Lynn canal, Alaska; pop. (entire) 85 in 1900.

Hair. See *Anatomy*.

Hair dressing. Many tribes had a distinctive mode of cutting and dressing the hair, and the style occasionally suggested the nickname by which the people were called by other tribes, as, for instance, in the case of the Pawnee, who cut the hair close to the head, except a ridge from the forehead to the crown, where the scalp-lock was parted off in a circle, stiffened with fat and paint, made to stand erect, and curved like a horn, hence the name *Pawnee*, derived from *pariki*, 'horn.' The same style of shaving the head and roaching the hair was common among eastern and western tribes, who braided and generally hung the scalp-lock with ornaments. The Dakota and other western tribes parted the hair in the middle from the forehead to the nape of the neck, the line, usually painted red, being broken by the circle that separated the scalp-lock, which was always finely plaited, the long hair on each side, braided and wrapped in strips of beaver or otter skin, hanging down in front over the chest. The Nez Percés of Idaho and neighboring tribes formerly wore the hair long and unconfined, falling loosely over the back and shoulders. In the S. W. among most of the Pueblo men the hair was cut short across the forehead, like a "bang," and knotted behind. The Eskimo wore the hair loose.

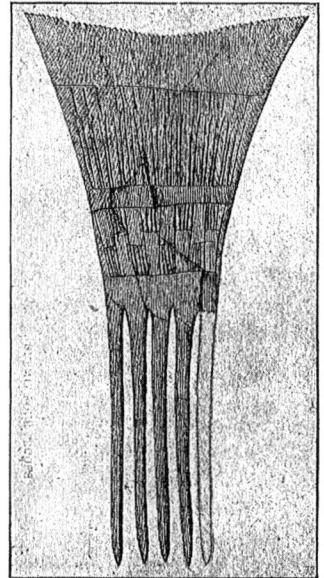

COMB OF BONE FROM A VIRGINIA MOUND; ABOUT ⅞. (FOWKE)

There was generally a difference in the manner of wearing the hair between the men and women of a tribe, and in some tribes the women dressed their hair differently before and after marriage, as with the Hopi, whose maidens arranged it in a whorl over each ear, symbolizing the flower of the squash, but after marriage wore it in simple braids. Aside from these ordinary modes of hair dressing there were styles that were totemic and others connected with religious observances or with shamanistic practices. Among the Omaha and some other tribes the child from 4 to 7 years of age formerly had its hair cut in a manner to indicate the totem of its gens; for instance, if the turtle was the totem, all the hair was cut

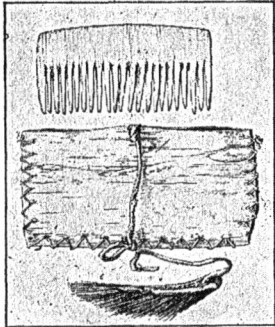

WOODEN COMB AND BIRCH-BARK CASE; HUDSON BAY ESKIMO. (TURNER)

off close, except a short fringe encircling the head, a little tuft being left on the forehead, one at the nape of the neck, and two tufts on each side; the bald crown above the fringe represented the shell of the turtle and the tufts its head, tail, and four legs. Generally speaking, the mode of wearing the hair was in former times not subject to passing fancies or fashions, but was representative of tribal kinship and beliefs.

ZUÑI HAIR-DRESSING. (STEVENSON)

The first cutting of the hair was usually attended with religious rites. Among the Kiowa and other southern Plains tribes a lock from the first clipping of the child's hair was tied to the forelock (Mooney). Among many tribes the hair was believed to be closely connected with a person's life. This was true in a religious sense of the scalp-lock. In some of the rituals used when the hair was first gathered up and cut from the crown of a boy's head the

teaching was set forth that this lock represents the life of the child, now placed wholly in the control of the mysterious and supernatural power that alone could will his death. The braided lock worn thereafter was a sign of this dedication and belief, and represented the man's life. On it he wore the ornaments that marked his achievements and honors, and for anyone to touch lightly this lock was regarded as a grave insult. As a war trophy the scalp-lock had a double meaning. It indicated the act of the supernatural power that had decreed the death of the man, and it served as tangible proof of the warrior's prowess in wresting it from the enemy. The scalper, however, was not always the killer or the first striker. The latter had the chief credit,

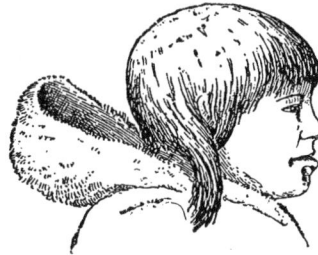

HAIR DRESSING; WESTERN ESKIMO MAN. (MURDOCH)

and frequently left others to do the killing and scalping. With the Eastern or timber tribes, the scalper was usually the killer, but this was not so often the case among the Plains Indians. The scalp was frequently left on the battle ground as a sacrifice. Among the Dakota a bit of the captured scalp-lock was preserved for a year, during which period the spirit was supposed to linger near; then, when the great death feast was held, the lock was destroyed and the spirit was freed thereby from its earthly ties (see *Scalp*). There are many beliefs connected with the hair, all of which are interwoven with the idea that it is mysteriously connected with a person's life and fortune. One can be bewitched and made subservient to the will of a person who becomes possessed of a bit of his hair; consequently combings are usually carefully

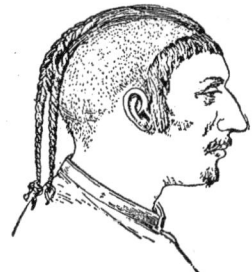

HEAD OF SEMINOLE MAN. (MACCAULEY)

burned. According to Hrdlicka the Pima, after killing an Apache, purified themselves with smoke from the burnt hair of the victim.

Personal joy or grief was manifested by the style of dressing the hair (see *Mourning*). Young men often spend much time over their locks, friends assisting friends in the toilet. The Pueblo and Plains tribes commonly used a stiff brush of spear grass for combing and dressing the hair, while the Eskimo and the N. W. coast tribes used combs. A pointed stick served for parting it and painting the line. These sticks were often carefully wrought, ornamented with embroidery on the handle, and kept in an embroidered case. Perfumes, as well as oils, were used, and wisps of sweet-grass were concealed in the hair of young men to add to their attractions. The Pima and Papago paint or stain the hair when it becomes bleached by the sun (Hrdlicka in Am. Anthrop., VIII, no. 1, 1906), and the former, as well as other tribes of the arid region, often coated the hair completely with river mud to destroy vermin.

Early French travelers in Texas and other Southern states mention a custom of the hostess to hasten to wash the head of a visitor with warm water, as a sign of good will and welcome. Among the Pueblo Indians the washing of the hair with the pounded root of the yucca plant prior to a religious rite was attended with much ceremony, and seems to correspond to the purification observances of the sweat lodge, which always preceded sacred rites among the tribes of the plains. See *Adornment*.   (A. C. F.)

Hairwork. One of the most useful materials known to the Indians of the United States was hair, which, as a textile material, was generally more available than vegetal fibers. Hair was obtained from the dog, buffalo, mountain sheep, mountain goat, moose, deer, reindeer, elk, antelope, opossum, rabbit, beaver, otter, lynx, and other animals, and human hair was also sometimes employed.

In more modern times horsehair was used to stuff balls, drumsticks, dolls, pads, pillows, etc., and tufts of it, frequently dyed, were attached as ornaments to costumes, pouches, harness, ceremonial objects, etc. False hair was worn by the Crows, Assiniboin, Mandan, Mohave, and Yuma; and ceremonial wigs of black wool and bangs of natural or dyed hair, especially horsehair, were made by the Pueblos. Twisted or sometimes braided into cord, hair had a most extensive use, satisfying the multifarious demands for string or rope of great tensile strength, and was combined with other fibers in the warp or weft of textiles and basketry. According to Grinnell cowskin pads stuffed with the hair of elk, antelope, buffalo, or mountain sheep were commonly used instead of saddles by some of the Plains tribes in running buffalo and in war. Bourke (9th Rep. B. A. E., 474, 1892) says that mantles made of votive hair are mentioned as having been in use among the Lower California or southern California tribes in the 18th century, and quotes Parkman (Jesuits in North America, lxxxiv, 1867) to the effect that the Algonquians believed in a female manito who wore a robe made of the hair of her

victims, for she caused death. See *Adornment, Featherwork, Hair dressing, Quillwork.* Consult Holmes in 13th Rep. B. A. E., 25, 37, 1896.   (W. H.)

Haisla (*Xa-islá*). One of the three Kwakiutl dialectic divisions, embracing the Kitamat (Haisla proper) and the Kitlope.—Boas in Rep. Nat. Mus., 328, 1895.

Haiwal ('acorn'). A clan of the Tonkawa.   (A. S. G.)

Hakan. The Fire clans of the Keresan pueblos of Acoma, Cochiti, Santa Ana, Sia, and San Felipe, N. Mex. That of Acoma is now extinct.
Háka-hánoqᶜʰ.—Hodge in Am. Anthrop., IX, 350, 1896 (Acoma form: *hánoqch* = 'people'). Hákan-háno.—Ibid. (Santa Ana and Sia form). Ha'-kan-ñi.—Stevenson in 11th Rep. B. A. E., 19, 1894 (Sia form). Hákanyi-háno.—Hodge, op. cit. (San Felipe form). Hákanyi-hánuch.—Ibid. (Cochiti form.)

Hakkyaiwal (*Hăk-kyäi'-wăl*). A Yaquina village on the s. side of Yaquina r., Oreg.—Dorsey in Jour. Am. Folk-lore, III, 229, 1890.

Hakouchirmiou (probably misprint for Hakouchiriniou). Mentioned by Dobbs (Hudson Bay, 23, 1744), as a tribe, on or near Bourbon (Nelson) r., Brit. Am., at war with the Maskegon. Possibly a division of the Cree or of the Assiniboin.

Halant. A Shuswap village 3 m. below Shuswap lake, Brit. Col.; pop. 152 in 1904.
Halant.—Can. Ind. Aff., 244, 1902. Ha-la-ut.—Ibid., 196, 1885. Kell-aout.—Ibid., 188, 1884. Naskantlines.—Ibid.,78, 1878. Neskainlith.—Ibid., pt. II, 68, 1902. Niskahnuith.—Ibid., 259, 1882. Niskainlith.—Ibid., map, 1891. South Thompson.—Ibid.

Halchis. A former village, presumably Costanoan, connected with Dolores mission, San Francisco, Cal.—Taylor in Cal. Farmer, Oct. 18, 1861.

Half Breed Band. Mentioned by Culbertson (Smithson. Rep. 1850, 143, 1851) as a local band of the Cheyenne (q. v.) in 1850, probably named from a chief; or perhaps the Sutaio.

Half-breeds. See *Métis, Mixed-bloods.*

Half King (Scruniyatha, Seruniyattha, Tanacharison, Tannghrishon, etc.). An Oneida chief; born about 1700; died at the house of John Harris, at the site of Harrisburg, Pa., Oct. 4, 1754. He appears to have first come into notice about 1748, at which time he lived at or in the vicinity of Logstown, Pa. (q. v.). According to some statements his residence was in this village, but according to others it was on Little Beaver cr., about 15 m. distant. It was to Half King that most of the official visitors to the Indians of the Ohio region, including Weiser, Gist, Croghan, and Washington, applied for information, advice, and assistance, Logstown being their stopping place for this purpose. He accompanied Washington both on his journey of 1753 and on his expedition of 1754.

Half King claimed that he killed Jumonville, the French officer, during the skirmish at Great Meadows, Pa., May 28, 1754, in revenge of the French, who, he declared, had killed, boiled, and eaten his father; and it was he who had advised Ensign Ward, when summoned by Contrœur, the French officer, to surrender Ft Necessity, at the site of Pittsburg, Pa., to reply that his rank did not invest him with power to do so, thus obtaining delay. Half King was a prominent figure on the Indian side in the treaty with the Virginia commissioners in 1752, and for this and other services was decorated by Gov. Dinwiddie and given the honorary name "Dinwiddie," which, it is said, he adopted with pride. On the advice of Croghan, he with other Indians removed to Aughquick (Oquaga) cr., Pa., in 1754. Half King has been confused with the Huron Half King of Sandusky, Ohio, known also as Pomoacan, and with his own successor, who bore the same popular title. His Delaware name was Monakatuatha. See Drake, Aborig. Races, 531, 1880; Rupp, Hist. West. Pa., 71, 1846; Dinwiddie Papers, I, 148, 1883; Col. Records Pa., v, 358, 1851. (C. T.)

Half King (Petawontakas, Dunquad, Daunghquat; Delaware name, Pomoacan). A Huron chief of Sandusky, Ohio, who flourished during the latter part of the Revolutionary war. Under employment by the British he aided the Delawares in their resistance to the encroachment of the white settlements beyond the Allegheny mts., and it was through his intervention that the Moravians of Lichtenau were saved from massacre by the Indians in 1777. According to Loskiel (Missions United Brethren, pt. 3, 127, 1794) he was joined by a large number of warriors, including Hurons, Ottawa, Chippewa, Shawnee, and others, besides some French, and his influence as a disciplinarian was such that he kept this mixed assemblage in good order, permitting no extravagance on their part. Sometimes more than 200 warriors lay all night close to Lichtenau, but they behaved so quietly that they were hardly perceived. Loskiel also says that Half King "was particularly attentive to prevent all drunkenness, knowing that bloodshed and murder would immediately follow." He insisted on the removal of the Christian Indians from the vicinity of Sandusky, believing it to be unsafe for them to remain there; he also protected the Moravians and their converts from maltreatment when the missionaries were sent to Detroit. Under the name Daunghquat he signed the treaty of Ft McIntosh, Ohio, Jan. 21, 1785. The treaties of Greenville, Ohio, Aug. 3, 1795; Ft McIntosh, July 4, 1805; Greenville, July 22, 1814, and Spring Wells, Sept. 8, 1815, were signed by Haroenyou (Harrowenyou), his son, not by himself; but the name "Dunquad or Half King" is appended to the treaty of Miami Rapids, Ohio, Sept. 29, 1817. (C. T.)

Halfway Town. A former Cherokee settlement on Little Tennessee r., about halfway between Sitiku and Chilhowee, about the boundary of the present Monroe and Loudon cos., E. Tenn.—Timberlake, Mem., map, 1765.

Halkaiktenok (*Ha′lx′aix·tēnôx*, 'killer whale'). A division of the Bellabella.—Boas in Rep. Nat. Mus., 328, 1895.

Halona (*Hálona I′tiwana*, 'middle place of happy fortune', 'middle ant-hill of the world', 'the ant-hill at the navel of the Earth Mother.'—Cushing). A former pueblo of the Zuñi and one of the Seven Cities of Cibola of the early Spanish chroniclers, said to have been situated on both sides of Zuñi r., on and opposite the site of the present Zuñi pueblo, w. N. Mex. Only the mound on the s. side of the stream is now traceable, and a part of this is occupied by modern buildings erected by white people. While there seems to be no question that Halona was inhabited by the Zuñi at the time of Coronado in 1540, it was not mentioned by name until Nov. 9, 1598, when the Zuñi made a vow of obedience and vassalage to Spain at Hawikuh, Halona being designated as Halonagu (*Halonakwin,* 'Halona-place'). A Franciscan mission was established there in 1629, but the murder by the Zuñi of their missionary in 1632 impelled the Indians to flee for protection to Thunder mtn., a mesa 3 m. away, where they remained for about 3 years. The mission was rehabilitated some time after 1643, and continued until the Pueblo outbreak of Aug., 1680, when the Zuñi murdered Fray Juan de Bal, the Halona missionary, and burned the church. The Zuñi again fled to Thunder mtn., where they remained until after the reconquest by Diego de Vargas in 1692. Meanwhile the pueblos in the valley, including Halona, had fallen in decay, and none of them was rebuilt. The present village of Zuñi was reared on the N. bank of Zuñi r., partly on the site of Halona, about the close of the 17th century. The population of Halona at the time of the revolt of 1680 was about 1,500, and Matsaki and Kiakima were visitas of its mission. See Bancroft, Ariz. and N. Mex., 1889; Bandelier (1) Doc. Hist. Zuñi Tribe, in Jour. Am. Eth. and Arch., III, 1892, (2) in Arch. Inst. Papers, III, IV, 1890–92; Cushing, Zuñi Creation Myths, 13th Rep. B. A. E., 1896; Vetancurt in Teatro Am., repr. 1871. (F. W. H.)

Alauna.—Jefferys, Am. Atlas, map no. 5, 1776. Alena.—Bowles, map Am., 1784. Aloma.—Vargas

(1692) quoted in Davis, Span. Conq. of N. Mex., 371, 1869. **Alomas.**—Mota-Padilla, Hist. de la Conquista (possibly the same; Acoma (q. v.), however, seems more likely). **Alona.**—De l'Isle, Carte Mexique et Floride, 1703; Vetancurt (1693) in Teatro Mex., III, 320, 1871. **Alonas.**—Rivera, Diario y Derrotero, leg. 950, 1736 (referring to the inhabitants). **Ant Hill.**—Cushing, Zuñi Folk Tales, 7, 1901 (Hálonawan, or). **Ant Hill of the Middle.**—Ibid., 31. **Concepcion de Alona.**—Vetancurt (1693), Menolog. Fran., 275, 1871 (mission name). **Halona.**—Cushing in Millstone, IX, 55, Apr. 1884 (Zuñi name). **Halonagu.**—Oñate (1598) in Doc. Inéd., XVI, 133, 1871 (corruption of Halonakwin, *kwin* being the locative). **Halona I'tiwana.**—Cushing in Millstone, IX, 55, Apr. 1884. **Hálona-ítiwana.**—Cushing, Zuñi Folk Tales, 7, 1901. **Halona-kue.**—Bandelier in Arch. Inst. Papers, V, 171, 1890 (given as the name of the pueblo; but *kue*= 'people'). **Halona Kuin.**—Bandelier, ibid., IV, 337, 1892 (*kuin*=locative). **Hal-onan.**—Ibid., 335. **Halona-quin.**—Bandelier in Jour. Am. Ethnol. and Archæol., III, 84, 1892. **Hal-on-aua.**—Bandelier in Arch. Inst. Papers, III, 260, 1890. **Há-lo-na-wa.**—Cushing in Compte-rendu Internat. Cong. Am., VII, 156, 1890 (or Há-lo-na). **Hálonawan.**—Cushing, Zuñi Folk Tales, 7, 1901. **La Purificacion de la Virgen de Alona.**—Bandelier in Arch. Inst. Papers, IV, 337, 1892 (mission name). **Middle Ant Hill.**—Cushing, Zuñi Folk Tales, 31, 1901. **Middle Ant Hill of the World.**—Ibid., 55. **Middle Place.**—Ibid., 34. **Purificacion.**—D'Anville, map Am. Sept., 1746 (intended for mission name).

Halpadalgi (*hálpada* 'alligator', *algi* 'people'). A Creek clan.
Hálpadalgi—Gatschet, Creek Migr. Leg., I, 155, 1884. **Kal-pŭt'-lŭ.**—Morgan, Anc. Soc., 161, 1877.

Hamalakyauae. An ancestor of a Nimkish gens, after whom it was sometimes called.—Boas in Petermanns Mitt., pt. 5, 130, 1887.

Hamanao (*Xámanáô*). A gens of the Quatsino tribe of the Kwakiutl, q. v.—Boas in Rep. Nat. Mus., 329, 1895.

Hamechuwa. A former Luiseño village in the neighborhood of San Luis Rey mission, s. Cal.—Taylor in Cal. Farmer, May 11, 1860.

Hameyisath (*Ha'mēyisath*). A sept of the Seshat, a Nootka tribe.—Boas in 6th Rep. N. W. Tribes Can., 32, 1890.

Hami. The Tobacco clans of Sia and San Felipe pueblos, N. Mex.
Háami-háno.—Hodge in Am. Anthrop., IX, 352, 1896 (Sia form: *háno*='people'). **Há-mi.**—Stevenson in 11th Rep. B. A. E., 19, 1894 (Sia form). **Hámi-hano.**—Hodge, op. cit. (San Felipe form).

Hamilton Creek. The local name for a body of Salish of Kamloops-Okanagan agency, Brit. Col.; pop. 38 in 1901 (Can. Ind. Aff. for 1901, pt. II, 166), after which date the name does not occur.

Hamitinwoliyu. A former Nishinam village in the valley of Bear r., Cal.
Hameting-Woleyuh.—Powers in Overland Mo., XII, 22, 1874. **Ha'-mi-ting-Wo'-li-yuh.**—Powers in Cont. N. A. Ethnol., III, 316, 1877.

Hammers. Few implements are of so much importance to primitive men as the stone hammer and the several closely allied forms—the sledge, the maul, and the stone-head club, which may be described here rather than under the caption *Clubs*. All of these implements are employed, like the ordinary club, in striking blows that stun, break, crush, or drive, the only distinction to be drawn between the hafted hammer and the club being that the one carries the weight chiefly in the extremity or head, which is usually of heavier or harder material than the handle, while the other has the weight distributed along the shaft. Although the several implements comprised in this group have many features in common, they are somewhat clearly differentiated in shape and use. All

DISCOIDAL CHIPPING HAMMERS. *a*, OHIO; *b*, CALIFORNIA. (ABOUT 1-6)

are made of hard, heavy, tough materials, including stone, bone, ivory, antler, shell, and metal. Some are never hafted, while perhaps nearly all on occasion are used unhafted, one or both hands being employed according to the weight of the implement. Haftings vary with the form and use of the object as well as with the region and the people.

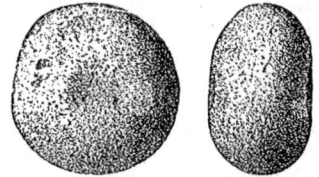

PITTED HAMMER. (ABOUT 1-5)

Hammers employed in shaping stone, especially in the more advanced stages of the work, are usually unhafted and are held tightly in the hand for delivering heavy blows, or lightly between the thumb and fingertips for flaking or pecking. They may be natural pebbles, bowlders, or fragments, but by prolonged use they assume definite shapes or are intentionally

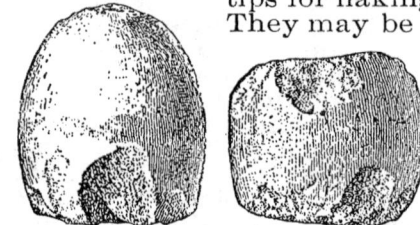

SLEDGE HEADS FROM THE COPPER MINES, MICHIGAN. (ABOUT 1-5)

modified to better fit them for their purpose. Globular and discoidal forms prevail, and the variety employed in pecking and for other light uses often has shallow depressions centrally placed at opposite sides to render the finger hold more secure. The pecking and flaking work is accomplished by strokes with the periphery, which is round or slightly angular in profile to suit the requirements of the particular work.

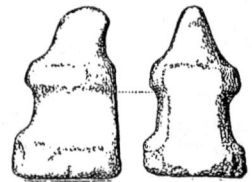

HEAVY HAMMER; BRITISH COLUMBIA. (LENGTH 6 3-4 IN.)

Hammers intended for breaking, driving, and killing are generally hafted to increase their effectiveness. Sledge hammers, used in mining and quarrying, were usually heavy, often rudely shaped, and the haft was a pliable stick or withe bent around the body of the implement, which was sometimes grooved for the purpose. The fastening was made secure by the application of thongs or rawhide coverings. In the flint quarries and copper mines great numbers of hammers or sledges were required; indeed, it may be said that in and about the ancient copper mines of McCargolscove, Isle Royale, Mich., there are to be seen tens of thousands of wornout and abandoned sledge heads. In an ancient paint mine in Missouri, recently exposed by the opening of an iron mine, upward of 1,200 rude stone sledges were thrown out by the workmen. Heavy grooved and hafted hammers, resembling somewhat the mining sledges, though much more highly specialized, were in general use among the tribes of the great plains and served an important purpose in breaking up the bones of large game animals, in pounding pemmican,

HEAVY HAMMER OF THE PLAINS TRIBES. (ABOUT 1-8)

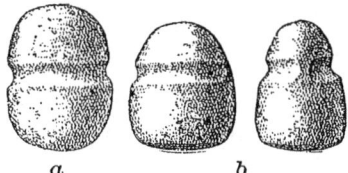

GROOVED STONE HAMMERS. *a*, NEW MEXICO; *b*, DAKOTA

flint, and seeds, in driving tipi pegs, etc. A lighter hammer, usually referred to as a war-club, was and is in common use among the western tribes. It is a globular or doubly conical stone, carefully finished and often grooved, the haft being strengthened by binding with rawhide. Closely allied to this weapon is a kind of slung hammer, the roundish stone being

BONE MAUL WITH WOODEN HANDLE. (1-6) ESKIMO. (MURDOCH)

held in place at the end of the handle by a covering of rawhide that extends the full length of the haft. These are very effectual implements, and decked with streamers of horsehair and other ornaments have been devoted, at least in recent years, to ceremony and show.

Heavy hammers, often tastefully carved, were and are used by the tribes of the N. W. for driving wedges in splitting wood, for driving piles, and for other heavy work; they are usually called mauls, or pile-drivers. Many of the larger specimens have handles or finger holes carved

in the stone, while others are provided with handles of wood. The Eskimo also have hammers for various purposes, made of stone, bone, and ivory, with haftings ingeniously attached.

The literature of this topic is voluminous, but much scattered, references to the various kinds of hammers occurring in nearly all works dealing with the archeology and ethnology of N. America. For an extended article on the stone hammer, see McGuire in Am. Anthropologist, IV, no. 4, 1891.   (W. H. H.)

Hammonasset. A small band, headed by a chief named Sebequanash ('the man who weeps'), formerly living about Hammonasset r., near Guilford, Middlesex co., Conn. They were probably a part of the Quinnipiac.—De Forest, Hist. Inds. Conn., 52, 1853.

Hamnulik. A former Aleut village on Agattu id., Alaska, one of the Near id. group of the Aleutians, now uninhabited.

Hampasawan ('tented village,' from *hampone*, 'tent'). A former Zuñi pueblo, the ruins of which are still visible 6 m. w. of the present Zuñi, Valencia co., N. Mex. Regarded by Cushing as probably one of the seven cities of Cibola. See Mindeleff in 8th Rep. B. A. E., 83, 1891, and the authors cited below.

Haínpassawan.—ten Kate, Reizen in N. A., 291, 1885 (after Cushing; misprint). Hámpasawan.—Cushing, Zuñi Folk Tales, 6, 1901. Ham-pas-sa-wan.—Cushing in Millstone, IX, 55, 1884. Tented Pueblo.—Cushing, Zuñi Folk Tales, 6, 1901. Village of the White Flowering Herbs.—Cushing, Zuñi Folk Tales, 104, 1901 (probably the same).

Hampton Normal and Agricultural Institute. A school for negroes and Indians, situated 2 m. from Fort Monroe and Old Point Comfort, Va. Established in 1868 by Gen. S. C. Armstrong for the industrial and agricultural education of freedmen, it was the first school in the United States of a practical industrial nature. After 10 years of success in training and establishing negroes as teachers and farmers, it responded to the call of 14 young Indians, who had been prisoners of war at St Augustine, Fla., for three years, and thus opened its doors to the Indian race. Since then 1,100 Indian girls and boys have had more or less training at Hampton, and to-day five-sixths of those now living are industrious and civilized, working with their own hands for the support of themselves and their families.

The school is not a government institution, but is controlled by a board of 17 trustees, and is entirely nonsectarian in character. It is supported by the income of a partial endowment and by certain government funds distributed by the state of Virginia, but its chief support is derived from the donations of its friends.

The academic course covers a period of 4 years, and includes English branches in both grammar and high school grades.

Normal courses are given in business, agriculture, and the trades, as well as in kindergarten and public school teaching. Agriculture begins in the primary department of the training school, and becomes so important a branch of the academic work that at the end of the course the student is prepared to conduct intelligent farming. In addition to the model farm, dairy, orchards, poultry yards, and experiment garden, the school has a dairy and stock farm of 600 acres a few miles away. The trades taught the boys are carpentry, wood turning, bricklaying, plastering, painting, wheelwrighting, blacksmithing, machine work, steam fitting, tailoring, shoe and harness making, tinsmithing, upholstering, and printing. A large and well equipped trade school, with mechanical-drawing room, offers excellent facilities for the practical instruction given. The domestic-science building and the school kitchens and laundries give opportunity for instruction in all kinds of domestic work, and each girl is required to complete a practical course in every branch of housekeeping, cooking, dairying, and gardening.

The school has about 60 buildings for housing and educating its 900 boarding students. These include a church, library, dormitories, recitation halls, trade school, domestic science and agricultural building, hospital, printing office, greenhouses, barn, workshops, laundry, offices, and dwellings for the officers and teachers. All the young men receive instruction in military tactics, which has proved of great value in instilling habits of promptness, neatness, and obedience.

The Government pays $167 a year for each of its 120 Indian pupils; all expenses in excess of this must be provided by philanthropic friends. The Indians and colored students have separate dormitory buildings, and the pupils of the two races also occupy separate tables in the dining rooms, but work together in classes and shops with mutual good feeling and helpfulness.

The record of Indians returned to their homes is carefully kept. For the year ending in May, 1906, there were 183 doing an excellent grade of work as teachers in schoolroom, shop, or on farms; as doctors, lawyers, or ethnologists; 306 were living civilized lives, setting examples of industry and temperance; 80 were doing fairly well under hard conditions; 28 were doing poorly, and 4 were bad. This gives so large a proportion of satisfactory results that Hampton considers her work for Indians in every way a success.

The school publishes a monthly magazine called *The Southern Workman*, devoted to the interests of the negro and the Indian. The Indians publish a small paper, *Talks and Thoughts*, now in its nineteenth year; all its contributors are Indians, and many of the articles are valuable additions to Indian literature and ethnology. (C. M. F.)

Hamtsit (*Hámtsīt*, 'having food', named from an ancestor). A Bellacoola division at Talio, Brit. Col.—Boas in 7th Rep. N. W. Tribes Can., 3, 1891.

Han. An unidentified tribe living on a part of the island of Malhado (Galveston id.?), Texas, on which Cabeza de Vaca suffered shipwreck in 1528. The language of the Han differed from that of their neighbors, the Capoque (probably Coaque), but they had customs in common. They possibly formed the westernmost band of the Attacapa. See Cabeza de Vaca, Narr., Smith trans., 82, 1871; Gatschet, Karankawa Inds., 34, 1891.

Han ('night'). A Kansa gens. Its subgentes are Hannikashinga and Dakanmanyin.
Haⁿ.—Dorsey in Am. Nat., 671, 1885.

Hana ('dog'). A subphratry or gens of the Menominee.—Hoffman in 14th Rep. B. A. E., pt. I, 42, 1896.

Hanahawunena ('rock men.'—Kroeber). A division of the Northern Arapaho, now practically extinct.
Aanû'hawă.—Mooney in 14th Rep. B. A. E., 956, 1896. Ha'nahawunĕna.—Ibid. Hăⁿanaxawüune'-naⁿ.—Kroeber in Bull. Am. Mus. Nat. Hist., XVIII, pt. 1, 6, 1902.

Hanakwa. A former pueblo of the Jemez in New Mexico, the exact site of which is not known.
Ham-a-qua.—Bandelier in Arch. Inst. Papers, IV, 207, 1892. Han-a-kwá.—Hodge, field notes, B. A. E., 1895.

Hanaya. A former Chumashan village in Mission canyon, near Santa Barbara mission, Cal.
Ha'-na-ya.—Henshaw, Santa Barbara MS. vocab., B. A. E., 1884. Janaya.—Taylor in Cal. Farmer, Apr. 24, 1863.

Hanehewedl (*Xanexewéʼ*, 'stone by or near the trail'). A village of the Nicola band of the Ntlakyapamuk, near Nicola r., 27 m. above Spences Bridge, Brit. Col.—Teit in Mem. Am. Mus. Nat. Hist., II, 174, 1900.

Hanga ('leader'). A gens of the Hangashenu division of the Omaha.
Foremost.—Dorsey in Bull. Philos. Soc. Wash., 129, 1880. Hañga.—Dorsey in 3d Rep. B. A. E., 233, 1884. Hunga.—Morgan, Anc. Soc., 155, 1877. Hunguh.—Long, Exped. Rocky Mts., I, 327, 1823. Large Hanga.—Dorsey in Am. Nat., 674, 1885. Medicine.—Morgan, op. cit., 155.

Hangashenu ('young men of the leaders.'—Fletcher). One of the two divisions of the Omaha, composed of the Wezhinshte, Inkesabe, Hanga, Dhatada, and Kanze gentes.
Hañgacenu.—Dorsey in 3d Rep. B. A. E., 219, 1884; 15th Rep. B. A. E., 226, 1897. Hongashan.—Jackson (1877) quoted by Donaldson in Smithson. Rep., 1885, pt. 2, 74, 1886. Hon-ga-sha-no.—Long, Exped. Rocky Mts., I, 325, 1823.

Hangatanga ('large Hanga'). A Kansa gens.
Black eagle.—Morgan. Anc. Soc., 156, 1877. Dăsin'-ja-hă-gă.—Ibid. ('Deer tail'). Hañga tanga.—Dorsey in 15th Rep. B. A. E., 231, 1897. Hañga

utanandji.—Ibid. ('Hanga apart from the rest'). **Hûng-ga ni-ka-shing-ga.**—Stubbs, Kaw MS. vocab., B. A. E., 25, 1877. **Hun-go-tin'-ga.**—Morgan, Anc. Soc., 156, 1877. **Ta nika-shing-ga.**—Stubbs, op. cit. **Ta sindje qaga.**—Dorsey in 15th Rep. B. A. E., 231, 1897.

Hanging-maw (*Uskwá'lĭ-gû'tă*, 'his stomach hangs down'). A prominent Cherokee chief of the Revolutionary period.—Mooney in 19th Rep. B. A. E., 543, 1900.

Hanginihkashina ('night people'). A subdivision of the Tsishu division of the Osage. Its subdivisions in turn are Haninihkashina and Wasape.
Haⁿ i'niųk'ăcin'a.—Dorsey in 15th Rep. B. A. E., 234, 1897. **Huinihkaciⁿa.**—Dorsey, Osage MS. vocab., B. A. E., 1883. **Tse'ǫañka'.**—Dorsey in 15th Rep. B. A. E., 234, 1897. **Tsi'ou we'haxiǫe.**—Ibid.

Hangka ('leader'). One of the three divisions of the Osage, the last to join the tribe, dividing with the Wazhazhe the right or war side of the camp circle.
Hañxa.—Dorsey in 15th Rep. B. A. E., 233, 1897.

Hangkaahutun ('Hangka having wings'). A gens of the Hangka division of the Osage, in two subgentes, Husadtawanun and Husadta.
Eagle people.—Dorsey, Osage MS. vocab., B. A. E., 1883. **Hañ'xa a'hü tüⁿ'.**—Dorsey in 15th Rep. B. A. E., 234, 1897. **Hü'saȝa.**—Ibid. ('limbs stretched stiff'). **Qŭǫ i'niųk'ăcin'a.**—Ibid. ('white eagle people').

Hangkaenikashika ('those who became human beings by means of the ancestral animal'). A Quapaw gens.
Ancestral gens.—Dorsey in 15th Rep. B. A. E., 229, 1897. **Hañxa e'nikaci'xa.**—Ibid.

Hangkautadhantsi ('Hangka apart from the rest'). A gens on the Hangka side of the Osage tribal circle.
Hañxa uta'ǫanȝsi.—Dorsey in 15th Rep. B. A. E., 234, 1897. **Qŭǫa'qtsi i'niųk'ăcin'a.**—Ibid. ('real eagle people'). **War eagle people.**—Dorsey, Osage MS. vocab., B. A. E., 1883.

Hangnikashinga ('night people'). A subgens of the Han gens of the Kansa.
Haⁿ nikaciⁿga.—Dorsey in 15th Rep. B. A. E., 231, 1897.

Hanilik. A former Aleut village on Agattu id., Alaska, one of the Near id. group of the Aleutians, now uninhabited.

Haninihkashina ('night people proper'). A subdivision of the Haninihkashina division of the Osage.—Dorsey in 15th Rep. B. A. E., 234, 1897.

Hankutchin ('river people'). A Kutchin tribe on upper Yukon r. below Klondike r., Alaska. They make baskets of tamarack roots with hair and porcupine quills tastefully woven into them. When these are used for cooking, the water is boiled by putting red-hot stones into them. The Hankutchin are noted for their skill in catching large salmon. Gibbs stated that 60 hunters visited Ft Yukon in 1854. They still trade at that post. Subdivisions are Katshikotin, Takon, and Tsitoklinotin. Villages are Fetutlin, Johnnys, Nuklako, Tadush, and Tutchonekutchin.
Ai-yan.—Schwatka, Rep. on Alaska, 82, 1885. **Ai-ya'-na.**—Dawson in Rep. Geol. Surv. Can., 200-B, 1887. **An-Kutchin.**—Whymper, Alaska, 223, 1868. **Au Kotchins.**—Raymond quoted by Colyer in Ind. Aff. Rep. 1869, 593, 1870. **Ayans.**—Schwatka in Century Mag., 821, Sept. 1885. **Gens de Bois.**—Dall in Proc. A. A. A. S., XVIII, 271, 1870. **Gens-de-fine.**—Raymond quoted by Colyer in Ind. Aff. Rep. 1869, 593, 1870. **Gens de Fou.**—Hardisty in Smithson. Rep. 1866, 311, 1872. **Gens de Foux.**—Whymper in Jour. Roy. Geog. Soc., 233, 1868. **Gens des Bois.**—Raymond in Sen. Ex. Doc. 12, 42d Cong., 1st sess., 34, 1871. **Gens des faux.**—Petroff, Alaska, 160, 1884. **Hai-ankutchin.**—Dall in Proc. A. A. A. S., XXXIV, 376, 1886. **Han-kutchi.**—Richardson, Arct. Exped., I, 396, 1851. **Han kutchin.**—Dall in Proc. A. A. A. S., XVIII, 271, 1870. **Hăn-Kŭtchin.**—Dall in Cont. N. A. Ethnol., I, 31, 1877. **Han-kuttchin.**—Petitot, Dict. Dènè-Dindjié, xx, 1876. **Hong-Kutchin.**—Jones in Smithson. Rep. 1866, 321, 1872. **Hun-koo-chin.**—Hardisty, ibid., 311. **Hun-Kutchin.**—Raymond in Sen. Ex. Doc. 12, 42d Cong., 1st sess., 34, 1871. **Hŭn'kŭtch-ĭn.**—Ross, MS. notes on Tinne, B. A. E. (trans.: 'people of the river country'). **Lower Gens de fou.**—Ibid. **Wood people.**—Dall in Proc. A. A. A. S., XVIII, 271, 1870.

Hannakallal. A tribe or band, probably Athapascan, numbering 600 in 1804, and dwelling s. of the 'Luckkarso' (Kosotshe) on the Pacific coast; possibly the Khainanaitetunne or the Henaggi.
Hannakalals.—Lewis and Clark, Exped., II, 119, 1814. **Hannakallah.**—Schoolcraft, Ind. Tribes, III, 571, 1853. **Han-na-kal-lal.**—Orig. Jour. Lewis and Clark, VI, 117, 1905.

Hano (contracted from *Anopi*, 'eastern people.'—Fewkes). The easternmost pueblo of Tusayan, N. E. Ariz., and familiarly spoken of as one of the Hopi villages; it is, however, occupied by Tewa people, whose ancestors, early in the 18th century, migrated from the upper Rio Grande, in New Mexico, principally from an ancient pueblo known as Tsawarii, above the present town of Santa Cruz, where the hamlet of La Puebla now stands (Hodge). The Hano people have largely intermarried with the Hopi. In 1782 the population was 110 families; in 1893 it numbered 163 individuals, including 23 husbands of Hano women. In addition, there were 16 Hano people living in the Hopi pueblos. The clans represented at Hano are the Ke (Bear), Kun (Corn), Sa (Tobacco), Tenyo (Pine), Okuwa (Cloud), Nang (Earth), Kachina, and Tang (Sun). Formerly there were also the Kapulo (Crane), Pe (Timber), Kopeli (Pink conch), Pohulo (Herb), Kuyanwe (Turquoise ear pendant), Ku (Stone), and Ta (Grass) clans, but these have become extinct since the Hano people settled in Tusayan. Consult Fewkes (1) in 17th Rep. B. A. E., 636, 1898; (2) in 19th Rep. B. A. E., 612, 1900; (3) in Am. Anthrop., VII, 162, 1894; Mindeleff in 8th Rep. B. A. E., 62, 1891.
Háno. Gatschet in Wheeler Surv. Rep., VII, 412, 1879. **Hánoki.**—Ibid. **Hánom.**—ten Kate, Reizen in N. A., 259, 1885 (Hopi name for the people). **Há-no-me.**—ten Kate, Synonymie, 7, 1884 (Hopi name for the people). **Hánomuh.**—Stephen and Mindeleff in 8th Rep. B. A. E., 36, 1891. **Harno.**—Ten Broeck in Schoolcraft, Ind. Tribes, IV, map, 24–25, 87, 1854. **Haro.**—Keane in Stanford, Compend., 515, 1878. **Iano.**—Taylor in Cal. Farmer, June 19, 1863. **Jano.**—Garcés (1776), Diary, 394, 1900. **Janogualpa.**—Garcés quoted by Bancroft, Ariz. and N. Mex., 137, 395, 1889 (Hano and Walpi combined). **Koyóshtu.**—Hodge, field notes, B. A. E., 1895 (Acoma name). **Na-cá-ci-kĭn.**—Stephen, MS., B. A. E., 1887 (Navaho name: 'foreign bear people's house'). **Nah-shah-shaı.**—Eaton in

Schoolcraft, Ind. Tribes, IV, 220, 1854 (Navaho name). **Tano.**—Ward quoted by Donaldson, Moqui Pueblo Inds., 14, 1893. **Tanoí.**—Hodge, field notes, B. A. E., 1895 (Isleta name). **Tanoquevi.**—Schoolcraft, Ind. Tribes, I, 519, 1853. **Tanoquibi.**—Calhoun quoted by Donaldson, Moqui Pueblo Inds., 14, 1893. **Tanos.**—Villa-Señor, Theatro Am., pt. 2, 425, 1748. **Tanus.**—Escudero, Noticias de Chihuahua, 231, 1834. **Taucos.**—Cortez (1799) in Whipple, Pac. R. R. Rep., III, pt. 3, 121, 1856. **Té-é-wŭn-nà.**—Whipple, ibid., 13, 1856 (Zuñi name). **Teh-wa.**—Stephen in Donaldson, Moqui Pueblo Inds., 14, 1893. **Tewa.**—Popular but incorrect name for the pueblo (see *Tewa*). **Tewe.**—Shipley in Ind. Aff. Rep., 310, 1891. **Towas.**—Davis, El Gringo, 115, 1857.

Hanocoucouaij. A village on the E. coast of Florida, N. of C. Cañaveral, in the 16th century.—De Bry, Brev. Nar., II, map, 1591.

Hantiwi. A Shastan tribe or band formerly living in Warm Spring valley, Modoc co., Cal.
Han-te'-wa.—Powers in Cont. N. A. Ethnol., III, 267, 1877.

Hanut Cochiti (*hanut*, 'above', + Cochiti, q. v.). The sixth town successively occupied by the people of Cochiti; situated about 12 m. N. W. of Cochiti pueblo, in the Potrero Viejo, N. Mex.
Há-nut Cochití.—Lummis in Scribner's Monthly, 100, 1893.

Hapaluya. A former large village in upper Florida, visited by De Soto in 1539.—Gentl. of Elvas (1557) in French, Hist. Coll. La., II, 133, 1850.

Hapanyi. The Oak clans of the Keresan pueblos of Laguna, Acoma, Sia, San Felipe, and Cochiti, N. Mex. The Oak clan of Laguna claims to have come originally from Rio Grande pueblos, by way of Mt Taylor, and to form a phratry with the Mokaich (Mountain Lion) clan; while that of Acoma claims phratral relationship with the Showwiti (Parrot) and Tanyi (Calabash) clans. The Oak clan of Sia is extinct. (F. W. H.)
Hápai-hánoᶜʰ.—Hodge in Am. Anthrop., IX, 351, 1896 (Laguna form; *hánoch* = 'people'). **Hápan-háno.**—Ibid. (Sia form). **Ha-pan-ñi.**—Stevenson in 11th Rep. B. A. E., 19, 1894 (Sia form). **Hápanyi-háno.**—Hodge, op. cit. (San Felipe form). **Hápanyi-hánoqᶜʰ.**—Ibid. (Acoma form). **Hápanyi-hánuch.**—Ibid. (Cochiti form).

Hapes. A small tribe found by Spanish explorers on the lower Rio Grande in the vicinity of Eagle Pass, Tex., although Uhde (1861) places it near Lampazos, in Nueva Leon, Mexico, some distance farther W. They numbered 490 in 85 huts in 1688, but an epidemic of smallpox raged among them soon afterward, and in 1689 the survivors were attacked by coast Indians and exterminated, with the exception of some boys who were carried off. (J. R. S.)
Apes.—Fernando del Bosque (1675) in Nat. Geog. Mag., XIV, 9, 347, 1903. **Apis.**—Manzanet (1689) in Tex. Hist. Ass. Quar., II, 25, 1898. **Hapes.**—De León (1689), ibid., VIII, 205, 1905. **Iapies.**—Linschoten, Descr. de l'Amér., map, 1, 1638. **Japies.**—De Laet, Hist. Nouv. Monde, 234, 1640. **Jeapes.**—Fernando del Bosque, op. cit. **Xapes.**—Uhde, Länder, 121, 1861. **Xapies.**—Navarette, Memorial y Noticias Sacras, 104, 1646.

Hapkug. A former Aleut village on Agattu id., Alaska, one of the Near id. group of the Aleutians, now uninhabited.

Happy Hunting Ground. See *Popular fallacies*.

Haqihana ('wolves'). A local band of the Arapaho, q. v.

Haqui. A Caddoan (?) tribe, apparently in N. E. Texas, mentioned in 1687 as at war with the "Cœnis" or main body of the Caddo confederacy. Perhaps the Adai.
Aquis.—Joutel (1687) in Margry, Déc., III, 409, 1878. **Hakesians.**—Hennepin, New Discov., 41, 1698. **Haquis.**—Douay (1687) quoted by Shea, Discov. Miss. Val., 217, 1852.

Harahey. One of the various forms of the name of a province of which Coronado, while among the New Mexico pueblos in 1540–41, learned from a native thereof who said that it lay beyond Quivira (the Wichita country of E. central Kansas), and contained much gold. This Indian, who was known as The Turk (q. v.) and who served as a guide to Coronado's army, became a traitor to the Spaniards by leading them astray on the buffalo plains of Texas. After 12 days' journey from Pecos r. in New Mexico the Spaniards, then on the Staked plain, were informed by The Turk that Haxa, or Haya, was one or two days' journey toward sunrise. A party was sent forward to find it, and although settlements of Indians were found, amongst them Cona, occupied by the Teya (Texas?), Haxa does not appear to have been reached; it is therefore possible that Haxa, or Haya, is but another form of Harahey, which was far N. of where the Spaniards then were. Arriving at Quivira, Coronado learned more of Harahey, which was the next province beyond. The Spaniards did not visit it, but sent for their chief, named Tatarrax, who came with 200 warriors, "all naked, with bows, and some sort of things on their heads." From the characteristic headdress of The Turk and the other members of the tribe, and their proximity and apparent relationship with the Quivira, or Wichita, the Harahey people may have been the Pawnee, and their habitat at this date (1542) in the vicinity of Kansas r. in E. Kansas. See Brower, Quivira, 1898; Hodge, Coronado's March, in Brower, Harahey, 1899; Winship, Coronado Exped., 14th Rep. B. A. E., 1896. (F. W. H.)
Araal.—Barcia, Ensayo, 21, 1723. **Arache.**—Jaramillo (after 1542) in 14th Rep. B. A. E., 588, 1896. **Arae.**—Rel. del Suceso (ca. 1542), ibid., 577, 1896. **Arahei.**—Jaramillo, op. cit. **Arche.**—Castañeda (ca. 1565) in 14th Rep. B. A. E., 503, 1896. **Axa.**—Gomara (1553) quoted by Winship in 14th Rep. B. A. E., 492, 1896. **Axaas.**—Volney, America, map, 1804. **Axas.**—Güssefeld, Charte Nord America, 1797. **Harae.**—Herrera, Historia, VI, 206, 1728. **Harahey.**—Jaramillo, op. cit., 590. **Harale.**—Rel. del Suceso, op. cit. **Harall.**—Doc. of 1541 in Doc. Inéd., XIV, 325, 1870. **Haxa.**—Castañeda (ca. 1565) in 14th Rep B. A. E., 505, 1896. **Haya.**—Ibid. **Hurall.**—Bancroft, Ariz. and N. Mex., 51, 1889. **Xaqueuira.**—Galvano (1563) in Hakluyt Soc. Publ., XXX, 227, 1862 (apparently Axa and Quivira confused).

Harames. A former tribe of Coahuila, N. E. Mexico, gathered into the mission of San Juan Bautista.   Probably of Coahuiltecan stock.

Jarames.—Morfi (1777) quoted by Bancroft, Nat. Races, I, 612, 1886.   **Xarames.**—Revillagigedo (1793) quoted by Bancroft, ibid., 611.

Harasgna.   A former Gabrieleño rancheria in Los Angeles co., Cal.—Ried (1852) quoted by Taylor in Cal. Farmer, June 8, 1860.

Hard-mush.   See *Big-mush.*

Harooka (*Näyuhäru′kĕñ,* 'forked reed.—Hewitt).   A Tuscarora village in North Carolina in 1701.—Lawson (1709), Carolina, 383, 1860.

Harpaha.   A former Timucua village near the mouth of St Johns r., Fla.—Laudonnière (1565) in French, Hist. Coll. La., n. s., 349, 1869.

Harpoons.   Piercing and retrieving weapons with a movable head—probably the most ingenious and complicated device invented by the North American aborigines.   Before the natives came into contact with the whites, they made harpoons of wood, bone, walrus ivory, shell, stone, sinew, and hide.   The several structural parts consisted of the shaft, foreshaft, loose shaft, ice pick, head, hinge, connecting line, assembling line, main line, hand rest, eyelet, float, and detachers.   Besides these there were a multitude of accessories, such as stools, decoys, ice scoops, and canoes.   The technic of every part represented the Indian's best skill in a number of handicrafts—wood working, bone and ivory carving, chipping and grinding stone; shredding, twisting, and braiding sinew; and dressing hides or floats, canoes, and the toughest possible thongs or lines, and other parts.

There are two quite different varieties of harpoons, based on the shape of the head—the barbed harpoon and the toggle harpoon.   The head of the barbed harpoon is attached to the shaft by means of a connecting line tied to the butt or tang of the head.   The toggle head is attached to the line or sling by means of a hole bored through the body; the head is driven entirely into the animal, and, toggling under the skin, gives firm hold.   These two types merge into each other, and some harpoons possess the characteristics of both.

The parts of a barbed harpoon are:

Head.—Of various materials, the specific characters being the same as those of barbed arrows; they differ in that the tang fits loosely into a socket and is roughened, notched, or pierced for the hingeing or connecting line.

BARBED-HEAD HARPOON; WESTERN ESKIMO

Foreshaft.—That of the harpoon, as compared with the arrow, is heavier, and has a socket in front for the wedge-shaped, conical, or spindle-shaped tang of the head.

Shaft.—Length, from a few inches to many feet; thickness, from one-fourth of an inch to an inch or more; outer end spliced or socketed to the foreshaft; center of gravity furnished with hand rest; inner end pointed, pitted for hook of throwing stick, notched for a bowstring, with or without feathers, or furnished with ice pick.

Connecting line.—Of string or thong rudely tied to head and shaft or, in the finest specimens, attached at one end through a hole in the tang, the other end being bifurcated and fastened like a martingale to the ends of the shaft.   When the animal is struck by the hurled harpoon the head is withdrawn, the foreshaft sinks by its gravity, and the shaft acts as a drag to impede the progress of the game (see Nat. Mus. Rep. 1900, pl. 11).

The parts of a toggle harpoon are:

Toggle head.—Consisting of body; blade of slate, chipped stone, ivory, or metal, usually fitted into a slit in front; line hole or opening through the body for the sling or leader of hide on which the toggle head hinges; line grooves channeled backward from the line hole to protect the leader; barbs projecting backward at the butt of the toggle head to catch into the flesh and make the head revolve 90 degrees, forming a T with the line; shaft socket, a conoid pit in the butt of the toggle head to receive front end of loose shaft; and leader or sling, not always separate, but

TOGGLE-HEAD HARPOON; ESKIMO

DETAIL OF TOGGLE-HEAD HARPOON; ESKIMO

when so, either spliced to the main line or joined by an ingenious detacher, which is sometimes prettily carved.

Loose shaft.—A spindle-shaped piece of ivory socketed to toggle head and foreshaft and attached as a hinge to the leader or the foreshaft. Its object is to catch the strain caused by convulsive movements in the game and to render certain the speedy detachment of the toggle head.

One of the most interesting studies in connection with harpoons is environment in relation to culture—the play between the needy and ingenious man and the resources of game, materials, and tools. In E. Greenland is found the hinged toggle by the side of old forms; in W. Greenland a great variety of types from the very primitive and coarse to those having feathers of ivory and the hooks on the shaft. In the latter area are also throwing sticks of two kinds. On the W. side of Davis strait harpoons are heavy and coarse, showing contact of the natives with whalers, especially the Ungava Eskimo examples. There also are flat types suggestive of N. Asia. From the Mackenzie r. country the harpoons are small and under the influence of the white trader. The harpoons of the Pt Barrow Eskimo are exhaustively discussed by Murdoch, and those from Pt Barrow southward by Nelson.

From Mount St Elias southward, within the timber belt, where wood is easily obtainable, harpoon shafts are longer, but all the parts are reduced to their simplest form. For example, the Ntlakyapamuk of British Columbia make the toggle heads of their two-pronged harpoons by neatly lashing the parts together and to the sennit leaders. The Makah of Washington formerly made the blade of the head from shell, but now use metal; the leader is tied to a

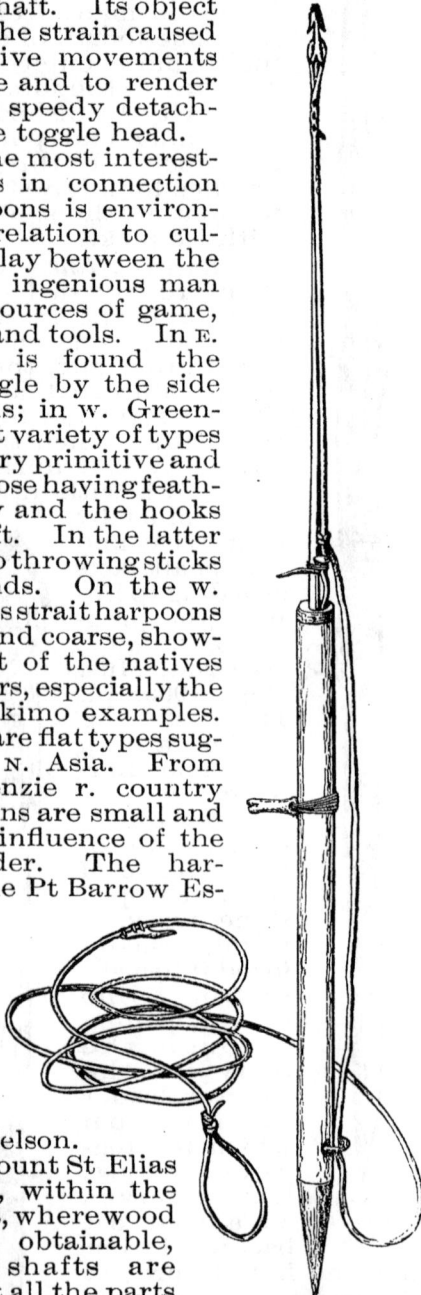

ESKIMO HARPOON MODIFIED BY CONTACT WITH WHITES

large, painted float of sealskin, the shaft being free. The Quinaielt of Washington have the bifurcated shaft, but no float. The Naltunne of Oregon have a barbed harpoon, with prongs on the blade as well as on the shank, while their cousins, the Hupa of N. California make the toggle, as do the Vancouver tribes, by attaching the parts of the head to a strip of rawhide.

See Boas in 6th Rep. B. A. E., 1888; Goddard in Publ. Univ. Cal., Am. Archæol. and Ethnol., I, no. 1, 1903; Holm, Ethnol. Skizz., 1887; Mason in Rep. Nat. Mus. 1900, 1902; Morice in Trans. Can. Inst., IV, 1895; Murdoch in 9th Rep. B. A. E., 1892; Nelson in 18th Rep. B. A. E., 1899; Niblack in Rep. Nat. Mus. 1888, 1890; Powers in Cont. N. A. Ethnol., III, 1877; Teit in Mem. Am. Mus. Nat. Hist., II, Anthrop. I, 1900; Turner in 11th Rep. B. A. E., 1894.   (O. T. M.)

Harrison River. The local name for a body of Cowichan near lower Fraser r., Brit. Col. (Can. Ind. Aff. for 1878, 78); evidently the Scowlitz, or the Chehalis, or both.

Harsanykuk (*Hársanykük*, 'saguaro cactus standing'). A Pima village at Sacaton Flats, s. Ariz.—Russell, Pima MS., B. A. E., 18, 1902.

Hartwell. An Algonquian settlement, containing 25 persons in 1884, in Ottawa co., Quebec.—Can. Ind. Aff., 1884.

Harutawaqui (*Haroñtawă''kon*, 'He holds the tree.'—Hewitt). A Tuscarora village in North Carolina in 1701.—Lawson (1709), Carolina, 383, 1860.

Hasatch ('place to the east'). A former summer village of the Lagunas, now a permanently occupied pueblo; situated 3 m. E. of Laguna pueblo, N. Mex.
Hasatch.—Loew in Wheeler Survey Rep., VII, 345, 1879. Hasátyï.—Hodge, field notes, B. A. E., 1895 (proper native name). Mesita.—Ind. Aff. Rep. 1904, 256, 1905 ('little mesa': common Spanish name). Mesita Negra.—Hodge (after Pradt) in Am. Anthrop., IV, 346, 1891 (Span.: 'little black mesa').

Hashkushtun (*Ha'-ckŭc-tŭn*). A former Takelma village on the s. side of Rogue r., Oreg.—Dorsey in Jour. Am. Folk-lore, III, 235, 1890.

Haslinding. A small Hupa village, recently deserted, on the E. side of Trinity r., Cal., at the mouth of a creek of the same name, 3 m. s. of Hupa valley.   (P. E. G.)
Has-lintah.—Gibbs in Schoolcraft, Ind. Tribes, III, 139, 1853. Hass-lin'-tung.—Powers in Cont. N. A. Ethnol., III, 73, 1877. Kas-lin-ta.—McKee (1851) in Sen. Ex. Doc. 4, 32d Cong., spec. sess., 194, 1853. Xaslindiñ.—Goddard, Life and Culture of the Hupa, 12, 1903.

Hasoomale. One of the Diegueño rancherias represented in the treaty of 1852 at Santa Isabel, s. Cal.—H. R. Ex. Doc. 76, 34th Cong., 3d sess., 133, 1857.

Hassanamesit ('at the place of small stones.'—Gookin). A village of Christian Indians established in 1654 at Grafton, Worcester co., Mass., in Nipmuc territory.

The last of the pure Indians died about 1825, but in 1830 there were still 14 persons there of mixed Indian and negro blood. It was the third of the praying towns "in order, dignity, and antiquity." Cf. *Hassimanisco.*　　　　　　　(J. M.)

Hasanameset.—Hubbard (1680) in Mass. Hist. Soc. Coll., 2d s, v, 544, 1815. **Hasanamoset.**—Gookin (1677) in Trans. Am. Antiq. Soc., II, 447, 1836. **Hasanemesett.**—Leverett (1677) in N. Y. Doc. Col. Hist., XIII, 513, 1881. **Hassanamasasitt.**—Salisbury (1677) ibid., 526. **Hassanamaskett.**—Writer of 1676 in Drake, Ind. Chron., 17, 1836. **Hassanamesitt.**—Gookin (1674) in Mass. Hist. Soc. Coll., 1st s., I, 184, 1806. **Hassana-misco.**—Barber, Hist. Coll. Mass., 568, 1839. **Hassanamset.**—Gookin (1677) in Trans. Am. Antiq. Soc., II, 467, 1836. **Hassanemesit.**—Rawson (1675) in Drake, Ind. Chron., 17, 1836. **Hassannamesit.**—Gookin (1677) in Trans. Am. Antiq. Soc., II, 435, 1836. **Hassenemassit.**—Harris in Mass. Hist. Soc. Coll., 1st s., IX, 198, 1804. **Hassinammisco.**—Drake, Bk. Inds., bk, 2, 51, 1848. **Hassunnimesut.**—Eliot quoted by Tooker, Algonq. Ser., x, 24, 1901. **Hessamesit.**—Writer of 1675 in Mass. Hist. Soc. Coll., 1st s., VI, 205, 1800. **Hussanamesit.**—Drake, Ind. Chron., 166, 1836.

Hassasei. A rancheria, probably Diegueño, on the coast of Lower California; it was under the mission of San Miguel de la Frontera, which was in lat. 32°.—Taylor in Cal. Farmer, May 18, 1860.

Hassimanisco. A former Indian village in Connecticut, probably near Connecticut r. In 1764 there were only 5 Indians left.—Stiles (1764) in Mass. Hist. Soc. Coll., 1st s., x, 105, 1809. Cf. *Hassanamesit.*

Hassinunga. A tribe of the Manahoac confederacy living about 1610 on the headwaters of Rappahannock r., Va.

Hasinninga.—Smith (1629), Virginia, I, 186, repr. 1819. **Hassaninga.**—Ibid., 74. **Hassiniengas.**—Boudinot, Star in the West, 126, 1816. **Hassinugas.**—Strachey (*ca.* 1612), Virginia, 104, 1849. **Hassinungaes.**—Smith, op. cit., 74.

Hastings Saw Mill. A local name for a body of Squawmish of Fraser River agency, Brit. Col.; pop. 91 in 1898, the last time the name is mentioned.

Haisting's Saw Mills.—Can. Ind. Aff. for 1889, 268. **Hastings Saw-mill.**—Ibid., 1898, 413. **Hastings Saw Mills.**—Ibid., 1886, 229.

Hastwiana ('he was a little man.'—Hewitt). A former Onondaga settlement on the site of the present village of Onondaga Valley, Onondaga co., N. Y.

Cis-twc·ah′-na.—Morgan, League Iroq., 421, 1851. **Häs-twi′-ä′-nä.**—Hewitt, inf'n, 1886 (Onondaga form). **Touenho.**—Denonville (1688) in N. Y. Doc. Col. Hist., IX, 375, 1855.

Hata. A Tsawatenok village at the head of Bond sd., Brit. Col.

Hä-tä.—Dawson in Can. Geol. Surv., map, 1888.

Hataam ('rider'). A Diegueño rancheria in N. W. Lower California, near Santo Tomas mission; visited in 1867 by Wm. Gabb, who obtained a vocabulary published in Ztschr. f. Ethnologie, 1877.

Hatakfushi ('bird'). A Chickasaw clan of the Koi phratry.

Fushi.—Gatschet, Creek Migr. Leg., I, 96, 1884. **Hä-täk-fu-shi.**—Morgan, Anc. Soc., 163, 1877.

Hatawa. A former Luiseño village in the neighborhood of San Luis Rey mission, s. Cal. (Taylor in Cal. Farmer, May 11, 1860). Possibly the same as Ehutewa.

Hatchcalamocha. A former Seminole village near Drum swamp, 18 m. w. of New Mickasuky town; probably in the present Lafayette co., Fla.—H. R. Ex. Doc. 74 (1823), 19th Cong., 1st sess., 27, 1826.

Hatchets. These implements, made of iron or steel, and hafted with wood, were an important factor in the colonization of northern America, and the value of the hatchet, as well as that of the ax, was soon recognized by the natives, who obtained these tools through trade. Large numbers of hatchets and axes of both French and English manufacture are obtained from aboriginal dwelling sites. It is not known with certainty just what aboriginal implements and weapons were supplanted by the European hatchet, but it probably superseded, in large part, the grooved ax, the celt, and probably the

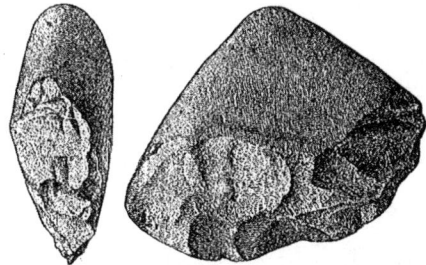

COMMON FORM OF HATCHET—A SHARPENED BOWLDER; VIRGINIA

tomahawk or war club among tribes that used these implements. So far as can be judged by the forms, the term "hatchet" may be applied with equal propriety to both the hafted ax and the hafted celt, as both were wielded usually with one hand and were equally effectual in war and in the arts of peace. So far as colonial literature refers to the uses of these implements, it would appear that the tomahawk or club, among the eastern tribes, was the weapon of war par excellence, while the ax and the celt were employed more especially in domestic work and for other ordinary industrial purposes (McCulloch). Both the hatchet and the war club doubtless rose on occasion to the dignity of ceremonial objects.

It is clear, not only from the practice of the living tribes and of primitive peoples generally, but from traces of handles remaining on both stone and copper

CELT-HATCHET WITH WOODEN HANDLE, FROM A MICHIGAN MOUND. (DODGE COLL.)

specimens obtained from the mounds, that the celt was hafted after the manner of the hatchet. An interesting group of implements showing that this was the archaic method of hafting celt-like objects, are the monolithic hatchets in which the blade and the handle are carved of a single piece of stone. Several specimens of this type are on record; one, found by

MONOLITHIC HATCHET OF GREENSTONE, FROM A TENNESSEE MOUND. LENGTH 13 1-2 IN. (JONES)

Joseph Jones, in Tennessee, is made of greenstone, and is 13½ in. in length; another, from a mound in York district, S. C., now in the National Museum, is also of greenstone; the third is from Mississippi co., Ark., and is owned by Mr Morris of that county (Thruston); the fourth, from a mound in Alabama, and now in possession of Mr C. B. Moore,

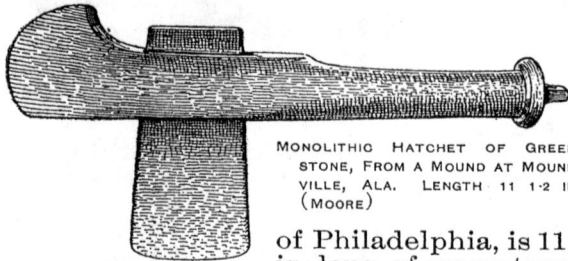

MONOLITHIC HATCHET OF GREENSTONE, FROM A MOUND AT MOUNDVILLE, ALA. LENGTH 11 1-2 IN. (MOORE)

of Philadelphia, is 11½ in. long, of greenstone, and a superb example of native lapidarian work. Specimens of this class are much more numerous in the Bahamas and the West Indies. As all are carefully finished, some being provided with a perforated knob or projection at the end of the handle for the insertion of a thong, it is probable that they served as maces or for some other ceremonial use. On the Pacific coast the stone war club sometimes took the form of a monolithic hatchet (Niblack).

The combination of the iron hatchet with the tobacco pipe as a single implement, often called the tomahawk pipe, became very general in colonial and later times, and as no counterpart of this device is found in aboriginal art, it was probably devised by the whites as a useful and profitable combination of the symbols of peace and war. To "take up the hatchet" was to declare war, and "to bury the hatchet" was to conclude peace. According to some authors the hatchet pipe was a formidable weapon in war, but in the forms known to-day it is too light and fragile to have taken the place of the stone ax or the iron hatchet. It has passed entirely out of the realm of weapons. See *Axes, Calumet, Cells, Pipes, Tomahawks.*

Consult C. C. Jones, Antiq. So. Inds., 1873; Jos. Jones, Aboriginal Remains of Tenn., 1876; McCulloch, Researches, 1829; McGuire in Rep. Nat. Mus., 1897; Moore, various memoirs in Jour. Acad. Nat. Sci. Phila., 1894–1905; Morgan, League of the Iroquois, 1904; Niblack in Rep. Nat. Mus. 1888, 1890; Thruston, Antiq. of Tenn., 1897; Wilson in Rep. Nat. Mus. 1896, 1898. (w. h. h.)

Hatcheuxhau.—A former Upper Creek village near the site of La Grange, Troup co., Ga.—Royce in 18th Rep. B. A. E., Ga. map, 1899.

Hatchichapa ('half-way creek'). A former branch settlement of the Upper Creek town Kailaidshi, between Coosa and Tallapoosa rs., Ala. Hawkins states that the Creeks hostile to the United States burned it in 1813, but it was probably rebuilt as it is mentioned in Parsons' census list of 1832 as having 62 heads of families.
Halchuchubb.—U. S. Ind. Treat. (1827), 420, 1837. **Half-way Creek.**—Gatschet, Creek Migr. Leg., I, 131, 1884. **Hatchchi chubba.**—Parsons (1832) in Schoolcraft, Ind. Tribes, IV, 578, 1854. **Hatchechubba.**—Corley (1835) in H. R. Doc. 452, 25th Cong., 2d sess., 66, 1838. **Hat-che chub-bau.**—Hawkins (1799), Sketch, 49, 1848. **Hatchechubbee.**—Creek paper (1836) in H. R. Rep. 37, 31st Cong., 2d sess., 122, 1851. **Hatch ee chub ba.**—Abbott (1832) in Schoolcraft, Ind. Tribes, IV, 580, 1854. **Hatcheechubbas.**—Simpson (1836) in H. R. Doc. 80, 27th Cong., 3d sess., 50, 1843. **Hatchi tchapa.**—Gatschet, Creek Migr. Leg., I, 131, 1884.

Hatchichapa. A township in the Creek Nation, Ind. T., near North fork of Canadian r.

Hatch Point. A local name for a body of Salish of Cowichan agency, Vancouver id.; pop. 4 in 1896, the last time reported.
Haitch Point.—Can. Ind. Aff. for 1896, 433. **Hatch Point.**—Ibid., 1883, 197.

Hatchukuni ('wolf'). A Tonkawa clan.
Hátchukuni.—Gatschet, Tonkawe MS. vocab., B. A. E., 1884.

Hathawekela. A principal division of the Shawnee, the name of which is of uncertain etymology. They emigrated from the S. about 1697, together with other Shawnee bands, and settled with them, partly on Susquehanna and partly on Allegheny r., Pa., where they are mentioned in 1731. Sewickley, Pa., probably takes its name from them. According to W. H. Shawnee, an educated member of the tribe, the proper form is Ha-ṭha-we-ke-lah, and they constitute one of the original 5 principal divisions of the Shawnee. Together with the Bicowetha (*Piqua*) and Kispokotha (*Kispococoke*) divisions they removed about 1793 to what was then Spanish territory in e. Missouri, thence into Arkansas, and in 1832 into Texas, where with other tribes they settled for a time near Saline r. Being afterward driven out by the new Texas government they removed to the present Oklahoma, where the 3 united bands are now known as

Absentee Shawnee, from having been absent from the more recent treaties made with the rest of the tribe. The Hathawekela claim to be the "elder brothers" among the Shawnee, as being the first created of the tribe. The band formerly under Black Bob (q. v.) are a portion of this division. See Halbert and Shawnee in Gulf States Hist. Mag., I, no. 6, 413–418, 1903.   (J. M.)

Asseekales.—Cartlidge (1731) in Pa. Archives, I, 305, 1852. Assekelaes.—Gordon (1731) quoted by Brinton, Lenape Legends, 32, 1885. Assiwikales.—Brinton, ibid. Asswekales.—Davenport (1731) in Pa. Archives, I, 299, 1852. Asswikales.—Gov. Pa. (1731), ibid., 302. Asswikalus.—Le Tort (1731), ibid., 300. Elder Brothers.—W. H. Shawnee, op. cit., 417. Ha-tha-we-ke-lah.—Ibid., 415. Ha-tha-we-ki-lah.—Ibid., 417.

Hathletukhish (*Haçl′-t′ŭ-qĭc′*). A former Yaquina village on the s. side of Yaquina r., Oreg.—Dorsey in Jour. Am. Folk-lore, III, 229, 1890.

Hatsi. The extinct Earth clans of Laguna and San Felipe pueblos, N. Mex. The Earth clan of Laguna claimed to have come originally from Jemez and to have formed a phratry with the Meyo (Lizard), Skurshka (Water-snake), and Shruhwi (Rattlesnake) clans.   (F. W. H.)

Háatsü-háno.—Hodge in Am. Anthrop., IX, 350, 1896 (San Felipe form: háno = 'people'). Hátsi-hánoᶜʰ.—Ibid. (Laguna form).

Hatsinawan (*hawe* 'leaves', *tsinawe* 'marks,' 'paintings', *wan* 'place of': 'town of the (fossil?) leaf-marks.'—Cushing). A ruined pueblo formerly inhabited by the Zuñi, situated N. N. W. of Hawikuh and s. w. of the present Zuñi pueblo, N. Mex.—Cushing, inf'n, 1891.

Hatschi-na-wha.—Fewkes in Jour. Am. Ethnol. and Archæol., I, 101, 1891 (probably identical).

Hatteras. An Algonquian tribe living in 1701 on the sand banks about C. Hatteras, N. C., E. of Pamlico sound, and frequenting Roanoke id. Their single village, Sandbanks, had then only about 80 inhabitants. They showed traces of white blood and claimed that some of their ancestors were white. They may have been identical with the Croatan Indians (q. v.), with whom Raleigh's colonists at Roanoke id. are supposed to have taken refuge.   (J. M.)

Hatarask.—Lane (1586) in Smith (1629), Virginia, I, 92, 1819 (place name). Hatorask.—Ibid. Hatteras Indians.—Lawson (1714), Carolina, 108, 1860.

Hauenayo. A clan of the Apohola phratry of the ancient Timucua of Florida.—Pareja (*ca.* 1614) quoted by Gatschet in Am. Philos. Soc. Proc., XVII, 492, 1878.

Haukoma. A Pomo division or band on the w. side of Clear lake, Cal., numbering 40 in 1851.

How-ku-ma.—Gibbs (1851) in Schoolcraft, Ind. Tribes, III, 109, 1853. How-ru-ma.—McKee (1851) in Sen. Ex. Doc. 4, 32d Cong., spec. sess., 136, 1853.

Hauwiyat (*Hau-wĭ-yät′*). A former Siuslaw village on or near Siuslaw r., Oreg.—Dorsey in Jour. Am. Folk-lore, III, 230, 1890.

Hauzaurni. A former Costanoan village near Santa Cruz mission, Cal.—Taylor in Cal. Farmer, Apr. 5, 1860.

Havasupai ('blue or green water people'). A small isolated tribe of the Yuman stock

HAVASUPAI MAN. (AM. MUS. NAT. HIST.)

(the nucleus of which is believed to have descended from the Walapai) who occupy Cataract canyon of the Rio Colorado in N.

HAVASUPAI WOMAN. (AM. MUS. NAT. HIST.)

w. Arizona. Whipple (Pac. R. R. Rep., III, pt. I, 82, 1856) was informed in 1850 that the "Cosninos" roamed from the

Sierra Mogollon to the San Francisco mts. and along the valley of the Colorado Chiquito. The tribe is a peculiarly interesting one, since of all the Yuman tribes it is the only one which has developed or borrowed a culture similar to, though less advanced than, that of the Pueblo peoples; indeed, according to tradition, the Havasupai (or more probably a Pueblo clan or tribe that became incorporated with them) formerly built and occupied villages of a permanent character on the Colorado Chiquito E. of the San Francisco mts., where ruins were pointed out to Powell by a Havasupai chief as the former homes of his people. As the result of war with tribes farther E., they abandoned these villages and took refuge in the San Francisco mts., subsequently leaving these for their present abode. In this connection it is of interest to note that the Cosnino caves on the upper Rio Verde, near the N. edge of Tonto basin, central Arizona, were named from this tribe, because of their supposed early occupancy by them. Their present village, composed of temporary cabins or shelters of wattled canes and branches and earth in summer, and of the natural caves and crevices in winter, is situated 115 m. N. of Prescott and 7 m. s. of the Grand canyon. The Havasupai are well formed, though of medium stature. They are skilled in the manufacture and use of implements, and especially in preparing raw material, like buckskin. The men are expert hunters, the women adept in the manufacture of baskets which, when lined with clay, serve also as cooking utensils. Like the other Yuman tribes, until affected by white influences during recent years, their clothing consisted chiefly of deerskin and, for the sake of ornament, both men and women painted their faces with thick, smooth coatings of fine red ocher or blue paint prepared from wild indigo; tattooing and scarification for ornament were also sometimes practised. In summer they subsist chiefly on corn, calabashes, sunflower seeds, melons, peaches, and apricots, which they cultivate by means of irrigation, and also the wild datila and mescal, in winter principally upon the flesh of game, which they hunt in the surrounding uplands and mountains. While a strictly sedentary people, they are unskilled in the manufacture of earthenware and obtain their more modern implements and utensils, except basketry, by barter with the Hopi, with which people they seem always to have had closer affiliation than with their Yuman kindred. Their weapons in war and the chase were rude clubs and pikes of hard wood, bows and arrows, and, formerly, slings; but firearms have practically replaced these more primitive appliances. The gentile system of descent or organization seems to be absent among the Havasupai, their society consanguineally being patriarchal. They are polygamists, the number of wives a man shall have being limited apparently only by his means for supporting them. Betrothals by purchase are common, and divorces are granted only on the ground of unfaithfulness. The Havasupai occupy a reservation of about 38,400 acres, set aside by Executive order in 1880 and 1882. Their population was 300 in 1869, 233 in 1902, 174 in 1905. (H. W. H.)

Agua Supais.—Hodge, Arizona, 169, 1877. Ah-Supai.—Bourke, Moquis of Ariz., 80, 1884. Ăk'-ba-sū'-pai.—Gilbert, Yuma vocab., B. A. E., 64, 1878 (Walapai form). Akuesú-pai.—Gatschet in Ztschr. f. Ethnol., XV, 127, 1885. Ava-Supies.—Bancroft, Ariz. and N. Mex., 547, 1889. Avĕsúpai.—Gatschet, op. cit., 123. Casinos.—Ind. Aff. Rep. 1869, 91, 1870. Casnino.—Taylor in Cal. Farmer, Mar. 27, 1863. Co-a-ni-nis.—Powell in Scribner's Mag., 213, Dec. 1875. Cochineans.—Emory, Recon., 96, 1848 (trans. 'dirty fellows'). Cochnichnos.—Bartlett, Pers. Narr., II, 178, 1854. Coçoninos.—Cushing in Atlantic Mo., 544, Oct. 1882. Cohoninos.—Bourke, Moquis of Ariz., 80, 1884. Cojnino.—Sitgreaves, Expedition, 15, 1853 (name by which a Havĕsúpai called himself). Cojonina.—Scott in Donaldson, Moqui Pueblo Inds., 52, 1893. Cominas.—Vargas (1692), cited by Davis, Span. Conq. N. Mex., 370, 1869. Cominos.—Browne, Apache Country, 290, 1869 (mentioned as a branch of Gila Apache). Coninas.—Rivera, Diario y Derrotero, leg. 950, 1736. Conninos.—Pumpelly, Across America and Asia, map, 1870. Cosninas.—Garcés (1776), Diary, 472, 1900. Cosninos.—Whipple, Pac. R. R. Rep., III, pt.I, 82, 1856. Cuesninas.—Garcés (1776), Diary, 445, 1900 (erroneously said to be Maricopa name for Mohave). Cuismer.—Orozco y Berra, Geografía, 59, 1864 (misquoting Garcés). Cuisnurs.—Garcés (1776), Diary, 446, 1900. Culisnisna.—Ibid., 473 (erroneously said to be applied to Mohave). Culisnurs.—Ibid. (erroneously said to be applied to the Mohave). Habasopis.—Gibbs, MS. map of Colorado tribes, B. A. E., no. 282. Haha-vasu-pai.—James, Inds. Painted Desert, 195, 199, 1903 ('people of the blue water'). Havasopi.—Thomas, MS., no. 602, B. A. E., 1868. 'Havasua Pai.—Ewing in Great Divide, 203, Dec. 1892. Ha-va-su-pai.—Cushing in Atlantic Mo., L, 374, Sept. 1882. Hava-su-pay.—Bandelier in Arch. Inst. Papers, IV, 366, 1892. Havesu-pai.—Ewing, op. cit. 'Havisua Pai.—Ibid. Jabesúa.—Garcés (1776), Diary, 340, 1900. Java Supais.—Baxter in Harper's Mag., June 1882. Javeusa.—Escudero, Noticias de Chihuahua, 228, 1834 (misquoting Garcés). Kochninakwe.—ten Kate, Reizen in N. A., 300, 1885 (Zuñi name: 'Piñon nut people'?). Kochoníno.—Ibid., 259. Ko'-hni'-na.—Gilbert, Yuma vocab., B. A. E., 64, 1878 (Hopi name). Kóhonino.—Voth, Traditions of the Hopi, 19, 1905 (Hopi name). Kokoninos.—Gatschet in Zeitschr. f. Ethnol., XVIII, 97, 1886. Kónino.—Ibid., xv, 124, 1883 (Hopi name). Koχ-nina'kwe.—ten Kate, Synonymie, 7, 1884 (Zuñi name, borrowed from the Hopi). Kóχniname.—Ibid. (Hopi name). Kúchnikwe.—ten Kate, Reizen in N. A., 300, 1885 (Zuñi name: 'Piñon nut people'?). Kuhni kwe.—Cushing in Atlantic Mo., L, 362, Sept. 1882 (Zuñi name; kwe='people'). Ku'h-nis.—Escudero, Noticias de Chihuahua, 228, 1834 (misquoting Garcés, 1776). Kúχni-kue.—Gatschet in Zeitschr. f. Ethnol., XV, 124, 1883 (Zuñi name). Nation of the Willows.—Cushing in Atlantic Mo., L, 362, 541, 1882. Nävĕsú-pai.—Gatschet, op. cit., XV, 127, 1883 (a Walapai form). People of the Willows.—Powell in 3d Rep. B. A. E., XIX, 1884. Supais.—Cushing in Atlantic Mo., 544, Oct. 1882 (after "Arizona Miner"). Supies.—Hinton, Handbook to Arizona, 353, 1878. Supis.—Orozco y Berra, Geografía, 59, 386, 1864 (erroneously given as part of Faraon Apache). Suppai.—Ind. Aff. Rep., lxxxi, 1886. **Tonto Cosnino.**—Möllhausen, Tagebuch, II, 196, 1858. **Yabipais Jabesua.**—Garcés (1776), Diary, 414, 1900. **Yavai Suppai.**—Arthur (1882) in Ind Aff. Rep., 297, 1886. **Yavipai Jabesua.**—Bandelier in Arch. Inst. Papers, III, 112, 1890 (after Garcés). **Yavipai javesua.**—Orozco y Berra, Geog., 41, 1864 (after Garcés). **Yuva-Supai.**—Corbusier in Am. Antiq., 276, Sept. 1886.

Haverstraw (Dutch: *haverstroo*, 'oatstraw'). The name applied by the Dutch to a small tribe or band (according to Ruttenber, a division) of the Unami Delawares, formerly living on the w. bank of the lower Hudson, in Rockland co., N. Y. The name they applied to themselves is lost, but it may have been Reweghnome or Rumachenanck.

Haverstraw.—Van Couwenhoven (1664) in N. Y. Doc. Col. Hist., XIII, 364, 1881. **Haverstroo.**—De Laet (1633) quoted by Ruttenber, Tribes Hudson R., 71, 1872. **Rewechnongh.**—Treaty of 1664 in N. Y. Doc. Col. Hist., XIII, 375, 1881 ('Rewechnongh or Haverstraw'). **Rumachenanck.**—Treaty of 1660, ibid., 147 (apparently given as the tribal name).

Hawai. A former Diegueño rancheria under the Dominican mission of San Miguel de la Frontera, w. coast of Lower California, about 30 m. s. of San Diego, Cal. (A. S. G.)

Hawaiian influence. The establishment of the whale and seal fisheries of the N. Pacific coast led to the presence in that region of sailors and adventurers of the most diverse races and nationalities, many of whom came into more or less lasting contact with the natives of the country. Toward the middle of the 19th century (Hale, Oregon Trade Language, 19, 1890) the Hawaiian language was spoken by about 100 Sandwich Islanders employed as laborers about Ft Vancouver, Wash. Doubtless some intermixture of these with the Indians took place. In 1891 there lived among the Kutenai an Indian nicknamed Kanaka. Murdoch (9th Rep. B. A. E., 55, 1892) notes that several Hawaiian words have crept into the jargon as used by the western Eskimo and white whalers and traders who come into contact with them, and one or two of these words have even come to be employed by the Pt Barrow Eskimo among themselves; but there is no evidence that the Chinook jargon contains a Hawaiian element. Swanton suggests that it is barely possible that the Haida custom of tattooing may have come from some Polynesian island, as its introduction is always said by the natives to be recent. Whether the idea of a ladder made of a chain of arrows, which occurs among the myths of Polynesians and the people of the N. W. coast, could have had a similar origin may be doubted, but it is nevertheless possible. The theory of Polynesian-American contact has been maintained by Ratzel, Schultz, and others, stress being laid on resemblances in art as exemplified by clubs, masks, etc., and in other ways. (A. F. C.)

Hawikuh (*hawe* 'leaves', *wiku* 'gum'). A former pueblo of the Zuñi and one of the Seven Cities of Cibola of early Spanish times, situated about 15 m. s. w. of the present Zuñi pueblo, N. Mex., near the summer village of Ojo Caliente. Hawikuh was seen in 1539 by Fray Marcos de Niza, who viewed it from an adjacent height a few days after the murder, by the Zuñi of Hawikuh, of Estevanico, the former negro companion of Cabeza de Vaca. Fray Marcos referred to it by the name of Ahacus. In the following year Francisco Vasquez Coronado visited the pueblo with his advance guard, and as its inhabitants offered resistance, the village was stormed and captured, most of its people fleeing for safety to Taaiyalone, a mesa E. of the present Zuñi. Coronado referred to Hawikuh, under the name Granada, as the chief pueblo of Cibola, containing about 200 houses, and from there wrote his account of the journey to the viceroy Mendoza, Aug. 15, 1540. A Franciscan mission was established at Hawikuh in 1629, at which time the pueblo contained about 110 houses. Owing to Navaho or Apache depredations in Oct., 1670, when many of the Zuñi as well as the missionary of Hawikuh were killed, the pueblo was abandoned and never afterward permanently occupied. It is said that the roof timbers of the old church at Zuñi, which was erected about 1705, were those used previously in the Hawikuh chapel. A portion of the adobe walls of the latter building were still standing until about 1894, when the adobes were taken by the Indians to Ojo Caliente and there used in the construction of new houses. See Mindeleff in 8th Rep. B. A. E., 80, 1891; Bandelier (1) Final Rep., pts. I, II, 1890, 1892; (2) Doc. Hist. Zuñi Tribe, 1892; Cushing in 13th Rep. B. A. E., 1896; Hodge in Am. Anthrop., VIII, 142, 1895. (F. W. H.)

Abacu.—Heylyn, Cosmog., 968, 1703. **Abacus.**—Blaeu, Atlas, XII, first map, 1667. **Aguas Calientes.**—Bandelier in Arch. Inst. Papers, III, 133, 1890 (Ha-ui-cu, or). **Aguascobi.**—Zarate - Salmeron (ca. 1629) quoted by Bandelier in Mag. West. Hist., 663, 1886. **Aguico.**—Cushing in Millstone, IX, 20, Feb. 1884 (misquoting Coronado). **Aguicobi.**—Oñate (1598) in Doc. Inéd., XVI, 133, 1871. **Aguscobi.**—Ibid., 132. **Ahacus.**—Niça (1539) in Hakluyt, Voy., 443, 1600. **Apacus.**—Davis, Span. Conq. N. Mex., 128, 1869 (misquoting Marcos de Niza). **Aquico.**—Espejo (1583) in Doc. Inéd., XV, 118, 181, 1871. **Auuico.**—MS. of 1676 quoted by Bandelier in Arch. Inst. Papers, IV, 338, 1892. **Aviou.**—Cushing in Compte-rendu Internat. Cong. Am., VII, 156, 1890 (given as an early Spanish form). **Cibola.**—Castañeda (ca. 1565) in 14th Rep. B. A. E., 483, 1896. **Granada.**—Coronado (1540) in Hakluyt, Voy., III, 449, 451, 1600. **Granade.**—Gomara, Hist. Gen., 467b, 1606. **Granado.**—Purchas, Pilgrimes, 648, 1613; v, 853, 1626. **Granata.**—Coronado (1540) in Ramusio, Nav. et Viaggi, 361, 363, 1565. **Grenada.**—Simpson in Smithson. Rep. 1869, 330, 1871. **Grenade.**—Sanson, map l'Amérique, 28, 1657. **Hahauien.**—Peet in Am. Antiq., XVII, 352, 1895 (misprint). **Ha Huico.**—Zarate-Salmeron (1629) cited by Bancroft, Ariz. and N. Mex., 154, 1889 (Havico or). **Haicu.**—

Bandelier in Arch. Inst. Papers, IV, 326, 1892 (misprint). **Ha-ui-ca.**—Bandelier quoted in Arch. Inst. Rep., V, 43, 1884. **Ha-ui-cu.**—Bandelier in Revue d'Ethnog., 202, 1886. **Havico.**—Zarate-Salmeron (*ca.* 1629), Relacion, in Land of Sunshine, 47, Dec. 1899. **Ha-vi-cu.**—Bandelier in Mag. West. Hist., 668, Sept. 1886. **Ha-wi-k'hu.**—Cushing in Millstone, X, 4, Jan. 1885. **Há-wi-k'uh.**—Ibid., 19, Feb. 1884. **Há-wi-k'uh-ians.**—Ibid., 20 (=the people of Hawikuh). **Ha-wi-kuhs.**—Powell, 2d Rep. B. A. E., XXVII, 1883. **Hay-way-ku.**—Fewkes in Jour. Am. Ethnol. and Archæol., I, 100, 1891. **Hay-we-cu.**—Ibid., map. **Jahuicu.**—Escalante (1778) quoted by Bandelier in Arch. Inst. Papers, IV, 257, 1892. **Kuikawkuk.**—Peet in Am. Antiq., XVII, 352, 1895 (misprint). **La Concepcion de Aguico.**—Vetancurt (1693) in Teatro Mex., 320, 1871. **Nueua Granada.**—Galvano (1563) in Hakluyt Soc. Publ., XXX, 227, 1862. **Nueva Granada.**—Barcia, Ensayo, 21, 1723. **Ojo-caliente.**—Alcedo, Dic. Geog., III, 370, 1788 (doubtless identical). **Rosa Hawicuii.**—Villaseñor misquoted by Bancroft, Ariz. and N. Mex., 252, 1889 (confused with Abiquiu). **Santa Rosa de Hauicui.**—Alcedo, Dic. Geog., II, 355, 1787. **Santa Rosa Havicuii.**—Villaseñor, Theatro Am., pt. 2, 413, 1748. **Tzibola.**—Mota-Padilla (1742), Hist. Nueva España, 111, 1871. **Zibola.**—Perea, Verdadera Rel., 4, 1632.

Hawmanao (*Xámanáô*).   A gens of the Quatsino, a Kwakiutl tribe.—Boas in Rep. Nat. Mus. for 1895, 329.

Hayah (*Hä-yäh*).   The Snake clan of the Pecos tribe of New Mexico.—Hewett in Am. Anthrop., VI, 439, 1904.

Head deformation.   See *Artificial head deformation.*

Heakdhetanwan (*Hé-aɲŧĕ taⁿwaⁿ'*).   An ancient Osage village on Spring cr., a branch of Neosho r., Indian Ter.—Dorsey, Osage MS. vocab., B. A. E., 1883.

Health and Disease. There is little evidence to show what diseases prevailed among the Indians N. of Mexico prior to the advent of white people. The traditions of the Indians, the existence among them of elaborate healing rites of undoubtedly ancient origin, their plant-lore, in which curative properties are attributed to many vegetal substances, and the presence among them of a numerous class of professed healers, honored, feared, and usually well paid, would seem to indicate that diseases were not rare, but actual knowledge and even tradition as to their nature are wanting. The condition of the skeletal remains, the testimony of early observers, and the present state of some of the tribes in this regard, warrant the conclusion that on the whole the Indian race was a comparatively healthy one. It was probably spared at least some of the epidemics and diseases of the Old World, such as smallpox and rachitis, while other scourges, such as tuberculosis, syphilis (precolumbian), typhus, cholera, scarlet fever, cancer, etc., were rare, if occurring at all. Taking into consideration the warlike nature of many of the tribes and the evidence presented by their bones (especially the skulls), injuries, etc., particularly those received by offensive weapons, must have been common, although fractures are less frequent than among white people.

At the time of the discovery the Indians on the whole were probably slowly increasing in numbers. Frequent wars, however, had a marked effect in limiting this increase. Since their contact with whites most of the tribes have gradually diminished in strength, while some of the smaller tribes have disappeared entirely. Very few tribes have shown an increase or even maintained their former numbers. The most remarkable example of steady gain is the Navaho tribe. The causes of decrease were the introduction of diseases (particularly smallpox), the spread of alcoholism, syphilis, and especially tuberculosis, destructive wars with the whites, and increased mortality due to changes in the habits of the people through the encroachment of civilization. During recent years a slow augmentation in population has been noticed among a number of tribes, and as more attention is paid to the hygienic conditions of the Indians, an increase comparable to that in whites may be expected in many sections. The least hopeful conditions in this respect prevail among the Dakota and other tribes of the colder northern regions, where pulmonary tuberculosis and scrofula are very common. (See *Population.*)

While preserving much of their robust constitution, the Indians—particularly those of mixed blood—are at present subject to many disorders and diseases known to the whites, although the pure bloods are still free from most of the serious morbid conditions and tendencies due to defective inheritance. They suffer little from insanity, idiocy, and rachitis. Cretinism is exceedingly rare, and general paresis, with a large number of serious nervous affections, has not yet been recorded among them. Diseases of the heart, arteries, and veins, serious affection of the liver and kidneys, as well as typhoid and scarlet fever are infrequent. Congenital malformations are very rare, although it is commonly heard among the Indians themselves that they do sometimes occur, but that the afflicted infants are not allowed to live. Fractures, and diseases of the bones in general, as well as dental caries, are less frequent than among the whites. There is considerable doubt whether cancer occurs in any form. Venereal diseases, while predominant among the more degraded Indians, are more or less effectually guarded against by others.

The most common disorders of health now experienced among Indians generally are those of the gastro-intestinal tract, which in infancy are due to improper feeding and particularly to the universal consumption of raw, unripe fruit and vegetables, and in later life to the lack of or overindulgence in food, irregular meals, the preference for fat, crudely prepared food, and, recently, the misuse of inferior baking powders and excessive use of coffee. While most of the disorders thus introduced are of a minor character, others, particularly in infants, are frequently fatal. Other more common diseases are various forms of malaria, bronchitis, pneumonia, pleurisy, and measles in the young. Whooping cough is also met with. Inflammation of the conjunctivæ is common and often leads to ulceration, opacity, and defect in or even total loss of vision. Defective hearing is occasionally found in the aged, and there are rare instances of deaf mutes. Eczema, favus, and acnæ are among the more ordinary affections of the skin. Tuberculosis of the lungs, and glandular tuberculosis, or scrofula, are frequent in many localities and are especially common among the reservation Indians in the colder parts of the United States, particularly in North Dakota, South Dakota, and Montana, due to their present mode of life. They live in small, insanitary hovels, which in cold weather are ill ventilated and often overheated and crowded, while their dress is heavier than formerly, their daily life less active, their food changed, and, what is most important, there is complete ignorance of the contagious nature of consumption. Some of these conditions, however, are being gradually bettered.

Goiter is widely distributed, though seldom prevalent; it is found particularly among some bands of the Sioux, and it occurs also with some frequency among the Menominee, Oneida, Crows, and White Mountain Apache. Albinism occurs among a number of the tribes; the cases, however, are quite isolated, except among the Hopi and to a lesser degree the Zuñi. In 1903 there were 12 cases of albinism in the former and 4 in the latter tribe, all of the complete variety. Vitiligo is much more scattered, but the cases are few. Diseases and functional disturbances peculiar to women, including those of the puerperium, are much less common among Indians than among the white women of this country. Of diseases peculiar to old age, senile arthritis, which affects particularly the spine, and occasional dementia, are found. Senility proceeds slowly in the pure-blood Indian, and the number of individuals above 80 years of age, according to census returns (which, however, should be regarded with caution), is relatively greater than among the whites. See *Anatomy, Physiology.*

Consult Bancroft, Native Races (with bibliographical references), I–V, 1882; Hrdlicka, Physiological and Medical Observations Among the Indians (with bibliography), Bull. 33, B. A. E., 1906; Jesuit Relations, Thwaites ed., I–LXXIII, 1896–1901; Josselyn, New-England's Rarities (1672), repr. 1865; Reports of the Commissioner of Indian Affairs; Report on Indians, Eleventh U. S. Census (1890), 1894; Schoolcraft, Indian Tribes, I–VI, 1851–57.   (A. H.)

Heashkowa. A prehistoric pueblo of the Red Corn (Kukinish-yaka) clan of Acoma, situated at the foot of a mesa about 2 m. s. E. of the present Acoma pueblo, N. Mex. According to tradition it was built by the Red Corn clan when the tribe entered its present valley from the N. and settled at Tapitsiama. It is said that when the village was abandoned some of the inhabitants joined the main body of the tribe while the remainder migrated southward.   (F. W. H.)

Hebron. A Moravian Eskimo mission, founded in 1830, on the E. Labrador coast, lat. 58°.—Hind., Lab. Penin., II, 199, 1863.

Hecatari. A former Nevome pueblo of Sonora, Mexico, with 127 inhabitants in 1730; situated probably at or near the junction of the w. branch of the Rio Yaqui with the main stream, about lat. 28° 30′. Orozco y Berra classes it as a pueblo of the upper Pima.

Hecatari.—Rivera (1678) quoted by Bancroft, No. Mex. States, I, 513, 1884. Hecatazi.—Orozco y Berra, Geog., 347, 1864.

Heda-haidagai (*Xē′daxā′-idᴀga-i*, 'people living on the low ground'). A subdivision of the Stawas-haidagai, a Haida family of the Eagle clan; named from the character of the ground on which their houses stood in the town of Cumshewa. The town chief belonged to this subdivision.—Swanton, Cont. Haida, 273, 1905.

Hediondo (Span.: 'fetid'). A Huichol rancheria about 2½ m. w. of Ratontita, in Jalisco, Mexico.—Lumholtz, Unknown Mex., II, 271, 1902.

Rancho Hediondo.—Lumholtz, ibid.

Hegan. According to Pike (N. H. Hist. Soc. Coll., III, 56, 1832) some English near Kittery, York co., Me., were attacked in 1706 "by their good friends, the Hegans." This may mean some relatives of Hogkins or Hawkins, a chief of the hostile Pennacook, formerly living in that vicinity. It can hardly mean the Mohegan, who were not hostile and who did not live in the neighborhood.   (J. M.)

Hehametawe (*Hē′ha′mē′tawē*, 'descendants of Hametawe'). A subdivision of the Laalaksentaio, a Kwakiutl gens.—Boas in Rep. Nat. Mus. for 1895, 332.

Hehlkoan ('people of Foam'). A Tlingit division at Wrangell, Alaska, belonging to the Wolf clan. They are named from a place called Foam (*Xēɫ*), close to Loring, where they lived before joining the Stikine.

Chrēlch-kōn.—Krause, Tlinkit Ind., 120, 1885. Qētlk·oan.—Boas, 5th Rep. N. W. Tribes Can., 25, 1889. Xēɫkoan—Swanton, field notes, B. A. E., 1904.

Heiltsuk (*He'-ilt-suq*). A dialect of Kwakiutl embracing the Bellabella (after whose native name it is called), the China Hat, Somehulitk, Nohunitk, and Wikeno. The number of Indians speaking the dialect was about 500 in 1904.   (J. R. S.)

Heitotowa. A Choctaw town in the Choctaw Nation, Ind. T., situated at the later Sculleville.
Hei-to-to-wee.—Möllhausen, Journey, I, 32, 1858.

Hekhalanois (*Hēχalǟ'nois*). The ancestor of a Koskimo gens, after whom it was sometimes called.—Boas in Petermanns Mitt., pt. 5, 131, 1887.

Hekpa. The Fir clan of the Honau (Bear) phratry of the Hopi.
He'k-pa.—Stephen in 8th Rep. B. A. E., 38, 1891.

Helapoonuch. A former Chumashan village situated about 15 m. from Santa Barbara mission, Cal.—Father Timeno (1856) quoted by Taylor in Cal. Farmer, May 4, 1860.

Helicopile. A village, named after a chief, on lower St Johns r., Fla., in 1564, probably belonging to Saturiwa's confederacy.
Helicopilé.—Laudonnière (1567) in French, Hist. Coll. La., n. s., 349, 1869. Hilicopile.—Gourgue (1568), ibid., 2d s., II, 280, 1875.

Helikilika. An ancestor of a gens of the Nakomgilisala tribe of Kwakiutl.—Boas in Petermanns Mitt., pt. 5, 131, 1887.

Hellelt. A Salish tribe on Chimenes r., s. w. Vancouver id., speaking the Cowichan dialect; pop. 28 in 1904.
Hal-alt.—Can. Ind. Aff., 308, 1879. Haltalt.—Ibid., 79, 1878. Hel-alt.—Ibid., 1883, pt. I, 190. Hellal.—Ibid., 1892, 313. Hel-lalt.—Ibid., 1889, 269. Hellelt.—Ibid., 1901, pt. II, 164. Qalǟ'ltq.—Boas, MS., B. A. E., 1887.

Hello (*Hĕl-lo'*). A former Chumashan village on Mooris id., w. of Santa Barbara, Cal.—Henshaw, Buenaventura MS. vocab., B. A. E., 1884.

Helshen ('sandy beach'; lit., 'soft to the foot'). A Squawmish village community on Burrard inlet, Brit. Col.
Hĕlcen.—Hill-Tout in Rep. Brit. A. A. S., 475, 1900.

Heluta. A former Cholovone village in San Joaquin co., Cal., near San Joaquin r.—Pinart, Cholovone MS., B. A. E., 1880.

Hematite. An iron ore much used by the native tribes for implements, ornaments, and small objects of problematical use. It is found in many parts of the country and in great abundance in the Iron Mountain district of Missouri and in the Marquette region of Michigan. It occurs as a massive ore, as nodules, and in other forms, distributed through rocks of various classes, and is usually dark in color, showing various shades of gray, brown, and red. The specular varieties are generally rather gray, and have a metallic luster. The red, earthy varieties, when compact, are known as red chalk, and when much disintegrated and pulverulent, as red ocher. They were, and are, much used as paint by the aborigines, and small quantities, either in lumps or as powder, are commonly found in ancient graves, placed there for personal embellishment in the future existence. The highly siliceous varieties are often very hard, heavy, and tough, and make excellent implements. They were used especially in the manufacture of celts, axes, scrapers, etc., and for the rudely shaped hammers and sledges that served in mining work, as in the iron mines at Leslie, Mo. (Holmes). Many of the celts and celt-like implements are quite small, and in some cases probably served as amulets. Grooved axes of this material are of somewhat rare occurrence, but objects of problematical use, such as cones, hemispheres, and plummets, are common, and on account of their high finish, richness of color, and luster, are much prized by collectors. Hematite objects are found in mounds and on dwelling sites in the middle Mississippi valley region, in the Ohio valley, and extending into E. Kentucky and Tennessee to w. North Carolina, and to a limited extent in the S., in the Pueblo country, and on the Pacific coast. A small, well-shaped figure of this material, representing a bird, and neatly inlaid with turquoise and white shell, is among the collections obtained by Pepper from the Pueblo Bonito ruin, New Mexico. Hematite is not always readily distinguishable from limonite (which is generally yellowish or brownish in tint), and from some other forms of iron ore. See *Mines and Quarries.*

References to hematite objects are widely distributed throughout the literature of American archeology. Among others the following authors may be consulted: Douglass in Bull. Am. Mus. Nat. Hist., VIII, 1896; Fewkes (1) in 17th Rep. B. A. E., 730, 1898, (2) in 21st Rep. B. A. E., 77, 1903; Fowke in 13th Rep. B. A. E., 1896; Holmes in Smithson. Rep. 1903, 1904; Moorehead, Prehist. Impls., 1900; Pepper in Am. Anthrop., VII, 195, 1905.   (W. H. H.)

Hembem. A former Maidu village on the E. side of North fork of American r., about 6 m. s. E. of Colfax, Placer co., Cal.—Dixon in Bull. Am. Mus. Nat. Hist., XVII, pl. XXXVIII, 1905.

Hemispheres, Spheres. Small objects, usually of polished stone, the use of which has not been fully determined; they are therefore classed with problematical objects. The more typical forms, found in the mounds, are often of hematite and, like the cones, rarely exceed a few ounces in weight. Hemispheres are comparatively numerous, but spheres referable to this group are rare. Hammerstones and stones used as club-heads (see *Clubs, Hammers*) are often spherical, but usually they are not well finished, and occasionally large cannonball-like stones are found which can not be properly classed with the smaller polished objects. The base of the hemispheres is flat, rarely slightly hollowed out, and varies from a circle to a decided ellipse, while the vertical section departs considerably from a true semicircle. Typical objects of this group are most plentiful in the middle Ohio valley. It is surmised that they served in playing some game, as talismans or charms, or for some special shamanistic purpose. According to Grinnell (inf'n, 1906) small balls of stone are still used by some Plains tribes in a game. Little girls roll them on the ice in winter, trying to move a small stick resting on the ice in front of the opposing party, perhaps 20 ft distant. If the stick is touched and moved, the side which rolls the ball may roll it again, and a point is counted. If the stick is not moved, the ball is rolled by one of the opposing party who endeavors to move the stick which rests on the ice in front of her opponent.

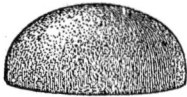

HEMISPHERE OF HEMATITE; WEST VIRGINIA. (1-3)

A small stone sphere was used by the Pima of Arizona in a kicked ball game, and numerous small spheres, usually of soft stone, are found in prehistoric ruins in Salt river valley of the same territory.

Consult Rau in Smithson. Cont., XXII, 1877; Fowke (1) in 13th Rep. B. A. E., 1896, (2) Archæol. Hist. Ohio, 1902; Hrdlicka in Am. Anthrop., VIII, no. 1, 1906; Moorehead, Prehist. Impls. 1900; Cushing in Compte-rendu Internat. Cong. Am., VII, 178, 1890.   (W. H. H.)

Hemptown (translation of the native name, *Gatûñ'lti'yĭ*). A former Cherokee settlement on a creek of the same name, near the present Morganton, Fannin co., Ga.—Mooney in 19th Rep. B. A. E., 519, 1900.

Henaggi. An Athapascan tribe or band residing, according to Powers (Cont. N. A. Ethnol., III, 65, 1877), on Smith r., Cal. A treaty was made with them Aug. 17, 1857. It is said they were exceedingly hostile to the neighboring bands to whom they were related, but this hostility was probably only a temporary feud. They are seemingly extinct.
Engnas.—Ind. Aff. Rep. 1856, 219, 1857 (possibly identical). Hanags.—Taylor in Cal. Farmer, June 8, 1860. Haynaggi.—Keane in Stanford, Compend., 665, 1878. Haynargee.—Gibbs, letter to Hazen, B. A. E., 1856. Hay-narg-ger.—A. W. Hamilton, MS. vocab., B. A. E. Hé-nag-gi.—Powers in Cont. N. A. Ethnol., III, 65, 1877. Hé-narger.—Hamilton, vocab., op. cit.

Henakyalaso (*Hē'nakyalasō*). An ancestor of a gens of the Kwakiutl tribe Tlatlasikoala, after whom it was sometimes called.—Boas in Petermanns Mitt., pt. 5, 131, 1887.

Hendrick. A Mohawk chief, son of The Wolf, a Mohegan, and a Mohawk woman; often called King Hendrick. With many of his men he participated in the campaign against the French in 1755, and notwithstanding the strong tendency of Braddock's defeat in that year to draw the Indians to the side of the French, Hendrick, at the request of Gen. Johnson, joined the English army, which met 2,000 French under Gen. Dieskau at Lake George, N. Y. At the battle which there took place, Sept. 8, 1755, Hendrick and many of his followers were killed. He was then less than 70 years of age.

Henicohio. Mentioned, in connection with Puaray, apparently as a pueblo of the Tigua in New Mexico in 1598.—Oñate (1598) in Doc. Inéd., XVI, 115, 1871.

Heniocane. A former tribe in s. Texas, encountered by Fernando del Bosque in 1675 and said to number 178, including 65 warriors. They were probably related to the Coahuiltecan tribes.
Geniocane.—Fernando del Bosque (1675), in Nat. Geog. Mag., XIV, 346, 1903.

Henry, William. See *Gelelemend*.

Hens. Seemingly derived from a New England Indian cognate of Algonkin, Chippewa, and Cree *ens*, 'a shell,' especially a small shell, with which may be compared the Natick *anna* (?*anns*) and the Abnaki *als* (*l* = *n*). The early English colonists of New England by prefixing *h* formed *hens*, which they applied to the *quahaug, quahock*, or *poquahock*, 'a little thick shellfish' (*Venus mercenaria*), from an interior portion of the shell of which the New England Indians manufactured *suckauhock*, 'black or purple beads,' commonly called purple wampum. See *Wampum*.   (J. N. B. H.)

Henuti. The extinct Cloud clan of the pueblo of Sia, N. Mex.
Hĕn'-na-ti.—Stevenson in 11th Rep. B. A. E., 19, 1894. Hĕ'nüti-háno.—Hodge in Am. Anthrop., IX, 349, 1896 (*háno* = 'people').

Henya. A Tlingit tribe on the w. coast of Prince of Wales id., Alaska, between Tlevak narrows and Sumner strait; pop. 300 in 1869, 500 in 1881, 262 in 1890, and about the same in 1900. Their chief town is Klawak; other towns are Shakan and Tuxican. The social divisions of the tribe are Ganahadi, Hlkoayedi, Kakos hit tan, Kuhinedi, Shunkukedi, Takwanedi, and Tanedi.   (J. R. S.)
Anega. Mahony (1869) in Sen. Ex. Doc. 68, 41st Cong., 2d sess., 19, 1870. Genuvskoe.—Veniaminoff, Zapiski, II, pt. 3, 30, 1840. Hanaga.—Kane, Wand. N. A., app., 1859. Hanega.—11th Census, Alaska, 158, 1890. Hanieas.—Borrows in H. R. Ex. Doc. 197, 42d Cong., 2d sess., 4, 1872 (probably identical). Henja-kŏn.—Krause, Tlinkit Ind., 111, 1885. Hennĕ-gā-kŏn.—Ibid., 120. Hennegas.—Ibid., 111. Henya qoan.—Swanton, field notes, B. A. E., 1904.

Hepowwoo. A former Luiseño village in the neighborhood of San Luis Rey mission, s. Cal.—Taylor in Cal. Farmer, May 11, 1860.

Heraldry. Among the tribes of the great plains, and perhaps of other sections, there existed a well-defined system of military and family designation comparable with the heraldic system of Europe. It found its chief expression in the painting and other decoration of the shield and tipi, with the body paint and adornment of the warrior himself, and was guarded by means of religious tabu and other ceremonial regulations. The heraldic tipis, which might number one-tenth of the whole body, usually belonged to prominent families by hereditary descent. The shield belonged to the individual warrior, but several warriors might carry shields of the same origin and pattern at the same time, while so far as known the heraldic tipi had no contemporary duplicate. Both tipi and shield were claimed as the inspiration of a vision, and the design and decoration were held to be in accordance with the instructions imparted to the first maker by the protecting spirit of his dream. The tipi is commonly named from the most notable feature of the painting, as the 'buffalo tipi,' 'star tipi,' etc. The shield was more often known by the name of the originator and maker of the series, but certain more noted series were known as the 'buffalo shield,' 'bird shield,' 'sun shield,' etc., the 'medicine' or protecting power being believed to come from the buffalo, bird, or sun spirits respectively. Shields of the same origin were usually but not necessarily retained in the possession of members of the family of the original maker, and handed down in time to younger members of the family, unless buried with the owner. A certain price must be paid and certain tabus constantly observed by the owner of either shield or tipi. Thus the heir to a certain heraldic tipi in the Kiowa tribe must pay for it a captive taken in war, while those who carried the bird shield were forbidden to approach a dead bird, and were under obligation on killing their first enemy in battle to eat a portion of his heart. Those of the same shield generally used a similar body paint and headdress, pony decorations, and war cry, all having direct reference to the spirit of the original vision, but no such regulation appears to have existed in connection with any tipi. The flag carried on the upper Columbia by the followers of the prophet Smohalla is an instance of the adaptation of Indian symbolism to the white man's usage (Mooney in 14th Rep. B. A. E., 1896).

Among the Haida and some other tribes of the N. W. coast, according to Swanton and other authorities, is found the germ of a similar system. Here, in many cases, the clan totem, or perhaps the personal manito of the individual, has evolved into a crest which persons of the highest rank, i. e. of greatest wealth, are privileged to figure by carving or painting upon their totem poles, houses, or other belongings, tattooing upon their bodies, or painting upon their bodies in the dance, on payment of a sufficient number of "potlatch" gifts to secure recognition as chiefs or leading members of the tribe. The privilege is not hereditary, the successor of the owner, usually his sister's son, being obliged to make the same ceremonial payment to secure the continuance of the privilege.   (J. M.)

Hermho (*Herm'-ho*, 'once'). A Pima village on the N. side of Salt r., 3 m. from Mesa, Maricopa co., s. Ariz.—Russell, Pima MS., B. A. E., 1902.
Â'mû Â'kimûlt.—Russell, ibid.

Hero Myths. See *Mythology, Religion*.

Herring Pond. A former settlement on a reserve established for Christian Indians in 1655 at Herring Pond, Plymouth co., Mass. It is probably identical with Comassakumkanit, mentioned by Bourne in 1674, and the Indians there seem to have been considered a distinct tribe. In 1825 there were but 40 left, and these were of mixed blood.   (J. M.)

Heshokta ('ancient town of the cliffs'). A ruined pueblo, formerly inhabited by the Zuñi, on a mesa about 5 m. N. W. of Zuñi pueblo, N. Mex. Cf. *Shopakia*.
Heshohtakwin.—ten Kate, Reizen in N. A., 291, 1885 (Heshoktakwin, or). Héshokta.—Cushing, Zuñi Folk Tales, 365, 1901. Hesh-o-ta-thlu-al-la.—Fewkes in Jour. Am. Ethnol. and Archæol., I, 111, 1891.

Heshota Ayahltona ('ancient buildings above'). The ruins of a group of stone houses on the summit of Taaiyalana, or Seed mtn., commonly called Thunder mtn., about 4 m. s. E. of Zuñi pueblo, N. Mex. This mesa has been a place of refuge for the Zuñi at various periods since they have been known to history, Coronado mentioning it as such, although not by name, in 1540. In 1632, after having killed their first missionary, the Zuñi fled to the heights, remaining there until 1635. The ruined pueblo now to be seen on the summit was built probably about 1680, on the site of the ancient fortifications alluded to by Coronado, as a refuge against Spanish invasion during the Pueblo revolt of that year, when the villages in the valley below—those that remained of the Seven Cities of Cibola—were abandoned. The tribe doubtless occupied this stronghold uninterruptedly for at least 12 years during the Pueblo revolt, being found there by Vargas in 1692. In 1703 the Zuñi again fled to their mesa village, after having killed 4 Spanish soldiers. This time they remained until 1705, when they returned to the valley and began to build the pres-

ent Zuñi pueblo on a part of the site of Halona. The ruins of Heshota Ayahltona have been mistakenly regarded by some writers as the ancient Cibola, hence are often noted on maps as Old Zuñi. See Mindeleff in 8th Rep. B. A. E., 89, 1891; Bandelier (1) in Arch. Inst. Papers, III, 134, 1890; IV, 335, 1892, (2) Doc. Hist. Zuñi, in Jour. Am. Ethnol. and Archæol., III, 1892; Cushing, Zuñi Creation Myths, in 13th Rep. B. A. E., 1896; Winship, Coronado Exped., in 14th Rep. B. A. E., 1896.
(F. W. H.)
He-sho-ta A'-yathl-to-na.—Cushing, inf'n, 1891. **Mesa de Galisteo.**—Vargas (1692) quoted by Bancroft, Ariz. and N. Mex., 200, 1889 (referring to the mesa). **Old Tuni.**—Wallace, Land of Pueblos, 238, 1888 (misprint). **Old Zuñi.**—Common map form. **Tâa-ái-yal-a-na-wan.**—Cushing, inf'n, 1891 (lit. 'abiding place above on mountain-of-all-seed'). **Tâaiyá'hltona 'Hlúelawa.**—Cushing in 13th Rep. B. A. E., 429, 1896 (lit. 'towns-all-above of-the-seed-all'). **Toillenny.**—Donaldson, Moqui Pueblo Inds., 127, 1893 (refers to the mesa). **To-yo-a-la-na**—Bandelier in Arch. Inst. Papers, III, pt. 1, 134, 1890. **Zuñi Vieja.**—Domenech, Deserts, I, 211, 1860.

Heshota Hluptsina (*Héshota-'hlúp-tsina*, 'ancient village of the yellow rocks'). A prehistoric ruined stone pueblo of the Zuñi, situated between the "gateway" and the summer village of Pescado, 7 m. E. of Zuñi pueblo, N. Mex. (F. W. H.)
Heshota Ihluctzina.—Bandelier in Rev. d'Ethnog., 200, 1886 (misprint). **Hesh-o-ta-sop-si-na.**—Fewkes in Jour. Am. Ethnol. and Archæol., I, map, 1891. **Heshota Thluc-tzinan.**—Bandelier in Arch. Inst. Papers, IV, 333, 1892. **Heshotathlu'ptsina.** — ten Kate, Reizen in N. A., 291, 1885. **Village of the Yellow Rocks.**—Cushing, Zuñi Folk Tales, 104, 1901.

Heshota Imkoskwin ('ancient town surrounded by mountains'). A ruined pueblo near Tawyakwin, or Nutria, anciently occupied by the northern clans of the Zuñi.—Cushing, inf'n, 1891.
He-sho-ta Im'-k'os-kwi-a.—Cushing, inf'n, 1891 (another form). **Heshota Im-quosh-kuin.**—Bandelier in Arch. Inst. Papers, IV, 340, 1892. **Heshota Im-quosh-quin.**—Bandelier in Rev. d' Ethnog., 202, 1886. **Hesh-o-ta-inkos-qua.**—Fewkes in Jour. Am. Ethnol. and Archæol., I, 100, 1891. **Heshota Mimkuosh-kuin.**—Bandelier in Arch. Inst. Papers, IV, 340, 1892. **Hesho-ta Mimquoshk-kuin.**—Ibid., 329.

Heshota Uhla (*Héshota-ú'hla*, 'ancient town of the embrasure'). A prehistoric ruined stone pueblo of the elliptical type, supposed to be of Zuñi origin; situated at the base of a mesa on Zuñi r., about 5 m. w. of the Zuñi summer village of Ojo Pescado, or Heshotatsina, N. Mex. So named, according to Cushing, because it was embraced by hills, and by the turn of a northern trail. (F. W. H.)
Heshota Uthia.—Bandelier in Arch. Inst. Papers, IV, 22, 1892 (misprint). **Hesho-ta U-thla.**—Ibid., 329. **Heshotau'thla.**—ten Kate, Reizen in N. A., 291, 1885.

Heshque. The principal village of the Hesquiat (q. v.), on Hesquiat harbor, Vancouver id.—Can. Ind. Aff., 264, 1902.

Hespatingh. A village in 1657, probably belonging to the Unami Delawares, and apparently in N. New Jersey (Deed of 1657 in N. Y. Doc. Col. Hist., XIV, 393,

1883). A clue to the locality is given by Nelson (Inds. N. J., 124, 1894), who records Espatingh, or Ispatingh, as the name of a hill back of Bergen, or about Union Hill, in 1650.

Hesquiat. A Nootka tribe on Hesquiat harbor and the coast to the westward, Vancouver id.; pop. 162 in 1901, 150 in 1904. Their principal village is Heshque.
Esquiates.—Jewitt, Narr., 37, 1849. **He'okwiath.**—Boas in 6th Rep. N. W. Tribes Can., 31, 1890. **Hesh-que-aht.**—Can. Ind. Aff., 188, 1883. **Hesquiaht.**—Ibid., 131, 1879. **Hesquiat.**—Ibid., pt. 2, 158, 1901. **Hishquayaht.**—Sproat, Sav. Life, 308, 1868. **Hosh-que-aht.**—Can. Ind. Aff., 186, 1884.

Heuchi. A Yokuts tribe formerly living in the plains on or s. of Fresno r., N. central Cal., and on Fresno reserve in 1861, when they numbered 18.
Hawitches.—Barbour et al. (1851) in Sen. Ex. Doc. 4, 32d Cong., spec. sess , 61, 1853. **Haw-on-chee.**—Ind. Com'r Jour. (1851), ibid., 61. **Heuchi.**—A. L. Kroeber, inf'n, 1906 (correct form). **Hou-et-chus.**—Johnston (1851) in Sen. Ex. Doc. 61, 32d Cong., 1st sess., 22, 1852. **How-ach-ees.**—Barbour (1852), op. cit., 252. **How-a-chez.**—Lewis in Ind. Aff. Rep., 399, 1857. **Howchees.**—Ind. Aff. Rep., 219, 1861. **How-ech-ee.**—Royce in 18th Rep. B. A. E., 782, 1899. **How-ech-es.**—McKee (1851) in Sen. Ex. Doc. 4, 32d Cong., spec. sess., 74, 1853.

Heudao (*Xe-uda'o*, 'the village that fishes toward the south'). A Haida town of the Kaidju-kegawai on the E. side of Gull pt., Prevost id., Queen Charlotte ids., Brit. Col.—Swanton, Cont. Haida, 277, 1905.

Hevhaitanio (*Hévhaitä'nio*, 'hair men', 'fur men'; sing., *Hévhaitän*). A principal division of the Cheyenne, q. v.
Hairy-Men's band.—G. A. Dorsey in Field Columb. Mus. Pub. no. 99, 13, 1905 (also Hairy-Men band). **Hév'ä tän i u.**—Grinnell, Social Org. Cheyennes, 136, 1905 (trans. 'hairy men'). **Hev'-hai-ta-ni-o.**—Hayden, Ethnog. and Philol. Mo. Val., 290, 1862 ('hairy people'). **Hévhaitä'nio.**—Mooney, inf'n, 1905 (see p. 254 of this Handbook). **Héwä-tä'-niuw'.**—Mooney in 14th Rep. B. A. E., 1025, 1896.

Heviqsnipahis (*Heviqs'-ni''pahis*, 'aortas closed, by burning'; sing., *Heviqs'-ni'pa*). A principal division of the Cheyenne, q. v.
Aorta band—G. A. Dorsey in Field Columb. Mus. Pub., no. 99, 13, 1905. **Eví'sts-uní' pahis.**—Mooney in 14th Rep. B. A. E., 1025, 1896 (it does not mean 'smoky lodges', as stated in the Clark MS). **Heviqs-ni''kpahis.**—Mooney, inf'n, 1905 (see p. 254 of this Handbook). **I vístś tsí níh' pah.**—Grinnell, Social Org. Cheyennes, 136, 1905 (trans. 'small wind-pipes'). **We hee skeu (chien).**—Clark (1804) in Orig. Jour. Lewis and Clark, I, 190, 1904.

Hewut. The village of the Umpqua on upper Umpqua r., Oreg.
Hay-woot.—Milhau, Umpqua Val. MS. vocab., B. A. E. **He'-wŭt.**—Milhau, Hewŭt MS. vocab., B. A. E.

Hia ('band of Cree'). A former Arikara band under chief Cherenakuta, or Yellow Wolf.
Hi'-a.—Hayden, Ethnog. and Philol., 357, 1862.

Hiabu. A tribe met by De Leon, in company with the Hapes, Jumenes (Jumano), and Mescales, near the Rio Grande, not far from the present Laredo, Tex., in 1696. It was probably a Coahuiltecan tribe.
Xiabu.—De Leon (1696) in Texas Hist. Ass. Quar., VIII, 205, 1905.

Hiamonee. A former Seminole village 5 m. from the Georgia boundary, on the E. bank of Okloknee r., probably on the present L. Lamony, Leon co., Fla.
Hiamonce.—H. R. Ex. Doc. 74 (1823), 19th Cong., 1st sess., 27, 1826.

Hianagouy. Mentioned by Joutel (Margry, Déc., III, 409, 1878) as a tribe living probably in E. Texas in 1687, and hostile to the Kadohadacho.

Hiantatsi. Mentioned by Joutel (Margry, Déc., III, 409, 1878) as a tribe living probably in E. Texas in 1687, and hostile to the Kadohadacho.

Hiaqua. Shell money and ornaments, composed of strings of dentalia, used by Indians of the N. Pacific coast. This word, which has been variously spelled *haiqua, hioqua, hiqua, hykwa, iokwa, ioqua,* etc., and even *Iroquois,* is derived from the name for dentalium in the Chinook jargon. (A. F. C.)

Hiatam (*Hi'-a-tam,* 'sea-sand place,' from *Hiakatcik*). A Pima village N. of Maricopa station on the S. P. R. R., s. Ariz.—Russell, Pima MS., B. A. E., 18, 1902.

Hiawatha (*Haion'hwa''tha'*, 'he makes rivers'). A name and a title of a chieftainship hereditary in the Tortoise clan of the Mohawk tribe; it is the second on the roll of federal chieftainships of the Iroquois confederation. The first known person to bear the name was a noted reformer, statesman, legislator, and magician, justly celebrated as one of the founders of the League of the Iroquois, the Confederation of Five Nations. Tradition makes him a prophet also. He probably flourished about 1570, A. D., and was the disciple and active coadjutor of Dekanawida. These two sought to bring about reforms which had for their object the ending of all strife, murder, and war, and the promotion of universal peace and well-being. Of these one was the regulation to abolish the wasting evils of intratribal blood-feud by fixing a more or less arbitrary price—10 strings of wampum, a cubit in length—as the value of a human life. It was decreed that the murderer or his kin or family must offer to pay the bereaved family not only for the dead person, but also for the life of the murderer who by his sinister act had forfeited his life to them, and that therefore 20 strings of wampum should be the legal tender to the bereaved family for the settlement of the homicide of a co-tribesman. By birth Hiawatha was probably a Mohawk, but he began the work of reform among the Onondaga, where he encountered bitter opposition from one of their most crafty and remorseless tyrants, Wathatotarho (Atotarho). After three fruitless attempts to unfold his scheme of reform in council, being thwarted by the craft of his formidable antagonist (who for revenge destroyed his opponent's daughters), Hiawatha left the Onondaga and, exiling himself, sought the aid of the Mohawk and other tribes. But, meeting with little success among the former, he continued his mission to the Oneida, who willingly assented to his plans on condition that the Mohawk should do the same. The Mohawk, the Cayuga, and the Oneida finally formed a tentative union for the purpose of persuading the Onondaga to adopt the plan of confederation, and the latter accepted it on condition that the Seneca should also be included. A portion of the Seneca finally joined the confederation, whereon the Onondaga, through Wathatotarho, accepted the proposed union. As the Onondaga chieftain was regarded as a great sorcerer, it was inferred that in this matter he had been overcome by superior magic power exercised by Hiawatha and Dekanawida, for they had brought Wathatotarho under the dominion of law and convention for the common welfare. Hence in time the character of Hiawatha became enveloped in mystery, and he was reputed to have done things which properly belong to some of the chief gods of the Iroquois. In this mystified form he became the central figure of a cycle of interrelated legends. Longfellow has made the name of Hiawatha everywhere familiar, but not so the character of the great reformer. Schoolcraft, in his Algic Researches, embodied a large number of legends relating to Chippewa gods and demigods, and, while compiling his Notes on the Iroquois, J. V. H. Clark communicated to him this cycle of mythic legends misapplied to Hiawatha. Charmed with the poetic setting of these tales, Schoolcraft confused Hiawatha with Manabozho, a Chippewa deity, and it is to these two collections of mythic and legendary lore that the English language owes the charming poem of Longfellow, in which there is not a single fact or fiction relating to the great Iroquoian reformer and statesman. For further published information see Hale (1) Iroquois Book of Rites, (2) A Lawgiver of the Stone Age; Hewitt in Am. Anthrop., Apr. 1892. (J. N. B. H.)

Hicaranaou. An ancient Timuquanan village in N. Florida.—De Bry, Brev. Nar., II, map, 1591.

Hiccora, Hiccory. See *Hickory.*

Hichakhshepara ('eagle'). A subgens of the Waninkikikarachada, the Bird gens of the Winnebago.
Hi-tca-qce-pa-ră.—Dorsey in 15th Rep. B. A. E., 240, 1897.

Hichucio. A subdivision or settlement of the Tehueco, probably inhabiting the lower Rio Fuerte or the Fuerte-Mayo divide, in N. W. Sinaloa, Mex.—Orozco y Berra, Geog., 58, 1864.

Hickerau. A small Santee village on a branch of Santee r., S. C., in 1701.

Black house.—Lawson (1714), Hist. Carolina, 45, 1860 (so called by traders). **Hickerau.**—Ibid.

Hickory. A walnut tree belonging to any one of several species of the genus *Hicoria*. The word is spelled by early writers in a great variety of ways: *po-hickery* (Farrar, 1653), *pekickery* (Shrigley, 1669), *peckikery, pokickery, hickorie, hiccora, hiccory, hickory* (1682), etc. Capt. John Smith (Hist. Va., II, 26, 1624) describes *pawcohiccora*, a food of the Algonquian Indians of Virginia, as a preparation of pounded walnut kernels with water. From the cluster words *paw-cohiccora*, etc., transferred by the whites from the food to the tree, has been derived *hickory*. Derivative words and terms are: Hickory-borer (*Cyllene picta*), hickory-elm (*Ulmus racemosa*), hickory-eucalyptus (*Eucalyptus punctata*), hickory-girdler (*Oncideres cingulatus*), hickory-head (the ruddy duck), hickory nut (the nut of the hickory, specifically of *Hicoria ovata* or *H. laciniosa*), hickory-oak (*Quercus chrysolepis*), hickory-pine (*Pinus balfouriana* and *P. pungens*), hickory pole (a Democratic party emblem), hickory poplar (*Liriodendron tulipifera*), hickory-shad (the gizzard-shad), hickory shirt (a coarse cotton shirt). As an adjective the word hickory took on the sense of firm, unyielding, stubborn, as applied to religious sectarians, members of a political party, etc. Gen. Andrew Jackson was called "Old Hickory." In Waterloo co., Ontario, according to W. J. Wintemberg, the German residents call a Pennsylvania German a *Hickory*, possibly in reference to their fellows in Pennsylvania having voted the Jackson ticket. (A. F. C.)

Hickory Indians. A small band formerly occupying a village near Lancaster, Pa. (Day, Penn., 397, 1843). Probably a part of the Delawares.

Hickory Log. A former Cherokee settlement on Etowah r., a short distance above Canton, Cherokee co., Ga.—Mooney in 19th Rep. B. A. E., 545, 1900. **Wane'-asûñ'tlûñyĭ.**—Mooney, ibid. ('hickory foot-log place': native name).

Hickorytown. A former Munsee and Delaware village, probably about East Hickory or West Hickory, Forest co., Pa. On account of the hostility of the western tribes the Indians here removed in 1791 to the Seneca and were by them settled near Cattaraugus, N. Y. (J. M.) **Hickory town.**—Procter (1791) in Am. State Papers, Ind. Aff., I, 154, 1832. **Munsee settlement.**—Ibid., 153.

Hictoba. One of the 5 divisions of the Dakota recorded by Pachot (Margry, Déc., VI, 518, 1886) about 1722. Unidentified. **Scioux de la chasse.**—Ibid.

Hidatsa. A Siouan tribe living, since first known to the whites, in the vicinity of the junction of Knife r. with the Missouri, North Dakota, in intimate connection with the Mandan and Arikara. Their language is closely akin to that of the Crows, with whom they claim to have been united until some time before the historic period, when the two separated in consequence of a quarrel over the division of some game, the Crows then drawing off farther to the w.

The name Hidatsa, by which they now call themselves, has been said, with doubtful authority, to mean 'willows,' and is stated by Matthews to have been originally the name only of a principal village of the tribe in their old home on Knife r. (see *Elahsa*). It probably came to be used as the tribe name, after the smallpox epi-

HIDATSA (CHESHAKHADAKHI, LEAN WOLF)

demic of 1837, from the consolidation of the survivors of the other two villages with those of Hidatsa. By the Mandan they are known as Minitarí, signifying 'they crossed the water,' traditionally said to refer to their having crossed Missouri r. from the E. The Sioux call them Hewaktokto, said to mean 'dwellers on a ridge,' but more probably signifying 'spreading tipis,' or 'tipis in a row,' the name by which they are known to the Cheyenne and Arapaho. The sign gesture in each case would be nearly the same (Mooney). The Crows call them Amashi, 'earth lodges,' and they are now officially known as Gros Ventres (q. v.), a name applied also to the Atsina, a detached tribe of the Arapaho.

According to their own tradition the Hidatsa came from the neighborhood of a lake N. E. of their later home, and identified by some of their traditionists with Mini-wakan or Devils lake, N. Dak. They had here the circular earth-covered log house, in use also by the Mandan, Arikara, and other tribes living close along the upper Missouri, in addition to the skin tipi occupied when on the hunt. Removing from there, perhaps in consequence of attacks by the Sioux, they moved S. W. and allied themselves with the Mandan, who then lived on the W. side of the Missouri, about the mouth of Heart r. The three tribes, Hidatsa, Mandan, and Arikara were all living in this vicinity about 1765. From the Mandan the Hidatsa learned agriculture. Some time before 1796 these two tribes moved up the river to the vicinity of Knife r., where they were found by Lewis and Clark in 1804, the Hidatsa being then in three villages immediately on Knife r., while the Mandan, in two villages, were a few miles lower down, on the Missouri. The largest of the three villages of the tribe was called Hidatsa and was on the N. bank of Knife r. The other two, Amatiha and Amahami, or Mahaha, were on the S. side. The last named was occupied by the Amahami (Ahnahaway of Lewis and Clark), formerly a distinct but closely related tribe. In consequence of the inroads of the Sioux they had been so far reduced that they had been compelled to unite with the Hidatsa, and have long since been completely absorbed. The three villages together had a population of about 600 warriors, equivalent to about 2,100 souls. Of these the Amahami counted about 50 warriors. There was no change in the location of the villages until after the terrible smallpox epidemic of 1837, which so greatly reduced the Indian population of the upper Missouri, and in consequence of which the survivors of the three villages consolidated into one. In 1845 they, and about the same time the remnant of the Mandan also, moved up the river and established themselves in a new village (see *Hidatsati*) close to the trading post of Ft Berthold, on the N. bank of the Missouri and some distance below the entrance of the Little Missouri, in North Dakota. In 1862 the Arikara moved up to the same location, the three tribes now occupying a reservation of 884,780 acres on the N. E. side of the Missouri, including the site of the village. In 1905 the Hidatsa (Gros Ventres) were officially reported to number only 471.

Early writers describe the Hidatsa as somewhat superior intellectually and physically to their neighbors, although according to Matthews this is not so evident in later days. In home life, religious beliefs and customs, house building, agriculture, the use of the skin boat, and general arts, they closely resembled the Mandan with whom they were associated. Their great ceremony was the Sun dance, called by them Da-ħpi-ke, which was accompanied with various forms of torture. Their warriors were organized into various military societies, as is the case with the Plains tribes generally.

Morgan (Anc. Soc., 159, 1877) gives a list of 7 Hidatsa "gentes," which were probably really original village names, or possibly society names, viz: Mit-che-ro′-ka ('knife'), Min-ne-pä-ta ('water'), Bä-ho-hä′-ta ('lodge'), Seech-ka-be-ruh-pä′-ka ('prairie chicken'), E-tish-sho′-ka ('hill people'), Aħ-naħ-ha-nä′-me-te (an unknown animal), E-ku′-pä-be-ka ('bonnet'). The list of "bands" given by Culbertson (Smithson. Rep. 1850, 143, 1851) is really a list of military societies, viz: Fox, Foolish Dog, Old Dog, Bull, and Black-tailed Deers.

Consult Clark, Ind. Sign Lang., 1885; Coues, Exped. Lewis and Clark, 1893; Orig. Jour. Lewis and Clark, I–VIII, 1904–05; Dorsey in 15th Rep. B. A. E., 1897; Hayden, Ethnog. and Philol. Mo. Val., 1867; Matthews, Ethnog. and Philol. Hidatsa, 1877; Maximilian, Trav., 1843; McGee in 15th Rep. B. A. E., 1897. (J. M.)

A-gutch-a-ninne.—Tanner, Narr., 58, 1830. A-gutch-a-ninne-wug.—Ibid. ('the settled people': Chippewa name). A-me-she′.—Hayden, Ethnog. and Philol., 402, 1862 ('people who live in earth houses': Crow name). Ar-me-shay.—Anon. MS. Crow vocab., B. A. E. Belantse-etea.—U. S. Ind. Treaties, 354, 1826. Belautse-etea.—Cass (1834) in Schoolcraft, Ind. Tribes, III, 609, 1853. E-nät′-zä.—Morgan in N. A. Rev., 47, Jan. 1870 (national name; cf. *Ehartsar*). Gi-aucth-in-in-e-wug.—Warren in Minn. Hist. Coll., V, 178, 1885 ('men of the olden time': Chippewa name). Gi-aucth-in-e-wug.—Ibid., 261. Grosventres.—For various forms of this name applied to the Hidatsa, see *Gros Ventres*. Hedatse.—Hamilton in Trans. Nebr. Hist. Soc., I, 75, 1885. He-wa′-kto-kta.—Cook, Yankton, MS. vocab., B. A. E., 184, 1882. Hewaktokto.—Matthews, Ethnog. and Philol., 36, 1877 (Dakota name). He-war-tuk-tay.—Corliss, Lacotah MS. vocab., B. A. E., 106, 1874. Hidatsa.—Matthews. Ethnog. and Philol., 3, 1877 (own name). Hidatza.—Baxter in Harper's Mag., June, 1882. Hidhatsa.—Dorsey in Am. Nat., 829, 1882. Manetores.—Ramsey in Ind. Aff. Rep., 75, 1849. Maniataris.—Du Lac, Voy. dans La., 225, 1805. Manitaries.—Maximilian, Trav., vii, 1843. Mannatures.—Cumming in H. R. Ex. Doc. 65, 34th Cong., 1st sess., 8, 1856. Menetare.—Lewis and Clark, Discov., 26, 1806. Me-ne-ta-rees.—Orig. Jour. Lewis and Clark (1805), I, 249, 1904. Menetarres.—Lewis and Clark, Discov., 25, 1806. Me ne tar res.—Orig. Jour. Lewis and Clark (1805), I, 248, 1904 (also Mene tar rés). Metaharta.—Lewis and Clark, Exped., I, 121, 1814. Miditadi.—Matthews, Ethnog. and Philol., 193, 1887. Mimetari.—Meigs in Smithson. Rep. 1867, 414, 1868. Minataree.—Clark and Cass in H. R. Ex. Doc. 117, 20th Cong., 2d sess., 98, 1829. Minatarees.—Bradbury, Trav., 109, 1817. Minatares.—Brown, West. Gaz., 215, 1817. Minatories.—Dougherty in H. R. Ex. Doc. 276, 25th Cong., 2d sess., 16, 1838. Minetaire.—Drake, Bk. Inds., vi, 1848. Minetarees.—Lewis and Clark, Exped., I, 163, 1817. Minetares.—Orig. Jour. Lewis and Clark (1805), I, 324, 1904. Minetari.—Prichard, Phys. Hist. Man., v, 409, 1847. **Minetaries.**—Gallatin in Trans. Am. Antiq. Soc., II, 125, 1836. **Minetarre.**—Lewis and Clark, Exped., I, map, 1814. **Minetarries.**—Orig. Jour. Lewis and Clark (1805), I, 283, 1904. **Minitare.**—Latham in Jour. Ethnol. Soc. Lond., I, 160, 1848. **Minitarees.**—Orig. Jour. Lewis and Clark (1804), I, 216, 1904. **Minitares.**—Ibid., 10. **Minitari.**—Brownell, Ind. Races N. Am., 466, 1853 (Mandan name). **Minitarres.**—Orig. Jour. Lewis and Clark, I, 13, 1904. **Minnetahrees.**—Tanner, Narr., 316, 1830. **Minnetahse.**—Ibid., 325 (misprint). **Mĭn-nĕ-tȧ-rĕ.**—Long, Exped. Rocky Mts., II, lxx, 1823. **Minnetarees.**—Lewis and Clark, Exped., I, 115, 1814. **Minnetarees Metaharta.**—Ibid., 131. **Minnetarees of the Willows.**—Ibid. **Minnetares of the Knife R.**—Orig. Jour. Lewis and Clark (1805), I, 283, 1904. **Minnetaroes.**—Lewis and Clark, Exped., I, 164, 1817. **Minnetarres.**—Warren, Nebr. and Ariz., 50, 1875. **Minnitarees.**—Hayden, Ethnog. and Philol. Mo. Val., 420, 1862. **Minnitarees Metaharta.**—Lewis and Clark, Exped., I, 131, 1814. **Minnitarees of the Willows.**—Ibid. **Minnitaris.**—Am. Nat., 829, 1882. **Minntaree.**—Trans. Anthrop. Soc. Wash., III, 65, 1885. **Mœnnitarris.**—Maximilian, Trav., 337, 1843. **Quehatsa.**—Brown, West. Gaz., 213, 1817. **Stationary Minetares.**—Gallatin in Trans. Am. Antiq. Soc., II, 125, 1836 (as distinguished from "Minitarees of Fort de Prairie," i. e., the Atsina). **Wa-nuk'-e-ye'-na.**—Hayden, Ethnog. and Philol. Mo. Val., 326, 1862 ('lodges planted together': Arapaho name). **Wetitsaán.**—Matthews, Ethnog. and Philol. Hidatsa, 36, 1877 (Arikara name). **Winetaries.**—Orig. Jour. Lewis and Clark (1804), I, 220, 1904. **Wi-tets'-han.**—Hayden, op. cit., 357 ('well-dressed people': Arikara name).

Hidatsati (from *Hidatsa* and *ati:* 'dwelling of the Hidatsa Indians'). The Hidatsa village formerly at Ft Berthold, N. Dak. In 1872 it contained 71 Arikara and 104 Hidatsa and Mandan dwellings. See *Elahsa.*

Berthold Indian Village.—Royce in 18th Rep. B. A. E., pl. cxviii, 1899. **Hi dá tsa ti.**—Matthews, Ethnog. and Philol. Hidatsa, 211, 1877.

Hidlis Hadjo. See *Hillis Hadjo.*

Highahwixon. One of several tribes displaced by the whites in 1651 from their homes in Charles and St Mary cos., Md., and given a tract at the head of the Wicomoco. They were probably Conoy.— Bozman, Maryland, II, 421, 1837.

High Tower Forks. A former Cherokee settlement mentioned in a document of 1799 (Royce in 5th Rep. B. A. E., 144, 1887). It was probably one of the places called Etowah (*I'tăwă*), q. v.

Higos (*Indios de los Higos*, Span.: 'Fig Indians'). A tribe of s. Texas, so named by Cabeza de Vaca in 1528 (Smith trans., 84, 1851) from their custom of subsisting on the prickly pear, or tuna, in its season. Cabeza de Vaca states that they counted the seasons by the ripening of the fruits, the "dying" or (according to Smith) the biting of the fish, and by the appearance of certain constellations. Nothing is known of their ethnic relations. (A. C. F.)

Higtiguk. A former Aleut village on Agattu id., Alaska, one of the Near id. group of the Aleutians, now uninhabited.

Hihagee. An unidentified Lower Creek town mentioned in a census list of 1833.— Schoolcraft, Ind. Tribes, IV, 578, 1854.

Hihakanhanhanwin ('women the skin of whose teeth dangles'). A band of the Brulé Teton Sioux.

Hi-ha kaṇhaṇhaṇ wiṇ.—Dorsey (after Cleveland) in 15th Rep. B. A. E., 219, 1897. **Hi-ha kaⁿhaⁿhaⁿ wiⁿ.**—Ibid.

Hihames. A former tribe of Coahuila, N. E. Mexico, which was gathered into the mission of El Santo Nombre de Jesus Peyotes when it was refounded in 1698. This tribe probably belonged to the Coahuiltecan family.

Gijames.—Morfi (1777) quoted by Bancroft, Nat. Races, I, 611, 1886. **Hijames.**—Revillagigedo (1793), ibid. **Xijames.**—Ibid.

Hilakwitiyus (*Hĭl-ȧ-kwĭ-tĭ-yŭs'*). A former Siuslaw village on or near Siuslaw r., Oreg.—Dorsey in Jour. Am. Folk-lore, III, 230, 1890.

Hilksuk. A former Aleut village on Agattu id., Alaska, one of the Near id. group of the Aleutians, now uninhabited.

Hillabi (pron. *hi'-la-pi*). A former Upper Creek town near the present Ashland, Clay co., Ala., in the "central district" between Coosa and Tallapoosa rs., on Koufadi cr., a branch of Hillabee cr. Most of the Hillabi people had settled before 1799 in the 4 villages called Hlanudshiapala, Anatichapko, Istudshilaika, and Uktahasasi. In the vicinity of Hillabi town its inhabitants, with other "Red Sticks," or hostiles, were vanquished by Jackson's army, Nov. 18, 1813, when 316 of them were killed or captured and their town devastated. (A. S. G.)

Halibee.—Drake, Bk. Inds., bk. IV, 54, 1848. **Hallebac.**—Jefferys, Am. Atlas, map 5, 1776 (on w. bank of Loucushatchee [Tallapoosa] r.). **Hallibees.**—Drake, Ind. Chron., 198, 1836. **Hĭ'-la-pi.**—Gatschet, Creek. Migr. Leg., I, 131, 1884 (proper pronunciation). **Hillaba.**—Bartram, Travels, 462, 1791 (on a branch of Coosa r.). **Hillabees.**—Swan (1791) in Schoolcraft, Ind. Tribes, v, 262, 1855. **Hillabys.**—Woodward, Reminiscences, 96, 1859. **Hill-au-bee.**—Hawkins (1799), Sketch, 43, 1848. **Hillebese.**—Cornell (1793) in Am. State Papers, Ind. Aff., I, 385, 1832.

Hillabi. A town of the Creek Nation, s. w. of Eufaula, between North fork and Canadian r., Ind. T.—Gatschet, Creek Migr. Leg., II, 185, 1888.

Hílabi.—Gatschet, ibid.

Hillis Hadjo. (*hilis* 'medicine', *hadsho* 'crazy', an official at the busk, q. v.). A noted Seminole leader in the early part of the 19th century, usually known among the whites as Francis the Prophet, and whose name is also recorded as Hidlis Hadjo, Hillishago, Hillishager, etc. He took an active part in the Seminole war, and is accused of having been one of the chief instigators of the second uprising. He seems to have come into public notice as early as 1814, as on Apr. 18 of that year Gen. Jackson wrote from his camp at the junction of Coosa and Tallapoosa rs., Ala., that "Hillishagee, their [the Seminole's] great prophet, has absconded." Led by some abandoned English traders to believe that the treaty of Ghent in 1814 provided for the restoration of the Seminole country, and in the hope of obtaining aid for his tribe against the Americans, he went to England, where he received much attention. An English journal thus mentions his arrival: ''The sound of trumpets announced the approach of the patriot Francis, who fought so gloriously in our cause in America during the late war. Being dressed in a most splendid suit of red and gold, and wearing a tomahawk set with gold, gave him a highly imposing appearance.'' His mission led to no practical result. Near the close of 1817 an American named McKrimmon, who had been captured by a Seminole party, was taken to Mikasuki, where dwelt Hillis Hadjo, who ordered him to be burned to death, but at the last moment his life was saved by the entreaties of Milly (q. v.), the chief's daughter, who, when her father wavered, showed her determination to perish with him. Francis shortly thereafter fell into the hands of the Americans and was hanged. His wife and several daughters afterward surrendered to the Americans at St Marks, Fla., where Milly received much attention from the whites, but refused McKrimmon's offer of marriage until assured that it was not because of his obligation to her for saving his life.   (c. t.)

Hiluys. An unidentified tribe, said to have lived on Laredo channel, Brit. Col., about lat. 52° 30′ (Scott in Ind. Aff. Rep., 316, 1868). This is in the country of the Kittizoo.

Himatanohis (*Hímátanóhís*, 'bowstring men'). A warrior society of the Cheyenne, q. v.   (j. m.)
Bow-String (Society).—Dorsey in Field Columb. Mus. Pub., no. 99, 15, 1905. Inverted (Society).—Ibid.

Himoiyoqis (*Hí'moiyóqís*, a word of doubtful meaning). A warrior society of the Cheyenne (q. v.); also sometimes known as Oómi-nŭ'tqiu, 'Coyote warriors.'   (j. m.)
Coyote (Society).—Dorsey in Field Columb. Mus. Pub., no. 99, 15, 1905.

Hinama (*Hí'námá*, referring to the head of a variety of fish). A former Maricopa village whose people now live on the s. bank of Salt r., E. of the Mormon settlement of Lehi, Maricopa co., s. Ariz.—Russell, Pima MS., B. A. E., 16, 1902.

Hinanashiu (*Hinanä'shiu*, 'golden eagle'). A gens of the Kineuwidishianun or Eagle phratry of the Menominee.—Hoffman in 14th Rep. B. A. E., pt. I, 42, 1896.

Hinauhan's Village. A summer camp of a Stikine chief on Stikine r., Alaska. In 1880, 31 people were there.—Petroff in Tenth Census, Alaska, 32, 1884.

Hinhanshunwapa ('toward the owl feather'). A band of the Brulé Teton Sioux.
Hinhaⁿ-cŭⁿ-wapa.—Dorsey (after Cleveland) in 15th Rep. B. A. E., 219, 1897. Hiŋhaŋ-ṣun-wapa.—Ibid.

Hiocaia. A former village, governed by a female chieftain, situated 12 leagues N. of Charlefort, the French fort on St Johns r., Fla., in the 16th century.
Hiocaia.—Laudonnière (1564) in French, Hist. Coll. La., n. s., 286, 1869. Hiouacara.—De Bry, Brev. Narr., II, map, 1591.

Hioqua. See *Hiaqua.*

Hios. A branch of the Nevome who lived 8 leagues E. of the pueblo of Tepahue, in Sonora, Mexico (Orozco y Berra, Geog., 58, 351, 1864). The name doubtless properly belongs to their village.

Hipinimtch (*hipi* 'prairie', *nimtch* 'road,' 'portage'). A former Chitimacha village on the w. side of Grand lake, at Fausse Pointe, near Bayou Gosselin, La.
Hipinimtch námu.—Gatschet in Trans. Anthrop. Soc. Wash., II, 152, 1883 (*námu*='village').

Hiqua. See *Hiaqua.*

Hirrihigua. A province and town, presumably Timuquanan, on the w. coast of Florida, on or near Tampa bay, where De Soto landed in May, 1539. Possibly the same as Ucita.
Harriga.—Shipp, De Soto and Fla., 257, 1881. Hihirrigua.—Garcilasso de la Vega, Hist. Fla., 30, 1723. Hirriga.—Shipp, op. cit., 683.

Hisada ('legs stretched out stiff', referring to a dead quadruped). A Ponca gens on the Chinzhu side of the camp circle.
Hisada.—Dorsey in 15th Rep. B. A. E., 228, 1897. Thunder people.—Ibid.

Hishkowits (*Híshkowí'ts*, 'porcupine', known to the whites as Harvey Whiteshield). A Southern Cheyenne interpreter, born in w. Oklahoma in 1867; eldest son of the chief White-shield (see *Wopowats*). After 5 years' attendance at the agency schools he entered Carlisle School, Pa., in 1881, afterward attending other schools at Ft Wayne, Hanover (Ind.), and Lawrence (Kan.). In 1893 he became assistant teacher in the Mennonite mission school among the Cheyenne at Cantonment, Okla., which position he held for 4 years. He still serves as interpreter for the mission and has been chief assistant of the Rev. Rudolph Petter, missionary in charge, in the preparation of a number of translations and a manuscript dictionary of the Cheyenne language.   (j. m.)

Hisiometanio (*Hísíometä'nio*, 'ridge men'; sing., *Hísíometä'n*). A principal division of the Cheyenne, q. v.
Hísíometa'nio.—Mooney, inf'n, 1905 (see p. 255 of this Handbook). Hǐssí o mé tän i u.—Grinnell, Social Org. Cheyennes, 136, 1905. Ǐ' sium-itä' niuw'.—Mooney in 14th Rep. B. A. E., 1025, 1896.

Histapenumanke. A Mandan band, the first, according to their mythology, to come above ground from the subterranean lake.
E-sta-pa'.—Morgan, Anc. Soc., 158, 1877 ('those with the tattooed faces'). Flat-head.—Ibid. Hista pe' nu-mañ'-ke.—Dorsey in 15th Rep. B. A. E., 241, 1897. Histoppa.—Maximilian, Trav., 366, 1843.

Hitchapuksassi. A former Seminole town about 20 m. from the head of Tampa bay, in what is now Hillsboro co., Fla.

Hechapususse.—Bell in Morse, Rep. to Sec. War, 307, 1822. **Helch-puck[sasy].**—H. R. Ex. Doc. 74 (1823), 19th Cong., 1st sess., 23, 1826 (the last two syllables of this name are joined to the next town name, -*chicu-chaty*.) **Hich-a-pue-susse.**—Bell, op. cit. **Hichipucksassa.**—Taylor, War map, 1839.

Hitchiti (Creek: *ahitchita*, 'to look up-stream'). A Muskhogean tribe formerly residing chiefly in a town of the same name on the E. bank of Chattahoochee r., 4 m. below Chiaha, and possessing a narrow strip of good land bordering on the river, in W. Georgia. When Hawkins visited them in 1799 they had spread out into two branch settlements—one, the Hitchitudshi, or Little Hitchiti, on both sides of Flint r. below the junction of Kinchafoonee cr., which passes through a country named after it; the other, Tutalosi, on a branch of Kinchafoonee cr., 20 m. W. of Hitchitudshi. The tribe is not often mentioned in history, and appears for the first time in 1733, when two of its delegates, with the Lower Creek chiefs, met Gov. Oglethorpe at Savannah. The language appears to have extended beyond the limits of the tribe as here defined, as it was spoken not only in the towns on the Chattahoochee, as Chiaha, Chiahudshi, Hitchiti, Oconee, Sawokli, Sawokliudshi, and Apalachicola, and in those on Flint r., but by the Mikasuki, and, as traceable by the local names, over considerable portions of Georgia and Florida. The Seminole are also said to have been a half Creek and half Hitchiti speaking people, although their language is now almost identical with Creek; and it is supposed that the Yamasi likewise spoke the Hitchiti language. This language, like the Creek, has an archaic form called "woman's talk," or female language. The Hitchiti were absorbed into and became an integral part of the Creek Nation, though preserving to a large extent their own language and peculiar customs. See *Creeks.*　　　(A. S. G.)

Achilia.—Jefferys, French Dom. Am., I, 134, map, 1761 (incorrectly located; false orthography). **At-pasha-shliha.**—Gatschet, Koasati MS., B. A. E. (Koasati name: 'mean people'). **Echeetees.**—Carver, Travels, map, 1778. **Echeles.**—Jefferys, Am. Atlas, 7, 1776 (town on Apalachicola r., Ga.). **Echeta.**—Bartram, Trav., 462, 1791. **Echetas.**—Drake, Bk. Inds., bk. IV, 29, 1848. **Echetee.**—Lattré, map, U. S., 1784 (1, on Chattahoochee; 2, on Altamaha). **Echetes.**—Jefferys, French Dom. Am., I, 134, map 1761 (two towns, incorrectly located). **Echeti.**—Mandrillon, Spectateur Américain, map, 1785. **Echetil.**—Alcedo, Dic. Geog., II, 00, 1787 (on Echesii r., Ga.). **Echitis.**—Ibid. (on Apalachicola r.). **Echitos.**—Penière in Morse, Rep. to Sec. War, 311, 1822. Doc. of 1747 in McCall, Hist. Ga., I, 367, 1811. **Etichita.**—Jones, Hist. Ga., I, 134, 1873. **Euchitaws.**—Gatschet, Creek Migr. Leg., II, 9, 1888. **Hatchita.**—Robin, Voy., I, map, 1807. **Hichetas.**—Woodward, Reminiscenses, 25, 38, 1859. **Hilchittees.**—Stevens, Hist. Ga., 51, 1847. **Hitchatees.**—Swan (1791) in Schoolcraft, Ind. Tribes, V, 262, 1855. **Hitchetaws.**—U. S. Ind. Treat. (1779), 69, 1837. **Hit-che-tee.**—Hawkins (1799), Sketch, 64, 1848. **Hitchies.**—Schoolcraft, Ind. Tribes, I, 239, 1851. **Hitchittees.**—Drake, Bk. Inds., bk. VIII, 1848. **Hitch-ity.**—Duval (1894) in

Sen. Ex. Doc. 49, 31st Cong., 1st sess., 144, 1850. **Ichiti.**—Rafinesque, introd. Marshall, Ky., I, 24, 1824. **Kitaheeta.**—Barnard (1792) in Am. State Papers, Ind. Aff., I, 309, 1832 (misprint).

Hitchiti. A town of the Creek Nation, Ind. Ter., on Deep fork of Canadian r., about midway between Eufaula and Ocmulgee.

Hitchita.—P. O. Guide, 367, 1904. **Hitchiti.**—Gatschet, Creek Migr. Leg., II, 185, 1888.

Hitchitipusy. A former village, probably Seminole, a few miles S. E. of Ft Alabama, and the same distance N. E. of Ft Brooke, both of which forts were on Hillsboro r., Fla.—H. R. Doc. 78, 25th Cong., 2d sess., 768–9, map, 1838.

Hitchitudshi. A branch settlement of Hitchiti on Flint r., Ga., below its junction with Kinchafoonee cr.

Hitchatooche.—Royce in 18th Rep. B. A. E., Ga. map, 1900. **Hit-che-too-che.**—Hawkins (1779), Sketch, 65, 1848. **Hitchitúdshi.**—Gatschet, Creek Migr. Leg., I, 77, 131, 1884. **Little Hit-chetee.**—Hawkins, op. cit. **Little Hitchiti.**—Gatschet, op. cit.

Hitschowon. A former Chumashan village on the harbor of Santa Cruz id., off the coast of California.

Hits-tcö'-wön.—Henshaw, Buenaventura MS. vocab., B. A. E., 1884.

Hitshinsuwit. A former Yaquina village on the S. side of Yaquina r., Oreg.

Hi'-ɢoïn-su'-wĭt.—Dorsey in Jour. Am. Folk-lore, III, 229, 1890.

Hittoya ('westerners.'—Kroeber). A division of the Miwok on upper Chowchilla r., Mariposa co., Cal.

Heth-to'-ya.—Powers in Cont. N. A. Ethnol., III, 349, 1877. **Hittoya.**—A. L. Kroeber, inf'n, 1903.

Hiwaitthe. A former Yaquina village on the S. side of Yaquina r., Oreg.

Hi'-wai-i'-t'çě.—Dorsey in Jour. Am. Folk-lore, III, 229, 1890.

Hiwassee (*Ayuhwa'sĭ*, 'savanna,' 'meadow'). The name of several former Cherokee settlements. The most important, commonly distinguished by the Cherokee as Ayuhwa'sĭ Egwâ'hĭ, or Great Hiwassee, was on the N. bank of Hiwassee r., at the present Savannah ford, above Columbus, Polk co., Tenn. Another was farther up the same river, at the junction of Peachtree cr., above Murphy, Cherokee co., N. C.—Mooney in 19th Rep. B. A. E., 512, 1900.

Ayuhwa'sĭ.—Mooney, op. cit. **Euforsee.**—Doc. of 1755 quoted by Royce in 5th Rep. B. A. E., 142, 1887. **Highwassee.**—Doc. of 1799 quoted by Royce, ibid., 144. **Hiwasse.**—Bartram, Travels, 371, 1792. **Owassa.**—Lanman quoted by Mooney, op. cit.

Hiyaraba ('panther'). A clan of the Achcha phratry of the ancient Timucua of Florida.—Pareja (c a. 1614) quoted by Gatschet in Am. Philos. Soc. Proc., XVII, 492, 1878.

Hiyayulge ('tree trunk'). A former Maricopa village on Gila r., S. Ariz.

Hiyayulge.—ten Kate, inf'n, 1888. **Uskök.**—Ibid. (Pima name).

Hizo. A division of the Varohio which occupied the pueblo of Taraichi in Chinipas valley, W. Chihuahua, Mexico.—Orozco y Berra, Geog., 58, 324, 1864.

Hlagi (*Ḷă′gî*). A town of the Kaidju-kegawai family of the Haida, on an island near the E. end of Houston Stewart channel, Queen Charlotte ids., Brit. Col.—Swanton, Cont. Haida, 277, 1905.

Hlahayik (*Ḷă′xayîk*, 'inside of Hlaha [*Ḷă′xa*]'). A former Yakutat town on Yakutat bay, Alaska, back of an island called Hlaha, whence the name. The Clach-ă-jĕk of Krause seems to be indentical with the town of Yakutat.
(J. R. S.)

Hlahloakalga ('*Lá′lo-akálga*, 'fish ponds'). A Creek town in the Creek Nation, Ind. T., near Hilabee, between North fork and Canadian r.
Fish Ponds.—Gatschet, Creek Migr. Leg., II, 185, 1888. 'Lá′lo akálga.—Ibid.

Hlahloalgi ('fish people'). An extinct Creek clan.
Hŭ′-hlo.—Morgan, Anc. Soc., 161, 1877. 'Lá′lo-algi.—Gatschet, Creek Migr. Leg., I, 155, 1884.

Hlahlokalka ('*Lá′lo-kálka: ′lá′lo* 'fish', *akálgäs* 'I am separated from'). A former Upper Creek settlement established by the Okchayi on a small river forming ponds, 4 m. above Oakfuskee, Cleburne co., Ala.
(A. S. G.)
Fish pond.—Bartram, Travels, 462, 1791 (traders' name). Fish ponds.—Hawkins (1799), Sketch, 49, 1848. Fish-Pond Town.—Parsons (1833) in Schoolcraft, Ind. Tribes, IV, 578, 1854. 'Lá′lo-kálka.—Gatschet, Creek Migr. Leg., I, 137, 1884. Slaka-gulgas.—Swan (1791) in Schoolcraft, op. cit., v, 262, 1855. Tatloulgees.—Woodward, Reminis., 83, 1859. Thlatlogulgau.—Schoolcraft, op. cit., IV, 381. Thlot-lo-gul-gau.—Hawkins (1799), Sketch, 49, 1848.

Hlakeguns (*Ḷaqē′gᴧns*). A town of the Kuna-lanas on Yagun r., at the head of Masset inlet, Queen Charlotte ids., Brit. Col.—Swanton, Cont. Haida, 281, 1905.

Hlanudshiapala ('*láni* 'mountain', *udshi* dim. suffix, *apála* 'on the other side': 'on the other side of a little mountain'). A former Upper Creek settlement, one of the four Hillabi villages, with a town square, situated on the N. w. branch of Hillabi cr., Ala., 15 m. from Hillabi town.
(A. S. G.)
'Lánudshi apála.—Gatschet, Creek Migr. Leg., I, 137, 1884. Thla-noo-che au-bau-lau.—Hawkins (1799), Sketch, 43, 1848.

Hlaphlako ('*Láp-′láko*, 'tall cane'). Two former Upper Creek villages on or near Cupiahatchee cr., in Macon co., Ala., with 81 and 66 heads of families, respectively, in 1832.
James Bay.—H. R. Ex. Doc. 276, 24th Cong., 1st sess., 131, 1836 (misprint). Jim Boy's.—Campbell (1836) in H. R. Doc. 274, 25th Cong., 2d sess., 20, 1838. 'Láp-′láko.—Gatschet, Creek Migr. Leg., I, 137, 1884. Thabloc-ko.—H. R. Ex. Doc. 276, op. cit. Thloblocco-town.—Jesup (1836) in H. R. Doc. 78, 25th Cong., 2d sess., 48, 1838. Thlobthlocco.—H. R. Doc. 274, op. cit. Thlob Thlocko.—Sen. Ex. Doc. 425, 24th Cong., 1st sess., 257, 1836. Thlop-thlocco.—Woodward, Reminis., 91, 1859.

Hlaphlako. A town of the Creek Nation, on Alabama cr., N. of the North fork of Canadian r., Okla.—Gatschet, Creek Migr. Leg., II, 185, 1888.

Hlauhla ('*Hla′-u′hla*, 'surrounded by arrow-shaft bushes'). The ruins of a small but traditionally important Zuñi pueblo near a small spring about 10 m. N. N. E. of Zuñi, N. Mex.   (F. H. C.)
Clan-utsh-la.—Fewkes in Jour. Am. Ethnol. and Archæol., I, 100, 1891. 'Hla′-u′hla.—Cushing, inf'n, 1891.

Hlaukwima ('*Hlaukwi′ma*). The native name of the South town of Taos pueblo, N. Mex.   (F. W. H.)

Hlauuma ('*Hlauu′ma*). The native name of the North town of Taos pueblo, N. Mex.   (F. W. H.)

Hleetakwe ('*Hle′-e-tâ-kwe*). The northwestern migration of the Bear, Crane, Frog, Deer, Yellow-wood, and other clans of the ancestral pueblo of Zuñi.—Cushing quoted by Powell, 4th Rep. B. A. E., xxxviii, 1886. See *Pishla Ateuna*.

Hlekatchka ('*Le-kátchka*, or '*Li-i-kátchka*, from '*le* or '*li*, 'arrow', *kátchka*, 'broken': 'broken arrow'). A former Lower Creek town on a trail ford crossing Chattahoochee r., 12 m. below Kasihta, on the w. side of the river, probably in Russell co., Ala. According to Hawkins (Am. State Papers, Ind. Aff., I, 858, 1832) the settlement was destroyed in 1814; but it was apparently reestablished, as it was represented in the treaty of Nov. 15, 1827, and a census of 1832 (Schoolcraft, Ind. Tribes, IV, 578, 1854) gives the number of families as 331 in that year.   (A. S. G.)
Broken Arrow.—Carey (1792) in Am. State Papers, Ind. Aff., I, 329, 1832. Broken Arrow Old Field.—Robertson (1796), ibid., 600. Chalagatsca.—Swan (1791) in Schoolcraft, Ind. Tribes, v, 262, 1855. Horse-path-town.—Sen. Ex. Doc. 425, 24th Cong., 1st sess., 135, 1836. 'Lèkátchka.—Gatschet, Creek Migr. Leg., I, 137, 1884. 'Li-i-kátchka.—Ibid. Tauthlacotchcau.—Hawkins (1814) in Am. State Papers, op. cit., 858. Theacatckkah.—Drake, Bk. Inds., bk. 4, 54, 1848. Thlakatchka.—Census of 1832 in Schoolcraft, Ind. Tribes, IV, 578, 1854. Thleacatska.—Woodward, Reminis., 35, 1859. Thlu-katch-ka.—Sen. Ex. Doc. 425, 24th Cong., 1st sess., 135, 1836.

Hlekatska ('*Le kátska*). The settlement of an offshoot of the Kawita on Arkansas r., almost opposite Wialaka and near Coweta (Kawita), in the Creek Nation, Okla.—Gatschet, Creek Migr. Leg., II, 185, 1888.

Hlgadun (*Ḷgadᴧ′n*, 'suffering from overwork'). A town of the Skidai-lanas on Moresby id., opposite and facing Anthony id., Queen Charlotte group, Brit. Col. It is prominent in Haida mythology.—Swanton, Cont. Haida, 277, 1905.

Hlgaedlin (*Ḷgă′-iḷn*, probably 'where they wash the frames upon which salal berries are dried'). A Haida town occupied by a branch of the Kona-kegawai called Sus-haidagai; situated on the s. side of Tanoo id., s. E. Queen Charlotte ids., Brit. Col.—Swanton, Cont. Haida, 278, 1905.

Hlgagilda-kegawai (*Ḷgagî′lda qē′gawa-i*, 'those born at Hlgagilda,' i. e., Skidegate). A subdivision of the Hlgaiu-lanas family of the Haida.—Swanton, Cont. Haida, 269, 1905.

Hlgahet (*Ɫgā'xet*, 'pebble town'.) A former Haida town near Skidegate, Queen Charlotte ids., Brit. Col. It was purchased from its earlier owners, the Kogangas, by a branch of the Yaku-lanas who were afterward known as the Hlgahetgu-lanas, from the name of their town.　　　　　　　　　(J. R. S.)
Kil-káit-hādē.—Krause, Tlinkit Indianer, 304, 1885 ('people of Hlgahet'). Tlg·ā'it.—Boas, 12th Rep. N. W. Tribes Can., 24, 1898 (misapplied to to Old Gold Harbor).

Hlgahet-gitinai (*Ɫgā'xet gitînā'-i*, 'Gitins of Pebble-town'). A division of the Eagle clan of the Haida, for which Gitins was a second name. They moved from Hlgahet, the old town near Skidegate, to Chaahl on the w. coast, along with other families (see *Hlgahetgu-lanas*). Originally they and the Gitins of Skidegate constituted one family. The Djahui-hlgahet-kegawai, Yaku-gitinai, Hlgahet-kegawai, and Gweundus were subdivisions.　　　　　　　　(J. R. S.)
Ɫgā'xet gitînā'-i.—Swanton, Cont. Haida, 274, 1905. Tlg·ā'it gyit'inai'.—Boas, 12th Rep. N. W. Tribes Can., 24, 1898.

Hlgahetgu-lanas (*Ɫgā'xet-gu-lā'nas*, 'people of Pebble-town'). The most important division of the Raven clan of the Haida, on the w. coast of Queen Charlotte ids., Brit. Col. It received its name from an old town near Skidegate, where the people formerly lived. Before this they were part of the Yaku-lanas and lived at Lawn hill, but trouble arising, they were driven away and purchased the town of Hlgahet from the Kogangas. Later another war forced them to move to the w. coast.　　　　　　(J. R. S.)
Ɫgā'xet-gu-lā'nas.—Swanton, Cont. Haida, 270, 1905. Lth'ait Lennas.—Harrison in Proc. and Trans. Roy. Soc. Can., sec. II, 125, 1895. Tlg·ā'itgu lā'nas.—Boas, 12th Rep. N. W. Tribes Can., 24, 1898.

Hlgahet-kegawai (*Ɫgā'xet-qē'gawa-i*, 'those born at Pebble-town'). A subdivision of the Hlgahet-gitinai, a family of the Eagle clan of the Haida, or only another name for that family.—Swanton, Cont. Haida, 274, 1905.

Hlgai (*Ɫgā'i*). Said to have been the name of a town at the head of Skedans bay, w. coast of the Queen Charlotte ids., Brit. Col.—Swanton, Cont. Haida, 279, 1905.

Hlgaiha (*Ɫga'-ixa*, from *ɫgai* 'to dig', *xa* 'to put in'). A semi-legendary Haida town N. of Dead Tree pt., at the entrance of Skidegate inlet, Queen Charlotte ids., Brit. Col. From this place the great Gitins family of Skidegate is said to have sprung.—Swanton, Cont. Haida, 99, 1905.

Hlgaiu (*Ɫgāi-u'*, probably 'place of stones'). A town and camping place of the Djahui-skwahladagai of the Haida,

s. of Dead Tree pt., at the entrance to Skidegate inlet, Queen Charlotte ids., Brit. Col. One of the names of the town of Skidegate is said to have been derived from this.　　　　　　　　(J. R. S.)
Kit-hai-uáss hādē.—Krause, Tlinkit Indianer, 304, 1885 (possibly identical). Ɫgāi-u'.—Swanton, Cont. Haida, 279, 1905.

Hlgaiu-lanas (*Ɫgai-ū' lā'nas*, 'Skidegate town people'). A division of the Raven clan of the Haida who originally owned the town of Skidegate, Brit. Col., and hence came to be called by the Haida name of the town. Later they gave the town to the Gitins in payment for an injury inflicted on one of the latter, and moved to Gaodjaos, farther up the inlet. A subdivision was called Hlgagilda-kegawai.　　　　　　　　(J. R. S.)
Ɫgai-ū' lā'nas.—Swanton, Cont. Haida, 269, 1905. Tlaiyū Hāadē.—Harrison in Proc. and Trans. Roy. Soc. Can., sec. II, 125, 1895 (erroneously assigned to Old Gold Harbor). Tlg·aio lā'nas.—Boas, 12th Rep. N. W. Tribes Can., 24, 1898. Tlqaiu lā'nas.—Boas, 5th Rep. of same, 26, 1889.

Hlgan (*Ɫgẟn*, 'killer-whale's dorsal fin'). A Haida town s. of Tigun, on the w. coast of Graham id., Queen Charlotte group, Brit. Col., occupied by the Dostlan-lnagai. The Koetas are said to have lived at this place before they moved to Alaska, and the town is said to have been so named on account of a rock which stands up in front of it like the dorsal fin of a killer-whale.　　(J. R. S.)
Ɫgẟn.—Swanton, Cont. Haida, 280, 1905. Ɫᵍẟn.—Swanton, inf'n, 1905 (another form).

Hlgihla-ala (*Ɫgĭ'ɫɅ ála*, probably 'town of the ditches'). A former Haida town N. of Cape Ball, E. shore of Graham id., Queen Charlotte group, Brit. Col. It was occupied by the Naikun-kegawai.—Swanton, Cont. Haida, 280, 1905.

Hlielung (*Ɫi'elɅñ*). A former Haida town of the Kuna-lanas family on the right bank of a river of the same name (Hi-ellen on Dawson's chart), which flows into Dixon entrance at the foot of Tow hill, N. coast of Queen Charlotte ids., Brit. Col. The town was erroneously thought by Dawson (Queen Charlotte Ids., 165B, 1880) to be the Ne-coon of John Work.　　　　　　　　(J. R. S.)
Hieller.—Deans, Tales from Hidery, 92, 1899. Ia'gEn.—Boas, 12th Rep. N. W. Tribes Can., 23, 1898. Ɫi'elɅñ.—Swanton, Cont. Haida, 280, 1905.

Hlielung-keawai (*Ɫi'elɅñ qē'awa-i*, 'those born at the town of Hlielung'). A subdivision of the Stustas, a family of the Eagle clan of the Haida, occupying a town at the mouth of Hiellen (Hlielung) r., Graham id., Queen Charlotte group, Brit. Col.　　　　(J. R. S.)
Dl'iā'lEn k·ēowai'.—Boas, 12th Rep. N. W. Tribes Can., 23, 1898. Ɫi'elɅñ qē'awa-i.—Swanton, Cont. Haida, 276, 1905. Lthyhellun Kiiwē.—Harrison in Proc. and Trans. Roy. Soc. Can., sec. II, 125, 1895.

Hlielungkun-lnagai (*Ɫi'elɅñ kun lnagā'-i*, 'Ɫi'elɅñ river point town-people'). A town of the Kuna-lanas, belonging to the **Raven clan** of the Haida, situated on a river of the same name (called Hiellen on Dawson's map).　　　(J. R. S.)

Dl'iā'lɛn kunîlnagai'.—Boas, 12th Rep. N. W. Tribes Can., 23, 1898. **Łi'elAñ kun lnagā'-i.**—Swanton, Cont. Haida, 270, 1905.

Hlielung-stustae (*Łi'elAñ stAstā'-i*, 'Stustas of Hlielung'). A subdivision of the Stustas, an important family of the Eagle clan of the Haida, occupying the town at the mouth of Hlielung or Hiellen r., Queen Charlotte ids., Brit. Col. Possibly a synonym of Hlielung-keawai.—Swanton, Cont. Haida, 276, 1905.

Hlimulnaas-hadai (*ŁimA'l na'as xā'-da-i*, 'hlimul-skin-house people'). A subdivision of the Salendas, a Haida family of the Eagle clan. They were so called from one of their houses; *hlimul* was a name applied to the skins of certain mainland animals.—Swanton, Cont. Haida, 276, 1905.

Hlingwainaas-hadai (*Łingwā'-i na'as xā'da-i*, 'world-house people'). A subdivision of the Aokeawai, a family of the Raven clan of the Haida; probably named from a house.—Swanton, Cont. Haida, 272, 1905.

Hlkaonedis (Tlingit: *Łqa'onedis*, 'people of Łqao river'). A subdivision of the Koetas, a family of the Raven clan of the Haida, living principally in Alaska. They may have received their name from a camping place.—Swanton, Cont. Haida, 272, 1905.

Hlkia (*Łklïä'*, 'chicken-hawk town' or 'saw-bill town') A former Haida town on the outer side of Lyell id., Queen Charlotte ids., Brit. Col. It was occupied by the Kona-kegawai.—Swanton, Cont. Haida, 278, 1905.

Hlkoayedi (*Łqo'ayedi*). A Tlingit division at Klawak, Alaska, said to be part of the Shunkukedi, q. v.　　　(J. R. S.)

Hlukahadi. A division of the Raven phratry of the Chilkat, formerly living in the town of Yendestake, Alaska. According to the Chilkat themselves the name means 'quick people', but according to informants at Wrangell, 'people of Hlukak' (*Łuqā'x*), a creek near Wrangell.

Chlukŏach-adĭ.—Krause, Tlinkit Ind., 116, 1885. **Kădŭwot-kĕdi.**—Ibid. (given as a distinct social group). **Łuqā'xadĭ.**—Swanton, field notes, B. A. E., 1904.

Hlukkuhoan (*ŁAxqluxo-ān*, 'town where people do not sleep much'). A former Tlingit town in Alaska.　　　(J. R. S.)

Hluln (*Łꜰuln*). A former Haida town in Naden harbor, Graham id., Queen Charlotte group, Brit. Col.—Swanton, Cont. Haida, 281, 1905.

Hoabonoma. Evidently the Pima or Maricopa name of a tribe of which Father Kino learned while on the lower Rio Gila, Ariz., in 1700. Unidentified, although probably Yuman. They have sometimes been loosely classed as a part of the Cocopa. **Heabenomas.**—Consag (1746) quoted by Taylor in Cal. Farmer, Dec. 6, 1861. **Hebonumas.**—Venegas, Hist. Cal., II, 171, 1759. **Hoabonoma.**—Kino (1700) quoted by Coues, Garcés Diary, 548, 1900. **Hoahonómos.**—Mayer, Mexico, II, 38, 1853. **Hobonomas.**—Venegas, Hist. Cal., I, 301, 1759. **Oaboponoma.**—Kino (1700) in Doc. Hist. Mex., 4th s., I, 349, 1856.

Hoaiels. Mentioned by Baudry des Lozières (Voy. Louisiane, 242, 1802) in a list of tribes with no indication of habitat. Possibly intended for Theloel, a name given sometimes to part, at others to all the Natchez.

Hoako. A former Maidu village on the w. bank of Feather r., below Marysville, Sutter co., Cal.　　　(R. B. D.)

Hoak.—Wozencraft (1851) in Sen. Ex. Doc. 4, 32d Cong., spec. sess., 206, 1853. **Hoako.**—Dixon in Bull. Am. Mus. Nat. Hist., XVII, pt. 3, map, 124, 1905. **Hock.**—Powers in Cont. N. A. Ethnol., III, 282, 1877. **Hocks.**—Ind. Aff. Rep., 129, 1850. **Hoka.**—Curtin, MS. vocab., B. A. E., 1885. **Huk.**—Hale, Ethnol. and Philol., VI, 631, 1846.

Hobatinequasi. A clan of the Acheha phratry of the ancient Timucua of Florida.—Pareja (*ca.* 1614) quoted by Gatschet in Am. Philos. Soc. Proc., XVII, 492, 1878.

Hobbamock, Hobbamoco. See *Hobomok, Hobomoko.*

Hobeckentopa. A locality, possibly a town, where a treaty with the Choctaw was concluded Aug. 31, 1803. It was on Tombigbee r., in the E. part of Washington co., Ala., perhaps on or near a bluff of the same name upon which St Stephens now stands.　　　(H. W. H.)

Hobeckenlopa.—Am. State Papers, Ind. Aff. (1805), I, 749, 1832. **Hoe-Buckin-too-pa.**—U. S. Ind. Treat. (1803), 103, 1837.

Hobnuts. A folk-etymological corruption of *hobbenis*, the name of a tuberous root (*Orontium aquaticum*) in the Delaware dialect of Algonquian. Rev. A. Hesselius (cited by Nelson, Inds. of N. J., 78, 1894), writing in the early years of the 18th century in New Jersey, mentions "the first fruits of roots, which grow in swamps, not unlike nuts, called *tachis*, or by the English *hopnuts*." The Delaware *hobbenis* is a diminutive of *hobbin*, which was afterward applied by these Indians to the potato. The Swedish colonists called this root *hopnis*.　　　(A. F. C.)

Hobomok. A chief of the Wampanoag who was the life-long friend of the English, from the time he met them at Plymouth in 1621. He helped to strengthen the friendship of Massasoit for the colonists, but, unlike Massasoit, he became a Christian, and died, before 1642, as a member of the English settlement at Plymouth. He was of great service to the English in warning them of Indian conspiracies. He was present at some of the battles in which Standish performed valorous deeds, but was not an active participant. The name is identical with Abbamocho, Hobbamoco, Habamouk, Hobbamock, Hobomoko, etc. See the following.　　　(A. F. C.)

Hobomoko. Whittier, in the notes to his Poems (464, 1891) cites the saying concerning John Bonython:

Here lies Bonython, the Sagamore of Saco,
He lived a rogue and died a knave, and went to Hobomoko.

Mentioned by early writers as an evil deity of the Massachuset and closely related Algonquian tribes.   (A. F. C.)

Hoccanum. Mentioned as a band formerly in East Hartford township, Hartford co., Conn., where they remained, according to Stiles, until about 1745. They were probably identical with or a part of the Podunk (q. v.). De Forest locates the Podunk here, but does not mention the Hoccanum.

Hoccanums.—Stiles (1761) in Mass. Hist. Soc. Coll., 1st s., X, 105, 1809. Hockanoanco.—Mason (1659) ibid., 4th s., VII, 423, 1865 (perhaps the name of the village).

Hochelaga (dialectic form of *Hochelayi,* 'at the place of the [beaver] dam'). A former Iroquoian town, strongly palisaded, situated in 1535 on Montreal id., Canada, about a mile from the mountain first called "Mont Royal" by Cartier. At that time it contained about 50 typical Iroquoian lodges, each 50 or more paces in length and 12 or 15 in breadth, built of wood and covered with very broad strips of bark, neatly and deftly joined. Estimating 12 fires and 24 firesides, each of three persons, to every lodge, the total population would have been about 3,600. The upper portion of the lodges was used for storing corn, beans, and dried fruits. The inhabitants pounded corn in wooden mortars with pestles and made a paste of the meal, which was molded into cakes that were cooked on large hot rocks and covered with hot pebbles. They also made many soups of corn, beans, and peas, of which they had a sufficiency. In the lodges were large vessels in which smoked fish was stored for winter use. They were not travelers like those of "Canada" and "Saguenay," although, according to Cartier, "the said Canadians are subject to them with 8 or 9 other peoples along the river."

(J. N. B. H.)

Hochelaga.—Cartier (1545), Bref Récit, 9, 1863. Hochelagenses.—De Laet (1633) quoted by Barton, New Views, xlii, 1798 (Latin name of the inhabitants). Ochelaga.—Map (*ca.* 1543) in Maine Hist. Soc. Coll., I, 354, 1869; Jes. Rel. 1642, 36, 1858.

Hochelayi ('at the place of the [beaver] dam'). A former Iroquoian town, situated in 1535 in a flat country not far from the junction of Jacques Cartier r. with the St Lawrence, and probably near the present Pt Platon, Quebec.   (J. N. B. H.)

Achelaci.—Cartier (1535), Bref Récit, 56a, 1863. Achelacy.—Ibid. Achelaiy.—Ibid. Achelayy.—Ibid. Hochelai.—Cartier (1535) quoted by Hakluyt, Voy., II, 115, 1889. Hochelay.—Ibid., 129. Ochelay.—Cartier, Bref Récit, op. cit.

Hochonchapa ('alligator'). A Chickasaw clan of the Ishpanee phratry.

Ho-chon-chab-ba.—Morgan, Anc. Soc., 163, 1877.

Hotchon tchápa.—Gatschet, Creek Migr. Leg., I, 96, 1884.

Hockhocken ('place of gourds.'—Hewitt). A former Delaware village on Hocking r., Ohio.

Hackhocken.—La Tour, map, 1779. Hockhocken.—Ibid., 1782. Hoekhocken.—Lattré, map, 1784. Mockhoeken.—Esnauts and Rapilly, map, 1777 (misprint).

Hoes and Spades. Agricultural implements in general are referred to under Agriculture (q. v.), special mention being here made of certain numerous, large, bladelike, chipped implements of flint found in the rich alluvial bottom lands of the middle Mississippi valley, whose polished surfaces in many cases unmistakably indicate long-continued use in digging operations; and this, in connection with their suggestive shape, has caused them to be classified as hoes and spades. Extensive quarries of the flint nodules from which implements of this class were shaped, have been located in Union co., Ill. (see *Quarries*). Great numbers of the hoes and spades, originating in these or in similar quarries, are distributed over an extensive area in Missouri, Illinois, and the neighboring states. The most common form has an oval, or elliptical outline, with ends either rounded or somewhat pointed; a modified form has the lower end strongly curved, with the sides in straight or slightly concave lines and the same pointed top. Beginning with the extremes of this type, it is possible to arrange a series which will pass by insensible gradations into small scrapers and scraper-like celts. Another type, not unusual, has a semi-elliptical blade with a square or flat top, in the sides of which deep notches are cut for securing the handle. An allied form is without the notches but has projecting points at the top, which answer the same purpose. The larger implements of this class, often reaching a foot in length, are generally denominated spades, and the shorter, or notched, forms hoes; but as both had the handles put on either parallel with the longer axis or at an angle with it, allowing all alike to be used in the same manner, the distinction is without particular significance.

Consult Fowke in 13th Rep. B. A. E., 1896; Moorehead, Prehist. Implements, 1900; Rau, Archæol. Coll. Nat. Mus., 1876; Thruston, Antiquities of Tenn., 1897; Willoughby in Am. Anthrop., VIII, 130, 1906.   (G. F. W. H. H.)

Hog. See *Quahog*.

Hogan. A Navaho house; adapted from *qoghán* (Mindeleff in 17th Rep. B. A. E., 475, 1898), in the Navaho dialect of the Athapascan stock. See *Habitations*.

Hog Creek. A former Shawnee settlement on a branch of Ottawa r., in Allen co., Ohio. The Indians sold their reservation there in 1831 and removed w. of the Mississippi.   (J. M.)

Hogologes. A former Yuchi town on Apalachicola r., at the junction of Chattahoochee and Flint rs., in Georgia.
Hagaligis.—Bartram, Voy., I, map, 1799. Hogohegees.—Jefferys, Am. Atlas, map 8, 1776. Hogoleeges.—Romans, Fla., I, 280, 1775. Hogoleegis.—Roberts, Fla., 13, 90, 1763. Hogoligis.—Alcedo, Dic. Geog., II, 364, 1787. Hogologes.—Jefferys, Am. Atlas, map 5, 1776. Ogolegees.—Lattré, Map U. S., 1784.

Hogstown. Described as an old (Delaware) village between Venango and Buffalo cr., Pa., in 1791 (Proctor in Am. St. Papers, Ind. Aff., I, 153, 1832). Perhaps wrongly located and identical with Kuskuski.

Hoh. A band of the Quileute living at the mouth of Hoh r., about 15 m. s. of Lapush, the main seat of the tribe on the w. coast of Washington. They are under the jurisdiction of the Neah Bay agency. Pop. 62 in 1905.   (L. F.)
Hohs.—McKenney in Ind. Aff. Rep. 1869, 131, 1870. Holes.—Hill, ibid., 1867, 48, 1868. Hooch.—Swan, N. W. Coast, 211, 1857. Hooh.—Ibid. Hüch.—Gibbs in Cont. N. A. Ethnol., I, 173, 1877. Kwääksat.—Ibid.

Hohandika ('earth eaters'). A Shoshoni division inhabiting the region w. of Great Salt lake, Utah. They suffered a severe defeat in 1862 at the hands of California volunteers.
Diggers.—Gatschet in Geog. Surv. W. 100 M., 409, 1879. Earth Eaters.—Hoffman in Proc. Am. Philos. Soc., XXIII, 298, 1886. Hóhandíka.—Ibid. Hokan-dik'-ah.—Stuart, Montana, 81, 1865. Hokanti ͨkara.—Gatschet, op. cit. Salt Lake Diggers.—Stuart, op. cit.

Hohe ('Assiniboin'). A band of the Sihasapa division of the Teton Sioux.—Dorsey in 15th Rep. B. A. E., 219, 1897.

Hohilpo. Said by Lewis and Clark (Exped., I, map, 1814; II, 596, 1817) to be a tribe of the Tushepaw (q. v.) residing on Clarke r., above the Micksucksealton, in the Rocky mts., and numbering 300 in 25 lodges in 1805.
Ho hill pos.—Orig. Jour. Lewis and Clark, VI, 114, 1905. Ho-hil-pos.—Ibid., 120. Ho-pil-po.—Lewis and Clark misquoted by Gibbs in Pac. R. R. Rep., I, 417, 1855.

Hohio. Mentioned by Coxe (Carolana, 12, 1741) as a nation living on the Wabash. Unidentified, and probably imaginary as a tribe, although the name is the same as Ohio.

Hohopa (Ho-ho-pa). A Koeksotenok village on the w. coast of Baker id., Brit. Col.—Dawson in Trans. Roy. Soc. Can., sec. 2, 73, 1887.

Hohota. Mentioned by Oñate (Doc. Inéd., XVI, 113, 1871) as a pueblo of New Mexico in 1598; at that time doubtless situated in the country of the Salinas, in the vicinity of Abo, E. of the Rio Grande, and evidently occupied by the Tigua or the Piros.   (F. W. H.)

Hoindarhonon ('island people.'—Hewitt). The Huron name of a tribe subordinate to the Ottawa.—Sagard (1632), Canada, IV, cap. 'Nations,' 1866.

Hoitda. A division of the Maidu living on Rock cr., in the N. part of Butte co., Cal.
Hocktem.—Chever in Bull. Essex Inst., II, 28, 1871. Hoitda.—Curtin, MS. vocab., B. A. E., 1885.

Hokarutcha ('skunk'). A band or society of the Crows.
Ho-ka-rut'-cha.—Morgan, Anc. Soc., 159, 1877. Pole-cat band.—Culbertson in Smithson. Rep. 1850, 144, 1851.

Hokedi (Xŏq!e′dî, 'people of Xŏq!'). A Tlingit clan at Wrangell, Alaska, belonging to the Wolf phratry. They are named from a place (Xŏq!) opposite Old Wrangell.
Kook-a-tee.—Kane, Wand. in N. A., app., 1859. Qŏkē′dĕ.—Boas, 5th Rep. N. W. Tribes of Can., 25, 1889. Rohŭch-ē′di.—Krause, Tlinkit Ind., 120, 1885. Xŏq!e′dî.—Swanton, field notes, B. A. E., 1904.

Hoko. A Clallam village on Okeho r., Wash. Under the name Okeno its inhabitants participated in the treaty of Point No Point, Wash., in 1855.
Hoko.—Swan, letter, B. A. E., Feb. 1886. Ocha.—Gibbs in Pac. R. R. Rep., I, 429, 1855. Ocho.—Stevens in Ind. Aff. Rep., 450, 1854. Okeho.—Ibid. Okeno.—U. S. Ind. Treat. (1855), 800, 1873.

Hoko. The Juniper clan of the Kokop (Wood) phratry of the Hopi.
Hóhu.—Voth, Hopi Proper Names, 78, 1905. Hoko wiñwû.—Fewkes in 19th Rep. B. A. E., 584, 1900 (wiñwû='clan'). Ho′-ko wüñ-wû.—Fewkes in Am. Anthrop., VII, 404, 1894.

Hokokwito. A former village of the Awani division of the Miwok, opposite Yosemite falls, in Yosemite valley, Mariposa co., Cal. The hotel now occupies its site.
Hocócwedoc.—Powers in Overland Mo., X, 333, 1874. Hok-ok′-wi-dok.—Powers in Cont. N. A. Ethnol., III, 365, 1877. Hokokwito.—A. L. Kroeber, inf'n, 1905.

Hokomo. A former Maidu village on the E. side of Middle fork of Feather r., almost due N. of Mooretown, Butte co., Cal.—Dixon in Bull. Am. Mus. Nat. Hist., XVII, pl. xxxviii, 1905.

Hokwaits (Ho-kwaits). A band of Paiute formerly living near Ivanpah, s. E. Cal. (Powell in Ind. Aff. Rep. 1873, 51, 1874). Cf. Hakwiche, the Mohave name of the Kawia, q. v.

Holatamico, popularly known as Billy Bowlegs. The last Seminole chief of prominence to leave Florida and remove with his people to the W. He was born about 1808, and after the first Seminole removal became the recognized chief of the remnant in 1842, and was the leader of hostilities in 1855 to 1858. Although but 25 years of age, and not then a chief, he was one of the signers of the treaty of Payne's Landing, May 9, 1832, by which the Seminole agreed to remove to Indian Ter., but it was not until May, 1858, that he and his band, numbering 164 persons, departed. See Bowlegs.   (C. T.)

Holeclame. One of several tribes formerly occupying "the country from Buena Vista and Carises lakes, and Kern r. to the Sierra Nevada and Coast range,"

Cal. (Barbour in Sen. Ex. Doc. 4, 32d Cong., spec. sess., 256, 1853). By treaty of June 10, 1851, these tribes reserved a tract between Tejon pass and Kern r., and ceded the remainder of their lands to the United States. Probably Mariposan (Yokuts), though possibly Chumashan. Cf. *Holkoma, Holmiuk*.

Hole-in-the-day (*Bagwŭnagijĭk*, 'hole, opening, rift in the sky.'—W. J.). A Chippewa chief, a member of the warlike Noka (Bear) clan. He succeeded Curlyhead (q. v.) as war chief in 1825. He had already been recognized as a chief by the Government for his bravery and fidelity to the Americans in the war of 1812. His whole subsequent life was spent in fighting the Sioux, and he ended the struggle that had lasted for centuries over the possession of the fisheries and hunting grounds of the L. Superior region by definitively driving the hereditary enemy across the Mississippi. Had not the Government intervened to compel the warring tribes to accept a line of demarkation, he threatened to plant his village on Minnesota r. and pursue the Sioux into the western plains. At Prairie du Chien he acknowledged the ancient possession by the Sioux of the territory from the Mississippi to Green bay and the head of L. Superior, but claimed it for the Chippewa by right of conquest. The Chippewa had the advantage of the earlier possession of firearms, but in the later feuds which Hole-in-the-day carried on the two peoples were equally armed. George Copway, who valued the friendship of Hole-in-the-day and once ran 270 miles in 4 days to apprise him of a Sioux raid, relates how he almost converted the old chief, who promised to embrace Christianity and advise his people to do so "after one more battle with the Sioux." He was succeeded as head chief of the Chippewa on his death in 1846 by his son, who bore his father's name and who carried on in Minnesota the ancient feud with the Dakota tribes. At the time of the Sioux rising in 1862 he was accused of planning a similar revolt. The second Hole-in-the-day was murdered by men of his own tribe at Crow Wing, Minn., June 27, 1868. (F. H.)

Holholto. A former Maidu village a few miles s. of Mooretown, Butte co., Cal.
Helto.—Powers in Cont. N. A. Ethnol., III, 282, 1877. Holholto.—Dixon in Bull. Am. Mus. Nat. Hist., XVII, pl. xxxviii, 1905.

Holkoma. A Mono tribe on Sycamore cr. and Big cr., N. of Kings r., Cal. There is some doubt as to its proper name.
Hol-cu-ma.—Royce in 18th Rep. B. A. E., 782, 1899. Ho-len-mahs.—Johnston (1851) in Sen. Ex. Doc 61, 32d Cong., 1st sess., 22, 1852. Hol-en-nas.—Barbour (1852) in Sen. Ex. Doc. 4, 32d Cong., spec. sess., 254, 1853. Hol'-ko-mah.—Merriam in Science, XIX, 916, June 15, 1904. Hol-o'-kommah.—Ibid. To-win-che'-bă.—Ibid.

Hollow-horn Bear. A Brulé Sioux chief, born in Sheridan co., Nebr., in Mar., 1850. When but 16 years of age he accompanied a band led by his father against the Pawnee, whom they fought on the present site of Genoa, Nebr. In 1868 he joined a band of Brulés in an attack on United States troops in Wyoming, and in another where now is situated the Crow agency, Mont.; and in the following year participated in a raid on the laborers who were constructing the Union Pacific R. R. Subsequently he became captain of police at Rosebud agency, S. Dak., and arrested his predecessor, Crow Dog, for the murder of Spotted Tail. Five years later he resigned and was appointed second lieutenant under Agent Spencer, but was again compelled to resign on account of ill health. When Gen. Crook was sent with a commission to Rosebud, in 1889, to make an agreement with the Indians there, Hollow-horn Bear was chosen by the Sioux as their speaker, being considered an orator of unusual ability. He took part in the parade at the inauguration of President Roosevelt at Washington, Mar. 4, 1905. (C. T.)

Holmiuk. One of the tribes formerly occupying "the country from Buena Vista and Carises lakes, and Kern r. to the Sierra Nevada and Coast range," Cal. By treaty of June 10, 1851, these tribes reserved a tract between Tejon pass and Kern r. and ceded the remainder of their land to the United States. Probably of Mariposan (Yokuts) or Shoshonean stock. Cf. *Holeclame, Holkoma*.
Hol-mie-uhs.—Barbour (1852) in Sen. Ex. Doc. 4, 32d Cong., spec. sess., 256, 1853. Holmiuk.—Royce in 18th Rep. B. A. E., 782, 1899.

Holstenborg. A missionary station on Davis str., w. Greenland.
Holsteinberg.—Crantz, Hist. Greenland, I, 13, 1767. Holstensborg.—Meddelelser om Grönland, XXV, map, 1902.

Holtrochtac. A Costanoan village formerly connected with Santa Cruz mission, Cal.—Taylor in Cal. Farmer, Apr. 5, 1860.

Holukhik (*Ho-lŭq'-ĭk*). A Yaquina village on the N. side of Yaquina r., Oreg.—Dorsey in Jour. Am. Folk-lore, III, 229, 1890.

Homalko. A Salish tribe on the E. side of Bute inlet, Brit. Col., speaking the Comox dialect; pop. 89 in 1904.
Em-alcom.—Can. Ind. Aff. for 1884, 187. Homalco.—Ibid., 1891, map. Homalko.—Ibid., 1901, pt. II, 158. Qoē'qomatlxo.—Boas, MS., B. A. E., 1887.

Homayine (*Ho'ma yiñ'-e*, 'young elk'). A subgens of the Khotachi, the Elk gens of the Iowa.—Dorsey in 15th Rep. B. A. E., 238, 1897.

Homayo. A large ruined pueblo of the Tewa on the w. bank of Rio Ojo Caliente, a small w. tributary of the Rio Grande, in Rio Arriba co., N. Mex. See Bandelier in Arch. Inst. Papers, IV, 37, 1892; Hewett in Bull. 32, B. A. E., 39, 1906.

Homhoabit. Given by Rev. J. Caballeria (Hist. San Bernardino Val., 1902) as a former village, probably of the Serranos, at a place now called Homoa, near San Bernardino, s. Cal.

Hominy. From the Algonquian dialects of New England or Virginia, applied to a dish prepared from Indian corn pounded or cracked and boiled, or the kernels merely hulled by steeping first in lye or ashes and afterward boiled, with or without fish or meat to season it. The first mention of the name in print occurs in Capt. John Smith's True Travels, 43, 1630. Some forms of the name given by early writers are *tackhummin*, 'to grind corn (or grain),' and *pokhommin*, 'to beat or thresh out.' Josselyn (N. E. Rar., 53, 1672) defined *hominy* as what was left after the flour had been sifted out of cornmeal. Beverley (Virginia, bk. 3, 1722) says that *homony* is "Indian corn, broken in a mortar, husked, and then boiled in water over a gentle fire for ten or more hours to the consistency of furmity." The name "hominy grits" is sometimes applied to the cracked variety. Tooker suggests as the radicals *ahäm*, 'he beats or pounds'; *min*, 'berry or fruit,' 'grain.' The name may be a reduction of some of the words in which it occurs, as *rockohominy*. Dr Wm. Jones (inf'n, 1906) says: "It is plain that the form of the word *hominy* is but an abbreviation, for what is left is the designative suffix *-min*, 'grain,' and part of a preceding modifying stem." For a discussion of the etymology see Gerard in Am. Anthrop., VI, 314, 1904; VII, 226, 1905; Tooker, ibid., VI, 682. See *Samp.*
(A. F. C.   J. N. B. H.)

Homna (*Ho-mna*, 'smelling like fish'). A division of the Brulé Teton Sioux.—Dorsey in 15th Rep. B. A. E., 218, 1897.

Homnipa. Given as a Karok village on Klamath r., N. W. Cal., inhabited in 1860.
Home-nip-pah.—Taylor in Cal. Farmer, Mar. 23, 1860.

Homolobi (*Hō-mōl'-ōbi*, 'place of the breast-like elevation'). A group of ruined pueblos near Winslow, Ariz., which were occupied by the ancestors of various Hopi clans. See Fewkes in 22d Rep. B. A. E., 23, et seq., 1904; Mindeleff in 8th Rep. B. A. E., 29, 1891.

Homolua. A former Timucua village, situated, according to Laudonnière, on the s. side of St Johns r., Fla., at its mouth, in 1564. De Gourgues placed a town of similar name about 60 leagues inland on the same river.
Emola.—Laudonnière (1564) in French, Hist. Coll. La., n. s., 306, 1869. Homoloa.—Ibid., 331. Homoloua.—De Bry, Brev. Nar., map, 1590. Molloua.—Laudonnière, op. cit., 242. Moloa.—Fontaneda (1575), ibid., 2d s., 264, 1875. Molona.—Laudonnière, op. cit., 245. Monloua.—Gourges, ibid., 2d s., 275, 1875. Omoloa.—Laudonnière, op. cit., 253.

Homosassa ('abundance of pepper'). A Seminole town in Hernando co., Fla., in 1837. There are now a river and a town of the same name in that locality.
Homa Susa.—Drake, Ind. Chron., 215, 1836.

Homuarup. A former Karok village on Klamath r., Cal.
Home-war-roop.—Taylor in Cal. Farmer, Mar. 23, 1860.

Homulchison. A Squawmish village community at Capilano cr., Burrard inlet, Brit. Col.; the former headquarters of the supreme chief of the tribe. Pop. 45 in 1904.
Capalino.—Can. Ind. Aff., 276, 1894. Capitano Creek.—Can. Ind. Aff., 308, 1879. Hōmu'ltcison.—Hill-Tout in Rep. Brit. A. A. S., 475, 1900. Kapilano.—Can. Ind. Aff., 357, 1897.

Honabanou. Coxe (Carolana, 14, 1741) says that "fifteen leagues above the Hohio . . . to the w. is the river Honabanou, upon which dwells a nation of the same name, and another called Amicoa." On the map accompanying his work this river is represented as in s. E. Missouri, entering the Mississippi immediately above or nearly opposite the mouth of the Ohio. As there is no stream on the w. side between the mouth of the Ohio and St Genevieve co. that can be called a river, and no Indians of the names mentioned are known to have resided in that section, both must be rejected as unauthentic, and indeed mythical so far as the locality is concerned. This river has evidently been laid down from Hennepin's map of 1697, relating to the "New Discovery," which is admitted to be unauthentic so far as it relates to the region s. of the mouth of Illinois r. It is evident, however, that Coxe has attempted to give the name Ouabano (q. v.), which La Salle applied to some Indians who visited Ft St Louis, on Matagorda bay, Texas, from a westerly section.
(J. M.   C. T.)

Honani. The Badger phratry of the Hopi, comprising the Honani (Badger), Muinyan (Porcupine), Wishoko (Turkeybuzzard), Buli (Butterfly), Buliso (Evening Primrose), and Kachina (Sacred Dancer) clans. According to Fewkes this people settled at Kishyuba, a spring sacred to the Kachinas, before going to Tusayan. The Honani and Kachina phratries are intimately associated. The former settled Walpi when the village was on the old site, and some of them went on to Awatobi, whence they returned after the fall of that pueblo. The arrival of the Honani in Tusayan was probably not earlier than the latter part of the 17th century.
Ho-na-ni-nyû-mû.—Fewkes in Am. Anthrop., VII, 405, 1894 (*nyû-mû*='phratry').

Honani. The Badger clan of the Hopi.
Honáni.—Bourke, Snake Dance, 117, 1884. Honani wiñwû.—Fewkes in 19th Rep. B. A. E., 584, 1900 (*wiñwû*='clan'). Ho-na'-ni wüñ-wü.—Fewkes in Am. Anthrop., VII, 405, 1894. Hon'-wüñ-wü.—Ibid., 404.

Honanki (Hopi: 'bear house'). A prehistoric cliff-village, attributed to the Hopi, in the valley of Oak cr., in the "red-rock" country s. of Flagstaff, Ariz.—Fewkes in 17th Rep. B. A. E., 558–569, 1898.

Honau (*Hó'-na-u*). The Bear phratry of the Hopi, comprising the Honau (Bear), Tokochi (Wild-cat), Chosro (Bird [blue]), Kokyan (Spider), and Hekpa (Fir) clans. According to Fewkes these people are traditionally said to have been the first to arrive in Tusayan. Although reputed to be the oldest people in Walpi they are now almost extinct in that pueblo, and are not represented in Sichomovi. They exist however at Mishongnovi.
Honau.—Fewkes in 19th Rep. B. A. E., 584, 1900. Ho'-nau-üh.—Fewkes in Am. Anthrop., VII, 404, 1894. Hónin nyumu.—Stephen in 8th Rep. B. A. E., 38, 1891 (*nyumu*='phratry'). Hon-ñamu.—Voth, Traditions of the Hopi, 36, 1905.

Honau. The Bear clan of the Hopi.
Honan.—Bourke, Snake Dance, 117, 1884 (misprint). Ho'-nau.—Stephen in 8th Rep. B. A. E., 39, 1891. Honau winwû.—Fewkes in 19th Rep. B. A. E., 584, 1900. Honawuu.—Dorsey and Voth, Mishongnovi Ceremonies, 175, 1902.

Honayawus. See *Farmer's Brother*.

Honeoye ('his finger lies.'—Hewitt). A former Seneca settlement on Honeoye cr., near Honeoye lake, N. Y.; destroyed by Sullivan in 1779.
Anagangaw.—Livermore (1779) in N. H. Hist. Soc. Coll., VI, 327–329, 1850. Anjageen.—Pouchot, map (1758) in N. Y. Doc. Col. Hist., X, 694, 1858. Annagaugaw.—Livermore, op.cit. Anyayea.—Hubley (1779) quoted by Conover, Kanadega and Geneva MS., B. A. E. Hannayaye.—Sullivan (1779) quoted by Conover, ibid. Hanneyaye.—Nukerck (1779), ibid. Haunyauya.—Grant (1779), ibid. Honeyoye.—Dearborn (1779), ibid. Honneyayea.—Fellows (1779), ibid. Onnayayou.—McKendry (1779), ibid. Onyauyah.—Barton (1779), ibid.

Honest John. See *Tedyuskung*.

Honetaparteenwaz. Given as a division of the Yankton of the North under chief Tattunggarweeteco in 1804, but probably intended for the Hunkpatina.
Hone-ta-par-teen-waz.—Lewis and Clark, Discov., 34, 1806; Orig. Jour. Lewis and Clark, VI, 99, 1905.

Honkut. A division of Maidu living near the mouth of Honcut cr., Yuba co., Cal.
Hoancuts.—Powers in Overland Mo., XII, 420, 1874. Hoan'-kut.—Powers in Cont. N. A. Ethnol., III, 282, 1877. Honcut.—Bancroft, Nat. Races, I, 450, 1874.

Honmoyaushu (*Hon-mo-yau'-cu*). A former Chumashan village at El Barranco, near San Pedro, Ventura co., Cal.—Henshaw, Buenaventura MS. vocab., B. A. E., 1884.

Honniasontkeronon (Iroquois: 'people of the place of crook-necked squashes,' or 'people of the place where they wear crosses'). An unidentified people of whom Gallinée was informed by the Iroquois as living on Ohio r., above the falls at Louisville, Ky. On a map of De l'Isle, dated 1722, a small lake called L. Oniasont, around which are the words 'les Oniasontke,' is placed on the s. side, apparently, of the "Ouabache, otherwise called Ohio or Beautiful river," and the outlet of L. Oniasont is made to flow into the Ouabache. It may be inferred that the Iroquois statement as to the location of this people was substantially correct; that is, that they lived on a small lake E. of Wabash r. and having an outlet into that stream, although Honniasontke'ronⁿ is an Iroquois euphemism for the land of departed spirits. (J. N. B. H.)
Honniasontkeronons.—Gallinée (1669) in Margry Déc., I, 116; 1875. Oniasontke.—De l'Isle, map, 1772. Oniasont-Keronons.—Fernow, Ohio Valley, 32, 1890.

Honosonayo ('white deer'). A clan of the ancient Timucua of Florida.
Honoso Nayo.—Pareja (ca. 1613) quoted by Gatschet in Am. Philos. Soc. Proc., XVII, 492, 1878.

Honowa (*Hó'nowă*, 'poor people'; sing., *Hó'nów*). A principal division of the Cheyenne, q. v.
Hóf nowa.—Grinnell, Social Org. Cheyennes, 136, 1905. Hó'nowă.—Mooney, inf'n, 1905. Poor.—Dorsey in Field Columb. Mus. Pub., no. 103, 62, 1905.

Honsading. A former Hupa village situated on the right bank of Trinity r., Cal., near the entrance of the canyon through which the river flows after leaving Hupa valley. (P. E. G.)
Aknutl.—Goddard, inf'n, 1903 (Yurok name). Hoonselton.—Ind. Aff. Rep., 66, 1872. Hoonsolton.—Ind. Aff. Rep., 82, 1870. Hun'-sa-tung.—Powers in Cont. N. A. Ethnol., III, 73, 1877. Loonsolton.—H. R. Rep. 98, 42d Cong., 3d sess., 428, 1873. Okähno.—Meyer, Nachdem Sacramento, 282, 1855. Oka-no.—McKee in Sen. Ex. Doc. 4, 32d Cong., spec. sess., 194, 1853. Oke-noke.—Gibbs in Schoolcraft, Ind. Tribes, III, 139, 1853. Okenope.—Gibbs, MS., B. A. E., 1852.

Honwee Vallecito. A Diegueño rancheria represented in the treaty of 1852 at Santa Isabel, s. Cal.—H. R. Ex. Doc. 76, 34th Cong., 3d sess., 132, 1857.

Hook. One of the small tribes or bands formerly living in South Carolina on the lower Pedee and its affluents, and possibly of Siouan stock. Lawson (Hist. Car., 45, 1860) refers to them as foes of the Santee and as living in 1701 about the mouth of Winyaw bay, S. C. Consult Mooney, Siouan Tribes of the East, Bull. B. A. E., 1895. See *Backhook*.

Hooka (*Ho'-o-ka*). The Dove clans of the Keresan pueblos of Santa Ana, San Felipe, and Sia, New Mexico. That of the last-mentioned village is extinct.
Hóhoka-háno.—Hodge in Am. Anthrop., IX, 350, 1896 (Sia form; *háno* = 'people'). Hóoka-háno.—Ibid. (Santa Ana form). Húuka-háno. Ibid. (San Felipe form).

Hook-stones. A variety of prehistoric artifacts to which no particular purpose can be assigned. They are heavy, hook-like objects, from 1 to 4 or 5 in. in length and of diversified proportions. The principal variety standing on the heavy rounded base resembles somewhat the letter Z; others are longer and more slender, with the base less developed, but with the hook more pronounced. An example with hook at both ends, probably not properly included in this group, is given by Yates in Morehead's Prehistoric Implements. They are usually made of soapstone and other soft rock, and occur in burials in s. California, on the islands as well as on the mainland, and no doubt had symbolic use (see *Problematical objects*). A number of these objects, now in the Peabody Museum, are described by Putnam, who prefers to regard them as implements, and mentions signs of use. Two examples were obtained from a grave at the ancient soapstone quarry of Santa Catalina id. in 1902 (Holmes), and a deposit of about 50 specimens was discovered at Redondo beach, Cal., in 1903 (Palmer).

HOOK-STONE; S. CALIFORNIA. (PALMER)

Consult Holmes in Rep. Nat. Mus. 1900, 1902; Moorehead, op. cit.; Palmer in 2d Bull. S. W. Soc. Archæol. Inst. Am., 1905; Putnam in Surv. W. 100th Merid., 7, 1879.   (w. h. h.)

Hoolatassa. A former Choctaw town 4 m. from Abihka, probably in the present Kemper co., Miss.—Romans, Fla., 310, 1775.

Hoolikan. See *Eulachon*.

Hoonebooey. One of the Shoshoni tribes or bands said to have dwelt E. of the Cascade and s. of the Blue mts. of Oregon, in 1865. Not identified.
Hoonebooey.—Huntington in Ind. Aff. Rep., 466, 1865. Hoo-ne-boo-ly.—Ibid., 471.

Hooshkal (*Hoosh-kal*). A former Chehalis village on the N. shore of Grays harbor, Wash.—Gibbs, MS., no. 248, B. A. E.

Hopahka Choctaw. The Choctaw formerly residing in Hopahka town in s. Mississippi, w. of Pearl r., who are spoken of as the most intelligent and influential of the tribe. Known also as Cobb Indians, from their leader.—Claiborne (1843) in Sen. Doc. 168, 28th Cong., 1st sess., 39, 65, 1844.

Hopedale. A Moravian Eskimo mission village on the E. coast of Labrador, established in 1782 (Hind, Lab. Penin., II, 199, 1863). Pop. about 155.

Hopehood. A Norridgewock chief, known among his people as Wahowa, or Wohawa, who acquired considerable notoriety in E. New England in the latter part of the 17th century. He was the son of a chief called Robinhood. Hopehood's career is pronounced by Drake (Ind. Biog., 130, 1832) to have been one of long and bloody exploits. He first appears as a participant in King Philip's war, when he made an attack on a house filled with women and children at Newichawanoc, about the site of Berwick, Me.; all escaped, however, except two children and the woman who bravely barred and defended the door. In 1676 he was one of the leaders of the E. New England tribes who held consultation with the English at Taconnet, Me. In 1685 he joined Kankamagus and other sachems in a letter to Gov. Cranfield of New Hampshire, protesting against the endeavor of the English to urge the Mohawk to attack them. On Mar. 18, 1690, he joined the French under Hertel in a massacre at Salmon falls, and in May attacked Fox Point, N. H., burning several houses, killing 14 persons, and carrying away 6 others. Not long afterward he penetrated the Iroquois country, where some Canadian Indians, mistaking him for an Iroquois, slew him and several of his companions. Hopehood was at one time a captive in the hands of the English and served as a slave for a season in Boston.   (c. t.)

Hopi (contraction of *Hópitu*, 'peaceful ones,' or *Hópitu-shínumu*, 'peaceful all people': their own name). A body of Indians, speaking a Shoshonean dialect, occupying 6 pueblos on a reservation of 2,472,320 acres in N. E. Arizona. The name "Moqui," or "Moki," by which they have been popularly known, means 'dead' in their own language, but as a tribal name it is seemingly of alien origin and of undetermined signification—perhaps from the Keresan language (Mósïcha in Laguna, Mo-ts in Acoma, Mótsï in Sia, Cochiti, and San Felipe), whence Espejo's "Mohace" and "Mohoce" (1583) and Oñate's "Mohoqui" (1598). Bandelier and Cushing believed the Hopi country, the later province of Tusayan, to be identical with the Totonteac of Fray Marcos de Niza.

History.—The Hopi first became known to white men in the summer of 1540, when Coronado, then at Cibola (Zuñi), dispatched Pedro de Tobar and Fray Juan de Padilla to visit 7 villages, constituting the province of Tusayan, toward the w. or N. w. The Spaniards were not received with friendliness at first, but the opposition of the natives was soon overcome and the party remained among the Hopi several days, learning from them of the existence of the Grand canyon of the Colorado, which Cardenas was later ordered to visit. The names of the Tusayan towns are not recorded by Coronado's chroniclers, so that with the exception of Oraibi, Shongopovi, Mishongnovi, Walpi, and Awatobi, it is not known with certainty what villages were inhabited when the Hopi first became known to the Spaniards. Omitting Awatobi, which was destroyed in 1700, with the possible exception of Oraibi none of these towns now occupies its 16th century site.

Francisco Sanchez Chamuscado visited Zuñi in 1581 and speaks of the Hopi country as Asay or Osay, but he did not visit it on account of the snow. Two years later, however, the province was visited by Antonio de Espejo, who journeyed 28 leagues from Zuñi to the first of the Hopi pueblos in 4 days. The Mohoce, or Mohace, of this explorer consisted of 5 large villages, the population of one of which, Aguato (Ahuato, Zaguato=Awatobi) he estimated at 50,000, a figure perhaps 25 times too great. The names of the other towns are not given. The natives had evidently forgotten the horses of Tobar and Cardenas of 43 years before, as they now became frightened at these strange animals. The Hopi presented Espejo with quantities of cotton "towels," perhaps kilts, for which they were celebrated then as now.

The next Spaniard to visit the "Mohoqui" was Juan de Oñate, governor and colonizer of New Mexico, who took possession of the country and made the Indians swear to obedience and vassalage on Nov. 15, 1598. Their spiritual welfare was assigned to Fray Juan de Claros, although no active missions were established among the Hopi until nearly a generation later. The 5 villages at this time, so far as it is possible to determine them, were Aguato or Aguatuybá (Awatobi), Gaspe (Gualpe=Walpi), Comupaví or Xumupamí (Shongopovi), Majananí (Mishongnovi), and Olalla or Naybí (Oraibi).

The first actual missionary work undertaken among the Hopi was in 1629, on Aug. 20 of which year Francisco de Porras, Andrés Gutierrez, Cristobal de la Concepcion, and Francisco de San Buenaventura, escorted by 12 soldiers, reached Awatobi, where the mission of San Bernardino was founded in honor of the day, followed by the establishment of missions also at Walpi, Shongopovi, Mishongnovi, and Oraibi. Porras was poisoned by the natives of Awatobi in 1633. All the Hopi missions seem to have led a precarious existence until 1680, when in the general Pueblo revolt of that year four resident missionaries were killed and the churches destroyed. Henceforward no attempt was made to reestablish any of the missions save that of Awatobi in 1700, which so incensed the other Hopi that they fell upon it in the night, killing many of its people and compelling its permanent abandonment. . Before the rebellion Mishongnovi and Walpi had become reduced to visitas of the missions of Shongopovi and Oraibi respectively. At the time of the outbreak the population of Awatobi was given as 800, Shongopovi 500, and Walpi 1,200. Oraibi, it is said, had 14,000 gentiles before their conversion, but that they were consumed by pestilence. This number is doubtless greatly exaggerated.

The pueblos of Walpi, Mishongnovi, and Shongopovi, situated in the foothills, were probably abandoned about the time of the Pueblo rebellion, and new villages

built on the adjacent mesas for the purpose of defense against the Spaniards, whose vengeance was needlessly feared. The reconquest of the New Mexican pueblos led many of their inhabitants to seek protection among the Hopi toward the close of the 17th century. Some of these built the pueblo of Payupki, on the Middle mesa, but were taken back and settled in Sandia about the middle of the 18th century. About the year 1700 Hano

WIKI, CHIEF PRIEST OF THE ANTELOPE SOCIETY; PUEBLO OF WALPI. (VROMAN, PHOTO.)

was established on the East mesa, near Walpi, by Tewa from near Abiquiu, N. Mex., who came on the invitation of the Walpians. Here they have lived uninterruptedly, and although they have intermarried extensively with the Hopi, they retain their native speech and many of their distinctive tribal rites and customs. Two other pueblos, Sichomovi on the First mesa, built by Asa clans (q. v.)

from the Rio Grande, and Shipaulovi, founded by a colony from Shongopovi on the Second or Middle mesa, are both of comparatively modern origin, having been established about the middle of the 18th century, or about the time the Payupki people returned to their old home. Thus the pueblos of the ancient province of Tusayan now consist of the following: Walpi, Sichomovi, and Hano, on the First or East mesa; pop. (1900) 205, 119, and 160, respectively, exclusive of about 20 who have established homes in the plain; total 504. Mishongnovi, Shongopovi, and Shupaulovi, on the Second or Middle mesa; estimated pop. 244, 225, and 126; total 595. Oraibi, on the Third or West mesa; pop. (1890) 905. Total Hopi population (1904) officially given as 2,338, including about 160 Tewa of Hano.

Social organization.—The Hopi people are divided into several phratries, consisting of numerous clans, each of which preserves its distinct legends, ceremonies, and ceremonial paraphernalia. Out of

HOPI MAN AND WIFE; PUEBLO OF MISHONGNOVI. (VROMAN, PHOTO.)

these clan organizations have sprung religious fraternities, the head-men of which are still members of the dominant clan in each phratry. The relative importance of the clans varies in different pueblos; many that are extinct in some villages are powerful in others. The 12 phratries and their dependent clans as represented in the East Mesa villages are as follows:

1. *Ala-Lengya* (Horn-flute) *phratry:* Ala (Horn), Pangwa (Mountain sheep), Sowiinwa (Deer), Chubio (Antelope), Chaizra (Elk), Lehu (Seed grass), Shiwanu (Ant), Anu (Red-ant), Tokoanu (Black-ant), Wukoanu (Great-ant), Leliotu (Tiny-ant), Shakwalengya (Blue flute), Masilengya (Drab or All-colors flute).

2. *Patki* (Water-house or Cloud) *phratry:* Patki (Water-house), Kau (Corn), Omauwu (Rain-cloud), Tanaka (Rainbow), Talawipiki (Lightning), Kwan (Agave), Siwapi ('Rabbit-brush'), Pawikya (aquatic animal [Duck]), Pakwa (Frog), Pavatiya (Tadpole), Murzibusi (Bean), Kawaibatunya (Watermelon), Yoki (Rain).

3. *Chua* (Snake) *phratry:* Chua (Snake), Tohouh (Puma), Huwi (Dove), Ushu (Columnar cactus), Puna (Cactus fruit), Yungyu (Opuntia), Nabowu (Opuntia frutescens), Pivwani (Marmot), Pihcha (Skunk), Kalashiavu (Raccoon), Tubish (Sorrow), Patung (Squash), Atoko (Crane), Kele (Pigeon-hawk), Chinunga (Thistle). The last 5 are extinct.

4. *Pakab* (Reed) *phratry:* Pakab (Reed), Kwahu (Eagle), Kwayo (Hawk), Koyonya (Turkey), Tawa (Sun), Paluna (Twin-brother of Puhukonghoya), Shohu (Star), Massikwayo (Chicken-hawk), Kahabi (Willow), Tebi (Greasewood).

5. *Kokop* (Wood) *phratry:* Kokop (Wood), Ishauu (Coyote), Kwewu (Wolf), Sikyataiyo (Yellow-fox), Letaiyo (Gray-fox), Zrohona (small mammal), Masi (Masauu, dead, skeleton, Ruler of the Dead), Tuvou (Piñon), Hoko (Juniper), Awata (Bow), Sikyachi (small yellow bird), Tuvuchi (small red bird).

6. *Tabo* (Cottontail rabbit) *phratry:* Tabo (Cottontail rabbit), Sowi (Jackrabbit).

7. *Tuwa* (Sand or Earth) *phratry:* Kukuch, Bachipkwasi, Nananawi, Momobi (varieties of lizard), Pisa (White sand), Tuwa (Red sand), Chukai (Mud), Sihu (Flower), Nanawu (small striped squirrel).

8. *Honau* (Bear) *phratry:* Honau (Bear), Tokochi (Wild-cat), Chosro (Blue-bird), Kokyan (Spider), Hekpa (Fir).

9. *Kachina* (Sacred dancer) *phratry:* Kachina (Sacred dancer), Gyazru (Paroquet), Angwusi (Raven), Sikyachi (Yellow bird), Tawamana (Blackbird), Salabi (Spruce), Suhubi (Cottonwood).

10. *Asa* (Tansy mustard) *phratry:* Asa (Tansy mustard), Chakwaina (Black-earth Kachina), Kwingyap (Oak), Hosboa (Chapparal cock), Posiwu (Magpie), Chisro (Snow-bunting), Puchkohu (Boomerang rabbit-stick), Pisha (Field-mouse).

11. *Piba* (Tobacco) *phratry:* Piba (Tobacco), Chongyo (Pipe).

12. *Honani* (Badger) *phratry:* Honani (Badger), Muinyawu (Porcupine), Wishoko (Turkey-buzzard), Buli (Butterfly), Buliso (Evening Primrose), Kachina (Sacred dancer).

Most of the above clans occur in the other Hopi pueblos, but not in Hano. There are a few clans in the Middle Mesa villages and in Oraibi that are not now represented at Walpi. For the Hano clans see *Hano*.

The Honau (Bear) clan is represented on each mesa and is supposed to be the oldest in Tusayan. It is said to have come originally from the Rio Grande valley, but on the East mesa the clan is now so reduced as to be threatened with extinction at Walpi within a generation.

The Chua (Snake) people were among the earliest to settle in Tusayan, joining the Bears and living with them when Walpi was in the foot-hills. The legends of this people declare that they came from pueblos in the N., near Navaho mt., on the Rio Colorado. In their northern home they were united with the Ala (Horn) people, who separated from them in their southerly migration and united with the Flute people at the now-ruined pueblo of Lengyanobi, N. of the East mesa. The combined Snake and Ala people control the Antelope and Snake fraternities, and possess the fetishes and other paraphernalia of the famous Snake dance. The palladium of this people is kept at Walpi, thus leading to the belief that this was the first Hopi home of the Snake and kindred people.

The Lengya (Flute) people, once very strong, are now almost extinct at the East mesa, but are numerous in some of the other pueblos. They are said to have lived formerly at Lengyanobi and to have come to Tusayan from the S., or from pueblos along Little Colorado r. The chief of the Flute priesthood controls the Flute ceremony, which occurs biennially, alternating with the Snake dance. There are two divisions in the Flute fraternity, one known as the Drab Flute and the other as the Blue Flute, the former being extinct at Walpi. Sichomovi and Hano have no representatives of this phratry, but it is represented in all the other Hopi villages.

There are Ala, or Horn, people in most of the Hopi pueblos, and clans belonging to this phratry are named generally after horned animals. Their ancestors came to Walpi with the Flute people and were well received, because they had formerly lived with the Snake people in the N. They now join the Snake priest in the Antelope rites of the Snake dance.

The Patki (Water-house, or Cloud) phratry includes a number of clans that came to the Hopi country from the S., and the now ruined villages along the Little Colorado are claimed by this people to have been their former homes. They were comparatively late arrivals, and brought a high form of sun and serpent worship that is still prominent in the Winter Solstice ceremony. The Sun priests, who are well represented in most of the

Hopi pueblos and are especially strong at Walpi, accompanied this people. Others, as the Piba or Tobacco clan, came to Walpi from Awatobi on the destruction of the latter pueblo in 1700.

The Pakab (Reed) people also came from Awatobi, settling first at the base of the Middle mesa, whence they went to Walpi. They control the Warrior society called Kalektaka.

The Kokop (Wood) phratry came from Sikyatki and have a few representatives in Walpi and in the other villages. The traditional home of the Kokop and allied clans was Jemez (q. v.), in New Mexico.

The Honani or Badger phratry originally lived at Awatobi, and after the destruction of that pueblo went to Oraibi and Walpi. It is now largely represented in Sichomovi, which village it joined the Asa in founding. The Buli, or Butterfly, clan is closely related to the Honani people, and both are probably of Keresan or of Tewa origin.

HOPI SNAKE CEREMONY

The Kachina phratry is also of New Mexican origin, and in some of the pueblos shares with the Honani the control of the masked dance organization called Kachinas; but it is not strong in Walpi.

The Asa people were Tewa in kin, coming originally from the Rio Grande valley and settling successively at Zuñi and in the Canyon de Chelly. This people, with the Honani, founded Sichomovi, and is now one of the strongest clans on the East mesa. Only one or two members now live at Walpi; a few live in the Middle Mesa villages, but none at Oraibi.

Archeology.—The erection and final abandonment of their villages by the various Hopi clans during their migrations and successive shiftings have left many ruins, now consisting largely of mounds, both within their present territory and remote from it. Ruins of villages which the traditions of the Hopi ascribe to their ancestors are found as far N. as the Rio Colorado, w. to Flagstaff, Ariz., s. to the Verde valley, Tonto basin, and the Rio Gila, and E. to the Rio Grande in New Mexico. Therefore, although Shoshonean in language, the present Hopi population and culture are composite, made up of accretions from widely divergent sources and from people of different linguistic stocks. Some of the Hopi ruins have been explored by the Bureau of American Ethnology, the National Museum, and the Field Museum of Natural History. One of the most celebrated of these is Awatobi (q. v.) on Jeditoh or Antelope mesa, the walls of whose mission church, built probably in 1629, are still partly standing.

Sikyatki (q.v.), another large and now well-known ruin, in the foot-hills of the East mesa, was occupied in prehistoric times by Kokop clans of Keresan people from the Rio Grande country. They had attained a highly artistic development as exhibited by their pottery, which is probably the finest ware ever manufactured by Indians N. of Mexico.

The original clans of Walpi are said to have occupied three sites after their arrival in the Hopi country, settling first on the terrace w. of the East mesa, then higher up and toward the s., where the foundation walls of a Spanish mission church can still be traced. From this point they moved to the present Walpi on the summit of the mesa, apparently soon after the Pueblo revolt of 1680. See *Kisakobi, Kuchaptuvela.*

Payupki, a picturesque ruin on the Middle mesa, was settled by Tanoan people (apparently Tigua) about the year 1700 and abandoned about 1742, when the inhabitants were taken back to the Rio Grande and settled at Sandia.

Chukubi, a prehistoric pueblo midway between Payupki and Shupaulovi, also on the Middle mesa, was built probably by southern clans whose descendants form most of the present population of the Middle mesa villages.

Old Shongopovi lay in the foot-hills at the base of the Middle mesa, below the present pueblo of that name. This town was inhabited at the time of the Spanish advent, and near it was built a church the walls of which, up to a few years ago, served as a sheep corral. Its original inhabitants came from the Little Colorado valley.

The ruins of Old Mishongnovi are on the terrace below the present pueblo. Its walls are barely traceable. From its cemetery beautiful pottery, resembling that of Sikyatki, has been exhumed.

Some of the most important ruins of the Hopi country are situated on the rim of Antelope mesa, not far from Awatobi, and are remains of Keresan pueblos. Among these are Kawaika and Chakpa-

hu. In the same neighborhood are the ruins of Kokopki, once occupied by the Wood clan, originally from Jemez. North of the present Hopi mesas are ruins at Kishuba, where the Kachina clan once lived, and at Lengyanobi, the home of the Flute people. The ruins along the lower Little Colorado, near Black falls, known as Wukoki, and those called Homolobi, near Winslow, are likewise claimed by the Hopi as the homes of ancestral clans. Wukoki may have been inhabited by the Snake people, while the inhabitants of Homolobi were related to southern clans that went to Walpi and Zuñi.

Characteristics and customs.—The Hopi are rather small of stature, but muscular and agile. Both sexes have reddish-brown skin, high cheek-bones, straight broad nose, slanting eyes, and large mouths with gentle expression. As a rule the occiput exhibits cradle-board flattening (see *Artificial head deformation*). The proportion of albinos is large. The hair is usually straight and black, but in some individuals it is brownish and in others it is wavy. The hair of the men is commonly "banged" in front or cut in "terraces"; the long hair behind is gathered in a sort of short queue and tied at the neck. The matrons wear their hair in two coils which hang in front. On reaching puberty the girls dress their hair in whorls at the sides of the head, in imitation of the squash blossom, the symbol of fertility (see illustration). The women tend to corpulency and age rapidly; they are prolific, but the infant mortality is very great (see *Health and Disease*). Boys and girls usually have fine features, and the latter mature early, often being married at the age of 15 or 16 years. Bachelors and spinsters are rare. A few men dress as women and perform women's work.

In mental traits the Hopi are the equal of any Indian tribe. They possess a highly artistic sense, exhibited by their pottery, basketry, and weaving. They are industrious, imitative, keen in bargaining, have some inventive genius, and are quick of perception. Among themselves they are often merry, greatly appreciating jests and practical jokes. They rarely forget a kindness or an injury, and often act from impulse and in a childlike way. They are tractable, docile, hospitable, and frugal, and have always sought to be peaceable, as their tribal name indicates. They believe in witchcraft, and recognize many omens of good and bad.

The Hopi are monogamists, and as a rule are faithful in their marital relations. Murder is unknown, theft is rare, and lying is universally condemned. Children are respectful and obedient to their elders and are never flogged except when ceremonially initiated as kachinas. From their earliest years they are taught industry and the necessity of leading upright lives.

The clothing of the Hopi men consists of a calico shirt and short pantaloons, and breechcloth, moccasins, and hair bands. Bracelets, necklaces of shell, turquoise, or silver, and earrings, are commonly worn.

HOPI MAIDEN.   (MOONEY, PHOTO.)

The women wear a dark-blue woolen blanket of native weave, tied with an embroidered belt, and a calico manta or shawl over one shoulder; their moccasins, which are worn only occasionally, are made of ox-hide and buckskin, like those of the men, to which are attached leggings of the same material, but now often replaced by sheepskin. The ear-pendants of the women and girls consist of small wooden disks, ornamented with turquoise mosaic on one side. Small

children generally run about naked, and old men while working in the fields or taking part in ceremonies divest themselves of all clothing except the breechcloth.

The governing body of the Hopi is a council of hereditary clan elders and chiefs of religious fraternities. Among these officials there is recognized a speaker chief and a war chief, but there has never been a supreme chief of all the Hopi. Following ancient custom, various activities inhere in certain clans; for instance, one clan controls the warrior society, while another observes the sun and determines the calendar. Each pueblo has an hereditary village chief, who directs certain necessary communal work, such as the cleaning of springs, etc. There seems to be no punishment for crime except sorcery, to which, under Hopi law, all transgressions may be reduced. No punishment of a witch or wizard is known to have been inflicted at Walpi in recent years, but there are traditions of imprisonment and of the significant and mysterious disappearance of those accused of witchcraft in former times.

The Hopi possess a rich mythology and folklore, inherited from a remote past. They recognize a large number of supernatural beings, the identification of which is sometimes most difficult. Their mythology is poetic and highly imaginative, and their philosophy replete with inconsistency. Their songs and prayers, some of which are in foreign languages, as the Keresan and Tewa, are sometimes very beautiful. They have peculiar marriage customs, and elaborate rites in which children are dedicated to the sun. The bodies of the dead are sewed in blankets and deposited with food offerings among the rocks of the mesas. The Hopi believe in a future life in an underworld, but have no idea of future punishment. They smoke straight pipes in ceremonies, but on secular occasions prefer cigarettes of tobacco wrapped in corn-husks. They never invented an intoxicating drink, and until within recent years none of them had any desire for such. Although they have seasons of ceremonial gaming, they do not gamble; and they have no oaths, but many, especially among the elders, are garrulous and fond of gossip.

Maize being the basis of their subsistence, agriculture is the principal industry of the Hopi. On the average 2,500 acres are yearly planted in this cereal, the yield in 1904 being estimated at 25,000 bushels. Perhaps one-third of the annual crop is preserved in event of future failure through drought or other causes. There are also about 1,000 acres in peach orchards and 1,500 acres in beans, melons, squashes, pumpkins, onions, chile, sunflowers, etc. Cotton, wheat, and tobacco are also raised in small quantities, but in early times native cotton was extensively grown. In years of stress desert plants, which have always been utilized to some extent for food, form an important part of the diet.

The Hopi have of late become more or less pastoral. Flocks (officially estimated in 1904 at 56,000 sheep and 15,000 goats), acquired originally from the Spaniards, supply wool and skins. They own also about 1,500 head of cattle, and 4,350 horses, burros, and mules. Dogs, chickens, hogs, and turkeys are their only other domesticated animals. All small desert animals are eaten; formerly antelope, elk, and deer were captured by being driven into pitfalls or corrals. Communal rabbit hunts are common, the animals being killed with wooden clubs shaped like boomerangs (see *Rabbit sticks*). Prairie dogs are drowned out of their burrows, coyotes are caught in pitfalls made of stones, and small birds are captured in snares.

The Hopi are skilled in weaving, dyeing, and embroidering blankets, belts, and kilts. Their textile work is durable, and shows a great variety of weaves. The dark-blue blanket of the Hopi woman is an important article of commerce among the Pueblos, and their embroidered ceremonial blankets, sashes, and kilts made of cotton have a ready sale among neighboring tribes. Although the Hopi ceramic art has somewhat deteriorated in modern times, fair pottery is still made among the people of Hano, where one family has revived the superior art of the earlier villagers. They weave basketry in a great variety of ways at the Middle Mesa pueblos and in Oraibi; but, with the exception of the familiar sacred-meal plaques, which are well made and brightly colored, the workmanship is crude. The Hopi are clever in making masks and other religious paraphernalia from hides, and excel in carving and painting dolls, representing kachinas, which are adorned with bright feathers and cloth. They likewise manufacture mechanical toys, which are exhibited in some of their dramatic entertainments. Nowhere among the aborigines of North America are the Hopi excelled in dramaturgic exhibitions, in some of which their imitations of birds and other animals are marvelously realistic.

The Hopi language is classified as Shoshonean; but, according to Gatschet, it "seems to contain many archaic words and forms not encountered in the other dialects, and many vocables of its own." The published vocabularies are very limited, and comparatively little is known of the grammatical structure of the language; but it is evident that it contains many words of Keresan, Tewa, Pima, Zuñi, Ute, Navaho, and Apache derivation. As among other Southwestern tribes a number of words are modified Spanish, as those for horse, sheep, melon, and the names for other intrusive articles and objects. Slight dialectic differences are noticeable in the speech of Oraibi and Walpi, but the language of the other pueblos is practically uniform. The Hopi language is melodious and the enunciation clear. The speech of the people of Awatobi is said to have had a nasal intonation, while the Oraibi speak drawlingly. Although they accompany their speech with gestures, few of the Hopi understand the sign language. The Keresan people have furnished many songs, with their words, and Zuñi and Pima songs have also been introduced. Some of the prayers also have archaic Tanoan or Keresan words.

The Hopi are preëminently a religious people, much of their time, especially in winter, being devoted to ceremonies for rain and the growth of crops. Their mythology is a polytheism largely tinged with ancestor worship and permeated with fetishism. They originally had no conception of a great spirit corresponding to God, nor were they ever monotheists; and, although they have accepted the teachings of Christian missionaries, these have not had the effect of altering their primitive beliefs. Their greatest gods are deified nature powers, as the Mother Earth and the Sky god—the former mother, and the latter father, of the races of men and of marvelous animals, which are conceived of as closely allied.

The earth is spoken of as having always existed. In Hopi mythology the human race was not created, but generated from the earth, from which man emerged through an opening called the *sipapu*, now typified by the Grand canyon of the Colorado. The dead are supposed to return to the underworld. The Sky Father and the Earth Mother have many names and are personated in many ways; the latter is represented by a spider; the former by a bird—a hawk or an eagle. Such names as Fire god, Germ god, and others are attributal designations of the great male powers of nature, or its male germinative principle. All supernatural beings are supposed to influence the rain and consequently the growth of crops. Every clan religion exhibits strong ancestral worship, in which a male and a female ancestral tutelary of the clan, called by a distinctive clan name, is preëminent. The Great Horned or Plumed Serpent, a form of sky god, derived from the S., and introduced by the Patki and other southern clans, is prominent in sun ceremonies. The number of subordinate supernatural personages is almost unlimited. These are known as "kachinas," a term referring to the magic power inherent in every natural object for good or for bad. Many of these kachinas are personations of clan ancestors, others are simply beings of unknown relationship but endowed with magic powers. Each kachina possesses individual characteristics, and is represented in at least six different symbolic colors. The world-quarters, or six cardinal points, play an important rôle in Hopi mythology and ritual. Fetishes, amulets, charms, and mascots are commonly used to insure luck in daily occupations, and for health and success in hunting, racing, gaming, and secular performances. The Hopi ceremonial calendar consists of a number of monthly festivals, ordinarily of 9 days' duration, of which the first 8 are devoted to secret rites in kivas (q. v.) or in rooms set apart for that purpose, the final day being generally devoted to a spectacular public ceremony or "dance." Every great festival is held under the auspices of a special religious fraternity or fraternities, and is accompanied with minor events indicating a former duration of 20 days. Among the most important religious fraternities are the Snake, Antelope, Flute, Sun, Lalakontu, Owakultu, Mamzrautu, Kachina, Tataukyamu, Wuwuchimtu, Aaltu, Kwakwautu, and Kalektaka. There are also other organized priesthoods, as the Yaya and the Poshwympkia, whose functions are mainly those of doctors or healers. Several ancient priesthoods, known by the names Koyimsi, Paiakyamu, and Chukuwympkia, function as clowns or fun-makers during the sacred dances of the Kachinas. The ceremonial year is divided into two parts, every great ceremony having a major and a minor performance occurring about 6 months apart; and every 4 years, when initiations occur, most ceremonies are celebrated in extenso. The so-called Snake and Flute dances are performed biennially at all the pueblos except Sichomovi and Hano, and alternate with each other. Ceremonies are also divided into those with masked and those with unmasked participants, the former, designated kachinas, extending from January to July, the latter occurring in the remaining months of the year. The chief of each fraternity has a badge of his office and conducts both the secret and the open features of the ceremony. The fetishes and idols used in the sacred rites are owned by the priesthood and are arranged by its chief in temporary altars (q. v.), in front of which dry-paintings (q. v.) are made. The Hopi ritual is extraordinarily complex and time-consuming, and the paraphernalia required

is extensive. Although the Hopi cultus has become highly modified by a semi-arid environment, it consisted originally of ancestor worship, embracing worship of the great powers of nature—sky, sun, moon, fire, rain, and earth. A confusion of effect and cause and an elaboration of the doctrine of signatures pervade all their rites, which in the main may be regarded as sympathetic magic.

Consult Dorsey and Voth in the publications of the Field Columbian Museum; Fewkes in Reports of the Bureau of American Ethnology and in various papers in the American Anthropologist, the Journal of American Folk-lore, and the Journal of American Ethnology and Archæology; Mindeleff in 8th Rep. B. A. E., 1891. See *Pueblos, Shoshonean*, and the pueblos above named. (J. W. F.)

A-ar-ke.—White, MS. Hist. Apaches, B. A. E., 1875 (Apache name). **Ah-mo-kái.**—Eaton in Schoolcraft, Ind. Tribes, IV, 221, 1854 (Zuñi name). **Ai-yah-kín-nee.**—Ibid., 220 (Navaho name). **Alo-qui.**—Escalante (1775–1776) quoted by Bancroft, Ariz. and N. Mex., 185, 1889. **Amaques.**—Short, N. Am. of Antiq., 332, 1880 (wrong identification). **Amaqui.**—Ibid. **A'moekwikwe.**—ten Kate, Reizen in N. Am., 264, 1885 ('smallpox-folk': Zuñi name). **A-mo-kini.**—Bowman in Ind. Aff. Rep., 136, 1884 (Zuñi. name; 'kini'=*kwe*, 'people'). **A-mo-kwi.**—Vandever in Ind. Aff. Rep., 168, 1890 (Zuñi name). **A'-mu-kwi-kwe.**—ten Kate, Synonymie, 7, 1884 ('smallpox people': Zuñi name). **Asay.**—Bustamante and Gallegos (1582) in Doc. Inéd., XV, 86, 1871 (also Osay, p. 93). **Bokeaí.**—Hodge, field notes, B. A. E., 1895 (Sandia Tigua name). **Buhk'hérk.**—Ibid. (Isleta Tigua name for Tusayan). **Búkïn.**—Ibid. (Isleta name for the people). **Chinouns.**—Hoffman in Bull. Soc. d'Anthrop. Paris, 206, 1883 (='Moquis de l'Arizona'). **Cí-nyu-múh.**—Fewkes in Jour. Am. Folk-lore, V, 33, 1892 ('people': own name; *c*=*sh*). **Cummoaquí.**—Viceroy Monterey (*ca.* 1602) in Doc. Inéd., XVI, 60, 1871. **Cummooqui.**—Viceroy Monterey cited by Duro, Don Diego de Peñalosa, 24, 1882. **E-***ar'***-ke.**—White, Apache Names of Ind. Tribes, MS., B. A. E., 2, n. d. (='live high up on top of the mesas': Apache name). **Eyakíni diné.**—Gatschet, MS., B. A. E. (Navaho name). **Hape-ka.**—Hodge, Arizona, 169, 1877 (=Hépekyakwe, 'excrement people': a Zuñi name). **Hapitus.**—Bowman in Ind. Aff. Rep., 136, 1884 (given as their own name). **Ho-pees.**—Dellenbaugh in Bull. Buffalo Soc. Nat. Sci., 170, 1877 ('our people': own name). **Hopi.**—Fewkes in Am. Anthrop., V, 9, 1892. **Hopii.**—Bourke, Moquis of Ariz., 117, 1884 (own name). **Hopite.**—ten Kate, Reizen in N. Am., 259, 1885 ('the good ones?': own name). **Hópitû.**—Ibid. **Hopituh.**—Mindeleff in 8th Rep. B. A. E., 17, 1891 (own name). **Hó-pi-tûh-ci'-nu-múh.**—Fewkes in Am. Anthrop., V, 9, 1892 ('peaceful people': own name; *c*=*sh*). **Hó-pi-tûh-ci-nyu-múh.**—Fewkes in Jour. Am. Folk-lore, V, 33, 1892. **Ho-pi-tuh-lei-nyu-muh.**—Donaldson, Moqui Pueblo Inds., 13, 1893 (misprint). **Húpi.**—Lummis quoted by Donaldson, ibid., 71. **Joso.**—Fewkes in 10th Rep. B. A. E., 612, 1900 (Tewa name). **Khoso.**—Hodge cited in 17th Rep. B. A. E., 642, 1898 (Santa Clara name). **Koco.**—Fewkes in 17th Rep. B. A. E., 642, 1898 (Hano Tewa name; *c*=*sh*). **Koso.**—Ibid. **K'o-so-o.**—Hodge, field notes, B. A. E., 1895 (San Ildefonso Tewa name). **Maastoetsjkwe.**—ten Kate, Reizen in N. Am., 260, 1885 ('the land of Másawé,' god of the earth: given as the name of their country). **Macueques.**—Arricivita, Cronica Seráfica, II, 424, 1792 (probably identical). **Magui.**—Ten Broeck in Schoolcraft, Ind. Tribes, IV, 81, 1854 (misprint). **Makis.**—Bowman in Ind. Aff. Rep., 136, 1884. **Maqui.**—Venegas, Hist. Cal., II, 194, 1759. **Mastutc'-kwe.**—ten Kate, Synonymie, 6, 1884 ('the country of Ma-sa-wĕ': given as the Hopi name for their country). **Mawkeys.**—Bartlett in Trans. Am. Ethnol. Soc., II, 17, 1848; Squier in Am. Review, 523, Nov. 1848 (traders' corruption of 'Moqui'). **Miqui.**—Johnston in Emory, Recon., 569, 1848. **Mocas.**—Schoolcraft, Ind. Tribes, I, 561, 1851. **Mochi.**—Clavijero, Storia della California, map, 1789. **Mochies.**—Calhoun (1849) in Cal. Mess. and Corresp., 221, 1850. **Mogeris.**—Ruxton misquoted by Simpson, Report, 57, 1850. **Mogin.**—Wilkins (1859) in H. R. Ex. Doc. 69, 36th Cong., 1st sess., 6, 1860 (misprint). **Mogui.**—Ogilby, America, map, 1671. **Mohace.**—Espejo (1583) in Doc. Inéd., XV, 119, 1871. **Mohoce.**—Ibid. **Mohóce.**—Oñate (1598), ibid., XVI, 307, 1871. **Mohoqui.**—Ibid., 115. **Mohotze.**—Hakluyt, Voyages, 462, 1600. **Moke.**—Gatschet in Mag. Am. Hist., 260, 1882. **Mokee.**—Pattie, Pers. Narr., 91, 1833. **Moki.**—Hervas, Idea dell' Universo, XVII, 76, 1784. **Monkey Indians.**—Wilkes, U. S. Expl. Exped., IV, 472, 1845. **Monquoi.**—Prichard, Physical Hist. Mankind, v, 430, 1847. **Mooqui.**—Zarate-Salmeron(ca.1629), Relacion, in Land of Sunshine, 48, Dec. 1899. **Mo-o-tzä.**—Bandelier in Jour. Am. Ethnol. and Archæol., III, 67, 1892 (Keresan name). **Moq.**—Saldivar (1618) quoted by Prince, N. Mex., 176, 1883. **Moqni.**—ten Kate, Reizen in N. Am., 260, 1885 (misprint). **Moqua.**—Palmer in Am. Nat., XII, 310, 1878. **Moques.**—Blaeu, Atlas, XII, 62, 1667. **Moqui.**—Benavides, Memorial, 33, 1630. **Moquian Pueblos.**—Shufeldt, Ind. Types of Beauty, 14, 1891. **Moquinas.**—Villa-Señor, Theatro Am., pt. 2, 426, 1748. **Moquinos.**—Kino (1697) in Doc. Hist Mex., 4th s., I, 285, 1856; Rivera, Diario, leg. 950, 1736. **Moquins.**—Poston in Ind. Aff. Rep. 1863, 388, 1864. **Moquitch.**—Barber in Am. Nat., II, 593, 1877 (Ute name). **Moquois.**—Holmes in 10th Rep. Hayden Surv., 403, 1878. **Moquy.**—Duro, Don Diego de Peñalosa, 63, 1882. **Morqui.**—Hoffman in Jour. Anthrop. Inst., IX, 465, 1880. **Mósï.**—Hodge, field notes, B. A. E., 1895 (Laguna name for Tusayan). **Mósïcha.**—Ibid. (Laguna name for the Hopi). **Mosquies.**—Calhoun in Ind. Aff. Rep., 65, 1850. **Mó-ts.**—Hodge, field notes, B. A. E., 1895 (Acoma name for the Hopi). **Mo'-tsï.**—Ibid. (Cochiti name). **Mouguis.**—Taylor in Cal. Farmer, May 18, 1860. **Moxi.**—Palou, Relacion Hist., 251, 1787. **Muca.**—Garcés cited by Escudero, Noticias Estad. de Chihuahua, 228, 1834. **Mu-gua.**—Bandelier, Gilded Man, 149, 1893 (misprint). **Mú-kĕ.**—Corbusier, Yavapai MS. vocab., B. A. E., 27, 1873–75 (Yavapai name). **Munchies.**—Sage, Scenes in Rocky Mts., 198, 1846. **Muqui.**—Garcés (1775–76) cited by Bancroft, Ariz. and N. Mex., 137, 395, 1889. **Opii.**—Bourke, Moquis of Ariz., 117, 1884 (given as their own name). **Osaij.**—Bandelier in Jour. Am. Ethnol. and Archæol., III, 62, 1892 (misprint of the following). **Osay.**—Bustamante and Gallegos (1582) in Doc. Inéd., XV, 93, 1871 (also Asay, p. 86). **Pokkenvolk.**—ten Kate, Reizen in N. Am., 264, 1885 (Dutch: 'smallpox-folk,' trans. of Zuñi name; see A'moek-wikwe, above). **Shē-noma.**—Gatschet in Wheeler Surv. Rep., VII, 412, 1879 (trans., 'towns people'). **Shínome.**—ten Kate, Reizen in N. Am., 259, 1885 (Shinumo, or). **Shi-nu-mos.**—Powell in Scribner's Mag., 202, 212, 1875 (own name: trans., 'we, the wise'). **Shumi.**—Bourke, Moquis of Ariz., 118, 1884 (given as the sacred name for themselves). **Ta-sa-ûn.**—Vandever in Ind. Aff. Rep., 168, 1890 ('the place of isolated buttes': Navaho name of surrounding country). **Tesayan.**—Prince, N. Mex., 125, 1883. **Tonteac.**—Sanson, L'Amérique, 30, 1657. **Tonteaca.**—Mota-Padilla, Hist. de la Conquista, 111, 1742. **Tontonteac.**—Wytfliet, Hist. des Indes, map, 66–67, 1605. **Topin-keua.**—Cushing cited by Bandelier in Archæol. Inst. Papers, IV, 368, 1892 (or Topin-teua; given as the Zuñi name of which 'Totonteac' is a corruption). **Top-in-te-ua.**—Bandelier, ibid., v, 175, 1890; IV, 368, 1892. **Totanteac.**—Marcos de Niça (1539) in Hakluyt, Voy., 443, 1600 (misprint). **Totonteac.**—Ibid., 440; Coronado (1540), ibid., 452 (see Bandelier in Arch. Inst. Papers, III, 114; v, 175, 1890). **Totonteal.**—Loew (1875) in Wheeler Surv. Rep., VII, 333, 1879 (misprint). **Totontoac.**—Alarcon (1540) in Ternaux-Compans, Voy., IX, 315, 1838. **Totōteac.**—Visscher, Americæ Nova Descr., first map, 1601. **Tuçan.**—Writer of 1542 in Smith, Colec. Doc. Fla.,

I, 149, 1857. **Tucano.**—Coronado (1542) in Hakluyt, Voy., III, 453, 1600. **Tucayan.**—Castaneda (ca. 1565) in Ternaux-Compans, Voy., IX, 181, 1838; Jaramillo, ibid., 370. **Tuchano.**—Zaltieri, map (1566) in Winsor, Hist. Am., II, 451, 1886; Wytfliet, Hist. des Indes, map, 114–116, 1605. **Tusan.**—Coronado (1540) quoted by Bancroft, Ariz. and N. Mex., 46, 137, 1889. **Tusayan.**—Castañeda (ca. 1565) in Ternaux-Compans, Voy., IX, 58, 1838. **Tusayan Moqui.**—Bandelier in Arch. Inst. Papers, III, 115, 1890. **Tu-se-an.**—Bowman in Ind. Aff. Rep., 136, 1884 (said to be the Navaho name for the Rocky mts.). **Tusyan.**—Stevenson in 2d Rep. B. A. E., 328, 1883. **Tuzan.**—Coronado (1540) in Doc. Inéd., XIV, 320, 1870. **Usaya.**—Bandelier in Arch. Inst. Papers, v, 170, 1890 (or Usayan; "names given anciently by the Zuñis to the principal pueblos of Moqui"). **Usaya-kue.**—Ibid., 115 (= 'people of Usaya,' the Zuñi name of "two of the largest Moqui villages"; hence T-usayan). **Usayan.**—Ibid., 170. **Welsh Indians.**—Prichard, Phys. Hist. Mankind, v, 431, 1847. **White Indians.**—Sage, Scenes in Rocky Mts., 198, 1846. **Whiwunai.**—Hodge, field notes, B. A. E., 1895 (Sandia Tigua name).

Hopitsewah. Mentioned as a "sacred town" of the "Laguna" Indians, a Pomo band on the w. shore of Clear lake, Mendocino co., Cal.—Revere, Tour of Duty, 130, 1849.

Hopkins, Sarah. See *Winnemucca*.

Hopnis, Hopnuts. See *Hobnuts*.

Hopnomkoyo. A former Maidu village on Lights cr., in the N. part of Plumas co., Cal.—Dixon in Bull. Am. Mus. Nat. Hist., XVII, pl. xxxviii, 1905.

Hopocan ('[tobacco] pipe'). A Delaware chief, known to the whites as Captain Pipe, and after 1763 among his people as Konieschguanokee ('Maker of Daylight'). An hereditary sachem of the Wolf division of the Delawares, he was war chief of the tribe. He was also prominent in council, having a reputation for wisdom and a remarkable gift of oratory. In the French war he fought against the English with courage and skill. He was present at the conference with Geo. Croghan at Ft Pitt in 1759, and in 1763 or 1764 tried to take the fort by strategem, but failed, and was captured. After peace was concluded he settled with his clan on upper Muskingum r., Ohio, and in 1771 sent a "speech" to Gov. Penn. He attended the councils of the tribe at the Turtle village and at Ft Pitt until the Revolutionary war broke out, when he accepted British pay and fought the Americans and the friendly Indians, but told the British commander at Detroit that he would not act savagely toward the whites, having no interest in the quarrel, save to procure subsistence for his people, and expecting that when the English made peace with the colonists the Indians would be punished for any excesses that they committed. Col. William Crawford, however, in retaliation for the massacre of Moravian Indians by a party of white men, was put to torture when he fell into Captain Pipe's hands after the ignominious rout of his regiment of volunteers near the upper Sandusky in May,

1782. Pipe signed the treaty of Ft Pitt, Pa., Sept. 17, 1778, the first treaty between the United States and the Indians; he was also a signer of the treaties of Ft McIntosh, Ohio, Jan. 21, 1785, and Ft Harmar, Ohio, Jan. 9, 1787. In 1780 he removed from his home on Walhonding cr., at or near White Woman's town, to old Upper Sandusky, or Cranestown, Ohio, thence to Captain Pipe's village, about 10 m. s. e. of Upper Sandusky, on land that was ceded to the United States in 1829. He died in 1794. See Drake, Hist. Ind., 534, 1880; Darlington, Jour. of Col. May, 94, 1873; Pa. Archives, IV, 441, 1833.

Hoquiam. A Chehalis village on a creek of the same name, N. shore of Grays harbor, Wash.
Ho-ki-um.—Ross in Ind. Aff. Rep., 18, 1870. **Hokwaimits.**— Gibbs, MS., No. 248, B. A. E. (Chehalis name). **Hoquiam.**—Land Office map of Washington, 1891. **Hoquium.**—Gibbs, op. cit.

Horicon. Marked on a map of 1671 as a people living on the headwaters of Hudson r., N. Y., w. of L. Champlain, and placed by others in the same general region. Ruttenber says they were a part of the Mahican who occupied the L. George district, but Shea considers the word a mere misprint for Hirocoi, Hierocoyes, or Iroquois, which is doubtful.
Herechenes.—Gatschet in Am. Antiq., III, 321, 1881. **Herechenes.**—Fleet (1632) quoted, ibid. **Horicons.**—Ruttenber, Tribes Hudson R., 41, 1872. **Horikans.**—Ogilby, America, map, 1671.

Hormiguero (Span.: 'ant hill'). A village, probably of the Pima, on the Pima and Maricopa res., Gila r., Ariz.; pop. 510 in 1860, 514 in 1869. Cf. *Ormejea.*
Herringuen.—Browne, Apache Country, 290, 1869. **Hormiguero.**—Taylor in Cal. Farmer, June 19, 1863.

Hornotlimed. A Seminole chief who came into notice chiefly through a single incident of the Seminole war of 1817–18. He resided at the Fowl Town, in N. w. Florida, at the beginning of hostilities, but was forced to flee to Mikasuki. On Nov. 30, 1817, three vessels arrived at the mouth of Apalachicola r. with supplies for the garrison farther up the stream, but on account of contrary winds were unable to ascend. Lieut. Scott was sent to their assistance with a boat and 40 men, who, on their return from the vessels, were ambushed by Hornotlimed and a band of warriors, all being killed except 6 soldiers, who jumped overboard and swam to the opposite shore. Twenty soldiers who had been left to aid the vessels, and an equal number of women and sick who were with them, fell into the hands of Hornotlimed and his warriors and were slain and scalped. The scalps were carried to Mikasuki and displayed on red sticks as tokens of the victory. Mikasuki was soon afterward visited by American troops and, although most of the Indians escaped, Hornotlimed was captured and immediately hanged. Gen. Jackson

called him "Homattlemico, the old Redstick," the latter name being applied because he was a chief of the Mikasuki band, known also as Red-sticks, because they erected red-painted poles in their village.   (C. T.)

Horocroc. A former village, presumably Costanoan, connected with Dolores mission, San Francisco, Cal.—Taylor in Cal. Farmer, Oct. 18, 1861.

Horses. The first horses seen by the mainland Indians were those of the Spanish invaders of Mexico. A few years later De Soto brought the horse into Florida and westward to the Mississippi, while Coronado, on his march to Quivira in 1541, introduced it to the Indians of the great plains. When the Aztec saw the mounted men of Cortés they supposed horse and man to be one and were greatly alarmed at the strange animal. The classical Centaur owed its origin to a like misconception. A tradition existed among the Pawnee that their ancestors mistook a mule ridden by a man for a single animal and shot at it from concealment, capturing the mule when the man fell.

The horse was a marvel to the Indians and came to be regarded as sacred. For a long time it was worshiped by the Aztec, and by most of the tribes was considered to have a mysterious or sacred character. Its origin was explained by a number of myths representing horses to have come out of the earth through lakes and springs or from the sun. When Antonio de Espejo visited the Hopi of Arizona in 1583, the Indians spread cotton scarfs or kilts on the ground for the horses to walk on, believing the latter to be sacred. This sacred character is sometimes shown in the names given to the horse, as the Dakota *súnka wákan,* 'mysterious dog.' Its use in transportation accounts for the term 'dog' often applied to it, as the Siksika *ponokámita,* 'elk dog'; Cree *mistatīm,* 'big dog'; Shawnee *mishäwä,* 'elk.' (See Chamberlain in Am Ur-Quell, 1894.)

The southern plains proved very favorable, and horses greatly multiplied. Stray and escaped horses formed wild herds, and, as they had few carnivorous enemies, their increase and spread were astonishingly rapid. The movement of the horse was from s. to N., at about an equal rate on both sides of the mountains. It moved northward in three ways: (1) The increase of the wild horses and their dispersal into new regions was rapid. (2) For 150 years before the first exploration of the W. by residents of the United States, Spaniards from the Mexican provinces had been making long journeys northward and eastward to trade with the Indians, even, it is said, as far N. as the camps of the Kiowa, when these were living on Tongue r. (3) As soon as the Indians nearest to the Spanish settlements appreciated the uses of the horse, they began to make raiding expeditions to capture horses, and as knowledge of the animal extended, the tribes still farther to the N. began to procure horses from those next S. of them. So it was that tribes in the S. had the first horses and always had the greatest number, while the tribes farthest N. obtained them last and always had fewer of them. Some tribes declare that they possessed horses for some time before they learned the uses to which they could be put.

On the N. Atlantic coast horses were imported early in the 17th century, and the Iroquois possessed them toward the end of that century and were regularly breeding them prior to 1736. For the northern plains they seem to have been first obtained from the region w. of the Rocky mts., the Siksika having obtained their first horses from the Kutenai, Shoshoni, and other tribes across the mountains, about the year 1800. W. T. Hamilton, who met the Nez Percés, Cayuse, and other tribes of the Columbia region between 1840 and 1850, tells of the tradition among them of the time when they had no horses; but having learned of their existence in the S., of the purposes for which they were used, and of their abundance, they made up a strong war party, went S., and captured horses. It is impossible to fix the dates at which any tribes procured their horses, and, since many of the Plains tribes wandered in small bodies which seldom met, it is likely that some bands acquired the horse a long time before other sections of the same tribe. The Cheyenne relate variously that they procured their first horses from the Arapaho, from the Kiowa, and from the Shoshoni, and all these statements may be true for different bodies. A very definite statement is made that they received their first horses from the Kiowa at the time when the Kiowa lived on Tongue r. The Cheyenne did not cross the Missouri until toward the end of the 17th century. For some time they resided on that stream, and their progress in working westward and southwestward to the Black-hills, Powder r., and Tongue r. was slow. They probably did not encounter the Kiowa on Tongue r. long before the middle of the 18th century, and it is possible that the Kiowa did not then possess horses. Black Moccasin, reputed trustworthy in his knowledge and his dates, declared that the Cheyenne obtained horses about 1780. The Pawnee are known to have had horses and to have used them in hunting early in the 18th century. Carver makes no mention of

seeing horses among the Sioux that he met in 1767 in w. Minnesota; but in 1776 the elder Alexander Henry saw them among the Assiniboin, while Umfreville a few years later spoke of horses as common, some being branded, showing that they had been taken from Spanish settlements.

The possession of the horse had an important influence on the culture of the Indians and speedily changed the mode of life of many tribes. The dog had previously been the Indian's only domestic animal, his companion in the hunt, and to some extent his assistant as a burden bearer, yet not to a very great degree, since the power of the dog to carry or to haul loads was not great. Before they had horses the Indians were footmen, making short journeys and transporting their possessions mostly on their backs. The hunting Indians possessed an insignificant amount of property, since the quantity that they could carry was small. Now all this was changed. An animal had been found which could carry burdens and drag loads. The Indians soon realized that the possession of such an animal would increase their freedom of movement and enable them to increase their property, since one horse could carry the load of several men. Besides this, it insured a food supply and made the moving of camp easy and swift and long journeys possible. In addition to the use of the horse as a burden bearer and as a means of moving rapidly from place to place, it was used as a medium of exchange.

The introduction of the horse led to new intertribal relations; systematic war parties were sent forth, the purpose of which was the capture of horses. This at once became a recognized industry, followed by the bravest and most energetic young men. Many of the tribes, before they secured horses, obtained guns, which gave them new boldness, and horse and gun soon transformed those who, a generation before, had been timid foot wanderers, to daring and ferocious raiders.

On the plains and in the S. W. horses were frequently used as food, but not ordinarily when other flesh could be obtained, although it is said that the Chiricahua Apache preferred mule meat to any other. It frequently happened that war parties on horse-stealing expeditions killed and ate horses. When this was done the leader of the party was always careful to warn his men to wash themselves thoroughly with sand or mud and water before they went near the enemy's camp. Horses greatly dread the smell of horse flesh or horse fat and will not suffer the approach of any one smelling of it.

The horse had no uniform value, for obviously no two horses were alike. A war pony or a buffalo horse had a high, an old pack pony a low, value. A rich old man might send fifteen or twenty horses to the tipi of the girl he wished to marry, while a poor young man might send but one. A doctor might charge a fee of one horse or five, according to the patient's means. People paid as they could. Among the Sioux and the Cheyenne the plumage of two eagles used to be regarded as worth a good horse. Forty horses have been given for a medicine pipe.

Indian saddles varied greatly. The old saddle of Moorish type, having the high peaked pommel and cantle made of wood or horn covered with raw buffalo hide, was common, and was the kind almost always used by women; but there was another type, low in front and behind, often having a horn, the prong of a deer's antler, for a rope. The Indians rode with a short stirrup—the bareback seat. To-day the young Indians ride the cowboy saddle, with the cowboy seat—the long leg. Cow-skin pads stuffed with the hair of deer, elk, antelope, buffalo, or mountain sheep were commonly used instead of saddles by some of the tribes in running buffalo or in war, but among a number of tribes the horse was stripped for chasing buffalo and for battle. Some tribes on their horse-stealing expeditions carried with them small empty pads, to be stuffed with grass and used as saddles after the horses had been secured. The Indians of other tribes scorned such luxury and rode the horse naked, reaching home chafed and scarred.

Horse racing, like foot racing, is a favorite amusement, and much property is wagered on these races. The Indians were great jockeys and trained and handled their horses with skill. When visiting another tribe they sometimes took race horses with them and won or lost large sums. The Plains tribes were extremely good horsemen, in war hiding themselves behind the bodies of their mounts so that only a foot and an arm showed, and on occasion giving exhibitions of wonderful daring and skill. During the campaign of 1865 on Powder r., after Gen. Conner's drawn battle with a large force of Arapaho and Cheyenne, an Arapaho rode up and down in front of the command within a few hundred yards, and while his horse was galloping was seen to swing himself down under his horse's neck, come up on the other side, and resume his seat, repeating the feat many times.

The horse was usually killed at the grave of its owner, just as his arms were buried with him, in order that he might be equipped for the journey that he was about to take. A number of Plains tribes

practised a horse dance. There were songs about horses, and prayers were made in their behalf. On the whole, however, the horse's place in ceremony was only incidental. On the occasion of great gatherings horses were led into the circle of the dancers and there given away, the donor counting a coup as he passed over the gift to the recipient. In modern times the marriage gift sent by a suitor to a girl's family consisted in part of horses. Among some tribes a father gave away a horse when his son killed his first big game or on other important family occasions. In the dances of the soldier-band societies of most tribes 2, 4, or 6 chosen men ride horses during the dance. Their horses are painted, the tails are tied up as for war, hawk or owl feathers are tied to the forelock or tail, and frequently a scalp, or something representing it, hangs from the lower jaw. The painting represents wounds received by the rider's horse, or often there is painted the print of a hand on either side of the neck to show that an enemy on foot has been ridden down. In preparing to go into a formal battle the horse as well as his rider received protective treatment. It was ceremonially painted and adorned, as described above, and certain herbs and medicines were rubbed or blown over it to give it endurance and strength.

Among some of the Plains tribes there was a guild of horse doctors who devoted themselves especially to protecting and healing horses. They doctored horses before going into battle or to the buffalo hunt, so that they should not fall, and doctored those wounded in battle or on the hunt, as well as the men hurt in the hunt. In intertribal horse races they "doctored" in behalf of the horses of their own tribe and against those of their rivals. See *Commerce, Domestication, Travel and Transportation.*   (G. B. G.)

Hosboa. The Road-runner or Pheasant clan of the Hopi, q. v.
Hoc'-bo-a.—Stephen in 8th Rep. B. A. E., 39, 1891. Hoo'-bo-a wuñ-wû.—Fewkes in Am. Anthrop., VII, 405, 1894 (*wuñ-wû* = 'clan'). Hosboa winwû.—Fewkes in 19th Rep. B. A. E., 584, 1900. Huspoa.—Bourke, Snake Dance, 117, 1884.

Hosmite. A former Cholovone village on lower San Joaquin r., Cal.
Hosmite.—Pinart, Cholovone MS., B. A. E., 1880. Kosmitas.—Chamisso in Kotzebue, Voy., III, 51, 1821. Kosmiti.—Choris, Voy. Pitt., 5, 1822.

Hospitality. Hospitality, distinguished from charity, was a cardinal principle in every Indian tribe. The narratives of many pioneer explorers and settlers, from De Soto and Coronado, Amidas and Barlow, John Smith and the Pilgrims, down to the most recent period, are full of instances of wholesale hospitality toward the white strangers, sometimes at considerable cost to the hosts. Gift dances were a feature in every tribe, and it was no uncommon occurrence on the plains during the summer season for large dancing parties to make the round of the tribes, returning in the course of a month or two with hundreds of ponies given in return for their entertainment. Every ceremonial gathering was made the occasion of the most lavish hospitality, both in feasting and the giving of presents. In some languages there was but one word for both generosity and bravery, and either one was a sure avenue to distinction. A notable exemplification of this was the institution of the *potlatch* (q. v.) among the tribes of the N. W. coast, by which a man saved for half a lifetime in order to give away his accumulated wealth in one grand distribution, which would entitle him and his descendants to rank thereafter among the chiefs. In tribes where the clan system prevailed the duty of hospitality and mutual assistance within the clan was inculcated and sacredly observed, anyone feeling at liberty to call on a fellow-clansman for help in an emergency without thought of refusal. The same obligation existed in the case of formal comradeship between two men. Among the Aleut, according to Veniaminoff, the stranger received no invitation on arriving, but decided for himself at which house he chose to be a guest, and was sure to receive there every attention as long as he might stay, with food for the journey on his departure.

On the other hand it can not be said that the Indian was strictly charitable, in the sense of extending help to those unable to reciprocate either for themselves or for their tribes. The life of the savage was precarious at best, and those who had outlived their usefulness were very apt to be neglected, even by their own nearest relatives. Hospitality as between equals was a tribal rule; charity to the helpless depended on the disposition and ability of the individual. See *Ethics and Morals, Feasts*.   (J. M.)

Hostayuntwa (*Ho-'stă-yón-twän'*, 'there he cast a lean thing into the fire.'—Hewitt). An Oneida village that stood on the site of Camden, N. Y.
Ho-'stă-yón-twän'.—J. N. B. Hewitt, inf'n, 1906. Ho-stä-yun'-twä.—Morgan, League Iroq., 473, 1851.

Hosukhaunu ('foolish dogs'). Given as an Arikara band under chief Sithauche about 1855, but properly a dance society.
Foolish Dogs.—Culbertson in Smithson. Rep. 1850, 143, 1851. Ho-sŭk'-hau-nu.—Hayden, Ethnog. and Philol., 357, 1862.

Hosukhaunukarerihu ('little foolish dogs'). Given as an Arikara band under chief Tigaranish about 1855, but properly a dance society.
Ho-sŭk'-hau-nu-ka-re'-ri-hu.— Hayden, Ethnog. and Philol., 357, 1862. Little Foolish Dogs.—Ibid.

Hotachi ('elk'). A Missouri gens, coordinate with the Khotachi gens of the Iowa.
Ho-ma'.—Dorsey in 15th Rep. B. A. E., 240, 1897. Hoo'-ma.—Morgan, Anc. Soc., 156, 1877. Ho-ta'-tci.—Dorsey, op. cit.

Hotagastlas-hadai (*Xṓᴛᴀɢᴀsᴛʟᴀs xā' da-i*, 'people who run about in crowds'). A subdivision of the Chaahl-lanas, a family of the Eagle clan of the Haida, settled in Alaska. They are said to have been thus named because they were so numerous that when visitors came great crowds ran to meet them.—Swanton, Cont. Haida, 276, 1905.

Hotalihuyana (Creek: *hótali, hútali,* 'wind,' 'gust,' 'hurricane'; *huyána,* 'passing'; hence 'Hurricane town'). A former Lower Creek or Seminole town in Dougherty co., Ga., established by Indians of Chiaha on the E. bank of Flint r., 6 m. below the junction of Kitchofooni cr. Settlers from the adjacent Osotchi had mingled with the 20 families of the village in Hawkins' time (1799). It had 27 families in 1832.   (A. S. G.)
Fatehennyaha.—Brinton, Florida Penin., 145, 1859. Holatlahoanna.—H. R. Ex. Doc. 276, 24th Cong., 1st sess., 300, 1836. Ho tal le ho yar nar.—Schoolcraft, Ind. Tribes, IV, 578, 1854. O-tel-le-who-yau-nau.—Hawkins (1799), Sketch, 64, 1848. Otellewhoyonnee.—U. S. Ind. Treat. (1814), 163, 1837. Talehanas.—Ibid. (1797), 68. Taléhouyana.—Penière in Morse, Rep. to Sec. War, 311, 1822. Talle-wheanas.—Ibid., 364. Telhuanas.—Kinnard (1792) in Am. State Papers, Ind. Aff., I, 313, 1832. Tellihuana.—Ibid., 383. Telluiana.—Ibid.

Hotamimsaw (*Hotám-ĭmsáw,* 'foolish or crazy dogs'). A warrior society of the Cheyenne, q. v.
Hotă'mi măssaŭ.—Grinnell, inf'n, 1906 (lit. 'dogs crazy'). Hotám-ĭmsáw.—Mooney, inf'n, 1905.

Hotamitanio (*Hotámitä'nio,* 'dog men'; sing., *Hotámitä'n*). A warrior society of the Cheyenne (q. v.), commonly known to the whites as Dog Soldiers. See *Military Societies*.   (J. M.)
Dog Men's.—G. A. Dorsey, The Cheyenne, 15, 1905. Dog Soldier band.—Culbertson in Smithson. Rep. 1850, 143, 1851. Hotámitä'nio.—Mooney, inf'n, 1905 (see p. 256 of this Handbook). Ho-tum'-i-ta'-ni-o.—Hayden, Ethnog. and Philol. Mo. Val., 281, 1862 (incorrectly given as the name of a dance, but properly intended for the dance of this society). Mi'stävii'nût.—Mooney in 14th Rep. B. A. E., 1026, 1896 (='heavy eyebrows': another name).

Hotao (*Xṓ'tao*). A legendary Haida town that is said to have stood on the s. w. coast of Maude id., Queen Charlotte group, Brit. Col. From this place, according to one account, came the ancestress of the Hlgaiu-lanas.—Swanton, Cont. Haida, 279, 1905.

Hotdjihoas (*Xṓ'tdjixoa's,* 'hair seals at low tide'). A former Haida town on Lyell id., near the N. end of Darwin sd., Queen Charlotte ids., Brit. Col. It was occupied by the Hagi-lanas.—Swanton, Cont. Haida, 277, 1905.

Hothlepoya. See *Menewa*.

Hotnas-hadaĭ (*ᵍot nas xadá'-i,* 'box-house people'). Given by Boas (Fifth

Rep. N. W. Tribes Can., 27, 1889) as the name of a subdivision of the Yaku-lanas, a family of the Raven clan of the Haida in Alaska. It is in reality only a house name belonging to that family. (J. R. S.)

Hot Springs. A summer camp of the Sitka Indians on Baranoff id., Alaska. There were 26 people there in 1880.—Petroff in Tenth Census, Alaska, 32, 1884.

Hottrochtac. A Costanoan village situated in 1819 within 10 m. of Santa Cruz mission, Cal.—Taylor in Cal. Farmer, Apr. 5, 1860.

Houaneiha. An unidentified village or tribe mentioned to Joutel (Margry, Déc., III, 409, 1878) in 1687, while he was staying with the Kadohadacho on Red r. of Louisiana, by the chief of that tribe as being among his enemies.

Houattoehronon (Huron: *Kwathoge'-rónon*, 'people of the sunsetting or of the west'). One of a number of tribes, mentioned in the Jesuit Relation for 1640, which were reputed to be sedentary, populous, and agricultural. Later the form Quatoghe, or Quadoge, is found as the name of the s. end of L. Michigan, being so employed on Mitchell's map of the British Colonies in N. A., of 1755, and on Jefferys' and D'Anville's maps, the one of 1777 and the other of 1775. Meaning simply 'people of the west', it was evidently the name of some people living in the w., at the s. end of L. Michigan. For some unknown reason the name Quatoghees or Quatoghies was applied to the Tionontati by Colden, and by Gallatin, Schoolcraft, and others who followed him; but this is an apparent error, as the Tionontati, or Hurons du Petun, never lived at the s. end of L. Michigan. In the famous deed of the hunting grounds of the Five Nations to the King of England, in 1701, Quadoge is given as the western boundary, at a point w. of the Miami. Father Potier, who resided at Detroit in 1751, says that 8atoeronnon (Ouatoieronon and Quatokeronon being cognate forms) was the Huron name for the Sauk. (J. N. B. H.)
Houattoehronon.—Jes. Rel., index, 1858. Hvat-toehronon.—Jes. Rel. 1640, 35, 1858. Satoeronnon.—Potier, Rac. Hur. et Gram., MS., 1751.

Houjets. An unidentified tribe containing 40 men described as of fine stature, living on a branch of Red r. of Louisiana, 6 leagues from the main stream, at the beginning of the 19th century.—Baudry des Lozières, Voy. a la Louisiane, 242, 249, 1802.

Houtgna. A former Gabrieleño rancheria in Los Angeles co., Cal., at a locality later called Ranchito de Lugo.—Taylor in Cal. Farmer, June 8, 1860.

Howakeeas. Mentioned with the Choctaw as forming a small party which was defeated by the Creeks (Oglethorpe, 1743,

in N. Y. Doc. Col. Hist. VI, 242, 1855). Possibly a bad misprint for Timucua.

Howiri. A ruined pueblo, formerly occupied by the Tewa, at the Rito Colorado, about 10 m. w. of the Hot Springs, near Abiquiu, Rio Arriba co., N. Mex. See Bandelier in Arch. Inst. Papers, III, 61, 1890; IV, 22, 1892; Hewett in Bull. 32, B. A. E., 40, 1906.
Ho-ui-ri.—Bandelier, op. cit.

Howkan (ᵍa'ok!ian, a Tlingit word probably referring to a stone which stood up in front of the town, although some derive it from *qōwakā'n*, 'deer,' deer being numerous there). A Haida town on Long id., facing Dall id., Alaska, below which a great canoe fight took place, resulting in the occupancy of part of Prince of Wales id. by the Kaigani Haida. It was the seat of several families, but the Chaahl-lanas owned it. According to John Work's estimate (1836–41) there were 27 houses and 458 inhabitants. Petroff gave the population as 287 in 1880–81; in 1890 there were 90; in 1900, 145, including whites. (J. R. S.)
Hau kan hade.—Krause, Tlinkit Indianer, 304, 1885. Hou a guan.—Schoolcraft, Ind. Tribes, V, 489, 1855 (after Work, 1836–41). Houkan Hāadē.—Harrison in Proc. and Trans. Roy. Soc. Can., sec. II, 125, 1895. How-a-guan.—Dawson, Q. Charlotte Ids., 173B, 1880 (after Work). Howakan.—Petroff in 10th Census, Alaska, 32, 1884. Howkan.—Eleventh Census, Alaska, 31, 1890. Uon-a-gan.—Kane, Wand. in N. A., app., 1859 (misprint from Work).

Howungkut. A Hupa village of the southern division, nearly due s. of Medilding, from which it is separated by Trinity r., Cal. At this village the first day's dancing of the white deer-skin dance of the Hupa takes place. (P. E. G.)
Wang'-kat.—Powers in Cont. N. A. Ethnol., III, 73, 1877. Xōwûñkût.—Goddard, Life and Culture of the Hupa, 12, 1903.

Hoya. The name of a chief and also of a former settlement on or near the s. coast of South Carolina, visited by Jean Ribault in 1562. Apparently the Ahoya mentioned by Vandera in 1567. The people were friendly with and were possibly related to the Edisto, q. v.
Ahoya.—Vandera (1567) in Smith, Colec. Doc. Fla., 16, 1857. Hoya.—Ribault (1562) in Hakluyt, Voy., 1600, 379, 1800.

Hoya (*Xō'ya*, 'raven' in the Skidegate dialect). One of the two great phratries or clans into which the Haida are divided. (J. R. S.)
K·'oā'la.—Boas, Fifth and Twelfth Reps. N. W. Tribes Canada, *passim* (improperly applied; *K·oā'la* or *K!oa'las* means simply 'people of another clan'). Yêhl.—Swanton, inf'n, 1900 (name in Masset dialect).

Hoyagundla (*Xō'ya ga'nLa*, 'raven creek'). A Haida town on a stream of the same name which flows into Hecate str. a short distance s. of C. Fife, Queen Charlotte ids., Brit. Col. It was occupied by the Djahui-gitinai.—Swanton, Cont. Haida, 280, 1905.

Hoyalas ('the troubled ones'). A Kwakiutl tribe formerly occupying the upper shores of Quatsino sd.; they were exterminated by the Koskimo.

Ho-ya.—Dawson in Trans. Roy. Soc. Can. for 1897, sec. II, 70. **Xō'yalas.**—Boas in Mem. Am. Mus. Nat. Hist., v, pt. 2, 401, 1902. **Xoyā'les.**—Boas in Rep. Nat. Mus. for 1895, 332.

Hoyima. A former Yokuts (Mariposan) tribe on San Joaquin r., Cal.—A. L. Kroeber, inf'n, 1906.

Huachi. A former Costanoan village near Santa Cruz mission, Cal.—Taylor in Cal. Farmer, Apr. 5, 1860.

Huachinera (so called on account of the tascal wood found there in abundance.—Rudo Ensayo). An Opata pueblo and seat of a Spanish mission, founded about 1645, which afterward became a visita of Baseraca; situated on Tesorobabi cr., a branch of Rio Bavispe, E. Sonora, Mexico, near the Chihuahua border. Population 538 in 1678; 285 in 1730, but as it became the place of refuge of the inhabitants of Baquigopa and Batesopa on the abandonment of those villages later in the 18th century, the population was augmented. Total pop. 337 in 1900. (F. W. H.)

Guatzinera.—Rudo Ensayo (ca. 1763), Guiteras trans., 217, 1894. **Huachinera.**—Bandelier in Arch. Inst. Papers, III, pt. 1, 59, 1890. **San Juan Guachirita.**—Orozco y Berra, Geog., 343, 1864 (mentioned as if distinct from Huachinera). **S. Juan de Guachinela.**—Rivera, Diario, leg. 1444, 1736. **S. Juan Guachinera.**—Zapata (1678) quoted by Bancroft, No. Mex. States, I, 246, 1884.

Huadjinaas-hadai. (Xū'Adjî na'as xā'da-i, 'people of grizzly-bear house'). A subdivision of the Koetas family of the Kaigani Haida of British Columbia.—Swanton, Cont. Haida, 272, 1905.

Huados (Xuadō's, 'standing-water people,' in allusion to the swampy nature of the land around their towns). A division of the Raven clan of the Haida, formerly occupying the E. shore of Graham id., Queen Charlotte group, Brit. Col. Originally they were settled at Naikun, but on account of wars they moved to C. Ball, thence to Skidegate. The Naikunkegawai seem to have been a sort of aristocratic branch of this family. (J. R. S.)

Qua'dōs.—Boas, 12th Rep. N. W. Tribes Canada, 24, 1898. **Xuadō's.**—Swanton, Cont. Haida, 270, 1905.

Huados. A small Haida town, inhabited by a family bearing the same name, near the town of Hlgihla-ala, N. of C. Ball, Queen Charlotte ids., Brit. Col.—Swanton, Cont. Haida, 280, 1905.

Hualga. Given by Bourke (Jour. Am. Folk-lore, II, 180, 1889) as the Moon clan of the Mohave; but according to Kroeber, so far as known the Mohave do not name their clans, and their name for moon is *halya*.

Hualimea. A former Cochimi rancheria under San Ignacio mission, Lower California, about lat. 28° 40'.—Taylor in Cal. Farmer, Jan. 17, 1862.

Hualquilme. A former Costanoan village near Santa Cruz mission, Cal.—Taylor in Cal. Farmer, Apr. 5, 1860.

Huanes. A former tribe of s. Texas, mentioned with the Pampoas, Mesquites, Pastias, Camamas, Cacanas, and Canas, as a tribe for which mission San José at San Antonio had been founded.

Xuanes.—Solis, Diario, 1767–68, cited by H. E. Bolton, inf'n, 1906.

Huaque. Mentioned by Oviedo (Hist. Gen. Indies, III, 628, 1853) as one of the provinces or villages visited by Ayllon in 1520. Probably on the South Carolina coast.

Huascari. A tribe or band, probably Paiute, living in 1775 in lat. 38° 3', doubtless in s. Utah.—Dominguez and Escalante in Doc. Hist. Mex., 2d s., I, 537, 1854.

Huashpatzena (*huashpa* = 'dance-kilt'). A pueblo occupied after 1605 by the ancestors of the inhabitants of Santo Domingo pueblo, near the present site of the latter, on the E. bank of the Rio Grande, N. central New Mexico. The pueblo was erected after the destruction, by a freshet, of the second Gipuy (q. v.) to the eastward. A part of Huashpatzena was also carried away by flood, compelling the villagers to move farther east, where they built the pueblo of Kiua—the present Santo Domingo, q. v.

Huash-pa Tzen-a.—Bandelier in Arch. Inst. Papers, IV, 187, 1892. **Uash-pa Tze-na.**—Ibid., III, 34, 1890.

Huasna. A former Chumashan village near Purísima mission, Santa Barbara co., Cal.—Taylor in Cal. Farmer, Oct. 18, 1861.

Huatabampo. One of the principal settlements of the Mayo, in Sonora, Mexico; pop. 1,553 in 1900.—Censo del Estado de Sonora, 96, 1901.

Huaxicori. A former Tepehuane pueblo in lat. 23°, long. 105° 30', Sinaloa, Mexico.

Huajicori.—Orozco y Berra, Geog., map, 1864. **Huaxicori.**—Ibid., 281.

Huchiltchik (Hü'tcĭlttcĭk, 'round clearing'). A Pima village below Santa Ana, on the N. bank of the Gila, in s. Arizona.

Hörltohöletchök.—ten Kate quoted by Gatschet, MS., B. A. E., XX, 199, 1888 (trans. 'plain'). **Hü'tcĭlttcĭk.**—Russell, Pima MS., B. A. E., 1902. **Buen Llano.**—Bailey in Ind. Aff. Rep., 208, 1858. **Llano.**—Brown, Apache Country, 270, 1869.

Huchnom. A division of the Yuki of N. California, speaking a dialect divergent from that of the Round Valley Indians. They lived on South Eel r. above its confluence with the middle fork of Eel r., or in adjacent territories, and on the headwaters of Russian r. in upper Potter valley. To the N. of them were the Witukomnom Yuki, to the E. the Wintun, and on the other sides were Pomo tribes. The Pomo call them Tatu, the whites Redwoods, from Redwood cr.

Hūch'-nom.—Powers in Cont. N. A. Ethnol., III, 126, 1877 (trans. 'outside the valley'). **Redwoods.**—Ind. Aff. Rep., 75, 1870. **Tahtoos.**—Powers in Overland Mo., IX, 507, 1872. **Tá-tu.**—Powers in Cont. N. A. Ethnol., op. cit., 139 (so called by Pomo of Potter valley).

Huda ('wind'). A Yuchi clan.

Hudá tahá.—Gatschet, Uchee MS., B. A. E., 70, 1885.

Huddoh. A local name of the hump-backed salmon (*Salmo proteus*); also known as haddo, from *huddo*, the name of this fish in Niskwalli (Rep. U. S. Comm. Fish., 1872–73, p. 99), of the Salishan stock.   (A. F. C.)

Hudedut (*Hûdedût'*). A former Takilman village at the forks of Rogue r. and Applegate cr., Oreg.
Howtetech.—Latham in Trans. Philol. Soc. Lond., 76, 1856 (misprint). How-te-te'-oh.—Gibbs in Schoolcraft, Ind. Tribes, III, 423, 1853 (possibly the same, or mistaken for the Kikaktsik). Hû-de-dût'.—Dorsey in Jour. Am. Folk-lore, III, 235, 1890.

Huehuerigita. A former Opata pueblo at Casas Grandes, at the w. foot of the Sierra Madre, Chihuahua, Mexico. It was already deserted in the 16th century. Bandelier, Gilded Man, 142, 1893.

Huelemin. A former Chumashan village near Santa Barbara, Cal.—Taylor in Cal. Farmer, Apr. 24, 1863.

Huenejel. A former Chumashan village near Purísima mission, Santa Barbara co., Cal.—Taylor in Cal. Farmer, Oct. 18, 1861. Mentioned as if distinct from Huenepel.

Hueneme. A former Chumashan village on the coast, a few miles s. of Saticoy r., Ventura co., Cal.
Hueneme.—Taylor in Cal. Farmer, July 24, 1863. We-ne'-mu.—Henshaw, Buenaventura MS. vocab., B. A. E., 1884.

Huenepel. A former Chumashan village near Purísima mission, Santa Barbara co., Cal.—Taylor in Cal. Farmer, Oct. 18, 1861. Mentioned as if distinct from Huenejel.

Huepac. A Teguima Opata pueblo and the seat of a Spanish mission founded in 1639; situated in Sonora, Mexico, on the E. bank of Rio Sonora, below lat. 30°. Pop. 268 in 1678, 71 in 1730. In addition to its civilized Opata population it contained 10 Yaqui in 1900.
Guipaca.—Kino, map (1702) in Stöcklein, Neue Welt-Bott, 1726. Huépac.—Davila, Sonora Histórico, 317, 1894. Huepaca.—Orozco y Berra, Geog., 344, 1864. San Lorenzo Guepaca.—Ibid., 343. San Lorenzo Huepaca.—Zapata (1678) quoted by Bancroft, No. Mex. States, 514, 1884.

Huertas (*Las Huertas;* Span.: 'the orchards' or 'kitchen gardens'). A cluster of ruined pueblos 4 m. below Socorro, N. Mex. (Abert in Emory, Recon., 495, 1848); probably originally inhabited by the Piros.

Hueso Parado (Span.: 'bone set up' or 'standing bone'). A former Pima and Maricopa village on the Pima and Maricopa res., Gila r., Ariz.; pop. 263 Pima and 314 Maricopa in 1858.
El Juez Farado.—Bell in Jour Ethnol. Soc. Lond., I, 231, 1869 (misquoting Bailey). El Juez Tarado.—Bailey in Ind. Aff. Rep., 207, 208, 1858. Hueso Parrado.—Taylor in Cal. Farmer, June 19, 1863.

Huexotitlan. A pueblo in Chihuahua, Mexico, and the seat of a Spanish mission with a mixed population of Nevome, Tepehuane, and Tarahumare. Its inhabitants are now civilized.

Huejotitán.—Present name. Huexotitlan.—Bancroft, No. Mex. States, I, 598, 1884. San Gerónimo Huexotitlan.—Orozco y Berra, Geog., 324, 1864.

Huhilp (*Huh-ilp*, 'on the edge'). A village of the Fountain band of Upper Lillooet, on Fountain cr., an E. affluent of upper Fraser r., Brit. Col.—Dawson in Trans. Roy. Soc. Can. for 1891, sec. II, 44.

Huhlitaiga (*Hú'li-täíga*, 'war ford'). A lower Creek village on Chattahoochee r., about the present Georgia-Alabama boundary, the inhabitants of which in or prior to 1799 removed to Oakfuski, settling on the opposite side of the Tallapoosa.
Hohtatoga.—Swan (1791) in Schoolcraft, Ind. Tribes, V, 262, 1855. Ho-ith-le-ti-gau.—Hawkins (1799), Sketch, 45, 1848. Hothletega.—Bartram, Travels, 462, 1791. Hothtetoga.—Swan misquoted by Gatschet, Creek Migr. Leg., I, 131, 1884. Hu'li-täíga.—Ibid. (correct form).

Huhliwahli ('to apportion war'). A former Upper Creek town on the right bank of Tallapoosa r., 5 m. below Atasi, in Macon co., Ala. It obtained its name from the privilege of declaring war which was accorded to it, the declaration being sent from this town to Tukabatchi, thence to the other villages.   (A. S. G.)
Cawalla.—H. R. Ex. Doc. 276, 24th Cong., 1st sess., 150, 1836. Chiwalle.—Ibid., 131. Cleewallees.—U. S. Ind. Treat. (1797), 68, 1837. Cleu wathta.—Parsons in Schoolcraft, Ind. Tribes, IV, 575, 1854. Clewalla.—U. S. Ind. Treat. (1827), 420, 1837. Clewauleys.—Swan (1791) in Schoolcraft, Ind. Tribes, V, 262, 1855. Clewella.—Devereux in H. R. Doc. 274, 25th Cong., 2d sess., 8, 1838. Clewulla.—Schoolcraft, Ind. Tribes, IV, 578, 1854. Cleyali.—Alcedo, Dic. Geog., I, 589, 1786. Cluale.—Bartram, Travels, 461, 1791. Cuwally.—Woodward, Reminiscences, 14, 1859. Elewalies.—Weatherford (1793) in Am. State Pap., Ind. Aff., I, 385, 1832. Hoithlewalee.—Flint, Ind. Wars, 205, 1833. Ho-ith-le Waule.—Hawkins (1799), Sketch, 32, 1848. Hothleawally.—Woodward, Reminiscences, 76, 1858. Hú'li Wa'hli.—Gatschet, Creek Migr. Leg., I, 131, 1884. Rolling Bullet.—Woodward, op. cit. Sdewaetes.—Weatherford (1793) in Am. State Pap., Ind. Aff., I, 385, 1832. Teguales.—Barcia (1693), Ensayo, 313, 1723 (called a Talapoosa town). Tekeewaulees.—Doyell (1813) in Am. State Pap., Ind. Aff., I, 841, 1832. Thlea Walla.—Woodward, Reminiscences, 14, 75, 1858 ("Rolling Bullet").

Huhliwahli. A town in the Creek Nation, on North fork of Canadian r., above Hillabi, Okla.
Hú'li-Wá'li.—Gatschet, Creek Migr. Leg., II, 185, 1888. 'Liwá'hli.—Ibid.

Huhunata (*Hu-hu'-na-ta*). A former Chumashan village near Santa Inés mission, Santa Barbara co., Cal.—Henshaw, Santa Inez MS. vocab., B. A. E., 1884.

Huiauulch.—A Clallam village, the modern Jamestown, 5 m. E. of Dungeness, Puget sd., Wash.
Hui-au-ultc.—Eells, letter, B. A. E., May 21, 1886. Jamestown.—Ibid.

Huichol. A tribe of the Piman stock, numbering 3,000 to 4,000, living in the rugged Sierra Madre of N. w. Jalisco, Mexico. Their neighbors on the E. are the Tepecano, on the w. the Cora; in the N. their territory was formerly bounded by that of the Tepehuane, and in the s. by the Jalisco tribes proper, but these have largely given way to a Mexican and mixed population. In many respects the Huichol are closely related to the Cora; they are alike physically, speak cognate dialects, and exhibit many similarities in culture, thus leading some early writers to confuse the two tribes.

Their country, drained chiefly by the Rio Chapalagana, is divided into three principal districts, with the villages of

HUICHOL MAN. (Am. Mus. Nat. Hist.)

Santa Catarina, San Sebastian, and San Andrés Coamiata as their respective central seats of government. There is little political unity in the tribe. Each of the three districts controls the land within definite boundaries and annually elects officers of its own, consisting of a governor, an alcalde, a captain, a majordomo, and some minor officials—an acquisition from the Spaniards. These officials reside in the central village, which is also a religious center. The farming season is spent in isolated rancherias, and here indeed some of the natives live during the entire year.

The Huichol are of medium stature, three-fourths of the men ranging between 160 and 170 cm.; they are predominantly brachycephalic (the cephalic index of 70 percent of the men exceeding 80), with rather short face and slightly platyrhinic nose. The body is generally well developed, deformity being extremely rare. They are healthy and prolific, and gain their livelihood by farming, hunting, fishing, and by gathering wild fruits. The wealthier Indians own good cattle. They maintain their independence with great jealousy, but they are generally peaceable and mild tempered, and show marked fondness for music, dancing,

flowers, and personal finery. The women are adept in weaving and embroidery.

Their houses are quadrangular, and are built of loose stones, or of stone and mud, with thatched roofs. The dress of the men, now slightly modified, consisted of a poncho made of brown, blue, or white woolen fabric, tightened at the waist with one to three handsomely embroidered girdles, and short breeches of poorly dressed deerskin without hair, at the lower edges of which were strung a number of leathern thongs. To-day these are supplanted by trousers of white cotton. The males wear straw hats handsomely decorated in many ways. Pouches woven of wool or cotton in great variety of design form a part of their costume. Several such bags generally hang from a woven string around the waist; on ceremonial occasions as many as a dozen may be thus worn. The women wear short skirts and ponchos of cotton cloth, sometimes nicely embroidered. Both the men and the women wear over their shoulders, on gala occasions, a small cotton shawl, richly embroidered with red or red and blue thread. Sandals are worn by men. The men tie the hair in a sort of queue

HUICHOL WOMAN. (Am. Mus. Nat. Hist.)

with a colored hair ribbon, or confine it at the neck behind. The women usually wear the hair loose.

The Huichol are polygamists. They preserve their aboriginal religious beliefs, which however show some Christian admixture owing to the teachings of the friars which began after the Spanish conquest of 1722. They have numerous small temples, shrines, and sacrificial caves. Each year a party of men makes a pilgrimage to

San Luis Potosi to gather peyote and to procure holy water, and their return is followed by an elaborate ceremony. Justice is administered almost entirely by the Indians themselves. Thieves are punished by enforced restitution; other criminals by whipping and confinement without food; sorcerers are sometimes killed. The dead are buried in graves or deposited in caves.

The Huichol villages and rancherias, past or present, include Bastita, Chonacate, Guadalupe y Ocotan, Guayabas, Hediondo, Kiatate, Nogal, Ocota, Pedernales, Pochotita, Popotita, San Andrés Coamiata, San José, San Sebastian, Santa Catarina, Santa Gertrudis, Soledad, and Texompa.　　　　　　　　　　(A. H.)
Huicholas.—Bancroft, Nat. Races, I, 621, 1882. Huitcole.—Ibid., III, 719, 1886. Vi-ra-ri-ka.—Lumholtz, Huichol Inds., 2, 1898 (given as their own name). Vishálika.—Lumholtz, Unknown Mexico, II, 21, 1902.

Huikuayaken. Given as a gens of the Squawmish on Howe sd., Brit. Col.
Xuikuā'yaxēn.—Boas, MS., B. A. E., 1887.

Huilacatlan (Nahuatl: 'place of the reeds'). A former settlement of the Tepecano, situated in the valley of the Rio de Bolaños, a short distance from the town of Bolaños, in Jalisco, Mexico.—Hrdlicka in Am. Anthrop., v, 409, 1903.
Huila.—Hrdlicka, ibid.

Huililoc. A former Chumashan village near Santa Barbara, Cal.
Hĕl-i-ok.—Henshaw, Buenaventura MS. vocab., B. A. E., 1884. Huililoc.—Taylor in Cal. Farmer, Apr. 24, 1863.

Huimen. A former Costañoan rancheria connected with Dolores mission, San Francisco, Cal.—Taylor in Cal. Farmer, Oct. 18, 1861.

Huinihkashina (*Hu i'niŋk'ǎciⁿ'a*, 'fish people'). A division of the Washashewanun gens of the Osage.—Dorsey in 15th Rep. B. A. E., 234, 1897.

Huinikashika. A Quapaw gens.
Fish gens.—Dorsey in 15th Rep. B. A. E., 229, 1897. Hu i'nikaci'ᶍa.—Ibid.

Huinyirren. A former Costanoan village whose people were connected with San Juan Bautista mission, Cal.
Huiñirren.—Arroyo de la Cuesta, Idiomas Californias, 1821, MS. trans., B. A. E.

Huirivis. A settlement of the Yaqui on the N. bank of the lower Rio Yaqui, s. w. Sonora, Mexico.
Huadíbis.—Mühlenpfordt quoted by Bancroft, Nat. Races, I, 608, 1882. Huiris.—Orozco y Berra, Geog., 332, 1864. Huirivis.—Velasco (1850) quoted by Bancroft, op. cit.

Huite (Cahita: 'archer'). A small tribe or subdivision of the Cahita group, formerly living, according to Orozco y Berra, in the mountains of N. Sinaloa, Mexico, 7 leagues from the "Sinaloas." They are described as having been anthropophagous, at open war with all their neighbors, and as barbarous and naked, but through the efforts of the missionaries they were gradually reformed

and were gathered into a pueblo where they afterward became confounded with the "Sinaloas." Whether they spoke a dialect different from that of the other subdivisions of the Cahita is uncertain, although from statements by Father Perez de Ribas, in 1645, it may be inferred that they did. They became extinct as a tribe at an early date, probably through absorption by the Sinaloa.
Huites.—Ribas, Hist. Triumphos, 211, 1645. Santiago Huires.—Orozco y Berra, Geog. 333, 1864 (mission name of settlement). Vites.—Ibid.

Huititnom. The branch of the Yuki of N. California who held the s. fork of the middle fork of Eel r.　　　(A. L. K.)

Huixapapa. A former Chumashan village near Santa Barbara, Cal.—Bancroft, Nat. Races, I, 459, 1874.

Hukanuwu(*Xak nuwū'*). An old Tlingit town on the N. side of Cross sd., Alaska, between the mainland and Chichagof id. Distinct from Kukanuwu.　　(J. R. S.)

Huldanggats (*Xaldā'ngats*, 'slaves'). A division of the Hagi-lanas, an important part of the Raven clan among the Ninstints Haida of Queen Charlotte ids., Brit. Col. The native story told to account for their name relates that a chief's wife was once giving these people food, and since they never seemed to have enough, she finally said, "Are you slaves?" The name clung to them ever after.　　(J. R. S.)
Qaldā'ngasal.—Boas, 12th Rep. N. W. Tribes Canada, 25, 1898. Xaldā'ñgats.—Swanton, Cont. Haida, 268, 1905.

Hullooetell. Reported to Lewis and Clark as a numerous nation living N. of Columbia r., on Coweliskee (Cowlitz) r., above the Skilloot, and on Chahwahnahiooks (Lewis) r., in 1806. It was either a Chinookan or a Salishan tribe.
Hull-loo-el-lell.—Orig. Jour. Lewis and Clark, vi, 117, 1905. Hullooellell.—Lewis and Clark, Exped., II, 591, 1817. Hullooetell.—Ibid., II, 209, 1814. Hulloo-et-tell.—Orig. Jour. Lewis and Clark, iv, 206, 1905. Hul-lu-et-tell.—Ibid., 214.

Huma ('red'). A Choctaw tribe living during the earlier period of the French colonization of Louisiana, 7 leagues above Red r. on the E. bank of the Mississippi, their settlement in 1699 containing 140 cabins and 350 families. A red pole (see *Baton Rouge*) marked the boundary between them and the Bayogoula on the s. In 1706 the Tonika fled to them from the Chickasaw, but later rose against them and killed more than half, after which the remainder established themselves near the site of New Orleans. Later they lived along Bayou La Fourche and in the neighborhood of the present Houma, La., which bears their name and where they are still represented by several hundred mixedbloods.
Homas.—La Harpe (1719) in Margry, Déc., VI, 244, 1886. Houma.—Gatschet, op. cit. Omats.—Letter of 1682 in Margry, Déc., II, 205, 1877. Ommas.—Iberville (1699), ibid., IV, 448, 1880. Ouma.—La Salle, ibid., I, 563, 1875.

Humalija. A former Chumashan village near Santa Barbara, Cal.—Taylor in Cal. Farmer, Apr. 24, 1863.

Humarisa (from *húmashi*, 'to run'). A rancheria of 288 Tarahumare, not far from Norogachic, Chihuahua, Mexico.—Lumholtz, inf'n, 1894.

Humawhi. A Shastan tribe or subtribe formerly living on the s. fork of Pit r., Modoc co., Cal. According to Curtin they were a portion of the Ilmawi, living a short distance N. of Hot Spring, Modoc co.

Häma'wi.—Curtin, Ilmawi vocab., B. A. E., 1889. Hu-mâ'-whi.—Powers in Cont. N. A. Ethnol., III, 267, 1877.

Humbo. A New Hampshire word for maple syrup. Horatio Hale sought to bring it into relation with *ombigamisige* in Chippewa and closely related Algonquian dialects, a term signifying ' he makes the maple syrup boil,' or 'boiled sugar drink,' the chief element being the radical *omb*, 'to boil.' (A. F. C.)

Humboldt Indians. The Paviotso living around Humboldt lake, Nev.—Simpson, Rep. of Explor. Across Utah, 38, 1876.

Hume. A former tribe of s. Texas, probably Coahuiltecan, the chief of which was encountered in 1675 by Fernando del Bosque 7 leagues beyond the Rio Grande.

Jume.—Fernando del Bosque (1675) in Nat. Geog. Mag., XIV, 344, 1903. Jumees.—Revillagigedo, MS. (1793) quoted by Orozco y Berra, Geog., 306, 1864.

Humelsom (*HumElsom*). A Squawmish village community on Burrard inlet, Brit. Col.—Hill-Tout in Rep. Brit. A. A. S., 475, 1900.

Humkak (*Hum-kak'*). An important Chumashan village formerly near Pt Conception, Santa Barbara co., Cal.—Henshaw, Buenaventura MS. vocab., B. A. E., 1884.

Humor. It has been so commonly the fashion to describe the American Indian as "the stoic of the woods without a tear," that he has generally been denied as well the possession of a sense of humor. That he does not lack such, however, will readily be admitted by any one who has come to know the Indian as he is, has shared his meals and his camp fire, and had the opportunity of enjoying the real wit and humor abounding in common speech and in ancient legend. The pun, the jest of all kinds, the practical joke, the double-entendre, of which he is sometimes past-master, are all known to him. Particularly does the awkward action or the inexpert movement of the white man incite him to laughter. Like the white man, he has a fund of wit at the expense of the weaker sex and its peculiarities. The Eskimo and the Pueblos especially are merry, laughing people, who jest and trifle through all the grades from quiet sarcasm to the loudest joke. This appears in their songs and legends, in which humor and satire are constantly cropping out. That the Micmac and closely related Indian tribes of the Algonquian stock in N. E. North America have a keen sense of the humorous and ridiculous any one may convince himself by reading some of the tales in Leland and Prince's Kuloskap (1902), especially the episode of the master and the babe, and the story of the wizard and the Christian priest. The mythic trickster is, in fact, found in every tribe, sometimes as a misshapen personage, sometimes as a supernatural coyote, rabbit, or other animal, and the relation of his adventures provokes the greatest mirth. Around their camp fires, and " when the spirit moves them," the Chippewa and related tribes can jest and trifle in real fashion. The episodes in many of their tales and legends also prove their possession of wit and humor. The Cherokee sense of humor is proved by their myths and legends (Mooney in 19th Rep. B. A. E., 1900), and that of the Zuñi by the folklore of that tribe (Cushing, Zuñi Folk Tales, 1901). The Kutenai of British Columbia and Idaho are not without the virtues of humor and sarcasm (Chamberlain, Rep. on N. W. Tribes of Can., 70, 1892). Puns and mistakes in pronunciation easily set them into fits of laughter. The Pueblos, Iroquois, Apache, some of the Plains tribes, and those of the N. W. Pacific coast had regular clowns or funmakers at some of their dances and other ceremonies. Some Plains tribes had the custom of marking the spot where any amusing accident occurred while on the march in order that later travelers might inquire and learn the joke. See *Amusements.* (A. F. C.)

Humptulips (said to mean 'chilly region'). A body of Chehalis on a river of the same name emptying into Chehalis r., Wash. They are under the supervision of the Puyallup school superintendent and numbered 21 in 1904.

Hamtolops.—Keane in Stanford, Compend., 574, 1878. Humptulip.—Ind. Aff. Rep., pt. I, 702, 1901. Hump-tu-lups.—Ross in Ind. Aff. Rep., 18, 1870. Um-too-leaux.—Ford, ibid., 250, 1858.

Huna. A Tlingit tribe on Cross sd., Alaska, camping in summer northward to and beyond Lituya bay. Pop. 1,300 in 1870, 908 in 1880, and 592 in 1890. For 1900 the entire population of Gaudekan, the chief Huna village, was given as 447. Other towns in their country are Akvetskoe, Hukanuwu, Klughuggue, Kukanuwu, and Tlushashakian. Their social divisions are Chukanedi, Koskedi, Takdentan, and Wushketan.

Chūna-kŏn.—Krause, Tlinkit Ind., 118, 1885. Cross Sound Indians.—Kane, Wand N. A., app., 1859 (traders' name). Grass Sound Indians.—Colyer in Ind. Aff. Rep., 535, 1870. Hoonah Kow.—Emmons in Mem. Am. Mus. Nat. Hist., III, 232, 1903. Hoone-ahs.—Scott in Ind. Aff. Rep., 314, 1868. Hoone-aks.—Halleck in Rep. Sec. War, pt. I, 39, 1868. Hooniahs.—Scidmore, Alaska, 127, 1885. Hoonid.—Colyer in Ind. Aff. Rep., 535, 1870. Hoonyah.—Petroff in Tenth Census, Alaska,

31, 1884. **Humros.**—Scott in Ind. Aff. Rep., 314, 1868. **Huna.**—Pfeiffer, Second Journ. Around World, 314, 1856. **Huna cow.**—Schoolcraft, Ind. Tribes, v, 489, 1855 (after Kane; misprint). **Hūna-kŏn.**—Krause, Tlinkit Ind., 118, 1885. **Hunnas.**—Halleck in Rep. Sec. War, pt. I, 39, 1868 **Ueena-caw.**—Kane, Wand in N. A., app., 1859. **Whinega.**—Mahony (1869) in Sen. Ex. Doc. 68, 41st Cong., 2d sess., 19, 1870.

Hunawurp (*Hu-na-wûrp*). One of the Chumashan villages formerly near Santa Inés mission, Santa Barbara co., Cal.— Henshaw, Santa Inez MS. vocab., B. A. E., 1884.

Hunctu. A former village, presumably Costanoan, connected with Dolores mission, San Francisco, Cal.—Taylor in Cal. Farmer, Oct. 18, 1861.

Hungopavi (Navaho: 'crooked nose'). An important pueblo ruin 2 m. above Pueblo Bonito, on the N. side of Chaco canyon, at the base of the canyon wall, in N. w. New Mexico. It is built around 3 sides of a court, the extremities of the wings being connected by a semicircular double wall and the space between these walls divided into rooms. The length of the main building is 309 ft; of the 2 wings, 136 ft each. The building was 4 stories high. There is a circular kiva in the court and another inclosed within the walls of the main building. The one inclosed is 23 ft in diameter. The masonry of Hungopavi is exceptionally good; the material is fine-grained, grayish-yellow sandstone, compactly laid in thin mud mortar. The exterior walls of the first story are 3 ft thick. Walls still stand to a height of 30 ft, and deterioration has proceeded very slowly since the ruin was first described. See Hardacre in Scribner's Mag., Dec. 1878; Jackson in 10th Rep. Hayden Surv., 438, 1879, and the writers mentioned below.   (E. L. H.)
Hungo Parie.—Domenech, Deserts, I, 200, 1860 (misprint). **Hungo Pavia.**—Morgan in Rep. Peabody Mus., XII, 549, 1880. **Hungo Pavie.**—Simpson, Exped. Navaho Country, 79, 1850. **Hunyo Pavie.**—Cope in Rep. Wheeler Surv., app. LL, 173, 1875.

Huning ruin. A large, rectangular, prehistoric ruin on the ranch of Henry Huning at Showlow, Navajo co., Ariz., on a rock table above Showlow cr. The pottery found on the site is of red and gray ware, not of very fine quality. The masonry of the walls is good, but the remains of the pueblo do not indicate very long occupancy.—Hough in Rep. Nat. Mus. 1901, 301, 1903.

Hunkkhwitik (*Hŭñ kqwi' tĭk*). A former Yaquina village on the N. side of Yaquina r., Oreg.—Dorsey in Jour. Am. Folk-lore, III, 229, 1890.

Hunkpapa (variously interpreted 'at the entrance,' 'at the head end of the circle,' 'those who camp by themselves,' and 'wanderers'). A division of the Teton Sioux. From the meager data relating to the history of this band it seems probable that it is one of comparatively modern formation. When Hennepin, in 1680,

found what are believed to have been the Teton as far E. as the banks of the upper Mississippi, no mention of the Hunkpapa at that early date or for 100 years thereafter can be found unless it be under some name yet unidentified. Their name is not mentioned by Lewis and Clark, though it is possible that the tribe is included in the Tetons Saone of those explorers. The name first appears as Honkpapa, and it is properly written Hunkpapa in the treaty of 1825. It is evident that the tribe was then well known, although its history previous to this date is undetermined. The Tetons Saone were located by Lewis and Clark, in 1804, on both sides of the Missouri below Beaver cr., N. Dak., and were estimated at 300 men or 900 souls in 120 tipis. Ramsey (1849) gave their location as near Cannonball r. Culbertson (1850) gave their range as on the Cheyenne, Moreau, Grand, and Cannonball rs., and estimated them at 320 tipis. Gen. Warren (1855) said that they lived on the Missouri near the mouth of the Moreau and roamed from the Big Cheyenne up to the Yellowstone, and w. to the Black-hills. He states that they formerly intermarried extensively with the Cheyenne. His estimate of population is 365 tipis, 2,920 souls. He adds that many of the depredations along the Platte "are committed by the Unkpapas and Sihasapas." It is indicative of their character that they were among the last of the Dakota to be brought upon reservations. The Indian agent, writing in 1854, says: "All the bands of Sioux have already received their presents with great appearance of friendship, excepting the Minnecowzues (Miniconjou), Blackfeet (Sihasapa), and Honepapas (Hunkpapa). The former band are daily expected at the fort, and will gladly receive their annuities; but the Blackfeet and Honepapas still persist in refusing any annuities, and are constantly violating all the stipulations of the treaty. They are continually warring and committing depredations on whites and neighboring tribes, killing men and stealing horses. They even defy the Great Father, the President, and declare their intention to murder indiscriminately all that come within their reach. They, of all Indians, are now the most dreaded on the Missouri." And when the agent finally succeeded in reaching them and holding a council with their chiefs at Ft Clark, they refused to receive the presents sent by the Government, stating that they did not want them, but preferred the liberty to take scalps and commit whatever depredations they pleased. They took part in most of the subsequent conflicts with the whites, as that at Ft Phil. Kearney and that with Custer on the Little Bighorn. The number of the band in 1891 was 571;

these were gathered on Standing Rock res., N. and S. Dak. The population is no longer given separately. The noted Sitting Bull was chief of this tribe, though in making treaties he signed also for the Oglala.

Their subdivisions as given by J. O. Dorsey are: (1) Chankaokhan, (2) Cheokhba, (3) Tinazipeshicha, (4) Talonapin, (5) Kiglashka, (6) Chegnakeokisela, (7) Shikshichela, (8) Wakan, and (9) Hunskachantozhuha. Culbertson (Smithson. Rep. 1850, 141, 1851) mentions the following bands: Devil's medicine-man band (Wakan), Half breechclout people (Chegnakeokisela), Fresh meat necklace people (Talonapin), Sleepy Kettle band (Cheokhba), Sore backs (Chankaokhan), Bad bows (Tinazipeshicha), and Those that carry. Fire-Heart's band (Chantaapeta's band) is supposed to be a part of the Hunkpapa.

Ampapa.—Smet, Miss.de l'Oregon, 264, 848. Ampapes.—Smet, Letters, 23, 1843. Aukpapas.—Ind. Aff. Rep., 297, 1854. Hankpapes.—Parker, Jour., 44, 1840. Honepapas.—Ind. Aff. Rep., 295, 1854. Honk pa pa.—Ex. Doc. 56, 18th Cong., 1st sess., 9, 1824. Houkpapas.—Ind. Aff. Rep., 471, 1838. Hunkappas.—Ramsey in Ind. Aff. Rep. 1849, 86, 1850 (misprint). Huŋkpapa.—Riggs, Dakota Gram. and Dict., viii, 1852. Hunkpapas.—U. S. Ind. Treat. (1825), 346, 1826. Hunkpa-te-dans.—Ramsey in Ind. Aff. Rep. 1849, 86, 1850 (mistake). Nicpapa.—Hare in Spirit of Missions, 586, 1885 (misprint). Oak-pa-pas.—Hoffman in H. R. Ex. Doc. 36, 33d Cong., 2d sess., 3, 1855. Oncapapas.—Corliss, Lacotah MS. vocab., B. A. E., 107, 1874. Onch-pa-pah.—Culbertson in Smithson. Rep. 1850, 141, 1851. Onc-pah-pa.—Donaldson in Smithson. Rep. 1885, pt. 2, 57, 1886. Oncpapa.—Catlin, N. Am. Inds., I, 223, 1844. One-capapa.—Donaldson in Smithson. Rep., 1885, pt. 2, 57, 1886. Onkpahpah.—U. S. Ind. Treat. (1886), 899, 1873. Onkpapah.—Schoolcraft, Ind. Tribes, v, 494, 1855. Ouh-papas.—Vaughan in H. R. Doc. 36, 33d Cong., 2d sess., 6, 1855. Uncpapa.—Terry in Rep. Sec. War for 1869, pt. 1, 34. Unc Papas.—Ind. Aff. Rep. 1856, 7, 1857. Uncpappas.—Keane in Stanford, Compend., 541, 1878. Unkpapa Dakotas.—Hayden, Ethnog. and Philol. Mo. Val., map, 1862. Unkpapas.—Warren, Dacota Country, 16, 1855.

Hunkpatina ('campers at the end of the circle'). One of the two primary divisions of the Yanktonai Sioux, commonly known as Lower Yanktonai, from their former range on lower James r. of E. South Dakota. The Hunkpatina are seemingly referred to for the first time, in whole or in part, by Lewis and Clark, in 1804, under the name Honetaparteen, as a division of the Yankton of the N. They were on intimate terms with the Upper Yanktonai, who ranged about the upper waters of the James. They are now chiefly on Crow Creek res., S. Dak., where they numbered 1,009 in 1905. In 1866 they were estimated at 2,100. Some others appear to be attached to Standing Rock agency, N. Dak. Their bands, as given by J. O. Dorsey (15th Rep. B. A. E., 218, 1897), are: Putetemini (Sweat-lips), Shungikcheka (Common dogs), Takhuhayuta (Eat-the-scrapings-of-hides), Sangona (Shot-at-some-white-object), Ihasha (Red-lips), Iteghu (Burnt-face), Pteyuteshni (Eat-no-buffalo-cows).

Amkepatines.—Smet, Letters, 23, 1843. Hen-ta-pahtus.—Prescott in Schoolcraft, Ind. Tribes, II, 169, note, 1852. Hen-tee-pah-tees.—Ibid. Ho in de borto.—Clark (1804) in Orig. Jour. Lewis and Clark, I, 132, 1904. Honcpatela band.—Sen. Ex. Doc. 94, 34th Cong., 1st sess., 11, 1856. Honepatela Yanctonnais.—H. R. Ex. Doc. 130, 34th Cong., 1st sess., 7, 1856. Honeta-par-teen.—Lewis and Clark, Discov., 34, 1806. Hunk-pate.—Ind. Aff. Rep., 71, 1858. Hunkpatee.—Cleveland in Our Church Work, Dec. 4, 1875. Hunkpatidan.—Schoolcraft, Ind. Tribes, I, 248, 1851. Huŋkpatidaŋs.—Riggs, Dak. Gram. and Dict., xvi, 1852. Hunkplatin.—Brown in Ind. Aff. Rep. 1859, 92, 1860. Lower Yanctonais.—Ind. Aff. Rep., 371, 1866. Lower Yanctonnais.—Ibid., 1871, 525, 1872. Lower Yanctonai.—Robinson, letter to Dorsey, 1879. Lower Yanktonnais.—Ind. Aff. Rep., 27, 1878. Unc-pah-te.—Ind. Aff. Rep. 1867, 231, 1868. Uncpatina.—Alderson in Ind. Aff. Rep., 266, 1874. Unkepatines.—Smet, Letters, 37, note, 1843.

Hunkuwanicha ('without a mother'). A band of the Brulé Teton Sioux.

Huŋku-waniċa.—Dorsey (after Cleveland) in 15th Rep. B. A. E., 219, 1897. Hŭňku-wanitca.—Ibid.

Hunnint. A Clallam village in N. w. Washington which participated in the treaty of Point No Point in 1855.—U. S. Ind. Treat., 800, 1873.

Hunskachantozhuha ('legging tobacco pouches'). A band of the Hunkpapa Teton Sioux.

Huŋska-ċaŋtożuha.—Dorsey in 15th Rep. B. A. E., 221, 1897. Hŭňska-tcaⁿtojuha.—Ibid.

Hunting. The pursuit of game may be divided into two sets of activities, which correspond to military strategy and tactics, the one including the whole series of traps, the other hunting weapons and processes. Beginning with the latter, the following 9 classes embrace all the hunting activities of the American Indians:

(1) Taking animals with the hand without the aid of apparatus. Examples of this are picking up marine animals on the beach to eat on the spot, robbing birds' nests, and seizing birds on their roosts on dark nights. Such unskilled taking developed the utmost cunning, agility, and strength for pursuing, seizing, climbing, diving, stealing upon, and deceiving, and the same qualities were useful also in the pursuit with weapons. The climax of this first class was the communal game drive, in which a whole band or tribe would surround a herd of animals and coax or force them into a gorge, a corral, or natural cul-de-sac.

(2) Gathering with devices. To this class of activities belong substitutes for the fingers or palms, such as rakes for drawing or piling up sea food; a sharp stick for getting worms by forcing them out of the ground; nets and scoops for taking animals from the water (see Fishing, Nets); also dulls, reatas, and bolas for reaching out and grasping. This class reached its climax in the partnership or communal net, used by the Eskimo and other tribes for taking seal and also small fish.

(3) The employment of apparatus for

striking, bruising, or breaking bones, including stones held in the hands, clubs with grips, and hard objects at the end of a line or handle, like a slung shot. The N. Pacific tribes took great pains with their clubs, carving on them their symbolism.

(4) Slashing or stabbing with edged weapons. The Indians had little to do with metals and were given almost altogether to the use of stone, bone, reeds, and wood for stabbing and slashing. Both chipped and ground weapons were used, either without a handle, with a grip, or at the end of a shaft. Every Eskimo had a quiver of daggers for use at close quarters, and so had the Indian his side arms. Edged weapons, however, were not so common as the weapons of the next class.

(5) Hunting with piercing weapons, the most common of all Indian methods of taking animals. The implements include the pointed stick or stone, the lance, the spear, the harpoon, and the arrow (q. v.). Weapons of this class were held in the hand, hurled from the hand, shot from a bow or a blowgun, or slung from the throwing stick. Each of the varieties went through a multitude of transformations, depending on game, materials at hand, the skill of the maker, etc.

(6) The use of traps, pits, and snares (see Traps). The Tenankutchin of Alaska capture deer, moose, and caribou by means of a brush fence, extended many miles, in which at intervals snares are set; and the same custom was practised by many other tribes in hunting the larger game. The Plains tribes and the ancient Pueblos captured deer, antelope, and wolves by means of pitfalls.

(7) Capturing game by means of dogs or other hunting animals. Indian tribes, with few exceptions, had no hunting dogs regularly trained to pursue game, but the common dog was very efficient. Fowls of the air, marine animals, and especially carnivorous animals, such as the coyote, by their noises and movements gave the cue which aided the cunning and observant hunter to identify, locate, and follow his game. (See Domestication.)

(8) Hunting by means of fire and smoke. In America, as throughout the world, as soon as men came into possession of fire the conquest of the animal kingdom was practically assured. The Indians used smoke to drive animals out of hiding, torches to dazzle the eyes of deer and to attract fish and birds to their canoes, and firebrands and prairie fires for game drives.

(9) Taking animals by means of drugs. The bark of walnut root served to asphyxiate fish in fresh-water pools in the Southern states; in other sections soap root and buckeyes were used.

In connection with hunting processes there were accessory activities in which the Indian had to be versed. There were foods to eat and foods tabued, clothing and masks to wear, shelters and hiding places to provide, and not only must the hunter be familiar with calls, imitations, decoys, whistles, and the like, but acquainted with the appropriate hunting songs, ceremonies, and fetishes, and with formulas for every act in the process, the time for the chase of the various animals, the laws for the division of game, and the clan names connected with hunting. Besides, there were numberless employments and conveniences associated therewith. In order to use the harpoon it was necessary to have a canoe, and with every method of hunting were connected other employments which taxed the ingenuity of the savage mind. There were also certain activities which were the result of hunting. Questions presented themselves regarding transportation, receptacles, the discrimination of useful species, and the construction of fences. A slight knowledge of anatomy was necessary in order to know where to strike and how to cut up game. All these gave excellent training in perception, skill, and cooperative effort. See Buffalo, Fishing, Food, Fur trade, Horse, etc., and the various subjects above referred to.

Consult Allen, Rep. on Alaska, 138, 1885; Boas, Central Eskimo, 6th Rep. B. A. E., 1888; Catlin, N. A. Inds., I-II, 1844; Dixon in Bull. Am. Mus. Nat. Hist., XVII, pt. 3, 1905; Hoffman, Menomini Inds., 14th Rep. B. A. E., 1896; Mason, various articles in Rep. Smithson. Inst. and Nat. Mus.; Maximilian, Travels, 1849; Murdoch, Ethnological Results of the Point Barrow Exped., 9th Rep. B. A. E., 1892; Nelson, Eskimo about Bering Strait, 18th Rep. B. A. E., 1899; Schoolcraft, Indian Tribes, I-VI, 1851-57.　　(O. T. M.)

Huntlatin. A division of the Tenankutchin on Tanana r., Alaska.
Hautlatin.—Dawson (after Allen) in Rep. Geol. Surv. Can., 203B, 1887. Huntlatin.—Allen, Rep. on Alaska, 137, 1887.

Hunxapa. A former Chumashan village near Santa Barbara, Cal.
Huixapa.—Bancroft, Nat. Races, I, 459, 1874. Hunxapa.—Taylor in Cal. Farmer, Apr. 24, 1863.

Huocom. A former Costanoan village near Santa Cruz mission, Cal.—Taylor in Cal. Farmer, Apr. 5, 1860.

Hupa. An Athapascan tribe formerly occupying the valley of Trinity r., Cal., from South fork to its junction with the Klamath, including Hupa valley. They were first mentioned by Gibbs in 1852; a military post was established in their territory in 1855 and maintained until 1892; and a reservation 12 m. square, including nearly all the Hupa habitat, was set apart in Aug., 1864. The population in 1888 was given as 650; in 1900, 430; in 1905, 412. They are at present self-supporting, depending on agriculture and

HUPA WOMAN.   (GODDARD)

stock raising. When they first came in contact with the whites, in 1850, the Hupa were all under the control of a chief called Ahrookoos by the Yurok (McKee in Sen. Ex. Doc. 4, 32d Cong., spec. sess., 161, 1853), whose authority is said to have extended to other peoples southward along Trinity r. The position of chief depended on the possession of wealth, which usually remained in the family, causing the chieftainship to descend from father to son. In feasts and dances a division of the Hupa into two parts is manifest, but this division seems to have no validity outside of religious matters. The tribe occupied the following permanent villages: Cheindekhotding, Djishtangading, Haslinding, Honsading, Howungkut, Kinchuwhikut, Medilding,

Miskut, Takimilding, Tlelding, Toltsasding, and Tsewenalding. Powers (Cont. N. A. Ethnol., III, 73, 1877) gave Chailkutkaituh, Wissomanchuh, and Misketoiitok, which have not been identified with any of the foregoing; Gibbs (MS. on Klamath river, B. A. E., 1852), on information furnished by the Yurok, gave Wangullewutlekauh, Wangullewatl, Sehachpeya, and (Schoolcraft, Ind. Tribes, III, 139, 1853) Tashuanta, Sokeakeit (Sokchit), and Meyemma.

The houses of the Hupa were built of cedar slabs set on end, the walls being 4 ft high on the sides and rising to more than 6 ft at the ends to accommodate the slope of the roof, inclosing a place about 20 ft square, the central part of which was excavated to form the principal chamber, which was about 12 ft square and 5 ft deep. The entrance was a hole 18 or 20 in. in diameter and about a foot above the ground. This was the storehouse for the family goods and the sleeping place of the women. The men occupied sweat houses at night. The Hupa depended for food on the deer and elk of the mountains, the salmon and lamprey of the

HUPA MAN.   (GODDARD)

river, and the acorns and other vegetal foods growing plentifully about them. They are noted for the beautiful twined baskets produced by the women and the fine pipes and implements executed by the men. The yew bows they used to make, only about 3 ft long, strengthened with sinew fastened to the back with sturgeon glue, were effective up to 75 yds. and could inflict a serious wound at 100 yds. Their arrows, made of syringa shoots wound with sinew, into which foreshafts of juneberry wood were inserted, feathered with three split hawk feathers and pointed with sharp heads of obsidian, flint, bone, or iron, sometimes passed entirely through a deer. The hunter, disguised in the skin of the deer or elk, the odor of his body removed by ablution and smoking with green fir boughs, simulated so perfectly the movements of the animal in order to get within bowshot that a panther sometimes pounced upon his back, but withdrew when he felt the sharp pins that, for the very purpose of warding off such an attack, were thrust through the man's hair gathered in a bunch at the back of the neck. The Hupa took deer also with snares of a strong rope made from the fiber of the iris, or chased them into the water with dogs and pursued them in canoes. Meat was roasted before the fire or on the coals or incased in the stomach and buried in the ashes until cooked, or was boiled in water-tight baskets by dropping in hot stones. Meat and fish were preserved by smoking. Salmon were caught in latticed weirs stretched across the river or in seines or poundnets, or were speared with barbs that detached but were made fast to the pole by lines. Dried acorns were ground into flour, leached in a pit to extract the bitter taste, and boiled into a mush.

The men wore ordinarily a breechclout of deerskin or of skins of small animals joined together, and leggings of painted deerskin with the seam in front hidden by a fringe that hung from the top, which was turned down at the knee. Moccasins of deerskin with soles of elk hide were sometimes worn. The dance robes of the men were made of two deerskins sewn together along one side, the necks meeting over the left shoulder and the tails nearly touching the ground. Panther skins were sometimes used. The hair was tied into two clubs, one hanging down on each side of the head, or into one which hung behind. Bands of deerskin, sometimes ornamented with woodpeckers' crests, were worn about the head in dances, and occasionally feathers or feathered darts were stuck in the hair. The nose was not pierced, but in the ears were often worn dentalium shells with tassels of woodpeckers' feathers. A quiver of handsome skin filled with arrows was a part of gala dress, and one of plain buckskin or a skin pouch or sack of netting was carried as a pocket for small articles. Women wore a skirt of deerskin reaching to the knees, with a long, thick fringe hanging below and a short fringe at the waist. When soiled it was washed with the soap plant. At the opening of the skirt in front an apron was worn underneath. The skirts worn in dances were ornamented with strings of shell beads, pieces of abalone shell, and flakes of obsidian fastened to the upper and of shells of pine nuts inserted at intervals in the lower fringe. The apron for common wear was made of long strands of pine-nut shells and braided leaves attached to a belt. The dance aprons had strands of shells and pendants cut from abalone shells. Small dentalium and olivella shells, pine-nut shells, and small black fruits were strung for necklaces. A robe of deerskin or of wildcat fur was worn with the hair next to the body as a protection against the cold and in rainy weather with the hair side out. The head covering was a cap of fine basket work, which protected the forehead from the carrying strap whereby burdens and baby baskets were borne. Women, except widows, wore their hair long and tied in queues that hung down in front of the ears, and were ornamented with strips of mink skin, sometimes covered with woodpeckers' crests, and shell pendants, and sometimes perfumed with stems of yerba buena. From their ears hung pendants of abalone shell attached to twine. All adult women were tattooed with vertical black marks on the chin and sometimes curved marks were added at the corners of the mouth.

The imagination of the Hupa has peopled the regions E., W., S., and above with mortals known as Kihunai. The underworld is the abode of the dead. Their creator or culture hero, Yimantuwingyai, dwells with Kihunai across the ocean toward the N. A salmon feast is held by the southern divison in the spring and an acorn feast by the northern division in the fall. They formerly celebrated three dances each year: the spring dance, the white-deerskin dance, and the jumping dance. They have a large and varied folklore and many very interesting medicine formulas. See Goddard, Life and Culture of the Hupa, Univ. Cal. Pub., 1903; Hupa Texts, ibid., 1904.   (P. E. G.)

Cha′parahihu.—A. L. Kroeber, inf'n, 1903 (Shasta name). Híuh′hu.—Kroeber, inf'n, 1903 (Chimariko name). Hoopa.—Gatschet in Beach, Ind. Miscel., 440, 1877. Hoo-pah.—Gibbs in Schoolcraft, Ind. Tribes, III, 139, 1853. Ho-pah.—Gibbs, MS., B. A. E., 1852. Hupá.—Powers in Cont. N. A. Ethnol., III, 73, 1877. Húpô.—Gatschet in Beach, Ind. Miscel., 440, 1877. Kishakevira.—Kroeber, inf'n, 1903 (Karok name). Nabiltse.—Gibbs, Nabiltse MS. vocab., B. A. E., 1857 (trans. 'man'). Nabil-tse.—Gibbs in Schoolcraft, Ind. Tribes, III, 423, 1853. Nabittse.—Latham in Proc. Philol. Soc. Lond., VI, 84, 1854. Natano.—Ray in Am. Nat., 832, 1886. Noh-tin-oah.—Azpell, MS., B. A. E. (own name). Num-ee-muss.—Ibid. (Yurok name). Trinity Indians.—McKee (1851) in Sen. Ex. Doc.

4, 32d Cong., spec. sess., 161, 1858. **Up-pa.**—Hazen quoted by Gibbs, Nabiltse MS. vocab., B. A. E.

Huron (lexically from French *huré*, 'bristly,' 'bristled,' from *hure*, 'rough hair' (of the head), head of man or beast, wild boar's head; old French, 'muzzle of the wolf, lion,' etc., 'the scalp,' 'a wig'; Norman French, *huré*, 'rugged'; Roumanian, *hurée*, 'rough earth,' and the suffix *-on*, expressive of depreciation and employed to form nouns referring to persons). The name *Huron*, frequently with an added epithet, like *vilain*, 'base,' was in use in France as early as 1358 (La Curne de Sainte-Palaye in Dict. Hist. de l'Ancien Langage Françoise, 1880) as a name expressive of contumely, contempt, and insult, signifying approximately an unkempt person, knave, ruffian, lout, wretch. The peasants who rebelled against the nobility during the captivity of King John in England in 1358 were called both *Hurons* and *Jacques* or *Jacques bons hommes*, the latter signifying approximately 'simpleton Jacks,' and so the term *Jacquerie* was applied to this revolt of the peasants. But Father Lalement (Jes. Rel. for 1639, 51, 1858), in attempting to give the origin of the name *Huron*, says that about 40 years previous to his time, i. e., about 1600, when these people first reached the French trading posts on the St Lawrence, a French soldier or sailor, seeing some of these barbarians wearing their hair cropped and roached, gave them the name Hurons, their heads suggesting those of wild boars. Lalement declares that while what he had advanced concerning the origin of the name was the most authentic, "others attribute it to some other though similar origin." But it certainly does not appear that the rebellious French peasants in 1358, mentioned above, were called Hurons because they had a similar or an identical manner of wearing the hair; for, as has been stated, the name had, long previous to the arrival of the French in America, a well-known derogatory signification in France. So it is quite probable that the name was applied to the Indians in the sense of 'an unkempt person,' 'a bristly savage,' 'a wretch or lout,' 'a ruffian.'

A confederation of 4 highly organized Iroquoian tribes with several small dependent communities, which, when first known in 1615, occupied a limited territory, sometimes called Huronia, around L. Simcoe and s. and E. of Georgian bay, Ontario. According to the Jesuit Relation for 1639 the names of these tribes, which were independent in local affairs only, were the Attignaouantan (Bear people), the Attigneenongnahac (Cord people), the Arendahronon (Rock people), and the Tohontaenrat (*Atahonta'enrat* or *Tohonta'enrat*, White-eared or Deer people). Two of the dependent peoples were the Bowl people and the Ataronchronon. Later, to escape destruction by the Iroquois, the Wenrohronon, an Iroquoian tribe, in 1639, and the Atontrataronnon, an Algonquian people, in 1644, sought asylum with the Huron confederation. In the Huron tongue the common and general name of this confederation of tribes and dependent peoples was *Wendat* (8endat), a designation of doubtful analysis and signification, the most obvious meaning being 'the islanders' or 'dwellers on a peninsula.' According to a definite tradition recorded in the Jesuit Relation for 1639, the era of the formation of this confederation was at that period comparatively recent, at least in so far as the date of membership of the last two tribes mentioned therein is concerned. According to the same authority the Rock people were adopted about 50 years and the Deer people about 30 years (traditional time) previous to 1639, thus carrying back to about 1590 the date of the immigration of the Rock people into the *Huron* country. The first two principal tribes in 1639, regarding themselves as the original inhabitants of the land, claimed that they knew with certainty the dwelling places and village sites of their ancestors in the country for a period exceeding 200 years. Having received and adopted the other two into their country and state, they were the more important. Officially and in their councils they addressed each other by the formal political terms 'brother' and 'sister'; they were also the more populous, having incorporated many persons, families, clans, and peoples, who, preserving the name and memory of their own founders, lived among the tribes which adopted them as small dependent communities, maintaining the general name and having the community of certain local rights, and enjoyed the powerful protection and shared with it the community of certain other rights, interests, and obligations of the great Wendat commonwealth.

The provenience and the course of migration of the Rock and Deer tribes to the Huron country appear to furnish a reason for the prevalent but erroneous belief that all the Iroquoian tribes came into this continent from the valley of the lower St Lawrence. There is presumptive evidence that the Rock and the Deer tribes came into Huronia from the middle and upper St Lawrence valley, and they appear to have been expelled therefrom by the Iroquois, hence the expulsion of the Rock and the Deer people from lower St Lawrence valley has been mistaken for the migration of the entire stock from that region.

In his voyages to the St Lawrence in 1534–43, Jacques Cartier found on the present sites of Quebec and Montreal, and along both banks of this river above the Saguenay on the N. and above Gaspé peninsula on the s. bank, tribes speaking Iroquoian tongues, for there were at least two dialects, a fact well established by the vocabularies which Cartier recorded. Lexical comparison with known Iroquoian dialects indicates that those spoken on the St Lawrence at that early date were Huron or Wendat. Cartier further learned that these St Lawrence tribes were in fierce combat with peoples dwelling southward from them, and his hosts complained bitterly of the cruel attacks made on them by their southern foes, whom they called Toudamani (Trudamans or Trudamani) and Agouionda (*Oñkhiion'thǎ'* is an Onondaga form), the latter signifying 'those who attack us.' Although he may have recorded the native names as nearly phonetically as he was able, yet the former is not a distant approach to the well-known Tsonnontowanen of the early French writers, a name which Champlain printed *Chouontouaroüon* (probably written Chonontouaroñon), the name of the Seneca, which was sometimes extended to include the Cayuga and Onondaga as a geographical group. Lescarbot, failing to find in Canada in his time the tongues recorded by Cartier, concluded that "the change of language in Canada" was due "to a destruction of people," and in 1603 he declared (Nova Francia, 170, 1609): "For it is some 8 years since the Iroquois did assemble themselves to the number of 8,000 men, and discomfited all their enemies, whom they surprised in their enclosures;" and (p. 290) "by such surprises the Iroquois, being in number 8,000 men, have heretofore exterminated the Algoumequins, them of Hochelaga, and others bordering upon the great river." So it is probable that the southern foes of the tribes along the St Lawrence in Cartier's time were the Iroquois tribes anterior to the formation of their historical league, for he was also informed that these Agouionda "doe continually warre one against another"—a condition of affairs which ceased with the formation of the league. Between the time of the last voyage of Cartier to the St Lawrence, in 1543, and the arrival of Champlain on this river in 1603, nothing definite is known of these tribes and their wars. Champlain found the dwelling places of the tribes discovered by Cartier on the St Lawrence deserted and the region traversed only rarely by war parties from extralimital Algonquian tribes which dwelt on the borders of the former territory of the expelled Iroquoian tribes. Against the aforesaid Iroquoian tribes the Iroquois were still waging relentless warfare, which Champlain learned in 1622 had then lasted more than 50 years.

Such was the origin of the confederation of tribes strictly called Hurons by the French and Wendat (8endat) in their own tongue. But the name Hurons was applied in a general way to the Tionontati, or Tobacco tribe, under the form "Huron du Pétun," and also, although rarely, to the Attiwendaronk in the form "Huron de la Nation Neutre." After the destruction of the Huron or Wendat confederation and the more or less thorough dispersal of the several tribes composing it, the people who, as political units, were originally called Huron and Wendat, ceased to exist. The Tionontati, or Tobacco tribe, with the few Huron fugitives, received the name "Huron du Pétun" from the French, but they became known to the English as Wendat, corrupted to Yendat, Guyandotte, and finally to Wyandot. The Jesuit Relation for 1667 says: "The Tionnontateheronnons of to-day are the same people who heretofore were called the Hurons de la nation du pétun." These were the so-called Tobacco nation, and not the Wendat tribes of the Huron confederation. So the name Huron was employed only after these Laurentian tribes became settled in the region around L. Simcoe and Georgian bay. Champlain and his French contemporaries, after becoming acquainted with the Iroquois tribes of New York, called the Hurons *les bons Iroquois*, 'the good Iroquois,' to distinguish them from the hostile Iroquois tribes. The Algonquian allies of the French called the Hurons and the Iroquois tribes *Nadowek*, 'adders,' and *Iriⁿkhowek*, 'real serpents,' hence, 'bitter enemies.' The singular *Iriⁿkowi*, with the French suffix -*ois*, has become the familiar "Iroquois." The term *Nadowe* in various forms (e. g., Nottaway) was applied by the Algonquian tribes generally to all alien and hostile peoples. Champlain also called the Hurons *Ochateguin* and *Charioquois*, from the names of prominent chiefs. The Delawares called them *Talamatan*, while the peoples of the "Neutral Nation" and of the Huron tribes applied to each other the term *Attiwendaronk*, literally, 'their speech is awry,' but freely, 'they are stammerers,' referring facetiously to the dialectic difference between the tongues of the two peoples.

In 1615 Champlain found all the tribes which he later called Hurons, with the exception of the Wenrohronon and the Atontrataronon, dwelling in Huronia and waging war against the Iroquois tribes in New York. When Cartier explored the St Lawrence valley, in 1534–43,

Iroquoian tribes occupied the N. bank of the river indefinitely northward and from Saguenay r. eastward to Georgian bay, with no intrusive alien bands (despite the subsequent but doubtful claim of the Onontcharonon to a former possession of the island of Montreal), and also the s. watershed from the Bay of Gaspé w. to the contiguous territory of the Iroquois confederation on the line of the E. watershed of L. Champlain.

The known names of towns of these Laurentian Iroquois are Araste, Hagonchenda, Hochelaga, Hochelay, Satadin, Stadacona, Starnatan, Tailla, Teguenondahi, and Tutonaguy. But Cartier, in speaking of the people of Hochelaga, remarks: "Notwithstanding, the said Canadians are subject to them with eight or nine other peoples who are on the said river." All these towns and villages were abandoned previous to the arrival of Champlain on the St Lawrence in 1603. Of the towns of the Hurons, Sagard says: "There are about 20 or 25 towns and villages, of which some are not at all shut, nor closed [palisaded], and others are fortified with long pieces of timber in triple ranks, interlaced one with another to the height of a long pike [16 ft], and reenforced on the inside with broad, coarse strips of bark, 8 or 9 ft in height; below there are large trees, with their branches lopped off, laid lengthwise on very short trunks of trees, forked at one end, to keep them in place; then above these stakes and bulwarks there are galleries or platforms, called *ondaqua* ('box'), which are furnished with stones to be hurled against an enemy in time of war, and with water to extinguish any fire which might be kindled against them. Persons ascend to these by means of ladders quite poorly made and difficult, which are made of long pieces of timber wrought by many hatchet strokes to hold the foot firm in ascending." Champlain says that these palisades were 35 ft in height. In accord with the latter authority, Sagard says that these towns were in a measure permanent, and were removed to new sites only when they became too distant from fuel and when their fields, for lack of manuring, became worn out, which occurred every 10, 20, 30, or 40 years, more or less, according to the situation of the country, the richness of the soil, and the distance of the forest, in the middle of which they always built their towns and villages. Champlain says the Hurons planted large quantities of several kinds of corn, which grew finely, squashes, tobacco, many varieties of beans, and sunflowers, and that from the seeds of the last they extracted an oil with which they anointed their heads and employed for various other purposes.

The government of these tribes was vested by law in a definite number of executive officers, called "chiefs" (q. v.) in English, who were chosen by the suffrage of the child-bearing women and organized by law or council decree into councils for legislative and judicial purposes. There were five units in the social and political organization of these tribes, namely, the family, clan, phratry, tribe, and confederation, which severally expressed their will through councils coordinate with their several jurisdictions and which made necessary various grades of chiefs in civil affairs. In these communities the civil affairs of government were entirely differentiated from the military, the former being exercised by civil officers, the latter by military officers. It sometimes happened that the same person performed the one or the other kind of function, but to do so he must temporarily resign his civil authority should it be incumbent on him to engage in military affairs, and when this emergency was past he would resume his civil function or authority.

In almost every family one or more chiefship titles, known by particular names, were hereditary, and there might even be two or three different grades of chiefs therein. But the candidate for the incumbency of any one of these dignities was chosen only by the suffrage of the mothers among the women of his family. The selection of the candidate thus made was then submitted for confirmation to the clan council, then to the tribal council, and lastly to the great federal council composed of the accredited delegates from the various allied tribes.

The tribes composing the Hurons recognized and enforced, among others, the rights of ownership and inheritance of property and dignities, of liberty and security of person, in names, of marriage, in personal adornment, of hunting and fishing in specified territory, of precedence in migration and encampment and in the council room, and rights of religion and of the blood feud. They regarded theft, adultery, maiming, sorcery with evil intent, treason, and the murder of a kinsman or a co-tribesman as crimes which consisted solely in the violation of the rights of a kinsman by blood or adoption, for the alien had no rights which Indian justice and equity recognized, unless by treaty or solemn compact. If an assassination were committed or a solemnly sworn peace with another people violated by the caprice of an individual, it was not the rule to punish directly the guilty person, for this would have been to assume over him a jurisdiction which no one would think of claiming; on the contrary, presents designed to "cover the death" or to restore peace were offered to the aggrieved party by the offender and his kindred. The greatest punishment that could be inflicted on a guilty person by his kindred was to refuse to defend him, thus placing him outside the rights of the blood feud and allowing those whom he had offended the liberty to take vengeance on him, but at their own risk and peril.

The religion of these tribes consisted in the worship of all material objects, the elements and bodies of nature, and many creatures of a teeming fancy, which in their view directly or remotely affected or controlled their well-being. These objects of their faith and worship were regarded as man-beings or anthropic persons possessed of life, volition, and orenda (q. v.) or magic power of different kind and degree peculiar to each. In this religion ethics or morals as such received only a secondary, if any, consideration. The status and interrelations of the persons of their pantheon one to another were fixed and governed by rules and customs assumed to be similar to those of the social and the political organization of the people, and so there was, therefore, at least among the principal gods, a kinship system patterned after that of the people themselves. They expressed their public religious worship in elaborate ceremonies performed at stated annual festivals, lasting from a day to fifteen days, and governed by the change of seasons. Besides the stated gatherings there were many minor meetings, in all of which there were dancing and thanksgiving for the blessings of life. They believed in a life hereafter, which was but a reflex of the present life, but their ideas regarding it were not very definite. The bodies of the dead were wrapped in furs, neatly covered with flexible bark, and then placed on a platform resting on four pillars, which was then entirely covered with bark; or the body, after being prepared for burial, was placed in a grave and over it were laid small pieces of timber, covered with strong pieces of bark and then with earth. Over the grave a cabin was usually erected. At the great feast of the dead, which occurred at intervals of 8 or 10 years, the bodies of those who had died in the interim, from all the villages participating in the feast, were brought together and buried in a common grave with elaborate and solemn public ceremonies.

In 1615, when the Hurons were first visited by the French under Champlain, he estimated from the statements of the Indians themselves that they numbered 30,000, distributed in 18 towns and villages, of which 8 were palisaded; but in a subsequent edition of his work Cham-

plain reduces this estimate to 20,000. A little later Sagard estimated their population at 30,000, while Brebeuf gave their number as 35,000. But these figures are evidently only guesses and perhaps much above rather than below the actual population, which, in 1648, was probably not far from 20,000.

When the French established trading posts on the St Lawrence at Three Rivers and elsewhere, the Hurons and neighboring tribes made annual trips down Ottawa r. or down the Trent to these posts for the purpose of trading both with the Europeans and with the Montagnais of the lower St Lawrence who came up to meet them. The chief place of trade at this time was, according to Sagard (Histoire, I, 170, 1866), in the harbor of Cape Victory, in L. St Peter of St Lawrence r., about 50 miles below Montreal, just above the outlet of the lake, where, on Sagard's arrival, there were "already lodged a great number of savages of various nations for the trade of beavers with the French. The Indians who were not sectarians in religion invited the missionaries into their country. In 1615 the Récollect fathers accepted the invitation, and Father Le Caron spent the year 1615–16 in Huronia, and was again there in 1623–24. Father Poulain was among the Hurons in 1622, Father Viel from 1623 to 1625, and Father De la Roche Daillion in 1626–28. The labors of the Jesuits began with the advent of Father Brebeuf in Huronia in 1626, but their missions ended in 1650 with the destruction of the Huron commonwealth by the Iroquois. In all, 4 Récollect and 25 Jesuit fathers had labored in the Huron mission during its existence, which at its prime was the most important in the French dominions in North America. As the first historian of the mission, Fr. Sagard, though not a priest, deserves honorable mention.

From the Jesuit Relation for 1640 it is learned that the Hurons had had cruel wars with the Tionontati, but that at the date given they had recently made peace, renewed their former friendship, and entered into an alliance against their common enemies. Sagard is authority for the statement that the Hurons were in the habit of sending large war parties to ravage the country of the Iroquois. The well-known hostility and intermittent warfare between the Iroquois and the Huron tribes date from prehistoric times, so that the invasion and destruction of the Huron country and confederation in 1648–50 by the Iroquois were not a sudden, unprovoked attack, but the final blow in a struggle which was already in progress when the French under Cartier in 1535 first explored the St Lawrence. The acquirement of firearms by the Iroquois from the Dutch was an important factor in their subsequent successes. By 1643 they had obtained about 400 guns, while, on the other hand, as late as the final invasion of their country the Hurons had but very few guns, a lack that was the direct cause of their feeble resistance and the final conquest by the Iroquois confederation of half of the country E. of the Mississippi and N. of the Ohio. In July, 1648, having perfected their plans for the final struggle for supremacy with the Hurons, the Iroquois began open hostility by sacking two or three frontier towns and Teanaustayaé (St Joseph), the major portion of the invading warriors wintering in the Huron country unknown to the Hurons; and in March, 1649, these Iroquois warriors destroyed Taenhatentaron (St Ignace) and St Louis, and carried into captivity hundreds of Hurons. These disasters completely demoralized and disorganized the Huron tribes, for the greater portion of their people were killed or led into captivity among the several Iroquoian tribes, or perished from hunger and exposure in their precipitate flight in all directions, while of the remainder some escaped to the Neutral Nation, or "Hurons de la Nation Neutre," some to the Tobacco or Tionontati tribe, some to the Erie, and others to the French settlements near Quebec on the island of Orleans. The Tohontaenrat, forming the populous town of Scanonaenrat, and a portion of the Arendahronon of the town of St-Jean-Baptiste surrendered to the Seneca and were adopted by them with the privilege of occupying a village by themselves, which was named Gandougarae (St Michel). As soon as the Iroquois learned of the Huron colony on Orleans id., they at once sought to persuade these Hurons to migrate to their country. Of these the Bear people, together with the Bowl band and the Rock people, having in an evil day promised to remove thither, were finally, in 1656, compelled to choose between fighting and migrating to the Iroquois country. They chose the latter course, the Bear people going to the Mohawk and the Rock people to the Onondaga. The Cord people alone had the courage to remain with the French.

The adopted inhabitants of the new town of St Michel (Gandougarae) were mostly Christian Hurons who preserved their faith under adverse conditions, as did a large number of other Huron captives who were adopted into other Iroquois tribes. In 1653 Father Le Moine found more than 1,000 Christian Hurons among the Onondaga. The number of Hurons then among the Mohawk, Oneida, and Cayuga is not known.

Among the most unfortunate of the Huron fugitives were those who sought asylum among the Erie, where their presence excited the jealousy and perhaps the fear of their neighbors, the Iroquois, with whom the Erie did not fraternize. It is also claimed that the Huron fugitives strove to foment war between their protectors and the Iroquois, with the result that notwithstanding the reputed 4,000 warriors of the Erie and their skill in the use of the bow and arrow (permitting them dextrously to shoot 8 or 9 arrows while the enemy could fire an arquebus but once), the Erie and the unfortunate Huron fugitives were entirely defeated in 1653–56 and dispersed or carried away into captivity. But most pathetic and cruel was the fate of those unfortunate Hurons who, trusting in the long-standing neutrality of the Neutral Nation which the Iroquois had not theretofore violated, fled to that tribe, only to be held, with the other portion of the Huron people still remaining in their country, into harsh captivity (Jes. Rel. 1659–60).

A portion of the defeated Hurons escaped to the Tionontati or "Huron du Pétun," then dwelling directly westward from them. But in 1649, when the Iroquois had sacked one of the Tionontati palisaded towns, the remainder of the tribe, in company with the refugee Hurons, sought an asylum on the Island of St Joseph, the present Charity or Christian id., in Georgian bay. It is this group of refugees who became the Wyandots of later history. Finding that this place did not secure them from the Iroquois, the majority fled to Michilimakinac, Mich., near which place they found fertile lands, good hunting, and abundant fishing. But even here the Iroquois would not permit them to rest, so they retreated farther westward to Manitoulin id., called Ekaentoton by the Hurons. Thence they were driven to Ile Huronne (Potawatomi id., because formerly occupied by that tribe), at the entrance to Green bay, Wis., where the Ottawa and their allies from Saginaw bay and Thunder bay, Manitoulin, and Michilimakinac, sought shelter with them. From this point the fugitive Hurons, with some of the Ottawa and their allies, moved farther westward 7 or 8 leagues to the Potawatomi, while most of the Ottawa went into what is now Wisconsin and N. W. Michigan among the Winnebago and the Menominee. Here, in 1657, in the Potawatomi country, the Hurons, numbering about 500 persons, erected a stout palisade. The Potawatomi received the fugitives the more readily since they themselves spoke a language cognate with that of the Ottawa and also were animated by a bitter hatred of the Iroquois who had in former times driven them from their native country, the N. peninsula of Michigan. This first flight of the Potawatomi must have taken place anterior to the visit by Nicollet in 1634.

Having murdered a party of Iroquois scouts through a plot devised by their chief Anahotaha, and fearing the vengeance of the Iroquois, the Hurons remained here only a few months longer. Some migrated to their compatriots on Orleans id., near Quebec, and the others, in 1659–60, fled farther w. to the Illinois country, on the Mississippi, where they were well received. Anahotaha was killed in 1659 in a fight at the Long Sault of Ottawa r., above Montreal, in which a party of 17 French militia under Sieur Dolard, 6 Algonkin under Mitameg, and 40 Huron warriors under Anahotaha (the last being the flower of the Huron colony then remaining on Orleans id.) were surrounded by 700 Iroquois and all killed with the exception of 5 Frenchmen and 4 Hurons, who were captured. It was not long before the Hurons found new enemies in the Illinois country. The Sioux brooked no rivals, much less meddlesome, weak neighbors; and as the Hurons numbered fewer than 500, whose native spirit and energy had been shaken by their many misfortunes, they could not maintain their position against these new foes, and therefore withdrew to the source of Black r., Wis., where they were found in 1660. At last they decided to join the Ottawa, their companions in their first removals, who were then settled at Chequamigon bay, on the s. shore of L. Superior, and chose a site opposite the Ottawa village. In 1665 Father Allouez, the founder of the principal western missions, met them here and established the mission of La Pointe du Saint Esprit between the Huron and the Ottawa villages. He labored among them 3 years, but his success was not marked, for these Tionontati Hurons, never fully converted, had relapsed into paganism. The Ottawa and the Hurons fraternized the more readily here since the two peoples dwelt in contiguous areas s. of Georgian bay before the Iroquois invasion in 1648–49. Father Marquette succeeded Father Allouez in 1669 and founded the missions of the Sault Ste Marie and St François-Xavier de la Baie des Puants. The Sioux, however, sought every possible pretext to assail the settlements of the Hurons and the Ottawa, and their numbers and known cruelty caused them to be so feared that the latter tribes during Marquette's régime withdrew to the French settlements, since the treaty of peace between the French and the Iroquois in 1666 had delivered them from their chief enemies. The Ottawa, however, returned to Manitoulin id., where the mission of

St Simon was founded, while the Hurons, who had not forgotten the advantageous situation which Michilimakinac had previously afforded them, removed about 1670 to a point opposite the island, where they built a palisaded village and where Marquette established the mission of St Ignace. Later, some of the Hurons here settled moved to Sandusky, Ohio, others to Detroit, and still others to Sandwich, Ontario. The last probably became what was latterly known as the Anderdon band of Wyandots, but which is now entirely dissipated, with the possible exception of a very few persons.

In 1745 a considerable party of Hurons under the leadership of the war chief Orontony, or Nicholas, removed from Detroit r. to the marsh lands of Sandusky bay. Orontony was a wily savage whose enmity was greatly to be feared, and he commanded men who formed an alert, unscrupulous, and powerful body. The French having provoked the bitter hatred of Nicholas, which was fomented by English agents, he conspired to destroy the French, not only at Detroit but at the upper posts, and by Aug., 1747, the "Iroquois of the West," the Hurons, Ottawa, Abnaki, Potawatomi, "Ouabash," Sauteurs, Missisauga, Foxes, Sioux, Sauk, "Sarastau," Loups, Shawnee, and Miami, indeed all the tribes of the middle W., with the exception of those of the Illinois country, had entered into the conspiracy; but through the treachery of a Huron woman the plot was revealed to a Jesuit priest, who communicated the information to Longueuil, the French commandant at Detroit, who in turn notified all the other French posts, and although a desultory warfare broke out, resulting in a number of murders, there was no concerted action. Orontony, finding that he had been deserted by his allies, and seeing the activity and determination of the French not to suffer English encroachments on what they called French territory, finally, in Apr., 1748, destroyed his villages and palisade at Sandusky, and removed, with 119 warriors and their families, to White r., Ind. Not long after he withdrew to the Illinois country on Ohio r., near the Indiana line, where he died in the autumn of 1748. The inflexible and determined conduct of Longueuil toward most of the conspiring tribes brought the coalition to an end by May, 1748.

After this trouble the Hurons seem to have returned to Detroit and Sandusky, where they became known as Wyandots and gradually acquired a paramount influence in the Ohio valley and the lake region. They laid claim to the greater part of Ohio, and the settlement of the Shawnee and Delawares within that area was with their consent; they exercised the right to light the council fire at all intertribal councils, and although few in number they joined all the Indian movements in the Ohio valley and the lake region and supported the British against the Americans. After the peace of 1815 a large tract in Ohio and Michigan was confirmed to them, but they sold a large part of it in 1819, under treaty provisions, reserving a small portion near Upper Sandusky, Ohio, and a smaller area on Huron r., near Detroit, until 1842, when these tracts also were sold and the tribe removed to Wyandotte co., Kans. By the terms of the treaty of 1855 they were declared to be citizens, but by the treaty of 1867 their tribal organization was restored and they were placed on a small tract, still occupied by them, in the N. E. corner of Oklahoma.

That portion of the Hurons who withdrew in 1650 and later to the French colony, were accompanied by their missionaries. The mission of La Conception, which was founded by them, although often changed in name and situation, has survived to the present time. The Hurons who wintered in Quebec in 1649 did not return to their country after learning of its desolation by the Iroquois, but were placed on land belonging to the Jesuits at Beauport, and when the Huron fugitives came down to Quebec to seek protection, the others followed these in May, 1651, to Orleans id., settling on the lands of Madamoiselle de Grand Maison that had been bought for them. Here a mission house was erected near their stockaded bark lodges. In 1654 they numbered between 500 and 600 persons. But again the Iroquois followed them, seeking through every misrepresentation to draw the Hurons into their own country to take the place of those who had fallen in their various wars. By this means a large number of the Hurons, remnants of the Bear, Rock, and Bowl tribes, were persuaded in 1656 to migrate to the Iroquois country, a movement that met with such success that the Iroquois even ventured to show themselves under the guns of Quebec. In the same year they mortally wounded Father Garreau, near Montreal, and captured and put to death 71 Hurons on Orleans id. These misfortunes caused the Hurons to draw nearer to Quebec, wherein they were given asylum until peace was concluded between the French and the Iroquois in 1666. The Hurons then withdrew from the town about 5 m., where in the following year the mission of Notre Dame de Foye was founded. In 1693 the Hurons moved 5 m. farther away on account of the lack of wood and the need of

richer lands; here the missionaries arranged the lodges around a square and built in the middle of it a church, to which Father Chaumonot added a chapel, patterned after the Casa Sancta of Lorette in Italy, and now known as Old Lorette. Some years later the mission was transferred a short distance away, where a new village, Younger Lorette, or La Jeune Lorette, was built. About the remains of this mission still dwell the so-called Hurons of Lorette.

The old estimates of Huron population have been previously given. After the dispersal of the Huron tribes in 1649–50, the Hurons who fled w. never seem to have exceeded 500 persons in one body. Later estimates are 1,000, with 300 more at Lorette (1736), 500 (1748), 850 (1748), 1,250 (1765), 1,500 (1794–95), 1,000 (1812), 1,250 (1812). Only the first of these estimates is inclusive of the "Hurons of Lorette," Quebec, who were estimated at 300 in 1736, but at 455, officially, in 1904. In 1885 those in Indian Ter. (Oklahoma) numbered 251, and in 1905, 378, making a total of 832 in Canada and the United States.

Nothing definite was known of the clans of the Hurons until the appearance of Morgan's Ancient Society in 1877, Powell's Wyandot Government (1st Rep. B. A. E., 1881), and Connolley's The Wyandots (Archæol. Rep. Ontario, 92, 1899). From the last writer, who corrects the work of the former authorities, the following list of Huron clans is taken: Great Turtle, Little Water Turtle, Mud Turtle, Wolf, Bear, Beaver, Deer, Porcupine, Striped Turtle, Highland Turtle, Snake, and Hawk. These, according to Powell, were organized into four phratries or clan brotherhoods, but Connolley denies that four phratries ever existed. The evidence appears to indicate, however, that the four-phratry organization was merged into one of three, of which the Wolf clan constituted one and acted as executive and presiding officer.

The Huron villages were Andiata, Angoutenc, Anonatea, Arendaonatia, Arente, Arontaen, Brownstown, Cahiague, Carhagouha, Carmaron, Cranetown (2 villages), Ekhiondatsaan, Endarahy, Iaenhouton, Ihonatiria (St Joseph II), Jeune Lorette, Junqusindundeh(?), Junundat, Khioetoa, Karenhassa, Khinonascarant (3 small villages so called), Lorette, Onentisati, Ossossané, Ouenrio, Sandusky, Ste Agnes, Ste Anne, St Antoine, Ste Barbe, Ste Catherine, Ste Cècile, St Charles (2 villages), St Denys, St Etienne, St François Xavier, St Geneviève, St Joachim, St Louis, St Martin, Ste Marie (2 villages), Ste Térèse, Scanonaenrat, Taenhatentaron (St Ignace I, II), Teanaustayaé (St Joseph I), Teandewiata, Toanche, Touaguainchain (Ste Madeleine), and Tondakhra.

For sources of information consult Bressany, Relation-Abregée (1653), 1852; Connolley in Archæol. Rep. Ontario 1899, 1900; Jesuit Relations, I-III, 1858, and also the Thwaites edition, I-LXXIII, 1896–1901; Journal of Capt. William Trent (1752), 1871; Morgan, Ancient Society, 1878; N. Y. Doc. Col. Hist., I-XV, 1853–87; Perrot, Mémoire, Tailhan ed., 1864; Powell in 1st Rep. B. A. E., 1881. (J. N. B. H.)

Ahouandate.—Schoolcraft, Ind. Tribes, III, 522, 1853. Ahwāndate. — Featherstonhaugh, Canoe Voy., I, 108, 1847. Atti8endaronk.—Jes. Rel. 1641, 72, 1858. Bons Irocois.—Champlain (1603), Œuvres, II, 47, 1870. Charioquois.—Ibid. (1611), III, 244 (probably from the name of a chief). Delamattanoes.—Post (1758) in Proud, Pa., II, app., 120, 1798 (Delaware name). Delamattenoos.—Loskiel, Hist. United Breth., pt. 3, 16, 103, 1794. Delemattanoes.—Post (1758) quoted by Rupp, West. Pa., app., 118, 1846. Dellamattanoes.—Barton, New Views, app., 8, 1798. Ekeenteeronnon.—Potier, Rac. Huron et Gram., MS., 1761 (Huron name of Hurons of Lorette). Euyrons.—Van der Donck (1656) in N. Y. Hist. Soc. Coll., 2d s., I, 209, 1841. Garennajenhaga.—Bruyas, Radices, 69, 1863. Guyandot.—Parkman, Pioneers, xxiv, 1883. Gyandottes.—Gallatin in Trans. Am. Ethnol. Soc., II, 103, 1848. Hah8endagerha.—Bruyas, Radices, 55, 1863. Harones.—Rasle (1724) in Mass. Hist. Soc. Coll., 2d s., II, 246, 1814. Hatindia8ointen.—Potier, Rac. Huron et Gram., MS., 1761 (Huron name of Hurons of Lorette). Hiroons.—Gorges (1658) in Maine Hist. Soc. Coll., II, 67, 1847. Houandates.—Sagard (1632), Canada (Dict.), IV, 1866. Hounondate.—Coxe, Carolana, 44, 1741. Hourons.—Tonti (1682) in French, Hist. Coll. La., 169, 1846. Huron.—Jesuit Relation 1632, 14, 1858. Hurones.—Vaillant (1688) in N. Y. Doc. Col. Hist., III, 524, 1853. Huronnes. — Hildreth, Pioneer Hist., 9, 1848. Hurrons.—Writer of 1761 in Mass. Hist. Soc. Coll., 4th s., IX, 427, 1871. Lamatan.—Rafinesque, Am. Nations, I, 139, 1836 (Delaware name). Little Mingoes.—Pownall, map of N. Am., 1776. Menchón.—Duro, Don Diego de Peñalosa, 43, 1882. Nadowa.—For forms of this name applied to the Hurons see Nadowa. Ochasteguin.—Champlain (1609), Œuvres, III, 176, 1870 (from name of chief). Ochatagin.—Ibid., 219. Ochataiguin.—Ibid., 174. Ochategin.—Ibid. (1632), v, pt. 1, 177. Ochateguin.—Ibid. (1609), III, 175. Ochatequins.—Ibid., 198. Ouaouackecinatouek.—Potier quoted by Parkman, Pioneers, xxiv, 1883. Ouendat.—Jes. Rel. 1640, 35, 1858. 8endat.—Jes. Rel. 1639, 50, 1858. Owandats.—Weiser (1748) quoted by Rupp, West. Pa., app., 16, 1846. Owendaets.—Peters (1750) in N. Y. Doc. Col. Hist., VI, 596, 1855. Owendats.—Croghan (1750) quoted by Rupp, West. Pa., app., 26, 1846. Owendot.—Hamilton (1760) in Mass. Hist. Soc. Coll., 4th s., IX, 279, 1871. Pemedeniek.—Vetromile in Hist. Mag., 1st s., IV, 369, 1860 (Abnaki name). Quatoges.—Albany conf. (1726) in N. Y. Doc. Col. Hist., V, 791, 1855. Quatoghees.—Ibid., VI, 391, note, 1855. Quatoghies.—Garangula (1684) in Williams, Vermont, I, 504, 1809. Quatoghies of Loretto.—Colden, Five Nations, I, 197, 1755. Sastaghretsy.—Post (1758) in Proud, Pa., II, app., 113, 1798. Sastharhetsi.—La Potherie, Hist. Am. Sept., III, 223, 1753 (Iroquois name). Talamatan.—Walam Olum (1833) in Brinton, Lenape Leg., 200, 1885. Talamatun.—Squier in Beach, Ind. Miscel., 28, 1877. ꞁelamaꝛenoⁿ.—Hewitt after Journeycake, a Delaware ("Coming out of a mountain or cave": Delaware name). Telematinos.—Document of 1759 in Brinton, Lenape Leg., 231, 1885. ꞁhăsꝛchetcï'.—Hewitt, Onondaga MS., B. A. E., 1888 (Onondaga name). Viandots.—Maximilian, Travels, 382, 184. Wanats.—Barton, New Views, xlii, 1798. Wandats.—Weiser (1748) quoted by Rupp, West. Pa., app., 15, 1846. Wandots.—Ibid., 18. Wantats.—Weiser in Schoolcraft, Ind. Tribes, IV, 605, 1854. Wayandotts.—

Hamilton (1749) in N. Y. Doc. Col. Hist., VI, 531, 1855. Wayondots.—Croghan (1759) in Proud, Pa., II, 296, 1798. Wayondotts.—Croghan, Jour., 37, 1831. Wayundatts.—Doc. of 1749 in N. Y. Doc. Col. Hist., VI, 533, 1855. Wayundotts.—Ibid. Weandots.—Buchanan, N. Am. Inds., 156, 1824. Wendats.—Shea, Miss. Val., preface, 59, 1852. Weyandotts.—Croghan (1760) in Mass. Hist. Soc. Coll., 4th s., IX, 262, 1871. Weyondotts.—Ibid., 249. Wiandotts.—Ft Johnson conf. (1756) in N. Y. Doc. Col. Hist., VII, 236, 1856. Wiondots.—Edwards (1788) in Mass. Hist. Soc. Coll., 1st s., IX, 95, 1804. Wiyandotts.—Morse, Modern Geog., I, 196, 1814. Wyandote.—Morgan in N. Am. Rev., 52, Jan. 1870. Wyandotte.—Garrard, Wahtoyah, 2, 1850. Wyandotts.—Croghan (1754) quoted by Rupp, West. Pa., app., 51, 1846. Wyondats.—Croghan (1765) in N. Y. Doc. Col. Hist., VII, 782, 1856. Wyondotts.—Croghan, Jour., 34, 1831. Yendat.—Parkman, Pioneers, xxiv, 1883. Yendots.—Schoolcraft in N. Y. Hist. Soc. Proc., 86, 1844.

Hurriparacussi. A village near which De Soto landed from Tampa bay, Fla., in 1539. According to Gatschet the name is properly the title of the principal chief, from two Timucua words signifying 'war chief.'

Hurripacuxi.—Biedma in Smith, Colec. Doc. Fla., 48, 1857. Paracossi.—Gentl. of Elvas (1557) in French, Hist. Coll. La., II, 128, 1850. Parocossi.—Gentl. of Elvas in Hakluyt Soc. Pub., IX, 32, 1851. Urriba cuxi.—French, op. cit., 98, note. Urribaracuxi.—Garcilasso de la Vega cited in Hakluyt Soc. Pub., op. cit, 32. Vrribarracuxi.—Garcilasso de la Vega, Florida, 37, 1723.

Hurst tablet. See Notched plates.

Husada ('legs stretched out stiff'.). A subgens of the Khuya gens of the Kansa.

Hüsada.—Dorsey in 15th Rep. B. A. E., 231, 1897. Qüyunikaciⁿga.—Ibid. ('White-eagle people').

Husadta (Hüsaꝗa, 'limbs stretched stiff'). A subgens of the Hangkaahutun gens of the Osage, one of the original fireplaces of the Hangka division.—Dorsey in 15th Rep. B. A. E., 234, 1897.

Husadtawanu (Hü'saꝗa Wanü^{n'}, 'elder Husadta'). A subgens of the Hangkaahutun gens of the Osage, one of the original fireplaces of the Hangka division.—Dorsey in 15th Rep. B. A. E., 234, 1897.

Husam. A former winter village of the Hahamatses at the mouth of Salmon r., Brit. Col.; now the seat of a salmon fishery.

H'usam.—Boas in Bull. Am. Geog. Soc., 230, 1887. Koo-sām.—Dawson in Trans. Roy. Soc. Can. for 1887, sec. II, 65.

Hushkoni ('skunk'). A Chickasaw clan of the Ishpanee phratry.

Hushkoni.—Morgan, Anc. Soc., 163, 1877. Huskóni.—Gatschet, Creek Migr. Leg., I, 96, 1884.

Hushkovi. A traditional village about 2 m. N. W. of Oraibi, N. E. Ariz. According to Hopi story Hushkovi and Pivanhonkapi were destroyed by a fire that had been kindled in the San Francisco mts., 90 m. away, at the instance of the chief of Pivanhonkapi and with the aid of the Yayaponchatu people who are said to have been in league with supernatural forces, because the inhabitants of Pivanhonkapi had become degenerates through gambling. Most of the inhabitants were also destroyed; the survivors moved away, occupying several temporary villages during their wanderings, the ruins of which are still to be seen.　See Voth, Traditions of the Hopi, 241, 1905.

Hŭ′ckovi.—Voth, op. cit.

Husistaic. A former Chumashan village near Purísima mission, Santa Barbara co., Cal.—Taylor in Cal. Farmer, Oct. 18, 1861.

Huskanaw. An Algonquian word applied to certain initiation ceremonies of the Virginia Indians, performed on boys at puberty, which were accompanied by fasting and the use of narcotics. The whites applied the term *to huskanaw* (Beverley, Hist. Va., III, 32, 39, 1705) in a figurative sense. Thus Jefferson (Corresp., II, 342) wrote: "He has the air of being *huskanoyed*, i. e., out of his element." The term is derived from the language of the Powhatan. Gerard (Am. Anthrop., VII, 242, 1905) etymologizes the word as follows: "Powhatan *uskinaweu*, 'he has a new body', from *uski* 'new', *naw* 'body', *eu* 'has he', said of a youth who had reached the age of puberty". But the word is rather from the Powhatan equivalent of the Massachuset *wuskenœ*, 'he is young', and does not necessarily contain the root *iaw* (not *naw*) 'body'. It has no connection with the English word "husky," as some have supposed. For an account of the "solemnity of *huskanawing*" see Beverley, op. cit., and cf. Heckewelder (1817), Indian Nations, 245, 1876. See *Child life, Ordeals.*　　　(A. F. C.)

Husky. According to Julian Ralph (Sun, N. Y., July 14, 1895), "the common and only name of the wolf-like dogs of both the white and red men of our northern frontier and of western Canada." *Husky* was originally one of the names by which the English settlers in Labrador have long known the Eskimo (q. v.). The word, which seems to be a corruption of one of the names of this people, identical with our 'Eskimo' in the northern Algonquian dialects, has been transferred from man to the dog.　　　(A. F. C.)

Husoron. A former division or pueblo of the Varohio, probably in the Chinipas valley, in w. Chihuahua, Mexico.—Orozco y Berra, Geog., 58, 1864.

Huspah. A Yamasi band living in South Carolina under a chief of the same name about the year 1700.　　(A. S. G.)

Hussliakatna. A Koyukukhotana village, of 14 people in 1885, on the right bank of Koyukuk r., Alaska, 2 m. above the s. end of Dall id.

Hussleakátna.—Allen, Rep. on Alaska, 122, 1887. **Hussliakatna.**—Ibid., 141.

Hutalgalgi (*hútali* 'wind', *algi* 'people'). A principal Creek clan.

Ho-tor′-lee.—Morgan, Anc. Soc., 161, 1877. **Hotulgee.**—Pickett, Hist. Ala., I, 96, 1851. **Hútalgalgi.**—Gatschet, Creek Migr. Leg., I, 155, 1884. **Wind Family.**—Woodward, Reminiscences, 19, 20, 1859.

Hutatchl (Hut-tát-ch'l). A former Lummi village at the s. e. end of Orcas id.,

of the San Juan group, Wash.—Gibbs, Clallam and Lummi, 38, 1863.

Huthutkawedl (*X·ú′tx·útkawêɪ*, 'holes by or near the trail'). A village of the Nicola band of the Ntlakyapamuk, near Nicola r., 23 m. above Spences Bridge, Brit. Col.

N'hothotkō′as.—Hill-Tout in Rep. Ethnol. Surv. Can., 4, 1899. **X·û′tx·útkawêɪ.**—Teit in Mem. Am. Mus. Nat. Hist., II, 174, 1900.

Hutsawap. One of the divisions or subtribes of the Choptank, formerly in Dorchester co., Md.—Bozman, Maryland, I, 115, 1837.

Hutsnuwu ('grizzly bear fort'). A Tlingit tribe on the w. and s. coasts of Admiralty id., Alaska; pop. estimated at 300 in 1840, and given as 666 in 1880 and 420 in 1890. Their former towns were Angun and Nahltushkan, but they now live at Killisnoo. Their social divisions are Ankakehittan, Daktlawedi, Deshuhittan, Tekoedi, and Wushketan.　　(J. R. S.)

Chūts-ta-kŏn.—Krause, Tlinkit Ind., 118, 1885. **Chútznou.**—Holmberg, Ethnog. Skizz., map facing 142, 1855. **Contznoos.**—Borrows in H. R. Ex. Doc. 197, 42d Cong., 2d sess., 4, 1872. **Hoidxnous.**—Scott in Ind. Aff. Rep., 313, 1868. **Hoochenoos.**—Ball in Sen. Ex. Doc. 105, 46th Cong., 1st sess., 30, 1880. **Hoochinoo.**—Wright, Among the Alaskans, 151, 1883. **Hoodchenoo.**—George in Sen. Ex. Doc. 105, 46th Cong., 1st sess., 29, 1880. **Hoodsinoo.**—Colyer, ibid., 1869, 575, 1870. **Hoodsna.**—Hallock in Rep. Sec. War, pt. I, 39, 1868. **Hoods-Nahoos.**—Scott in Ind. Aff. Rep., 309, 1868. **Hookchenoo.**—Ball in Sen. Ex. Doc. 105, 46th Cong., 1st sess., 30, 1880. **Hoonchenoo.**—George, ibid., 29. **Hootsinoo.**—Kane, Wand. N. A., app., 1859. **Hootz-ahtar-qwan.**—Emmons in Mem. Am. Mus. Nat. Hist., III, 232, 1903. **Khootznahoo.**—Petroff in Tenth Census, Alaska, 32, 1884. **Khutsno.**—Tikhmenief, Russ. Am. Co., II, 341, 1863. **Khutsnu.**—Ibid. **Koo-tche-noos.**—Beardslee in Sen. Ex. Doc. 105, 46th Cong., 1st sess., 29, 1880. **Kootsenoos.**—Mahoney in Ind. Aff. Rep. 1869, 576, 1870. **Kootsnovskie.**—Elliott, Cond. Aff. Alaska, 227, 1875 (transliterated from Veniaminoff). **Kootznahoo.**—Niblack, Coast Indians of S. Alaska, chart I, 1890. **Kootznoos.**—Seward, Speeches on Alaska, 5, 1869. **Kootznov.**—Colyer in Ind. Aff. Rep., 587, 1870. **Koushnous.**—Halleck in Rep. Sec. War, I, 38, 1868. **Koutzenoos.**—Beardslee in Sen. Ex. Doc. 105, 46th Cong., 1st sess., 31, 1880. **Koutznous.**—Halleck in Rep. Sec. War, pt. I, 38, 1868. **Kutsnovskoe.**—Veniaminoff, Zapiski, II, pt. 3, 30, 1840. **X̱û′adji-nao.**—Swanton, field notes, 1900-01 (according to the Haida). **X̱ûts!nuwū′.**—Ibid., 1904, B. A. E. (own name).

Hutucgna. A former Gabrieleño rancheria in Los Angeles co., Cal., at a place later called Santa Ana (Yorbas).

Hutucgna.—Taylor in Cal. Farmer, June 8, 1860. **Hutuk.**—Kroeber, inf'n, 1905 (Luiseño name).

Huvaguere. A Nevome division, described as adjoining the Hio, who were settled 8 leagues E. of Tepahue, in Sonora, Mexico (Orozco y Berra, Geog., 58, 1864). The name doubtless properly belongs to their village.

Huwaka. The Sky clan of Acoma pueblo, N. Mex., which, with the Osach (Sun) clan, forms a phratry.

Huwáka-hanoqᶜʰ.—Hodge in Am. Anthrop., IX, 352, 1896 (*hanoqch*='people').

Huwanikikarachada ('those who call themselves after the elk'). A Winnebago gens.

Elk.—Morgan, Anc. Soc., 157, 1877.　**Hoo-wun′-nä.**—

Ibid. **Hu-waⁿ-i-ki′-ka-ra′-tca-da.**—Dorsey in 15th Rep. B. A. E., 240, 1897.

Huwi. The Dove clan of the Chua (Rattlesnake) phratry of the Hopi.
Hé-wi.—Stephen in 8th Rep. B.A.E.,38,1891. **Hüwi wiñwû.**—Fewkes in 19th Rep. B. A. E., 582, 1901 (*wiñwû*=‘clan’). **Hü′-wi wuñ-wü.**—Fewkes in Am. Anthrop., VII, 402, 1894.

Hwades (*X̱udē′s*, ‘cut beach’). The principal village of the Koskimo and Koprino at Quatsino narrows, Vancouver id.
Hwat-ēs′.—Dawson in Trans. Roy. Soc. Can. for 1887, sec. II, 65, 1888. **Hwot-es.**—Dawson in Can. Geol. Surv., map, 1887. **X̱udē′s.**—Boas, inf'n, 1906.

Hwahwatl (*Qwā′qwatl*). A Salish tribe on Englishman r., Vancouver id., speaking the Puntlatsh dialect.—Boas, MS. B. A. E., 1887.

Hwotat. A Hwotsotenne village on the E. side of Babine lake, near its outlet, in British Columbia.
Hwo′-tat.—Morice in Trans. Roy. Soc. Can., X, 109, 1893. **Whalatt.**—Downie in Mayne, Brit. Col., 453, 1861 (misprint). **Whatatt.**—Downie in Jour. Roy. Geog. Soc., XXXI, 253, 1861. **Wut-at.**—Dawson in Geol. Surv. Can., 26B, 1881.

Hwotsotenne (‘people of Spider river’). A Takulli tribe, belonging to the Babine branch, living on Bulkley r. and hunting as far as François lake, Brit. Col. They are somewhat mixed with their immediate neighbors, the Kitksan (Morice in Trans. Can. Inst., 27, 1893). Their villages are Hagwilget, Hwotat, Keyerhwotket, Lachalsap, Tsechah, and Tselkazkwo.
Akwilgét.—Morice, Notes on W. Dénés, 27, 1893 (‘well dressed’: Kitksan name). **Hwotso′tenne.**—Morice in Trans. Roy. Soc. Can., map, 1892. **Outsotin.**—British Columbia map, 1872.

Hykehah. A former Chickasaw town, one of a settlement of five, probably in or near Pontotoc co., Miss.
Hikihaw.—Romans, Florida, 63, 1775. **Hikkihaw.**—W. Florida map, ca. 1775. **Hykehah.**—Adair, Am. Ind., 352, 1775.

Hykwa. See *Hiakwa*.

Hyperboreans (Greek). Applied by Bancroft (Nat. Races, I, 37, 1882) to the tribes of extreme N. w. America, N. of lat. 55°, including western and southern Eskimo, Aleut, Tlingit, and Athapascan tribes; by others the name is employed to designate all the circumpolar tribes of both the Old and the New World.

Hyukkeni. A former Choctaw settlement, noted by Romans in 1775, but not located on his map unless it be an unnumbered town on the E. side of Buckatunna cr., N. E. of Yowani, in the present Mississippi.—Halbert in Miss. Hist. Soc. Pub., VI, 432, 1902.

Iahenhouton (‘at the caves.’—Hewitt). A Huron village in Ontario in 1637.—Jes. Rel. for 1637, 159, 1858.

Ialamma. A former Chumashan village subordinate to Purísima mission, Santa Barbara co., Cal.—Taylor in Cal. Farmer, Oct. 18, 1861.

Ialamne. A former Chumashan village subordinate to Santa Inés mission, Santa Barbara co., Cal. (Taylor in Cal. Farmer,

Oct. 18, 1861). Possibly the same as Ialamma.

Ialmuk (*Ia′lmuq*). A Squawmish village community at Jericho, Burrard inlet, Brit. Col.—Hill-Tout in Rep. B. A. A. S., 475, 1900.

Ialostimot (*Ialo′stimōt*, ‘making good fire’). A Talio division among the Bellacoola of British Columbia; named from a reputed ancestor.
Ialo′stimōt.—Boas in 7th Rep. N. W. Tribes Canada, 3, 1891. **T′ā′t′Entsāit.**—Ibid. (‘a cave protecting from rain’: secret society name).

Iana (*Ia′na*). The Corn clan of the pueblo of Taos, N. Mex.
Iána-tañina.—Hodge, field notes, B. A. E., 1895 (*tañina* = ‘people’).

Ibache (‘holds the firebrand to sacred pipes’). A Kansa gens. Its subgentes are Khuyeguzhinga and Mikaunikashinga.
Hañga jiñga.—Dorsey in 15th Rep. B. A. E., 231, 1897 (‘small Hanga’). **Ibato′ĕ.**—Ibid.

Ibin. A former Aleut village on Agattu id., Alaska, one of the Near id. group of the Aleutians, now uninhabited.

Ibitoupa. A small tribe of unknown affinity, but the theory that they were connected with the Chickasaw has more arguments in its favor than any other. In 1699 they formed one of the villages mentioned by Iberville (Margry, Déc., IV, 180, 1880) as situated on Yazoo r., Ibitoupa being near the upper end of the group between the Chaquesauma (Chakchiuma) and the Thysia (Tioux), according to the order named, which appears to be substantially correct, although Coxe (Carolana, 10, 1741) who omits Thysia, makes the Ibitoupa settlement expressly the uppermost of the series. The Ibitoupa and Chakchiuma, together with the Tapoucha (Taposa), were united in one village on the upper Yazoo by 1798. What eventually became of them is not known, but it is probable that they were absorbed by the Chickasaw. See *Itomapa*.
(A. S. G.)

Bitoupas.—Pénicaut (1700) in French, Hist. Coll. La., n. s., I, 61, 1869. **Epitoupa.**—Coxe, Carolana, 10, map, 1741. **Ouitoupas.**—Penicaut (1700) in Margry, Déc., V, 401, 1883. **Outapa.**—Iberville (1699), ibid., IV, 180, 1880. **Outaypes.**—Martin, Hist. La., I, 249, 1827. **Witoupo.**—Alcedo, Dic. Geog., V, 343, 1789 (misprint). **Witowpa.**—Esnauts et Rapilly, map, 1777. **Witowpo.**—Philippeaux, map of English Col., 1781. **Ybitoopas.**—Romans, Fla., I, 101, 1775. **Ybitoupas.**—Baudry des Lozières, Voy. à la Louisiane, 245, 1802.

Icayme. Given as the native name of the site on which San Luis Rey mission, s. California, was founded; perhaps also the name of a neighboring Diegueño village.—Taylor in Cal. Farmer, Feb. 22, 1860.

Ichenta. A village of the Chalone division of the Costanoan family, formerly near Soledad mission, Cal.
Ichenta.—Taylor in Cal. Farmer, Apr. 20, 1860. **San José.**—Ibid.

Ichuarumpats (*I'-chu-ar'-rum-pats*, 'people of cactus plains'). A Paiute tribe formerly in or near Moapa valley, s. E. Nev., numbering 35 in 1873.—Powell in Ind. Aff. Rep. 1873, 50, 1874.

Icosans. Mentioned by Bartram (Trav., 54, 1792) in connection with the Ogeeche, Santee, Utina, Wapoo, Yamasi, etc., as having been attacked by the Creeks, and "who then surrounded and cramped the English possessions." The reference is to the early colonial period of South Carolina and Georgia.

Idakariuke. Mentioned as a Shasta band of Shasta valley, N. Cal., in 1851, but it is really only a man's personal name. (R. B. D.)
Ida-kara-wak-a-ha.—McKee (1851) in Sen. Ex. Doc. 4, 32d Cong., spec. sess., 221, 1853 (seemingly identical). Ida-ka-riúke.—Gibbs (1851) in Schoolcraft, Ind. Tribes, III, 171, 1853. I-do-ka-rai-uke.—McKee, ibid., 171.

Idelabuú ('mesas of the mountains'). A rancheria, probably Cochimi, connected with Purísima (Cadegomo) mission, Lower California, in the 18th century.—Doc. Hist. Mex., 4th s., v, 189, 1857.

Idelibinagá ('high mountains'). A rancheria, probably Cochimi, connected with Purísima mission, Lower California, in the 18th century.—Doc. Hist. Mex., 4th s., v, 189, 1857.

Idiuteling. An Eskimo settlement on the N. shore of Home bay, Baffin land, where the Akudnirmiut Eskimo gather to hunt bear in the spring.
Ipiutelling.—Boas in 6th Rep. B. A. E., 441, 1888 (misprint). Ipnitelling.—Ibid., map (misprint).

Idjorituaktuin ('with grass'). A village of the Talirpingmiut division of the Okomiut Eskimo on the w. shore of Cumberland sd.; pop. 11 in 1883.
Ejujuajuin.—Kumlien in Bull. Nat. Mus., no. 15, 15, 1879. Idjorituaktuin.—Boas in Deutsche Geog. Blätt., VIII, 33, 1885. Idjorituaqtuin.—Boas in 6th Rep. B. A. E., 426, 1888. Idjorituaχtuin.—Boas in Petermanns Mitt., no. 80, 70, 1885.

Idjuniving. A spring settlement of Padlimiut Eskimo near the s. end of Home bay, Baffin land —Boas in 6th Rep. B. A. E., map, 1888.

Iebathu. The White-corn clan of the Tigua pueblo of Isleta, N. Mex.
Íebathú-t'aínin.—Lummis quoted by Hodge in Am. Anthrop., IX, 349, 1896 (*t'aínin*='people').

Iechur. The Yellow-corn clan of the Tigua pueblo of Isleta, N. Mex.
Íechúr-t'aínin.—Lummis quoted by Hodge in Am. Anthrop., IX, 349, 1896 (*t'aínin*='people').

Iefeu. The Red-corn clan of the Tigua pueblo of Isleta, N. Mex.
Íefë'u-t'aínin.—Lummis quoted by Hodge in Am. Anthrop., IX, 349, 1896 (*t'aínin*='people').

Iekidhe (*Iekiǵě*, 'criers'). A gens of the Inkesabe division of the Omaha.—Dorsey in 15th Rep. B. A. E., 227, 1897.

Ieshur. The Blue-corn clan of the Tigua pueblo of Isleta, N. Mex.
Íeshur-t'aínin.—Lummis quoted by Hodge in Am. Anthrop., IX, 349, 1896 (*t'aínin*='people').

Ieskachincha ('child of one who speaks Dakota'). The ordinary name for the mixed-blood element among the western Sioux. Given by J. O. Dorsey as a Brulé gens composed of half-breeds.
Ieskaċiŋċa.—Dorsey (after Cleveland) in 15th Rep. B. A. E., 219, 1897. Ieska-tciⁿtca.—Ibid.

Ieskachincha. A modern Oglala Dakota band, composed of half-breeds.
Ieska ċiŋċa.—Cleveland, letter to Dorsey, 1884. Ieska-tciⁿtca.—Dorsey (after Cleveland) in 15th Rep. B. A. E., 221, 1897.

Ietan. A term which, with "Tetau" and other forms of the name, was applied by writers of the early part of the 19th century to several western tribes. Mooney (17th Rep. B. A. E., 167, 1898) explains its application as follows: "The Ute of the mountain region at the headwaters of the Platte and the Arkansas, being a powerful and aggressive tribe, were well known to all the Indians of the plains, who usually called them by some form of their proper name, *Yútawáts*, or, in its root form, *Yúta*, whence we get Eutaw, Utah, and Ute. Among the Kiowa the name becomes *Iátä*(*-go*), while the Siouan tribes seem to have nasalized it so that the early French traders wrote it as Ayutan, Iatan, or Ietan. By prefixing the French article it became L'Iatan, and afterward Aliatan, while by misreading of the manuscript word we get Jatan, Jetan, and finally Tetau. Moreover, as the early traders and explorers knew but little of the mountain tribes, they frequently confounded those of the same generic stock, so that almost any of these forms may mean Shoshoni, Ute, or Comanche, according to the general context of the description." By reason of the varied applications of Ietan and its equivalents, the name is here treated separately.
Aliatâ.—Lewis and Clark, Discov., 60, 1806 (so called by the French). Aliatan.—Drake, Bk. Inds., vi, 1848. Aliatans, of La Playes.—Lewis, Travels, 181, 1809. Aliatans, of the West.—Lewis and Clark, Discov., 63, 1806. Aliatons.—Lewis and Clark, Jour., 139, 1840. Aliatons of the West.—Brown, West. Gaz., 213, 1817. Alitan.—Lewis and Clark, Discov., 23, 1806. Aliton.—Am. State Papers, Ind. Aff., I, 710, 1832. Alliatan.—Lewis and Clark, Exped., II, 131, 1814. Alliatans of the west.—Brown, West. Gaz., 215, 1817. Ayutan.—Brackenridge, Views of Louisiana, 80, 1814 (also called 'Camanches'). Halisanes.—Du Lac, Voy. Louisianes, 261, 1805. Halitanes.—Ibid., 309. Hietanes.—Orozco y Berra, Geog., 40, 1864. Hietans.—Pénicaut (1720) in French, Hist. Coll. La., I, 156, 1869. I-â'-kâr.—Lewis and Clark, Discov., 60, 1806. Iatan.—Gregg, Comm. Prairies, I, 21, 1844. I-a-tans.—Bonner, Life of Beckwourth, 34, 1856. Iotans.—Boudinot, Star in West, 126, 1816 (misprint). Ielan.—Morse, Rep. to Sec. War, 1822 (misprint). Ietam.—Cass in H. R. Ex. Doc. 117, 20th Cong., 2d sess., 102, 1829. Ietan.—Pike, Travels, xiv, 1811. Ietanes.—Orozco y Berra, Geog., 40, 1864. Ietans.—Pike, Exped., 3d map, 1810. Iotan.—Pattie, Pers. Narr., 36, 1833. Itean.—M'Kenney, Memoirs, II, 94, 1846 (misprint). Jetam.—Cass quoted by Schoolcraft, Ind. Tribes, III, 609, 1853 (misprint). Jetans.—Pénicaut (1720) in French, Hist. Coll. La., I, 156, note, 1869 (misprint). Jetans.—Mayer, Mexico, II, 39, 1853 (misprint). Jotans.—Pattie, Pers. Narr., 37, 1833 (misprint). Laitanes.—Mallet (1740) in Margry, Déc., VI, 457, 1886 (French form). La Kar.—Fisher, New Trav., 175, 1812. La Litanes.—Ibid.

Lee-ha-taus.—Hunter, Captivity, 68, 1823. **Liahtan Band.**—Morse, Rep. to Sec. War, map, 1822. **L'Iatan.**—Mooney in 14th Rep. B. A. E., 1043, 1896 (French form of *Iatan* above). **Tetaus.**—Pike, Exped., 109, 1810 (misprint). **Yetans.**—Keane in Stanford, Compend., 545, 1878 (misprint).

Iewatse (*I-e-wat-se'*, 'mouth men'). The Crow name for some unidentified tribe.—Hayden, Ethnog. and Philol. Mo. Val., 402, 1862.

Ift. A Karok village on Klamath r., Cal., inhabited in 1860.
If-terram.—Taylor in Cal. Farmer, Mar. 23, 1860.

Igagik. An Aglemiut Eskimo settlement at the mouth of Ugaguk r., Alaska; pop. 120 in 1880, 60 in 1890, 203 in 1900.
Igagik.—Petroff, 10th Census, Alaska, 17, 1884. **Ugaguk.**—Baker, Geog. Dict. Alaska, 1902.

Igak. A former Kaniagmiut Eskimo village on Afognak id., Alaska, E. of Afognak, whither it seems to have been moved.
Igagmjut.—Holmberg, Ethnog. Skizz., map, 1855. **Kaljukischwigmjut.**—Ibid.

Igamansabe (*Igamaⁿsábĕ*, 'black paint,' Kansa name for Big Blue r., Kans.). One of the villages occupied by the Kansa, probably before 1820.—Dorsey, MS. Kansas vocab., B. A. E., 1882.

Igdlorpait. A Danish post and Eskimo village in s. w. Greenland, lat. 60° 28'.
Igdlopait.—Koldewey, German Arct. Exped., 182, 1870. **Igdlorpait.**—Meddelelser om Grönland, XVI, map, 1896.

Igdluluarsuk. A village of the southern group of East Greenland Eskimo, on the coast between lat. 63° and 64°.—Nansen, First Crossing, 383, 1890.

Igiak. A Magemiut Eskimo village inland from Scammon bay, Alaska; pop. 10 in 1880.
Igiagagamute.—Petroff, Rep. on Alaska, 1884. **Igiogagamut.**—Nelson in 18th Rep. B. A. E., 1899. **Igragamiut.**—Nelson cited by Baker, Geog. Dict. Alaska, 212, 1901.

Igiakchak. A village of the Kuskwogmiut Eskimo in the Kuskokwim district, Alaska; pop. 81 in 1890.
Ighiakchaghamiut.—11th Census, Alaska, 6, 1893. **Igiakchak.**—Ibid.

Igivachok. A Nushagagmiut Eskimo village in the Nushagak district, Alaska; pop. 31 in 1890.
Igivachochamiut.—11th Census, Alaska, 164, 1893.

Iglakatekhila ('refuses to move camp'). A division of the Oglala Teton Sioux.
Iglaka tehila.—Dorsey (after Cleveland) in 15th Rep. B. A. E., 220, 1897. **Iglaka-teqila.**—Ibid.

Iglu. A snow house of the Eskimo: from *igdlu*, its name in the E. Eskimo dialects. See *Habitations*. (A. F. C.)

Igludahoming. An Ita Eskimo settlement on Smith sd., Greenland.
Igloodahominy.—Mrs Peary, My Arct. Jour., 81, 1893. **Igludahoming.**—Heilprin, Peary Relief Exped., 133, 1893.

Igluduasuin (*Igludŭă'hsuin*, 'place of houses'). An Ita Eskimo village in N. Greenland, lat. 77° 50'.—Stein in Petermanns Mitt., no. 9, map, 1902.

Iglulik. A winter settlement of the Aivilirmiut Eskimo at the head of Lyon inlet, Hudson bay.
Igdlulik.—Rink in Jour. Anthrop. Inst., XV, 240, 1886. **Igdlumiut.**—Boas in 6th Rep. B. A. E., map, 1888 (the inhabitants). **Igloolik.**—Parry, Sec. Voy.,

404, 1824. **Igloolip.**—Gilder, Schwatka's Search, 253, 1881.

Iglulik. A town of the Iglulirmiut Eskimo, on an island of the same name, near the E. end of Fury and Hecla straits.—Boas in Zeitschr. Ges. f. Erdk., 226, 1883.

Iglulirmiut ('people of the place with houses'). A tribe of central Eskimo living on both sides of Fury and Hecla straits. They kill walrus in winter on Iglulik and other islands, harpoon seal in the fjords in early spring, and throughout the summer hunt deer in Baffin land or Melville peninsula. Their settlements are Akuli, Arlagnuk, Iglulik, Kangertluk, Krimerksumalek, Pilig, Pingitkalik, and Uglirn.—Boas in 6th Rep. B. A. E., 444, 1888.
Iglulingmiut.—Boas in Trans. Anthrop. Soc. Wash., III, 96, 1885.

Ignok. An Ikogmiut Eskimo village on the right bank of the lower Yukon, Alaska; pop. 175 in 1880.
Ignokhatskomute.—Petroff in 10th Census, Alaska, 57, 1884. **Ingekasagmi.**—Raymond (1869), quoted by Baker, Geog. Dict. Alaska, 1902.

Ignokhatskamut. A village on lower Yukon r., adjacent to the Bering coast Eskimo, the inhabitants of which are probably of Athapascan and Eskimo mixture.—Nelson in 18th Rep. B. A. E., pl. ii, 1900.

Igpirto. A fall settlement of Talirpingmiut Eskimo of the Okomiut tribe at the head of Nettilling fjord, Cumberland sd.—Boas in 6th Rep. B. A. E., map, 1888.

Igualali (*Ig-wa'-la-li*, 'a hole'). A small rancheria of the Tarahumare, not far from Norogachic, Chihuahua, Mexico.—Lumholtz, inf'n, 1894.

Iguanes. A tribe of whom Father Kino heard, in 1699, while near the mouth of the Rio Gila in s. w. Arizona. As they are mentioned in connection with the Alchedoma and Yuma, they were probably a Yuman tribe.
Iguanas.—Venegas, Hist. Cal., I, 57, 1759. **Iguanes.**—Kino (1699) quoted by Coues, Garcés Diary, 544, 1900. **Yuanes.**—Orozco y Berra, Geog., 59, 1864.

Iguik. An Unaligmiut Eskimo village on Norton sd., Alaska; pop. 8 in 1880, 51 in 1890.
Agowik.—11th Census, Alaska, 165, 1893. **Egowik.**—Dall in Cont. N. A. Ethnol., I, map, 1877. **Igauik.**—Nelson in 18th Rep. B. A. E., map, 1899. **Igawik.**—Petroff in 10th Census, Alaska, 59, 1884. **Iguik.**—Baker, Geog. Dict. Alaska, 165, 1893.

Igushik. A Nushagagmiut Eskimo village on Igushik r., Alaska; pop. 74 in 1880.
Igushek.—Petroff in 10th Census, Alaska, 17, 1884. **Igushik.**—Baker, Geog. Dict. Alaska, 1901.

Ihaisdaye (*Iha-isdaye*, 'mouth-greasers'). A band of the Yankton Sioux.—Dorsey in 15th Rep. B. A. E., 217, 1897.

Ihamba (*I'ha-mba*). An ancient pueblo of the Tewa on the s. side of Pojoaque r., between Pojoaque and San Ildefonso pueblos, N. New Mex.—Bandelier in Arch. Inst. Papers, IV, 85, 1892.

Ihanktonwan ('Yankton'). A band of the Brulé Teton Sioux, so called because descended from Yankton women.

Ihanktonwan.—Dorsey in 15th Rep. B. A. E., 218, 1897. **Ihaṅktoⁿwaⁿ.**—Ibid.

Ihasha ('red lips'). A band of the Hunkpatina or Lower Yanktonai Sioux.
Iha-ca.—Dorsey in 15th Rep. B. A. E., 218, 1897. **Iha-śa.**—Ibid.

Ihonatiria. A former Huron village in Simcoe co., Ontario, built about 1634 and depopulated by pestilence in 1636. The Jesuits established there the mission of Immaculate Conception.
Ihonatiria.—Jes. Rel. for 1635, 30, 1858. **Ihonat-tiria.**—Jes. Rel. for 1637, 153, 1858. **Immaculate Conception.**—Shea, Cath. Miss., 173, 1855.

Ijelirtung. The northernmost summer settlement of the Akudnirmiut Eskimo of Baffin land.—Boas in 6th Rep. B. A. E., 441, 1888.

Ijirang. A fabulous people of central Eskimo mythology.—Boas in 6th Rep. B. A. E., 640, 1888.

Ika. A Cochimi tribe of Lower California, said by Father Baegert to have lived about 40 m. inland from Magdalena bay in the 18th century.
Ica.—Mühlenpfordt, Mexico, II, 2, 443, 1844. **Ikas.**—Baegert, Nachrichten, 96, 1773.

Ikak. An Aglemiut Eskimo village near Naknek lake, Alaska; pop. 162 in 1880.
Ik-khagmute.—Petroff in 10th Census, Alaska, 17, 1884. **Savonoski.**—Spurr and Post (1898) quoted by Baker, Geog. Dict. Alaska, 1902. **Ukak.**—Dall, Alaska, map, 1870.

Ikalu. A winter village of the Ita Eskimo on Whale sd., N. Greenland.
Idkalloo.—Markham in Trans. Ethnol. Soc. Lond., 129, 1866. **Ikă′rlo.**—Stein in Petermanns Mitt., no. 9, map, 1902.

Ikanachaka (*ikana* 'ground', *atchaka* 'reserved,' 'set apart,' 'beloved,' 'sacred'). A former Upper Creek town, located by Meek (Romantic Passages in S. W. Hist., 278, 1857) on the s. side of Alabama r., between Pintlala and Big Swamp cr., in Lowndes co., Ala. It was built on "holy ground" and hence was thought to be exempt from hostile inroads. Weatherford and the "prophet" Hillis Hadjo resided there, and the Creek forces were defeated there Dec. 23, 1813, at which date it contained 200 houses and included some Shawnee.   (H. W. H.)
Eckanachacu.—Claybourne (1814) in Boudinot, Star in the West, 254, 1816. **Eckanakaka.**—Drake, Bk. Inds., bk. IV, 58, 1848. **Econachaca.**—Pickett, Hist. Ala., II, 323, 1851. **E-cun-cha-ta.**—Royce in 18th Rep. B. A. E., Ala., map, 1899. **Holy Ground.**—Claybourne (1814) in Boudinot, op. cit. **Ikanatch-áka.**—Gatschet, Creek Migr. Leg., I, 132, 1884.

Ikanhatki ('white ground'). A former Upper Creek town on the right bank of lower Tallapoosa r., Montgomery co., Ala., immediately below Kulumi town. Swan, who passed there in 1791, says it had been settled by Shawnee, who had 4 villages in the vicinity, and they are called by him Shawnee refugees, but Bartram (1775) states that they spoke Muscogee. Under the name Ekundutske the village was said to contain 47 families in 1832.   (A. S. G.)

Cunhutke.—Bartram, Trav., 461, 1791. **Econa-tckky.**—Sen. Ex. Doc. 425, 24th Cong., 1st sess., 255, 1836. **Econautske.**—Ibid. **E-cun-hut-ke.**—Hawkins (1799), Sketch, 34, 1848. **Ecunhutlee.**—Schoolcraft, Ind. Tribes, IV, 380, 1854. **E kun duts ke.**—Census of 1832, ibid., 578. **Ekunhutke.**—Pickett, Hist. Ala., II, 267, 1851 (inhabited by Shawanese). **Ikan'-hátki.**—Gatschet, Creek Migr. Leg., I, 132, 1884. **Kenhulka.**—Swan (1791) in Schoolcraft, op. cit., v, 262, 1855. **White Ground.**—Finnelson (1792) in Am. State Pap., Ind. Aff., I, 289, 1832.

Ikaruck. Mentioned as a Shasta band of Shasta valley, N. Cal., in 1851, but it is really a man's personal name. (R. B. D.)
I-ka-nuck.—McKee (1851) in Sen. Ex. Doc. 4, 32d Cong., spec. sess., 171, 1853. **Ika-ruck.**—Gibbs (1851) in Schoolcraft, Ind. Tribes, III, 171, 1853.

Ikatchiocata. A former Choctaw town between the headwaters of Chicasawhay and Tombigbee rs., Miss.
Ikachiocata.—Lattré, map U. S., 1784. **Ikechipou-ta.**—Philippeaux, map, 1781.

Ikatek. An Angmagsalingmiut Eskimo village on Sermilik fjord, E. Greenland; pop. 58 in 1884.—Meddelelser om Grönland, x, map, 1888.

Ikatikunahita (*ikă′tĭ* 'swamp', *kŭnahi′ta* 'long': Long Swamp town). A Cherokee settlement, about the period of the removal in 1839, situated on Long Swamp cr., about the boundary of Forsyth and Cherokee cos., N. w. Ga.   (J. M.)
Long Swamp Village.—Royce in 5th Rep. B. A. E., map, 1887.

Ikatlek. An Ikogmiut Eskimo village on Yukon r., Alaska, 30 m. below Anvik; pop. 9 in 1880.
Ikaklagmüte.—Raymond in Sen. Ex. Doc. 12, 42d Cong., 1st sess., 25, 1871. **Ikatlegomut.**—Nelson in 18th Rep. B. A. E., map, 1899. **Ikatlego-mute.**—Petroff in 10th Census, Alaska, map, 1884. **Ikoklag′müt.**—Dall in Cont. N. A. Ethnol., I, 17, 1877.

Ikerasak. A northern settlement of the Angmagsalingmiut Eskimo of E. Greenland, lat. 66°.—Meddelelser om Grönland, XXVII, 22, 1902.

Ikherkhamut (*I-qĕr-qa-mŭt′*, 'end of river people': Kaniagmiut name). A division of the Ahtena near the mouth of Copper r., Alaska.—Hoffman, MS., B. A. E., 1882.

Ikmun (referring to an animal of the cat kind). A band of the Yankton Sioux.
Ikmuŋ.—Dorsey in 15th Rep. B. A. E., 217, 1897. **Ikmuⁿ.**—Ibid.

Iknetuk. A Kaviagmiut Eskimo village on Golofnin bay, Alaska; pop. 100 in 1880.
Ignituk.—Nelson in 18th Rep. B. A. E., map, 1899. **Iknetuk.**—Baker, Geog. Dict. Alaska, 1901. **Kniktag′emüt.**—Dall in Cont. N. A. Ethnol., I, 16, 1877.

Ikogmiut. A tribe of Alaskan Eskimo inhabiting both banks of the Yukon as far as Makak. They have hairy bodies and strong beards and exhibit a marked variation in physique, customs, and dialect from the Eskimo N. and E. of Norton sd., being more nearly allied to the other fishing tribes s. of them. Dall estimated their number at 1,000 in 1870, including the Chnagmiut. In 1890 there were 172

Ikogmiut proper. Holmberg divided the natives of the delta into the Kwikpagmiut and the Kwikluagmiut, living respectively on the Kwikpak and Kwikluak passes. The villages are Asko, Bazhi, Ignok, Ikatlek, Ikogmiut, Ingahame, Ingrakak, Katagkag, Kenunimik, Kikhkat, Koko, Koserefski, Kuyikanuikpul, Kvikak, Makak, Narosigak, Nukluak, Nunaikak, Nunaktak, Paimute, Pogoreshapka, and Uglovaia.

Ekŏg′mūt.—Dall in Cont. N. A. Ethnol., I, 17, 1877. Ekógmuts.—Dall, Alaska, 407, 1870. Hekjnxtana.—Doroschin in Radloff, Wörterbuch°d. Kinai-Spr., 29, 1874 (Kinai name). Ikogmjut.—Holmberg, Ethnog. Skizz., map, 142, 1855. Ikvogmutes.—Schwatka, Milit. Recon., Explor. in Alaska, 353, 1900. Kahvichpaks.—Elliott, Cond. Aff. in Alaska, 29, 1874. Koikhpagamute.—Petroff in Am. Nat., XVI, 570, 1882 (Eskimo: 'people of the Kwikpak, the big river'). Kuwichpackmüten.—Wrangell, Ethnog. Nachr., 122, 1839. Kvikhpagmute.—Zagoskin quoted by Petroff in 10th Census, Alaska, 37, 1884. Kwichljuagmjuten.—Holmberg, Ethnog. Skizz., 5, 1855. Kwichpacker.—Wrangell, Ethnog. Nachr., 122, 1839. Kwiohpagmjuten.—Holmberg, Ethnog. Skizz., 5, 1855. Kwichpak.—Whymper, Trav. in Alaska, map, 1868. Kwikhpăg-mūt.—Dall in Cont. N. A. Ethnol., I, 17, 1877.

Ikogmiut. An Ikogmiut Eskimo village on the lower Yukon, Alaska, where the Russians established a mission about 1843. Pop. 148 in 1880, 140 in 1890, 166 in 1900.

Icogmute.—Bruce, Alaska, map, 1885. Ikoghmiout.—Zagoskine in Nouv. Ann. Voy., 5th s., XXI, map, 1850. Ikogmut.—Nelson in 18th Rep. B. A. E., pl. ii, 1899. Ikogmute.—Petroff, Rep. on Alaska, map, 1884. Ikuagmjut.—Holmberg, Ethnog. Skizz., map, 1855.

Ikolga. A former Aleut village on Unalaska, Aleutian ids., Alaska.—Coxe, Russian Discov., 164, 1787.

Iktigalik. A Kaiyuhkhotana village on Unalaklik r., Alaska, having 10 houses in 1866.

Igtigalik.—Whymper in Jour. Roy. Geog. Soc., 225, 1868. Iktigalik.—Dall, Alaska, 26, 1870. New Ulukuk.—Whymper, Trav. in Alaska, 175, 1869. Nove Ulukuk.—Ibid. (Russian name).

Ikuak. A Chnagmiut village on the lower Yukon, Alaska, near the head of the delta; pop. 65 in 1890.

Iko-agmiut.—11th Census, Alaska, 165, 1893. Ikuagmiut.—Tikhmenief (1861) quoted by Baker, Geog. Dict. Alaska, 1901. Ikuak.—Baker, ibid. Yukagamut.—Raymond (1869), quoted by Baker, ibid.

Ikwopsum. A Squawmish village community on the left bank of Squawmisht r., Brit. Col.

Eukwhatsum.—Survey map, U. S. Hydrog. Office. Ikwo′psum.—Hill-Tout in Rep. Brit. A. A. S., 475, 1900. Yik′oā′psan.—Boas, MS., B. A. E., 1887.

Ilamatech. A former Tepehuane pueblo in Durango, Mexico, and the seat of a mission.

S. Antonio Ilamatech.—Orozco y Berra, Geog., 319, 1864.

Ildjunai-hadai (Î′ldjuna-i xă′da-i, 'valuable-house people'). A subdivision of the Yadus, a family of the Eagle clan of the Haida in w. British Columbia. The name is derived from that of a house.—Swanton, Cont. Haida, 276, 1905.

Ile Percée. A French mission, probably among the Micmac, on the Gulf of St Lawrence in the 17th century.—Shea, Miss. Val., 85, 1852.

Ilex cassine. See *Black drink.*

Iliamna. A Kaniagmiut Eskimo village on the s. shore of Iliamna lake, Alaska; pop. 49 in 1880, 76 in 1890.

Iliamna.—11th Census, Alaska, 95, 1893. Ilyamna.—Petroff, 10th Census, Alaska, 17, 1884.

Ilis ('spread-legs beach'). A Nimkish Kwakiutl village on Cormorant id., Alert bay, Brit. Col., opposite Vancouver id. Some Kwakiutl proper come here during the salmon season.—Boas in Bull. Am. Geog. Soc., 227, 1887.

I-lis.—Dawson in Trans. Roy. Soc. Can., sec. II, 65, 1887.

Ilisees. Mentioned by Ker (Travels, 98, 1816) as the native name of a tribe, numbering about 2,000, which he says he met on upper Red r. of Louisiana, apparently in the N. E. corner of Texas. Their chief village was said to be Wascoo. Both the tribe and the village are seemingly imaginary.

Iliuliuk (Aleut: 'harmony'). A town on Unalaska id., Alaska, the headquarters of the commercial interests of the Aleutians (Schwatka, Mil. Recon., 115, 1885). Pop. 196 in 1831, 406 in 1880, 317 in 1890.

Gavanskoe.—Veniaminoff, Zapiski, II, 202, 1840 (Russian: 'harbor'). Gavanskoi.—Elliott, Cond. Aff. Alaska, 1875. Gawanskoje.—Holmberg, Ethnog. Skizz., map, 1855. Iljljuljuk.—Ibid. Illoolook.—Elliott, Our Arct. Prov., map, 1886. Oonalaska.—Schwatka, Mil. Recon., 115, 1885. Unalaska.—11th Census, Alaska, 88, 1893.

Iliutak. A Kuskwogmiut Eskimo village on Kuskokwim bay, Alaska; pop. 40 in 1880.

Iliutagamute.—Petroff, Rep. on Alaska, 53, 1884.

Ilkatsho ('the big fattening'). A village of the Ntshaautin on the lake at the head of Blackwater r., Brit. Col. The population is a mixed one of Takulli and Bellacoola descent.

ɋl′katoo.—Morice in Trans. Roy. Soc. Can., 109, 1892. Ṭ′ka-too.—Morice, Notes on W. Dénés, 25, 1893. Uhlchako.—Can. Ind. Aff., 285, 1902.

Illinois (*Iliniwek*, from *ilini* 'man', *iw* 'is', *ek* plural termination, changed by the French to *ois*). A confederacy of Algonquian tribes, formerly occupying s. Wisconsin, N. Illinois, and sections of Iowa and Missouri, comprising the Cahokia, Kaskaskia, Michigamea, Moingwena, Peoria, and Tamaroa.

The Jesuit Relation for 1660 represents them as living s. w. of Green bay, Wis., in 60 villages, and gives an extravagant estimate of the population, 20,000 men, or 70,000 souls. The statement in the Jesuit Relations that they came from the border of a great sea in the far W. arose, no doubt (as Tailhan suggests), from a misunderstanding of the term "great water," given by the Indians, which in fact referred to the Mississippi. Their exact location when first heard of by the whites can not be determined with certainty, as the tribes and bands were more or less scattered over s. Wisconsin, N. Illinois, and along the w. bank of the Mississippi as far s. as Des Moines r., Iowa. The whites first came in actual contact with them (unless it be true that Nicollet visited them) at La Pointe (Shaugawaumikong), where Allouez met a party in 1667, which was visiting that point for purposes of trade. In 1670 the same priest found a number of them at the Mascoutin village on upper Fox r., some 9 m. from where Portage City now stands, but this band then contemplated joining their brethren on the Mississippi. The conflicting statements regarding the number of their villages at this period and the indefiniteness as to localities render it difficult to reach a satisfactory conclusion on these points. It appears that some villages were situated on the w. side of the Mississippi, in what is now Iowa, yet the major portion of the tribes belonging to the confederacy resided at points in N. Illinois, chiefly on Illinois r. When Marquette journeyed down the Mississippi in 1673 he found the Peoria and Moingwena on the w. side, about the mouth of Des Moines r. On his return, 2 months later, he found them on Illinois r., near the present city of Peoria. Thence he passed N. to the village of Kaskaskia, then on upper Illinois r., within the present Lasalle co. At this time the village consisted of 74 cabins and was occupied by one tribe only. Hennepin estimated them, about 1680, at 400 houses and 1,800 warriors, or about 6,500 souls. A few years later (1690–94) missionaries reported it to consist of 350 cabins, occupied by 8 tribes or bands. Father Sébastian Rasles, who visited the village in 1692, placed the number of cabins at 300, each of 4 "fires," with 2 families to a fire, indicating a population of about 9,000—perhaps an excessive estimate. The evidence, however, indicates that a large part of the confederacy was gathered at this point for a while. The Kaskaskia at this time were in somewhat intimate relation with the Peoria, since Gravier, who returned to their village in 1700, says he found them preparing to start s., and believed that if he could have arrived sooner "the Kaskaskians would not thus have separated from the Peouaroua [Peoria] and other Illinois." By his persuasion they were induced to stop in s. Illinois at the point to which their name was given. The Cahokia and Tamaroa were at this time living at their historic seats on the Mississippi in s. Illinois. The Illinois were almost constantly harassed by the Sioux, Foxes, and other northern tribes; it was probably on this account that they concentrated, about the time of La Salle's visit, on Illinois r. About the same time the Iroquois waged war

against them, which lasted several years, and greatly reduced their numbers, while liquor obtained from the French tended still further to weaken them. About the year 1750 they were still estimated at from 1,500 to 2,000 souls. The murder of the celebrated chief Pontiac, by a Kaskaskia Indian, about 1769, provoked the vengeance of the Lake tribes on the Illinois, and a war of extermination was begun which, in a few years, reduced them to a mere handful, who took refuge with the French settlers at Kaskaskia, while the Sauk, Foxes, Kickapoo, and Potawatomi took possession of their country. In 1778 the Kaskaskia still numbered 210, living in a village 3 m. N. of Kaskaskia, while the Peoria and Michigamea together numbered 170 on the Mississippi, a few miles farther up. Both bands had become demoralized and generally worthless through the use of liquor. In 1800 there were only about 150 left. In 1833 the survivors, represented by the Kaskaskia and Peoria, sold their lands in Illinois and removed w. of the Mississippi, and are now in the N. E. corner of Oklahoma, consolidated with the Wea and Piankashaw. In 1885 the consolidated Peoria, Kaskaskia, Wea, and Piankashaw numbered but 149, and even these are much mixed with white blood. In 1905 their number was 195.

Nothing definite is known of their tribal divisions or clans. In 1736, according to Chauvignerie (N. Y. Doc. Col. Hist., IX, 1056, 1855), the totem of the Kaskaskia was a feather of an arrow, notched, or two arrows fixed like a St Andrew's cross; while the Illinois as a whole had the crane, bear, white hind, fork, and tortoise totems.

In addition to the principal tribes or divisions above mentioned, the following are given by early writers as seemingly belonging to the Illinois: Albivi, Amonokoa, Chepoussa, Chinko, Coiracoentanon, Espeminkia, and Tapouara. In general their villages bore the names of the tribes occupying them, and were constantly varying in number and shifting in location.

The Illinois are described by early writers as tall and robust, with pleasant visages. The descriptions of their character given by the early missionaries differ widely, but altogether they appear to have been timid, easily driven from their homes by their enemies, fickle, and treacherous. They were counted excellent archers, and, besides the bow, used in war a kind of lance and a wooden club. Polygamy was common among them, a man sometimes taking several sisters as wives. Unfaithfulness of a wife was punished, as among the Miami, the Sioux, the Apache, and other tribes, by cutting off the nose of the offending woman, and as the men were very jealous, this punishment was often inflicted on mere suspicion.

It was not the custom of the Illinois, at the time the whites first became acquainted with them, to bury their dead. The body was wrapped in skins and attached by the feet and head to trees. There is reason, however, to believe, from discoveries that have been made in mounds and ancient graves, which appear to be attributable to some of the Illinois tribes, that the skeletons, after the flesh had rotted away, were buried, often in rude stone sepulchers. Prisoners of war were usually sold to other tribes.

According to Hennepin, the cabins of the more northerly tribes were made like long arbors and covered with double mats of flat flags or rushes, so well sewed that they were never penetrated by wind, snow, or rain. To each cabin were 4 or 5 fires, and to each fire 2 families, indicating that each dwelling housed some 8 or 10 families. Their towns were not inclosed.

The villages of the confederacy noted in history are Cahokia (mission), Immaculate Conception (mission), Kaskaskia, Matchinkoa, Moingwena, Peoria, and Pimitoui.　　　(J. M. C. T.)

Abimiouec.—Doc. of 1660 in Margry, Déc., I, 54, 1875 (b=l). Abimi8ec.—Jes. Rel. 1660, 12, 1858 (b=l). Alimouek.—Ibid., 1667, 21. Alimouk.—Ibid., III, index, 1858. Aliniouek.—Ibid., 1658, 21. Alini8ek.—Ibid., 1660, 12 (correction in errata). Alinouecks.—Coxe, Carolana, 19, 1741. Allinoueoks.—Ibid., 49. Chicktaghicks.—Colden (1727), Five Nations, 30, 1747 (Iroquois name). Chictaghicks.—Smith in Williams, Vermont, I, 501, 1809. Chigtaghcicks.—Colden, op. cit., 31. Chiktachiks.—Homann, map, 1756. Eriniouai.—Jes. Rel. 1640, 35, 1858. Eriniwek.—Ibid., III, index, 1858. Geghdageghroano.—Post (1758) in Proud, Pa., II, app., 113, 1798. Geghtigeghroones.—Canajoharie conf. (1759) in N. Y. Doc. Col. Hist., VII, 384, 1856. Hilini.—Brinton, Lenape Leg., 213, 1885. Hiliniki.—Rafinesque, Am. Nations, I, 139, 1836 (Delaware name). Ilimouek.—Jes. Rel. 1670, 101, 1858. Iliné.—Hervas (1785) in Vater, Mith., pt. 3, sec. 3, 347, 1816 (Italian form). Ilinese.—La Hontan, New Voy., I, 217, 1703. Ilinesen.—Walch, map, 1805 (German form). Iliniöuek.—Jes. Rel. 1667, 18, 1858. Ilinois.—Ibid., 1670, 86. Ilinoüets.—Ibid., 1670, 92. Ilinoüetz.—Ibid., 101. Ilionois.—Proud, Pa., II, 296, 1798. Illenois.—Morse, North Am., map, 1776. Illenonecks.—Ibid., 255. Illicoueck.—Coxe, Carolana, 17, 1741. Illimoüec.—Jes. Rel. 1667, 21, 1858. Illinese.—Hennepin, Cont. of New Discov., 88, 1698. Illinesen.—Vater, Mith., pt. 3, sec. 3, 341, 1816 (German form). Il-li-ni.—Hough in Indiana Geol. Rep., map, 1883. Illiniens.—Hennepin, op. cit. 45b. Illiniwek.—Shea, Cath. Miss., 348, 1855. Illinoias.—Niles (1761?) in Mass. Hist. Soc. Coll., 4th s., V, 541, 1861. Illinois.—Prise de Possession (1671) in Margry, Déc., I, 96, 1875. Illinoix.—Brackenridge, La., 132, 1815. Illinonecks.—Morse, North Am., 255, 1798. Illinoneeks.—Doc. of 1719 in N. C. Rec., II, 351, 1886. Illinouecks.—Coxe, Carolana, 49, 1741. Illonese.—Schermerhorn (1812) in Mass. Hist. Soc. Coll., 2d s., II, 3, 1814. Illonois.—Campbell (1761), ibid., 4th s., IX, 423, 1871. Illuni.—Allouez (1665) quoted by Ramsey in Ind. Aff. Rep., 71, 1850. Irinions.—Jes. Rel. 1642, 97, 1858. Isle aux Noix.—Lapham, Ind's of Wis., 4, 1870 ('Walnut island': a form used by some author, who probably mistook Illinois for a corrupted French word). Islinois.—La Salle (1680) in Margry, Déc., II, 33, 1877. Kichtages.—Maryland treaty (1682) in N. Y. Doc.

Col. Hist., III, 325, 1853. Kicktages.—Albany conf. (1726), ibid., V, 791, 1855. Kighetawkigh Roanu.—Dobbs, Hudson Bay, 28, 1744 (Iroquois name). Kightages.—Livingston (1720) in N. Y. Doc. Col. Hist., V, 567, 1855. Lazars.—Croghan (1759) in Rupp, West. Pa., 146, 1846. Lezar.—Croghan quoted by Jefferson, Notes, 145, 1825 (probably the Illinois). Liniouok.—Jes. Rel. 1656, 39, 1858. Linneways.—Brice, Ft Wayne, 121, 1868. Linways.—Croghan, op. cit. Minneways.—Brice, Ft Wayne, 121, 1868. Ondataouatouat.—Potier MS. cited in Charlevoix, New France, II, 270, note, 1866 (first applied by the Wyandot to the Ottawa, afterward to the Illinois). Willinis.—Proud, Pa., II, 296, 1798. Witishaχtánu.—Gatschet, Wyandot MS., B. A. E., 1881 (from Ushaχtáno, 'Illinois r.,' Huron name for the Peoria, Kaskaskia, Wea, and Piankashaw).

Illumination. The employment of artificial light among the Indians was limited by their simple habits and needs to the camp-fire and the torch, in which respect they are found in the same culture grade as the Malay, the Negro, and the majority of uncivilized peoples. The camp-fire, built for the purpose of cooking food or furnishing heat, supplied most of the needed light. On special occasions large bonfires were made when ceremonies were held and nocturnal illumination was required. As a makeshift for the torch, a brand was taken from the camp-fire. When a continuous light was desired the fire was fed with slivers of wood set up in a circle and fed from one end where a gap was left in the circle, as among the Cherokee; or when a temporary light was wanted among

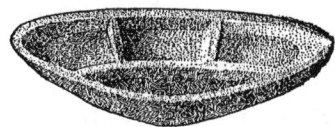

ESKIMO LAMP, 24 IN. LONG. (NELSON)

the Indians of British Columbia a little oil was thrown on the coals. The torches were of pine knots, rolls of bark, cane, or other inflammable material, but bundles of resinous wood, or masses of resin were almost never made, the form of the Indian torch being of the most primitive character. They were used by night for hunting and fishing; for instance, deer were "weequashed," or "jacked," by means of torches, and fish were speared and birds captured by light from pine knots, especially among the eastern Indians. Lamps, however, have been possessed from time immemorial by the Eskimo, and they are the only aborigines of the hemisphere who had such utensils. In s. Alaska the lamp has a narrow wick-edge and is in the shape of a flat-iron; along the tundra N. of St Michael it is a saucer of clay or stone; northward to Point Barrow it is gibbous, with wide wick-edge and made of soapstone. The length of the wick-edge of the Eskimo lamp has been observed to vary with the latitude, that is, the higher the latitude the longer the night, hence the greater need for light, which is met by lengthening the margin of the lamp on which the moss wick is placed, so that while in s.

Alaska the wick edge is 2 or 3 in. long, in Smith sd. it is 36 in. in length, and between these geographical extremes there is an increase in the size of the lamp from lower to higher latitudes. In at least two localities in the United States the bodies of fish were burned for light— the candle-fish of the N. W. coast and a fresh-water fish of Penobscot r. in Maine.

Torches and fires were used for signaling at night; the Apache set fire to the resinous spines of the saguaro, or giant cactus, for this purpose. The picturesque and remarkable Fire-dance of the Navaho described by Matthews is a good example of the use of illumination in ceremonies. Among many tribes fire forms an essential part of a ceremony; in some cases, where Indians have been induced to rehearse a night ceremony by day, they do not omit the fire, though artificial light is not required. A law of the Iroquois League required that a messenger approaching a camp-fire or village at night should carry a torch in order to show the absence of hostile intent. See *Fire-making*.

Consult Hough (1) Development of Illumination, Smithson. Rep. 1901, 1902, (2) The Range of the Eskimo Lamp, Am. Anthrop., Apr. 1898, (3) The Lamp of the Eskimo, Rep. Nat. Mus. 1896, 1898; Matthews, Mountain Chant, 5th Rep. B. A. E., 1887. (W. H.)

Ilmawi (own name; from *ilma*, 'river'). A tribe of the Achomawi division of the Shastan family, formerly living on the s. side of Pit r., opposite Ft Crook, Shasta co., Cal.

Illmawees.—Powers in Overland Mo., XII, 412, 1874. Il-mâ′-wi.—Powers in Cont. N. A. Ethnol., III, 267, 1877.

Ilrak (*I′rak*). A former village of the Ntshaautin sept of the Takulli of British Columbia.—Morice in Trans. Can. Inst., IV, 25, 1893.

Ilsethlthawaiame. A former village of the Mishikhwutmetunne on Coquille r., Oreg.

Il′-seçl ça-waí-ă-mě.—Dorsey in Jour. Am. Folk-lore, III, 232, 1890.

Iluilek. An Eskimo village, now deserted, on the E. coast of Greenland, lat. 60° 20′.

Illuidlek.—Das Ausland, 162, 1886. Iluilek.—Meddelelser om Grönland, XXV, 23, 1902.

Imagnee. A former Aleut village on Summer bay, Unalaska, E. Aleutian ids.; pop. 32 in 1830, 34 in 1884.

Imagnak.—Petroff in 10th Census, Alaska, 34, 1884. Imagnee.—Baker, Geog. Dict. Alaska, 215, 1902. Imagninskoe.—Veniaminoff, Zapiski, II, 202, 1840. Sinagnia.—Sarichef (1790) quoted by Baker, op. cit.

Imaha. A Quapaw village mentioned by La Metairie in 1682 and by Iberville in 1699, and visited by La Harpe in 1719. It was situated on a s. w. branch of Arkansas r. In the wars and contentions of the 18th and 19th centuries some of the Quapaw tribe fled from their more northerly villages and took refuge among the Caddo, finally becoming a recognized division of the confederacy. These were called Imaha, but whether the people composing this division were from the village Imaha, mentioned by the early French travelers, is not absolutely known. The people of the Imaha division of the Caddo confederacy for some time retained their own language, which was Siouan. See Mooney in 14th Rep. B. A. E., 1092, 1896. (A. C. F.)

Imaham.—La Harpe (1719) in French, Hist. Coll. La., pt III, 73, 1851. Imahans.—Jefferys, Am. Atlas, map 5, 1776. Imahao.—Iberville (1699) in Margry, Déc., IV, 179, 1880.

Imaklimiut. An Eskimo tribe occupying Big Diomede id., Bering strait. See *Okiogmiut*.

Achjuch-Aliat.—Dall in Smithson. Cont., XXII, 2, 1880. Imach-leet.—Jackson, Reindeer in Alaska, map, 145, 1894. Imăh-kli-mŭt.—Dall in Proc. A. A. A. S., XXXIV, 377, 1886. Imakleet.—Wells and Kelly, Eskimo-English and Eng.-Esk. Vocabs., chart, 1890. Imaklitgmut.—Zagoskin, Desc. Russ. Poss. in Am., I, 73, 1847. Inalugmiut.—Woolfe in 11th Census, Alaska, 130, 1893 (given to inhabitants of both islands; see *Inalik*). Yıkırga′ulıt.—Bogoras, Chukchee, 21, 1904 (Chukchi name for inhabitants of Diomede ids.).

Imarsivik. An Eskimo village of 21 people on the E. coast of Greenland.—Nansen, Eskimo Life, 124, 1894.

Imekpung (*Imě′kpŭñ*). An Utkiavinmiut Eskimo camp near Pt Barrow, Alaska.—Murdoch in 9th Rep. B. A. E., 274, 1892.

Imiak. A Togiagmiut village at the outlet of Aleknagik lake, Alaska.—Tebenkof (1849) quoted by Baker, Geog. Dict. Alaska, 1902.

Imiche. A Californian tribe cited several times and mentioned once as on Kaweah r., Cal., which location, if correct, would make it part of the Mariposan stock. The Wimilchi of Kings r. may have been meant.

Eemitches.—Bancroft, Nat. Races, I, 363, 1874. Y-Mitches.—Henley in Ind. Aff. Rep., 511, 1854 (at Four rivers, near Tulare r.). Ymitches.—Bancroft, op. cit., I, 456 (misquoted from Henley).

Imigen ('fresh water'). One of the two winter villages of the Kinguamiut, a branch of the Okomiut Eskimo, on an island at the head of Cumberland sd.; pop. 17 in 1883.—Boas in 6th Rep. B. A. E., map, 1888.

Imik. A former Aleut village on Agattu id., Alaska, one of the Near id. group of the Aleutians, now uninhabited.

Immaculate Conception. A mission established by Marquette in 1674 among the Kaskaskia, near Rockford, Ill.

Immaculate Conception.—Shea, Cath. Miss., 406, 1855. Immaculée Conception de Notre Dame aux Illinois.—Gravier(?) (1694) quoted by Shea, ibid., 419.

Immahal. A former Chumashan village in Ventura co., Cal., "not far from José Carrillo's rancho" in 1856.—Taylor in Cal. Farmer, May 4, 1860.

Imnangana. The southernmost winter settlement of the Ita Eskimo, situated at C. York, N. Greenland.

Ekadlŭ′hsuin.—Stein in Petermanns Mitt., no. 9, map, 1902 (='salmon fishery'). **Ignanine.**—Heilprin, Peary Relief Exped., 102, 1893. **Imangen.**—Markham in Trans. Ethnol. Soc. Lond., 127, 1866. **Imnagen.**—Ibid., 129. **Imnangana.**—Kroeber in Bull. Am. Mus. Nat. Hist., XII, 269, 1899. **Imuanak.**—Hayes, Arct. Boat Journ., 182, 1860.

Imnarkuan ('where we make maple sugar'). A Passamaquoddy village formerly on the site of Pembroke, Washington co., Me.—Vetromile, Abnakis, 56, 1866.

Imoktegokshuk. A Kaviagmiut Eskimo village at C. Nome, Alaska; pop. 30 in 1880.
Imokhtagokhshuk.—Petroff in 10th Census, Alaska, 11, 1884. **Imokhtegokhshuk.**—Ibid., map. **Imoktegokhshuk.**—Baker, Geog. Dict. Alaska, 1902.

Imongalasha (*Imoklasha*, 'their people are there'). A former Choctaw settlement, sometimes called West Imongalasha to distinguish it from Imongalasha Skatane, and also popularly known as Mokalusha. It was situated on the headwaters of Talasha cr., Neshoba co., Miss., and was the most important Choctaw town in that region, the name appearing often in early government records. Tecumseh visited it in 1811 and held a council there. In 1824 it was almost abandoned owing to the ravages of smallpox. The houses of the settlement, with the small fields intervening, covered an area of 3 m. N. and S., and 1½ m. E. and W. It consisted of a number of hamlets, the names of which, from S. to N., were Yaneka, Chukkilissa, Onaheli, Nanihaba, and Bihikonlo.—Halbert in Miss. Hist. Soc. Publ., VI, 431, 1902. **Imuklásha.**—Gatschet, Creek Migr. Leg., I, 138, 1884.

Imongalasha Skatane (*Imoklasha Iskitini*, 'Little Imongalasha'). A former Choctaw town on the E. prong of Yazoo cr., now known as Flat cr., a N. affluent of Petickfa cr., Kemper co., Miss.—Halbert in Miss. Hist. Soc. Pub., VI, 423, 1902.
East Moka-Lassa.—Romans, Florida, 310, 1775. **Imongolasha Skatani.**—West Fla. map., ca. 1775.

Implements, Tools, Utensils. While a tool is that with which something is made, an implement that with which work is done, and a utensil that in or on which something is prepared or used up, they can not always be distinguished among primitive peoples, who utilize one thing for many purposes. Many forms are discussed under *Arts and Industries* and in articles devoted to special activities. It must be borne in mind that all such devices were helpers of the skilful hand and a vast deal of excellent work was done with it alone.

The Indians of North America were in the stone age and therefore every device with which the arts of life were carried on, whether implement, tool, or utensil, was in harmony with this grade of culture. The archeologist finds of such objects in ancient remains and sites either their substantial portions, or the perishable parts that have been accidentally preserved, or impressions of them left on pottery. By comparing these relics with implements, tools, and utensils found in actual use among the Indians one is able to partially reconstruct ancient industry and read far backward into history. The moment that the savages saw implements, tools, and utensils of metal in the hands of Europeans, they recognized the superiority of these and adopted them. It is interesting to note the modifications that were made in hafting and using, in order to adapt the new devices to old habits and customs. As of old, manual parts were still carved, painted, and hung with symbols, without which they were thought to be ineffectual.

The instruments of handicraft were of two classes—general, for common purposes, and special, for particular industries. The general implements, tools, and utensils may be described in detail (Holmes in Rep. Nat. Mus. 1901, 501, 1903):

Hammers.—These were made of stone or other hard substance, with or without handles. There were sledges, mauls, and pile-drivers for two or more men.

Knives.—These were made commonly of chipped or ground stone. Teeth, bone, shell, and wood were also used for the purpose (McGuire in Am. Anthrop., IV, 1891).

Saws.—These were of serrated stones, shells, or other materials, and were worked by rubbing with the edge, often with the aid of sand with or without water.

Borers.—Many natural objects were used for making holes in hard and soft objects, either by pressure, striking, vibrating, or revolving. They were held directly in the hand or were hafted; were grasped by one hand or by both hands; held between the palms or were worked by means of strap, bow, or pump (McGuire in Rep. Nat. Mus. 1894, 623, 1896). (See *Drills and Drilling*.)

Axes.—The stone ax, rudely flaked or highly polished, plain or grooved, ranging in weight from a few ounces to many pounds in the ceremonial ax, was universal. It was held in the hand or attached in various ways to a handle by means of rawhide, but was never furnished with an eye for a helve. Other substances were occasionally used, as shell, iron ore, and copper, but the stone ax was the main reliance. The blade could be easily turned at right angles, and then the implement became an adz. (See *Adzes, Axes, Celts*.)

Scrapers.—The scraper was also a tool of wide dispersion. In shape it resembled a chisel blade with a beveled edge. The rudest were sharp spalls of siliceous stone, held in the hand with or without padding; others were of smooth materials set into handles or grips that snugly fitted the workwoman's hand. One variety was made for scraping hides, another for scraping wood.

Nippers.—These include all devices for holding tightly an object or holding parts together while being worked. Hinged varieties were not known, but the Eskimo, especially, had several inventions to do the work of clamps, pincers, tweezers, or the vise with the aid of wedges.

The simple mechanical powers, the wedge, the lever, and the inclined plane, were universally understood. The screw was employed but sparingly, if at all. The N. W. coast tribes used rollers, skids, and parbuckles to move great house beams into place, and the Alaskan Eskimo, according to Elliott, landed the walrus by means of a sliding tackle looped over pegs driven into cracks in the rocks and run through slits in the hide. The wheel and axle were entirely unknown, save in their most primitive form, the spindle. Power for doing work with the devices just described was derived from the muscle of the worker. The wind was utilized here and there, blowing upon a fixed mat erected for a sail, but nothing was known of shifting sails. The Indians made good use of fire in clearing ground for planting, in felling trees, excavating canoes, and making pitch and glue. Bellows were not used, but the blowtube existed. Water wheels were unknown, and in the matter of using nature's forces for work northern America was in a primitive state of culture. The special implements, tools, and utensils employed in the various aboriginal industries are enumerated below. They are also treated more fully in separate articles.

Agriculture.—Digging sticks, hardened in fire and sharpened, and often weighted; dibbles, hoes, scarecrows, harvesting devices, husking pegs, granaries, and caches were common. For harvesting both wild and cultivated produce various tribes had tongs for picking the cactus fruit, stone implements for opening hulls or shells, baskets for gathering, carrying, and storing, poles for reaching fruit, harvesting apparatus for grass seed, wild rice, camas, wokas, coonti, maize, etc. (See *Agriculture, Food.*)

Bark work.—Peelers, shredders, twisters, sewing tools, pitching tools.

Boat building.—Axes, adzes, saws, borers, hammers, knives, pitch and paint brushes, and fire.

Carrying.—Packing baskets, hide cases, walking sticks, special costumes, and a provision of compact food, as pemmican, dried fish, and crisp bread. The making up of burdens into neat loads for handling and for the back was understood and further completed by means of headbands, breast straps, and shoulder straps. The dog was here and there a pack beast and harness was devised.

Cooking.—Besides open roasting, grilling frames of wood, and pits for baking and steaming, there were stone slabs for parching seeds and for baking bread; pottery and baskets for boiling (the latter by the help of heated stones), and soapstone utensils for preparing meat and other food. (See *Food.*)

Curing food.—Drying frames, smoking devices.

Fishing.—Besides fishing implements proper, the fisher's outfit included canoes, paddles, weirs, dams, anchor stones, etc.

Plastic art.—In the technic of this industry belong all tools and implements used in quarrying clays and preparing them for the potter, all devices employed in building up, smoothing, polishing, and decorating ware, and the apparatus for burning. (See *Pottery.*)

Quarrying, mining, and stone working.—Digging sticks, mauls, hammers, edge tools for making lamps, and dishes and other receptacles of soapstone, chipping and other shaping tools and implements, carrying apparatus, flakers, chippers, polishers.

Textile industries.—All implements and tools needed in gathering roots, stems, and leaves as materials, and those used in preparing these for matting, bagging, basketry, blankets, robes, lacework, network, thread, string, and rope; finally all inventions employed in manufacturing these products. (See *Basketry, Blankets, Weaving.*)

Whaling.—Suit of water-tight clothing; kaiak and paddle; harpoon, with line; skin floats; lance.

Woodcraft.—Ax, knife, saw, adz, chisel, borers, rasps, polishers, paint brushes, rollers, moving and setting up devices. (See *Woodwork.*)

For serving and consuming food, knives were necessary; spoons were fashioned of natural objects, especially of wood, horn, and gourd, but there were no forks or individual dishes or tables. Much food was consumed on the spot where it was found. The Indians had manifold apparatus for making, preserving, and using fire; for cooking, lighting, and heating. Shovels were used for baking bread. The outfit for harvesting and preparing acorns included gathering basket, for which the woman's hat was often used, carrying hamper, granary, hulling mill, mortar, hopper basket, meal mat, leaching pit, cooking basket, mush basket, and eating bowls. Milling implements in general included natural bowlders and pebbles; mortars of wood, stone, bone, or hide; pestles of the same materials;

metates of varying degrees of texture, with manos to correspond; baskets to serve as hoppers and to catch meal, and brooms. Hunters' implements included a vast number of accessory apparatus for making weapons effectual.

Devices for binding or permanently holding two parts together, pegs, lashings, and cement were used (see *Cement*). In the absence of metal and rattan, rawhide, sinew, roots of evergreen trees, splits of tough wood, pitch, and animal glue performed the necessary function. In the aboriginal economy no great stones were moved, but large logs were sometimes transported many miles.

Metric devices of the North Americans were very crude compared with modern standards, but were exactly adapted to their needs. A man fitted his boat and all its appurtenances to his body, just as he did his clothing. The hunter, basket maker, potter, tentmaker, weighed and measured by means of the same standard. For securing uniform thickness the N. W. coast tribes bored holes through hulls of dugouts, and ran slender plugs into them which were used as gauges. Usually the parts of the body were the only gauges. (See *Measurements*.)

Straighteners were made of wood, stone, horn, or ivory for bending wood and other substances to shape. Digging sticks, dibbles, and the whole class of implements for making holes in the ground were used also for working in quarries, for getting worms and the like from the beach or the earth, and for digging roots for food or for textile and other industrial purposes. Tongs were employed in moving hot stones, in gathering cactus fruit, and in capturing snakes.

Dwellings were of such varying types and forms that their construction in different areas required the services of different kinds of work—that of the tentmaker, the joiner, the mason, or the snow worker, with their different implements, including shovels, axes, trowels, adzes, levers, parbuckles, etc. (see *Architecture, Habitations*). The joiner's outfit included many devices, from those for hafting to those for house building, tent framing, boat fitting, and the use of roots and thongs. Puncheons were hewn out, but there was no mortising. Hafting, the joining of the working part of a tool to the manual part, was accomplished variously by driving in, groove, splice, socket, tongue-and-groove, or mortising, and the fastening was done with pegs or lashing.

For the shaping arts, the working of stone, wood, and other hard substances, the apparatus varied with the material, and consisted of knives, hammers, wedges, saws, files, polishers, borers, adzes, and chisels, made out of materials best suited always to their uses. (See *Art, Sculpture, Stonework, Woodwork*.)

The propelling of all sorts of water craft was done by paddling, by poling, by dragging over mud, and by towing. No oars or rudders were used. Vessels were made water-tight with pitch or by the swelling of the wood. The rope or rawhide line for dragging a canoe along shore is known as a cordelle, the French-Canadian term. Portage, the moving of a bark canoe from one body of water to another, was accomplished by carrying load and canoe separately, sliding the empty canoe over mud, or shooting rapids in it. (See *Boats, Commerce, Travel and Transportation*.)

The making of snowshoes was an important occupation in the N., requiring great skill and manifold tools and devices. Ice and snow implements and utensils used in the higher latitudes include picks with ivory or stone blades, shovels with wooden blade and ivory edge, creepers for the boots, boat hooks for warding off and drawing canoes, sleds, and the indispensable snowshoes. The Eskimo were ingenious in devising such implements. They had shovels with edges of walrus ivory, walking sticks for going over the snow, snow goggles, snowshoes, and snow trowels and knives for housebuilding; also ice picks and crowbars and hooks and scoops for cutting and moving ice.

See *Arts and Industries*, and the subjects cited thereunder; also the articles describing special types of implements, tools, and utensils, and the materials from which they are made.　　　(O. T. M.)

Imtuk. A Yuit Eskimo village near Indian pt., N. E. Siberia; pop. 43 in 9 houses about 1895, 65 in 12 houses in 1901. Most of its people are of the Aiwan division, but 4 families are from Cherinak.

I'mtuk.—Bogoras, Chukchee, 29, 1904. I'mtun.—Ibid. (Chukchi name).

Imukfa (Hitchiti: 'shell,' also referring to a metallic ornament of concave shape; applied possibly in allusion to the bend in the river). A subordinate settlement of the Upper Creek town Oakfuski, on a creek of the same name, a short distance w. of Tallapoosa r., Ala. A battle was fought there Jan. 24, 1814, in the Creek war, and the celebrated battle of the Horseshoe Bend, on Mar. 25 of the same year, took place in the immediate vicinity.　　　(A. S. G.)

Emucfau.—Schoolcraft, Ind. Tribes, VI, 371, 1857. Emuckfau.—Pickett, Hist. Ala., II, 332–339, 1859. Emuckfaw.—Drake, Bk. Inds., bk. IV, 50, 1848. Emukfau.—Ibid., 59. Im-mook-fau.—Hawkins (1799), Sketch, 46, 1848.

Imuris. Given by early authorities as a Pima rancheria near the E. bank of Rio San Ignacio (or Magdalena), lat. 30° 50′, long. 110° 50′, in the present Sonora, Mexico. Orozco y Berra mentions the Himeris (who are evidently the inhabitants of this settlement), with the Opata. If they belonged to the latter, Imures was doubtless the last Opata settlement toward the N., and the earlier writers did not, in this case, distinguish the Opata from the Pima. Imuris was visited by Father Kino as early as 1699, and the bell in its church bears the date 1680. It was afterward a visita of San Ignacio mission (Rudo Ensayo, *ca.* 1762, 153, 1863), with 80 inhabitants in 1730. It is now a civilized pueblo. Of its 637 inhabitants in 1900, 74 were Mayo and 32 Yaqui.   (F. W. H.)

Himares.—Kino, map, in Stöcklein, Neue Welt-Bott, 74, 1726. **Himeris.**—Orozco y Berra, Geog., 58, 344, 1864. **Himuri.**—Rudo Ensayo (*ca.* 1762), 153, 1863. **Imoris.**—Box, Adventures, 277, 1869. **Imures.**—Kino (1696) in Doc. Hist. Mex., 4th s., I, 267, 1856. **Imurez.**—Hardy, Travels, 427, 1829. **Imuri.**—Kino (*ca.* 1699) in Doc. Hist. Mex., 4th s., I, 348, 1856. **Imuris.**—Font, map (1777) in Bancroft, Ariz. and N. Mex., 393, 1889. **Imuriz.**—Hardy, Travels, 432, 1829. **S. José Imuri.**—Rivera (1730) in Bancroft, No. Mex. States, I, 514, 1884. **Uburiqui.**—Kino (*ca.* 1699) in Doc. Hist. Mex., 4th s., I, 348, 1856. **Ymúrez.**—Bandelier, Gilded Man, 179, 1893.

Inajalaihu. A former Chumashan village near Santa Barbara, Cal.—Bancroft, Nat. Races, I, 459, 1874.

Inalik. An Inguklimiut village on Little Diomede id., Alaska. The name of the people was extended by Woolfe (11th Census, Alaska, 130, 1893) to include the inhabitants of both islands.—Nelson, 18th Rep. B. A. E., map, 1899.

Inam. The best known village of the upper division of the Karok, speaking the Karakuka dialect. Situated on Klamath r., at or near the mouth of Clear cr., N. W. Cal. It was the scene of the Deerskin dance and of an annual "world-making" ceremony.   (A. L. K.)

E-nam.—Taylor in Cal. Farmer, Mar. 23, 1860.

Inaqtek (*Inä′khtek*, 'raven'). A sub-phratry or gens of the Menominee.—Hoffman in 14th Rep. B. A. E., pt. I, 42, 1896.

Inaspetsum. One of the tribes included by the early fur traders under the term Nez Percé (Ross, Fur Hunters, I, 185, 1855). They lived on Columbia r., above the mouth of the Snake, in Washington. Perhaps they were the Winatshipum or the Kalispel.   (L. F.)

Incense. Incense, from the Latin *incendere*, 'to burn,' is defined as anything burned to produce a pleasant sweet smell during religious rites. It may be regarded as direct sacrifice, as symbolic of ascending prayer, or as an aid to spiritual exaltation. Incense has been in almost universal use from the earliest historic period, particularly in the more highly organized ancient religions. In Mexico and adjacent parts various resinous gums known collectively under the Aztec name of *copalli*, or copal, were used. North of the Rio Grande the plant substances most commonly employed for the same purpose

were tobacco, in various native varieties; the dried tops of *Thuja*, and other cedars; spruce and pine needles, particularly those of *Abies* and *Pinus ponderosa;* sweet grass (*Savastana odorata*), Artemisia, and the root of the balsam-root (*Balsamorrhiza*). Tobacco was used in one way or another in important ceremonials over almost the whole area of the United States and along the N. W. coast, and in the Canadian interior. Pine needles were most commonly used among the Pueblos and other tribes of the S. W. In the noted Hopi snake dance the smoke of burning juniper tops was blown through tubes known as "cloud-blowers" until the kiva was filled with the pleasing fragrance. Cedar tops, sweet grass, and wild sage were more common in ceremonies of the Plains Indians, especially the Peyote rite, and parcels of the dried substance were sometimes attached to sacrifice poles or deposited with the corpse in the grave or on the scaffold. With some tribes the twigs and leaves of the plant were differentiated as male and female. The balsam root was burned in small quantities in every great sweat-house rite among the Plains tribes and was held so precious that sometimes a horse was given for a single root. Among the Siksika, according to Wissler, every tipi contains an altar—a small excavation in the earth—where sweet gum is burned daily.

There were also a number of vegetal perfumes used for personal gratification, either by rubbing the juice of the crushed plant over the skin or by wearing the leaves or dried tops in little bags attached to the clothing. The Southern Ute mother placed sweet-smelling herbs under the pillow of her baby. One of the ingredients of the secret medicine employed by the Buffalo doctors among the Plains tribes in treating wounds is believed to have been the strong smelling musk of the beaver.   (J. M.)

Incha. An unidentified tribe said to have lived where there were Spanish settlements and to have been at war with the Mantons (Mento) of Arkansas r. in 1700.

Icca.—Iberville (1702) in Margry, Déc., IV, 561, 1880. **Incha.**—Ibid., 599.

Inchi (*In′tci*, 'stone lodge'). A village occupied by the Kansa in their migration up Kansas r.—J. O. Dorsey, inf'n, 1882.

Incomecanetook (*Income-can-étook*). Given by Ross (Advent., 290, 1847) as an Okinagan tribe.

Indak. A former Maidu village on the site of Placerville, Eldorado co., Cal.—Dixon in Bull. Am. Mus. Nat. Hist., XVII, pl. xxxviii, 1905.

Indelchidnti ('pine'). An Apache clan or band at San Carlos agency and Ft Apache, Ariz., in 1881 (Bourke in Jour. Am. Folk-lore, III, 111, 1890); identical with Indilche-dentiene, 'Live in country with large pine trees' (White, Apache Names of Indian Tribes, MS., B. A. E.), a band formerly under chief Narchubeulecolte.

Indian. The common designation of the aborigines of America. The name first occurs in a letter of Columbus dated Feb., 1493, wherein the discoverer speaks of the Indios he had with him (F. F. Hilder in Am. Anthrop., n. s., i, 545, 1899). It was the general belief of the day, shared by Columbus, that in his voyage across the Atlantic he had reached India. This term, in spite of its misleading connotation, has passed into the languages of the civilized world: *Indio* in Spanish, Portuguese, and Italian; *Indien* in French; *Indianer* in German, etc. The term American Indian, for which it has been proposed to substitute *Amerind* (q. v.), is however in common use; less so the objectionable term redskins, to which correspond the French *Peaux-rouges*, the German *Rothhäute*. Brinton titled his book on the aborigines of the New World, "The *American* Race," but this return to an early use of the word *American* can hardly be successful. In geographical nomenclature the Indian is well remembered. There are Indian Territory, Indiana, Indianapolis, Indianola, Indio. Besides these, the maps and gazetteers record Indian arm, bay, bayou, beach, bottom, branch, brook, camp, castle, cove, creek, crossing, diggings, draft, fall, field, fields, ford, gap, grove, gulch, harbor, head, hill, hills, island, lake, mills, mound, mountain, neck, orchard, pass, point, pond, ridge, river, rock, run, spring, springs, swamp, town, trace, trail, valley, village, and wells, in various parts of the United States and Canada. The term Red Indian, applied to the Beothuk, has given Newfoundland a number of place names.

Many wild plants have been called "Indian" in order to mark them off from familiar sorts. Use by Indians has been the origin of another class of such terms. The following plants have been called after the Indian:

Indian apple.—The May apple, or wild mandrake (*Podophyllum peltatum*).

Indian arrow.—The burning bush, or wahoo (*Euonymus atropurpureus*).

Indian arrow-wood.—The flowering dogwood, or cornelian tree (*Cornus florida*).

Indian balm.—The erect trillium, or ill-scented wake-robin (*Trillium erectum*).

Indian bark.—The laurel magnolia, or sweet bay (*Magnolia virginiana*).

Indian bean.—(1) The catalpa, or bean-tree (*Catalpa catalpa*). (2) A New Jersey name of the groundnut (*Apios apios*).

Indian beard-grass.—The bushy beard-grass (*Andropogon glomeratus*).

Indian bitters.—A North Carolina name of the Fraser umbrella or cucumber tree (*Magnolia fraseri*).

Indian black drink.—The cassena, yaupon, black drink (q. v.), or Carolina tea (*Ilex cassine*).

Indian boys and girls.—A western name of the Dutchman's breeches (*Bikukulla cucullaria*).

Indian bread.—The tuckahoe (*Sclerotium giganteum*).

Indian bread-root.—The prairie turnip, or pomme blanche (*Psoralea esculenta*).

Indian cedar.—The hop-hornbeam, or ironwood (*Ostrya virginiana*).

Indian cherry.—(1) The service-berry, or june-berry (*Amelanchier canadensis*). (2) The Carolina buckthorn (*Rhamnus caroliniana*).

Indian chickweed.—The carpet-weed (*Mollugo verticillata*).

Indian chief.—A western name of the American cowslip or shooting-star (*Dodecatheon meadia*).

Indian cigar tree.—The common catalpa (*Catalpa catalpa*), a name in use in Pennsylvania, Maryland, and the District of Columbia. See *Indian bean*, above.

Indian corn.—Maize (*Zea mays*), for which an early name was Indian wheat.

Indian cucumber.—*Medeola virginiana*, also known as Indian cucumber-root.

Indian cup.—(1) The common pitcher-plant (*Sarracenia purpurea*). (2) The cup-plant (*Silphium perfoliatum*).

Indian currant.—The coral-berry (*Symphoricarpos vulgaris*).

Indian dye.—The yellow puccoon or orange-root (*Hydrastis canadensis*); also known as yellow-root.

Indian elm.—The slippery-elm (*Ulmus fulva*).

Indian fig.—(1) The eastern prickly pear (*Opuntia opuntia*). (2) *Cereus giganteus*, or saguaro, the giant cereus of Arizona, California, Mexico, and New Mexico.

Indian fog.—The crooked yellow stonecrop or dwarf houseleek (*Sedum reflexum*).

Indian gravel-root.—The tall boneset or joe-pye-weed (*Eupatorium purpureum*).

Indian hemp.—(1) The army-root (*Apocynum cannabinum*), called also black Indian hemp. (2) The swamp milkweed (*Asclepias incarnata*) and the hairy milkweed (*A. pulchra*), called also white Indian hemp. (3) A West Virginia name for the yellow toad-flax (*Linaria linaria*). (4) The velvet-leaf (*Abutilon abutilon*), called also Indian mallow.

Indian hippo.—The bowman's-root (*Porteranthus trifoliatus*), called also Indian physic.

Indian lemonade.—A California name, according to Bergen, for the fragrant sumac (*Rhus trilobata*).

Indian lettuce.—The round-leaved wintergreen (*Pyrola rotundifolia*).

Indian mallow.—(1) The velvet-leaf (*Abutilon abutilon*), also known as Indian hemp. (2) The prickly sida (*Sida spinosa*).

Indian melon.—A Colorado name of a species of *Echinocactus*.

Indian millet.—The silky oryzopsis (*Oryzopsis cuspidata*).

Indian moccasin.—The stemless lady's-slipper or moccasin-flower (*Cypripedium acaule*).

Indian mozemize, or moose misse.—The American mountain-ash or dogberry (*Sorbus americana*).

Indian paint.—(1) The strawberry-blite (*Blitum capitatum*). (2) The hoary puccoon (*Lithospermum canescens*). (3) A Wisconsin name, according to Bergen, for a species of *Tradescantia*. (4) Bloodroot (*Sanguinaria canadensis*), called red Indian paint. (5) The yellow puccoon (*Hydrastis canadensis*), called yellow Indian paint.

Indian paint-brush.—The scarlet-painted cup (*Castilleja coccinea*).

Indian peach.—Ungrafted peach trees, according to Bartlett, which are considered to be more thrifty and said to bear larger fruit. In the South a specific variety of clingstone peach.

Indian pear.—The service-berry (*Amelanchier canadensis*), called also wild Indian pear.

Indian physic.—(1) The bowman's-root (*Porteranthus trifoliatus*), called also Indian hippo. (2) American ipecac (*Porteranthus stipulatus*). (3) Fraser's magnolia, the long-leaved umbrella-tree (*Magnolia fraseri*).

Indian pine.—The loblolly, or old-field pine (*Pinus taeda*).

Indian pink.—(1) The Carolina pink, or worm-grass (*Spigelia marylandica*). (2) The cypress-vine (*Quamoclit quamoclit*). (3) The fire pink (*Silene virginica*). (4) The cuckoo-flower, or ragged-robin (*Lychnis flos-cuculi*). (5) The fringed milkwort, or polygala (*Polygala paucifolia*). (6) The scarlet-painted cup (*Castilleja coccinea*). (7) The wild pink (*Silene pennsylvanica*). (8) *Silene californica*.

Indian pipe.—The corpse-plant or ghost-flower (*Monotropa uniflora*).

Indian pitcher.—The pitcher-plant or side-saddle flower (*Sarracenia purpurea*).

Indian plantain.—(1) The great Indian plantain or wild collard (*Mesadenia reniformis*). (2) The pale Indian plantain (*M. atriplicifolia*). (3) The tuberous Indian plantain (*M. tuberosa*). (4) The sweet-scented Indian plantain (*Synosma suaveolens*).

Indian poke.—(1) American white hellebore (*Veratrum viride*). (2) False hellebore (*V. woodii*).

Indian posey.—(1) Sweet life-everlasting (*Gnaphalium obtusifolium*). (2) Large-flowered everlasting (*Anaphalis margaritacea*). (3) The butterfly-weed (*Asclepias tuberosa*).

Indian potato.—(1) The groundnut (*Apios apios*). (2) A western name for the squirrel-corn (*Bikukulla canadensis*). (3) A California name, according to Bergen, for *Brodiaea capitata;* but according to Barrett (inf'n, 1906) the term is indiscriminately given to many different species of bulbs and corms, which formed a considerable item in the food supply of the Californian Indians.

Indian puccoon.—The hoary puccoon (*Lithospermum canescens*).

Indian red-root.—The red-root (*Gyrotheca capitata*).

Indian rhubarb.—A California name, according to Bergen, for *Saxifraga peltata*.

Indian rice.—Wild rice (*Zizania aquatica*).

Indian root.—The American spikenard (*Aralia racemosa*).

Indian sage.—The common thoroughwort or boneset (*Eupatorium perfoliatum*).

Indian shamrock.—The ill-scented wake-robin, or erect trillium (*Trillium erectum*).

Indian shoe.—The large yellow lady's-slipper (*Cypripedium hirsutum*).

Indian slipper.—The pink lady's-slipper, or moccasin-flower (*Cypripedium acaule*).

Indian soap-plant.—The soap-berry, or wild China-tree (*Sapindus marginatus*).

Indian strawberry.—The strawberry-blite (*Blitum capitatum*).

Indian tea.—Plants, the leaves, etc., of which have been infused by the Indians, and after them by whites; also the decoction made therefrom, for example, Labrador tea (*Ledum grœlandicum*), which in Labrador is called Indian tea.

Indian tobacco.—(1) The wild tobacco (*Lobelia inflata*). (2) Wild tobacco (*Nicotiana rustica*). (3) The plantain-leaf everlasting (*Antennaria plantaginifolia*). (4) A New Jersey name, according to Bartlett, of the common mullein (*Verbascum thapsus*).

Indian turmeric.—The yellow puccoon, or orange-root (*Hydrastis canadensis*).

Indian turnip.—(1) The jack-in-the-pulpit (*Arisaema triphyllum*), also called three-leaved Indian turnip. (2) The prairie potato, or pomme blanche (*Psoralea esculenta*).

Indian vervain.—A Newfoundland name, according to Bergen, for the shining club-moss (*Lycopodium lucidulum*).

Indian warrior.—A California name for *Pedicularis densiflora*.

Indian weed.—An early term for tobacco.

Indian wheat.—An early term for maize, or Indian corn.

Indian whort.—A Labrador and Newfoundland name for the red bearberry or kinnikinnik (*Arctostaphylos uva-ursi*).

Indian wickup.—The great willow-herb or fireweed (*Epilobium augustifolium*), although Algonquian Indians called the basswood (*Tilia americana*) wickup.

There are, besides, the *Indian's dream*, the purple-stemmed cliff-brake (*Pellaea atropurpurea*), and the *Indian's plume*, Oswego tea (*Monarda didyma*).

Another series of terms in which the Indian is remembered is the following:

Indian bed.—A simple method of roasting clams, by placing them, hinges uppermost, on the ground, and building over them a fire of brushwood.

Indian bread.—Bread made of maize meal or of maize and rye meal.

Indian-corn hills.—(1) In Essex co., Mass., according to Bartlett, hummocky land resembling hills of Indian corn. (2) Hillocks covering broad fields near the ancient mounds and earthworks of Ohio, Wisconsin, etc. (Lapham, Antiquities of Wisconsin).

Indian dab.—A Pennsylvania name for a sort of battercake.

Indian file.—Single file; the order in which Indians march.

Indian fort.—A name given to aboriginal earthworks in w. New York, in Ohio, and elsewhere.

Indian gift.—Something reclaimed after having been given, in reference to the alleged custom among Indians of expecting an equivalent for a gift or otherwise its return.

Indian giver.—A repentant giver.

Indian ladder.—A ladder made by trimming a small tree, the part of the branches near the stem being left as steps.

Indian liquor.—A Western term for whisky or rum adulterated for sale to the Indians.

Indian meal.—Maize or corn meal. A mixture of wheat and maize flour was called in earlier days "wheat and indian"; one of maize and rye flour, "rye and indian."

Indian orchard.—According to Bartlett, a term used in New York and Massachusetts to designate an old orchard of ungrafted apple trees, the time of planting being unknown.

Indian pipestone.—A name for catlinite (q. v.), the stone of which tribes in the region of the upper Mississippi made their tobacco pipes.

Indian pudding.—A pudding made of cornmeal, molasses, etc.

Indian reservation or *reserve*.—A tract of land reserved by Government for the Indians.

Indian sign.—A Western colloquialism of the earlier settlement days for a trace of the recent presence of Indians.

Indian sugar.—One of the earlier names for maple sugar.

Indian summer.—The short season of pleasant weather usually occurring about the middle of November, corresponding to the European St Marthas summer, or summer of All Saints (Albert Matthews in Monthly Weather Rev., Jan., 1902).

The name Indian appears sometimes in children's games (Chamberlain in Jour. Am. Folk-lore, xv, 107–116, 1902). In Canadian French the usual term applied to the Indian was "sauvage" (savage); and hence are met such terms as "botte sauvage," "traîne sauvage," "tabagane," "thé sauvage." The "Siwash" of the Pacific coast and in the Chinook jargon is only a corruption of the "sauvage" of French-Canadian trappers and adventurers.   (A. F. C.)

Indian Affairs. See *Office of Indian Affairs*.

Indian Commissioners. See *United States Board of Indian Commissioners*.

"Indian Helper." See *Carlisle School*.

Indian Industries League. A philanthropic organization, originally the Indian industries department of the National Indian Association, but incorporated as an independent body at Boston, Mass., in 1901. Its object is "to open individual opportunities of work, or of education to be used for self-support, to individual Indians, and to build up self-supporting industries in Indian communities." As a department of the national organization the Indian industries gained its first important impetus in 1892, when it held at the Mechanics' Fair, in Boston, an exhibition of Indian beadwork and of class-room work in iron, tin, wood, leather, and lace. It has been instrumental in the education of two Indian girls, who were graduated with credit from the Boston High School, and has helped individual educated Indians toward self-support, having in view the fact that the progress of the Indians toward civilization is in proportion to the number of their young people who have seen and practised the white man's life at its best. It has also helped to foster a beadwork industry; aided in developing the native moccasin to suit the white man; bought baskets of native manufacture, paying therefor a fair price to the Pima and Mission Indians, the basket-making tribes of Washington, and others, and has obtained for these products places for exhibit and sale. The league also erected an industrial room for the Navaho on San Juan r., N Mex., which was disposed of when the plant became a mission station. In 1905 the president of the league officially visited the Mission Indians of California and others, his report on the former resulting in the amelioration of their extreme poverty by bringing to them governmental and private aid. The league strives to aid the Indians in any way that offers even temporary self-support, like that derived from their aboriginal industries. It believes in the assimilation of the Indians into the national life, in the abolishment of reservations, and in the freedom of the Indians to live and work where they please.   (F. C. S.)

Indian Point. A village on the site of Lisbon, N. Y., occupied after the Revolution by Catholic Iroquois removed thither by the English Government until they were dispersed in 1806, when they retired to Onondaga and St Regis.—Shea, Cath. Miss., 342, 1855.

Indian Rights Association. A nonpolitical, nonsectarian body organized in Philadelphia, Dec. 15, 1882, by gentlemen who met in response to an invitation of Mr John Welsh to consider the best method of producing such public feeling and Congressional action as should secure civil rights and education to the Indians, and in time bring about their civilization and admission to citizenship. When the association began its work much of the country over which the Indians roamed was sparsely settled; outbreaks had been frequent; comparatively little attention was paid to the Indians' rights and wrongs, and ignorance concerning Indian affairs was widespread. When the tide of emigration swept westward, and settlers, good and bad, began crowding the Indians more and more, it was evident that measures should be adopted whereby the Indian could be adapted to his new artificial environment. The work confronting the association was one of magnitude. It was necessary to procure accurate knowledge of actual conditions, which could be done only by frequent visits to the Indian country. The information thus obtained had to be brought to the attention of the public in order that sufficient pressure might be exerted on Congress and the Executive. This was done by dissemination of information in pamphlets and leaflets, by public addresses, and by announcements through the public press. The association gradually won the respect and confidence of the public. The accuracy of its statements is rarely questioned now, and an appeal to the press on any matter requiring attention from Congress or the public usually meets with ready response. In the beginning the association was regarded by a few as maintaining visionary theories, and was viewed by some Government officials as a meddlesome and irresponsible body; but the Office of Indian Affairs came to regard it as a friendly critic and welcomed its aid. The association has a representative in Washington to cooperate with the Office of Indian Affairs, to bring to the attention of the Commissioner matters requiring adjustment, to scrutinize legislation relating to Indian affairs, and to inform members of Congress regarding the merits or demerits of pending bills. Vicious legislation, when it can not be defeated in committee, is vigorously fought in Congress through personal presentation and by letters and pamphlets, with frequent appeals to the Executive.

Many of the laws enacted by Congress with a view of improving the condition of the Indian have been prompted by the association. Among those of a general nature is the statute of Feb. 8, 1887, known as the "general severalty act," which authorizes allotments. Under this law the title to Indian lands is held by the Government in most cases for 25 years, but in the meantime the allottee is subject to the laws in common with other citizens. More recent is the enactment of a statute, drafted by the association, designed to defeat the monopoly that has so largely controlled Indian trade, the law now providing that any person of good moral character shall be granted a license on application.

The courts have frequently been appealed to by the association in the endeavor to secure justice. The Warner Ranch (Mission Indian) case, appealed from the local courts of California to the Supreme Court of the United States, was in its inception espoused by the association and prosecuted by it to the final decree of the highest tribunal, the necessary funds for the prosecution of the case being advanced by the association. The celebrated "Lone Wolf" case was appealed by the association to the United States Supreme Court in the hope that the policy of recognizing the validity and sacredness of the Government's treaty obligations with the Indian tribes, followed since the adoption of the Constitution, would be upheld. The adverse decision in this case marked the beginning of a new era in the management of the Indians. The appeal made to the association by friends of Spotted Hawk and Little Whirlwind, of the Northern Cheyenne in Montana, under sentence of death and life imprisonment, respectively, for the alleged murder of a sheep herder, was responded to by the association, which employed counsel to present the case on appeal to the supreme court of Montana. The effort resulted in securing the liberty of both young men, and a subsequent confession by the person guilty of the crime charged to them fully exonerated them and showed the need of watchfulness to prevent great wrongs against Indians by reason of local prejudice. The exposure by the association of the anomalous conditions in Indian Territory resulted in directing the attention of the people and of Congress to the need of better safeguarding the rights of the Five Civilized Tribes.

Considerable attention has been given by the association to exposing the wrongdoing of Government officials where such unfortunately existed, usually by the class of employees who obtained their positions through political influence. The association has also strenuously urged that the appointment of Indian agents be made solely on the ground of efficiency, and it was through its efforts that the civil-service rules were extended to the Indian service.

At the time of the organization of the Indian Rights Association, Congress, owing largely to misunderstanding of the Indians' needs, failed to make adequate appropriations for schools, but by informing the public of the nature and possibilities of this work, a vigorous sentiment was created in its favor (see *Education*). The fact that an organization exists solely to guard the rights of the Indians acts as a powerful deterrent to persons seeking the exploitation of the Indians' estate.

The association has printed and distributed about 600,000 copies of various publications. Among those that have attracted much attention are: The Indian Before the Law, by Henry S. Pancoast; The Indian Question Past and Present, by Herbert Welsh; Indian Wardship, by Charles E. Pancoast; Civilization Among the Sioux, by Herbert Welsh; The Mission Indians, by C. C. Painter; Latest Studies on Indian Reservations, by J. B. Harrison; and A New Indian Policy, by S. M. Brosius.　　　　(M. K. S.　S. M. B.)

Indian River. A summer camp of the Sitka Indians of Alaska, containing 43 persons in 1880.—Petroff in Tenth Census, Alaska, 32, 1884.

"Indian's Friend." See *National Indian Association.*

Indian Village. A former Micmac village near L. Badger, Fogo co., Newfoundland.—Vetromile, Abnakis, 56, 1866.

Industries. See *Arts and Industries*, and the various industries thereunder mentioned.

I n e w a k h u b e a d h i n (*In'ĕ-waqube-aɸin*, 'keepers of the mysterious stones'). A subgens of the Mandhinkagaghe gens of the Omaha.—Dorsey in 15th Rep. B. A. E., 228, 1897.

Ingahame. An Ikogmiut Eskimo village on lower Yukon r., Alaska; pop. 63 in 1880, 50 in 1890.
Ingahamé.—Petroff in 10th Census, Alaska, 12, 1884. Ingahameh.—Ibid, map. Ingahamiut.—11th Census, Alaska, 165, 1893.

Ingalik ('having louse's eggs'). An Eskimo term for Indian, applied first to the Kaiyukhotana of Yukon r., and extended by the Russians to all Kaiyukhotana, sometimes to Athapascan tribes in general. Pop. 635 in 1890: 312 males and 323 females. The villages are Anvik, Chagvagchat, Chinik, Kagokakat, Kaiakak, Kaltag, Khatnotoutze, Khogoltlinde, Khulikakat, Klamasqualtin, Koserefski, Kunkhogliak, Kutul, Lofka, Nunakhtagamut, Tanakot, Tutago, Taguta, and Wolasatux.
Ingaleek.—Elliott, Cond. Aff. Alaska, 29, 1874. Ingaleet.—Dall in Cont. N. A. Ethnol., I, 26, 1877. Ingalete.—Whymper, Alaska, 153, 1868. Ing'-aliki.—Dall, op. cit., 25 (Russian form). Ingalit.—Petroff in 10th Census, Alaska, 5, 1884. Ingekasagmi.—Raymond in Sen. Ex. Doc. 12, 42d Cong., 1st sess., 25, 1871. Ingeletes.—Ibid., 31. In'-kalik.—Dall, op. cit., 25. Inkalite.—Latham in Jour. Ethnol. Soc. Lond., I, 183, 1848. Inkaliten.—Glasunoff in Baer and Helmersen, Beiträge, I, 120, 1839. Inkilik.—Schott in Erman, Archiv, VII, 480, 1849. Inkiliken.—Holmberg, Ethnog. Skizz., 7, 1855.

Ingamatsha. A Chugachigmiut village on Chenega id., Prince William sd., Alaska; pop. 80 in 1880, 73 in 1890, 140 in 1900.
Chenega.—Petroff in 10th Census, Alaska, 29, 1884. Ingamatsha.—Eleventh Census, Alaska, 67, 1893.

Ingdhezhide ('red dung'). An Omaha gens on the Inshtasanda side of the tribal circle.
Iñgɸe-jide.—Dorsey in 3d Rep. B. A. E., 219, 1885. Iñgdhe-zhide.—Dorsey in Bull. Philos. Soc. Wash., 130, 1880. Ing-gera-je-da.—Long, Exped. Rocky Mts., I, 327, 1823. In-grä'-zhe-da.—Morgan, Anc. Soc., 155, 1877 (trans. 'red').

Inger. A Nunivagmiut Eskimo village on Nunivak id., Alaska; pop. 35 in 1890.
Ingeramut.—Nelson in 18th Rep. B. A. E., map, 1899.

Ingichuk. A Chnagmiut village in the delta of the Yukon, Alaska; pop. 8 in 1880.
Ingechuk.—Elliott, Our Arct. Prov., map, 1886. Ingichuk.—Nelson (1878) quoted by Baker, Geog. Dict. Alaska, 1902.

Ingkdhunkashinka ('small cat'). A subgens of the Wasapetun gens of the Hangka division of the Osage.
Iñxɸuñ'ka oiñ'xa.—Dorsey in 15th Rep. B. A. E., 234, 1897.

Inglutaligemiut (*Inglŭtāl'igemŭt*). A subdivision of Malemiut Eskimo dwelling on Inglutalik r., Alaska.—Dall in Cont. N. A. Ethnol., I, 16, 1877.

Ingmikertok. An East Greenland Eskimo village on a small island in Angmagsalik fjord.—Meddelelser om Grönland, IX, 379, 1889.

Ingrakak. An Ikogmiut Eskimo village on lower Yukon r., Alaska.
Ingrakaghamiut.—Coast Surv. officers, 1898. Ingrakak.—Baker, Geog. Dict. Alaska, 1902.

Inguklimiut. An Eskimo tribe occupying Little Diomede id., Bering strait. Their village is Inalik. See *Okiogmiut*.
Achjuch-Aliat.—Dall in Smithson. Cont., XXII, 2, 1878 (Chukchi name). Inalugmiut.—Woolfe in 11th Census, Alaska, 130, 1893 (given to inhabitants of both islands). Ing-ŭh-kli-mūt.—Dall in Trans. A. A. S., XXXIV, 377, 1885. Inugleet.—Jackson in Rep. Bur. Education, 145, map, 1894. Yikirga'ulit.—Bogoras, Chukchee, 21, 1904 (Chukchi name: 'large-mouthed,' referring to their labrets).

Iniahico. A principal Apalachee village in 1539, near the site of Tallahassee, Fla.

Anaica Apalache.—Gentleman of Elvas in Hakluyt Soc. Pub., IX, 43, 1851. **Anhayca.**—Gallatin in Trans. Am. Antiq. Soc., II, 102, 1836. **Aniaca Apalache.**—Shipp, De Soto and Florida, 684, 1881 (misprint). **Iniahico.**—Biedma (1544) in Ternaux-Compans, Voy., XX, 57, 1841.

Inigsalik. A southern settlement of the Angmagsalingmiut Eskimo of E. Greenland, where they find soft stone of which they fashion pots and lamps.—Meddelelser om Grönland, X, 368, 1888.

Inigsuarsak. An Eskimo village in lat. 72° 45′, w. Greenland.—Science, XI, map, 259, 1888.

Inisiguanin. Mentioned as one of the towns or provinces apparently on or in the vicinity of the South Carolina coast, visited by Ayllon in 1520.
Inisiguanin.—Oviedo, Hist. Gen. Indias, III, 628, 1853. **Yncignavin.**—Barcia, Ensayo, 5, 1723.

Initkilly. A Tikeramiut Eskimo village near the coal veins E. of C. Lisburne, Alaska.—Coast Surv. map, 1890.

Inkalich. The Eskimo name of a division of the Kaiyuhkhotana on Innoko r., Alaska. Paltchikatno and Tigshelde were probably two of the villages.
Inchulukhlaites.—Latham, Essays, 271, 1860. **Inkālichljüaten.**—Holmberg quoted by Dall in Cont. N. A. Ethnol., I, 25, 1877. **Inkülüchlüaten.**—Wrangell quoted by Baer and Helmersen, Beiträge, I, 118, 1839. **Inkulukhlaites.**—Latham, op. cit., 267. **Inkuluklaities.**—Ibid., 272.

Inkesabe ('black shoulder'). An Omaha gens of the Hangashenu division, the custodian of the tribal pipes. The subgentes are Iekidhe, Nonhdeitazhi, Wadhigizhe, and Watanzizhidedhatazhi.
Black.—Morgan, Anc. Soc., 155, 1877. **Enk-ka-saba.**—Long, Exped. Rocky Mts., I, 326, 1823. **Inkka'-sa-ba.**—Morgan, Anc. Soc., 155, 1877. **Iñkesabĕ.**—Dorsey in 3d Rep. B. A. E., 219, 1885.

Inkillis Tamaha ('English town'). One of the former so-called Choctaw Sixtowns in the N. W. part of Jasper co., Miss. It gave its name to a considerable tract in that part of the county and extending into Newton co. It is said to have received this name from the fact that the English made a distribution of property there in early times.—Halbert in Ala. Hist. Soc., Misc. Coll., I, 382, 1901.
Killis-tamaha.—Gatschet, Creek Migr. Leg., I, 109, 1884.

Inkpa. A band of the Wahpeton Sioux, living in 1886 at Big Stone lake, Minn., and probably at Cormorant pt., Mille Lacs, in 1862.
Big Stone Lake band.—Ind. Aff. Rep., 102, 1859. **Inkpatonwan.**—Ashley, letter to Dorsey, Jan. 1886. **Inpaton.**—Ibid.

Innoka. A Kaiyuhkhotana village on Tlegon r., Alaska.—Petroff, Rep. on Alaska, 37, 1884.

Inojey. A former Chumashan village near Santa Barbara, Cal.—Taylor in Cal. Farmer, Apr. 24, 1863.

Inomassi. A former Diegueño rancheria belonging to San Miguel de la Frontera mission, w. coast of Lower California, about lat. 32° 10′.—Taylor in Cal. Farmer, May 18, 1860.

Inoschuochn ('bear berry'). An Apache clan or band at San Carlos agency and Ft Apache, Ariz., in 1881.
Inoschujóchen.—Bourke in Jour. Am. Folk-lore, III, 112, 1890.

Inotuks. Given as a Karok village on Klamath r., Cal.; inhabited in 1860.
E-no-tucks.—Taylor in Cal. Farmer, Mar. 23, 1860.

Insanity. See *Health and Disease.*

Inscribed tablets. Objects, generally of soft stone, usually shale or sandstone, containing various lines and formal characters incised or in relief. Some of them are undoubtedly prehistoric and susceptible of interpretation in the light of aboriginal ornamentation and symbolism; others are forgeries. While it would perhaps be too much to say that there exists N. of Mexico no tablet or other ancient article that contains other than a pictorial or pictographic record, it is safe to assert that no authentic specimen has yet been brought to public notice. Any object claimed to be of pre-Columbian age and showing hieroglyphic or other characters that denote a degree of culture higher than that of the known tribes, is to be viewed with suspicion and all the circumstances connected with its discovery subjected to rigid scrutiny. The same remarks apply to engraved copper plates. In the latter material, the uneven surface produced by natural corrosion is often mistaken for attempts at inscriptions. See *Grave Creek mound, Pictography.*

GRAVE CREEK TABLET; LENGTH 1 3-4 IN.

Consult Farquharson in Proc. Davenport Acad. Sci., II, 1877–80; Fowke, Archæol. Hist. Ohio, 1902; McLean, Mound Builders, 1879; Mallory in 10th Rep. B. A. E., 1893; Mercer, The Lenape Stone, 1885; Moorehead, Prehist. Impls., 1900; Schoolcraft, Ind. Tribes, I–IV, 1851-57; Squier and Davis, Ancient Monuments, 1848; Thomas in 12th Rep. B. A. E., 632, 1894. (G. F.)

Inscription Rock. See *El Morro.*

Inselnostlinde. A Kaiyuhkhotana village of the Jugelnute division on Shageluk r., Alaska.—Zagoskin, Descr. Russ. Poss. Am., map, 1842.

Inshtasanda (*inshta*, 'eye' or 'eyes'; *sanda*, an archaic and untranslatable term.—Fletcher). One of the 2 divisions of the Omaha, containing the Mandhinkagaghe, Tesinde, Tapa, Ingdhezhide, and Inshtasanda gentes.
Grey Eyes.—Jackson (1877) quoted by Donaldson in Smithson. Rep. 1885, pt. 2, 74, 1886. **Ictasanda.**—Dorsey in 3d Rep. B. A. E., 219, 1885. **Inshtasanda.**—A. C. Fletcher, Inf'n, 1906. **Ish-ta-sun'-da.**—Long, Exped. Rocky Mts., I, 325, 1823. **Istasunda.**—Jackson (1877), op. cit., 74.

Inshtasanda. An Omaha gens, belonging to the Inshtasanda division. The subdivisions are Ninibatan, Real Inshtasanda, Washetan, and Real Thunder people.
Ictasanda.—Dorsey in 3d Rep. B. A. E., 220, 1885. **Inshtasanda.**—A. C. Fletcher, inf'n, 1906. **Ish-**

dä′-sun-da.—Morgan, Anc. Soc., 155, 1877 (trans. 'thunder'). **Thunder.**—Ibid. **Wash-a-tung.**—Long, Exped. Rocky Mts., I, 327, 1823 (mistaking a Hangashenu gens for the Inshtasanda division).

Insiachak. A Nushagagmiut Eskimo village in the Nushagak district, Alaska; pop. 42 in 1890.
Insiachamiut.—Eleventh Census, Alaska, 164, 1893.

Intanto. A former Nishinam village in the valley of Bear r., Cal.—Powers in Cont. N. A. Ethnol., III, 316, 1877.

Intapupshe (*I^{n}tahpupcĕ′*, 'curved stone'). An ancient Osage village on upper Osage r., above the mouth of Sac r., Mo.—Dorsey, Osage MS. vocab., B. A. E., 1883.

Intatchkalgi ('people of the beaver dams.'—Gatschet). A former Yuchi town on Opihlako cr., 28 m. above its junction with Flint r., probably in Dooly co., Ga. It contained 14 families in 1799.
Intatchkálgi.—Gatschet, Creek Migr. Leg., I, 132, 1884. In-tuch-cul-gau.—Hawkins (1799), Sketch, 62, 1848.

Intenleiden. A Kaiyuhkhotana village of the Jugelnute division on the E. bank of Shageluk r., Alaska.
Iltenleiden.—Zagoskin quoted by Petroff in 10th Census, Alaska, 37, 1884. Imtelleïden.—Zagoskin in Nouv. Ann. Voy., 5th s., XXI, map, 1850. Intenleiden.—Zagoskin, Descr. Russ. Poss. Am., map, 1842.

Interpreters. See *Agency system*.

Intietook (*Inti-etook*). Given by Ross (Advent., 290, 1847) as an Okinagan tribe.

Intimbich. A Mono band in Mill Creek valley, some miles s. of its junction with Kings r., Cal.
Em-tim′-bitch.—Merriam in Science, XIX, 916, June 15, 1904. Entimbich.—A. L. Kroeber, Inf'n, 1906 (correct form). Eu-tem-pe-che's.—Wessells (1853) in H. R. Ex. Doc. 76, 34th Cong., 3d sess., 32, 1857. In-tem-peach-es.—Johnston (1851) in Sen. Ex. Doc. 61, 32d Cong., 1st sess., 22, 1852. Intim-peach.—Royce in 18th Rep. B. A. E., 782, 1899. In-tim-peches.—Barbour (1852) in Sen. Ex. Doc. 4, 32d Cong., spec. sess., 254, 1853. Ytimpabiches.—Dominguez and Escalante (1776) in Doc. Hist. Mex., 2d s., I, 537, 1854.

Inuarudligang. A race of dwarfs who figure in the mythology of the Central Eskimo. They are supposed to inhabit cliffs that overhang the sea.—Boas in 6th Rep. B. A. E., 640, 1888.

Inugsiut. An Eskimo settlement in E. Greenland, about lat. 61° 50′; pop. 32 in 1884.—Das Ausland, 163, 1886.

Inugsulik. A summer settlement of the Aivilirmiut Eskimo on the N. coast of Repulse bay, N. of Hudson bay.
Enook-sha-lig.—Ross, Second Voy., 430, 1835. Inugsulik.—Boas in 6th Rep. B. A. E., map, 1888.

Inuhksoyistamiks (*In-uhk′ oo yi stam iks*, 'long tail lodge poles'). A band of the Kainah division of the Siksika.—Grinnell, Blackfoot Lodge Tales, 209, 1892.

Inuissuitmiut. An Eskimo tribe that occupied Depot id. and the adjacent coast of Hudson bay before 1800. The last descendant died some years ago.—Boas in Bull. Am. Mus. Nat. Hist., xv, 6, 1901.

Inuksikahkopwaiks (*I-nuk-si′-kah-ko-pwa-iks*, 'small brittle fat'). A division of the Piegan Siksika.—Grinnell, Blackfoot Lodge Tales, 209, 225, 1892.

Inuksiks ('small robes'). A former division of the Piegan Siksika.
A-miks′-eks.—Hayden, Ethnog. and Philol. Mo. Val., 264, 1862. I-nuks′-iks.—Grinnell, Blackfoot Lodge Tales, 209, 1892. **Little Robes.**—Culbertson in Smithson. Rep. 1850, 144, 1851. **Small Robes.**—Grinnell, op. cit., 225.

Invention. In the language of the Patent Office "an invention is something new and useful." The word applies to the apparatus of human activities and to the processes involved. The life of culture from the lowest savagery to the highest civilization is an increase in the artificialities of life. There were no tribes in America without culture, and the lowest of them had inventions. For instance, the Fuegians had learned to convert the fish-spear into a barbed harpoon by fastening the detachable head, which was set loosely in the socket, to the end of a shaft by means of a short piece of rawhide. They had also invented a canoe of bark made in three pieces. When they wished to move to a new bay or inlet between which and the last there was a dangerous headland, they could take the canoe apart, carry it over the intervening mountain, and unite the parts by lashing, covering the joints with pitch. The most ingenious savages on the continent, however, were the Eskimo, all of whose apparatus used in their various activities show innumerable additions and changes, which are inventions. They lived surrounded by the largest animals in the world, which they were able to capture by their ingenuity. Their snow domes, waterproof clothing, skin canoes, sinew-backed bows, snowshoes, traps and snares in myriad varieties, some of which they shared with neighboring Indian tribes, amaze those who study them. Among other ingenious devices which would pass under the name of inventions are: the use of skids by the N. W. coast natives for rolling logs into place in building their immense communal dwellings; the employment of the parbuckle to assist in the work of moving logs; the use of a separate fly of rawhide at the top of the tipi, which could be moved by means of a pole with one end resting on the ground, so that the wind would not drive the smoke back into the tipi; driving a peg of known length into the side of a canoe as a gauge for the adzman in chipping out the inside; the boiling of food in baskets or utensils of wood, gourd, or rawhide, by means of hot stones; the attachment of inflated sealskins to the end of a harpoon line to impede the progress of game through the water after it was struck; the sinew-backed bow, which enabled the Eskimo hunter to employ brittle wood for the rigid portion and sinew string for propulsion; the continuous motion spindle; the reciprocating drill; the sand saw for hard stone, and all sorts of signaling and sign language. See *Arts and Indus-*

tries and *Implements*, and the separate articles cited thereunder.

Consult Mason (1) Aboriginal American Mechanics, Mem. Internat. Cong. Anthrop., Chicago, 1894; (2) Origins of Invention, 1895; McGuire, A Study of the Primitive Methods of Drilling, Rep. U. S. Nat. Mus. 1894, 1896; Holmes, Development of the Shaping Arts, Smithson. Rep. 1902. See also the various Reports of the Bureau of American Ethnology. (O. T. M.)

Inyaha. A Diegueño village in w. San Diego co., Cal. Its inhabitants, who numbered 53 in 1883, 32 in 1891, and 42 in 1902, occupy a reservation comprising 280 acres of poor land, which has been patented to them.
Anaha.—Jackson and Kinney, Rep. Miss. Ind., 24, 1883. Anahuac.—Ind. Aff. Rep., 175, 1902. Ineja.—Ibid., II, 72, 1891. Injaya.—Ibid., 146, 1903. Inyaha.—Ibid., 175, 1902.

Inyancheyaka-atonwan ('village at the dam or rapids'). A Wahpeton Sioux band or division residing in 1859 at Little Rapids, Sand Prairie, and Minnesota r., not far from Belleplaine, Minn. Mazomani was their chief in 1862.
Inya^n-tceyaka-ato^{n}wa^n.—Dorsey (after Ashley) in 15th Rep. B. A. E., 216, 1897. Little Falls Band.—Ind. Aff. Rep. 1859, 102, 1860. Little Rapids.—Parker, Minn. Handbk., 140, 1857. Lower Wahpeton.—Ind. Aff. Rep. 1859, 102, 1860. Lower Wakpatons.—Minn. Hist. Coll., III, 250, 1880.

Inyangmani. A Wahpeton Sioux band, named after its chief, living on Yellow Medicine cr., Minn., in 1862.
Inyangmani.—Ashley, letter to J. O. Dorsey, 1886. Yellow Medicine's band.—McKusick in Ind. Aff. Rep. 1863, 315, 1864.

Inyanhaoin ('musselshell earring'). A band of the Miniconjou Teton Sioux.
I-na-ha'-o-wín.—Hayden, Ethnog. and Philol. Mo. Val., 376, 1862 (trans. 'stone earring band'). I^{n}ya^n-ha-oi^n.—Dorsey in 15th Rep. B. A. E., 220, 1897. Iηyaη-h-oiη.—Ibid. Shell earring band.—Culbertson in Smithson. Rep. 1850, 142, 1851.

Iokwa. See *Hiaqua*.

Ionata. Apparently two former Chumashan villages connected with Santa Inés mission, Santa Barbara co., Cal.
Ionata.—Taylor in Cal. Farmer, Oct. 18, 1861. Jonatas.—Gatschet in Chief Eng. Rep., pt. III, 553, 1876.

Ioqua. See *Hiaqua*.

Iowa ('sleepy ones'). One of the southwestern Siouan tribes included by J. O. Dorsey with the Oto and Missouri in his Chiwere group. Traditional and linguistic evidence proves that the Iowa sprang from the Winnebago stem, which appears to have been the mother stock of some other of the southwestern Siouan tribes; but the closest affinity of the Iowa is with the Oto and Missouri, the difference in language being merely dialectic. Iowa chiefs informed Dorsey in 1883 that their people and the Oto, Missouri, Omaha, and Ponca "once formed part of the Winnebago nation." According to the traditions of these tribes, at an early period they came with the Winnebago from their priscan home N. of the great lakes, but that the Winnebago stopped on the shore of a great lake (L. Michigan), attracted by the abundant fish, while the others continued southwestward to the Mississippi. Here another band, the Iowa, separated from the main group, "and received the name of Pahoja, or Gray Snow, which they still retain, but are known to the white people by the name of Ioways, or Aiaouez. The first stopping place of the Iowa, after parting from the Winnebago, as noted in the tradition, appears to have been on Rock r., Ill., near its junction with the Mississippi. Another tradition places them farther N. In 1848 a map was drawn by a member of the tribe showing their movements from the mouth of Rock r. to the place where they were then living. According to this their first move was to the banks of Des Moines r., some distance above its mouth; the second was to the vicinity of the pipestone quarry in s. w. Minnesota, although on the map it was placed erroneously high up on the Missouri; thence they descended to the mouth of Platte r., and later moved successively to the headwaters of Little Platte r., Mo.; to the w. bank of the Mississippi, slightly above the mouth of Des Moines r., a short distance farther up on the same side of the Mississippi; again southwestwardly, stopping on Salt r., thence going to its extreme headwaters; to the upper part of Chariton r.; to Grand r.; thence to Missouri r., opposite Ft Leavenworth, where they lived at the time the map was drawn. These successive movements, which are of comparatively recent date, are generally accepted as substantially correct. The Sioux have a tradition (Williamson in Minn. Hist. Coll., I, 296) that when their ancestors first came to the falls of St Anthony, the Iowa occupied the country about the mouth of Minnesota r., while the Cheyenne dwelt higher up on the same stream. The Iowa appear to have been in the vicinity of the mouth of Blue Earth r., Minn., just before the arrival there of Le Sueur in 1701 for the purpose of erecting his fort. His messengers, sent to invite them to settle in the vicinity of the fort because they were good farmers, found that they had recently removed toward Missouri r., near the Maha (Omaha), who dwelt in that region. The Sioux informed Le Sueur that Blue Earth r. belonged to the Scioux of the West (Dakota), the Ayavois (Iowas), and Otoctatas (Oto), who lived a little farther off. Father Marest (La Harpe, Jour., 39, 1851) says that the Iowa were about this date associated with the Sioux in their war against the Sauk. This does not accord with the general tradition that the Dakota were always enemies of the Iowa, nevertheless the name Nadoessi Mascouteins seems to have been applied to the Iowa by the early missionaries because of their relations for a time with the Sioux. Père Andre thus designated them in 1676, when they were living 200 leagues w. of Green Bay, Wis. Perrot (Mém., 63, 1864) apparently located them in the vicinity of the Pawnee, on the plains, in 1685. Father Membré (1680) placed the Anthoutantas (Oto) and Nadouessious Maskoutens (Iowa) about 130 leagues from the Illinois, in 3 great villages built near a river which empties into the river Colbert (Mississippi) on the w. side, above the Illinois, almost opposite the mouth of the Wisconsin. He appears to locate a part of the Ainoves (perhaps intended for Aioües), on the w. side of Milwaukee r., in Wisconsin. On Marquette's map (1674–79) the Pahoutet (Iowa), the Otontanta (Oto), and Maha (Omaha) are placed on Missouri r., evidently by mere guess. La Salle knew of the Oto and the Iowa, and in his letter in regard to Hennepin, Aug. 22, 1682, mentions them under the names Otoutanta and Aiounouea, but his statement that Accault, one of his company, knew the languages of these tribes is doubtful. It is probable that in 1700, when Le Sueur furnished them with their first firearms, the Iowa resided on the extreme headwaters of Des Moines r., but it appears from this explorer's journal that they and the Oto removed and "established themselves toward the Missouri river, near the Maha." Jefferys (Fr. Dom. in Am., 1761) placed them on the E. side of the Missouri, w. of the sources of Des Moines r., above the Oto, who were on the w. side of the Missouri and below the Omaha; but in the text of his work they are located on the Mississippi in lat. 43° 30′. In 1804, according to Lewis and Clark (Orig. Jour., VI, 91–92, 1905), they occupied a single village of 200 warriors or 800 souls, 18 leagues up Platte r., on the S. E. side, although they formerly lived on the Missouri above the Platte. They conducted traffic with traders from St Louis at their posts on Platte and Grand Nemaha r., as well as at the Iowa village, the chief trade being skins of beaver, otter, raccoon, deer, and bear. They also cultivated corn, beans, etc. In 1829 (Rep. Sec. War) they were on Platte r., Iowa., 15 m. from the Missouri state line. Schoolcraft (1853) placed them on Nemaha r., Nebr., a mile above its mouth. By 1880 they were brought under the agencies.

The visiting and marriage customs of the Iowa did not differ from those of cognate tribes, nor was their management of children unlike that of the Dakota, the Omaha, and others. They appear to have been cultivators of the soil at an early date, as Le Sueur tried to persuade them to fix their village near Ft L'Huillier because they were "industrious and accustomed to cultivate the earth." Pike says that they cultivated corn, but proportionately not so much as the Sauk and Foxes. He also affirms that the Iowa were less civilized than the latter. Father André (Jes. Rel., 1676, Thwaites ed., LX, 203, 1900) says that although their village was very large, they were poor, their greatest wealth consisting of "ox-hides and red calumets," indicating that the Iowa early manufactured and traded catlinite pipes. Some small mounds in Minnesota and Iowa have been ascribed to them by two distinct traditions.

IOWA. (DAVID TOHEE)

In 1824 they ceded all their lands in Missouri, and in 1836 were assigned a reservation in N. E. Kansas, from which a part of the tribe moved later to another tract in central Oklahoma, which by agreement in 1890 was allotted to them in severalty, the surplus acreage being opened to settlement by whites.

Various estimates of the population of the Iowa at different dates are as follows: In 1760, 1,100 souls; by Lewis and Clark in 1804, 800, smallpox having carried off 100 men besides women and children in 1803; the Secretary of War gives the number in 1829 as 1,000; Catlin in 1832 at about 1,400, but in 1836 at 992; the Indian Affairs Report of 1843 gives their number as 470; the number at the Potawatomi and Great Nemaha agency in

Kansas was 143 in 1884, 138 in 1885, 143 in 1886, and 225 in 1905. At the latter date they were under the jurisdiction of the Kickapoo School. At the Sauk and Fox agency, Okla., in 1885 they numbered 88; in 1901, 88; in 1905, 89.

The Iowa camp circle was divided into half circles, occupied by two phratries of four gentes each. These were:

First phratry. (1) Tunanpin, Black Bear; (2) Michirache, Wolf; (3) Cheghita, Eagle and Thunder-being; (4) Khotachi, Elk.

Second phratry. (5) Pakhtha, Beaver; (6) Ruche, Pigeon; (7) Arukhwa, Buffalo; (8) Wakan, Snake; (9) Mankoke, Owl. The last-named gens is extinct.

There was an Iowa village called Wolf village.

See Catlin, Iowa Inds., 1844; Dorsey (1) in 11th Rep. B. A. E., 1894, and 15th Rep. B. A. E., 1897, (2) Trans. Anthrop. Soc. Wash., II, 1883; Hamilton and Irvin, Ioway Gram., 1848; Hayden, Ethnog. and Philol. Mo. Val., 1862; Lewis and Clark, Orig. Jour., I–VIII, 1904–05; Long, Exped. Rocky Mts., I, 1823; Minn. Hist. Soc. Coll., I, 1872; Sen. Doc. 452, 57th Cong., 1st sess., II, 1903. (J. O. D. C. T.)

Agones.—Boudinot, Star in the West, 125, 1816. Agouais.—De Ligney (1726) in Wis. Hist. Soc. Coll., I, 22, 1854. Agoual.—Chauvignerie (1736) quoted by Schoolcraft, Ind. Tribes, III, 557, 1853. Agoues.—Hutchins (1764), ibid. Ah-e-o-war.—Orig. Jour. Lewis and Clark, VI, 91, 1905. Aiaoua.—Perrot (1689), Mém., 196, 1864. Aiaouais.—Ibid., index. Aiaouez.—Jefferys, French Dom. in Am., I, 139, 1761. Aiauway.—Orig. Jour. Lewis and Clark (1804), I, 61, 1904. Aiavvis.—Le Sueur quoted by Ramsey in Minn. Hist. Coll., I, 45, 1872. Aieways.—Orig. Jour. Lewis and Clark (1804), I, 45, 1904. Aijoues.—Schoolcraft, Ind. Tribes, III, 522, 1853. Ainones.—Membre (1680) quoted by Hayden, Ethnog. and Philol. Mo. Val., 445, 1862. Ainoves.—Hennepin, New Discov., 132, 1698. Aioaez.—Coues, Lewis and Clark Exped., I, 19, note, 43, 1893. Aiouez.—Charlevoix (1723) in Margry, Déc., VI, 526, 1886. Aiounouea.—Hennepin (1680–82) in Margry, Déc., II, 258, 1877. Aiowais.—Pike, Trav., 134, 1811. Aisnous.—McKenney and Hall, Ind. Tribes, III, 80, 1854. Ajaouez.—Jefferys, Fr. Dom. Am., pt 1, map 1, 1761. Ajouas.—Smet, Miss. de l'Oregon, 108, 1848. Ajoues.—Bowles, map Am., ca. 1750. Ajouez.—Perrot, Mém., index, 1864. Anjoues.—Buchanan, N. Am. Inds., 155, 1824. Aöais.—N. Y. Doc. Col. Hist., x, 630, 1858. Aonays.—Smet, Letters, 38, note, 1843 (misprint). Aouas.—Cabeça de Vaca misquoted by Schoolcraft, Ind. Tribes, II, 37, 1852 (error). Avauwais.—Lewis and Clark, Trav., 14, 1807. Avoy.—Neill, Hist. Minn., 200, 1858. Avoys.—Wis. Hist. Soc. Coll., I, 32, 1854. Ayahwa.—Coues, Lewis and Clark Exped., I, 20, note, 1893. Ayauais.—Drake, Bk. Inds., vi, 1848. Ayauvai.—Coues, Lewis and Clark Exped., I, 19, note, 1893. Ayauwais.—Lewis and Clark, Discov., 17, 1806. Ayauwas.—Lapham, Blossom, and Dousman, Inds. Wis., 3, 1870. Ayauwaus.—Orig. Jour. Lewis and Clark, I, 91, 1904. Ayauway.—Ibid., 45. Ayavois.—La Harpe and Le Sueur (1699) quoted by Long, Exped. St Peter's R., II, 320, 1824. Ayawai.—Coues, Lewis and Clark Exped., I, 19, note, 1893. Ayaways.—Lewis and Clark, Trav., II, 442, 1814. Ayeouais.—Neill, Hist. Minn., 197, 1858. Aye8ais.—N. Y. Doc. Col. Hist., x, 608, 1858. Ayoa.—Martin, Hist. La., 301, 1882. Ayoes.—Perrot (1689) in Minn. Hist. Coll., II, pt 2, 24, 1864. Ayoois.—Bienville (1722) in Margry, Déc., VI, 407, 1886. Ayoouais.—Beauharnois and Hocquart (1731) in Margry, Déc., VI, 570, 1886. Ayooués.—Iberville (1702) quoted by Neill, Hist. Minn., 172, 1858.

Ayo8ois.—N. Y. Doc. Col. Hist., IX, 1055, 1855. Ayoua.—Adelung, Mithridates, III, 271, 1816. Ayouahs.—Domenech, Deserts N. Am., II, 34, 1860. Ayoues.—Neill, Hist. Minn., 173, 1858. Ayouez.—Lamothe Cadillac (1695) in Margry, Déc., v, 124, 1883. Ayouwa.—Pike, Trav., map, 1811. Ayouwais.—Lewis and Clark, Discov., 49, 1806. Ayouways.—Ibid., 29. Ayovai.—Coues, Lewis and Clark Exped., I, 20, note, 1893. Ayovois.—Bienville (1722) in Margry, Déc., VI, 396, 1886. Ayowa.—Gatschet, Kaw MS. vocab., B. A. E., 27, 1878 (Kansa name). Ayowäs.—Maximilian, Travels, 507, 1843. Ayoway.—Lewis and Clark, Exped., I, 487, 1817. Ayuhba.—Riggs, Dak. Gram. and Dict., 278, 1852. Ayuhuwahak.—Gatschet, Fox MS., B. A. E. (Fox name). Ayukba.—Williamson in Minn. Hist. Coll., I, 299, 1872. Ayuwas.—Brackenridge, Views of La., 83, 1815. Dusty Nose.—Schoolcraft, Ind. Tribes, III, 262, 1853. Ho-wah.—Ramsey in Ind. Aff. Rep. 1849, 74, 1850 (Mdewakanton name). Iawai.—Coues, Lewis and Clark Exped., I, 20, note, 1893. Iawas.—La Harpe and Le Sueur (1699) quoted by Long, Exped. S. Peter's R., II, 320, 1824. Iaways.—Orig. Jour. Lewis and Clark, VI, 91, 1905. Ihoway.—Sen. Doc. 21, 18th Cong., 2d sess., 5, 1825. Ioewaig.—Tanner, Narr., 316, 1830 (Ottawa name). Iowa.—Pike, Trav., 134, 1811. Ioway.—Pike, Exped., 112, 1810. Iyakhba.—Williamson in Minn. Geol. Rep. for 1884, 106 (Santee Dakota name). Iyakhwa.—Ibid. (Teton name). Iyuhba.—Riggs, Dak. Gram. and Dict., 278, 1852 (trans. 'sleepy ones'). Jowai.—Ann de la Propag. de la Foi, III, 569, 1828. Jowas.—Pike, Trav., 123, 1811. Joways.—Schermerhorn (1812) in Mass. Hist. Coll., 2d s. II, 39, 1814. Máqude.—Dorsey, Çegiha MS. Dict., B. A. E. 1878 (Omaha and Ponca name). Minowas.—Rafinesque in Marshall, Hist. Ky., I, 28, 1824 (confounding Iowa with Missouri). Nadoessi Mascouteins.—Jes. Rel. 1676–77, Thwaites ed., LX, 203, 1900. Nadouessi-Maskoutens.—Perrot, Mém., index, 1864. Nadouessioux des prairies.—Ibid., 237. Nadouessioux Maskoutens.—Minn. Hist. Coll., II, pt 2, 30, note, 1864 ('Sioux of the prairies': Algonkin name). Ne persa.—Orig. Jour. Lewis and Clark, VI, 91, 1905 (i.e., Nez Percés; given as traders' nickname). Ovas.—Barcia, Ensayo, 238, 1723. Oyoa.—Du Lac, Voy. dans les Louisianes, 232, 1805. Pa-ho-cha.—Hamilton in Trans. Nebr. Hist. Soc., I, 47, 1885 (trans. 'dusty men'). Pa-ho-dje.—Maximilian, Trav., 507, 1843 (trans. 'dust-noses'). Pa-ho-ja.—Long. Exped. Rocky Mts., I, 339, 1823 (trans. 'gray snow'). Pah8tet.—Marquette (1673) in Shea, Discov., 268, map, 1852. Pahucæ.—Hamilton and Irwin, Ioway Gram., 17, 1848. Pa-hu-cha.—Schoolcraft, Ind. Tribes, III, 262, 1853. Pä-kuh'-thä.—Morgan, Anc. Soc., 156, 1877. Paoté.—La Salle (1682) in Margry, Déc., II, 215, 1877. Paoutées.—La Harpe, from Le Sueur's Jour. (1700) in Shea, Early Voy., 93, 1861. Paoutés.—Le Sueur (1700) in Margry, Déc., VI, 70, 1886. Paoutez.—Jefferys, Am. Atlas, map 5, 1776. Paqocte.—Dorsey in Trans. Anthrop. Soc. Wash., II, 10, 1883. Pa'-qo-tce.—Dorsey, Kansa MS. vocab., B. A. E., 1882 (Kansa name). Pa'-qu-tĕ.—Dorsey, Kwapa MS. vocab., B. A. E., 1881 (Quapaw name). Páquïsĕ.—Dorsey, Osage MS. vocab., B. A. E., 1883 (Osage name). Pashóhan.—Gatschet, Pawnee MS., B. A. E. (Pawnee name). Passinchan.—Doc. 1720 quoted by Bandelier in Arch. Inst. Pap., v, 203, 1890. Pauhoochees.—McKenney and Hall, Ind. Tribes, II, 209, 1854. Páχodshe.—Gatschet, Kaw MS. vocab., B. A. E., 27, 1878 (Kansa name). Pierced Noses.—Long, Exped. Rocky Mts., I, 339, 1823. Wa-qôtc'.—Dorsey, Winnebago MS. vocab., B. A. E., 1886 (Winnebago name). Yahowa.—Beltrami, Ptlgrimage, II, 151, 1828. Yoways.—De l'Isle, map of La., in Neill, Hist. Minn., 164, 1858. Yuahés.—Iberville (1700) in Margry, Déc., IV, 440, 1880 (identical?). Zaivvois.—Haldimand, according to Catlin, quoted by Donaldson in Smithson. Rep. for 1885, pt. 2, 145, 1886.

Ipec. A former Chumashan village near Santa Barbara mission, Cal.—Taylor in Cal. Farmer, Apr. 24, 1863.

Ipersua. A summer village of the Utkiavimiut Eskimo in N. Alaska.—Murdoch in 9th Rep. B. A. E., 83, 1892.

Ipik. An Eskimo village in s. w. Greenland, lat. 60° 31'.—Meddelelser om Grönland, XVI, map, 1896.

Ipisogi. A subordinate settlement of the Upper Creek town Oakfuski, on a creek of the same name which enters the Tallapoosa from the E., opposite Oakfuski, Ala. According to Hawkins it had 40 settlers in 1799.
E-pe-sau-gee.—Hawkins (1799), Sketch, 47, 1848. Ipisógi.—Gatschet, Creek Migr. Leg., I, 133, 1884.

Ipnot. A Nunatogmiut Eskimo village at C. Thomson, Alaska; pop. 40 in 1880.
Ip-Not.—Petroff in 10th Census, Alaska, 59, 1884.

Ipoksimaiks (*I'-pok-si-maiks*, 'fat roasters'). A division of the Piegan.
E-pōh'-si-miks.—Hayden, Ethnog. and Philol. Mo. Val., 264, 1862 (= 'the band that fries fat'). **Fat Roasters.**—Grinnell, Blackfoot Lodge Tales, 225, 1892. Ih-po'-se-mä.—Morgan, Anc. Soc., 171, 1877 (= 'webfat'). I'-pok-si-maiks.—Grinnell, op. cit., 209.

Ippo (*Ip-po'*, 'mesa'). A Tarahumare rancheria in Chihuahua, Mexico.—Lumholtz, inf'n, 1894.

Iptugik. A former Aleut village on Agattu id., Alaska, one of the Near id. group of the Aleutians, now uninhabited.

Iratae. A village, presumably Costanoan, formerly connected with San Juan Bautista mission, Cal.—Taylor in Cal. Farmer, Nov. 23, 1860.

Irihibano ('war councilors'). The progenitors of the Fish clan of the ancient Timucua of Florida.—Pareja (*ca.* 1613) quoted by Gatschet in Am. Philos. Soc. Proc., XVII, 492, 1878.

Iron. The use of iron by the American aborigines and especially by the tribes N. of Mexico was very limited as compared with their use of copper. The compact ores were sometimes used, and were flaked, pecked, or ground into shape, as were the harder varieties of stone. Implements, ornaments, and symbolic objects of hematite ore are found in great numbers in mounds and in burial places and on dwelling sites over a large part of the country. Since smelting was unknown to the natives, the only form of metallic iron available to them and sufficiently malleable to be shaped by hammering is of meteoric origin, and numerous examples of implements shaped from it have been recovered from the mounds. A series of celts of ordinary form, along with partly shaped pieces and natural masses of the metal, were found by Moorehead in a mound of the Hopewell group near Chillicothe, Ohio, and these are now in the Field Museum of Natural History, Chicago. The Turner mounds, in Hamilton co., Ohio, have perhaps yielded the most interesting relics of this class. Putnam describes these, in enumerating the various objects found on one of the earthen altars, as follows: "But by far the most important things found on this altar were the several masses of meteoric iron and the ornaments made from this metal. One of

them is half of a spool-shaped ear ornament, like those made of copper with which it was associated. Another ear ornament of copper is covered with a thin plating of iron, in the same manner as others were covered with silver. Three of the masses of iron have been more or less hammered into bars, as if for the purpose of making some ornament or implement, and another is apparently in the natural shape in which it was found" (16th Rep. Peabody Museum, III, 171, 1884; see also Putnam in Proc. Am. Antiq. Soc., II, 349, 1883). Ross records the fact that the Eskimo of Smith sd. used meteoric iron. Small bits of this metal beaten out and set in a row in an ivory handle made effective knives. See *Hematite, Metal work.*

Consult Kroeber in Bull. Am. Mus. Nat. Hist., XII, 285, 1899; Ross, Voyage of Discovery, 1819; Thomas in 12th Rep. B. A. E., 319, 336, 1894.   (W. H. H.)

Iroquoian Family. A linguistic stock consisting of the following tribes and tribal groups: the Hurons composed of the Attignaouantan (Bear people), the Attigneenongnahac (Cord people), the Arendahronon (Rock people), the Tohontaenrat (Atahontaenrat or Tohontaenrat, White-eared or Deer people), the Wenrohronon, the Ataronchronon, and the Atonthrataronon (Otter people, an Algonquian tribe); the Tionontati or Tobacco people or nation; the confederation of the Attiwendaronk or Neutrals, composed of the Neutrals proper, the Aondironon, the Ongniarahronon, and the Atiragenratka (Atiraguenrek); the Conkhandeenrhonon; the Iroquois confederation composed of the Mohawk, the Oneida, the Onondaga, the Cayuga, and the Seneca, with the Tuscarora after 1726; and in later times the incorporated remnants of a number of alien tribes, such as the Tutelo, the Saponi, the Nanticoke, the Conoy, and the Muskwaki or Foxes; the Conestoga or Susquehanna of at least three tribes, of which one was the Akhrakouaehronon or Atrakouaehronon; the Erie or Cat nation of at least two allied peoples; the Tuscarora confederation, composed of several leagued tribes, the names of which are now unknown; the Nottaway; the Meherrin; and the Cherokee composed of at least three divisions, the Elati, the Middle Cherokee, and the Atali; and the Onnontioga consisting of the Iroquois-Catholic seceders on the St Lawrence.

Each tribe was an independent political unit, except those which formed leagues in which the constituent tribes, while enjoying local self-government, acted jointly in common affairs. For this reason there was no general name for themselves common to all the tribes.

Jacques Cartier, in 1534, met on the

shore of Gaspé basin people of the Iroquoian stock, whom in the following year he again encountered in their home on the site of the city of Quebec, Canada. He found both banks of the St Lawrence above Quebec, as far as the site of Montreal, occupied by people of this family. He visited the villages Hagonchenda, Hochelaga, Hochelayi, Stadacona, and Tutonaguy. This was the first known habitat of an Iroquoian people. Champlain found these territories entirely deserted 70 years later, and Lescarbot found people roving over this area speaking an entirely different language from that recorded by Cartier. He believed that this change of languages was due to "a destruction of people," because, he writes, "some years ago the Iroquois assembled themselves to the number of 8,000 men and destroyed all their enemies, whom they surprised in their enclosures." The new language which he recorded was Algonquian, spoken by bands that passed over this region on warlike forays.

The early occupants of the St Lawrence were probably the Arendahronon and Tohontaenrat, tribes of the Hurons. Their lands bordered on those of the Iroquois, whose territory extended westward to that of the Neutrals, neighbors of the Tionontati and western Huron tribes to the N. and the Erie to the s. and w. The Conestoga occupied the middle and lower basin of the Susquehanna, s. of the Iroquois. The N. Iroquoian area, which Algonquian tribes surrounded on nearly every side, therefore embraced nearly the entire valley of the St Lawrence, the basins of L. Ontario and L. Erie, the s. E. shores of L. Huron and Georgian bay, all of the present New York state except the lower Hudson valley, all of central Pennsylvania, and the shores of Chesapeake bay in Maryland as far as Choptank and Patuxent rs. In the S. the Cherokee area, surrounded by Algonquian tribes on the N., Siouan on the E., and Muskhogean and Uchean tribes on the s. and w., embraced the valleys of the Tennessee and upper Savannah rs. and the mountainous parts of Virginia, the Carolinas, and Alabama. Separated from the Cherokee by the territory of the eastern Siouan tribes was the area occupied by the Tuscarora in E. North Carolina and by the Meherrin and Nottoway N. of them in s. E. Virginia.

The northern Iroquoian tribes, especially the Five Nations so called, were second to no other Indian people N. of Mexico in political organization, statecraft, and military prowess. Their leaders were astute diplomats, as the wily French and English statesmen with whom they treated soon discovered. In war they practised ferocious cruelty toward their prisoners, burning even their unadopted women and infant prisoners; but, far from being a race of rude and savage warriors, they were a kindly and affectionate people, full of keen sympathy for kin and friends in distress, kind and deferential to their women, exceedingly fond of their children, anxiously striving for peace and good will among men, and profoundly imbued with a just reverence for the constitution of their commonwealth and for its founders. Their wars were waged primarily to secure and perpetuate their political life and independence. The fundamental principles of their confederation, persistently maintained for centuries by force of arms and by compacts with other peoples, were based primarily on blood relationship, and they shaped and directed their foreign and internal polity in consonance with these principles. The underlying motive for the institution of the Iroquois league was to secure universal peace and welfare (*ne'' skĕñ'non'*) among men by the recognition and enforcement of the forms of civil government (*ne'' gā'i'hwiio*) through the direction and regulation of personal and public conduct and thought in accordance with beneficent customs and council degrees; by the stopping of bloodshed in the bloodfeud through the tender of the prescribed price for the killing of a cotribesman; by abstaining from eating human flesh; and, lastly, through the maintenance and necessary exercise of power (*ne'' gă'shăsdon''sä'*), not only military but also magic power believed to be embodied in the forms of their ceremonial activities. The tender by the homicide and his family for the murder or killing by accident of a cotribesman was twenty strings of wampum—ten for the dead person, and ten for the forfeited life of the homicide.

The religious activities of these tribes expressed themselves in the worship of all environing elements and bodies and many creatures of a teeming fancy, which, directly or remotely affecting their welfare, were regarded as man-beings or anthropic personages endowed with life, volition, and peculiar individual *orenda*, or magic power. In the practice of this religion, ethics or morals, as such, far from having a primary had only a secondary, if any, consideration. The status and personal relations of the personages of their pantheon were fixed and regulated by rules and customs similar to those in vogue in the social and political organization of the people, and there was, therefore, among at least the principal gods, a kinship system patterned on that of the people themselves.

The mental superiority of the Hurons (q. v.) over their Algonquian neighbors is frequently mentioned by the early

French missionaries. A remainder of the Tionontati, with a few refugee Hurons among them, having fled to the region of the upper lakes, along with certain Ottawa tribes, to escape the Iroquois invasion in 1649, maintained among their fellow refugees a predominating influence. This was largely because, like other Iroquoian tribes, they had been highly organized socially and politically, and were therefore trained in definite parliamentary customs and procedure. The fact that, although but a small tribe, the Hurons claimed and exercised the right of lighting the council fire at all general gatherings, shows the esteem in which they were held by their neighbors. The Cherokee were the first tribe to adopt a constitutional form of government, embodied in a code of laws written in their own language in an alphabet based on the Roman characters adapted by one of them (see *Sequoya*), though in weighing these facts their large infusion of white blood must be considered.

The social organization of the Iroquoian tribes was in some respects similar to that of some other Indians, but it was much more complex and cohesive, and there was a notable difference in regard to the important position accorded the women. Among the Cherokee, the Iroquois, the Hurons, and probably among the other tribes, the women performed important and essential functions in their government. Every chief was chosen and retained his position, and every important measure was enacted by the consent and cooperation of the child-bearing women, and the candidate for a chiefship was nominated by the suffrages of the matrons of this group. His selection by them from among their sons had to be confirmed by the tribal and the federal councils respectively, and finally he was installed into office by federal officers. Lands and houses belonged solely to the women.

All the Iroquoian tribes were sedentary and agricultural, depending on the chase for only a small part of their subsistence. The northern tribes were especially noted for their skill in fortification and house-building. Their so-called castles were solid log structures, with platforms running around the top on the inside, from which stones and other missiles could be hurled down upon besiegers.

For the population of the tribes composing the Iroquoian family see *Iroquois*, and the descriptions of the various Iroquoian tribes.   (J. N. B. H.)

>Chelekees.—Keane in Stanford, Compend., Cent. and So. Am., app., 472, 1878 (or Cherokees). >Cherokees.—Gallatin in Am. Antiq. Soc., II, 89, 306, 1836 (kept apart from Iroquois, though probable affinity asserted); Bancroft, Hist. U. S., III, 246, 1840; Prichard, Phys. Hist. Mankind, v, 401, 1847; Gallatin in Trans. Am. Ethnol. Soc., II, pt.

1, xcix, 77, 1848; Latham. in Trans. Philol. Soc. Lond., 58, 1856 (a separate group, perhaps to be classed with Iroquois and Sioux); Gallatin in Schoolcraft, Ind. Tribes, III, 401, 1853; Latham, Opuscula, 327, 1860; Keane in Stanford, Compend., Cent. and So. Am., app., 460, 472, 1878 (same as Chelekees or Tsalagi—"apparently entirely distinct from all other American tongues"). >Cheroki.—Gatschet, Creek Migr. Leg., I, 24, 1884; Gatschet in Science, 413, Apr. 29, 1887. =Huron-Cherokee.—Hale in Am. Antiq., 20, Jan., 1883 (proposed as a family name instead of Huron-Iroquois; relationship to Iroquois affirmed). <Huron-Iroquois.—Bancroft, Hi t. U. S., III, 243, 1840. >Irokesen.—Berghaus (1845), Physik. Atlas, map 17, 1848; ibid., 1852. ×Irokesen.—Berghaus, Physik. Atlas, map 72, 1887 (includes Kataba and said to be derived from Dakota). =Iroquoian.—Powell in 7th Rep. B. A. E., 77, 1891. >Iroquois.—Gallatin in Trans. Am. Antiq. Soc., II, 21, 23, 305, 1836 (excludes Cherokee); Prichard, Phys. Hist. Mankind, v, 381, 1847 (follows Gallatin); Gallatin in Trans. Am. Ethnol. Soc., II, pt. 1, xcix, 77, 1848 (as in 1836); Gallatin in Schoolcraft, Ind. Tribes, III, 401, 1853. Latham in Trans. Philol. Soc. Lond., 58, 1856; Latham, Opuscula, 327, 1860; Latham, Elements Comp. Philol., 463, 1862. >Tschirokies.—Berghaus (1845), Physik. Atlas, map 17, 1848. >Wyandot-Iroquois.—Keane in Stanford, Compend., Cent. and So. Am., app., 460, 468, 1878.

Iroquois (Algonkin: *Irinakhoiw*, 'real adders', with the French suffix -*ois*). The confederation of Iroquoian tribes known in history, among other names, by that of the Five Nations, comprising the Cayuga, Mohawk, Oneida, Onondaga, and Seneca. Their name for themselves as a political body was *Oñgwanonsioñni'*, 'we are of the extended lodge.' Among the Iroquoian tribes kinship is traced through the blood of the woman only; kinship means membership in a family, and this in turn constitutes citizenship in the tribe, conferring certain social, political, and religious privileges, duties, and rights which are denied to persons of alien blood; but, by a legal fiction embodied in the right of adoption, the blood of the alien may be figuratively changed into one of the strains of the Iroquoian blood, and thus citizenship may be conferred on a person of alien lineage. In an Iroquoian tribe the legislative, judicial, and executive functions are usually exercised by one and the same class of persons, commonly called chiefs in English, who are organized into councils. There are three grades of chiefs. The chiefship is hereditary in certain of the simplest political units in the government of the tribe; a chief is nominated by the suffrages of the matrons of this unit, and the nomination is confirmed by the tribal and the federal councils. The functions of the three grades of chiefs are defined in the rules of procedure. When the five Iroquoian tribes were organized into a confederation, its government was only a development of that of the separate tribes, just as the government of each of the constituent tribes was a development of that of the several clans of which it was composed. The government of the clan was a development of that of the several brood families of which it was composed, and the brood family, strictly speaking, was composed of the progeny of a woman and her female descendants, counting through the female line only; hence the clan may be described as a permanent body of kindred, socially and politically organized, who trace actual and theoretical descent through the female line only. The simpler units surrendered part of their autonomy to the next higher units in such wise that the whole was closely interdependent and cohesive. The establishment of the higher unit created new rights, privileges, and duties. This was the principle of organization of the confederation of the five Iroquoian tribes. The date of the formation of this confederation (probably not the first, but the last of a series of attempts to unite the several tribes in a federal union) was not earlier than about the year 1570, which is some 30 years anterior to that of the Huron tribes.

The Delawares gave them the name Mingwe. The northern and western Algonquians called them Nadowa, 'adders'. The Powhatan called them Massawomekes. The English knew them as the Confederation of the Five Nations, and after the admission of the Tuscarora in 1722, as the Six Nations. Moreover, the names Maqua, Mohawk, Seneca, and Tsonnontowan, by which their leading tribes were called, were also applied to them collectively. The League of the Iroquois, when first known to Europeans, was composed of the five tribes, and occupied the territory extending from the E. watershed of L. Champlain to the w. watershed of Genesee r., and from the Adirondacks southward to the territory of the Conestoga. The date of the formation of the league is not certain, but there is evidence that it took place about 1570, occasioned by wars with Algonquian and Huron tribes. The confederated Iroquois immediately began to make their united power felt. After the coming of the Dutch, from whom they procured firearms, they were able to extend their conquests over all the neighboring tribes until their dominion was acknowledged from Ottawa r. to the Tennessee and from the Kennebec to Illinois r. and L. Michigan. Their westward advance was checked by the Chippewa; the Cherokee and the Catawba proved an effectual barrier in the S., while in the N. they were hampered by the operations of the French in Canada. Champlain on one of his early expeditions joined a party of Canadian Indians against the Iroquois. This made them bitter enemies of the French, whom they afterward opposed at every step to the close of the French

régime in Canada in 1763, while they were firm allies of the English. The French made several attempts through their missionaries to win over the Iroquois, and were so far successful that a considerable number of individuals from the different tribes, most of them Mohawk and Onondaga, withdrew from the several tribes and formed Catholic settlements at Caughnawaga, St Regis, and Oka, on the St Lawrence. The tribes of the league repeatedly tried, but without success, to induce them to return, and finally, in 1684, declared them to be traitors. In later wars the Catholic Iroquois took part with the French against their former brethren. On the breaking out of the American Revolution the League of the Iroquois decided not to take part in the conflict, but to allow each tribe to decide for itself what action to take. All the tribes, with the exception of the Oneida and about half of the Tuscarora, joined the English. After the revolution the Mohawk and Cayuga, with other Iroquoian tribes that were in the English interest, after several temporary assignments, were finally settled by the Canadian government on a reservation on Grand r., Ontario, where they still reside, although a few individuals emigrated to Gibson, Bay of Quinté, Caughnawaga, and St Thomas, Ontario. All the Iroquois in the United States are on reservations in New York with the exception of the Oneida, who are settled near Green Bay, Wis. The so-called Seneca of Oklahoma are composed of the remnants of many tribes, among which may be mentioned the Conestoga and Hurons, and of emigrants from all the tribes of the Iroquoian confederation. It is very probable that the nucleus of these Seneca was the remnant of the ancient Erie. The Catholic Iroquois of Caughnawaga, St Regis, and Oka, although having no connection with the confederation, supplied many recruits to the fur trade, and a large number of them have become permanently resident among the northwestern tribes of the United States and Canada.

The number of the Iroquois villages varied greatly at different periods and from decade to decade. In 1657 there were about 24, but after the conquest of the Erie the entire country from the Genesee to the w. watershed of L. Erie came into possession of the Iroquoian tribes, which afterward settled colonies on the upper waters of the Allegheny and Susquehanna and on the N. shore of L. Ontario, so that by 1750 their villages may have numbered about 50. The population of the Iroquois also varied much at different periods. Their constant wars greatly weakened them. In

1689 it was estimated that they had 2,250 warriors, who were reduced by war, disease, and defections to Canada, to 1,230 in 1698. Their losses were largely made up by their system of wholesale adoption, which was carried on to such an extent that at one time their adopted aliens were reported to equal or exceed the number of native Iroquois. Disregarding the extraordinary estimates of some early writers, it is evident that the modern Iroquois, instead of decreasing in population, have increased, and number more at present than at any former period. On account of the defection of the Catholic Iroquois and the omission of the Tuscarora from the estimates it was impossible to get a statement of the full strength of the Iroquois until within recent times. About the middle of the 17th century the Five Nations were supposed to have reached their highest point, and in 1677 and 1685 they were estimated at about 16,000. In 1689 they were estimated at about 12,850, but in the next 9 years they lost more than half by war and by desertions to Canada. The most accurate estimates for the 18th century gave to the Six Nations and their colonies about 10,000 or 12,000 souls. In 1774 they were estimated at 10,000 to 12,500. In 1904 they numbered about 16,100, including more than 3,000 mixed-bloods, as follows:

In Ontario: Iroquois and Algonkin at Watha (Gibson), 139 (about one-half Iroquois); Mohawk of the Bay of Quinté, 1,271; Oneida of the Thames, 770; Six Nations on Grand r., 4,195 (including about 150 Delawares). In Quebec: Iroquois of Caughnawaga, 2,074; of St Regis, 1,426; of Lake of Two Mountains, 393. Total in Canada, about 10,418.

The Iroquois of New York in 1904 were distributed as follows: Onondaga and Seneca on Allegany res., 1,041; Cayuga, Onondaga, and Seneca on Cattaraugus res., 1,456; Oneida on Oneida res., 150; Oneida and Onondaga on Onondaga res., 513; St Regis res., 1,208; Cayuga and Seneca on Tonawanda res., 512; Onondaga and Tuscarora on Tuscarora res., 410. Total, 5,290.

In 1905 there were also 366 Indians classed as Seneca under the Seneca School, Okla.

The Algonquian and other Indians included with the Iroquois are probably outnumbered by the Caughnawaga and others in the Canadian N. W. who are not separately enumerated.

The following villages were Iroquois, but the particular tribes to which they belonged are either unknown or are collective: Adjouquay, Allaquippa, Anpuaqun, Aquatsagana, Aratumquat, Awegen, Blackleg's Village, Buckaloon, Cahun-ghage, Canowdowsa, Caughnawaga, Chartierstown, Chemegaide, Chenango, Chinklacamoose, Chugnut, Churamuk, Codocoraren, Cokanuck, Conaquanosshan, Conejoholo, Conemaugh, Conihunta, Connosomothdian, Conoytown (mixed Conoy and Iroquois), Coreorgonel (mixed), Cowawago, Cussewago, Ganadoga, Ganagarahhare, Ganasarage, Ganeraske, Ganneious, Gannentaha, Glasswanoge, Goshgoshunk (mixed), Grand River Indians, Hickorytown (mixed), Janundat, Jedakne, Johnstown, Jonondes, Juniata, Juraken (2), Kahendohon, Kanaghsaws, Kannawalohalla, Kanesadageh, Karaken, Karhationni, Karhawenradon, Kayehkwarageh, Kaygen, Kenté, Kickenapawling, Kiskiminetas, Kittaning, Kuskuski (mixed), Lawunkhannek, Logstown, Loyalhannon (?), Mahusquechikoken, Mahican, Mahoning, Manckatawangum, Matchasaung, Middletown, Mingo Town, Mohanet, Nescopeck, Newtown (4 settlements), Newtychaning, Octageron, Ohrekionni, Onaweron, Onkwe Iyede, Opolopong, Oquaga, Osewingo, Oskawaserenhon, Ostonwackin, Oswegatchie, Otiahanague, Otskwirakeron, Ousagwentera, Owego, Paille Coupée, Pluggy's Town, Punxatawney, Quinaouatoua, Runonvea, Saint Regis, Sawcunk, Schoharie, Schohorage, Sconassi, Scoutash's Town, Seneca Town, Sevegé, Sewickly's Old Town, Shamokin, Shannopin, Shenango, Sheshequin, Sheoquage, Sittawingo, Skannayutenate, Skehandowa, Solocka, Swahadowri, Taiaiagon, Tewanondadon, Tioga, Tohoguses Cabins, Tonihata, Tullihas, Tuscarora, Tuskokogie, Tutelo, Unadilla, Venango, Wakatomica, Wakerhon, Wauteghe, Yoghroonwago, Youcham. Catholic missions among the Iroquois were: Caughnawaga, Indian Point, La Montagne, La Prairie, Oka, Oswegatchie, St Regis, and Sault au Recollet. For the other Iroquois settlements, see under the several tribal names.   (J. N. B. H.)

Acquinoshionee.—Schoolcraft, Ind. Tribes, III, 517, 1853. Acquinushionee.—Schoolcraft in Proc. N. Y. Hist. Soc., 80, 1844. Aganuschioni.—Macauley, N. Y., II, 185, 1829. Agoneaseah.—Ibid. Agonnonsionni.—Charlevoix (1744) quoted by Drake, Bk. Inds., bk. v, 3, 1848. Agonnousioni.—McKenney and Hall, Ind. Tribes, III, 79, 1854. Agonnsionni.—Clark, Onondaga, I, 19, 1849. Akononsionni.—Brinton, Lenape Leg., 255, 1885. Akwinoshioni.—Schoolcraft, Ind. Tribes, VI, 138, 1857. Aquanoschioni.—Barton, New Views, app., 7, 1798. Aquanuschioni.—Drake, Bk. Inds., bk. v, 4, 1848. Aquanuschionig.—Vater, Mith., pt. 3, sec. 3, 309, 1816. Aquinoshioni.—Schoolcraft, Ind. Tribes, VI, 188, 1857. Aquinushionee.—Ibid., III, 532, 1853. Caenoestoery.—Schuyler (1699) in N. Y. Doc. Col. Hist., IV, 563, 1854. Canaghkonje.—Dellius (1697), ibid., 280. Canaghkouse.—Ibid. Cannassoone.—Doc. of 1695, ibid., 122. Cannissoone.—Ibid., 120. Canossoene.—Gov. of Can. (1695), ibid., 122, note. Canossoené.—Doc. of 1695, ibid., 120. Canossoone.—Ibid. Canton Indians.—Fletcher (1693), ibid., 33. Coenossoeny.—Ibid., 563, note. Confederate Indians.—Johnson (1760), ibid., VII, 432. Confederate Nations.—Mt Johnson conf.

(1755), ibid., VI, 983, 1855. **Confederates.**—Johnson (1763), ibid., VII, 582, 1856. **Erocoise.**—Morton (*ca.* 1650) in Me. Hist. Soc. Coll., III, 34, 1853. **Five Canton Nations.**—Jamison (1696) in N. Y. Doc. Col. Hist., IV, 235, 1854. **Five Indian Cantons.**—Hunter (1711), ibid., V, 252, 1855. **Five Mohawk Nations.**—Carver, Trav., 173, 1778. **Five Nations.**—Andros (1690) in R. I. Col. Rec., III, 284, 1858. **Gwhunnughshonee.**—Macauley, N. Y., II, 185, 1829. **Haughgoghnuchshionee.**—Ibid., 185. **Hirocoi.**—Shea, Cath. Miss., 215, 1855. **Hiroquais.**—Ibid., 205 (first applied by French to both Hurons and Iroquois). **Hiroquois.**—Jes. Rel. for 1632, 14, 1858. **Ho-de′-no-sau-nee.**—Morgan, League Iroq., 51, 1851. **Ho-di-noⁿ'syoⁿ'ni′.**—Hewitt, inf'n, 1886 ('they are of the house': own name, Seneca form). **Honontonchionni.**—Millet (1693) in N. Y. Doc. Col. Hist., IV, 78, 1854. **Hotinnonchiendi.**—Jes. Rel. for 1654, 11, 1858. **Hotinnonsionni.**—Shea, Cath. Miss., 205, 1855. **Hotinonsionni.**—Bruyas (*ca.* 1700) quoted in Charlevoix, New France, II, 189, note, 1866 (Mohawk form). **Hyroquoise.**—Sagard (1636) in note to Champlain, Œuv., III, 220, 1870. **Hyroquoyse.**—Ibid. **Inquoi.**—Boyd, Ind. Local Names, 1885 (misprint). **Irecoies.**—Lovelace (1670) in N. Y. Doc. Col. Hist., III, 190, 1853. **Irequois.**—Brickell, N. C., 283, 1737. **Iriquoi.**—Boyd, Ind. Local Names, 30, 1885. **Iriquois.**—Thornton in Me. Hist. Soc. Coll., V, 175, 1857. **Irocois.**—Champlain (1603), Œuv., II, 9, 1870. **Irocquois.**—Doc. of 1666 in N. Y. Doc. Col. Hist., III, 134, 1853. **Irognas.**—Rasle (1724) in Mass. Hist. Soc. Coll., 2d s., VIII, 246, 1819. **Irokesen.**—Vater, Mith., pt. 3, sec. 3, 303, 1816 (German form). **Ironois.**—Hennepin, Cont. of New Discov., map, 1698. **Iroquaes.**—Bayard (1698) in N. Y. Doc. Col. Hist., IV, 353, 1854. **Iroque.**—Smith (1799) quoted by Drake, Trag. Wild., 254, 1841. **Iroquese.**—Hennepin (1683) quoted by Harris, Voy. and Trav., II, 906, 1705. **Iroqueze.**—Harris, ibid., I, 811, 1705. **Iroquiese.**—Hennepin, New Discov., 19, 1698. **Iroquoi.**—Baraga, Eng.-Otch. Dict., 147, 1878. **Iroquois.**—Jes. Rel. for 1645, 2, 1858. **Iroquos.**—Drake, Bk. Inds., bk. v, 41, 1848. **Irriquois.**—Pike, Trav., 130, 1811. **Irroquois.**—Talon (1671) in Margry, Déc., I, 100, 1875. **Irroquoys.**—La Montagne (1658) in N. Y. Doc. Col. Hist., XIII, 89, 1881. **Ke-nunctioni.**—Macauley, N. Y., II, 174, 1829. **Konoshioni.**—Gale, Upper Miss., 159, 1867. **Konossioni.**—Dellius (1694) in N. Y. Doc. Col. Hist., IV, 78, 1854. **Konungzi Oniĝa.**—Vater, Mith., pt 3, sec.3, 309, 1816. **Let-e-nugh-shonee.**—Macauley, N. Y., II, 185, 1829. **Mahongwis.**—Rafinesque, Am. Nations, I, 157, 1836. **Masawomekes.**—Smith (1629), Va., I, 120, 1819. **Massawamacs.**—Keane in Stanford, Compend., 521, 1878. **Massawomacs.**—Jefferson, Notes, 279, 1825. **Massawomecks.**—Strachey (*ca.* 1612), Va., 40, 1849. **Massawomees.**—Rafinesque, introd. to Marshall, Ky., I, 33, 1824. **Massawomekes.**—Smith (1629), Va., I, 74, 1819. **Massawonacks.**—Schoolcraft, Ind. Tribes, VI, 130, 1857. **Massawonaes.**—Boudinot, Star in the West, 127, 1816. **Massowomeks.**—Smith (1629), Va., I, 119, 1819. **Mat-che-naw-to-waig.**—Tanner, Narr., 316, 1830 ('bad snakes': Ottawa name for the Iroquois, in contradistinction to the Hurons, called the 'good snakes'). **Matchinadoaek.**—La Hontan (1703) quoted by Vater, Mith., pt 3, sec. 3, 264, 1816 ('bad people': Algonquian name). **Mengua.**—Heckewelder (1819) quoted by Thompson, Long Id., I, 767, 1843. **Mengues.**—Bozman, Md., II, 481, 1837. **Menguy.**—Rafinesque, introd. to Marshall, Ky., I, 31, 1824. **Mengwe.**—Heckewelder (1819) in Me. Hist. Soc. Coll., VI, 216, 1859. **Mengwee.**—Macauley, N. Y., II, 185, 1829. **Mengwi.**—Rafinesque, Am. Nations, I, 157, 1836. **Messawomes.**—Am. Pion., II, 189, 1843. **Minckquas.**—Smitt (1660) in N. Y. Doc. Col. Hist., XIII, 164, 1881. **Mincquaas.**—Doc. of 1660, ibid., 184. **Mingaes.**—Doc. of 1659, ibid., 106. **Mingoe.**—Conestoga council (1721) quoted by Proud, Penn., II, 132, 1797. **Mingos.**—Homann Heirs map, 1756. **Mingwee.**—Macauley, N. Y., II, 185, 1829. **Minquaas.**—Doc. of 1660 in N. Y. Doc. Col. Hist., XIII, 181, 1881 (also applied to the Mingo on Ohio r., on map in Mandrillon, Spectateur Américain, 1785). **Minquaes.**—Doc. of 1658, ibid. 95. **Minquas.**—Van der Donck (1656) quoted by Ruttenber, Tribes Hudson R., 51, 1872. **Mungwas.**—Schoolcraft, Ind. Tribes, V, 147, 1855 (Chippewa mame, and may mean the Mundua). **Nä-do-wage′.**—

Morgan in N. Am. Rev., 52, 1870. **Nadowaig.**—Schoolcraft, Ind. Tribes, V, 39, 1855. **Nadowas.**—Schoolcraft, Pers. Mem., 446, 1851. **Nâdowé.**—Baraga, Engl.-Otch. Dict., 147, 1878 (Chippewa name). **Nah-dah-waig.**—Schoolcraft, Ind Tribes, V, 193, 1855. **Nahdooways.**—Jones, Ojebway Inds., 32, 1861. **Nahdoways.**—Ibid., 111. **Natuági.**—Gatschet, Creek Migr. Leg., I, 61, 1884 (Creek name). **Naud-o-waig.**—Warren (1852) in Minn. Hist. Soc. Coll., V, 83, 1885. **Naudoways.**—Tanner, Narr., 88, 1830. **Nautowaig.**—Ibid., 316 (Ottawa name). **Nautowas.**—Schoolcraft, Ind. Tribes, I, 304, 1853. **Nautoway.**—Tanner, Narr., 310, 1830. **Nodowaig.**—Ind. Aff. Rep., 90, 1850. **Nodoways.**—Schoolcraft, Ind. Tribes, II, 149, 1852. **Nodswaig.**—Ind. Aff. Rep., 83, 1850. **Notinnonchioni.**—Millet (1693) in N. Y. Doc. Col. Hist., IV, 79, 1854. **Nottawagees.**—Glen (1750), ibid., VI, 588, 1855. **Nottawegas.**—Mitchel in Hist. Mag., 1st s., IV, 358, 1860. **Notteweges.**—McCall, Hist. Ga., I, 243, 1811. **Oñ-gwä-noⁿ'syoⁿ'ni′.**—Hewitt, inf'n, 1886 (Seneca form). **Rodinunchsiouni.**—Colden (1727) quoted in Charlevoix, New France, II, 189, note, 1866. **Sechs Nationen.**—Güssefeld, map, 1784 (German: 'Six Nations'). **Six Allied Nations.**—Sharpe (1754) in Mass. Hist. Soc. Coll., 3d s., V, 16, 1836. **Six Nations.**—Albany conf. (1724) in N. Y. Doc. Col. Hist. V, 713, 1855. **Trokesen.**—Heckewelder (1819) quoted by Thompson, Long Id., I, 76, 1843 (Dutch form; misprint). **Troquois.**—Gorges (1658) in Me. Hist. Soc. Coll., II, 66, 1847 (misprint). **Tudamanes.**—Barcia, Ensayo, 16, 1723. **Wassawomees.**—Rafinesque, introd. to Marshall, Ky., I, 33, 1824. **Yäⁿkwä-näⁿ-'syäñ-ni′.**—Hewitt, inf'n, 1886 (Tuscarora form). **Yrocois.**—Champlain (1632), Œuv., V, pt 2, 46, 1870. **Yrokoise.**—Vaudreuil (1760) in N. Y. Doc. Col. Hist., X, 1092, 1858. **Yroquois.**—Champlain (1632), Œuv., V, pt 2, 47, 1870.

Iroquoise Chippeways. The Catholic Iroquois and Nipissing settled at Oka, Quebec.—Schermerhorn (1812) in Mass. Hist. Soc. Coll., 2d s., II, 11, 1814.

Iroquois Supérieurs (French: 'upper Iroquois'). A geographical group of Iroquois, embracing the Oneida, Onondaga, Cayuga, and Seneca, occupying, in the 17th century, an inland country farther from St Lawrence r. than the Mohawk, who were called Iroquois Inférieurs.—Jes. Rel. for 1656, 7, 1858.

Irrigation. It was once assumed that irrigation was not practised by the Indians of the arid region, except to a very limited extent, until after they came under the influence of Spanish missionaries; but recent systematic study of the archeologic remains in the S. W. has removed all doubt that agriculture was conducted in prehistoric times with the aid of extensive irrigation canals, reservoirs, and dams. The most important of these works are in the valleys of the Gila and its tributaries, in s. Arizona, where scores of miles of ditches are still traceable, in instances extending more than 10 m. from the stream from which the water was diverted; according to some observers there are individual canals that traverse a total distance of 25 m. In the Salt River valley alone it is estimated that from 200,000 to 250,000 acres were made available for cultivation by means of irrigation before the arrival of white men. Some of the ancient canals were about 7 ft deep and 4 ft wide at the bottom, but the sides sloped gradually, rising in steps, giving the acequia a width of about 30 ft at the surface. Both the bed and the sides were carefully tamped and plastered with clay to prevent waste through seepage. Remains of what are believed to have been wooden head gates have been exposed by excavation. Where canal depressions have disappeared, owing to cultivation or to sand drift, the canals are still traceable by the innumerable bowlders and water-worn concretions that line the banks; these, according to Cushing, having been placed there by the natives as "water-tamers" to direct the streams to the thirsty fields. The irrigation works in the valleys mentioned probably indicate greater engineering skill than any aboriginal remains that have been discovered N. of Mexico. Several of the old canal beds have been utilized for miles by modern ditch builders; in one instance a saving of $20,000 to $25,000 was effected at the Mormon settlement of Mesa, Maricopa co., Ariz., by employing an ancient acequia that traversed a volcanic knoll for 3 m. and which at one point was excavated to a depth of 20 to 25 ft in the rock for several hundred feet. The remains of ditches the building of which necessitated overcoming similar though less serious obstacles exist in the valley of the Rio Verde; and on the Hassayampa, N. w. of Phœnix, a canal from that stream traverses a lava mesa for several miles and falls abruptly into a valley 40 or 50 ft. below, the water in its descent having cut away the rocky mesa walls for several feet.

Even where the water supply of a pueblo settlement situated several miles from a stream was obtained by means of canals, each house cluster was provided with a reservoir; and in many instances through the S. W., reservoirs, sometimes covering an area measuring 1 m. by ½ m., designed for the storage of rain water, were the sole means of water supply both for domestic purposes and for irrigation. In the valleys of the Rio Grande and its tributaries, in New Mexico, small reservoirs were the chief means of supplying water to the ancient villages; and even to-day only the rudest methods of irrigation are employed by the Pueblo tribes. The ancient occupants of Peñasco Blanco, one of the Chaco canyon group of ancient ruins in the Navaho desert in N. w. New Mexico, diverted water from the Chaco by means of a ditch which supplied a reservoir built in sand, and partially prevented seepage by lining its bed with slabs of stones and clay. The neighboring pueblos of Una Vida, Pueblo Bonito, Kinklazhin, Kinbineola, and Kinyaah, also were artificially provided with water for irrigation. Kinbineola, however, exhibits the best example of irrigation works of any of the Chaco group of villages, water having been diverted from the sandy wash to a large natural depression and thence conducted to the fields, 2 m. away, by a ditch dug around a mesa and along a series of sand hills on a fairly uniform grade. This ditch was mainly earthwork, but where necessary the lower border was reenforced with retaining walls of stone. Kinyaah is said to have been provided with two large reservoirs and a canal 25 to 30 ft wide and in places 3 to 4 ft deep.

Hand irrigation is still practised by the Pueblo Indians. The Zuñi women, in order to raise their small crops of onions, chile, etc., are obliged to carry water in jars on their heads, sometimes for several hundred yards; it is then poured on the individual plants with a gourd ladle. At the Middle Mesa villages of the Hopi, garden patches are watered in much the same way, except that here the gardens are within easier reach of the springs and are irrigated by means of a gourd vessel fastened to the end of a long pole. Both the Hopi of to-day and the ancient inhabitants of the vicinity of the present Solomonville, on the Gila, constructed reservoirs on the mesa sides from which terraced gardens below were readily irrigated, the reservoirs being supplied by impounding storm water. Throughout the S. W. where pueblos occupied the summits of mesas, reservoirs were provided, and according to tradition some of these were filled in winter by rolling into them immense snowballs. For hundred of years the pueblo of Acoma (q. v.) has derived its entire water supply for domestic purposes from a natural depression in the rock which receives the rainfall from the mesa summit.

Consult Cushing (1), Zuñi Breadstuff, 1884–85, (2) in Compte-rendu Internat. Cong. Amér., VII, 163, 1890; Fewkes in 22d Rep. B. A. E., 1904; Hewett in Records of the Past, IV, no. 9, 1905; Hodge in Am. Anthrop., VI, 323, 1893; Mindeleff in 13th Rep. B. A. E., 1896; Wilson in 13th Rep. U. S. Geol. Surv., 133, 1893. (F. W. H.)

Irrupiens. A village on a river of the same name, an affluent of Trinity r., Tex., at which St Denis and his party stopped in 1717. Herds of buffalo were encountered there. The region was in the main occupied by tribes of the Caddoan family, but bordered the country occupied by intrusive tribes of other stocks. Consult Derbanne in Margry, Déc., VI, 204, 1886; La Harpe in French, Hist. Coll. La., III, 48, 1851. Cf. *Ervipiames.*
(A. C. F.)

Iruwaitsu (*Iruai'tsu*, 'Scott valley people'). One of the 4 divisions of the main body of Shasta, living in Scott valley, Siskiyou co., Cal. In 1851 the entire Indian population of Scott valley occupied 7 villages and was estimated by Gibbs (Schoolcraft, Ind. Tribes, III, 171, 1853) to number 420. One of these settlements was apparently Watsaghika.

Iruai'tsu.—R. B. Dixon, inf'n, 1903 (correct name). I'ruwai.—Curtin, MS. vocab., B. A. E., 1885. Scott's Valley Indians.—McKee (1851) in Sen. Ex. Doc. 4, 32d Cong., spec. sess., 170, 1853. Scott Valley Indians.—Steele in Ind. Aff. Rep. 1864, 120, 1865.

Isalwakten. A body of Salish of Fraser superintendency, Brit. Col.

Isalwakten.—Can. Ind. Aff., 79, 1878. Isalwalken.—Ibid., 138, 1879.

Isamis. A body of Salish of Fraser superintendency, Brit. Col.—Can. Ind. Aff., 78, 1878.

Isamuck. A body of Salish of Fraser superintendency, Brit. Col.

Isammuck.—Can. Ind. Aff., 138, 1879. Isamuck.—Ibid., 78, 1878.

Isanthcogna. A former Gabrieleño rancheria in Los Angeles co., Cal., at a locality later called Mission Vieja.—Ried (1852) quoted by Hoffman in Bull. Essex Inst., XVII, 2, 1885.

Isanyati ('Santee'). A Brulé Sioux band, probably originally Santee.

Isaŋyati.—Cleveland quoted by Dorsey in 15th Rep. B. A. E., 219, 1897. Isaⁿyati.—Ibid.

Isfanalgi. An extinct clan of the Creeks, said by Gatschet to be seemingly analogous to the Ishpani phratry and clan of the Chickasaw.

Is-fä-nŭl'-ke.—Morgan, Anc. Soc., 161, 1877. Ishfánalgi.—Gatschet, Creek Migr. Leg., I, 156, 1884.

Isha. A former populous Chumashan village near San Pedro, Ventura co., Cal.

I-ca'.—Henshaw, Buenaventura MS. vocab., B. A. E., 1884.

Ishauu. The Coyote clan of the Hopi.

I'-sau-üh wüñ-wü.—Fewkes in Am. Anthrop., VII, 403, 1894 (wüñ-wü= 'clan'). Isauû wiñwû.—Fewkes in 19th Rep. B. A. E., 584, 1900. Ish.—Voth, Oraibi Summer Snake Ceremony, 282, 1903. I-sha-hue.—Bourke, Snake Dance, 171, 1884. Ishawu.—Dorsey and Voth, Oraibi Soyal, 12, 1901. I'shawuu.—Voth, Hopi Proper Names, 81, 1905. Shahue.—Donaldson, Moqui Pueblo Inds., 65, 1893 (misquoting Bourke).

Ishgua. A former Chumashan village located by Taylor near the mouth of Saticoy r., Ventura co., Cal. Perhaps the same as Isha.

Ishgua.—Taylor in Cal. Farmer, July 24, 1863. Ishguaget.—Ibid.

Ishipishi. A Karok village on the w. bank of Klamath r., N. w. Cal., a mile above the mouth of the Salmon, opposite Katimin, and, like it, burned by the whites in 1852.

Ish-e-pish-e.—Taylor in Cal. Farmer, Mar. 23, 1860. Ishipishi.—A. L. Kroeber, inf'n, 1904 (Karok name). Isshe-pishe-rah.—Gibbs, MS. Misc., B. A. E., 1852. Kepar.—Kroeber, inf'n, 1904 (Yurok name).

Ishpani ('Spanish'). A Chickasaw phratry and clan.

Ish-pän-ee.—Morgan, Anc. Soc., 163, 1877. Ishpáni.—Gatschet, Creek Migr. Leg., I, 96, 1884. Ispáni.—Ibid., 156.

Ishtakhechiduba (Icta'qe tci dúba, 'four white men's houses'). One of the later villages occupied by the Kansa in their migration up Kansas r.—Dorsey, Kansa MS. vocab., B. A. E., 1883.

Ishtowa. The extinct Arrow clans of Sia and San Felipe pueblos, N. Mex.

Ish'to-háno.—Hodge in Am. Anthrop., IX, 348, 1896 (San Felipe form; háno = 'people'). Ishtówaháno.—Ibid. (Sia form).

Ishtua Yene (Keresan: ishtoa, 'arrow'). A place above Santo Domingo, N. Mex., whence fled the Cochiti inhabitants of Kuapa when pursued in prehistoric times by the mythical Pinini (q. v.), or pygmies, according to San Felipe tradition. The place is so called on account of numerous arrow points found there.—Bandelier in Arch. Inst. Papers, IV, 166, 1892.

Isht-ua Yen-e.—Bandelier, op. cit.

Ishtunga ('right side'). The name applied to those divisions of the Kansa that camped on the right side of the tribal circle.

Ictŭñga.—Dorsey in 15th Rep. B. A. E., 230, 1897.

Ishwidip. A Karok village on Klamath r., Cal., inhabited in 1860.

E-swhedip.—Taylor in Cal. Farmer, Mar. 23, 1860. Ishwidip.—A. L. Kroeber, inf'n, 1905.

Isi (a red and white flower). A clan of San Felipe pueblo, N. Mex., of which there was but a single survivor in 1895.

I'si-háno.—Hodge in Am. Anthrop., IX, 350, 1896 (háno = 'people').

Isisokasimiks (I-sis'-o-kas-im-iks, 'hair shirts'). A division of the Kainah.

Hair Shirts.—Grinnell, Blackfoot Lodge Tales, 209, 1892. I-sis'-o-kas-im-iks.—Ibid. The Robes with Hair on the outside.—Culbertson in Smithson. Rep. 1850, 144, 1851.

Isituchi. A former Aleut village on Agattu id., Alaska, one of the Near id. group of the Aleutians, now uninhabited.

Iskutani ('small' [people]). A Choctaw clan of the Watakihulata phratry.

Iskulani.—Morgan, Anc. Soc., 162, 1878 (misprint).

Isle aux Tourtes (French: 'turtle-dove island'). A French Sulpitian mission station, probably on Ottawa r., Quebec, begun for the Algonkin and Nipissing about 1720, but shortly afterward removed to Oka, q. v.—Shea, Cath. Miss., 333, 1855.

Isle of St John's. A village or resort of a band of Micmac, probably in Nova Scotia, in 1760.—Frye (1760) in Mass. Hist. Soc. Coll., 1st s., x, 115, 1809.

Isleta (Span: 'islet', so named from the location of the old village on a delta or island between the bed of a mountain torrent and the Rio Grande. The native name of the pueblo is Shiewhibak, 'knife laid on the ground to play whib,' whib being a native foot race. The name was perhaps suggested by the knife-like shape of the lava ridge on which the pueblo is built.—Lummis). A Tigua pueblo on the w. bank of the Rio Grande, about 12 m. s. of Albuquerque, N. Mex. According to Lummis it stands on the site it occupied at the time of the Spanish discovery in 1540, when it formed one of the villages of the province of Tiguex of Coronado's chroniclers. It was the seat of the Franciscan mission of San Antonio de Isleta from prior to 1629, and about 1675 received accessions from the Tigua pueblos of Quarai, Tajique, and others, E. of the Rio Grande, when those pueblos were abandoned in consequence of Apache depredations. In 1680 the population of Isleta was about 2,000. As the Spanish settlers along the lower Rio Grande took refuge in this pueblo when the uprising occurred in the year named, and thus in-

ISLETA WOMAN.   (VROMAN, PHOTO.)

terrupted communication between its inhabitants and the seat of war at the northern villages, they did not participate in the massacre of the colonists and missionaries in the vicinity. When Gov. Otermin retreated from Santa Fé, however, he found Isleta abandoned, the inhabitants having joined the rebels. The

year following (1681) Otermin surprised and captured the pueblo, and on his return from the N. took with him 519 captives, of whom 115 afterward escaped. The remainder were settled on the N. E. bank of the Rio Grande, a few miles below El Paso, Tex., the name Isleta del Sur ('Isleta of the South') being applied to their pueblo. The date of the refounding of the northern Isleta is somewhat in doubt. According to Bancroft the present pueblo was built in 1709 by some scattered families of Tigua gathered by missionary Juan de la Peña, while Bandelier asserts that the pueblo "remained vacant and in ruins until 1718, when it was repeopled with Tiguas who had returned from the Moquis [Hopi], to whom the majority of the tribe had fled during

VICENTE JIRON, FORMER GOVERNOR OF ISLETA

the 12 years of Pueblo 'independence,'" 1680–92. The name of the mission (San Antonio de la Isleta) seems also to have been transferred to the new pueblo in the s., and on the reestablishment of the northern Isleta the latter became the mission of San Agustin. The Genizaros pueblos of Belen and Tomé were visitas of this mission in 1788. It has been learned by Lummis that a generation ago about 150 Queres from Acoma and Laguna were forced to leave their homes on account of drought and to settle at Isleta, where they still form a permanent part of that village and are recognized by representation in its civil and religious government. Pop. 1,110. (Consult Bandelier in Arch. Inst. Papers, IV, 233, et seq., 1892.)

According to Lummis (inf'n, 1896) the Isleta people have the following clans: Kim (Mountain lion), Pashir (Water pebble), Num (Earth), T'hur (Sun), Shiu (Eagle), Tam (Antelope), Pim (Deer), Churehu (Mole), Shumuyu (Turquoise), Kurni (Goose), Tuim (Wolf), Iebathu (White corn), Iefeu (Red corn), Ieshur (Blue corn), Iechur (Yellow corn), and Parrot. According to Gatschet the tribe is divided into the Churan and Shifunin fraternities or parties—the 'Red Eyes' and the 'Black Eyes'—but these may be merely phratral designations. See *Pueblos, Tigua.*   (F. W. H.)

Alameda la Isleta.—Jefferys, Am. Atlas, map 5, 1776. Gleta.—Calhoun (1849) in Cal. Mess. and Corresp., 211, 1850 (misprint). Hanichiná.—Hodge, field notes, B. A. E., 1895 ('eastern river': Laguna name). Ilet.—D'Anville, map N. A., 1752. Iseta.—Segura in Ind. Aff. Rep., 172, 1890 (misprint). Islella.—Morse, Hist. Am., map, 1798 (misprint). Isleta.—De l'Isle, carte Mexique et Floride, 1703. Isletabuh.—Ward (1864) in Donaldson, Moqui Pueblo Inds., 81, 1893. Isletans.—Lummis, N. Mex. David, 98, 1891. Isleteños.—Lummis, Man Who Married the Moon, 133, 1894. Isletta.—Kitchin, map N. Am., 1787. Isoletta.—Emory, Recon., 41, 1848. Jsleta.—Humboldt, Atlas Nouv.-Espagne, carte 1, 1811. Lleta.—Senex, map, 1710 (misprint). San Agustin del Isleta.—Alencaster (1805) quoted by Prince, N. Mex., 37, 1883. San Antonio de la Isleta.—Benavides, Memorial, 20, 1630. San Augustin de la Isleta.—Villa-Señor, Theatro Am., pt. 2, 418, 422, 1748. San Augustin del Isleta.—Alencaster (1805) in Meline, Two Thousand Miles, 212, 1867. Shee-ah-whib-bahk.—Lummis in St Nicholas, XVIII, 834, Sept. 1891 (native name). Shee-ah-whib-bak.—Ibid., 829. Shee-e-huib-bac.—Lummis in Scribner's Mag., 478, Apr. 1893. Shee-eh-whib-bak.—Lummis, Man Who Married the Moon, 4, 1894. Shiewhibak.—Hodge, field notes, B. A. E., 1895. Shye-ui-beg.—Century Cyclop. of Names, art. "Isleta," 1894. Siwhipa.—Hodge, field notes, B. A. E., 1895 (Acoma form). Táyude.—Gatschet, Isleta MS. vocab., 1882 ('one of the people': proper name of an Isleta Indian; pl. Táyun or Tá-iun). Tchi-ha-hui-pah.—Jouvenceau in Cath. Pion., I, no. 9, 13, 1906. Tshi-a-uip-a.—Bandelier in Arch. Inst. Papers, IV, 220, 1892. Tshya-ui-pa.—Bandelier in Arch. Inst. Rep., V, 37, 1884. Tü-ei.—Gatschet, Isleta MS. vocab., 1882 ('town': given as their own name for the pueblo). Yoletta.—Columbus Memorial Vol., 156, 1893 (misprint). Ysleta.—Rivera, Diario, leg. 756, 1736. Yslete.—Buschmann, N. Mex., 277, 1858. Ystete.—Lane (1854) in Schoolcraft, Ind. Tribes, V, 689, 1855.

Isleta del Sur (Span.: 'Isleta of the south'). A Tigua pueblo on the N. E. bank of the Rio Grande, a few miles below El Paso, Tex. It was established in 1681 by some 400 Indian captives from Isleta, N. Mex., taken thence by Gov. Otermin on his return from the attempted reconquest of the Pueblos after their revolt in Aug., 1680. It was the seat of a Franciscan mission from 1682, containing a church dedicated to San Antonio de Pádua. The mission name San Antonio applied to Isleta del Sur belonged to the northern Isleta until its abandonment in consequence of the revolt, and when the latter was resettled in 1709 or 1718, the mission was named San Agustin de la Isleta. The few inhabitants of Isleta del Sur are now almost completely Mexicanized. See authors cited below; also Fewkes in Am. Anthrop., IV, no. 1, 1902.   (F. W. H.)

Corpus Christi de Isleta.—Otermin (1682) quoted by Bancroft, Ariz. and N. Mex., 191, 1889. Ilesta.—De l'Isle, Atlas Nouveau, map, 59, 1733. Iselle.—Vaugondy, map Amér., 1778. Isla.—Escudero, Noticias Nuevo-Méx., 14, 1849. Isleta del Paso.—Gatschet in Mag. Am. Hist., 259, Apr. 1882. Isleta-del-Paso.—ten Kate, Synonymie, 8, 1884. Isleta del Sur.—Bandelier in Arch. Inst. Papers, III, 86, 1890. Isleta of the South.—Davis, El Gringo, 115, 1857. Isletta.—Ind. Aff. Rep., 128, 1850. Islettas.—Calhoun (1849) in Cal. Mess. and Corresp., 211, 1850. San Antonio de la Isleta.—Bell in Jour. Ethnol. Soc. Lond., I, 224, 1869. Ysleta.—Rivera, Diario, leg. 684, 1736.

Islets de Jeremie. An Indian mission, probably Montagnais, on the lower St Lawrence, Quebec, in 1863.—Hind, Lab. Penin., II, 179, 1863.

Islyamen. A village w. of the Tlaamen and N. of Texada id., on the mainland of British Columbia.—Brit. Col. map, Ind. Aff., Victoria, 1872.

Ismiquilpas. A tribe or band of w. Texas, allied with the Jumano in 1699.—Iberville (1702) in Margry, Déc., IV, 316, 1880.

Ismuracanes. One of the tribes formerly connected with San Carlos mission, near Monterey, Cal.—Galiano, Relacion, 164, 1802.

Isoguichic. A Tarahumare settlement in Chihuahua, Mexico (Orozco y Berra, Geog., 323, 1864); possibly the same as Sisoquichi, located on some maps near the headwaters of Rio Conchos, lat. 27° 48'.

Ispipewhumaugh. One of the tribes included by the early fur traders under the term Nez Percés (Ross, Fur Hunters, I, 185, 1855). They lived on Columbia r., above the mouth of Snake r., Wash. They were possibly of Shahaptian stock, but are not otherwise identifiable.

Isquepah. A Sumass village on the N. bank of Fraser r., Brit. Col., opposite the lake.—Brit. Col. map, Ind. Aff., Victoria, 1872.

Issi ('deer'). A clan of the Koi phratry of the Chickasaw.—Morgan, Anc. Soc., 163, 1877.

Issui (*Is'-sui*, 'tails that can be seen from the front,' in allusion to a buffalo-tail worn on the hip.—Wissler). A society of the Ikunuhkahtsi, or All Comrades, among the Piegan Siksika. It is composed of old men who dress like and dance with and like the Emitaks, though forming a different society.—Grinnell, Blackfoot Lodge Tales, 221, 1892.

Istapoga (*isti* 'people', *apókita* 'to reside'). An Upper Creek settlement, not recorded in the earlier documents; but probably in the neighborhood of the present Eastaboga, Talladega co., Ala.—Gatschet, Creek Migr. Leg., I, 133, 1884.

Istsikainah (*Is-tsi'-kai-nah*, 'woods Bloods'). A division of the Kainah. Is-tsi'-kai-nah.—Grinnell, Blackfoot Lodge Tales, 209, 1892. Woods Bloods.—Ibid.

Istudshilaika (*I'studshi-läi'ka*, 'where a young thing was found.'—Hawkins). One of the 4 Hillabi villages formerly on the left side of Hillabi cr., 4 m. below Hillabi, Ala.

E-chuse-is-li-gau.—Hawkins (1799), Sketch, 43, 1848. **Ístudshi-läíka.**—Gatschet, Creek Migr. Leg., I, 133, 1884.

Isutkwa (*Isútkwa*). An ancient Nuwukmiut village on the site of the U. S. Signal station at Pt Barrow, Alaska.—Murdoch in 9th Rep. B. A. E., pl. ii, 1892.

Ita. A tribe of Eskimo between lat. 76° and 78° 18′, w. Greenland. Their principal village (Etah), from which they take their name, is at Foulke fjord; their chief hunting grounds are Whale and Wolstenholme sds. When first visited by Ross in 1818 they possessed neither canoes nor arrows. The art of building kaiaks, long forgotten, was introduced after 1873 by immigrants from Baffin land, who came by way of Ellesmere land. They hunt seal, their principal food, on the floes of the bays and walrus at the floe edges, and in summer they kill caribou in the mountains. They live in almost complete isolation, without salt, with scarcely any substance of vegetal origin, in the northernmost climate inhabited by human beings, having no food besides meat, blood, and blubber; no clothing except the skins of birds and animals. Pop. in 1854, according to Kane, 140; in 1884, according to Nourse, 80; Peary enumerated 253 in 1895, reduced by disease to 234 in 1897. Their villages and camping places at various times are: Akpan, Anoatok, Etah, Igludahoming, Igluduasuin, Ikalu, Imnangana, Iterlesoa, Itibling, Kana, Kangerdluksoa, Kangidli, Karmenak, Karsuit, Kiatang, Kingatok, Koinsun, Kukan, Navialik, Netlek, Nutun, Pikirlu, Pituarvik, Sarfalik, Udluhsen, Umana, and Uwarosuk. See Kroeber, cited below.

Arctic Highlanders.—Ross, Voy. of Discov., 183, 1819. **Etah.**—Hayes, Arct. Boat. Jour., 197, 1860. **Ita-Eskimos.**—Boas in Trans. Anthrop. Soc. Wash., III, 102, 1885. **Ítă'mi.**—Stein in Petermanns Mitt., 198, 1902. **Itaner.**—Bessells, Amer. Nordpol. Exped., 351, 1879. **Itanese.**—Bessells in Am. Nat., XVIII, 863, 1884. **Smith Sound Eskimo.**—Kroeber in Bull. Am. Mus. Nat. Hist., XII, 266, 1899.

Itaanyadi (*Ita anyadi*, 'deer people'). A Biloxi clan.—Dorsey in 15th Rep. B. A. E., 243, 1897.

Itaes.—A former Chumashan rancheria connected with Dolores mission, San Francisco, Cal.—Taylor in Cal. Farmer, Oct. 18, 1861.

Itafi. A district of Florida where one of the Timuquanan dialects was spoken.—Pareja (*ca.* 1614), Arte Leng. Timuq., xxi, 1886.

Itahasiwaki ('old log'). A former Lower Creek town on lower Chattahoochee r., 3 m. above Ft Gaines, Ga., with 100 inhabitants in 1820.

Eto-husse-wakkes.—Morse, Rep. to Sec. War, 364, 1822.

Itamalgi. A Creek clan.

Ítamalgi.—Gatschet, Creek Migr. Leg., I, 155, 1884. **Támalgi.**—Ibid. **Tä-mul'-kee.**—Morgan, Anc. Soc., 161, 1877.

Itamameou. A Montagnais mission in 1854, E. of Natashquan, on the N. bank of the St Lawrence, Quebec province.

Itamameóu.—Arnaud (1854) in Hind, Lab. Penin., II, 178, 1863. **Itamamiou.**—Hind, ibid., 180.

Itara. A former village in N. Florida, visited by De Soto's troops in 1539.

Ytara.—Gentl. of Elvas (1557) in French, Hist. Coll. La., II, 130, 1850.

Itaywiy. A former Luiseño village in the neighborhood of San Luis Rey mission, S. Cal.—Taylor in Cal. Farmer, May 11, 1860.

Itazipcho ('without bows'). A band of the Sans Arcs Sioux, the same as Minishala, though the two were originally distinct.

Itazipĉo-hĉa.—Dorsey in 15th Rep. B. A. E., 219, 1897. **Itaziptco-qtca.**—Ibid. **Me-ne-sharne.**—Lewis and Clark, Discov., 34, 1806 (given as a Brulé division). **Mini-cala.**—Dorsey, op. cit. **Mini-ŝala.**—Ibid. **Min-i-sha'.**—Hayden, Ethnog. and Philol. Mo. Val., 375, 1862. **Red water band.**—Culbertson in Smithson. Rep. 1850, 142, 1851.

Itchadak. A former Aleut village on one of the E. Aleutian ids., Alaska.—Coxe, Russ. Discov., 165, 1787.

Itchhasualgi (*itchhasua* 'beaver', *algi* 'people'). A Creek clan.—Gatschet, Creek Migr. Leg., I, 155, 1884.

Itchualgi (*itchu* 'deer', *algi* 'people'). A Creek clan.

E'-cho.—Morgan, Anc. Soc., 161, 1877. **Itchúalgi.**—Gatschet, Creek Migr. Leg., I, 155, 1884.

Iteghu ('burnt faces'). A band of the Hunkpatina or Lower Yanktonai Sioux.

Ite ġu.—Dorsey in 15th Rep. B. A. E., 218, 1897. **Ite-xu.**—Ibid.

Iterlesoa (*Iterlĕ'hsoa*, 'bay'). An Ita Eskimo settlement on Granville bay, lat. 76° 50′, N. Greenland.—Stein in Petermanns Mitt., no. 9, map, 1902.

Iteshicha ('bad face'). A band of the Oglala Sioux.

Bad Faces.—Brackett in Smithson. Rep. 1876, 467, 1877. **E-tach-e-cha.**—Ibid. **Ite-citca.**—Dorsey in 15th Rep. B. A. E., 220, 1897. **Ite-śiĉa.**—Ibid. **Oglala-qtca.**—Ibid. ('real Oglala').

Iteshichaetanhan ('from bad face'). A band of the Oglala Sioux.

Ite-citca-etaⁿhaⁿ.—Dorsey (after Cleveland) in 15th Rep. B. A. E., 220, 1897. **Ite-śiĉa-etaɳhaɳ.**—Ibid.

Ithkyemamits. A tribe or band of doubtful linguistic affinity, either Chinookan or Shahaptian, living in 1812 on Columbia r. in Klickitat co., Wash., nearly opposite The Dalles. Their number was estimated at 600.

Iltte-Kaï-Mamits.—Stuart in Nouv. Ann. Voy., XII, 26, 1821. **Ithkyemamits.**—Morse, Rep. to Sec. War, 368, 1822.

Itibleng ('portage'). An Ita Eskimo village at the entrance of Inglefield gulf, N. W. Greenland.

Ĭ'tibleng.—Stein in Petermanns Mitt., 198, 1902. **Ittibloo.**—Peary in Geog. Jour., II, 224, 1898. **Ittiblu.**—Peary, My Arct. Jour., 80, 1898. **Ittiblu-Netlik.**—Sharp, Arct. Highlanders, II, 244, ——.

Iticha. A Yokuts (Mariposan) tribe on Kings r., Cal., below the Choinimni and above the Wichikik.

Aiticha.—A. L. Kroeber, inf'n, 1906 (correct form). **I-tach-ee.**—Royce in 18th Rep. B. A. E., 782, 1899. **Itaches.**—Johnston (1851) in Sen. Ex. Doc. 61, 32d Cong. 1st sess., 22, 1852. **I-te-che.**—Wessells (1853) in H. R. Ex. Doc. 76, 34th Cong., 3d sess., 31, 1857.

I-techees.—McKee et al. (1851) in Sen. Ex. Doc. 4, 32d Cong., spec. sess., 75, 1853. **It-i′-cha.**—Powers in Cont. N. A. Ethnol., III, 370, 1877. **I-to-ches.**—Barbour (1852) in Sen. Ex. Doc. 4, 32d Cong., spec. sess., 252, 1852. **Ituchas.**—Lewis in Ind. Aff. Rep., 399, 1858 (a band of the Wattokes high up on Kings r.).

Itijarelling. A summer settlement of Padlimiut Eskimo on Exeter sd., Baffin land.—Boas in 6th Rep. B. A. E., map, 1888.

Itivimiut ('people of the farther side,' so called by the Eskimo of Labrador proper). A tribe of Labrador Eskimo inhabiting the E. coast of Hudson bay, from lat. 53° to 58°; pop. estimated at 500. These people hunt in the interior halfway across the peninsula, continually scouring the coast for seal and the plains and hills for caribou to obtain necessary food and clothing.
Itivimiut.—Turner in Trans. Roy. Soc. Can., II, 99, 1888. **Thiviment.**—Boas in Am. Antiq., 40, 1888 (misprint).

Itivliarsuk. An Eskimo village in w. Greenland, lat. 73° 30′.—Science, XI, map, 259, 1888.

Itiwa Ateuna ('those of the midmost all'). A Zuñi phratry embracing the Pichi or Mula (Parrot or Macaw), Taa (Seed or Corn), and Yatokya (Sun) clans.—Cushing, inf'n, 1891.

Itliok. A Squawmish village community on the left bank of Squawmisht r., Brit. Col.
Itli′ōq.—Hill-Tout in Rep. Brit. A. A. S., 474, 1900. **Yîtlē′q.**—Boas, MS., B. A. E., 1887.

Itokakhtina ('dwellers at the south'). A band of the Sisseton Sioux; an offshoot of the Basdecheshni.
Itokah-tina.—Dorsey in 15th Rep. B. A. E., 217, 1897. **Itokaq-tina.**—Ibid.

Itomapa. Mentioned by Martin (Hist. La., I, 252, 1820) as a tribe, on the w. side of the lower Mississippi, which sent a deputation to the village of the Acolapissa in 1717 to meet Bienville. Cf. *Ibitoupa.*

Itrahani. The Cottonwood clan of Cochiti pueblo, N. Mex.
Hiits Hanyi.—Bandelier, Delight Makers, 256, 1890 (same ?). **Y′traháni hánuch.**—Hodge in Am. Anthrop., IX, 350, 1896 (*hanuch*='people').

Itsaatiaga (*It-sa′-a-ti-a-ga*). A Paviotso band formerly living about Unionville, w. Nev.—Powell, Paviotso MS., B. A. E., 1881.

Itscheabine. A division of the Assiniboin, numbering 850, including 250 warriors, in 100 tipis, when seen by Lewis and Clark in 1804, at which time they roved on the headwaters of Mouse (Souris), Qu'Appelle, and Assiniboine rs., in the United States and Canada. In 1808, according to Henry (Coues, New Light, II, 522, 1897), they were at enmity with the Dakota, Shoshoni, and with some of the Arikara and other tribes, but were friendly with the Cree. They lived by hunting, conducting trade with the Hudson's Bay, Northwest, and X. Y. fur companies, whose posts were 150 m. N. of Ft Mandan. They are said to have paid little attention to their engagements and were great drunkards. In 1853 they numbered 10 lodges under chief Les Yeux Gris. (F. W. H.)
Gens de Feuilles.—Lewis and Clark, Exped., I, 217, 1893. **Gens de la Feuille.**—Badin (1830) in Ann. de la Prop. de la Foi, IV, 536, 1843 (same?). **Gens des fees or Girls.**—Orig. Jour. Lewis and Clark, VI, 104, 1905 (given as traders' nickname). **Gens des filles.**—Maximilian, Trav., 194, 1843. **Gens des Tee.**—Orig. Jour. Lewis and Clark, op. cit. **Girls' band.**—Hayden quoted by Dorsey in 15th Rep. B. A. E., 222, 1897. **Itscheabinè.**—Maximilian, op. cit. **Little Girl Assiniboines.**—Coues, Henry and Thompson Jour. (1808), II, 522, 1897. **Na-co′-tah O-see-gah.**—Orig. Jour. Lewis and Clark, op. cit. **Osgeegah.**—Ibid. **We-che-ap-pe-nah.**—Denig (1853) quoted by Dorsey, op. cit. **Wi-io′-ap-i-naḣ.**—Hayden, Ethnog. and Philol. Mo. Val., 387, 1862. **Witcinya·npina.**—Dorsey in 15th Rep. B. A. E., 223, 1897.

Itseyi (*Itséyĭ,* 'new green place,' or 'place of fresh green'; often falsely rendered 'Brasstown,' from the confusion of *Itséyĭ* and *Ûñtsaiyĭ′,* the latter term signifying 'brass'). The name of several former Cherokee settlements. One was on Brasstown cr. of Tugaloo r., in Oconee co., S. C.; another was on Little Tennessee r., near the present Franklin, Macon co., N. C., and probably about the junction of Cartoogaja cr.; a third, known to the whites as Brasstown, was on upper Brasstown cr. of Hiwassee r., Towns co., Ga.—Mooney in 19th Rep. B. A. E., 523, 1900.
Echay.—Mouzon map quoted by Royce in 5th Rep. B. A. E., 143, 1887. **Echia.**—Mooney, op. cit. **Echoe.**—Bartram, Travels, 371, 1792. **Echoee.**—Doc. of 1755 quoted by Royce, op. cit. **Etchoe.**—Scaife, Hist. Catawba, 7, 1896. **Etchowee.**—Mooney, op. cit.

Ittatso. The principal village of the Ucluelet (q v.) on Ucluelet arm of Barclay sd., w. coast of Vancouver id.—Can. Ind. Aff., 263, 1902.

Ituc. A former Chumashan village near Santa Barbara, Cal.—Taylor in Cal. Farmer, Apr. 24, 1863.

Itukemuk. A former Luiseño village in the neighborhood of San Luis Rey mission, s. Cal.—Taylor in Cal. Farmer, May 11, 1860.

Ivan. A Kaiyuhkhotana village on the divide between Unalaklik and Yukon rs., Alaska. Allen (Rep. Alaska, 131, 1877) gave the population as 69.
Ivan's barrábora.—Dall, Alaska, 531, 1870.

Ivigtite. A variety of paragonite. According to Dana (Text-book of Mineral., 354, 1888) it occurs in yellow scales, also granular, with cryolite from Greenland. It was named from Ivigtuk, Greenland, where it was discovered, a place-name derived from the Eskimo language. The *-ite* is an English suffix. (A. F. C.)

Ivigtut. A settlement of Europeans and Eskimo in s. w. Greenland, lat. 61° 15′.—Nansen, First Crossing, II, 182, 1890.

Ivikat. A missionary station 16 m. N. of Julianehaab, s. Greenland.—Koldewey, German Arct. Exped., 203, 1874.

Ivimiut. An Eskimo settlement near Lindenov fjord, E. Greenland, with 12 inhabitants in 1829.—Graah, Exped., 114, 1837.

Ivitachuco. A former principal town of the Apalachee, possibly near the present Wacahotee, Fla.
Attachooka.—Archdale (1707) in Carroll, Hist. Coll. S. C., II, 352, 1836. **Ibitachka.**—Ibid., 575. **Ivitachma.**—Bancroft, Hist. U. S., II, 194, 1884. **Ivitachua.**—Jefferys, Fr. Dom. Am., West Indies map, 1761. **Ivi-ta-chuco.** — Biedma (1544) in French, Hist. Coll. La., II, 99, 1850. **Ivitanoa.**—Jefferys, Fr. Dom. Am., 135, map, 1761. **Vitachuco.**—Gentl. of Elvas (1557) in French, Hist. Coll. La., II, 134, 1850. **Yvitachua.** — Bartram, Trav., I, map, 1799.

Ivory. See *Bonework.*

Ivy Log. A Cherokee settlement, about the period of the removal of the tribe to Indian Ter. in 1839, on Ivy Log cr., Union co., N. Ga. (J. M.)

Iwai. A former Yaquina village on the N. side of Yaquina r., Oreg.
I-wai′.—Dorsey in Jour. Am. Folk-lore, III, 229, 1890.

Iwayusota ('uses up by begging for'; 'uses up with the mouth'). A band of the Oglala Sioux.—Dorsey (after Cleveland) in 15th Rep. B. A. E., 220, 1897.

Iwi. The Eagle gens of the Kadohadacho.—Mooney in 14th Rep. B. A. E., 1093, 1896.

Ixtacan. A pueblo of the Cora and the seat of a mission; situated on the s. bank of the Rio San Pedro, about lat. 22°, Tepic, Mexico.
Diskatan.—Hrdlicka, inf'n, 1906. **S. Pedro de Ixtacan.**—Orozco y Berra, Geog., 280, 1864.

Iyaaye (*I-ya-áye*, 'sunflower'). An Apache clan or band at San Carlos agency and Ft Apache in 1881.—Bourke in Jour. Am. Folk-lore, III, 111, 1890. See *Yachin.*

Iyakoza ('wart on a horse's leg'). A band of the Brulé Teton Sioux.
A-á-ko-za.—Hayden, Ethnog. and Philol. Mo. Val., 376, 1862. **Big Ankle band.**—Ibid. **Big-legged horses.**—Culbertson in Smithson. Rep. 1850, 141, 1851. **Iyakoza.**—Dorsey in 15th Rep. B. A. E., 218, 1897. **Iyak'oza.**—Ibid.

Iyama Ateuna ('those of the uppermost'). A phratry embracing the Kyakyali (Eagle) and Ana (Tobacco) clans of the Zuñi.—Cushing, inf'n, 1891.

Iyis. A Karok village on Klamath r., Cal., inhabited in 1860.
I-yiss.—Taylor in Cal. Farmer, Mar. 23, 1860.

Iza. A settlement of which Coronado was informed by the Indian known as The Turk, while on the Rio Grande in New Mexico in 1540–41, as a place, 6 or 7 days' journey distant, at which the army could obtain provisions on its way to "Copala" and Quivira. It was possibly imaginary; if not, it may have been a settlement of the Eyish, a Caddoan tribe of Texas. See Mota-Padilla (1742), Nueva Galicia, 164, 1870. (F. W. H.)

Iztacans. A name adopted by Rafinesque (introd. to Marshall, Ky., I, 26, 1824) for an imaginary prehistoric race of the United States.

Jack. See *Kintpuash.*

Jackash. A name of the American mink (*Putorius vison*) in use in the fur country (Coues, N. Am. Must., 172, 1877). From *atchákas*, the name of this animal in the Cree dialect of Algonquian. This word Lacombe (Dict., 316, 1874) explains as a diminutive of *wittakäy*, signifying 'genitals,' in reference to the glands of the creature. (A. F. C.)

Jack Indians. An unidentified tribe mentioned by Dobbs (Hudson Bay, 13, 1744), who states that in 1731 they came to trade at the mouth of Albany r., N. W. Ter., Canada. Named as distinct from Moose River Indians (Monsoni), Sturgeon Indians (Nameuilini), and French Indians.

Jackquyome (*Jack-quy-ome*). A body of Salish of Kamloops agency, Brit. Col.; pop. 257 in 1884, when their name appears for the last time.—Can. Ind. Aff. for 1884, 188.

Jacobs Cabins. A settlement on Youghiogheny r. in 1753 (Gist in Mass. Hist. Soc. Coll., 3d s., v. 102, 1836). It may have been near Jacobs cr., Fayette co., Pa., and was perhaps named from Captain Jacobs. (J. M.)

Jacobs, Captain. A Delaware chief who participated in the ambush of Gen. Braddock's army, and a leader in conjunction with Shingis in the raids and massacres on the frontiers of the settlements of Pennsylvania that followed the British disaster. A price was set on both their heads. They had a rendezvous at Kittanning, Pa., whither they took their spoils and captives. Col. John Armstrong marched against this place and assailed it at daybreak on Sept. 8, 1756. The Pennsylvanians surrounded the village and the Indians defended themselves bravely but hopelessly from their burning wigwams. Jacobs was killed with all his family.—Drake, Bk. Inds., 534, 1880.

Jacona (Span. form of Tewa *Sákona*). A former small Tewa pueblo situated with Cuyamunque a short distance w. of Nambe, on the s. side of Pojoaque r., Santa Fé co., N. Mex. At the time of the Pueblo rebellion of 1680 it was a visita of Nambe mission. It was abandoned in 1696, its inhabitants settling among the other Tewa pueblos, and in 1702 the grant of land that had been made to it by Spain became the property of Ignacio de Roybal. See Bandelier in Arch. Inst. Papers, IV, 85, 1892. (F. W. H.)
Iacona.—Buschmann, Neu-Mex., 230, 1858. **Jacoma.**—Davis, El Gringo, 88, 1857. **Jacona.**—Vetancurt (1693) Teatro Mex., III, 317, 1871. **Sacona.**—Bandelier in Arch. Inst. Papers, IV, 85, 1892 (Jacona, or). **Sa'kona.**—Hodge, field notes, B. A. E., 1885 (Tewa pronunciation). **S. Domingo de Xacomo.**—Jefferys, Am. Atlas, map 5, 1776. **S. Domingo de Xacoms.**—Walch, Charte America, 1805. **S. Domingo de Xacona.**—D'Anville, map Am. Sept., 1746. **Xacona.**—De l'Isle, carte Mexique et Floride, 1703. **Xacono.**—De l'Isle, Atlas Nouveau, map 60, 1733.

Jacuencacahel. A former rancheria under the mission of San Francisco Xavier de Biaundo, in Lower California.—Writer of 1728 in Doc. Hist. Mex., 4th s., v, 187, 1857.

Jade. See *Nephrite*.

Jagavans. The name of a small tribe formerly on the Texas coast; mentioned by Harris (Coll. Voy., i, 802, 1705) as one of those visited about 1530 by Cabeza de Vaca, as not far from the Chorruco, and as neighbors of the Mariames. Possibly the Yguases of Cabeza de Vaca's Relation (Smith trans., 92, 1871).

Jagaya. A former village in a well-watered country 50 leagues from Santa Helena and 20 leagues from the sea, in N. W. South Carolina; visited by Juan Pardo in 1565.—Vandera (1567) in Smith, Colec. Doc. Fla., i, 16, 1857.

Jakobshavn. A Danish missionary station and trading post on Disko bay, w. Greenland, established in 1741. Pop. 300 in 1867.
Jacobs-haven.—Crantz, Hist. of Greenland, i, 15, 1767.

Jamac. A former rancheria, probably of the Sobaipuri of s. Arizona, and a visita of the mission of Guevavi in 1732.—Alegre quoted by Bancroft, No. Mex. States, i, 524, 1884.

Jamaica. A former pueblo of the Opata in N. E. Sonora, Mexico, under the jurisdiction of the municipality of Cumpus, in the district of Moctezuma (Orozco y Berra, Geog., 343, 1864). It contained 9 civilized inhabitants in 1900.

Jameco. The supposed name of "a small tribe or family of Indians subject to some other," thought to have dwelt formerly on Long Island, N. Y., near Jamaica, which derives its name from the band.
Jameco.—Thompson, Long Id., 382, 1839. Jemaco.—Flint, Early Long Id., 198, 1896.

Janemo. See *Ninigret*.

Janos. An extinct tribe which, with the Jocomes, inhabited the region of Chihuahua, Mexico, between Casas Grandes, Chihuahua, and Fronteras. Bandelier (Nation, July 2, 1885) classes them as the most southerly band of the Apache, called after presidio Janos in N. W. Chihuahua. He believes that the tribe slowly arose after 1684 and was composed of Lipan, Mescalero, and other Apache stragglers, together with renegade Suma, Toboso, Tarahumare, and Opata Indians, and Spanish captives. Missions were established among them at an early date at Janos and Carretas, but were abandoned on account of the incursions of the Apache proper, with whom the Janos were subsequently merged. Frequent mention is made of the Janos by Jesuit missionaries during the first half of the 18th century, but of their language and customs almost nothing is known.
Hanes.—Linschoten, Descr. de l'Am., map 1, 1638. Hanos.—Benavides, Memorial, 7, 1630. Jamos.—

Duro, Peñalosa, 63, 1882. Janeros.—Bandelier in N. Y. Nation, July 2, 1885. Janos.—Kino (1690) in Doc. Hist. Mex., 4th s., i, 230, 1856. Yanos.—Mühlenpfordt, Mejico, ii, 521, 1844.

Jantamais. Mentioned by Domenech (Deserts of N. Am., i, 441, 1860) in a list of tribes without further notice. Possibly the Yanktonai; otherwise unknown.

Japazaws. A Powhatan Indian, chief of Potomac and a friend of the English. In 1611 he inveigled Pocahontas on board an English ship to be detained as a hostage for the good behavior of Powhatan, her father.—Drake, Bk. Inds., 357, 1880.

Jappayon. A former village connected with San Carlos mission, Cal., and said to have been Esselen.—Taylor in Cal. Farmer, Apr. 20, 1860.

Japul. Given by the Yavapai to Fray Francisco Garcés in 1776 (Diary, 405, 1900) as the name, seemingly, of a Yuman tribe; locality not recorded, but possibly in the vicinity of the Rio Colorado.
Japiel.—Orozco y Berra, Geog., 349, 1864 (misprinting Garcés). Japui.—Garcés, op. cit., 444. Tapiel.—Cortez (1799) in Whipple, Pac. R. R. Rep., iii, pt. 3, 126, 1856 (misprint).

Jars. See *Dishes, Pottery, Receptacles*.

Jasniga. A former village, presumably Costanoan, connected with San Juan Bautista mission, Cal.—Taylor in Cal. Farmer, Nov. 25, 1860.

Jasper. An impure, opaque form of chalcedony displaying various shades of color, the yellow, red, and brown hues predominating. When grayish or greenish and mottled with red the name bloodstone is sometimes applied. It was much used by the native tribes for flaked implements of several varieties, and more rarely for hammers, celts, axes, and ornaments. It occurs in irregular masses, or pockets, in connection with other formations in many sections of the United States, and was often obtained by the Indians in the form of fugitive pebbles and bowlders; but in Pennsylvania, and perhaps in other states, it was quarried from the original beds. The best known quarries are in Bucks, Lehigh, and Berks cos., E. Pa. Jasper was extensively worked by the ancient inhabitants of Converse and neighboring counties of Wyoming, who found this material as well as the translucent varieties of chalcedony in connection with the quartzite of the region. See *Chalcedony*.

Consult Dorsey in Field Columb. Mus. Pub., Anthrop. ser., ii, no. 4, 1900; Holmes in 15th Rep. B. A. E., 1897; Mercer in Am. Anthrop., vii, 80, 1894.
(w. h. h.)

Jatonabine ('people of the rocks'). An Assiniboin band living in 1808 in N. W. Manitoba, and having 40 tipis.
E-an-to-ah.—Denig quoted by Dorsey in 15th Rep. B. A. E., 222, 1897 ('Stone Indians': "the original appellation for the whole nation"). Eascab.—Franklin, Narr., 104, 1823. Gens de Roche.—Ibid., 306. Gens des Roches.—Hayden, Ethnog. and Philol. Mo. Val., 387, 1862. Gens des rosches.—Ind.

Aff. Rep., 289, 1854. **I'-aŋ-to'-an.**—Hayden, Ethnog. and Philol. Mo. Val., 387, 1862. **Ie-ska-pi.**—Am. Natur., 829, 1882. **Inyantonwan.**—Dorsey in 15th Rep. B. A. E., 223, 1897 (= 'stone village'). **Jatonabinè.**—Maximilian, Trav., 194, 1843. **Rocks.**—Larpenteur (1829), Narr., I, 109, 1898. **Stone Indians.**—Maximilian, Trav., 194, 843 (so called by the English).

Jaumalturgo. A rancheria of the Pima or the Sobaipuri in 1697, s. of the ruin of Casa Grande, in the present Arizona.
San Gregoris Jaumalturgo.—Mange quoted by Schoolcraft, Ind. Tribes, III, 301, 1853 (Gregoris = Gregorio).

Jeaga. A village at the s. extremity of Florida, about 1570.
Caga.—Fontaneda (ca. 1575) in Ternaux-Compans, Voy., xx, 32, 1841. **Feaga.**—Shipp, Hist. Fla., 587, 1881. **Jaega.**—Fontaneda, Narr., Smith trans., 21, 1854. **Teaga.**—Fontaneda in Ternaux-Compans, op. cit., 23. **Teago.**—Ibid., 32.

Jeboaltae. A former village, presumably Costanoan, near San Juan Bautista mission, Cal.
Jeboaltae.—Taylor in Cal. Farmer, Nov. 23, 1860. **Teboaltac.**—Engelhardt, Franciscans in Cal., 398, 1897.

Jedakne. A village, Iroquois or Delaware, that existed in the 18th century on the w. branch of Susquehanna r., probably on the site of Dewart, Northumberland co., Pa. (J. N. B. H.)
Jedacne.—Lattré, map, 1784. **Jedakne.**—Homann Heirs' map, 1756.

Jedandago. A former Seneca hamlet, E. of Irondequoit bay, L. Ontario, N. Y.—Doc. of 1687 in N. Y. Doc. Col. Hist., III, 434, 1853.

Jemez (from *Hä'-mish*, or *Hae'-mish*, the Keresan name of the pueblo.—Bandelier). A village on the N. bank of Jemez r., about 20 m. N. w. of Bernalillo, N. Mex. According to tradition the Jemez had their origin in the N., at a lagoon called Uabunatota (apparently identical with the Shipapulima and Cibobe of other Pueblo tribes), whence they slowly drifted into the valleys of the upper tributaries of the Rio Jemez—the Guadalupe and San Diego—where they resided in a number of villages, and finally into the sandy valley of the Jemez proper, which they now occupy, their habitat being bounded on the s. by the range of the w. division of the Rio Grande Keresan tribes—the Sia and Santa Ana. Castañeda, the chronicler of Coronado's expedition of 1541, speaks of 7 pueblos of the Jemez tribe in addition to 3 others in the province of Aguas Calientes, identified by Simpson with the Jemez Hot Springs region. Espejo in 1583 also mentions that 7 villages were occupied by the Jemez, while in 1598 Oñate heard of 11 but saw only 8. In the opinion of Bandelier it is probable that 10 pueblos were inhabited by the tribe in the early part of the 16th century.

Following is a list of the pueblos formerly occupied by the Jemez people so far as known. The names include those given by Oñate, which may be identical with some of the others: Amushungkwa, Anyukwinu, Astialakwa, Bulitzequa, Catroo, Ceca, Guatitruti, Guayoguia, Gyusiwa, Hanakwa, Kiashita, Kiatsukwa, Mecastria, Nokyuntseleta, Nonyishagi, Ostyalakwa, Patoqua, Pebulikwa, Pekwiligii, Potre, Seshukwa, Setokwa, Towakwa, Trea, Tyajuindena, Tyasoliwa, Uahatzaa, Wabakwa, Yjar, Zolatungzezhii.

Doubtless the reason for the division of the tribe into so many lesser village communities instead of aggregating in a single pueblo for defense against the persistent aggressiveness of the Navaho, according to Bandelier, was the fact that cultivable areas in the sandy valley of the Jemez and its lower tributaries are small and at somewhat considerable distances from one another; but another and perhaps even more significant reason was that the Navaho were apparently not troublesome to the Pueblos at the time of the Spanish conquest. On the establishment of Spanish missions in this section and the introduction of improved methods of utilizing the water for irrigation, however, the

JEMEZ MAN AND WIFE. (VROMAN, PHOTO.)

Jemez were induced to abandon their pueblos one by one, until about the year 1622 they became consolidated into the two settlements of Gyusiwa and probably Astialakwa, mainly through the efforts of Fray Martin de Arvide. These pueblos are supposed to have been the seats of the missions of San Diego and San Joseph, respectively, and both contained chapels probably from 1618. Astialakwa was permanently abandoned prior to the Pueblo revolt of 1680, but in the meantime another pueblo (probably Patoqua) seems to have been established, which became the mission of San Juan de los Jemez. About the middle of the 17th century the Jemez conspired with the Navaho against the Spaniards, but the outbreak plotted was repressed by the hanging of 29 of the Jemez. A few years later the Jemez were again confederated with the Navaho and some Tigua against the Spaniards, but the contemplated rebellion was again quelled, the Navaho soon resuming their hostility toward the village dwellers. In the revolt of the Pueblos in Aug., 1680, the Jemez took a prominent part. They murdered the missionary at Gyusiwa (San Diego de Jemez), but the missionary at San Juan de los Jemez, with the alcalde mayor and three soldiers, succeeded in escaping. In 1681, when Gov. Otermin attempted to regain possession of New Mexico, the Jemez retreated to the mesas, but returned to their village on the evacuation of the region by the Spaniards. Here they probably remained until 1688, when Cruzate appeared, causing them to flee again to the heights. When Vargas came in 1692 the Jemez were found on the mesa in a large pueblo, but they were induced to descend and to promise the Spaniards their support. The Jemez, however, failed to keep their word, but waged war during 1693 and 1694 against their Keresan neighbors on account of their fidelity to the Spaniards. Vargas returned to the Jemez in 1693, when they reiterated their false promises. In July, 1694, he again went to Jemez with 120 Spaniards and some allies from Santa Ana and Sia. The mesa was stormed, and after a desperate engagement, in which 84 natives were killed, the pueblo was captured. In the month following, Vargas (after destroying this village, another on a mesa some distance below, and one built by their Santo Domingo allies 3 leagues N.) returned to Santa Fé with 361 prisoners and a large quantity of stores. From this time the only then existing pueblo of the Jemez reoccupied was San Diego, or Gyusiwa, which was inhabited until 1696, when the second revolt occurred, the Indians killing their missionary and again fleeing to the mesas, where they constructed temporary shelters. Here they were joined by some Navaho, Zuñi, and Acoma allies, and made hostile demonstrations toward the Sia, Santa Ana, and San Felipe people, but in June of the year mentioned they were repulsed by a small detachment of Spaniards from Bernalillo and Sia with a loss of 30 men, 8 of whom were Acoma. The defeated Jemez this time fled to the Navaho country, where they remained several years, finally returning to their former home and constructing the present village, called by them Walatoa, "Village of the Bear." In 1728, 108 of the inhabitants died of pestilence. In 1782 Jemez was made a visita of the mission of Sia.

The Jemez clans are: Waha (Cloud), Seh (Eagle), Sonsa (Badger), Daahl (Earth), Kyiahl (Crow), Pe (Sun), Kyunu (Corn), Sungki (Turquoise), Weha (Calabash), Yang (Coyote), Kio (Pine).

The population of the tribe in 1890 was 428; in 1904, 498, including a score of descendants of the remnant of the Pecos (q. v.), who left their old home on the upper Rio Pecos in 1838 to join their kindred.

Consult Bancroft, Arizona and N. Mex., 1889; Bandelier in Arch. Inst. Papers, IV, 200–217, 1892; Hewett in Bull. 32, B. A. E., 1906; Holmes in Am. Anthrop., VII, no. 2, 1905. See also *Pecos, Pueblos, Tanoan.* (F. W. H.)

Amayes.—Duro, Don Diego de Peñalosa, 128, 1882. **Ameges.**—Siguenza quoted by Buschmann, Neu-Mex., 228, 264, 1858. **Ameias.** Espejo (1583) quoted by Mendoza (1586) in Hakluyt Soc. Pub., XV, 245, 1854. **Ameies.**—Mendoza in Hakluyt, Voy., III, 469, 1600. **Amejes.**—Ibid., 462. **Ameries.**—Squier in Am. Review, 523, Nov. 1848. **Amies.**—Davis, Span. Conq. N. Mex., 252, 1869. **Amios.**—Ibid., map. **Amires.**—Ogilby, Amer., 294, 1671. **Djémez.**—Gallatin in Nouv. Ann. Voy., 5th s., XXVII, 280, 1851. **Emeaes.**—Bandelier in Arch. Inst. Papers, IV, 206, 1892. **Emeges.**—Espejo (1583) in Doc. Inéd., XV, 179, 1871. **Emenes.**—Bancroft, Ariz. and N. Mex., 132, 1889. **Emes.**—Cordova (1619) in Ternaux-Compans, Voy., X, 444, 1838. **Emès.**—Villagran, Hist. Nueva Mex., 155, 1610. **Emexes.**—Espejo (1583) in Doc. Inéd., XV, 116, 1871. **Emmes.**—Oñate (1598), ibid., XVI, 102, 260, 1871. **Euimes.**—Columbus Memorial Vol., 155, 1893. **Gemes.**—Villa-Señor, Theatro Am., pt. 2, 421, 1748. **Gemex.**—Zárate-Salmeron (*ca.* 1629) quoted by Bancroft, Nat. Races, I, 600, 1882. **Gemez.**—Humboldt, Atlas Nouv. Espagne, carte 1, 1811. **Gomez.**—Arrowsmith, map N. A., 1795, ed. 1814. **Hae-mish.**—Bandelier in Revue d'Ethnog., 203, 1886 (Queres name). **Hä-mish.**—Bandelier in N. Y. Staatszeitung, June 28, 1885 (Queres name). **Ha-waw-wah-lah-too-waw.**—Simpson in Rep. Sec. War, 143, 1850 (proper name of pueblo). **He'-mai.**—Hodge, field notes, B. A. E., 1895 (Isleta name). **Hemeos.**—Zárate-Salmeron (1629) quoted by Bandelier in Arch. Inst. Papers, IV, 205, 1892. **Hemes.**—Castañeda (*ca.* 1565) in Ternaux-Compans, Voy., IX, 138, 1838. **Hémès.**—Benavides (1630) quoted by Gallatin in Nouv. Ann. Voy., 5th s., XXVII, 305, 1851. **Hemeshítse.**—Hodge, field notes, B. A. E., 1895 (Laguna and San Felipe name). **He'-me-shu-tsa.**—Hodge, field notes, B. A. E., 1895 (Sia form). **Hemez.**—Squier in Am. Review, 522, Nov. 1848 (misquoting Castañeda). **He'mi.**—Hodge, field notes, B. A. E., 1895 ((Santa Ana name). **He-mi-ma'.**—Ibid. (Picuris name). **Hémishitz.**—Ibid. (Acoma name). **Henex.**—Zárate-Salmeron (*ca.* 1629) quoted by Bandelier in Arch. Inst. Papers, IV, 205, 1892. **Hermes.**—Curtis, Children of the Sun, 121, 1883 (misquoting Coronado). **Hernes.**—Kern in Schoolcraft, Ind. Tribes, IV, 32, 39, 1854. **He''-wâ'.**—Hodge, field notes, B. A. E., 1895 (Pecos name of pueblo). **Hiem-ai.**—Gatschet, Isleta MS. vocab., B. A. E., 1885 (Isleta name of pueblo). **Hiémide.**—Ibid. (pl. Híemnin; Isleta name for the people). **James.**—Marcy in Rep. Sec. War, 196, 1850. **Jamez.**—Gallegas (1844) in Emory, Recon., 478, 1848. **Jemas.**—Wislizenus, Memoir, 24, 1848. **Jemes.**—Mendoza (1742) in Meline, Two Thousand Miles, 213, 1867. **Jemex.**—Taylor in Cal. Farmer, June 12, 1863. **Jemez.**—Simpson in Rep. Sec. War, 59, 1850. **Jemmes.**—Peet in Am. Antiq., XVII, 354, 1895. **Jemos.**—Loew (1875) in Wheeler Surv. Rep., VII, 345, 1879. **Jenies.**—Calhoun in Schoolcraft, Ind. Tribes, III, 633, 1853. **Jermz.**—Kern, ibid., IV, 39, 1854. **Jeures.**—Ward in Ind. Aff. Rep. 1867, 210, 1868. **Jimenez.**—Escudero, Not. Estad. Chihuahua, 180, 1834. **Jumez.**—Arch. Inst. Rep., V, 37, 1884. **Maí-děc-kǐž-ne.**—ten Kate, Synonymie, 6, 1884 ('Wolf neck': Navaho name). **Tames.**—Brackenridge, Early Spanish Discov., 19, 1857. **Temes.**—Gatschet in Mag. Am. Hist., 259, Apr. 1882. **Temez.**—Alegre, Hist. Comp. Jesus, I, 336, 1841. **Tuhoa.**—Bandelier in Ausland, 813, 1882 (='houses': proper name of the pueblo). **Tu'-wa.**—Hodge, field notes, B. A. E., 1895 (own name of pueblo). **Uala-to-hua.**—Bandelier in Arch. Inst. Papers, III, 260, 1890 ('village of the bear': own name of pueblo). **Ual-to-hua.**—Ibid., IV, 203, 1892. **Vallatoa.**—Loew in Wheeler Surv. Rep., VII,

344, 1879. **Wa-la-nah.**—Jouvenceau in Cath. Pion., I, no. 9, 13, 1906. **Walatoa.**—Gatschet in Mag. Am. Hist., 259, Apr. 1882. **Wa'-la-tu-wa.**—Hodge, field notes, B. A. E., 1895. **Wöng'-ge'.**—Ibid. ('Navaho place': Santa Clara and San Ildefonso name). **Xemes.**—Rivera, Diario, leg. 950, 1736. χemes.—ten Kate, Synonymie, 6, 1884. **Xeméz.**—Ruxton, Adventures, 194, 1848. **Yemez.**—Latham, Var. of Man, 396, 1850. **Zemas.**—Simpson in Jour. Am. Geog. Soc., v, 195, 1874.

Jennesedaga.—A former Seneca village on the right bank of Allegheny r., 17 m. above Warren, Pa., which in 1816 was the residence of the celebrated Cornplanter; it then consisted of 12 houses.—Day, Hist. Coll. Pa., 656, 1853.

Jenzenaque. A former Natchez village. Dumont (Mémoire, II, 97, 1753) mentions it in addition to Great, Flour, Apple, and Gray villages, in the early part of the 18th century. The fifth village, mentioned by most authors of his period, is Terre Blanche, and Jenzenaque may be its Natchez name.

Jerome Big Eagle. See *Wamdetanka*.

Jeromestown. A former Delaware village near the present Jeromesville, Ashland co., Ohio, on a section of land set aside for the use of the Delawares by act of Mar. 3, 1807, but ceded to the United States by treaty of Sept. 29, 1817. It received its name from Jean Baptiste Jerome, an early French trader. See Brown, West. Gaz., 314, 1817; Howe, Hist. Coll. Ohio, I, 255, 1898; Royce in 18th Rep. B. A. E., Ohio map, 1899.

Jesus María. A pueblo of the Cora on the E. bank of Rio San Pedro, here known as the Rio Jesus María, in the N. part of the Territory of Tepic, about lat. 22° 40′, Mexico. It was the seat of a mission, of which San Francisco was a visita. See Orozco y Berra, Geog., 380, 1864; Lumholtz, Unknown Mexico, I, 487; II, 16, map, 1902.

Jesus María y José. A Franciscan mission founded by Fathers Casañas and Bordoy, in 1690, in the vicinity of and as an adjunct to the mission of San Francisco de los Tejas (q. v.) in Texas, and abandoned in 1693. Its history is the same as that of the parent mission. See Bancroft, No. Mex. States, I, 417–418, 666, 1886; Garrison, Texas, 1903.
Santa María.—Bancroft, op. cit. **Santísimo Nombre de María.**—Ibid.

Jet, Lignite, Anthracite, Cannel coal. Carbonaceous materials used to some extent by Indians. Jet of excellent quality occurs in Colorado, and the Indians of the arid region employ it for jewelry and various carvings. Good examples of lignite ornaments were obtained by Fewkes from the ancient ruins of Arizona, and of jet by Pepper from the ruins of Chaco canyon, N. Mex. Among the latter is a well-sculptured frog decorated with inlaid designs in turquoise and shell. Cannelcoal objects are found in the Ohio valley mounds, but few specimens carved from anthracite are known. A small, well-carved human head of jet-like stone was obtained by Smith from a shell heap on lower Frazer r., Brit. Col., and Niblack says that the N. W. coast tribes pulverize lignite and mix it with oil for paint.

Consult Fewkes in 22d Rep. B. A. E., 1903; Niblack in Rep. Nat. Mus. 1888, 1890; Pepper in Am. Anthrop., VII, 1905; Smith in Mem. Am. Mus. Nat. Hist., IV, 1903.　　　(W. H. H.)

Jetti. A former Cochimi rancheria 3 leagues N. of Loreto mission, Lower California.—Picolo (1702) in Lettres Édifiantes, II, 63, 1841.

Jews and Indians. See *Lost Ten Tribes, Popular fallacies.*

Jiaspi. A former rancheria of the Sobaipuri, visited by Father Kino about 1697 and by him named Rosario. It was situated on the w. bank of Rio San Pedro, probably in the vicinity of the present village of Prospect, s. Arizona.　(F. W. H.)
Jiaspi.—Kino (1697) in Doc. Hist. Mex., 4th s., I, 279, 1856. **Rosario.**—Bernal (1697) quoted by Bancroft, Ariz. and N. Mex., 356, 1887, (Jiaspi, or).

Jicamorachic. A former Tarahumare settlement in Chihuahua, Mexico.—Orozco y Berra, Geog., 323, 1864.

Jicara. (Mex. Span.: 'small gourd vessel or basket'). A former Tepehuane pueblo in Durango, Mexico, and the seat of a Spanish mission.
S. Pedro Jícara.—Orozco y Berra, Geog., 319, 1864.

Jicarilla (Mex. Span.: 'little basket'). An Athapascan tribe, first so called by Spaniards because of their expertness in making vessels of basketry. They apparently formed a part of the Vaqueros of early Spanish chronicles, although, according to their creation legend, they have occupied from the earliest period the mountainous region of s. E. Colorado and N. New Mexico, their range at various periods extending eastward to w. Kansas and Oklahoma, and into N. w. Texas. The Arkansas, Rio Grande, and Canadian rs. figure in their genesis myth (Mooney in Am. Anthrop., XI, 200, 1898), but their traditions seem to center about Taos and the heads of Arkansas r. They regard the kindred Mescaleros and also the Navaho as enemies, and, according to Mooney, their alliances and blood mixture have been with the Ute and Taos. In language they are more closely related to the Mescaleros than to the Navaho or the Arizona Apache. The Jicarillas were first mentioned by this name early in the 18th century. Later, their different bands were designated Carlanes, Calchufines, Quartelejos, etc., after their habitat or chieftains. The Spaniards established a mission among them within a few leagues of Taos, N. Mex., in 1733, which prospered for only a short time. They were regarded as a worthless people by both the Spanish settlers of New Mexico and their American successors, in raids for plunder the worst of the Apache tribes, more treacherous and cruel and less brave and energetic warriors than the Ute, but equally fond of intoxicants. While they sometimes planted on a small scale, they regarded theft as a natural means of support. The governor of New Mexico in 1853 induced 250 of the tribe to settle on Rio Puerco, but failure to ratify the treaty caused them to go on the warpath, maintaining hostility until their defeat by United States troops in 1854. Henceforward they were nominally at peace, although committing many petty thefts. In 1870 they resided on the Maxwell grant in N. E. New Mexico, the sale of which necessitated their removal. In 1872 and again in 1878 an attempt was made to move them s. to Ft Stanton, but

JICARILLA. (AGUSTIN VIJIL)

most of them were permitted to go to the Tierra Amarilla, on the N. confines of the territory, on a reservation of 900 sq. m. set aside in 1874. Their annuities being suspended in 1878 on account of their refusal to move southward in accordance with an act of Congress of that year, they resorted to thieving. In 1880 the act of 1878 was repealed, and a new reservation was set aside on the Rio Navajo, to which they were removed. Here they remained until 1883, when they were transferred to Ft Stanton, but in 1887 were again returned to the reservation set aside for them in the Tierra Amarilla region by Executive order of Feb. 11 of that year, where they have since resided. Of this reservation 129,313.35 acres have been allotted

to the Indians, and 280.44 acres reserved for mission, school, and agency purposes; the remainder, comprising 286,400 acres, is unallotted. Their population in 1905 was 795. The present divisions of the Jicarilla, as recorded by Mooney (MS., B. A. E., 1897), are: Apatsiltlizhihi, Dachizhozhin, Golkahin, Ketsilind, and Saitinde. (F. W. H.)

Apaches Xicarillas.—Cortez (1799) in Pac. R. R. Rep., III, 119, 1856. Bĕ'-χai.—ten Kate, Synonymie, 6, 1884 (Navaho name). Gicarillas.—MS. of 1784 quoted by Bandelier in Arch. Inst. Papers, V, 184, 1890. Hickory.—Coues, Garcés Diary, 222, 1900. Icarilla Apaches.—Arny in Ind. Aff. Rep. 1867, 204, 1868. Iccarilla Apaches.—Ibid., 217, 1861. Icharilla Apaches.—Ibid., 1864, 495, 1865. Iicarrillas.—Bent (1846) in H. R. Ex. Doc. 76, 30th Cong., 1st sess., 11, 1848. Jacarilla Apaches.—Ind. Aff. Rep., 328, 1875. Jacarrilla Apaches.—Bell, New Tracks in N. Am., I, 184, 1869. Jecorilla.—Latham in Proc. Ethnol. Soc. Lond., VI, 74, 1854. Jicaras.—Gibbs, Letter to Higgins, B. A. E., 1866. Jicarello Apaches.—Meriwether in Sen. Ex. Doc. 69, 34th Cong., 1st sess., 15, 1856. Jicarila Apache.—Taylor in Cal. Farmer, June 12, 1863. Jicarilla.—Rivera, Diario y Derrotero, leg. 950, 1736. Jicarilla Apaches.—Ind. Aff. Rep. 434, 1853. Jicarilleros.—Keane in Stanford, Compend., 464, 1878. Jicarillos.—Morgan in N. Am. Rev., 58, 1870. Jiccarilla Apache.—Sen. Ex. Doc. 55, 35th Cong., 1st sess., 11, 1858. Jiccarrilla Apaches.—Bell in Jour. Ethnol. Soc. Lond., I, 240, 1869. Jickorie.—Higgins, MS. notes on Apache, B. A. E., 1866. Jicorilla.—Schoolcraft, Ind. Tribes, I, 243, 1851. Jicorilla Apaches.—Simpson, MS. vocab., B. A. E. Kiñyá-indé.—Mooney, field notes, B. A. E., 1897 (Mescalero name). K'op-tagúi.—Ibid. ('mountain Apache': Kiowa name). Northern Apaches.—Ind. Aff. Rep., 142, 1850. Pe+χ'-gĕ.—ten Kate, Synonymie, 6, 1884 (Navaho name). Pi'-ke-e-wai-i-ne.—Hodge, field notes, B. A. E., 1895 (Picuris name). Tan-nah-shisen.—Yarrow in Wheeler Surv. Rep., VII, 470, 1879 ('men of the woodland'). Tashi'nĕ.—Mooney, field notes, B. A. E., 1897 (Mescalero name, possibly from tashi, 'above,' 'beyond'). Ticorillas.—Simpson in Rep. Sec. War, 57, 1850 (misprint). Tïndé.—Hodge, field notes, B. A. E., 1895 (own name). Tu-sa-be'.—ten Kate, Synonymie, 8, 1884 (Tesuque name). Xicarillas.—MS. of 1724 quoted by Bandelier in Arch. Inst. Papers, V, 192, 1890.

Jitisorichi. A former pueblo, apparently of the Teguima Opata, on the upper Rio Sonora between Bacuachi and Arizpe, in Sonora, Mexico. It was doubtless abandoned prior to the 17th century.
Jitisorichi.—Bandelier in Arch. Inst. Papers, IV, 489, 1892. Ti-ji-só-ri-chi.—Bandelier, Gilded Man, 182, 1893 (misprint).

Jlaacs. A former Chumashan village near Purísima mission, Santa Barbara co., Cal.
Jlaacs.—Taylor in Cal. Farmer, Oct. 18, 1861. Jlacus.—Ibid.

Joasseh ('heron'). An Iroquois clan.
Jo-äs'-seh.—Morgan, League Iroq., 80, 1851 (Seneca form). Otinanchahé.—French writer (1666) in N. Y. Doc. Col. Hist., IX, 47, 1855.

Jocomes. A warlike nomadic tribe of the 17th and 18th centuries which, with the Janos, ranged to the N. of the Casas Grandes in Chihuahua, Mexico, and westward to Fronteras, Sonora, later becoming absorbed by the Apache (Bandelier in Arch. Inst. Papers, III, 91, 1890). Orozco y Berra (Geog., 59, 1864) classes them as a part of the Faraon Apache and as distinct from the Jacomis, who, however, were doubtless the same. (F. W. H.)

Hojomes.—De l'Isle, Carte Mex. et Floride, 1703. **Jacome.**—Humboldt, Atlas, 1st map, 1811. **Jacomis.**—Orozco y Berra, Geog., 59, 1864. **Jocomeos.**—Doc. *ca.* 1702 in Doc. Hist. Mex., 4th s., v, 129, 1857. **Jocomes.**—Kino (1690), ibid. I, 230, 1856. **Jocomis.**—Rudo Ensayo (*ca.* 1763), 154, 1863. **Xôcomes.**—Rivera, Diario, leg. 591, 1736.

Joconostla. A former Tepehuane pueblo in Durango, Mexico, and the seat of a Spanish mission.

S. José de Joconostla.—Orozco y Berra, Geog., 318, 1864.

John Day. A Shahaptian tribe, speaking the Tenino language, formerly living on John Day r., Oreg., having their principal village 4 m. above the mouth. By treaty of 1855 they were placed on Warm Springs res., Oreg., where there are about 50 survivors. (L. F.)

Dock-spus.—U. S. Stat., XII, 963, 1863. **John Days.**—Thompson in Ind. Aff. Rep., 285, 1854. **John Day's river.**—Gibbs in Pac. R. R. Rep., I, 417, 1855. **Tûkspû'sh.**—Mooney in 14th Rep. B. A. E., 743, 1896 (Tenino name for John Day r.). **Tûkspû'sh-'lĕma.**—Ibid. (sig.: 'people of John Day r.').

John Hicks' Town. A former Seminole settlement w. of Payne's savanna, in N. Florida, occupied by Mikasuki Indians.—Bell in Morse, Rep. to Sec. War, 307, 1822.

Johnnys. A Hankutchin village situated on Yukon r., Alaska, where the mining camp of Eagle now is. It was the village of the Katshikotin, whose chief was known as John.—Schwatka, Recon. in Alaska, 87, 1885.

Johnson, John. See *Enmegahbowh.*

Johnstown. A former Cherokee settlement on the upper waters of Chattahoochee r., probably in the N. part of Hall co., Georgia.

John's Town.—Royce in 18th Rep. B. A. E., map, 1887.

Johnstown. A new settlement "where the Iroquois were thereafter to speak," instead of at Orange or New Albany, N. Y.—Doc. of 18th cent. in N. Y. Doc. Col. Hist., x, 98, 1858.

Jolee. A former Seminole town in Florida, on the w. bank of Apalachicola r., 60 m. above its mouth, apparently at or near the present Iola in Calhoun co.—H. R. Ex. Doc. 74 (1823), 19th Cong., 1st sess., 27, 1826.

Jolly, John. A Cherokee chief, noted as the adopted father of Gen. Samuel Houston, and later chief of the Arkansas band of Cherokee. His native name was Ahúludégĭ, 'He throws away the drum.' His early life was spent in Tennessee, near the mouth of the Hiwassee, where an island still preserves his name, and it was here that Houston came to live with him, remaining 3 years and acquiring a lifelong friendship for his adopted people. In 1818 Jolly removed to the other side of the Mississippi and joined the Arkansas band, whose chief he became a few years later on the death of Tollunteeskee.—Mooney in 19th Rep. B. A. E., 507, 1900.

Jonatas. A former Chumashan village, tributary to Santa Inés mission, Santa Barbara co., Cal.—Gatschet in Chief Engrs. Rep., pt. III, 553, 1876.

Joneadih (*Jo'-ne-a-dih,* 'beyond the point.'—Hewitt). A former Seneca village on Allegheny r., nearly opposite Salamanca, N. Y.—Morgan, League Iroq., 466, 1851.

Jones, Peter (Kahkewaquonaby, Kahkewagwonnaby). A mixed-blood Missisauga chief, missionary, and author; born Jan. 1, 1802, died June 29, 1856. His father was a white man of Welsh descent named Augustus Jones, who maintained the closest friendship with Brant during the latter's life. Peter's mother was Tuhbenahneeguay, daughter of Wahbanosay, a chief of the Missisauga on Credit r., at the extreme w. end of L. Ontario, where, on a tract of land known as Burlington heights, Peter and his brother John were born. He remained with his tribe, following their customs and accompanying them on their excursions, until his 16th year, when his father, who was then a government surveyor, had him baptized by Rev. Ralph Leeming, an English Episcopal minister, at the Mohawk church on Grand r., near Brantford, Ont. Having professed religion at a campmeeting held near Ancaster, Ont., and taken an active part in the religious exercises of the Wesleyan Methodist Church, Peter was sent on a missionary tour, in 1827, to L. Simcoe, St Clair, Muncey, and other points in w. Ontario, although not yet ordained. He had by this time entered upon his literary work, as in this year was published a hymn book translated by him into Chippewa. He was constituted a deacon of the Wesleyan Methodist conference in 1830, and as minister by Rev. George Marsden at the Toronto conference in 1833. The remainder of his life was devoted chiefly to missionary work among the Missisauga and Chippewa, and to some extent among the Iroquois. His position as a Christian pastor and ruling chief of his tribe gave him great influence, not only among his own people, but among all the Chippewa tribes. He visited England and New York, and made repeated journeys to Toronto in the prosecution of his work and in behalf of his people. It was largely through his efforts that the titles of the Credit Indians to their lands were perfected. Although inured to out-door life and of a somewhat robust frame, his constitution began to yield to excessive exposures, resulting in his death, near Brantford, in 1856. A monument was erected to his memory, in 1857, with the inscription: "Erected by the Ojibeway and other Indian tribes to their revered and beloved chief, Kahkewaquonaby (the

Rev. Peter Jones)." A memorial tablet was placed by his family in the Indian church at the New Credit settlement.

Ryerson (Ojebway Indians, 18, 1861) describes Jones as "a man of athletic frame, as well as of masculine intellect; a man of clear perception, good judgment, great decision of character; a sound preacher, fervent and powerful in his appeals; very well informed on general subjects, extensively acquainted with men and things." His wife was an English woman, who with 4 sons survived him. His seventh son, Peter E. Jones, who bore his father's name (Kah-ke-wa-quo-na-by), was editor of a periodical, *The Indian*, published at Hagersville, Ont., in 1885–86.

In addition to the volume of hymns, first printed in 1829, republished in 1836, and in various enlarged editions in later years, Jones translated also into Chippewa a volume of Additional Hymns (1861), an Ojibway Spelling Book (1828), Part of the New Testament (1829), The First Book of Moses (1835), and Part of the Discipline of the Wesleyan Methodist Church in Canada (1835). He also wrote the Life and Journals of Kah-ke-wa-quo-na-by (Rev. Peter Jones), 1860, and a History of the Ojebway Indians, with Especial Reference to their Conversion to Christianity, 1861. Consult Pilling, Bibliog. Algonq. Lang., Bull. B. A. E., 1891.

Jones' River. A village of Christian Indians in Kingston township, Plymouth co., Mass., in 1703.—Cotton (1703) in Mass. Hist. Soc. Coll., 3d s., II, 244, 1830.

Jonondes (*Diionon'dese'*, 'at the high mountain'). A former Iroquois village belonging to the Bear clan; location unknown.   (J. N. B. H.)
Jonondese.—Hale, Iroquois Book of Rites, 120, 1833. Jonondeseh.—Ibid., 121.

Joquizara. A former village, presumably Costanoan, connected with Dolores mission, San Francisco, Cal.—Taylor in Cal. Farmer, Oct. 18, 1861. Cf. *Josquigard*.

Jore (probably from *Ayā'li'yĭ*, 'little place,' i. e., 'little town'; abbreviated *Ayā'li*). A former Cherokee settlement on Iola cr., an upper branch of Little Tennessee r., N. C.   (J. M.)
Iola.—Present map form. Jore.—Bartram, Travels, 371, 372, 1792. Joree.—Doc. of 1755 cited by Royce in 5th Rep. B. A. E., 142, 1887.

Joseph. The leader of the Nez Percés in the hostilities of 1877. His mother was a Nez Percé, his father a Cayuse, who received the name Joseph from his teacher, the missionary Spalding, who was with Dr Whitman and who went to the Idaho country in the late thirties of the 19th century. Chief Joseph's native name was Hinmaton-yalatkit (*hinmaton*, 'thunder'; *yalatkit*, 'coming from the water up over the land.'—Miss McBeth), but both he and his brother Ollicot were often called Joseph, as if it were a family name. Joseph was a man of fine presence and impressive features, and was one of the most remarkable Indians within the borders of the Union. The treaty of 1863, by which the whites obtained a right to the Wallowa valley, the ancient home of Joseph's band in N. E. Oregon, was not recognized by Joseph and the Indians sympathizing with him, who continued to dwell there in spite of collisions between the Indians and the whites, which became more and more frequent. The matter of removing these Indians to the Lapwai res. in Idaho, after the failure of a commission the previous year, was proceeding to a peaceful settlement when outrageous acts on the part of the white settlers caused the Nez Percés to break loose and attack the set-

CHIEF JOSEPH

tlements. War was declared. After several engagements, in which the whites lost severely, Joseph displayed remarkable generalship in a retreat worthy to be remembered with that of Xenophon's ten thousand (Mooney in 14th Rep. B. A. E., 714, 1896). In spite of the fact that in front of him was Col. Miles, behind Gen. Howard, on his flank Col. Sturgis and his Indian scouts, Joseph brought his little band, incommoded with women and children, to within 50 miles of the Canadian border, their objective point, when they were cut off by fresh troops in front and forced to surrender conditionally on Oct. 5, 1877. Not only the conduct of the Nez Percés during this retreat of more than 1,000 miles, but also the military and tactical skill displayed by their leader, won unstinted praise from their conquerors. The promises made to Joseph and his people were ignored, and the Indians, numbering 431, were removed to Ft Leavenworth, Kans., and afterward to Indian Ter., where they remained for several years, always yearning for the mountains and valleys of Idaho. In 1883 a party of 33 women and children were allowed to go back to their old home, and were followed the next year by 118 others. Joseph and the remaining members of his band, however, numbering 150, were not permitted to return to Idaho, but were sent to the Colville res., Wash. He lived to visit President Roosevelt and Gen. Miles at Washington in Mar., 1903, but died at Nespelim, on the Colville res., Wash., Sept. 21, 1904. According to the Indian agent he had become reconciled to civilization in his last years, lending his aid in the education of the children of his tribe, and discouraging gambling and drunkenness.

Josquigard. A former village, presumably Costanoan, connected with Dolores mission, San Francisco, Cal.—Taylor in Cal. Farmer, Oct. 18, 1861. Cf. *Joquizara.*

Jotars. An unidentified tribe of Texas, mentioned in the Mezières MS. of 1779, together with the Kichai and Nasoni, from whom an epidemic had spread to the Tawakoni, Caddo, and other tribes. The Jotars lived in a locality remote from Nacogdoches, probably toward the N. W. (H. E. B.)

Jova. A former Opata division inhabiting principally the valley of the stream on which Sahuaripa (lat. 29°, lon. 109°) is situated, in Sonora, Mexico, and extending E. into Chihuahua, to and including the village of Dolores on a s. tributary of Rio Aros. Its members are now completely Mexicanized. The language spoken differed dialectically from the Opata proper and the Eudeve. The Jova settlements were Arivechi, Chamada, Natora, Ponida, Sahuaripa (in part), San Mateo, Malzura, Santa María de los Dolores, Santo Tomas, Satechi (?), Servas, Setasura, and Teopari. (F. W. H.)
Jaba.—Davila, Sonora Hist., 316, 1894. Joba.— Ibid., 317. Jobal.—Orozco y Berra, Geog., 345, 1864. Jobales.—Ibid. Jova.—Ibid. Ovas.—Ibid. Sahuaripas.—Ibid.

Joytudachi. Apparently a former village of the Opata in the Sierra de Baserac, one of the N. W. spurs of the Sierra Madre, in N. E. Sonora, Mexico.—Bandelier in Arch. Inst. Papers, III, 58, 1890.

Joyvan. Mentioned by La Harpe (Margry, Déc., VI, 277, 1886), together with the Quidehais, Naouydiches, Huanchanés, and others, as a wandering tribe, apparently W. of southern Arkansas in 1719. Unidentified.

Juajona. A former rancheria, probably Papago, near San Xavier del Bac in s. Arizona; visited by Kino and Mange in 1699.—Mange quoted by Bancroft, Ariz. and N. Mex., 358, 1889.

Juan Bautista. A Kawia village of the Cabezon division, in San Bernardino co., Cal.—Burton in H. R. Ex. Doc. 76, 34th Cong., 3d sess., 117, 1857.

Juaneños. A Shoshonean division on the California coast, named from San Juan Capistrano mission (q. v.), at which they were principally gathered, extending N. to Alisos cr. and s. to a point between San Onofre and Las Flores crs. Their language forms one group with those of the Luiseños, Kawia, and Aguas Calientes (q. v.). According to Ames (Rep. Mission Inds., 5, 1873) there were only 40 individuals in the neighborhood in 1873; of these most are now dead and the remainder scattered.
Gaitchim.—Gatschet in Rep. Chief of Engrs., pt. 3, 555, 1876. Juaneños.—Kroeber, inf'n, 1905 (so called by the Indians and Spaniards). Netela.— Hale, Ethnog. and Philol., 222, 1846 (sig. 'my language').

Judac. The largest of three large Pima rancherias on Gila r., s. Ariz., in the 18th century, now probably known by some other name.—Villa-Señor, Theatro Am., pt. 2, 404, 1748.

Judosa. A village or community E. of the mouth of Trinity r., Tex., in a region generally controlled by tribes of the Attacapan family in the 17th century.
Jacdoas.—Uhde, Länder, 159, 1861. Judosa.—De l'Isle, map (1700) in Winsor, Hist. Am., II, 294, 1886.

Jugelnute. A Kaiyuhkhotana division on Shageluk and Innoko rs., Alaska; pop. 150 in 1880. It included the villages of Anilukhtakpak, Inselnostlinde, Intenleiden, Khuligichakat, Kuingshtetakten, Kvigimpainagmute, and Vagitchitchate.
Chageluk settlements.—Petroff in 10th Census, Alaska, 12, 1884. Inkalit-Ingelnut.—Schott in Erman, Archiv, VII, 480, 1849 (misprint). Jugelnuten.—Holmberg, Ethnog. Skizz., 7, 1855. Jugelnuts.—Keane in Stanford, Compend., 517, 1878. Ounagountchaguéliougïout.—Zagoskin in Nouv. Ann. Voy., 5th s., XXI, map, 1850. Shagelook—Whymper, Alaska, map, 1869. Shageluk.— Schwatka, Rep. on Alaska, 101, 1885. Shaglook.— Whymper, Alaska, 265, 1869. Tākai'-yākhōtān'ā.—Dall in Cont. N. A. Ethnol., I, 26, 1877 (Athapascan name). Yugelnut.—Zagoskin (1842) quoted by Petroff in 10th Census, Alaska, 37, 1884.

Juichun. A Costanoan division or village in California, speaking a dialect very similar to that of the Mutsun.—Arroyo de la Cuesta, Idiomas Californias, MS. trans., B. A. E.

Jukiusme. The Moquelumnan Indians on whose land the San Rafael mission, Cal., was built. Their language was identical with the Chokuyem, and their name may be a distorted form of the same word.
Joukiousmé.—Duflot de Mofras, Expl., II, 391, 1844. Jouskiousmé.—Shea, Catholic Miss., 109, 1855. San Rafael Indians.—Powers in Cont. N. A. Ethnol., III, 195, 1877. Yonkiousme.—Latham in Trans. Philol. Soc. Lond., 82, 1856 (misquoted).

Julianehaab. A Danish colony and Eskimo settlement on a small island, lat. 60° 43', s. Greenland.

Julianehaab.—Graah, Exped. Greenland, map, 1837. **Kakortok.**—Meddelelser om Grönland, XVI, map, 1896.

Julimeños. A former tribe in N. E. Mexico, probably of the Coahuiltecan linguistic family, which was gathered into the mission of San Francisco Vizarron de los Pausanes, in Coahuila, in 1737.—Orozco y Berra, Geog., 303, 1864.

Jumano. A tribe of unknown affinity, first seen, although not mentioned by name, about the beginning of 1536 by Cabeza de Vaca and his companions in the vicinity of the junction of the Conchos with the Rio Grande, or northward to about the s. boundary of New Mexico. They were next visited in 1582 by Antonio de Espejo, who called them Jumanos and Patarabueyes, stating that they numbered 10,000 in five villages along the Rio Grande from the Conchos junction northward for 12 days' journey. Most of their houses were built of sod or earth and grass, with flat roofs; they cultivated maize, beans, calabashes, etc. When visited in 1598 by Juan de Oñate, who called them Rayados on account of their striated faces, a part at least of the Jumano resided in several villages near the Salinas, E. of the Rio Grande, in New Mexico, the four principal ones being called Atripuy, Genobey, Quelotetrey, and Pataotrey. From about 1622 these were ministered to by the Franciscan Fray Juan de Salas, missionary at the Tigua pueblo of Isleta, N. Mex. In response to the request of 50 Jumano, who visited Isleta in July, 1629, an independent mission, under the name San Isidore, was established among them in the Salinas, but the main body of the tribe at this time seems to have resided 300 m. E. of Santa Fé, probably on the Arkansas, within the present Kansas, where they were said to be also in 1632. Forty years later there were Jumano 15 leagues E. of the Piros and Tigua villages of the Salinas, not far from Pecos r., who were ministered to by the priest at Quarai. About this time the Salinas pueblos were abandoned on account of Apache depredations. The Jumano did not participate in the Pueblo rebellion of 1680–92, but before it was quelled, i. e., in Oct., 1683, 200 of the tribe visited the Spaniards at El Paso, to request missionaries, but owing to the unsettled condition of affairs by reason of the revolt in the N., the request was not granted. In the following year friars visited the Jumano in s. Texas, and within this decade they became known to the French under the name Choumans. Various references to them are made during the 18th century, including the perhaps significant statement by Cabello (Informe, 1784, MS. cited by H. E. Bolton, inf'n, 1906) that "the Taguayazes (Wichita) are known in New Mexico by the name of Jumanes also." As late as the middle of the 19th century they are mentioned in connection with the Kiowa, and again as living near Lampazas, Nuevo Leon, Mexico. The tribal name was once applied to the Wichita mts. in Oklahoma, and it is still preserved in the "Mesa Jumanes" of New Mexico. See Bandelier in Arch. Inst. Papers, IV, 268, 1892; Benavides, Memorial (1630), in Land of Sunshine, XIV, 46, 51, 1901; Vetancurt (1693), Teatro Americana, III, 304, repr. 1871. (F. W. H.)

Aumanes.—Uhde, Länder, 121, 1861 (near Lampazos, N. Leon). **Borrados.**—Doc. of 1796 quoted by Orozco y Berra, Geog., 382, 1864 'striped'; same?). **Chaumenes.**—Charlevoix, New France, Shea ed., IV, 78, 1870. **Chomanes.**—Barcia, Ensayo, 264, 1723. **Chomans.**—Doc. of 1699 in Margry, Déc., IV, 316, 1880. **Chomenes.**—Barcia, op. cit., 271. **Chouman.**—Joutel (1687) in Margry, Déc., III, 299, 1878. **Choumanes.**—Barcia, op. cit., 283. **Choümans.**—Douay (ca. 1687) quoted by Shea, Discov., 205, 1852. **Choumay.**—Joutel (1687) in Margry, Déc., III, 410, 1878. **Choumenes.**—Joutel (1687) in French, Hist. Coll. La., I, 137, 1846. **Desumanas.**—Duro, Don Diego de Peñalosa, 63, 1882. **Humanas.**—Perea, Verdadera Rel., 2, 1632. **Humanas de Tompires.**—Brion de la Tour, Map N. Am., 1779 (confounded with Tompiros). **Humanas de Tompires.**—Jefferys, Am. Atlas, map 5, 1776. **Humanos.**—Schoolcraft, Ind. Tribes, II, 28, 1852. **Humas.**—Orozco y Berra, Geog., 70, 1864 (believed by Bandelier to be identical; see *Xumas* below). **Humunas de Tompires.**—Morse, Atlas, map 52, 1812. **Ipataragüites.**—Mota-Padilla, Hist. de la Conquista, 169, 1742 (probably identical). **Iúmanes.**—Buschmann, Neu-Mexico, 228, 264, 1858 (after Siguenza, 1691–93). **Iumanes.**—Sanson, L'Amérique, map, 27, 1657. **Iumanos.**—Mendoça (1586) in Hakluyt, Voy., 459, 466, 1600. **Jumanas.**—Espejo (1582) in Doc. Inéd., XV, 186, 1871. **Jumanes.**—Whipple, Pac. R. R. Rep., III, pt. 3, 113, 1856 (misquoting Hakluyt). **Jumanoes.**—Schoolcraft, Ind. Tribes, II, 29, 1852. **Jumanos.**—Dobbs, Hudson Bay, 163, 1744. **Jumas.**—Orozco y Berra (1864) quoted in Arch. Inst. Bul., I, 31, 1883. **Lumanos.**—Davis, Span. Conq. N. Mex., 242, 1869. **Parabuyeis.**—De l'Isle, Atlas Nouveau, map 59, 1733. **Patarabueges.**—Bell in Jour. Ethnol. Soc. Lond., I, 263, 1869. **Patarabueyes.**—Espejo (1582) in Doc. Inéd., XV, 168, 1871. **Patarabuyes.**—Mendoça (1586) in Hakluyt, Voy., 459, 1600. **Patarabyes.**—Heylen, Cosmog., 1072, 1703. **Rayados.**—Oñate (1598) in Doc. Inéd., XVI, 266, 1871. **Rrayados.**—Ibid. **Sumanas.**—Duro, Don Diego de Peñalosa, 56, 1882. **Tarra-Iumanes.**—Linschoten, Description de l'Amérique, map 1, 1638 (confused with Tarahumare?). **Tatarabueyes.**—Rodriguez, Relacion, in Doc. Inéd., XV, 97, 1871. **Umanos.**—Schoolcraft, Ind. Tribes, I, 519, 1851 (misidentified with Yumas). **Xoumanes.**—Doc. of 1699 in Margry, Déc., IV, 316, 1880. **Xumanas.**—Oñate (1598) in Doc. Inéd., XVI, 114, 1871. **Xumanes.**—Del'Isle, Map Am. Septentrionale, 1700. **Xumarias.**—Espejo (1582) in Doc. Inéd., XV, 168, 1871. **Xumas.**—Bandelier in Arch. Inst. Bul., I, 31, 1883 (said to be a 16th century name). **Xumáses.**—Oñate (1598) in Doc. Inéd., XVI, 266, 1871. **Yumanos.**—Bent (1846) in Schoolcraft, Ind. Tribes, I, 242, 1851. **Zumanas.**—Vetancurt (1693), Teatro Mex., III, 308, 1871.

Junaluska (corruption of *Tsunúlăhúnskĭ*, 'he tries repeatedly, but fails'). A former noted chief of the East Cherokee in North Carolina. In the Creek war of 1813–14 he led a detachment of warriors to the support of Gen. Jackson, and did good service at the bloody battle of the Horseshoe Bend. Having boasted on setting out that he would exterminate the Creeks, he was obliged to confess on his return that some of that tribe were still alive, whence the name jokingly bestowed upon him by his friends. He went west with his people in the removal of 1838, but returned to North Carolina, and as a special recognition of his past services was given citizenship rights and a tract of land at Cheowa, near the present Robbinsville, Graham co., N. C., where he died in 1858. See Mooney in 19th Rep. B. A. E., 97, 164–5, 1900.

Junatca. A former tribe or village, presumably Costanoan, from which Dolores mission, San Francisco, Cal., drew some of its neophytes.—Taylor in Cal. Farmer, Oct. 18, 1861.

Junetre. A ruined pueblo of the Tewa in Rio Arriba co., N. Mex.—Bandelier in Ritch, N. Mex., 201, 1885. See *Tajique.*

Juniamuc. A former village, presumably Costanoan, connected with Dolores mission, San Francisco, Cal.—Taylor in Cal. Farmer, Oct. 18, 1861.

Juniata (from *Tyu'naⁿyate*, 'projecting rock,' in the Seneca and other Iroquois dialects, a name said to refer to a standing stone to which the Indians paid reverence.—Hewitt). An unidentified tribe that lived at and about the mouth of Juniata r., Pa. Their village, known by the same name, was situated on Duncan id., in the Susquehanna. About 1648 they were the forced auxiliaries of the Conestoga. (J. M.)
Ihon-a-Does.—Writer (ca. 1648) quoted by Proud, Penn., I, 114, 1797. Iottecas.—Map (ca. 1614) in N. Y. Doc. Col. Hist., I, 1856. John-a-does.—Sanford, U. S., cxlviii, 1819. Juneauta.—Brainerd (1745) quoted by Day, Penn., 275, 1843 (the village).

Junostaca. A former rancheria, probably Papago, visited by Kino and Mange in 1699; situated near San Xavier del Bac, in the present s. Arizona.—Mange quoted by Bancroft, Ariz. and N. Mex., 358, 1889.

Junqueindundeh ('it has a rock.'—Hewitt). A village, probably of the Hurons, situated in 1766 on Sandusky r., Ohio, 24 m. above its mouth.—Smith, Bouquet Exped., 67, 1766.

Junundat ('one hill.'—Hewitt). A Huron village in 1756 on a small creek that empties into a little lake below the mouth of Sandusky r., Seneca co., Ohio.
Ayonontouns.—La Jonquière (1751) in N. Y. Doc. Col. Hist., X, 240, 1858. Ayonontout.—Ibid., VI, 733, 1855. Canundageh.—Guy Park conf. (1775), ibid., VIII, 556, 1857. Chenunda.—Croghan (1759) quoted by Rupp, West. Penn., 146, 1846. Chenundea.—Croghan (1759) quoted by Proud, Penn., II, 206, 1798. Chinundeda.—Croghan (1760) in Mass. Hist. Soc. Coll., 4th s., IX, 261, 1871. Junundat.—Peters (1760), ibid., 258. Sunyendeand.—Smith (1799) quoted by Drake, Trag. Wild., 201, 1841. Wyandot Town.—Hutchins, map in Smith, Bouquet Exped., 1766.

Juraken. Two former villages under Iroquois rule, one situated on the right bank of Susquehanna r., just below the fork, at the site of Sunbury, Pa., the other on the left bank of the E. branch of the Susquehanna.—Popple, Nouv. Carte Particulière de l'Amérique [n. d.].
(J. N. B. H.)

Juris. A former village, presumably Costanoan, connected with Dolores mission, San Francisco, Cal.—Taylor in Cal. Farmer, Oct. 18, 1861.

Jurlanoca. A former village on the Indian trail of N. Florida, 8 m. E. of Alachua. Jefferys (Topog. N. Am., chart, 67, 1762) has here a river joining the St Johns from the s. w.

Jurumpa. Given by Rev. J. Caballeria (Hist. San Bernardino Val., 1902) as a former village, probably Serrano, at Riverside, s. California. The Spanish Rancho Jurupa shows the same name.

Jutun. A Calusa village on the s. w. coast of Florida, about 1570.
Futun.—Fontaneda as quoted by Shipp, De Soto and Fla., 586, 1881 (misprint). Jutun.—Fontaneda Memoir (ca. 1575), Smith trans., 19, 1854.

Juyubit. A former rancheria connected with San Gabriel mission, Los Angeles co., Cal. The locative ending, *bit*, shows the name to be Serrano rather than Gabrieleño.
Jujubit.—Latham in Proc. Philol. Soc. Lond., VI, 76, 1854. Juyubit.—Duflot de Mofras, Explor., I, 394, 1844.

Kaadnaas-hadai (*Q!ā'ad na'as Xadā'-i*, 'dogfish house people'). A subdivision of the Yaku-lanas, a family of the Raven clan of the Haida, living in s. w. Alaska. The name is probably derived from that of a particular house. (J. R. S.)
K·'at nas :had'ā'i.—Boas, 5th Rep. N. W. Tribes Canada, 26, 1898. Q!ā'ad na'as Xadā'-i.—Swanton, Cont. Haida, 271, 1905.

Kaake (*Qā'āqē*). A Salish tribe which formerly occupied the s. E. coast of Valdez id. Brit. Col., and spoke the Comox dialect. It is now extinct.—Boas, MS., B. A. E., 1887.

Kaana. The Corncob clan of the pueblo of Taos, N. Mex.
Kââna-taïina.—Hodge, field notes, B. A. E., 1899 (*taïina*='people').

Kaayahunik. A Squawmish village on the w. bank of Squawmisht r., Brit. Col.—Brit. Adm. chart, no. 1917.

Kaayu (*Ka-ä-yu*). A pueblo built, occupied, and abandoned by the Nambe tribe prior to the Spanish advent in the 16th century. Situated with Agawano in the vicinity of the "Santuario," in the mountains about 7 m. E. of the Rio Grande, on Rio Santa Cruz, Santa Fé co., N. Mex.—Bandelier in Arch. Inst. Papers, IV, 84, 1892.

Kabahseh ('sturgeon'). A gens of the Abnaki.
Kä-bäh'-seh.—Morgan. Anc. Soc., 174, 1877. Kabasa.—J. Dyneley Prince, inf'n, 1905 (modern St Francis Abnaki form).

Kabaye. A tribe or village formerly in the country lying between Matagorda bay and Maligne (Colorado) r., Tex. Joutel in 1687 obtained the name from the Ebahamo Indians, who were probably closely affiliated to Karankawan tribes living in this region. They are probably identical with the Cabia of Manzanet. See Joutel in French, Hist. Coll. La., I,

137, 152, 1846, and in Margry, Déc., III, 288, 1878; Gatschet, Karankawa Indians, 23, 25, 1891. Cf. *Kiabaha*. (A. C. F.)

Cabaies.—Barcia, Ensayo, 271, 1723. Cabia.—Massanet (1690), MS., cited by Bolton, inf'n, 1906. Kabayes.—Joutel, Jour. Voy., 90, 1719.

Kachegaret. A Kaviagmiut village at Port Clarence, Alaska.—11th Census, Alaska, 162, 1893.

Kachgiya ('the raven'). A Knaiakhotana division residing on Cook inlet, Alaska.—Richardson, Arctic Exped., I, 406, 1851.

Kachina. A term applied by the Hopi to "supernatural beings impersonated by men wearing masks or by statuettes in imitation of the same"; also to the dances in which these masks figure. See *Masks*. Consult Fewkes (1) in 15th Rep. B. A. E., 25, 1897; (2) 21st Rep. B. A. E., 3, 1903; Voth in various pubs. Field Columbian Museum.

Kachina. The Sacred Dancer phratry of the Hopi, comprising the Kachina, Gyazru (Paroquet) Angwusi (Raven), Sikyachi (Yellow bird), Tawamana (Black bird), Salabi (Spruce), and Suhubi (Cottonwood) clans. They claim to have come from the Rio Grande, but lived for some time near the now ruined pueblo of Sikyatki.

Ka-tci'-na.—Stephen in 8th Rep. B. A. E., 39, 1891 (*tc* = *ch*). Ka-tci'-na nyû-mû.—Fewkes in Am. Anthrop., VII, 404, 1894 (*nyû-mû* = 'phratry').

Kachina. The name of two distinct Sacred Dancer clans of the Hopi, one belonging to the Kachina, the other to the Honani (Badger) phratry. The Tewa pueblo of Hano has a similar clan.

Kachína-tówa.—Hodge in Am. Anthrop., IX, 351, 1896 (Tewa name: *tówa* = 'people'). Ka-tci-na.—Stephen in 8th Rep. B. A. E., 39, 1891. Katcina wiñwû.—Fewkes in 19th Rep. B. A. E., 584, 1900 (*wiñwû* = 'clan'). Ka-tci'-na wüñ-wü.—Fewkes in Am. Anthrop., VII, 404, 1894.

Kachinba ('sacred-dancer spring'). A small ruin at a spring 6 m. from Sikyatki and about E. of Walpi pueblo, N. E. Arizona. It was one of the stopping places of the Kachina clan of the Hopi, whence the name.—Fewkes in 17th Rep. B. A. E., 589, 1898.

Kachisupal. A former Chumashan village connected with Purísima mission, Santa Barbara co., Cal.—Taylor in Cal. Farmer, Oct. 18, 1861.

Kachnawaacharege. A former fishing station of the Onondaga, situated w. of Oneida lake. At this place Col. Schuyler held a conference with the Onondaga chiefs, Apr. 25, 1700. (J. N. B. H.)

Kachnawaacharege.—Doc. of 1700 in N. Y. Doc. Col. Hist., IV, 657, 1854. Kachnawarage.—Ibid., 799. Kagnewagrage.—Ibid., 805.

Kachyayakuch (*Katc-ya-yá'-kutc*). A former Chumashan village at Alazumita, near San Buenaventura, Ventura co., Cal.—Henshaw, Buenaventura MS. vocab., B. A. E., 1884.

Kadadjans (*Q!adadja'ns*, said to be applied to a person who gets angry with another and talks of him behind his back; a backbiter). A town of the Hagilanas of the Haida, on the N. w. end of Anthony id., Queen Charlotte ids., Brit. Col., on which also stood the town of Ninstints.—Swanton, Cont. Haida, 277, 1905.

Kadakaman. A Laimon tribe or band that lived between the old missions of San Fernando and Santa Rosalia Mulege, Lower California.—Taylor in Browne, Res. Pac. Slope, app., 54, 1869. See *San Ignacio de Kadakaman*.

Kadishan's Village. A summer settlement of a Stikine chief named Katishan, on Stikine r., Alaska; 27 people were there in 1880.—Petroff in Tenth Census, Alaska, 32, 1884.

Kadohadacho (*Kä'dohadä'cho*, 'real Caddo,' 'Caddo proper'). A tribe of the Caddo confederacy, sometimes confused with the confederacy itself. Their dialect is closely allied to that of the Hainai and Anadarko, and is one of the two dialects dominant to-day among the remnant of the confederacy.

The Kadohadacho seem to have developed, as a tribe, on Red r. of Louisiana and in its immediate vicinity, and not to have migrated with their kindred to any distance either N. or S. Their first knowledge of the white race was in 1541, when De Soto and his followers stayed with some of the subtribes on Washita r. and near the Mississippi. The Spaniards never penetrated during the 16th and 17th centuries to their villages in the lake region of N. w. Louisiana, but the people came in contact with Spanish soldiers and settlers from the w. by joining the war parties of other tribes. Various articles of European manufacture were brought home as trophies of war. The tribe was not unfamiliar with horses, but had not come into possession of firearms when the survivors of La Salle's party visited them on their way N. in 1687. For nearly two years La Salle had previous direct relations with tribes of the Caddo confederacy who were living in what is now Texas, so that when the approach of the French was reported the visitors were regarded as friends rather than as strangers. The chief of the Kadohadacho, with his warriors, taking the calumet, went a league to meet the travelers, and escorted them with marks of honor to the village on Red r. On arrival, "the women," says Douay, "as is their wont, washed our heads and feet in warm water and then placed us on a platform covered with very neat white mats. Then followed banquets, the calumet dance, and other rejoicing day and night." The friendly relations then begun with the French were never abandoned. A trading post was established and a flour mill built at their village by the French early in the 18th century, but both were given up in a few years owing to the unsettled state of affairs between the Spaniards and the French. These disturbances, added to the enmity of tribes who were being pushed from their homes by the increasing number of white settlers, together with the introduction of new diseases, particularly smallpox and measles, brought about much distress and a great reduction in the population. During the last quarter of the 18th century the Kadohadacho abondoned their villages in the vicinity of the lakes in N. W. Louisiana, descended the river, and settled not far from their kindred, the Nachitoches. By the beginning of the 19th century their importance as a distinct tribe was at an end; the people became merged with the other tribes of the confederacy and shared their misfortune. In customs and ceremonies they resembled the other Caddo tribes.

The tribes of the Caddo confederacy, including the Kadohadacho, have 10 clans, according to Mooney, viz.: Suko (Sun), Kagahanin (Thunder), Iwi (Eagle), Kishi (Panther), Oat (Raccoon), Tao (Beaver), Kagaih (Crow), Nawotsi (Bear), Tasha (Wolf), Tanaha (Buffalo). The Buffalo clan was sometimes called Koho (Alligator), "because both animals bellow in the same way." The members of a group did not kill the animal from which the group took its name, except the eagle, whose feathers were necessary for regalia and in sacred ceremonies; but the bird was killed only by certain men initiated to perform this ceremonial act. The rituals and songs attending the rite of preparation for the killing of eagles have passed away with their last keeper, and the people have now to depend on other tribes for the needed feathers (see Mooney in 14th Rep. B. A. E., 1093, 1896).   (A. C. F.)

At'-ta-wits.—ten Kate, Synonymie, 10, 1884 (Comanche name). Cadadoquis.—Tonti (1690) in French, Hist. Coll. La., I, 73, 1846. Cadaquis.—Joutel (1687) in Margry, Déc., III, 409, 1878. Cadaudachos.—Barreiro, Ojeada, 7, 1832. Cadaux.—Sibley, Hist. Sketches, 136, 1806 (so called by the French). Caddo-dacho.—Espinosa (1746) quoted by Buschmann, Spuren, d. aztec. Spr., 417, 1854. Caddoe.—Nuttall, Jour., 288, 1821. Caddokies.—Gallatin in Trans. Am. Antiq. Soc., II, 116, 1836. Caddons.—Keane in Stanford, Compend., 504, 1878. Caddoques.—Sibley, Hist. Sketches, 66, 1806. Caddoquies.—Ibid., 105. Caddoquis.—Brackenridge, Views of La., 80, 1815. Caddos.—Sibley, Hist. Sketches, 66, 1806. Caddow.—Sen. Ex. Doc. 21, 18th Cong., 2d sess., table, 5, 1825. Cadeaux.—Sibley, Hist. Sketches, 162, 1806. Cadloes.—Keane in Stanford, Compend., 504, 1878. Cado.—Long, Exped. Rocky Mts., II, 310, 1823. Cadodaccho.—Hennepin, New Discov., pt. 2, 41, 1698. Cadodache.—Drake, Bk. Inds., vi, 1848. Cadodachos.—De l'Isle, map, 1700. Cadodaguios.—Carver, Trav., map, 1778. Cadodakis.—Güssefeld, Charte U. S., 1784. Cadodaquinons.—Keane in Stanford, Compend., 504, 1878. Cadodaquio.—Joutel (1687) in French, Hist. Coll. La., I, 168, 1846. Cadodaquiou.—Joutel (1687) in Margry, Déc., III, 408, 1878. Cadodaquioux.—Pénicaut (1701) in French, Hist. Coll. La., n. s., I, 73, 1869. Cadodaquis.—Joutel (1687) in Margry, Déc., III, 409, 1878. Cadoes.—Ker, Trav., 83, 1816. Cadogdachos.—Morfi, Mem. de Texas, 1792. Ca-do-

ha-da-cho.—Pénicaut (1701) in French, Hist. Coll. La., n. s., I, 73, note, 1869. Cadojodacho.—Linares (1716) in Margry, Déc., VI, 217, 1886. Cadoux.—Lewis and Clark, Jour., 193, 1840. Cadrons.—Schoolcraft, Ind. Tribes, VI, 34, 1857. Candadacho.—Altamira (1714) quoted by Yoakum, Hist. Texas, I, 386, 1855. Caodacho.—Tex. State Arch., Nov. 17, 1763. Catcho.—Joutel (1687) in Margry, Déc., III, 409, 1878. Chadadoquis.—Sibley, Hist. Sketches, 134, 1806. Coddoque.—Brackenridge, Views of La., 87, 1815. Codogdachos.—Morfi quoted by Shea in Charlevoix, New France, IV, 80, note, 1870. Dä'sha-i.—Mooney in 14th Rep. B. A. E., 1092, 1896 (Wichita name). Datcho.—Joutel (1687) in Margry, Déc., III, 409, 1878. Dĕ'sa.—Mooney, op. cit. (another form of Dä'sha-i). Édawika.—Gatschet, MS., B. A. E. (Pawnee name, sing.). Érawika.—Ibid. Kaddo.—Möllhausen, Journ. to Pac., 95, 1858. Ka'-di.—Gatschet, Caddo and Yatassi MS., B. A. E. ('chief': original name). Kado.—Bruyère (1742) in Margry, Déc., VI, 483, 1886. Kadodakio.—Gravier (1701) quoted by Shea, Early Voy., 149, 1861. Kadodakious.—Bruyère (1742) in Margry, Déc., VI, 474, 1886. Kadodaquious.—Ibid., 483. Kä'dohädä'cho.—Mooney in 14th Rep. B. A. E., 1092, 1896 (own name). Ka-lŏχ-la'-tce.—ten Kate, Synonymie, 11, 1884 (Choctaw form). Kalu-χnádshu.—Gatschet, Tonkawa MS., B. A. E. (Tonkawa form). Karo-χnádshu.—Ibid. Kássēya.—Ibid. (Tonkawa name). Kasseye'-i.—Ibid. (Tonkawa name). Kul-hŭl-atsĭ.—Grayson, MS. vocab., B. A. E., 1885 (Creek name). Ma'se'p.—Mooney in 14th Rep. B. A. E., 1092, 1896 ('pierced nose': Kiowa name). Mósi.—ten Kate, Reizen in N. Am., 375, 1885 (Kiowa name). Ni'rĭs-hări's-kĭ'riki.—Mooney in 14th Rep. B. A. E., 1092, 1896 (another Wichita name). Otä's-itä'niuw'.—Ibid. ('pierced-nose people': Cheyenne name). Quadodaquees.—Boudinot, Star in the West, 128, 1816. Quadodaquious.—Le Page du Pratz, Hist. La., map, 1758. Quodadiquio.—Barcia, Ensayo, 288, 1723. Soudayé.—La Harpe (1722) in Margry, Déc., VI, 363, 1886 (Fr. form of Quapaw name). Su'-dʒĕ.—Dorsey, Kwapa MS. vocab., B. A. E., 1891 (Quapaw name). Tani'bänĕn.—Mooney in 14th Rep. B. A. E., 1092, 1896 ('pierced-nose people': Arapaho name). Tani'bänĕnina.—Ibid. Tani'bätha.—Ibid. Táshash.—Gatschet, Wichita MS., B. A. E. (Wichita name). Táwitskash.—Ibid. (Wichita name for a Caddo). U-tai-si'-ta.—ten Kate, Synonymie, 9, 1884 ('pierced noses': Cheyenne name). Utá-sĕta.—Gatschet, MS., B. A. E. (Cheyenne name). Witúne.—Gatschet, Comanche MS. vocab., B. A. E., 9, 1884 (Comanche name).

Kadusgo (*Q!ā'dʌsgo*). A Haida town or camp on Louise id., Queen Charlotte group, Brit. Col., at the mouth of a creek bearing the same name, which flows into Cumshewa inlet from the s. The family which occupied it came to be called Kadusgo-kegawai ('those born at Kadusgo').—Swanton, Cont. Haida, 278, 1905.

Kadusgo-kegawai (*Q!ā'dʌsgo qē'gawa-i*, 'those born at Kadusgo creek'). A family belonging to the Raven clan of the Haida, residing in the town of Kloo, Queen Charlotte ids., Brit. Col. The name was derived from that of an old camping place on the N. side of Louise id., and the people claimed descent from the Hlgahetgu-lanas of Old Gold Harbor; but until recent years they occupied a low position socially. At present they form one of the most numerous of the surviving family groups of the tribe.   (J. R. S.)
K''adas ke'ē'owai.—Boas, 12th Rep. N. W. Tribes Canada, 25, 1898. Q!ā'dʌsgo qē'gawa-i.—Swanton, Cont. Haida, 269, 1905.

Kae (*Qā-i*, 'sea-lion town'). A former Haida town on Skotsgai bay, above Skidegatɕ, Queen Charlotte ids., Brit. Col. It was occupied by the Kaiahl-lanas, who took their name from the place before they moved to Kaisun. (J. R. S.)

Kaekibi. A traditionary pueblo of the Asa people of the Hopi, who were of Tewa origin; situated on the Rio Chama, N. Mex., near the present Abiquiu.—Stephen in 8th Rep. B. A. E., 30, 1891.

Kaersok. An Eskimo village and trading post in w. Greenland, lat. 72° 39'.—Meddelelser om Grönland, VIII, map, 1889.

Kaffetalaya (*Kafi-talaia*, 'sa: safras thicket'). A former Choctaw town on Owl cr., Neshoba co., Miss. The name was extended to cover a large district in that territory.—Halbert in Miss. Hist. Soc. Pub., VI, 427, 1902.
Cofetalaya.—Gatschet, Creek Migr. Leg., I, 108, 1884. Coffadeliah.—West Florida map, ca. 1775. Kaffi.talaya.—Romans, Florida, map, 1775.

Kagahanin (*Ka'găhănin*). The Thunder clan of the Caddo.—Mooney in 14th Rep. B. A. E., 1093, 1896.

Kagaih (*Ka'g'aih*). The Crow clan of the Caddo.—Mooney in 14th Rep. B. A. E., 1093, 1896.

Kagakwisuwug (*Kägă'kwisuwągi*, 'they go by the name of pigeon-hawk'). A Thunder gens of the Sauk and Foxes.
Kägä'kwisuwągi.—Wm. Jones, inf'n, 1906. Kä-kä-kwis'-so-uk.—Morgan, Anc. Soc., 170, 1877.

Kaganhittan ('sun-house people'). Given by Boas as a social group of the Tlingit at Wrangell, Alaska, but it is actually only the name of the people of a house belonging to the Kiksadi, q. v.
Gagū'nhît tān.—Swanton, field notes, B. A. E., 1904. K·agan hit tan.—Boas, 5th Rep. N. W. Tribes of Can., 25, 1889.

Kagials-kegawai (*Qă'gials qē'gawa-i*, 'those born at Kagials'). An important family of the Raven clan of the Haida, which derives its name from a reef near Lawn hill, at the mouth of Skidegate inlet, Queen Charlotte ids., Brit. Col., where some of the people formerly lived. A second name was Ḷqe'noḷ-lā'nas, 'people of [the town of] Cumshewa', whence one portion of the Kagials-kegawai is said to have moved. Their own town was Skedans, and their chief was one of the most influential on the islands. Subdivisions of the family were the Kils-haidagai and Kogaahl-lanas, the latter being of low social rank. The Kagials-kegawai claim to have sprung from a woman who floated ashore at Hot Springs id. in a cockleshell. They were closely connected with the Tadji-lanas, who appear to have originated in the same locality. (J. R. S.)
K·agyalsk·ē'owai.—Boas, 12th Rep. N. W. Tribes Can., 24, 1898. Ḷqe'noḷ lā'nas.—Swanton, Cont. Haida, 269, 1905. Qă'gials qē'gawa-i.—Ibid. Tlk·î'notl lā'nas.—Boas, op. cit.

Kagokakat. A village of the Ingalik division of the Kaiyuhkhotana, at the mouth of Medicine cr., N. bank of Yukon r., Alaska; pop. 9 in 1843, 115 in 1880.
Kagokhakat.—Zagoskin in Nouv. Ann. Voy., 5th s., XX, map, 1850. Kakagokhakat.—Zagoskin

quoted by Petroff in 10th Census, Alaska, 37, 1884. Khatnotoutze.—Petroff, ibid., 12.

Kagoughsage (Seneca: *Kakoñ'să'-ge*, 'at false-face place'). The Iroquois name of a Shawnee village, known also as Akonwarage (Akoñwară'-ge, the Mohawk equivalent), in 1774, apparently in Ohio or w. Pa. (J. N. B. H.)
Agonwarage.—Johnson Hall conf. (1774) in N. Y. Doc. Col. Hist., VIII, 426, 1857. Akonwarage.—Ibid. Kagoughsage.—Ibid.

Kagsersuak. An Eskimo village and trading post in w. Greenland, lat. 73° 5'.
Kagerssauk.—Science, XI, 259, 1888. Kagsersuak.—Meddelelser om Grönland, VIII, map, 1889. Kasarsoak.—Kane, Arct. Explor., II, 293, 1853.

Kaguyak. A Kaniagmiut Eskimo village on the s. w. coast of Kodiak id., Alaska; pop. 109 in 1880, 112 in 1890.
Alsentia.—Coast Surv. map, 1898. Kaguiak.—Petroff in 10th Census, Alaska, 29, 1884. Kaguyak.—Coast Surv. map, 11th Census, Alaska, 1893. Kaniag-miut.—Russ.-Am. Co. map, 1849. Kaniagmjut.—Holmberg, Ethnog. Skizz., 142, map, 1855. Kawnjagmjut.—Ibid.

Kaguyak. A Kaniagmiut Eskimo village on Shelikof strait, Alaska; pop. 85 in 1890.
Douglas.—11th Census, Alaska, map, 1893. Kaiaiak.—Tebenkof (1849) quoted by Baker, Geog. Dict. Alaska, 1902. Kaiayakak.—Lutke (1835), quoted, ibid. Kayayak.—Coast Surv. charts prior to 1884, quoted, ibid.

Kagwantan ('burnt [house] people'). A large and important Tlingit division at Sitka, Chilkat, Huna, and Yakutat, Alaska, being especially strong at the two first-mentioned places. It belongs to the Wolf phratry.
Kagontān.—Krause, Tlinkit Ind., 116, 118, 1885. Kā'gwantān.—Swanton, field notes, 1904, B. A. E. Kar-gwan-ton.—Emmons in Mem. Am. Mus. Nat. Hist., III, pl. vi, 1903. Kokvontan.—Lutke, Voy. Autour du Monde, I, 195, 1835. Koukhontans.—Ibid.

Kahabi (*Ka-ha'-bi*). The Willow clan of the Pakab (Reed) phratry of the Hopi.—Stephen in 8th Rep. B. A. E., 39, 1891.

Kahansuk. Marked as a Delaware tribe on the E. bank of lower Delaware r., about Low cr., Cumberland co., N. J., on Herrman's map (1670) in Maps to Accompany the Report of the Commissioners on the Boundary line between Virginia and Maryland, 1873.

Kahendohon (*Kă'hě'ñdo'-hon*). A former Iroquois village belonging to the Two-clans of the Turtle. The locality is not known. (J. N. B. H.)
Kahhendohhon.—Hale, Iroquois Book of Rites, 118, 1883. Kah ken doh hon.—Ibid., 119.

Kahesarahera ('a rotten log lying on the top of it.'—Hewitt). A Seneca village in New York in 1691; location unknown.—Markham (1691) in N. Y. Doc. Col. Hist., III, 805, 1853.

Kah-ge-ga-gah-bowh. See *Copway*.

Kahl. The Forehead clan of the Hopi, represented in their pueblo of Mishongnovi.
Kahl.—Dorsey and Voth, Mishongnovi Ceremonies, 175, 1902. Kál-ñamu.—Voth, Trad. of the Hopi, 58, 1905.

Kahlchanedi (*Q!Aɫcʌne'dĭ*, 'people of Kahlchan r.'). An extinct Tlingit division formerly living at Kake, Alaska. It was of the Raven phratry.   (J. R. S.)

Kahlchatlan (*Qǎ'ttcaʟ!an*). A town occupied by the Stikine before moving to the present site of Wrangell, Alaska, and consequently called Old Wrangell by the whites.   (J. R. S.)

Kahlguihlgahet-gitinai (*Qaɫguǐ'-ǐgǎ'xet gǐtǐna'-i*, 'the Pebble-town Gǐtǐ'ns living on the side of the town up the inlet'). A small branch of a Haida family called Hlgahet-gitinai living on the w. coast of Queen Charlotte ids., Brit. Col.—Swanton, Cont. Haida, 284, 1905.

Kahligua-haidagai (*Qǎ'tiguaxǎ'-idₐga-i*, 'people living at the end of the town up the inlet'). A subdivision of the Stawas-haidagai, a family of the Eagle clan of the Haida in Brit. Col., so named from the position of their houses in the town.—Swanton, Cont. Haida, 273, 1905.

Kahmetahwungaguma ('lake of the sandy waters.'—Warren). The Chippewa name of Sandy lake, on the upper Mississippi r., in Cass co., Minn. The Chippewa built a village on this lake about 1730, which was their first settlement on the headwaters of the Mississippi. The band residing here was commonly known as the Sandy Lake band. Some of them removed about 1807 to Pembina r. at the persuasion of the Northwest Fur Company.   (J. M.)
Chippeways of Sand Lake.—Lewis and Clark, Travels, 28, 1806.   Kah-me-tah-wung-a-guma.—Warren (1852) in Minn. Hist. Soc. Coll., V, 177, 1885. Kāmi'tāwₐngāgamāg.—Wm. Jones, inf'n, 1906 (correct form).   Sandy Lake Indians.—Morse, Rep. to Sec. War, 33, 1822.

Kahmitaiks ('buffalo dung'). A division of the Piegan tribe of the Siksika.
Buffalo Dung.—Grinnell, Blackfoot Lodge Tales, 225, 1892.   Kah'-mi-taiks.—Ibid., 209.

Kahmiut. A Kuskwogmiut Eskimo village in the Kuskokwim district, Alaska; pop. 40 in 1890.—11th Census, Alaska, 164, 1893.

Kahra ('wild rice'). One of the two modern divisions of the Sisseton Sioux. They had no permanent residence, but frequently visited L. Traverse, Minn., their hunting grounds being on Red r. of the North. Long (Exped. St Peters R., I, 378, 1824) said that they dwelt in fine skin tipis, the skins being well prepared and handsomely painted.
Caree.—Drake, Book Inds., vi, 1848 (identical?). Carees.—Domenech, Deserts of N. Am., I, 440, 1860 (identical?).   Uarrees.—Pike, Trav., 127, 1811. Cawras.—McIntosh, Origin of N. Am. Inds., 202, 1853.   Caw-ree.—Lewis and Clark, Discov., 34, 1806. Lac Traverse band.—Ind. Aff. Rep. 1859, 102, 1860. North Susseeton.—Ind. Aff. Rep., 497, 1839. Sussitongs of Roche Blanche.—Pike, Trav., 127, 1811. Upper Seesetoans.—Sibley (1852) in Sen. Ex. Doc. 29, pt. 2, 32d Cong., 2d sess., 9, 1853.

Kahtai. A former Clallam village at Port Townsend, Wash., in territory formerly occupied by the Chemakum.
Kahti—Gibbs in Pac. R. R. Rep., I, 429, 1855. Ká-tai.—Gibbs, Clallam and Lummi, 20, 1863.

Kai ('willows'). A Navaho clan. Cf. *Kaihatin.*
Kài-ɉine —Matthews in Jour. Am. Folk-lore, III, 103, 1890 (='people of the willows').   Káidǐne'.— Matthews, Navaho Legends, 30, 1897.

Kaiachim. A former Pomo village in Russian r. valley, Sonoma co., Cal.
Kajatschim.—Wrangell, Ethnog. Nachr., 80, 1839.

Kaiahl-lanas (*Qǎ'-iat lǎ'nas*, 'people of sea-lion town'). A family of the Eagle clan of the Haida, so called from the town which they formerly occupied on Skotsgai bay, near Skidegate, Queen Charlotte ids., Brit. Col. After difficulties with their neighbors they moved to the w. coast, where they built the town of Kaisun. The remnant is now at Skidegate. They claimed community of origin with the Kona-kegawai, Djiguaahl-lanas, and Stawas-haidagai.   (J. R. S.)
K·ai'atl lā'nas.—Boas in 12th Rep. N. W. Tribes Can., 24, 1898.   Qā'-iat lā'nas.—Swanton, Cont. Haida, 274, 1905.   Qā'-ita lā'nas.—Ibid.

Kaiak, kayak. The men's boat of the Eskimo of N. E. North America, from *qajaq* (*q*=German *ch*), the name in the eastern dialects of the Eskimo language. See *Boats.*   (A. F. C.)

Kaiakak. A village of the Ingalik division of the Kaiyuhkhotana, with 134 natives in 1880, on the w. bank of Yukon r., Alaska.—Petroff in 10th Census, Alaska, 12, 1884.

Kaiaksekawik ('place for making kaiaks'). A Utukamiut village on the N. side of Icy cape, Alaska.
Kaiaksekawik.—Eleventh Census, Alaska, 162, 1893.   Kayakshigvikg.—Zagoskin, Descr. Russ. Poss. in Am., pt. 1, 74, 1847.

Kaialigmiut. An Eskimo tribe N. of the Kuskwogmiut, extending on the mainland from Kuguktik r. to C. Romanzof, Alaska. In the lakes and streams of the tundra they obtain an abundant supply of fresh fish at the season when the coast natives often hunger. They are therefore a more vigorous people, living still in primitive simplicity. Their villages are Agiukchuk, Askinuk, Chininak, Kaialik, Kaliukluk, Kashigalak, Kushunuk, Kvigatluk, Nuloktolok, Nunvogulukhluguk, Sfaganuk, Ukak, Ukuk, and Unakagak.
Kaialigamut.—Nelson in 18th Rep. B. A. E., map, 1899.   Kai-á-lig-mūt.—Dall in Proc. Am. A. A. S., XXXIV, 18, 1886.

Kaialik. A Kaialigmiut Eskimo village in the Yukon delta near Azun r., Alaska; pop. 100 in 1880, 157 in 1890.
Kaialigumiut.—Nelson (1868) quoted by Baker, Geog. Dict. Alaska, 1902.   Kailwigamiut.—Eleventh Census, Alaska, 164, 1893.   Kialigamiut.—Ibid., 110.

Kaibab (prob. 'on the mountain,' from *kaib* or *kaiba*, 'mountain,' and the locative ending *ab* or *ba*.—Kroeber). A division of the Paiute, numbering 171 in 1873, when they were in the vicinity of Kanab, s. w. Utah. Powell gave their name to the Kaibab plateau, N. w. Ariz. In 1903 their number was given as 140, of which 30 were at Cedar City, Utah, and 110 under a special agent.   In 1905 there were 109 reported, not under an agent.

Kai-bäb-bit.—Ind. Aff. Rep. 251, 1877. **Kaibabits.**—Ingalls in H. R. Ex. Doc. 66, 42d Cong., 3d sess., 2, 1873. **Kaivavwit.**—Powell in Ind. Aff. Rep. 1873, 50, 1874. **Kai-vwav-uai Nu-ints.**—Sen. Ex. Doc. 42, 43d Cong., 1st sess., 15, 1874.

Kaidatoiabie (*Kai-da-toi-ab-ie*). A Paviotso tribe of 6 bands formerly living in N. E. Nevada; pop. 425 in 1873.—Powell in Ind. Aff. Rep. 1873, 52, 1874.

Kaidju (*Qai'dju*, 'songs-of-victory town'). A Haida town on a point opposite Danger rocks, Moresby id., Queen Charlotte ids., Brit. Col., occupied by the Tadji-lanas. The Kaidju-kegawai, a subdivision of the Tadji-lanas, took its name from this town.—Swanton, Cont. Haida, 277, 1905.

Kaidju. A Haida town in Hewlett bay, on the E. coast of Moresby id., Queen Charlotte ids. Brit. Col. It was occupied by the Kas-lanas.—Swanton, Cont. Haida, 277, 1905.

Kaidjudal (*Qai'djudal*). A former Haida town on Moresby id., opposite Hot Spring id., Queen Charlotte group, Brit. Col. It was occupied by the Huldanggats.—Swanton, Cont. Haida, 278, 1905.

Kaidju-kegawai (*Qai'dju qē'gawa-i*, 'those born at Songs-of-victory town'). A subdivision of the Tadji-lanas, a family belonging to the Gunghet-haidagai (Ninstints people) of the Haida of British Columbia.—Swanton, Cont. Haida, 269, 1905.

Kaigani (*K!aigā'ni*). A division of the Haida, living in Alaska. Their name is derived from that of a camping place or summer settlement where they were accustomed to assemble to meet incoming vesels and to trade with the whites. The Kaigani emigrated from the N. w. end of Queen Charlotte ids. between 150 and 200 years ago, drove the Tlingit (Koluschan) from the s. end of Prince of Wales id., and took possession of their towns. The most important of these settlements were Sukwan, Klinkwan, Howkan, and Kasaan, which bear their old Tlingit names. The last three are still inhabited. Like many Tlingit tribes, but unlike other Haida, the Kaigani subdivisions often took their names from the name given to some individual house. About 1840 the population was estimated at 1,735. According to Petroff's report (10th Census, Alaska) they numbered 788 in 1880; in 1890 the population was given as 391. Their present number probably does not exceed 300.   (J. R. S.)

Kaiaganies.—Halleck (1869) in Morris, Resources of Alaska, 67, 1879. **Kaigan.**—Terry in Rep. Sec. War, I, 40, 1868–69. **Kaigani.**—Dawson, Queen Charlotte Ids., 104B, 1880. **Kegarnie.**—Dunn, Hist. Oregon, 281, 1844. **Kiganis.**—Duflot de Mofras, Oregon, I, 335, 336, 1844. **Kigarnee.**—Ludewig, Aborig. Lang. America, 157, 1860. **Kigenes.**—Am. Pioneer, II, 189, 1843. **Kygani.**—Dall in Proc. A. A. A. S., 269, 1869. **Kyganies.**—Scouler in Jour. Geog. Soc.

Lond., I, 219, 1841. **Kygany.**—Gibbs after Anderson in Hist. Mag., 74, 1863. **Kygargey.**—Schoolcraft, Ind. Tribes, v, 489, 1855 (after Work, 1836–41). **Kygarney.**—Kane, Wand. N. A., app., 1859 (after Work, 1836–41).

Kaigani. An important Haida summer town or camping place at the s. E. end of Dall id., s. w. Alaska. Most of the families which moved from the Queen Charlotte ids. formerly gathered here to meet trading vessels, for which reason they came to be known to the whites as Kaigani. The dominant family in this town is said to have been the Yakulanas.   (J. R. S.)

Kaigwu (Kiowa proper). The oldest tribal division of the Kiowa, from which the tribe derives its name. To it belongs the keeping of the medicine tipi, in which is the grand medicine of the tribe.—Mooney in 14th Rep. B. A. E., 1079, 1896.

Kaihatin ('willow'). A clan or band of the Coyotero and also of the Pinaleño Apache at San Carlos and Ft Apache agencies, Ariz.; coordinate with the Kai clan of the Navaho.

Kayjatin.—Bourke in Jour. Am. Folk-lore, III, 112, 1890. **Kay-tzen-lin.**—Ibid.

Kaiihl-lanas (*Qai-ĭt lā'nas*). A subdivision of the Dostlan-lnagai, a family group of the Haida, named from a camping place on the w. coast of Queen Charlotte ids., Brit. Col.   (J. R. S.)

Kailaidshi. A former Upper Creek town in the central district, on a creek of the same name, which joins Oakjoy cr., a w. tributary of Tallapoosa r., probably in the N. w. part of the present Elmore co., Ala. Atchinahatchi and Hatchichapa were dependent villages of this town, the name of which probably has reference to a warrior's head-dress.   (A. S. G.)

Caileedjee.—Robin, Voy., II, map, 1807. **Cieligees.**—Woodward, Reminiscences, 83, 1859. **Ka-iläidshi.**—Gatschet, Creek Migr. Leg., I, 133, 1884. **Kealeegees.**—U. S. Ind. Treat. (1779), 69, 1837. **Keilijah.**—H. R. Ex. Doc. 276, 24th Cong., 1st sess., 318, 1836. **Kialajahs.**—Simpson (1836) in H. R. Doc. 80, 27th Cong., 3d sess., 50, 1843. **Kialechies.**—H. R. Ex. Doc. 276, 24th Cong., 1st sess., 124, 1836. **Kialeegees.**—U. S. Ind. Treaties (1779), 69, 1837. **Kialega.**—Crawford (1836) in H. R. Doc. 274, 25th Cong., 2d sess., 24, 1838. **Kialgie.**—Shorter (1835) in H. R. Doc. 452, 25th Cong., 2d sess., 65, 1838. **Kialiages.**—Ore (1792) in Am. State Pap., Ind. Aff., I, 274, 1832. **Kialiga's.**—Campbell (1836) in H. R. Doc. 274, 25th Cong., 2d sess., 20, 1838. **Kialige.**—Creek paper (1836) in H. R. Rep. 87, 31st Cong., 2d sess., 122, 1851. **Kialigee.**—H. R. Doc. 274, 25th Cong., 2d sess., 149, 1838. **Ki-a-li-jee.**—Hawkins (1799), Sketch, 48, 1848. **Kiolichee.**—Sen. Ex. Doc. 425, 24th Cong., 1st sess., 181, 1836. **Kiliga.**—Gatschet, Creek Migr. Leg., I, 133, 1884 (an early form). **Killeegko.**—Swan (1791) in Schoolcraft, Ind. Tribes, v, 262, 1855. **Kiolege.**—Bartram (1778), Travels, 462, 1791. **Kuyalegees.**—U. S. Ind. Treat. (1797), 68, 1837. **Ogoleegees.**—Lattré, map of U. S., 1784 (probably identical). **Pialeges.**—Weatherford (1793) in Am. State Pap., Ind. Aff., I, 386, 1832.

Kailaidshi. A town of the Creek Nation on Canadian r., E. of Hilabi, Okla.

Ka-ilä'idshi.—Gatschet, Creek Migr. Leg., II, 185, 1888.

Kaime (*Kai-me'*). A Pomo tribe occupying Russian r. valley, Cal., from Cloverdale to Geyserville.—Powers in Cont. N. A. Ethnol., III, 183, 1877.

Kainah (*Ah-kai-nah*, 'many chiefs', from *a-kai-im* 'many', *ni'-nah* 'chiefs'). A division of the Siksika (q. v.), or Blackfeet, now living on a reservation under the Blood agency in Alberta, Canada, between Belly and St Mary rs. The subtribes or bands are Ahkaiksumiks, Ahkaipokaks, Ahkotashiks, Ahkwonistsists, Anepo, Apikaiyiks, Aputosikainah, Inuhksoyistamiks, Isisokasimiks, Istsikainah, Mameoya, Nitikskiks, Ponokix, Saksinahmahyiks, Siksahpuniks, and Siksinokaks. According to the Report of the Commissioner of Indian Affairs for 1858, there were then 300 tipis and 2,400 persons. In 1904 there were 1,196 persons on the reservation, of whom 958 were classed as pagans.

Bloodies.—Hind, Red R. Exped., 157, 1860 (so called by half-breeds). **Blood Indians.**—Writer of 1786 in Mass. Hist. Soc. Coll., 1st s., III, 24, 1794. **Blood People.**—Morgan, Consang. and Affin., 289, 1871. **Blut Indianer.**—Walch, map, 1805 (German form). **Ede-but-say.**—Anon. Crow MS. vocab., B. A. E. (Crow name). **Gens du Sang.**—Duflot de Mofras, Expl., II, 342, 1844. **Indiens du Sang.**—Ibid., 339. **Kaënna.**—Maximilian, Travels, 245, 1843. **Kahna.**—Ibid. **Kai'-e-na.**—Hayden, Ethnog. and Philol. Mo. Val., 256, 1862. **Kaimè.**—Browne in Beach, Ind. Miscel., 81, 1877. **Kai'-na.**—Clark Wissler, inf'n, 1905 (Piegan dialectic form). **Kai'nau.**—Tims, Blackfoot Gram. and Dict., 113, 1889 (Siksika name). **Kainœ'-koon.**—Franklin, Journ. Polar Sea, I, 170, 1824 (own name). **Kam'-ne.**—Hayden, op. cit., 402 (Crow name). **Ke'na.**—Hale, Ethnol. and Philol., 219, 1846 (sing., Keneku'n). **Ki-na.**—Morgan, Consang. and Affin., 289, 1871 (trans.: 'high minded people'). **Kine-ne-ai-koon.**—Henry, MS. vocab., 1808. **Ki'-no.**—Morgan, Anc. Soc., 171, 1877. **Meethco-thinyoowuc.**—Franklin, Journ. Polar Sea, I, 170, 1824. **We'-wi-ca-sa.**—Cook, Yankton MS. vocab., B. A. E., 1882 (Yankton name).

Kaisun (*Qai'sun*). A former Haida town on the N. w. coast of Moresby id., Queen Charlotte group, Brit. Col. It belonged to the Kaiahl-lanas, who settled there after moving from Skidegate inlet, but before that time the Kas-lanas are said to have occupied it. By the whites Kaisun was sometimes called Gold Harbor, or, to distinguish it from the town afterward built on Maude id. by the west-coast people, Old Gold Harbor; but this term is properly applicable to Skaito, a camp on Gold Harbor, itself occupied by Haida from all parts of the Queen Charlotte ids. during the time of the gold excitement. Kaisun is the Kish-a-win of John Work's list, which was accredited by him with 18 houses and 329 people in 1836–41. Since the old people can still remember 17 houses, Work's figures would appear to be trustworthy. The few survivors of Kaisun now live at Skidegate. (J. R. S.)

Kaishun.—Dawson, Q. Charlotte Ids., 168, 1880. **K·ai's'un.**—Boas, Twelfth Report N. W. Tribes Canada, 24, 1880. **Kaiswun Hááde.**—Harrison in Proc. and Trans. Roy. Soc. Can., sec. II, 125, 1895. **Kish-a-win.**—Schoolcraft, Ind. Tribes, V,

489, 1855 (after Work, 1836–41). **Qai'sun.**—Swanton, Cont. Haida, 287, 1905.

Kaivanungavidukw (*Kai-va-nung-av'-i-dukw.*) A band of the Paviotso, popularly called Paiute, formerly living in Surprise valley, N. E. Cal.—Powell, Paviotso MS., B. A. E., 1881.

Kaiyau ('head'). A name applied by all the Pomo about Clear lake to those living about the N. end of the lake, in Upper Lake and Bachelor valleys, Lake co., Cal. (S. A. B.)

Kaiyuhkhotana. The westernmost Athapascan tribe of Alaska, living on the banks of Yukon r. between Anvik and Koyukuk rs. They have been supplanted in the w. part of their old habitat by Eskimo. Since hostilities between them and the Eskimo have ceased they have become assimilated with the latter, adopting a fish diet and differing from all their congeners in acquiring a liking for oil. The tribe is distinguished from its neighbors also by its language, they being unable to converse with the Kutchin. The southernmost settlements subsist principally by fishing and trading. They dry fish and are very expert in making wooden ware and strong birch canoes. Those of upper Yukon, Shageluk, and Kuskokwim rs. combine hunting with these pursuits. The Kaiyuhkhotana build permanent villages which they sometimes leave during the summer. The pointed hunting shirts formerly worn have been largely replaced by the clothing of the whites. They do not appear to have adopted a totemic system, and follow the Eskimo custom of giving elaborate feasts. Zagoskin in 1844 estimated their population at 923. Petroff (10th Census, Alaska, 1884) gave their number as 805 on the Yukon and 148 on the Kuskokwim. Allen (Report on Alaska, 1887) gave the population as about 1,300. The 11th Census (158, 1893) gives the population of the Yukon district as 753 and of the Kuskokwim as 386; total, 1,139. The following are Kaiyuhkhotana villages, exclusive of those of the Jugelnute division: Anvik, Chagvagchat, Chinik, Iktigalik, Innoka, Ivan, Kagokakat, Kaiakak, Kaltag, Khaigamute, Khogoltlinde, Khulikakat, Khunanilinde, Klamaskwaltin, Koserefski, Kunkhogliak, Kutul, Lofka, Nulato, Paltchikatno, Taguta, Tanakot, Terentief, Tigshelde, Tutago, Ulukakhotana, and Wolaеatux. The local divisions were Ingalik, Inkalich, Jugelnute, Kaiyuhkhotana, Nulato, Takaiak, Tlegonkhotana, Taiyanyanokhotana, and Ulukakhotana.

Danè.—Petitot, Autour du lac des Esclaves, 361, 1891. **Ingaliks.**—Dall in Proc. Am. A. A. S., XVIII, 270, 1870. **Kaeyah-Khatana.**—Bancroft, Nat. Races, I, 133, 1874. **Kaiyuhkatana.**—Ibid., 148, 1882. **Kaiyuhkho-tana.**—Dall, Alaska, 431, 1870. **Kaiyukhotana.**—Allen, Rep., 143, 1887. **Kkρayou-Kouttànœ.**—Petitot, Autour du lac des Esclaves, 361,

1891 ('people of the willows'). **Lowlanders.**—Dall in Proc. Am. A. A. S., XVIII, 270, 1870.

Kaiyuhkhotana. A division of the Kaiyukhkhotana, living on Kaiyuh r. Their village was Kutul.
Kainhkhotana.—Petroff in 10th Census, Alaska, 161, 1884 (misprint). Kaiyŭk'ā-kho-tān'ā.—Dall in Cont. N. A. Ethnol., I, 26, 1877.

Kaiyuwuntsunitthai ('rocky land'). A former Kuitsh village on lower Umpqua r., Oreg.
Kai'-yŭ-wun-ts'u'-nĭt t'ɕai'.—Dorsey in Jour. Am. Folk-lore, III, 231, 1890.

Kajechadi. (*Kä-jēch-adĭ*). Given by Krause (Tlinkit-Ind., 116, 1885) as a Tlingit division living in the town of Chilkoot, Alaska. Unidentified.

Kajienatroene ('eagle people.'—Hewitt). One of the 6 "castles" of the Ottawa near Michilimackinac, Mich., in 1723.—Albany conf. (1723) in N. Y. Doc. Col. Hist., v, 693, 1855.

Kaka ('crows'). A band or society of the Arikara.
Crows.—Culbertson in Smithson. Rep. 1850, 143, 1851. Ka-ka'.—Hayden, Ethnog. and Philol., 357, 1862.

Kakagshe (*Kä-käg'-she*, 'crow'). A gens of the Potawatomi.—Morgan, Anc. Soc., 167, 1877.

Kakake(*Kakáke*, 'crow'). A subphratry or gens of the Menominee.—Hoffman in 14th Rep. B. A. E., pt. I, 42, 1896.

Kakake. Given as the Pigeon-hawk gens of the Chippewa, but really the Raven (Kagigi) gens of that tribe.
Kagagi.—Wm. Jones, inf'n, 1906. Ka-kaik.—Tanner, Narr., 314, 1830 ('hen hawk'). Ka-kake'.—Morgan, Anc. Soc., 166, 1877 ('pigeon hawk').

Kakanatzatia. A former village of the Sia (q. v.), opposite the present Sia pueblo, on Jemez r., N. central N. Mex. According to Sia tradition, war broke out between the inhabitants of this village and those of Kohasaya, the former being driven southward by an attempt of the latter to burn their pueblo, the Kohasaya afterward moving to the site of Sia. It is not improbable that one of the two pueblos mentioned was occupied at the time of Espejo's visit in 1583, and thus formed one of the villages of his province of Punames.
Ka-kan A-tza Tia.—Bandelier in Arch. Inst. Papers, IV, 198, 1892.

Kakapoya ('inside fat.'—Morgan). Given as a division of the Piegan tribe of the Siksika. Perhaps the same as Inuksikahkopwaiks, q. v.
Inside Fat.—Morgan, Anc. Soc., 171, 1877. Ka-ka'-po-ya.—Ibid.

Kakawatilikya (*Qä'qawatilik·a*). A gens of the Tsawatenok, a Kwakiutl tribe.—Boas in Rep. Nat. Mus. 1895, 331, 1897.

Kake. A Tlingit tribe on Kupreanof id., Alaska. The designation is often extended to include the people of Kuiu and Sumdum (q. v.). Their winter village is Koke, near Hamilton harbor. Pop., including probably the Kuiu people, 234 in 1890. Their social divisions are

Kahlchanedi (extinct), Katchadi, Nesadi, Sakutenedi, Shunkukedi, Tsaguedi, Tanedi, and Was-hinedi. (J. R. S.)
Cakes.—Seward, Speeches on Alaska, 5, 1869. Kaacks.—Crosbie in H. R. Ex. Doc. 77, 36th Cong., 1st sess., 8, 1860. Kake.—Kane, Wand. in N. A., app., 1859. Kakus.—Halleck in Rep. Sec. War, pt. 1, 38, 1868. Kates.—Colyer (Louthan) in Ind. Aff. Rep., 573, 1870. Kaykovskie.—Elliott, Cond. Aff. Alaska, 227, 1875 (transliterated from Veniaminoff). Kehk.—Petroff in 10th Census, Alaska, 32, 1884. Kehons.—Scott in Ind. Aff. Rep., 313, 1868 (name on Russian charts). Kek.—Tikhmenieff, Russ. Am. Co., II, 341, 1863. Kēkch-kŏn.—Krause, Tlinkit Ind., 120, 1885. Kekuvskoe.—Veniaminoff, Zapiski, II, pt. 3, 30, 1840. Kēq!—Swanton, field notes, B. A. E., 1904. Khēkhu.—Holmberg, Ethnog. Skizz., map, 1855. Kyacks.—Scott in Ind. Aff. Rep., 314, 1868. Rat tribe.—Mahony (1869) in Sen. Ex. Doc. 68, 41st Cong., 2d sess., 20, 1870.

Kake. The modern name of the village of the Kake Indians on the N. w. coast of Kupreanof id., Alaska; pop. 234 in 1890.
Kēq!.—Swanton, field notes, B. A. E., 1904. Klukwan.—Petroff in Tenth Census, Alaska, 32, 1884. S!îkAnAxsā'nî.—Swanton, op. cit. (said to be proper name of the town, perhaps meaning 'from a black bear town').

Kakegha ('making a grating noise'). A division of the Brulé Teton Sioux.
Kakeɡa.—Dorsey (after Cleveland) in 15th Rep. B. A. E., 219, 1897. Kak'exa.—Ibid.

Kakekt (*Xäx'ēqt*). An extinct Salish tribe which formerly lived at C. Lazo, E. coast of Vancouver id., and spoke the Comox dialect.—Boas, MS., B. A. E., 1887.

Kakhan. The Wolf clan of the Keresan pueblo of Laguna, N. Mex. It claims to have come originally from Sandia.
Ka-kan.—Bandelier in Arch. Inst. Papers, III, 293, 1890 (given as name of the wolf fetish). Kákhan-hanoᶜʰ.—Hodge in Am. Anthrop., IX, 352, 1896 (*hanoch* = 'people').

Kakhmiatonwan ('village at the bend'). A division of the Sisseton Sioux.
Kahmi-atoŋwaŋ.—Dorsey in 15th Rep. B. A. E., 217, 1897. Kaqmi-atoⁿwaⁿ.—Ibid.

Kakhtshanwaish. A former Alsea village on the N. side of Alsea r., Oreg.
Kăq-tcaⁿ-waic'.—Dorsey in Jour. Am. Folk-lore, III, 230, 1890.

Kakick. According to Coxe a tribe formerly on an island of the same name in Tennessee r., above the Chickasaw; possibly Creek. See *Cochali*.
Kakick.—Coxe, Carolana, map, 1741. Kakigue.—Ibid., 14.

Kakinonba. A tribe mentioned by several early French writers about the close of the 18th century as living apparently on Tennessee or Cumberland r., although the exact locality and the relationship of the tribe can not be determined. Marquette's map places them E. of the Mississippi, about the region of Kentucky, in 1674. The Senex map of 1710 locates them along the middle of Tennessee r. St Cosme speaks of them as in s. Illinois in 1699. Tennessee r. was called Casquinambeaux, Casquinampo, and Kaskinenpo by early French explorers.
Cakinonpas.—Sauvole (1701) in French, Hist. Coll. La., III, 238, 1851. Caskinampo.—Senex, map of N. Am., 1710. Kakinonba.—Marquette's map (*ca.* 1674) in Shea, Discov. Miss., 1852. Karkinonpols.—

St Cosme (1699) in Shea, Early Voy., 60, 1861.
Kasquinanipo.—Tonti (*ca.* 1690) in French, Hist.
Coll. La., I, 82, 1846.

Kakliaklia. A Koyukukhotana village
of 26 people on the Koyukuk, at the mouth
of Sukloseanti r., Alaska.
Kakhlyakhlyakakat.—Zagoskin, Desc. Russ. Poss.
Am., map, 1848. **Kakliakhliakat.**—Zagoskin
quoted by Petroff in 10th Census, Alaska, 37, 1884.
Kakliaklia.—Baker, Geog. Dict. Alaska, 1902.
Kakliakliakat.—Tikhmenief (1861) quoted by
Baker, ibid. **Kikliakliakakate.**—Zagoskin in
Nouv. Ann. Voy., 5th s., XXI, map, 1850.

Kakonak. A Kiatagmiut Eskimo village on the s. shore of Iliamna lake, Alaska; pop. 28 in 1890.
Kakhonak.—Eleventh Census, Alaska, 164, 1893.

Kakonkaruk (*kakon*, a species of hawk;
ka, locative; *ruk,* 'house.'—Kroeber).
A village of the Rumsen, a division of the
Costanoan family, formerly at Sur, on the
coast, 20 m. s. of Monterey, Cal.
Cakanaruk.—Taylor in Cal. Farmer, Apr. 20, 1860.
Kakontaruk.—A. L. Kroeber, inf'n, 1906.

Kakos-hit-tan (*Qaq!ō′s hit tän,* 'people
of man's-feet house'). A subdivision of
the Shunkukedi (q. v.), a Tlingit division
at Klawak, Alaska. (J. R. S.)

Kakouchaki (from *kakou,* 'porcupine').
A small Montagnais tribe formerly living
on St John lake, Quebec. They frequently
visited Tadoussac with other northern
tribes and were occasionally visited in
their country by the missionaries.
Kacouchakhi.—Can. Ind. Aff., 40, 1879. **Kak8a-
zakhi.**—Jes. Rel. for 1641, 57, 1858. **Kakouchac.**—
Ibid., 1672, 44. **Kakouchakhi.**—Ibid., 1643, 38.
Kakouchaki.—Champlain, Œuvres, II, 21, note,
1870. **Nation des Porc epics.**—Jes. Rel. for 1638, 24,
1858. **Nation of the Porcupine.**—Winsor, Cartier to
Frontenac, 171, 1894. **Porcupine Tribe.**—Charlevoix, Hist. N. France, II, 118, 1866.

Kaksine (*Qāk·sinē*). A Squawmish village community on Mamukum cr., left
bank of Squawmisht r., Brit. Col.—Hill-
Tout in Rep. Brit. A. A. S., 474, 1900.

Kaku (*Ká-k'u*). A former Yaquina
village on the s. side of Yaquina r., Oreg.—
Dorsey in Jour. Am. Folk-lore, III, 229,
1890.

Kakuak. A Nushagagmiut Eskimo village 60 m. up Nushagak r., Alaska; pop.
104 in 1880, 45 in 1890.
Kakuak.—Petroff, Rep. on Alaska, 47, 1881. **Kak-
wok.**—Coast Surv. map, 11th Census, Alaska, 1893.

Kakuguk. A former Aleut village on
Agattu id., Alaska, one of the Near id.
group of the Aleutians, now uninhabited.

Kakuiak. A Kuskwogmiut Eskimo village on Kuskokwim r., Alaska; pop. 8 in
1880.
Kakhuiyagamute.—Petroff in 10th Census, Alaska,
17, 1884.

Kalanunyi (*Kâ′lanûñ′yi,* 'raven place').
One of the five districts or "towns" which
Col. William H. Thomas, in his capacity of
agent for the Eastern Cherokee, laid off
on the E. Cherokee res., in Swain and
Jackson cos., N. C., after the removal of
the rest of the tribe to Indian Ter. in 1838.
The name is still retained. (J. M.)
Big Cove.—Mooney in 19th Rep., B. A. E., 161, 524,
1900. **Kâ′lanûñ′yĭ.**—Ibid. (Cherokee name: 'Raven place'). **Raventown.**—Ibid.

Kalapooian Family. A group of tribes formerly occupying the valley of Willamette
r., N. W. Oreg., and speaking a distinct
stock language (see Powell in 7th Rep. B.
A. E., 81, 1891). Little is known of their
history, but they seem to have confined
themselves to the territory mentioned,
except in the case of one tribe, the Yonkalla, which pushed southward to the valley of the Umpqua. The earliest accounts
describe a numerous population in Willamette valley, which is one of the most
fertile in the N. W.; but the Kalapooian
tribes appear to have suffered severe losses
by epidemic disease about 1824, and since
that time they have been numerically
weak. They are also described as being
indolent and sluggish in character, yet
they seem to have been able to hold their
territory against the attempts of surrounding tribes to dispossess them. They were
at constant war with the coast peoples
and also suffered much at the hands of
the white pioneers. Game, in which the
country abounded, and roots of various
kinds constituted their chief food supply.
Unlike most of the Indians of that region
they did not depend on salmon, which
are unable to ascend the Willamette above
the falls, and at which point the Kalapooian territory ended. Of the general
customs of the group there is little information. Slavery existed in a modified
form, marriage was by purchase and was
accompanied by certain curious ceremonials (Gatschet in Jour. Am. Folk-lore,
XII, 212, 1899), and flattening of the head
by fronto-occipital pressure was practised.
The language is sonorous, the verb excessively complex, few prefixes being
used, and the words are distinguished by
consonantal endings.

By treaty of Calapooia cr., Oreg., Nov.
29, 1854, the Umpqua and Kalapooian
tribes of Umpqua valley ceded their lands
to the United States, the tract, however,
to constitute a reserve for these and other
tribes, unless the President should decide
to locate them elsewhere. This removal
was effected, and the entire tract was regarded as ceded. By treaty at Dayton,
Oreg., Jan. 22, 1855, the Calapooya and
confederated bands of Willamette valley
ceded the entire drainage area of Willamette r., the Grande Ronde res. being
set aside for them and other bands by
Executive order of June 30, 1857. By
agreement June 27, 1901, confirmed Apr.
21, 1904, the Indians of Grande Ronde
res. ceded all the unallotted lands of said
reservation. The Kalapooian bands at
Grande Ronde numbered 351 in 1880,
164 in 1890, 130 in 1905. There are also
a few representatives of the stock under
the Siletz agency.

It is probable that in early times the
tribes and divisions of this family were

more numerous, but the following are the chief ones of which there is definite information: Ahantchuyuk or Pudding River, Atfalati or Tualati, Calapooya, Chelamela, Chepenafa, Lakmiut, Santiam, Yamel, and Yonkalla.

The following are presumed to be Kalapooian tribes or bands, but have not been fully identified: Chemapho, Chemeketas, Chillychandize, Laptambif, Leeshtelosh, Peeyou, Shehees, Shookany, and Winnefelly. See *Calapooya*. (L. F.)

>**Calapooya.**—Bancroft, Nat. Races, III, 565, 629, 1882. ×**Chinooks.**—Keane in Stanford, Compend., Cent. and So. Am., app., 474, 1878 (includes Calapooyas and Yamkally). =**Kalapooiah.**—Scouler in Jour. Roy. Geog. Soc. Lond., XI, 225, 1841 (includes Kalapooiah and Yamkallie; thinks the Umpqua and Cathlascon languages are related); Buschmann, Spuren der aztek. Sprache, 599, 617, 1859 (follows Scouler). =**Kalapooian.**—Powell in 7th Rep. B. A. E., 81, 1891. =**Kalapuya.**—Hale in U. S. Expl. Exped., VI, 217, 564, 1846 (of Willamet valley above falls); Gallatin in Trans. Am. Ethnol. Soc., II, pt. 1, c, 17, 77, 1848; Berghaus (1851), Physik. Atlas, map 17, 1852; Gallatin in Schoolcraft, Ind. Tribes, III, 402, 1853; Latham in Trans. Philol. Soc. Lond., 73, 1856; Buschmann, Spuren der aztek. Sprache, 617, 1859; Latham, Opuscula, 340, 1860; Gatschet in Mag. Am. Hist., 167, 1877; Gatschet in Beach, Ind. Miscel., 442, 1877. >**Yamkally.**—Bancroft, Nat. Races, III, 565, 630, 1882 (bears a certain relationship to Calapooya).

Kalashiauu (*Ka-la'-ci-au-u*). The Raccoon clan of the Chua (Snake) phratry of the Hopi.—Stephen in 8th Rep. B. A. E., 38, 1891.

Kalawashuk (*Ka-la-wa'-cŭk*). One of the Chumashan villages connected with the former Santa Inés mission, Santa Barbara co., Cal.—Henshaw, Santa Inez MS. vocab., B. A. E., 1884.

Kalawatset. A geographical group of tribes of different families in w. Oregon, embracing particularly the Coos, Kuitsh, and Siuslaw.

Kala-Walset.—Mannypenny in H. R. Ex. Doc. 37, 34th Cong., 3d sess., 9, 1857. **Kalawatset.**—Milhau, MS. vocab. Coast Inds., B. A. E. **Kalawatshet.**—Gibbs, MS., B. A. E. **Kiliwatsal.**—Framboise, quoted by Gairdner (1835) in Jour. Geog. Soc. Lond., XI, 255, 1841. **Kiliwátshat.**—Hale, Ethnol. and Philol., 221, 1846. **Killawat.**—Drake, Bk. Inds., viii, 1848. **Killewatsis.**—Armstrong, Oreg., 116, 1857. **Killiwashat.**—Latham (1853) in Proc. Philol. Soc. Lond., VI, 82, 1854. **Killiwatshat.**—Hamilton quoted by Gibbs, MS., B. A. E. **K'qlo-qwec'ʋŭnnĕ.**—Dorsey, MS. Chasta Costa vocab., B. A. E., 1884 (Chastacosta name). **Ral-la-wat-sets.**—Drew in H. R. Ex. Doc. 93, 34th Cong., 1st sess., 127, 1856.

Kalbauvane. A former Delaware (?) village on the headwaters of the w. branch of Susquehanna r., Pa.—Pouchot map (1758) in N. Y. Doc. Col. Hist., x, 694, 1858.

Kalbusht ('where the water rolls'). A former Alsea village on the s. side of Alsea r., Oreg.

ɥäl'-bŭct'.—Dorsey in Jour. Am. Folk-lore, III, 230, 1890.

Kalekhta. A former Aleut village on Unalaska, Aleutian ids., Alaska, containing 14 persons about 1825.

Kahlechtenskoi.—Elliott, Cond. Aff. Alaska, 225, 1875. **Kalaktak.**—Coxe, Russian Discov., 167, 1787. **Kalechtinskoje.**—Holmberg, Ethnog. Skizz., map, 1885. **Kalekhtinskoe.**—Veniaminoff, Zapiski, II, 202, 1840.

Kalelk (*Ka'-lelk*). A former Modoc settlement on the n. shore of Tule or Rhett lake, s. w. Oregon.—Gatschet in Cont. N. A. Ethnol., II, pt. 1, xxxii, 1890.

Kali ('fishermen'). A Knaiakhotana clan living on Cook inlet, Alaska.—Richardson, Arct. Exped., I, 407, 1851.

Kalignak. A Nushagagmiut village on a tributary of Nushagak r., Alaska; pop. 91 in 1880.—Petroff, Rep. on Alaska, 47, 1880.

Kaliko. A Yuit Eskimo village on the Siberian coast E. of Iskagan bay.—Krause in Deutsche Geog. Blätt., v, 80, map, 1882.

Kalindaruk (*kalin* 'ocean', *ta* 'at', *ruk* 'houses.'—Kroeber). A village near the mouth of Salinas r., Cal. The name has been used, whether or not with justification, to designate the group of Indians inhabiting the villages on lower Pajaro r., and between it and the Salinas, near the coast. Indians from this area were taken both to San Carlos and to San Juan Bautista missions. Among the villages attributed to this region are Alcoz, Animpayamo, Kapanai, Kulul, Lukaiasta, Mustak, Nutnur, Paisin, Poitokwis, Tiubta, and Ymunakam.

Calendaruc.—Engelhardt, Franciscans in Cal., 398, 1897. **Kalindaruk.**—A. L. Kroeber, inf'n, 1906 (proper form). **Kathlendaruc.**—Taylor in Cal. Farmer, Nov. 25, 1860. **Katlendarukas.**—Ibid., Apr. 20, 1860.

Kalispel (popularly known as Pend d'Oreilles, 'ear drops'). A Salish tribe around the lake and along the river of the same name in the extreme N. part of Idaho and N. E. Washington. Gibbs divided them into the Kalispelms or Pend d'Oreilles of the Lower Lake and the Slka-tkml-schi or Pend d'Oreilles of the Upper Lake, and according to Dr Dart the former numbered 520 in 1851, the latter 480 (Pac. R. R. Rep. I, 415, 1855). McVickar (Hist. Exped. Lewis and Clark, II, 386, note, 1842) made three divisions: Upper Pend d'Oreilles, Lower Pend d'Oreilles, and Micksucksealton. Lewis and Clark estimated their number at 1,600 in 30 lodges in 1805. In 1905 there were 640 Upper Pend d'Oreilles and 197 Kalispel under the Flathead agency, Mont., and 98 Kalispel under the Colville agency, Wash.

The subdivisions, being seldom referred to, are disregarded in the synonymy.

Ach-min-de-cou-may.—Anon. Crow MS. vocab., B. A. E. (Crow name). **Ak-min'-e-shu'-me.**—Hayden, Ethnog. and Philol., 402, 1862 ('the tribe that uses canoes': Crow name). **Calapelins.**—Schoolcraft, Ind. Tribes, VI, 686, 1857. **Calespelin.**—Lane (1849) in Sen. Ex. Doc. 52, 31st Cong., 1st sess., 170, 1850. **Calespell.**—Johnson and Winter, Rocky Mts., 34, 1846. **Calespin.**—Lane (1849) in Sen. Ex. Doc. 52, op. cit., 170. **Calispells.**—Keane in Stanford, Compend., 504, 1878. **Colespelin.**—Schoolcraft, Ind. Tribes, VI, 701, 1857. **Colespells.**—H. R. Ex. Doc. 102, 43d Cong., 1st sess., I, 1874. **Coopspellar.**—Drake, Bk. Inds., vii, 1848. **Coospellar.**—Lewis and Clark Exped., II, 475, 1814. **Coos-pel-lar's Nation.**—Orig. Jour. Lewis and Clark, VI, 119, 1905. **Ear Rings.**—De Smet, Letters, 62, 1843. **Flathead Kootanie.**—Tolmie and Dawson,

Comp. Vocabs., 124B, 1884 (erroneously so called). **Hanging Ears.**—Irving, Rocky Mts., I, 127, 1837. **Kah-lis-pelm.**—Stevens in Ind. Aff. Rep., 461, 1854. **Kale pel.**—Ibid., 418. **Kälespilum.**—Gatschet, MS., B. A. E. (Okinagan name). **Kalispel.**—Ind. Aff. Rep. 1901, 692, 1902 (own name). **Kalispelines.**—Stevens in Ind. Aff. Rep., 418, 1854. **Kalispelms.**—Gibbs in Pac. R. R. Rep., I, 415, 1855. **Kalispels.**—Smet, Letters, 170, 1843. **Kalispelum.**—Stevens in Ind. Aff. Rep., 419, 1854. **Kalispelu ses.**—Ibid., 418. **Ka'nōqtla'tlăm.**—Chamberlain in 8th Rep. N. W. Tribes Can., 8, 1892 (Kutenai name: 'compress side of head'). **Kellespem.**—Duflot de Mofras, Expl., II, 101, 335, 1844. **Klanoh-klatk!am.**—Tolmie and Dawson, Comp. Vocabs., 124B, 1884 (Kutenai name). **Kul as Palus.**—Warre and Vavasseur in Martin, Hudson Bay Ter., 82, 1849. **Kullespelm.**—Hale in U. S. Expl. Exped., VI, 205, 1846. **Kullespen.**—Gallatin in Trans. Am. Ethnol. Soc., II, 27, 1848. **Kúshpĕlu.**—Mooney in 14th Rep. B. A. E., 731, 1896 (a Yakima or Paloos form). **Kuttelspelm.**—Latham, Comp. Philol., 399, 1862. **Lower Pend d'Oreilles.**—Gibbs in Pac. R. R. Rep., I, 415, 1855. **Ni-he-ta-te-tup'i-o.**—Hayden, Ethnog. and Philol., 264, 1862 (Siksika name). **Papshpûn'lĕma.**—Mooney in 14th Rep. B. A. E., 731, 1896 (Yakima name: 'people of the great fir trees'). **Peaux d'Oreilles.**—Audouard, Le Far West, 204, 1869. **Pend d'Oreilles of the Lower Lake.**—Gibbs in Pac. R. R. Rep., I, 415, 1855. **Pend d'Oreilles of the Upper Lake.**—Ibid. **Pends-d'oreilles.**—Smet, Letters, viii, 1843. **Pendı Oreilles.**—Irving, Rocky Mts., I, 121, 1837. **Pond d'Oreilles.**—Price in Sen. Ex. Doc. 44, 47th Cong., 2d sess., 2, 1883. **Pondecas.**—McVickar, Hist. Exped. Lewis and Clark, II, 386, note, 1842. **Pondera.**—Parker, Jour., 293, 1840. **Ponderas.**—Robertson (1846) in H. R. Ex. Doc. 76, 30th Cong., 1st sess., 8, 1848. **Ponderays.**—Hale in U. S. Expl. Exped., VI, 569, 1846. **Po d Orrilles.**—Dart in Ind. Aff. Rep., 216, 1851. **Ponduras.**—Lane (1849) in Sen. Ex. Doc. 52, 31st Cong., 1st sess., 170, 1850. **Pouderas.**—Lane in Ind. Aff. Rep., 159, 1850. **Sar-lit-hu.**—Suckley in Pac. R. R. Rep., I, 300, 1855. **Slka-tkml-schi.**—Gibbs, ibid., I, **Upper Pend d'Oreilles.**—Com'r. Ind. Aff. in Sen. Misc. Doc. 136, 41st Cong., 2d sess., 11, 1870.

Kaliukluk. A Kaialigmiut Eskimo village s. of C. Vancouver, Nelson id., Alaska; pop. 30 in 1880. **Kaliokhlogamute.**—Nelson quoted by Baker, Geog. Dict. Alaska, 1902. **Kaliookhlogamute.**—Petroff in 10th Census, Alaska, 54, 1884. **Kaliukluk.**—Baker, op. cit.

Kalkalya. A former Maidu village on the site of Mooretown, Butte co., Cal.—Dixon in Bull. Am. Mus. Nat. Hist., XVII, pl. xxxviii, 1905.

Kalokta. The Crane clan of the Zuñi of New Mexico. **Kâ'loktā-kwe.**—Cushing in 13th Rep. B. A. E., 368, 1896 (*kwe*='people'). **tKo-ōh-lōk-tā-que.**—Stevenson in 5th Rep. B. A. E., 541, 1887.

Kalokwis (*Qā'logwis*, 'crooked beach'). A village of the Tlauitsis on Turner id., Brit. Col. It was the legendary home of the Kwakiutl tribe at which all the transformations of animals took place. **Kā-loo-kwis.**—Dawson in Trans. Roy. Soc. Can. for 1887, sec. II, 72. **Kar-luk-wees.**—Boas in Bull. Am. Geog. Soc., 229, 1887. **Qā'logwis.**—Boas, inf'n, 1906 (= 'crooked beach'). **Qalukwis.**—Boas in Bull. Am. Geog. Soc., op. cit.

Kalopaling (pl. *Kalopalit*). A merman of Eskimo mythology; also called Mitiling ('with eider ducks'). He wears a jacket of eider-duck skins spotted with their black heads, and into the enormous hood he puts drowned hunters when kaiaks capsize. His feet are as big as sealskin floats. The Central Eskimo believe that once there were many Kalopalit, while now only few are left, but they imagine that they still see one occasionally swimming far out at sea and splashing the water with his legs and arms, or basking on a rock, or sitting in winter on the edge of a floe. They are supposed to delight in overturning kaiaks, and hunters tell stories of stealing up to Kalopalit while they lie asleep on the water and killing them with walrus harpoons, but one must shut his eyes as he makes the cast, else the Kalopaling will overset the kaiak and drown all on board. The flesh of the Kalopalit is said to be poisonous, but it can be fed to dogs.—Boas in 6th Rep. B. A. E., 620, 1888.

Kaltag. A Kaiyuhkhotana village on the left bank of the Yukon, Alaska; pop. 45 in 1880. **Coltog.**—Whymper, Alaska, 190, 1869. **Kahltog.**—Raymond in Sen. Ex. Doc. 12, 42d Cong., 1st sess., 25, 1871. **Kaltag.**—Dall, Alaska, 41, 1870. **K-kaltat.**—Zagoskin quoted by Petroff in 10th Census, Alaska, 37, 1884. **Kkhaltel.**—Tikhmenief (1861) quoted by Baker, Geog. Dict. Alaska, 1902.

Kaltat. A Koyukukhotana village on an island in Yukon r., not far from its junction with Koyukuk r., Alaska; pop. 9 in 1842. **Khaltat's village.**—Allen, Rep. on Alaska, 110, 1887. **K-khaltat.**—Zagoskin quoted by Petroff in 10th Census, Alaska, 37, 1884.

Kaltsergheatunne ('people on a point of land extending far into the ocean'). A division of the Tututni, formerly residing at Port Orford, on the coast of Oregon. **Kăl-ts'e'-rxe-a ɂûnnĕ'.**—Dorsey in Jour. Am. Folk-lore, III, 233, 1890 (own name). **Port Orford Indians.**—Palmer in Ind. Aff. Rep. 1856, 214, 1857. **Port Orfords.**—Ind. Aff. Rep., 470, 1865. **Qwûc-tcu'-mĭçl-tûn ɂûnn'ĕ.**—Dorsey in Jour. Am. Folk-lore, III, 233, 1890 (Naltunnetunne name). **Tsa-re-ar-to-ny.**—Abbott, MS. Coquille census, B. A. E., 1855. **Ts'e-rxi'-à ɂûnnĕ.**—Dorsey, Coquille MS. vocab., B. A. E., 1884. **Tse-xi'-ä tĕne'.**—Everette, Tutu MS. vocab., B. A. E., 1883 (= 'people by C. Foulweather').

Kaltshak. A Kuskwogmiut Eskimo village on the right bank of Kuskokwim r., about lon. 161°; pop. 106 in 1880, 29 in 1890. **Kakhilgagh-miut.**—Zagoskin in Nouv. Ann. Voy., 5th s., XXI, map, 1850. **Kalkhagamute.**—Hallock in Nat. Geog. Mag., IX, 90, 1898. **Kalthagamute.**—Petroff in 10th Census, Alaska, map, 1884. **Kaltkagamut.**—Eleventh Census, Alaska, 164, 1893. **Kaltkhagamute.**—Petroff, op. cit., 53. **Kaltshagamut.**—Spurr and Post quoted by Baker, Geog. Dict. Alaska, 1902. **Kaltshak.**—Baker, ibid. **Kchaljkagmjut.**—Holmberg, Ethnog. Skizz., map, 1855.

Kaluiak. A Kaniagmiut Eskimo village and fishing station on Chignik bay, Alaska; pop. 30 in 1880, 193 in 1890. **Chignik Bay.**—Eleventh Census, Alaska, 163, 1893. **Kaluiak.**—Petroff in 10th Census, Alaska, 28, 1884.

Kaluktuk. An Eskimo village in the Kuskokwim district, Alaska; pop. 29 in 1893. **Kahlukhtughamiut.**—Eleventh Census, Alaska, 164, 1893.

Kalulaadlek (*Kalulaā'ᴌEX*, 'small house of owl'). A village of the Ntlakyapamuk on the E. side of Fraser r., about 24 m. above Yale, Brit. Col.—Teit in Mem. Am. Mus. Nat. Hist., II, 169, 1900.

Kalulek. A Kaviagmiut Eskimo village at Port Clarence, Alaska.

Kalulegeet.—Eleventh Census, Alaska, 162, 1893.

Kaluplo (*Ka'-lu-plo.*) A former Nishinam village in the valley of Bear r., Cal.—Powers in Cont. N. A. Ethnol., III, 316, 1877.

Kamaiakan (*Kamai'äkan*). The principal chief of the Yakima and confederate tribes of E. Washington under the treaty of 1855, and leader in the war which began a few months later and continued for 3 years. He appears to have been himself a Yakima. In consequence of the heavy immigration to Oregon and the discovery of gold in the Colville and Cœur d'Alêne country of N. E. Washington and adjacent Idaho, in the spring of 1855, Gov. Stevens, of Washington, was instructed to negotiate treaties for cession of territory with the various tribes of the region, with the purpose of limiting them to reservations. Led by Kamaiakan the Indians offered strong opposition to any arrangement which would deprive them of any portion of the lands or allow right of way to the whites. After considerable difficulty treaties were made with a number of the tribes, largely through the assistance of a majority of the Nez Percés, but it soon became evident that practically the entire body of the Cayuse, Yakima, Wallawalla, Paloos, Spokan, and others were bitterly opposed to removal from their homes or confinement to reservations. In the meantime, although the treaties were not yet ratified and no time had been designated for the removal, settlers and miners began to overrun the Indian lands and collisions became frequent. In Sept., 1855, the war began with the killing of special agent Bolon while on his way to arrange a conference with Kamaiakan, who now publicly declared his intention to keep all whites out of the upper country by force and to make war also on any tribe refusing to join him. The first regular engagement occurred, Oct. 4 and 5, on the southern edge of Simcoe valley, between a detachment of 84 regulars under Maj. Haller and a large force of Indians led by Kamaiakan himself. The troops were finally obliged to retire, although the Indian loss was thought to be the greater.

By this time it was believed that 1,500 hostiles were in the field, and the rising now spread to the tribes in w. Washington as well as among those of s. Oregon, and even including some of the coast Indians of s. Alaska. The principal leader in w. Washington was Leschi (q. v.). In Sept., 1856, another conference was held near Wallawalla with some of the chiefs, but to no purpose, Kamaiakan refusing to attend and those present refusing all terms except the evacuation of the territory by the whites. The war went on, with numerous raids, murders, and small engagements by regulars and volunteers. In the next year, 1857, the rising was brought under control w. of the Cascade mts., several of the leaders being hanged. An incident of the war in this quarter was a determined attack on Seattle, Jan. 25, 1856, which was repulsed by a naval force stationed in the harbor at the time.

On May 17, 1858, a strong force of dragoons under Col. Steptoe was defeated a few miles from the present site of Colfax, N. W. Washington, by a combined force of Paloos, Spokan, and Skitswish (Cœur d'Alênes), but a few months later the war was brought to a close by two decisive defeats inflicted by Col. George Wright, with more than 700 cavalry, infantry, and artillery, on the main body of the hostiles led by Kamaiakan himself. The engagements took place Sept. 1 and 5 near Four Lakes, on a s. tributary of Spokane r. Besides their killed and wounded, the Indians lost 800 horses, having already lost large quantities of winter supplies, and burned their own village to save it from capture. Kamaiakan was among the wounded. On the 17th Wright dictated terms to the hostiles at a conference near Cœur d'Alêne mission. The defeated Indians, being no longer capable of resistance, were treated with great severity, 24 of the leading chiefs of the various tribes being either hanged or shot. Kamaiakan refused to sue for peace, but crossed the border into Brttish Columbia, where he finally ended his days. Consult Bancroft, Hist. Wash., Idaho, and Montana, 1890, and authorities cited; Stevens, Life of I. I. Stevens, 1900.   (J. M.)

Kamass. See *Camas.*

Kamatukwucha (*Kā'matúk wü'tcá,* 'below the Estrella mts.'). A Pima village at Gila crossing, s. Ariz.—Russell, Pima MS., B. A. E., 18, 1902.

Kamegli. A Kuskwogmiut Eskimo village on the right bank of Kuskokwim r., above Bethel, Alaska.

Kameglimut.—Kilbuck (1898) quoted by Baker, Geog. Dict. Alaska, 1902.

Kamenakshtchat. A former important Chitimacha town at Bayou du Plomb, near Bayou Chêne, 18 m. N. of Charenton, La.

Káme náksh tchāt námu.—Gatschet in Trans. Anthrop. Soc. Wash., II, 152, 1883 (*tchāt,* 'bayou'; *námu,* 'village').

Kamiah. A Nez Percé band formerly living at the site of the present town of Kamiah, Idaho. It is mentioned by Lewis and Clark in 1805 as a band of the Chopunnish and numbering 800 people who lived in large lodges.

Kamia.—Gatschet, MS., B. A. E., 1878. Kamiah.—Howard, Nez Percé Joseph, 19, 1885. Kimmooenim.—Morse, Rep. to Sec. War, 369, 1822. Kimoenims.—Drake, Bk. Inds., vii, 1848. Kimooenim.—Lewis and Clark, Exped., II, 471, 1814. Ki-moo-e-nim.—Orig. Jour. Lewis and Clark, VI, 115, 1905.

Kamiaken. See *Kamaiakan.*

Kamit (*Kä'mĭt*, 'back'). A former Pima village in s. Arizona.—Russell, Pima MS., B. A. E., 16, 1902.

Kamloops ('point between the rivers'). A village at the junction of Thompson and North Thompson rs., Brit. Col., occupied by Shuswap Salish; pop. 244 in 1904. It gave its name to Kamloops Indian agency, now united with that of Okanagan as Kamloops-Okanagan.

Kam-a-loo'-pa.—Dawson in Trans. Roy. Soc. Can. for 1891, sec. II, 7 (native name). Kameloups.—Smet, Oregon Miss., 100, 1847. Kamloops.—Cox, Columbia River, II, 87, 1831. Salst Kamlúps.—Gatschet, MS., B. A. E. (Okinagan name, from Sälst, 'people').

Kammatwa (*Kammát'wa*). One of the four divisions of the main body of the Shasta, occupying Klamath valley from Scott r. to Seiad valley, N. w. Cal. According to Steele the native name of these Hamburg Indians, so-called, is T-ka, but this is apparently a misprint of I-ka, properly Aika, their name for Hamburg bar.   (R. B. D.)

Hamburg Indians.—Steele in Ind. Aff. Rep. 1864, 120, 1865. T-ka.—Ibid. (misprint).

Kammuck. A former body of Salish of Fraser superintendency, Brit. Col.

Kammack.—Can. Ind. Aff. for 1879, 138. Kammuck.—Ibid., 1878, 79.

Kamuksusik. A former Aleut village on Agattu id., one of the Near id. group of the Aleutians, now uninhabited.

Kamulas. A former Chumashan village situated at or near the present Camulos, near the mouth of the Piru, in Ventura co., Cal.

Kamulas.—Taylor in Cal. Farmer, July 24, 1863. Ka-mu'-lŭs.—Henshaw, Buenaventura MS. vocab., B. A. E., 1884.

Kana. An Ita Eskimo settlement on Murchison sd., N. Greenland.

Kă'na.—Stein in Petermanns Mitt., no. 9, map, 1902. Karnah.—Mrs Peary, My Arct. Jour., 190, 1893.

Kanadasero. One of the two Seneca villages, locality unknown, which in 1763 were still in the English interest.—Johnson (1763) in N. Y. Doc. Col. Hist., VII, 582, 1856.

Kanagak. An Eskimo village in the Kuskokwim district, Alaska; pop. 35 in 1890.

Kanagamiut.—Eleventh Census, Alaska, 164, 1893.

Kanagaro (*Kanákaro'*, 'a pole in the water'). A Mohawk town situated in 1677 on the N. side of Mohawk r., in Montgomery or Herkimer co., N. Y. In the year named it had a single stockade, with four ports, and contained 16 houses. Megapolensis mentions it as early as 1644, but no reference is made to it after 1693.   (J. N. B. H.)

Andagaron.—Parkman, Jesuits, 222, note, 1883. Andaraqué.—Parkman, Old Rég., 197, 1883. Banagiro.—Megapolensis (1644) in N.Y. Doc. Col. Hist., III, 250, 1853. Kanagaro.—Conf. of 1674, ibid., II, 712, 1858. Kanagiro.—N. Y. Doc. Col. Hist., III, 250, 1853. Kanákaro'.—Hewitt, inf'n (Mohawk and Cayuga form).

Kanagaro. A former Seneca town on Boughton hill, directly s. of Victor, N. Y. For a long period it was the capital of the Seneca tribe. Greenhalgh states that in 1677 it contained 150 houses, 50 to 60 ft in length, with 13 or 14 fires to the house. Here Greenhalgh saw 9 prisoners (4 men, 4 women, and a boy) burned, the torture lasting about seven hours. This shows that the Iroquois as well as the Neuters burned their unadopted women prisoners, but the Jesuit Relation for 1641 says the Huron do not burn their women captives. On the approach of Denonville, in 1687, this town was burned by its inhabitants, who, like those of the neighboring Kanagaro, the foreign colony, removed about 20 m. s. E. to Kanadasega, where the foreign element became known by the name Seneca. In the early part of the 19th century the Seneca formed a village approximately on the site of the burned Kanagaro, which they called Gaonsageon ('basswood bark lying around'), referring, it is said, to gutters of this material employed to convey water from a neighboring spring. Another settlement existed in 1740 in the vicinity of the old site, which was called Chinoshahgeh.

(J. N. B. H.)

Cahacarague.—Lattré, map, 1784. Cahaquonaghe.—Esnauts and Rapilly, map, 1777. Canagaroh.—Greenhalgh (1677) in N. Y. Doc. Col. Hist., III, 251, 1853. Canagora.—Ibid., 250. Cangaro.—Ibid. Gaensera.—Belmont (1687) quoted by Conover, Kanadega and Geneva MS., B. A. E. Ganagaro.—La Salle (1682) in Margry, Déc., II, 217, 1877. Gandagan.—Jes. Rel. for 1657, 45, 1858. Gandagaro.—Jes. Rel. for 1670, 23, 1858. Gannagaro.—Denonville (1687) in N. Y. Doc. Col. Hist., IX, 367, 1855. Kanákao'.—Hewitt, inf'n (Seneca and Onondaga form). Kohoseraghe.—Cortland (1687) in N. Y. Doc. Col. Hist., III, 434, 1853. Onnutague.—Belmont (1687) quoted by Conover, op. cit. Saint Jacques.—Jes. Rel. for 1671, 20, 1858. Saint James.—N. Y. Doc. Col. Hist., IX, 367, 1855.

Kanagaro. A former town belonging to the Seneca, situated at different times at different sites from 1½ to 4 m. s. of Kanagaro, the Seneca capital, and s. E. from Victor, on the E. side of Mud cr., N. Y. According to Greenhalgh it contained about 30 houses in 1677. The inhabitants of this town, according to the Jesuit Relation for 1670, were chiefly incorporated captives and their descendants of three tribes, the Onnontioga, the Neuters, and the Hurons. Its situation thus placed its inhabitants directly under the eyes of the federal chiefs dwelling in the capital town of Kanagaro. Here in 1656 the Jesuits established the mission of the Tohontaenrat at Scanonenrat, which surrendered in a body to the Seneca in 1649. On account of these associations the missionaries gave it their special attention, with such success that it became known as the Christian town of the Seneca. Like all the principal Seneca towns it was destroyed by Denonville in 1687. The inhabitants of the western towns, Totiakton and Gandachiragon, removed s. and then w. to Genesee r., where their settlements were destroyed by Sullivan in 1779; those of the eastern towns, Gandagaro

(Kanagaro) and Gandougarae, removed to the E., where their settlements at Canandaigua and near Geneva, N. Y., were also destroyed by Sullivan's army.

(J. N. B. H.)

Canoenada.—Greenhalgh (1677) in N. Y. Doc. Col. Hist., III, 250, 1883. Gandagarae.—Jes. Rel. for 1670, 77, 1858. Gandougaraé.—Denonville (1687) quoted by Conover, MS., B. A. E. Gannogarae.—Denonville (1687) in N. Y. Doc. Col. Hist., IX, 366, 1855. Gannongarae.—Doc. 1687, ibid., 334. Gannougarae.—Denonville quoted by Conover, MS., B. A. E. Saint Michael's.—Shea, Cath. Miss., 291, 1855. Saint Michel.—Jes. Rel. for 1670, 77, 1858.

Kanaghsaws. An Iroquois town of 18 houses, situated in 1779 about 1 m. N. W. of Conesus Center, N. Y. Grant, one of Sullivan's officers, says: "Captain Sunfish, a negro, resided here, a very bold, enterprising fellow, who commanded the town." Chief Bigtree (Karontowanen) is said to have resided here also.—Jour. Mil. Exped. of Gen. Sullivan (1779), 131, 1887. (J. N. B. H.)

Kanajormiut. An Eskimo village in s. w. Greenland.—Meddelelser om Grönland, XVI, map, 1896.

Kanak. An Alaskan Eskimo village in the Kuskokwim district, Alaska; pop. 41 in 1893.

Kanagmiut.—11th Census, Alaska, 164, 1893.

Kanakanak. A Nushagagmiut village on Nushagak bay, near which are two salmon canneries; pop. 53 in 1890, 145 in 1900.

Kanakanak.—11th Census, Alaska, 93, 1893. Knakanak.—12th Census Rep., I, 426, 1901.

Kanakuk. A Kickapoo prophet. When the Kickapoo in 1819 ceded their lands,

KANAKUK, THE KICKAPOO PROPHET. (AFTER CATLIN)

covering nearly half the state of Illinois, they could not go to the reservation assigned to them in Missouri because it

was still occupied by the hostile Osage. Half the tribe emigrated instead to Spanish territory in Texas, and the rest were ready to follow when the Government agents intervened, endeavoring to induce them to remove to Missouri. Kanakuk, inspired with the ideas that had moved Tenskwatawa, exhorted them to remain where they were, promising that if they lived worthily, abandoning their native superstitions, avoiding quarrels among themselves and infractions of the white man's law, and resisting the seduction of alcohol, they would at last inherit a land of plenty clear of enemies. He was accepted as the chief of the remnant who remained in Illinois, and many of the Potawatomi of Michigan became his disciples. He displayed a chart of the path, leading through fire and water, which the virtuous must pursue to reach the "happy hunting grounds," and furnished his followers with prayer-sticks graven with religious symbols. When in the end the Kickapoo were removed to Kansas he accompanied them and remained their chief, still keeping drink away from them, until he died of smallpox in 1852. See Mooney in 14th Rep. B. A. E., 692–700, 1896.

Kanani (*Ka'nàni*, 'living arrows'). A Navaho clan.—Matthews in Jour. Am. Folk-lore, III, 104, 1890.

Kanapima ('one who is talked of'). An Ottawa chief, born about 40 m. s. of Mackinaw, Mich., July 12, 1813, and christened as Augustin Hammelin, jr. He was sent with his younger brother, Macoda Binnasee (The Blackbird), in 1829 to be educated in the Catholic seminary at Cincinnati, where the two boys remained for 3 years without making marked progress in their studies. In 1832 both were sent to Rome to continue their education in the college of the Propaganda Fide, with the view of entering the priesthood. This object in Kanapima's case was defeated from the usual causes. After his brother died at the end of two years he ceased his studies, returned to America, became chief of his branch of the tribe, and resumed the costume and habits of his people, except when he went among white people, as in 1835, to make a treaty for the Ottawa with the Government at Washington, but he does not appear to have been a signer of any Ottawa treaty. On such occasions he exhibited the ease and polish of a man of the world.

Kanastunyi (*Kănastûñ'yĭ*). A traditionary Cherokee settlement on the headwaters of French Broad r., near the present Brevard, in Transylvania co., N. C. A settlement called Cannostee or Cannastion is mentioned as existing on Hiawassee r. in 1776. (J. M.)

Conastee.—Doc. of 1755 quoted by Royce in 5th Rep. B. A. E., 142, 1887. Kăna'sta.—Mooney in

19th Rep. B. A. E., 480, 524, 1900 (abbreviated form). **Kănastûñ'yĭ.**—Ibid.

Kanatak. A Kaniagmiut Eskimo village on Shelikof strait, Alaska; pop. 26 in 1890 (11th Census, Alaska, 163, 1893).

Kanatakowa ('great village.'—Hewitt). The village of the Onondaga situated at the place still called Onondaga Castle, N. Y. It was the principal village of the tribe as early as 1654.   (J. M.)
Kä-nä-tä-go'-wä.—Morgan, League Iroq., 471, 1851. **Kä-nä-tä'-ko'-wä'.**—Hewitt, inf'n, 1886 (Onondaga form). **Onondaga.**—Greenhalgh (1677) quoted by Morgan, League Iroq., 316, 1851. **Onondaga Castle.**—Ibid., 471 (common English name). **Onondaghara.**—Macauley, N. Y., II, 177, 1829. **Onondagharie.**—Ibid.

Kanatiochtiage ('place of wild rice'). A former Iroquois settlement or village on the N. shore of L. Ontario, inhabited chiefly by "Dowaganhaes," and reputed to be "near the Sennekes [Seneca] country." It was situated near Tchojachiage, or approximately on the site of Darlington or Port Hope, in the New Castle district, Ontario. Three nations, composing 16 "castles", came to settle there by Iroquois permission.   (J. N. B. H.)
Ganadatsiagon.—Frontenac (1673) in N. Y. Doc. Col. Hist., IX, 112, 1855. **Ganatcheskiagon.**—Ibid., note. **Ganatoheskiagon.**—Ibid. **Kanatiochtiage.**—Doc. of 1700, ibid., IV, 694, 1854.

Kanchati ('red ground,' 'red earth'). A name applied to several places, one of the best known being the principal village of the Alibamu, formerly on the E. bank of Alabama r., below Koasati and a little w. of Montgomery, Ala. Hawkins described it in 1799 as a small village on the left bank of Alabama r., with its fields on the right side in a cane swamp, and its people poor and indolent. A census of 1832 (Schoolcraft, Ind. Tribes, IV, 578, 1854) gave the number of families as 55. The name has been applied also to a township in the Creek Nation, Okla., and to a village a few miles N. w. of Talladega, Ala.   (A. S. G.)
Con chante ti.—Census of 1832 in Schoolcraft, Ind. Tribes, IV, 578, 1854. **Con-chant-ti.**—Gatschet, Creek Migr. Leg., I, 133, 1884. **Conchart-ee.**—H. R. Ex. Doc. 276, 24th Cong., 1st sess., 312, 1836. **Ecanchatty.**—Woodward, Reminiscences, 12, 1859. **Ecumchate.**—Schoolcraft, Ind. Tribes, IV, 380, 1854. **E-cun-cha-ta.**—Royce in 18th Rep. B. A. E., Ala. map, 1899. **E-cun-chate.**—Hawkins (1799), Sketch, 36, 1848. **Ikan-tcháti.**—Gatschet, Creek Migr. Leg., I, 88, 1884. **Kansháde.**—Ibid., 133. **O-cun-cha-ta.**—Bell in Morse, Rep. to Sec. War, 307, 1822. **Red Grounds.**—Ibid., 364.

Kandoucho. A former village of the Neutrals in Ontario, near the Huron country.
Kandoucho.—Jes. Rel. for 1641, 75, 1858. **Tous les Saints.**—Ibid. (mission name).

Kaneenda. A former fishing station of the Onondaga, situated at the fork of Seneca and Onondaga rs., N. Y., 8 m. from their palisaded village. It was also their landing place when they returned from hunting on the N. side of L. Ontario.   (J. N. B. H.)
Kanienda.—Doc. of 1700 in N. Y. Doc. Col. Hist., IV, 649, 1854.

Kanesadageh (*Kane'sădă'ge'*). A former Iroquois village belonging to the Two-clans of the Turtle; location unknown.   (J. N. B. H.)
Kaneghsadakeh.—Hale, Iroquois Book of Rites, 118, 1883. **Kanesadakeh.**—Ibid, 119.

Kanestio. A village occupied by Delawares and others, subject to the Iroquois, formerly on the upper Susquehanna, near Kanestio cr., in Steuben co., N. Y. It was burned by the Iroquois in 1764, on account of hostilities committed by the inhabitants against the whites. It then contained about 60 houses.
Canestio.—Vaudreuil (1757) in N. Y. Doc. Col. Hist., X, 588, 1858 (name of the creek). **Kanestio.**—Pouchot, map (1758), ibid., 694.

Kang. The Mountain Lion clans of the Tewa pueblos of San Juan, San Ildefonso, and Nambe, N. Mex.
Chang Doa.—Bandelier, Delight Makers, 464, 1890. **Kän-tdóa.**—Hodge in Am. Anthrop., IX, 351, 1896 (San Juan and San Ildefonso form; *tdóa* = 'people'). **Qën-tdóa.**—Ibid. (Nambe form; *q* = German *ch*).

Kangarsik. A village of the Angmagsalingmiut on a large island at the mouth of Angmagsalik fjord, Greenland, lat. 65° 33'; pop. 34 in 1884.—Meddelelser om Grönland, IX, 379, 1889.

Kangek. An Eskimo settlement 10 m. s. of Godthaab, w. Greenland, lat. 64° 10'.—Nansen, Eskimo Life, 166, 1894.

Kangerdluksoa ('the great fjord'). An Ita Eskimo settlement in Inglefield gulf, N. Greenland.
Kangerdlooksoah.—Wychoff in Scribner's Mag., XXVIII, 447, 1900. **Kangerdlü'hsoa.**—Stein in Petermanns Mitt., IX, map, 1902.

Kangertloaping ('remarkable fjord'). A summer settlement of Okomiut Eskimo of Saumia, at the head of an inlet emptying into Cumberland sd., Baffin land.—Boas in 6th Rep. B. A. E., map, 1888.

Kangertluk ('fjord'). A spring and fall settlement of Iglulirmiut Eskimo on N. Melville penin. near the Fox Basin coast.—Boas in 6th Rep. B. A. E., map, 1888.

Kangertlukdjuaq ('great fjord'). A summer settlement of Okomiut Eskimo of Saumia, at the head of an inlet emptying into Cumberland sd., Baffin land.—Boas in 6th Rep. B. A. E., map, 1888.

Kangertlung ('fjord'). A summer settlement of Talirpia Okomiut Eskimo on the s. w. coast of Cumberland sd.—Boas in 6th Rep. B. A. E., map, 1888.

Kangguatl-lanas (*Qā'ñguaL lā'nas*). An extinct subdivision of the Stustas, a family of the Eagle clan of the Haida of British Columbia.   (J. R. S.)
K·anguatl lā'nai.—Boas, 12th Rep. N. W. Tribes Can., 22, 1898. **Qā'ñguaL lā'nas.**—Swanton, Cont. Haida, 276, 1905.

Kanghishunpegnaka ('those who wear crow feathers in their hair'). A division of the Sihasapa or Blackfoot Sioux.
Kaŋgi-śuŋ-pegnaka.—Dorsey in 15th Rep. B. A. E., 219, 1897. **Kaⁿxi-cŭⁿ-pegnaka.**—Ibid.

Kanghiyuha ('crow keepers'). A division of the Brulé Teton Sioux.
Kaŋ-gi yu-ha.—Tatankawakan, letter to Dorsey, 1880. **Kaŋgi-yuha.**—Dorsey in 15th Rep. B. A. E., 218, 1897. **Kaⁿxi-yuha.**—Ibid. **Those that eat crows.**—Culbertson in Smithson. Rep. 1850, 141, 1851.

Kangiartsoak. An Eskimo village and Danish settlement in w. Greenland, lat. 72° 47′.—Kane, Arctic Exped., 472, 1854.

Kangidli. An Ita Eskimo village at C. York, N. Greenland.—Stein in Petermanns Mitt., IX, map, 1902.

Kangigdlek. An Angmagsalingmiut Eskimo village on Angmagsalik fjord, E. Greenland, lat. 65° 40′.—Meddelelser om Grönland, XVI, map, 1896.

Kangikhlukhmut (*Kang-iq-xlu-q'mūt*, 'head-of-the-rapid-river people': Kaniagmiut name). A division of the Ahtena at the head of Copper r., Alaska.—Hoffman, MS. vocab. B. A. E., 1882.

Kangisunka. See *Crow Dog*.

Kangivamiut ('people at the head'). A subtribe of the Sukinimiut Eskimo, living in the region of George r., N. Labrador.
Kangivamiut.—Boas in 6th Rep. B. A. E., map, 1888. Kan'gûkélua'luksoagmyut.—Turner in 11th Rep. B. A. E., 176, 1894 (='people of the great bay'). Kañûktlualuksoagmyut.—Turner in Trans. Roy. Soc. Can., V, 99, 1888.

Kangmaligmiut ('distant ones'). An Arctic Eskimo tribe between Manning pt and Herschel id. The name has been attached to different local groups all the way from Pt Hope to Mackenzie r.
Kudjakians.—Rink in Jour. Anthrop. Inst., XV, 240, 1886. Kakmalikg.—Zagoskin, Descr. Russ. Poss. Am., pt. I, 74, 1847. Kangiugdlit.—Rink, op. cit., 240. Kangmali-enyüin.—Richardson, Polar Regions, 300, 1861. Kangmaligmeut.—Murdoch in Ninth Rep. B. A. E., 46, 1892. Kăngmāli'gmūt.—Dall in Cont. N. A. Ethnol., I, 10, 1877. Kangmaliinnuin.—Simpson quoted by Dall, ibid. Kangmalik.—Woolfe in 11th Census, Alaska, 130, 1893. Kangnialis.—Keane in Stanford, Compend., 517, 1878. Kanmali-enyuin.—Murdoch in 9th Rep. B. A. E., 46, 1892. Kûnmû'd'liñ.—Ibid., 43, 46. Western Mackenzie Innuit.—Dall in Cont. N. A. Ethnol., I, 12, 1877 (collective term including Kopagmiut and Kangmaligmiut).

Kangormiut ('goose people'). A tribe of Central Eskimo living in Victoria land.
Kang-orr-Mœoot.—Franklin, Journ. to Polar Sea, II, 43, 1824. Kanq-or-mì-ut.—Richardson, Arct. Exped., I, 362, 1851. Kañρ-meut.—Petitot in Bib. Ling. et Ethnol. Am., III, 11, 1876 (Chiglit name). White-Goose Eskimos.—Franklin, op. cit., 42.

Kanhada (*G·anháda*, meaning obscure). One of the 4 clans or phratries into which all Indians of the Chimmesyan stock are divided. It is also applied specifically to various local subdivisions of the clan. One such is found in the Niska town of Lakkulzap and one in each of the Kitksan towns—Kitwingach, Kitzegukla, and Kishpiyeoux.—Boas in 10th Rep. N. W. Tribes Can., 49–50, 1895.

Kanhanghton. A former Delaware village about the mouth of Chemung r., in the N. part of Bradford co., Pa. It was destroyed by the Iroquois in 1764 on account of the hostility of its inhabitants to the whites.—Johnson (1764) in N. Y. Doc. Col. Hist., VII, 625, 1856.

Kaniagmiut ('people of Kodiak'). The largest and most powerful Eskimo tribe on the Alaskan coast, inhabiting Kodiak id. and the mainland from Iliamna lake to Ugashik r., the s. coast to lon. 159° w. The tribe numbered 1,154 in 1890. Their villages are Afognak, Aiaktalik, Akhiok, Aleksashkina, Alexandrovsk, Ashivak, Chiniak, Fugitive, Igak, Iliamna, Kaguyak, Kaluiak, Kanatak, Karluk, Katmai, Kattak, Kiliuda, Kodiak, Kuiukuk, Kukak, Liesnoi, Mitrofania, Nauklak, Nunamiut, Nuniliak, Orlova, Ostrovki, Seldovia, Sutkum, Three Saints, Uganik, Uhaiak, Uhaskek, Ukshivikak, Uyak, Uzinki, Yalik, and Yelovoi.
Achkugmjuten.—Holmberg, Ethnog. Skizz., 4, 1855 (applied to Aglemiut and Kaniagmiut by the people of Norton sd.;='inhabitants of the warm country'). Kadiagmuts.—Am. Nat., XV, 156, 1881. Kadjacken.—Wrangell, Ethnol. Nach., 117, 1839. Kanagist.—Coxe, Russ. Disc., 135, 1787. Kăniăg'-mūt.—Dall in Cont. N. A. Ethnol., I, 20, 1877. Kaniagmut.—Rink, Eskimo Tribes, 32, 1887. Kinaghi.—Morse, Syst. of Mod. Geog., I, 74, 1814. Konagens.—Drake, Bk. of Inds., viii, 1848. Konagis.—Latham in Jour. Ethnol. Soc. Lond., I, 183, 1848. Konasgi.—Prichard, Phys. Hist., Man, 371, 1847. Koniagi.—Humboldt, New Spain, II, 392, 1811. Koniágmutes.—Dall in Proc. Am. A. A. S., XVIII, 267, 1870. Konjagen.—Holmberg, Ethnog. Skizz., 4, 1855. Southern Eskimos.—Form used by various English writers.

Kanig. A former Chnagmiut village on the N. bank of Yukon r., Alaska, near its mouth.
Kanig-mïout.—Zagoskin in Nouv. Ann. Voy., 5th s., XXI, map, 1850. Kanygmjut.—Holmberg, Ethnog. Skizz., map, 1855.

Kanikaligamut (*Ka'ni-qa-li-ga-mut*, 'people close to the river': Chugachigmiut name). An unidentified division of the Knaiakhotana living on Cook inlet, Alaska.—Hoffman, MS., B. A. E., 1882.

Kanikluk. A Chugachigmiut village on the N. shore of Prince William sd., Alaska; pop. 54 in 1880, 73 in 1890.
Kanikhluk.—Petroff in 10th Census, Alaska, 29, 1884. Kanikluk.—Baker, Geog. Dict. Alaska, 229, 1902.

Kanlax (*Nxō'istɛn*, 'the point'). An Upper Lillooet town at the junction of Bridge and Fraser rs., interior of British Columbia; pop. 104 in 1904.
Bridge river.—Can. Ind. Aff. Rep. 1904, pt. 2, 72, 1905. Kan-lax'.—Dawson in Trans. Roy. Soc. Can. for 1891, sec. II, 44. Nxō'istɛn.—Boas, inf'n, 1906.

Kanna ('eel'). A clan of the Tuscarora. According to Morgan (League Iroq., 70, 1877) an Eel clan is found among the Tuscarora, the Onondaga, and the Cayuga.
Eel.—Morgan, op. cit. Kä'n'-nä.—Hewitt, inf'n, 1886 (Tuscarora form).

Kannawalohalla ('a head fastened to the end of an object.'—Hewitt). An Iroquois village on the site of Elmira, N. Y., which was destroyed by Sullivan in Aug., 1779.—Jour. Mil. Exped. Gen. Sullivan (1779), 232, 1887.

Kannehouan. An unidentified tribe, possibly of Caddoan affinity, heard of by La Salle's party in 1687 as living to the w. or N. w. of Maligne (Colorado) r., Tex. Cf. *Cahinnio, Kanohatino*.
Caniouis.—Alcedo, Dic. Geog., I, 341, 1786 (possibly identical). Cannaha.—Joutel (1687) in Margry, Déc., III, 409, 1878. Cannahios.—Ibid. Cannehovanes.—Barcia, Ensayo, 271, 1723. Kannehonan.—Joutel (1687), Jour. Voy., 90, 1719. Kannehouan.—Joutel

(1687) in Margry, Déc., III, 288, 1878. **Kaouanoua.**— 17th cent. Doc. in Margry, ibid., 602. **Ouanahinan.**— De l'Isle, map (1703) in Winsor, Hist. Am., II, 294, 1886 (possibly identical; misprint *O* for *C*). **Quayneos.**—Jefferys, Am. Atlas, map 5, 1776. **Tahiannihouq.**—Joutel (1687) in Margry, Déc., III, 409, 1878.

Kanohatino ('red river'). The Caddo name for the Red r. of Louisiana, and, according to Gatschet, for the Colorado r. of Texas. It was supposed by the companions of La Salle to be the name of a tribe encountered by them in the neighborhood of the Colorado or the Brazos. From the alternative name given, "Ayano," or "Ayona," it has been erroneously assumed that this tribe was the Hainai. "Ayano," however, is evidently the general Caddo word for "man." Although a Caddo tribe may have been living or camping in the region indicated when La Salle passed, the fact that they were not mentioned when León advanced to the Caddo country a few years later would seem to discredit the theory. The only alternative supposition is that the Wichita or one of their branches, the Tawakoni or the Waco, were camping considerably to the s. of their customary habitat at that time. This would explain the warfare that was found to exist between the Caddo and the Kanohatino in which some of La Salle's former companions took part.   (J. R. S.)

Aiano.—Barcia, Ensayo, 271, 1723. **Ayano.**—Joutel (1687) in Margry, Déc., III, 299, 1878. **Ayona.**— Joutel in French, Hist. Coll. La., I, 138, 1846. **Canatino.**—Anville, map N. Am., 1752. **Cannohatinno.**—Joutel (1687) in Margry, Déc., III, 299, 1878. **Cannohatino.**—Barcia, Ensayo, 271, 1723. **Cannokantimo.**—Joutel (1687) in French, Hist. Coll. La., I, 148, 1846. **Canoatinno.**—Joutel (1687) in Margry, Déc., III, 409, 1878. **Canoatinos.**—Iberville (1700), ibid., IV, 374, 1880. **Canohatinno.**—Shea, Early Voy., 36, note, 1861. **Canohatino.**—Joutel, Jour. Voy., 90, 1719. **Canouhanans.**—Baudry des Lozières, Voy. a la Le., 242, 1802. **Conoatinos.**—Bienville (1700) in Margry, Déc., IV, 442, 1880. **Kanaatino.**— Brion de la Tour, Carte Gen. des Col. Angl., 1781. **Kanoatinas.**—Boudinot, Star in the West, 127, 1816. **Kanoatinnos.**—Hennepin, New Discov., pt. 2, 32, 1698. **Kanoatino.**—Le Page du Pratz (1757), Hist. La., map, 1774. **Kano Hatino.**—Mooney, inf'n (Caddo: 'red river'). **Kanoutinoa.**—Cavelier (1688) in Shea, Early Voy., 36, 1861. **Konatines.**— Coxe, Carolana, map, 1741. **Konoatinnos.**—Ibid., 38. **Quanoatinno.**—Douay (*ca.* 1688) in Shea, Discov., 211, 1852. **Quanoatinos.**—McKenney and Hall, Ind. Tribes, III, 81, 1854. **Quanoouatinos.**— Tonti (1690) in French, Hist. Coll. La., I, 76, 1846. **Quanouatins.**—Ibid., 74. **Quoanantino.**—Barcia, Ensayo, 302, 1723. **Quonantino.**—McKenney and Hall, Ind. Tribes, III, 87, 1854. **Quonoatinnos.**— Coxe, Carolana, 38, 1741.

Kansa. A southwestern Siouan tribe; one of the five, according to Dorsey's arrangement, of the Dhegiha group. Their linguistic relations are closest with the Osage, and are close with the Quapaw. In the traditional migration of the group, after the Quapaw had first separated therefrom, the main body divided at the mouth of Osage r., the Osage moving up that stream and the Omaha and Ponca crossing Missouri r. and proceeding northward, while the Kansa ascended

the Missouri on the s. side to the mouth of Kansas r. Here a brief halt was made, after which they ascended the Missouri on the s. side until they reached the present N. boundary of Kansas, where they were attacked by the Cheyenne and compelled to retrace their steps. They settled again at the mouth of Kansas r., where the Big Knives, as they called the whites, came with gifts and induced them to go farther w. The native narrators of this tradition give an account of about 20 villages occupied successively along Kansas r. before the settlement at Council

KANSA. (KAKEBASHA)

Grove, Kans., whence they were finally removed to their reservation in Indian Ter. Marquette's autograph map, drawn probably as early as 1674, places the Kansa a considerable distance directly w. of the Osage and some distance s. of the Omaha, indicating that they were then on Kansas r. The earliest recorded notice of the Kansa is by Juan de Oñate, who went from San Gabriel, N. Mex., in 1601, till he met the "Escansaques," who lived 100 leagues to the N. E., near the "Panana," or Pawnee. It is known that the Kansa moved up Kansas r. in historic times as far as Big Blue r., and thence went to Council Grove in 1847. The move to the Big Blue must have taken place after 1723, for at that date Bourgmont speaks of the large village of the Quans (Kansa) as on a small river flowing from the N. 30 leagues above Kansas r. and near the Missouri. The village of the Missouri tribe was then 30 leagues below Kansas r. and 60 leagues from the Quans village. Iberville estimated them at 1,500 families in 1702. A treaty of peace and friendship was made with them by the United States, Oct. 28, 1815. They were then on Kansas r. at the mouth of Saline r., having been forced back from the Missouri by the Dakota. They occupied 130 earth lodges, and their number was estimated at 1,500. According to Lewis and Clark, they resided in 1804 on Kansas r., in two villages, one about 20 and the other 40 leagues from its mouth, with a population of 300 men. These explorers say that they formerly lived on the s. bank of Missouri r. about 24 leagues above the mouth of the Kansas, and were more numerous, but were reduced by the attacks of the Sauk and the Iowa. O'Fallon estimated their number in 1822 at 1,850. By the treaty of St Louis, June 3, 1825, they ceded to the United States their lands in N. Kansas and S. E. Nebraska, and relinquished all claims they might have to lands in Missouri, but reserving for their use a tract on Kansas r. Here they were subject to attacks by the Pawnee, and on their hunts by other tribes, whereby their number was considerably reduced. Porter estimated their number in 1829 at 1,200; according to the Report of the Indian Office for 1843 the population was 1,588. By treaty at Methodist Mission, Kans., Jan. 14, 1846, they ceded to the United States 2,000,000 acres of the E. portion of their reservation, and a new reservation was assigned them at Council Grove, on Neosho r., Morris co., Kans., where they remained until 1873. As this tract was overrun by settlers, it was sold, and with the funds another reservation was bought for them in Indian Ter. next to the Osage; with the exception of 160 acres, reserved for school purposes, all their lands have now been allotted in severalty. The population diminished from about 1,700 in 1850 to 209 in 1905, of whom only about 90 were full-bloods. Much of this decrease has been due to epidemics. In the winter of 1852–53 smallpox alone carried off more than 400 of the tribe at Council Grove.

The Kansa figured but slightly in the history of the country until after the beginning of the 19th century, and they never played an important part in frontier affairs. During the 26 years which the Kansa spent at Council Grove, efforts were made to civilize them, but with little success. Mission schools were conducted by the Methodists in 1850–54, and by the Quakers in 1869–73, but the conservatism of the tribesmen prevented the attendance of the children, believing it to be degrading and ruinous to Indian character to adopt the white man's ways. According to T. S. Huffaker, who lived among them, chiefly as teacher, from 1850 to 1873, only one Indian of the tribe was converted to Christianity during that period, while the influence of frontier settlers and traders, with the introduction of liquor, stood in the way of the good that the schools might otherwise have accomplished. While at Council Grove they subsisted largely by hunting the buffalo, until the extinction of the herds, when they took up desultory farming under the instruction of Government teachers, because driven to it by necessity; but the houses erected by the Government for their use they refused to occupy, regarding their own lodges as more healthful and comfortable (G. P. Morehouse, inf'n, 1906).

Say's account, perhaps the most accurate of the earlier notices (Long, Exped. Rocky Mts., 1823), describes the ordinary dress of the men as consisting of a breech-clout of blue or red cloth secured in its place by a girdle, leggings and moccasins without ornamentation, and a blanket thrown over the shoulders. The hair of the chiefs and warriors, except a small lock at the back, was scrupulously removed. The dress of the females consisted of a piece of cloth secured at the waist by a girdle, the sides meeting on the outside of the right thigh, the whole extending downward to the knee. In cold weather or for full dress a similar piece of cloth was thrown over the left shoulder, and leggings of cloth, with a broad protecting border on the outside, and moccasins were worn. They were cultivators of the soil. Tattooing was formerly practised to a limited extent. The chastity of the females was guarded to a greater extent than was usual among the western tribes. The mode of constructing their principal permanent dwellings is described by Say as follows: "The roof is supported by two series of pillars, or rough vertical posts, forked at top for the reception of the transverse connecting pieces of each series; 12 of these posts form the outer series, placed in a circle; and 8 longer ones, the inner series, also describing a circle; the outer wall, of rude frame-work, placed a proper distance from the exterior series of pillars, is 5 or 6 ft high. Poles as thick as the leg at base rest with their butts upon the wall, extending on the crosspieces, which are upheld by the pillars of the two series, and are of sufficient length to reach nearly to the summit. These poles are very numerous, and, agreeably to the position which we have indicated, they are placed all round in a radiating manner, and support the roof like rafters. Across these are laid long and slender sticks or twigs, attached parallel to each other by means of bark cord; these are covered by mats made of long grass, or reeds, or with the bark of trees; the whole is then covered completely over with earth, which, near the ground, is banked up to the eaves. A hole is permitted to remain in the middle of the roof to give exit to the smoke [see *Earth lodge*]. Around the walls of the interior a continuous series of mats are suspended; these are of neat workmanship, composed of a soft reed united by bark cord in straight or undulated lines, between which lines of black paint sometimes occur. The bedsteads are elevated to the height of a common seat from the ground, and are about 6 ft wide; they extend in an uninterrupted line around three-fourths of the circumference of the apartment, and are formed in the simplest manner of numerous sticks or slender pieces of wood, resting at their ends on crosspieces, which are supported by short notched or forked posts driven into the ground; bison skins supply them with a comfortable bedding.'' Restriction of marriage according to gentes has always been strictly observed by the Kansa. When the eldest daughter of a family married, she controlled the lodge, her mother, and all her sisters, the latter being always the wives of the same man. On the death of the husband the widow became the wife of his eldest brother without ceremony; if there was no brother the widow was left free to select her next husband.

The Kansa gentes as given by Dorsey (15th Rep. B. A. E., 230, 1897) are: 1, Manyinka (earth lodge); 2, Ta (deer); 3, Panka (Ponca); 4, Kanze (Kansa); 5, Wasabe (black bear); 6, Wanaghe (ghost); 7, Kekin (carries a turtle on his back); 8, Minkin (carries the sun on his back); 9, Upan (elk); 10, Khuya (white eagle); 11, Han (night); 12, Ibache (holds the firebrand to sacred pipes); 13, Hangatanga (large Hanga); 14, Chedunga (buffalo bull); 15, Chizhuwashtage (Chizhu peacemaker); 16, Lunikashinga (thunderbeing people). These gentes constitute 7 phratries.

The following were some of the Kansa villages, their names having been gained chiefly through the investigations of Rev. J. O. Dorsey, but in only a few cases are their locations known: Bahekhube, Cheghulin (2), Djestyedje, Gakhulin, Gakhu-

linulinbe, Igamansabe, Inchi, Ishtakhechiduba, Manhazitanman, Manhazulin, Manhazulintanman, Manyinkatuhuudje, Neblazhetama, Niudje, Padjegadjin, Pasulin, Tanmangile, Waheheyingetseyabe, Wazhazhepa, Yuzhemakancheubukhpaye, Zandjezhinga, Zandjulin, and Zhanichi.

Alähó.—Mooney, inf'n (Kiowa name). **Ansaus.**—Trumbull, Ind. Wars, 185, 1851 (misprint). **Canceze.**—Coues, Lewis and Clark Exped., I, xxv, note, 1893. **Cancezs.**—Lewis (1806) in Orig. Jour. Lewis and Clark, VII, 336, 1905. **Canchez.**—Le Page Du Pratz, Hist. La., II, 251, 1758. **Canips.**—Lewis, Trav., 3, 1809. **Cans.**—Maximilian, Trav., 119, 1843 (so called by the French). **Cansa.**—Harris, Voy. and Trav., I, map, 685, 1705. **Canses.**—Smith, Bouquet Exped., 70, 1766. **Cansés.**—Iberville (1702) in Margry, Déc., IV, 601, 1880. **Cansez.**—Charlevoix, Voy. N. Am., II, 168, 1766. **Canzas.**—Le Page Du Pratz, Hist. La., 301, 1774. **Canzés.**—Bienville (1722) in Margry, Déc., VI, 387, 1886. **Canzez.**—Le Page Du Pratz, Hist. La., I, 324, 1758. **Caugh.**—Whitehouse (1804) in Orig. Jour. Lewis and Clark, VII, 40, 1905. **Cauzes.**—Trumbull, Ind. Wars, 185, 1851. **Caw.**—Farnham, Trav. West. Prairies, 14, 1843. **Ercansaques.**—Salmeron quoted by Dunbar in Mag. Am. Hist., IV, 280, 1880. **Escanjaques.**—Vetancurt (1693), Teatro Mex., III, 303, repr. 1871. **Escansaques.**—Zarate-Salmeron (*ca.* 1629), Relacion, in Land of Sunshine, 45, Dec. 1899 (the original form of this name; possibly the Kansa). **Escanxaques.**—Shea (1662), Peñalosa, 29, 1882 (supposed by Shea to be Comanche). **Esquansaques.**—Ladd, Story of N. Mex., 109, 1891. **Estanxaques.**—Shea, Peñalosa, 83, 1882. **Excanjaque.**—Zarate-Salmeron quoted by Bancroft, Nat. Races, I, 599, 1882. **Excausaquex.**—Columbus Memor., 157, 1893 (misprint). **Hútañga.**—Dorsey, Kansa MS. vocab., B. A. E., 1882 (own name). **Ka Anjou.**—Bowen, Am. Discov. by the Welsh, 92, 1876. **Ka Anzou.**—Ibid. (called Chickasaw name; trans. 'first men'). **Kah.**—Orig. Jour. Lewis and Clark, VI, 81, 1905 (given as French traders' name). **Kâh.**—Lewis and Clark, Discov., 13, 1806. **Kamse.**—N. Y. Doc. Col. Hist., IX, 1057, 1855. **Kancas.**—La Potherie, Hist. Am., II, 271, 1753. **Kancès.**—Du Lac, Voy. dans les Louisianes, VI, 1805. **Kans.**—Pike, Exped., 123, 1810. **Kansa.**—Ex. Doc. 56, 18th Cong., 1st sess, 9, 1824. **Kansæ.**—Coxe, Carolana, 11, 1741. **Kansas.**—Orig. Jour. Lewis and Clark (1804), I, 60, 1904. **Kansé.**—La Harpe (1722) in Margry, Déc., VI, 365, 1886. **Kaⁿsĕ.**—Dorsey, Osage MS. vocab., B. A. E., 1883 (Osage and Quapaw name). **Kanses.**—Iberville (1702) in Margry, Déc., IV, 599, 1880. **Kansez.**—Anville, map N. Am., 1752. **Kansies.**—Schoolcraft, Ind. Tribes, III, 557, 1853. **Kantha.**—Hamilton in Trans. Nebr. Hist. Soc., I, 73, 1885 (Iowa name). **Kants.**—Smet, Oregon Miss., 161, 1847. **Kanzas.**—Orig. Jour. Lewis and Clark (1804), I, 67, 1904. **Kanzeis.**—Whitehouse (1805), ibid., VII, 189, 1905. **Kanzes.**—Lewis and Clark, ibid., VI, 84. **Kar'sa.**—Lewis and Clark, Discov., 13, 1806. **Karsea.**—Orig. Jour. Lewis and Clark, VI, 84, 1905 (given as their own name). **Kasas.**—Schoolcraft, Ind. Tribes, II, 37, 1853. **Kathági.**—Gatschet, MS., B. A. E. (Shawnee name). **Kausas.**—Dorsey in Am. Antiq., I, 186, 1879 (misprint). **Kauzau.**—M'Coy, Ann. Reg., no. 2, 4, 1836. **Kaws.**—Gregg, Commerce of Prairies, I, 41, 1844. **Kaw'-sä.**—Huffaker (1873), inf'n communicated by G. P. Morehouse, 1906 (own name). **Kaw'-zǎ.**—Morgan, Anc. Soc., 156, 1877. **Konaz—.**—Latham, Philol. and Ethnol. Essays, 296, 1860 (misprint). **Konsa.**—Gatschet, Kaw vocab., 27, B. A. E., 1878. **Kon-ses.**—Hunter, Captiv. among Inds., 18, 1823. **Konza.**—Maximilian Trav., 119, 1843. **Konzas.**—Long, Exped. Rocky Mts., I, 111, 1823. **Les pancaké.**—Shea, Peñalosa, 21, note, 1882 (=Les kançaké=Escanxaques). **Móhtawas.**—ten Kate, Reizen in N. Am., 383, 1885 (Comanche name). **Mo"tawâs.**—ten Kate, Synonymie, 9, 1884 (Comanche name: 'without a lock of hair on the forehead'). **Okames.**—Morgan in N. Am. Rev., 45, 1870. **Okams.**—N. Y. Doc. Col. Hist., IX, 1057, 1855. **Okanis.**—Schoolcraft, Ind. Tribes, III, 557, 1853.

Quans.—Bourgmont (1723) in Margry, Déc., VI, 393, 1886. **Ukasa.**—Gatschet, MS., B. A. E. (Fox name). **Ukasak.**—Ibid.

Kansaki (*Gănsâ'gĭ, Gănsâ'giyĭ*). The name of several distinct Cherokee settlements: (1) on Tuckasegee r., a short distance above the present Webster, in Jackson co., N. C.; (2) on the lower part of Canasauga cr., in McMinn co., Tenn.; (3) at the junction of Conasauga and Coosawatee rs., where afterward was situated the Cherokee capital, New Echota, in Gordon co., Ga.; (4) mentioned in the De Soto narratives as Canasoga or Canasagua, in 1540, on Chattahoochee r., possibly in the neighborhood of Kenesaw mtn., Ga. (J. M.)

Canasagua.—Gentl. of Elvas (1557) in Hakluyt Soc. Pub., IX, 61, 1851. **Canasauga.**—Royce in 5th Rep. B. A. E., map, 1887. **Gănsâ'gĭ.**—Mooney in 19th Rep. B. A. E., 518, 1900. **Gănsâgiyĭ.**—Ibid.

Kanse ('Kansa'). The 14th Hangka Osage gens and 7th on the right side of the tribal circle. See *Kanze.*

A'k'a íniᵤak'ǎciⁿ'a.—Dorsey in 15th Rep. B. A. E., 234, 1797 ('south wind people'). **I'dats'ě.**—Ibid. ('holds a firebrand to the sacred pipes to light them'). **Kansa.**—Ibid. **Kaⁿ'se.**—Ibid. **Pe'ᵤse i'niᵤk'ǎciⁿ'a.**—Ibid. ('fire people'). **Taᵤse' i'niᵤk'ǎc-ⁿ'a.**—Ibid. ('wind people').

Kantico, Kanticoy. See *Cantico.*

Kanulik. A Nushagagmiut Eskimo village on the left bank of Nushagak r., near its mouth, in Alaska; pop. 142 in 1880, 54 in 1890. Carmel mission is here.

Kanoolik.—Petroff, Rep. on Alaska, 47, 1880. **Kanulik.**—Petroff in 10th Census, Alaska, 17, 1884. **Karulik.**—Elliott, Our Arct. Prov., map, 1886.

Kanutaluhi (*Kanu'tălû'hĭ*, 'dogwood place'). A Cherokee settlement in N. Georgia about the period of the removal of the tribe in 1839. (J. M.)

Kanuti. A Koyukukhotana village on Koyukuk r., Alaska, lat. 66° 18', with 13 inhabitants in 1885.

Kanuti.—Baker, Geog. Dict. Alaska, 1902. **Konoótená.**—Allen, Rep. Alaska, 97, 1887.

Kanwaiakaku (*Kan-wai'-a-ka-ku*). A former Chumashan village near the mission of San Buenaventura, Cal.—Henshaw, Buenaventura MS. vocab., B. A. E., 1884.

Kanwasowaua (*Kănwăsowäuᵃ*, 'long tail'). The panther gens of the Miami.

Ka-no-zä'-wa.—Morgan, Anc. Soc., 168, 1877. **Kănwăsowäuᵃ.**—Wm. Jones, inf'n, 1906.

Kanyuksa Istichati (*i-kan-sa* 'ground', *i-yuk-sa* 'point' or 'tip', i. e., point of ground, or peninsula, *is-ti-tca-ti* 'red men'). The native name of that branch of the Seminole, numbering 136 in 1881, residing s. of Caloosahatchee r., at Miami and Big Cypress Swamp settlements, Fla.—MacCauley in 5th Rep. B. A. E., 509, 1887.

Kanze (archaic and untranslatable; rendered by Dorsey 'wind people'). The 5th gens on the Hangashenu side of the Omaha tribal circle. See *Kanse.*

ᵤaⁿze.—Dorsey in 3d Rep. B. A. E., 220, 1885. **Kon-za.**—Long, Exped. Rocky Mts., I, 327, 1823. **Kun'-zä.**—Morgan, Anc. Soc., 155, 1877.

Kanze (Kansa). Given by J. O. Dorsey as the 4th Kansa gens, consisting of the Tdjeunikashinga and Tadjezhinga subgentes.

Ic'-hä-she.—Morgan, Anc. Soc., 156, 1877 (trans. 'tent'). **Kaⁿze.**—Dorsey in 15th Rep. B. A. E., 231, 1897. **Last-lodge.**—Ibid. **Lodge-in-the-rear.**—Ibid. **Tci haciⁿ.**—Ibid.

Kapachichin ('sandy shore'). A Ntlakyapamuk town on the w. side of Fraser r., about 28 m. above Yale, Brit. Col.; pop. 52 in 1901.

Kapatci'tcin.—Teit in Mem. Am. Mus. Nat. Hist., II, 169, 1900. **Kapatsitsan.**—Can. Ind. Aff. for 1901, pt. II, 164. **Klapatcī'tcin.**—Hill-Tout in Rep. Ethnol. Surv. Can., 5, 1899. **Kopachichin.**—Brit. Col. map, Ind. Aff., Victoria, 1872. **North Bend.**—Teit, op. cit. (name given by whites).

Kapaits. The conservative party among the Lagunas of New Mexico (Loew in Wheeler Surv. Rep., VII, 339, 1879). According to Bandelier this party constitutes a phratry. See *Kayomasho.*

Kapaka (*Ka'-pa-ka*). A former Nishinam village in the valley of Bear r., N. Cal.—Powers in Cont. N. A. Ethnol., III, 316, 1877.

Kapanai. A former village of the same Costanoan group as Kalindaruk, and connected with San Carlos mission, Cal.

Capanay.—Taylor in Cal. Farmer, Apr. 20, 1860. **Kapanai.**—A. L. Kroeber, inf'n, 1905.

Kaparoktolik. A summer settlement of Tununirusirmiut Eskimo near the entrance to Ponds inlet, Baffin land.—McClintock, Voy. of Fox, 162, 1859.

Kapaslok (*K·apaslôq*, 'sand roof'). A village of Ntlakyapamuk on Fraser r., above Suk, Brit. Col. It was formerly a large settlement.—Hill-Tout in Rep. Ethnol. Surv. Can., 5, 1899.

Kapawnich. A village of the Powhatan confederacy on the N. bank of the Rappahannock, about Corotoman r., Lancaster co., Va., in 1608.—Smith (1629), Va., I, map, repr. 1819.

Kapiminakouetiik. Mentioned in the Jesuit Relations (26, 1646) as a tribe living at some distance N. of Three Rivers, Can. Doubtless Montagnais, and possibly the Papinachois, q. v.

Kapisilik. An Eskimo village not far from Godthaab, N. Greenland.—Nansen, First Crossing of Greenland, II, 219, 1890.

Kapkapetlp (*Qapqapētlp*, 'place of cedar' [?]). A Squawmish village community at Point Grey, Burrard inlet, Brit. Col.—Hill-Tout in Rep. Brit. A. A. S., 475, 1900.

Kapozha ('not encumbered with much baggage'). A Mdewakanton Sioux band. In 1811 they lived between Cannon r. and Minnesota r., and their village, known as Kaposia, was on the E. bank of the Mississippi 15 m. below the mouth of the Minnesota. At that time the chief was Little Crow (Chetanwakanmani), q. v. In 1830 their village was said to be 3 leagues below the mouth of Minnesota r. Another Little Crow, who was chief in 1862, was killed at the close of the Sioux outbreak.

Ca-po-cia band.—Smithson. Misc. Coll., XIV, art. 6, 1878. **His-scarlet-people.**—Neill, Hist. Minn., 144, note, 1858. **Kah-po-sia.**—Prescott in Schoolcraft, Ind. Tribes, pt. 2, 171, 1852. **Kahpozhah.**—Snelling,

Tales of N. W., 197, 1830. **Kahpozhay.**—McKenney and Hall, Ind. Tribes, I, 303, 1854. **Kapoga.**—Neill in Minn. Hist. Coll., I, 263, 1872. **Kapoja.**—Long, Exped. St Peters R., I, 383, 1824. **Kapo'ja.**—Dorsey in 15th Rep. B. A. E., 215, 1897. **Ka-po-sias.**—Ramsay in Ind. Aff. Rep., 81, 1850. **Kapota.**—Ausland, 462, 1887. **Ka-po'-ża.**—Riggs, Dak. Gram. and Dict., 118, 1852. '**Kapozha.**—Williamson in Minn. Geol. Rep., 107, 1884. **Little Crow's band.**—Ind. Aff. Rep., 118, 1850. **Petit Corbeau's band.**—Long, Exped. St Peters R., 380, 1824. **Tahohyahtaydootah.**—Neill, Hist. Minn., 589, 1858 ('his scarlet people': real name of Little Crow). **Ta-o-ya-te-du-ta.**—Ibid., 144, note.

Kapozha. A band of the Sisseton Sioux. **Kap'oja.**—Dorsey in 15th Rep. B. A. E., 217, 1897. **Kapoża.**—Riggs quoted by Dorsey, ibid.

Kapulo. The now extinct Crane clan of the Tewa of Hano pueblo, N. L. Arizona. **Ka-pu'-lo.**—Fewkes in Am. Anthrop., VII, 166, 1894. **Kapúlo-tówa.**—Hodge, ibid., IX, 350, 1896 (*towa*='people').

Kaquaith. A former Clallam village at Port Discovery, Wash. **Ká-kaitl.**—Gibbs, Clallam and Lummi, 20, 1863. **Ka-quaith.**—Stevens in Ind. Aff. Rep., 457, 1854. **Ka-quaitl.**—Gibbs in Pac. R. R. Rep., I, 435, 1855. **Skwá-kwel.**—Gibbs, Clallam and Lummi, 20, 1863. **Squah-quaihtl.**—U. S. Ind. Treat., 800, 1873. **Squa-que-hl.**—Gibbs in Pac. R. R. Rep., I, 429, 1855.

Karaken (*Karä'kĕn*, 'it is white'). A traditional Iroquois town belonging to the Bear clan and designated as one of recent formation. (J. N. B. H.) **Karakenh.**—Hale, Iroquois Book of Rites, 120, 1883. **Ka ra ken.**—Ibid., 121.

Karakuka. The name given by the main body of the Karok (q. v.) to the divergent dialect spoken on Clear cr. and at Happy Camp, Cal.—A. L. Kroeber, inf'n, 1905.

Karankawa. A term that seems to have been given originally to a small tribe near Matagorda bay, Texas, but its application has been extended to include a number of related tribes between Galveston bay and Padre id. The signification of the name has not been ascertained. Although the linguistic material obtained is not sufficient to show positive relation to any other language, there are very strong indications of affinity with the dialects of the Pakawa group—Pakawa, Comecrudo, and Cotonam—still recognized as a part of the Coahuiltecan family. On the other side they were probably connected with the Tonkawa. If any of the coast tribes mentioned by Cabeza de Vaca was identical with the Karankawa, which is not unlikely, it is impossible to determine the fact. The first positive notice of them is found in the accounts of La Salle's ill-fated visit to that section. It was on Matagorda bay, in the country of the tribe at that time, that this French explorer built his Ft St Louis. Joutel (1687) mentions them under the name Koïenkahé (Margry, Déc., III, 288, 1878), probably a misprint for Korenkake, which is also given. They are represented as living at that time chiefly between St Louis bay (a part of Matagorda bay) and Maligne (Colorado) r., but are the Indians, though mentioned under the

name Clamcöets, who massacred all except 5 of the people left by La Salle at his fort in 1687. If the Ebahamo, Hebobiamos, Bahamos, or Bracamos were identical with the Karankawa or with a portion of the tribe, which is probable, they were living on St Louis or St Bernard bay in 1707 (De l'Isle's map in Winsor, Hist. Am., II, 294, 1886), and are noticed as living at the same place in 1719-21. Their abode is spoken of as an island or peninsula in St Bernard bay (French, Hist. Coll., II, 11, note, 1875). It appears from documents in the Texas archives that in 1793 a part of the Karankawa had become christianized and were then living at the mission of Nuestra Señora del Refugio (q. v.), established in 1791 at the mouth of Mission r. emptying into Aransas bay. The pagan portion of the tribe lived at that time contiguous to the Lipan. Later a number of the tribe were living at the mission of Espíritu Santo de Zúñiga. According to Orozco y Berra (Geog., 382, 1864) the territory of the Lipan near the lower Rio Grande bordered that occupied by the Karankawa in 1796. An incident in the history of the tribe was a fierce battle with Lafitte's band of pirates in consequence of the abduction of one of their women by one of the former; the Indians, however, were forced to retreat before the heavy fire of the buccaneers. With the settlement made by Stephen Austin on the Brazos in 1823 began the decline of the tribe. Conflicts between the settlers and the Indians were frequent, and finally a battle was fought in which about half the tribe were slain, the other portion fleeing for refuge to La Bahia presidio on San Antonio r. They took sides with the Americans in the Texan war of independence, in which their chief, José Maria, was killed, as were most of his warriors, amounting, however, to only about 20. Mention is made of 10 or 12 families living between 1839 and 1851 on Aransas bay and Nueces r. According to Bonnell (Topog. Descrip. Texas, 137, 1840) the Karankawa in 1840 had become reduced to 100, living on Lavaca bay. In 1844, having murdered one of the whites on Guadalupe r., they fled toward the mouth of the Rio Grande, one part stopping on Padre id. and the other passing into Mexico. But few references are made to them after this date, and these are conflicting. A report quoted by Gatschet says the history of these Indians terminates with an attack made on them in 1858 by Juan Nepomuceno Cortina with other rancheros, when they were surprised at their hiding place in Texas and exterminated.

The men are described as very tall and well formed, the women as shorter and fleshier. Their hair was unusually coarse, and worn so long by many of the men that it reached to the waist. Agriculture was not practised by these Indians, their food supply being obtained from the waters, the chase, and wild plants, and, to a limited extent, human flesh; for, like most of the tribes of the Texas coast, they were cannibals. Travel among them was almost wholly by the canoe, or dugout, for they seldom left the coast. Head-flattening and tattooing were practised to a considerable extent. Little is known in regard to their tribal government, further than that they had civil and war chiefs, the former being hereditary in the male line. (See Gatschet, Karankawa Inds., 1891.)

The following tribes or villages were probably Karankawan: Coaque, Ebahamo, Emet, Kouyam, Meracouman, Quara, and Quinet. The following were in the country of the Karankawa, but whether linguistically connected with them is not certain: Ahehouen, Ahouerhopiheim, Arhau, Chorruco, Doguenes, Kabaye, Kiabaha, Kopano, Las Mulas, Mariames, Mendica, Mora, Ointemarhen, Omenaosse, Pataquilla, Quevenes, San Francisco, and Spichehat. See *Nuestra Señora del Rosario*. (A. C. F. J. R. S.)

Caramanes.—Mezières (1778) quoted by Bancroft, No. Mex. States, I, 661, 1886 (distinct from the Xaramanes=Aramanes). Carancaguacas.—Doc. of 1796 quoted by Orozco y Berra, Geog., 382, 1864. Carancaguazes.—Rivera, Diario, leg. 2602, 1736. Carancahuas.—Maillard, Hist. Tex., 238, 251, 1842. Carancahuases.—Doc. of 1828 in Soc. Geog. Mex., 504, 1869. Carancahuazes.—Doc. of 1793 quoted by Gatschet, Karankawa Inds., 28, 1891. Carancanay.—Robin, Voy. Louisiane, III, 15, 1807. Carancouas.—Latham in Trans. Philol. Soc. Lond., 101, 1856. Caranhouas.—Lewis and Clark, Jour., 155, 1840. Carankahuas.—Latham in Trans. Philol. Soc. Lond., 103, 1856. Carankawaes.—French, Hist. Coll. La., II, 11, note, 1875. Carankonas.—Domenech, Deserts N. A., I, 440, 1860. Carankouas.—Sibley, Hist. Sketches, 72, 1806. Carankoways.—Schoolcraft, Ind. Tribes, V, 571, 1855. Cazancanay.—Robin, Voy. Louisiane, III, 14, 1807. Charankoua.—Schoolcraft, Ind. Tribes, III, 544, 1853. Clamcoets.—Joutel, Jour. du Dernier Voy. de La Salle, 74, 1713. Coiencanes.—Barcia, Ensayo, 271, 1723. Coran-canas.—Schermerhorn (1812) in Mass. Hist. Coll., 2d s., II, 25, 1814. Corankoua.—Brackenridge, Views La., 81, 1814. Coronkawa.—Morse, Rep. to Sec. War, 374, 1822. Coronks.—A popular abbreviation in Texas for Karankawa. Curancahuases.—Escudero, Not. de Chihuahua, 231, 1834. Karankaways.—Ind. Aff. Rep., 30, 1850. Karankoas.—Sanford, Hist. U. S., clxvii, 1819. Karankoo-as.—Brackenridge, Views La., 87, 1814. Kéles.—Gatschet, MS., B. A. E. ('wrestlers': Tonkawa name). Kikanonas.—Barcia, Ensayo, 263, 1723. Kironnonas.—French, Hist. Coll. La., II, 11, note, 1875. Kironomes.—Charlevoix, New France, Shea ed., IV, 88, 1870. Kirononas.—Coxe, Carolana, 38, 1741. Koïenkahe.—Joutel (1687) in Margry, Déc., III, 288, 1878. Korenkake.—Joutel (1687) in French, Hist. Coll. La., I, 187, 1846. Koronks.—Bollaert (1849) quoted by Gatschet, Karankawa Inds., 35, 1891. Nda kun-dadéhe.—Gatschet, Lipan MS., B. A. E., 1884 (Lipan name: *ndá* 'people', *kun* 'water', *dadéhe* 'going walking': 'people walking in the water'). Quelamoueches.—De l'Isle map (*ca.* 1707) in Winsor, Hist. Am., II, 294, 1886. Quĕlancouchis.—Iberville (1699) in Margry, Déc., IV, 316, 1880. Quelanhubeches.—Barcia, Ensayo, 294, 1723 (probably identical). Quineres.—

Ibid., 259 (identical?). Quinets.—Douay in Shea, Discov., 207, 210, 1852 (identical?). Tampacuases.—Reports of the Mex. Border Commission, 406, 1873. Tarancahuases.—Doc. of 1828 quoted by Gatschet, Karankawa Inds., 34, 1891. Yákokon kápai.—Gatschet, Tonkawa MS., B. A. E., 145 ('without moccasins': Tonkawa name, including also the Coahuiltecan coast tribes).

Karankawan Family. A family established by Powell (7th Rep. B. A. E., 82, 1891) on the language of the Karankawa tribe as determined by Gatschet. Although this and the related tribes are extinct, investigation has led to the conclusion that the Coaque, Ebahamo, and other tribes or settlements of the Texas coast mentioned under Karankawa (q. v.) should be included in the family.

Karezi. An unidentified tribe mentioned as living w. of L. Superior and distinct from the Cree.—Jes. Rel. 1667, 23, 1858.

Karhadage ('in the forest.'—Hewitt). An unidentified tribe, band, or village, probably in Canada, with which the Iroquois affirmed they had made peace in 1701. Mentioned with the Chippewa, Missisauga, Nipissing, and others (Livingston in N. Y. Doc. Col. Hist., IV, 899, 1854). Cf. *Karhagaghrooney, Karigouistes, Karrihaet*. (J. M.)

Karhagaghrooney (*Karhagaronon,* 'people of the woods'). According to Sir Wm. Johnson a name applied by the Iroquois to wandering Indians N. of Quebec; but as he suggests Carillon on Ottawa r. as the best point for a post of trade with them, they were probably more to the westward. Dobbs located them N. of L. Huron. The term is a collective one, referring to wandering bands of different tribes, possibly to the Têtes de Boule, and to those called O'pimittish Ininiwac by Henry.

Karhagaghrooneys.—Johnson (1764) in N. Y. Doc. Col. Hist., VII, 658, 1856. Kirhawguagh Roanu.—Dobbs, Hudson Bay, 28, 1744.

Karhationni (*Kărhătioñ'nĭ',* 'a forest lying extended lengthwise'). A traditionary Iroquois village belonging to the Wolf clan; location unknown. (J. N. B. H.)

Karhatyonni.—Hale, Iroquois Book of Rites, 118, 1883. Karhetyonni.—Ibid., 119.

Karhawenradonh (*Karhawĕn'hră'don'*). A traditionary Iroquois town belonging to the Bear clan and to those towns designated as cf recent formation; location unknown. (J. N. B. H.)

Karhawenghradongh.—Hale, Iroquois Book of Rites, 120, 1883. Ka rho wengh ra don.—Ibid., 121.

Kariak. An Eskimo settlement close to Amaralik fjord, w. Greenland.—Crantz, Hist. Greenland, I, 8, 1767.

Kariak. A summer settlement of Aivilirmiut Eskimo on Lyon inlet, N. end of Hudson bay.—Boas in 6th Rep. B. A. E., 450, 1888.

Karigouistes. The name given by the Iroquois to the Catholic Indians of Canada, probably more especially to the

Caughnawaga. The name seems to have reference to a long dress, possibly the gowns worn by the priests. (J. N. B. H.)

Caraguists.—Colden (1727), Five Nations, 163, 1747. **Karigouistes.**—Bacqueville de la Potherie, III, 200, 1753. **Karig8stes.**—Dellins (1694) in N. Y. Doc. Col. Hist., IV, 95, 1854.

Karkin. A division of the Costanoan Indians inhabiting the country s. of Carquinez straits, San Francisco bay, Cal., the name of the straits being derived from that of the Indians. According to Kotzebue they extended E. as far as the mouth of San Joaquin r.

Carquin.—Taylor in Cal. Farmer, Oct. 18, 1861. **Jarquin.**—Ibid. **Karkin.**—Arroyo de la Cuesta, Idiomas Californias, MS. trans., B. A. E. **Karquines.**—Taylor in Cal. Farmer, Oct. 18, 1861. **Korekins.**—Kotzebue, New Voy. (1823–26), II, 141, 1830.

Karluk. A Kaniagmiut village on the N. coast of Kodiak id., Alaska, where there are large salmon canneries; pop. 302 in 1880, 1,123 in 1890, 1,864 in 1900.

Carlook.—Lisianski (1805), quoted by Baker, Geog. Dict. Alaska, 1902. **Karlooch.**—Ibid. **Karluta.**—Coxe, after Shelikof, quoted by Baker, ibid. **Nunakachwak.**—Holmberg, Ethnog. Skizz., map, 1855.

Karmakdjuin (*Qarmaqdjuin,* 'large huts'). A summer settlement of the Akudnirmiut Eskimo on Home bay, Baffin land.—Boas in 6th Rep. B. A. E., 441, 1888.

Karmakdjuin. A village of Padlimiut Eskimo on the coast just N. of Exeter sd., Baffin land.—Boas in 6th Rep. B. A. E., map, 1888.

Karmang (*Qarmang,* 'hut'). A summer settlement of Talirpingmiut Okomiut Eskimo at the N. w. end of Nettilling lake, w. of Cumberland sd.—Boas in 6th Rep. B. A. E., map, 1888.

Karmenak. An Ita Eskimo settlement in N. Greenland.—Kane, Arct. Explor., II, 127, 1856.

Karmentaruka. A former village of the Rumsen, connected with San Carlos mission, Cal.

Carmentaruka.—Taylor in Cal. Farmer, Apr. 20, 1860.

Karok (*karuk,* 'upstream'; they have no name for themselves other than that for 'men' or 'people', *arar,* whence *Arra-arra, Ara-ara,* etc.). The name by which the Indians of the Quoratean family have, as a tribe, been generally called. They lived on Klamath r. from Redcap cr. to Indian cr., N. w. Cal. Below them on the river were the Yurok, above them the Shasta, to their E. were other Shastan tribes, while on the w. they were separated by a spur of the Siskiyou mts. from the Yurok and the Athapascan Tolowa. Salmon r., a tributary of the Klamath, was not Karok territory except for about 5 m. from its mouth, but was held mainly by Shastan tribes. While the Karok language is fundamentally different from the languages of the adjacent Hupa and Yurok, the Karok people closely resemble these two tribes in mode of life and culture, and any description given of the latter will apply to the Karok. They differ from the Yurok principally in two points: One, that owing to the absence of redwood they do not make canoes but buy them from the Yurok; the other, that they celebrate a series of annual ceremonies called "making the world," which are held at Panamenik, Katimin, and Inam, with a similar observance at Amaikiara, while the Yurok possess no strictly analogous performances. The Karok had no divisions other than villages, and while these extended along the entire extent of their territory, three important clusters are recognizable, in each of which there was one village at which certain ceremonies were held that were observed nowhere else. Panamenik, on the site of Orleans Bar, and several other settlements formed the first group; the second was about the mouth of Salmon r. and comprised Amaikiara, Ashipak, Ishipishi, Katimin, Shanamkarak, and others; in the third and northernmost group the most important villages were Inam, at the mouth of Clear cr., and Asisufuunuk at Happy Camp. In the first two groups a single dialect was spoken; in the last, the farthest upstream, a divergent dialect called Karakuka was employed.

Following is a list of the Karok villages: Amaikiara, Aperger, Apyu, Aranimokw, Ashipak, Asisufuunuk, Chainiki, Chawakoni, Chinits, Couth, Homnipa, Homuarup, Ift, Inam, Inotuks, Ishipishi, Ishwidip, Iyis, Katimin, Katipiara, Kokaman, Kworatem, Ohetur, Olegel, Oler, Opegoi, Panamenik, Pasara, Sawuara, Shanamkarak, Shegoashkwu, Sumaun, Sunum, Supasip, Tishrawa, Tsano, Tsofkara, Tui, Uchapa, Unharik, Wetsitsiko, Wopum, and Yutoyara.

Ara.—Gatschet in Cont. N. A. Ethnol., II, pt. 1, xlvi, 1890 (sig. 'man'). **Ara-ara.**—Ibid. **Arra.**—Crook, ibid., III, 447, 1877. **Cahroos.**—Powers in Overland Mo., IX, 157, 1872. **Cahroes.**—Keane in Stanford, Compend., 504, 1878. **Cisquiouws.**—Meek in H. R. Ex. Doc. 76, 30th Cong. 1st sess., 10, 1848 (may include also Yurok and Shasta). **Ivap'i.**—A. L. Kroeber, inf'n, 1903 (Shasta name). **Kahruk.**—Gibbs (1851) in Schoolcraft, Ind. Tribes, III, 151, 1853. **Karok.**—Powers in Cont. N. A. Ethnol., III, 19, 1877. **Orleans Indians.**—Kroeber, inf'n, 1903 (sometimes locally used, especially downstream from the Karok territory). **Patesick.**—McKee (1851) in Sen. Ex. Doc. 4, 32d Cong., spec. sess., 194, 1853. **Patih-riks.**—Meyer, Nach dem Sacramento, 282, 1855. **Peh-tsik.**—Gibbs (1851) in Schoolcraft, Ind. Tribes, III, 138, 1853 (Yurok name; sig. 'upstream'—Kroeber). **Petit-sick.**—McKee, op. cit., 161. **Petsikla.**—Kroeber, inf'n, 1903 (Yurok name). **Upper Klamath.**—McKee, op. cit., 194.

Karrihaet. Given as the name of a tribe, probably in Canada, with whom the Iroquois made peace in 1701. Mentioned with the Chippewa, Missisauga, Nipissing, and others.—Livingston (1701) in N. Y. Doc. Col. Hist., IV, 899, 1854. Cf. *Karigouistes, Karhadage.*

Karsok. An Eskimo village in w. Greenland, lat. 72° 40′.
Karsok.—Science, XI, 259, 1888. Karsuk.—Kane, Arct. Explor., I, 458, 1856.

Karsuit. A village of Ita Eskimo on Inglefield gulf, N. Greenland.
Karsioot.—Kane, Arct. Explor., II, 212, 1856. Karsooit.—Hayes, Arct. Boat. Journ., 307, 1860.

Karsukan. A spring settlement of Okomiut Eskimo of Saumia, on the coast of Baffin land, N. of Cumberland sd.—Boas in 6th Rep. B. A. E., map, 1888.

Karusuit ('the caves'). A village of the Talirpingmiut Okomiut Eskimo on Nettilling fjord, w. shore of Cumberland sd.; pop. 29 in 1883.
Kaiossuit.—Boas in Deutsche Geog. Blätt., VIII, 32, 1885. K'arussuit.—Boas in Petermanns Mitt., no. 80, 70, 1885. Kemasuit.—Kumlien in Bull. Nat. Mus., no. 15, 15, 1879. Kemesuit.—Ibid. Kimmocksowick.—Wareham in Jour. Roy. Geog. Soc., XII, 24, 1842. Qarussuit.—Boas in 6th Rep. B. A. E., 426, 1888.

Karusuk. An Eskimo settlement near Ameralik fjord, lat. 64° 20′, w. Greenland.—Nansen, First Crossing of Greenland, II, 416, 1890.

Kasaan (pronounced by Haida GAsa'n, but said to be from Tlingit Kā'sĭ-ăn, 'pretty town'). One of the three towns in Alaska still occupied by the Haida; situated on Skowl arm of Kasaan bay, E. coast of Prince of Wales id. Chatchee-nie, the name of a Kaigani town in John Work's list of 1836–41, was either a camping place of the people of Kasaan or a town occupied by them before moving to the latter place. In Work's time it had 18 houses and 249 people. Petroff gives the population of Kasaan (and "Skowl") in 1880 as 173, and the Census of 1890 as 46; the present number is insignificant. The family that settled here was the Tadjilanas. (J. R. S.)
GAsā'n.—Swanton, Cont. Haida, 282, 1905. Kasaan.—U. S. Coast Surv. map of Alaska, southeast sec., Apr. 1898. Kassan.—Petroff in 10th Census, Alaska, 32, 1884. Kassan Häadē.—Harrison in Proc. and Trans. Roy. Soc. Can., sec. II, 125, 1895.

Kasaktikat (Ka-sak-ti'-kat). A former Chumashan village at a place called Bajada de la Cañada, in Ventura co., Cal.—Henshaw, Buenaventura MS. vocab., B. A. E., 1884.

Kasenos (Ka'-se-nos). A village, probably of the Cathlacumup, formerly situated where Scappoose cr. empties into Willamette slough, Oreg.—Gibbs, MS. 248, B. A. E.

Kashahara. The Karok name of the Wintun of Trinity r., N. Cal. (Kroeber, inf'n, 1903). The Trinity r. Wintun consisted of the Normuk, Tientien, and Waikenmuk.

Kashaiak. A Togiagamiut Eskimo village on Togiak r., near its junction with the Kashaiak, Alaska; pop. 181 in 1880.
Kashaiak.—Baker, Geog. Dict. Alaska, 1902. Kashaiyak.—Spurr and Post quoted by Baker, ibid. Kissaiakh.—Petroff in 10th Census, Alaska, 17, 1884. Kissiak.—Petroff, Rep. on Alaska, 49, 1880. Kissiakh.—Nelson in 18th Rep. B. A. E., map, 1900.

Kashiga. An Aleut village on Unalaska id., Alaska. Pop. 41 in 1833 (at which date it was the headquarters of the foreman of the Russian-American Co. for the w. half of Unalaska), according to Veniaminoff; 74 in 1874, according to Shiesnekov; 73 in 1880; 46 in 1890.
Kashega.—Sarichef (1792) quoted by Baker, Geog. Dict. Alaska, 1902. Kashiga.—11th Census, Alaska, 89, 1893. Kashigin.—Ibid. Koschiginskoje.—Holmberg, Ethnog. Skizz., map, 142, 1855. Koshegenskoi.—Elliott, Cond. Aff. Alaska, 225, 1875. Koshigin.—Petroff, Rep. on Alaska, 20, 1880. Koshiginskoe.—Veniaminoff, Zapiski, II, 202, 1840.

Kashigalak. A Kaialigmiut Eskimo village in the middle of Nelson id., Alaska; pop. 10 in 1880.
Kashigalagamute.—Petroff, Rep. on Alaska, 54, 1881. Kashigalogamut.—Nelson (1878) quoted by Baker, Geog. Dict. Alaska, 1902. Kashigalogumut.—Nelson in 18th Rep. B. A. E., map, 1900. Kashigaluk.—Baker, op. cit.

Kashiwe (Kas-hi'-we). A former Chumashan village near Newhall, Ventura co., Cal., at a place now called Cuesta Santa Susána.—Henshaw, Buenaventura MS. vocab., B. A. E., 1884.

Kashkachuti (Kash-kach'-u-ti). A pueblo of the Acoma which, according to tradition, was inhabited in prehistoric times during the migration of the tribe from the mythic Shipapu in the indefinite N.—Hodge in Century Mag., LVI, 15, May, 1898.

Kashkekoan ('people of [the r.] Kãshk'). A Tlingit division at Yakutat, Alaska, that is said to have migrated from the Athapascan country on the upper part of Copper r. It belongs to the Raven phratry.
Kâck!ē qoan.—Swanton, field notes, B. A. E., 1904. Kāschke-kon.—Krause, Tlinkit Ind., 116, 1885.

Kashong. A former Seneca settlement on Kashong cr., at its entrance into Seneca lake. It is first mentioned in 1765, and contained 14 houses when destroyed by Sullivan in Sept., 1779. (J. M.)
Cashaem.—MS. Jour. of 1787 quoted by Conover, Kanadasega and Geneva MS., B. A. E. Cashong.—Ibid. Gaghasieanhgwe.—Ibid. Gaghsiungua.—Ibid. Gaghsonghgwa.—Ibid. Gaghsonshwa.—Kirkland (1765) quoted by Conover, ibid. Gagsonghwa.—Ibid. Gahasieanhgwe.—Ibid. Garhawquash.—Morgan, League Iroq., map, 1851. Gathsiungua.—Jour. of 1687 quoted by Conover, MS., B. A. E. Gothescunqueon.—Ibid. Gothsenquean.—Ibid. Gothseunquean.—Ibid. Gothsinquea.—Ibid. Kashanquash.—Ibid. Kashong.—Ibid. Kashonquash.—Ibid. Kershong.—Ibid. Kushang.—Ibid. Shenawaga.—Ibid.

Kash's Village. A summer camp of a Stikine chief on Etolin id., Alaska; 40 people were there in 1880.—Petroff in 10th Census, Alaska, 32, 1884.

Kashtata (K'ac-ta'-tă). A former Takelma village on the s. side of Rogue r., above Leaf cr. and Galice cr., Oreg.—Dorsey in Jour. Am. Folk-lore, III, 235, 1890.

Kashtok (Kac-tö'k). A former Chumashan village in the interior of Ventura co., Cal.—Henshaw, Buenaventura MS. vocab., B. A. E., 1884.

Kashtu (Kac-tú). A former Chumashan village on the Piru, a tributary of Santa Clara r., Ventura co., Cal.—Henshaw, Buenaventura MS. vocab., B. A. E., 1884.

Kashunuk. A Magemiut Eskimo village on the Kashunuk outlet of Yukon r., Alaska; pop. 125 in 1880, 232 in 1890, 208 in 1900.

Kashunahmiut.—11th Census, Alaska, 111, 1893. Kashunok.—Petroff in 10th Census, Alaska, 54, 1884. Kashunuk.—Nelson (1878) quoted by Baker, Geog. Dict. Alaska, 1902. Kesuna.—12th Census Rep.

Kashutuk.—A Chnagmiut Eskimo village on an island of the Yukon delta, Alaska; pop. 18 in 1880.

Kachutok.—Petroff in 10th Census, Alaska, map, 1884. Kashutuk.—Nelson (1878) quoted by Baker, Geog. Dict. Alaska, 1902. Kushutuk.—Nelson in 18th Rep. B. A. E., map, 1899.

Kasigianguit ('little freshwater seals.'— Boas). An Eskimo village near Ameralik fjord, w. Greenland, lat. 64° 10′.—Nansen, First Crossing of Greenland, II, 376, 1890.

Kasihta. A former Lower Creek town on the E. bank of Chattahoochee r., in Chattahoochee co., Ga., 2½ m. below Kawita, its branch settlements extending along the w. side of the river. It was visited by De Soto in 1540, and is referred to under the name Casiste by the Gentleman of Elvas as a great town. In 1799 it was considered the largest of the Lower Creek towns, containing, with its dependencies, 180 warriors and in 1832 it had 620 families and 10 chiefs. Hawkins (Sketch, 58, 1843), in 1799, described a large conical mound, with the "old Cussetah town" near it, which afterward was settled by the Chickasaw. Apatai, now spelled Upatoie, was a branch village. The Kasihta people believed they were descended from the sun, and a curious migration legend, preserved by Von Reck, existed among them (see Gatschet, Creek Migr. Leg., I, 133–34, 1884), from which it appears that the Kawita were originally the same people as those of Kasihta, and that they separated in very ancient times. Cusseta, a variant of Kasihta, is now the name of a town in Chambers co., Ala., and another is in Chattahoochee co., Ga. A district in the Creek Nation, Okla., was once called Cuseta.   (A. S. G.)

Casawda.—Crawford (1836) in H. R. Doc. 274, 25th Cong., 2d sess., 24, 1838. Caseltas.—Boudinot, Star in the West, 126, 1816. Casica.—Barcia (1693), Ensayo, 287, 1723. Casista.—Ibid., 333. Casiste.— Gentleman of Elvas (1557) in French, Hist. Coll. La., II, 155, 1850. Cassetash.—White (1787) in Am. State Pap., Ind. Aff., I, 21, 1832. Cassita.—Swan (1791) in Schoolcraft, Ind. Tribes, V, 254, 1855. Cuseta.—Ind. Aff. Rep., 365, 1854. Cusetahs.—U. S. Ind. Treat. (1779), 69, 1837. Cusetas.—Lattré, Carte des Etats-Unis, 1784. Cushetaus.—Coxe, Carolana, 23, 1741. Cusitas.—Alcedo, Dic. Geog., I, 738, 1786. Cusitash.—White (1787) in Am. State Pap., Ind. Aff., I, 20, 1832. Cusseta.—Gatschet, Creek Migr. Leg., II, 180, 1888. Cussetahs.—McGillivray (1787) in Am. State Pap., Ind. Aff., I, 18, 1832. Cussetas.— Pickett, Hist. Ala., passim, 1851. Cussetau.—U. S. Ind. Treat. (1814), 162, 1837. Cussetaw.—Census of 1832 in Schoolcraft, Ind. Tribes, IV, 578, 1854. Cusse-tuh.—Hawkins (1799), Sketch, 25, 57, 1848. Cussitahs.—Swan (1791) in Schoolcraft, Ind. Tribes, V, 262, 1855. Cussito.—Romans, Florida, I, 280, 1775. Cussutas.—Boudinot, Star in the West, 126, 1816. Kacistas.—Milfort, Mémoire, 118, 1802. Old Cusetaw.—Woodward, Reminis., 14, 1859. Usseta.— Bartram, Travels, 457, 1791.

Kasilof. A Knaiakhotana village on the E. coast of Cook inlet, at the mouth of Kasilof r., Alaska. A settlement was planted there by the Russians in 1786, called St George. Pop. 31 in 1880; 117, in 7 houses, in 1890.

Georgiefskaia.—Russian map cited by Baker, Geog. Dict. Alaska, 232, 1902. Kassilo.—Petroff in 10th Census, Alaska, 29, 1884. Kassilof.—Ibid., map. Kussilof.—Post route map, 1903.

Kasispa (kasi's 'a point', pä locative: 'at the point'). A Paloos village at Ainsworth, at the junction of Snake and Columbia rs., Wash.

Cosispa.—Ross, Fur Hunters, I, 185, 1855. Kasī′spä.—Mooney in 14th Rep. B. A. E., 735, 1896.

Kaska. Given by Dawson (Rep. Geol. Surv. Can., 199B, 1889) as a division of the Nahane, comprising the Achetotena (Etchareottine) and Dahotena (Etagottine) tribes. They are described as undersized and of poor physique, have the reputation of being timid, and are lazy and untrustworthy, but are comparatively prosperous, as their country yields good furs in abundance. According to Morice (Trans. Can. Inst., VII, 519, 1892–93), however, "Kaska is the name of no tribe or subtribe, but McDane cr. is called by the Nahane Kasha . . . and this is the real word which, corrupted into Cassiar by the whites, has since a score of years or more served to designate the whole mining region from the Coast range to the Rocky mts., along and particularly to the N. of the Stickeen r." The name Kaska is not recognized by the Indians themselves, who form the third division of Morice's classification of the Nahane. They number about 200.   (A. F. C.)

Kaskakoedi ('people of Kaskek'). A division of the Raven phratry of the Tlingit, living at Wrangell, Alaska. They are said to have come from among the Masset Haida and to have received their name from a place (Kāsq!ē′kⁿ) where they camped during the migration.

Kaas-ka-qua-tee.—Kane, Wand. in N. A., app., 1859. K·asq'aguē′dē.—Boas, 5th Rep. N. W. Tribes of Can., 25, 1889. Kāsq!akue′dî.—Swanton, field notes, B. A. E., 1904. Kassra-kŭēdi.—Krause, Tlinkit Ind., 120, 1885.

Kaskanak. A Kiatagmiut Eskimo village on Kvichak r., where it flows from L. Iliamna, Alaska; pop. 119 in 1880, 66 in 1890.

Kaskanakh.—Post route map, 1903. Kaskanek.— Petroff, Rep. on Alaska, map, 1880. Kaskinakh.— Ibid., 45.

Kaskaskia (perhaps akin to kaskaskahamwᵃ, 'he scrapes it off by means of a tool.' The Foxes have always held the Peoria in low esteem, and in their traditions claim to have destroyed most of them on a rocky island in a river.—Wm. Jones). Once the leading tribe of the Illinois confederacy, and perhaps rightly to be considered as the elder brother of the group. Although the first knowledge of this confederacy obtained by the whites related, in all probability, to the Peoria while they yet resided on the Mississippi, it is probable that the references to them in the Jesuit Relations of 1670 and 1671, from the reports of Father Allouez, apply to the Kaskaskia on upper Illinois r. and possibly to some minor tribes or bands connected therewith whose names have not been preserved. Although it has been asserted that earlier visits than that of Marquette in 1673 were made to this people by the whites, there is no satisfactory evidence to justify this conclusion. Their chief village, which had the same name as that of the tribe, is supposed to have been situated about the present site of Utica, La Salle co., Ill. Marquette states that at the time of his first visit the village was composed of 74 cabins. He returned again in the spring of 1674 and established the mission of Immaculate Conception among them. It appears that by this time the village had increased to somewhat more than a hundred cabins. Allouez, who followed as the next missionary, states that when he came to the place in 1677 the village contained 351 cabins, and that while the village formerly consisted of but one nation (tribe), at the time of his visit it was composed of 8 tribes or peoples, the additional ones having come up from the neighborhood of the Mississippi. Although the known Peoria village was some distance away, it may be that at this time this tribe and the Moingwena resided at the Kaskaskia village. This is implied in an expression by Gravier, who speaks of the Mugulasha "forming a village with the Baiougoula [Bayogoula] as the Pioüaroüa [Peoria] do with the Kaskaskia." This, however, would lead to the supposition, if the statement by Allouez be accepted as correct, that there were other bands or tribes collected here at the time of his mission whose names have not survived. Possibly they may have been bands of the Mascoutin or the Miami. Kaskaskia was the village of the Illinois which La Salle reached about the close of Dec., 1679, on his first visit southward from the lakes. He found it unoccupied, however, the inhabitants being on a hunting expedition. The French mission was maintained at this place under Fathers Rasles, Gravier, Binneteau, Pinet, and Marest, until about the close of 1700. At that time the Kaskaskia, influenced by a desire to join the French in Louisiana, resolved to separate from their brethren and migrate to the lower Mississippi. Gravier was much opposed to this movement, and although he arrived on the ground too late to prevent their departure, he was successful in checking the blow which the indignant Peoria and Moingwena were about to inflict on them. It was also through his influence that

they were induced to halt at the mouth of Kaskaskia r., where they made their home, on or near the site of the present town of Kaskaskia, Randolph co., Ill., until their removal w. of the Mississippi under the treaty of Oct. 27, 1832. According to Hutchins, in 1764 the Kaskaskia numbered 600, but he gives the number in 1778 as 210 individuals, including 60 warriors. They were then in a village about 3 m. N. of the present town of Kaskaskia, greatly degenerated and debauched. The tribe participated in the treaties of Greenville, Ohio, Aug. 3, 1795, and Ft Wayne, Ind., June 7, 1803, made by the tribes of the N. W. with Anthony Wayne and William H. Harrison. In the treaty of Aug. 13, 1803, at Vincennes, Ind., it is stated that the tribe constitutes "the remains of and rightfully represents all the tribes of the Illinois Indians, originally called the Kaskaskia, Mitchigamia, Cahokia, and Tamaroi." By this treaty they were taken under the immediate care and patronage of the United States and promised protection against the other Indians. By treaty made at Castor Hill, Mo., Oct. 27, 1832, they ceded to the United States all their lands E. of the Mississippi except a single tract reserved to Ellen Ducoigne, the daughter of their late chief. Previous to this, however, the remnants of the various tribes of the Illinois confederacy had consolidated with the Kaskaskia and Peoria. By the treaty of Washington, May 30, 1854, the consolidated tribes ceded to the United States part of the tracts held by them under the treaty of 1832, above mentioned, and under the treaty with the Piankashaw and Wea, Oct. 29, 1832, reserving 160 acres for each member of the tribe and 10 sections as a tribal reserve. By the treaty of Washington, Feb. 23, 1867, land was assigned them in the N. E. corner of Indian Ter.

The consolidated bands, including also the remnant of the Wea and Piankashaw and now known officially as Peoria, numbered altogether in 1905 only 195, hardly one of whom was of pure Indian blood.

Their totem or crest was an arrow notched at the feather, or two arrows supporting each other like a St Andrew's cross.   (J. M. C. T.)

Cacachias.—La Salle (1682) in Margry, Déc., II, 96, 1877. **Carcarilica.**—Hennepin, New Discov., 310, 1698 (? an Illinois division about 1680). **Cas.**—Marain (1753) in Margry, Déc., VI, 654, 1886. **Cascachias.**—Memoir of 1718 in N. Y. Doc. Col. Hist., IX, 891, 1855. **Cascacia.**—La Salle (1682) in Margry, Déc., I, 508, 1875. **Cascakias.**—La Harpe (1719), ibid., VI, 310, 1886. **Cascaqu'as.**—Güssefeld, map, 1784. **Cascaschia.**—La Salle (1681) in Margry, Déc., II, 134, 1877. **Cascaskias.**—Perkins and Peck, Annals of the West, 55, 1850. **Cascasquia.**—Joutel (1687) in Margry, Déc., III, 476, 1878. **Caskaguias.**—De l'Isle map (ca. 1710) in Neill, Minn., 1858. **Caskaquias.**—Doc. of 1748 in N. Y. Doc. Col. Hist., X, 142, 1858. **Casquasquia.**—Joutel (1687) in Margry, Déc., III, 481, 1878. **Casquiars.**—Writer in Smith, Bouquet Exped., 66, 1766. **Casquias.**—Smith, ibid. **Huskhuskeys.**—Croghan (1765) in Monthly Am. Jour. Geol., 272, 1831. **Kacaskias.**—La Harpe (1719) in Margry, Déc., VI, 309, 1886. **Kachkach-kia.**—Allouez (1677) in Shea, Miss. Val., 74, 1852. **Kachkaska.**—Marquette map (ca. 1678) in Shea, ibid. **Kakaskígi.**—Gatschet, Shawnee MS., B. A. E., 1879 (Shawnee name, sing., Kakaskí). **Kakasky.**—Imlay, West. Ter., 364, 1797. **Karhaski.**—Loskiel (1794) quoted by Ruttenber, Tribes Hudson r., 336, 1872. **Karkadia.**—Perkins and Peck, Annals of the West, 64, 1850. **Kasgresquios.**—Buchanan, N. Am. Inds., 155, 1824. **Kaskaisas.**—Doc. of 1717 in N. Y. Doc. Col. Hist., IX, 876, 1855. **Kaskaiskas.**—Jefferys, French Doms., pt. 1, map, 1761. **Kaskakias.**—Chauvignerie (1736) in N. Y. Doc. Col. Hist., IX, 1056, 1855. **Kaskakiés.**—Vaudreuil (1760), ibid., x, 1092, 1858. **Kaskascia.**—La Salle (1680) in Margry, Déc., II, 121, 1877. **Kaskasia.**—Burton, City of the Saints, 117, 1861. **Kaskaskia.**—La Salle (1682) in Margry, Déc., II, 201, 1877. **Kaskaskians.**—U. S. Ind. Treat. (1795), 184, 1873. **Kaskaskies.**—Greenville treaty (1795) in Harris, Tour, 241, 1805. **Kaskasquia.**—Charlevoix (1724) in Schoolcraft, Travels, 136, 1821. **Kaskkasies.**—Boudinot, Star in the West, 127, 1816. **Kasqui.**—Coxe, Carolana, 13, 1741 (identical?). **Kasquias.**—Vater, Mith., pt. 3, sec. 3, 351, 1816. **Kasquuasquias.**—Smyth, Tour in U.S., I, 347, 1784. **Keskeskias.**—Doc. of 1764 in N. Y. Doc. Col. Hist., VII, 641, 1856. **Kiskuskias.**—Smyth, Tour in U. S., II, 247, 1784 (place name). **Kuilka.**—Hennepin, New Discov. (1698), II, 667, 1903. **Kuskeiskees.**—Johnson (1767) in N. Y. Doc. Col. Hist., VII, 966, 1856. **Kuskuske.**—Adair, Am. Inds., 371, 1775. **Quasquens.**—Iberville(ca. 1701) in Margry, Déc., IV, 544, 1880. **Roinsac.**—Memoir of 1718 in N. Y. Doc. Col. Hist., IX, 891, 1855 (village). **Rouinsac.**—Ibid., 886 (said in note to be Kaskaskia village). **Tchatchakigouas.**—La Salle (1679-81) in Margry, Déc., I, 481, 1877.

Kas-lanas (Q!ās lā'nas, 'pitch-town people'). A family of the Raven clan of the Haida. They inhabited the w. coast of Moresby id., Queen Charlotte group, Brit. Col., had no crests like the other Haida divisions, and were regarded as barbarous by the latter. Their principal town was in Tasoo harbor.—Swanton, Cont. Haida, 270, 1905.

Kaslukug. A former Aleut village on Agattu id., Alaska, one of the Near id. group of the Aleutians, now uninhabited.

Kasnatchin. A Knaiakhotana village at Anchor pt., Kenai penin., Alaska; pop. 29 in 1880.
Kasnatchin.—Baker, Geog. Dict. Alaska, 75, 1902. **Laida.**—Petroff in 10th Census, Alaska, 37, 1884. **Laidennoj.**—Baker, op. cit. (Russian name: 'icy').

Kaso (Kā'so). A former Chumashan village at Cañada del Diablo, Ventura co., Cal.—Henshaw, Buenaventura MS. vocab., B. A. E., 1884.

Kasoongkta. A tribe or band conquered by the Iroquois and settled among the Onondaga. — Clark, Onondaga, I, 305, 1849.

Kassiank. A Togiagamiut village on Togiak r., Alaska, having two dance houses; pop. 615 in 1880, 50 in 1890.
Kassiachamiut.—Eleventh Census, Alaska, 164, 1893. **Kassianmute.**—Petroff in 10th Census, Alaska, 17, 1884.

Kassigiakdjuak (Qassigiaqdjuaq). A winter settlement of Nugumiut Eskimo on Frobisher bay, S. E. Baffin land.—Boas in 6th Rep. B. A. E., map, 1888.

Kassovo (from Gashowu, pl. of Gashwusha.—Kroeber). A Yokuts tribe for-

merly living on Dry cr., Fresno co., Cal. Several families of survivors now live in Winchell gulch, near Pollasky.
Car-soos.—Johnston (1851) in Sen. Ex. Doc. 61, 32d Cong., 1st sess., 23, 1852. **Cas-sans.**—Barbour (1852) in Sen. Ex. Doc. 4, 32d Cong., spec. sess., 252, 1853. **Cas-soes.**—McKee et al. in Ind. Aff. Rep., 223, 1851. **Casson.**—Royce in 18th Rep. B. A. E., 782, 1899. **Cassoos.**—Johnston (1851) in Sen. Ex. Doc. 61, 32d Cong., 1st sess., 22, 1852. **Cosos.**—Taylor in Cal. Farmer, May 18, 1863 (same?). **Costrowers.**—Henley in Ind. Aff. Rep., 512, 1854. **Coswas.**—Lewis in Ind. Aff. Rep., 1857, 399, 1858. **Gashowu.**—A. L. Kroeber, inf'n, 1906 (correct form; pl. Gashwusha). **Gosh'-sho-o.**—Merriam in Science, XIX, 915, June 15, 1904. **Kash-ă-woosh-ah.**—Ibid., 916 (Wiksachi name). **Kas-so'-vo.**—Powers in Cont. N. A. Ethnol., III, 370, 1877. **Kosh-sho'-o.**—Merriam, op. cit.

Kasta (Q!ā'sta). A legendary Haida town on Copper bay, Moresby id., Queen Charlotte group, Brit. Col. It was named for the creek (Skidegate cr.), which ran near it, and was occupied by the Daiyuahllanas.—Swanton, Cont. Haida, 279, 1905.

Kastitchewanuk. A Cree band on Albany r. of Hudson bay in 1770.—Hutchins (1770) in Richardson, Arctic Exped., II, 37, 1851.

Kata (K'át'a, 'biters,' referring to the Arikara). A tribal division of the Kiowa; so called, not because of Arikara origin, but because they were more intimate with that tribe in trade and otherwise when the Kiowa lived in the N.—Mooney in 14th Rep. B. A. E., 1079, 1896.

Katagemane (Kä-ta'-ge-mă-ne, 'starving'). Given by Morgan (Anc. Soc., 171, 1877) as a division of the Piegan tribe of the Siksika, q. v.

Katagkak. An Ikogmiut Eskimo village on Innoko r., above its junction with the Yukon, Alaska.
Ighelkostlende.—Zagoskin in Nouv. Ann. Voy., 5th s., XXI, map, 1850. **Katagkag-mioute.**—Ibid.

Katagwadi (KАtagwA'dĭ). A Tlingit division formerly resident at Sitka, Alaska, but now almost extinct.　　(J. R. S.)

Katahuac. A former Chumashan village connected with Santa Inés mission, Santa Barbara co., Cal.—Taylor in Cal. Farmer, Oct. 18, 1861.

Katamoonchink ('hazelnut grove.'—Lewis). The Indian name of the site of Whiteland, Chester co., Pa., and perhaps also of a Delaware (?) village formerly near West Whiteland. Mentioned by Lewis (1824) in Day, Penn., 222, 1843.

Katana (K!ā'tana). A former Haida town on Louise id., Queen Charlotte group, Brit. Col., in possession of the Kagials-kegawai.—Swanton, Cont. Haida, 279, 1905.

Katchadi (people of Katch, a creek on Admiralty id.). A Tlingit division at Kake and Wrangell, Alaska. Some of them intermarried with the Athapascans on the upper Stikine.
Kaadg ett ee.—Schoolcraft, Ind. Tribes, V, 489, 1855 (after Kane; misprint). **Kaady-ett-ee.**—Kane, Wand. in N. A., app., 1859. **K'atc'a'dē.**—Boas, Fifth Rep. N. W. Tribes Can., 25, 1889. **Kätschadi.**—Krause, Tlinkit Ind., 120, 1885. **Qā'tcadĭ.**—Swanton, field notes, B. A. E., 1904.

Katchanaak (*QătcxA′na-ăk!*, 'Hip lake'). The native name for the Tlingit town now known as Wrangell, the winter town of the Stikine Indians of Alaska. It was so named because the mountain behind it resembles a human hip and the inner harbor is so shut in as to appear like a lake. Indian pop. 228 in 1890; total population (white and Indian) 868 in 1900. (J. R. S.)

Katearas. One of the principal villages of the Tuscarora in 1669, "a place of great Indian trade and commerce"; situated on a s. branch of Roanoke r., N. C.
Katearas.—Lederer (1672), Discov., 22, 1902. Kateras.—Ibid., map.

Katernuna (perhaps jargon 'Kater land'). A Talirpingmiut Eskimo village of the Okomiut tribe on Cumberland sd., Baffin land.—Howgate, Cruise of Florence, 84, 1879.

Kathio. A large village of the eastern Dakota, the Mdewakanton, Wahpekute, Sisseton, and Wahpeton, who were gathered about Mille Lac in the 17th and 18th centuries. Brower (Kathio, 33, 1901) locates the village at the outlet of Mille Lac, Minn., and thinks it was a Mdewakanton settlement. It was visited in 1659 by Radisson; in 1679 by Du Luth, who speaks of it as a great village; and by Hennepin in 1680. According to Warren (Hist. Ojibways, 160, 1885) it was destroyed by the Chippewa about 1750. See Du Luth in N. Y. Doc. Col. Hist., ix, 795, 1855.

Kathlaram. A body of Salish formerly under Fraser superintendency, British Columbia; now no longer officially reported.
Kathlaram.—Canadian Ind. Aff., 79, 1878. Kathlarem.—Ibid., 138, 1879.

Katimin. A Karok village in N. w. Cal., on the E. bank of Klamath r., a mile above the mouth of the Salmon, opposite Ishipishi. It was believed by the Karok to be the center of the world, contained a sacred house and sweat-house, and was the scene of the deer-skin dance and of an annual ceremony called "making the world." The village was burned by the whites in 1852.
Sche-woh.—Gibbs (1851) in Schoolcraft, Ind. Tribes, III, 151, 1853. Se-wah.—McKee (1851) in Sen. Ex. Doc. 4, 32d Cong., spec. sess., 164, 1853. Shegwuu.—A. L. Kroeber, inf'n, 1903 (Yurok name). Si-wahs.—McKee, op. cit., 211.

Katipiara. A Karok village of two houses on the s. bank of Klamath r., Cal., nearly opposite Orleans Bar; described by Gibbs in 1852. See *Tsana*.
Kah-tee-pee-rah.—Gibbs, MS. Miscel., B. A. E., 1852. Katipiara.—A. L. Kroeber, inf'n, 1904.

Katiru (*Ka-ti′-ru*). One of the 4 divisions of the main body of the Shasta, living in Klamath valley, from Seiad valley to Happy Camp, N. Cal. (R. B. D.)

Katkaayi ('island people', from an island at the mouth of Alsek r.). A Tlingit division at Sitka belonging to the Raven phratry.

Chrátka-âri.—Krause, Tlinket Ind., 118, 1885. Q!A′tkaayî—Swanton, field notes, B. A. E., 1904.

Katkwaahltu ('town on the point of a hill'). A Tlingit town about 6 m. above the mouth of Chilkat r., Alaska; pop. 125 in 1880.
Katkwaltú.—Krause, Tlinkit Ind., 100, 1885. Kutkwutlu.—Petroff in 10th Census, Alaska, 31, 1884. Qātq!wā′ạltū′.—Swanton, field notes, B. A. E., 1904.

Katlagulak (*KLă′gulaq*). A Chinookan tribe formerly living on the s. bank of Columbia r., in Columbia co., Oreg., 2 m. below Rainier.—Boas, Kathlamet Texts, 6, 1901.

Katlaminimin. A Chinookan tribe formerly occupying the s. end of Sauvies id., Multnomah co., Oreg. Their principal village was on the s. w. side of the island, in Willamette r. In 1806 Lewis and Clark estimated their number at 280 in 12 houses. In 1850 they were said by Lane to be associated with the Cathlacumup and Namoit.
Cathlaminimims.—Stuart in Nouv. Ann. Voy., x, 23, 1821. Cathlanamenamens.—Morse, Rep. to Sec. War, 368, 1822. Cathlanaminim.—Franchère, Narr., 135, 1854. Cathlanaminimins.—Stuart, op. cit., 115. Clam-nah-min-na-mun.—Lewis and Clark Exped., Coues ed., 913, note, 1893. Clanaminamums.—Lewis and Clark Exped., II, 212, 1814. Clanaminanums.—Ibid., II, 268, 1817. Clannahhminamun.—Ibid., II, 226, 1814. Clan-nar-min-a-mon's.—Clark (1806) in Orig. Jour. Lewis and Clark, IV, 220, 1905. Clannarminimuns.—Drake, Bk. Inds., vii, 1848. Clan-nar-minna-mon.—Clark (1806) in Orig. Jour. Lewis and Clark, IV, 216, 1905. Clannarminnamuns.—Lewis and Clark Exped., II, 473, 1814. Kathlaminimim.—Framboise quoted by Gairdner in Jour. Geog. Soc. Lond., XI, 255, 1841. Namanamin.—Lane in Sen. Ex. Doc. 52, 31st Cong., 1st sess., 172, 1850. Namananim.—Lane in Ind. Aff. Rep., 161, 1850.

Katlamoik. Said by Boas (Kathlamet Texts, 6, 1901) to be a Chinookan tribe formerly living at the site of the present town of Rainier, Columbia co., Oreg., but later (inf'n, 1904) given as the Chinook name of the locality of the modern Rainier, and of Rainier itself.
GaLiă′moix.—Boas, inf'n, 1904. KLă′mōix.—Boas, Kathlamet Texts, 6, 1901.

Katlany's Village. A summer camp of one of the Taku chiefs of the Tlingit named Qālā′nî; 106 people were there in 1880.—Petroff in 10th Census, Alaska, 32, 1884.

Katlian. The principal chief at Sitka, Alaska, at the time it was settled by the Russians under Baranoff. Also called Kotlian. The first fort established by Baranoff in 1799 was destroyed by the natives under Katlian's leadership, and they afterward entrenched themselves so strongly in a palisaded fort reinforced by stone that the Russians, returning 5 years later, had great difficulty in dislodging them. The name is that usually borne by the chief of the Kiksadi clan of the Tlingit. (J. R. S.)

Katluchtna ('lovers of glass beads'). A Knaiakhotana clan.—Richardson, Arct. Exped., I, 407, 1851.

Katmai. A Kaniagmiut Eskimo village on the s. E. coast of Alaska penin.; pop. 218 in 1880, 132 in 1890.—Petroff in 10th Census, Alaska, 28, 1884.

Kato. A Kuneste tribe or band formerly living in Cahto and Long valleys, Mendocino co., Cal. These were probably the people mentioned by McKee as occupying the second large valley of Eel r., numbering about 500 in 1851, and differing in language from the Pomo, a fact which has long been lost sight of. Powers divides them into Kai Pomo, Kastel Pomo, and Kato Pomo, and gives a Kulanapan vocabulary. They have recently been found to belong to the Athapascan stock, and closely related to the Wailaki, although they resemble the Pomo in culture.   (P. E. G.)
Batemdaikai.— Latham in Trans. Philol. Soc. Lond., 77, 1856. Batem-da-kai-ee.—Gibbs in Schoolcraft, Ind. Tribes, III, 434, 1853. Ba-tem-da-kaii.—Powell in Cont. N. A. Ethnol., III, 491, 1877. Batin-da-kia.—Ind. Aff. Rep., 240, 1851. Cabadilapo.—McKee (1851) in Sen. Ex. Doc. 4, 32d Cong., spec. sess., 148, 1853. Cahto Pomo.—Powers in Overland Mo., IX, 500, 1872. Kai Po-mo.—Powers in Cont. N. A. Ethnol., III, 148, 1877. Ká-to-Po-mo.—Ibid., 150. Ki-Pomas.—Ind. Aff. Rep. 1864, 119, 1865. Laleshiknom.—A. L. Kroeber, inf'n, 1903 (Yuki name). Tlokeang.—Kroeber, Coast Yuki MS., Univ. Cal. (own name).

Katomemetunne ('people by the deep water'). A former village of the Mishikhwutmetunne on Coquille r., Oreg.
Ka'-to-mĕ'-me ʒûn'nĕ.—Dorsey in Jour. Am. Folklore, III, 232, 1890.

Katsalgi (*kátsa* 'panther', *algi* 'people'). A Creek clan.
Kat'-chŭ.—Morgan, Anc. Soc., 161, 1877 ('Tiger'). Kátsalgi.—Gatschet, Creek Migr. Leg., I, 155, 1884.

Katsey. A Cowichan tribe occupying the villages of Seltsas and Shuwalethet, on Pitt lake and river emptying into the lower Fraser, Brit. Col.; pop. 79 in 1904.
Kaitze.—Brit. Adm. Chart, no. 1917. Katezie.—Can. Ind. Aff. for 1878, 79. Katsey.—Can. Ind. Rep. 1901, pt. 2, 158. K·ë'ėtsē.—Boas in Rep. 64th Meeting Brit. A. A. S., 454, 1894. Ke'tsī.—Hill-Tout in Ethnol. Surv. Can., 54, 1902.

Katshikotin. A part of the Hankutchin living on Yukon r., a short distance below Fortymile cr., near the Yukon-Alaska boundary.
Ka-tshik-otin.—Dawson in Rep. Geol. Surv. Can. for 1888, 202B, 1889. Klat-ol-klin.—Schwatka, Rep. on Alaska, 86, 1885 (name given by Russian half-breeds).

Katstayot (*Kat-sta'-yŏt*). A former Chumashan village between Pt Conception and Santa Barbara, Cal., at a locality now called Santa Anita.—Henshaw, Buenaventura MS. vocab., B. A. E., 1884.

Kattak. A former Kaniagmiut village on Afognak id., E. of Afognak, Alaska.
Katak.—Baker, Geog. Dict. Alaska, 1902. Kattagmiut.—Russ.-Am. map (1849) quoted by Baker, ibid. Kattagmjut.—Holmberg, Ethnog. Skizz., map, 1855.

Katzik. Two Indian settlements on the s. bank of lower Fraser r., below Sumass lake, Brit. Col. (Brit. Col. map, Ind. Aff., Victoria, 1872.) Perhaps the name refers to the Katsey tribe.

Katzimo (*Ka-tzi'-mo*). The Keresan name of a precipitous mesa rising 430 ft

above the basin of Acoma, and about 3 m. N. E. of the latter pueblo, in Valencia co., N. Mex. According to tradition its summit was the site of one of several prehistoric villages which the Acoma people successively occupied during their southwesterly movement from the mythic Shipapu in the indefinite N. The tradition relates that during a storm a part of the rock fell and some of the inhabitants, cut off from the valley beneath, perished. The site was henceforth abandoned, the survivors moving to another mesa on the summit of which they erected the present Acoma pueblo (q. v.). Katzimo mesa is inaccessible by ordinary means, but it was scaled in 1897 by a party representing the Bureau of American Ethnology and evidences of its former occupancy observed, thus verifying the native tradition. See Bandelier in Century Cyclop. of Names, 1894; Hodge (1) in Century Mag., LVI, 15, May, 1898, (2) in Am. Anthrop., Sept. 1897, and the references noted below.   (F. W. H.)
Enchanted Mesa.—Lummis, New Mexico David, 39, 1891. Katzim-a.—Bandelier in Arch. Inst. Pap., IV, 314, 1892. Mesa Encantada.—Pullen in Harper's Weekly, 594, Aug. 2, 1890. Rock of Katzimo.—Lummis, op. cit., 40.

Kau. The Corn clan of the Patki (Water House) phratry of the Hopi.
Ká-ah.—Bourke, Snake Dance, 117, 1884. Ka'i-e.—Stephen in 8th Rep. B. A. E., 39, 1891. Kaü wiñwû.—Fewkes in 19th Rep. B. A. E., 583, 1901 (*wiñwû* = 'clan'). Ka'-ü wüñ-wû.—Fewkes in Am. Anthrop,, VII, 402, 1894.

Kaudjukdjuak (*Qaudjuqdjuaq*). A winter settlement of the Akudnirmiut Eskimo between Frobisher bay and Cumberland sd., Baffin land.—Boas in 6th Rep. B. A. E., map, 1888.

Kaughii. A former Chumashan village at La Cañada del Corral, about 22 m. from Santa Barbara, Cal.
Ka-h·ö'.—Henshaw, Buenaventura MS. vocab., B. A. E., 1884. Kaughii.—Father Timeno (1856) quoted by Taylor in Cal. Farmer, May 4, 1860.

Kauhuk ('high place'). A former Alsea village on the s. side of Alsea r., Oreg.; noted by Lewis and Clark as containing 100 inhabitants in 1806, and as existing on the coast.
Kahuncle.—Lewis and Clark, Exped., II, 473, 1814. Kahunkle.—Ibid., II, 188, 1814. Ka-hun-kle's.—Orig. Jour. Lewis and Clark, VI, 117, 1905. Kau'-hük.—Dorsey in Jour. Am. Folk-lore, III, 230, 1890.

Kaukhwan. A former Alsea village on the N. side of Alsea r., Oreg., at Beaver cr.
Kau'-qwan.—Dorsey in Jour. Am. Folk-lore, III, 230, 1890.

Kauldaw. The Kitksan division and town lying farthest inland toward the headwaters of Skeena r., under the Babine and Skeena River agency, Brit. Col.; pop. 37 in 1904.
Culdoah.—Horetzky, Canada on Pac., 212, 1874. Gal-doe.—Can. Ind. Aff. Rep., 431, 1896. Gal Doe.—Ibid., 252, 1891. Gol-doe.—Ibid., 280, 1894. Kaldoe.—Ibid., 415, 1898. Kaul-daw.—Dorsey in Am. Antiq., XIX, 278, 1897. Kuldo.—Brit. Col. map, 1872. Kuldoe.—Can. Ind. Aff., pt. II, 160, 1901. Kuldōs.—Tolmie and Dawson, Vocabs. Brit. Col., 114B, 1884.

Kaumauangmiut (from the lake of the same name, around which they chiefly dwell). An Eskimo tribe in s. e. Baffin land, probably closely related to the Nugumiut.

Karmowong.—Hall, Arctic Researches, 294, 1865. Kaumanang.—Boas in Deutsche Geog. Blätt., viii, 32, 1885 (misprint). K'aumauangmiut.—Boas in Petermanns Mitt., no. 80, 70, 1885. Quaumauangmiut.—Boas in 6th Rep. B. A. E., 421, 1888.

Kaunaumeek. A former Stockbridge village in Rensselaer co. (?), N. Y., about halfway between Albany and Stockbridge, Mass., to which latter place the inhabitants removed in 1744.—Brainerd (ca. 1745) quoted by Ruttenber, Tribes Hudson R., 198, 1872.

Kautas. A Koyukukhotana village on Koyukuk r., Alaska, with 10 inhabitants in 1885.

Cawtaskákat.—Allen, Rep. on Alaska, 141, 1887.

Kauten (Kau'ten). A Squawmish village community on the right bank of Squawmisht r., Brit. Col.—Hill-Tout in Rep. Brit. A. A. S., 474, 1900.

Kauweh. An unidentified village on Klamath r., Cal., below its junction with the Trinity, and therefore in Yurok territory.—McKee (1851) in Schoolcraft, Ind. Tribes, iii, 138, 1853.

Kaveazruk. A Kaviagmiut village at Port Clarence, Alaska.—Eleventh Census, Alaska, 162, 1893.

Kaviagmiut. An Eskimo tribe occupying the s. part of Kaviak penin., Alaska, from Norton bay w. Many winter on the e. shore of Norton sd. Dall includes the Kinugumiut, whose lawless life and enterprise have been copied by the Kaviagmiut remaining in their old home. This was once a populous country, but the extermination of the arctic hare and the marmot, the disappearance of the reindeer, and the raids of the Kinugumiut have depopulated the peninsula and caused the inhabitants to migrate to other parts of arctic Alaska and become merged in other tribes. Local subdivisions of the existing Kaviagmiut, who numbered 427 in 1890, are as follows: Aziagmiut, of Sledge id.; Kaviazagmiut, at the head of Port Clarence; Kniktagemiut, of Golofnin bay, and Ukivogmiut, of King id. Their villages are Aiacheruk, Akpaliut, Anelo, Anlik, Atnuk, Ayak, Aziak, Chaik, Chainruk, Chinik, Chiukak, Iknetuk, Imoktegokshuk, Kachegaret, Kalulek, Kaveazruk, Kaviak, Kogluk, Kovogzruk, Metukatoak, Netsekawik, Niktak, Okinoyoktokawik, Opiktulik, Perebluk, Senikave, Shinnapago, Siningmon, Sinuk, Sitnazuak, Sunvalluk, Takchuk, Tubuktulik, Uinuk, Ukivak, Ukodliut, and Ukviktulik.

Anligmuts.—Holmberg quoted by Dall, Alaska, 408, 1870. Anlygmüten.—Wrangell, Ethnog. Nach., 122, 1839. Kavea.—Kelly, Arct. Eskimo, 9, 1890. Kaveaks.—Whymper, Trav. in Alaska, 143, 1868. Kaverong Mutes.—Kelly, Arct. Eskimo, chart, 1890. Kaviacks.—Raymond in Ind. Aff. Rep. 1869, 591,

1870. Kaviagmut.—Nelson in 18th Rep. B. A. E., map, 1899. Kaviágmuts.—Dall, Alaska, 408, 1870. Kaviagmyut.—Turner in 11th Rep. B. A. E., 178, 1894. Kaviaks.—Dall in Proc. Cal. Acad. Sci., iv, 35, 1869.

Kaviak. A Kaviagmiut village s. e. of Port Clarence, Alaska; pop. 200 in 1880.—Baker, Geog. Dict. Alaska, 1902.

Kaviazagmiut. A subdivision of the Kaviagmiut, q. v.

Kaviagamute.—Petroff, 10th Census, Alaska, map, 1884. Kaviazagamute.—Ibid., 11. Kāviāzā'gemut.—Dall in Cont. N. A. Ethnol., i, map, 1887.

Kavinish. A former Kawia village in Coahuila valley, Riverside co., Cal.

Ka-vi-nish.—Barrows, Ethno.-Bot. Coahuilla Ind., 34, 1900. Indian Wells.—Ibid.

Kawa (Káwa, 'eel spring'). A Modoc camp at Yaneks, on Sprague r., s. Oreg.

Kaúa.—Gatschet in Cont. N. A. Ethnol., ii, pt. 1, 31; pt. 2, 122, 1890. Káwa.—Ibid.

Kawaibatunya (Ka-wái-ba-tuñ-a). Given as the Watermelon clan of the Patki (Cloud) phratry of the Hopi.—Stephen in 8th Rep. B. A. E., 39, 1891.

Kawaiisu. The most westerly subdivision of the Ute-Chemehuevi linguistic division of the Shoshonean family. They occupy an isolated area on both sides of the Tehachapi mts., Cal., but particularly the w. side around Paiute mts., and the valleys of Walker basin and Caliente and Kelso crs. as far s. as Tehachapi.

Cobajais.—Garcés (1776), Diary, 489, 1900. Cobaji.—Ibid., 304, 445. Covaji.—Keane in Stanford, Compend., 510, 1878. Kah-wis'-sah.—Merriam in Science, xix, 916, June 15, 1904. Kawaiisu.—Kroeber, inf'n, 1905 (Yokuts name). Kâ-wi'-a-suh.—Powers in Cont. N. A. Ethnol., iii, 393, 1877 (Yokuts name). Kawishm.—Kroeber, inf'n, 1905 (Tubatulabal name). Kow-ā'-sah.—Merriam, op. cit. Kubakhye.—Kroeber, inf'n, 1905 (Mohave name). Newoo'-ah.—Merriam, op.cit.(='people'). Noches Colteches.—Garcés, op. cit., 295, 304 (so called by Mariposa people). Ta-hi-cha-pa-han-na.—Powers in Cont. N. A. Ethnol., iii, 393, 1877 (division around mtns. of same name). Ta-hichp'.—Ibid. (so called by Kern r. people).

Kawaika. A ruined pueblo, attributed by the Hopi to the Kawaika people, a name also applied by them to the pueblo of Laguna, N. Mex., and by the Lagunas themselves to designate their village; situated a short distance w. of the Keam's Canyon road, on the top of a mesa between two gorges tributary to Jeditoh valley, in the Hopi country, n. e. Arizona. The ruin was surveyed and first described by V. Mindeleff in 1885, under the name Mishiptonga, apparently through confusion with Nesheptanga, another ruin near by. The ruin has been largely rifled of its art remains by Navaho diggers and the results mostly lost to science, but systematic excavation was conducted in the undisturbed portion by the National Museum in 1901. See Mindeleff in 8th Rep. B. A. E., 52, pl. 9, 1891; Mooney in Am. Anthrop., July, 1893; Fewkes in 17th Rep. B. A. E., 590, 622, 1898; Hough in Rep. Nat. Mus. 1901, 339, 1903.

Kawaíka.—Mooney, op. cit. Kawaiokuh.—Hough op. cit. Mishiptonga.—Mindeleff, op. cit.

Kawaiki (Hitchiti: *oki* 'water', *awäiki* 'hauling', 'carrying' [place]: 'water-carrying place'). A former Lower Creek town at the junction of the present Cowikee cr. and Chattahoochee r., in the N. E. corner of Barbour co., Ala. It had 45 heads of families in 1833. (A. S. G.)

Cow ye ka.—Census of 1833 in Schoolcraft, Ind. Tribes, IV, 578, 1854. **Kawäiki.**—Gatschet, Creek Migr. Leg., I, 134, 1884.

Kawanunyi (*Kâwanûñyî*, from *kâwănă* 'duck', *yi* locative: 'duck place'). A former Cherokee settlement about the present Ducktown, Polk co., S. E. Tennessee. (J. M.)

Cowanneh.—Royce in 5th Rep. B. A. E., map, 1887. Duck-town.—Doc. of 1799 quoted by Royce, ibid., 144.

Kawarakish (*Ka-wa-ra'-kish*). One of the two divisions of the Pitahauerat, or Tapaje Pawnee, the other being the Pitahauerat proper.—Grinnell, Pawnee Hero Stories, 241, 1889.

Kawas (*K!ä'was*, 'fish eggs'). A subdivision of the Stustas, an important family of the Eagle clan of the Haida. One of their chiefs is said to have been blown across to the Stikine country, where he became a chief among the Stikine. (J. R. S.)

K'ā'was.—Boas, 12th Rep. N. W. Tribes Canada, 22, 1898. K!ä'was.—Swanton, Cont., Haida, 275, 1905. Kouas.—Harrison in Proc. and Trans. Roy. Soc. Can., sec. II, 125, 1895.

Kawchodinne (*ka* 'hare', *cho* 'great', *dinne* 'people': 'people of the great hares'). An Athapascan tribe dwelling N. of Great Bear lake, Mackenzie Ter., Canada, on Mackenzie r., the lakes E. of it, and Anderson r. Mackenzie (Voy., I, 206, 1802) said they were a small tribe residing on Peace r., who spoke the language of the Chipewyan and derived their name from the Arctic hare, their chief means of support. At another time (Mass. Hist. Coll., II, 43, 1814) he placed them on Porcupine r., Alaska. Franklin (Journ. to Polar Sea, 261, 1824) placed them immediately N. of the Thlingchadinne on the N. side of the outlet of Bear lake. Back (Journal, 497, 1833–35) located them on Mackenzie r. as far N. as 68°. Richardson (Arct. Exped., II, 3, 1851) gave their habitat as the banks of Mackenzie r. from Slave lake downward. Hind (Lab. Penin., II, 261, 1863) said they resorted to Ft Norman and Ft Good Hope on the Mackenzie, and also to Ft Yukon, Alaska. Ross (MS., B. A. E.) said they resided in 1859 in the country surrounding Ft Good Hope on Mackenzie r., extending beyond the Arctic circle, where they came in contact with the Kutchin, with whom by intermarriage they have formed the tribe of Bastard Loucheux (Nellagottine). Petitot (Dict. Dènè-Dindjié, xx, 1876) said the Kawchodinne lived on the lower Mackenzie from Ft Norman to the Arctic ocean. They are described as a thickset people, who subsist partly on fish and reindeer, but obtain their clothing and most of their food from the hares that abound in their country. Their language differs little from that of the Etchareottine, while their style of dress and their customs are the same, although through long intercourse with the traders, for whom they have great respect, most of the old customs and beliefs of the tribe have become extinct. They are on friendly terms with the Eskimo. The Kawchodinne have a legend of the formation of the earth by the muskrat and the beaver. The dead are deposited in a rude cage built above ground, the body being wrapped in a blanket or a moose skin; the property of relatives is destroyed, and their hair is cut as a sign of mourning. When the supply of hares becomes exhausted, as it frequently does, they believe these mount to the sky by means of the trees and return in the same way when they reappear. Polygamy is now rare. They are a peaceable tribe, contrasting with their Kutchin neighbors. In personal combat they grasp each other by their hair, which they twist round and round until one of the contestants falls to the ground. They are not so numerous as formerly, a great many having died from starvation in 1841, at which time numerous acts of cannibalism are said to have occurred. In 1858 Ross (MS., B. A. E.) gave the population as 467; 291 males, 176 females. Of these 103 resorted to Ft Norman and 364 to Ft Good Hope. Petitot (Dict. Dènè-Dindjié, xx, 1876) arranged them in five subdivisions: Nigottine, Katagottine, Katchogottine, Satchotugottine, and Nellagottine. In another list (Bull. Soc. Géog. Paris, 1875) instead of Nigottine he has Etatchogottine and Chintagottine. In a later grouping (Autour du lac des Esclaves, 362, 1891) Petitot identifies Katagottine with Chintagottine, suppresses Satchotugottine, and adds Kfwetragottine.

Dènè.—Petitot, Hare MS. vocab., B. A. E., 1869. Dènè Peaux-de-Lièvre.—Petitot, Autour du lac des Esclaves, 289, 1891. Harefoot Indians.—Chappell, Hudson Bay, 166, 1817. Hare Indians.—Mackenzie, Voy., I, 206, 1802. Hareskins.—Petitot in Jour. Roy. Geog. Soc., 650, 1883. Kā-cho-'dtinnè.—Richardson, Arct. Exped., II, 3, 1851. Kah-cho tinne.—Ross quoted by Gibbs, MS., B. A. E. ('Arctic hare people'). Kan:ho.—Gallatin in Trans. Am. Antiq. Soc., II, 19, 1836. Kat'a-gottiné.—Petitot, MS. vocab., B. A. E., 1867. K'a-t'a-gottiné.—Petitot, Dict. Dènè-Dindjié, xx, 1876 ('people among the hares'). Kawchodinneh.—Franklin, Journ. to Polar Sea, 261, 1824. Kha-t'a-ottinè.—Petitot in Bull. Soc. Géog. Paris, chart, 1875. Khatρa-Gottine.—Petitot, Autour du lac des Esclaves, 362, 1891 ('people among the rabbits'). Kkρayttchare ottiné.—Petitot, Hare MS. vocab., B. A. E., 1869 (Chipewyan name). Nouga.—Macfarlane (1857) in Hind, Lab. Penin., II, 258, 1863 ('spittle': Eskimo name). Peau de Lièvre.—Petitot in Bull. Soc. Géog. Paris, chart, 1875. Peaux-de-Lièvres.—Petitot, Autour du lac des Esclaves, 362, 1891. Rabbitskins.—McLean, Hudson Bay, II, 243, 1849. Slave.—Richardson, Arct. Exped., I, 242, 1851. Tä-nä-tin-ne.—Morgan, Consang. and Affin., 289, 1871.

Kawchogottine ('dwellers among the large hares'). A division of the Kawchodinne. Petitot, in 1867 (MS., B. A. E.), located them on the border of the wooded region N. E. of Ft Good Hope, and in 1875 (Bull. Soc. de Géog. Paris, chart, 1875) on the headwaters of Anderson r., N. of Great Bear lake. The same authority (Autour du lac des Esclaves, 362, 1891) says their habitat is on the large lakes of the interior E. of Mackenzie r.

K'a-tchô-gottiné.—Petitot, Dict. Dènè-Dindjié, xx, 1876. Katchô-Ottiné.—Petitot in Can. Rec. Sci., I, 49, 1884. Kha-tchô-gottinè.—Petitot in Bul. Soc. de Géog. Paris, chart, 1875. Natlé-tρa-Gottine.—Petitot, Autour du lac des Esclaves, 362, 1891 (='people among the little reindeer').

Kawia. The name, of uncertain derivation, of a Shoshonean division in s. California, affiliated linguistically with the Aguas Calientes, Juaneños, and Luiseños. They inhabit the N. tongue of the Colorado desert from Banning s. E. at least as far as Salton, as also the headwaters of Santa Margarita r., where the Kawia res. is situated. Formerly they are said to have extended into San Bernardino valley, but it seems more likely that this

KAWIA MAN

was occupied, as at present, by the Serranos. They are not to be confounded with a Yokuts tribe bearing the same name. They were first visited in 1776 by Fray Francisco Garcés, who referred to them under their Mohave name, "Jecuich," obtained from his guide. At this time they lived about the N. slopes of the San Jacinto mts. and to the northward, and roamed E. to the Colorado, but their

principal seat was about San Gorgonio pass. Burton (H. R. Ex. Doc. 76, 34th Cong., 3d sess., 115, 1857) gave 3,500 as the number of men alone in 1856, evidently an exaggeration. There were 793 Indians assembled under the name "Coahuila" at all the Mission reservations in 1885, while the Indians on Cahuilla res. under the Mission Tule r. agency in 1894 numbered 151, and in 1902, 159. This reser-

KAWIA WOMAN

vation consists of 18,240 acres of unpatented land. Villages: Duasno, Juan Bautista, Kavinish, Kawia, Kwaleki, Lawilvan, Malki, Pachawal, Palseta, Paltewat, Panachsa, San Sebastian, Sechi, Sokut Menyil, Temalwahish, Torres, Tova, and Wewutnowhu.

Caguillas.—Duflot de Mofras, I, 349, 1844. Cagullas.—Duflot de Mofras misquoted by Latham in Proc. Philol. Soc. Lond., VI, 76, 1854. Cahnilla.—Tolmie and Dawson, Comp. Vocabs., 128, 1884. Cahnillo.—Ibid., 129. Cahuilla.—Ind. Aff. Rep., 175, 1902 (applied to res.). Cahuillos.—Ludwig, Abor. Lang., 26, 1816. Cah-wée-os.—Whipple, Exped. from San Diego, 17, 1851. Cah-wilias.—Heintzelman (1853) in H. R. Ex. Doc. 76, 34th Cong., 3d sess., 44, 1857. Carvillas.—Burton, ibid., 114. Cavīos.—Gatschet in Rep. Chief Engrs., pt. 3, 553, 1876. Cawéos.—Ibid. Coahuilas.—Stanley in Ind. Aff. Rep. 1869, 194, 1870. Coguifa.—Garcés (1775–76), Diary, 289, 1900 (identical?). Cohuillas.—Stanley in Ind. Aff. Rep., 119, 1865. Cohuilles.—Greene in Ind. Aff. Rep., 93, 1870. Cowela.—Henley in Ind. Aff. Rep. 1856, 243, 1857. Cowillas.—Beale in Sen. Ex. Doc. 4, 32d Cong., spec. sess., 378, 1853. Dancers.—Coues, Garcés Diary, 42, 1900. Danzarines.—Ibid., 204, 423. Gecuiches.—Ibid., 423. Hakwiche.—Kroeber, inf'n, 1905 (Mohave name). Jecuches.—Coues, Garcés Diary, index, 1900. Jecuéche.—Garcés (1776), Diary, 444, 1900. Jecuich.—Ibid., 451. Jequiches.—Ibid. Kahuilla.—Kingsley, Stand. Nat. Hist., pt. 6, 189, 1883. Kahweaks.—Sen. Misc. Doc. 53, 45th Cong., 3d sess., 70, 1879. Kah-we-as.—Wozencraft in Ex. Doc. 4, 32d Cong., spec. sess., 289, 1853. Kahweyahs.—

Schumacher in Rep. Peabody Mus., XII, 521, 1880. **Kauvuyas.**—Loew in Rep. Chief Engrs., pt. 3, 542, 1876. **Kau-yai'-chits.**—Powell in Ind. Aff. Rep. 1873, 51, 1874. **Kavayos.**—Gatschet in Rep. Chief Engrs., pt. 3, 553, 1876. **Kavwaru-maup.**—Ingalls (1872) in H. R. Ex. Doc. 66, 42d Cong., 3d sess., 2, 1873. **Koahualla.**—Ind. Aff. Rep. 1877, 246, 1878. **Tecuiche.**—Cortez (1799) in Pac. R. R. Rep., III, pt. 3, 125, 1856 (misquoting Garcés).

Kawia. A Yokuts tribe formerly living on the edge of the plains on the N. side of Kaweah r., Cal., but now extinct. They were hostile to the American settlers. By agreement of May 13, 1851 (which was not confirmed), a reserve was set aside for this and other tribes between Kaweah and Chowchilla rs., Cal., which at the same time ceded their unreserved lands. This tribe is to be distinguished from the Kawia (Coahuila, Cahuillo, etc.), a Shoshonean tribe in Riverside co., Cal.
Cah-was.—Johnston (1851) in Sen. Ex. Doc. 61, 32d Cong., 1st. sess., 23, 1852. **Cahwia.**—Barbour in Ind. Aff. Rep., 232, 1851. **Cah-wi-ah.**—Wessells (1853) in H. R. Ex. Doc. 76, 34th Cong., 3d sess., 32, 1857. **Cowhuillas.**—Taylor in Cal. Farmer, June 8, 1860. **Cowiahs.**—Henley in Ind. Aff. Rep., 511, 1854. **Cow-illers.**—Lewis, ibid., 400, 1858. **Cowwillas.**—Dole, ibid., 219, 1861. **Gawia.**—A. L. Kroeber, inf'n, 1906 (the more strictly correct form). **Kahweahs.**—Bancroft, Nat. Races, I, 456, 1874. **Kauia.**—Powers in Cont. N. A. Ethnol., III, 370, 1877. **Kawia.**—Ind. Aff. Rep. 1903, 508, 1904. **Keawahs.**—Maltby in Ind. Aff. Rep., 381, 1872. **Keweah.**—Ind. Aff. Rep., 284, 1884.

Kawia. A Kawia village on Cahuilla res., near the headwaters of Santa Margarita r., s. Cal.
Cahuilla.—Ind. Aff. Rep. 1902, 175, 1903.

Kawírasanachi ('white hill'). A Tarahumare rancheria in Chihuahua, Mexico.—Lumholtz, inf'n, 1894.

Kawita. The name of two former Lower Creek towns on Chattahoochee r., in Russell co., Ala. They were situated 2½ m. apart and were commonly distinguished as Upper Kawita and Kawita Talahasi ('Kawita old town'), in various forms of spelling. The former was situated on the w. bank of the river, 3 m. below its falls, the latter ½ m. from the stream. Kawita Talahasi, or Old Kawita, was the "public establishment" of the Lower Creeks and the headquarters of the agent. In 1799 it could muster 66 warriors, and about the year 1833 the town contained 289 families. It was an offshoot from Kasihta, and in turn gave origin to Wetumpka, on Big Uchee cr. From the fact that Kawita was regarded as the assembly place and treaty capital of the Lower Creeks, the name was frequently used synonymously with Lower Creeks; as Kusa, the name of the capital of the Upper Creeks, was sometimes used to designate that portion of the tribe. In 1775 Bartram (Trav., 387, 1792) spoke of Kawita Talahasi as "the bloody town, where the micos, chiefs, and warriors assemble when a general war is proposed; and here captives and state malefactors are put to death." (A. S. G.)
Akowetako.—Squier in Beach, Ind. Miscel., 34, 1877 (traditional name, fide the Walam-Olum).

Ani'-Kawi'tă.—Mooney in 19th Rep. B. A. E., 508, 1900 (Cherokee name of Lower Creeks, from their former principal town on Chattahoochee r.). **Cabetas.**—Barcia, Ensayo, 313, 1723. **Cabuitta.**—Jefferys, Am. Atlas, 5, 1776. **Cacouïtas.**—Baudry des Lozières, Voy. à la Le., 242, 1802. **Cahouita.**—Penière in Morse, Rep. to Sec. War, 311, 1822. **Cahouitas.**—La Harpe (1703) in French, Hist. Coll. La., III, 29, 1851. **Cahuita.**—Jefferys, Fr. Dom., 134, map, 1761. **Canitas.**—Smith (1785) in Schoolcraft, Ind. Tribes, III, 557, 1853. **Caoitas.**—Charlevoix, New France, Shea's ed., VI, 147, 1866. **Caonetas.**—Boudinot, Star in the West, 126, 1816. **Caonites.**—Ibid. **Caouikas.**—Smith, Bouquet's Exped., 70, 1766. **Caouitas.**—Du Pratz, La., II, 208, 1758. **Caveta.**—Barcia, Ensayo, 287, 1723. **Cawidas.**—N. Y. Doc. Col. Hist. (1753), VI, 797, 1855. **Cawittas.**—Romans, Florida, 90, 1775. **Cawittaws.**—Carroll, Hist. Coll. S. C., I, 190, 1836. **Cohuntas.**—Martin, Hist. La., I, 161, 1827. **Coneta.**—Morse, N. Am., 218, 1776 (misprint). **Conetta.**—Jefferys, Am. Atlas, 5, 1776 (town on headwaters of Ocmulgee r.). **Conetuhs.**—Hawkins (1799), Sketch, 19, 1848. **Couetta.**—Jefferys, Am. Atlas, 5, 1776. **Couitias.**—Brinton, Florida Pen., 144, 1859. **Couueta.**—Alcedo, Dic. Geog., I, 676, 1876. **Coweeta.**—Drake, Bk. Inds., bk. IV, 29, 1848. **Coweitas.**—Güssefeld, map U. S., 1784. **Coweta.**—Bartram, Travels, 387, 1792. **Cowetah.**—Gallatin in Trans. Am. Antiq. Soc., II, 95, 1836. **Cow-e-tah Tallahassee.**—Royce in 18th Rep. B. A. E., Ga. map, 1899. **Cowetas.**—Lincoln (1789) in Am. State Pap., Ind. Aff., I, 78, 1832. **Cowetau.**—U. S. Ind. Treat. (1814), 162, 1837. **Cowetaw.**—Drake, Bk. Inds., bk. IV, 51, 1848. **Cowettas.**—Romans, Florida, I, 280, 1775. **Cow-e-tugh.**—Hawkins (1799), Sketch, 52, 1848. **Cow-e-tuh.**—Ibid., 25, 55. **Cow-e-tuh Tal-lau-has-see.**—Ibid., 55. **Grand Coweta.**—Robin, Voy., I, map, 1807. **Kaioutais.**—Lozières, Voy. à la Le., 242, 1802. **Kaouitas.**—Gayarré, Hist. La., II, 40, 1852. **Kaoutyas.**—McKenney and Hall, Ind. Tribes, III, 79, 1854. **Kawíta Talahássi.**—Gatschet, Creek Migr. Leg., I, 135, 1884. **Kawuytas.**—Bossu (1759), Travels, I, 229, 1771. **Kawytas.**—Ibid., 271. **Kow-he'-tah.**—Adair, Am. Ind., 257, 1775. **Lahouita.**—Morse, Rep. to Sec. War, 149, 1822. **Powebas.**—Lattré, Carte des Etats-Unis, 1784. **Pt. Coweta.**—Robin, Voy., I, map, 1807. **Upper Cowetas town.**—Seagrove (1793) in Am. State Pap., Ind. Aff., I, 427, 1832.

Kawita. A town of the Creek Nation on the N. side of Arkansas r., Okla.
Coweta.—U. S. P. O. Guide, 367, 1904. **Kawíta.**—Gatschet, Creek Migr. Leg., II, 185, 1888.

Kawoltukwucha (*Káwoltŭk' wŭtca*, 'hill below'). A Pima village w. of the Maricopa and Phœnix R. R., in Maricopa co., Ariz.—Russell, Pima MS., B. A. E., 18, 1902.
Káwerkewötche.—ten Kate quoted by Gatschet, MS., B. A. E., XX, 199, 1888.

Kayak. See *Kaiak.*

Kayashkidetan ('people of the house with a high foundation'). A Tlingit division at Wrangell, Alaska, belonging to the Wolf phratry and closely connected with the Nanyaayi and Hokedi.
Harā'c hit tan.—Boas, 5th Rep. N. W. Tribes Can., 25, 1889. **Kā-rasch-kídetan.**—Krause, Tlinkit Ind., 120, 1885. **Kayā'ckidêtān.**—Swanton, field notes, B. A. E., 1904.

Kayehkwarageh (*Kāie'kwărā'ge'*). A traditional Iroquois village belonging to the Two-clans of the Turtle; locality unknown. (J. N. B. H.)
Kah he kwa ke.—Hale, Iroq. Book of Rites, 119, 1883. **Kayyhekwarakeh.**—Ibid, 118.

Kayepu. A prehistoric ruined pueblo of the compact, communal type, situated about 5 m. s. of Galisteo, Santa Fé co., N. Mex. The Tanos now living with the Queres of Santo Domingo claim that it was a village of their tribe.

Ka-ye Pu.—Bandelier in Arch. Inst. Papers, IV, 106, 1892 (native name). **Pueble Blanco.**—Bandelier in Ritch, N. Mex., 201, 1885 (misprint). **Pueblo Blanco.**—Ibid. (Span.: 'white house').

Kaygen. A Seneca village on the s. bank of Chemung r., below Kanestio r., N. Y.—Pouchot, map (1758) in N. Y. Doc. Col. Hist., x, 694, 1858.

Kaynaguntl ('people at the mouth of the canyon'). An Apache clan or band at San Carlos agency and Ft Apache, Ariz., in 1881.—Bourke in Jour. Am. Folk-lore, III, 111, 1890.

Kayomasho. The progressive party in Laguna pueblo, N. Mex. (Loew in Wheeler Survey Rep., VII, 339, 1879). According to Bandelier this party constitutes a phratry. See *Kapaits*.

Kayung (*Q!ayā'ñ*). A Haida town on Masset inlet, Queen Charlotte ids., Brit. Col., just above Masset. It was occupied by the Kuna-lanas, who owned the place, and the Sagui-gitunai. John Work does not give separate figures for the population of this town in 1836–41, but the old people estimate the number of houses at 14, which would indicate about 175 people. The place was at one time entirely abandoned, but two or three families have recently returned to it.

(J. R. S.)

K·'āya'ng.—Boas, 12th Rep. N. W. Tribes Can., 23, 1898. **Kayung.**—Dawson, Queen Charlotte Ids., 163B, 1880. **Q!ayā'ñ Inagā'-i.**—Swanton, Cont. Haida, 281, 1905 (the people).

Kchegagonggo (*K'chi-gä-gong'-go*, 'pigeon-hawk'). A gens of the Abnaki (q. v.).—Morgan, Anc. Soc., 174, 1877.

Kdhun ('thunder being'). The 7th Tsichu gens of the Osage tribe.

Ḵǫaⁿ.—Dorsey, Osage MS. vocab., B. A. E., 1883. **Ḵǫuⁿ.**—Dorsey in 15th Rep. B. A. E., 234, 1897. **Ma'xe.**—Ibid. ('upper-world people'). **Niʠ'ka wakan'ʠaxǐ.**—Ibid. ('mysterious male being'). **Thunder People.**—Dorsey in Am. Nat., 114, 1884. **Tsi'haciⁿ.**—Dorsey in 15th Rep., op cit. ('camp last').

Ke. The Bear clan of the Tewa pueblo of Nambe, N. Mex., and of Hano, Ariz.

Cac.—Stephen in 8th Rep. B. A. E., 39, 1891 (Navaho name). **Ho'-nau.**—Ibid. (Hopi name). **Ke.**—Ibid. (Tewa name). **Ke-tdóa.**—Hodge in Am. Anthrop., IX, 349, 1896 (Nambe form; *tdóa*='people'). **Ke'-to-wa.**—Fewkes in Am. Anthrop., VII, 166, 1894.

Kechayi. A division of the Yokuts, formerly living on San Joaquin r., Cal.

Kechayi.—A. L. Kroeber, inf'n, 1906. **Kech-eel.**—Ind. Aff. Rep., 223, 1851 (same?).

Kechemeches. A division of the New Jersey Delawares mentioned by Evelin (Proud, Pa., I, 113, 1797; Smith, Hist. N. J., 29, 1765, rep. 1890) as living in 1648 in the s. part of the state, at the mouth of Delaware r., and numbering 50 men. Some old authorities locate here the Naraticon.

Kechemudluk. A Kevalingamiut village at C. Seppings on the Arctic coast of Alaska; pop. 50 in 1880.

Cape Sepping.—Petroff, Rep. on Alaska, 59, 1900. **Cape Seppings.**—Nelson in 18th Rep. B. A. E., map, 1899. **Kechemudluk.**—Hydrog. chart cited by Baker, Geog. Dict. Alaska, 115, 1902. **Kivalinge.**—Eleventh Census, Alaska, 162, 1893.

Kechepukwaiwah. A former Chippewa village on a lake of the same name, near Chippewa r., Wis.—Warren (1852) in Minn. Hist. Soc. Coll., v, 314, 1885.

Kechipauan ('town of the spread-out grit'; evidently referring to the sandstone mesa). A former pueblo of the Zuñi on a mesa E. of Ojo Caliente, or Kyapkwaina-kwin, 15 m. s. w. of Zuñi pueblo, N. Mex. According to Cushing it was called also Kyanawe, which Bandelier identifies with the Canabi of Oñate in 1598, and therefore regards it as one of the Seven Cities of Cibola of Marcos de Niza and Coronado in 1539–42. Spanish Franciscans evidently began the establishment of a mission at this pueblo, probably in 1629, when the first missionaries resided among the Zuñi, but judging from the character of the church building, the walls of which are still standing, it was never finished. See Mindeleff in 8th Rep. B. A. E., 81, 1891, and authorities cited below. (F. W. H.)

Cánabe.—Cushing in Compte-rendu Internat. Cong. Am., VII, 156, 1890 (misprint of early Spanish form). **Canabi.**—Oñate (1598) in Doc. Inéd., XVI, 133, 1871. **Chan-a-hue.**—Bandelier in Arch. Inst. Papers, III, 133, 1890.—Ibid., v, 171, 1891; IV, 338, 1892. **Chyanaue.**—Ibid., III, 133, note, 1890. **Chek-e-pā-wha.**—Fewkes in Jour. Am. Eth. and Arch., I, 101, 1891. **Ké·tchi-na.**—Cushing in Millstone, IX, 55, Apr. 1884. **Ketchip-a-huan.**—Bandelier in 10th Rep. Arch. Inst. Am., 107, 1889. **Ketchip-a-uan.**—Bandelier in Arch. Inst. Papers, III, 133, 1890; IV, 329, 1892; v, 171, 1891 (recorded as distinct from Kyanawe). **Kia'anaän.**—ten Kate, Reizen in N. A., 291, 1885. **Kiá-na-wa.**—Cushing in Millstone, IX, 55, Apr. 1884. **K'yá-na-we.**—Cushing in Compte-rendu Internat. Cong. Am., VII, 156, 1890. **Village of Odd Waters.**—Cushing, Zuñi Folk-tales, 104, 1901 (possibly identical).

Kecoughtan. A small tribe of the Powhatan confederacy residing in 1607 at the mouth of James r., in what is now Elizabeth City co., Va. According to Capt. John Smith their fighting men did not exceed 20.—Smith (1629), Hist. Va., I, 116, map, repr. 1819.

Keda-lanas (*Q!ē'da lā'nas*, 'strait people'). A subdivision of the Hagi-lanas, a family of Ninstints belonging to the Raven clan of the Haida. They received their name from a narrow strait in front of the town.—Swanton, Cont. Haida, 268, 1905.

Kedlamik (*Qê'ᴛamix*, 'broad patch of bushes'). An Okinagan village near Nicola lake, Brit. Col.

Lkaᴛamix.—Teit in Mem. Am. Mus. Nat. Hist., II, 174, 1900. **Qê'ᴛamix.**—Ibid.

Keeches. Mentioned by Barbour (Sen. Ex. Doc. 4, 32d Cong., spec. sess., 61, 1853) as a hostile tribe living N. and E. of San Joaquin r., among the foot-hills of the Sierra Nevada, on the headwaters of the Tuolumne, Merced, and Mariposa rs., Cal., in 1851. It was probably of Moquelumnan stock.

Kegi. The House clan of the Tewa of Hano pueblo, N. E. Ariz.

Ke'gi.—Stephen in 8th Rep. B. A. E., 39, 1891. **Ki-a'-ni.**—Ibid. (Navaho name). **Ki'-hu.**—Ibid. (Hopi name).

Kegiktowrigemiut (*Kĕgiktowrig'emūt*). A subdivision of the Unaligmiut Eskimo whose chief village is Kiktaguk.—Dall in Cont. N. A. Ethnol., I, 17, 1877.

Keguayo. A pueblo built, occupied, and abandoned by the Nambe tribe prior to the Spanish advent in the 16th century. Situated in the vicinity of the Chupaderos, a cluster of springs in a mountain gorge, about 4 m. E. of Nambe pueblo, N. N. Mex.—Bandelier in Arch. Inst. Papers, IV, 84, 1892.

Kehsidatsoos (*Keh-sid-ats-oos*). A former summer village of the Makah of Washington.—Gibbs, MS. 248, B. A. E.

Kein ('turtle carriers,' because they have the ceremonies connected with the turtle.—Fletcher). A subgens of the Dhatada gens of the Omaha.
Kaetage.—Balbi, Atlas Ethnog., 56, 1826. Ka-e-ta-je.—Long, Exped. Rocky Mts., I, 327, 1823 ('those who do not touch turtles'). Kä'-ih.—Morgan, Anc. Soc., 155, 1877. ꞯe'iⁿ.—Dorsey in 15th Rep. B. A. E., 226, 1897.

Keinouche (*Kĭnōzhäⁿ*, 'pickerel'). One of the divisions or chief bands of the Ottawa, q. v. The Jesuit Relation of 1640 locates them at that time, under the name Kinounchepirini, s. of the Isle of the Algonquins (Allumette id.) in Ottawa r. This would place them, if taken literally, some distance E. of L. Huron; but as the knowledge then possessed by the French was very imperfect, it is probable that the Relation of 1643, which places them on L. Huron, is more nearly correct. In 1658 they appear to have lived along the N. shore of the lake. Between 1660–70 they, with the Kiskakon and Sinago, were attached to the mission at Shaugawaumikong (now Bayfield), on the s. shore of L. Superior. It is probable, however, that at the time of Father Menard's visit, in 1660, they were at Keweenaw bay, Mich. In 1670–71 they returned to Mackinaw, some passing on to Manitoulin id.; but it is probable that the latter, or a part of them, were included in the Sable band, q. v.   (J. M.   C. T.)
Keinouché.—Jes. Rel. 1670, 87, 1858. Kinonchepiirinik.—Ibid., 1658, 22, 1858. Kinonchepirinik.—Ibid., 1643, 61, 1858. Kinouché.—Marquette (1670) quoted by Shea, Miss. Val., xlix, 1852. Kinouchebiiriniouek.—Jes. Rel. 1646, 34, 1858. Kinounchepirini.—Ibid., 1640, 34, 1858. Quenongebin.—Champlain (1613), Œuvres, III, 298, 1870.

Kekayeken (*Kˑĕkˑä'yĕkˑⁿ*). A Songish division residing between Esquimalt and Beecher bay, s. end of Vancouver id.—Boas in 6th Rep. N. W. Tribes Can., 17, 1890.

Kekelun (*Kˑĕ'kⁿ*). A Squawmish village community on the w. side of Howe sd., Brit. Col.—Hill-Tout in Rep. Brit. A. A. S., 474, 1900.

Kekertakdjuin (*Qeqertaqdjuin*, 'big island'). A spring settlement of Padlimiut Eskimo at the end of Howe bay, Baffin land.—Boas in 6th Rep. B. A. E., map, 1888.

Kekertarsuarak. An Eskimo village on an islet off the s. w. coast of Greenland, lat. 60° 50'.—Meddelelser om Grönland, XVI, map, 1896.

Kekertaujang (*Qeqertaujang*, 'like an island'). A winter village of the Saumingmiut, a subtribe of the Okomiut Eskimo, on Cumberland penin., Baffin land.—Boas in 6th Rep. B. A. E., map, 1888.

Kekerten ('islands'). The winter village of the Kingnaitmiut Eskimo on the E. side of Cumberland id., Baffin land; pop. 82 in 1883.
K'exerten.—Boas in Petermanns Mitt., no. 80, 70, 1885. Kikkerton.—Kumlien in Bull. U. S. Nat. Mus., no. 15, 15, 1879. Qeqerten.—Boas in 6th Rep. B. A. E., 425, 1888.

Kekertukjuak (*Qeqertuqdjuaq*, 'big island'). A spring settlement of Nugumiut Eskimo on an island in Frobisher bay, s. E. Baffin land.—Boas in 6th Rep. B. A. E., map, 1888.

Kekin (*Ke k'in'*, 'turtle carriers'). A division of the Washashewanun gens of the Osage.—Dorsey in 15th Rep. B. A. E., 234, 1897.

Kekin. A Kansa gens.
Do-hä-kel'-yă.—Morgan, Anc. Soc., 156, 1877 (trans. 'turtle'). Ke.—Dorsey in Am. Nat., 671, 1885 ('turtle'). Ke-k'iⁿ.—Dorsey in 15th Rep. B. A. E., 231, 1897 (trans. 'carries a turtle on his back'). Ke nika-shing-ga.—Stubbs, Kaw MS. vocab., B. A. E., 25, 1877.

Kekionga. The principal village of the Miami, formerly situated on the E. bank of St Joseph r., in Allen co., Ind., opposite Ft Wayne. It was often designated as "Miami town" and "Great Miami village." Several other settlements were in the vicinity. It was burned in 1790, and the tract on which it stood, an area 6 m. square, was ceded to the United States by the treaty of Greenville, Aug. 3, 1795. See *Maumee Towns.*   (J. M.)
Great Miami village.—Drake, Bk. Inds., bk. 5, 189, 1848. Kegaiogue.—Harmon (1790) in Rupp, West. Pa., app., 228, 1846. Kegniogue.—Ibid. Ke-ke-on-gay.—Hough, map in Indiana Geol. Rep., 1883. Ke-ki-on-ga.—Royce in 1st Rep. B. A. E., map, 1881. Ke-ki-on-go.—Royce in 18th Rep. B. A. E., Ind. map, 1899. Miami town.—Gamelin (1790) in Am. State Papers, Ind. Aff., I, 93, 1832.

Kekios. A Squawmish village community on the right bank of Squawmisht r., w. Brit. Col.
Qaqiō's.—Boas, MS., B. A. E., 1887. Qē'qiōs.—Hill-Tout in Rep. Brit. A. A. S., 474, 1900.

Kekwaiakin (*Qɛk·wai'akin*). A Squawmish village community on the left bank of Squawmisht r., Brit. Col.—Hill-Tout in Rep. Brit. A. A. S., 474, 1900.

Kekwaii (*Ke-kwai'-i'*). A village occupied in ancient times by the Nambe people of New Mexico; situated near Agawana (q. v.). Distinct from Keguayo.   (F. W. H.)

Kelatl (*Qɛlä'tl*). The uppermost Cowichan subtribe on Fraser r., Brit. Col. Their town was Asilao, above Yale.—Boas in Rep. Brit. A. A. S., 454, 1894.

Kele. The extinct Pigeon-hawk clan of

the Chua (Snake) phratry of the Hopi. Distinct from the Hawk (Kwayo) and Chicken-hawk (Massikwayo) clans.

Kē-le'-nyu-mûh.—Fewkes in Am. Anthrop., v, 223, 1892 (nyu-mûh=‘people’; usually employed by this author to denote phratry). Kele wiñwû.—Fewkes in 19th Rep. B. A. E., 583, 1901 (wiñ-wū= ‘clan’). Ke'-le wuñ-wü.—Fewkes in Am. Anthrop., VII, 403, 1894.

Kelemanturuk. An Utukamiut Eskimo village near Icy cape, Alaska.—Eleventh Census, Alaska, 162, 1893.

Keles (Qē'lɛs). A Chilliwack town on upper Chilliwack r., Brit. Col.—Boas in 64th Rep. Brit. A. A. S., 454, 1894.

Keliopoma. The name, in their own language, of the northernmost branch of the Pomo, bordering on the coast Yuki and the Athapascan Kato, and inhabiting the country from Sherwood to the coast near Cleone, Cal., to which place they gave its name. They were also called Shibalna Pomo.

Chiabel-na-poma.—Tobin in Ind. Aff. Rep. 1857, 404, 1858. Ku-lá Kai Pó-mo.—Powers in Cont. N. A. Ethnol., III, 155, 1877. She-bal-ne Pomas.—Wiley in Ind. Aff. Rep. 1864, 119, 1865. Shi-bal'-ni Po'-mo.—Powers, op. cit. (Kaito Pomo name: ‘neighbor people’).

Kelketos (Qē'lkɛtōs, ‘painted’). A Squawmish village community on the E. coast of Howe sd., Brit. Col.—Hill-Tout in Rep. Brit. A. A. S., 474, 1900.

Kelsemaht (‘rhubarb people’). A Nootka tribe on Clayoquot sd., Vancouver id.; pop. 76 in 1904. Their principal village is Yahksis.

Kel-seem-aht.—Can. Ind. Aff., 186, 1884. Kel-sem-aht.—Ibid., 357, 1897. K·eltsmā'ath.—Boas in 6th Rep. N. W. Tribes Can., 31, 1890. Killsmaht.—Sproat, Savage Life, 308, 1868. Kilsämāt.—Mayne, Brit. Col., 251, 1861.

Keltakkaua (Kɛ'ltāqk·aua). A division of the Nuhalk, a Bellacoola tribe of the coast of British Columbia.—Boas in 7th Rep. N. W. Tribes Can., 3, 1891.

Kemanks. A body of Salish of Fraser superintendency, Brit. Col. (Can. Ind. Aff., 138, 1879), no longer officially reported.

Kemisak. An Eskimo village on the E. coast of Greenland, about lat. 63° 40′; pop. 90 in 1829.—Graah, Exped. Greenland, map, 1837.

Kenabig (Kinäbĭk, ‘snake’). A gens of the Chippewa.

Che-she-gwa.—Warren (1852) in Minn. Hist. Soc. Coll., v, 45, 1885 (‘rattlesnake’). Ke-na'-big.—Morgan, Anc. Soc., 166, 1877 (‘snake’). Kinäbik.—Wm. Jones, inf'n, 1906. She-she-gwah.—Tanner, Narrative, 175, 1830. She-she-gwun.—Ibid., 315 (‘rattlesnake’).

Kenachananak. A Kuskwogmiut Eskimo village on the seashore opposite Nunivak id., Alaska; pop. 181, in 8 dwellings, in 1890.

Kenachananak.—Baker, Geog. Dict. Alaska, 236, 1902. Kennachananaghamiut.—Eleventh Census, Alaska, 109, 1893.

Kenai. A Knaiakhotana settlement and trading post of 44 people on the E. side of Cook inlet, Alaska, at the mouth of Kaknu r. The population in 1890 was 263 in 30 houses. The Russians erected

here the redoubt of St Nicholas in 1791, and a Russian orthodox mission was established about 1900, the Knaiakhotana here being devoted members of the Russian church. A large salmon cannery has been in operation for many years.

Fort Kenai.—Baker, Geog. Dict. Alaska, 236, 1902. Kenai redoute.—Petroff in 10th Census, Alaska, 29, 1884. Pavlovskaia.—Russian map (1802) cited by Baker, op. cit. St. Nicholas.—Ibid. St. Nicolas.—Ibid. St. Nikolas.—Ibid.

Kenapacomaqua. The principal village of the Wea, formerly on the w. bank of Eel r., near its mouth, 6 m. above Logansport, Cass co., Ind. From its situation on Eel r. (Anguille in French) it was called L'Anguille by the French. It was destroyed by Gen. Wilkinson in 1791.

(J. M.)

Kenapacomaqua.—Wilkinson (1791) in Am. State Papers, Ind. Aff., I, 134, 1832. Ke-na-pe-com-a-qua.—Hough in Indiana Geol. Rep., map, 1851. L'Anguille.—Rupp, West. Pa., 264, 1846.

Kendaia (‘it is an orchard.’—Hewitt). A former Seneca settlement situated at about the site of Kendaia, Seneca co., N. Y. Before its destruction by Gen. Sullivan in Sept., 1779, it contained about 20 houses. (J. M.)

Appletown.—Livermore (1779) in N. H. Hist. Soc. Coll., VI, 326, 1850. Canadia.—Hubley (1779) quoted by Conover, Kanadega and Geneva MS., B. A. E. Candaia.—Norris quoted by Conover, ibid. Candia.—Machin, map, ibid. Conday.—Livermore, op. cit. Kahonta'yoⁿ.—Hewitt, inf'n, 1890 (Seneca form). Kandaia.—Nukerck (1779) quoted by Conover, Kanadega and Geneva MS., B. A. E. Kendaes.—Pouchot, map (1758) in N. Y. Doc. Col. Hist., X, 694, 1858. Kindais.—Pemberton (1792) in Mass. Hist. Soc. Coll., 1st s., II, 176, 1810. Saint Coy.—McKendry (1779) quoted by Conover, Kanadega and Geneva MS., B. A. E.

Kendawa (Ken-da-wă', ‘eagle’). A gens of the Miami (q.v.).—Morgan, Anc. Soc., 168, 1877.

Kenek. A Yurok village on lower Klamath r., 5 or 6 m. below the mouth of Trinity r., Cal. It plays a prominent part in Yurok myths, but does not appear to have been important in historic times.

Kenek.—A. L. Kroeber, inf'n, 1904 (Yurok name). Shwufum.—Ibid. (Karok name.)

Kenikashika (‘those who became human beings by the aid of a turtle’). A Quapaw gens.

Ke-ni'kaci'ᴋa.—Dorsey in 15th Rep. B. A. E., 229, 1897. Turtle gens.—Ibid.

Kenim Lake. A Shuswap village or band on Kenim lake, which flows into North Thompson r., interior of British Columbia; pop. 87 in 1902, 67 in 1904.

Kanim Lake.—Can. Ind. Aff., 274, 1902. Kaninim Lake.—Ibid., 271, 1889. Kaninis' Tribe.—Ibid., 190, 1884. Kenim Lake.—Ibid., pt. II, 72, 1902.

Kenipsim. A Cowichan tribe in Cowitchin valley, near the s. E. end of Vancouver id.; pop. 53 in 1904.

Ka-nip-sum.—Can. Ind. Aff., 308, 1879. Kee-nip-saim.—Ibid., 302, 1893. Kee-nip-sim.—Ibid., 231, 1886. Ke-nip-sim.—Ibid., 190, 1883. Khenipsim.—Ibid., pt. II, 164, 1901. Khenipsin.—Ibid., pt. II, 69, 1904. Qē'nipsen.—Boas, MS., B. A. E., 1887.

Kennebec (‘at the long water’). A former village, probably of the Norridgewock division of the Abnaki, on Kennebec r. between Augusta and Winslow, Me.

Mentioned by Capt. John Smith in 1616 and visited by Druillettes in 1646.

Kénébec.—Maurault, Hist. Abenakis, 120, 1866. **Kenebecka.**—Smith (1629), Hist. Va., II, 177, 1819. **Kenebeke.**—Ibid., 183. **Kinibeki.**—Jes. Rel. (1647), Thwaites ed., XXXI, 189, 1898.

Kennebunker. A word local in the Maine lumbering regions, defined (Dialect Notes, 390, 1895) as a "valise in which clothes are put by lumbermen when they go into camp for a 'winter operation.'" This term, of quite recent origin, has been formed, with the English suffix -er, from *Kennebunk*, a river and port in Maine; derived from the Passamaquoddy or a closely related dialect of Algonquian, probably signifying 'at the long water.' (A. F. C.)

Kenozhe (*Kʻinozhän*, 'pickerel'). A gens of the Chippewa. Cf. *Keinouche*.

Ke-noushay.—Warren (1852) in Minn. Hist. Soc. Coll., V, 44, 1885 (trans. 'pike'). **Ke-no-zha.**—Tanner, Narrative, 314, 1830 ('pickerel'). **Ke-no'-zhe.**—Morgan, Anc. Soc., 166, 1877 ('pike'). **Kinōjän.**—Wm. Jones, inf'n, 1906.

Kenta (probably from *kéntʻa*, 'field', 'meadow.'—Hewitt). A Tuscarora village in North Carolina in 1701.—Lawson (1714), Carolina, 383, 1860.

Kentanuska. A Tuscarora village in North Carolina in 1701.—Lawson (1714), Carolina, 383, 1860.

Kente (*kéntʻa*, 'field', 'meadow'). A Cayuga village existing about 1670 on Quinté bay of L. Ontario, Ontario.

Kanté.—Bruyas (1673) in N. Y. Doc. Col. Hist., IX, 792, 1855. **Kenté.**—Frontenac (1673), ibid., 96. **Kentsia.**—Homann Heirs' map, 1756. **Kentsio.**—Lotter, map, *ca.* 1770. **Quentè.**—La Honton, New Voy., I, 32, 1703. **Quintay.**—Frontenac (1672), op. cit., 93. **Quinté.**—Doc. of 1698 in N. Y. Doc. Col. Hist., IX, 681, 1855.

Kenunimik. An Ikogmiut Eskimo village on the right bank of the lower Yukon, Alaska (Coast Surv. chart, 1898), 15 m. above Andreafski. Perhaps the same as Ankachak.

Keokuk (*Kiyoʻkagᵃ*, 'one who moves about alert'). A Sauk leader, a member of the Fox clan, born on Rock r., Ill., about 1780. He was not a chief by birth, but rose to the command of his people through marked ability, force of character, and oratorical power. His mother is said to have been half French. At an early age he was a member of the Sauk council, which he graced, but at first played only a subordinate role therein. He stepped into prominence later on when he was made tribal guest-keeper. While holding this office he was supplied at tribal expense with all the means of rendering hospitality, and played the part of a genial host with such pleasing effect that his lodge became a center for all things social and political. Quick to see the possibilities of this office he made use of the opportunity to further his own ambitions.

Keokuk was well aware of the fact that the rigid social organization of his people offered a barrier to the realization of his cherished desire, which was to become the foremost man of his tribe. Contrary to the manner of men of his training, environment, and tradition, he had no scruples against doing away with a practice if thereby he might reap profit for himself; and he worked his will against custom, not in an open, aggressive way, but by veiled, diplomatic methods. He was continually involved in intrigue; standing always in the background, he secretly played one faction against another. In time he became the leading councilor in the Sauk assembly, and enjoyed great popularity among his people. But the situation assumed a different aspect when the troubled period of the so-called Black Hawk war arrived. The immediate cause of this conflict grew out

KEOKUK

of an agreement first entered into between the Government and a small band of Sauk who, under their leader Kwaskwamia, were in winter camp near the trading post of St Louis. By this compact the Sauk were to give up the Rock River country. As soon as the agreement became noised abroad among all the Sauk there was strong opposition, particularly to the form in which it had been made. Throughout the affair Keokuk assumed so passive an attitude that he lost at once both social and political prestige. Those of the Sauk who favored an appeal to arms then turned to a man of the Thunder clan, Black-big-chest, known to the whites under the name of Black Hawk (q. v.), who became their leader. Just at this critical period the feeble bond of political union between the Sauk and the Foxes was broken, this result being due largely to internal dissensions brought on by the intrigues of Keokuk, who, with a following of unpatriotic Sauk, sought and obtained protection from the Foxes under their chief, Paweshik. The fighting began before Black Hawk was ready, and he was forced to take the field with but a small number of those on whose support he had depended. With his depleted forces he could not successfully contend against the Illinois militia and their Indian allies.

Keokuk loomed up again during the final negotiations growing out of the war, and played so deftly into the hands of the Government officials that he was made chief of the Sauk. It is said that the announcement of his elevation to supreme power was made in open council, and that it so aroused the anger and contempt of Black Hawk that he whipped off his clout and slapped Keokuk across the face with it. The act of creating Keokuk chief of the Sauk has always been regarded with ridicule by both the Sauk and the Foxes, for the reason that he was not of the ruling clan. But the one great occasion for which both the Sauk and the Foxes honor Keokuk was when, in the city of Washington, in debate with the representatives of the Sioux and other tribes before Government officials, he established the claim of the Sauk and Foxes to the territory comprised in what is now the state of Iowa. He based this claim primarily on conquest.

On his death, in 1848, in Kansas, whither he had moved three years before, the chieftainship, with its unsavory associations, went to his son, Moses Keokuk (Wunagisä^a, 'he leaps up quickly from his lair'), who displayed many of the mental characteristics of the father. Those who knew them both maintain that the son was even the superior intellectually, and of higher ethics. He was fond of debate, being always cool, deliberate, and clear-headed. In argument he was more than a match for any Government officer with whom he ever came in contact at the agency. He bore an intense hatred for the Foxes, which was returned with more than full measure. Moses Keokuk was acknowledged the purest speaker of the Sauk dialect. The Sauk were never tired of his eloquence; it was always simple, clear, and pleasing. Late in life he embraced Christianity and was baptized a Baptist; but he never ceased to cherish a sincere regard for the old-time life and its fond associations. He succeeded in turning aside much of the odium that had early surrounded his office, and though he met with more po-

litical opposition during his whole life, yet when he died, at Sauk and Fox agency, Okla., in Aug. 1903, his death was regarded by the Sauk as a tribal calamity.

In 1883 the remains of the elder Keokuk were removed from Kansas to Keokuk, Iowa, where they were reinterred in the city park and a monument erected over his grave by the citizens of the town. A bronze bust of Keokuk stands in the Capitol at Washington. (w. J.)

Keotuc (prob. for *Kiwätŭg*, 'he whose voice is heard roaming about.'—W. J.). A Potawatomi band, probably taking its name from the chief, living in Kansas in 1857.—Baldwin in Ind. Aff. Rep. 1857, 163, 1858.

Keowee (according to Wafford, *Kuwáhiyĭ*, or, in abbreviated form, *Kuwáhi*, 'mulberry grove place'). The name of two or more former Cherokee settlements. One, sometimes distinguished as Old Keowee, the principal of the Lower Cherokee towns, was on the river of the same name, near the present Port George, in Oconee co., S. C. Another, distinguished as New Keowee, was on the headwaters of Twelve-mile cr., in Pickens co., S. C.—Mooney in 19th Rep. B. A. E., 525, 1900.
Keowe.—Bartram, Travels, 372, 1792. **New Keowee.**—Mouzon's map quoted by Royce in 5th Rep. B. A. E., 143, 1887.

Kepatawangachik. Given as the name of a tribe formerly living near L. St John, Quebec, but driven off by the Iroquois (Jes. Rel. 1660, 12, 1858). Named in connection with Abittibi and Ouakouiechidek (Chisedec). Possibly the Papinachois.

Kepel. A Yurok village on lower Klamath r., about 12 m. below the mouth of the Trinity, in N. California. It was the only place in Yurok territory, besides Loolego, at which a fish dam was erected across the river.
Akharatipikam.—A. L. Kroeber, inf'n, 1904 (Karok name). **Capel.**—Gibbs in Schoolcraft, Ind. Tribes, III, 138, 1853. **Cap-pel.**—McKee in Sen. Ex. Doc. 4, 32d Cong., spec. sess., 161, 1853. **Kai-petl.**—Gibbs, op. cit.

Kerahocak. A former village of the Powhatan confederacy on the N. bank of the Rappahannock, in King George co., Va.—Smith (1629), Virginia, I, map, repr. 1819.

Kerechun (*ke-re-tcŭⁿ*, probably 'hawk'). A subgens of the Waninkikikarachada, the Bird gens of the Winnebago.—Dorsey in 15th Rep. B. A. E., 240, 1897.

Keremen. A village or tribe formerly in the country between Matagorda bay and Maligne (Colorado) r., Tex. The name seems to have been given Joutel in 1687 by the Ebahamo, who were probably affiliated to the neighboring Karankawa. They are probably the Aranama (q. v.) of the Spanish chroniclers. See Gatschet, Karankawa Inds., 23, 35, 46, 1891. (A. C. F.)

Keremen.—Joutel (1687) in French, Hist. Coll. La., I, 137, 1846. Korimen.—Joutel (1687) in Margry, Déc., III, 288, 1878 (mentioned as distinct from Keremen, but probably a duplication).

Keremeus. A Similkameen band of the Okinagan; pop. 55 in 1897, when last separately enumerated.

Kerem-eeos.—Can. Ind. Aff. for 1883, 191. Keremeoos.—Ibid., 1892, 313. Keremeus.—Ibid., 1897, 364. Kêremya'uz.—Teit in Mem. Am. Mus. Nat. Hist., II, 174, 1900.

Keresan Family (adapted from *K'eres*, the aboriginal name). A linguistic family of Pueblo Indians including the inhabitants of several villages on the Rio Grande, in N. central New Mexico, between the Rito de los Frijoles (where, before being confined to reservations, they joined the Tewa on the N.) and the Rio Jemez, as well as on the latter stream from the pueblo of Sia to its mouth. The w. division, comprising Acoma and Laguna pueblos, are situated westward from the Rio Grande, the latter on the Rio San José. Like the other Pueblo tribes of New Mexico, the Keresan Indians maintain that they had their origin at the mythical Shipapu and that they slowly drifted southward to the Rio Grande, taking up their abode in the Rito de los Frijoles, or Tyuonyi, and constructing there the cliff-dwellings found to-day excavated in the friable volcanic tufa. Long before the coming of the Spaniards they had abandoned the Rito, and, moving farther southward, separated into a number of autonomous village communities. According to Coronado, who visited the "Quirix" province in 1540, these Indians occupied 7 pueblos; 40 years later Espejo found 5; while in 1630 Benavides described the stock as numbering 4,000 people, in 7 towns extending 10 leagues along the Rio Grande. See Bandelier (1) in Arch. Inst. Papers, I, 114, 1883, (2) ibid., IV, 139 et seq., 1892, (3) Delight Makers, 1890.

According to Loew this stock constitutes two dialectic groups, the first or Queres group comprising the inhabitants of Santo Domingo, Santa Ana, Sia, San Felipe, and Cochiti; the other, the Sitsime or Kawaiko group, comprehending Laguna and Acoma with their outlying villages.

The Keresan settlements are as follows, those marked with an asterisk being extinct: Acoma, Acomita, Casa Blanca, Cieneguilla*, Cochiti, Cubero*, Cueva Pintada*, Encinal, Gipuy*, Haatze*, Hasatch, Heashkowa*, Huashpatzena*, Kakanatzatia*, Kashkachuti*, Katzimo*, Kohasaya*, Kowina*, Kuapa*, Kuchtya*, Laguna, Moquino*, Paguate, Pueblito, Puerto (?)*, Punyistyi, Rito*, San Felipe, Santa Ana, Santo Domingo, Seemunah, Shumasitscha*, Sia, Tapitsiama*, Tipoti*, Tsiama, Wapuchuseamma, Washpashuka*, Yapashi*. The following pueblos,

now extinct, were perhaps also Keresan: Alipoti, Ayqui, Cebolleta, Pelchiu, Pueblo del Encierro, San Mateo, Tashkatze, Tojagua.   (F. W. H.)

Bierni'n.—Hodge, field notes, B. A. E., 1895 (Sandia name). Cherechos.—Oñate (1598) in Doc. Inéd., XVII, 102, 1871. Cheres.—Ibid., XVI, 114. Chu-chacas.—Lane (1854) in Schoolcraft, Ind. Tribes, V, 689, 1855 (applied to the language). Chu-chachas.—Keane in Stanford, Compend., 479, 1878 (after Lane, misprint). Cueres.—Humboldt, Atlas Nouv. Espagne, carte 1, 1811. Cuerez.—Simpson in Smithson. Rep. 1869, 334, 1871. Drinkers of the Dew.—Cushing in Johnson's Cyclop., IV, 891, 1896 (given as Zuñi traditional name). Gueres.—Ogilby, America, 295, 1671. Hores.—Oñate (1598) in Doc. Inéd., XVI, 265, 1871 (probably identical). Ing-wë-pi'-ran-di-vi-he-man.—Hodge, field notes, B. A. E., 1895 (San Ildefonso Tewa name). Jerez.—Loew (1875) in Wheeler Survey Rep., VII, 338, 1879 (probably identical). Kera.—Hervas, Idea dell' Universo, XVII, 76, 1784. Kéran.—Powell in Am. Nat., XIV, 604, Aug. 1880. Keras.—Malte-Brun, Geog., V, 318, 1826. Keres.—Pike, Expeditions, 220, 1810. Kes-whaw-hay.—Lane (1854) in Schoolcraft, Ind. Tribes, V, 689, 1855 (applied to language). Kwéres.—Petitot, Dict. Dènè-Dindjié, XVII, 1876. Pabierni'n.—Hodge, field notes, B. A. E., 1895 (Isleta name). Qq'uêres.—Bandelier in Arch. Inst. Papers, I, 114, 1883. Quera.—Hervas (1784) quoted by Prichard, Phys. Hist. Mankind, V, 341, 1847. Quéra.—Bandelier in Arch. Inst. Papers, I, 114, 1883. Queres.—Benavides, Memorial, 20, 1630. Quéres.—Villagran, Hist. Neuva Mex., 155, 1610. Quérés.—Benavides (1630) quoted by Gallatin in Nouv. Ann. Voy., 5th s., XXVII, 305, 1851. Quereses.—Sosa (1591) in Doc. Inéd., XV, 248, 1871. Querez.—Rivera, Diario y Derrot., leg. 784, 1736. Quéris.—Bandelier in Revue d'Ethnog., 203, 1886. Queros.—Walch, Charte America, 1805. Quingas.—Graves (1854) in H. R. Misc. Doc. 38, 33d Cong., 1st sess., 7, 1854. Quires.—Espejo (1583) in Doc. Inéd., XV, 122, 1871. Quirex.—Simpson in Smithson. Rep. 1869, map, 1871. Quiria.—Gallatin in Trans. Am. Ethnol. Soc., II, lxxi, 1848. Quirix.—Castañeda (ca. 1565) in Ternaux-Compans, Voy., IX, 110, 1838. Quiros.—Dobbs, Hudson Bay, 163, 1744. Quivix.—Castañeda (ca. 1565) in Ternaux-Compans, Voy., IX, 182, 1838. Xeres.—Rivera, Diario y Derrot., leg. 950, 1736. Zures.—Vetancurt (1693), Crónica, 315, 1871.

Kernertok. A settlement of East Greenland Eskimo near Frederiksdal.—Meddelelser om Grönland, XXV, 246, 1902.

Kern River Shoshoneans. A small Shoshonean group in S. California which differs so much linguistically from all other peoples of this family as to form a major division, although numerically insignificant. It includes the Tubatulabal, who occupy the valley of Kern r. above the falls, and the Bankalachi of upper Deer cr.

Keroff. Mentioned among a number of Upper Creek towns in H. R. Ex. Doc. 276, 24th Cong., 1st sess., 162, 1836. It probably is a badly mutilated abbreviation of the name of a known Creek town, but is not identifiable in this form. The settlement appears to have been on the upper course of Coosa r., Ala.

Kershaw. See *Cashaw*.

Kesa (*Qê'sa*). A Haida town on the w. coast of Graham id., Queen Charlotte group, Brit. Col. It was occupied by the Tadji-lanas before moving to Alaska.—Swanton, Cont. Haida, 281, 1905.

Keshkunuwu (*Q!eckunuwŭ'*, 'bluejay fort'). A former Tlingit village in the Sitka country, Alaska.   (J. R. S.)

Keshlakchuis (*Kĕ'sh-lăktchuish*). A former Modoc settlement on the s. E. side of Tule (Rhett) lake, Modoc co., N E. Cal.—Gatschet in Cont. N. A. Ethnol., II, pt. 1, xxxii, 1890.

Keskaechquerem. Mentioned as if a former Canarsee village near Maspeth, on the w. end of Long id., N. Y., in deed of 1638.—N. Y. Doc. Col. Hist., XIV, 14, 1883.

Keskistkonk. A former Nochpeem village which seems to have been on Hudson r., s. of the Highlands, in Putnam co., N. Y. **Keskistkonck.**—Van der Donck (1656) quoted by Ruttenber, Tribes Hudson R., 80, 1872. **Kis Kightkonck.**—Doc. of 1663 in N. Y. Doc. Col. Hist., XIII, 303, 1881 (used for the Nochpeem tribe).

Kesmali (*Kĕs-mä-li*). A former village of the San Luis Obispo Indians of the Chumashan family, at Pt Sal, San Luis Obispo co., Cal.—Schumacher in Smithson. Rep. 1874, 340, 1875.

Kespoogwit ('land's end'). One of the two divisions of the territory of the Micmac as recognized by themselves. According to Rand it includes the districts of Eskegawaage, Shubenacadie, and Annapolis (q. v.), embracing all of s. and E. Nova Scotia. In Frye's list of 1760, Kashpugowitk and Keshpugowitk are mentioned as two of 14 Micmac bands or villages. These are evidently duplicates, as the same chief was over both, and were intended for the Kespoogwit division. The inhabitants are called Kespoogwitunak. See *Micmac.*   (J. M.)
Kashpugowitk.—Frye (1760) in Mass. Hist. Soc. Coll., 1st s., X, 115–116, 1809. **Keshpugowitk.**—Ibid. (mentioned separately, but evidently the same). **Kespoogwit.**—Rand, First Micmac Reading Book, 81, 1875. **Kespoogwitunâ'k.**—Ibid. (the people of Kespoogwit).

Kestaubuinck. A former Sintsink village in Westchester co., N. Y., between Singsing cr. and Croton r.; mentioned by Van der Donck in 1656.—Ruttenber, Tribes Hudson R., 72, 79, 1872.

Ket (*Q!ĕt*, 'narrow strait'). A Haida town on Burnaby str., Moresby id., Queen Charlotte group, Brit. Col. It was occupied by a branch of the Hagi-lanas, who from their town were called Keda-lanas.—Swanton, Cont. Haida, 277, 1905.

Ketangheanycke. A village, probably of the Abnaki, near the mouth of Kennebec r., Me., in 1602–09.—Purchas (1625) quoted in Me. Hist. Soc. Coll., v, 156, 1857.

Ketchewaundaugenink ('large lick at.'—Hewitt). A former Chippewa village on Shiawassee r., on the trail between Detroit and Saginaw bay, in lower Michigan, on a reservation sold in 1837.   (J. M.)
Big Lick.—Detroit treaty (1837) in U. S. Ind. Treat., 245, 1873. **Big salt lick.**—Williams (1872) in Mich. Pion. Coll., II, 476, 1880. **Che-won-der-goning.**—Ibid., 477. **Ke-che-wan-dor-goning.**—Ibid., 476. **Kech-e-waun-dau-gu-mink.**—Royce in 18th Rep. B. A. E., Mich. map, 765, 1899. **Ketchewaundaugenink.**—Saginaw treaty (proclaimed 1820) in U. S. Ind. Treat., 142, 1873. **Ketchewaundaugumink.**—Detroit treaty, op. cit. **Ketchiwāwiyändāganing.**—Wm. Jones, inf'n, 1905. **Keth-e-wandon-gon-ing.**—Williams, op. cit., 481. **Saline.**—Ibid., 476 (French name). **Wan-dor-gon-ing.**—Ibid., 477.

Ketchigumiwisuwugi (*Ke'tcigamiwisuwągi*, 'they go by the name of the sea'). A Sauk gens.
Kǎ-che-kone-a-we'-so-uk.—Morgan, Anc. Soc., 170, 1877 (trans. 'sea'). **Ke'tcigamiwisuwągi.**—Wm. Jones, inf'n, 1906.

Ketgohittan ('people of small-shark house'). Given as a subdivision of the Tlingit clan Nanyaayi, but in reality simply the name of those inhabiting a certain house.
K·'ē'tgo hit tan.—Boas, 5th Rep. N. W. Tribes Can., 25, 1889. **Q!A'tgu hît tān.**—Swanton, field notes, B. A. E., 1904.

Ketlalsm (*Kē'tlals'm*, 'nipping grass', so called because deer come here in spring to eat the fresh grass). A Squawmish village community on the E. side of Howe sd., Brit. Col.—Hill-Tout in Rep. Brit. A. A. S., 474, 1900.

Ketlaynup. A body of Salish of Vancouver id., speaking the Cowichan dialect; pop. 24 in 1882.—Can. Ind. Aff. for 1882, 258.

Ketnas-hadai (*K·'ētnas :had'ä'i*, 'sea-lion house people' [?]). Given by Boas (Fifth Rep. N. W. Tribes Canada, 27, 1889) as the name of a subdivision of the Yakulanas, a family of the Raven clan of the Haida of s. w. Alaska; but it is in reality only a house name belonging to that family. There seems to be an error in the designation, the word for 'sea-lion' being *qa-i*.   (J. R. S.)

Ketsilind (*Kĕtsĭlĭ'nd*, 'people of the Rio Chiquito ruin'). A division of the Jicarilla who claim that their former home was s. of Taos pueblo, N. Mex. They are possibly of mixed Picuris descent.
   (J. M.)

Keuchishkeni (*Ke-utchishχē'ni*, 'where the wolf rock stands'). A former Modoc camping place on Hot cr., near Little Klamath lake, N. Cal.—Gatschet in Cont. N. A. Ethnol., II, pt. 1, xxxii, 1890.

Kevalingamiut. A tribe of Eskimo whose country extended from C. Seppings and C. Krusenstern, Alaska, inland to Nunatak r. They were an offshoot of the Nunatogmiut, reenforced by outlaws from the Kinugumiut and Kaviagmiut. The main body of the tribe is now found about Pt Hope and farther N., having emigrated on account of disease and lack of food, and expelled the Tigaramiut from their northern hunting grounds. Their villages are Kechemudluk, Kivualinak, and Ulezara.
Kevalinye Mutes.—Kelly, Arct. Eskimos, chart, 1890. **Kevalinyes.** — Ibid., 13. **Kivalinag-miut** (Tikhmenief (1861) quoted by Baker, Geog. Dict. Alaska, 115, 1902.

Kevilkivashalah. A body of Salish of Victoria superintendency, Vancouver id. Pop. 31 in 1882, when last separately enumerated.
Kevil-kiva-sha-lah.—Can. Ind. Aff. for 1882, 258.

Kewatsana (*Kewátsăna*, 'no ribs'). An extinct division of the Comanche.—Mooney in 14th Rep. B. A. E., 1045, 1896.

Kewaughtohenemach. Given as a division of the Okinagan that lived 30 m. above Priests rapids, on Columbia r., Wash.

Ke-waught-chen-unaughs.—Ross, Adventures, 290, 1849. Ke-waugh-tohen-emachs.—Ibid., 137.

Kewigoshkeem. A former Chippewa or Ottawa village, named after a chief who flourished in the latter part of the 18th century; situated on Grand r., at or near the present Grand Rapids, Mich., on land ceded to the United States by the treaty of Chicago, Aug. 29, 1821, proclaimed Mar. 25, 1832. Under this treaty half a section of land near the village was granted to Charles and Medart Beaubien, sons of Mannabenaqua.

Ke-wi-go-shkeem.—Treaty (proclaimed 1832) in U. S. Ind. Treat., 154, 1873. Ke-wi-go-sh-kum.—Royce in 18th Rep. B. A. E., Mich. map, 1899. Kewigushkum.—Bennett (1779) in Mich. Pion. Coll., IX, 393, 1886 (the chief).

Keya. The Badger clan of the Tewa pueblos of San Juan, Santa Clara, and San Ildefonso, N. Mex.—Hodge in Am. Anthrop., IX, 349, 1896.

Keyatiwankwi (*K'éyatiwankwi*, 'place of upturning or elevation'). The first of the mythic settling places of the Zuñi after their emergence from the underworld.—Cushing in 13th Rep. B. A. E., 388, 1896.

Keyauwee. A small tribe formerly living in North Carolina, affiliated with the Tutelo, Saponi, and Occaneechi. Nothing remains of their language, but they perhaps belonged to the Siouan family, from the fact of their intimate association with well known Siouan tribes of the E. In 1701 Lawson (Carolina, 1714, 87–89, repr. 1860) found them in a palisaded village about 30 m. N. E. of Yadkin r., near the present Highpoint, Guilford co., N. C. Around the village were large fields of corn. At that time they were about equal in number to the Saponi and had, as chief, Keyauwee Jack, who was by birth a Congaree, but had obtained the chieftaincy by marriage with their "queen." Lawson says most of the men wore mustaches or whiskers, an unusual custom for Indians. At the time of this traveler's visit the Keyauwee were on the point of joining the Tutelo and Saponi for better protection against their enemies. Shortly afterward they, together with the Tutelo, Saponi, Occaneechi, and Shakori, moved down toward the settlements about Albemarle sd., the five tribes with one or two others not named numbering then only about 750 souls. In 1716 Gov. Spotswood of Virginia proposed to settle the Keyauwee with the Eno and Sara at Enotown on the frontier of North Carolina, but was prevented by the opposition of that colony. They moved southward with the Sara, and perhaps also the Eno, to Pedee r., S. C., some time in 1733. On Jefferys' map of 1761 their village is marked on the Pedee above that of the Sara, about the boundary between the two Carolinas. With this notice they disappear from history, having probably been absorbed by the Catawba. (J. M.)

Keawe.—Jefferys, Fr. Dom. Am., I, 134, map, 1761. Keawee.—Bowen, map of the Brit. Am. Plantations, 1760. Keeawawes.—Doc. of 1716 in N. C. Rec., 242, 1886. Keeowaws.—Ibid., 243. Keeowee.—Vaugondy, map Partie de l'Amér. Sept., 1755. Keiauwees.—Lawson (1701), Carolina, 384, 1860. Keomee.—Moll, map of Car., 1720 (misprint). Kewawees.—Byrd (1733), Hist. Div. Line, II, 22, 1866. Keyauwee.—Lawson (1701), Carolina, 87, repr. 1860. Keyawees.—Brickell, Nat. Hist. N. Car., 343, 1737.

Keyerhwotket ('old village'). A village of the Hwotsotenne on Bulkley r., Brit. Col., lat. 55°.

Kéyər-hwotqət.—Morice, Notes on W. Dénés, 27, 1902. 'ʜeyəɹhwotqət.—Morice in Trans. Roy. Soc. Can., X, map, 1892. Kyahuntgate.—Tolmie and Dawson, Vocabs. B. C., map, 1884. Kyahwilgate.—Dawson in Rep. Geol. Surv. Can., 20B, 1881.

Keyukee. A former Cherokee town; locality undetermined.—Doc. of 1799 quoted by Royce in 5th Rep. B. A. E., 144, 1887.

Kezche. A Tatshiautin village on Taché r., Brit. Col., under the Babine and Upper Skeena River agency; pop. 24 in 1904.

Grand Rapids.—Can. Ind. Aff., pt. 2, 70, 1902. 'Keztce.—Morice, Notes on W. Dénés, 26, 1902. Kus-chë-o-tin.—Dawson in Rep. Can. Geol. Surv., 30B, 1881. Kustsheotin.—Tolmie and Dawson, Vocabs. B. C., 123B, 1884.

Keze ('barbed like a fishhook,' a derisive name, alluding to their cross disposition). A band of the Sisseton Sioux, an offshoot of the Kakhmiatonwan.—Dorsey in 15th Rep. B. A. E., 217, 1897.

Kezonlathut. A Takulli village on McLeod lake, Brit. Col.; pop. 96 in 1904.

McLeod's Lake.—Can. Ind. Aff., 1904, pt. II, 74, 1905. Qézoñlathût.—Morice in Trans. Roy. Soc. Can., X, 109, 1892.

Kfwetragottine ('mountain people'). A division of the Kawchodinne living s. of Ft Good Hope, along Mackenzie r., Mackenzie Ter., Can.

Kfwè-tρa-Gottinè.—Petitot, Autour du lac des Esclaves, 362, 1891.

Khaamotene. Given, seemingly in error, as a subdivision of the Tolowa formerly dwelling at the mouth of Smith r., Cal., in the village of Khoonkhwuttunne, and at the forks in a village called Khosatunne.

Qa'-a-mo' te'-ne.—Dorsey in Jour. Am. Folk-lore, III, 236, 1890. Smith River Indians.—Ibid.

Khaap. A body of Ntlakyapamuk under the Kamloops-Okanagan agency, Brit. Col.; pop. 23 in 1901, the last time the name appears.

Khaap.—Can. Ind. Aff. 1901, pt. 2, 166. Skaap.—Ibid., 1885, 196.

Khabemadolil. A Pomo village on upper Clear lake, Cal.—Kroeber, MS., Univ. Cal., 1903.

Khabenapo ('stone village', or 'stone people'). A Pomo division or band on Kelsey cr., in Big valley, on the w. side of Clear lake, Cal. They numbered 195 in 1851.

Ca-ba-na-po.—McKee (1851) in Sen. Ex. Doc. 4, 32d Cong., spec. sess., 136, 1853. Habe-napo.—Gibbs (1851) in Schoolcraft, Ind. Tribes, III, 109,

1853. **Ha-bi-na-pa.**—McKee, op. cit. **Ká-bi-na-pek.**—Powers in Cont. N. A. Ethnol., III, 204, 1877.

Khachtais. A former Siuslaw village on Siuslaw r., Oreg.
K'qătc-ɹais'.—Dorsey in Jour. Am. Folk-lore, III, 230, 1890.

Khahitan (*Gha-hitä'n*, pl. *Gha-hitä'neo*, 'ermine people', from *gha-ĭ* 'ermine', *hitä'neo* 'people'). The Cheyenne name of an unidentified Pueblo tribe of the Rio Grande, known to the Cheyenne through visits and trade intercourse. They formerly accompanied Mexican traders in their journeys to the camps of the Plains tribes, and used Spanish as well as their own language. They formerly cut their hair across below the ears, with a short side plait wrapped with strings of white ermine skin, but have now adopted the ordinary hairdress style of the Plains tribes. From information of Cheyenne who met some of them on a recent visit to Taos, N. Mex., it is known that they are distinct from Ute, Navaho, Jicarilla, or Taos Indians, and live farther s. than any of these. They may possibly be the Picuris. (J. M.)
Ghá-hi-täneo.—Mooney, MS. Cheyenne notes, B. A. E., 1906. *Ka-he'-ta-ni-o.*—Hayden, Ethnog. and Philol. Mo. Val., 290, 1862.

Khaik. A Chnagmiut Eskimo village on the Yukon, Alaska.
Khaigamut.—Nelson in 18th Rep. B. A. E., map, 1899. *Khaigamute.*—Petroff in 10th Census, Alaska, map, 1884.

Khaikuchum. A former Siuslaw village on Siuslaw r., Oreg.
K'qai'-kŭ-tc'ûm'.—Dorsey in Jour. Am. Folk-lore, III, 230, 1890.

Khainanaitetunne. A former village of the Tututni, the inhabitants of which were exterminated, except two boys, one of whom was an old man at Siletz agency, Oreg., in 1884.
Qa'-i-na'-na-i-tĕ' ɹûnnĕ.—Dorsey in Jour. Am. Folk-lore, III, 236, 1890.

Khaishuk. A former Yaquina village on the N. side of Yaquina r., Oreg.
Kqai'-cŭk.—Dorsey in Jour. Am. Folk-lore, III, 229, 1890.

Khaiyukkhai. A former Yaquina village on the s. side of Yaquina r., Oreg.
Kqai-yûk'-kqai.—Dorsey in Jour. Am. Folk-lore, III, 229, 1890.

Khaiyumitu. A former Siuslaw village on Siuslaw r., Oreg.
K'qai-yu'-mi-ɹû.—Dorsey in Jour. Am. Folk-lore, III, 230, 1890.

Khakaiauwa. Said to be a collective name for the Pomo villages on upper Clear lake, Cal.—Kroeber, MS., Univ. Cal., 1903. Cf. *Khana.*

Khakhaich. A former Siuslaw village on Siuslaw r., Oreg.
Kqa-kqaitc'.—Dorsey in Jour. Am. Folk-lore, III, 230, 1890.

Khalakw. A former Siuslaw village on Siuslaw r., Oreg.
Qa-lăk'w'.—Dorsey in Jour. Am. Folk-lore, III, 230, 1890.

Khaltso ('yellow bodies'). A Navaho clan, the descendants of two daughters of an Apache father.

Háltso.—Matthews, Navaho Legends, 30, 1897. *Háltsodĭne'.*—Ibid. **Qàlto.**—Matthews in Jour. Am. Folk-lore, III, 103, 1890. **Qaltsoǿine.**—Ibid.

Khana (Pomo: 'on the water', or 'on [Clear] lake'). A term which seems to have been descriptively applied to the Pomo of Clear lake, Cal. Bartlett (1854) gives a H'hana vocabulary, which is Pomo, as coming from the upper Sacramento, but obtained it from a stray Pomo at San Diego.
H'hana.—Bartlett in Cont. N. A. Ethnol., III, 492, 1877. **Khana.**—S. A. Barrett, inf'n, 1906.

Kharatanumanke. Given as a Mandan gens, but evidently merely a band.
Ho-ra-ta'-mŭ-make.—Morgan, Anc. Soc., 158, 1877. *Qa-ra-ta' nu-mañ'-ke.*—Dorsey in 15th Rep. B. A. E., 241, 1897 (given with a query). **Wolf.**—Morgan, op. cit.

Khashhlizhni ('mud'). A Navaho clan.
Haslĭ'zdĭne'.—Matthews, Navaho Legends, 30, 1897. *Haslĭ'zni.*—Ibid. **Qaclíj.**—Matthews in Jour. Am. Folk-lore, III, 103, 1890. **Qaclíjni.**—Ibid.

Khaskankhatso ('much yucca'). A Navaho clan.
Haskánhatso.—Matthews, Navaho Legends, 30, 1897. *Haskanhatsódĭne'.*—Ibid. **Qackàⁿqatsò.**—Matthews in Jour. Am. Folk-lore, III, 103, 1890. **Qackàⁿqatsòǿine.**—Ibid.

Khauweshetawes ('spread-out irrigation ditch'). A Maricopa rancheria on the Rio Gila, s. Ariz.—ten Kate, inf'n, 1888.

Khawina ('on the water'). The name, in the Upper Clear Lake dialect, of the Lower Clear Lake Pomo village at Sulphur Bank, Lake co., Cal.—Kroeber, MS., Univ. Cal., 1903.

Khdhasiukdhin ('dwelling place among the yellow flowers'; i. e., 'sunflower place' [?]). An ancient Osage village on Neosho r., Kans.
Qǿási úɹǿiⁿ.—Dorsey, Osage MS. vocab., B. A. E., 1883. **Qdhasi ukdhiⁿ.**—Ibid.

Kheerghia. A former Tututni village on the coast of Oregon, about 25 m. s. of the mouth of Pistol r.
Mûn-kqĕ'-tûn.—Dorsey in Jour. Am. Folk-lore, III, 236, 1890. **Qé-e-rxi'-a.**—Ibid.

Khemnichan ('mountain-water wood,' from a hill covered with timber that appears to rise out of the water). A band of the Mdewakanton Sioux. According to Pike they were living in 1811 in a village near the head of L. Pepin, Minn., on the site of the present Red Wing, under chief Tatankamani ('Walking Buffalo'); in 1820 they lived on L. Pepin, under chief Red Wing. Long, in 1824, found them in two small villages, one on Mississippi r., the other on Cannon r., aggregating 150 people in 20 lodges. Shakea was then their chief, subordinate to Wabeshaw of the Kiyuksa. They were under Wakute ('Shooter') at the time of the Sioux outbreak in 1862.
Eambosandata.—Neill in Minn. Hist. Coll., I, 263, 1858 (trans. 'mountain beside the water'). **Eanbosandata.**—Long, Exped. St Peter's R., I, 380, 1824. **Hamine-chan.**—Prescott in Schoolcraft, Ind. Tribes, II, 171, 1852. **He-mini-ćaŋ.**—Dorsey in 15th Rep. B. A. E., 215, 1897. **Hemnića.**—Ibid. **He-**

mni′-ċaŋ.—Riggs, Dak. Gram. and Dict., 73, 1852. **Ki-mni-oan.**—Ramsey in Ind. Aff. Rep., 81, 1850 (trans. 'those who live about the tree on the mountain near the water'). **Qe-mini-tca**ⁿ.—Dorsey, op. cit. **Qemnitca.**—Ibid. **Raymneecha.**—Neill, Hist. Minn., xliv, 589, 1858 (so designated because their village was near a hill, *ha;* 'water,' *min;* and 'wood,' *chan*). **Red Wing's.**—Long, Exped. St Peters R., I, 380, 1824. **Reminica Band.**—Smithson. Misc. Coll., xiv, art. 5, 8, 1878. **Remnica.**—Neill, Hist. Minn., 84, 1858. **Remnichah.**—Ibid., 327. **Shooter.**—Ibid., 144, note (trans. of Wakute, name of the chief). **Talangamanae.**—Shea, Discov., 111, 1852. **Wahcoota band.**—Ind. Aff. Rep., 282, 1854. **Wah-koo-tay.**—Neill, Hist. Minn., 589, 1858 (chief's name). **Wahkuti band.**—Ind. Aff. Rep. 1855, 64, 1856. **Wahute band.**—McKusick in Ind. Aff. Rep.1863, 314, 1864. **Wakootay's band.**—Pike (1806) quoted by Neill, Hist. Minn., 289, 1858 (cf. Coues, Pike's Exped., I, 62, 69, 88, 1895). **Wakuta band.**—Gale, Upper Miss., 252, 1867. **Wa-ku-te.**—Neill, Hist. Minn., 144, note, 1858. **Wakute's band.**—McKusick in Ind. Aff. Rep. 1863, 316, 1864. **Waukouta band.**—Warren in Minn. Hist. Coll., v, 156, 1885. **Weakaote.**—Long, Exped. St Peter's R., 380, 1824.

Kheyataotonwe ('village back from the river'). A Mdewakanton Sioux band formerly occupying the country near Harriet and Calhoun lakes, Minn., driven, according to Neill (Hist. Minn., 590, 1858), from L. Calhoun by the Chippewa and settled in 1858 near Oak Grove, Minn. Ḣeyata-otoŋwe.—Dorsey in 15th Rep. B. A. E., 215, 1897. Ḣeyata tonwan.—Riggs, letter to Dorsey, Mar.28, 1884. **Lake Calhoun band.**—Parker, Minn. Handbook, 140, 1857. **Ma-rpi-wi-ca-xta.**—Neill, Hist. Minn., 144, note, 1858 (name of the chief). Qeyata-otoⁿwe.—Hakewashte quoted by Dorsey, op. cit. Qeyata-toⁿwaⁿ.—Riggs quoted by Dorsey, op.cit. **Reyataotonwe.**—Neill in Minn. Hist. Coll., I, 263, 1872 ('island people'). **Ri-ga-ta-a-ta-wa.**—Smithson. Misc. Coll., xiv, art. 6, 8, 1878. **Sky-Man.**—Neill, Hist. Minn., 144, note, 1858.

Kheyatawichasha ('people back from the river'). The Brulé Teton Sioux who formerly inhabitĕd the sand hills and high country on the Nebraska-Dakota border, subsequently placed under the Rosebud agency, under the name Upper Brulés. The Indian Report for 1885 gives their number (including the Loafer or Waglughe and the Wazhazha) as 6,918. Ḣeyata wiċaṡa.—Dorsey in 15th Rep. B. A. E., 218, 1897. **Highland Brulé.**—Robinson, letter to Dorsey, 1879. **Highland Sicangu.**—Ibid. **Northern Brule.**—Ind.Aff. Rep., 178, 1875. Qeyata-witcaca.—Dorsey, op. cit. **Sicangu.**—Cleveland, letter to Dorsey, 1884 (erroneously refers only to the Upper Brulés, the Lower Brulés being called Kutawicasa). **Upper Brules.**—Ibid. **Upper Platte Indians.**—Ind. Aff. Rep., 209, 1866 (includes most, probably all, the Upper Brulés).

Khidhenikashika (*Qidₑ e′nikaci′γa,* 'eagle people'). A gens of the Quapaw.—Dorsey in 15th Rep. B. A. E., 229, 1897.

Khiltat. A Tenankutchin village on Tanana r. at the mouth of Nabesna r., lat. 63° 40′, Alaska.

Khilukh. A former Yaquina village on the N. side of Yaquina r., Oreg. **K′qil′-ŭq.**—Dorsey in Jour. Am. Folk-lore, III, 229, 1890.

Khinonascarant ('at the base of the mountain.'—Hewitt). A Huron village in Ontario in 1637.—Jes. Rel. for 1637, 126, 1858.

Khinukhtunne ('people among the small undergrowth'). A former village of the Mishikhwutmetunne on Coquille r., Oreg.

K′qi-nuq′ ɹûnnĕ′.—Dorsey in Jour. Am. Folk-lore, III, 232, 1890.

Khioetoa. A former village of the Neutrals, apparently situated a short distance E. of the present Sandwich, Ontario, Canada. (J. N. B. H.) **Khioetoa.**—Jes. Rel. for 1641, 80, 1858. **Kioetoa.**—Jes. Rel., III, index, 1858. **St. Michel.**—Jes. Rel. for 1641, 80, 1858 (mission name).

Khitalaitthe. A former Yaquina village on the s. side of Yaquina r., Oreg. **Kqi′-ɹä-lai′-t′çĕ.**—Dorsey in Jour. Am. Folk-lore, III, 229, 1890.

Khitanumanke ('eagle'). Mentioned as a Mandan gens, but evidently only a band. **Ki-tä′-ne-mäke.**—Morgan, Anc. Soc., 158, 1877. **Qi-ta′ nu-mañ′-ke.**—Dorsey in 15th Rep. B. A. E., 241, 1897 (given with a query).

Khlimkwaish ('man goes along with the current'). A former Alsea village on the s. side of Alsea r., Oreg. **Kqlĭm-kwaic′.**—Dorsey in Jour. Am. Folk-lore, III, 230, 1890.

Khlokhwaiyutslu ('deep lake'). A former Alsea village on the N. side of Alsea r., Oreg. **Kqlo′-qwai yu-tslu.**—Dorsey in Jour. Am. Folklore, III, 230, 1890.

Khloshlekhwuche. A former village of the Chastacosta on Rogue r., Oreg. **K′qloc′-le-qwŭt′-tcĕ.**—Dorsey in Jour. Am. Folklore, III, 234, 1890.

Khoalek. A Pomo village on upper Clear lake, Cal.—Kroeber, MS., Univ. Cal., 1903.

Khoghanhlani ('many huts'). A Navaho clan. *Hoganláni.*—Matthews, Navaho Legends, 31, 1897. **Qo-ganlàni.**—Matthews in Jour. Am. Folk-lore, III, 104, 1890.

Khogoltlinde. A Kaiyuhkhotana village on Yukon r., Alaska; pop. 60 in 1844. **Khogoltlinde.**—Zagoskin quoted by Petroff in 10th Census, Alaska, 37, 1844. **Khogotlinde.**—Zagoskin, Desc. Russ. Poss. Am., map, 1844.

Kholkh. A former Yaquina village on the s. side of Yaquina r., Oreg. **K′qōlq.**—Dorsey in Jour. Am. Folk-lore, III, 229, 1890.

Khomtinin ('southerners'). A generic term applied by all Yokuts tribes to those s. of them, especially if of their own linguistic family. Cf. *Khosminin.*

Khonagani ('place of walking'). A Navaho clan. *Honagá′ni.*—Matthews Návaho Legends, 30, 1897. **Qonagá′ni.**—Matthews in Jour. Am. Folk-lore, III, 104, 1890.

Khoonkhwuttunne. A former village of the Tolowa at the mouth of Smith r., Cal.; incorrectly given by Dorsey as a Khaamotene village. **Qo-on′-qwût-ɹûn′nĕ.**—Dorsey in Jour. Folklore, III, 236, 1890 (Tututni name). **Qû-wûn′-kqwût.**—Ibid. (Naltunne name).

Khosatunne. A former village of the Tolowa on the forks of Smith r., Cal., near the Oregon line. **Q′o′-sa ɹûn′nĕ.**—Dorsey in Jour. Am. Folk-lore, III, 236, 1890 (Tututni name). **Qwa**ⁿ**-s′a-a′-tûn.**—Ibid. (Naltunne name).

Khosminin ('northerners'). A generic term applied by all Yokuts tribes to those N. of them, whether of their own or of alien stock. Cf. *Khomtinin.*

Josimnin.—Arroyo de la Cuesta, Idiomas Californias, 1821, MS. trans., B. A. E. **Khosminin.**—A. L. Kroeber, inf'n, 1905.

Khotachi ('elk'). An extinct Iowa gens, coordinate with the Hotachi gens of the Missouri. Its subgentes were Unpeghakhanye, Unpeghayine, Unpeghathrecheyine, and Homayine.

Ho'-dash.—Morgan, Anc. Soc., 156, 1877. Ho'-tatci.—Dorsey, Tciwere MS. vocab., B. A. E., 1879. Qo'-ta-tci.—Dorsey in 15th Rep. B. A. E., 238, 1897.

Khotana. A name applied to several Athapascan tribes of lower Yukon r., Cook's inlet, and Koyukuk r., Alaska, as the Kaiyuhkhotana, Knaiakhotana, Unakhotana, and Koyukukhotana; and sometimes to these tribes collectively. The name contains the term for 'people' in their dialects.   (J. R. S.)

Khotltacheche. A former village of the Chastacosta on Rogue r., Oreg.

Qōtl'-ta-tce'-tcĕ.—Dorsey in Jour. Am. Folk-lore, III, 234, 1890.

Khoughitchate. A village, probably of an Athapascan tribe, above the N. mouth of Innoko r., w. Alaska.—Zagoskin in Nouv. Ann. Voy., 5th s., XXI, map, 1850.

Khra ('eagle'). A subgens of the Cheghita gens of the Missouri.

Kha'-ă.—Morgan, Anc. Soc., 156, 1877 (Eagle). Khu-a nika-shing-ga.—Stubbs, Kaw MS. vocab., B. A. E., 25, 1877. Qra.—Dorsey in 15th Rep. B. A. E., 246, 1897.

Khrahune (Qra' hŭñ'-e, 'ancestral or gray eagle'). A subgens of the Cheghita gens of the Iowa.—Dorsey in 15th Rep. B. A. E., 238, 1897.

Khrakreye (Qra'qre'-ye, 'spotted eagle'). A subgens of the Cheghita gens of the Iowa.—Dorsey in 15th Rep. B. A. E., 238, 1897.

Khrapathan (Qra' pa çan, 'bald eagle'). A subgens of the Cheghita gens of the Iowa.—Dorsey in 15th Rep. B. A. E., 238, 1897.

Khtalutlitunne. A former village of the Chastacosta on Rogue r., Oreg.

Qta'-lût-li' ʒûnnĕ.—Dorsey in Jour. Am. Folk-lore, III, 234, 1890.

Khube (Qube, 'mysterious'). A subgens of the Mandhinkagaghe gens of the Omaha.—Dorsey in 15th Rep. B. A. E., 228, 1897.

Khudhapasan ('bald eagle'). A subgens of the Tsishuwashtake gens of the Osage.

ọansan'u'niqk'ăcin'a.—Dorsey in 15th Rep. B. A. E., 234, 1897 (Sycamore people). Qüça' pa san.—Ibid.

Khulhanshtauk. A former Yaquina village on Yaquina r., at the site of Elk City, Benton co., Oreg.

Kqûl-hanc't-auk.—Dorsey in Jour. Am. Folk-lore, III, 229, 1890.

Khuligichakat. A Jugelnute village on Shageluk r., Alaska.

Khuligichagat.—Zagoskin, Descr. Russ. Poss. Am., map, 1844. Khuligichakat.—Zagoskin quoted by Petroffin, 10th Census, Alaska, 37, 1884.

Khulikakat. A Kaiyuhkhotana village on Yukon r., Alaska; pop. 11 in 1844.—Zagoskin quoted by Petroff in 10th Census, Alaska, 37, 1884.

Khulpuni. A former Cholovone village on lower San Joaquin r., Cal.

Chulpun.—Chamisso in Kotzebue, Voy., III, 51, 1821. Guylpunes.—Taylor in Cal. Farmer, Oct. 18, 1861. Hulpunes.—Kotzebue, New Voy., 146, 1830. Khoulpouni.—Choris, Voy. Pitt., 5, 1822.

Khunanilinde. A Kaiyuhkhotana village near the headwaters of Kuskokwim r., w. Alaska; pop. 9 in 1880.

Khounanilinde.—Zagoskin in Nouv. Ann. Voy., 5e s., XXI, map, 1850. Khunanilinde.—Zagoskin as quoted by Petroff in 10th Census, Alaska, 37, 1884.

Khundjalan (Qŭndj-alan, 'wear red cedar on their heads'). A subgens of the Ponka gens of the Kansa.—Dorsey in 15th Rep. B. A. E., 231, 1897.

Khundtse (Qŭnʒse', 'red cedar'). A subgens of the Panhkawashtake gens of the Osage.—Dorsey in 15th Rep. B. A. E., 234, 1897.

Khunechuta. A former Tututni village on the N. side of Rogue r., Oreg.

Qûn-e'-tcu-ʒa'.—Dorsey in Jour. Am. Folk-lore, III, 233, 1890.

Khuniliikhwut. A former Chetco village on the S. side of Chetco cr., Oreg.

Q'ŭ'-ni-li-i'-kqwût.—Dorsey in Jour. Am. Folk-lore, III, 236, 1890.

Khuwaihus. A former Kuitsh village on lower Umpqua r., Oreg.

Çlti'-ai-äm'-nḷọ kqu-wai'-hu.—Dorsey in Jour. Am. Folk-lore, III, 1890. Kqu-wai'-hus.—Ibid.

Khuya ('white eagle'). The 10th Kansa gens. Its subgentes are Husada and Wabinizhupye.

Eagle.—Dorsey in Am. Nat., 671, 1885. Hu-e'-yă.—Morgan, Anc. Soc., 156, 1877. Qüya.—Dorsey, op. cit. White Eagle.—Dorsey in 15th Rep. B. A. E., 231, 1897.

Khuyeguzhinga ('hawk that has a tail like a king eagle'). A subgens of the Ibache gens of the Kansa.

Chicken-hawk.—Dorsey in Am. Nat., 674, July 1885. Qüyegu jiñga.—Dorsey in 15th Rep. B. A. E., 231, 1897.

Khwaishtunnetunne ('people of the gravel'). A former Tututni village near the mouth of a small stream locally called Wishtenatin, after the name of the settlement, that enters the Pacific in s. w. Oregon about 10 m. s. of Pistol r., at a place later known as Hustenate, also from the aboriginal village name. The inhabitants, who numbered 66 in 1854, claimed the country as far as a small trading post known as the Whale's Head, about 27 m. s. of the mouth of Rogue r. If there are any survivors they reside on Siletz res., Oreg.

Khust-e-nēt.—Schumacher in Bull. G. and G. Surv., III, 31, 1877. Khust-e-nēte.—Ibid., 33. Qwai'-ctûn-ne' ʒûnnĕ.—Dorsey in Jour. Am. Folk-lore, III, 236, 1890 ('people among the gravel': own name). Qwin'-ctûn-ne'-tûn.—Ibid. (Naltunne name.) Whash-to-na-ton.—Abbott, MS. Coquille census, B. A. E., 1858. Whish-ten-eh-ten.—Gibbs, MS. on coast tribes, B. A. E. Whistanatin.—Schoolcraft, Ind. Tribes, VI, 702, 1857. Wish-ta-nah-tin.—Kautz, MS. Toutouten census, B. A. E., 1855. Wishtanatan.—Taylor in Cal. Farmer, June 18, 1860. Wish-te-na-tin.—Parrish in Ind. Aff. Rep., 495, 1854. Wis'-tûn-ä-ti' tĕne.—Everette, Tututĕne MS. vocab., B. A. E., 1883 (trans: 'people by the springs').

Khwakhamaiu. The Pomo who lived about Ft Ross, the early Russian settlement on the coast in Sonoma co., Cal. The origin of the name is not known.

(S. A. B.)

Chwachamaju.—Wrangell, Ethnol. Nach., 80, 1839. Chwachmaja.—Ludewig, Aborig. Lang., 170, 1858. Khwakhamaiu.—S. A. Barrett, inf'n, 1905. Northerners.—Ibid. Severnovskia.—Ibid. Severnovze.—Ibid. Severnovzer.—Ibid. Severnovzi.—Ibid.

Khweshtunne. A former Mishikhwutmetunne village on Coquille r., Oreg., next above Coquille city.

Qwec' ʒûnnĕ.—Dorsey in Jour. Am. Folk-lore, III, 232, 1890.

Khwunrghunme. Seemingly the Tolowa name of a Yurok village on the coast of California, just s. of the mouth of Klamath r.

Kal'-ă-qu-ni-me'-ne tûn'-nĕ.— Dorsey, Chetco MS. vocab., B. A. E., 183, 1884 (Chetco name). Kal-hwûn'-ûn-me'-ĕ-ni te'-ne.—Dorsey, Smith River MS. vocab., B. A. E., 1884. Qwûn-rxûn'-me.—Dorsey in Jour. Am. Folk-lore, III, 237, 1890 (Naltunne name).

Kiabaha. A village or tribe, now extinct, said to have existed between Matagorda bay and Maligne [Colorado] r., Tex. The name seems to have been given to Joutel in 1687 by the Ebahamo Indians, probably closely affiliated to the Karankawa, whose domain was in this region. A rancheria called Cabras (apparently the same name as Kiabaha), with 26 inhabitants, was mentioned in 1785 as being near the presidio of Bahia and the mission of Espíritu Santo de Zúñiga (q. v.) on the lower Rio San Antonio (Bancroft, No. Mex. States, I, 659, 1886). See Gatschet, Karankawa Ind., 23, 35, 1891. Cf. *Kabaye*.

(A. C. F.)

Cabras.—Bancroft, op. cit. Kiabaha.—Joutel (1687) in Margry, Déc., III, 288, 1878. Kiaboha.—Shea, note in Charlevoix, New France, IV, 78, 1870. Kiahoba.—Joutel (1687) in French, Hist. Coll. La., I, 137, 1846. Kiobobas.—Barcia, Ensayo, 271, 1723. Niabaha.—Joutel (1687) in French, op. cit., 152.

Kiaken (*K·ĭāke'n*, 'palisade' or 'fenced village'). Two Squawmish village communities in British Columbia; one on the left bank of Squawmish r., the other on Burrard inlet.—Hill-Tout in Rep. Brit. A. A. S., 474, 475, 1900.

Kiakima (*K'yä'kima*, 'home of the eagles'). A former Zuñi pueblo at the s. w. base of Thunder mtn., 4 m. s. E. of Zuñi pueblo, w. N. Mex. It was occupied in the 16th and 17th centuries as one of the "Seven Cities of Cibola," and, according to Zuñi tradition, was the scene of the death of the negro Estevanico, who had been a companion of Cabeza de Vaca, and had accompanied Fray Marcos de Niza on his journey from Mexico in 1539; but historical evidence places that event at Hawikuh. It was a visita of the mission of Halona, probably from 1629, and contained about 800 inhabitants, but on the insurrection of the Pueblos against Spanish authority in 1680, Kiakima was permanently abandoned, the inhabitants fleeing to Thunder mtn. for safety. See Bandelier, cited below; Mindeleff in 8th Rep.

B. A. E., 85, 1891; Lowery, Span. Settlements in U. S., 1901. (F. W. H.)

Caquima.—Vetancurt (1693) in Teatro Mex., III, 320, 1871. Caquimay.—Doc. of 1635 quoted by Bandelier in Arch. Inst. Papers, v, 165, 1890. Caquineco.—Ladd, Story of N. Mex., 34, 1891. Coaqueria.—Oñate (1598) in Doc. Inéd., XVI, 133, 1871. Coquimas.—Pike, Exped., 3d map, 1810. Coquimo.—Bandelier quoted in The Millstone, IX, 55, Apr. 1884. Heshota O'aquima.—Bandelier, Gilded Man, 159, 1893 (misprint). Ke'iá-kí-me.—Powell, 2d Rep. B. A. E., XXVI, 1883. K'iä-ki-me.—Cushing in The Millstone, IX, 55, Apr. 1884. K'iä' ki me.—Ibid., 225, Dec. 1884. K'iákime.—Cushing, Zuñi Folk Tales, 65, 1901. Kyakima.—Bandelier in Arch. Inst. Papers, III, 133, 1890. K'yä'-ki-me.—Cushing in Compte-rendu Internat. Cong. Am., VII, 156, 1890. O'aquima.—Bandelier, Gilded Man, 158, 1893 (misprint). Qa-quima.—Bandelier in Revue d'Ethnog., 201, 1886. Quaguina.—Senex, map, 1710. Quaquima.—Bandelier in Arch. Inst. Rep., v, 41, 1884. Quaquina.—De l'Isle, Carte Mex. et Floride, 1703. Quiaquima.—Bandelier in Jour. Am. Ethnol. and Archæol., III, 16, 1892. Quia-Quima.—Ibid., 29. Quiquimo.—Güssefeld, Charte Nord Am., 1797.

Kialdagwuns (*K!ia'ldagwAns*, 'Sandpipers'). A subdivision of the Saguigitunai, a family belonging to the Eagle clan of the Haida.

K!ia'ldagwAns.—Swanton, Cont. Haida, 274, 1905. Kyiä'ltkoangas.—Boas, 12th Rep. N. W. Tribes of Canada, 23, 1898.

Kialegak. A Yuit Eskimo village near Southeast cape, St Lawrence id., Bering sea.

Kahgallegak.—Elliott, Our Arct. Prov., map, 1886. Kgallegak.—Tebenkof (1849) quoted by Baker, Geog. Dict. Alaska, 1902. Kialegak.—Russ. chart. quoted by Baker, ibid. Kiallegak.—Nelson in 18th Rep. B. A. E., map, 1899.

Kialinek. A former village of the Angmagsalingmiut on the E. coast of Greenland, lat. 66° 50′, where they hunted the narwhal and the bear throughout the year. Some of its people are said to have emigrated northward.—Meddelelser om Grönland, IX, 382, 1889.

Kiamisha. A former Caddo village at the junction of Kiamichi and Red rs., in the present Choctaw nation, Okla. It contained 20 families in 1818.

Cayameechee.—Bell in Morse, Rep. to Sec. War, 255, 1822 (the river). Kamissi—Thevenot quoted by Shea, Discov., 268, 1852 (identical?). Kiamisha.—Trimble (1818) in Morse, op. cit., 259 (the river). Kio Michie.—Rublo (1840) in H. R. Doc. 25, 27th Cong., 2d sess., 14, 1841.

Kianusili (*Kia'nusili*, 'cod people'). A family belonging to the Raven clan of the Haida. *Kiän* is the name for the common cod. This family group formerly lived on the w. coast of Queen Charlotte ids., near Hippa id., Brit. Col. (J. R. S.)

Kiānōsilī.—Harrison in Proc. and Trans. Roy. Soc. Canada, II, 123, 1895. Kiä'nusilī.—Swanton, Cont. Haida, 271, 1905. Kyä'nusla.—Boas, 12th Rep. N. W. Tribes Canada, 22, 1898.

Kiashita. A former pueblo of the Jemez in Guadalupe canyon, N. of Jemez pueblo, N. Mex.

Kiashita.—Hodge, field notes, B. A. E., 1895. Quia-shi-dshi.—Bandelier in Arch. Inst. Papers, IV, 207, 1892.

Kiaskusis ('small gulls'). A small Cree band residing in 1856 around the fourth lake from Lac Qu'Apelle, N. W. Ter.,

Canada. They were formerly numerous, but had become reduced to 30 or 40 families owing to persistent Blackfeet raids.—Hayden, Ethnog. and Philol. Mo. Val., 237, 1862.

Kiasutha (alias Guyasuta, 'it sets up a cross.'—Hewitt). A chief of some prominence as an orator in the Ohio region about 1760–1790. Although called a Seneca, he probably belonged to the mixed band of detached Iroquois in Ohio commonly known as Mingo, who sided with the French while their kinsmen of the New York confederacy acted as allies of the English. As a young warrior he accompanied Washington and Gist on their visit to the French forts on the Allegheny in 1753. After Braddock's defeat in 1755 he visited Montreal in company with a French interpreter and in 1759 was present at Croghan's conference with the Indians at Ft Pitt (now Pittsburg). He is mentioned also at the Lancaster conference in 1762, and in 1768 was a leading advocate of peace with the English both at the treaty of Ft Pitt in May and at Bouquet's conference there six months later. Washington visited him while on a hunting tour in Ohio in 1770. He is noted as at other conferences up to the time of the Revolution, and in 1782 is mentioned as leading an Indian raid on one of the frontier settlements. His name occurs last in 1790, when he sent a written message to some friends in Philadelphia. See Darlington, Christopher Gist's Journal, 1893.

Kiatagmiut. A division of the Aglemiut Eskimo of Alaska, inhabiting the banks of Kvichivak r. and Iliamna lake. They numbered 214 in 1890. Their villages are Chikak, Kakonak, Kaskanak, Kichik, Kogiung, Kvichak, and Nogeling.
Kiatagmiut.—Schanz in 11th Census, Alaska, 95, 1893. **Kiatagmute.**—Petroff in 10th Census, Alaska, 135, 1884. **Kiatenes.**—Lutke, Voyage, I, 181, 1835. **Kijataigmjuten.**—Holmberg, Ethnog. Skizz., 5, 1855. **Kijataigmüten.**—Wrangell, Ethnog. Nachr., 121, 1839. **Kijaten.**—Ibid. **Kiyataigmeuten.**—Richardson, Arct. Exped., I, 370, 1851. **Kiyaten.**—Ibid. **Kwichăgmūt.**—Dall in Cont. N. A. Ethnol., I, 19, 1877.

Kiatang ('shoulder'). A village of the Ita Eskimo on Northumberland id., Whale sd., N. Greenland.
Keate.—Peary, Northward, 113, 1898. **Keati.**—Mrs Peary, My Arct. Jour., 84, 1893. **Kiĕ'teng.**—Stein in Petermanns Mitt., 198, 1902. **Kujata.**—Ibid.

Kiatate. A group of ruins in the Sierra de los Huicholes, about 10 m. N. W. of San Andrés Coamiata, in the territory of the Huichol, Jalisco, Mexico.—Lumholtz, Unknown Mex., II, 16, map, 1902.

Kiatsukwa. A former pueblo of the Jemez in New Mexico, the exact site of the ruins of which is not known.
Kiatsúkwa.—Hodge, field notes, B. A. E., 1895. **Quia-tzo-qua.**—Bandelier in Arch. Inst. Papers, IV, 207, 1892.

Kiawaw. A small tribe, of unknown affinity, formerly on Kiawah id., Charles-

ton co., S. C., but long extinct. They were regarded as one of the tribes of the Cusabo group.
Cayawah.—Moll, map, 1715. **Cayawash.**—Moll, map in Humphrey, Acct., 1730. **Keawaw.**—Mills, Stat. S. C., 459, 1826. **Kiawaw.**—Rivers, Hist. S. C., 38, 1856. **Kyewaw.**—Deed of 1675 quoted by Mills, op. cit., app., 1, 1826.

Kiawetnau. The Yokuts name of the territory about Porterville, Cal. Given by Powers (Cont. N. A. Ethnol., III, 370, 1877) as the name of a tribe (Ki-a-wét-ni, which lacks the locative suffix -au).

Kichai (from *Kitsäsh*, their own name). A Caddoan tribe whose language is more closely allied to the Pawnee than to the other Caddoan groups. In 1701 they were met by the French on the upper waters of the Red r. of Louisiana and had spread southward to upper Trinity

KICHAI MAN

r. in Texas. In 1712 a portion of them were at war with the Hainai, who dwelt lower down the Trinity. They were already in possession of horses, as all the Kichai warriors were mounted. They seem to have been allies of the northern and western tribes of the Caddoan confederacy and to have intermarried with the Kadohadacho. In 1719 La Harpe met some of the Kichai on Canadian r., in company with other Caddoan tribes, on their way toward New Mexico to wage war against the Apache. At that time they pledged friendship to the French, to whom they seem to have remained faithful. In common with all the other tribes they suffered from the introduction of new diseases and from the conflicts incident to the contention of the Spaniards, French, and English for control of the country, and became greatly reduced in numbers. In 1772 the main Kichai village was E. of Trinity r., not far from Palestine, perhaps a little N. E. At that time it was composed of 30 houses, occupied by 80 warriors, "for the most part young." In 1778 there was another village, "separated from the main body of the tribe," farther s. and in nearly a direct line from San Pedro to the Tawakoni villages, probably on the site of the present Salt City. The junta de guerra held in the same year estimated the strength of the Kichai at 100 fighting men (Bolton, inf'n, 1906). With several other small Texas tribes they were assigned by the United States Government to a reservation on Brazos r. in 1855, but on the dispersal of the Indians by the Texans three years later they fled N. and joined the Wichita, with whom they have since been associated, and whom they resemble in their agriculture, house-building, and general customs. About 50 souls still keep the tribal name and language.

See Pénicaut in French, Hist. Coll. La., n. s., 73, 120, 1869; La Harpe in Margry, Déc., VI, 277–8, 1886; Rep. Com. Ind. Aff., 1846, 1849, 1851, 1872, 1901. (A. C. F.)

Cachies.—Arbuckle in H. R. Doc. 434, 25th Cong., 2d sess., 5, 1838. Cassia.—Joutel (1687) in Margry, Déc., III, 409, 1878. Gíts'ajĭ.—Dorsey, Kansa MS. vocab., B. A. E., 1882 (Kansa name). Guichais.— Tex. State Arch., 1792. Guitzeis.—Morfi, MS. Historia, bk. 2, cited by Bolton, infn, 1906. Hitchi.— Latham in Trans. Philol. Soc. Lond., 104, 1856 (misprint). Hitchies.—Burnet (1847) in Schoolcraft, Ind. Tribes, I, 239, 1851. Kăjĭ.—McCoy, Annual Register, no. 4, 27, 1838. Kechies.—Alvord in Sen. Ex. Doc. 18, 40th Cong., 3d sess., 6, 1869. Kechies.— Marcy, Explor. Red r., 93, 1854. Kechis.—Latham, Essays, 399, 1860. Keechers.—Ind. Aff. Rep., 144, 1850. Keechi.—Whiting in Rep. Sec. War, 242, 1850. Keechies.—Ind. Aff. Rep., 894, 1846. Keechy.—Sen. Ex. Conf. Doc. 13, 29th Cong., 2d sess., 1, 1846. Keetsas.—Arbuckle (1845) in Sen. Ex. Doc. 14, 32d Cong., 2d sess., 134, 1853. Kekies.—Ind. Aff. Rep. 1871, 191, 1872. Kerchi.—Ibid., 263, 1851. Ketcheyes.—Edward, Hist. Texas, 92, 1836. Ketchies.— Bollaert in Jour. Ethnol. Soc. Lond., II, 265, 1850. Keycchies.—Lewis and Clark, Journal, 142, 1840. Keyche.—Drake, Bk. Inds., viii, 1848. Keychies.— Pénicaut (1701) in French, Hist. Coll. La., n. s., I, 73, 1869. Keyes.—Sibley, Hist. Sketches, 70, 1806. Keyeshees.—Brackenridge, Views of La., 87, 1815. Keys.—Lewis and Clark, Journal, 145, 1840. Kichae.—Bol. Soc. Geogr. Mex., 267, 1870. Kichais.—Whipple in Pac. R. R. Rep., III, pt. 3, 76, 1856. Kiche.—Wallace (1840) in H. R. Doc. 25, 27th Cong., 2d sess., 5, 1841. Kichis.—Sen. Ex. Doc. 14, 32d Cong., 2d sess., 16, 1853. Ki-ḍi'-tcac.—Dorsey, Çegiha MS. dict., B. A. E., 1878 (Omaha name). Kiechee.—Ind. Aff. Rep. 1849, 36, 1850. Kiétsash.— Gatschet, Wichita MS., B. A. E. (Wichita name). Kishais.—H. R. Rep. 299, 44th Cong., 1st sess., 1, 1876. Kitaesches.—Pénicaut (1714) in Margry, Déc., v, 502, 1883. Kitaesechis.—Pénicaut (1714) in French, Hist. Coll. La., n. s., I, 120, 1869. Ki'tchas.— Gatschet, Tonkawa MS., B. A. E. (Tonkawa name). Ki'-tchĕsh.—Gatschet, Caddo and Yatassi MS., 65, B. A. E. (Caddo name). Kitchies.— Schoolcraft, Ind. Tribes, I, 237, 1851. Kítsaoi.— Dorsey, Osage MS. vocab., B. A. E., 1883 (Osage name). Kitsaiches.—Bruyère (1742) in Margry, Déc., VI, 492, 1886. Ki'tsäsh.—Mooney in 14th Rep. B. A. E., 1095, 1896 (own name). Kitsasĭ.—Grayson, Creek MS. vocab., B. A. E., 1885 (Creek name). Kits de Singes.—Robin, Voyages, III, 5, 1807. Kitsoss.— Arbuckle in H. R. Doc. 434, 25th Cong., 2d sess., 5, 1838. Ki'tsu.—Gatschet, MS., B. A. E. (Pawnee and Wichita name). Koechies.—Schoolcraft, Ind.

Tribes, I, 518, 1851. Kyis.—Brackenridge, Views of La., 81, 1815. Queyches.—Jefferys, Am. Atlas, map 5, 1776. Quichaais.—Census of 1790 in Tex. State Arch. Quichais.—Ybarbo (1778), letter cited by Bolton, inf'n, 1906. Quicheigno.—Ripperdá (1774), ibid. Quiches.—Anville, Carte des Isles de l'Amérique, 1731. Quidaho.—La Harpe (1719) in French, Hist. Coll. La., III, 72, 1851. Quidehaio.—Ibid. Quidehais.—La Harpe (1719) in Margry, Déc., VI, 277, 1886 (probably identical). Quitoeis.—Mezières (1778) quoted by Bancroft, No. Mex. States, I, 661, 1886. Quitres.—Mezières (1779), letter cited by Bolton, inf'n, 1906. Quitreys.—Ibid. Quitseigus.— Ripperdá (1776), letter, ibid. Quitseings.—Ripperdá (1777), letter, ibid. Quitseis.—Doc. of 1771–2 quoted by Bolton in Tex. Hist. Quar., IX, 91, 1905. Quituchiis.—Villa-Señor, Theatro Am., II, 413, 1748. Quitxix.—Fran. de Jesus María (1691), Relacion cited by Bolton, inf'n, 1906. Quitzaené.—Pimentel, Cuadro Descr., II, 347, 1865 (given as a Comanche division). Quizi.—Fran. de Jesus María (1691) cited by Bolton, inf'n, 1906.

Kicham (_K·'tcā'm_). A Squawmish village community on Burrard inlet, Brit. Col.—Hill-Tout in Rep. Brit. A. A. S., 475, 1900.

Kichesipirini ('men of the great river,' from _kiche_ 'great', _sipi_ 'river', _iriniouek_ 'men.' By the Huron they were called Ehonkeronon; from the place of their residence they were often designated Algonquins of the Island, and Savages of the Island. Once an important tribe living on Allumette id., in Ottawa r., Quebec province. They were considered as the typical Algonkin, and in order to distinguish them from the other tribes included under the term in this restricted sense were called "Algonquins of the Island," a name first applied by Champlain (see _Algonkin_). As Ottawa r. was the line of travel between the upper-lake country and the French settlements, the position of the tribe made it at times troublesome to traders and voyageurs, although as a rule they appear to have been peaceable. In 1645 they, together with the Hurons, made a treaty of peace with the Iroquois; but it was of short duration, for 5 years later both the Hurons and the Kichesipirini fled for safety to more distant regions. What became of them is not known. It is probable that they were consolidated with the Ottawa or with some other northwestern Algonquian tribe. (J. M. J. N. B. H.)

Algommequin de l'Isle.—Champlain (1632), Œuvres, v, pt. 2, 193, 1870 (see _Algonkin_ for various forms of the word). Ehonkeronons.—Jes. Rel. 1639, 88, 1858. Héhonqueronon.—Sagard (1632), Hist. Can., IV, cap. 'Nations,' 1866. Honqueronons.—Sagard (1636), ibid., III, 620. Honquerons.—Ibid., I, 247. Kichesipiiriniouek.—Jes. Rel. 1658, 22, 1858. Kichesipirini.—Ibid., 1640, 34, 1858. Kichesipiriniwek.—Ibid., 1646, 34, 1858. Nation de l' Isle.— Ibid., 1633, 34, 1858. Sauvages de l' Isle.—Ibid., 1646, 34, 1858.

Kichik. A Kiatagmiut village on a lake of the same name E. of Iliamna lake, Alaska; pop. 91 in 1880.—Tenth Census, Alaska, map, 1884.

Kichye ('where there is much _ki-ke_,' a lily root used for glue). A small rancheria of the Tarahumare in the Sierra Madre, w. Chihuahua, Mexico.—Lumholtz, inf'n, 1894.

Kickapoo (from *Kiwĭgapawᵃ*, 'he stands about,' or 'he moves about, standing now here, now there'). A tribe of the central Algonquian group, forming a division with the Sauk and Foxes, with whom they have close ethnic and linguistic connection. The relation of this division is rather with the Miami, Shawnee, Menominee, and Peoria than with the Chippewa, Potawatomi, and Ottawa.

History.—The people of this tribe, unless they are hidden under a name not yet known to be synonymous, first appear in history about 1667–70. At this

KICKAPOO MAN

time they were found by Allouez near the portage between Fox and Wisconsin rs. Verwyst (Missionary Labors, 1886) suggests Alloa, Columbia co., Wis., as the probable locality, about 12 m. s. of the mixed village of the Mascouten, Miami, and Wea. No tradition of their former home or previous wanderings has been recorded; but if the name Outitchakouk mentioned by Druillettes (Jes. Rel. 1658, 21, 1858) refers to the Kickapoo, which seems probable, the first mention of them is carried back a few years, but they were then in the same locality. Le Sueur

(1699) mentions, in his voyage up the Mississippi, the river of the Quincapous (Kickapoo), above the mouth of the Wisconsin, which he says was "so called from the name of a nation which formerly dwelt on its banks." This probably refers to Kickapoo r., Crawford co., Wis., though it empties into the Wisconsin, and not into the Mississippi. Rock r., Ill., was for a time denominated the "River of the Kickapoos," but this is much too far s. to agree with the stream mentioned by Le Sueur. A few years later a part at least of the tribe appears to have moved s. and settled somewhere about Milwaukee r. They entered into the plot of the Foxes in 1712 to burn the fort at Detroit. On the destruction of the Illinois confederacy, about 1765, by the combined forces of the tribes N. of them, the conquered country was partitioned among the victors, the Sauk and Foxes moving down to the Rock r. country, while the Kickapoo went farther s., fixing their headquarters for a time at Peoria. They appear to have gradually extended their range, a portion centering about Sangamon r., while another part pressed toward the E., establishing themselves on the waters of the Wabash, despite the opposition of the Miami and Piankashaw. The western band became known as the Prairie band, while the others were denominated the Vermilion band, from their residence on Vermilion r., a branch of the Wabash. They played a prominent part in the history of this region up to the close of the War of 1812, aiding Tecumseh in his efforts against the United States, while many Kickapoo fought with Black Hawk in 1832. In 1837 Kickapoo warriors to the number of 100 were engaged by the United States to go, in connection with other western Indians, to fight the Seminole of Florida. In 1809 they ceded to the United States their lands on Wabash and Vermilion rs., and in 1819 all their claims to the central portion of Illinois. Of this land, as stated in the treaty, they "claim a large portion by descent from their ancestors, and the balance by conquest from the Illinois nation, and uninterrupted possession for more than half a century." They afterward removed to Missouri and thence to Kansas. About the year 1852 a large party left the main body, together with some Potawatomi, and went to Texas and thence to Mexico, where they became known as "Mexican Kickapoo." In 1863 they were joined by another dissatisfied party from the tribe. The Mexican band proved a constant source of annoyance to the border settlements, and efforts were made to induce them to return, which were so far successful that in 1873 a number were brought back and settled in Indian Ter. Others have come in since, but the remainder, constituting at present nearly half the tribe, are now settled on a reservation, granted them by the Mexican government, in the Santa Rosa mts. of E. Chihuahua.

Customs and Beliefs.—The Kickapoo lived in fixed villages, occupying bark houses in the summer and flag-reed oval lodges during the winter. They raised corn, beans, and squashes, and while dwelling on the E. side of the Mississippi they often wandered out on the plains to hunt buffalo. On these hunting trips they came to know the horse, and previous to the Civil war they had gone as far as Texas for the sole purpose of stealing horses and mules from the Comanche. No other Alg. nquians of the central group were more familiar with the Indians of the plains than the Kickapoo; and yet, with all this contact, their culture has remained essentially the same as that of the Sauk and the Foxes.

Like the Sauk and Foxes they believe in a cosmic substance prevailing throughout all nature, and the objects endowed with the mystic property are given special reverence. Far in the past they claim to have practised the *Midéwiwin;* but to-day their most sacred ceremony is the *Kigänowini*, the feast dance of the clans. The dog is held in special veneration and is made an object of sacrifice and offering to the manitos. The mythology is rich, and is characterized by a mass of beast fable. The great cosmic myth centers about the death of the younger brother of the culture-hero, whose name is Wisa käⁿ. To him they attribute all the good things of this world and the hope of life in the spirit world, over which the younger brother presides. The brothers are idealized as youths.

The gentile system prevailed, and marriage was outside of the gens. The name had an intimate connection with the gens, and children followed the gens of the father. The gentes to-day are Water, Tree, Berry, Thunder, Man, Bear, Elk, Turkey, Bald-eagle, Wolf, and Fox.

Population.—In 1759 the population of the Kickapoo was estimated at about 3,000; in 1817 at 2,000, and in 1825 at 2,200. Since the last-mentioned date they have greatly decreased. In 1875 those in Kansas and Indian Ter. together, including all of those recently brought from Mexico, were officially reported to number 706, while 100 more were supposed to be in Mexico, making a total for the tribe of about 800. In 1885 those in the United States numbered about 500, of whom 235 were in Kansas, while the Mexican band in Indian Ter. (including some Potawatomi) numbered about 325. It is supposed that there were at the same time about 200 living in Mexico. Those in the United States in 1905 were officially reported at 432, of whom 247 were in Oklahoma and 185 in Kansas. There are supposed to be about 400 or more in Mexico. Within the last two years there has been considerable effort by private parties to procure the removal of the Oklahoma band also to Mexico.

The following are known as Kickapoo villages: Etnataek (with Sauk and Foxes), Kickapougowi, and Neconga.

(J. M. W. J.)

A'-uyaχ.—Gatschet, Tonkawe MS., B. A. E., 1884 ('deer eaters,' from *a'-u* deer, *ya'χa* 'to eat': Tonkawa name). Gîgabu.—Gatschet, Fox MS., B. A. E., 1882 (Fox name; plural Gîgabuhak). Gikapu.—Gatschet, ibid. (Fox name). Gokapatagans.—Bacqueville de la Potherie, Hist. de l'Amér, IV, 224, 1753 (perhaps identical). Hígabu.—Dorsey, Ꞓegiha MS. vocab., B. A. E., 1878 (Omaha and Ponca name). Hiꞧa'pu.—Dorsey, Tciwere MS. vocab., B. A. E., 1879 (Iowa, Oto, and Missouri name). I'-ka-dŭ'.—Dorsey, MS. Osage vocab., B. A. E., 1883 (Osage name). Kackapoes.—Dalton (1783) in Mass. Hist. Soc. Coll., 1st s., X, 123, 1809. Kecapos.—Croghan (1759) in Rupp, West. Pa., app., 132, 1846. Kecopes.—Croghan, (1760) in Mass. Hist. Soc. Coll., 4th s., IX, 250, 1871. Ke-ga-boge.—Morgan, Consang. and Affin., 288, 1871. Kehabous.—McKenney and Hall, Ind. Tribes, III, 79, 1854 (misprint). Kekapos.—Croghan (1759) in Rupp, West. Pa., app., 134, 1846. Kekapou.—Doc. of 1695 in N. Y. Doc. Col. Hist., IX, 619, 1855. Kekaupoag.—Tanner, Narrative, 315, 1830 (Ottawa name). Kicapoos.—Croghan (1765) in Craig, Olden Time, 409, 1846. Kicapous.—Johnson (1772) in N. Y. Doc. Col. Hist., VIII, 292, 1857. Kicapoux.—Doc. of 1748, ibid., X, 150, 1858. Kicapus.—Rafinesque, introd. Marshall, Ky., I, 38, 1824. Kiccapoos.—Croghan (1765) in Monthly Am. Jour. Geol., 263, 1831. Kichapacs.—Writer of 1786 in Mass. Hist. Soc. Coll., 1st s., III, 26, 1794. Kickapoos.—Croghan (1765) in N. Y. Doc. Col. Hist., VII, 780, 1856. Kickapos.—German Flats conf. (1770), ibid., VIII, 244, 1857. Kickapous.—Chauvignerie (1736), ibid., IX, 1055, 1855. Kickipoo.—Gale, Upper Miss., map, 1867. Kicoagoves.—Barcia, Ensayo, 238, 1723 (mentioned with Miami and Mascoutin). Kicoapous.—Tonti, Rel. de la Louisiane, 82, 1720. Kicopoux.—Chauvignerie (1736) in Schoolcraft, Ind. Tribes, III, 554, 1853. Kikabeux.—Marquette, Discov., 322, 1698. Kikabons.—Bacqueville de la Potherie, Hist. de l'Amér., II, 49, 1753. Kikabou.—Jes. Rel. 1670, 100, 1858. Kikaboua.—Jes. Rel. 1672, LVIII, 40, 1899. Kikábu.—Dorsey, Kansa MS. vocab., B. A. E., 1882 (Kansa name). Kikapaus.—Hennepin, Cont. of New Discov., map, 1698. Kikapoes.—Vincennes treaty (1803) in U. S. Ind. Treat., 383, 1873. Kikapoos.—Vater, Mith., pt. 3, sec. 3, 351, 1816. Kikapous.—Hennepin, New Discov., 132, 1698. Kikap8s.—Vaudreuil (1719) in N. Y. Doc. Col. Hist., IX, 893, 1855. Kikapoux.—Frontenac (1682), ibid., 182. Kikapouz.—Coxe, Carolana, 18, 1741. Kikapu.—Gatschet, Potawatomi MS., B. A. E., 1878 (Potawatomi name; plural Kíkapug). Kikapus.—Loskiel, Hist. Miss. United Breth., pt. 1, 2, 1794. Kikkapoos.—Barton, New Views, xxxiii, 1798. Kikpouz.—Coxe, Carolana, 50, 1741. Kispapous.—Longueuil (1752) in N. Y. Doc. Col. Hist., X, 246, 1858 (misprint). Qnicapous —Tonti, Rel. de la Louisiane, 99, 1720 (misprint). Quicapause.—Lattré, map, 1784. Quicapons.—Esnauts and Rapilly, map, 1777 (misprint). Quicapous.—De Bourain (1700) in Margry, Déc., VI, 73, 1886. Quinaquois.—McKenney and Hall, Ind. Tribes, III, 80, 1854. Quincapous.—Iberville (1700) in Neill, Minn., 154, 1858. Ricapous.—Conf. of 1766 in N. Y. Doc. Col. Hist., VII, 860, 1856 (misprint). Rickapoos.—Croghan (1765), ibid. (misprint). Shack-a-po.—H. R. Rep. 299, 44th Cong., 1st sess., 1, 1876 ("known to us as Kickapoos"). Shake-kah-quah.—Marcy, Explor. Red R., 273, 1854 (Wichita name). Shígapo.—Gatschet, Apache MS., B. A. E., 1884 (so called by Apache and other southern tribes). **Shikapu.**—Ibid. (Apache name). **Sik'-a-pu.**—ten Kate, Synonymie, 10, 1884 (Comanche name). **Tékapu.**—Gatschet, Wyandot MS., B. A. E., 1881 (Huron name). **Yuⁿtara'ye-ru'nu.**—Ibid. ('tribe living around the lakes': another Huron name).

Kickapoos. According to Norton (Polit. Americanisms, 60, 1890), a secret Republican political organization in Oklahoma (1888); from the name of an Algonquian tribe.   (A. F. C.)

Kickapougowi. A former Kickapoo village on the Wabash, in Crawford co., Ill., about opposite the mouth of Turman cr.
Kick-a-pou-go-wi Town.—Hough, map in Ind. Geol. Rep., 1883. **Kikapouguoi.**—Gamelin (1790) in Am. State Papers, Ind. Aff., I, 93, 1832.

Kickenapawling. A former village of mixed Delawares and Iroquois, taking its name from the chief; situated 5 m. N. of the present Stoyestown, Pa., between or at the fork of Quemahoning and Stony crs. It was abandoned before 1758.
Keckkeknepolin.—Post (1758) in Rupp, West. Pa., app., 103, 1846. **Kickenapawling.**—Day, Penn., 182, 1843. **Kickenapawlings Old Town.**—Day, Pa. Hist. Coll., 182, 1843. **Kickenapawlings Village.**—Royce in 18th Rep. B. A. E., Pa. map, 1899.

Kicking Bear. A Sioux medicine-man of Cheyenne River agency, S. Dak., who acquired considerable notoriety as leader of a hostile band and priest of the Ghost-dance craze among the Sioux in 1890. He organized and led the first dance at Sitting Bull's camp on Standing Rock res., and was prominent in the later hostilities, for which he was afterward held for some time as a military prisoner. See Mooney in 14th Rep. B. A. E., 1896.

Kicking Bird (Tené-angpóte). A Kiowa chief. He was the grandson of a Crow captive who was adopted into the tribe, and early distinguished himself by his mental gifts. In tribal traditions and ceremonial rites he was a thorough adept, and as a warrior he won a name, but had the sagacity to see the hopelessness of the struggle with the whites and used all his influence to induce the tribe to submit to inevitable conditions. He signed the first agreement to accept a reservation on Aug. 15, 1865, at Wichita, and the treaty concluded at Medicine Lodge on Oct. 21, 1867, definitively fixing the Kiowa-Comanche-Apache res. in the present Oklahoma. In the resistance to removal to the reservation in 1868 and in the subsequent raids into Texas he took no part. When the Federal authorities in 1873 failed to carry out their agreement to release the Kiowa chiefs imprisoned in Texas, he lost faith in the Government and was tempted to join the expeditions against the Tonkawa tribe and the white buffalo-hunters of Texas in 1874; but when Lone Wolf decided to join the hostiles who were defying United States troops, Kicking Bird induced two-thirds of the tribe to return with him to the agency at Ft Sill, and was treated thenceforth as the

head chief of the Kiowa, Lone Wolf's offer to surrender and join the friendlies being refused. He invited and assisted in the establishment of the first school among the Kiowa in 1873. At one time when his constant advocacy of peace brought him into disrepute and the charges that he was a woman and a coward caused his counsels to be treated with contempt, he gathered a band for a Texas raid and fought a detachment of troops victoriously, regaining his old repute for courage and success in war. He died suddenly, by poison if the suspicions of his friends were just, on May 5, 1875, and at the request of his family was buried with Christian rites.—Mooney in 17th Rep., B. A. E., II, 190, 216, 252, 1898.

Kick in the Belly. Mentioned by Culbertson (Smithson. Rep. 1850, 144, 1851) as a Crow band.

Kiddekubbut. A Makah summer village 3 m. from Neah, N. w. Wash.
Kiddekubbut.—Swan in Smithson. Cont., XVI, 6, 1870. **Tehdakomit.**—Gibbs, MS. 248, B. A. E.

Kidnelik. A tribe of Central Eskimo living on Coronation bay, Canada.
Copper Eskimo.—Schwatka in Science, 543, 1884. **Kidelik.**—Rink, Eskimo Tribes, 33, 1887. **Kidnelik.**—Schwatka in Science, 543, 1884. **Qidneliq.**—Boas in 6th Rep. B. A. E., 470, 1888.

Kientpoos. See *Kintpuash*.

Kiequotank. A village of the Powhatan confederacy, at the present Hampton, Va., where Lord De la Warre built his Ft. Henry. It was nearly depopulated in 1722.
Kiequotank.—Beverley, Virginia, 199, 1722. **Kikotan.**—Herrman, map (1670), in Maps to Accompany the Rep. of the Comrs. on the Bndry. Line bet. Va. and Md., 1873.

Kigicapigiak ('the great establishment,' or 'great harbor'). A former Micmac village on Cascapediac r., Bonaventure co., Quebec.—Vetromile, Abnakis, 59, 1866.

Kigiktagmiut ('island people'). A tribe of Eskimo inhabiting the islands of Hudson bay off the Labrador coast, between lat. 56° and 61°. They wear the skins of seals and dogs instead of reindeer skins, use the bow and arrow and the spear instead of firearms, and often suffer for want of food.
Ki'gĭktag'myut.—Turner in 11th Rep. B. A. E., 180, 1894. **Kigukhtagmyut.**—Turner in Trans. Roy. Soc. Can., 1887, sec. II, 99.

Kiglashka ('they who tie their own'). A division of the Hunkpapa Teton Sioux.
Kiglacka.—Dorsey in 15th Rep. B. A. E., 221, 1897. **Kiglaśka.**—Ibid.

Kigsitatok. A former Aleut village on Agattu id., Alaska, one of the Near id. group of the Aleutians, now uninhabited.

Kihegashugah. See *Mohongo*.

Kik. The House clan of the Ala (Horn) phratry of the Hopi.
Kik-wüñ-wü.—Fewkes in Am. Anthrop., VII, 401, 1894 (*wüñ-wü* = 'clan').

Kikait (*Kĭkait*). A Kwantlen village at Brownsville, opposite New Westminster, on lower Fraser r., Brit. Col.; pop., together with the New Westminster village, 65 in 1902.—Hill-Tout in Ethnol. Surv. Can., 54, 1902.

Kikatsik (*Ki'-kat-sik*). One of the 4 divisions of the main body of Shasta, occupying Shasta valley and Klamath valley from Hot Springs to Scott r., N. Cal. They were early mentioned, under various forms of "Autire" and "Edhowe" (from *Ahótidĕ'ĕ*, the Shasta name of Shasta valley), as occupying 19 to 24 villages of about 60 inhabitants each, one of which was apparently Wiyahawir. There are now only a few survivors. (R. B. D.)
Autiré.— Curtin, MS. vocab., B. A. E., 1885. É'd-ohwe.—Ibid. Ho-te-day.—Steele in Ind. Aff. Rep. 1864, 120, 1865 (given as their own name). Id-do-a.—Ibid. (misapplied to the Iruwaitsu). O-de-eilah.—Gibbs (1851) in Schoolcraft, Ind. Tribes, III, 171, 1853. O-de-i-lah.— McKee (1851) in Sen. Ex. Doc. 4, 32d Cong., spec. sess., 221, 1853. Yeka.—Steele in Ind. Aff. Rep. 1864, 120, 1865 (given as proper name of Yreka = 'Shasta butte;' properly Waii'ka). Yrekas. — Taylor in Cal. Farmer, June 22, 1860.

Kikchik. A former Aleut village on Agattu id., Alaska, one of the Near id. group of the Aleutians, now uninhabited.

Kikertarsoak ('great island'). An Eskimo village in Greenland, about lat. 63° 30'; pop. 75 in 1829. Its harbor was formerly used by the Dutch in trading with the natives.
Kikkertarsoak.—Graah, Exped. E. Coast Greenland, map, 1837.

Kikhkat. A former Ikogmiut Eskimo village on the N. bank of Yukon r., near Ikogmiut, Alaska.—Zagoskin in Nouv. Ann. Voy., 5th s., XXI, map, 1850.

Kikiallu. A Skagit subtribe formerly living on the N. end of Whidbey id. and at the mouth of Skagit r., Wash., but now on Swinomish res. They participated in the treaty of Pt Elliott, Wash., Jan. 22, 1855.
Ke-ka-alns.—Fay in Ind. Aff. Rep., 238, 1858. Kickuallis.—Starling, ibid., 171, 1852. Kike-alans.— Simmons, ibid., 194, 1860. Kikiallis.—Gibbs in Pac. R. R. Rep., I, 436, 1825. Kikiallu.—Gibbs in Cont. N. A. Ethnol., I, 180, 1878. Kik-i-állus.—U. S. Ind. Treat. (1850), 378, 1873. Ki-kia-loos.—Mallet in Ind. Aff. Rep., 198, 1877. Kikial-tis.—Gibbs in Pac. R. R. Rep., I, 432, 1855.

Kikiktak. A Kowagmiut Eskimo summer village at the mouth of Hotham inlet, Kotzebue sd., Alaska; pop. 200 in 1880.
Kee-kik-tag-ameuts.—Hooper, Cruise of Corwin, 26, 1880. Kikikhtagyut.—Zagoskin, Descr. Russ. Poss. in Am., pt. I, 74, 1847. Kikiktagamute.—Petroff in 10th Census, Alaska, 4, 1884. Kikiktag-mut.—Nelson in 18th Rep. B. A. E., map, 1899. Kikiktak.—Baker, Geog. Dict. Alaska, 1902. Kot-zebue.—Post-route map, 1903.

Kikimi. A Pima village on the Gila River res., s. Ariz.—Dudley in Ind. Aff. Rep. 1871, 58, 1872.

Kiksadi ('people of Kîks'). One of the most important divisions of the Tlingit, belonging to the Raven phratry. They lived principally at Sitka and Wrangell, Alaska, but there were also some at Sanya.
Kaksatis.—Beardslee in Sen. Ex. Doc. 105, 46th Cong., 2d sess., 31, 1880. Kick-sa-tee.—Kane, Wand. in N. A., app., 1859. Kiks-ádi.—Krause, Tlinkit Ind., 118, 1885. Kîksạ'dî.—Swanton, field

notes, B. A. E., 1904. Kyiks'adē.—Boas, 5th Rep. N. W. Tribes Canada, 25, 1889.

Kiktaguk. An Unaligmiut Eskimo village on the s. coast of Norton sd., Alaska; pop. 20 in 1800, 23 in 1890.
Ikekik.—Eleventh Census, Alaska, map, 162, 1893. Ikikiktoik.—Coast Surv. chart, 1898. Kegickto-wruk.—Dall in Cont. N. A. Ethnol., I, map, 1877. Kegictowik.—Petroff in 10th Census, Alaska, map, 1884. Kēgiktow'rŭk.—Dall in Cont. N. A. Ethnol., I, 17, 1877. Kegokhtowik.—Petroff in 10th Census, Alaska, 11, 1881. Kiektaguk.—Tebenkof (1849) quoted by Baker, Geog. Dict. Alaska, 239, 1902. Kigh-Mioute.—Zagoskin in Nouv. Ann. Voy., 5th s., XXI, map, 1850. Kigikhtawik.—Petroff, Rep. on Alaska, 54, 1881. Kigiktauik.—Nelson in 18th Rep. B. A. E., map, 1899. Kikchtaguk.—Holmberg, Ethnog. Skizz., map, 1855. Kikhtaghouk.—Zagoskin in Nouv. Ann. Voy., 5th s., XXI, map, 1850. Kikhtangouk.—Ibid., 218. Kikiktowrik.—Eleventh Census, Alaska, 165, 1893. Kikiktowruk.—Kelly, Arct. Eskimos, 15, 1890. Kiktaguk.—Baker, Geog. Dict. Alaska, 1902.

Kiktak ('big island'). A Kuskwog-miut Eskimo village on an island in Kus-kokwim r., Alaska, 25 m. above Bethel; pop. 232 in 1880, 119 in 1890.
Kikikhtagamiut.—Eleventh Census, Alaska, 164, 1893. Kikkhlagamute.—Hallock in Nat. Geog. Mag., IX, 90, 1898. Kikkhtagamute.—Petroff, Rep. on Alaska, 53, 1880. Kiktak.—Baker, Geog. Dict. Alaska, 1902.

Kiktheswemud. A former Delaware (?) village near Anderson, Madison co., Ind. Marked as Kik-the-swe-mud on Hough's map (Ind. Geol. Rep., 1883). Perhaps identical with Buckstown, or with Little Munsee Town.

Kikuikak. A Kuskwogmiut Eskimo village at the mouth of Kuskokwim r., Alaska; pop. 9 in 1880.
Kik-khuïgagamute.—Petroff in 10th Census, Alaska, 17, 1884.

Kikun. A former Aleut village on Agattu id., Alaska, one of the Near id. group of the Aleutians, now uninhabited.

Kikwistok. A Nakoaktok village on Seymour inlet, Brit. Col.
Kē-ques-ta.—Boas in Bull. Am. Geog. Soc., 226, 1887. Kikwistoq.—Ibid. Tē'-kwok-stai-e.—Dawson in Trans. Roy. Soc. Can. for 1887, sec. II, 65.

Kil (*K!îl*, 'sand-spit-point [town]'). A small Haida town formerly on Shingle bay, Skidegate inlet, Queen Charlotte ids., Brit. Col. It was occupied by the Lanachaadus, who owned it, and the Gitingidjats, two family groups of very low social rank.—Swanton, Cont. Haida, 279, 1905.

Kilatika. A Miami division living with the Wea, Piankashaw, and others near Ft St Louis, on the upper Illinois, in 1684.
Kalatekoë.—Membré (1682) in Margry, Déc., II, 216, 1877. Kilataks.—Bacqueville de la Potherie, II, 261, 1753. Kilatica.—Franquelin map (1684) in Parkman, La Salle, 1883. Kilatika.—La Salle (1683) in Margry, Déc., II, 320, 1877. Kolatica.—La Salle (1682), ibid., 201.

Kilauutuksh. A former Yaquina village on the s. side of Yaquina r., Oreg.
Ki-lau'-u-tŭkc'.—Dorsey in Jour. Am. Folk-lore, III, 229, 1890.

Kilchik (from the native name of L. Clark). A Knaiakhotana village on L. Clark, Alaska; pop. 91 in 1880. It seems to have been consolidated with Nikhkak, 9 m. below, by 1904.

Keechik.—Petroff in 10th Census, Alaska, 46, 1884. **Kichik.**—Ibid., map. **Kilchikh.**—Eleventh Census, Alaska, 94, 1893.

Kilherhursh. A Tillamock village, named after a chief, at the entrance of Tillamook bay, Oreg., in 1805.
Kil-har-hurst's Town.—Orig. Jour. Lewis and Clark, VI, 71, 1905. **Kilherhursh.**—Lewis and Clark, Exped., II, 117, 1814.

Kilherner. A Tillamook village in 1805, named after a chief, on Tillamook bay, Oreg., at the mouth of a creek, 2 m. from Kilherhursh.
Kil-har-nar's town.—Orig. Jour. Lewis and Clark, VI, 71, 1905. **Kilherner.**—Lewis and Clark, Exped., II, 117, 1814.

Kilikunom. A division of the Witukomnom branch of the Yuki of N. California.   (A. L. K.)

Kilimantavie (from *Ke-lĕv'-a-tow-tin*, 'sling.'—Murdoch). A Kunmiut Eskimo village on the Arctic coast w. of Wainwright inlet, Alaska; pop. 45 in 1880.
Kelamantowruk.—U. S. Hydrog. chart 68 quoted by Baker, Geog. Dist. Alaska, 239, 1902. **Kē-lĕ'va-tow-tin.**—Murdoch quoted by Baker, ibid. **Kilametagag-miut.**—Tikhmenief (1861) quoted by Baker, ibid. **Kĭlauwitawĭñ.**—Murdoch in 9th Rep. B. A. E., 44, 1892. **Kilimantavie.**—Hydrog. charts, op. cit. **Kilyamigtagvik.**—Zagoskin, Descr. Russ. Poss. Am., pt. I, 74, 1847. **Kolumakturook.**—Petroff in 10th Census, Alaska, map, 1884. **Kolumatourok.**—Petroff, Rep. on Alaska, 59, 1880. **Kolumaturok.**—Nelson in 18th Rep. B. A. E., map, 1899.

Kilinigmiut ('people of the serrated country'). A subtribe of the Suhinimiut Eskimo inhabiting the region about C. Chidley, N. Labrador. Pop. fewer than 40.
Ki lĭn'ĭg myut.—Turner in 11th Rep. B. A. E., 176, 1894.

Kilistinons of the Nipisiriniens. Mentioned by the Jesuit Rel. of 1658 (Thwaites ed., XLIV, 249, 1899) as one of the 4 divisions of the Cree, so called because they traded with the Nipissing. They lived between L. Nipigon and Moose r., Canada, though they were not very stationary. Their population at the date given was estimated at 2,500.

Kiliuda (perhaps Aleut, from *kiliak* 'morning', *uda* 'bay'). A Kaniagmiut Eskimo village on the E. coast of Kodiak id., Alaska; pop. 36 in 1880, 22 in 1890.
Kiliuda.—Baker, Geog. Dict. Alaska, 1902. **Killuda.**—Petroff in 10th Census, Alaska, 29, 1884.

Kiliwi. A Yuman band of a dozen people who furnished Gabb a vocabulary when he visited them, in Apr. 1867, near Santo Tomás mission, 150 m. N. w. of Santa Borja, Lower California. The vocabulary is published in Zeitschr. f. Ethnologie, 1877. The Kiliwi were reported as still existing in 1906.

Killaxthokle. A Chinookan tribe or village, apparently named after its chief, on Shoalwater bay, Wash., in 1805. Mentioned by Lewis and Clark, from Indian information, who estimated the population at 100 in 8 houses. Distinct from Calasthocle, who are the Quileute.
GaLā'qstxoqL.—Boas, inf'n, 1905. **Killaxthocles.**—Coues, Lewis and Clark Exped., 1252, 1892. **Killaxt-ho-kle's T.**—Orig. Jour. Lewis and Clark (1805),

VI, 118, 1905. **Killaythocles.**—Schoolcraft, Ind. Tribes, III, 571, 1853.

Killbuck. See *Gelelemend*.

Killbuck's Town. A former Delaware town on the E. side of Killbuck cr., about 10 m. s. of Wooster, Wayne co., Ohio; occupied as early as 1764 by a chief named Killbuck, from whom it received the name.   (J. M.)

Killhag. A sort of trap, defined by Bartlett (Dict. Americanisms, 332, 1877) as "a wooden trap used by the hunters in Maine"; from *kilhigan* in the Malecite dialect of Algonquian, signifying 'trap', from the radical *kilh*, 'to catch or keep caught', and the suffix radical *igan*, 'instrument.'   (A. F. C.)

Killikinnick. See *Kinnikinnick*.

Killisnoo. A modern settlement of the Hutsnuwu on Killisnoo id., near Admiralty id., Alaska. They have been drawn there through the establishment of oil works by the whites.
Kănăs-nū.—Krause, Tlinkit Ind., 105, 1885. **Kenasnow.**—Ibid. (quoted).

Kilpanlus. A Cowichan tribe in Cowitchin valley, Vancouver id., consisting of only 4 people in 1904.
Kil-pan-hus.—Can. Ind. Aff. for 1883, 190. **Kilpanlus.**—Ibid., 1901, pt. 2, 164, 1902. **Tilpā'les.**—Boas, MS., B. A. E., 1887. **Tlip-pah-lis.**—Can. Ind. Aff. for 1880, 316. **Tlip-pat-lis.**—Ibid., 1879, 308.

Kils-haidagai (*Kĭ'ils xā'-idᴀga-i*, 'peninsula people'). A branch of the Kagialskegawai, a family group belonging to the Raven clan of the Haida. They took their name from a point at the outer end of the tongue of land on which Skedans formerly stood, and where were most of their houses.—Swanton, Cont. Haida, 269, 1905.

Kilstlai-djat-takinggalung (*Kĭ'lsᴌa-i djat t!ak!ĭ'ngalᴀñ*, 'chieftainess' children'). A subdivision of the Hlgahetgu-lanas, a family of the Raven clan of the Haida.—Swanton, Cont. Haida, 270, 1905.

Kilutsai (*Gyilōts'ä'ṛ*, 'people of the river's arm'). A Tsimshian family and town near Metlakahtla, on the N. w. coast of British Columbia.
Gyilōts'ä'ṛ.—Boas in Zeitschr. für Ethnol., 232, 188. **Kel-ut-sah.**—Kane, Wand. in N. A., app., 1859. **Kill, on, chan.**—Howard, Notes on Northern Tribes, 1854, MS., B. A. E. **Killoosa.**—Horetzky, Canada on Pacific, 212, 1874. **Killowitsa.**—Brit. Col. map, 1872. **Killūtsār.**—Krause, Tlinkit Ind., 318, 1885. **Kilootsā.**—Tolmie and Dawson, Vocabs. Brit. Col., 114B, 1884. **Kil-utsai.**—Dorsey in Am. Antiq., XIX, 281, 1897.

Kim. The Mountain Lion clan of the Tigua pueblo of Isleta, N. Mex.
Kim-t'aïnïn.—Hodge (after Lummis) in Am. Anthrop., IX, 351, 1896 (*t'aïnïn* = 'people').

Kimaksuk. A Kinguamiut Eskimo village on Cumberland sd., lat. 65°, Baffin land.—McDonald, Discovery of Hogarth's Sd., 86, 1841.

Kimestunne ('people opposite a cove of deep water'). A former village of the Mishikhwutmetunne on Coquille r., Oreg.
Ki-mĕs' tûnnĕ'.—Dorsey in Jour. Am. Folk-lore, III, 232, 1890. **Ku-mas' ᴊûnnĕ'.**—Ibid.

Kimissing (*Qimissing*). A fall settlement of Talirpingmiut Eskimo, of the Okomiut tribe, on the s. side of Cumberland sd., Baffin land.—Boas in 6th Rep. B. A. E., map, 1888.

Kimituk. A former Aleut village on Agattu id., Alaska, one of the Near id. group of the Aleutians, now uninhabited.

Kimsquit (probably from *Ki'm-kuitx*, applied to the Bellacoola of Deans channel by the Heiltsuk). Given as the name of part of the "Tallion nation" or Bellacoola.

Athlankenetis.—Brit. Col. map, Ind. Aff., Victoria, 1872. Kemsquits.—Ibid. Ki'mkuitq.—Boas in 7th Rep. N. W. Tribes Can., 3, 1891. Kinisquit.—Can. Ind. Aff., pt. II, 162, 1901 (perhaps identical). Kinisquitt.—Ibid., 272, 1889. Kui-much-qui-toch.—Kane, Wand. in N. A., app., 1859.

Kimus ('brow' or 'edge'). A village of the Ntlakyapamuk on the E. side of Fraser r., between Yale and Siska, Brit. Col. Pop. in 1901 (the last time the name appears), together with Suk, 74.

Kamus.—Can. Ind. Aff. for 1886, 230. Kîmu's.—Teit in Mem. Am. Mus. Nat. Hist., II, 169, 1900. Sk'mūo.—Hill-Tout in Rep. Brit. Ass. Adv. Sci., 5, 1899. Sook-kamus.—Can. Ind. Aff. for 1901, pt. 2, 164 (name combined with that of Suk, q. v.). Suuk-kamus.—Ibid., 418, 1898.

Kinaani ('high-standing house'). A Navaho clan, the descendants of several women given that tribe by the Asa phratry of the Hopi prior to 1680, when, on account of drought, the Asa people (q. v.) abandoned Hano pueblo and made their home in Canyon de Chelly, N. E. Arizona, afterward returning to Tusayan.

High-House people.—Vandiver in Ind. Aff. Rep., 159, 1890. Kiáini.—Stephen in 8th Rep. B. A. E., 30, 1891. Kiⁿaá'ni.—Matthews in Jour. Am. Folklore, III, 104, 1890 ('high-standing house'). Kinaá'ni.—Matthews, Navaho Legends, 30, 1897.

Kinagingeeg (*Gyinaχangyi'ek*, 'people of the mosquito place'). A Tsimshian town and local group near Metlakahtla, N. w. coast of British Columbia.

Gyinaχangyi'ek.—Boas in Zeitschr. für Ethnol., 232, 1888. Kenchenkieg.—Kane, Wand. in N. A., app., 1859. Kīnagingeeg.—Dorsey in Am. Antiq., XIX, 281, 1897. Kinahungik.—Tolmie and Dawson, Vocabs. Brit. Col., 114B, 1884. Kinkhankuk.—Howard, Notes on Northern Tribes, 1854, MS., B. A. E. Kĭn-nach-hangĭk.—Krause, Tlinkit Ind., 318, 1885. Kinnakangeok.—Brit. Col. map, 1872.

Kinak ('face'). A Kuskwogmiut Eskimo village on the N. bank of lower Kuskokwim r., Alaska; pop. 60 in 1880, 257 in 1890, 209 in 1900.

Kenaghamiut.—11th Census, Alaska, 108, 1893. Kinagamute.—Petroff in 10th Census, Alaska, 54, 1884.

Kinalik. An Eskimo village in s. w. Greenland, lat. 60° 34'.—Meddelelser om Grönland, XVI, map, 1896.

Kinapuke (*Kin-a-pu'-ke*). A former Chumashan village on San Buenaventura r., Ventura co., Cal., near its mouth.—Henshaw, Buenaventura MS. vocab., B. A. E., 1884.

Kinarbik. An Eskimo village in s. E. Greenland, about lat. 62° 50'; pop. 14 in 1829.—Graah, Exped. Greenland, map, 1837.

Kinbaskets. A body of Shuswap who forced themselves into the Kutenai country near Windermere, Brit. Col., from N. Thompson r., about 50 years ago and maintained themselves there with the help of the Assiniboin until the whites appeared and wars came to an end. Pop. 41 in 1891, 56 in 1904.

Kinbaskets.—Can. Ind. Aff. 1902, 253, 1903. Shuswap Band.—Ibid.

Kinbiniyol (Navaho: *kin* 'pueblo house', *bi* 'its', *niyol* 'whirlwind': 'Whirlwind pueblo.'—Matthews). One of the best preserved of the pueblo ruins of the Chaco canyon group in N. w. New Mexico. It is not in the canyon proper, but in the basin of an arroyo tributary to it. The ruin lies 500 yds. E. of the wash, at the base of a low mesa, about 10 m. w. and 5 m. s. of Pueblo Bonito. It is rectangular in form, having 3 wings extending to the s., one at the center and one at each extremity of the main building. The exterior dimensions of the parallelogram occupied by the building are approximately 320 by 270 ft. The 2 courts formed by the wings are 91 by 125 and 76 by 83 ft respectively, the former being inclosed by a low wall, the latter open. Ten circular kivas are built within the walls of the structure, the largest being 26 ft in diameter and the smallest 15 ft. The largest rectangular room is $16\frac{1}{2}$ by 17 ft, the smallest 7 by 11 ft. The walls of the ruin stand 30 ft above the plain. Of the N. exterior wall 120 ft are still standing to above the second story. Parts of a fourth story wall are still in place. Probably half the original walls are still standing. The doors average 22 by 34 in. in size, the windows 8 by 12 in. Walls and corners are true to the plummet and try-square, an exceptional occurrence in aboriginal structures. The remains of extensive irrigation works exist in close proximity, the most elaborate that have been observed in the San Juan drainage. (E. L. H.)

Kinchuwhikut ('on its nose'). A former large Hupa village, the name referring to its situation on a point of land on the E. bank of Trinity r., Cal., near the N. end of the valley. It is prominent in Hupa folk-lore. (P. E. G.)

Kintcūwhwikût.—Goddard, Life and Culture of the Hupa, 13, 1903.

Kincolith ('place of scalps'). A mission village on Nass inlet, Brit. Col., founded in 1867 and settled by the Niska. Pop. 267 in 1902, 251 in 1904.

Kinegnagak. A Kuskwogmiut Eskimo village in w. Alaska; pop. 92 in 1890.

Kinegnagamiut.—Eleventh Census, Alaska, 164, 1893.

Kinegnak. A Kuskwogmiut Eskimo village on C. Newenham, Alaska; pop. 76 in 1890. This is also the Eskimo name for Razboinski, q. v.

Kinegñagmiut.—Eleventh Census, Alaska, 99, 1893. Kniegnagamute.—Ibid., map.

Kineuwidishianun (*Kinĕ'u^v wi'dishi'a-nun*). The Eagle phratry of the Menominee, consisting of the Bald-eagle, Crow, Raven, Red-tail Hawk, Golden-eagle, and Fish-hawk gentes.—Hoffman in 14th Rep. B. A. E., pt. I, 42, 1896.

Kingaseareang (*Qingaseareang*). A spring settlement of Kinguamiut Eskimo on an island near the entrance to Nettilling fjord, Cumberland sd., Baffin land.—Boas in 6th Rep. B. A. E., map, 1888.

Kingatok. An Ita Eskimo village on Smith sd., N. Greenland.—Kane, Arct. Explor., I, 32, 1856.

Kingegan. The chief village of the Kinugumiut Eskimo, situated inland from C. Prince of Wales, Alaska. The dialect here spoken is the same as that used on the Diomede ids. Pop. 400 in 1880, 488 in 1900.
Ki'hi.—Bogoras, Chukchee, 21, 1904 (Yuit name). King-a-ghe.—Beechey (1827) quoted by Baker, Geog. Dict. Alaska, 241, 1902. Kingaghee.—Eleventh Census, Alaska, 165, 1893. King-a-khi.—Baker, ibid. (quoted). Kingigamute.—Petroff in 10th Census, Alaska, map, 1884. Kingeqan.—Dall, Alaska, map, 1875 (changed to Kingegan in errata, 628).

Kingep (*Kiñep*, 'big shields'). The largest and most important tribal division of the Kiowa.—Mooney in 14th Rep. B. A. E., 1079, 1896.

Kingiak. An Aglemiut village on the N. side of the mouth of Naknek r., Bristol bay, Alaska; pop. 51 in 1890.
Ft. Suwarof.—Post-route map, 1903. Kenigayat.—Petroff, Rep. on Alaska, 45, 1880. Kinghiak.—Petroff in 10th Census, Alaska, 17, 1884. Kiniaak.—Post-route map, 1903. Kinuyak.—Eleventh Census, Alaska, 164, 1893. Suworof.—Baker, Geog. Dict. Alaska, 1902.

Kingiktok. An Eskimo village in w. Greenland, lat. 72° 57'.
Kinggigtok.—Meddelelser om Grönland, VIII, map, 1889.

Kingmiktuk (*Qingmiktuq*). The winter settlement of the Ugjulirmiut in King William land.—Boas in 6th Rep. B. A. E., map, 1888.

Kingnaitmiut. One of the 4 branches of the Okomiut Eskimo of Baffin land, formerly settled at Pagnirtu and Kignait fiords, but now having their permanent village at Kekerten; pop. 86 in 1883. Their summer villages are Kitingujang, Kordlubing, Niutang, and Nirdlirn.—Boas in 6th Rep. B. A. E., 437, 1888.

Kingnelling. A spring settlement of Padlimiut Eskimo at the s. end of Home bay, Baffin land.—Boas in 6th Rep. B. A. E., map, 1888.

King Philip. Metacom, second son of Massasoit, sachem of the Wampanoag, who attained that office himself through the death of his father and elder brother in 1661–62, and to the English was better known as Philip of Pokanoket, or King Philip. He was the most remarkable of all the Indians of New England. For 9 years after his elevation to the chieftaincy, although accused of plotting against the

colonists, he seems to have devoted his energies to observation and preparation rather than to overt actions of a warlike nature. He even acknowledged himself the king's subject. But war with the English was inevitable, and the struggle called King Philip's war (1675–76) broke out, resulting in the practical extermination of the Indians after they had inflicted great losses upon the whites. The ability of King Philip is seen in the plans he made before the war began, the confederacy he formed, and the havoc he wrought among the white settlements. Of 90 towns, 52 were attacked and 12 were completely destroyed. The bravery of the Indians was in many cases remarkable. Only treachery among the natives in all probability

KING PHILIP. (AFTER CHURCH, FROM AN OLD ENGRAVING)

saved the colonists from extinction. In the decisive battle, a night attack, at a swamp fortress in Rhode Island, Aug. 12, 1676, the last force of the Indians was defeated with great slaughter, King Philip himself being among the slain. His body was subjected to the indignities usual at that time, and his head is said to have been exposed at Plymouth for 20 years. His wife and little son were sold as slaves in the West Indies. Widely divergent estimates of King Philip's character and achievements have been entertained by different authorities, but he can not but be considered a man of marked abilities. Weeden (Ind. Money, 12, 1884) says: "History has made him 'King Philip,' to commemorate the heroism of his life and death. He almost made himself a king by his marvelous energy and statecraft put forth among the New England tribes. Had the opposing power been a little weaker, he might have founded a temporary kingdom on the ashes of the colonies.'' King Philip has been the subject of several poems, tales, and histories. The literature includes: Church, History of King Philip's War, 1836; Apes, Eulogy on King Philip, 1836; Freeman, Civilization and Barbarism, 1878; Markham, Narrative History of King Philip's War, 1883.   (A. F. C.)

Kings River Indians. A collective term for Indians on Tule River res., Cal., in 1885, embracing the tribes formerly on and about Kings r., some at least of whom were the Choinimni, Wachahet, Iticha, Chukaimina, Michahai, Holkoma, Tuhukmache, Pohoniche, and Wimilche, according to Wessells (Sen. Ex. Doc. 76, 34th Cong., 3d sess., 31, 1853). The number gathered under this name, together with the Wikchamni and Kawia, was 135 in 1884.

King's River Indians.—McKee (1851) in Sen. Ex. Doc. 4, 32d Cong., spec. sess., 80, 1853.

Kingua ('its head'). A Kinguamiut Okomiut summer village at the head of Cumberland sd., s. E. Baffin land.

Kingawa.—Boas in Bull. Am. Mus. Nat. Hist., XV, pt. 1, 126, 1901. Kingoua.—McDonald, Discov. of Hogarth's Sd., 86, 1841. Qingua.—Boas in 6th Rep. B. A. E., map, 1888.

Kinguamiut ('inhabitants of its head'). A subtribe of the Okomiut Eskimo living in the villages of Anarnitung, Imigen, and Kingaseareang, at the head of Cumberland sd., and numbering 60 in 1883. Kimaksuk seems to have been a former village.

Kignuamiut.—Boas in Geog. Blätt., VIII, 33, 1885. K'inguamiut.—Boas in Petermanns Mitt., no. 80, 69, 1885. Qinguamiut.—Boas in 6th Rep. B. A. E., 426, 1888.

Kinhlitshi ('red house' [of stone]). A Navaho clan.

Kinlitci.—Matthews in Jour. Am. Folk-lore, III, 103, 1890. Kinlitcini.—Ibid. Kĭnłĭtsí.—Matthews, Navaho Legends, 30, 1897. Kĭnłĭtsídíne'.—Ibid.

Kinhlizhin (Navaho, 'black house'). An important pueblo ruin of the Chaco canyon group of N. w. New Mexico, 6½ m. w. and 2 m. s. of Pueblo Bonito. It is not in the canyon, but stands, facing E., on a sand hill 200 yds. w. of a dry wash which enters the Chaco about 4 m. below. Its length was 145 ft, greatest width 50 ft. A semicircular wall, 450 ft long, connects the N. E. and S. E. corners, inclosing an irregular court. In the wall at a point 285 ft from the S. E. corner of the building was a circular tower, 4 or 5 ft in diameter, which must have been from 20 to 30 ft high. On the w. side 50 ft of exterior wall still stands, 26 ft above the débris and 38 ft above ground. The wall is 36 in. thick at the base, diminishing in thickness a few inches at the base of each additional story. Portions of a fourth-story wall still stand; the original height was 5 stories. The masonry, which is of dark-brown sandstone, consists of alternating courses of large and small stones. There are 3 small windows, 6 by 8 in. Four circular kivas, 10 by 16 ft in diameter, are built within the walls, and one, 35 ft in diameter, partly within the front wall and partly within the court. The smaller kivas are built within rectangular rooms, and the space between the room and the kiva walls is filled in with masonry. An ancient system of irrigation works, consisting of stone dam, wasteway reservoir, and ditches, is plainly traceable.   (E. L. H.)

Kiniklik. A Chugachigmiut Eskimo village on the N. shore of Prince William sd., Alaska.

Kinicklick.—Schrader (1900) quoted by Baker, Geog. Dict. Alaska, 1902. Kiniklik.—Baker, ibid.

Kinipetu ('wet country'). A central Eskimo tribe on the w. coast of Hudson bay, extending s. from Chesterfield inlet 250 m. They hunt deer and muskoxen, using the skins for clothing and kaiak covers, coming to the coast only in winter when seals are easily taken.

Agutit.—Petitot in Bib. Ling. et Ethnog. Am., III, x, 1876. Kiaknukmiut.—Boas in Bull. Am. Mus. Nat. Hist., XV, 6, 1901 (own name). Kimnepatoo.—Schwatka in Century Mag., XXII, 76, 1881. Kinipetu.—Boas in 6th Rep. B. A. E., 450, 1888. Kinnepatu.—Boas in Trans. Anthrop. Soc. Wash., III, 96, 1885. Kinnipetu.—Boas in Petermanns Mitt., no. 80, 72, 1885.

Kinkash. A Potawatomi band, so named in treaties of 1832 and 1836. Their village or reservation, which was sold to the United States in 1836, was on Tippecanoe r., Kosciusko co., Ind.

Kin-Kash.—Tippecanoe treaty (1832) in U. S. Ind. Treaties, 701, 1873. Kin-krash.—Chippewaynaung treaty (1836), ibid., 713.

Kinkletsoi (Navaho: 'yellow house'). A small pueblo ruin about ¾ m. N. w. of Pueblo Bonito, on the N. side of the arroyo, at the base of the canyon wall, in Chaco canyon, N. w. N. Mex. Its ground-plan is a perfect parallelogram, with no inner court. Its dimensions are 135 by 100 ft, and originally it probably contained 4 stories; fragments of the third story walls are still standing from 20 to 25 ft above the ground. The masonry consists of blocks of yellow sandstone, averaging 8 by 5 by 3 in., fairly well shaped and laid in adobe mortar. The pueblo walls are from 18 to 24 in. thick. The remaining doorways, all interior, average 27 by 42 in. Three circular kivas, 18 to 22 ft in diameter, are built within the walls. It is Ruin No. 8 of Jackson (10th Rep. Hayden Surv., 1878).   (E. L. H.)

Kinnazinde (probably *Kinazhi*, or *Kiniazhi*, 'little pueblo'). The Navaho name of a small, ancient, circular pueblo near Kintyel (q. v.), Ariz.; believed to have been occupied by the people of the latter place as a summer settlement. See Mindeleff in 8th Rep. B. A. E., pl. LXVI, 91, 1891; Fewkes in 22d Rep. B. A. E., 134, 1904.

Kinna-zinde.—Mindeleff, op. cit. **Zïnni jïn'n ë.**—Cushing quoted by Powell in 4th Rep. B. A. E., xxxviii, 1886 (confused with Kintyel).

Kinnikinnick. An Indian preparation of tobacco, sumac leaves, and the inner bark of a species of dogwood, used for smoking by the Indians and the old settlers and hunters in the W. The preparation varied in different localities and with different tribes. Bartlett quotes Trumbull as saying: "I have smoked half a dozen varieties of kinnikinnick in the N. W., all genuine." The word, which has as variants, kinnik-kinnik, k'nickk'neck, kinnikinik, killikinnick, etc., is an apocopation of Chippewa *kinikinigán*, meaning '(what is) mixed by hand,' from the verb *kinikiniye*, 'he mixes by hand' (any two or more dry objects), but, more correctly, 'he jumbles by hand.' The name was applied also by the white hunters, traders, and settlers to various shrubs, etc., the bark or leaves of which are employed in the mixture: Red osier (*Co nus stolonifera*), bearberry (*Arctostaphylos uva-ursi*), silky cornel (*Cornus sericea*), ground dogwood (*C. canadensis*), as well as sumac and poke leaves, etc. Matthews (Am. Anthrop., v, 170, 1903) maintains that the ordinary source of kinnikinnick was not the red willow, as has often been said, but the silky cornel, a species of dogwood, bearing, especially in winter, a marked resemblance to the red-bark willow. See *Smoking, Tobacco.* (A. F. C. W. R. G.)

Kinship. The foundation of social organization, and hence of government, the tangible form of social organization, was originally the bond of real and legal blood kinship. The recognition and perpetuation of the ties of blood kinship were the first important steps in the permanent social organization of society.

Among the North American Indians kinship is primarily the relation subsisting between two or more persons whose blood is derived from common ancestors through lawful marriage. Persons between whom kinship subsists are called kin or kindred. Kinship may be lineal or collateral. By birth through the natural order of descent kindred are divided into generations or categories, which represent lineally and collaterally relationships or degrees of kinship, which in turn are sometimes modified by the age and the sex of the persons so affected. In noting the degrees of kinship in the direct line all systems appear to agree in assigning one degree to a generation. Thus is developed a complex system of relationships. The extent and the complexity of the system in any case vary with the social organization of the people. These degrees of kinship may be called relationships, and they define more or less clearly the station, rights, and obligations of the several individuals of the kinship group specified. The distinction between relationship and kinship must not be confused, for there are persons who are related but who do not belong to the same kin.

In speaking of the entire body of a group of kindred it is necessary that reference be made to some person, the propositus, as the starting point. In general every person belongs naturally to two distinct families (see *Family*) or kinship groups, namely, that of the father and that of the mother. These two groups of kindred, which before his birth were entirely distinct for the purposes of marriage and the inheritance of property and certain other rights, privileges, and obligations, unite in his person and thereafter form only subdivisions of his general group of kindred, and both these groups share with him the rights, privileges, and obligations of kindred.

There are two radically different methods of naming these relationships; the one is called the classificatory, the other the descriptive method. In the descriptive phrase the actual relationship becomes a matter of implication—that is, the relationship is made specific either by the primary terms of relationship or by a combination of them. Under the first, kindred are never described, but are classified into categories and the same term of relationship is applied to every person belonging to the same category. In the descriptive system of naming kinship degrees there is usually found a number of classificatory terms.

There has been prevalent hitherto among many ethnologists the opinion that the tracing of descent through the paternal line is in most cases a development from the system of tracing descent exclusively through females, and that, therefore, the latter system is antecedent and more primitive than the former. But it is not at all clear that there has been adduced in support of this contention any conclusive evidence that it is a fact or that either system has been transformed from the other; but it is evident that such an improbable procedure would have caused the disregard and rupture of a vast body of tabus—of tabus among the most sacred known, namely, the tabus of incest.

The kinship system in vogue among the Klamath Indians of California and Oregon is apparently typical of those tribes in which, like the Kiowa, both the clan and the gentile systems of kinship are wanting. This lack of either system, so far as known, is characteristic of nearly all the tribes of the plains, the Pacific slope, and the N. W. coast. The Klamath system recognizes only two degrees in ascending above and only two in descending below the propositus in the direct line, and four collateral degrees of the paternal line, that of father's brothers, that of father's uncles, and then that of father's sisters and that of father's aunts; and four collateral degrees of the maternal line, that of mother's sisters, that of mother's aunts, that of mother's brothers, and that of mother's uncles, or eight collateral degrees in all. Hence in reckoning descent below himself in the direct line the offspring of propositus recognizes one degree of kinship below the lower of the two admitted by his father; but in the ascending direct line, the offspring of propositus does not recognize as a relation the higher of the two admitted by his father. So that in this system the circle of relationships shifts with the person selected as the starting point of the reckoning. The father recognizes relations which his child does not admit, and the child recognizes relations which the father does not admit.

Where the blood ties appear to be so limited and so disregarded in the social organization, the cohesion of the tribe is accomplished more or less satisfactorily through military, religious, or other societies.

In North America those tribes among whom the clan system prevailed, with the tracing of descent through the female line, became the most important peoples of modern times. The Five Civilized Tribes of Oklahoma and the Iroquois peoples are examples of this.

Among the Omaha a man must not marry in his own gens. A law of membership requires that a child belong to its father's gens. This is descent in the male line, but children of white or black persons (negroes) belong to the gens of the mother, into which they are forbidden to marry. Moreover, a stranger can not belong to any gens of the tribe because there is no ceremony of adoption into a gens. A man is prohibited from marrying a woman of the gens of his father, as the women of this gens are his grandmothers, aunts, sisters, nieces, daughters, or granddaughters. For the same reason he can not marry a woman of the gens of his father's mother, but he can marry a woman belonging to any other gens of his paternal grandmother's phratry, as she would not be of his kindred.

Consanguineous or blood kinship embraces not only the gens of the father, but also that of the mother and grandmothers, and these kindred with reference to a man fall into fourteen groups, and with reference to a woman into fifteen groups.

Among the Omaha, within the phratry in which gentes exist, those who occupy the one side of the fire are not regarded as full kindred by those occupying the other side of the fire, and they are prohibited from intermarrying. But were it not for the institution of these gentes or quasi-kindred groups within the phratries, a man would be compelled to marry outside of his tribe, for the reason that all the women of the tribe would otherwise be his kindred through the previous intermarriages among the ten original "gentes" or phratries.

The Omaha kinship system may be taken as typical of the gentile organization, tracing descent through the male line. In this system the relationships are highly complex and the terms, or rather their approximate English equivalents, denotive of these relationships are employed with considerable latitude and in quite a different manner from their use in English. For example: If the propositus be a male or a female, he or she would call all men his or her 'fathers' whom his or her father would call 'brothers', or whom his or her mother would call her potential 'husbands.' He or she would call all women his or her 'mothers' whom his or her mother would call 'sisters', 'aunts', or 'nieces', or whom his or her father would call his potential 'wives.' Moreover, he or she would call all men 'brothers' who are the sons of such fathers or mothers, and their sisters would be his or her 'sisters.' He or she would call all men his or her 'grandfathers' who are the fathers or grandfathers of his or her fathers or mothers, or whom his or her fathers or mothers would call their mothers' 'brothers.' He or she would also call all women his or her 'grandmothers' who are the real or potential wives of his or her grandfathers, or who are the mothers or grandmothers of his or her fathers or mothers, or whom his or her fathers would call their fathers' 'sisters.'

If the propositus be a male he would call all males his 'sons' who are the sons of his brothers or of his potential wives, and the sisters of these sons are his 'daughters.' If the propositus be a female person she would call all children of her sisters her 'children', because their father is or their fathers are her potential or actual husband or husbands; and she would call those males her 'nephews' who are the sons of her brothers, and the daughters of her brothers would be her 'nieces.'

If the propositus be a male, he would call his sister's son his 'nephew' and her daughter his 'niece'; but whether male or female, the propositus would call all male and female persons who are the children of his sons, daughters, nephews, or nieces, 'grandchildren'; and, in like manner, he or she would call all men 'uncles' whom his or her mothers would call their 'brothers', and would call all female persons 'aunts' who are his or her father's sisters as well as those who are the wives of his or her uncles. But the father's sisters' husbands of a male person are his brothers-in-law, because they are the actual or potential husbands of his sisters; and when the propositus is a female person they are her actual or potential husbands.

Any female person whom a man's own wife calls 'elder sister' or 'younger sister', her father's sister, or her brother's daughter is his potential wife.

Any male person whom a man's wife would call 'elder brother' or 'younger brother' is his brother-in-law; also any other male person who is the brother of his wife's niece or of his brother's wife. But his wife's father's brother is his grandfather, not his brother-in-law, although his sister is his potential wife. When his brother-in-law is the husband of his father's sister or of his own sister, his sister is his grandchild, and not his potential wife. A male person is the brother-in-law of a man if he be the husband of the sister of the other's father, since that man could marry his (the other's own) sister, but his aunt's husband is not his brother-in-law when he is his own uncle or his mother's brother. Any male person is the brother-in-law of the man whose sister is his wife. But since his sister's niece's husband is his sister's potential or actual husband, he is his son-in-law, because he is his daughter's husband.

A male or female person would call any male person his or her 'son-in-law' who is the husband of his or her daughter, niece, or grandchild, and his father is his or her son-in-law. When a male person or a female person would call the father of his or her daughter-in-law his or her 'grandfather,' her brother is his or her grandson.

A male or female person would call any other female person who is the wife of his or her son, nephew, or grandson, his or her 'daughter-in-law'; and the mother of his or her son-in-law is so called by him or her.

The father, mother's brother, or grandfather of a man's wife, of his potential wife, or of his daughter-in-law (the last being the wife of his son, nephew, or grandson) is the grandfather (or father-in-law) of that man. Any female person who is the mother, mother's sister, or grandmother of a man's wife, of his potential wife, or of his daughter-in-law (a wife of his son, nephew, or of his grand-

son) is the grandmother (or mother-in-law) of that man.

By the institution of either the clan (q. v.) or the gens system of determining and fixing degrees of relationship, kinship through males or through females acquired increased importance, because under either form of organization it signified 'clan kin' or 'gentile kin' in contradistinction to non-gentile kin. The members of either were an organized body of consanguinei bearing a common clan or gentile name, and were bound together by ties of blood and by the further bond of mutual rights, privileges, and obligations characteristic of the clan or the gens. In either case, 'clan kin' or 'gentile kin' became superior to other kin, because it invested its members with the rights, privileges, and obligations of the clan or gens.

Where a man calls his mother's sister 'mother', and she in turn calls him her 'son', although she did not in fact give him birth, the relationship must in strictness be defined as a marriage relationship and not as a blood relationship. Under the clan or the gentile system of relationships kinship was traced equally through males and through females, but a broad distinction was made between the paternal and the maternal kindred, and the rights, privileges, and obligations of the members of the line through which descent was traced were far more real and extensive than were those of the other line. Among North American Indians kinship through males was recognized just as constantly as kinship through females. There were brothers and sisters, grandfathers and grandmothers, grandsons and granddaughters, traced through males as well as through females. While the mother of a child was readily ascertainable, the father was not, but because of this uncertainty, kinship through males was not therefore rejected, and probable fathers, probable brothers, and probable sons were placed in the category of real fathers, real brothers, and real sons.

In every Iroquois community the degree of security and of distinction which every member of the community enjoyed, depended chiefly on the number, the wealth, and the power of his kindred, hence the tie uniting the members of the kinship group was not lightly or arbitrarily broken.

It appears that where the clan organization is in vogue the adoption (q. v.) of alien persons was customary.

With descent in the female line a male person had in his clan grandfathers and grandmothers, mothers, brothers and sisters, uncles, rarely nephews and nieces, and grandsons and granddaughters, some lineal and some collateral; at the same time, with the exception of uncles, he had the same relationships outside of his clan, and fathers, aunts, sons and daughters, and cousins, in addition. A woman had the same relationships in the clan as a man, and in addition sons and daughters; and at the same time she had the same relationships outside of her clan as had the man.

In certain communities there are terms in use applied to polyandrous and polygynous marriage relations. For instance, in Klamath the term *p'tcekē'p* denotes (1) the relationship of the two or more wives of a man, and (2) the relationship of two or more men (who may be brothers) who marry sisters or a single woman among them. And in the Cree the term *n't'áyim*, employed by both men and women, signifies 'my (sexual) partner'; for example, a wife will apply this term to the cowife of the husband or husbands; and the term *nikusák* is applied by one man to another with whom he shares a wife or wives, or to whom he has loaned his own wife. This term is employed also as a term of friendship among men.

The distinction between one's own father and mother and the other persons so called was sometimes marked by the use of an explanatory adjective, 'real,' 'true,' or the like; sometimes by calling all the others 'little fathers' or 'little mothers.'

The following chart, which applies especially to the Haida, may be taken as typical of a two-clan system with female descent, self being male:

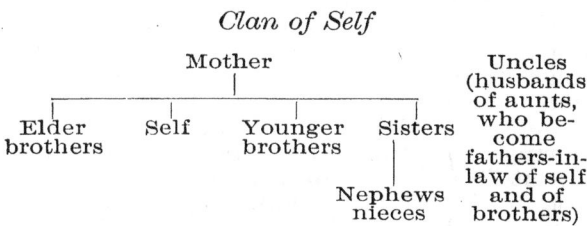

Clan of Self

In paternal succession analogous series of terms of relationship develop.

The persons belonging to one's own clan being accounted blood relations, marriage with any of them was not permitted, and where there were many clans this prohibition usually extended to the father's clan also. After marriage, terms of affinity corresponding to 'father-in-law,' 'mother-in-law,' 'brother-in-law,' and 'sister-in-law,' were applied not only to persons who could be so designated in English, but to all members of the same clans of corresponding age and sex as well. Where there were but two clans the terms of affinity might be applied to those who had previously been

known as uncles, aunts, uncles' children, nephews, and nieces, as indicated in the above table.

Where clans did not exist blood relationship was recognized on both sides as far as the connection could be remembered, and marriage with any person within this circle was, generally speaking, less usual than with one entirely outside, though such marriages were not everywhere prohibited, and in some cases were actually preferred. There was the same custom, however, of extending the terms of relationship to groups of individuals, such as the brothers of one's father, and the sisters of one's mother. Among the Salish tribes of British Columbia, who appear to have had a special fondness for recording genealogies, the number of terms of relationship is very greatly increased. Thus four or even five generations back of that of the parents and below that of the children are marked by distinct terms, and there are distinguishing terms for the first, second, third, and youngest child, and for the uncle, aunt, etc., according as one's father, mother, or other relative through whom the relationship exists is living or dead, and different terms for a living and a dead wife. There are thus 25 terms of relationship among the Lillooet, 28 among the Shuswap, and 31 among the Squawmish. By way of illustration, the kinship system of the last-mentioned tribe is subjoined (see Boas in Rep. on N. W. Tribes of Can., 136, 1890):

1. Direct relationship. *Haukwēyuk*, great-great-great grandparent or great-great grandchild; *tsopeyuk*, great-great-grandparent or great-great-grandchild; *stshamik*, great-grandparent or great-grandchild; *seel*, grandfather, grandmother, great-uncle, or great-aunt; *emats*, grandchild, grandnephew, or grandniece; *man*, father; *chisha*, mother; *men*, child; *seentl*, eldest child; *anontatsh*, second child; *menchechit*, third child; *saut*, youngest child; *kupkuopits*, brothers, sisters, and cousins together; *kuopits*, elder brother or sister, or father's or mother's elder brother's or sister's child; *skak*, younger brother or sister, or father's or mother's younger brother's or sister's child; *snchoitl*, cousin.

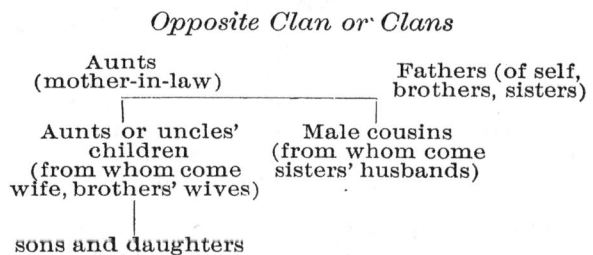

2. Indirect relationship. (A) When

the intermediate relative is alive: *sisi*, father's or mother's brother or sister; *staeatl*, brother's or sister's child; *chemash*, wife's or husband's cousin, brother, or sister; or cousin's brother's or sister's wife or husband; *saak*, son-in-law, daughter-in-law, father-in-law, or mother-in-law; *skuewas*, any relative of a husband or wife. (B) When the intermediate relative is dead: *uotsaeqoitl*, father's or mother's brother or sister; *suinemaitl*, brother's or sister's child; *chaiae*, wife's or husband's cousin, brother, or sister, or cousin's brother's or sister's wife or husband; *slikoaitl*, son-in-law, daughter-in-law, father-in-law, or mother-in-law.

3. Indirect affinity. *Skseel*, wife's grandfather or grandmother, or stepfather's or stepmother's father or mother; *skaman*, aunt's husband or stepfather; *skechisha*, uncle's wife or stepmother; *skemen*, stepchild; *skemats*, grandson's or granddaughter's wife or husband; *skesaak*, wife's or husband's stepfather or stepmother, or stepchild's husband or wife.

It will be noted that many of these are reciprocal terms, and such were very common in Indian kinship systems, used between persons of different generations, as above, or sometimes between persons of opposite sex of the same generation, such as husband and wife. Out of 14 terms in Klamath and Modoc 11 are reciprocal. On the other hand, persons of different sexes will often indicate the same relative, such as a father or a mother, by entirely different terms, and different terms are applied to those of a person's own phratry and to members of the opposite one, while the Iroquois use the equivalent for 'brother' for persons inside and outside the tribe indiscriminately. In all tribes, no matter how organized, a distinction is made between the elder and the younger members of the generation of self, at least between older and younger members of the same sex.

The terms corresponding to 'grandfather' and 'grandmother,' except among a few peoples, like the Salish, were extended to all those of a generation older than that of the parents and sometimes even to persons of that generation, while the term for 'grandchild' was applied to very young people by old ones quite indiscriminately. There were also terms to indicate the potential relationship of husband and wife, applied by a man to his wife's sisters, his aunt, or his niece, not because she was or had been, but because she might become, his wife, as usually happens to the wife's sister after the wife's death.

Besides the natural import of terms of kinship, they were employed metaphorically in a great number of ways, as to indicate respect, to avoid the use of a man's personal name, to indicate the clan or phratry to which a person belonged, or to indicate the possession of special privileges. Naturally enough, they often took the place of clan or even tribal designations, a fact which undoubtedly has led to serious errors in attempts to trace the history of Indian tribes. Again, they were applied to animals or supernatural beings, and with the Haida this use was intended to mark the fact that the being in question belonged to such and such a phratry or that a representation of it was used as a crest in that phratry. As this classification of animals by phratries or clans is often traced back to the intermarriage of a human being and an animal, we have an extension of the idea of kinship quite beyond any civilized conceptions. See *Clan and Gens, Family, Social Organization.*   (J. N. B. H.   J. R. S.)

Kintecaw, Kintecoy, Kinte Kaye, Kinticka.   See *Cantico.*

Kintpuash ('having the water-brash'— Gatschet; also spelled Keintpoos, but commonly known as Captain Jack). A subchief of the Modoc on the Oregon-California border, and leader of the hostile element in the Modoc war of 1872–73.

The Modoc, a warlike and aggressive offshoot from the Klamath tribe of S. E. Oregon, occupied the territory immediately to the S. of the latter, extending across the California border and including the Lost r. country and the famous Lava-bed region. They had been particularly hostile to the whites up to 1864, when, under the head chief Sconchin, they made a treaty agreeing to go upon a reservation established on Upper Klamath lake jointly for them and the Klamath tribe. The treaty remained unratified for several years, and in the meantime Jack, with a dissatisfied band numbering nearly half the tribe and including about 70 fighting men, continued to rove about the Lost r. country, committing frequent depredations and terrorizing the settlers. He claimed as his authority for remaining, in spite of the treaty, a permission given by an Indian agent on the California side. With some difficulty he was finally induced in the spring of 1870 to go with his band upon the reservation, where the rest of the tribe was already established under Sconchin. He remained but a short time, however, and soon left after killing an Indian doctor, who, he said, was responsible for two deaths in his own family. He returned to Lost r. demanding that a reservation be assigned to him there on the ground that it was his home country and that it was impossible to live on friendly terms with the Klamath. One or two conferences were arranged both by the military and civil authorities, but without shaking his purpose, and it became evident that he was planning for a treacherous outbreak at the first opportunity. At a final conference, Nov. 27, 1872, he absolutely refused to go on the reservation or to discuss the matter longer, and the attitude of the Indians was so threatening that an order was sent the military at Ft Klamath to put him and his head men under arrest. The attempt was made by Capt. Jackson with 36 cavalrymen at Jack's camp on Lost r., Oreg., Nov. 29, but the Indians resisted, killing or wounding 8 soldiers with a loss to themselves of 15. The Modoc, led by Jack, fled into the impenetrable Lava-beds on the s. shore of Rhett (Modoc or Tule) lake, just across the California border, killing a number of settlers on the way. Those under Sconchin remained quietly on the reservation.

KINTPUASH (AFTER MEACHAM)

The war was now begun, and volunteer companies were organized to assist the small body of troops available. A number of friendly Modoc, Klamath, and other Indians also enlisted. The Modoc position was so strong with rocks and caves and hidden passages that it was practically impossible for the troops to enter with any prospect of success. On Dec. 22, 1872, the Indians attacked a wagon train with ammunition supplies and a skirmish ensued in which one or two were killed on each side. On Jan. 17, 1873, an attempt was made by Col. Greer to storm the Modoc stronghold by the entire force of regulars and volunteers, numbering nearly 400 men, assisted by a howitzer battery, but after fighting all day among the rocks against a concealed foe the troops were obliged to retire with the loss of 9 killed and 30 wounded.

Soon afterward civil indictments for murder were procured by the settlers against 8 Modocs concerned in the killing of settlers. Another conference was appointed under a regular peace commission, consisting of Gen. E. R. S. Canby, Indian superintendent A. B. Meacham, Rev. E. Thomas, and Indian agent L. S. Dyar. By agreement with Jack, the commissioners, together with Frank F. Riddle and his Indian wife, Toby (Winema), as interpreters, met Jack and several of his men near the Modoc camp, Apr. 11, 1873, to debate terms of settlement. Hardly had the talk begun when, by premeditated treachery, Jack gave a signal, and drawing a revolver from his breast shot General Canby dead, while his companions attacked the other commissioners, killing Mr Thomas and putting 5 bullets into Meacham, who fell unconscious. The others escaped, pursued by the Indians until the latter were driven off by a detachment of troops who came up just in time, one of the officers having already been killed in the same treacherous fashion by another party of the same band.

Active measures were now put into operation and a company of Warmspring Indian scouts from N. Oregon, under Donald McKay, was secured to assist the troops in penetrating the maze of the Lava-beds. With these and the aid of the field guns the Modoc were soon compelled to vacate their stronghold and take refuge in the rocks farther along the lake shore. On Apr. 26 a search detachment of about 85 men, under Lieuts. Thomas and Wright, was suddenly attacked by the Indians from cover, with the loss of 26 killed, including both officers, besides 16 wounded. In consequence of this defeat Col. Jefferson C. Davis, in command of the Department of the Columbia, restored control of operations to Col. Wheaton, who had been temporarily superseded by another officer. Other minor encounters took place, in one of which Jack in person led the attack, clad in the uniform which he had stripped from Gen. Canby. By this time the Indians were tired of fighting, and many of Jack's warriors had deserted him, while he, with the rest, had vacated the Lava-beds entirely and taken up a new position about 20 m. farther s. The pursuit was kept up, and on May 22, 1873, a party of 65 hostiles surrendered, including several of the most prominent leaders. Others came in later, and on June 1 Jack himself, with his whole remaining party, surrendered to Capt. Perry at a camp some miles E. of Clear lake, N. w. Cal. The whole military force then opposed to him numbered 985 regulars and 71 Indians, while he himself had never had more than about 80 warriors, who were now reduced to 50, besides about 120 women and children. The whites had lost 65 killed, soldiers and civilians, including two Indian scouts, with 63 wounded, several mortally. The Modoc prisoners were removed to Ft Klamath, where, in July, 6 of the leaders were tried by court-martial for the murder of Gen. Canby, Mr Thomas, and the settlers, and 4 of them condemned, namely, Jack, young Sconchin, Black Jim, and Boston Charley, who were hanged together Oct. 3, 1873, thus closing what Bancroft calls "their brave and stubborn fight for their native land and liberty—a war in some respects the most remarkable that ever occurred in the history of aboriginal extermination." The remainder of the band were not permitted to rejoin their people on Klamath res., but were deported to the s. E. corner of Oklahoma, where a part of them still remain. See *Modoc*. Consult Bancroft, Hist. Oregon, II, 1888; Commissioner of Ind. Affs. Reports for 1872–73; Dunn, Massacres of the Mts., 1886; Gatschet in Cont. N. A. Ethnol., II, 1890. (J. M.)

Kintyel (Navaho: *Kíntyél*, or *Kíntyé'li*, from *kin* 'pueblo house', *tyel* 'broad': 'broad house.'—Matthews). An unusually large, ancient, circular pueblo ruin on Leroux wash, about 23 m. N. of Navajo station, on the S. F. Pac. R. R., Ariz. According to Zuñi tradition the village was built by the Hleetakwe, during the migration of the Bear, Crane, Frog, Deer, Yellow-wood, and other Zuñi clans. The Zuñi origin of the pueblo has been borne out by archeological study of the ruins. See Cushing in 4th Rep. B. A. E., xxxviii, 1886; Mindeleff in 8th Rep. B. A. E., 91–94, 1891; Fewkes in 22d Rep. B. A. E., 124, 1904.
Hé-sho-ta-páthl-táїe.—Cushing quoted by Powell in 4th Rep. B. A. E., xxxviii, 1886 (Zuñi name). K'in'i K'el.—Ibid. Kin-Tiel.—Mindeleff quoted in 5th Rep. B. A. E., xxiv, 1887. Pueblo Grande.—Mindeleff in 8th Rep. B. A. E., 91, 1891.

Kintyel. A ruined pueblo in Chaco canyon, N. W. N. Mex. It figures in Navaho legend as in course of erection during one of their early migratory movements, and later as a ruin. Its builders are not known.
Kintail.—Bickford in Century Mag., XL, 903, Oct. 1890. Kíntyél.—Matthews in Jour. Am. Folk-lore, III, 224, 1890. Kíntyê'li.—Ibid.

Kinugumiut. An Eskimo tribe of Alaska, inhabiting the region of C. Prince of Wales on Kaviak penin. About 1860 they overran the country as far as Selawik r., oppressing other tribes and collecting annual tribute from the Kaviagmiut. They now visit the shores of Kotzebue sd. to barter with the inland tribes, and are the keenest traders among the Eskimo and the most vicious, perhaps from longer intercourse with whalemen. Their dialect is more guttural than that of the Kaviag-

miut and other tribes of Alaska, resembling that of the Yuit. They numbered 400 in 1880, 652 in 1890. Their villages are: Eidenu, Kingegan, Mitletukeruk, Nuk, Pikta, Shishmaref, Sinar, and Takchuk. For illustrations of types see *Eskimo.*
Kinegans.—Kelly, Arct. Eskimo in Alaska, 9, 1890. Kingee'ga-mūt.—Dall in Cont. N. A. Ethnol., I, 16, 1877. Kiñugmut.—Rep. U. S. Bur. Ed., Circ. of Inf'n No. 2, chart, 1901. Kiñugumut.—Nelson in 18th Rep. B. A. E., map, 1899. Kinik Mute.—Rep. U. S. Bur. Ed., op. cit. Kǐ'xmi.—Bogoras, Chukchee, 21, 1904 (Yuit name: 'the inhabitant of Kihi,' i. e., of Prince of Wales id.).

Kinuhtoiah (*Gyidnadâ'eks*, 'people of the rapids'). A former Tsimshian division and town near Metlakatla, Brit. Col.
Gyidnadâ'eks.—Boas in Zeitsch. für Ethnol., 232, 1888. Keen-ath-toix.—Kane, Wand. in N. Am., app., 1859. Kenath tui ex.—Howard, Notes on Northern Tribes visited in 1854, MS., B. A. E. Kinnatō-iks.—Krause, Tlinkit Ind., 318, 1885. Kinnstoucks.—Brit. Col. map, 1872. Kinuhtōiah.—Tolmie and Dawson, Vocabs. Brit. Col., 114B, 1884.

Kinyaah (Navaho: *Kinaa'*, 'high house.'—Matthews). A small ruined pueblo about 30 m. s. and 5 m. w. of Pueblo Bonito, on the Thoreau road, N. W. New Mexico. It is in the Chaco drainage, but on an open plain. The ruin is rectangular, 165 by 90 ft, and without an inclosed court; the foundations are true to the cardinal points and a perfect parallelogram. Some circular depressions indicate the former presence of kivas. A small wing 30 ft square is at the s. E. corner of the building. A portion of the w. wall stands 30 ft high and partly incloses a large kiva which still stands 3 stories high. The material is dark-brown laminated sandstone, which must have been brought from the mountains 3 m. away. The stones used were the largest employed in the construction of any of the Chaco canyon group of buildings, to which group Kinyaah is evidently related by all cultural affinities that have been discovered. Some small pueblo ruins exist near by, and a large irrigation ditch and two reservoirs are discernible. (E. L. H.)

Kio. The Pine clan of the pueblo of Jemez, N. Mex. A corresponding clan existed also at the former related pueblo of Pecos.
Kíotsaá.—Hodge in Am. Anthrop., IX, 351, 1896 (*tsaá*, or *tsaásh*, = 'people'). K'ótsaä'.—Ibid. (Pecos form).

Kioch's Tribe. A body of Salish of Williams Lake agency, Brit. Col., numbering 45 in 1886, the last time the name appears.—Can. Ind. Aff. for 1886, 232.

Kiohero ('where reeds float.'—Hewitt). A former Cayuga settlement on the E. side of the N. end of Cayuga lake, N. Y. It was occupied by descendants of incorporated Hurons and other prisoners. In 1670 the French had there the mission of St Étienne. (J. M.)
Kiohero.—Jes. Rel. for 1670, 63, 1858. Saint Estienne.—Jes. Rel. for 1670, 63, 1858. Saint Stephen.—N. Y. Doc. Col. Hist., III, 251, 1853. Thi-

hero.—Conover, op. cit. **Tichero.**—Ibid. **Tiohero.**—Jes. Rel. for 1669, 14, 1858.

Ki-on-twog-ky. See *Cornplanter.*

Kiota. Mentioned in connection with the Shasta and several small Athapascan tribes of s. Oregon as being hostile to white settlers in 1854. They numbered only 8 and their name was possibly that of their leader.—Ambrose in H. R. Ex. Doc. 93, 34th Cong., 1st sess., 90, 1856.

Kiowa (from *Gá'-i-gwŭ,* or *Ká'-i-gwŭ,* 'principal people,' their own name). A tribe at one time residing about the upper Yellowstone and Missouri, but better

APIATAN (WOODEN LANCE)—KIOWA

known as centering about the upper Arkansas and Canadian in Colorado and Oklahoma, and constituting, so far as present knowledge goes, a distinct linguistic stock. They are noticed in Spanish records as early, at least, as 1732. Their oldest tradition, which agrees with the concurrent testimony of the Shoshoni and Arapaho, locates them about the junction of Jefferson, Madison, and Gallatin forks, at the extreme head of Missouri r., in the neighborhood of the present Virginia City, Mont. They afterward moved down from the mountains and formed an alliance with the Crows, with whom they have since continued on friendly terms. From here they drifted southward along the base of the mountains, driven by the Cheyenne and Arapaho, with whom they finally made peace about 1840, after which they commonly acted in concert with the latter tribes. The Sioux claim to have driven them out of the Black hills, and in 1805 they were reported by Lewis and Clark as

living on the North Platte. According to the Kiowa account, when they first reached Arkansas r. they found their passage opposed by the Comanche, who claimed all the country to the s. A war followed, but peace was finally concluded, when the Kiowa crossed over to the s. side of the Arkansas and formed a confederation with the Comanche, which continues to the present day. In connection with the Comanche they carried on a constant war upon the frontier settlements of Mexico and Texas, extending their incursions as far s., at least, as Durango. Among all the prairie tribes they were noted as the most predatory and bloodthirsty, and have probably killed more white men in proportion to their numbers than any of the others. They made their first treaty with the Government in 1837, and were put on their present reservation jointly with the Comanche and Kiowa Apache in 1868. Their last outbreak was in 1874-75 in connection with the Comanche, Kiowa Apache, and Cheyenne. While probably

KIOWA WOMAN.　(SOULE, PHOTO.)

never very numerous, they have been greatly reduced by war and disease. Their last terrible blow came in the spring of 1892, when measles and fever destroyed more than 300 of the three confederated tribes.

The Kiowa do not have the gentile system, and there is no restriction as to intermarriage among the divisions, of which they have six, including the Kiowa Apache associated with them, who form a component part of the Kiowa camp circle. A seventh division, the Kuato, is now extinct. The tribal divisions in the order of the camp circle, from the entrance at the E. southward, are Kata, Kogui, Kaigwu, Kingep, Semat (i. e., Apache), and Kongtalyui.

Although brave and warlike, the Kiowa are considered inferior in most respects to the Comanche. In person they are dark and heavily built, forming a marked

SLEEPING WOLF AND WIFE—KIOWA

contrast to the more slender and brighter complexioned prairie tribes farther N. Their language is full of nasal and choking sounds and is not well adapted to rhythmic composition. Their present chief is Gui-pägo, 'Lone Wolf,' but his title is disputed by Äpiatan. They occupied the same reservation with the Comanche and Kiowa Apache, between Washita and Red rs., in s. w. Oklahoma; but in 1901 their lands were allotted in severalty and the remainder opened to settlement. Pop. 1,165 in 1905. Consult Mooney, Ghost-dance Religion, 14th Rep. B. A. E., pt. I, 1896, and Calendar History of the Kiowa, 17th Rep. B. A. E., pt. I, 1898.   (J. M.)

Be'shīltchă.—Mooney in 14th Rep. B. A. E., 1078, 1896 (Kiowa Apache name). Cahiaguas.—Escudero, Noticias Nuevo Mexico, 87, 1849. Cahiguas.—Ibid., 83. Cai-a-was.—H. R. Rep. 299, 44th Cong., 1st sess., 1, 1876. Caigua.—Spanish doc. of 1735 cited in Rep. Columb. Hist. Expos. Madrid, 323, 1895. Caiguarás.—Pimentel, Cuadro Descr., II, 347, 1865 (given as Comanche division). Caihuas.—Doc. of 1828 in Bol. Soc. Geog. Mex., 265, 1870. Caiwas.—Amer. Pioneer, I, 257, 1842. Cargua.—Spanish doc. of 1732 cited in Rep. Columb. Hist. Expos. Madrid, 323, 1895 (for Caigua). Cayanwa.—Lewis, Travels, 15, 1809 (for Cayauwa). Cay-au-wa.—Orig. Jour. Lewis and Clark, VI, 100, 1905. Cay-au-wah.—Ibid. Cayouas.—Barreiro, Ojeada sobre Nuevo Mex., app., 10, 1832. Cayguas.—Villa Señor, Teatro Amer., pt. 2, 413, 1748 (common Spanish form, written also Caygüas). Cayohuas.—Bandelier in Jour. Am. Ethnol. and Archæol.,

III, 43, 1892. Cayugas.—Sen. Rep. 18, 31st Cong., 1st sess., 185, 1850 (for Cayguas). Ciawis.—H. R. Rep. 299, 44th Cong., 1st sess., 1, 1876. Datŭmpa'ta.—Mooney in 17th Rep. B. A. E., 148, 1898 (Hidatsa name, perhaps a form of Witapähätu or Witapätu). Gahe'wa.—Mooney in 14th Rep. B. A. E., 1078, 1896 (Wichita and Kichai name). Gâ'-igwŭ.—Mooney in 17th Rep. B. A. E., 148, 1898. Gai'wa.—La Flesche cited in 17th Rep. B. A. E., 148, 1898 (Omaha and Ponca name). Guazas.—Texas State archives, Nov. 15, 1785 (probably misprint of Caiguas). Kaiawas.—Gallatin in Trans. Am. Ethnol. Soc., II, 20, 1848. Kâ'igwŭ.—Mooney in 14th Rep. B. A. E., 1078, 1896 ('principal people': proper tribal name). Kaiowan.—Hodge, MS. Pueblo notes, B. A. E., 1895 (Sandia name). Kaî-ó-wás.—Whipple in Pac. R. R. Rep., III, pt. 1, 31, 1856. Kaiowē.—Gatschet cited in 6th Rep. B. A. E., xxxiv, 1888. Kaî-wa.—Mooney in 17th Rep. B. A. E., 148, 1898 (Comanche name; also Kai-wă, 14th Rep. B. A. E., 1078, 1896). Kai-wane'.—Hodge, MS. Pueblo notes, B. A. E., 1895 (Picuris name). Kawa.—La Flesche, inf'n. (Omaha name). Kawas.—Sen. Doc. 72, 20th Cong., 2d sess., 104, 1829. Kayaguas.—Bent (1846) in H. R. Doc. 76, 30th Cong., 1st sess., 11, 1848. Kayaways.—Pike, Exped., app., III, 73, 1810. Kayowa.—Gatschet, Kaw MS., B. A. E., 1878 (Kansa and Tonkawa name). Káyowe'.—Gatschet in Am. Antiquarian, IV, 281, 1881. Kayowŭ.—Grayson, Creek MS., B. A. E., 1885 (Creek name). Kayuguas.—Bent (1846) in Schoolcraft, Ind. Tribes, I, 244, 1851. Ka'yuwa.—Dorsey, Kansa MS. vocab., B. A. E., 1882 (Kansa name). Keawas.—Porter (1829) in Schoolcraft, Ind. Tribes, III, 596, 1853. Keaways.—Farnham, Travels, 29, 1843. Ki'-â-wâ.—Lewis and Clark, Discoveries, 37, 1806. Kiawas.—Pénicaut (1719) in French, Hist. Coll. La., n. s., I, 153, 1869. Kiaways.—Gallatin in Trans. Am. Ethnol. Soc., II, cvii, 1848. Ki-e-wah.—Orig. Jour. Lewis and Clark, I, 190, 1904. Kinawas.—Gallatin in Trans. Am. Antiq. Soc., II, 133, 1836 (misprint). Kiniwas.—Wilkes, U. S. Expl. Exped., IV, 473, 1845 (misprint). Kiohicans.—Philippeaux, Map of Engl. Col., 1781 (possibly the same; this and the 3 forms following are evidently from the early French form Quiouaha, etc.). Kiohuan.—Anville, Map of N. A., 1752. Kiohuhahans.—Jefferys, Am. Atlas, map 5, 1776. Kiouahaa.—Gravier (1700) quoted by Shea, Early Voy., 149, 1861 (possibly identical). Kiovas.—Möllhausen, Jour. to the

KIOWA MOTHER AND CHILD.   (RUSSELL, PHOTO.)

Pacific, I, 158, 1858 (misprint). Kiowahs.—Davis, El Gringo, 17, 1857. Kioway.—Ind. Aff. Rep., 240, 1834 (official geographic form; pron. Kai'-o-wa). Kioways.—Brackenridge, Views of La., 80, 1814. Kiwaa.—Kendall, Santa Fé Exped., I, 198, 1844 (given as pronunciation of Caygüa). Ko'mpabi'-anta.—Mooney in 17th Rep. B. A. E., 149, 1898 ('large tipi flaps': name sometimes used by the Kiowa). Kompa'go.—Ibid. (abbreviated form of Ko'mpabi'änta). Kuyawas.—Sage, Scenes in Rocky Mts., 167, 1846. Kwŭ'da.—Mooney in 14th Rep. B. A. E., 1078, 1896 ('going out': old name for themselves). Kyaways.—Pike (1807), Exped., app. II, 16, 1810. Manrhoat.—La Salle (ca. 1680) in

Margry, Déc., II, 201, 1877 (mentioned with Gattacka, or Kiowa Apache; believed by Mooney to be perhaps the Kiowa). **Manrhout.**—La Salle (*ca.* 1680), ibid., 168. **Mayoaho.**—Coxe, Carolana, map, 1741. **Na'la'ni.**—Mooney in 17th Rep. B. A. E., 149, 1898 ('many aliens': collective Navaho name for southern plains tribes, particularly the Comanche and Kiowa). **Ne-ċi'-he-nɛn-a.**—Hayden, Ethnog. and Philol. Mo. Val., 326, 1862. **Nĭ'-chihinĕ'na.**—Mooney in 14th Rep. B. A. E., 1078, 1896 ('river men': Arapaho name). **Nitchíhi.**—Gatschet in Am. Antiq., IV, 281, 1881. **Oways.**—Hildreth, Dragoon Campaigns, 162, 1836 (probable misprint of Kioways). **Quichuan.**—La Harpe (1719) in Margry, Déc., VI, 278, 1886 (probably identical: *c=o*). **Quiohohouans.**—Baudry des Lozières, Voy. à la Le., 244, 1802. **Quiouaha.**—Joutel (1687) in Margry, Déc., III, 409, 1878. **Quiouahan.**—Iberville, ibid., IV, 464, 1880. **Riana.**—Kennedy, Texas, I, 189, 1841 (misprint). **Ryawas.**—Morse, Rep. to Sec. War, app., 367, 1822 (misprint). **Ryuwas.**—Brackenridge, Views of La., 85, 1814 (misprint). **Shish-i-nu'-wut-tsit'-a-ni-o.** — Hayden, Ethnog. and Philol. Mo. Val., 290, 1862 (improperly given as the Cheyenne name and rendered 'rattlesnake people'; **Shĭ'shĭnóatsĭtä'neo**, 'snake people,'

KIOWA MAN AND WIFE (SANTA FE RAILWAY)

is the Cheyenne name for the Comanche). **Te'pdă'.**—Mooney in 17th Rep. B. A. E., 149, 1898 ('coming out': ancient name used to designate themselves; may have been substituted for K̇wu'-'da). **Tepk'i'ñago.**—Ibid. ('people coming out': another form of Te'pdă). **Tideing Indians.**—Orig. Jour. Lewis and Clark, I, 190, 1904. **Vi'täpätu'i.**—Mooney in 17th Rep. B. A. E., 149, 1898 (name used by the Sutaya Cheyenne). **Watahpahata.**—Mallery in 4th Rep. B. A. E., 109, 1886. **Wate-panatoes.**—Brackenridge, Views of La., 85, 1814 (misprint). **Watepaneto.**—Drake, Bk. of Inds., xii, 1848 (misprint). **Weta-hato.**—Lewis, Travels, 15, 1809 (misprint). **Wetapahato.**—Lewis and Clark, Exped., I, 34, map, 1814. **We-te-pâ-hâ'-to.**—Lewis and Clark, Travels, 36, 1806. **Wetopahata.**—Mallery in 4th Rep. B. A. E., 109, 1886. **Wettaphato.**—Morse, Rep. to Sec. War., app., 366, 1822. **Wĭ'-ta-pa-ha.**—Riggs-Dorsey, Dakota-Eng. Dict., 579, 1890. **Witapä'hat.**—Mooney in 14th Rep. B. A. E., 1078, 1898 (Cheyenne form of Witapähä'tu). **Wĭ'tapähä'tu.**—Ibid. ('island butte people': Dakota name). **Witapä'tu.**—Ibid. (Cheyenne form). **Wităp'ätu.**—Mooney in 17th Rep. B. A. E., 150, 1898. **Wi-tup-a'-tu.**—Hayden, Ethnog. and Philol. Mo. Val., 290, 1862 (Cheyenne name for Kiowa; incorrectly given as their name for the Comanche).

Kiowa Apache. A small Athapascan tribe, associated with the Kiowa from the earliest traditional period and forming a component part of the Kiowa tribal circle, although preserving its distinct language. They call themselves Na-i-shañ-dina, 'our people'. In the earliest French records of the 17th century, in Lewis and Clark's narrative, and in their first treaty in 1837, they are called by various forms of 'Gattacka', the name by which they are known to the Pawnee; and they are possibly the Kaskaia, 'Bad Hearts', of Long in 1820. The Kiowa call them by the contemptuous title Semät, 'Thieves', a recent substitute for the older generic term Tagúi, applied also to other Athapascan tribes. They are commonly known as Kiowa Apache, under the mistaken impression, arising from the fact of their Athapascan affinity, that they are a detached band of the Apache of Arizona. On the contrary, they have never had any political connection with the Apache proper, and were probably unaware of their existence until about a century ago. A few Mescalero Apache from New Mexico are now living with them, and individuals of the two tribes frequently exchange visits, but this friendly intimacy is of only 60 or 80 years' standing. The Kiowa Apache did not emigrate from the S. W. into the plains country, but came with the Kiowa from the N. w. plains region, where they lay the scene of their oldest traditions. It is probable that the Kiowa Apache, like the cognate Sarsi, have come down along the E. base of the Rocky mts. from the great Athapascan body of the Mackenzie r. basin instead of along the chain of the sierras, and that, finding themselves too weak to stand alone, they took refuge with the Kiowa, as the Sarsi have done with the Blackfeet. As they are practically a part of the Kiowa in everything but language, they need no extended separate notice. Their authentic history begins nearly 70 years earlier than that of the Kiowa, they being first mentioned under the name Gattacka by La Salle in 1681 or 1682, writing from a post in what is now Illinois. He says that the Pana (Pawnee) live more than 200 leagues to the w. on one of the tributaries of the Mississippi, and are "neighbors and allies of the Gattacka and Manrhoat, who are s. of their village and who sell to them horses which they probably steal from the Spaniards in New Mexico." It is therefore plain that the Kiowa Apache (and formerly also the Kiowa) ranged even at this early period in the same general region where they were known more than a century later, namely, between the Platte and the frontier of New Mexico, and that they already had horses taken from the Spanish settlements. It appears also that they were then in friendship with the Pawnee, unless, as seems more probable, by Pana is meant the Arikara, an offshoot of the Pawnee proper and old trading friends of the Kiowa and the Kiowa Apache. From the fact that they traded horses to other tribes, and that La Salle proposed to supply himself from them or their neighbors, it is not impossible that they sometimes visited the French post on Peoria lake. In 1719 La Harpe speaks of them, under the name of Quataquois, as living in connection with the Tawakoni and other affiliated tribes in a village on the Cimarron near its junction with the Arkansas, in the present Creek Nation, Okla. In 1805 Lewis and Clark described the Kiowa Apache as living between the

PACER ("PESO"), A KIOWA APACHE CHIEF

heads of the two forks of Cheyenne r. in the Black-hills region of N. E. Wyoming, and numbering 300 in 25 tipis. The Kiowa then lived on the North Platte, and both tribes had the same alliances and general customs. They were rich in horses, which they sold to the Arikara and Mandan. In 1837, in connection with the Kiowa and Tawakoni, the Kiowa Apache (under the name Kataka) made their first treaty with the Government. Their subsequent history is that of the Kiowa. In 1853 they are mentioned as a warlike band ranging the waters of Canadian r. in the same great plains occupied by the Comanche, with whom they often joined in raiding expeditions. By the treaty of Little Arkansas in 1865 they were detached at their own request

from the Kiowa and attached to the Cheyenne and Arapaho on account of the unfriendly attitude of the Kiowa toward the whites; but the arrangement had no practical force, and in the treaty of Medicine Lodge, in 1867, they were formally reunited with the Kiowa, although a part of them continued to live with the Cheyenne and Arapaho until after the readjustment at the close of the outbreak of 1874–75. In keeping with the general conduct of the tribe they remained peaceable and friendly throughout these troubles. In 1891 their population was 325; together with the Kiowa they suffered terribly in 1892 from an epidemic of measles and fever, losing more than one-fourth of their number. In 1905 they numbered only 155.   (J. M.)

Apaches.—Fitzpatrick in Ind. Aff. Rep., 52, 1850. Apaches of Arkansas River.—Whitfield in Ind. Aff. Rep., 255, 1855. Apaches of the Plains.—Pope (1854) in Pac. R. R. Surv., II, 17, 1855. Bad-hearts.—Long, Exped., II, 103, 1823. Cahata.—Lewis and Clark, Jour., 28, 1840 (misprint). Cancey.—This name in its various forms is the Caddo designation for the Apache of the plains, including the Kiowa Apache; it was usually applied, however, to the Lipan (q. v.). Cantajes.—Mota-Padilla, Hist. de la Conquista, 382, 1742. Cataha.—Lewis, Trav., 15, 1809. Ca'takâ.—Lewis and Clark, Discov., 38, 1806. Cattako.—Ibid., 23. Cuttako.—Am. State Papers, Ind. Aff., I, 710, 1832. Ésikwíta.—Mooney in 17th Rep. B. A. E., 245, 1898. Essaqueta.—Ind. Aff. Rep., 175, 1875. Essequeta.—Mooney in 17th Rep. B. A. E., 245, 1898 (sometimes but improperly applied). Gántsi.—Gatschet, Caddo MS., B. A. E., 65, 1884 ('liars': Caddo name). Gataea.—La Salle (1682) in Margry, Déc., II, 168, 1877. Gataka.—Harris, Coll. Voy., I, map, 685, 1705. Gáta'ka.—Mooney in 17th Rep. B. A. E., 245, 1898 (Pawnee name). Gattacka.—La Salle (1682) in Margry, Déc., II, 201, 1877. Gĭnä's.—Mooney in 17th Rep. B. A. E., 245, 1898 (Wichita name). Gû'ta'k.—La Flesche quoted by Mooney, ibid. (Omaha and Ponca name). Ha ka.—Orig. Jour. Lewis and Clark, VI, 101, 1905 (given, with a query, as a Canadian French nickname). Kántsi.—Mooney in 17th Rep. B. A. E., 245, 1898 ('liars': Caddo name for all Apache of the plains). K'á-pätop.—Ibid. ('knife-whetters': Kiowa name). Kareses.—McKenney and Hall, Ind. Tribes, III, 81, 1854 (misprint). Kaskaias.—Long, Exped., II, 101, 1823 ('bad hearts', possibly identical). Kaskaya.—Amer. Pioneer, II, 189, 1843. Kaskia.—Drake, Bk. of Inds., viii, 1848. Ka-ta-kas.—Ind. Aff. Rep., 527, 1837. Kataχka.—Gatschet, inf'n (Pawnee name). Kattekas.—Pénicaut (1719) in French, Hist. Coll. La., n. s., I, 153, note, 1869. Kiowa Apaches.—Clark, Ind. Sign Lang., 33, 1885. Kĭsínähĭs.—Mooney in 17th Rep. B. A. E., 245, 1898 (Kichai name). Matages.—Bancroft, N. Mex. States, I, 640, 1886 (misprint). Mûtsíãnä-täníu.—Mooney in 17th Rep. B. A. E., 245, 1898 ('whetstone people': Cheyenne name). Nadeicha.—Joutel (1687) in Margry, Déc., III, 409, 1878 (possibly identical). Nadíisha-déna.—Mooney in 17th Rep. B. A. E., 245, 1898 ('our people': own name). Na-i-shan-dina.—Mooney, inf'n, 1904. Na-ishi Apache.—Gatschet quoted by Powell in 6th Rep. B. A. E., xxxv, 1888. Nardichia.—Joutel (1687) in Margry, Déc., III, 409, 1878 (possibly identical). Natafé.—Garcés (1775) quoted by Orozco y Berra, Geog., 350, 1864. Natagees.—Mota-Padilla, Hist. de la Conquista, 516, 1742. Natages.—Sanchez (1757) in Doc. Hist. Mex., 4th s., I, 93, 1856. Natajeês.—Rivera, Diario y Derrotero, leg. 950, 1736. Natajes.—Bancroft, Nat. Races, III, 595, 1882. Natale.—18th century doc. quoted by Bancroft, ibid., 594. Pacer band of Apaches.—H. R. Ex. Doc. 43, 42d Cong., 3d sess., 3, 1872. Prairie Apaches.—Whitfield in Ind. Aff. Rep., 298, 1854. Quataquois.—La Harpe (1719) in Margry, Déc., VI, 289, 1886. Quataquon.—Beaurain, ibid., note. **Sádalsómte-k'íägo.**—Mooney in 17th Rep. B. A. E., 245, 1898 ('weasel people': Kiowa name). **Semät.**—Ibid. ('thieves': Kiowa name). **Tâ'gugála.**—Hodge, Pueblo MS. notes, 1895 (Jemez name for Apache tribes, including Kiowa Apache). **Tagúi.**—Mooney in 17th Rep. B. A. E., 245, 1898 (an old Kiowa name). **Tágukerísh.**—Hodge quoted by Mooney, ibid. (Pecos name for all Apache). **Tashĭn.**—Mooney, ibid. (Comanche name for all Apache). **Tha'káhinĕ'na.**—Mooney, ibid., 245 ('saw-fiddle men': Arapaho name). **Tha'káitän.** — Ibid. (Arapaho variant). **Yabipais Natagé.**—Garcés (1776), Diary, 452, 1900. **Yavipais-Natajé.**—Garcés (1776) quoted by Bandelier in Arch. Inst. Papers, III, pt. 1, 114, 1890.

Kiowan Family. A linguistic group first identified as a distinct stock by Albert Gallatin in 1853, but formally placed in the list of families by Powell (7th Rep. B. A. E., 84, 1891). The name is from *Kiowa* (q. v.), that of the only tribe included in the family. =**Kiaways.**—Gallatin in Schoolcraft, Ind. Tribes, III, 402, 1853. =**Kioway.**—Turner in Pac. R. R. Rep., III, pt. 3, 55, 80, 1856 (based on the Kioway, or Caigua, tribe only); Buschmann, Spuren der aztek. Sprache, 432, 433, 1859; Latham, Elem. Comp. Philol., 444, 1862 ("more Paduca than aught else"). =**Káyowē.**—Gatschet in Am. Antiq., 280, Oct. 1882.

Kipana. A former pueblo of the Tanos, s. of the hamlet of Tejon, lat. 35° 20′, Sandoval co., N. Mex. It was inhabited in 1598 when visited by Oñate, and probably as late as 1700. **Guipana.**— Columbus Memorial Vol., 155, 1893 (misprint). **Ki-pa-na.**—Bandelier in Arch. Inst. Papers, III, 125, 1890. **Ki-pan-na.**—Bandelier, ibid., IV, 109, 1892. **Quipana.**—Oñate (1598) in Doc. Inéd., XVI, 114, 1871.

Kipaya towns (also called "Red towns," "War towns"). A group of former Creek towns, governed by warriors only, and so called in contradistinction to the *Tálua-mikagi*, or peace towns. The following were said to belong to this division: Kawita, Tukabatchi, Hlaphlako, Atasi, Kailaidshi, Chiaha, Osotchi, Hotalihuyana, Alibamu, Eufaula, Hillabi, and Kitchopataki. (A. S. G.) **Ke-pau-yau.**—Hawkins (1799), Sketch, 52, 1848. **Kipáya towns.**—Gatschet, Creek Migr. Leg., I, 121, 1884. **Red (towns).**—Ibid.

Kipniak. A Magemiut Eskimo village at the mouth of the s. arm of Yukon r., Alaska. **Kip-naí-ăk.**—Dall quoted by Baker, Geog. Dict. Alaska, 1902. **Kipniaguk.**—Petroff in 10th Census, Alaska, map, 1884. **Kipniak.**—Baker, Geog. Dict. Alaska, 1902. **Kipnisk.**—Dall in Cont. N. A. Ethnol., I, map, 1877. **Kramalit.**—Rink, Eskimo Tribes, 33, 1887. **Kripniyukamiut.**—Coast Surv. chart cited by Baker, op. cit.

Kirishkitsu. A Wichita subtribe.— J. O. Dorsey, inf'n, 1881.

Kirokokhoche (*Kĭ'-ro-ko'-qo-tce*, 'reddish black bear cub'). A subgens of the Tunanpin gens of the Iowa.—Dorsey in 15th Rep. B. A. E., 238, 1897.

Kisakobi (Hopi: 'ladder-town place'). A former pueblo of the Hopi people of Walpi, at the N. W. base of the East mesa of Tusayan, N. E. Ariz. It was apparently occupied during the mission period (1629–1680), then abandoned and the present pueblo of Walpi built. The ruins

of the Franciscan mission here are called Nushaki by the Hopi, probably from the Spanish *misa*, 'mass,' and the Hopi *ki*, 'house.' See Fewkes in 19th Rep. B. A. E., 580, 1901, and articles cited below. **Kisákobi.**—Stephen in 8th Rep. B. A. E., 21, 1891. **Kisakovi.**—Fewkes in Am. Anthrop., VII, 395, 1894. **Nücaki.**—Ibid. **Nüshaki.**— Fewkes in 17th Rep. B. A. E., 578, 585, 1898. **Old Walpi.**—Ibid., 586.

Kishacoquillas. A Shawnee village, named after its chief, situated at the junction of Kishacoquillas cr. and Juniata r., at the site of Lewiston, Mifflin co., Pa. It existed before 1731 and was probably abandoned not long after the death of Kishacoquillas in 1754. **Kishakoquilla.**—Alden (1834) in Mass. Hist. Soc. Coll., 3d s., VI, 152, 1837 (in Crawford co.). **Kishequechkela.**—Lattré, Map, 1784 (in Huntingdon co.).

Kishgagass ('place of ancestor Gagass'). A Kitksan division and town on Babine r., an E. tributary of the Skeena, Brit. Col.; pop. 241 in 1904. **Kis-ge-gas.**—Can. Ind. Aff., 415, 1898. **Kisgegos.**—Can. Ind. Aff. 1904, pt. 2, 73, 1905. **Kis-go-gas.**—Ibid., 431, 1896. **Kish-ga-gass.**—Dorsey in Am. Antiq., XIX, 278, 1897. **Kishgahgahs.**—Brit. Col. map, 1872. **Kishke-gas.**—Can. Ind. Aff., 272, 1889. **Kiskagähs.**—Tolmie and Dawson, Vocabs. Brit. Col., 114B, 1884. **Kissgarrase.**—Horetzky, Canada on Pacific, 212, 1874. **Kiss-ge-gaas.**—Can. Ind. Aff., 252, 1891. **Kit-ka-gas.**—Dawson in Geol. Surv. Can., 20B, 1879–80. **Kitsagas.**—Scott in Ind. Aff. Rep. 1869, 563, 1870. **Kits-ge-goos.**—Can. Ind. Aff., 358, 1895. **Kits-go-gase.**—Ibid., 280, 1894.

Kishi. The Panther clan of the Caddo.— Mooney in 14th Rep. B. A. E., 1093, 1896.

Kishkakon (Chippewa: *kishki*, 'cut' (past participle); *ano*, from *anowe*, 'tail to have,' especially a bushy tail; hence, 'those who have cut tails,' referring to the naturally short tail of the bear.— Hewitt). The Bear gens or band of the Ottawa, usually found associated with two other bands, the Sinago or Black Squirrel, and the Keinouche or Pike. In 1658 the Kishkakon were allied with about 500 Christian Tionontati Hurons, who occupied contiguous territory, and they were neighbors of the Potawatomi, who at this time occupied the islands at the outlet of Green bay and the mainland to the southward along the w. shores of L. Michigan. Father Allouez found these three bands occupying a single village at La Pointe du Saint Esprit, near the present Bayfield, Wis., in 1668. For three years the Kishkakon refused to receive the gospel announced to them by Father Allouez; but in the autumn of 1688 they resolved in council to accept the teaching of the Christian doctrine. The Kishkakon, having been invited to winter near the chapel at La Pointe du Saint Esprit, left the other bands to draw near the mission house. Marquette found them divided into five "bourgades." In 1677 they were with the Hurons at Mackinaw, Mich., where in 1736 they had 180 warriors and about 200 in the vicinity of Detroit. They appear to have been more closely affiliated with the Sinago and the Keinouche than with the other Ottawa bands. For their history and customs, see *Ottawa*. (J. N. B. H.)

Culs-coupés.—Doc. of 1698 in N. Y. Doc. Col. Hist., IX, 683, 1855. Kescacons.—York (1700), ibid., IV, 749, 1854. Kichaoneiak.—Jes. Rel. 1672–3, LVII, 210, 1899. Kichaoueiak.—Shea, Cath. Miss., 358, 1855. Kichkagoneiak.—Jes. Rel. 1648, 62, 1858. Kichkankoueiak.—Ibid., 1658, 22, 1858. Kiokakons.—Bacqueville de la Potherie, Hist. de l'Amér., II, 64, 1753 (misprint). Kiscacones.—De Bougainville (1757) in N. Y. Doc. Col. Hist., x, 608, 1858. Kiscacons.—Vaudreuil conf. (1703), ibid., IX, 754, 1855. Kiscakons.—Du Chesneau (1681), ibid., 161. Kiscakous.—McKenney and Hall, Ind. Tribes, III, 82, 1858. Kishkako.—Kelton, Ft Mackinac, 15, 1884. Kiskacoueiak.—Jes. Rel. 1658, 21, 1858. Kiskakonk.—Ibid., 1670, 87, 1858. Kiskakons.—Du Chesneau (1681), op. cit., IX, 164, 1855. Kiskakoumac.—Jes. Rel. 1667, 17, 1858. Kiskakoüns.—Cadillac (1702) in Margry, Déc., V, 275, 1883. Kiskokans.—Chauvignerie (1736) in Schoolcraft, Ind. Tribes, III, 554, 1853. Queouës coupées.—Jes. Rel. 1669, 19, 1858. Queuës coupées.—N. Y. Doc. Col. Hist., IX, 161, note, 1855 (French name).

Kishkallen. A former Chehalis village on the N. shore of Grays harbor, Wash.—Gibbs, MS., B. A. E., No. 248.

Kishkat. A Wichita subtribe.—J. O. Dorsey, inf'n, 1881.

Kishkawbawee (*Kishkabawä*, probably 'broken by water.'—W. Jones). A former Chippewa village on Flint r., in lower Michigan (Saginaw treaty, 1820, in U. S. Ind. Treat., 141, 1873). The reservation was sold in 1837.

Kishpachlaots (*Gyiŝpeχlȧ'ots*, 'people of the place of the fruit of the cornus'). A Tsimshian division and town formerly at Metlakatla, Brit. Col. The people have now removed to Port Simpson.

Gpaughettes.—Howard, Notes on Northern Tribes visited in 1854, MS., B. A. E. Gyispaqlâ'ots.—Boas in 5th Rep. N. W. Tribes Canada, 35, 1889. Gyiŝpeχlȧ'ots.—Boas in Zeitschr. für Ethnol., 232, 1888. Kisch-pǎch-lä-óts.—Krause, Tlinkit Ind., 317, 1885. Kishpochalots.—Brit. Col. map, 1872. Kishpokalants.—Dorsey in Am. Antiq., XIX, 281, 1897. Kis-pa-cha-laidy.—Kane, Wand. in N. Am., app., 1859. Kispachlohts.—Gibbs in Cont. N. A. Ethnol., I, 143, 1877. Kitspukaloats.—Tolmie and Dawson, Vocabs. Brit. Col., 114B, 1884. Kyspyox.—Horetzky, Canada on the Pacific, 212, 1874.

Kishpiyeoux ('place of ancestor Piyeoux'). A Kitksan division and town at the junction of Kishpiyeux and Skeena rs., Brit. Col. According to Boas there were two clans there, Raven and Bear. Pop. 216 in 1904.

Gyîŝpayô'kᴄ.—Boas in 10th Rep. N. W. Tribes Canada, 50, 1895. Kish-pi-yeoux.—Dorsey in Am. Antiq., XIX, 278, 1897. Kispaioohs.—Tolmie and Dawson, Vocabs. Brit. Col., 114B, 1884. Kispiax.—Can. Ind. Aff. 1904, pt. 2, 73, 1905. Kish-pi-youx.—Jackson, Alaska, 300, 1880. Kispyaths.—Downie in Jour. Roy. Geog. Soc., XXXI, 253, 1861. Kispyox.—Tolmie and Dawson, Vocabs. Brit. Col., map, 1884. Kitspayuchs.—Scott in Ind. Aff. Rep. 1869, 563, 1870. Kits-piouse.—Can. Ind. Aff., 358, 1895. Kits-pioux.—Ibid., 359, 1897. Kits-piox.—Ibid., 415, 1898. Kits-pyonks.—Ibid., 304, 1893.

Kishqra. The extinct Reindeer (?) clan of Cochiti pueblo, N. Mex.

Kíshqra-hánuch.—Hodge in Am. Anthrop., IX, 351, 1896 (*hánuch* = 'people').

Kiskatomas. See *Kiskitomas*.

Kiski. A small division of the Maidu formerly residing on lower Sacramento r., Cal., probably within the limits of Sacramento co.

Kishey.—Bancroft, Nat. Races, I, 451, 1874. Kiski.—Latham in Proc. Philol. Soc. Lond., VI, 79, 1852–53. Kis Kies.—Taylor in Cal. Farmer, June 8, 1860. Kisky.—Hale, Ethnol. and Philol., VI, 631, 1846.

Kiskiminetas ('plenty of walnuts.'—Hewitt). A former Delaware village on the S. side of lower Kiskiminetas cr., near its mouth, in Westmoreland co., Pa. Cf. *Kiskominitoes*.

Gieschgumaníto.—Heckewelder in Trans. Am. Philos. Soc., n. s., IV, 371, 1834 (given as meaning 'make day light', 'cause it to become day light'). Kishkemanetas.—Jefferys, Am. Atlas, map 20, 1776. Kishkiminitas.—Royce in 18th Rep. B. A. E., Pa. map, 1899. Kiskaminetas.—Heckewelder, op. cit. Kiskemanitas.—Ibid. Kiskemeneco.—Post (1758) in Rupp, West Pa., app., 104, 1846.

Kiskitomas. A name for the walnut or hickory nut, formerly common in New Jersey and Long Island. The word has been variously spelled *kisky thomas*, *kiskatomas*, *kiskytom*, *cuscatomin*, etc. The Canadian French name is *noyer tendre* ('softnut'), referring to the shell of the nut; and J. H. Trumbull suggests connecting the word with the Abnaki *kouskádamen*, 'crack with the teeth' (given by Rasle), cognate with the Chippewa *kishkibidon*, 'tear with the teeth,' the Cree *kiskisikatew*, 'it is cut or gnawed.' The terms *kisky thomas* and *kisky thomnut* are folk-etymological corruptions of this Algonquian word. (A. F. C.)

Kiskominitoes ('plenty of walnuts.'—Hewitt). A former Delaware village on the N. bank of Ohio r., in Ohio, between Hocking and Scioto rs. The word seems to be identical with Kiskemeneco and Kiskiminetas (q. v.) in Pennsylvania. On Lattré's map "Kiskowanitas" is located on the S. E. side of Maumee r., Ohio.

Kiskominitoes.—Esnauts and Rapilly, map, 1777. Kiskomnitos.—La Tour, map, 1782. Kiskowanitas.—Lattré, map, 1784.

Kisky thomas, Kisky thomnut, Kiskytom. See *Kiskitomas*.

Kispokotha. One of the 5 divisions existing among the Shawnee, without reference to their gentes. See *Big Jim*.

Big Jim's Band.—Common official name. Ke-spico-tha.—W. H. Shawnee in Gulf States Hist. Mag., I, 417, 1903. Kickapoo.—McKenney and Hall, Ind. Tribes, III, 111, 1854 (not the Kickapoo). Kiscapocoke.—Johnston (1819) in Brinton, Lenape Leg., 30, 1885. Kiscopokes.—Drake, Tecumseh, 69, 1856. Kiskapocoke.—Morse, Rep. to Sec. War, app., 97, 1822. Kispogógi.—Gatschet, Shawnee MS., B. A. E., 1879. Ki-spo-ko-tha.—W. H. Shawnee, op. cit., 415.

Kisthemuwelgit. An old Niska town on the N. side of Nass r., Brit. Col., near its mouth, and numbering about 50 inhabitants. There is some question about the correctness of the name. See *Kitangata*.

Kis-themu-welgit.—Dorsey in Am. Antiq., XIX, 279, 1897.

Kitahon. A former Niska village on Nass r., Brit. Col., a few miles from tidewater.

Kit-a-hon.—Kane, Wand. in N. Am., app., 1859. Kitawn.—Horetzky, Canada on the Pacific, 132, 1874.

Kitaix. A Niska village near the mouth of Nass r., Brit. Col.; pop. 28 in 1903, the last time it was separately enumerated. In 1904 the combined strength of the Kitaix and Andeguale people was 80.
Git!ē′ks.—Swanton, field notes, 1900–01. **Kit-aix.**—Dorsey in Am. Antiq., XIX, 279, 1897. **Kitax.**—Can. Ind. Aff., 416, 1898. **Kitlax.**—Ibid., 280, 1894. **Kittak.**—Ibid., 251, 1891. **Kit-tek.**—Ibid., 360, 1897. **Kitten.**—Ibid., 1903, pt. 2, 72, 1904. **Kit-tex.**—Ibid., 432, 1896.

Kitak. A former Aleut village on Agattu id., Alaska, one of the Near id. group of the Aleutians, now uninhabited.

Kitamat. A northern Kwakiutl tribe living on Douglas channel, Brit. Col., and speaking the Heiltsuk dialect. They are divided into the Beaver, Eagle, Wolf, Salmon, Raven, and Killer-whale clans. Pop. 279 in 1904.
Gyit′amā′t.—Boas, 5th Rep. N. W. Tribes Can., 9, 1889 (Chimmesyan name). **Hai-shi-la.**—Dawson in Trans. Roy. Soc. Can., sec. II, 65, 1887. **Haishilla.**—Tolmie and Dawson, Vocabs. Brit. Col., 117B, 1884. **Hyshalla.**—Scouler (1846) in Jour. Ethnol. Soc. Lond., 233, 1848. **Ket a Mats.**—Colyer in Ind. Aff. Rep. 1869, 534, 1870. **Kitamah.**—Can. Ind. Aff. 1904, pt. 2, 70, 1905. **Kitamaht.**—Brit. Col. map, 1872. **Kitamat.**—Tolmie and Dawson, op. cit. **Kitamatt.**—Can. Ind. Aff., 244, 1890. **Kitimat.**—Ibid., pt. 2, 162, 1901. **Kit ta maat.**—Schoolcraft, Ind. Tribes, V, 487, 1855. **Kittamarks.**—Downie in Mayne, Brit. Col., app., 452, 1862. **Kit-ta-muat.**—Kane, Wand. in N. Am., app., 1859 (erroneously included under the Chimmesyan Sabassa). **Kittimat.**—Fleming, Can. Pac. R. R. Rep. Prog., 138, 1877. **Kittumarks.**—Horetzky, Can. on Pacific, 212, 1874. **Qāisla′.**—Boas, 6th Rep. N. W. Tribes Can., 52, 1890. **Xa-isla′.**—Boas in Rep. Nat. Mus. 1895, 328, 1897 (own name).

Kitami (*Kitä′mi*, 'porcupine'). A subphratry or gens of the Menominee.—Hoffman in 14th Rep. B. A. E., pt. I, 42, 1896.

Kitangata. A Niska town on Nass r. or inlet, Brit. Col.; pop. 30 in 1903, the last time the name appears. Probably identical with either Lakungida or Kisthemuwelgit.
Kitangata.—Can. Ind. Aff., pt. II, 68, 1902. **Kitangataa**—Ibid., 416, 1898.

Kitanmaiksh. An old town and division of the Kitksan just above the junction of Skeena and Bulkley rs., Brit. Col. The new town is now called Hazelton and has become a place of some importance, as it stands at the head of navigation on the Skeena. Pop. 241 in 1904.
Get-an-max.—Can. Ind. Aff., 415, 1898. **Git-an-max.**—Ibid., 252, 1891. **Git-au-max.**—Ibid., 304, 1893. **Gyît′anmā′kys.**—Boas in 10th Rep. N. W. Tribes Can., 50, 1895. **Kit-an-maiksh.**—Dorsey in Am. Antiq., XIX, 278, 1897. **Kitināhs.**—Tolmie and Dawson, Vocabs. Brit. Col., 114B, 1884.

Kitchawank (perhaps akin to Chippewa *Kichŭchĭwink*, 'at the great mountain.'— W. Jones). Apparently a band or small tribe, or, as Ruttenber designates it, a "chieftaincy" of the Wappinger confederacy, formerly residing on the E. bank of the Hudson in what is now Westchester co., N. Y. Their territory is believed to have extended from Croton r. to Anthony's Nose. Their principal village, Kitchawank, in 1650, appears to have been about the mouth of the Croton, though one authority (N. Y. Doc. Col. Hist., XIII, 14, 1881) locates it at Sleepy Hollow. They also had a village at Peekskill which they called Sackhoes. Their fort, or "castle," which stood at the mouth of Croton r., has been represented as one of the most formidable and ancient of the Indian fortresses s. of the Highlands. Its exact situation, according to Ruttenber, was at the neck of Teller's, called Senasqua. The Kitchawank were a party to the treaty of peace made with the Dutch, Aug. 30, 1645. (J. M. C. T.)
Kechtawangh.—Stuyvesant (1663) in N. Y. Doc. Col. Hist., XIII, 300, 1881. **Kichtawan.**—Doc. of 1664, ibid., 364. **Kichtawanc.**—Treaty of 1643, ibid., 14. **Kichtawanghs.**—Treaty of 1645, ibid., 18. **Kichtawons.**—Treaty of 1643 in Winfield, Hudson Co., 45, 1874. **Kichtewangh.**—Doc. of 1664 in N. Y. Doc. Col. Hist., XIII, 371, 1881. **Kichtowanghs.**—Stuyvesant (1663), ibid., 300. **Kicktawanc.**—Treaty of 1643 in Ruttenber, Tribes Hudson R., 78, 1872. **Kictawanc.**—Records (1643) in Winfield, Hudson Co., 42, 1874. **Kightewangh.**—Treaty of 1664 in N. Y. Doc. Col. Hist., XIII, 375, 1881. **Kightowan.**—Records of 1690 in Ruttenber, Tribes Hudson R., 178, 1872. **Kitchawanc.**—Treaty of 1643, ibid., 110. **Kitchawonck.**—Ruttenber, ibid., 79. **Kitchtawanghs.**—Treaty of 1645, ibid., 118.

Kitchigami ('great water,' from *kitchi* 'great,' *gami* 'water,' the Chippewa name for L. Superior). A tribe living in 1669–70, about central or s. w. Wisconsin, with the Kickapoo and Mascoutens, with which tribes they were ethnically and linguistically related. Little has been recorded in relation to the Kitchigami, and after a few brief notices of them, chiefly by Fathers Allouez and Marquette, they drop from history, having probably been absorbed by the Mascoutens or the Kickapoo. The first mention of them is in a letter written by Marquette, probably in the spring of 1670 (Jes. Rel. 1670, 90, 1858), in which he says: "The Illinois are thirty days' journey by land from La Pointe, the way being very difficult. They are southwestward from La Point du Saint Esprit. One passes by the nation of the Kitchigamis, who compose more than 20 large lodges, and live in the interior. After that the traveler passes through the country of the Miamiouek [Miami], and traversing great deserts (prairies) he arrives at the country of the Illinois." It appears from his statement that they were at this time at war with the Illinois. In the same Relation (p. 100) it is stated that along Wisconsin r. are numerous other nations; that 4 leagues from there "are the Kickapoos and the Kitchigamis, who speak the same language as the Mascoutens." Tailhan, who is inclined to associate them with the Illinois, says the above statement is confirmed by the inedited relation of P. Beschefer. As neither Marquette nor Allouez speaks of them when they reach the section indicated, but mention the Kickapoo, Mascouten, and Illinois, and as it appears that they had been at war with the Illinois, it is probable that the Kitchigami formed a part of the Kickapoo or the Mascoutens tribe. They are not noted on Marquette's true map, but are located on Thevenot's so-called Marquette map, under the name Kithigami, as immediately w. of the Mississippi, opposite the mouth of Wisconsin r. The fact that they drop so suddenly and entirely from history would indicate that they became known under some other name. (C. T.)

Ketchegamins.—Perrot (1718–20), Mémoire, 221, 1864. Ketchigamins.—Jes. Rel., index, 1858. Ketehigamins.—Ibid., 1670, 90, 1858. Kischigamins.—Jes. Rel. 1683, Thwaite's ed., LXII, 193, 1900. Kitchigamich.—Jes. Rel. 1670, 100, 1858. Kitchigamick.—Shea in Wis. Hist. Coll., III, 131, 1857. Kithigami.—Thevenot quoted by Shea, Discov. Miss., 268, 1852.

Kitchigumiwininiwug ('men of the great lake'). A collective term for those Chippewa formerly living on and near the shores of Lake Superior, in Michigan, Wisconsin, and Minnesota. By the treaty of Lapointe in 1854 the bands officially recognized as "Chippewas of Lake Superior" were declared to be those living at Fond du Lac (Minnesota), La Pointe, Lac du Flambeau, Lac Court Oreilles (Wisconsin), Desert lake, L'Anse, Ontonagon, Grand Portage, and Bois Forte (Michigan). Their history, except as regards treaty relations with the United States, is the same as that of the southern Chippewa (see *Chippewa*). By the treaty of Fond du Lac, Minn., Aug. 2, 1847, they joined the Chippewa of the Mississippi in relinquishing their claim to a tract of land about the mouth of Crow Wing r., Minn. By treaty of Lapointe, Wis., Sept. 3, 1854, they ceded all their lands in upper Michigan and N. Wisconsin, the United States agreeing to reserve for the use of each of said bands a specified tract within the ceded area. By act of June 5, 1872, the Secretary of the Interior was authorized to remove, with their consent, the bands from Lac du Flambeau, Lac Court d'Oreilles, and Fond du Lac res. to Bad River res., but this removal was not carried into effect, the Indians refusing permission. By Executive Order of Mar. 1, 1873, the reservation in Wisconsin selected for the Lac Court Oreilles band was approved. By order of Dec. 20, 1881, a reservation at Vermillion Lake, Minn., was set aside for the Bois Forte band. The Executive order of June 30, 1883, set apart the Deer Creek res., Minn., for the same band. By agreements of Oct. 24, Nov. 12, and Nov. 21, 1889, the Grand Portage, Bois Forte, and Fond du Lac bands ceded such of their lands at Red Lake, Fond du Lac, Bois Forte, and Deer Creek, as were not needed for allotment. In 1867 they were officially reported to number about 5,560; in 1880, 2,813; in 1905, 4,703.

(J. M. C. T.)

Chippewas of Lake Superior.—Lapointe treaty (1854) in U. S. Ind. Treat., 223, 1873. Kechegumme-winine-wug.—Ramsey in Ind. Aff. Rep., 84, 1850. Kéchékåmé Wénénéwåk.—Long, Exped. St. Peter's R., II, 153, 1824. Kitchigamiwininiwak.—Gatschet, Ojibwa MS., B. A. E., 1882. Kitcigamīwininiwag.—Wm. Jones, inf'n, 1906.

Kitchisibiwininiwug ('men of the great river,' from *kitchi* 'great', *sibiw* 'river', *ininiwug* 'men'). A collective term for the Chippewa living on the upper Mississippi, in N. E. Minnesota, S. E. of Leech lake. Their principal bands were Misisagakaniwininiwak at Sandy lake, Kahmetahwungaguma at Mille lac, the Rabbit Lake band at Rabbit lake, and the Gull Lake band at Gull lake. (J. M.)

Ke-che-se-be-win-in-e-wug. — Warren (1852) in Minn. Hist. Soc. Coll., V, 39, 1885. Ke-che-se-be-win-o-wing.—Ramsey in Ind. Aff. Rep., 86, 1850. Kitchisibi-wininiwak.—Gatschet, Ojibwa MS., B. A. E., 1882. Kitcisibiwininiwag.—Wm. Jones, inf'n, 1906. Mississippi bands.—Lapointe treaty (proclaimed 1843) in U. S. Ind. Treat., 218, 1873.

Kitchopataki (*kitchu* 'a block of wood to pound grain', *patáki* 'spreading out'). A former Upper Creek town, N. E. of Hillabi town, on a small affluent of upper Tallapoosa r., Randolph co., Ala. It had 48 families in 1832.

Hitch o par tar ga.—Census of 1832 in Schoolcraft, Ind. Tribes, IV, 578, 1854. Kitcho-patáki.—Gatschet, Creek Migr. Leg., I, 135, 1884.

Kitchopataki. A town of the Creek Nation on the point at the junction of Deep and North forks of Canadian r., Okla.—Gatschet, Creek Migr. Leg., II, 185, 1888.

Kitchu patáki.—Gatschet, ibid.

Kitegareut ('dwellers on reindeer mountains'). A tribe of Eskimo E. of Mackenzie r. on Anderson r. and at C. Bathurst, Can. They are the most easterly tribe wearing labrets. Their country is known as a source of stone utensils.

Anderson's River Esquimaux.—Hind, Labrador, II, 259, 1863. Kitiga'ru.—Murdoch in 9th Rep. B. A. E., 45, 1892. Kittè-gà-re-ut.—Richardson, Arct. Exped., I, 362, 1851. Kitte-garrœ-oot.—Richardson in Franklin, Second Exped., 174, 1828. Kit-tega'-ru.—Simpson quoted by Murdoch in 9th Rep. B. A. E., 48, 1892. Kρagmalit.—Petitot quoted by Murdoch, ibid. Kρagmalivéit.—Ibid. Kρagmalivéit.—Petitot in Bib. Ling. et Ethnog. Am., XI, 11, 1876 (= 'the real Kragmalit'). Kρamalit.)—Rink, Eskimo Tribes, 33, 1887. Kρavañaρtat.—Petitot in Bib. Ling. et Ethnog. Am., XI, 11, 1876 (='easterners'). Kρoteyoρéut.—Ibid.

Kithateen. A Chimmesyan division on Nass r., Brit. Col.—Kane, Wand. in N. A., app., 1850.

Kithathratts. Given by Downie (Jour. Roy. Geog. Soc., XXXI, 253, 1861) as a Chimmesyan village on the headwaters of Skeena r., Brit. Col., in the territory of the Kitksan; not identifiable with any present Kitksan town.

Kitingujang. A summer settlement of the Kingnaitmiut Eskimo at the head of Kingnait fjord, Cumberland sd.—Boas in 6th Rep. B. A. E., map, 1888.

Kitkadusshade. According to Krause (Tlinkit Indianer, 304, 1885), the name of a branch of the Haida. Unidentified.

Kitkahta ('people of the poles'; so called from their salmon weirs). A Tsimshian division and town on Douglas channel, N. w. coast of British Columbia. Although formerly a large town, its inhabitants are said by Boas to have been subject to the chief of the Kitwilgioks, to whom they paid tribute. Pop. 79 in 1904.

Gyitg·ā′ata.—Boas in 5th Rep. N.W. Tribes Canada, 9, 1889. **Hartley Bay.**—Can. Ind. Aff. 1904, pt. 2, 70, 1905. **Kil-cah-ta.**—Kane, Wand. in N. A., app., 1859. **Kitha-ata.**—Can. Ind. Aff., 271, 1889. **Kitka-ata.**—Ibid., 432, 1896. **Kitkāda.**—Tolmie and Dawson, Vocabs. Brit. Col., 114B, 1884. **Kĭtkăĕt.**—Krause, Tlinkit Ind., 318, 1885. **Kitkaht.**—Brit. Col. map, Victoria, 1872. **Kit-kahta.**—Dorsey in Am. Antiq., XIX, 280, 1897. **Kit-kats.**—Scott in Ind. Aff. Rep., 316, 1868.

Kitkatla ('people of the sea'). A leading Tsimshian division and town on Porcher id., N. w. coast of British Columbia; pop. 225 in 1902, 208 in 1904.

Gyitqā′tla.—Boas in 5th Rep. N. W. Tribes Canada, 9, 1889. **Keek heat la.**—Schoolcraft, Ind. Tribes, V, 487, 1855. **Keet-heat-la.**—Kane, Wand. in N. A., app., 1859. **Keethratlah.**—Mayne, Brit. Col., 279, 1861. **Kitatels.**—Scott in Ind. Aff. Rep., 312, 1868. **Kitcathla.**—Mohun in Can. Ind. Aff., 153, 1881. **Kit-chatlah.**—Scouler (1846) in Jour. Ethnol. Soc. Lond., I, 233, 1848. **Kithātlă.**—Tolmie and Dawson, Vocabs. Brit. Col., 114B, 1884. **Kithkatla.**—Can. Ind. Aff., 251, 1891. **Kitkathla.**—Brit. Col. map, Victoria, 1872. **Kitkatla.**—Can. Ind. Aff., 432, 1896. **Kitkhall-ah.**—Howard, Notes on Northern Tribes visited in 1854, MS., B. A. E. **Kit-khatla.**—Dorsey in Am. Antiq., XIX, 280, 1897. **Kitoonitza.**—Tolmie and Dawson, Vocabs. Brit. Col., 115B, 1884 (Kwakiutl name). **Kittrālchlă.**—Krause, Tlinkit Ind., 318, 1885. **Síbapa.**—Howard, Notes on Northern Tribes visited in 1854, MS., B. A. E. (probably the name of the chief, Djebasa).

Kitkehahki ('on a hill.'—Grinnell). One of the tribes of the Pawnee confederacy (q. v.), sometimes called Republican Pawnee, as their villages were at one time on Republican r. Their villages were always w. of those of the Chaui, or up stream, and were spoken of as the upper villages. The tribe lived with its kindred on Loup r., Nebr., where their reservation was established in 1857. In 1875 they were removed to Oklahoma, where they now dwell. In 1892 they took their lands in severalty and became citizens of the United States. In tribal organization, customs, and beliefs the Kitkehahki did not differ from their congeners. Grinnell (Pawnee Hero Stories, 241, 1889) mentions three divisions, the Great Kitkehahki, Little Kitkehahki, and Blackhead Kitkehahki.

(A. C. F.)

Kattahawkees.—Ind. Aff. Rep., 213, 1861. **Ket-kakesh.**—Long, Exped. Rocky Mts., II, lxxxv, 1823. **Kit′-kä.**—Morgan, Syst. Consan. and Affin., 286, 1871. **Kitkahä′ki.**—Gatschet, MS., B. A. E. **Kitkahoets.**—Keane in Stanford, Compend., 518, 1878. **Kit′-ke-hak-ī.**—Dunbar in Mag. Am. Hist., IV, 246, 1880. **Mítaháwiye.**—Dorsey, Kansa MS. vocab., B. A. E., 1882 (Kansa name). **Panea Republicans.**—Lewis, Travels, 13, 1809. **Pania Republican.**—Sibley, Hist. Sketches, 62, 1806. **Panias républicains.**—Gass, Voy., 417, 1810. **Panias Republican.**—Lewis and Clark, Discov., 17, 1806. **Panis Republican.**—Lewis and Clark, Travels, 14, 1807. **Paunee Republics.**—H. R. Ex. Doc. 117, 19th Cong., 1st sess., 7, 1826. **Pawnee republic.**—Pike, Travels, 190, 1811. **Pawnee Republican.**—Irving, Indian Sketches, II,

13, 1835. **Pawnees republic.**—Pike, Exped., 143, 1810. **Republic.**—Lewis and Clark, Discov., 18, 1806. **Republican Pawnees.**—Lewis and Clark, Exped., I, 33, 1814. **Republicans.**—Ind. Aff. Rep., 95, 1840. **Republick.**—Orig. Jour. Lewis and Clark, VI, 87, 1905 (name given by traders). **Républiques.**—Du Lac, Voy. dans les Louisianes, 225, 1805. **Ze-ka-ka.**—Long, Exped. Rocky Mts., II, lxxxv, 1823. **Zíka hákisi**[n].—Dorsey, Kansa MS. vocab., B. A. E., 1882 (Kansa name). **Zizíka áki¢isi**[n]′.—La Flesche quoted by Dorsey in Cont. N. A. Ethnol., VI, 397, 1892 (Omaha name). **Zizíka-ákisí.**—Sanssouci quoted, ibid. (Omaha name).

Kitksan ('people of Skeena [Ksian] river'). One of the three dialectic divisions of the Chimmesyan stock, affiliated more closely with the Niska than with the Tsimshian proper. The people speaking the dialect live along the upper waters of Skeena r., Brit. Col. Dorsey enumerates the following towns: Kauldaw, Kishgagass, Kishpiyeoux, Kitanmaiksh, Kitwingach, Kitwinskole, and Kitzegukla. To these must be added the modern mission town of Meamskinisht. A division is known as the Glen-Vowell Band. Pop. 1,120 in 1904.

Gyikshan.—Boas in 10th Rep. N. W. Tribes Can., 50, 1895. **Gyitksa′n.**—Boas in 5th Rep. N. W. Tribes Can., 8, 1889. **Gyitkshan.**—Boas in 10th Rep. ibid., 50, 1895. **Kiksàn.**—J. O. Dorsey in Am. Antiq., XIX, 277, 1897. **Kit-ih-shian.**—Tolmie and Dawson, Vocabs. Brit. Col., 114B, 1884. **Kitksa′n.**—Dorsey in Am. Antiq., XIX, 277, 1897. **Kit-ksum.**—Can. Ind. Aff., 359, 1897. **Kit-ksun.**—Can. Ind. Aff., 358, 1895.

Kitlakaous ('people on the sandy point'). A former Niska village on Nass r., Brit. Col., near its mouth. It was entirely abandoned in 1885.—Dorsey in Am. Antiq., XIX, 279, 1897.

Kitlakdamix. A division and town of the Niska on Nass r., Brit. Col., about 25 m. from tidewater; pop. 169 in 1898, 126 in 1904.

Gyît′laqdā′mikc.—Boas in 10th Rep. N. W. Tribes Can., 49, 1895. **Kilawalaks.**—Tolmie and Dawson, Vocabs. Brit. Col., map, 1884. **Kin-a-roa-lax.**—Kane, Wand. in N. A., app., 1859. **Kin-a-wa-lax.**—Schoolcraft, Ind. Tribes, V, 487, 1855. **Kinnewoolun.**—Brit. Col. map, 1872. **Kitlacdamax.**—Can. Ind. Aff. 1904, pt. 2, 69, 1905. **Kitlach-damak.**—Can. Ind. Aff., 271, 1889. **Kitlach-damax.**—Ibid., 416, 1898. **Kit-lak-damix.**—Dorsey in Am. Antiq., XIX, 280, 1897. **Kitlatamox.**—Horetzky, Canada on Pacific, 128, 1874.

Kitlani (*Gyitlä′n*, 'people who paddle stern first'). A former Tsimshian division and town near Metlakatla, N. w. coast of British Columbia; now at Port Simpson.

Gyitlä′n.—Boas in Zeitschr. für Ethnol., 232, 1888. **Ketlane.**—Kane, Wand. in N. A., app., 1859. **Kitlan.**—Tolmie and Dawson, Vocabs. Brit. Col., 114B, 1884. **Kitlani.**—Dorsey in Am. Antiq., XIX, 281, 1897. **Kitlan Kilwilpeyot.**—Brit. Col. map of Ind. Tribes, Victoria, 1872. **Kittlĕăn.**—Krause, Tlinkit Ind., 318, 1885.

Kitlope (Tsimshian: 'people of the rocks'). A Kwakiutl tribe living on Gardiner channel, Brit. Col.; pop. 84 in 1901, 71 in 1904.

Gī′manoîtx. — Boas in Rep. Nat. Mus. 1895, 328, 1897. **Gyimanoitq.**—Boas in 5th Rep. N. W. Tribes Can., 9, 1889. **Gyitlō′p.** — Ibid. **Keimanoeitoh.**—Tolmie and Dawson, Vocabs. Brit. Col., 117B, 1884. **Kitloop.**—Brit. Col. map, 1872. **Kitlop.**—Tolmie and Dawson, op. cit. **Kit-lope.**—Kane, Wand. in N. A., app., 1859 (wrongly classed as Sabassa). **Kittlope.**—Can. Ind. Aff., 315, 1892.

Xanā′ks'iala.—Boas in Rep. Nat. Mus. 1895, 328, 1897 (own name).

Kitrauaiiks (*Kĭtrău-ai-iks*). Given by Krause (Tlinkit Ind., 318, 1885) as a division of the Tsimshian on Skeena r., Brit. Col., and southward; they are not now identifiable.

Kitsalthlal (*Gyidzaχtlä′tl*, 'people of the salmon-berries'). A Tsimshian division and town on the coast of British Columbia, between Nass and Skeena rs., probably near Metlakatla.
Gyidzaχtlä′tl.—Boas in Zeitschr. für Ethnol., 232, 1888. **Kitch-a-clalth.**—Kane, Wand. in N. A., app., 1859. **Kitche kla la.**—Howard, Notes on Northern Tribes visited in 1854, MS., B. A. E. **Kīts-āch-lä-āl'ch.** — Krause, Tlinkit Ind., 317, 1885. **Kitsagatala.**—Downie in Jour. Roy. Geog. Soc., XXXI, 253, 1861. **Kitsalthlal.**—Tolmie and Dawson, Vocabs. Brit. Col., 114B, 1884.

Kitsanaka. Given by Dawson (Queen Charlotte Ids., 134, 1880) as the name of one of four Haida clans, the word being supposed to signify "crow." As there are only two Haida clans, the Raven (*Hoya*) and the Eagle (*Got*), and the word for crow is *k!áldjida*, it is evident that Dawson misunderstood his informant.   (J. R. S.)

Kittamaquindi (properly *Kittamaqueink*, 'place of the old great beaver.'—Hewitt). The principal village of the Conoy (Piscataway) in Maryland in 1639. In that year the Jesuits established there a mission, which was removed in 1642 to Potopaco on account of the inroads of the Conestoga and their allies. According to Brinton the village was at the junction of Tinkers cr. with the Piscataway, a few miles above the Potomac, in Prince George co.   (J. M.)
Kittamaque-ink.—Brinton, Lenape Leg., 27, 1885 (proper form). **Kittamaquindi.**—Writer of 1639 in White, Relatio Itineris, 63, 1874. **Kittamaqundi.**—White, ibid., 127, note.

Kittanning ('on the great stream', from *kit*, 'large, superior'; *hanne*, 'stream'; *ing*, the locative). An important village of mixed Iroquois, Delaware, and Caughnawaga, formerly about the site of the present Kittanning, on Allegheny r., in Armstrong co., Pa. It was destroyed by the Pennsylvanians in 1756 after a desperate fight. It seems to have consisted of two or three settlements. The most important, called Upper Kittanning, was on the E. side of the river. Middle Kittanning was on the w. bank.   (J. M.)
Adigie.—Guy Park conf. (1775) in N. Y. Doc. Col. Hist., VIII, 557, 1857. **Adigo.**—Johnson Hall conf. (1765), ibid., VII, 728, 1865 (perhaps the Iroquois name). **Atiga.**—Bellin, map, 1775. **Attigné.**—Céloron (1749) in Margry, Déc., VI, 685, 1886. **Attigua.**—Bellin, map, 1755 (marked as if distinct from Atiga). **Attiqué.**—Céloron, op. cit. **Cantanyans.**—Boudinot, Star in the West, 126, 1816 (used for the inhabitants). **Cattanyan.**—Smith (1799) in Drake, Trag. Wild., 263, 1841. **Kattaning.**—Harris, Tour, map, 1805. **Kitanning.**—Pa. Gazette (1756) quoted in Mass. Hist. Soc. Coll., 3d s., IV, 298, 1834. **Kithannink.**—Heckewelder in Trans. Am. Philos. Soc., n. s., IV, 368, 1834. **Kittaning.**—Johnson Hall conf., op. cit. **Kittanning.**—Croghan (?), ca. 1756, in Rupp, West. Pa., 116, 1846. **Kittaones.**—Lattré, map, 1784.

Kitteaumut. A village of Christian Indians in the s. part of Plymouth co., Mass., near Monument Ponds, in 1674, perhaps under the dominion of the Wampanoag. See Cotton (1674) in Mass. Hist. Soc. Coll., 1st s., I, 199, 1806.

Kittizoo. The southernmost division and town of the Tsimshian, on the s. side of Swindle id., N. w. of Millbank sd., Brit. Col. The town is now almost deserted.
Gyidesdzo′.—Boas in 5th Rep. N. W. Tribes Can., 9, 1889. **Ketyagoos.**—Colyer in Ind. Aff. Rep. 1869, 534, 1870. **Kitestues.**—Brit. Col. map, Victoria, 1872. **Kitistzoo.**—Tolmie and Dawson, Vocabs. Brit. Col., 114B, 1884. **Kit-tist-zū.**—Gibbs in Cont. N. A. Ethnol., I, 143, 1877. **Kit-tizoo.**—Dorsey in Am. Antiq., XIX, 280, 1897. **Kityagoos.**—Scott in Ind. Aff. Rep., 316, 1868. **Whīsklāleitoh.**—Tolmie and Dawson, Vocabs. Brit. Col., 114B, 1884 ('people across the sea': Heiltsuk name).

Kittsawat. A Ntlakyapamuk village near Lytton, Brit. Col., with 4 inhabitants in 1897 (Can. Ind. Aff. Rep.), the last time the name appears.

Kituhwa (*Kitúhwă*). A former important Cherokee settlement on Tuckasegee r., and extending from above the junction of the Oconaluftee nearly to the present Bryson City, Swain co., N. C. The name, which appears also as Kettooah, Kittoa, Kittowa, etc., has lost its meaning. The people of this and the subordinate settlements on the waters of the Tuckasegee were known as Aní-Kĭtúhwagĭ, and the name was frequently extended to include the whole tribe. For this reason it was adopted in later times as the name of the Cherokee secret organization, commonly known to the whites as the Ketoowah society, pledged to the defence of Cherokee autonomy.—Mooney in 19th Rep. B. A. E., 525, 1900.
Kautika.—Doc. of 1799 quoted by Royce in 5th Rep. B. A. E., 144, 1887. **Kettooah.**—Mooney, op. cit. **Kittoa.**—Ibid. **Kittowa.**—Doc. of 1755 quoted by Royce, op. cit., 143.

Kituitsach-hade. A name given by Krause (Tlinkit Indianer, 304, 1885) to a supposed branch of the Haida on Queen Charlotte ids., Brit. Col. Unidentified.

Kitunahan Family. A linguistic family established by Powell (7th Rep. B. A. E., 85, 1891) to include the single Kutenai tribe (q. v.). The name is adopted from Hale's term, Kitunaha, applied to the tribe. This family has since been found to consist of two tribes with slightly differing dialects, viz., the Upper Kutenai and the Lower Kutenai, the former being properly the Kitōnā′qā, the latter the Ȧqkȯqtl′-ātlqō. Certain other minor differences exist between these two sections. The following family synonyms are chronologic.   (A. F. C.)
=Kitunaha.—Hale in U. S. Expl. Exped., VI, 204, 555, 1846 (between the forks of the Columbia); Gallatin in Trans. Am. Ethnol. Soc., II, pt. 1, c. 10, 77, 1848 (Flatbow); Berghaus (1851), Physik. Atlas, map 17, 1852; Latham in Trans. Philol. Soc. Lond., 70, 1856; Latham, Opuscula, 338, 1860; Latham, Elem. Comp. Philol., 395, 1862 (between lat. 52° and 48°, w. of main ridge of Rocky mts.);

Gatschet in Mag. Am. Hist. 170, 1877 (on Kootenay r.). =**Coutanies.**—Hale in U.S. Expl. Exped., VI, 204, 1846 (=Kitunaha). =**Kutanis.**—Latham, Nat. Hist. Man, 316, 1850 (Kitunaha). =**Kituanaha.**—Gallatin in Schoolcraft, Ind. Tribes, III, 402, 1853 (Coutaria or Flatbows, N. of lat. 49°). =**Kootanies.**—Buschmann, Spuren der aztek. Sprache, 661, 1859. =**Kutani.**—Latham, Elem. Comp. Philol., 395, 1862 (or Kitunaha). =**Cootanie.**—Latham, ibid. (synonymous with Kitunaha). =**Kootenai.**—Gatschet in Mag. Am. Hist., 170, 1877 (defines area occupied); Gatschet in Beach, Ind. Miscel., 446, 1877; Bancroft, Nat. Races, III, 565, 1882. =**Kootenuha.**—Tolmie and Dawson, Comp. Vocabs. Brit. Col., 79–87, 1884 (vocabulary of Upper Kootenuha). =**Flatbow.**—Hale in U. S. Expl. Exped., VI, 204, 1846 (=Kitunaha); Gallatin in Trans. Am. Ethnol. Soc., II, pt. 1, 10, 77, 1848 (after Hale); Buschmann, Spuren der aztek. Sprache, 661, 1859; Latham, Elem. Comp. Philol., 395, 1862 (or Kitunaha); Gatschet in Mag. Am. Hist., 170, 1877. =**Flachbogen.**—Berghaus (1851), Physik. Atlas, map 17, 1852. ×**Shushwaps.**—Keane in Stanford Compend. (Cent. and So. Am.), app., 460, 474, 1878 (includes Kootenais Flatbows or Skalzi). =**Kitunahan.**—Powell in 7th Rep. B. A. E., 85, 1891.

Kitunto (*Gyit'endâ,* 'people of the stockaded town'). A Tsimshian division and town formerly near the mouth of Skeena r., Brit. Col. The people were related to the Kishpachlaots. **Gyit'Endâ.**—Boas in 5th Rep. N. W. Tribes Canada, 35, 1889. **Ket-an-dou.**—Kane, Wand. in N. A., app., 1859. **Kitadah.**—Dorsey in Am. Antiq., XIX, 281, 1897. **Kit, an, doh.**—Howard, Notes on Northern Tribes visited in 1854, MS., B. A. E. **Kittandô.**—Krause, Tlinkit Ind., 318, 1885. **Kitunto.**—Tolmie and Dawson, Vocabs. Brit. Col., 114B, 1884.

Kitwilgioks (*Gyitwulgyâ'ts,* 'people of the camping place'). A Tsimshian division in the neighborhood of the mouth of Skeena r., Brit. Col. Their chief outranked all other Tsimshian chiefs. **Gyitwulgyâ'ts.**—Boas in 5th Rep. N. W. Tribes Canada, 35, 1889. **Kitwilgiōks.**—Tolmie and Dawson, Vocabs. Brit. Col., 114B, 1884. **Kit-willcoits.**—Kane, Wand. in N. A., app., 1859. **Kitwill quoitz.**—Howard, Notes on Northern Tribes visited in 1854, MS., B. A. E. **Kit-wulg-jats.**—Krause, Tlinkit Ind., 317, 1885.

Kitwilksheba (*Gyitwulkṣẹbā'*). A Tsimshian division in the neighborhood of Metlakatla and the mouth of Skeena r., Brit. Col. In 1884 it was almost extinct. **Gyitwulkṣẹbā'.**—Boas in Zeitschr. für Ethnol., 232, 1888. **Ket-wilk-ci-pa.**—Kane, Wand. in N. A., app., 1859. **Kitwilksheba.**—Tolmie and Dawson, Vocabs. Brit. Col., 114B, 1884. **Kit, will, su, pat.**—Howard, Notes on Northern Tribes visited in 1854, MS., B. A. E. **Kit-wúlkse-bē.**—Krause, Tlinkit Ind., 318, 1885.

Kitwingach ('people of place of plenty of rabbits'). A division and town of the Kitksan on the N. bank of Skeena r., Brit. Col., just above the rapids; pop. 154 in 1904. **Gyitwung-ā'.**—Boas in 10th Rep. N. W. Tribes Canada, 50, 1895. **Kilgonwah.**—Brit. Col. map, Victoria, 1872. **Kitcoonsa.**—Downie in Jour. Roy. Geog. Soc., XXXI, 253, 1861. **Kitswingahs.**—Scott in Ind. Aff. Rep. 1869, 563, 1870. **Kit-wang-agh.**—Can. Ind. Aff., 415, 1898. **Kitwangar.**—Horetzky, Canada on the Pacific, 212, 1874. **Kit-win-gach.**—Dorsey in Am. Antiq., XIX, 279, 1897. **Kitwungā.**—Tolmie and Dawson, Vocabs. Brit. Col., 114B, 1884.

Kitwinshilk ('people of the place of lizards'). A Niska town on the middle course of Nass r., N. w. British Columbia. According to Boas there were four divisions: Laktiaktl, Lakloukst, Gyitsaek, and Gyisgahast. The first of these be-

longed to the Wolf clan, the second and third to the Eagle clan, and the fourth to the Bear clan. Pop. 77 in 1898, 62 in 1904. **Gyîtwunksē'tlk.**—Boas in 10th Rep. N. W. Tribes Canada, 49, 1895. **Ke toon ok shelk.**—Schoolcraft, Ind. Tribes, V, 487, 1855. **Kitwanshelt.**—Horetzky, Canada on the Pacific, 129, 1874. **Kit-win-shilk.**—Dorsey in Am. Antiq., XIX, 280, 1897. **Kitwintshieth.**—Can. Ind. Aff., 271, 1889. **Kitwintshilth.**—Ibid., 416, 1898.

Kitwinskole ('people where the narrows pass'). A Kitksan division and town on a w. branch of upper Skeena r., Brit. Col.; pop. 67 in 1904. **Gyîtwuntlkō'l.**—Boas in 10th Rep. N. W. Tribes Canada, 49, 1895. **Kitswinscolds.**—Scott in Ind. Aff. Rep. 1869, 563, 1870. **Kitwancole.**—Horetzky, Canada on the Pacific, 116, 1874. **Kit-wan-cool.**—Can. Ind. Aff., 415, 1898. **Kit-wan Cool.**—Ibid., 252, 1891. **Kit-win-skole.**—Dorsey in Am. Antiq., XIX, 279, 1897. **Kit-wun-kool.**—Dawson in Geol. Surv. of Can., 20B, 1879–80.

Kitzeesh (*Gyidzī's,* 'people of the salmon weir'). A Tsimshian division and town formerly near Metlakatla, Brit. Col. According to the Haida, this family was descended from a woman of their tribe. **Gittcī's.**—Swanton, field notes, 1900–01. **Gyidzī's.**—Boas in Zeitschr. f. Ethnol., 232, 1888. **Kee-ches.**—Schoolcraft, Ind. Tribes, V, 487, 1855. **Kee-chis.**—Kane, Wand. in N. A., app., 1859. **Keshase.**—Howard, Notes on Northern Tribes visited in 1854, MS., B. A. E. **Kitseesh.**—Brit. Col. map, Victoria, 1872. **Kīts-īsch.**—Krause, Tlinkit Ind., 318, 1885. **Kitsis.**—Tolmie and Dawson, Vocabs. Brit. Col., 114B, 1884. **Kitzeesh.**—Dorsey in Am. Antiq., XIX, 281, 1897.

Kitzegukla ('people of Zekukla mountain'). A Kitksan division and town on upper Skeena r., a short distance below Hazelton, Brit. Col. There is an old and also a new town of this name. According to Boas there were two clans here, Raven and Bear, the people of the latter being called specifically Gyîsg·ā'hast. Pop. of both, 91 in 1904. **Gyitsigyu'ktla.**—Boas in 10th Rep. N. W. Tribes Canada, 50, 1895. **Kitseguecla.**—Dawson in Geol. Surv. Canada, 20B, 1879–80. **Kitse-gukla.**—Can. Ind. Aff., 252, 1891. **Kitsenelah.**—Brit. Col. map, Victoria, 1872. **Kit-se-quahla.**—Can. Ind. Aff., 415, 1898. **Kit-se-quak-la.**—Ibid., 358, 1895. **Kitsigeuhlé.**—Horetzky, Canada on Pacific, 116, 1874. **Kitsiguchs.**—Scott in Ind. Aff. Rep. 1869, 563, 1870. **Kitsiguhli.**—Tolmie and Dawson, Vocabs. Brit. Col., 114B, 1884. **Kits-se-quec-la.**—Can. Ind Aff., 304, 1898. **Kitze-gukla.**—Dorsey in Am. Antiq., XIX, 278, 1897.

Kitzilas ('people of the canyon', i. e., of Skeena r.). A Tsimshian division. The two towns successively occupied by them bore their name. The first, just above the canyon of Skeena r., Brit. Col., has been abandoned, the people having moved, mainly in 1893, to New Kitzilas, just below the canyon. Pop. of the latter town, 144 in 1902; in 1904, together with Port Essington and Kitzimgaylum, 191. **Gyits'ala'ser.**—Boas in 5th Rep. N. W. Tribes Canada, 9, 1889. **Kisalas.**—Can. Ind. Aff., 416, 1898. **Kitalaska.**—Downie in Jour. Roy. Geog. Soc., XXXI, 252, 1861. **Kitchu lass.**—Howard, Notes on Northern Tribes visited in 1854, MS., B. A. E. **Kitsalas.**—Scott in Ind. Aff. Rep. 1869, 563, 1870. **Kitsallas.**—Can. Ind. Aff., 252, 1891. **Kitsallas.**—Brit. Col. map, Victoria, 1872. **Kit-se-lai-so.**—Kane, Wand. in N. A., app., 1859. **Kītselāssir.**—Krause, Tlinkit Ind., 318, 1885. **Kitsellase.**—Horetzky, Canada on Pacific, 212, 1874. **Kit zilas.**—Dorsey in Am. Antiq., XIX, 279, 1897. **Kit-zilass.**—Ibid., map.

Kitzimgaylum ('people on the upper part of the river.'—Boas). A Tsimshian division and town on the N. side of Skeena r., Brit. Col., below the canyon. These people were originally Tongas, of the Koluschan stock, who fled from Alaska on account of continual wars, and settled at this point. In course of time they came to speak the Tsimshian language. Pop. 69 in 1902; in 1904, together with Port Essington and Kitzilas, 191.
Gyits'umrä'lon.—Boas in 5th Rep. N. W. Tribes Canada, 9, 35, 1889. **Kee-chum-a-kai-lo.**—Kane, Wand. in N. A., app., 1859. **Kee-chum akarlo.**—Schoolcraft, Ind. Tribes, V, 487, 1855. **Kitchemkalem.**—Can. Ind. Aff., 271, 1889. **Kitchimkale.**—Howard, Notes on Northern Tribes visited in 1854, MS., B. A. E. **Kitsumkalem.**—Can. Ind. Aff., 416, 1898. **Kitsumkalum.**—Horetzky, Canada on Pacific, 212, 1874. **Kit-zim-gay-lum.**—Dorsey in Am. Antiq., XIX, 279, 1897.

Kiusta (*K!iū'sta*, 'where the trail comes out' [?]). A former Haida town on the N. w. coast of Moresby id., opposite North id., Queen Charlotte ids., Brit. Col. It was owned by the Stustas. Possibly the town given in John Work's list as "Lu-lan-na," with 20 houses and 296 inhabitants in 1836–40, included this place and the neighboring town of Yaku. The old people remember 9 houses as having stood here and 8 at Yaku. After the population of Kiusta had decreased considerably, the remainder went to Kung, in Naden harbor.   (J. R. S.)
Kioo-sta.—Dawson, Queen Charlotte Ids., 162, 1880. **Kūstā Hāadē.**—Harrison in Proc. and Trans. Roy. Soc. Can., sec. II, 125, 1895. **Ky'iū'st'a.**—Boas, 12th Rep. N. W. Tribes Canada, 22, 1898.

Kiva. The Hopi name of the sacred ceremonial, assembly, and lounging chamber, characteristic of ancient and modern Pueblo settlements of Arizona and New Mexico and the prehistoric pueblos of Colorado and Utah. They were first described by the early Spanish explorers of the S. W., who designated them *estufas*, meaning 'hot rooms,' evidently mistaking their chief use as that of sweat-houses. One of the kivas at the pueblo of Taos in 1540 is described by Castañeda (14th Rep. B. A. E., 1896) as containing "12 pillars, 4 of which, in the center, were as large as 2 men could reach around," while "some that were seen were large enough for a game of ball." The kivas of the Rio Grande villages

NAMBE KIVA. (VROMAN, PHOTO)

were described as "underground, square or round, with fine pillars," which is largely true to-day. The early Spaniards also state that "the young men lived in the estufas," that "if a man repudiated his woman he has to go to the estufa," and that "it is forbidden for women to sleep in the estufas, or to enter these for any purpose, except to give their husbands or sons something to eat," which is still the case save in the few instances in which kivas are used by women's religious societies or where women are witnesses of the ceremonies. "The kivas," says Castañeda, "belong to the men,

HOPI KIVA, SHONGOPOVI. (V. MINDELEFF)

while the houses belong to the women." Elsewhere he asserts that the kivas belong to the whole village, meaning that they are not the property of a single individual or household.

The oldest form of kiva seems to have been circular, and some of these are still used in Rio Grande pueblos, as Santo Domingo, Santa Clara, and Nambe, although in this section, where Spanish influence was strongest, the persistence of this type might be least expected. At Zuñi and in the Hopi villages, on the other hand, the kivas are rectangular, in the latter wholly or partly underground and usually isolated, in the former partly subterranean and forming part of the village cluster. Originally the Zuñi kivas were in the courtyards of the villages, but, probably by reason of Spanish restrictions, their situation was later hidden among the dwellings, where they are today. The number of kivas in a pueblo varied with its size and the number of the religious organizations using them. Oraibi alone has 13 kivas, while some of the smaller pueblos contain but one. Those of the Hopi, which number 33, are rectangular, and are generally so built that they are approximately on a N. and

s. line, the exceptions probably being due to the exigencies of the sites. This latter circumstance, however, is not permitted to interfere with the subterranean or semi-subterranean character of the kivas, for so persistently is this feature preserved that convenience of use is sacrificed for sites that admit of partial excavation in the rock or the sinking of the chamber below the surface of the mesa summit. Kivas contain few wall openings, and these are very small. The chambers are invariably entered by means of a ladder to the roof and another through a hatch-way. The roof is supported by beams covered with osiers or boards and adobe mortar well tamped; the floors consist usually of smooth sandstone slabs; the walls, which are sometimes decorated with symbolic paintings of directional animals in directional colors, are wholly or partly surrounded by a solid stone-capped adobe bench, and at one end, behind the ladder, is a low platform or dais. A shallow fire-pit occupies the center of the floor, the hatchway being the only means for the passage of the smoke. At the end of some kivas, facing the ladder, is a small round hole in a stone or slab of cottonwood—the *sipapu* or *shipapulima* (the name varying with the language of the tribes)—symbolizing the place of origin and the final place of departure of the Pueblo peoples and the medium of communication with the beings of the underworld. When not in use the *sipapu* is kept plugged. Behind this orifice an altar, varying with the society and the ceremony, is usually erected, and before it a dry-painting is sometimes made, and numerous symbolic paraphernalia are assembled in prescribed order. See *Altar, Ceremony, Pueblos, Shrines.*

Consult Bandelier in Arch. Inst. Papers, III, IV, 1890–92; Cushing in 13th Rep. B. A. E., 1896; Dorsey and Voth in Field Columbian Museum Pub., Anthrop. ser., III, VI, 1901–03; various papers by Fewkes in the reports of the B. A. E., and in Am. Anthrop. and Jour. Am. Folk-lore; Hewitt in Bull. 32, B. A. E., 1906; Mindeleff in 8th Rep. B. A. E., 1891; Nordenskiöld, Cliff-dwellers of the Mesa Verde, 1893; Mrs Stevenson in 11th and 23d Reps. B. A. E., 1894 and 1905; Winship in 14th Rep. B. A. E., 1896.　　　　(F. W. H.)

Kivezaku. A band, apparently of Yuman stock, formerly inhabiting the lower Rio Colorado valley in the present Arizona or California, and who were "conquered, absorbed, or driven out" by the Mohave, according to the tradition of the latter.
Kive-za-ku.—Bourke in Jour. Am. Folk-lore, II, 185, 1889.

Kivitung. A settlement of Akudnirmiut Eskimo on Padli fjord, Baffin land.
Qivitung.—Boas in 6th Rep. B. A. E., 441, 1888.

Kivualinak. A Kevalingamiut village near Pt Hope, Alaska.
Kivualinagmut.—Zagoskin, Desc. Russ. Poss. Am., pt. I, 74, 1847.

Kiyahani. An Apache clan or band at San Carlos and Ft Apache, Ariz., in 1881.
Ki-ya-hanni.—Bourke in Jour. Am. Folk-lore, III, 118, 1890. Ki-ya-jani.—Ibid., 111 (trans. 'alkali').

Kiyis (*Ki'yis,* 'dried meat'). A division of the Piegan tribe of the Siksika.—Grinnell, Blackfoot Lodge Tales, 209, 225, 1892.

Kiyuksa ('breakers,' so called because the members broke the marriage law by taking wives within prohibited degrees of kinship). A band of the Mdewakanton Sioux which lived in 1811, according to Pike, in a village on upper Iowa r., under chief Wabasha (Minn. Hist. Coll., II, 17, 1860); in 1820 they were on Mississippi r., above Prairie du Chien (Drake, Bk. Inds., bk. VIII, 1848). Long, in 1824, placed them in two villages, one on Iowa r. near the Mississippi, the other on L. Pepin. Their chief village was Winona, on the site of Winona, Minn., in 1858, and the other was where Wabasha is now.
Bounding-Wind.—Neill, Hist. Minn., 144, note, 1858 (English for Tatepsin, the name of the chief). Keoxa.—Long, Exped. St. Peter's R., I, 383, 1824. Ki-gu-ksa.—Smithson. Misc. Col., XIV, 7, 1878. Kiyu-ksa.—Ramsey in Ind. Aff. Rep., 81, 1850. Kiyuksan.—Williamson in Minn. Geol. Rep. for 1884, 112. La Feuille's band.—Long in Minn. Hist. Coll., II, 24, 1860. Ta-te-psin.—Neill, Hist. Minn., 144, note, 1858. Wabasha's band.—Sen. Ex. Doc. 90, 22d Cong., 1st sess., 64, 1832. Wabashaw band.—Ind. Aff. Rep., 282, 1854. Wabashaw's sub-band of Mede-wakant'wans.—Ramsey in Ind. Aff. Rep., 81, 1850. Wabushaw.—Prescott in Schoolcraft, Ind. Tribes, II, 169, 1852. Wa-ha-shaw's tribe.—U. S. Ind. Treaties (1836), 875, 1873. Wapasha's band.—Riggs, Dak. Gram. and Dict., 131, 1852. Wapashaw.—Neill, Hist. Minn., xliv, 1858 (chief's name). Wapashaw's village.—Throcmorton (1832) quoted by Drake, Bk. Inds., bk. v, 155, 1848. Wa-pa-shee.—Smithson. Misc. Coll., XIV, art. 6, 8, 1878. Wapatha.—Warren in Minn. Hist. Coll., v, 156, 1885. Wind people.—Dorsey in Am. Natur., 115, 1884.

Kiyuksa. A division of the Upper Yanktonai Sioux.
Kee-ark-sar.—Corliss, Lacotah MS. vocab., B. A. E., 106, 1874. Kee-uke-sah.—Lewis and Clark, Discov., 34, 1806; Orig. Jour. Lewis and Clark, VI, 99, 1905. Ku-ux-aws.—Prescott in Schoolcraft, Ind. Tribes, II, 169, 1852.

Kiyuksa. A division of the Brulé Teton Sioux.—Dorsey (after Cleveland) in 15th Rep. B. A. E., 219, 1897.

Kiyuksa. A division of the Oglala Teton Sioux.
Breakers of the custom.—Robinson, letter to Dorsey, 1879. Cut Offs.—Brackett in Smithson. Rep. 1876, 467, 1877. Ke-ax-as.—Ibid. Kiocsies.—Ind. Aff. Rep., 250, 1875. Kiyuksa.—Robinson (1880) quoted by Dorsey in 15th Rep. B. A. E., 220, 1897. Žuzeċa kiyaksa.—Cleveland (1884), ibid. (='bit the snake in two'). Zuzetca-kiyaksa.—Ibid.

Klahosaht. A Nootka tribe formerly living N. of Nootka sd., Vancouver id. (Sproat, Sav. Life, 308, 1869). Boas was unable to learn anything about them, but the name seems to occur in Jewitt's Narrative as the designation of a small tribe that had been "conquered and incorporated into that of Nootka."

Klahars.—Jewitt, Narr., 74, 1849. **Klahosaht.**—Sproat, Sav. Life, 308, 1869. **Tlahosath.**—Boas, 6th Rep. N. W. Tribes Can., 31, 1890.

Klahum. An Okinagan village where Astor's old fort stood, at the mouth of Okinakane r., Wash.—Gibbs in Pac. R. R. Rep., I, 413, 1855.

Klakaamu (*Kl'a-ka-a'-mu*). A former Chumashan village on Santa Cruz id., off the coast of California, E. of Punta del Diablo.—Henshaw, Buenaventura MS. vocab., B. A. E., 1884.

Klalakamish (*Kla-la'-ka-mish*). An extinct band of Lummi that resided on the E. side of San Juan id., N. W. Wash.—Gibbs, Clallam and Lummi, 39, 1863.

Klamaskwaltin. A Kaiyuhkhotana village on the N. bank of Yukon r., Alaska, near the mouth of Kaiyuh r.

Klamaskwaltin.—Baker, Geog. Dict. Alaska, 1902. **Klamasqualttin.**—Coast Survey cited by Baker, ibid.

Klamath (possibly from *máklaks*, the Lutuami term for 'Indians,' 'people,'

KLAMATH MEDICINE-MAN

'community'; lit. 'the encamped'). A Lutuamian tribe in s. w. Oregon. They call themselves Eukshikni or Auksni, 'people of the lake,' referring to the fact that their principal seats were on Upper Klamath lake. There were also important settlements on Williamson and Sprague rs. The Klamath are a hardy people and, unlike the other branch of the family, the Modoc, have always lived at peace with the whites. In 1864 they joined the Modoc in ceding the greater part of their territory to the United States and settled on Klamath res., where they numbered 755 in 1905, including, how-ever, many former slaves and members of other tribes who have become more or less assimilated with the Klamath since the establishment of the reservation. Slavery was a notable institution among the Klamath, and previous to the treaty of 1864 they accompanied the Modoc every year on a raid against the Achomawi of Pit r., Cal., for the capture of women and children whom they retained as slaves or bartered with the Chinook at The Dalles. The Klamath took no part in the Modoc war of 1872–73, and it is said that their contemptuous treatment of the Modoc was a main cause of the dissatisfaction of the latter with their homes on the reservation which led to their return to Lost r. and thus to the war. The following are the Klamath settlements and divisions so far as known: Awalokaksaksi, Kohashti, Kulshtgeush, Kuyamskaiks, Nilakshi, Shuyakeksh, Yaaga, and Yulalona. See also *Kumbatuash.* Consult Gatschet, Klamath Inds., Cont. N. A. Ethnol., II, 1890. (L. F.)

Aígspaluma.—Gatschet in Cont. N. A. Ethnol., II, pt. I, xxxiii, 1890 ('people of the chipmunks': Sahaptin name for all Indians on Klamath res. and vicinity; abbreviated to Aígspalo, Aíkspalu). **Alámmimakt ísh.**—Ibid., xxxiv (said to be the Achomawi name). **Athlámeth.**—Ibid. (Calapooya name). **Aúksiwash.**—Ibid. (so called in Yreka dialect of Shasta). **Ä-uksni.**—Ibid. (abbr. of É-ukshikni). **Ä'-ushkni.**—Ibid., pt. II, 31. **Clamaths.**—Lee and Frost, Oregon, 177, 1844. **Clamets.**—Hale in U. S. Expl. Exped., VI, 218, 1846. **Clamouths.**—Gallatin in Trans. Am. Antiq. Soc., II, map, 1836. **Clamuth.**—Johnson and Winter, Rocky Mts., 47, 1846. **Clamuts.**—White, Ten Years in Oregon, 259, 1850. **Climath.**—Spaulding in H. R. Rep. 830, 27th Cong., 2d sess., 59, 1842. **É-ukshikni.**—Gatschet in Cont. N. A. Ethnol., II, pt. I, xxxiv, 1890 (abbr. of the following). **É-ukshik-ni máklaks.**—Ibid. (own name: 'people at the lake'). **É-ukskni.**—Ibid. (abbr. of É-ukshikni). **É-ushkni.**—Ibid., pt. II, 31. **Ilamatt.**—H. R. Ex. Doc. 76, 30th Cong., 1st sess., 7, 1848 (misprint of Hale's Tlamatl). **Kalmaths.**—Dyar (1873) in H. R. Rep. 183, 44th Cong., 1st sess., 4, 1876 (misprint). **Klamacs.**—Duflot de Mofras, Explor. dans l'Oregon, II, 335, 1844. **Klamaks.**—Ibid., 357. **Klamat.**—Palmer, Rocky Mts., 103, 1852. **Klamath Lake Indians.**—Steele in Ind. Aff. Rep. 1864, 121, 1865. **Klamaths.**—Taylor in Cal. Farmer, June 8, 1860. **Klamatk.**—Gatschet misquoted in Congrès Internat. des Amér., IV, 284, 1881. **Klameth.**—Stanley in Smithson. Misc. Coll., II, 59, 1852. **Klamets.**—Farnham, Trav., 112, 1843. **Klawmuts.**—Meek in H. R. Ex. Doc. 76, 30th Cong., 1st sess., 10, 1848. **Makaítserk.**—Gatschet, op. cit., II, pt. I, xxxiv, 1890 (so called by western Shasta). **Muck-alucs.**—Powers quoted by Bancroft, Nat. Races, I, 351, 1882. **Muk'-a-luk.**—Powers in Cont. N. A. Ethnol., III, 254, 1877. **Okshee.**—Steele in Ind. Aff. Rep. 1864, 121, 1865. **Oukskenah.**—Taylor in Cal. Farmer, June 22, 1860. **Plaíkni.**—Gatschet, op. cit., II, pt. I, xxxv, 1890 (collective name for Klamath, Modoc, and Snakes on Sprague r.). **Sáyi.**—Ibid., xxiv (Snake name). **Tapaádji.**—Curtin, Ilmawi MS. vocab., B. A. E., 1889 (Ilmawi name). **Thlamalh.**—Tolmie and Dawson, Comp. Vocab., 11B, 1884. **Tlamath.**—Ruxton, Adventures, 244, 1848. **Tlamatl.**—Hale in U. S. Expl. Exped., VI, 218, 1846. **Tlameth.**—Thompson in Ind. Aff. Rep., 490, 1854.

Klamatuk. An old village, probably belonging to the Comox, on the E. coast of Vancouver id., opposite the s. end of Valdes id.

Kla-ma-took.—Dawson, Geol. Surv. Can., map, 1888.

Klaskino ('people of the ocean'). A Kwakiutl tribe on Klaskino inlet, N. w. coast of Vancouver id.; pop. 13 in 1888, when last separately enumerated.
Klarkinos.—Can. Ind. Aff., 145, 1879. Klās'-kaino.—Dawson in Trans. Roy. Soc. Can. for 1887, sec. II, 65. Klass-ki-no.—Can. Ind. Aff., 189, 1884. Ḷ'ā'sqʻēnôx.—Boas in Rep. Nat. Mus. for 1895, 329, 1897. Lǃā'sqǃēnoxᵘ.—Boas in Mem. Am. Mus. Nat. Hist., V, pt. 2, 354, 1902. Tla'sk'ēnoq.—Boas in 6th Rep. N. W. Tribes Canada, 53, 1890. Tlats'ē'noq.—Boas in Petermanns Mitt., pt. 5, 131, 1887 (misprint).

Klatanars. A band of Cowichan on Fraser r., Brit. Col. Pop. 36 in 1886, when last enumerated separately.
Klatanars.—Can. Ind. Aff. for 1886, 229. Klatawars.—Ibid. for 1879, 309.

Klatlawas. An ancient Clallam village on Puget sd., Wash. Its inhabitants participated in the treaty of Point no Point, Jan. 26, 1855.
Klatláwas.—Gibbs, Clallam and Lummi, 20, 1863. Klat-la-wash.—U. S. Ind. Treat. (1855), 800, 1873.

Klatwoat. A village on the w. bank of Harrison r., near its junction with Fraser r., Brit. Col.—Brit. Col. map, Ind. Aff., Victoria, 1872.

Klawak. The principal town of the Henya Tlingit on the w. coast of Prince of Wales id., Alaska. It is now inhabited largely by Haida. Pop. 261 in 1890, 131 in 1900.
Chla-wāk-kŏn.—Krause, Tlinkit Ind., 111, 1885 (kŏn=people). Klawak.—Eleventh Census, Alaska, 3, 1893. ᴸAwa'k.—Swanton, field notes, B. A. E., 1904. Thlewhákh.—Holmberg, Ethnog. Skizz., map, 1855.

Klchakuk. A Kuskwogmiut Eskimo village on the E. side of the entrance to Kuskokwim bay, Alaska; pop. 18 in 1880, 49 in 1890.
Klahangamut.—Nelson in 18th Rep. B. A. E., map, 1899. Klchakuk.—Baker, Geog. Dict. Alaska, 1902. Kl-changamute.—Petroff, Rep. on Alaska, 53, 1881.

Kleaukt (Klēau'kt, 'rocky bar'). A village of the Ntlakyapamuk on Fraser r., below North Bend, Brit. Col.—Hill-Tout in Rep. Ethnol. Surv. Can., 5, 1899.

Kleguchek. A Kuskwogmiut Eskimo village in Alaska, at the mouth of Kuskokwim r. on the right bank.
Kleguchek.—Baker, Geog. Dict. Alaska, 1902. Klegutshégamut.—Kilbuck (1898) quoted by Baker, ibid.

Klemiaksac.—A Chinookan village on Columbia r., Oreg., 25 m. below The Dalles.
Kle-miak-sac.—Lee and Frost, Oregon, 176, 1844.

Klikitat (Chinookan: 'beyond,' with reference to the Cascade mts.). A Shahaptian tribe whose former seat was at the headwaters of the Cowlitz, Lewis, White Salmon, and Klickitat rs., N. of Columbia r., in Klickitat and Skamania cos., Wash. Their eastern neighbors were the Yakima, who speak a closely related language, and on the w. they were met by various Salishan and Chinookan tribes. In 1805 Lewis and Clark reported them as wintering on Yakima and Klickitat rs., and estimated their number at about 700. Between 1820 and 1830 the tribes of Wil-

lamette valley were visited by an epidemic of fever and greatly reduced in numbers. Taking advantage of their weakness, the Klikitat crossed the Columbia and forced their way as far s. as the valley of the Umpqua. Their occupancy of this territory was temporary, however, and they were speedily compelled to retire to their old seat N. of the Columbia. The Klikitat were always active and enterprising traders, and from their favorable position became widely known as intermediaries between the coast tribes and those living E. of the Cascade range. They joined in the Yakima treaty at Camp Stevens, Wash., June 9, 1855, by which they ceded their lands to the United States. They are now almost wholly on Yakima res., Wash., where they have become so

KLIKITAT WOMAN. (SHACKELFORD COLL.)

merged with related tribes that an accurate estimate of their number is impossible. Of the groups still recognized on that reservation the Topinish are probably their nearest relatives (Mooney in 14th Rep. B. A. E., 738, 1896) and may be regarded as a branch of the Klikitat, and the Taitinapam, speaking the same tongue, as another minor branch. One of the settlements of the Klikitat was Wiltkun.   (L. F.)

Awi-adshi.—Gatschet, Molalla MS., B. A. E., 27, 1877 (Molala name). Chick-atat.—Lee and Frost, Oregon, 176, 1844. Chickitats.—Lane in Sen. Ex. Doc. 52, 31st Cong., 1st sess., 171, 1850. Chit-ah-hut.—Noble in H. R. Ex. Doc., 37, 34th Cong., 3d sess., 109, 1857. Chit-at-hut.—Ibid., 111. Click-a-hut.—Robie in Ind. Aff. Rep. 1857, 351, 1858. Clicka-tat.—Lee and Frost, Oregon, 99, 1844. Clicketats.—Armstrong, Oregon, 106, 1857. Clickitats.—Lane in

Ind. Aff. Rep., 160, 1850. **Clikatats.**—Stevens in Sen. Ex. Doc. 66, 34th Cong., 1st sess., 43, 1856. **Halthwypum.**—Coues, Henry and Thompson Jour., 827, 1897. **Kanatat.**—Gibbs in Pac. R. R. Rep., I, 418, 1855. **Klachatah.**—Nicolay, Oregon, 143, 1846. **Klackatacks.**—Wilkes, U. S. Expl. Exped., IV, 325, 1845. **Klackatucks.**—Slocum (1835) in H. R. Rep. 101, 25th Cong., 3d sess., 41, 1839. **Klakatacks.**—Farnham, Trav., 112, 1843. **Kleketat.**—Scouler (1846) in Jour. Ethnol. Soc. Lond., I, 231, 1848. **Klicatat.**—Parker, Jour., 238, 1840. **Klickataats.**—Kane, Wand. in N. Am., 173, 1859. **Klick-a-tacks.**—Catlin, N. Am. Ind., II, 113, 1866. **Klickatates.**—De Smet, Letters, 231, 1843. **Klickatats.**—Swan, Northwest Coast, 324, 1857. **Klickitats.**—Lyman in Oregon Hist. Soc. Quar., I, 170, 1900. **Klikalats.**—Gallatin in Trans. Am. Ethnol. Soc., II, 14, 1848. **Klikatat.**—Townsend, Narr., 174, 1839. **Kliketan.**—Scouler (1846) in Jour. Ethnol. Soc. Lond., I, 237, 1848. **Kliketat.**—Scouler in Jour. Geog. Soc. Lond., I, 225, 1841. **Klikitats.**—Ind. Aff. Rep. 1856, 17, 1857. **Kliquital.**—Ind. Aff. Rep. 1871, 131, 1872. **Kliû'kă-tät.**—Mooney in 14th Rep. B. A. E., 738, 1896. **Klûk-ha'-tät.**—Dorsey, Alsea MS. vocab., B. A. E., 1884 (Alsea name). **Lewis River Band.**—Milroy in Ind. Aff. Rep., 164, 1881. **Lûk'-a-ta+t.**—McCaw, Puyallup MS. vocab., B. A. E., 1885 (Puyallup name). **Máhane.**—Gatschet, Umpqua MS. vocab., B. A. E., 1887 (Umpqua name). **Mĭ'-çlauq'-tou-wûn'-ti.**—Dorsey, Alsea MS. vocab., B. A. E., 1884 ('scalpers': Alsea name). **Mûn-an'-nĕ-qai qûnnĕ.**—Dorsey, Naltunnetunne MS. vocab., B. A. E., 1884 ('inland people': Naltunnetunne name). **North Dale Indians.**—Meek in H. R. Ex. Doc. 76, 30th Cong., 1st sess., 10, 1848. **Qwû'lh-hwai-pûm.**—Mooney in 14th Rep. B. A. E., 738, 1896 ('prairie people': own name). **Rea Ratacks.**—Slocum in Sen. Doc. 24, 25th Cong., 2d sess., 15, 1838. **Roil-roil-pam.**—Pandosy in Shea, Lib. Am. Ling., VI, 7, 1862. **Shlakatats.**—Belcher, Voy., I, 307, 1843. **Tlakaï'-tat.**—Gatschet, MS., B. A. E., 1877 (Okinagan name). **Tlakatat.**—Hale in U. S. Expl. Exped., VI, 569, 1846. **Tlickitacks.**—Stanley in Smithson. Misc. Coll., II, 63, 1852. **T'likatat.**—Gibbs in Cont. N. A. Ethnol., I, 241, 1877. **Trile Kalets.**—Warre and Vavasour (1845) in Martin, Hudson's Bay Ter., 80, 1849. **Tsĕ 'la'kayāt amím.**—Gatschet, La'kmiut MS., B. A. E., 105 (Kalapuya name). **Tˌuwā'-nxa-îkc.**—Boas, Kathlamet Texts, 236, 1901 (Clatsop name). **Vancouvers.**—Dart in Ind. Aff. Rep., 215, 1851. **Wàhnookt.**—Gatschet, MS., B. A. E. (Cowlitz name). **White River Indians.**—Shaw in H. R. Ex. Doc. 37, 34th Cong., 3d sess., 112, 1857. **Whulwhaipum.**—Tolmie and Dawson, Comp. Vocabs. Brit. Col., 78, 1884. **Whulwhypum.**—Lord, Naturalist in Brit. Col., 245, 1866.

Kliksiwi (*Ḷîx·sī'wĕ⁶*, 'clover root at mouth of river.'—Boas). A former Kwakiutl village at the mouth of Kliksiwi r., on the E. side of Vancouver id. All traces of it have disappeared.
Klik-sī'-wi.—Dawson in Trans. Roy. Soc. Can. for 1887, sec. II, 72. **Ḷîx·sī'wĕ⁶.**—Boas, inf'n, 1905.

Klimmim. A former Chehalis village on the N. shore of Grays harbor, Wash.
Klimmím.—Gibbs, MS., no. 248, B. A. E. **Weh-ta-mich.**—Ibid.

Klinkwan (Tlingit: *Ḷingod'n*, 'shellfish town'; or 'town where they split yellow cedar bark into long strings [*tăn*]'). A Haida town, occupied by the Yaku-lanas, on Cordova bay, Prince of Wales id., Alaska. In John Work's list (1836–41) 26 houses and 417 inhabitants are assigned to a town called Click-ass. This is a camping place near Klinkwan, and the Klinkwan people are evidently intended. Petroff gives the population in 1880–81 as 125, and the census of 1890 as 19.　　　　　　　　　　　(J. R. S.)
Chlen-kŏ-ān hādĕ.—Krause, Tlinkit Indianer, 304, 1885. **Kliarakans.**—Halleck quoted by Morris, Res. of Alaska, 67, 1879. **Kliavakans.**—Halleck

quoted by Colyer in Ind. Aff. Rep. 1869, 562, 1870. **Klinkwan.**—U. S. Coast Survey, map of Alaska, S. E. section. **Klinquan.**—Eleventh Census, Alaska, 31, 1893. **Kliuquan.**—Petroff in 10th Census, Alaska, 32, 1884. **Tlinkwan Hāadĕ.**—Harrison in Proc. and Trans. Royal Soc. Can., sec. II, 125, 1895.

Klinquit. One of the bands or tribes taking part in the Yakima treaty of 1855 (U. S. Stat., XII, 951, 1863). They are not otherwise identifiable, and should not be confounded with the Tlingit.

Klkohtl (*Kl-kóh'tl*). The Chehalis name for an ancient village on the S. side of Grays harbor, Wash.—Gibbs, MS. no. 248, B. A. E.

Klochwatone. Mentioned as a Tlingit family under the leadership of Annahootz, residing in and near Sitka, Alaska, and consisting of 200 people in about 40 families. The name is said to mean 'warriors,' but in all probability it is a corruption of *Ḷû'koa-hît-tān*, 'people of the house on the point.' A house of this name stood on the point at Sitka, where Baranoff's fort was afterward built. It belonged to the Kiksadi and not to Annahootz's people, therefore possibly the word is corrupted from *Goch-hît-tān* ('wolf house people'), to whom Annahootz belonged.　　　　　　　　　　(J. R. S.)
Klochwatone.—Beardslee in Sen. Ex. Doc. 105, 46th Cong., 1st sess., 31, 1880. **Kluckwaton.**—Ibid., 32. **Kluckwatone**—Ibid.

Klodesseottine ('hay river people'). A division of the Etchareottine on Hay r., Mackenzie Ter., Canada. In 1904 there were 247 enumerated on the upper and 115 on the lower river.
Gens de la rivière au Foin.—Petitot, Dict. Dènè-Dindjié, XX, 1876. **Slaves of Lower Hay River.**—Can. Ind. Aff. 1904, pt. 2, 82, 1905. **Slaves of Upper Hay River.**—Ibid.

Klogi. A Navaho clan, named from an old pueblo.
Klògi.—Matthews in Jour. Am. Folk-lore, III, 103, 1890. **Klògiøine.**—Ibid (*øine*='people'). **Klògidíne'.**—Matthews, Navaho Legends, 30, 1897. **Klogni.**—Bourke, Moquis of Ariz., 279, 1884.

Klokadakaydn ('arrow reed'). An Apache clan or band at San Carlos agency and Ft Apache, Ariz., in 1875-81.
Clo-kar-da-ki-ein.—White, Apache Names for Ind. Tribes, MS., B. A. E., 1875. **Klokadakaydn.**—Bourke in Jour. Am. Folk-lore. III, 111, 1890. **Klugadu-cayn.**—Ibid., 112.

Klokegottine ('prairie people'). A Nahane division living between Mackenzie r. and lakes La Martre, Grandin, and Taché, Mackenzie Ter., Canada.
Klô-kkè-Gottinè.—Petitot, Autour du lac des Esclaves, 362, 1891. **Klô-kkè-ottinè.**—Petitot, MS. vocab., B. A. E., 1865. **Kl'o-ke-ottinè.**—Ibid. **Thlo-co-chassies.**—Campbell quoted by Dawson in Rep. Geol. Surv. Can., 200B, 1889. **Tˌòtœne.**—Morice, MS. letter, 1890 (Takulli name). **Tˌò-toⁿ-na.**—Ibid. (trans. 'grass people').

Klondike (el dorado, a rich strike, a fortune). This word, which entered the English language of America during the Alaskan gold fever of 1898–1900, is the name of a tributary of the Yukon in extreme N. w. Canada. Klondike is a corruption of the name of this stream in one of the Athapascan dialects prevailing in that region. In the literature of the day, 'Klondiker,' and even 'to Klon-dike,' also occur. Of the name Baker (Geog. Dict. Alaska, 244, 1902) says: "This [Klondike] river was named Deer river by the Western Union Telegraph Expedition, in 1867, and so appeared on various maps. Later it was called Raindeer and afterwards Reindeer. Ogilvie, writing September 6, 1896, from Cudahy, says: 'The river known here as the Klondike'; and in a footnote says: 'The correct name is Thron Duick.' It has also been called Clondyke and Chandik, or Deer." (A. F. C.)

Kloo (*Xe-u*, 'southeast,' the name of a town chief). A former Haida town at the E. end of Tanoo id., Queen Charlotte ids., Brit. Col. It was one of the largest towns in the Haida country and was occupied by three families, the Kona-kegawai, Djiguaahl-lanas, and Kadusgo-kegawai, to the first of which the town chief belonged. John Work (1836–41) assigned 40 houses and 545 inhabitants to this town; old people still remember 26 houses. Although abandoned, the houses and poles here are in better condition than in most uninhabited Haida villages. (J. R. S.)
Clew.—Can. Ind. Aff. 1894, 280, 1895. Cloo.—Schoolcraft, Ind. Tribes, V, 489, 1855 (after Work, 1836–41). Kloo.—Common geographic form. Klue.—Poole, Queen Charlotte Ids., passim, 1872. Klue's Village.—Dawson, Queen Charlotte Ids., 169, 1880 (so called from chief). Laχ-skik.—Ibid. (Chimmesyan name; *Laxskiyek* = 'those of the Eagle clan'). T'anó.—Boas in 12th Rep. N. W. Tribes Can., 25, 1898. Tanoo.—Dawson, op. cit. (own name; the name of a kind of sea grass). Tanū Hāadē.—Harrison in Proc. and Trans. Roy. Soc. Can., 125, 1895. Tlu.—Ibid.

Kloo. A temporary settlement on the N. side of Cumshewa inlet, occupied by Haida from the older town of Kloo for a few years before they passed on to Skidegate. (J. R. S.)

Klothchetunne (*K'loç-tcĕ'-ƚúnné*). A Chastacosta village on or in the vicinity of Rogue r., Oreg.—Dorsey in Jour. Am. Folk-lore, III, 234, 1890.

Kltlasen (*Qltlá'sEn*). A Songish band at McNeill bay, s. end of Vancouver id.—Boas in 6th Rep. N. W. Tribes Can., 17, 1890.

Kluckhaitkwu. A band of Okinagan formerly living at the falls of Okinakane r., Wash.
Kluck-hait-kwee.—Stevens in Ind. Aff. Rep., 445, 1854. Kluckhaitkwu.—Gibbs in Pac. R. R. Rep., I, 412, 1855.

Klughuggue. Given as a Huna village on Chichagof id., but probably identical with the Chlûl-chágu of Krause, which he places on the mainland opposite. It is perhaps also identical with Tlushashakian (q. v.). Pop. 108 in 1880.
Chlûl-chágu.—Krause, Tlinkit Ind., 104, 1885. Klughuggue.—Petroff in 10th Census, Alaska, 31, 1884.

Klukluuk (from *Lowû'q*, 'slides,' applied to places where gravel, small stones, or sand slides or falls down). A village

of the Spences Bridge band of the Ntlakyapamuk, on Nicola r., 8 m. from Spences Bridge, Brit. Col.
Klūklū'uk.—Hill-Tout in Rep. Ethnol. Surv. Can., 4, 1899. LoLowû'q.—Teit in Mem. Am. Mus. Nat. Hist., II, 173, 1900.

Klukwan ('old and celebrated place'). The principal Chilkat village on Chilkat r., 20 m. from its mouth. Indian pop. in 1890, 320.
Clokwon.—Willard, Life in Alaska, 78, 1884. Klakwan.—Eleventh Census, Alaska, 3, 1893. Klokwán.—Krause, Tlinkit Ind., 100, 1885. Kluckquan. Petroff in 10th Census, Alaska, 31, 1884. Lāku'-ān.—Swanton, field notes, B. A. E, 1904.

Klumaitumsh. Given by Gibbs (MS., B. A. E., *ca.* 1858) as the Chehalis name for an ancient village on the s. side of Grays harbor, Wash., but according to Boas it is an island near the entrance to Grays harbor. Lewis and Clark, in 1805, spoke of it as a tribe of about 260 people in 12 houses.
Clamochtomichs.—Lewis and Clark, Exped., II, 119, 1814. Clamoctomichs.—Ibid., 474. Clamoctomicks.—Domenech, Deserts, I, 441, 1860. Cla-moc-to-mick's.—Orig. Jour. Lewis and Clark, VI, 118, 1905. Cla-moi-to-micks.—Ibid., 70. Clamoitonnish.—Lewis and Clark, Reize, II, 350, 1817. LEmā'itEmc.—Boas, inf'n, 1905.

Klutak. An Eskimo village in the Kuskokwim district, Alaska; pop. 21 in 1890.
Klutagmiut.—Eleventh Census, Alaska, 164, 1893.

Knacto. A former Iroquois, probably Seneca, village on the N. bank of Chemung r., N. Y.—Pouchot, map (1758) in N. Y. Doc. Col. Hist., X, 694, 1858.

Knaiakhotana. An Athapascan tribe inhabiting Kenai penin., Alaska, the basins of Knik and Sushitna rs., and the shores of Iliamna and Cook lakes. It is the only northern Athapascan tribe occupying any large portion of the seacoast. They came in contact with the Russians at an early date and were subjugated only after much fighting; a permanent trading settlement was established in 1792 by Zaïkoff and Lastochkin, and in 1793 missionaries settled on Cook inlet. In the latter year Baranoff brought 30 convicts to teach agriculture to the people of Kenai penin.; the natives attacked him during his explorations, but were repulsed, the Russians losing 11 men. Father Juvenati in 1796 attempted to suppress polygamy among the natives, but was killed while preaching near Iliamna lake. Hostilities were resumed against Baranoff in 1801. An attempt to explore the region N. of Cook inlet was made in 1816 by the Russian-American Co., and in 1819 they had 4 settlements on Cook inlet. In 1838 an epidemic of smallpox carried off nearly half the native population. In 1861 Kenai penin. was designated one of the 7 missionary districts of the Russian church. The Knaiakhotana are taller and darker than their Eskimo neighbors, but their customs differ little from those of the neighboring tribes. Hunting and fishing are the chief occupations, birch-bark canoes being used for river journeys in the interior, while for coast voyages bidarkas are purchased from the Eskimo.

The Knaiakhotana are the most civilized of all the northern Athapascan tribes. They use dogs mainly for hunting, not harnessing them to their sleds even in the long journeys they perform in winter from one trapping ground to another. Occasionally in summer dogs are employed as pack animals. Their log houses are more solidly and warmly built than those of the moving Kutchin tribes; they are divided into an outer room for cooking and rough labor, and an inner sleeping apartment, floored and ceiled, lighted through a pane of glass or gut, and impenetrable to the outer air. In some villages the bedroom is used as a bathroom, being then heated with red-hot stones; but most villages have a bath hut or two. In the more primitive villages on the Sushitna and Knik rs. is found the old communal log house, occupied by several families, each having its separate sleeping apartment connected with the central structure by a hole in the wall. Provisions are kept out of the reach of dogs in a storehouse built of logs and elevated on posts (11th Census, Alaska, 167, 1893).

They bury their dead in wooden boxes, in which they put also the property of the deceased, and pile stones upon the grave. They express grief by smearing their faces with black paint, singeing their hair, and lacerating their bodies. Most of their clothing is made of the skin of the mountain goat, which they kill in large numbers. Their language is extremely guttural, compared with that of the Eskimo (Dall, Alaska, 430, 1870).

Richardson (Arct. Exped., i, 406, 1851) stated that the Knaiakhotana have two phratries, one containing 6 and the other 5 clans. The clans, according to their mythology, are descended from two women made by the raven, and are as follows: 1, Kachgiya (The Raven); 2, Tlachtana (Weavers of Grass Nets); 3, Montochtana (A Corner in the Back Part of the Hut); 4, Tschichgi (Color); 5, Nuchschi (Descended from Heaven); 6, Kali (Fishermen). 1, Tultschina (Bathers in Cold Water); 2, Katluchtna (Lovers of Glass Beads); 3, Schischlachtana (Deceivers Like the Raven); 4, Nutschichgi; 5, Zaltana (Mountain). Hoffman (Aijaluχamut MS., B. A. E., 1882) gives the following Chugachigmiut names for divisions of the Knaiakhotana: 1, Kanikaligamut (People Close to the River); 2, Maltshokamut (Valley People); 3, Nanualikɪnut (People Around the Lake). The same authority (Kadiak MS., B. A. E., 1882) gives the Kaniagmiut names

for 5 divisions: 1, Nanualuk (=Nanualikmut); 2, Kuinruk (Sea-hunting People); 3, Tuiunuk (=Tyonok, Marsh People); 4, Knikamut (=Knik, Fire-signal People); 5, Tigikpuk (People Living at the Base of a Volcano).

The Knaiakhotana villages are Chinila, Chuitna, Kasilof, Kasnatchin, Kenai, Kilchik, Knakatnuk, Knik, Kultuk, Kustatan, Nikhkak, Nikishka, Ninilchik, Nɪtak, Skilak, Skittok, Sushitna, Titukilsk, Tyonek, Tyonok, and Zdluiat.

The natives of Cook inlet in 1818 numbered 1,471, of whom 723 were males and 748 females. Baron Wrangell, in 1825, gave their population as 1,299, the females being slightly in excess. In 1839 Veniaminof made the number 1,628, and in 1860 the Holy Synod gave 937, declaring that the natives had become Christians. At the acquisition of Alaska by the United States in 1868, Gen. Halleck and Rev. Vincent Colyer erroneously estimated the Knaiakhotana at 25,000 (Petroff, Rep. on Alaska, 40, 1884). The population in 1880 consisted of 614 natives, and in 1890 they numbered 724 (11th Census, Alaska, 158, 1893).

Ilyamna people.—Petroff in 10th Census, Alaska, 164, 1884. Kaitānā.—De Meulen, Kenay MS. vocab., B. A. E., 1870. Kaneskies.—Colyer in Ind. Aff. Rep. 1869, 553, 1870. Kanisky.—Ibid., 575. Kankūnă.—Staffeief and Petroff, MS. vocab., B. A. E., 1885. Kankūnats kŏgtana.—Ibid. Kenai.—Gallatin in Schoolcraft, Ind. Tribes, iii, 401, 1853. Kenaians.—Terry in Rep. Sec. War, pt. i, 41, 1869. Kenáies.—Scouler in Jour. Geog. Soc. Lond., i, 218, 1841. Kenai-tená.—Dall, Alaska, 430, 1870. Kenaïtses.—Pinart in Rev. de Philol. et d'Ethnog., no. 2, 1, 1875. Kenaïtze.—Ludwig quoted by Dall in Cont. N. A. Ethnol., i, 35, 1877. Kenaïyer.—Richardson, Arct. Exped., i, 401, 1851. Kenaiyut.—Ibid. (Kaniagmiut name adopted by Russians). Kenaize.—Bancroft, Nat. Races, i, 116, 1874. Kenaizen.—Balbi, Atlas Ethnog., 855, 1826. Kenajer.—Erman, Archiv, vii, 128, 1849. Kenas.—Domenech, Deserts N. Am., i, 442, 1860. Kenay.—Latham in Jour. Ethnol. Soc. Lond., i, 160, 1841. Kenayern.—Wrangell in Baer and Helmersen, Beiträge, i, 103, 1839. Kenayzi.—Humboldt, Essai Polit., i, 347, 1811. Kiatenses.—Lutke, Voyage, i, 181, 1835 (probably identical). Kinætzi.—Prichard, Phys. Hist., v, 441, 1847. Kinai.—Vater, Mithridates, iii, 230, 1816. Kinaitsa.—Balbi, Atlas Ethnog., 1826. Kinaitze.—Vater, op. cit., 229. Kinaitzi.—Balbi, op. cit. Kinaizi.—Vater, op. cit., 228. Kinajut.—Wrangell in Baer and Helmersen, Beiträge, i, 103, 1839 (Kaniagmiut name). Kinnats.—Petroff in 10th Census, Alaska, 25, 1884. Kinnats-Khotana.—Ibid., 162. Kinnatz-kokhtana.—Ibid., 164. K'nai'-a-kho-tā'nă.—Dall in Cont. N. A. Ethnol., i, 35, 1877. Knaina.—Wrangell in Baer and Helmersen, Beiträge, i, 103, 1839. Knaiokhotana.—Eleventh Census, Alaska, 158, 1893. Koht-ana.—Liziansky, MS. vocab., B. A. E. Ougagliakmuzi-Kinaia.—Balbi, Atlas Ethnog., 1826. Taaš něi.—Doroschin in Radloff, Wörterbuch, 29, 1874 (Tenankutchin name). Tašne.—Pinart in Rev. de Philol. et d'Ethnog., no. 2, 6, 1875 (Tenankutchin name). Tehanin-Kutchin.—Dall, Alaska, 430, 1870 (Kaiyuhkhotana name). Tenahna.—Holmberg (1855) quoted by Dall in Proc. A. A. A. S., 1869, 270, 1870. Těnaina.—Radloff, Wörterbuch, 29, 1874 (own name). Thnaina.—Holmberg, Ethnog. Skizz., 6, 1855. Tinaina.—Hoffman, Kadiak MS., B. A. E., 1882. Tinina.—Hoffman, Aijaluχamūt MS., B. A. E., 1882. Tinnats.—Petroff in 10th Census, Alaska, 25, 1884. Tinnats-Khotana.—Ibid., 162. Tinnatz-Kokhtana.—Ibid., 164 (own name). Tnac.—Keane in Stanford, Compend., 539, 1878.

Tnai.—Dall in Cont. N. A. Ethnol., I, 35, 1877.
Tnaina.—Wrangell in Baer and Helmersen, Beiträge, I, 103, 1839 (derived from tnai, 'man').
Tnaina Ttynai.—Bancroft, Nat. Races, I, 116, 1874.
True Thnaina.—Holmberg quoted by Dall, Alaska, 430, 1870.

Knakatnuk. A Knaiakhotana village and trading post of 35 natives in 1880 on the w. side of Knik bay, at the head of Cook inlet, Alaska.

Knakatnuk.—Petroff in 10th Census, Alaska, 29, 1884. Knik Station.—Post route map, 1903.

Knatsomita (*Knăts-o-mĭ'-ta*, 'all crazy dogs'). A society of the Ikunuhkahtsi, or All Comrades, in the Piegan tribe; it is composed of men about 40 years of age.—Grinnell, Blackfoot Lodge Tales, 221, 1892.

K'nick K'neck. See *Kinnikinnick.*

Knik (Eskimo: 'fire,' a name given by the Eskimo of Kodiak because, having no seaworthy boats of their own, they signaled for other tribes across the bay to send aid). A Knaiakhotana settlement of several villages on Knik r., at the head of Cook inlet, Alaska. The chief village had 46 people in 1880 (Petroff, 10th Census, Alaska, 29, 1884); in 1900 the population was 160 in 31 houses. This branch of the tribe numbers altogether between 200 and 300, who obtain their subsistence by hunting and trapping and by bartering with the Ahtena, who bring fur skins over the divide between Knik and Copper rs. every winter and stay weeks or months with the Knik, who through this trade obtain the clothing, utensils, and even luxuries of the whites. Their houses are built above ground of logs tightly calked with moss and covered with bark (11th Census, Alaska, 70, 1893). They use the birch-bark canoe on the inland rivers, but purchase skin bidarkas of the Kenai or Nikishka people to fish and travel along the coast.

Kinik.—Petroff in 10th Census, Alaska, map, 1884. Kinnick.—Petroff, ibid., 39. K'niq'-a-mūt.—Hoffman, Kadiak MS., B. A. E., 1882.

Knives. Cutting tools are indispensable to primitive men, and the greatest ingenuity was exercised by the northern tribes in their manufacture. Every ma-

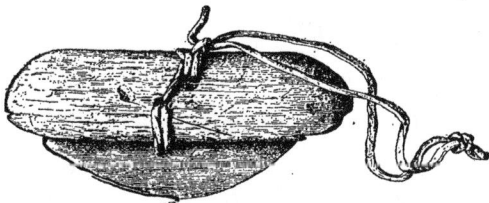

WOMAN'S SLATE KNIFE (ULU); ESKIMO (1-4). (MURDOCH)

terial capable of taking and retaining an edge was utilized—wood, reed, bone, antler, shell, stone, and metal. Teeth are nature's cutting tools, and the teeth of animals (shark, beaver, etc.) were much employed by primitive men, as also were sharp bits of stone and splinters of wood and bone, the natural edges of which

were artificially sharpened, and natural forms were modified to make them more effectual. The uses of the knife are innumerable; it served in war and was in-

OBSIDIAN CEREMONIAL BLADE, 21 IN. LONG; CALIFORNIA. (HOLMES)

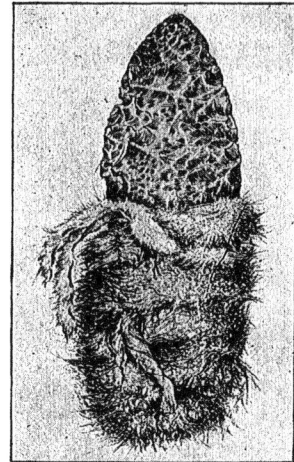

OBSIDIAN KNIFE WITH HANDLE OF OTTER SKIN, 7 1-4 IN. LONG; CALIFORNIA. (MASON)

dispensable in every branch of the arts of life, in acquiring raw materials, in preparing them for use, and in shaping whatever was made. Knives served also

JASPER BLADE, 8 3-4 IN. LONG; CALIFORNIA. (WILSON)

FLINT BLADE WITH BEVELED EDGE (1-2); OKLAHOMA. (HOLMES)

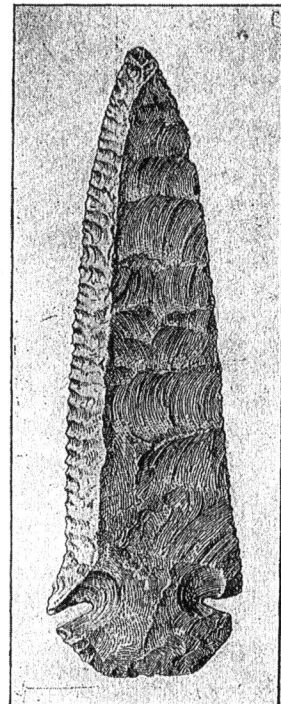

FLINT KNIFE WITH BEVELED EDGE (1-2); TENNESSEE

in symbolism and ceremony, and one of the most cherished symbols of rank and authority was the great stone knife chipped with consummate skill from obsidian or flint. According to Culin the stone knife is used among the Pueblos as a symbol of divinity, especially of the war gods, and is widely used in a healing ceremony called the "knife ceremony."

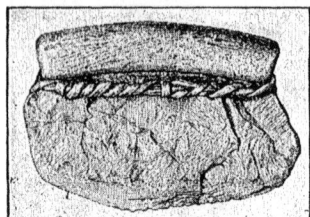

Differentiation of use combined with differences in material to give variety to the blade and its hafting; the so-called *ulu*, or woman's knife of the Eskimo, employed in various culinary arts, differs from the man's knife, which is used in carving wood and for various other purposes (Mason); and the bone snow knife of the Arctic regions is a species by itself (Nelson). The copper knife is distinct from the stone knife, and the latter takes a multitude of forms, passing from the normal types in one

WOMAN'S SLATE KNIFE (1-4); ESKIMO. (MURDOCH)

IRON KNIFE WITH WOODEN HANDLE (1-6); MAKAH

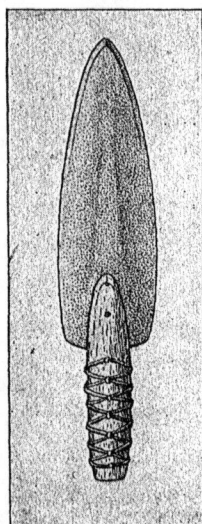

direction into the club or mace, in another into the scraper, and in another into the dagger; and it blends with the arrowhead and the spearhead so fully that no definite line can be drawn between them save when the complete

KNIFE OF NEPHRITE (1-6); ESKIMO. (NELSON)

KNIFE WITH BONE HANDLE; BRIT. COL. (SMITH)

haft is in evidence. The flaked knife blade of flint is straight like a spearhead or is curved like a hook or sickle, and it is frequently beveled on one or both edges. The ceremonial knife is often of large size and great beauty. Certain

Tennessee flint blades, believed to be of this class, though very slender, measure upward of 2 ft in length, while the beautiful red and black obsidian blades of California are hardly less noteworthy. Speaking of the latter, Powers says: "I have seen several which were 15 in.

CEREMONIAL KNIFE, LENGTH 24 1-2 IN.; KWAKIUTL. (BOAS)

or more in length and about 2½ in. wide in the widest part. Pieces as large as these are carried lifted in the hands in the dance, wrapped with skin or cloth to prevent the rough edges from lacerating the hands, but the smaller ones are mounted in wooden handles and glued fast. The large ones can not be purchased at any price." See *Implements*.

Two or three tribes of Indians, various clans, and some towns received their names from the knife, as Conshac ('reed knife'), a name for the Creeks; the town of Kusa among the Choctaw, and the Ntlakyapamuk of Thompson r., Brit. Col.

COPPER KNIFE OR DAGGER; HAIDA. (NIBLACK)

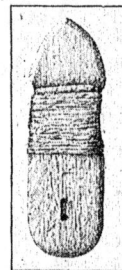

SLATE KNIFE WITH WOODEN HANDLE (1-5); ESKIMO. (MURDOCH)

Consult Boas (1) in 6th Rep. B. A. E., 1888, (2) in Nat. Mus. Rep. 1895, 1897; Fowke in 13th Rep. B. A. E., 1896; Goddard in Pub. Univ. of Cal., Anthrop. ser., I, 1903; Holmes in Nat. Mus. Rep. 1901, 1903; Mason (1) in Rep. Nat. Mus. 1890, 1891; (2) ibid., 1897, 1901; (3) ibid., 1886, 1889; Moorehead, Prehist. Impls., 1900; Murdoch in 9th Rep. B. A. E., 1892; Nelson in 18th Rep. B. A. E., 1899; Niblack in Rep. Nat. Mus. 1888, 1890; Powers in Cont. N. A. Ethnol., III, 1877; Rau in Smithson. Cont., XXII, 1876; Rust and Kroeber in Am. Anthrop., VII, 688, 1905; Thruston, Antiq. of Tenn., 1897; Wilson in Rep. Nat. Mus. 1897, 1899. (W. H. H.).

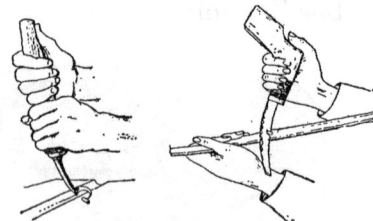

IRON CARVING KNIVES; ESKIMO. (MASON)

Knots. The Indians, and especially the Eskimo, whose difficulties with unfastening lines in a frozen area made them ingenious, tied for various purposes many kinds of knots and splices in bark, stems, roots, sinew thongs, strings, and ropes. There were knots and turk's heads in the ends of lines for buttons and toggles and for fastening work, loops and running nooses for bowstrings and tent fastenings, knots for attaching one line to another or to some object, the knots in netting for fish nets and the webbing in snowshoes and rackets, knots for attaching burdens and for packing and cinching, decorative knots in the dress of both sexes, and memorial knots used in calendars and for registering accounts and in religion. The bight, seen on Yuman carrying baskets, was universal, and the single, square, and granny knots and the half hitch were also quite common. In 1680 the Pueblo Indians communicated the number of days before their great uprising against the Spaniards by means of a knotted string, and some of their descendants still keep personal calendars by the same means, but in North America the *quipu* was nowhere so highly developed as it was in Peru. Boas (Bull. Am. Mus. Nat. Hist., xv, 1901) illustrates the many splices, hitches, loops, and knots of the Eskimo; Murdoch (9th Rep. B. A. E., 1892) has treated the knots used in nets, snowshoes, and sinew-backed bows; Dixon (Bull. Am. Mus. Nat. Hist., xvii, 1905) shows the knots of the northern Maidu of California; and Mason (Smithson. Rep. for 1893) gives details of those generally used on bows and arrows.　(o. t. m.)

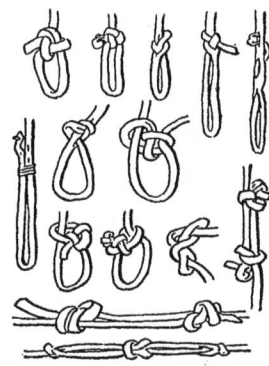

KNOTS OF THE CENTRAL ESKIMO. (BOAS)

Knou (*K'nou'*, 'eagle'). A gens of the Potawatomi, q. v.—Morgan, Anc. Soc., 167, 1877.

Knowilamowan. A former Chinookan village 25 m. from The Dalles, on Columbia r., Oreg.
Know-il-a-mow-an.—Lee and Frost, Oregon, 176, 1844.

Koagaogit (*Koaga'ogit*, 'wide and rushing waters'). A former Haida town on the N. shore of Bearskin bay, Skidegate inlet, Queen Charlotte ids., Brit. Col., in possession of the Djahui-gitinai.—Swanton, Cont. Haida, 279, 1905.

Koakotsalgi (*kóa-kótchi* 'wildcat,' *algi* 'people'). A clan of the Creeks.
Koákotsalgi.—Gatschet, Creek Migr. Leg., I, 155, 1884. Kŭ-wä'-ku-che.—Morgan, Anc. Soc., 161, 1877.

Koalcha (*Qōā'ltca*). A Squawmish village community at Linn cr., Burrard inlet, Brit. Col.—Hill-Tout in Rep. Brit. A. A. S., 475, 1900.

Koalekt (*Koā'lɛqt*). A Chehalis village at the headwaters of a w. tributary of Harrison r., in s. w. British Columbia.—Boas, MS., B. A. E., 1891.

Koanalalis (*Koanā'lalis*). The ancestor of a Nimkish gens after whom the gens was sometimes named.—Boas in Petermanns Mitt., pt. 5, 130, 1887.

Koapk (*Q'oa'px*). One of the Talio towns of the Bellacoola at the head of South Bentinck arm, coast of British Columbia.
K.'oa'pQ.—Boas in 7th Rep. N. W. Tribes Can., 3, 1891. Q'oa'px.—Boas in Mem. Am. Mus. Nat. Hist., II, 49, 1898.

Koas. Mentioned as a tribe residing with the Hutsnuwu, Chilkat, and others, in Sitka, Alaska (Beardslee in Sen. Ex. Doc. 105, 46th Cong., 1st sess., 31, 1880). It possibly refers to the Kuiu, otherwise the name is unidentifiable.

Koasati. An Upper Creek tribe speaking a dialect almost identical with Alibamu and evidently nothing more than a large division of that people. The name appears to contain the word for 'cane' or 'reed,' and Gatschet has suggested that it may signify 'white cane.' During the middle and latter part of the 18th century the Koasati lived, apparently in one principal village, on the right bank of Alabama r., 3 m. below the confluence of the Coosa and Tallapoosa, where the modern town of Coosada, Ala., perpetuates their name; but soon after w. Florida was ceded to Great Britain, in 1763, "two villages of Koasati" moved over to the Tombigbee and settled below the mouth of Sukenatcha cr. Romans and other writers always mention two settlements here, Sukta-loosa and Occhoy or Hychoy, the latter being evidently either Koasati or Alibamu. The Witumka Alibamu moved with them and established themselves lower down. Later the Koasati descended the river to a point a few miles above the junction of the Tombigbee and the Alabama, but, together with their Alibamu associates, they soon returned to their ancient seats on the upper Alabama. A "Coosawda" village existed on Tennessee r., near the site of Langston, Jackson co., Ala., in the early part of the 19th century, but it is uncertain whether its occupants were true Koasati. In 1799 Hawkins stated that part of the Koasati had recently crossed the Mississippi, and Sibley in 1805 informs us that these first settled on Bayou Chicot but 4 years later moved over to the E. bank of Sabine r., 80 m. s. of Natchitoches, La. Thence they spread over much of E. Texas as far as Trinity r., while a portion, or perhaps some of those who had remained in Alabama, obtained permission from the Caddo to settle on Red r. Schermerhorn (Mass. Hist. Soc. Coll., 2d s., II, 26, 1814) states that in 1812 the Koasati on Sabine r. numbered 600, and in 1820 Morse gave 350 on Red r., 50 on the Neches, 40 m. above its mouth, and 240 on the Trinity, 40 to 50 m. above its mouth. Bollaert (1850) estimated the number of warriors belonging to the Koasati on the lower Trinity as 500, in 2 villages, Colete and Batista. In 1870 50 were in Polk co., Tex., and 100 near Opelousas, La. They were honest, industrious, and peaceful, and still dressed in the Indian manner. Powell (7th Rep. B. A. E., 1891) says that in 1886 there were 4 families of Koasati, of about 25 individuals, near the town of Shepherd, San Jacinto co., Tex. As part of the true Alibamu were in this same region it is not improbable that some of them have been included in the above enumerations. Those of the Koasati who stayed in their original seats and subsequently moved to Indian Territory also remained near the Alibamu for the greater part, although they are found in several places in the Creek Nation, Okla. Two towns in the Creek Nation are named after them. (J. R. S.)

Aquas-saw-tee.—Schoolcraft, Ind. Tribes, I, 268, 1851. **Coashatay.**—Long, Exped. to Rocky Mts., II, 310, 1823. **Coashatta.**—Pike, Travels, map of La., 1811. **Coassattis.**—Trumbull in Johnson's Cyclopædia, II, 1156, 1877. **Cochatties.**—Le Branche (1839) in Sen. Ex. Doc. 14, 32d Cong. 2d sess., 27, 1853. **Colchattas.**—Keane in Stanford, Compend., 509, 1878. **Conchaques.**—Iberville (1702) in Margry, Déc., IV, 594, 1880. **Conchatas.**—Brackenridge, Views of La., 82, 1815. **Conchatez.**—De l'Isle, map (ca. 1710) in Winsor, Hist. Am., II, 294–295, 1886. **Conchati.**—d'Anville's map in Hamilton, Colonial Mobile, 158, 1897. **Conchattas.**—Sibley, Hist. Sketches, 81, 1806. **Conchttas.**—Lewis and Clark, Journal, 154, 1840. **Conshacs.**—Romans, Fla., 90, 1775. **Conshaes.**—Romans misquoted by Hawkins (1799), Sketch, 15, 1848. **Conshattas.**—Brown, West. Gaz., 152, 1817. **Coosadas.**—Romans, Fla., I, 332, 1775. **Coosadis.**—Ibid., 90. **Coosauda.**—Bartram, Travels, 461, 1791 (town of Tallapoosa; speak the Stincard language). **Coo-sau-dee.**—Hawkins (1779), Sketch, 35, 1848. **Coosawda.**—Pickett, Hist. Ala., II, 104, 1851. **Coosawda's.**—Campbell (1836) in H. R. Ex. Doc. 274, 25th Cong., 2d sess., 20, 1838. **Coosawder.**—Sen. Ex. Doc. 425, 24th Cong., 1st sess., 253, 1836. **Cooshates.**—Ind. Aff. Rep. 1849, 33, 1850. **Cooshatties.**—Whiteside in Ind. Aff. Rep., 327, 1870. **Coosidas.**—Schoolcraft, Ind. Tribes, V, 115, 1855. **Coowarsartdas.**—Woodward, Remin., 13, 1859. **Coowersortda.**—Ibid., 36. **Coshattas.**—Morse, Rep. to Sec. War, 257, 1822. **Coshattees.**—Schoolcraft, Ind. Tribes, III, 585, 1853. **Couchates.**—Berquin Duvallon, Travels, 97, 1806. **Cousatee.**—Jefferys, Am. Atlas, 5, 1776 (town on w. bank of Alabama r.). **Cousoudee.**—U. S. Ind. Treat. (1814), 163, 1837. **Coussac.**—Hutchins, Hist. Narr., 83, 1784 (probably identical). **Coussati.**—Alcedo, Dic. Geog., I, 676, 1786. **Coussehate.**—Milfort, Mémoire, 265, 1802. **Cunhates.**—Martin, Hist. La., II, 206, 1827. **Cushatees.**—Maillard, Hist. Texas, 252, 1842. **Cush-eh-tah.**—Schoolcraft, Ind. Tribes, I, 309, 1851. **Cussadies.**—Weatherford (1793) in Am. State Pap., Ind. Aff., I, 385, 1832. **Cusshetaes.**—Coxe, Carolana, 23, 1741. **Cutchates.**—Doc. of 1828 in Soc. Geog. Mex., 267, 1870 (live on E. bank of Trinidad [Trinity] r.). **Cuzadans.**—Rafinesque, introd. Marshall, Ky., I, 24, 1824. **Koo a sah te.**—Adair, Am. Ind., 169, 1775. **Ko-sa-te'haⁿ-ya.**—Dorsey, Biloxi MS. Dict., B.A.E., 1892 (Biloxi name). **Quaasada.**—U. S. Ind. Treat. (1827), 420, 1837. **Qua-saw-das.**—Ind. Aff. Rep., 279, 1846 (on Canadian r., Ind. Ter.). **Quesadas.**—Gallatin in Trans. Am. Antiq. Soc., II, 97, 1836. **Queseda.**—Schermerhorn (1812) in Mass. Hist. Coll., 2d s., II, 18, 1814. **Quezedans.**—Rafinesque,

introd., Marshall, Ky., I, 24, 1824. **Shati.**—Popular abbreviation of Koasati in Texas.

Koasati. Two towns of the Creek Nation, both in the s. part of their territory near Canadian r., one a few miles w. of Eufaula, the other w. of Hilabi, Okla.
Koassati.—Gatschet, Creek Migr. Leg., II, 185, 1888.

Koatlna (*Q'oā́'Lna*). A Bellacoola village on a bay of the same name at the s. entrance of Bentinck arm, coast of British Columbia.
K·oā́'tlna.—Boas in 7th Rep. N. W. Tribes Can., 3, 1891. **Q'oā́'Lna.**—Boas in Mem. Am. Mus. Nat. Hist., II, 48, 1898.

Kocheyali. A former Yokuts tribe that perhaps lived on Kings r., Cal.—A. L. Kroeber, inf'n, 1906. See *Mariposan Family.*

Kochinish-yaka. The Yellow-corn clan of the Keresan pueblos of Acoma and Laguna, N. Mex. See *Yaka.*
Kóchinish-yáka-hánoᶜʰ.—Hodge in Am. Anthrop., IX, 349, 1896 (Laguna form: *yáka*='corn'; *hanoch*= 'people'). **Kóchïnïshyáka-hánoqᶜʰ.**—Ibid. (Acoma form).

Kochkok. A Chnagmiut Eskimo village on the right bank of Yukon r., Alaska, near the Kuskokwim portage.
Kochkogamute.—Raymond (1869) quoted by Baker, Geog. Dict. Alaska, 1902. **Kokok.**—Baker, ibid.

Kodiak. A town on St Paul's harbor, at the E. end of Kodiak id., Alaska, established among the Eskimo by the Russians in 1789 as a center of the fur trade. Pop. 288 in 1880, 495 in 1890, 341 in 1900.
Kadiak.—Bruce, Alaska, map, 1885. **Pavlovsky gavan.**—Eleventh Census, Alaska, 75, 1893 (Russian: 'Paul's harbor'; natives still call it *Gavan*, 'the harbor'). **Saint Paul.**—Petroff, Rep. on Alaska, 28, 1884.

Kodlimarn (*Qodlimarn*). A summer settlement of the Eskimo of the plateau of Nugumiut, on the E. entrance to Frobisher bay, Baffin land.—Boas in 6th Rep. B. A. E., map, 1888.

Koeats. Given as a Ute band or tribe in N. central Nevada, but evidently Paviotso.—Powell in H. R. Ex. Doc. 86, 43d Cong., 1st sess., 1, 1874.

Koeentwakah. See *Cornplanter.*

Koekoaainok (*Qoḗ'qoaainôx*, 'people from the river Koais'). A gens of the Tenaktak, a Kwakiutl tribe.—Boas in Rep. Nat. Mus. for 1895, 331, 1897.

Koekoi (*K·ōḗ'kōi*). A Squawmish village community on the w. side of Howe sd., Brit. Col.—Hill-Tout in Rep. Brit. A. A. S., 474, 1900.

Koeksotenok ('people of the other side'). A Kwakiutl tribe on Gilford id., Brit. Col. The gentes are Naknahula, Memoggyins, Gyigyilkam, and Nenelpae. In 1885 they lived with the Mamalelekala in a town called Memkumlis. Kwakwakas was probably a former village. Pop. 50 in 1885, the last time the name appears.
K·wḗk·sōt́ēnoq.—Boas in 6th Rep. N. W. Tribes Can., 54, 1890. **Kwick-so-te-no.**—Can. Ind. Aff., 189, 1884. **Kwiksot'enoq.**—Boas in Bull. Am. Geog. Soc., 227, 1887. **Kwĩk'-so-tino.**—Dawson in Trans. Roy. Soc. Can. for 1887, sec. II, 74. **Qoḗ'xsōt́enôx.**—Boas in Rep. Nat. Mus. for 1895, 330, 1897. **Quick-**

sul-i-nut.—Kane, Wand. in N. Am., app., 1859. **Qwē'qᵘ sōt!ē'noxᵘ.**—Boas in Mem. Am. Mus. Nat. Hist., v, pt. 1, 156, 1902.

Koetas (*Q!oē'tas*, 'earth-eaters'). A family of the Raven clan belonging to the Kaigani or Alaskan branch of Haida. According to the southern Haida they derived their name from the fact that in a legendary Haida town whence all the Ravens came (see *Tadji-lanas*) they used to live near the trails. The Kaigani themselves, however, say that when they first settled at Hlgan, on the w. coast of Graham id., they were called, from the town, Hlun-staa-lanas (*Ł̣ᵍᴀn staᵍa lä'nas*, 'holding-up-the-fin-town-people'). Afterward they began to cook and eat a plant called hlkunit (*tk!u'nit*) which grows under the salmon-berry bushes. Some of them then joked at this, saying, "We are even eating earth," hence the name Koetas. On the Alaska mainland their town was Sukkwan. There were 5 subdivisions: Chats-hadai, Huadjinaas-hadai, Nakalas-hadai, Hlkaonedis, and Naden-hadai. (J. R. S.) **K·'oē'tas.**—Boas, 12th Rep. N. W. Tribes Can., 22, 1898. **Q!oē'tas.**—Swanton, Cont. Haida, 272, 1905.

Koetenok (*Q'oē'tenôx*, 'raven'). A clan of the Bellabella, a Kwakiutl tribe.—Boas in Rep. Nat. Mus. 1895, 328, 1897.

Koga (*Qō'ga*). A small Haida town formerly on McKay harbor, Cumshewa inlet, Queen Charlotte ids., Brit. Col., which was occupied by a family of the same name, of low social rank, who afterward moved to Skedans.—Swanton, Cont. Haida, 279, 1905.

Kogahl-lanas (*Qō'gał lä'nas*, 'people of the town of Koga'). A small division of the Kagials-kegawai family group of the Haida. They were of low social rank. Their town, called Koga, once stood in McKay harbor, and they are said to have been won in a gambling contest by the Kagials-kegawai.—Swanton, Cont. Haida, 269, 1905.

Kogals-kun (*K!ogä'ls kun*, 'sand-spit point'). A former Haida town on Masset inlet, Queen Charlotte ids., Brit. Col., occupied by the Aostlan-lnagai.—Swanton, Cont. Haida, 281, 1905.

Kogangas (*Qogä'ñas*, 'sea-otters'). An extinct family group belonging to the Raven clan of the Haida. Their towns stood near the modern town of Skidegate, Queen Charlotte ids., Brit. Col. (J. R. S.) **K·ōg·ā'ngas.**—Boas, 12th Rep. N. W. Tribes Canada, 24, 1898. **Qogä'ñas.**—Swanton, Cont. Haida, 269, 1905.

Kogiung. A Kiatagmiut Eskimo village at the mouth of Kvichak r., Bristol bay, Alaska; pop. 29 in 1880, 133 in 1890, 533 in 1900. **Koggiung.**—Petroff in 10th Census, Alaska, 17, 1884. **Kogiung.**—Baker, Geog. Dict. Alaska, 1902.

Kogluk. A Kaviagmiut village at C. Nome, Alaska.—Eleventh Census, Alaska, 162, 1893.

Koguethagechton. See *White-eyes*.

Kogui (*Kō'gúi*, 'elks'). A tribal division of the Kiowa.—Mooney in 14th Rep. B. A. E., 1079, 1896.

Kohamutkikatska (Creek: *kóha* 'cane', *mútki* 'cut off', *kátska* 'broken'). A former upper Creek town with 123 families in 1832. Location unknown. **Koho-mats-ka-catch-ka.**—Campbell (1836) in H. R. Doc. 274, 25th Cong., 2d sess., 20, 1838. **Ko ho mutki garts kar.**—Schoolcraft, Ind. Tribes, IV, 578, 1854. **Ko-ho-muts-ka-catch-ka.**—Crawford (1836) in H. R. Ex. Doc. 274, op. cit., 24. **Ko-ho-muts-kigar.**—H. R. Ex. Doc. 276, 24th Cong., 1st sess., 162, 1836. **Kohomutskigartokar.**—Sen. Ex. Doc. 425, 24th Cong., 1st sess., 299, 1836.

Kohani. A subtribe or band of the Karankawa. They are mentioned as late as 1824 in connection with the Coaques, from which it seems probable that they were one of the bands living near Colorado r., Texas. They may be identical with the Quevenes of Cabeza de Vaca. **Cobanes.**—Joutel quoted by Barcia, Ensayo, 271, 1723. **Cohannies.**—Texas Hist. Ass. Quar., VI, 250, 1903. **Coxanes.**—Solis (1768) cited by H. E. Bolton, inf'n, 1906. **Cujanes.**—Ripperdá (1777), ibid. **Cujanos.**—Bollaert in Jour. Ethnol. Soc. Lond., II, 276, 1850. **Cuyanes.**—Bollaert quoted by Gatschet, Karankawa Inds., 35, 1891. **Kouans.**—Joutel, Jour. Voy., 90, 1719. **Quevenes.**—Cabeza de Vaca (1555), Smith trans., 137, 1871 (possibly identical). **Qujanes.**—Ripperdá (1777) cited by H. E. Bolton, inf'n, 1906. **Quoan.**—Joutel (1687) in Margry, Déc., III, 288, 1878.

Kohasaya (*Ko-ha-say-a*). A former pueblo of the Sia, N. of the present Sia pueblo, N. Mex.—Bandelier in Arch. Inst. Papers, IV, 196, 1892. See *Kakanatzatia*.

Kohashti ('starting place of canoes'). A Klamath settlement, of 5 or 6 houses in 1890, at the N. E. end of Upper Klamath lake, Oreg., 3 m. N. of Yaaga; once the site of the Klamath Indian agency. **Koháshti.**—Gatschet in Cont. N. A. Ethnol., II, pt. I, xxx, 1890. **Ko-was-ta.**—Applegate in Ind. Aff. Rep., 89, 1866. **Kuhuáshti.**—Gatschet, op. cit. **Skohuáshki.**—Ibid.

Kohatsoath. A sept of the Toquart, a Nootka tribe.—Boas in 6th Rep. N. W. Tribes Canada, 32, 1890.

Kohhokking ('at the land of pines.'—Hewitt). A Delaware village in 1758 near "Painted Post," in Steuben co., N. Y., or Elmira, formerly called Painted Post, in Chemung co., N. Y. See Alden (1834) in Mass. Hist. Soc. Coll., 3d s., VI, 147, 1837.

Kohltiene's Village. The summer camp of a Stikine chief named Kåłtī'n on Stikine r., Alaska; 28 people were there in 1880.—Petroff in 10th Census, Alaska, 32, 1884.

Koi. A former Pomo village on Lower Lake id., Lake co., Cal. The island was known to the Indians by the same name. See *Makhelchel*. (S. A. B.)

Koi ('panther'). A Chickasaw phratry. **Kóa.**—Gibbs quoted by Gatschet, Creek Migr. Leg., I, 96, 1884. **Xoi.**—Copeland quoted by Morgan, Anc. Soc., 163, 1877.

Koiaum ('to pick berries'). A village

of the Ntlakyapamuk on the E. side of Fraser r., 25 m. above Yale, Brit. Col.

Boston Bar.—Name given by whites. **Koia´um.**—Teit in Mem. Am. Mus. Nat. Hist., II, 169, 1900. **Quiyone.**—Brit. Col. map, Ind. Aff., Victoria, 1872 (probably identical).

Koikahtenok (*Qoĭ´k·axtēnŏx*, 'whale people'). A clan of the Wikeno, a Kwakiutl tribe.—Boas in Rep. Nat. Mus. for 1895, 328, 1897.

Koikoi (*Xoē´xoē*, a supernatural being, sometimes described as living in ponds; used as a mask by the Lillooet, many coast Salish, and the southern Kwakiutl.—Boas). A Squawmish village community on Burrard inlet, Brit. Col.

Qoiqoi.—Hill-Tout in Rep. Brit. A. A. S., 474, 1900. **Xoē´xoē.**—Boas, inf'n, 1905.

Koinchush ('wild cat'). A Chickasaw clan of the Koi phratry.

Ko-in-chush.—Morgan, Anc. Soc., 163, 1877. **Kó-in-tchush.**—Gatschet, Creek Migr. Leg., I, 96, 1884.

Koinisun (*Kōinĭ´sun*). An Ita Eskimo settlement on Inglefield gulf, N. Greenland.—Stein in Petermanns Mitt., no. 9, map, 1902.

Koiskana (from *kōēs*, or *kwō´es*, a bush the bark of which is used for making twine; some say it is a Stuwigh or Athapascan name, but this seems doubtful). A village of the Nicola band of Ntlakyapamuk near Nicola r., 29 m. above Spences Bridge, Brit. Col.; pop. 52 in 1901, the last time the name appears.

Koaskunā´.—Hill-Tout in Rep. Ethnol. Surv. Can., 4, 1899. **Koiskana´.**—Teit in Mem. Am. Mus. Nat. Hist., II, 174, 1900. **Kuinskanaht.**—Can. Ind. Aff. for 1892, 313. **Kwois-kun-a´.**—Dawson in Trans. Roy. Soc. Can. for 1891, sec. II, 44. **Pitit Creek.**—Teit, op. cit. (name given by whites). **Qaiskana´.**—Teit, op. cit. **Quinskanaht.**—Can. Ind. Aff. for 1898, 419. **Quinskanht.**—Ibid. for 1901, 166. **Quis-kan-aht.**—Ibid. for 1886, 232. **Quss-kan-aht.**—Ibid. for 1883, 191.

Koiyo (*Kôi-yo*). A former Chumashan village at Cañada del Coyote, Ventura co., Cal.—Henshaw, Buenaventura MS. vocab., B. A. E., 1884.

Kojejewininewug (*Kuchĭchĭwĭnĭnĭwŭg*; from *kuchĭchĭw*, referring to the straits and bends of the rivers and lakes on which they resided; *ĭnĭnĭwŭg*, 'people'). A division of the Chippewa formerly living on Rainy lake and river on the N. boundary of Minnesota and in the adjacent part of British America. Cf. *Tecamamiouen*.

Algonquins of Rainy Lake.—Lewis and Clark, Travels, 55, 1806. **Kôchêchê Wenenewak.**—Long, Exped. St Peter's R., II, 153, 1824. **Ko-je-je-winin-e-wug.**—Warren (1852) in Minn. Hist. Soc. Coll., V, 84, 1885. **Kotchitchi-wininiwak.**—Gatschet, Ojibwa MS., B. A. E., 1882. **Kutcitciwininiwag.**—Wm. Jones, inf'n, 1906. **Lac la Pluie Indians.**—Hind, Red River Exped., I, 82, 1860. **Rainy-lake Indians.**—Schoolcraft (1838) in H. R. Doc. 107, 25th Cong., 3d sess., 9, 1839.

Kokaia (*Qō-qai´â*, 'maggot-fly,' because there are many found there in summer). An abandoned Chilliwack village on Chilliwack r., S. Brit. Col.—Hill-Tout in Rep. Ethnol. Surv. Can., 4, 1902.

Kokaitk. A division of the Bellabella, living on N. Millbank sd.

K'´ō´k'aitq.—Boas in 6th Rep. N. W. Tribes Can., 52, 1890. **Kok-wai-y-toch.**—Kane, Wand. in N. Am., app., 1859. **Kook-wai-wai-toh.**—Tolmie and

Dawson, Vocabs. Brit. Col., 117B, 1884. **Koqueightuk.**—Brit. Col. map, 1872. **Q'ō´qa-îtx.**—Boas in Rep. Nat. Mus. for 1895, 328, 1897.

Kokaman. Mentioned by writers between 1851 and 1855 as a Karok village on Klamath r., Humboldt co., Cal. In 1851 the chief's name was said to be Panamonee, but this is probably an error, as Panamenik is the Karok village at Orleans.

Coc-co-man.—McKee (1851) in Sen. Ex. Doc. 4, 32d Cong., spec. sess., 161, 1853 (upper Klamath tribe). **Cock-o-mans.**—Ibid., 215 (given as Hupa band). **Coc-ko-nan.**—Ibid., 194 (a Patesick band). **Cok-ka-mans.**—Meyer, Nach dem Sacramento, 282, 1855.

Kokhittan ('box-house people'). A Tlingit social group, forming a subdivision of the Kagwantan, q. v.

Kōk hĭt tän.—Swanton, field notes, B. A. E., 1904. **Kūkettän.**—Krause, Tlinkit Ind., 113, 1885. **Kukittan.**—Ibid.

Koknas-hadai (*K'ōk´-nas:had'ā´i*, 'snow-owl house people'). Given by Boas (5th Rep. N. W. Tribes Canada, 27, 1889) as a subdivision of the Yaku-lanas, a family of the Raven clan of the Alaskan Haida, but in reality it is only a house name belonging to that family group.   (J. R. S.)

Koko. An Ikogmiut Eskimo village on the N. bank of the Yukon, Alaska, below Ikogmiut.

Kochkomut.—Post route map, 1903. **Koko.**—Baker, Geog. Dict. Alaska, 1902.

Kokoaeuk (*Kōkoaē´uk·*). A village of the Matsqui tribe of Cowichan at the s. w. point of Sumass lake, near Fraser r., Brit. Col.—Boas in Rep. Brit. A. A. S., 454, 1894.

Kokob. The Burrowing-owl clan of the Hopi of Oraibi, Arizona.

Kokob.—Voth in Field Columb. Mus. Pub., no. 55, 13, 1901. **Kokop.**—Stephen quoted by Mindeleff in 8th Rep. B. A. E., 105, 1891 (cf. *Kokop*, the Firewood clan).

Kokoheba (*Ko-ko-he´-bă*). The name of a village which has come to be applied to an almost extinct Mono tribe in Burr valley, with one village over the divide, looking into the valley of Sycamore cr., N. of Kings r., Cal.—Merriam in Science, XIX, 916, June 17, 1904.

Kokoiap (*K'okōĭap´*, 'place of strawberries'). A village of the Ntlakyapamuk on Fraser r., above Siska, Brit. Col.—Hill-Tout in Rep. Ethnol. Surv. Can., 5, 1899.

Kokolik. A Kukpaurungmiut Eskimo village at Pt Lay, Arctic coast, Alaska, with 30 inhabitants in 1880.

Kokomo ('young grandmother'). A Miami village, named after a chief, that stood on the site of the present Kokomo, Ind.

Ko-ko-mah village.—Hough, map in Ind. Geol. Rep., 1883.

Kokop. The Firewood phratry of the Hopi, comprising the Kokop (Firewood), Ishauu (Coyote), Kwewu (Wolf), Sikyataiyo (Yellow Fox), Letaiyo (Gray Fox), Zrohona (small mammal, *sp. incog.*), Masi (Masauuh, a supernatural being), Tuvou (Piñon), Hoko (Juniper), Awata (Bow), Sikyachi (small yellow bird), and Tuvuchi (small red bird) clans. According to tradition they came from the Rio Grande, building the pueblo of Sikyatki, which they occupied until its destruction in late prehistoric times.

Ko'-kop nyû-mû.—Fewkes in Am. Anthrop., VII, 403, 1894 (nyû-mû='phratry').

Kokop. The Firewood clan of the Hopi, the ancestors of whom came from Jemez pueblo, New Mexico.

Kokop wiñwû.—Fewkes in 19th Rep. B. A. E., 584, 1900 (wiñwû='clan'). Ko-kop-wün-wû.—Fewkes in Am. Anthrop., VII, 403, 1894. Ku-ga.—Bourke, Snake Dance, 117, 1884 (given doubtfully).

Kokopki (Hopi: 'house of the Firewood people'). A large, ancient, ruined pueblo, attributed by the Hopi to the Firewood clan, originally a Jemez people; situated on a low mesa near Maupin's store, at Mormon John's spring, in Jeditoh valley, 2½ m. E. of Keam's Canyon school, Tusayan, N. E. Arizona. See Mindeleff in 8th Rep. B. A. E., 590, 1898; Hough in Rep. Nat. Mus. 1901, 333 et. seq., 1903.

Cottonwood ruin.—Hough, op. cit. (name given locally by whites). Delcalsacat.—Ibid. ('wild gourd': Navaho name). Horn House.—Mindeleff, op. cit. Kokopki.—Fewkes, inf'n, 1906 (ki = 'house'). Kokopnyama.—Hough, op. cit. ("name refers to the clans which lived here and is probably not the ancient designation of the village").

Kokoskeeg. An unidentified tribe which, according to Tanner (Narrative, 316, 1830), was known to the Ottawa and was so called by them.

Koksilah. A Cowichan tribe in Cowitchin valley, E. coast of Vancouver id., opposite Admiral id.; pop. 12 in 1904.

Cokesilah.—Can. Ind. Aff., lxi, 1877. Kokesailah.—Brit. Col. map, Ind. Aff., Victoria, 1872. Koksilah.—Can. Ind. Aff., pt. II, 164, 1901. Kulkuisála.—Boas, MS., B. A. E., 1887.

Koksoagmiut ('people of Big river'). A subtribe of the Sukinimiut Eskimo living on Koksoak (Big) r., N. Labrador. They numbered fewer than 30 individuals in 1893.

Koakramint.—Boas in Am. Antiq., 40, 1888 (misprint). Koksoagmyut.—Turner in 11th Rep. B. A. E., 176, 1894. Koksoak Innuit.—Ibid., 179. Koksoak river people.—Ibid. Kouksoarmiut.—Boas in 6th Rep. B. A. E., 463, 470, 1888.

Kokyan. The Spider clan of the Hopi.

Kóhkang.—Voth, Oraibi Summer Snake Ceremony, 282, 1903. Kohkañamu.—Dorsey and Voth, Oraibi Soyal, 9, 1901. Ko'-kyañ-a.—Stephen in 8th Rep. B. A. E., 38, 1891. Kokyan wiñwû.—Fewkes in 19th Rep. B. A. E., 584, 1900. Ko'-kyuñ-üh wüñwü.—Fewkes in Am. Anthrop., VII, 404, 1894.

Kolelakom (Qōlē'laQōm). A Squawmish village community on Bowen id., Howe sd., Brit. Col.—Hill-Tout in Rep. Brit. A. A. S., 474, 1900.

Kolmakof. A Moravian mission founded in 1885 among the Kuskwogmiut Eskimo on Kuskokwim r., Alaska, 200 m. from its mouth. It is on the site of a Russian redoubt and trading post, first established in 1832 by Ivan Simonson Lukeen, after whom it was named for a time. In 1841 it was partially destroyed by the Indians with fire, whereupon it was rebuilt by Alexander Kolmakof and took his name. The people are mixed Eskimo and Athapascan. See Baker, Geog. Dict. Alaska, 1902.

Kolmakof Redoubt.—Nelson in 18th Rep. B. A. E., map, 1899. Kolmakovsky.—Hallock in Nat. Geog. Mag., IX, 86, 1898.

Kolok. A former Chumashan village at the old mill in Carpinteria, E. of Santa Barbara, Cal.

K'-â'-lâk.—Henshaw, Buenaventura MS. vocab., B. A. E., 1884.

Koloma. A division of the Nishinam, at Coloma, between American r. and the s. fork of Yuba r., in Eldorado co., Cal.

Colomas.—Powers in Overland Mo., XII, 21, 1874. Ko-lo'-ma.—Powers in Cont. N. A. Ethnol., III, 315, 1877.

Koltsiowotl (K·oltsī'owotl). A division of the Nanaimo on the E. coast of Vancouver id.—Boas in 5th Rep. N. W. Tribes Can., 32, 1889.

Koluschan Family. A linguistic family embracing the Tlingit (q. v.). The name is said by Dall to be derived from Russian kalushka, 'a little trough,' but by others from the Aleut word kaluga, signifying 'a dish,' the allusion being to the concave dish-shaped labrets worn by the Tlingit women.

×Haidah.—Scouler in Jour. Roy. Geog. Soc., XI, 219, 1841 (same as his Northern). =Kaloshians.—Dall in Proc. Am. A. A. S., 375, 1885 (gives tribes and population). =Klen-e-kate.—Kane, Wanderings of an Artist, app., 1859 (a census of N. W. coast tribes classified by language). =Klen-ee-kate.—Schoolcraft, Ind. Tribes, V, 489, 1855. <Kolooch.—Latham in Trans. Philol. Soc. Lond., I, 31–50, 1846 (tends to merge Kolooch into Esquimaux); Latham in Jour. Ethnol. Soc. Lond., I, 163, 1848 (compared with Eskimo language); Latham, Opuscula, 259, 276, 1860. =Koloschen.—Berghaus (1845), Physik. Atlas, map 17, 1848; ibid., 1852; Buschmann Spuren der aztek. Sprache 680, 1859; Berghaus, Physik. Atlas, map 72, 1887. <Kolúch.—Latham, Nat. Hist. Man, 294, 1850 (more likely forms a subdivision of Eskimo than a separate class; includes Kenay of Cook inlet, Atna of Copper r., Koltshani, Ugalents, Sitkans, Tungaas, Inkhuluklait, Magimut, Inkalit; Dígothi and Nehanni are classed as a "doubtful Kolúches"). =Koluschan.—Powell in 7th Rep. B. A. E., 85, 1891. =Koluschen.—Gallatin in Trans. and Coll. Am. Antiq. Soc., II, 14, 1836 (islands and adjacent coast from 60° to 55° N. lat.). =Koluschians.—Prichard, Phys. Hist. Mankind, V, 433, 1847 (follows Gallatin); Scouler (1846) in Jour. Ethnol. Soc. Lond., I, 231, 1848. =Kolush.—Latham, Elem. Comp. Philol., 401, 1862 (mere mention of family with short vocabulary). =Koulischen.—Gallatin in Trans. and Coll. Am. Antiq. Soc., II, 306, 1836; Gallatin in Trans. Am. Ethnol. Soc., II, pt. 1, c, 77, 1848 (Koulischen and Sitka languages); Gallatin in Schoolcraft, Ind. Tribes, III, 402, 1853 (Sitka, bet. 52° and 59° lat.). ×Northern.—Scouler in Jour. Roy. Geog. Soc. Lond., XI, 218, 1841 (includes Koloshes and Tun Ghasse). =Thlinkeet.—Keane in Stanford, Compend., Cent. and So. Am., app., 460, 462, 1878 (from Mt St Elias to Nass r.; includes Ugalenzes, Yakutats, Chilkats, Hoodnids, Hoodsinoos, Takoos, Auks, Kakas, Stikines, Eeliknûs, Tungass, Sitkas); Bancroft, Nat. Races, III, 562, 570, 1882. =Thlinkets.—Dall in Proc. Am. A. A. S., XVIII, 268, 269, 1869 (divided into Sitka-kwan, Stahkin-kwan, "Yakutats"). =Thlinkit.—Tolmie and Dawson, Comp. Vocabs., 14, 1884 (vocab. of Skutkwan sept; also map showing distribution of family); Berghaus, Physik. Atlas, map 72, 1887. =Thlinkithen.—Holmberg in Finland Soc., 284, 1856, fide Buschmann, 676, 1859. =T'linkets.—Dall in Cont. N. A. Ethnol., I, 36, 1877 (divided into Yăk'ütăts, Chilkâht'kwăn, Sitka-kwan, Stăkhin'-kwăn, Kygăh'ni). =Thlinkit.—Dall in Proc. Am. A. A. S., 375, 1885 (enumerates tribes and gives population).

Komacho (Ko-ma'-cho). A name applied by Powers (Cont. N. A. Ethnol., III, 172, 1877) to the Pomo living in

Rancheria and Anderson valleys, Mendocino co., Cal., and said by him to have been derived from the name of their captain. The people living in these two valleys belonged to two different dialectic groups and in aboriginal times had no particular common interests. The connection of the two is probably entirely subsequent to white settlement. (s. A. B.)

Komarof. A Chnagmiut village at the N. mouth of Yukon r., Alaska; pop. 13 in 1880.—Petroff in 10th Census, Alaska, map, 1884.

Komarof.—Nelson in 18th Rep. B. A. E., map, 1899. Komarov Odinotchka.—Petroff, Rep. on Alaska, 57, 1880 (= 'Komaroff's trading post').

Komenok ('wealthy people'). An extinct sept of the Lekwiltok, a Kwakiutl tribe.

K·'ō'm'ēnoq.—Boas in 6th Rep. N. W. Tribes Can., 55, 1890. Q'ō'm'ēnôx.—Boas in Rep. Nat. Mus. for 1895, 332, 1897.

Komertkewotche (derived in part from *Kómert*, the Pima name of the Sierra Estrella). A Pima settlement on the Rio Gila., s. Ariz.—ten Kate quoted by Gatschet, MS., B. A. E., xx, 199, 1888.

Komkonatko ('head water', or 'head lake'). An Okinagan village 21 m. from the town of Kwilchana on Nicola lake, Brit. Col.

Fish Lake.—Teit in Mem. Am. Mus. Nat. Hist., II, 174, 1900 (name given by whites). Komkona'tko.—Ibid.

Komkutis (*Q'ō'mqūtis*). A Bellacoola village on the s. side of Bellacoola r., Brit. Col., near its mouth. It was one of the eight villages called Nuhalk.

K-ōmōtĒs.—Boas in 7th Rep. N. W. Tribes Can., 3, 1898. Kougotis.— Mayne, Brit. Col., 147, 1862. Q'ō'mqūtîs.—Boas in Mem. Am. Mus. Nat. Hist., II, 49, 1898.

Komkyutis ('the rich side'). A sept of the Kwakiutl proper, living at Ft Rupert, Brit. Col., and said to count 70 warriors in 1866. Boas in 1890 called them a gens of the Walaskwakiutl; in 1895 a sept of the tribe.

Cum-que-kis.—Kane, Wand. in N. Am., app., 1859. Komiū'tis.—Boas in Petermanns Mitt., 131, 1887. K·'ō'mkyūtis.—Boas in 6th Rep. N. W. Tribes Can., 54, 1890. Kum-cutes.—Lord, Natur. in Brit. Col., I, 165, 1866. Kumkewtis.—Brit. Col. map, 1872. Lō'kuili'la.—Boas in Petermanns Mitt., pt. 5, 131, 1887. Q'ō'mk·utis.—Boas in Rep. Nat. Mus. 1895, 330, 1897.

Komkyutis. A gens of the Goasila, q. v.

Komoyue ('the rich ones'). A division of the true Kwakiutl living at Ft Rupert, near the N. end of Vancouver id. They are more often known by the war name Kueha ('slayers'). The gentes are Gyigyilkam, Haailakyemae, Haanatlenok, Kukwakum, and Yaaihakemae. Pop. 42 in 1901, 25 in 1904.

Kueh'a.—Boas in Bull. Am. Geog. Soc., 227, 1887 ('murderers'). Kuē'qa.—Boas in 6th Rep. N. W. Tribes Can., 55, 1890. Kuē'xa.—Boas in Rep. Nat. Mus. for 1895, 330, 1897 (war name: 'the murderers'). Kuicha.—Boas in Petermanns Mitt., pt. 5, 131, 1887. Kwe-ah-kah.—Can. Ind. Aff., 189, 1884. Kwi-ah-kah.—Ibid., 364, 1897. Q'ō'moyuē.—Boas in Rep. Nat. Mus. for 1895, 330, 1897. Qua-kars.—Lord, Natur. in Brit. Col., I, 165, 1866. Queackar.—Can. Ind. Aff., 143, 1879. Quee ha Qna colt.—

Work quoted by Schoolcraft, Ind. Tribes, V, 488, 1855. Quee-ha-qua-coll.—Work (1836–41) in Kane, Wand. in N. Am., app., 1859 (= Kueha + Kwakiutl).

Komoyue. A gens of the Kueha division of the Lekwiltok. They live with the Wiweakam at the village of Tatapowis, on Hoskyn inlet, Brit. Col. Pop. 32 in 1887, the last time they were separately enumerated.

Ah-mah-oo.—Can. Ind. Aff. 1887, 309, 1888. K·'ō-mōyuē.—Boas in 6th Rep. N. W. Tribes Can., 55, 1890. Q'ō'moyuē.—Boas in Rep. Nat. Mus. for 1895, 331, 1897.

Komps (*Kōmps*). A Squawmish village community on the right bank of Squawmisht r., Brit. Col.—Hill-Tout in Rep. Brit. A. A. S., 474, 1900.

Kona (*Qoná*). A former Tlingit town in the Sitka country, Alaska. (J. R. S.)

Kona-kegawai (*Q!ō'na qē'gawa-i*, 'those born at Skedans'). One of the most important families of the Eagle clán of the Haida, part of whom lived at Skedans, while the remainder resided at Kloo, which was owned by their chief. The Kona-kegawai, Djiguaahl-lanas, Stawashaidagai, and Kaiahl-lanas claimed descent from one woman. (J. R. S.)

K·'unak·ē'owai.—Boas in 12th Rep. N. W. Tribes Can., 25, 1898. Q!ō'na qē'gawa-i.—Swanton, Cont. Haida, 272, 1905.

Kondiaronk. See *Adario*.

Konekonep. An Okinagan band formerly living on a creek known to the Indians by the same name, in Washington.

Kone-Konep.—Stevens in Ind. Aff. Rep., 445, 1854. Konekonl'p.—Gibbs in Pac. R. R. Rep., I, 412, 1855.

Konekotay. A division of the Delawares, formerly in New Jersey.—De Laet (*ca.* 1633) in N. Y. Hist. Soc. Coll., 2d s., I, 303, 1841.

Kongiganak. A Kuskwogmiut Eskimo village near the entrance to Kuskokwim bay, Alaska; pop. 175 in 1880.

Kongiganagamute.—Petroff in 10th Census, Alaska, 16, 1884. Koñigunugumut.—Nelson in 18th Rep. B. A. E., map, 1899.

Kongik. A Malemiut Eskimo village on Buckland or Konguk r., Seward penin., Alaska; pop. 90 in 1880, 54 in 1890.

Kangoot.—Kelly, Arct. Eskimos, 15, 1890. Kengugmiut.—Eleventh Census, Alaska, 165, 1893. Kongigamute.—Petroff in 10th Census, Alaska, 4, 1884. Kongik.—Baker, Geog. Dict. Alaska, 1902.

Konglo (*Kong'-lo*). The Corn clan of the Tewa of Hano pueblo, N. E. Ariz. They numbered 23 individuals in 1893. See *Kun*.

Ka'-ai.—Stephen in 8th Rep. B. A. E., 39, 1891 (Hopi name). Ko'n-lo.—Ibid. (Tewa name). Kulo^n-to-wa.—Fewkes in Am. Anthrop., VII, 166, 1894. Nata'n.—Stephen, op. cit. (Navaho name).

Kongtalyui (*Koñtä'lyui*, 'black boys'; sometimes also called *Sindiyúi*, 'Sindi's children'). A tribal division of the Kiowa, now practically extinct, whose members were said to be of darker color than the rest of the tribe, which, if true, might indicate foreign origin. Sindi is the great mythic hero of the Kiowa.—Mooney in 14th Rep. B. A. E., 1079, 1896.

Koni. A division of the Miwok s. of Cosumnes r., in Amador and Eldorado cos., Cal.

Cawnees.—Bancroft, Nat. Races, I, 456, 1874. Kâ'-ni.—Powers in Cont. N. A. Ethnol., III, 349, 1877. Koni.—A. L. Kroeber, inf'n, 1906.

Konkapot. A Mahican sachem who, in 1724, joined in the sale of the territory comprising the "upper and lower Housatonic townships"; his captain's commission was given him by Gov. Belcher in 1734, and he succeeded to the chieftaincy about 1744. He embraced Christianity and invited the Moravian missionaries to labor among his people, the Westenhuck, who became known as Stockbridge Indians after they were Christianized and removed to the mission, except such as went to join the Christian Indians in Pennsylvania. The chief, who received the Christian name John, and was recognized by the authorities at Albany and Boston as the head of the Mahican, they having had their council fire at Westenhuck, was long the patriarch of the Indian community at Stockbridge (Ruttenber, Tribes Hudson R., 88, 1872). The name survived as a family designation among the Stockbridges at least as late as 1864, a Levi Konkapot serving in the civil war (Nelson, Inds. N. J., 147, 1894).

Konkau (Kō'yŏang kâui, 'valley earth'). A formerly populous division of the Maidu, living in Butte co., Cal., in the valley of Concow cr., a tributary of the w. branch of Feather r. They are now on Round Valley res., Mendocino co., and numbered 171 in 1905.

Cancons.—Keane in Stanford, Compend., 505, 1878. Cancow.—Ind. Aff. Rep., 313, 1874. Caw-Caw.—Ibid., 1867, 111, 1868. Con-Con's.—Ibid., 75, 1870. Con-Cous.—Ibid., 1867, 121, 1868. Con-Cow.—Ibid., 1863, 93, 1864. Cou-cows.—Ibid., 1864, 119, 1865. Cow-Cow.—Ibid., 130, 1868. In'shin.—A. L. Kroeber, inf'n, 1903 (modern Yuki name). Kănkau.—Curtin, MS. vocab., B. A. E., 1885. Onocows.—Ind. Aff. Rep., 12, 1865 (misprint). Ooncows.—Ibid., 112.

Konomihu. A subsidiary tribe of the Shasta, living at the forks of Salmon r., Siskiyou co., Cal., extending 7 m. up the s. fork and 5 m. up the N. fork. Their language is very divergent from that of the main body of Shasta. (R. B. D.)

Konope. A Clatsop village on Columbia r., near its mouth, in Clatsop co., Oreg.

Konapee.—Lyman, Hist. Oregon, I, 171, 1903. Konō'pē.—Boas, Chinook Texts, 274, 1894.

Kontareahronon. The Huron name of a people mentioned in the 17th century as living s. of St Lawrence r., on the authority of Ragueneau's map. The name evidently designated the inhabitants of the Huron village of Contarea (q. v.). See Jes. Rel. 1640, 35, 1858. (J. N. B. H.)

Koo (Kŏ'-o, 'buffalo'). A clan of the Tewa pueblo of San Ildefonso, N. Mex.

Kóo-tdóa.—Hodge in Am. Anthrop., IX, 349, 1896 (tdóa == 'people').

Kooji ('wolf'). Given by Dawson (Queen Charlotte Ids., 134, 1880) as the name of one of the 4 Haida clans. There were only 2 clans, however, and the Wolf was not one of them. (J. R. S.)

Kookotlane (Kŏoqŏtlā'nē). A Bellacoola division at the town of Nuskelst, Bellacoola r., Brit. Col.—Boas in 7th Rep. N. W. Tribes Can., 3, 1891.

Kookupvansik (Kó-okúp Vánsĭk, 'medicine paraphernalia'). A former Pima village in s. Arizona.—Russell, Pima MS., B. A. E., 16, 1902.

Koonahmich. A body of Salish under the Victoria superintendency, Brit. Col. Pop. 15 in 1882, when last separately enumerated.

Koo-nah-mich.—Can. Ind. Aff., 258, 1882.

Koontie. See Coontie.

Kooskoo (Koos-koo', 'crane'). A gens of the Abnaki (q. v.).—Morgan, Anc. Soc., 174, 1877.

Koossawin ('hunters'). A term compounded from the Chippewa verb kiyusä-wĭn, 'hunting,' lit. 'the act of walking about' (Jones), and used by Schoolcraft (Ind. Tribes, VI, 582, 1857) to denote the hunting tribes.

Koot. The largest village of the Nunivagmiut, near C. Etolin, Nunivak id., Alaska; pop. 117 in 1890.—Eleventh Census, Alaska, 115, 1893.

Kootep (Ko'-o-tep). A Yurok village on lower Klamath r., Cal., near Klamath bluffs.—A. L. Kroeber, inf'n, 1905.

Kootpahl. A former village of the Atfalati at Forest Grove, Washington co., Oreg.—Lyman in Oreg. Hist. Soc. Quar. I, 323, 1900.

Koowahoke (Koo-wä-ho'-ke, 'pine region'). A subdivision of the Delawares (q. v.).—Morgan, Anc. Soc., 172, 1877.

Kooyah. A root (Valeriana edulis), also known as "tobacco root," from which a bread is made by some of the Indians of the Oregon region. The word is from one of the Shahaptian or Shoshonean dialects. (A. F. C.)

Kopaalk. A body of Salish under Fraser superintendency, Brit. Col. Can. Ind. Aff., 78, 1878.

Kopagmiut ('people of the great river'). An Eskimo tribe at the mouth of Mackenzie r., Canada. According to Dall they formerly extended up this river 200 m., but are now confined to islands at the mouth and the Arctic coast w. of Herschel id.

Añénépit.—Petitot in Bib. Ling. et Ethnol., III, 11, 1876 (= 'Eskimo of the east': so called by Hudson Bay, Labrador, and Greenland Eskimo). Chiglit.—Ibid., 10. Kopäg-müt.—Dall in Cont. N. A. Ethnol., I, 10, 1877. Kopäng'-meûn.—Richardson, Polar Regions, 1861. Kukhpagmiut.—Eleventh Census, Alaska, 130, 1893. Kupûnmiun.—Murdoch in 9th Rep. B. A. E., 45, 1854. Kurvik.—Petitot in Bul. Soc. de Géog., 6th s., X, 182, 1875. Mackenzie River Eskimo.—Richardson, Arct. Search. Exped., 354, 1851. Tareormeut.—Petitot, Monogr., map,

1876. **Taρeoρmeut.**—Ibid., 11 (= 'those who live by the sea'). **Tarrèor-meut.**—Dall in Cont. N. A. Ethnol., I, 10, 1877. **Tchiglit.**--Petitot, Monogr., 11 (applied to Mackenzie and Anderson r. tribes). **Tciglit.**—Ibid.

KOPAGMIUT GIRL.   (AM. MUS. NAT. HIST.)

Kopano. A small tribe formerly living on or near Copano Bay, s. Texas. There is no doubt that it belonged to the Karankawan linguistic stock, but it is seldom mentioned.
Coopanes.—Solis (1768) cited by H. E. Bolton, inf'n, 1906. **Copanes.**—Rivera, Diario, leg. 2602, 1737.

Kopeli. The extinct Pink Conch clan of the Tewa of Hano pueblo, N. E. Ariz.
Ko'-pe-li.—Fewkes in Am. Anthrop., VII, 166, 1894. **Kópeli-tówa.**—Hodge in Am. Anthrop., IX, 352, 1896 (*tówa* = 'people').

Kopiwari (*Ko-pi-wa'-ri*). An ancient village once occupied by the Nambe people, situated about 5 m. N. of the present Nambe pueblo, N. Mex.   (F. W. H.)

Koprino. A Kwakiutl tribe speaking the Koskimo subdialect. They lived formerly at the entrance of Quatsino sd., and were divided into the Koprino and Kotlenok clans, but they are now amalgamated with the Koskimo proper. Pop. 14 in 1884, the last time they were separately enumerated.
G·â'p!ēnoxᵘ.—Boas in Mem. Am. Mus. Nat. Hist., v, pt. 2, 393, 1902. **G·'ō'p'ēnŏx.**—Boas in Rep. Nat. Mus. 1895, 329, 1897. **Keope-e-no.**—Can. Ind. Aff., 190, 1883. **Keroopinough.**—Brit. Col. map, 1872. **Kiāwpino.**—Dawson in Trans. Roy. Soc. Can. for 1887, sec. II, 65. **Koprinos.**--Can. Ind. Aff., 145, 1879. **Kyŏ'p'ēnoq.**—Boas in 6th Rep. N. W. Tribes Can., 53, 1890.

Koprino. A gens of the Koprino, q. v.

Koquapilt. A Chilliwack town in lower Chilliwack valley, Brit. Col.; pop. 16 in 1904.
Co-qua-piet.—Can. Ind. Aff., pt. I, 268, 1889. **Coquopiet.**—Ibid., 309, 1879. **Coquopilt.**—Ibid., 74, 1878. **Koquahpilt.**—Ibid., 78. **Koquapilt.**—Brit. Col.

map, Ind. Aff., Victoria, 1872. **Kwaw-kwaw-apiet.**—Can. Ind. Aff., 413, 1898. **Kwawkwawapilt.**--Can. Ind. Aff., pt. II, 158, 1901.

Kordlubing. A summer settlement of the Kingnaitmiut Eskimo near the head of an inlet emptying into Cumberland sd. from the N. side.
Qordlubing.—Boas in 6th Rep. B. A. E., map, 1888.

Koremiut. An Eskimo settlement at Narket fjord, lat. 61° 17′, E. Greenland.—Nansen, First Crossing, I, 306, 1890.

Kornok. An Eskimo village in w. Greenland, lat. 64° 30′.—Nansen, First Crossing, II, 329, 1890.

Koroa. A small tribe, perhaps related to the Tonika, whose home was on the w. bank of the Mississippi below the Natchez, on the Yazoo, and in the country intervening westward from the Mississippi. They were visited early in 1682 by La Salle, who described their cabins as dome-shaped, about 15 ft high, formed chiefly of large canes, and without windows (Margry, Déc., I, 558, 1876). They were considered warlike, and were cruel and treacherous. In 1705 a party of them, hired by the French priest Foucault to convey him by water to the Yazoo, murdered him and two other Frenchmen. La Salle observed that their language differed from that of the Taensa and Natchez, but their customs were the same. All afterward moved to and settled on Yazoo r., Miss., where in 1742 they lived in the same village as the Yazoo. They were then allies of the Chickasaw, but were later merged with the Choctaw and their identity as a separate organization was lost. Allen Wright, whose grandfather was of this tribe, informed Gatschet (Creek Migr. Leg., I, 48, 1884) that the term Koroa, or Coroa, was neither Choctaw nor Chickasaw, and that the Koroa spoke a language differing entirely from the Choctaw.

Akoroa.—Marquette, map (1673) in Shea, Discov. Miss., 1852. **Coiras.**—Richebourg (*ca.* 1716) in French, Hist. Coll. La., III, 246, 1851. **Coloa.**—Iberville (1699) in Margry, Déc., IV, 179, 1880. **Coroa.**—Barcia, Ensayo, 246, 1723. **Coroha.**—Tonti (1684) in Margry, Déc., I, 603, 1876. **Corois.**—McKenney and Hall, Ind. Tribes, III, 81, 1854. **Corroas.**—Coxe, Carolana, 9, 1741. **Corrois.**—Charlevoix (1729), New France, VI, 85, 102, 1872. **Corroys.**—Le Petit quoted by Kip, Jesuit Missions, 289, 1866. **Couroas.**—Jefferys, French Dom., I, 144, 1761. **Courois.**—La Harpe (1699) in French, Hist. Coll. La., III, 19, 28, 1851. **Curois.**—Ibid., 32. **Ikouera.**—La Salle (1681) in Margry, Déc., II, 189, 198, 1877. **Kolwa.**—Gatschet, Creek Migr. Leg., I, 48, 1884 (Choctaw name). **Koroas.**—La Métairie (1682) quoted by French, Hist. Coll. La., II, 22, 1875. **Kouera.**—Proces verbal (1682) in French, Hist. Coll. La., I, 47, 1846. **Kourouas.**—Coxe, Carolana, 10, 1741. **Kourovas.**—Alcedo, Dic. Geog., V, 394, 1789. **Kowronas.**—Morse, N. Am., 254, 1776 (perhaps quoting Coxe). **Kúlua.**—Gatschet, Creek Migr. Leg., I, 48, 1884 (Choctaw name).

Korovinski. A former Aleut village on Atka id. at Korovin bay, which the natives deserted for Nazan across the island. The Russians built a church there in 1826 and made Atka the headquarters of the western district of the Aleutians.—Petroff in 10th Census, Alaska, 21, 1884.

Korovinski. An Aleut village on Korovin id., Alaska; pop. 44 in 1880, 41 in 1890.
Korovinsky.—Petroff, Rep. on Alaska, 25, 1881.

Korusi. A tribe of the Patwin division of the Copehan family, formerly living at Colusa, Colusa co., Cal. It was once comparatively populous, as Gen. Bidwell states that in 1849 the village of the Korusi contained at least 1,000 inhabitants (Powers in Cont. N. A. Ethnol., III, 219, 1877). They are spoken of as clannish, and fond of nursing family feuds. When a Korusi woman died, leaving a very young infant, her friends shook it to death in a skin or blanket. Powers (p. 226) says the Korusi hold that in the beginning of all things there was nothing but the Old Turtle swimming about in a limitless ocean, but that he dived down and brought up earth, with which he created the world.
Colouse.—Powers in Cont. N. A. Ethnol., III, 518, 1877. Colusa.—Ibid., 219. Colusi.—Taylor in Cal. Farmer, Mar. 23, 1860. Corusies.—Powers in Overland Mo., XIII, 543, 1874. Ko-rú-si.—Powers in Cont. N. A. Ethnol., III, 219, 1877.

Koserefski. A former Kaiyuhkhotana village, now an Ikogmiut settlement, on the left bank of the Yukon, near the mouth of Shageluk slough. It is the seat of the mission of the Holy Cross.
Koserefski.—Bruce, Alaska, map, 1885. Kozerevsky.—Eleventh Census, Alaska, 165, 1893. Kosyrof.—Map form cited by Baker, Geog. Dict. Alaska, 1902. Kozyrof.—Nelson in 18th Rep. B. A. E., map, 1899. Leather Village.—Dall, Alaska, 220, 1870.

Kosetah. Mentioned by Gibbs (Schoolcraft, Ind. Tribes, III, 171, 1853) as a Shasta band of Shasta valley, N. Cal., in 1851, but it is really a man's personal name. (R. B. D.)

Koshkogemut. A subdivision of the Chnagmiut Eskimo of Alaska.—Dall in Cont. N. A. Ethnol., I, 17, 1877.

Kosipatuwiwagaiyu (*Ko-si′-pa tu-wi′-wa-gai-yu*, 'muddy water place'). A Paviotso tribe formerly dwelling about Carson sink, w. Nev.
Ko-si′-pa tu-wi′-wa-gai-yu.—Powell, Paviotso MS., B. A. E., 1881. Ku′si-páh.—Powers, Inds. W. Nev., MS., B. A. E., 1876.

Koskedi. A Tlingit division at Gaudekan and Yakutat, belonging to the Raven phratry.
Kosk!ĕ′dî.—Swanton, field notes, B. A. E., 1904. Kusch-kē-ti.—Krause, Tlinkit Ind., 118, 1885. Kusk-edi.—Ibid.

Koskimo. An important Kwakiutl tribe inhabiting the shores of Quatsino sd., Vancouver id. The gentes are Gyekolekoa, Gyeksem, Gyeksemsanatl, Hekhalanois(?), Kwakukemalenok, Naenshya, Tsetsaa, and Wohuamis. Their winter village is Hwades; their summer village, Maate. Pop. 82 in 1904.
Kooskīmo.—Tolmie and Dawson, Vocabs. Brit. Col., 118B, 1884. Kosimo.—Can. Ind. Aff., 1904, pt. 2, 71, 1905. Kos-keemoe.—Ibid., 1884, 189, 1885.

Koskeemos.—Grant in Jour. Roy. Geog. Soc., 293, 1857. K·osk·ē′moq.—Boas, 6th Rep. N. W. Tribes Can., 53, 1890. Koskiemo.—Mayne, Brit. Col., 251, 1862. Kōs′-kĭ-mo.—Dawson in Trans. Roy. Soc. Can. for 1887, sec. II, 69. Koskimos.—Can. Ind.

KOSKIMO MAN. (AM. MUS. NAT. HIST.)

Aff., 145, 1879. Kos-ki-mu.—Ibid., 1894, 279, 1895. Koskumos.—Ibid., 113, 1879. Kus-ke-mu.—Kane, Wand. in N. Am., app., 1859. Qō′sqĕmox.—Boas in Rep. Nat. Mus. 1895, 329, 1897. Qósqīmō.—Boas in Petermanns Mitt., pt. 5, 131, 1887. Roskeemo.—Powell in Can. Ind. Aff., 130, 1879 (misprint).

KOSKIMO WOMAN. (AM. MUS. NAT. HIST.)

Koskimo. A Kwakiutl subdialect spoken by the Koprino, Klaskino, Koskimo, and Quatsino.

Kosotshe. A former village of the Tututni, identified by Dorsey with the Luckkarso nation of Lewis and Clark, who placed them on the Oregon coast s. of the Kusan territory, in 1805, and estimated their population at 1,200. Fifty years later Kautz said their village was on Flores cr., Oreg., about lat. 42° 50′; Dorsey fixed their habitat N. of Rogue r., between Port Orford and Sixes cr.

Kasoatcha.—Kautz, letter to Gibbs, B. A. E., ca. 1855. **Ko-so-a-cha.**—Gibbs, MS. on Coast tribes, B. A. E. **K͞ōs-o-tc͞ĕ′.**—Dorsey in Jour. Am. Folk-lore, III, 233, 1890 (Tututni name). **Ku-so-cha-to-ny.**—Abbott, MS. Coquille census, B. A. E., 1858. **Ku′-su-me′-t͡unn͞ĕ′.**—Dorsey, op. cit. (Naltunne-tunne name). **Luckasos.**—Lewis and Clark, Exped., II, 119, 1814. **Luckkarso.**—Ibid., 474. **Lukkarso.**—Drake, Bk. of Inds., ix, 1848. **Port Orford.**—Abbott, MS. Coquille census, B. A. E., 1858.

Kostuets (*K͞ŏ′s Tu͞ĕ′ts*, 'where pine trees stand'). A Shoshonean encampment 10 m. above Yaneks, or Yainax, on Sprague r., Klamath res., Oreg.—Gatschet in Cont. N. A. Ethnol., II, pt. 2, 143, 1890.

Kostun-hana (*Q!ō′stᴀn xā′na; q!ō′stᴀn* means 'crab'). A former Haida town, in possession of the Kogangas family group, a short distance E. of Skidegate, Queen Charlotte ids., Brit. Col. There does not appear to be space at this point for more than two or three houses.—Swanton, Cont. Haida, 279, 1905.

Kosunats. A Ute division formerly living on Uinta res., N. E. Utah, where Powell found 76 of them in 1873. They now form part of what are known as the Uinta Ute.

Kotasi. A former Maidu village in the N. part of Plumas co., Cal., about 3 m. E. of Greenville.—Dixon in Bull. Am. Mus. Nat. Hist., XVII, pl. xxxviii, 1905.

Kotil. A Koyukukhotana village at the junction of Kateel r. with Koyukuk r., Alaska; pop. 65 in 1844.

Khotilkakat.—Zagoskin quoted by Petroff in 10th Census, Alaska, 37, 1884. **Khotilkakate.**—Zagoskin in Nouv. Ann. Voy., 5th s., XXI, map, 1850. **Khotylnakat.**—Zagoskin, Desc. Russ. Poss. Am., map, 1844.

Kotlenok (*Q′ō′lēnŏx*). A gens of the Koprino, a Kwakiutl tribe.—Boas in Rep. Nat. Mus. 1895, 329, 1897.

Kotlian. See *Katlian.*

Kotlik ('breeches,' hence 'river fork'). A village of the Chnagmiut Eskimo on Kotlik r., Alaska; pop. 8 in 1880, 31 in 1890.

Coatlik.—Schwatka, Mil. Recon. in Alaska, 20, 1885. **Kotlik.**—Nelson in 18th Rep. B. A. E., map, 1899. **Kutlik.**—Post route map, 1903.

Kotlskaim (*Qotlskaim*, 'serpent pond'). A Squawmish village community on Burrard inlet, Brit. Col.—Hill-Tout in Rep. Brit. A. A. S., 475, 1900.

Kotsai (*Kotsái*). An extinct division of the Comanche.—Mooney in 14th Rep. B. A. E., 1045, 1896.

Kotsava (from *kozabi*, an insect used for food). A Mono band formerly living about Mono lake and Owens r. and lake, E. Cal., numbering 300 in 1870.

Caso.—Maltby in Ind. Aff. Rep., 94, 1866. **Cazaby**

Pah-Utes.—Campbell, ibid., 113, 1870. **Kots-a′-va.**—Powell, Paviotso MS., B. A. E., 1881. **Ko-za′-bi-ti-kut-teh.**—Powers, Ind. West Nev., MS., B. A. E., 1876 ('worm-eaters'). **Owen's River Indians.**—Maltby in Ind. Aff. Rep., 94, 1866.

Kotsoteka (*Kótso-tĕ′ka*, 'buffalo-eaters'). One of the principal divisions of the Comanche.

Buffalo Eater band.—Comanche and Kiowa treaty, Sen. Ex. Doc. O, 39th Cong., 1st sess., 4, 1866. **Buffalo Eaters.**—Butler in H. R. Doc. 76, 29th Cong., 2d sess., 6, 1847. **Buffalo Indians.**—Bell in Jour. Ethnol. Soc. Lond., I, 268, 1869. **Cash-chevatebka.**—Smith in H. R. Ex. Doc. 240, 41st Cong., 2d sess., 20, 1870. **Cashchokelka Comanches.**—Ibid., 21. **Castcheteghka-Comanches.**—Alvord in Sen. Ex. Doc. 18, 40th Cong., 3d sess., 35, 1869. **Co-che-ta-cah.**—Butler in H. R. Doc. 76, 29th Cong., 2d sess., 6, 1847. **Cochetakers.**—McKusker in Sen. Ex. Doc. 40, 40th Cong., 3d sess., 14, 1869. **Co-che-te-ka.**—Comanche and Kiowa treaty, Sen. Ex. Doc. O, 39th Cong., 1st sess., 4, 1866. **Cooch-chotellica.**—Sec. War in Sen. Ex. Doc. 7, 42d Cong., 3d sess., 1, 1872. **Cooch-cho-teth-ca.**—Sanders in H. R. Ex. Doc. 7, 42d Cong., 1st sess., 4, 1871. **Coocheetakas.**—Penney in Ind. Aff. Rep. 1869, 101, 1870. **Cools-on-tick-ara.**—Schoolcraft, Ind. Tribes, I, 250, 1853. **Coschotghta.**—Alvord in Sen. Ex. Doc, 18, 40th Cong., 3d sess., 6, 1869. **Cos-tche-tegh-kas.**—Ibid., 7. **Cstcheteghta Comanches.**—Alvord in H. R. Ex. Doc. 240, 41st Cong., 2d sess., 151, 1870. **Cuchanticas.**—Cortez (1799) in Pac. R. R. Rep., III, pt. 3, 121, 1856. **Cuechunticas.**—Pino, Not. Hist. Nuevo-Mex., 83, 1849. **Cuhtzuteca.**—Pimentel, Cuadro Descr., II, 347, 1865. **Curtoze-to-gah Comanches.**—Hazen in Sen. Ex. Doc. 18, 40th Cong., 3d sess., 31, 1869. **Curtz-e-Ticker Comanches.**—Ibid., 24. **E hunticas.**—Orozco y Berra, Geog., 59, 1864 (given as Apache). **Gū-shŏ-dŏj-ka.**—Butcher and Lyendecher, Comanche MS. vocab., B. A. E., 1867. **Koo-chee-ta-kee.**—Neighbors in Ind. Aff. Rep., 579, 1848. **Koo-che-ta-kers.**—Schoolcraft, Ind. Tribes, II, 128, 1852. **Koo-chi-ta-ker.**—Neighbors, op. cit., 578. **Koolsaticara.**—Schoolcraft, op. cit., VI, 687, 1857. **Koolsatik-ara.**—Ibid., I, 522, 1851. **Ko+s′-tco-te′-ka.**—ten Kate, Synonymie, 9, 1884. **Ko′stshote′ka.**—Hoffman in Proc. Am. Philos. Soc., XXIII, 299, 1886. **Ko′tso-tĕ′ka.**—Mooney in 14th Rep. B. A. E., 1045, 1896. **Ku′htche-téχka.**—Gatschet, Comanche MS. vocab., B. A. E.

Kotta ('mescal' or 'tobacco'). Given by Bourke (Jour. Am. Folk-lore, II, 181, 1889) as a clan of the Mohave, q. v.

Kouchnas-hadai (*Qō′utc nas :had′ā′i*, '[grizzly-] bear house people'). Given by Boas (Fifth Rep. N. W. Tribes Can., 27, 1889) as a subdivision of the Yakulanas, a family of the Raven clan of the Haida. It is in reality only a house name belonging to the family.

Koukdjuaq ('big river'). A Talirpingmiut Eskimo village of the Okomiut tribe formerly on L. Nettilling, Baffin land.—Boas in 6th Rep. B. A. E., map, 1888.

Kounaouons. A tribe or band, probably in Canada near the Maine frontier, mentioned as allies of the French in 1724.

K8na8ons.—Rasle (1724) in Mass. Hist. Soc. Coll., 2d s., VIII, 246, 1819.

Koungmiut ('river people'). An Eskimo tribe on the w. coast of Hudson bay, s. of the Kinipetu, in the region of Pt Churchill.—Boas in Bull. Am. Mus. Nat. Hist., XV, 6, 1901.

Kouse. A plant (*Peucedanum ambiguum*) used by the Indians of the Columbia-Oregon region for making bread. Lewis and Clark in 1804–06 used the form *cous.* Thornton (Oreg. and Cal., I, 355, 1849) speaks of "the *cowish* or biscuit root." The word is derived from *kowish*, the name of this root in the Nez Percé and closely related dialects of the Shahaptian stock. See *Roots*. (A. F. C.)

Kouyam. A village or tribe mentioned by Joutel in 1687 as being N. of Maligne (Colorado) r., Tex. It is probably the tribe called Caba by Manzanet, which may have been Coahuiltecan or Karankawan. See Gatschet, Karankawa Inds., 1891.
Cavaianes.—Barcia, Ensayo, 271, 1723. Kavagan.—Joutel (1687), Jour. Voy., 90, 1719. Kouayan.—Shea, note in Charlevoix, New France, IV, 78, 1870. Kouayon.—Joutel (1687) in French, Hist. Coll. La., I, 152, 1846. Kouyam.—Joutel in Margry, Déc., III, 288, 1878.

Kovogzruk. A Kaviagmiut village at Port Clarence, Alaska.—Eleventh Census, Alaska, 162, 1893.

Kowagmiuṭ ('big-river people'). A tribe of western Eskimo of Alaska, numbering 81 in 1890, dwelling on Kowak r. E. of Kotzebue sd. Their chief food besides fish and ptarmigan consists of marmots, but the number of these is rapidly decreasing. Their villages are Kikiktak, Kowak, Umokalukta, Unatak, and the summer settlement of Sheshalik. By some these Eskimo have been included in the Nunatogmiut; by others, together with the Selawigmiut, in the Malemiut.
Kooagamutes.—Petroff in 10th Census, Alaska, 60, map, 1884. Koo-og-ameuts.—Cooper, Cruise of Corwin, 26, 1880. Kowăg'-mŭt.—Dall in Cont. N. A. Ethnol., I, 12, 1877. Kowān'g-mĕŭn.—Simpson quoted by Dall, ibid. Kŭ-ăg'mŭt.—Dall in Proc. A. A. A. S., XXXIV, 377, 1886. Kuangmiut.—Woolfe in 11th Census, Alaska, 130, 1894. Kuwŭ'ñmiun.—Murdoch in 9th Rep. B. A. E., 44, 1892.

Kowailchew. A coast Salish tribe said by Gibbs (Pac. R. R. Rep., I, 433, 1855) to live N. of the Semiamo, principally if not altogether in Canada. Unless intended for the Cowichan they are not mentioned elsewhere.

Kowak (? 'great river'). A Kowagmiut village at the mouth of Kowak r., Alaska.
Koovuk.—Kelly, Arct. Eskimos, 15, 1890. Kubok.—Zagoskin, Desc. Russ. Poss. in Amer., pt. 1, 73, 1847.

Kowanga. A former Gabrieleño rancheria near San Fernando mission, Los Angeles co., Cal. Probably identical with Okowvinjha, or with Cahuenga, q. v.
Kowanga.—Taylor in Cal. Farmer, May 11, 1860. Owongos.—Lawson in Ind. Aff. Rep., 13, 1879.

Kowasayee. A small Shahaptian tribe, speaking the Tenino language and formerly living on the N. side of Columbia r., in Klickitat co., Wash., nearly opposite the mouth of the Umatilla. They were included in the Yakima treaty of 1855, and the survivors are on Yakima res., but their number is unknown.
K'kásăwi.—Mooney in 14th Rep. B. A. E., 739, 1896. Kowasayee.—Ind. Aff. Rep. 1856, 266, 1857. Kowwassayee.—U. S. Stat., XII, 951, 1863. Kowwassayes.—Keane in Stanford, Compend., 518, 1878.

Kowasikka. A village formerly occupied by the Eel River Miami until they removed, under the treaty of Feb. 11, 1828, to a reserve near the mouth of Eel r. It was on Sugar cr., near the present Thorntown, Boone co., Ind., and was commonly known as Thorntown. (J. M.)
Kow-a-sik-ka.—Hough in Ind. Geol. Rep., map, 1883. Thorntown.—Common name. Thorntown Miamies.—Drake, Ind. Chron., 205, 1836.

Kowina. A prehistoric circular pueblo on a low mesa opposite the spring at the head of Cebollita valley, about 15 m. w. of Acoma and 35 m. s. E. of Grant station on the Santa Fé Pac. R. R., Valencia co., N. Mex. The pueblo is attributed to the Calabash (Tanyi) clan of Acoma and is noted for the high class of masonry of its remaining walls. (F. W. H.)
Ka-uin-a.—Bandelier in Arch. Inst. Papers, IV, 324, 1892 (Acoma name). Kô-wí-na.—Hodge, field notes, B. A. E., 1895.

Kowsis. A tribe mentioned as roaming in the Tule r. country—territory occupied by Yokuts tribes—in s. central California in 1869 (Purcell in Ind. Aff. Rep. 1869, 193, 1870), but not further identifiable.

Koyeti. A Yokuts tribe formerly living in s. central California, in the vicinity of Tule r. and southward. Mentioned in 1852 as a friendly tribe on Paint (White) cr., and described as possessing unusual courage and intelligence. They are entirely extinct.
Co-ye-te.—Wessells (1853) in H. R. Ex. Doc. 76, 34th Cong., 3d sess., 32, 1857. Co-ye-tie.—Barbour (1852) in Sen. Ex. Doc. 4, 32d Cong., spec. sess., 256, 1853. Ko-ya-ta.—Johnston (1851) in Sen. Ex. Doc. 61, 32d Cong., 1st sess., 23, 1852. Ko-ya-te.—Barbour (1851) in Sen. Ex. Doc. 4, 32d Cong., spec. sess., 122, 1853. Ko-ya-tes.—Barbour in Ind. Aff. Rep., 232, 1851. Koyeti.—A. L. Kroeber, inf'n, 1906 (usual name among neighboring Yokuts tribes). Ko-ye-to.—Barbour in Sen. Ex. Doc. 4, 32d Cong., spec. sess., 255, 1853.

Koyonya. The Turkey clan of the Hopi.
Koyoña wiñwû.—Fewkes in 19th Rep. B. A. E., 584, 1900 (wiñwû='clan'). Ko-yo'-ño wüñ-wû.—Fewkes in Am. Anthrop., VII, 403, 1894.

Koyugmiut (*Koyŭg'mŭt*). A division of the Malemiut Eskimo on Koyuk r., Alaska.—Dall in Cont. N. A. Ethnol., I, 16, 1877.

Koyuhow (*Ko-yu-how'*). A Paviotso band formerly living about McDermit, N. Nev.—Powell, Paviotso MS., B. A. E., 1881.

Koyuktolik. A Malemiut Eskimo village on Koyuk r., Alaska.
Khoouchtioulik-mioute.—Zagoskin in Nouv. Ann. Voy., 5th s., XXI, map, 1850. Kuyuktolik.—Eleventh Census, Alaska, 162, 1893.

Koyukuk. A Koyukukhotana village, of 150 people in 1880, near the junction of Koyukuk and Yukon rs., Alaska. Petroff in 10th Census, Alaska, 12, 1884.

Koyukukhotana ('people of Koyukuk river'). A division of the Unakhotana inhabiting the basin of Koyukuk r., Alaska. Zagoskin in 1843 attempted to explore the Koyukuk country, but failed on account of the hostility of the natives. Lieut. Barnard in 1851 was killed by the Koyukukhotana, and Nulato destroyed because he sent for their chief. Maj. Kennicott also visited their territory, dying at Nulato, May 13, 1866. In the following year Dall explored the Koyukuk. Petroff visited the Koyukukhotana in 1880, and Allen made an exploration of their country in 1885. The Koyukukhotana were sedentary, but fierce and warlike, and hostile toward the Kaiyuhkhotana, although the manners, customs, and language of the two tribes are now similar. Their chief occupation is hunting deer and mountain sheep; they also act as middlemen in trade between the Malemiut and the Kaiyuhkhotana. They seem to have no system of totems (Dall in Cont. N. A. Ethnol., I, 27, 1877). Zagoskin found 289 living in permanent villages in 1843. In 1890 the population was given as 502: 242 males and 260 females, while the number in permanent villages was 174 in 32 houses. The villages are Batza, Bolshoigor, Dotle, Hussliakatna, Kakliaklia, Kaltat, Kanuti, Kautas, Kotil, Koyukuk, Mentokakat, Nohulchinta, Nok, Notaloten, Oonilgachtkhokh, Soonkakat, Tashoshgon, Tlialil, Tok, Zakatlatan, Zogliakten, and Zonagogliakten.

Coyoukons.—Whymper quoted by Dall in Cont. N. A. Ethnol., I, 27, 1877. Co-Yukon.—Whymper, Alaska, 182, 1868 (=Koyukukhotana and Unakhotana). Intsi-Dindjitch.—Petitot, Dict. Dènè-Dindjié, xx, 1876 (='men of iron'). Jūnnǎkāchotāna.—Holmberg quoted by Dall in Cont. N. A. Ethnol., I, 27, 1877. Koyoukon.—Elliott, Cond. Aff. Alaska, 29, 1874. Koyoukouk-kouttanæ.—Petitot, Autour du lac des Esclaves, 361, 1891. Koyū'-kŭkh-otā'nā.—Dall in Cont. N. A. Ethnol., I, 27, 1877 (='people of Koyukuk r.'). Koyūkŭns.—Ibid. (traders' name). Koyūkŭnskoi.—Ibid. (used by Russian traders). Kukunski.—Raymond in Bull. Am. Geog. Soc., III, 175, 1873. Kuyakinchi.—Raymond in Ind. Aff. Rep. 1869, 593, 1870. Kūyūkāntsi.—Worman quoted by Dall in Cont. N. A. Ethnol., I, 27, 1877. Kuyukuks.—Raymond in Sen. Ex. Doc. 12, 42d Cong., 1st sess., 31, 1871. Kuyukunski.—Ibid., 32. Yunnakakhotana.—Zagoskin quoted by Petroff in 10th Census, Alaska, 37, 1884.

Krayiragottine ('willow people'). A division of Etchaottine on Willow r., Mackenzie Ter., Can.

Kkρayiρa-Gottinè.—Petitot, Autour du lac des Esclaves, 319, 1891.

Kraylongottine ('people at the end of the willows'). A Nahane division living between Mackenzie r. and Willow lake, Mackenzie Ter., Canada. Their totem is the otter.

Kkᵣa-lon-Gottinè.—Petitot, Grand lac des Ours, 66, 1893 ('people at the end of the willows'). Kkρaylon-Gottinè.—Petitot, Autour du lac des Esclaves, 362, 1891.

Krentpoos. See *Kintpuash.*

Kretan ('hawk'). A subgens of the Cheghita gens of the Missouri tribe.

ɥre'-taⁿ.—Dorsey in 15th Rep. B. A. E., 240, 1897. K'ul-pa-ki'-a-ko.—ten Kate, Synonymie, 10, 1884 (Kiowa name: 'pearls people').

Krimerksumalek. An Iglulirmiut Eskimo village on the w. coast of Hudson bay.—McClintock, Voyage of Fox, 165, 1881.

Ksalokul (*Qsā'loqul*). A division of the Nanaimo on the E. coast of Vancouver

id.—Boas in 5th Rep. N. W. Tribes Can., 32, 1889.

Ksapsem (*Qsā'psEm*). A Songish division residing at Esquimalt, s. end of Vancouver id.—Boas in 6th Rep. N. W. Tribes Can., 17, 1890.

Kshiwukshiwu (*K'ciwuk'ciwu*). A former Chumashan village on Santa Rosa id., Cal.—Henshaw, Buenaventura MS. vocab., B. A. E., 1884.

Kthae (*K'çǎ'-ĕ*). A former Kuitsh village on lower Umpqua r., Oreg.—Dorsey in Jour. Am. Folk-lore, III, 321, 1890.

Kthelutlitunne (*Kçe'-lût-li' ɹ̇ûnnĕ'*, 'people at the forks'). A former village of the Chastacosta at the junction of Rogue r., Oreg., and a southern tributary.—Dorsey in Jour. Am. Folk-lore, III, 234, 1890.

Kthotaime (*K'ço-ɹai'-me*). A former Takelma village on the s. side of Rogue r., Oreg.—Dorsey in Jour. Am. Folk-lore, III, 235, 1890.

Kthukhwestunne (*K'çu-qwĕs' ɹ̇ûnnĕ'*, 'good-grass people'). A former village of the Mishikhwutmetunne on Coquille r., Oreg.—Dorsey in Jour. Am. Folk-lore, III, 232, 1890.

Kthukhwuttunne (*K'çu-qwût' ɹ̇ûnnĕ'*, 'people where good grass is'). A former village of the Tututni on the coast of Oregon, N. of Rogue r.—Dorsey in Jour. Am. Folk-lore, III, 233, 1890.

Kthunataachuntunne (*K'çu-na'-ta-a tcûn' ɹ̇ûnnĕ'*, 'people by a small grassy mountain'). A former village of the Mishikhwutmetunne on Coquille r., Oreg.—Dorsey in Jour. Am. Folk-lore, III, 232, 1890.

Kthutetmetseetuttun. A former village of the Tututni on the Pacific coast just N. of the mouth of Rogue r., Oreg.

K'çu-tĕt-me tse'-ĕ-tŭt'-tûn.—Dorsey in Jour. Am. Folk-lore, III, 233, 1890. ɥwi'-sŭt-qwŭt.—Ibid. Nu'-tcu-ma'-tûn ɹ̇ûn'nĕ.—Ibid. ('people in a land full of timber').

Ktlaeshatlkik ('people of Lgā'ĕcaLx'). A Cathlamet tribe named from a town on a creek of the same name, at the site of the present town of Cathlamet, Wahkiakum co., Wash.

Guithlia-ishalχi.—Gatschet, field notes, B. A. E. KLā'ecaLxîx·.—Boas, Kathlamet Texts, 6, 1901. Liā'icaLxē.—Boas, inf'n, 1905.

Ku. The Stone clan of the Tewa pueblos of San Ildefonso, N. Mex., and Hano, Ariz. That of the latter is extinct. Cf. *Nang.*

K'u-tdóa.—Hodge in Am. Anthrop., IX, 352, 1896 (San Ildefonso form; *tdóa*='people'). Ku-tówa.—Ibid. (Hano form).

Kua. The Bear clan of the pueblo of Taos, N. Mex.

Kŭa-tañina.—Hodge, field notes, B. A. E., 1899 (*tañina*='people').

Kuaiath. A division of the Seshat, a Nootka tribe.—Boas in 6th Rep. N. W. Tribes Can., 32, 1890.

Kuaiirnang. A winter residence of the Akuliarmiut on North bay, Baffin land.

K'uaiirnang.—Boas in Petermanns Mitt., no. 80, 67, 1885. **Quaiirnang.**—Boas in 6th Rep. B. A. E., 421, 1888.

Kuakaa. A prehistoric ruined pueblo of the Tanos on the s. bank of Arroyo Hondo, 5 m. s. of Santa Fé, N. Mex. It housed about 800 people. Not to be confounded with San Marcos, to which the same name was applied.

Cuâ-câ.—Bandelier, Gilded Man, 221, 1893. Cua-Kaa.—Ibid., 283. Kua-kaa.—Bandelier in Arch. Inst. Papers, IV, 90, 1892. Kua-kay.—Ibid.

Kuakumchen (*Kuā'kumtcẹn*). Given as a division of the Squawmish, on Howe sd., coast of British Columbia.—Boas, MS., B. A. E., 1887.

Kuapa. A ruined pueblo in the Cañada de Cochiti, 12 m. N. W. of Cochiti pueblo, N. Mex., by whose inhabitants it was formerly occupied and to whom are attributed the execution of the panther statues on the neighboring Potrero de los Idolos. It was the third place of settlement of the Cochiti after their abandonment of the Potrero de las Vacas, and from which they moved to their present pueblo.

Cŭa-pa.—Bandelier in Arch. Inst. Bul., I, 15, 1883. Cuá-pa.—Lummis in Scribner's Monthly, 98, 1893. Kua-pa.—Bandelier in Arch. Inst. Papers, IV, 162, 1892.

Kuapooge ('place of the shell beads near the water,' or 'mussel pearl place on the water'). A prehistoric Tewa pueblo which, with Analco, occupied the site of the present Santa Fé, N. Mex. Kuapooge was situated where old Ft Marcy was erected on the heights at the northern outskirts of the town by United States troops in 1847.

Apoga.—Ritch, New Mexico, 196, 1885. Apoge.—Ibid., 151. Cua P'Hoge.—Bandelier, Delight Makers, 453, 1890 (San Juan name). Cua-P'ho-o-ge.—Bandelier, Gilded Man, 284 1893. Cuâ-po-oge.—Ibid., 221. Cua-Po-o-qué.—Ladd, Story of N. Mex., 92, 1891. Kua-p'o-o-ge.—Bandelier in Arch. Inst. Papers, IV, 90, 1892. Oga P'Hoge.—Bandelier, Delight Makers, 453, 1890 (Santa Clara name). Og-a-p'o-ge.—Bandelier in Arch. Inst. Papers, IV, 90, 1892. Poga.—Ritch, New Mexico, 196, 1885. Poge.—Ibid., 151. Po-o-ge.—Bandelier in Ritch, ibid., 201.

Kuasse. An unidentified village or tribe mentioned by Joutel in 1687 as situated N. or N. W. of Maligne (Colorado) r., Tex. This region was controlled mainly by Coahuiltecan tribes, but Karankawan and Tonkawan Indians also roamed there. The name seems to have been given to Joutel by Ebahamo Indians, who were probably of Karankawan affinity. The Kuasse may possibly be identical with the Acafes and the Cacafes of Spanish writers and the Akasquy of Cavelier's narrative.

Kiaffess.—Joutel (1687) in French, Hist. Coll. La., I, 138, 1846 (cf. p. 152). Kiasses.—Shea, note in Charlevoix, New France, IV, 78, 1870. Kiasseschancres.—Barcia, Ensayo, 271, 1723 (combined with Chancres; see *Lipan*). Kuassé.—Joutel in Margry, Déc., III, 289, 1878.

Kuato (*K'uato*, 'pulling up from the ground, or a hole'). An extinct tribal division of the Kiowa, speaking a slightly different dialect, who were exterminated by the Sioux in battle about the year 1780. On this occasion, according to tradition, the Kiowa were attacked by an overwhelming force of Sioux and prepared to retreat, but the chief of the Kuato exhorted his people not to run, "because, if they did, their relatives in the other world would not receive them." So they stood their ground and were killed, while the others of the tribe escaped. Their place in the tribal camp circle is not known.—Mooney in 14th Rep. B. A. E., 1080, 1896.

Kuaua. A former Tigua pueblo, the ruins of which lie N. of the bridge across the Rio Grande above Bernalillo, N. Mex. According to Bandelier the main building, which is of adobe, is one of the largest pueblo houses in New Mexico, but whether or not the pueblo is historic is indeterminable. It is also known by the Spanish name Torreon, but should not be confounded with the Torreon E. of the Rio Grande, in lat. 34° 45'.

Kua-ua.—Bandelier in Arch. Inst. Papers, IV, 225, 1892. Torreon.—Ibid.

Kuaut. A Shuswap village at the head of Little Shuswap lake, interior of British Columbia; pop. 83 in 1904.

Knaut.—Can. Ind. Aff., supp., 60, 1902. Kroaout.—Can. Ind. Aff. for 1883, 189. Kualt.—Ibid., 1895, 361. Kuant.—Ibid., 1898, 419. Ku-a-ut.—Ibid., 1885, 196. Kwout.—Dawson in Trans. Roy. Soc. Can. for 1891, sec. II, 44, 1892. Little Shuswap —Can. Ind. Aff. for 1878, 74. Little Shuswap Lake.—Ibid., 1882, 259. Little Suswap Lake.—Ibid., 1879, 309. Sushwap.—Ibid., 1878, 78.

Kuchaptuvela ('ash-hill terrace'). A Hopi village, now in ruins, on the terrace of the East mesa of Tusayan, N. E. Arizona, below the present Walpi pueblo. It was occupied by the ancestors of the Hopi of Walpi evidently at the time of the arrival of the Spaniards in 1540. The occupants abandoned it in 1629, or shortly afterward, and moved to Kisakobi, farther up the mesa.

Küchaptüvela.—Fewkes in 17th Rep. B. A. E., 578, 585, 1898. Kwetcap tutwi.—Stephen in 8th Rep. B. A. E., 18, 1891. Old Walpi.—Ibid.

Kuchichi ('the small ones'). A small rancheria of the Tarahumare, not far from Norogachic, w. Chihuahua, Mexico.—Lumholtz, inf'n, 1894.

Kuchtya. A prehistoric Acoma pueblo which, according to tradition, was the third village built and occupied during the early migration of the tribe.—Hodge in Century Mag., LVI, 15, May 1898.

Kuechic ('small mountain'). A Tarahumare rancheria near Gumisachic, which is 20 m. N. E. of Norogachic, Chihuahua, Mexico.—Lumholtz, inf'n, 1894.

Kueha ('the murderers'). A division of the Lekwiltok living between Bute and Loughborough inlets, Brit. Col. They are divided into three gentes: Wiwekam, Komoyue, and Kueha. Pop. 25 in 1889. The Komoyue sept of the true Kwakiutl have this name for their war name.

Kuē′qa.—Boas in 6th Rep. N. W. Tribes Can., 606, 1891. **Kwe-ah-kah-Saich-kioie-tachs.**—Can. Ind. Aff. 1889, 227, 1890 (=Kueha Lekwiltok). **Kwiha.**—Tolmie and Dawson, Vocabs. Brit. Col., 119B, 1884. **Queeakahs.**—Brit. Col. map, 1872. **Quee-ha-ni-cul-ta.**—Work (1836–41) quoted by Kane, Wand. in N. A., app., 1859 (=Kueha Lekwiltok). **Quieha Ne cub ta.**—Work as quoted by Schoolcraft, Ind. Tribes, V, 488, 1855.

Kugaluk. A Malemiut Eskimo village on Spafarief bay, s. shore of Kotzebue sd., Alaska; pop. 12 in 1880.
Keewalik.—Post-route map, 1903. **Kualiug-miut.**—Baker, Geog. Dict. Alaska, 253, 1902 (Russian denotation in 1852). **Kualyugmut.**—Zagoskin, Desc. Russ. Poss. in Am., pt. 1, 73, 1847. **Kugaluk.**—Baker, Geog. Dict. Alaska, 1902. **Kugalukmut.**—Nelson in 18th Rep. B. A. E., map, 1899. **Kugalukmute.**—Petroff in 10th Census, Alaska, 4, 1884.

Kugaramiut. A subdivision of the Malemiut Eskimo on the s. shore of Kotzebue sd., Alaska.—Woolfe in 11th Census, Alaska, 130, 1893.

Kuhaia. The Bear clans of the Keresan pueblos of Laguna, San Felipe, Acoma, Sia, and Cochiti, N. Mex. The Bear clan of Laguna claims to have come originally from Acoma.
Ko-hai.—Stevenson in 11th Rep. B. A. E., 19, 1894 (Sia form). **Kohaía-hánoᶜʰ.**—Hodge in Am. Anthrop., IX, 349, 1896 (Laguna form). **Kóhai-háno.**—Ibid. (San Felipe form; háno = 'people'; Kohaí-hăno is the Sia form). **Kohaio.**—Bandelier, Delight Makers, 253, 1890. **Ko-ha-yo.**—Bandelier in Arch. Inst. Papers, III, 293, 1890. **Kúhaia-hánuch.**—Hodge, op. cit. (Cochiti form). **Kúwhaía-hánoqᶜʰ.**—Ibid. (Acoma form).

Kuhinedi ('martin people'). A Tlingit division at Klawak, Alaska, belonging to the Raven phratry.
K!ū′xînedî.—Swanton, field notes, B. A. E., 1904. **Uěch-ē-něětí.**—Krause, Tlinkit Ind., 120, 1885.

Kuhlahi (*Kû′lahĭ*, 'beech place,' from *kû′la* 'beech-tree'). A former Cherokee settlement in upper Georgia.   (J. M.)

Kuhlanapo (from *kuhla*, 'yellow waterlily' [*Nymphæa polysepala*], *napo*, 'village'). The name of one of the groups of people who formerly occupied Big valley on the s. shore of Clear lake, Lake co., Cal. Theirs was the w. part of the valley, extending from Adobe cr. on the E. into the foothills on the w., and their territory was definitely separated from that of the Khabenapo to the eastward. From this name Powell (7th Rep. B. A. E., 87, 1891) formed the stock name *Kulanapan*, which he applied to all of the Indians now usually known by the name of Pomo, and living chiefly in Sonoma, Mendocino, and Lake cos., with a small detached area in Colusa and Glenn cos.   S. A. B
Ghula′-napo.—A. L. Kroeber, inf'n, 1906. **Hulanapo.**—Gibbs (1851) in Schoolcraft, Ind. Tribes, III, 109, 1853. **Huta-napo.**—Ibid., 110 (misprint). **Kuhlanapo.**—S. A. Barrett, inf'n, 1906 (lit. 'yellow water-lily village'). **Kulanopo.**—Latham in Trans. Philol. Soc. Lond., 77, 1856.

Kuhpattikutteh (*Kuh′-pat-ti-kut′-teh*, 'squirrel-eaters'). A Paviotso band formerly living on Quinn r., w. Nev.—Powers, Inds. W. Nev., MS., B. A. E., 1876.

Kuilitsh (*Ku′-i-lĭtc′*). A former Kuitsh village on lower Umpqua r., Oreg.—Dorsey in Jour. Am. Folk-lore, III, 231, 1890.

Kuilkluk. A Kuskwogmiut Eskimo village on the left bank of Kuskokwim r., Alaska; pop. 75 in 1880. Perhaps identical with Quieclohchamiut (pop. 83), or with Quiechochlogamiut (pop. 65) in 11th Census, Alaska, 164, 1893.
Kuilkhlogamute.—Petroff in 10th Census, Alaska, map, 1884. **Kuilkluk.**—Baker, Geog. Dict. Alaska, 253, 1902. **Kulj-khlugamute.**—Ibid., 17.

Kuingshtetakten. A Jugelnute Eskimo village on Shageluk r., Alaska; pop. 37 in 1842.
Khuingetakhten.—Zagoskin, Desc. Russ. Poss. Am., map, 1844. **Khuingitatekhten.**—Zagoskin quoted by Petroff in 10th Census, Alaska, 37, 1884. **Kuingshtetakten.**—Tikhmenief (1861) quoted by Baker, Geog. Dict. Alaska, 365, 1900.

Kuinruk (*Kuin-rŭk*, 'sea-hunter people': Kodiak name). An unidentified division of the Knaiakhotana of Cook inlet, Alaska.—Hoffman, Kadiak MS., B. A. E., 1882.

Kuishkoshyaka. The extinct Blue-corn clan of Acoma pueblo, N. Mex. See *Yaka.*
Kŭ′ïshkŏshyáka-hánoqᶜʰ.—Hodge in Am. Anthrop., IX, 349, 1896 (*yáka* = 'corn', *hánoqch* = 'people').

Kuishtitiyaka. The extinct Brown-corn clan of Acoma pueblo, N. Mex. See *Yaka.*
Kŭ′ïshtᵗï′yáka-hánoqᶜʰ.—Hodge in Am. Anthrop., IX, 349, 1896 (*yáka* = 'corn', *hánoqch* = 'people').

Kuitsh. A small Yakonan tribe formerly living on lower Umpqua r., w. Oreg. A few survivors are on the Siletz res. According to Dorsey the former villages of the Kuitsh were Silela, Misun, Takhaiya, Chukhuiyathl, Chukukh, Thukhita, Tsunakthiamittha, Ntsiyamis, Khuwaihus, Skakhaus, Chupichnushkuch, Kaiyuwuntsunitthai, Tsiakhaus, Paiuiyunitthai, Tsetthim, Wuituthlaa, Chitlatamus, Kuilitsh, Tkimeye, Mikulitsh, and Kthae.
Ci-sta′-qwût-mê′ ʠûnnê′.—Dorsey in Jour. Am. Folk-lore, III, 231, 1890 (= 'people dwelling on the stream called Shista': Mishikwutmetunne name). **Ku-ītc′.**—Ibid., 230 (own name). **Lower Umpqua.**—Ind. Aff. Rep. 1857, 321, 1858. **Tŭ′kwĭl-mä′-k′ĭ.**—Dorsey, Alsea MS. vocab., B. A. E., 1884 (Alsea name). **Umpkwa.**—Bissell, MS. vocab., B. A. E., 1881. **Umpqua.**—Ibid.

Kuiu. A Tlingit tribe and town on an island, also called Kuiu, on the Alaskan coast. The town is in Port Beauclerc, and according to Petroff, who erroneously places it on Prince of Wales id. (unless indeed they were then living at Shakan), it contained 60 inhabitants in 1880. There has been no separate census of them since that time. They are said to have intermarried considerably with the Haida. Their social divisions are Kuyedi and Nastedi.   (J. R. S.)
Kouyou.—Petroff in 10th Census, Alaska, 32, 1884. **Koyu.**—Ibid., map. **Kuiu.**—Common spelling. **Kuyut-koe.**—Veniaminoff, Zapiski, II, pt. 3, 30, 1840.

Kuiukuk. A Kaniagmiut Eskimo village on the s. E. coast of Alaska penin., Alaska; pop. 18 in 1880, 62 in 1890.
Kuyukak.—Petroff in 10th Census, Alaska, 28, 1884. **Wrangell bay.**—Eleventh Census, Alaska, 163, 1893.

Kuiwanva (*Kui-wan′-va*). A traditionary settlement of the Bear clan of the Hopi, about 1 m. N. W. of Oraibi.—Voth, Traditions of the Hopi, 23, 1905.

Kuiyamu. (*Ku-ĭ'-ya'-mu*). One of the two former populous Chumashan villages, popularly known as Dos Pueblos, w. of Santa Barbara, Cal. (H. W. H.)

Kukak. A Kaniagmiut Eskimo village on Kukak bay, S. E. coast of Alaska penin., Alaska; pop. 37 in 1880.
Kukak.—Petroff in 10th Census, Alaska, 28, 1884. Toujajak.—Langsdorff, Voy., II, 235, 1814.

Kukamukamees. A Kyuquot village on Mission id., Kyuquot sd., w. coast of Vancouver id.—Can. Ind. Aff., 264, 1902.

Kukan ('finger-nail'). An Ita Eskimo settlement near McCormick bay, N. Greenland.—Heilprin, Peary Relief Exped., 128, 1893.

Kukanuwu (*KAq!anuwū'*). An old Tlingit town in the Huna country on the N. side of Cross sd., Alaskan coast. Distinct from Hukanuwu. (J. R. S.)

Kukinishyaka. The Red-corn clan of Acoma and Laguna pueblos, N. Mex. See *Yaka*.
Kŭ'kanïs'hyáka-hánoqᶜʰ.—Hodge in Am. Anthrop., IX, 349, 1896 (Acoma form; *yáka* = 'corn', *hánoqch* = 'people'). Kŭ'kinishyáka-hánoᶜʰ.—Ibid. (Laguna form).

Kukkuiks (*Kŭk-kŭiks'*, 'pigeons'). A society of the Ikunuhkahtsi, or All Comrades, in the Piegan tribe; it is made up of men who have been to war several times.—Grinnell, Blackfoot Lodge Tales, 221, 1892.

Kukluktuk. A Kuskwogmiut Eskimo village on the left bank of Kuskokwim r., 30 m. below Kolmakof, Alaska; pop. 51 in 1880, 20 in 1890.
Kochlogtogpagamiut.—Eleventh Census, Alaska, 164, 1893. Kokhlokhtokhpagamute.—Petroff in 10th Census, Alaska, 16, 1884. Kukluktuk.—Baker, Geog. Dict. Alaska, 254, 1902.

Kukoak (*Quqoā'q*). A Songish division at McNeill bay, S. end of Vancouver id.—Boas in 6th Rep. N. W. Tribes Can., 17, 1890.

Kukpaurungmiut. An Eskimo tribe that formerly occupied the country between Pt Belcher and C. Beaufort, Alaska, now much dwindled, having a village called Kokolik at Pt Lay with 30 inhabitants in 1880. In 1900 the tribe numbered 52.
Kookpovoros.—Kelly, Arctic Eskimos, 13, 1890. Koopowro Mutes.—Wells and Kelly in Rep. Bur. Ed. 1897, 1242, 1898. Kukpaurungmiut.—11th Census, Alaska, 158, 1893.

Kukuch. The Lizard clan of the Hopi.
Kókob.—Voth, Oraibi Summer Snake Ceremony, 283, 1903. Kŭ'-kü-tci.—Stephen in 8th Rep. B. A. E., 39, 1891. Kükŭto wiñwŭ.—Fewkes in 19th Rep. B. A. E., 583, 1901 (*wiñwŭ* = 'clan'). Kukuts.—Dorsey and Voth, Oraibi Soyal, 13, 1901. Kúkutsi.—Voth, Hopi Proper Names, 89, 1905.

Kukuchomo ('footprint mound'). A pueblo ruin, consisting of two conical mounds, on the East mesa of Tusayan, N. E. Arizona. It was built and occupied in prehistoric time by Hopi clans closely related to those of Sikyatki, with whom they are supposed to have removed to

Awatobi.—Fewkes in 17th Rep. B. A. E., 587–588, 1898.

Kukulek (*Ququ'lɛk*). A Songish division residing at Cadboro bay, s. end of Vancouver id.—Boas in 6th Rep. N. W. Tribes Can., 17, 1890.

Kukuliak. A Yuit Eskimo village on the N. shore of St Lawrence id., Bering sea.—Tebenkof (1849) quoted by Baker, Geog. Dict. Alaska, 1902.

Kukutwom. (*K·ukutwō'm*, 'waterfall'). A Squawmish village community on the E. side of Howe sd., Brit. Col.—Hill-Tout in Rep. Brit. A. A. S., 474, 1900.

Kukwakum ('the real Kwakiutl'). A gens of the Kwakiutl proper, consisting of two septs, the Guetela and the Komoyue.
K'kwā'kum.—Boas in 6th Rep. N. W. Tribes Can., 54, 1890. Kukwā'kum.—Boas in Rep. Nat. Mus. 1895, 330, 1897. Kwakoom.—Tolmie and Dawson, Vocabs. Brit. Col., 118B, 1884.

Kulahiyi (*Kŭ'láhi'yĭ*, or in the lower Cherokee dialect, *Kărăhi'yĭ*, from *kŭlá'hĭ*, a plant used as salad by the Cherokee). A former Cherokee town in N. E. Georgia, from which Currahee mtn. takes its name. (J. M.)

Kulaiapto. A former Maidu village between Mooretown and the village of Tsuka, Butte co., Cal.—Dixon in Bull. Am. Mus. Nat. Hist., XVII, pl. xxxviii, 1905.

Kulaken (*K·u'laqɛn*). A Squawmish village community on Burrard inlet, Brit. Col.—Hill-Tout in Rep. Brit. A. A. S., 475, 1900.

Kulanapan Family. Adopted by Powell (7th Rep. B. A. E., 87, 1891) as the name of a linguistic family in Sonoma, Lake, and Mendocino cos., Cal., comprising the group of tribes generally known as Pomo, q. v. See also *Kuhlanapo*.
×Kula-napo.—Gibbs in Schoolcraft, Ind. Tribes, III, 421, 1853 (the name of one of the Clear Lake bands). >Mendocino(?).—Latham in Trans. Philol. Soc. Lond., 77, 1856 (name suggested for Choweshak, Batemdaikai, Kulanapo, Yukai, and Khwaklamayu languages); Latham, Opuscula, 343, 1860; Latham, Elem. Comp. Philol., 410, 1862 (as above). >Pomo.—Powers in Overland Monthly, IX, 498, Dec. 1872 (general description of habitat and of family); Powers in Cont. N. A. Ethnol., III, 146, 1877; Powell, ibid., 491 (vocabularies of Gal-li-no-mé-ro, Yo-kai'-a, Ba-tem-da-kaii, Chau-i-shek, Yu-kai, Ku-la-na-po, H'hana, Venaambakaiia, Ka'-bi-na-pek, Chwachamaju); Gatschet in Mag. Am. Hist., 16, 1877 (gives habitat and enumerates tribes of family); Gatschet in Beach, Ind. Miscel., 436, 1877; Keane, in Stanford, Compend., Cent. and So. Am., app., 476, 1878 (includes Castel Pomos, Ki, Cahto, Choam, Chadela, Matomey Ki, Usal or Calamet, Shebalne Pomos, Gallinomeros, Sanels, Socoas, Lamas, Comachos). <Pomo.—Bancroft, Nat. Races, III, 566, 1882 (includes Ukiah, Gallinomero, Masallamagoon, Gualala, Matole, Kulanapo, Sanél, Yonios, Choweshak, Batemdakaie, Chocuyem, Olamentke, Kainamare, and Chwachamaju; of these, Chocuyem and Olamentke are Moquelumnan). =Kulanapan.—Powell in 7th Rep. B. A. E., 87, 1891.

Kulatsen (*Ku'latsɛn*). A Squawmish village community on the E. side of Howe sd., Brit. Col.—Hill-Tout in Rep. Brit. A. A. S., 474, 1900.

Kulchana ('strangers': Ahtena name), A nomadic Athapascan tribe in Alaska.

living about the headwaters of Kusko-kwim r., holding little intercourse with neighboring peoples. They are now a remnant, numbering about 300 (11th Census, Alaska, 156, 1893), but were once formidable enemies of the Russians. Khunanilinde and Tochotno were two of their villages known to Zagoskin in 1843. Calcharnies.—Allen, Rep., 132, 1887. Colcharney.—Ibid., note. Colching.—Mahoney in Ind. Aff. Rep. 1869, 574, 1870. Coltshanie.—Latham in Jour. Ethnol. Soc. Lond., I, 183, 1848. Galcäni.—Daw-dow in Radloff, Wörterb. d. Kinai-Spr., 29, 1874. Galtzanen.—Richardson, Arct. Exped., I, 402, 1851. Galzanen.—Holmberg, Ethnog. Skizz., 7, 1855. Gal-zani.—Scouler (1846) in Jour. Ethnol. Soc. Lond., I, 232, 1848. Ghuil-chan.—Petroff in 10th Census, Alaska, 164, 1884 (trans. 'tundra people'). Golt-zane.—Zagoskin quoted by Petroff, ibid., 37. Gol-zan.—Latham in Trans. Philol. Soc. Lond., 68, 1856. Golzanen.—Radloff, op. cit. Kal-chaina.—Dall in Proc. Am. A. A. S., 378, 1885. Kcäl tana.—Dawydow in Radloff, Wörterb. d. Kinai-Spr., 29, 1874. Khuil-chan.—Petroff in 10th Census, Alaska, 162, 1884. Khuilchana.—Ibid., map. Kolchane.—Ibid., 162. Kolchans.—Scouler in Jour. Geog. Soc. Lond., XI, 218, 1841. Kolchina.—Dall in Proc. A. A. S., 1869, 270, 1870 (Russian name). Kolshani.—Latham (1845) in Jour. Ethnol. Soc. Lond., 187, 1848. Koltchanes.—Petroff, Rep. on Alaska, 62, 1881. Koltschane.—Bancroft, Nat. Races, I, 134, 1874. Koltschanen.—Holmberg, Ethnog. Skizz., 7, 1855. Koltschaner.—Erman, Archiv, VII, 128, 1849. Kolt-shan.—Latham in Trans. Philol. Soc. Lond., 68, 1856. Koltshanen.—Richardson, Arct. Exped., I, 402, 1851. Koltshanes.—Bancroft, Nat. Races, I, 116, 1874. Koltshani.—Latham in Trans. Philol. Soc. Lond., 68, 1856. Koltshany.—Latham (1845) in Jour. Ethnol. Soc. Lond., I, 190, 1848. Ktzialtana.—Petroff in 10th Census, Alaska, 162, 1884. Kuskokwim.—Latham, Essays, 269, 1860. Kuskoquimers.—Ibid., 270. Ultschna.—Wrangell quoted by Baer and Helmersen, Beiträge, I, 110, 1839. Ultz-chna.—Petroff in 10th Census, Alaska, 164, 1884 (trans. 'slaves').

Kulkumish (*Kulkumic*). A former Maidu village near Colfax, Placer co., Cal.—Dixon in Bull. Am. Mus. Nat. Hist., XVII, pl. xxxviii, 1905.

Kullahan (*Kul-la'han*, 'stockade'). The site of an old village of the Semiahmoo.—Gibbs, Clallam and Lummi, 37, 1863.

Kulleets. A Cowichan tribe on Chimenes bay, Vancouver id.; pop. 68 in 1904. Ku-lees.—Can. Ind. Aff. for 1879, 308. Ku-leets.—Ibid., 1880, 316. Kulleets.—Ibid., 1901, pt. II, 164. Q'ale'ts.—Boas, MS., B. A. E., 1887.

Kulomum (*Ku-lo'-mum*). A division of Maidu living formerly at Susanville, Lassen co., Cal.—Powers in Cont. N. A. Ethnol., III, 282, 1877.

Kuloskap. See *Nanabozo*.

Kulsetsiyi (*Kúlsetsiyi*, 'honey-locust place'; but as *kúlsétsi*, the word for honey-locust, is also used for sugar, the local name has commonly been rendered Sugartown by traders). The name of several former settlement places in the old Cherokee country. One was on Keowee r., near the present Fall cr., in Oconee co., S. C.; another was on Sugartown or Cullasagee (Kulsétsi) cr., near the present Franklin, in Macon co., N. C.; a third was on Sugartown cr. near the present Morganton, in Fannin co., Ga.—Mooney in 19th Rep. B. A. E., 525, 1900.

Culsagee.—Common map form. Kulsage.—Bartram, Travels, 372, 1792.

Kulshtgeush ('badger standing in the water'). A Klamath settlement on Williamson r., Lake co., s. w. Oreg. Kúlsam-Tgé-us.—Gatschet in Cont. N. A. Ethnol., II, pt. I, xxix, 1890. Kúls-Tgé-ush.—Ibid.

Kulswa (*Kul-swä'*, 'sun'). A gens of the Miami (q. v.).—Morgan, Anc. Soc., 168, 1877.

Kultuk. A Knaiakhotana village, of 17 natives in 1880, on the E. side of Cook inlet, Alaska.—Petroff in 10th Census, Alaska, 29, 1884.

Kulukak. A Togiagmiut village on Kulukak bay, Alaska; pop. 65 in 1880. Kulluk.—Petroff in 10th Census, Alaska, 17, 1884.

Kulul. A former village of the Kalendaruk division of the Costanoan family, connected with San Carlos mission, Cal. Culul.—Taylor in Cal. Farmer, Apr. 20, 1860.

Kulumi. A former small upper Creek town on the right bank of lower Tallapoosa r., in N. Montgomery co., Ala., w. of and contiguous to Fusihatchi. Hawkins, in 1799, saw there a conical mound 30 ft in diameter opposite the town square. A part of the inhabitants had settled on Likasa cr. Remains of "Old Cool me town" were on the opposite side of Tallapoosa r. at the time of Bartram's visit in 1791. After the war of 1813–14 the inhabitants of Kulumi joined the Seminole in a body. (A. S. G.) Caloumas.—Bartram, Voy., I, map, 1799 (erroneously on the Chattahoochee). Colemmys.—Cornell (1793) in Am. State Pap., Ind. Aff., I, 384, 1832. Collamee.—Jefferys, Am. Atlas, map 5, 1776. Colomga.—Lattré, Carte des Etats-Unis, 1784. Colomiesk.—Robin, Voy., II, map, 1807. Coolamies.—Swan (1791) in Schoolcraft, Ind. Tribes, V, 262, 1855. Coolome.—Bartram, Travels, 394, 395, 448, 461, 1791. Coolooma.—Hawkins (1813) in Am. State Pap., Ind. Aff., I, 854, 1832. Coo-loo-me.—Hawkins (1799), Sketch, 25, 33, 52, 1848. Culloumas.—Alcedo, Dic. Geog., I, 719, 1786. Cullowes.—Güssefeld, Map of U. S., 1784 (wrongly placed on Chattahoochee). Kulumi.—Gatschet, Creek Migr. Leg., I, 136, 1884.

Kulushut (*Ku-lu'-shūt*, 'thieving people': Kaniagmiut name). A division of the Ahtena on Copper r., Alaska, next to the Ikherkhamiut.—Hoffman, MS., B. A. E., 1882.

Kulvagavik. A Kuskwogmiut Eskimo village on the w. shore of Kuskokwim bay, Alaska; pop. 10 in 1880. Koolvagavigamute. — Petroff in 10th Census, Alaska, map, 1884. Kulvagavik.—Baker, Geog. Dict. Alaska, 1902. Kulwoguwigumut.—Nelson in 18th Rep. B. A. E., map, 1899.

Kumachisi. A former Yokuts (Mariposan) tribe that lived on Tule or Kern r., Cal., or on one of the intervening streams.—A. L. Kroeber, inf'n, 1906.

Kumadha (*Kum-ad-ha*). Given by Bourke (Jour. Am. Folk-lore, II, 181, 1889) as a clan of the Mohave, q. v.

Kumaini. A village of the Awani formerly at the lower end of the Great Meadow, about a quarter of a mile from Yosemite falls, Mariposa co., Cal. Coomine.—Powers in Overland Monthly, X, 333, 1874. Ku-mai'-ni.—Powers in Cont. N. A. Ethnol., III, 365, 1877.

Kumarmiut. An Angmagsalingmiut Eskimo village on an island at the mouth of Angmagsalik fjord, Greenland, lat. 65° 45'; pop. 28 in 1884.—Meddelelser om Grönland, IX, 379, 1902.

Kumbatuash. The native name of the inhabitants of Kumbat, a rocky tract of land s. w. of Tule or Rhett lake, Cal., extending from the lake shore to the Lavabeds. These people are a mixture of Klamath Lake and Modoc Indians, and are said to have separated from these after 1830.
Cum-ba-twas.—Meacham, Wigwam and Warpath, 577, 1875. Gúmbatkni.—Gatschet in Cont. N. A. Ethnol., II, pt. II, 160 1890. Kúmbatkni.—Ibid. Kúmbatuash.—Ibid. Kúmbatuashkni.—Ibid. Kúmbatwash.—Ibid., pt. I, xxxiv, 1890. Rock Indians.—Meacham, op. cit., 610.

Kumiyus (*K'u'-mi-yŭs'*). A former Siuslaw village on Siuslaw r., Oreg.—Dorsey in Jour. Am. Folk-lore, III, 230, 1890.

Kumkwu (*K'úm-kwŭ'*). A former Siuslaw village on Siuslaw r., Oreg.—Dorsey in Jour. Am. Folk-lore, III, 230, 1890.

Kumsukwum (*K'úm'-sŭ-k'wúm*). A former Yaquina village on the s. side of Yaquina r., Oreg.—Dorsey in Jour. Am. Folk-lore, III, 229, 1890.

Kun. The Corn clans of the Tewa pueblos of San Juan and Santa Clara, N. Mex. See *Konglo*.
Khún-tdóa.—Hodge in Am. Anthrop., IX, 349, 1896 (Santa Clara form; *tdóa* = 'people'). Kún-tdóa.—Ibid. (San Juan form).

Kuna-lanas (*Ku'na lā'nas*, 'town people of the point'). An important family of the Raven clan of the Haida. According to one story it was so named because its people lived on a point in the legendary town of Skena (see *Tadji-lanas*); but more probably it refers to the point at Naikun where these people were at one time settled. The Teeskun-lnagai, Hlielungkun-lnagai, Saguikun-lnagai, and Yagunkun-lnagai were subdivisions. (J. R. S.)
Ku'na lānas.—Swanton, Cont. Haida, 270, 1905. Kun lā'nas.—Boas, 12th Rep. N. W. Tribes Canada, 23, 1898. Kwun lennas.—Harrison in Proc. and Trans. Roy. Soc. Canada, sec. II, 125, 1895.

Kundji (*Ku'ndji*). A legendary Haida town on the s. shore of Copper bay, Moresby id., Queen Charlotte group, Brit. Col. The family living there is said to have been the Daiyuahl-lanas. Another town of this name formerly stood on the w. side of Prevost id., in the Ninstints country.—Swanton, Cont. Haida, 270, 1905.

Kunechin (*Qunē'tcin*). A Seechelt sept which formerly lived at the head of Queen's reach, Jervis inlet, Brit. Col. The founder of this division is said to have come from Ft Rupert.—Hill-Tout in Jour. Anthr. Inst., 23, 1904.

Kuneste (Wailaki: 'Indian'). The southernmost Athapascan group on the Pacific coast, consisting of several tribes loosely or not at all connected politically, but speaking closely related dialects and possessing nearly the same culture. They occupied the greater part of Eel r. basin, including the whole of Van Duzen fork, the main Eel to within a few miles of Round valley, the s. fork and its tributaries to Long and Cahto valleys, and the coast from Bear River range s. to Usal. Their neighbors were the Wishosk on the N., the Wintun on the w., and on the s. the Yuki, whose territory they bisect at Cahto, where they penetrate to the Pomo country. The Kuneste subdivisions are Lassik, Wailaki, Sinkyone, Kato, and Mattole. (P. E. G.)
Ken'-es-ti.—Powers in Cont. N. A. Ethnol., III, 114, 1877 (own name). Kool.—A. L. Kroeber, inf'n, 1903 (Yuki name). Kuneste.—P. E. Goddard, inf'n, 1904 (Wailaki name).

Kung (*QAñ*). A former Haida town, owned by the Sakua-lanas, at the mouth of Naden harbor, Graham id., Queen Charlotte group, Brit. Col. Possibly this is the place referred to by John Work as Nigh-tasis (q. v.), where there were said to be 15 houses and 280 inhabitants in 1836–41. Old people remember 12 houses there. The inhabitants have all moved to Masset. (J. R. S.)
K'ang.—Boas, Twelfth Rep. N. W. Tribes Can., 23, 1898. Nigh-tasis.—Work (1836–41) in Dawson, Q. Charlotte Ids., 173B, 1880. QAñ.—Swanton, Cont. Haida, 281, 1905.

Kungaii. The Sweet-corn clan of San Ildefonso pueblo, N. Mex.
Kuⁿaii-tdóa.—Hodge in Am. Anthrop., IX, 349, 1896 (*tdóa*='people').

Kungfetdi. The Black-corn clan of San Ildefonso pueblo, N. Mex.
Kuⁿfetdi-tdóa.—Hodge in Am. Anthrop., IX, 349, 1896 (*tdóa*='people').

Kungga (*Q!A'ñga*, 'help received unexpectedly'). A former Haida town, occupied by the Kona-kegawai, on the s. shore of Dog id., Queen Charlotte group, Brit. Col. The inhabitants moved to Kloo.—Swanton, Cont. Haida, 278, 1905.

Kungielung (*K!u'ngielAñ*). A former Haida town on the w. side of the entrance to Masset inlet, Queen Charlotte ids., Brit. Col.—Swanton, Cont. Haida, 281, 1905.

Kungpi. The Red-corn clan of San Ildefonso pueblo, N. Mex.
Kuⁿpi-tdóa.—Hodge in Am. Anthrop., IX, 349, 1896 (*tdóa*='people').

Kungtsa. The White-corn clan of San Ildefonso pueblo, N. Mex.
Kuⁿtsa-tdóa.—Hodge in Am. Anthrop., IX, 349, 1896 (*tdóa*='people').

Kungtsei. The Yellow-corn clan of San Ildefonso pueblo, N. Mex.
Kuⁿtsei-tdóa.—Hodge in Am. Anthrop., IX, 349, 1896 (*tdóa*='people').

Kungtsoa. The Blue-corn clan of San Ildefonso pueblo, N. Mex.
Kuⁿtsoa-tdóa.—Hodge in Am. Anthrop., IX, 349, 1896 (*tdóa*='people').

Kungugemiut. A division of the Malemiut Eskimo on Buckland r., Alaska.
Kangoot Mutes.—Kelly, Arctic Eskimo, chart, 1890. Kanikgmut.—Zagoskin, Desc. Russ. Poss. in Am., pt. I, 73, 1847. Kongigamut.—Nelson in 18th Rep. B. A. E., map, 1899. Kongigamute.—Petroff in 10th Census, Alaska, 4, 1884. Kotsokhotana.—Zagoskin, Desc. Russ. Poss. in Am., pt. I, 73, 1847 (Tinneh name). Kungeeg-ameuts.—Hooper, Cruise of Corwin, 26, 1880. Küngŭgemūt.—Dall in Cont. N. A. Ethnol., I, 16, 1877.

Kungya. The Turquoise clans of the Tewa pueblos of San Juan, Santa Clara, San Ildefonso, and Tesuque, N. Mex. See *Kuyanwe*.
Koⁿyä-tdóa.—Hodge in Am. Anthrop., IX, 352, 1896 (Tesuque form; *tdóa*='people'). Kunyä-tdóa.—Ibid. (San Juan and Santa Clara form). Kuⁿye-tdóa.—Ibid. (San Ildefonso form).

Kungyi. The Ant clan of Nambe pueblo, N. Mex.
Kuⁿyi-tdóa.—Hodge in Am. Anthrop., IX, 348, 1896 (*tdóa*='people').

Kunhalas (*Ku'nxalas*). A former Haida town or camp just inside of Cumshewa pt., Queen Charlotte ids., Brit. Col. It belonged to the Kona-kegawai.—Swanton, Cont. Haida, 278, 1905.

Kunhittan (*Kūn-hittan*, 'people of flicker house'). Given by Krause (Tlinkit Ind., 120, 1885) as a Tlingit division, but in reality it is merely a name for the inhabitants of a house at Kuiu belonging to the Nastedi, q. v.

Kunipalgi (*k'uno, k'ono*, 'skunk'; *algi*, 'people'). A Creek clan.
Ku'-mu.—Morgan, Anc. Soc., 161, 1877. Kunipálgi.—Gatschet, Creek Migr. Leg., I, 155, 1884.

Kunjeskie. A Tlingit settlement in Alaska; location not given; pop. 150 in 1835, according to Veniaminoff.
Koonjeskie.—Elliott, Cond. Aff. Alaska, 227, 1875 (transl. from Veniaminoff).

Kunkhogliak. A Kaiyuhkhotana village on Yukon r., Alaska, containing 11 people in 1844.—Zagoskin quoted by Petroff in 10th Census, Alaska, 37, 1884.

Kunkia (*Q!A'nkia*). A former Haida town on the N. coast of North id., Queen Charlotte ids., Brit. Col.—Swanton, Cont. Haida, 281, 1905.

Kunmiut ('river people'). An Eskimo tribe living on Kok r. above Wainwright inlet, Alaska. They have been displaced by Nunatogmiut immigrants, and in 1890 had only 3 settlements left, each containing from 1 to 4 families. One of these was Kilimantavie.
Kĭlauwitawĭ'ñmiun.—Murdoch in 9th Rep. B. A. E., 44, 1892. Kooagomutes.—Elliott, Our Arct. Prov., map, 1886. Koogmute.—Kelly, Arct. Eskimos, 14, 1890. Kooq Mutes.—Ibid., chart. Kugmiut.—Eleventh Census, Alaska, 162, 1893. Ku'ñmiun.—Murdoch in 9th Rep. B. A. E., 44, 1892.

Kunnas-hadai (*Kun nas ːhad'ā'i*, 'whalehouse people'). Given by Boas (Fifth Report N. W. Tribes Canada, 27, 1889) as the name of a subdivision of the Yakulanas, a family of the Raven clan of the Haida, but in reality it is only a house name belonging to that group. (J. R. S.)

Kunnesee. See *Dragging-canoe*.

Kunniwunneme (*Kŭn-ni'-wŭn-ne'-me*). An Oregon tribe E. of the Tillamook (Dorsey, Naltûnnetûnne MS. vocab., B. A. E., 1884), identified as in Athapascan territory, but otherwise unknown.

Kunnupiyu (*K'ŭn-nŭ'-pi-yu'*). A former Yaquina village on the N. side of Yaquina r., Oreg.—Dorsey in Jour. Am. Folk-lore, III, 229, 1890.

Kunstamish (*Kun-sta-mish*). A village of the Guauaenok Kwakiutl on the E. side of Claydon bay, Wells passage, Brit. Col.—Dawson in Trans. Roy. Soc. Can. for 1887, sec. II, 73.

Kuosugru (*Kuosu'gru*). A summer village of the Utkiavinmiut Eskimo, on a dry place inland from Pt Barrow, Alaska.—Murdoch in 9th Rep. B. A. E., 83, 1892.

Kupimithlta (*Ku-di'-miçl-tă'*). A former Siuslaw village on Siuslaw r., Oreg.—Dorsey in Jour. Am. Folk-lore, III, 230, 1890.

Kuping. The Coral clans of the Tewa pueblos of San Juan, Santa Clara, San Ildefonso, and Tesuque, N. Mex. That of Tesuque is extinct.
Kopiⁿ-tdóa.—Hodge in Am. Anthrop., IX, 349, 1896 (San Juan form; *tdóa* = 'people'). Kupíⁿ-tdóa.—Ibid. (San Ildefonso form). Kupıⁿ-tdoa.—Ibid. (Tesuque form). Kupi-tóda.—Ibid. (Santa Clara form; *tóda* misprinted for *tdóa*).

Kupkipcock. A village of the Powhatan confederacy on Pamunkey r., King William co., Va., in 1608.
Kaposecocke.—Strachey (*ca.* 1612), Virginia, 62, 1849. Kupkipcock.—Smith (1629), Virginia, I, map, repr. 1819.

Kuptagok. A former Aleut village on Agattu id., Alaska, one of the Near id. group of the Aleutians, now uninhabited.

Kurni. The Goose clan of the Tigua pueblo of Isleta, N. Mex.
Kúrni-t'aínĭn.—Lummis quoted by Hodge in Am. Anthrop., IX, 350, 1896 (*t'aínĭn* = 'people').

Kurts. The Antelope clans of the Keresan pueblos of Laguna, Acoma, Sia, San Felipe, and Cochiti, N. Mex. The Antelope clan of Laguna claims to have come originally from Zuñi and to form a phratry with the Tsits (Water) clan, while that of Acoma forms a phratry with the Water clan of that pueblo. The Antelope clan of Cochiti is extinct. (F. W. H.)
Kŭr'ts-hánoqᶜʰ.—Hodge in Am. Anthrop., IX, 348, 1896 (Acoma form; *hánoqᶜʰ* = 'people'). Kŭr'tsi-hánoᶜʰ—Ibid. (Laguna form). Kurtz.—Stevenson in 11th Rep. B. A. E., 19, 1894 (Sia name). Kŭ'ts-háno.—Hodge, op. cit. (Sia form). Kŭ'ts-hánuch.—Ibid. (Cochiti form). Kúuts-háno.—Ibid. (San Felipe form).

Kusa (Gatschet suggests *kósa*, the name of a small forest bird resembling a sparrow, or *ō'sa, osá*, 'pokeweed,' as the origin of the word; but if the people of Kusa are identical with the Conshac of the French, the name would mean 'cane,' 'reed,' or 'reedbrake.' See *Conshac*). A former town of the Upper Creeks, on the high E. bank of Coosa r., between Columbiana and Talladega, in Talladega co., Ala., between the points where Talladega and Tallahatchie crs. join the Coosa, and on the site of the present Coosa station. The town was once regarded as an important center, a sort of capital. The De Soto expedition of 1540–41 saw it in its flourishing condition, but when Bartram passed it, about 1775, it was mostly in ruins and half deserted, a part of its inhabitants evidently having joined the Abikudshi, while the others went to the nearby Natchez town. Up to 1775, according to Adair, Kusa was a place of refuge for "those who kill undesignedly." The Upper Creeks were frequently called "Coosas," from the name of the town.

Coça.—Gentleman of Elvas (1557) in French, Hist. Coll. La., II, 141, 1850. **Cooca.**—French, ibid., 2d s., II, 247, 1875. **Coosa.**—Romans, Fla., 90, 1775. **Coosau.**—Hawkins (1799), Sketch, 41, 1848. **Coosaw.**—Martin, N. C., I, 194, 1829. **Coosee.**—Royce in 18th Rep. B. A. E., Ala. map, 1899. **Coosis.**—U. S. Ind. Treat. (1797), 68, 1837. **Corsas.**—Hawkins (1799), Sketch, 15, 1848. **Cosa**—Jefferys, French Dom. Am., map, 134, 1761. **Cossa.**—Vandera (1567) in Smith, Colec. Doc. Fla., I, 18, 1857. **Cousas.**—Mitchell, map (1755), cited in N. Y. Doc. Col. Hist., X, 219, 1858. **Coussa.**—Coxe, Carolana, map, 1741. **Cozas.**—Ibid., 25. **Curas.**—Rafinesque, introd. Marshall, Ky., I, 35, 1824. **Cuzans.**—Ibid., 24. **Koosah.**—Adair, Am. Ind., 159, 1775.

Kusan Family. A small linguistic stock formerly occupying villages on Coos r. and bay, and on lower Coquille r., Oreg. (see Powell in 7th Rep. B. A. E., 89, 1891). The name is from that of the tribe, Coos (q. v.) or Kusa, which is said to be taken from one of the Rogue River dialects in which it means 'lake,' 'lagoon,' or 'inland bay.' Within historic times there have been 4 villages in this region in which the Kusan language was spoken. It is probable that at an earlier period the family extended much farther inland along the tributaries of Coos bay, but had been gradually forced into the contracted area on the coast by the pressure of the Athapascan tribes on the S. and E. and the Yakonan on the N. The stock is now practically extinct; the few survivors, for the greater part of mixed blood, are on the Siletz res. in Oreg., whither they went after ceding their lands by (unconfirmed) treaty of 1855. Practically nothing is known of the customs of this people, but there is no reason to suppose that they differed markedly from their neighbors on the N. The social unit was apparently the village, and there is no trace of a clan or gentile system other than the relationships naturally arising in a locally restricted group. It is interesting to note also that the practice of deforming the head was not current among the Kusan, although prevalent among the Yakonan, their northern neighbors. The Kusan villages known to have existed are: Melukitz, N. side of Coos bay; Anasitch, S. side of Coos bay; Mulluk (speaking a different dialect), N. side of Coquille r.; Nasumi, S. side of Coquille r. (L. F.)

Kuseshyaka. The extinct White-corn clan of Acoma pueblo, N. Mex. See *Yaka*.

Küséshyáka-hánoq^ch.—Hodge in Am. Anthrop., IX, 349, 1896 (*yaka*='corn', *hánoqch*='people').

Kushapokla ('divided people'). One of the two Choctaw phratries, consisting of 4 clans: Kushiksa, Lawokla, Lulakiksa, and Linoklusha.

Kashápaokla.—ten Kate, Reizen in N. A., 402, 1885. **Kasháp-úkla.**—Gatschet, Creek Migr. Leg., I, 104, 1884. **Ku-shap'. Ok'-lä.**—Morgan, Anc. Soc., 162, 1877.

Kushetunne. A former village of the Tututni on the N. side of Rogue r., Oreg.

Cosatomy.—Palmer in Ind. Aff. Rep. 1856, 219, 1857. **Kas-so-teh-nie.**—Gibbs, MS. on coast tribes, B. A. E. **ʞûc-cĕ' ʇunnĕ'.**—Dorsey in Jour. Am. Folk-lore, III, 233, 1890. **Kwûs-se'-ʇûn.**—Dorsey, Naltûnne ʇûnnĕ MS. vocab., B. A. E., 1884 (Naltunnetunne name).

Kushiksa (*Kush-ik'-sä*). The Reed clan of the Choctaw, belonging to the Kushapokla or Divided people phratry.—Morgan, Anc. Soc., 162, 1877.

Kushletata (*Kŭc'-le-ta'-ta*). A former Chastacosta village on Rogue r., Oreg.—Dorsey in Jour. Am. Folk-lore, III, 234, 1890.

Kushuh ('cottonwood tree'). A former Chitimacha village on L. Mingaluak, near Bayou Chêne, La.

Kúshu'h námu.—Gatschet in Trans. Anthrop. Soc. Wash., II, 152, 1883 (*námu*='village').

Kusilvak. A Chnagmiut Eskimo village and Roman Catholic mission on Kusilvak id., at the mouth of Yukon r., Alaska.

Kusilvak.—Petroff in 10th Census, Alaska, map, 1884. **Kusilvuk.**—Bruce, Alaska, 1885.

Kuskok. A Kuskwogmiut Eskimo village on Kuskokwim r., Alaska, near its mouth; pop. 24 in 1880, 115 in 1890.

Kuskogamute.—Petroff in 10th Census, Alaska, map, 1884. **Kuskohkagamiut.**—Eleventh Census, Alaska, 164, 1893. **Kuskok.**—Baker, Geog. Dict. Alaska, 1902. **Kuskokvagamute.**—Petroff in 10th Census, Alaska, 17, 1884. **Kuskokvagmute.**—Petroff, Rep. on Alaska, 74, 1881. **Kuskokwagamute.**—Hallock in Nat. Geog. Mag., IX, 88, 1898.

Kuskokvak. A (former?) Kuskwogmiut Eskimo village on the W. bank of Kuskokwim r., Alaska, near its mouth.

Kuskokvakh.—Petroff in 10th Census, Alaska, map, 1884. **Kuskovak.**—Baker, Geog. Dict. Alaska, 1902. **Kuskovakh.**—Nelson (1879) cited by Baker, ibid.

Kuskunuk. A Kaialigamut Eskimo village on Hooper bay, Alaska.—Nelson in 18th Rep. B. A. E., map, 1899.

Kuskuski (seemingly from *kŭshkŭshkĭng*, 'hog place'). An important village of mixed Delawares and Iroquois, in 1753–1770, on Beaver cr., Pa., near Newcastle, in Lawrence co. A note in N. Y. Doc. Col. Hist. X, 949, says it was at the forks of Beaver cr., in Beaver co. Another authority (Darlington, Gist's Jour., 101, 1898) says it was on the W. bank of Mahoning r., 6 m. above the forks of Beaver cr. and just S. of the present Edinburg, Lawrence co. An older village of the same name had formerly stood on the Shenango, at the site of the present Newcastle. In 1758 Kuskuski was composed of 4 distinct settlements, having a total population of about 1,000 souls. (J. M.)

Cachecacheki.—Vaudreuil (1759) in N. Y. Doc. Col. Hist., x, 949, 1858. Cachekacheki.—Ibid. Cas,-cagh, sa, gey.—Clinton (1750), ibid., vi, 549, 1855. Coscosky.—Weiser (1748) in Rupp, West. Pa., app., 14, 1846. Cuschcushke.—Heckewelder in Trans. Am. Philos. Soc., n. s., iv, 395, 1834. Cuscuskie.—Croghan (1750) in Rupp, West. Pa., app., 27, 1846. Cuskcaskking.—Pa. Archives, iii, 525, 1853. Cuskuskus.—Rupp.; op. cit., 138 (pl. form used for the inhabitants). Cususkey.—Day, Pa., 62, 1843. Kaschkaschkung.—Leroy and Leininger (1755) in Pa. Mag. Hist. and Biog., xxix, 412, 1905. Kaskaskunk.—Loskiel, Miss. United Breth., pt. 3, 55, 1794. Kaskuskies.—Gist (1753) in Mass. Hist. Soc. Coll., 3d s., v, 103, 1836. Kishkuske.—Hutchin's map (1764) in Smith, Bouquet's Exped., 1766. Kshkushking.—Post (1758) in Rupp, West. Pa., app., 116, 1846 (u omitted). Kushcushkee.—Post (1758) in Drake, Bk. Inds., bk. 5, 39, 1848. Kushkushkee.—Post (1758) in Rupp, West. Pa., app., 80, 1846. Kushkushking.—Post (1758) in Rupp, West. Pa., app., 103, 1846. Kushkuskies.—Smith, Bouquet's Exped., 67, 1766. Kuskuschki.—Heckewelder in Trans. Am. Philos. Soc., n. s., iv, 366, 1834. Kuskuskas.—Washington (1753) in Rupp, West. Pa., app., 39, 1846. Kuskuskees.—N. Y. Doc. Col. Hist., x, 949, note, 1858. Kuskuskies.—Lotter, map, ca. 1770. Kuskuskin.—Alden (1834) in Mass. Hist. Soc. Coll., 3d s., vi, 144, 1837. Kuskusko Town.—Washington (1753) in Rupp, West. Pa., app., 41, 1846. Kuskusky.—Peters (1760) in Mass. Hist. Soc. Coll., 4th s., ix, 258, 1871. Murdering town.—Washington (1753) in Rupp, West. Pa., app., 48, 1846. Murthering Town.—Gist (1753) in Mass. Hist. Soc. Coll., 3d s., v, 103, 1836.

Kuskussu (*Kŭs'-kŭs-sŭ'*). A former Siuslaw village on Siuslaw r., Oreg.—Dorsey in Jour. Am. Folk-lore, iii, 230, 1890.

Kuskwogmiut. An Eskimo tribe inhabiting the shores of Kuskokwim bay and the banks of Kuskokwim r. and its tributaries as far as Kolmakof, Alaska. They are the most numerous of the tribes and the least modified through contact with whites. They live in underground huts, with frames of driftwood covered with sods. They hunt the walrus, the beluga, and the hair seal. Sea birds provide them with meat and eggs, and the feathered skins with clothing. The streams and lakes of the interior abound in trout, and herds of reindeer feed on the tundra. Their fuel is driftwood. They drink the foul water of the lagoons, yet are healthy and strong. Every male has a kaiak. Above tide water they use birch-bark canoes. They catch salmon and whitefish in wicker weirs, and trap foxes and otters. There is little that the natives can obtain to sell, and therefore they remain in their aboriginal condition. They are skillful carvers of ivory and wood. The dwellers on the tundra, where wild fowl and berries are plenty, repair with their kaiaks in the summer to trap and dry their winter supply of salmon. Villages on the upper reaches are built of wood, and each has its large ceremonial house in which masked dances take place in winter. Besides the summer houses roofed with sod there are the usual underground winter habitations reached by a tunnel.

The tribe numbered 3,287 in 1899. The Kuskwogmiut villages are as follows: Agomekelenanak, Agulakpak, Aguliak, Agumak, Akiachak, Akiak, Aklut, Akmiut, Anagok, Apahiachak, Apokak, Atchaluk, Bethel, Chimiak, Chuarlitilik, Ekaluktaluk, Etoluk, Igiakchak, Iliutak, Kahmiut, Kakuiak, Kakuikak, Kaltshak, Kaluktuk, Kamegli, Kanagak, Kanak, Kenachananak, Kiktak, Kinak, Kinegnagak, Kinegnak, Klchakuk, Kleguchek, Klutak, Kolmakof, Kongiganak, Kuilkluk, Kukluktuk, Kulvagavik, Kuskok, Kuskokvak, Kweleluk, Kwik, Kwikak, Kwilokuk, Kwinak, Lomavik, Mumtrak, Mumtrelek, Nak, Nakolkavik, Napai, Napaiskak, Napakiak, Nochak, Novoktolak, Okaganak, Oknagak, Oyak, Papka, Shevenak, Shiniak, Shokfak, Takiketak, Togiaratsorik, Tuklak, Tularka, Tuluksak, Tunagak, Ugovik, Uknavik, Ulokak, Vinasale, and Yakchilak.

Agŭlmūt.—Holmberg quoted by Dall in Cont. N. A. Ethnol., i, 18, 1877. Inkaliten.—Wrangell quoted by Dall, ibid. Koskoquims.—Elliott, Cond. Aff. in Alaska, 29, 1875. Kouskokhantses.—Lutke, Voyage, i, 191, 1835 (seemingly identical). Kuschkukohwak-müten.—Wrangell, Ethnog. Nachr., 127, 1839. Kushokwagmut.—Nelson in 18th Rep. B. A. E., map, 1899. Kusko kûax tana.—Doroschin in Radloff, Wörterb. d. Kinai-Spr., 29, 1874 (Kinai name). Kuskokwagmut.—Nelson in 18th Rep. B. A. E., pl. ii, 1899. Kuskokwigmjuten.—Holmberg, Ethnog. Skizz., 5, 1855. Kuskokwim.—Nelson in Soc. Roy. Belge de Geog., 318, 1901. Kuskokwimer.—Wrangell, Ethnog. Nachr., 121, 1839. Kuskokwimjuts.—Turner quoted by Dall in Cont. N. A. Ethnol., i, 18, 1877. Kuskokwims.—Latham (1845) in Jour. Ethnol. Soc. Lond., i, 185, 1848. Kuskokwimtsi.—Worman quoted by Dall in Cont. N. A. Ethnol., i, 18, 1877. Kuskutchewak.—Richardson, Arct. Exped., i, 364, 1851. Kuskutshewak.—Latham, Elem. Comp. Philol., 386, 1862. Kuskwógmuts.—Dall in Proc. A. A. A. S., 267, 1869.

Kustahekdaan (*Kʌstaxē'xda-ān*). A former Tlingit town in the Sitka country, Alaska. (J. R. S.)

Kustatan. A Knaiakhotana village, of 45 natives in 1890, on the w. side of Cook inlet, Alaska.—11th Census, Alaska, 163, 1893.

Kuta. Said to be a clan of the pueblo of Santo Domingo, N. Mex. The name refers to either the sagebrush or the sunflower.—Bourke, Moquis of Arizona, 13, 1884.

Shípi.—Bourke, ibid. (Kuta or).

Kutaiimiks (*Kut'-ai-ĭm-iks*, 'they do not laugh'). A division of the Piegan tribe of the Siksika, q. v.

Don't Laugh.—Grinnell, Blackfoot Lodge Tales, 225, 1892. Kä-ti'-ya-ye-mix.—Morgan, Anc. Soc., 171, 1877 (= 'never laugh'). Ko-te'-yi-miks.—Hayden, Ethnog. and Philol. Mo. Val., 264, 1862 (= 'the band that do not laugh'). Kut'-ai-ĭm-iks.—Grinnell, op. cit., 209. The People that don't laugh.—Culbertson in Smithson. Rep. 1850, 144, 1851.

Kutaisotsiman ('no parfleche'). A division of the Piegan tribe of the Siksika.

Kut-ai-sot'-si-man.—Grinnell, Blackfoot Lodge Tales, 209, 1892. No Parfleche.—Ibid., 225.

Kutauwa. A former Alsea village on the N. side of Alsea r., Oreg., at its mouth.

Kû-tau'-wă.—Dorsey in Jour. Am. Folk-lore, iii, 229, 1890. Necketo.—Lewis and Clark, Exped., ii,

118, 1814. **Necketoos.**—Ibid., II, 592, 1817. **Neekee-toos.**—Morse, Rep. to Sec. War, 371, 1822. **Neeke-toos.**—Lewis and Clark, Exped., II, 473, 1814.

Kutawichasha ('lowland people'). One of the two chief local divisions of the Brulé Teton Sioux, formerly inhabiting the bottom lands along Missouri r.
Coutah-wee-cha-cha.—Corliss, Lacotah MS. vocab., B. A. E., 106, 1874. **Kud-witcaca.**—Dorsey in 15th Rep. B. A. E., 218, 1897. **Ku^{n}ta-witcaca.**—Ibid. **Kunwica'sa.**—Iapi Oaye, XII, 12, 1884. **Kuta-witcaca.**—Dorsey, op. cit. **Lower Brulé.**—U. S. Stat., XIV, 699, 1868. **Lower Brusle.**—U. S. Ind. Treat., 892, 1873. **Lowland Brulé.**—Dorsey, op. cit. **Toncas.**—Corliss, Lacotah MS. vocab., B. A. E., 106, 1874.

Kutchakutchin ('giant people'). A Kutchin tribe in Alaska, inhabiting both banks of the Yukon from Birch cr. to Porcupine r., including the Ft Yukon district. In 1847 McMurray descended Porcupine r. to the Yukon and built Ft

SAVIAH, CHIEF OF THE KUTCHAKUTCHIN. (FROM RICHARD-SON, ARCTIC SEARCHING EXPED., 1851)

Yukon at the confluence. In 1860 Robert Kennicott wintered at Ft Yukon, and in 1866 Ketchum explored the country about the fort. In May, 1867, Dall and Whymper (Dall, Alaska, 277, 1870) visited Ft Yukon, being the first to reach that point by way of the river. The Kutchakutchin are somewhat nomadic, living principally by hunting and trapping the fox, marten, wolf, wolverene, deer, lynx, rabbit, marmot, and moose. They are traders, making little for themselves, but buying from the tribes which use Ft Yukon as a common trading post. *Nakieik*, their standard of value, consists of strings of beads, each string 7 ft long. A string is worth one or more beaver skins according to the kind of beads, and the whole *nakieik* is valued at 24 pelts. Their

dwellings, shaped like inverted teacups are of sewed deerskins fastened over curved poles. The women are said to perform most of the drudgery, but the men cook. Lacking pottery, their utensils are of wood, matting, sheep horns, or birch bark; their dishes are wooden troughs; and their spoons of wood or horn hold a pint. Kettles of woven tamarack roots are obtained from the Hankutchin. Jones says they are divided into three castes or clans: Tchitcheah (Chitsa), Tengeratsey (Tangesatsa), and Natsahi (Natesa). Formerly a man must marry into another clan, but this custom has fallen into disuse. Polygamy and slavery are practised among them. They formerly burned their dead, but now use a coffin placed upon a raised platform, a feast accompanying the funeral ceremony. Richardson (Arct. Exped., I, 386, 1851) placed the number of men at 90. They have a village at Ft Yukon. Senati, on the middle Yukon, was settled by them. The Tatsakutchin and Tennuthkutchin, offshoots of the main tribe, are extinct.
Eert-kai-lee.—Parry quoted by Murdoch in 9th Rep. B. A. E., 51, 1892. **Fort Indians.**—Ross, MS. notes on Tinne, B. A. E. **Ik-kil-lin.**—Gilder quoted by Murdoch in 9th Rep. B. A. E., 51, 1892. **Itch-ali.**—11th Census, Alaska, 154, 1893. **It-kagh-lie.**—Lyon quoted by Murdoch, op. cit. **It-ka-lya-rüin.**—Dall in Cont. N. A. Ethnol., I, 30, 1877 (Nuwukmiut Eskimo name). **I't-ka-lyi.**—Simpson quoted by Murdoch, op. cit. **Itkpe'lit.**—Petitot, Vocab. Français-Esquimau, 42, 1876. **Itkρé-léit.**—Ibid., xxiv. **Itku'dliñ.**—Murdoch, op. cit. **Koo-cha-koo-chin.**—Hardisty in Smithson. Rep., 311, 1866. **Kot-à-Kutchin.**—Bancroft, Nat. Races, I, 147, 1874. **Kotch-á-Kutchins.**—Whymper, Alaska, 247, 1869. **Koushcâ Kouttchin.**—Petitot, Autour du lac des Esclaves, 361, 1891. **Kutchaa Kuttchin.**—Petitot, MS. vocab., B. A. E., 1865. **Kutcha-kutchi.**—Richardson, Arct. Exped., I, 386, 1851. **Kutch a Kutchin.**—Kirkby (1862) in Hind, Lab. Penin., II, 254, 1863. **Kutchia-Kuttchin.**—Petitot, Dict. Dènè-Dindjié, xx, 1876 ('giant people'). **Kutsha-Ku-tshi.**—Latham, Nat. Races, 293, 1854. **Low-land-ers.**—Raymond in Sen. Ex. Doc. 12, 42d Cong., 1st sess., 34, 1871. **Lowland people.**—Whymper, Alaska, 254, 1869. **Na-Kotchρô-tschig-Kouttchin.**—Petitot, Autour du lac des Esclaves, 361, 1891 ('people of the river with gigantic banks'). **O-til'-tin.**—Dawson in Rep. Geol. Surv. Can., 202B, 1887. **Youkon Louchioux Indians.**—Ross, MS. notes on Tinne, B. A. E.

Kutchin ('people'). A group of Athapascan tribes in Alaska and British North America, inhabiting the region on the Yukon and its tributaries above Nuklukayet, the Peel r. basin, and the lower Mackenzie valley. They have decreased to half their former numbers owing to wars between the tribes and the killing of female children. Chiefs and medicine-men and those who possess rank acquired by property have two or more wives. They usually live in large parties, each headed by a chief and having one or more medicine-men, the latter acquiring an authority to which even the chiefs are subject. Their dances and chants are rhythmical and their games are more manly and rational than those of their congeners. They have wrestling bouts which are begun by little boys, those next in strength coming on in turn until the strongest or freshest man in the band remains the final victor, after which the

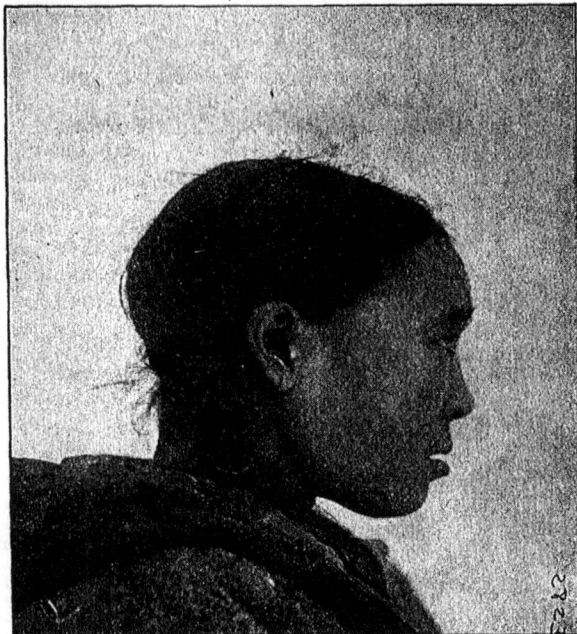

KUTCHIN WOMAN.   (AM. MUS. NAT. HIST.)

women go through the same progressive contest. They are exceedingly hospitable, keeping guests for months, and each head of a family takes his turn in feasting

KUTCHIN MAN.   (AM. MUS. NAT. HIST.)

the whole band, on which occasion etiquette requires him to fast until the guests have departed (Hardisty in Smithson. Rep. for 1866, 313). The Kutchin tribes

are Tenankutchin, Natsitkutchin, Kutchakutchin, Hankutchin, Trotsikkutchin, Tutchonekutchin, Vuntakutchin, Tukkuthkutchin, Tatlitkutchin, Nakotchokutchin, and Kwitchakutchin.

Déhkèwi.—Petitot, Kutchin MS. vocab., B. A. E., 1869 (Kawchodinneh name). Dendjyé.—Petitot, MS. vocab., B. A. E., 1865. Di-go-thi-tdinnè.—Richardson, Arct. Exped., I, 378, 1851 (Kawchodinneh name). Dindjiè.—Petitot in Bul. Soc. de Géog. Paris, chart, 1875. Dindjié.—Petitot, Autour du lac des Esclaves, 361, 1891. Dindjié Loucheux.—Ibid., 289. Erkiléït.—Ibid., 163 (Greenland Eskimo name). Irkρéléït.—Ibid. Koochin.—Anderson (1858) in Hind, Lab. Penin. II, 260, 1863. Koo-tchin'.—Morgan in N. Am. Rev., 58, 1870. Kūchin.—Ibid. Kutchin.—Richardson, Arct. Exped., 214, 1851. Ku-t'qin.—Morice, Notes on W. Dénés, 15, 1893. Kutshi.—Latham, Nat. Races, 293, 1854. Kutshin.—Ibid., 292. Loo-choos.—Schoolcraft, Ind. Tribes, II, 27, 1852. Loucheux.—Franklin, Journ. Polar Sea, II, 83, 1824 (Canadian French, 'squint-eyes'). Louchioux.—Ross, MS. notes on Tinne, B. A. E. Louchoux.—Ibid. Quarrelers.—Schoolcraft, Ind. Tribes, II, 27, 1852. Sharp-eyed Indians.—Richardson in Franklin, Second Exped. Polar Sea, 165, 1828. Squint Eyes.—Franklin, Journ. Polar Seas, II, 83, 1824. Zänker-Indianer.—Buschmann, Spuren der aztek. Sprache, 713, 1859.

Kutchlok. A former Aleut village on Unalaska, Aleutian ids., Alaska.
Ikutchlok.—Coxe, Russ. Discov., 160, 1787. Kutchlok.—Ibid., 158.

Kutek. A settlement of East Greenland Eskimo on the s. E. coast of Greenland, lat. 60° 45'.—Meddelelser om Grönland, x, 24, 1888.

Kutenai (corrupted form, possibly by way of the language of the Siksika, of *Kútonâqa*, one of their names for themselves). A people forming a distinct linguistic stock, the Kitunahan family of Powell, who inhabit parts of s. E. British Columbia and N. Montana and Idaho, from the lakes near the source of Columbia r. to Pend d'Oreille lake. Their legends and traditions indicate that they originally dwelt E. of the Rocky mts., probably in Montana, whence they were driven westward by the Siksika, their hereditary enemies. The two tribes now live on amicable terms, and some intermarriage has taken place. Before the buffalo disappeared from the plains they often had joint hunting expeditions. Recollection of the treatment of the Kutenai by the Siksika remains, however, in the name they give the latter, Sahantla ('bad people'). They entertained also a bad opinion of the Assiniboin (Tlutlamaeka, 'cut-throats'), and the Cree (Gutskiawe, 'liars').

The Kutenai language is spoken in two slightly differing dialects, Upper and Lower Kutenai. A few uncertain points of similarity in grammatical structure with the Shoshonean tongues seem to exist. The language is incorporative both with respect to the pronoun and the noun object. Prefixes and suffixes abound, the prefix $aq(k)$- in nouns occurring with remarkable frequency. As in the Algonquian tongues, the form of a word used in composition differs from that which it has independently. Reduplication is very rare, occurring only in a few nouns, some of which are possibly of foreign origin. There are a few loan-words from Salishan dialects.

The Upper Kutenai include the following subdivisions: Akiskenukinik, Akamnik, Akanekunik, and Akiyenik.

The Lower Kutenai are more primitive and nomadic, less under the influence of the Catholic church, and more given to gambling. They have long been river and lake Indians, and possess peculiar bark canoes that resemble some of those used in the Amur region in Asia (Mason in Rep. Nat. Mus., 1899). Of late years many of them have taken to horses and are skillful in their management. The Upper Kutenai keep nearer the settlements, often obtaining a living by serving the settlers and miners in various ways. Many of them have practically ceased to be canoemen and travel by horse. Both the Upper and the Lower Kutenai hunt and fish, the latter depending more on fish for food. Physically, the Kutenai are well developed and rank among the taller tribes of British Columbia. Indications of race mixture seem to be shown in the form of the head. Their general character from the time of De Smet has been reported good. Their morality, kindness, and hospitality are noteworthy, and more than any other Indians of the country they have avoided drunkenness and lewd intercourse with the whites. Their mental ability is comparatively high, and the efforts of the missionaries have been rewarded with success. They are not excessively given to emotional instability, do not lack a sense of interest, and can concentrate attention when necessary. Their social system is simple, and no evidence of the existence of totems or secret societies has been found. The chieftainship, now more or less elective, was probably hereditary, with limitations; slavery of war prisoners was formerly in vogue; and relatives were responsible for the debts of a deceased person. Marriage was originally polygamous; divorced women were allowed to marry again, and adultery was not severely punished. Adoption by marriage or by residence of more than a year was common. Women could hold certain kinds of property, such as tents and utensils. A wergild was customary. Religion was a sort of sun worship, and the belief in the ensoulment of all things and in reincarnation prevailed. The land of the dead was in the sun, from which at some time all the departed would descend to L. Pend d'Oreille to meet the Kutenai then living. In the old days the medicine-men were very powerful, their influence surviving most with the Lower Kutenai, who still paint their faces on dance occasions; but tattooing is rare. Except a sort of reed pipe, a bone flute, and the drum, musical instruments were unknown to them; but they had gambling, dancing, and medicine songs. The Lower Kutenai are still exceedingly addicted to gambling, their favorite being a noisy variety of the widespread guess-stick game. The Kutenai were in former days great buffalo hunters. Firearms have driven out the bow and arrow, save as children's toys or for killing birds. Spearing, the basket trap, and wicker weirs were much in use by the Lower Kutenai. Besides the bark canoe, they had dugouts; both skin and rush lodges were built; the sweat house was universal. Stone hammers were still in use in parts of their country, in the last years of the 19th century. The Lower Kutenai are still noted for their watertight baskets of split roots. In dress they originally resembled the Plains Indians rather than those of the coast; but contact with the whites has greatly modified their costume. While fond of the white man's tobacco, they have a sort of their own made of willow bark. A large part of their food supply is now obtained from the whites. For food, medicine, and economical purposes the Kutenai use a large number of the plant products of their environment (Chamberlain in Verh. d. Berl. Ges. f. Anthr., 551–6, 1895). They were gifted also with esthetic appreciation of several plants and flowers. The diseases from which the Kutenai suffer most are consumption and ophthalmic troubles; venereal diseases are rare. Interesting maturity ceremonies still survive in part. The mythology and folklore of the Kutenai consist chiefly of cosmic and ethnic myths, animal tales, etc. In the animal tales the coyote, as an adventurer and deceiver, is the most prominent figure, and with him are often associated the chicken-hawk, the grizzly bear, the fox, the cricket, and the wolf. Other creatures which appear in these stories are the beaver, buffalo, caribou, chipmunk, deer, dog, moose, mountain lion, rabbit, squirrel, skunk, duck, eagle, grouse, goose, magpie, owl, snowbird, tomtit, trout, whale, butterfly, mosquito, frog, toad, and turtle. Most of the cosmogonic legends seem to belong to the N. W. Pacific cycle; many of the coyote tales belong to the cycle of the Rocky mt. region, others have a Siouan or Algonquian aspect in some particulars. Their deluge myth is peculiar in several respects. A number of tales of giants occur, two of the legends, "Seven Heads" and "Lame Knee," suggesting Old World analogies. The story of the man in the moon is probably borrowed from French sources.

While few evidences of their artistic ability in the way of pictographs, birchbark drawings, etc., have been reported, the Kutenai are no mean draftsmen. Some of them possess an idea of map making and have a good sense of the physical features of the country. Some of their drawings of the horse and the buffalo are characteristically lifelike and quite accurate. The ornamentation of their moccasins and other articles, the work of the women, is often elaborate, one of the motives of their decorative art being the Oregon grape. They do not seem to have made pottery, nor to have indulged in wood carving to a large extent. The direct contact of the Kutenai with the whites is comparatively recent. Their word for white man, Sūyäpi, is identical with the Nez Percé Suēapo (Parker, Jour., 381, 1840), and is probably borrowed. Otherwise the white man is called Nūtlu'qenē, 'stranger.' They have had few serious troubles with the whites, and are not now a warlike people. As yet the Canadian Kutenai are not reservation Indians. The United States seems to have made no direct treaty with the tribe for the extinguishment of their territorial rights (Royce in 18th Rep. B. A. E., 856).

Within the Kutenai area, on the Columbia lakes, live a colony of Shushwap (Salishan) known as Kinbaskets, numbering 56 in 1904. In that year the Kutenai in British territory were reported to number 553, as follows: Lower Columbia Lake, 80; Lower Kutenai (Flatbow), 172; St Mary's (Ft Steele), 216; Tobacco Plains, 61; Arrow Lake (West Kutenai), 24. These returns indicate a decrease of about 150 in 13 years. The United States census of 1890 gave the number of Kutenai in Idaho and Montana as 400 to 500; in 1905 those under the Flathead agency, Mont., were reported to number 554. The Kutenai have given their name to Kootenai r., the districts of East, West, and North Kootenay, Brit. Col., Kootenai lake, Brit. Col., Kootanie pass in the Rocky mts., Kootenai co. and the town of Kootenai, Idaho, and to other places on both sides of the international boundary (Am. Anthrop., IV, 348–350, 1902).

Consult Boas, First Gen. Rep. on the Inds. of Brit. Col. in Rep. B. A. A. S., 1889; Chamberlain, Rep. on the Kootenay Inds. in Rep. B. A. A. S., 1892, also various articles by the same author since 1892 in Am. Anthrop., Jour. Am. Foik-lore, and Am. Antiq.; Hale in U. S. Expl. Exped., VI, 1846; Maclean, Canadian Savage Folk, 1896; Smet (1) Oregon Missions, 1847, (2) New Indian Sketches, 1863; Tolmie and Dawson, Comp. Vocabs. Brit. Col., 1884.   (A. F. C.)

Catanoneaux.—Schermerhorn (1812) in Mass. Hist. Soc. Coll., 2d s., II, 42, 1814 (wrongly applied to Piegan; corrupt Indian with French termination). Catawahays.—Moore in Ind. Aff. Rep., 292, 1846, (misprint). Cat-tan-a-hâws.—Lewis and Clark, Discov., 57, 1806 (said to be their own name). Cattanahâws.—Ibid. (so called by the French). Cattanahowes. — Mackenzie, Voy., map, 1801. Cautonee.—Harmon, Jour., map, 1820. Cautonies.—Ibid., 313. Contamis.—Schoolcraft, Ind. Tribes, I, 457, 1851 (probably a misprint). Contenay.—Lane in Ind. Aff. Rep., 158, 1850. Contonnés.—Catlin, N. Am. Ind., passim, 1844 (said to be French name). Cootanais.—Ross, Advent., 213, 1849. Cootanies.—Parker, Jour., 307, 1840. Cootneys.—Milroy in H. R. Misc. Doc. 122, 43d Cong., 1st sess., 5, 1875. Cootomies.—Wilkes, Hist. Oregon, 44, 1845. Cootonaikoon.—Henry, MS. vocab., 1808 (so called by the Blackfeet). Cootonais.—Cox, Advent., II, 75, 1831. Cootonay.—Ibid., 154. Cootounies.—Robertson, Oregon, 129, 1846. Cotones.—Hind, Red River Exped., II, 152, 1860. Cottonois.—Irving, Rocky Mts., I, 187, 1837. Counarrha.—Vocabulaire des Kootenays Counarrha ou Skalza, 1883, cited by Pilling, Proof Sheets, 1885. Coutanies.—Hale in U. S. Expl. Exped., VI, 204, 1846. Coutaria.—Schoolcraft, Ind. Tribes, III, 402, 1853. Coutenay.—Lane (1849) in Sen. Ex. Doc. 52, 31st Cong., 1st sess., 169, 1850. Coutnees.—Bonner, Life of Beckwourth, 226, 1856. Coutonais.—Maximilian, Trav., 509, 1843. Coutonois.—Pendleton in H. R. Rep. 830, 27th Cong., 2d sess., 21, 1842. Coutouns.—Morse, Rep. to Sec. War, 34, 1822. Flatbows.—See Lower Kutenai. Kattanahaws.—Keane in Stanford, Compend., 470, 1878 (applies to Upper Kutenai only). Ki'tōnā'qa.—Chamberlain, 8th Rep. N. W. Tribes, 6, 1892. Kit-too-nuh'-a.—Tolmie and Dawson, Comp. Vocabs., 124B, 1884 (applied to Upper Kutenai). Kituanaha.—Schoolcraft, Ind. Tribes, III, 402, 1853. Kitunaha.—Hale in U. S. Expl. Exped., VI, 204, 535, 1846. Kitunana.—Stevens, Rep. on N. Pac. R. R., 440, 1854. Kitunáxa.—Ibid., 535. Kodenees.—Meek in H. R. Ex. Doc. 76, 30th Cong., 1st sess., 10, 1848. Koeetenays.—De Smet, Letters, 170, 1843. Koetenais.—Ibid., 183. Koetenay.—Ibid., 203. Koetinays.—De Smet quoted in H. R. Ex. Doc. 65, 36th Cong., 1st sess., 141, 1860. Koo-tames.—Gibbs in Pac. R. R. Rep., I, 417, 1855. Kootanaise. — Mayne, Brit. Col., 298, 1862. Kootanay.—Taylor in Cal. Farmer, Feb. 27, 1863. Kootamies.—Stevens in Ind. Aff. Rep., 460, 1854. Kootanie.—Nicolet, Oregon, 143, 1846. Kootenai.—Brown in Beach, Ind. Misc., 77, 1877. Kootenaies.—Gibbs in Rep. N. Pac. R. R., 437, 1854. Kootenays.—De Smet, Letters, 37, 1843. Kootenia.—Emerson, Indian Myths, 404, 1884. Kootenuha.—Tolmie and Dawson, Comp. Vocabs., 124B, 1884. Koote-nuha.—Ibid., 5B. Kootones.—Henry (1811) quoted by Maclean, Canad. Sav. Folk, 138, 1896. Kootoonais.—Stevens in Ind. Aff. Rep., 461, 1854. Koutaines.—Ibid., 462. Koutanis.—Duflot de Mofras, Explor., II, 173, 1844. Koutonais.—H. R. Rep. 98, 42d Cong., 3d sess., 429, 1873. Kúspēlu.—Gatschet, MS., B. A. E. (Nez Percé name: 'water people'). Kutanä'.—Maximilian, Reise, II, 511, 1841. Kutanas.—Maximilian, Trav., 242, 1843. Kútani.—Latham, Elem. Comp. Philol., 395, 1862. Kútanis.—Latham, Nat. Hist. Man, 316, 1860. Kutenae.—Maclean, Canad. Sav. Folk, 137, 1896 (Siksika name; sing., Kutenaekwan). Kutenai.—Mason in Rep. Nat. Mus. 1899, 529, 1901. Kutenay.—Brinton, Amer. Race, 108, 1891. Kutnehä'.—Maxmilian, Reise, II, 511, 1841. Kutnehas.—Maximilian, Trav., 242, 1843. Kútona.—Hayden, Ethnog. and Philol. Mo. Val., 256, 1862. Kutonacha.—Maximilian, Trav., 500, 1843. Kutona'qa.—Boas, 5th Rep. N. W. Tribes, 10, 1889. Kutonas.—Maximilian, Trav., 245, 1848. Skaisi.—Schoolcraft, Ind. Tribes, III, map, 200, 1853. Skalza.—Gibbs in Pac. R. R. Rep., I, 416, 1855. Skalzi.—De Smet Letters, 224, 1843. Skalzy.—Ibid., 203. Skelsá-ulk.—Gatschet, MS., B. A. E. (Salish name: 'water people'). Skolsa.—Gibbs in Pac. R. R. Rep., I, 416, 1855.

Kutshamakin. One of the Massachuset sachems who signed the treaties of 1643 and 1645. He was properly the sachem of the country about Dorchester, Mass., part of which he sold to the English. It was his people to whom John Eliot first preached. Though at first opposed to the English, Kutshamakin afterward became Christianized and served them in many ways, particularly as interpreter. To his killing and scalping a Pequot Indian in 1636 has been attributed (Drake, Inds. of N. A., 116, 1880) the outbreak of a horrible war. (A. F. C.)

Kutshittan ('bear house people'). Given as a subdivision of the Tlingit group Nanyaayi (q. v.), but in reality it is merely the name of the occupants of a certain house.
Qūts hit tan.—Boas in 5th Rep. N. W. Tribes Canada, 25, 1889. Xūtsǃ hît tān.—Swanton, field notes, B. A. E., 1904.

Kutshundika ('buffalo eaters'). A band of the Bannock.
Buffalo-Eaters.—Schoolcraft, Ind. Tribes, I, 522, 1853. Kutsh'undika.—Hoffman in Proc. Am. Philos. Soc., XXXIII, 299, 1886.

Kutshuwitthe (*Ku'-ɔu-wi'-t'çĕ*). A former Yaquina village on the s. side of Yaquina r., Oreg.—Dorsey in Jour. Am. Folk-lore, III, 229, 1890.

Kutssemhaath (*Ku'tssɛmhaath*). A division of the Seshart, a Nootka tribe.— Boas in 6th Rep. N. W. Tribes Canada, 32, 1890.

Kutul. A Kaiyuhkhotana village on Yukon r., Alaska, 50 m. above Anvik; pop. 16 in 1844.
Hultulkakut.—Raymond in Sen. Ex. Doc. 12, 42d Cong., 1st sess., 25, 1871. Khutulkakat.—Zagoskin quoted by Petroff in 10th Census, Alaska, 37, 1884. Kutul.—Baker, Geog. Dict. Alaska, 1902.

Kuuanguala. A former pueblo of the Pecos tribe, more commonly known as Las Ruedas (Span.: 'the wheels'), situated a few miles s. E. of Pecos, near Arroyo Amarillo, at the present site of the village of Rowe, N. Mex. In the opinion of Bandelier it is not unlikely that this pueblo, together with Seyupaella, was occupied at the time of Espejo's visit in 1583.
Ku-uäng-ual-a.—Bandelier in Arch. Inst. Papers, IV, 125, 1892. Kuuang Ua-la.—Ibid., III, 128, 1890. Pueblo de las Ruedas.—Ibid.

Kuu-lana (*Kǃū'u lă'na*). A Haida town occupied by the Koetas, in Naden harbor, Graham id., Queen Charlotte ids., Brit. Col.—Swanton, Cont. Haida, 281, 1905.

Kuyama. A former Chumashan village near Santa Inez mission, Santa Barbara co., Cal.
Cuyama.—Taylor in Cal. Farmer, Oct. 18, 1861. Kuyam.—Ibid.

Kuyamskaiks (*Kuyám-Skä-iks*, 'crawfish trail'). A branch of the Klamath settlement of Yaaga, on Williamson r., Lake co., Oreg.—Gatschet in Cont. N. A. Ethnol., II, pt. I, xxix, 1890.

Kuyanwe. The extinct Turquoise Earpendant clan of the Tewa pueblo of Hano, N. E. Ariz. See *Kungya*.

Ku-yan-we.—Fewkes in Am. Anthrop., VII, 166, 1894. Kuyanwe-tó-wa.—Hodge, ibid., IX, 352, 1896 (*tó-wa* = 'people').

Kuyedi ('people of Kuiu'). A Tlingit division on the Alaskan island which bears their name.
Kujĕĕdi.—Krause, Tlinkit Ind., 120, 1885.

Kuyikanuikpul. An Ikogmiut Eskimo village on the right bank of Yukon r., below Koserefski, Alaska.—Raymond (1869) quoted by Baker, Geog. Dict. Alaska, 1902.

Kuyuidika ('sucker-eaters'). A Paviotso band formerly living near the site of Wadsworth, on Truckee r., w. Nev.
Coo-er-ee.—Campbell in Ind. Aff. Rep., 119, 1866. Coóyuweeweit.—Powers in Smithson. Rep., 450, 1876. Ku-yu-i'-di-ka.—Powell, Paviotso MS. vocab., B. A. E., 1881. Wun-a-muc-a's (the Second) band.—Ind. Aff. Rep. 1859, 374, 1860.

Kvichak. An Aglemiut Eskimo village on the river of the same name in Alaska; pop. 37 in 1890.
Kivichakh.—Eleventh Census, Alaska, 164, 1893. Kvichak.—Baker, Geog. Dict. Alaska, 1902.

Kvigatluk. A Kaialigmiut Eskimo village in the lake district N. w. of Kuskokwim r., Alaska; pop. 30 in 1880.
Kvigathlogamute.—Petroff in 10th Census, Alaska, map, 1884. Kvigatluk.—Baker, Geog. Dict. Alaska, 1902. Kwigathlogamute.—Petroff, Rep. on Alaska, 54, 1881. Kwigathlogumut.—Nelson in 18th Rep. B. A. E., map, 1899.

Kvigimpainag. A Jugelnute Eskimo village, of 71 persons in 1844, on the E. bank of the Yukon, 20 m. from Kvikak, Alaska.
Kvigimpainagmute.—Zagoskin quoted by Petroff in 10th Census, Alaska, 37, 1884 (the people).

Kviguk. A Malemiut Eskimo village at the mouth of Kviguk r., N. shore of Norton bay, Alaska.
Kvieg-miut.—Tikhmenief (1861) quoted by Baker, Geog. Dict. Alaska, 1902. Kvi guk-miut.—Ibid. Kviguk.—Baker, ibid. Kvigukmut.—Zagoskin, Desc. Russ. Poss. Am., pt. I, 72, 1847.

Kvikak. An Ikogmiut Eskimo village on Yukon r., 30 m. above Anvik, Alaska; formerly a Kaiyukhotana village.
Kvikak.—Baker, Geog. Dict. Alaska, 1902. Kvikhagamut.—Nelson in 18th Rep. B. A. E., map, 1900.

Kvinkak. A Malemiut Eskimo village on a river of the same name at the upper end of Norton sd., Alaska; pop. 20 in 1880.
Kvinghak-mioute.—Zagoskin in Nouv. Ann. Voy., XXI, map, 1850. Kvinkhakmut.—Zagoskin, Descr. Russ. Poss. Am., pt. 1, 72, 1847. Ogowinagak.—Nelson in 18th Rep. B. A. E., map, 1899. Ogowinanagak.—Petroff, Rep. on Alaska, 59, 1881.

Kwachelanokumae. The name of an ancestor of a gens of the Mamalelekala, a Kwakiutl tribe; also applied to the gens itself.—Boas in Petermanns Mitt., pt. 5, 130, 1887.

Kwae (*Kwā'-e*). A summer village of the Tsawatenok at the head of Kingcome inlet, Brit. Col.—Dawson in Trans. Roy. Soc. Can. for 1887, sec. II, 73.

Kwahari ('antelopes'). An important division of the Comanche, whose members frequented the prairie country and Staked plains of Texas, hence the name. They were the last to come in after the surrender in 1874. (J. M.)

Antelope-eaters.—Robinson, letter to J. O. Dorsey, 10, 1879. **Antelope Skinners.**—Leavenworth in H. R. Misc. Doc. 139, 41st Cong., 2d sess., 6, 1870. **Kua'hadi.**—Hoffman in Proc. Am. Philos. Soc., XXIII, 300, 1886. **Kwa'hădi.**—Mooney in 14th Rep. B. A. E., 1045, 1896. **Kwahare tetchaχane.**—Gatschet, Comanche MS. vocab., B. A. E., 1884 ('antelope skinners'). **Kwa'hări.**—Mooney, op. cit. **Llaneros.**—Mayer, Mexico, II, 123, 1853. **Noonah.**—Butler and Lewis (1846) in H. R. Doc. 76, 29th Cong., 2d sess., 6, 1847 (probably identical). **People of the Desert.**—Ibid. **Quaahda.**—Sec. War in Sen. Ex. Doc. 7, 42d Cong., 3d sess., 1, 1872. **Quahada Comanches.**—Battey, Advent., 83, 1876. **Quahadas.**—Ind. Aff. Rep. 1869, 101, 1870. **Quahade-Comanches.**—Alvord in Sen. Ex. Doc. 18, 40th Cong., 3d sess., 35, 1869. **Quaha-dede-chatz-Kenna.**—Ibid., 9 (a careless combination of Kwahari, or Kwahadi, and Ditsakana). **Qua-ha-de-dechutz-Kenna.**—Ibid., 6. **Quahades.**—Ibid., 10. **Qua-ho-dahs.**—Hazen, ibid., 38. **Quarrydechocos.**—Walkley, ibid., 19. **Quor-ra-da-chor-koes.**—Leavenworth in H. R. Misc. Doc. 139, 41st Cong., 2d sess., 6, 1870. **Staked Plain Indians.**—Ibid. **Staked Plains Omaions.**—Hazen in Sen. Ex. Doc. 18, 40th Cong., 3d sess., 38, 1869. **Staked Plains Onawas.**—Hazen (1868) in H. R. Ex. Doc. 240, 41st Cong., 2d sess., 150, 1870.

Kwahlaonan (*Kwa-'hlǎonan*). A division of one of the clans of the pueblo of Taos, N. Mex. (F. W. H.)

Kwahu. The Eagle clan of the Pakab (Reed) phratry of the Hopi.
Kuája.—Bourke, Snake Dance, 117, 1884. **Kwa.**—Voth, Oraibi Summer Snake Ceremony, 283, 1903. **Kwa'-hü.**—Stephen in 8th Rep. B. A. E., 39, 1891. **Kwahu wiñwû.**—Fewkes in 19th Rep. B. A. E., 584, 1900. **Kwa'-hü wüñ-wû.**—Fewkes in Am. Anthrop., VII, 403, 1894.

Kwaiailk. A body of Salish on the upper course of Chehalis r., above the Satsop and on the Cowlitz, Wash. In 1855, according to Gibbs, they numbered 216, but were becoming amalgamated with the Cowlitz.
Kwai-aílk.—Eells in letter, B. A. E., Feb. 1886 (own name). **Kwü-teh-ni.**—Gibbs in Cont. N. A. Ethnol., I, 172, 1877 (Kwalhioqua name). **Nü-so-lupsh.**—Ibid. (so called by Sound Indians, referring to the rapids of their stream). **Stak-ta-mish.**—Ibid. ('forest people'). **Staktomish.**—Schoolcraft, Ind. Tribes, V, 701, 1855. **Upper Chihalis.**—Gibbs in Pac. R. R. Rep., I, 435, 1855. **Upper Tsihalis.**—Gibbs in Cont. N. A. Ethnol., I, 172, 1877.

Kwaiantikwokets ('on the other side of the river'). An isolated Paiute band, formerly living in N. W. Arizona, E. of Colorado r. Pop. 62 in 1873. They affiliated largely with the Navaho.
Kuraintu-kwakats.—Ingalis in H. R. Ex. Doc. 66, 42d Cong., 3d sess., 2, 1873 (misprint). **Kwai-an'-ti-twok-ets.**—Powell in Ind. Aff. Rep. 1873, 50, 1874.

Kwaitshi (*Kwa-ai'-tc'ĭ*). A former Yaquina village on the s. side of Yaquina r., Oreg.—Dorsey in Jour. Am. Folk-lore, III, 229, 1890.

Kwaituki. The ruins of a former village of the Hopi, on the w. side of Oraibi arroyo, 14 m. above Oraibi, N. E. Ariz.—Mindeleff in 8th Rep. B. A. E., 57, 1891.

Kwakina ('town of the entrance place'). A ruined pueblo of the Zuñi, 7 m. s. w. of Zuñi pueblo, w. N. Mex. It formed one of the Seven Cities of Cibola, and was possibly the Aquinsa of Oñate, in 1598. The town is mentioned in Zárate-Salmeron's relation, ca. 1629, hence must have been abandoned subsequently to that date and prior to 1680, when but 4 of the cities of Cibola remained. Cf. *Pinawan.*
Aguinsa.—Bancroft, Ariz. and N. Mex., 136, 1889 (misquoting Oñate). **Aquinsa.**—Oñate (1598) in Doc. inéd. XVI, 133, 1871. **Cuakyina.**—Bandelier in Arch. Inst. Pap., III, 133, 1890. **Kua-kyi-na.**—Ibid., V, 171, 1890. **Kwá-ki-na.**—Cushing in Compterendu Internat. Cong. Amér., VII, 156, 1890. **Kyakuina.**—Bandelier in Arch. Inst. Pap., IV, 339, 1892. **Quakyina.**—Ibid., III, 133, 1890. **Quat-china.**—Fewkes in Jour. Am. Eth. and Arch., I, 101, 1891.

Kwakinawan ('town of the entrance place'). A former Zuñi pueblo s. s. E. of Thunder mt., which lies about 4 m. E. of Zuñi pueblo, N. Mex. It is distinct from Kwakina, although not unlikely it was built and for a time inhabited by the people formerly occupying the latter village after one of the descents of the Zuñi from their stronghold on Thunder mt. and the abandonment of the Seven Cities of Cibola. (F. H. C.)

KWAKIUTL MAN. (AM. MUS. NAT. HIST.)

Kwakiutl (according to their own folketymology the name signifies 'smoke of the world', but with more probability it means 'beach at the north side of the river'). In its original and most restricted sense this term is applied to a group of closely related tribes or septs living in the neighborhood of Ft Rupert, Brit. Col. These septs are the Guetela, Komkutis, Komoyue, and Walaskwakiutl, and their principal village Tsahis, surrounding Ft Rupert. Other former towns were Kalokwis, Kliksiwi, Noohtamuh, Tsaite, and Whulk, of which the last two were summer villages shared with the Nimkish during the salmon season. Those who encamped at Tsaite belonged to the Komoyue sept. In comparatively recent times a portion of the Kwakiutl separated from the rest and are known as Matilpe. These and the Komoyue are enumerated separately by the Canadian Department of Indian Affairs, thus limiting the term Kwakiutl to the Guetela, Komkutis, and Walaskwakiutl. In one place it is applied to the Guetela alone. The population of the Kwakiutl proper in 1904 was 163.

KWAKIUTL CHIEFTAINESS IN CEREMONIAL COSTUME.   (BOAS)

In more extended senses the term Kwakiutl is applied to one of the two great division of the Wakashan linguistic stock (the other being the Nootka), and to a dialect and a subdialect under this. The following is a complete classification of the Kwakuitl divisions and subdivisions, based on the investigations of Boas: HAISLA DIALECT—Kitamat and Kitlope. HEILTSUK DIALECT—Bellabella, China Hat, Nohuntsitk, Somehulitk, and Wikeno. KWAKIUTL DIALECT—*Koskimo subdialect*— Klaskino, Koprino, Koskimo, and Quatsino. *Nawiti subdialect*—Nakomgilisala

and Tlatlasikoala. *Kwakiutl subdialect*— Awaitlala, Goasila, Guauaenok, Hahuamis, Koeksotenok, Kwakiutl (including Matilpe), Lekwiltok, Mamalelekala, Nakoaktok, Nimkish, Tenaktak, Tlauitsis, and Tsawatenok. The Hoyalas were an extinct Kwakiutl division the minor affinities of which are unknown.

The total population of the Kwakiutl branch of the Wakashan stock in 1904 was 2,173, and it appears to be steadily decreasing.

Consult Boas, Kwakiutl Inds., Rep. Nat. Mus. 1895, 1897. For further illustrations, see *Koskimo*.   (J. R. S.)

Coquilths.—Dunn, Hist. Oregon, 239, 1844. Fort Rupert Indians.—Scott in H. R. Ex. Doc. 65, 36th Cong., 1st sess., 115, 1860. Kwā'g·uɫ.—Boas in Mem. Am. Mus. Nat. Hist., v, pt. 2, 271, 1902. Kwagutl.—Eighty-first Rep. Brit. and For. Bib. Soc., 380, 1885. Kwahkewlth.—Powell in Can. Ind. Aff., 119, 1880. Kwakiool.—Tolmie and Dawson, Vocabs. Brit. Col., 118B, 1884. Kwa'-kiutl'.—Gibbs in Cont. N. A. Ethnol., I, 144, 1877. Kwā-kuhl.—Tolmie and Dawson, Vocabs. Brit. Col., 118B, 1884. Kwat-kewlth.—Sproat in Can. Ind. Aff., 147, 1879. Kwaw-kewlth.—Can. Ind. Aff., 270, 1889. Kwawkwelch.—Ibid., 189, 1884. Qā gūtl.—Hall, St. John in Qā-gutl, Lond., 1884. Quackeweth.—Can. Ind. Aff., 316, 1880. Quackewlth.—Can. Ind. Aff., 92, 1876. Quackolls.—Grant in Jour. Roy. Geog. Soc., 293, 1857. Qua-colth.—Kane, Wand. in N. Am., app., 1859. Quacós.—Galiano, Relacion, 103, 1802. Quagheuil.—Scouler in Jour. Ethnol. Soc. Lond., I, 233, 1848. Quahkeulth.—Can. Ind. Aff., 52, 1875. Qualquilths.—Lord, Natur. in Brit. Col., I, 165, 1866. Quaquiolts.—Taylor in Cal. Farmer, July 19, 1862. Quawguults.—Mayne, Brit. Col., 251, 1861. Quoquoulth.—Sproat, Savage Life, 311, 1868.

Kwakokutl (*Kwā'kōk·ūL*). A gens of the Nakoaktok, a Kwakiutl tribe.—Boas in Rep. Nat. Mus. 1895, 330, 1897.

Kwakowenok (*Kwā'kōwēnôx*). A gens of the Guauaenok, a Kwakiutl tribe.—Boas in Rep. Nat. Mus. 1895, 331, 1897.

Kwakukemlaenok (*KwākūqEmāl'ēnôx*). A gens of the Koskimo, a Kwakiutl tribe. —Boas in Rep. Nat. Mus. 1895, 329, 1897.

Kwakwakas (*Kwa-kwa-kas*). A former village on the w. coast of Gilford id., Brit. Col., probably belonging to the Koeksotenok.—Dawson in Can. Geol. Surv., map, 1887.

Kwaleki (*Kwā-le-ki*). A former Kawia village in the San Jacinto mts., s. Cal.—Barrows, Coahuilla Ind., 27, 1900.

Kwalewia (*Qwalē'wia*; named from a large bowlder in the stream close by). A former village or camp of the Pilalt, a Cowichan tribe of lower Chilliwack r., Brit. Col.—Hill-Tout in Ethnol. Surv. Can., 48, 1902.

Kwalhioqua (from *Tkulxiyo-goā'ikc :kulxi*, 'at a lonely place in the woods', their Chinook name.—Boas). An Athapascan tribe which formerly lived on the upper course of Willopah r., w. Wash. Gibbs extends their habitat E. into the upper Chehalis, but Boas does not believe they extended E. of the Coast range. They have been confounded by Gibbs and others with a Chinookan tribe on the lower course of the river called Willopah (q. v.). The place where they generally lived was called Nq!ulā′was. The Kwalhioqua and Willopah have ceded their land to the United States (Royce in 18th Rep. B. A. E., pt. 2, 832, 1899). In 1850 two males and several females survived. Hale (Ethnog. and Philol., 204, 1846), who estimated them at about 100, said that they built no permanent habitations, but wandered in the woods, subsisting on game, berries, and roots, and were bolder, hardier, and more savage than the river and coast tribes.

GiLā′q!ulawas.—Boas, letter, 1904 (from name of the place where they generally lived, Nq!ulā′was). **Kivalhioqua.**—Buschmann in König. Akad. der Wiss. zu Berlin, III, 546–86, 1860. **Kwalhiokwas.**—Morice in Trans. Can. Inst., IV, 13, 1893. **Kwalhioqua.**—Hale, Ethnog. and Philol., 204, 1846. **Kwaliokwa.**—Latham in Trans. Philol. Soc. Lond., 70, 1856. **Ouillequegaws.**—Schoolcraft, Ind. Tribes, III, map, 96, 1853. **Owhillapsh.**—Gibbs in Cont. N. A. Ethnol., I, 164, 1877 (applied erroneously; see *Willopah*). **Ówilapsh.**—Gatschet, Kalapuya MS., 280, B. A. E. (erroneously given as Kalapuya name; see *Willopah*). **Qualhioqua.**—Keane in Stanford, Compend., 532, 1878. **Qualioguas.**—Hale, Ethnog. and Philol., 198, 1846. **Qualquioqua.**—Kingsley, Stand. Nat. Hist., pt. G, 142, 1885. **Quilleoueoquas.**—Schoolcraft, Ind. Tribes, III, map, 200, 1853. **Quillequaquas.**—Ind. Aff. Rep., 214, 1851. **Quillequeognas.**—Pres. Mess. in Ex. Doc. 39, 32d Cong., 1st sess., 5, 1852. **Quillequeoqua.**—Dart in Ex. Doc. 53, 32d Cong., 1st sess., 2, 1852. **Tilhalumma.**—Scouler (1846) in Jour. Ethnol. Soc. Lond., I, 235, 1848 (probably this tribe). **TkulHiyogoā′iko.**—Boas in 10th Rep. N. W. Tribes Can., 67, 1895 (Chinook name). **Tkulx̣iyogoā′íko.**—Boas, inf'n, 1904.

Kwalwhut. A rancheria in N. Lower California, whose occupants speak the Hataam dialect of Diegueño.—Henshaw, MS. vocab., B. A. E., 1884.

Kwamk (*Kwămk′*). A former Alsea village on the s. side of Alsea r., Oreg.—Dorsey in Jour. Am. Folk-lore, III, 230, 1890.

Kwan. The Agave clan of the Patki (Water-house) phratry of the Hopi.

Kwan wiñwû.—Fewkes in 19th Rep. B. A. E., 583, 1901 (*wiñwû*='clan'). **Kwan wüñ-wû.**—Fewkes in Am. Anthrop., VII, 402, 1894.

Kwanaken (*Kwāna′ken*, 'hollow in mountain'). A Squawmish village community on Squawmisht r., Brit. Col.—Hill-Tout in Rep. Brit. A. A. S., 474, 1900.

Kwane (*Kwā-nē*). A former village at C. Scott, N. end of Vancouver id., probably occupied by the Nakomgilisala.—Dawson in Can. Geol. Surv., map, 1887.

Kwantlen. An important Cowichan tribe between Stave r. and the mouth of the s. arm of Fraser r., Brit. Col. Pop. 125 in 1904. Villages: Kikait, Kwantlen, Skaiametl, Skaiets, and Wharnock. Kikait and Skaiametl were the original Kwantlen towns before the advent of the Hudson's Bay Company. (J. R. S.)

Kaitlen.—Dall, after Gibbs, in Cont. N. A. Ethnol., I, 241, 1877. **Koā′antEl.**—Boas in Rep. 64th Meeting B. A. A. S., 454, 1894. **Kuôôlt-e.**—Wilson in Jour. Ethnol. Soc. Lond., 329, 1866. **Kwahnt-len.**—Gibbs, MS. vocab., B. A. E., no. 281. **Kwaitlens.**—De Smet, Oregon Miss., 58, 1847. **Kwa′ntlEn.**—Hill-Tout in Ethnol. Surv. Can., 53, 1902. **Kwantlin.**—

Tolmie and Dawson, Vocabs. Brit. Col., 120B, 1884. **Kwantlum.**—Mayne, Brit. Col., 243, 1861. **Kwantlun.**—Ibid., 295. **Quaitlin.**—Scouler (1846) in Jour. Ethnol. Soc. Lond., I, 234, 1848. **Quant-lums.**—Fitzhugh in Ind. Aff. Rep. 1857, 329, 1858. **Quā′tl.**—Wilson in Jour. Ethnol. Soc. Lond., 278, 1866.

Kwantlen. The main Kwantlen village, situated at Ft Langley, on lower Fraser r., Brit. Col.; pop. 39 in 1904.

Kwa′ntlEn.—Hill-Tout in Ethnol. Surv. Can., 54, 1902. **Langley.**—Can. Ind. Aff., pt. II, 72, 1902.

Kwapahag. Mentioned in a letter sent by the Abnaki to the governor of New England, in 1721, as one of the divisions of their tribe.

K8apahag.—Abnaki letter (1721) in Mass. Hist. Soc. Coll., 2d s., VIII, 262, 1819.

Kwashkinawan ('is-there-no-water town'). A ruined Zuñi pueblo not far from the Manuelito road, 15 m. N. W. of Zuñi pueblo, near the Arizona and New Mexico boundary. (F. H. C.)

Kwatami ('on the gulf'). A subdivision of the Tututni, formerly living on or near Sixes r., Oreg., but now on Siletz res. Parker (Jour., 257, 1840) regarded them as a part of the Umpqua. Parrish (Ind. Aff. Rep. 1854, 496, 1855) placed them in 3 villages on the Pacific coast s. of Coquille r., near the mouth of Flores cr., at Sixes r., and at Port Orford. In 1854 they were governed by a principal chief, Hahhultalah, living at Sixes r., and a subchief, Tayonecia, residing at Port Orford. This band claimed all the country between the coast and the summit of the Coast range, from the s. boundary of the Nasumi to Humbug mt., 12 m. s. of Port Orford. In 1854 (Ind. Aff. Rep., 495, 1855) the Kwatami consisted of 53 men, 45 women, 22 boys, and 23 girls; total, 143. In 1877 (Ind. Aff. Rep., 300, 1877) they numbered 72.

Godamyon.—Framboise (1835) quoted by Gairdner in Jour. Geog. Soc. Lond., XI, 256, 1841. **Klantlalas.**—Ind. Aff. Rep. 1856, 219, 1857 (possibly identical). **Kwa′-ʒa′-me ʒûnnĕ′.**—Dorsey in Jour. Am. Folk-lore, III, 233, 1890 ('people on the gulf'). **Kwa-ʒa′-mi.**—Ibid. **K′watûmáti′-tĕne′.**—Everett, Tututĕne MS. vocab., B. A. E., 183, 1882 (='people by the little creek'). **Port Orford Indians proper.**—Kautz, MS. Census, B. A. E., 1855. **Quahtah-mah.**—Ibid. **Quah-to-mah.**—Parrish in Ind. Aff. Rep. 1854, 495, 1855. **Quakoumwahs.**—Domenech, Deserts N. Am., I, map, 1860. **Quakouwahs.**—Schoolcraft, Ind. Tribes, III, 96, map, 1853. **Quatomah.**—Hubbard (1856) in Cal. Farmer, June 8, 1860. **Qua-tou-wah.**—Dart (1851) in Ex. Doc. 57, 32d Cong., 1st sess., 59, 1852. **Quattamya.**—Parker, Jour., 257, 1840. **Saquaacha.**—Schoolcraft, Ind. Tribes, VI, 702, 1857. **Sequalchin.**—Dorsey in Jour. Am. Folk-lore, III, 233, 1890 (popular name). **Sequarchin.**—Ibid. **Se-queh-cha.**—Gibbs, MS. on Coast tribes, B. A. E. **Shix river.**—Abbott in Ind. Aff. Rep. 1854, 482, 1855. **Sik′ses-tĕne′.**—Everett, Tututene MS. vocab., 183, 1882 ('people by the far north country'). **Siquitchib.**—Gairdner (1835) in Jour. Geog. Soc. Lond., XI, 256, 1841. **Six.**—Ind. Aff. Rep. 300, 1877. **Sixes.**—Abbott, MS. Census, B. A. E., 1858. **Suc-qua-cha-to-ny.**—Ibid. **Sûk-kwe′-tĕ.**—Dorsey in Jour. Am. Folk-lore, III, 233, 1890 (Naltunne name). **T′ĕ-ʒa′ ʒûnnĕ.**—Dorsey, Chetco MS. vocab., B. A. E., 1884 (='northern language': Chetco name).

Kwatanakyanaan (*Kwá-tá-na K′ya-na-an*, 'town of the cave-enclosed spring'). A ruined pueblo of the Zuñi, about 40 m. s. w. of Zuñi pueblo, N. Mex. (F. H. C.)

Kwatchampedau ('petota [a plant] lying on the ground'). A Maricopa village on the Rio Gila, Ariz.—ten Kate, inf'n, 1888.

Kwatsei. The Shell-bead clan of San Ildefonso pueblo, N. Mex.
Kwatsei-tdóa.—Hodge in Am. Anthrop., IX, 352, 1896 (tdóa='people').

Kwatsi. A Kwakiutl village at Pt Macdonald, Knight inlet, Brit. Col., inhabited by the Tenaktak and Awaitlala; pop. 171 in 1885.
Kwā-tsi.—Dawson in Trans. Roy. Soc. Can. for 1887, sec. II, 65. Qoatse.—Boas in Bul. Am. Geog. Soc., 229, 1887.

Kwaustums (Gwā'ᵉyasdᴇmsē, 'feasting place.'—Boas). A winter village of the Koeksotenok on Gilford id., Brit. Col.; pop. 263 in 1885.
Gwā'ᵉyasdᴇmsē.—Boas in Mem. Am. Mus. Nat. Hist., V, pt. 1, 156, 1902. Kwā-us-tums.—Dawson in Trans. Roy. Soc. Can. for 1887, sec. II, 73. Qoaiastems.—Boas in Bul. Am. Geog. Soc., 228, 1887. Qua-ya-stums.—Ibid.

Kwayo. The Hawk clan of the Pakab phratry of the Hopi.
Kwa'-yo.—Stephen in 8th Rep. B. A. E., 39, 1891. Kwayo wiñwû.—Fewkes in 19th Rep. B. A. E., 584, 1900 (wiñwû='clan'). Kwa'-yo wüñ-wû.—Fewkes in Am. Anthrop., VII, 403, 1894.

Kwazackmash. Mentioned as one of the tribes that participated in the treaty of Pt Elliott, Wash., in 1855. Perhaps the Suquamish. They numbered 42 in 1870.
Kwa-zackmash.—Ross in Ind. Aff. Rep., 17, 1870.

Kweakpak. A Magemiut Eskimo village in the tundra s. of the Yukon delta, Alaska; pop. 75 in 1890.
Queakhpaghamiut.—Eleventh Census, Alaska, 110, 1893.

Kwehtlmamish. A Salish division on upper branches of Snohomish r., Wash., now officially included under the Snohomish on Tulalip res. Pop. 66 in 1870.
Kwehtl-ma-mish.—Gibbs in Cont. N. A. Ethnol., I, 179, 1877. Kwent-le-ah-mish.—Winans in Ind. Aff. Rep., 17, 1870. N'Quentl-ma-mish.—U.S. Ind. Treat., 378, 1873. N'Quentlmaymish.—Taylor in Sen. Ex. Doc. 4, 40th Cong., spec. sess., 3, 1867. N'quutl-ma-mish.—Stevens in Ind. Aff. Rep., 458, 1854. Nugh-Kwetle-babish.—Mallet, ibid., 198, 1877. Qunkma-mish.—Gibbs in Pac. R. R. Rep., I, 436, 1855.

Kwekweakwet ('blue'). A Shuswap village near upper Fraser r., 11 m. above Kelley cr., Brit. Col. Probably the town of the High Bar band, which numbered 54 in 1904.
High Bar.—Can. Ind. Aff., 274, 1902. Kwē-kwē-a-kwēt'.—Dawson in Trans. Roy. Soc. Can., sec. II, 44, 1891.

Kweleluk. A Kuskwogmiut Eskimo village on a small river in the tundra N. of Kuskokwim bay, Alaska; pop. 112 in 1890.
Kweleluk.—Baker, Geog. Dict. Alaska, 1902. Quelelochamiut.—Eleventh Census, Alaska, 109, 1893.

Kwengyauinge (Tewa: 'blue turquoise house'). A large pueblo ruin, attributed to the Tewa, situated on a conical hill, about 150 ft high, overlooking Chama r. at a point known as La Puenta, about 3 m. below Abiquiu, Rio Arriba co., N. Mex.—Hewett in Bull. 32, B. A. E., 26, 1906.

Kwesh. One of the divisions of the Tonkawa. (A. S. G.)

Kweundlas (Q!wē ᵍ'ᴀnʟas, 'muddy stream'). A former Haida town on the w. coast of Long id., Alaska. It appears in John Work's list (1836–41) as Quia-han-less, with 8 houses and 148 people. Petroff gives the number of inhabitants in 1880–81 as 62, but the town site is now used only for potato patches. It was occupied by the Yehlnaas-hadai, a branch of the Yaku-lanas. (J. R. S.)
Gu-ai-hendlas-hādē.—Krause, Tlinkit Indianer, 304, 1885. Koianglas.—Petroff in 10th Census, Alaska, 32, 1884. Kwaihāntlas Hāadē.—Harrison in Proc. and Trans. Roy. Soc. Can., sec. II, 125, 1895. Qui a han less.—Schoolcraft, Ind. Tribes, V, 489, 1855 (after Work, 1836–41). Q!wē ᵍᴀ'nʟas.—Swanton, Cont. Haida, 282, 1905.

Kwewu. The Wolf clan of the Hopi.
Kwe'-wû-üh wüñ-wû.—Fewkes in Am. Anthrop., VII, 403, 1894 wiñwû='clan'). Kwewû wñwû.—Fewkes in 19th Rep. B. A. E., 584, 1900 (misprint).

Kwiahok. A Chnagmiut Eskimo village at the s. mouth of the Kwikluak pass of the Yukon, Alaska.
Kweé-ahogemut.—Dall, Alaska, 264, 1870.

Kwichtenem (Kwi'tctenᴇm). A Squawmish village community on the w. side of Howe sd., Brit. Col.—Hill-Tout in Rep. Brit. A. A. S., 474, 1900.

Kwiengomats (Kwi-en'-go-mats). A Paiute band, numbering 18 in 1873, at which time they dwelt at Indian spring, s. Nev.—Powell in Ind. Aff. Rep. 1873, 50, 1874.

Kwigunts. A Paiute band in s. Utah.—Ingalls in H. R. Ex. Doc. 66, 42d Cong., 3d sess., 2, 1873.

Kwik ('river'). A Kuskwogmiut Eskimo village on the right bank of Kuskokwim r., Alaska, 10 m. above Bethel; pop. 215 in 1880.
Kooigamute.—Petroff in 10th Census, Alaska, 17, 1884. Kwégamut.—Kilbuck cited by Baker, Geog. Dict. Alaska, 1902. Kwigamute.—Petroff, op. cit., map. Kwik.—Baker, Geog. Dict. Alaska, 1902.

Kwik. A Malemiut Eskimo village on a stream near the head of Norton sd., Alaska; pop. 30 in 1880.
Kooigamute.—Petroff, Rep. on Alaska, 53, 1881. Kuikli.—Map cited by Baker, Geog. Dict. Alaska, 259, 1902. Kvigmut.—Zagoskin, Desc. Russ. Poss. in Am., pt. 1, 72, 1847. Kvikh.—Petroff in 10th Census, Alaska, map, 1884. Kviougmioute.—Zagoskin in Nouv. Ann. Voy., 5th s., XXI, map, 1850. Kwik.—Baker, op. cit. Kwikh.—Petroff in 10th Census, Alaska, map, 1884.

Kwik. A Malemiut village on the w. side of Bald Head, Norton bay, Alaska.
Isaacs.—Map cited by Baker, Geog. Dict. Alaska, 1902. Kwik.—Ibid.

Kwik. A Nunivagmiut Eskimo village on the s. shore of Nunivak id., Alaska; pop. 43 in 1890.
Kweegamute.—Eleventh Census, Alaska, map, 1893. Kwigamiut.—Ibid., 111. Kwik.—Baker, Geog. Dict. Alaska, 1902.

Kwikak. A Kuskwogmiut Eskimo village on upper Kuskokwim r., Alaska; pop. 314 in 1880.
Kwigalogamut.—Nelson in 18th Rep. B. A. E., map, 1899. Kwigalogamute.—Petroff in 10th Census, Alaska, 17, 1884. Kwikagamut.—Geol. Surv. quoted by Baker, Geog. Dict. Alaska, 1902. Kwikak.—Baker, ibid. Queékagamut.—Kilbuck quoted by Baker, ibid.

Kwikak. A Chnagmiut Eskimo village on the coast of the Yukon delta, s. of Black r., Alaska.

Kwikagamiut.—Coast Surv. (1898) quoted by Baker, Geog. Dict. Alaska, 1902. Kwikak.—Baker, ibid.

Kwikluagmiut. One of the two divisions into which Holmberg divided the Ikogmiut of the Yukon delta; so named because they inhabit Kwikluak slough or pass.

Kwikhluágemut.—Dall, Alaska, 407, 1870. Kwithluǎg'emūt.—Holmberg quoted by Dall in Cont. N. A. Ethnol., I, 17, 1877.

Kwikoaenok (*Kwi'koaēnóx*, 'those at the lower end of the village'). A gens of the Guauaenok, a Kwakiutl tribe.—Boas in Rep. Nat. Mus. 1895, 331, 1897.

Kwikooi. A Shuswap village at the outlet of Adams lake, at the head of Thompson r., interior of British Columbia; pop., with Slahaltkam (q. v.), 190 in 1904.

Adams Lake.—Can. Ind. Aff., 259, 1882. Kwī-kooi'.—Dawson in Trans. Roy. Soc. Can. for 1891, sec. II, 44.

Kwikpagmiut. One of the two divisions into which Holmberg divided the Ikogmiut of the Yukon delta, Alaska; so named because they inhabit Kwikpak slough or pass. The name has also been applied to the Ikogmiut generally.

Kwikhpag'emūt.—Holmberg quoted by Dall in Cont. N. A. Ethnol., I, 17, 1877. Kwikhpágmut.—Dall, Alaska, 407, 1870.

Kwilaishauk (*Kwĭl-aic'-auk*). A former Yaquina village on the s. side of Yaquina r., Oreg.—Dorsey in Jour. Am. Folk-lore, III, 229, 1890.

Kwilchana (*Qwĭltca'na*, sig. doubtful). A village of the Nicola band of the Ntlakyapamuk, on Nicola lake, Brit. Col.; pop. 111 in 1901, the last time the name appears.

Kinsaatin.—Can. Ind. Aff., 302, 1893. Kōiltca'na.—Hill-Tout in Rep. Ethnol. Surv. Can., 4, 1899. Kuisaatin.—Can. Ind. Aff., 313, 1892. Quinshaatin.—Ibid., pt. II, 166, 1901. Qwĭltca'na.—Teit in Mem. Am. Mus. Nat. Hist., II, 174, 1900.

Kwilokuk. An Eskimo village in the Kuskokwim district, Alaska; pop. 12 in 1890.

Quilochugamiut.—Eleventh Census, Alaska, 164, 1893.

Kwilsieton. A division of the Chasta on Rogue r., Oreg., in 1854, which J. O. Dorsey (MS., B. A. E.) thought may be identical with the Kushetunne of the Tututni.

Quil-si-eton.—U. S. Ind. Treat. (1854), 23, 1873.

Kwinak. A Kuskwogmiut Eskimo village and Moravian mission in Alaska, on the E. side of Kuskokwim r., at its mouth; pop. 83 in 1880, 109 in 1890.

Kwinak.—Sarichef (1826) quoted by Baker, Geog. Dist. Alaska, 1902. Kwygyschpainagmjut.—Holmberg, Ethnog. Skizz., 5, 1855. Quinchaha.—Postroute map, 1903. Quinehaha.—Bruce, Alaska, map, 1885. Quinehahamute.—Petroff, Rep. on Alaska, 53, 1881. Quinhaghamiut.—Eleventh Census, Alaska, 100, 1893.

Kwineekcha (*Kwin-eek'-cha*, 'long body'). A subclan of the Delawares (q. v.).—Morgan, Anc. Soc., 172, 1877.

Kwingyap. The Oak clan of the Asa phratry of the Hopi.

Kwi'ñobi.—Stephen in 8th Rep. B. A. E., 39, 1891. Kwiñ-yap wüñ-wû.—Fewkes in Am. Anthrop., VII, 405, 1894 (wüñ-wû='clan'). Quingoi.—Bourke, Snake Dance, 117, 1884.

Kwisaesekeesto (*Kwis-aese-kees'-to*, 'deer'). A subclan of the Delawares (q. v.).—Morgan, Anc. Soc., 172, 1877.

Kwitchakutchin ('people of the steppes'). A Kutchin tribe inhabiting the country between Mackenzie and Anderson rs., lat. 68°, British America.

Kodhell-vén-Kouttchin.—Petitot, Autour du lac des Esclaves, 361, 1891 (='people of the margin of the sterile Eskimo lands'). Kǔtch'-ä kǔtch'ĭn.—Ross, MS. notes on Tinne, B.A.E. (='people in a country without mountains'). Kwitcha-Kuttchin.—Petitot, Dict. Dènè-Dindjié, xx, 1876. Kwitchia-Kutchin.—Petitot, in Bul. Soc. de Géog. Paris, chart, 1875.

Kwiumpus ('bear river people'). A Paiute tribe formerly living in the vicinity of Beaver, s. w. Utah; pop. 29 in 1873.—Powell in Ind. Aff. Rep. 1873, 50, 1874. Cf. *Cumumbah*.

Kwohitsauk. See *Wovoka*.

Kwolan (*K·wo'lān*, 'ear'). A Squawmish village community on the right bank of Squawmisht r., Brit. Col.—Hill-Tout in Rep. Brit. A. A. S., 474, 1900.

Kwoneatshatka. An unidentified division of the Nootka near the N. end of Vancouver id.—Hale in U. S. Expl. Exped., VI, 569, 1846.

Kworatem. A locality and a camp or village at the confluence of Klamath and Salmon rs., N. w. Cal., on the E. bank of the former and the s. bank of the latter. The name is not Karok, in whose territory the place is situated, but from the Yurok language spoken farther down Klamath r. According to the Yurok custom, Kworatem, being the name of the place nearest the mouth of Salmon r., was used for the river itself, though always with the addition of a term like *umerneri*, 'stream.' The name Quoratem was erroneously used by Gibbs for the Karok Indians, and was adopted by Powell in the adjectival form Quoratean (q. v.) as the name of the linguistic family constituted by the Karok.   (A. L. K.)

Cor-a-tem.—McKee (1851) in Sen. Ex. Doc. 4, 32d Cong., spec. sess., 163, 1853. Quoratem.—Gibbs (1851) in Schoolcraft, Ind. Tribes, III, 151, 1853. Quoratems—Ibid.

Kwotoa. A division of the Maidu at Placerville, Eldorado co., Cal.

Kwo-to'-a.—Powers in Cont. N. A. Ethnol., III, 315, 1877. Quotoas.—Powers in Overland Mo., XII, 22, 1874.

Kwsichichu (*Kwsi'-ɿci-ɿcu'*). A former Siuslaw village s. of Eugene City, Oreg.—Dorsey in Jour. Am. Folk-lore, III, 230, 1890.

Kwulaishauik (*Kwŭl-ai'-cau-ɿk*). A former Yaquina village on the N. side of Yaquina r., Oreg.—Dorsey in Jour. Am. Folk-lore, III, 229, 1890.

Kwulchichicheshk (*Kwŭl-tci'-tci-tcĕck*). A former Yaquina village on the s. side

of Yaquina r., below Elk City, Oreg.—
Dorsey in Jour. Am. Folk-lore, III, 229,
1890.

Kwulhauunnich (*Kwŭl-hau'-ŭn-nītc'*).
A former Siuslaw village on Siuslaw r.,
Oreg.—Dorsey in Jour. Am. Folk-lore,
III, 230, 1890.

Kwulisit (*Kwû-li'-sĭt*). A former Alsea
village on the s. side of Alsea r., Oreg.—
Dorsey in Jour. Am. Folk-lore, III, 230,
1890.

Kwullaish (*Kwŭl-laic'*). A former Ya-
quina village on the s. side of Yaquina r.,
Oreg.—Dorsey in Jour. Am. Folk-lore,
III, 922, 1890.

Kwullakhtauik (*Kwŭl'-laq-t'au'ĭk*). A
former Yaquina village on the s. side of
Yaquina r., Oreg.—Dorsey in Jour. Am.
Folk-lore, III, 229, 1890.

Kwultsaiya (*Kwŭl-ısai'-yă*). A former
Siuslaw village on Siuslaw r., Oreg.—Dorsey in Jour. Am. Folk-lore, III, 230, 1890.

Kwunnumis (*Kwŭn'-nŭ-mĭs'*). A former
Siuslaw village on Siuslaw r., Oreg.—
Dorsey in Jour. Am. Folk-lore, III, 230,
1890.

Kwusathlkhuntunne ('people who eat
mussels'). A former village of the Tu-
tutni. Kautz, in 1855, placed it at the
mouth of Mussel cr., 5 m. s. of Mt Humbug, Oreg. In 1854 (Ind. Aff. Rep., 495,
1855) it numbered 27 persons. If any
survive they live on Siletz res., Oreg.
Co-soott-hen-ten.—Kautz, MS. Toutouten Census,
B. A. E., 1855. Cosotoul.—Palmer in Ind. Aff.
Rep., 217, 1856. Cosulhentan.—Schoolcraft, Ind.
Tribes, VI, 702, 1857. Cosulhenten.—Taylor in Cal.
Farmer, June 8, 1860. Cosutheuten.—Parrish in
Ind. Aff. Rep. 1854, 496, 1855. Co-sutt-heu-tun.—
Ibid., 495. Ko-sul-te-me.—Gibbs, MS. on coast
tribes, B. A. E. Kwûs-açl' qûn ıûnnĕ'.—Dorsey in
Jour. Am. Folk-lore, III, 233, 1890.

Kwuskwemus (*K'wŭs'-k'wê-mŭs'*). A
former Siuslaw village on Siuslaw r.,
Oreg.—Dorsey in Jour. Am. Folk-lore,
III, 230, 1890.

Kwutichuntthe (*Kwût'-ti-tcun'-t'çĕ*). A
former Yaquina village on the s. side of
Yaquina r., Oreg.—Dorsey in Jour. Am.
Folk-lore, III, 229, 1890.

Kyakyali. The Eagle clan of the Zuñi
of New Mexico.
K'yä'k'yäli-kwe.—Cushing in 13th Rep. B. A. E.,
368, 1896 (*kwe*='people').

Kyalishi-ateuna (*K'yälishi-áteuna*,
'those of the westernmost'). A phratry
embracing the Suski (Coyote) and Poye
(Chaparral-cock) clans of the Zuñi of
New Mexico.   (F. H. C.)

Kyamaisu (*Kyä-mai'-su*). A former
Alsea village at the mouth of Alsea r.,
Oreg., on the N. side.—Dorsey in Jour.
Am. Folk-lore, III, 229, 1890.

Kyamakyakwe ('snail-shell houses').
A massive ruined pueblo, built of lava
blocks, situated 47 m. s. s. w. of Zuñi, N.
Mex. According to Zuñi tradition this
settlement, together with Pikyaiawan and
Kyatsutuma, was the northernmost home
of the Snail people, whose dance is an-

nually performed by members of the
Black-corn clan of the Zuñi, who claim
descent from the Kyamakyakwe people.
The towns mentioned formed the northern outposts of the "Kingdom of Marata" (see *Matyata*), and were conquered
by the Zuñi prior to Coronado's visit in
1540, the "Corn captives" being spared
on account of their ceremonies and their
advancement in agriculture. (F. H. C.)
Cha-ma-kia.—Fewkes in Jour. Am. Eth. and Arch.,
I, 100, 1891. Kyamakyakwe.—Cushing, inf'n, 1892.

Kyana. The extinct Water clan of Zuñi
pueblo, N. Mex.
K'yána-kwe.—Cushing in 13th Rep. B. A. E., 368,
1896 (*kwe*='people').

Kyatiikya (*K'yätiik'ya*, 'water drops
come out'). A ruined pueblo at the
mouth of the canyon opposite the E. end
of Thunder mt., near Zuñi, N. Mex.; so
named because the water on which its
inhabitants depended oozed from the canyon walls.   (F. H. C.)
Chat-e-cha.—Fewkes in Jour. Am. Eth. and Arch.,
I, 100, 1891. K'yätiik'ya.—Cushing, inf'n, 1892.

Kyatsutuma (*K'yä-tsu-tu-ma*, 'town of
the dewdrops'). A former town which,
with Kyamakyakwe and Pikyaiawan,
was the northernmost home of the Snail
people and one of the outposts or strongholds of Matyata (q. v.), which were conquered by the Zuñi in late prehistoric
times.   (F. H. C.)

Kyaukuhu (*Kyau'-ku-hu*). A former Ya-
quina village on the N. side of Yaquina r.,
Oreg.—Dorsey in Jour. Am. Folk-lore,
III, 229, 1890.

Kyawana-tehuatsana (*K'yáwana-téhua-
tsana*, 'little gateway of Zuñi river'). A
prehistoric Zuñi village, now in ruins,
about 7 m. E. of Zuñi pueblo, on a mesa
above the "gateway," whence its name.
Cha-wa-na.—Fewkes in Jour. Am. Eth. and Arch.,
I, 100, 1891. Ky-a-wa-na Tehua-tsana.—Ibid., 96.
K'yawana Tehua-tsana.—Cushing, Zuñi Folk Tales,
297, 1901.

Kyekykyenok (*K·ek·k·"ēnóx*). A gens
of the Awaitlala, a Kwakiutl tribe.—Boas
in Rep. Nat. Mus. 1895, 331, 1897.

Kyiahl. The Crow clan of Jemez
pueblo, N. Mex. A corresponding clan
existed at the former related pueblo of
Pecos.
Kyiá'hl+.—Hodge in Am. Anthrop., IX, 350, 1896
(Pecos name; +=*ash*, or *tsaásh*, 'people').
Kyialish.—Ibid. (Jemez name).

Kyunggang. The Hawk clan of San
Ildefonso pueblo, N. Mex.
Kyuⁿgäⁿ-tdóa.—Hodge in Am. Anthrop., IX, 351,
1896 (*tdóa*='people').

Kyunu. The Corn clan of Jemez
pueblo, N. Mex. A corresponding clan
existed at the former related pueblo of
Pecos.
Kyunu'+.—Hodge in Am. Anthrop., IX, 349, 1896
(Pecos form; +=*ash*, or *tsaásh*, 'people'). Kyu-
nutsa-ásh.—Ibid. (Jemez form).

Kyuquot. A Nootka tribe on Kyuquot
sd., w. coast of Vancouver id.; pop. 305
in 1902, 281 in 1904. Its principal villages are Aktese and Kukamukamees.

Cayoquits.—Armstrong, Oregon, 136, 1857. **Cayu-quets.**—Jewitt, Narr., 77, 1849. **Kayŏ'kath.**—Boas in 6th Rep. N. W. Tribes Can., 31, 1890. **Kayo-kuaht.**—Brit. Col. map, 1872. **Kȳcŭ-cūt.**—Mayne, Brit. Col., 251, 1861. **Ky-u-kaht.**—Can. Ind. Aff., 276, 1894. **Ky-uk-ahts.**—Ibid., 52, 1875. **Kyuquot.**—Swan, MS., B. A. E. **Ky-wk-aht.**—Can. Ind. Aff., 188, 1883. **Ky-yoh-quaht.**—Sproat, Sav. Life, 308, 1868.

Kyuwatkal (*Kyu'-wăt-kăl*). A former Yaquina village on the N. side of Yaquina r., Oreg.—Dorsey in Jour. Am. Folk-lore, III, 229, 1890.

Laalaksentaio. A gens of the true Kwakiutl, embracing the subdivisions Laalaksentaio, Alkunwea, and Hehametawe. **Laa'laqsᴇnt'aiō.**—Boas in 6th Rep. N. W. Tribes Can., 54, 1890. **Lā'alaxsᴇnt'aiō.**—Boas in Rep. Nat. Mus. 1895, 330, 1897. **Lálachsent'aiō.**—Boas in Petermanns Mitt., pt. 5, 131, 1887.

Labor, Division of. The common impression that the Indian woman was a mere slave and drudge for her husband is an error due to ignorance of the Indian division of labor in accordance with the necessities of savage life. Briefly stated, it was the man's business to provide meat and skins from the forest and plain and to protect the home from enemies, while the woman attended to the household duties of preparing the food, arranging the house interior, and caring for the children. The preparation of the food implied also the principal work of cultivation among the agricultural tribes, with the bringing of the wood and water, while household work included the making of pottery, basketry, and mats. The men themselves frequently made their own buckskin dress, and almost always their ceremonial costume. Among the Pueblos the greater part of the buckskin clothing, including leggings and moccasins, for both sexes, was made by the men. The heavier part of the Pueblo weaving also was the work of the men, the women confining themselves for the greater part to the production of belts and other small pieces. Among the Navaho, on the other hand, the weaving work was about evenly divided. The men fashioned their weapons, and the articles of more laborious construction, as stone hatchets, canoes, fish weirs, etc. As tribes were constantly at war one with another and the pursuit of game carried the hunter into disputed territory, the first business of every man was to be a warrior, forever on the alert for danger. This condition left him very little leisure for other pursuits excepting during the season when his enemies also were unable to travel. His wife, recognizing this fact, took up her share of the burden cheerfully, and would have scorned as effeminate the husband who took any other view of the situation. Among the more sedentary and agricultural tribes, where the procuring of food did not necessitate hostile collision with other tribes, the men usually did their fair share of the home work, laboring in the fields together with the women. In general, it may be said that the man assumed the dangerous duty, the woman the safer routine work. The frequent sacrifice ordeals, intended to win the favor of the gods of the tribe, were borne almost entirely by the men, the part of the women being chiefly that of applauding spectators. The woman remained mistress of the home, and in spite of the variety of her duties, the number of women's games furnish testimony that she enjoyed her leisure in her own way. See *Popular fallacies, Women.* (J. M.)

Labrets. Ornaments worn in holes that are pierced through the lips. Cabeza de Vaca notes of Indians of the Texas coast: "They likewise have the nether lip bored, and within the same they carry a piece of thin cane about half a finger thick." It is quite certain that this custom prevailed for some distance inland along the Colorado r. of Texas and in neighboring regions, while large labrets were also found by Cushing among the remains on the w. coast of Florida. Outside of this region they were almost restricted to an area in the N. W., the habitat of the Aleut, Haida, Heiltsuk, Tlingit, Tsimshian, and Eskimo tribes, extending from Dean inlet to Anderson r. on the Arctic coast. They were also adopted by some of the western Athapascans. Here the lower lip alone was pierced. While the southern tribes made a single aperture in the middle of the lip, and consequently used but one labret, the Aleut and Eskimo usually punctured a hole below each corner of the mouth and inserted two. Moreover, among the southern tribes the ornament was worn only by women, while Aleut men used it occasionally and Eskimo men more and more generally, as one proceeded northward, until beyond the Yukon the use of labrets was confined to males. Among the Haida, Heiltsuk, Tlingit, and Tsimshian the labret was a mark of high birth, superseding in this respect the head-flattening of the tribes living farther s. The piercing was consequently done during potlatches, a small aperture being bored first, which was enlarged from year to year until it sometimes became so great that the lip proper was reduced to a narrow ribbon, which was liable to break, and sometimes did. The labrets were made of wood, stone, bone, or abalone shell, often inlaid, and present two general types, namely, a long piece inserted into the lip at one end, or a round or oval stud hollowed on each side and protruding but slightly from the face. George Dixon noted one of this latter type that was $3\frac{7}{8}$ in. long by $2\frac{5}{8}$ in. broad. The last labrets used were small plugs of silver, and the custom has now been entirely abandoned. On account of the use of these ornaments the Tlingit were called Kolosch by their northern neighbors and the Russians, whence the name Koluschan, adopted for the linguistic stock.

Among the Eskimo and Aleut bone labrets predominated, though some very precious specimens were of jade. They were shaped like buttons or studs, or, in the case of some worn by women, like sickles. The lips of men were pierced only at puberty, and the holes were enlarged successively by means of plugs,

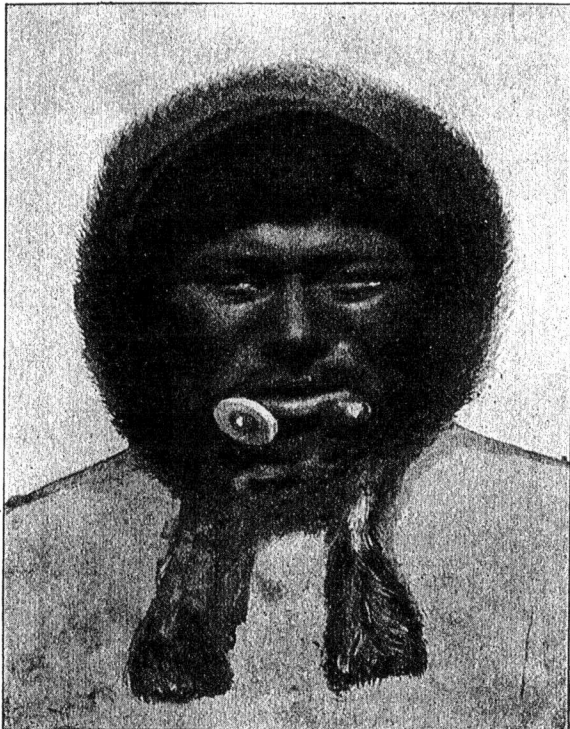

LABRETS, WESTERN ESKIMO.　(NELSON)

which were often strung together afterward and preserved. For further illustration of the use of labrets, see *Adornment*.

Consult Dall (1) in 3d Rep. B. A. E., 1884, (2) in Cont. N. A. Ethnol., I, 1877; Dawson, Rep. on Queen Charlotte Ids., Geol. Surv. Canada, 1880; Murdoch in 9th Rep. B. A. E., 1892; Nelson in 18th Rep. B. A. E., 1899.　　　　(J. R. S.)

Lacame. A province visited by Moscoso, of De Soto's expedition, toward the close of the year 1542; probably in s. w. Arkansas.
Lacame.—Biedma (1544) in French, Hist. Coll. La., II, 108, 1850. Lacane.—Gentl. of Elvas in Hakluyt Soc. Pub., IX, 135, 1851.

Lacayamu. Two former Chumashan villages, one on Santa Cruz id., the other in Ventura co., Cal.
Lacayamu.—Taylor in Cal. Farmer, Apr. 24, July 24, 1863. Lucuyumu.—Bancroft, Native Races, I, 459, 1874.

Lac Court Oreilles. A Chippewa band, named from the lake on which they lived, at the headwaters of Chippewa r., in Sawyer co., Wis. In 1852 they formed a part of the Betonukeengainubejig division of the Chippewa, and in 1854 were assigned a reservation. In 1905 they were officially reported to number 1,214, to whom lands had been allotted in severalty.
Lac Court d'Oreille band.—Ind. Aff. Rep., 254, 1877. Lac Court Oreille band.—U. S. Stat. L., X, 223, 1854. Lac Court Orielles.—La Pointe treaty (1854) in U. S. Ind. Treat., 224, 1873. Lac Court, Orville.— Fitch in Ind. Aff. Rep. 1857, 28, 1858. Lac Coutereille.—Warren (1852) in Minn. Hist. Soc. Coll., v, 191, 1885. Ottawa lake men.—Ibid., 39.

Lachalsap. A village of the Hwotsotenne on Bulkley r., Brit. Col.; pop. 157 in 1904.
Lachalsap.—Can. Ind. Aff., pt. 2, 70, 1902. Lackalsap.—Ibid., 1903, pt. 2, 73, 1904. Moricetown.— Ibid., 70, 1902.

Lackawanna. A variety of coal. From *Lackawanna*, the name of a tributary of the Susquehanna and a county in Pennsylvania, which represents *lechauwanne* in the Lenape (Delaware) dialect, signifying 'the stream forks'; from *lechau*, 'fork', and -*hanne*, 'stream,' 'river'. (A. F. C.)

Lackawaxen (*Lechauwéksink*, 'the forks of the road'). Mentioned by Alcedo (Dic. Geog., II, 565, 1787) as a former Indian (Delaware?) settlement on the E. branch of Delaware r., Pa. The E. branch of the Delaware is in New York, and the settlement, if ever existing, was probably on Lackawaxen cr., a tributary of the Delaware in N. E. Pennsylvania. Heckewelder (Trans. Am. Philos. Soc., IV, 359, 1834) mentions this as the Delaware name for two places, one in Wayne co. and the other in Northampton co., Pa.
Lechavaksein.—Alcedo, op. cit. Lechawaxen.— Heckewelder, op. cit.

Lacrosse. See *Ball play*.

Ladles.—See *Dishes, Gourds, Receptacles.*

Lady Rebecca. See *Pocahontas*.

Laenukhuma (*Laĕ′nuχuma*). Given by Boas (Petermanns Mitt., pt. 5, 131, 1887) as the ancestor of a gens of the Quatsino; also applied to the gens itself.

La Flesche, Francis. Son of Estamaza, or Joseph La Flesche, former head chief of the Omaha, born in Thurston co., Nebr., Dec. 25, 1857. He attended the Presbyterian mission school on the Omaha res., where he laid the foundation of his later education. In 1878–79 he accompanied the Ponca chief Standing Bear on his eastern tour and interpreted his presentation of the wrongs his people had suffered in the removal from their home in South Dakota. During an investigation of the Ponca removal by a committee of the U. S. Senate he served again as interpreter and attracted the attention of the chairman by the impartial manner in which he performed his work. In

1881, when Hon. S. J. Kirkwood, the chairman of that committee, became Secretary of the Interior, he called Mr La Flesche to Washington and gave him a position in the Office of Indian Affairs, where he remains. In 1893 he was graduated from the National University Law School. The memory of the tribal life of his childhood stimulated him to study his people, for which his father's position gave him unusual advantage. His mastery of English has enabled him accurately to set forth the results of his ethnological investigations, in which he is still actively engaged. His published writings have appeared in the Journal of American Folk-lore and other scientific periodicals, in the "Study of Omaha Indian Music," by Alice C. Fletcher (Peabody Museum Pub.), and in popular magazines. He is the author also of "The Middle Five," a book giving the story of his school days. Mr La Flesche has made ethnological collections for the University of Berlin, the University of California, the Peabody Museum of American Archæology and Ethnology, and other institutions of learning. He is a fellow of the American Association for the Advancement of Science, and a member of the American Anthropological Association and of the Anthropological Society of Washington. In 1906 Mr La Flesche married Miss Rosa Bourassa, of Chippewa descent.   (A. C. F.)

La Flesche, Susette. See *Bright Eyes.*

Lagcay. A former Chumashan village near Santa Barbara, Cal.
Laco.—Taylor in Cal. Farmer, Apr. 24, 1863. Lagcay.—Ibid.

Lagrimas de San Pedro (Span.: 'tears of St Peter'). A former group of Alchedoma rancherias, on or near the Rio Colorado, in California, more than 50 m. below the mouth of Bill Williams fork. They were visited and so named by Fray Francisco Garcés in 1776.—Garcés, Diary, 427, 1900.

Laguna (Span.: 'lagoon', on account of a large pond west of the pueblo; aboriginal name Ka-waik′, an old Keresan word of unknown signification). A Keresan tribe whose principal pueblo, which bears the same popular name, is situated on the s. bank of San José r., Valencia co., N. Mex., about 45 m. w. of Albuquerque. It was formerly the seat of a Spanish mission, dating from its establishment as a pueblo in July, 1699, and having Acoma as a visita after 1782. The lands of the Lagunas consist of a Spanish grant of 125,225 acres, mostly of desert land. The Laguna people are composed of 19 clans, as follows, those marked with an asterisk being extinct: Kohaia (Bear), Ohshahch (Sun), Chopi (Badger), Tyami (Eagle), Skurshka (Water-snake), Sqowi (Rattlesnake), Tsushki (Coyote), Yaka (Corn; divided into Kochinish-yaka, or

Yellow-corn, and Kukinish-yaka, or Redcorn), Sits (Water), Tsina (Turkey), Kakhan (Wolf), Hatsi (Earth)*, Mokaiqch (Mountain lion)*, Shawiti (Parrot), Shuwimi (Turquoise), Shiaska (Chaparralcock), Kurtsi (Antelope), Meyo (Lizard), Hapai (Oak). Most of the clans constitute phratral groups, as follows: (1) Bear, Badger, Coyote, and Wolf; (2) Mountain-lion and Oak; (3) Water-snake, Rattlesnake, Lizard, and Earth; (4) Antelope and Water. According to Laguna tradition, the Bear, Eagle, Water, Turkey, and Corn clans, together with some members of the Coyote clan, came originally from Acoma; the Badger, Parrot, Chaparralcock, and Antelope clans, and some members of the Coyote clan, came from Zuñi; the Sun people originated probably in San Felipe; the Water-snake in Sia; the

JOSÉ PAISANO—LAGUNA

Rattlesnake probably in Oraibi; the Wolf and Turquoise in Sandia; the Earth clan in Jemez; the Mountain-lion and Oak people claim to have come from Mt Taylor; the Lizard clan is of unknown origin. Laguna therefore is not only the most recent of the New Mexican pueblos, but its inhabitants are of mixed origin, being composed of at least four linguistic stocks—Keresan, Tanoan, Shoshonean, and Zuñian. It is said that formerly the people were divided into two social groups, or phratries, known as Kapaits and Kayomasho, but these are now practically political parties, one progressive, the other conservative. Until 1871 the tribe occupied, except during the summer season, the single pueblo of Laguna, but this village is gradually becoming depopulated, the inhabitants establishing permanent residences in the former summer villages of Casa Blanca, Cubero, Hasatch, Paguate, Encinal, Santa Ana, Paraje, Tsiama, and Puertecito. Of these, Paguate is the oldest and most populous, containing 350 to 400 inhabitants in 1891. Former villages were Shinats and Shunaiki. The Laguna people numbered 1,384 in 1905. See *Keresan Family, Moquino, Pueblos, Rito, Shumasitscha,* and the villages above named. (F. W. H.)

Biérai.—Gatschet, Isleta MS. vocab., 1885 (Isleta name of pueblo). Biéride.—Ibid. (pl. Biérnin; Isleta name of people). Ka-hua-i-ko.—Jouvenceau in Cath. Pion., I, no. 9, 13, 1906. Kairaikome.—Kingsley, Stand. Nat. Hist., VI, 183, 1885. Kaiwáika.—Stephen in 8th Rep. B. A. E., 30, 1891 (Hopi name of pueblo). Kan-Ayko.—Loew in Wheeler Surv. Rep., app. LL, 178, 1875 (Laguna name of pueblo, *n*=*u*). Ka-uay-ko.—Bandelier in Arch. Inst. Papers, III, 260, 1890 (Laguna name of pueblo). Kawáhykaka.—Voth, Traditions of the Hopi, 11, 1895 (Hopi name). Kawaíhkaa.—Ibid., 143. Kawaík'.—Hodge, field notes, B. A. E., 1895 (Laguna name of pueblo). Ka-waik'.—ten Kate, Synonymie, 7, 1884 (Laguna name of pueblo). Ka-waikă'.—Ibid. Káwaıkama.—Hodge, field notes, B. A. E., 1895 (Santa Ana name of tribe). Kawáikăme.—ten Kate, Reizen in N. A., 230, 1885 (Laguna name of tribe). Kawaik'-ka-me.—ten Kate, Synonymie, 7, 1884 (Laguna name of tribe). Kawaikome.—Powell in Am. Nat., XIV, 604, Aug. 1880 (mentioned distinctly from Laguna). Kóiks.—Lummis, Man who Married the Moon, 202, 1894 (native name of Laguna). Ko-stété.—Loew in Wheeler Surv. Rep., VII, 339, 1879 (given as proper name of pueblo). Kŭhkweaí.—Hodge, field notes, B. A. E., 1895 (Isleta and Sandia name: see *Bierai,* above). K'ya-na-thlana-kwe.—Cushing, inf'n, 1891 (Zuñi name: 'people of the great pool or pond'). Lagana.—Gatschet in Wheeler Surv. Rep., VII, 405, 1879 (misprint). Lagouna.—Gallatin in Nouv. Ann. Voy., 5th s., XXVII, 297, 1851. Laguna.—MS. of 1702 quoted by Bandelier in Arch. Inst. Papers, V, 189, 1890; Villa-Señor, Theatro Am., pt. 2, 421, 1748. Lagune.—Gatschet in Mag. Am. Hist., 263, Apr. 1882. Lagunes.—Simpson in Rep. Sec. War, 150, 1850. Lagunians.—ten Broeck (1852) in Schoolcraft, Ind. Tribes, IV, 81, 88, 1854. La haguna.—Domenech, Deserts N. Am., I, 443, 1860. Layma.—ten Broeck in Schoolcraft, Ind. Tribes, IV, 77, 1854 (misprint). Saguna.—Klett in Pop. Sci. Monthly, V, 584, 1874 (misprint). San José de la Laguna.—Ward in Ind. Aff. Rep. 1867, 213, 1868 (mission name). San Josef de La Laguna.—Alencaster (1805) in Prince, N. Mex., 37, 1883. Seguna.—Pike, Exped., 3d map, 1810 (misprint). Sitsimé.—Gatschet in Mag. Am. Hist., 263, Apr. 1882 (Laguna name for themselves). Taguna.—Wallace, Land of the Pueblos, 45, 1888 (misprint). To-zăn'-ne'.—ten Kate, Synonymie, 6, 1884 ('much water': Navaho name). Tozjánne.—ten Kate, Reizen in N. A., 231, 1885 (Navaho name). Tuzhláni.—Hodge, field notes, B. A. E., 1895 (Navaho name of people).

Laguna. A Pomo band on the w. shore of Clear lake, Cal.—Revere, Tour of Duty, 120, 1849. See *Clear Lake Indians.*

Laguna. A Diegueño village in w. San Diego co., Cal. (Jackson and Kinney, Rep. Miss. Ind., 24, 1883). The name is now applied to one of the so-called Campo reservations, comprising 320 acres, mostly of desert land, and containing only 5 inhabitants in 1906 (Kelsey, Rep., 25, 1906).

Lahanna. A name applied by Lewis and Clark in 1805 to a body of Indians, said to number 2,000 in 120 houses, on both sides of

Columbia r. about Clarke's fork. This is in the country of the Pend d'Oreilles and Senijextee, but Lahanna corresponds to no known division.

Lahama.—Bancroft, Nat. Races, I, 314, 1882 (misquoting Morse). Lahanna.—Lewis and Clark, Exped., II, 475, 1814. La-hânna.—Orig. Jour. Lewis and Clark, VI, 119, 1905.

Lahaui (*Lā'qauī*). A village of the Nicomen tribe of Cowichan at the mouth of Wilson cr., on the s. side of Fraser r., Brit. Col.—Boas in Rep. Brit. A. A. S., 454, 1894.

Lahoocat. Mentioned by Lewis and Clark as an old Arikara village, occupied in 1797, abandoned about 1800. It was situated on an island in Missouri r., below the present Cheyenne River agency, S. Dak., and when occupied consisted of 17 lodges arranged in a circle and walled.

Lahoocat.—Lewis and Clark, Exped., I, 97, 1814. La hoo catt.—Orig. Jour. Lewis and Clark, I, 179, 1904.

Laidukatuwiwait (*Lai'-du-ka-tu-wi-wait*). A Paviotso band formerly living about the sink of the Humboldt, in w. Nevada.—Powell, Paviotso MS., B. A. E., 1881.

Laimon. Venegas (Hist. Cal., I, 55, 1759) states that the Indians of Loreto-Concho mission have specific names for the tribes of Lower California according to the regions occupied by them, as the Edu, Eduu, or Edues in the s.; that they call themselves Monquis, and those N. of Loreto are called Laymones; the latter are in fact Cochimi, the Edues virtually Pericui, though both, the Edues and the Laymones, contain some tribes of the Monquis. Cagnaguet and Kadakaman are given as Laimon divisions.

Lamoines.—Taylor in Cal. Farmer, May 18, 1860. Layamon.—Latham in Trans. Philol. Soc. Lond., 88, 1856. Laymon.—Prichard, Nat. Hist. Man., II, 553, 1855. Laymóna.—Baegert in Smithson. Rep. 1864, 393, 1865. Laymones.—Venegas, Hist. Cal., I, 55, 1759. Limonies.—Taylor in Browne, Res. Pac. Slope, app., 54, 1869.

Lajas (Span.: 'stone slabs,' translation of the native name). A Tepehuane pueblo, of 900 inhabitants, in the extreme N. part of the territory of Tepic, Mexico, about lat. 23°, lon. 105°. The children of the town, who prior to about 1890 had never seen a white person, are now instructed in Spanish and the rudiments of civilization and Christianity.

Eityam.—Lumholtz, Unknown Mexico, I, 457, 1902 (native name). Lajas.—Orozco y Berra, Geog., 319, 1864. San Francisco Lajas.—Ibid. (full Spanish name).

La Joya (Span.: 'the jewel'). A Luiseño village N. of San Luis Rey, in San Diego co., Cal., from which 180 Indians are said to have been present at the Temecula meeting in 1865 (Lovett in Rep. Ind. Aff., 124, 1865). The settlement is now on Potrero res., 75 m. from Mission Tule River agency.

La Jolla.—Jackson and Kinney, Rep. Mission Inds., 29, 1883. La Joya.—Hayes (1850) quoted by Bancroft, Nat. Races, I, 460, 1882.

Lajuchu. A former Chumashan village near Purísima mission, Santa Barbara co., Cal.—Taylor in Cal. Farmer, Oct. 18, 1861.

Lake Indians. A term used by English writers of the 18th century to designate the Indians living on the great lakes, especially the Chippewa and the Ottawa.

Lakisumne. A village of California whose language, according to Pinart, showed differences from that of the Cholovone (Mariposan stock), but was understood by them. If not related to the Cholovone, this village was probably Moquelumnan.
Lacquesumne.—Pinart, Cholovone MS., B. A. E., 1880. Lakisumne.—Bancroft, Nat. Races, I, 450, 1874. Sakisimme.—Ibid.

Lakkulzap ('on the town'). A modern Chimmesyan town, founded in 1872 by a Mr Green from Niska, the inhabitants having been drawn from the villages of Kitaix and Kitkahta. Pop. 183 in 1902, 145 in 1904.
Greenville.—Can. Ind. Aff. for 1889, 272 (name given by whites). Kach-als-ap.—Dorsey in Am. Antiq., XIX, 281, 1897 (misquoted from Can. Ind. Aff.). Lachalsap.—Can. Ind. Aff., 416, 1898. Lack-al-sap.—Ibid., 272, 1889. Lak-kul-zap.—Dorsey in Am. Antiq., XIX, 281, 1897.

Lakloukst (*Laqlō'ukst*). A Niska division of the Lakskiyek clan, living in the town of Kitwinhilk, on Nass r., Brit. Col.—Boas in 10th Rep. N. W. Tribes Can., 49, 1895.

Lakmiut. A Kalapooian tribe formerly residing on a river of the same name, a western tributary of the Willamette, in Oregon. They are now on Grande Ronde res., where they were officially stated to number 28 in 1905. They are steadily decreasing. The following were Lakmiut bands as ascertained by Gatschet in 1877: Ampalamuyu, Chantkaip, Chepenafa, Mohawk, Tsalakmiut, Tsampiak, Tsantatawa, and Tsantuisha.
Alakĕma'yuk.—Gatschet, Atfalati MS., B. A. E. (Atfalati name). Chelukamanches.—Ind. Aff. Rep. 1864, 503, 1865. Chelukimaukes.—Ind. Aff. Rep., 221, 1861. Lákmiuk. — Gatschet in Jour. Am. Folk-lore, XII, 213, 1899. Lakmiut.—Gatschet, Atfalati MS., B. A. E., 1877 (own name). Luck-a-mi-ute.—Pres. Mess., Sen. Ex. Doc. 39, 32d Cong., 1st sess., 2, 1852. Luckamuke.—Palmer in Ind. Aff. Rep. 1856, 196, 1857. Luckamutes.—Keane in Stanford, Compend., 519, 1878. Luckiamut.—Smith in Ind. Aff. Rep., 56, 1875. Luckiamute.—Victor in Overland Monthly, VII, 346, 1871. Luckimiute.—McClane in Ind. Aff. Rep., 184, 1887. Luckimute.—Huntington in Ind. Aff. Rep. 1867, 62, 1868. Lukemayuk.—Gatschet, Atfalati MS., B. A. E., 1877 (Atfalati name). Sackanoir.—Schoolcraft, Ind. Tribes, VI, 701, 1857 (after Lane). Suchamier.—Ibid., 689. Suck-a-mier.—Lane in Ind. Aff. Rep., 161, 1850.

Lakseel (*Laqsē'el*, 'on the ocean'). A Niska division belonging to the Kanhada clan, living in the towns of Andeguale and Kitlakdamix on Nass r., Brit. Col.—Boas in 10th Rep. N. W. Tribes Can., 49, 1895.

Lakskiyek (*Laqskī'yek*, 'on the eagle'). One of the 4 Chimmesyan clans. Local subdivisions bearing the same name are found in the Niska towns of Lakkulzap and Kitlakdamix, and in the Kitksan town of Kitwingach.—Boas in 10th Rep. N. W. Tribes Can., 49, 50, 1895.

Laktiaktl (*Laqt'iă'k·tl*). A Niska division of the Lakyebo (Wolf) clan, settled in the town of Kitwinshilk, on Nass r., Brit. Col.—Boas in 10th Rep. N. W. Tribes Can., 49, 1895.

Laktsemelik (*Laqts'Emē'liH*, 'on the beaver'). A Niska division of the Lakskiyek clan, living in the town of Kitlakdamix, on Nass r., Brit. Col.—Boas in 10th Rep. N. W. Tribes Can., 49, 1895.

Lakungida (perhaps a Haida name). A Niska town near the mouth of Nass r., Brit. Col. In 1870 its inhabitants exceeded 400, but in 1897 it contained not more than 50.—Dorsey in Am. Antiq., XIX, 279, 1897.

Lakweip (Niska: *Lāq'uyî'p*, 'on the prairie.'—Boas). An isolated Athapascan tribe, related to the Tahltan, formerly living on Portland canal, Alaska, but having quarreled with the Niska are now on the headwaters of Stikine r., Brit. Col. Their chief village is Gunakhe.
Lackweips.—Scott in Ind. Aff. Rep. 1869, 563, 1870. Laq'uyî'p.—Boas in 10th Rep. N. W. Tribes Can., 34, 1895. Naqkyina.—Ibid. (Tsetsaut name: 'on the other side').

Lakyebo (*Laqkyebō*, 'on the wolf'). One of the 4 clans into which all the Chimmesyan are divided. The name is applied specifically to various local subdivisions as well, there being one such in the Niska town of Lakkulzap and another in the Kitksan town of Kishpiyeoux.—Boas in 10th Rep. N. W. Tribes Can., 49, 50, 1895.

Lalauitlela (*Lā'lăuiLɐla*, 'always crossing the sea'). A gens of the Tlatlasikoala, subdivided into the Gyegyote and Hahekolatl.—Boas in Rep. Nat. Mus. 1895, 329, 1897.

Lamasconson. One of several tribes or bands displaced from their homes in St Mary and Charles cos., Md., in 1651, and settled on a reservation at the head of Wicomico r. (Bozman, Maryland, II, 421, 1837). Perhaps a small branch of the Conoy.

Lamochattee. See *Weatherford, William.*

La Montagne (Fr.: 'the mountain'). A mission village established in 1677 for Caughnawaga and other Catholic Iroquois on a hill on Montreal id., Quebec. They were afterward joined by others, many of whom were not Christians. The village was temporarily deserted in 1689 on account of the Iroquois. In 1696 a part of the converts established a new mission village at Sault au Recollet, and were joined by the others until in 1704 La Montagne was finally abandoned.   (J. M.)
The Mountain.—Shea, Cath. Miss., 309, 1855.

Lamps. See *Illumination.*

Lamsim. A former village, presumably Costanoan, connected with Dolores mission, San Francisco, Cal.—Taylor in Cal. Farmer, Oct. 18, 1861.

Lamtama. A Nez Percé band living on White Bird cr., a tributary of Salmon r., Idaho, so called from the native name of the stream.—Gatschet, MS.,1878, B. A. E.
Buffalo Indiens.—Owen in Ind. Aff. Rep. 1859, 424, 1860. Lamtama.—Gatschet, MS.,1878, B. A. E. White Bird Nez Percés.—Ibid. (so called from the name of their chief).

Lana-chaadus (*Lă′na tcă′adAs*). A family of low social rank belonging to the Eagle clan of the Haida. Before becoming extinct they occupied, with the Gitingidjats, a town on Shingle bay, Queen Charlotte ids., Brit. Col. Some are said to have lived with the Kaiiahl-lanas.— Swanton, Cont. Haida, 274, 1905.

Lanadagunga (*Lă′na dă′gAña*, 'bad [or common] village'). A former Haida town, owned by the Saki-kegawai, on the coast of Moresby id., s. of Tangle cove, Queen Charlotte ids., Brit. Col. It was so called by the people of Hagi, opposite, because the Lanadagunga people used to talk against them.—Swanton, Cont. Haida, 277, 1905.

Lanagahlkehoda (*Lănă′ga łqē′xoda*, 'town that the sun does not shine on'). A Haida town on a small island opposite Kaisun, w. coast of Moresby id., Queen Charlotte ids., Brit. Col. It was so named because it faces N. This is a semi-mythical town, said to have been occupied by the Kas-lanas.—Swanton, Cont. Haida, 280, 1905.

Lanagukunhlin-hadai (*Lă′na gu qA′nłin xă′da-i*, 'resting-the-breast-on-a-town people'). A subdivision of the Chaahllanas, a family of the Eagle clan of the Haida. Lanagukunhlin was the name of a chief.—Swanton, Cont. Haida, 276, 1905.

Lanahawa (*Lă′na xă′wa*, 'swampy village'). A former Haida town on the w. coast of Graham id., opposite Hippa id., Queen Charlotte group, Brit. Col. It was also called Lanaheguns (*Lă′-na xē′-gAns*, 'town where there is a noise [of drums]') and Lanahltungua (*Lă′-na łłA′ngua*, 'town where there are plenty of feathers'). It was occupied by the Skwahladas and Nasto-kegawai before they moved to Rennell sd., and afterward by the Kianusili.—Swanton, Cont. Haida, 280, 1905.

Lanahawa. A former Haida town on the w. coast of Burnaby id., Queen Charlotte ids., Brit. Col., s. of the Ninstints town of Ket.—Swanton, Cont. Haida, 278, 1905.

Lanahilduns (*Lă′na hĭ′ldAns*, 'moving village'; also called Chahlolnagai, from the name of the inlet on which it was situated). A former Haida town on the s. w. side of Rennell sd., Graham id., Queen Charlotte group, Brit. Col.; occupied by the Nasto-kegawai or the Skwahladas family group.—Swanton, Cont. Haida, 280, 1905.

Lanaslnagai (*Lă′nas lnagă′-i*, 'peoples' town'). The name of three distinct Haida towns on Queen Charlotte ids., Brit. Col. One stood on the E. coast of Graham id., s. of C. Ball, and was owned by the Naikun-kegawai; another belonged to the Kuna-lanas and was on the w. side of Masset inlet where it broadens out; the third, which belonged to the Yagunstlanlnagai, was on Yagun r.—Swanton, Cont. Haida, 280, 281, 1905.

Lanaungsuls (*Lă′na ᵍA′ñsAls*, 'town [that] hides itself'). A Haida town on Masset inlet, Queen Charlotte ids., Brit. Col., belonging to the Aoyaku-lnagai.— Swanton, Cont. Haida, 281, 1905.

Lances. As an implement of the chase or of war the lance had a wide distribution among the ancient and the modern tribes of the United States. Though none of the objects of chipped stone called lance-heads that have been found in numbers on widely separated archeological sites are attached to shafts, there is reason to believe that many of the leaf-shaped blades were lance-heads. The only survivals of the use of the ancient lance are found among the Hupa of California and the western Eskimo, but earlier writers have mentioned their existence among various tribes. Lances for the chase were used occasionally in war by the Eskimo, but the Plains Indians, whenever possible, used two distinct varieties for war and for hunting, the hunting lance blade being shorter and heavier. The lance

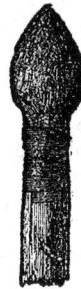

LANCE HEAD; WESTERN ESKIMO. (MURDOCH)

appears to have originated through the need of striking animals from some distance in order to escape personal danger and to produce surer results than were possible with a stone knife or other implement used at close quarters. The efficiency and range of the lance when thrown from the hand was increased by the throwing stick (q. v.), and the original lance or spear developed into a number of varieties under the influences of environment, the habits of animals, acculturation, etc. The greatest number of forms sprang up among the Eskimo, whose environment was characterized by a great variety and alternation of animal life, while in most other regions a simple lance was perpetuated.

The Plains tribes, as a rule, living in a region conducive to warfare and aggression through its lack of physical boundaries, made more use of the lance in war than did coast, woodland, desert, or mountain tribes. Since the general occupancy of the plains appears to have been coincident with the introduction of the horse, the use of the war lance has been associated with that animal, but it is evident that the tribes that occupied the plains were acquainted with the lance with a stone head as a hunting implement before they entered this vast region. A Kiowa lance in the National Museum is headed with a part of a sword blade and is reputed to have killed 16 persons.

In accord with the tendency of objects designed for especially important usage to take on a religious significance, the lance has become an accessory of ceremonies among the Plains Indians. Elaborately decorated sheaths were made for lances, varying according to the society or office of the owner. At home the lance was leaned against the shield tripod, tied horizontally above the tipi door, or fastened lengthwise to an upright pole behind the tipi. In both earlier and recent times offerings of lance-heads were made to springs, exquisitely formed specimens having been taken from a sulphur spring at Afton, Okla.

Consult Holmes (1) in 15th Rep. B. A. E., 1897, (2) in Am. Anthrop., IV, 108–129, 1902; Mooney in 14th Rep. B. A. E., 988–990, 1896. See *Arrowheads, Hunting, Spears, War and War discipline.* (w. h.)

Land tenure. The Indian conceived of the earth as mother, and as mother she provided food for her children. The words in the various languages which refer to the land as "mother" were used only in a sacred or religious sense. In this primitive and religious sense land was not regarded as property; it was like the air, it was something necessary to the life of the race, and therefore not to be appropriated by any individual or group of individuals to the permanent exclusion of all others. Other words referring to the earth as "soil" to be used and cultivated by man, mark a change in the manner of living and the growth of the idea of a secular relation to the earth. Instead of depending on the spontaneous products of the land the Indian began to sow seeds and to care for the plants. In order to do this he had to remain on the soil he cultivated. Thus occupancy gradually established a claim or right to possess the tract from which a tribe or an individual derived food. This occupancy was the only land tenure recognized by the Indian; he never of himself reached the conception of land as merchantable, this view having been forced on his acceptance through his relations with the white race. Tecumseh claimed that the Northwest Territory, occupied by allied tribes, belonged to the tribes in common, hence a sale of land to the whites by one tribe did not convey title unless confirmed by other tribes. Furthermore, among most of the Algonquian tribes, at least, according to Dr William Jones, if land were ceded to the whites, the cession could not be regarded as absolute, i. e., the whites could hold only to a certain depth in the earth such as was needful for sustenance. Each tribe had its village sites and contiguous hunting or fishing grounds; as long as the people lived on these sites and regularly went to their hunting grounds, they could claim them against all intruders. This claim often had to be maintained by battling with tribes less favorably situated. The struggle over the right to hunting grounds was the cause of most Indian wars. In some tribes garden spots were claimed by clans, each family working on its own particular patch. In other tribes the favorable localities were preempted by individuals regardless of clan relations. As long as a person planted a certain tract the claim was not disputed, but if its cultivation were neglected anyone who chose might take it. Among the Zuñi, according to Cushing, if a man, either before or after marriage, takes up a field of unappropriated land, it belongs strictly to him, but is spoken of as the property of his clan, or on his death it may be cultivated by any member of that clan, though preferably by near relatives, but not by his wife or children, who must be of another clan. Moreover, a man cultivating land at one Zuñi farming settlement of the tribe can not give even of his own fields to a tribesman belonging to another farming village unless that person should be a member of his clan; nor can a man living at one village take up land at another without the consent of the body politic of the latter settlement; and no one, whatever his rank, can grant land to any member of another tribe without consent of the Corn and certain other clans.

During the early settlement of the country absolute title was vested in the Crown by virtue of discovery or conquest, yet the English acknowledged the Indian's right of occupancy, as is shown by the purchase of these rights both by Lord Baltimore in 1635 and by William Penn in 1682, although colonizing under royal grants. The Puritans, however, coming without royal authority, were necessitated to bargain with the Indians. Absolute right to the Indian lands was fully stated in a proclamation by George III in 1763. In 1783 the Colonial Congress forbade private purchase or acceptance of lands from Indians. On the adoption of the Constitution the right of eminent domain became vested in the United States, and Congress alone had the power to extinguish the Indian's right of occupancy. The ordinance of 1787, relative to all territory n. w. of the Ohio, made the consent of the Indians requisite to the cession of their lands. Until the passage of the act of Mar. 3, 1871, all cession was by treaty, the United States negotiating with the tribes as with foreign nations; since then agreements have been less formal, and a recent decision of the U. S. Supreme Court makes even the agreement or consent of the Indians unnecessary. The tribes living in Arizona, California, Nevada, New Mexico, and Utah came under the provisions of the treaty of Guadalupe Hidalgo, most of the Pueblos holding their lands under Spanish grants. All Indian reservations have been established either by treaty or by order of the President, but in both cases the Indian's tenure is that of occupancy only. "They may not cut growing timber, open mines, quarry stone, etc., to obtain lumber, coal, building material, etc., solely for the purpose of sale or speculation. In short, what a tenant for life may do upon the lands of a remainder-man the Indians may do upon their reservations, but no more." In a few cases reservations have been patented to tribes, as those of the Five Civilized Tribes, and a limited number of tribes have had their lands apportioned and received patents for individual holdings, yet no general change in the Indian land tenure took place until the passage of the severalty act in 1887. This act provided for the allotment to each man, woman, and child of a certain portion of the tribal land and the issuance of a patent by which the United States holds the allotment in trust, free of taxation and encumbrance, for 25 years, when the allottee is entitled to a patent in fee simple. On the approval of their allotments by the Secretary of the Interior the Indians become citizens of the United States and subject to its laws. Seventy-three tribes already hold their lands under this tenure. See *Governmental policy, Legal status, Reservations, Treaties, Social organization.*

Consult Adair, Hist. Am. Indians, 282, 1775; Bandelier in Archæol. Inst. Papers, III, 201, 272, 1890; Cushing in Millstone, IX, 55, 1884; Dawson, Queen Charlotte Islands, 117, 1878; Fletcher, Indian Education and Civilization, 1888; Grinnell in Am. Anthrop., IX, no. 1, 1907; Jenks in 19th Rep. B. A. E., 1900; Powell in 7th Rep. B. A. E., 39–41, 1891; Royce, Indian Land Cessions, 18th Rep. B. A. E., 1889; Willoughby in Am. Anthrop., VIII, no. 1, 1906.   (A. C. F.)

Languages. The American languages show considerable variety in phonetics and structure. While some are vocalic and appear melodious to our ear, others contain many consonant sounds to which we are unaccustomed and which seem to give them a harsh character. Particularly frequent are sounds produced by contact between the base of the tongue and the soft palate, similar to the Scotch *ch* in *loch*, and a number of explosive *l's*, which are produced by pressing the tongue against the palate and suddenly expelling the air between the teeth. Harshness produced by clustering consonants is peculiar to the N. W. coast of America. Sonorous vocalic languages are found in a large part of the Mississippi basin and in California. Peculiar to many American languages is a slurring of terminal syllables, which makes the recording of grammatical forms difficult.

Contrary to the prevalent notion, the vocabularies are rich and their grammatical structure is systematic and intricate. Owing to the wealth of derivatives it is difficult to estimate the number of words in any American language; but it is certain that in every one there are a couple of thousand of stem words and many thousand words, as that term is defined in English dictionaries.

A considerable variety of grammatical structure exists, but there are a few common traits that seem to be characteristic of most American languages. The complexity of grammar is often great because many ideas expressed by separate words in the languages of other continents are expressed by grammatical processes in the languages of the Indians. The classification of words differs somewhat from the familiar grouping in Indo-European languages. The demarcation between noun and verb is often indistinct, many expressions being both denominative and predicative. Often the intransitive verb and the noun are identical in form, while the transitive verb only is truly verbal in character. In other languages the transitive verb is nominal, while the intransitive only is truly verbal. These phenomena are generally accompanied by the use of possessive pronouns with the nominal and of personal pronouns with the verbal class of words. In other cases the verbal forms are differentiated from the noun, but the close relationship between the two classes is indicated by the similarity of the pronominal forms. The intransitive verb generally includes the ideas which Indo-European languages express by means of adjectives. Independent pronouns are often compounds, and the pronoun appears in most cases subordinated to the verb.

In the singular are distinguished self (or speaker), person addressed, and person spoken of; in the plural, corresponding to our first person, are often distinguished the combination of speaker and persons addressed, and speaker and persons spoken of, the so-called inclusive and exclusive forms.

The demonstrative pronouns are analogous to the personal pronoun in that they are generally developed in three forms, indicating respectively the thing near me, near thee, near him. Their development is sometimes even more exuberant, visibility and invisibility, present and past, or location to the right, left, front and back of, and above and below the speaker, being distinguished.

The subordination of the pronoun to the verb is often carried to extremes. In many languages the pronominal subject, the object, and the indirect object are incorporated in the verb, for which reason American languages have often been called "incorporating languages." There are, however, numerous languages in which this pronominal subordination does not occur. In some the process of incorporation does not cease with the pronoun; but the noun, particularly the nominal object, is treated in the same manner. Where such incorporation is found the development of nominal cases is slight, since the incorporation renders this unnecessary.

The occurrence of other classes of words depends largely on the development of another feature of American languages, which is probably common to them all, namely, the expression of a great number of special ideas by means of either affixes or stem modification. On account of the exuberance of such elements American languages have been called "polysynthetic." The character of the subordinated elements shows great variations. In some languages most of the ideas that are subordinated are instrumental (with the hand, the foot, or the like; with the point or the edge of something, etc.); in others they include all kinds of qualifying ideas, such as are generally expressed by auxiliary verbs, verbal compounds, and adverbs. The Eskimo, for instance, by composition of other elements with the stem "to see," may express "he only orders him to go and see"; a Chimmesyan composition with the verb to go is, "he went with him upward in the dark and came against an obstacle." The existence of numerous subordinate elements of this kind has a strong effect in determining the series of stem words in a language. Whenever this method of composition is highly developed many special ideas are expressed by stems of very general significance, combined with qualifying elements. Their occurrence is also the cause of the obviousness of Indian etymologies. These elements also occur sometimes independently, so that the process is rather one of coordinate composition than of subordination. The forms of words that enter composition of this kind sometimes undergo considerable phonetic modification by losing affixes or by other processes. In such cases composition apparently is brought about by

apocope, or decapitation of words; but most of these seem to be reducible to regular processes. In many languages polysynthesis is so highly developed that it almost entirely suppresses adverbs, prepositions, and conjunctions.

The categories of Indo-European languages do not correspond strictly to those of Indian languages. This is true particularly of the ideas of gender and plurality. Grammatical gender based on sex distinction is very rare in America. It is based on other qualities, as animate and inanimate, or noble and ignoble, and often relates only to shape, as round, long, or flat. Complete absence of such classification is frequent. Plurality is seldom clearly developed; it is often absent even in the pronoun; its place is taken by the ideas of collectivity and distribution, which are expressed more often than plurality. Tense is also weakly developed in many languages, although others have a complex system of tenses. Like other adverbial ideas tense is often expressed by affixes. Moods and voice of the verb are also sometimes undeveloped and are expressed by adverbial elements.

In the use of grammatical processes there is great diversity. Suffixes occur almost everywhere; prefixes are not quite so frequent. Infixes seem to be confined to the Siouan languages, although infixation by metathesis occurs in other languages also. Reduplication is frequent, sometimes extending to triplication; but in some groups of languages it does not occur at all. Other forms of modification of stem also occur.

Indian languages tend to express ideas with much graphic detail in regard to localization and form, although other determining elements which Indo-European languages require may be absent. Those languages are, therefore, not so well adapted to generalized statements as to lively description. The power to form abstract ideas is nevertheless not lacking, and the development of abstract thought would find in every one of the languages a ready means of expression. Yet, since the Indian is not given to purely abstract speculation, his abstract terms always appear in close connection with concrete thought; for instance, qualities are often expressed by nominal terms, but are never used without possessive pronouns.

According to the types of culture served by the languages we find holophrastic terms, expressing complex groups of ideas. These, however, are not due to a lack of power to classify, but are rather expressions of form of culture, single terms being intended for those ideas that are of prime importance to the people.

The differentiation of stocks into dialects shows great variation, some stocks comprising only one dialect, while others embrace many that are mutually unintelligible. While the Eskimo have retained their language in all its minor features for centuries, that of the Salish, who are confined to a small area in the N. Pacific region, is split up into innumerable dialects. The fate of each stock is probably due as much to the morphological traits of the language itself as to the effects of its contact with other languages. Wherever abundant reduplication, phonetic changes in the stem, and strong phonetic modifications in composition occur, changes seem to be more rapid than where grammatical processes are based on simple laws of composition. Contact with other languages has had a far-reaching effect through assimilation of syntactic structure and, to a certain extent, of phonetic type. There is, however, no historical proof of the change of any Indian language since the time of the discovery comparable with that of the language of England between the 10th and 13th centuries.

A few peculiarities of language are worth mentioning. As various parts of the population speaking modern English differ somewhat in their forms of expression, so similar variations are found in American languages. One of the frequent types of difference is that between the language of men and that of women. This difference may be one of pronunciation, as among some Eskimo tribes, or may consist in the use of different sets of imperative and declarative particles, as among the Sioux, or in other differences of vocabulary; or it may be more fundamental, due to the foreign origin of the women of the tribe. In incantations and in the formal speeches of priests and shamans a peculiar vocabulary is sometimes used, containing many archaic and symbolic terms. See *Chinook jargon, Linguistic families, Sign language.*   (F. B.)

Languntennenk. A village of Moravian Delawares founded in 1770 on Beaver r., probably near the present Darlington, in Beaver co., Pa., by Indians who removed from Lawunkhannek. In 1773 they abandoned the village and joined the other Moravians on the Muskingum, in Ohio. The missionaries called it Friedensstadt, q. v.   (J. M.)

Langundowi-Oteey.—Loskiel (1794) cited by Rupp, West. Pa., 47, 1846. Languntennenk.—Crantz cited, ibid., 47. Languntouenünk.—Zeisberger (1791), Diary, II, 234, 1885. Languntoutenuenk.—Crantz, Hist. of the Brethren, 594, 1780.

Lansing Man. The name given to a partially dismembered human skeleton found in 1902 under 20 ft of undisturbed silt, 70 ft from the face of the Missouri r. bluff, near Lansing, Kans. The remains lay partly under a large limestone slab imbedded in a mass of talus at the foot of a shale and limestone cliff, against which the silt was deposited. The position of the bones denoted an intentional burial, and not the accidental lodgment of a body at this point. In the walls of the excavations made in the formation there was no indication of slipping, sliding, caving, or prolonged surface wash from a higher level; no indication of direct wind or wave action, except a narrow thin layer of dark clay at one part; no distinct lamination, stratification, or assortment of material; no indication that vegetation had ever taken hold; in short, no evidence that the mass of silt was due to any other process than a slow, steady accumulation, mainly or wholly in quiet water. There were small patches of gravel at irregular intervals, many snail shells, angular fragments of limestone up to 3 or 4 in. thick, small scraps of shale, a few pebbles of glacial drift origin, and a number of pieces of charcoal, some with

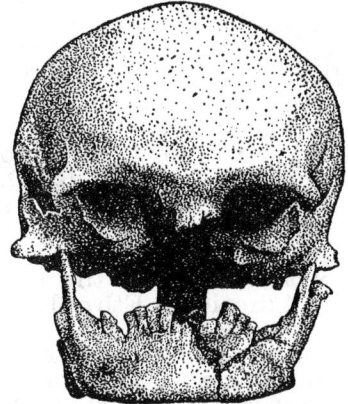

LANSING SKULL, FRONTAL VIEW

fractures and angles not in the least worn. These facts point to an upbuilding partly by wash, partly by winds, partly by creep from the adjacent hills, and partly by sediment from the Missouri. It appears that this deposit could have accumulated within a comparatively short period. Even allowing the utmost limit of time that can be reasonably claimed, namely, that the river has cut its way from the top of the silt deposit to its present grade, the time necessary for accomplishing this will fall very far within the period that must have elapsed since the existing to-

SECTION OF BLUFF SHOWING LOCATION OF SKELETON
(*a*, ENTRANCE TO TUNNEL; *b*, POSITION OF REMAINS)

pography was created, in part at least by streams that could not begin their work until after glacial floods had ceased to act. The bones themselves do not favor the theory of great antiquity for the remains. According to Hrdlicka (Am. Anthrop., v, 323, 1903) the skull and bones are not perceptibly fossilized, and are practically identical in their physical characters with the crania and bones of some of the historic Indians of the general region. The cranium has been placed for safe-keeping in the U. S. National

Museum by its owner, Mr M. C. Long, of Kansas City, Mo.

As the geologists who examined the site when the deep trenches cut by the Bureau of American Ethnology were open hold widely divergent opinions with respect to the age of the formation inclosing the remains, some of them considering it true loess, further investigation is necessary ere the question of antiquity can be finally settled.

Of the geologists referred to, those favoring great antiquity are Upham (Am. Antiq., XXIV, 413, 1902, and Am. Geologist, Sept. 1902, 135); Winchell (Am. Geologist, Sept. 1902); Williston (Science, Aug. 1, 1902), and Erasmus Haworth, Professor of Geology, University of Kansas. Those favoring a comparatively recent date are Chamberlin (Jour. of Geology, X, 745, 1903); Holmes (Smithson. Rep., 455, 1902); R. D. Salisbury, Professor of Geology, University of Chicago; Samuel Calvin, State Geologist of Iowa, and Gerard Fowke, who conducted the excavations on the site for the Bureau of American Ethnology. See *Antiquity, Archeology*. (G. F.)

Lapapu. A former Miwok village on Tuolumne r., Tuolumne co., Cal.
La-pap-poos.—Johnson in Schoolcraft, Ind. Tribes, IV, 407, 1854. Lapappu.—Latham in Trans. Philol. Soc. Lond., 81, 1856.

La Piche. A small rancheria, probably Luiseño, on Potrero res., 75 m. from Mission Tule River agency, s. Cal. With La Joya the population was officially given as 225 in 1903. Cf. *Apeche*.

La Posta (Span.; probably here meaning 'post station'). A reservation of 238.88 acres of unpatented desert land occupied by 19 so-called Mission Indians, situated 170 m. from Mission Tule River agency, s. Cal.

Lappawinze ('getting provisions'). A Delaware chief—one of those who were induced to sign at Philadelphia the treaty of 1737, known as the "walking purchase," confirming a reputed treaty of 1686, which granted to the whites land extending from Neshaminy cr. as far as a man could go in a day and a half. When the survey was made under this stipulation the governor of Pennsylvania had a road built inland and employed a trained runner, a proceeding that the Delawares denounced as a fraud. See Pa. Archives, 1st ser., I, 541, 1852; Thomson, Enquiry into Alienation of Delaware and Shawanese Inds., 69, 1759.

La Prairie. The first mission village of the Catholic Iroquois, established in 1668 on the s. bank of the St Lawrence, at La Prairie, La Prairie co., Quebec. The first occupants were chiefly Oneida with other Iroquois, but it soon contained members of all the neighboring Iroquoian and Algonquian tribes. The Mohawk, from Caughnawaga, N. Y., finally gained the leading position and their language came into vogue in the settlement. In 1676 the Indians removed to Portage r., a few miles distant, and built the present Caughnawaga, q. v.
Laprairie.—Shea, Cath. Miss., 262, 1855. La Prairie de la Madelaine.—Frontenac (1674) in N. Y. Doc. Col. Hist., IX, 116, 1855. Laprairie de la Madelaine.—Letter of 1756, ibid., X, 480, 1858. La Prairie de la Magdelaine.—La Barre (1683), ibid., IX, 202, 1855. Saint-François-Xavier-des-Prés.—Jes. Rel., III, index, 1858. St. Francis Xavier des Près.—Shea, Cath. Miss., 268, 1855 (mission name). St. François Xavier à Laprairie de la Magdeleine.—Jes. Rel. (1675) quoted by Shea, Cath. Miss., 304, 1855. S. Xavier des Praiz.—Jes. Rel. 1671, 12, 1858. S. Xavier des Prez.—Ibid., 1672, 16, 1858.

Laptambif. Probably a band of the Calapooya proper. In 1877 the name was borne by "Old Ben," at Grande Ronde res., Oreg., who came from Mohawk r., Lane co.

LAPPAWINZE. (McKenney and Hall)

Laptambif.—Gatschet, Atfalati MS., B. A. E., 368, 1877. Long-tongue-buff.—Ross, Adventures, 236, 1849.

La Punta (Span.: 'the point'). A former Diegueño rancheria near San Diego, s. Cal.—Ortega (1775) quoted by Bancroft, Hist. Cal., I, 253, 1884.

Lapwai. A Nez Percé band formerly living near the mouth of Lapwai cr., Idaho, now under the Lapwai school superintendent.

Las Flores (Span.: 'the flowers'). A former Luiseño village in N. San Diego co., Cal. (Hayes, 1850, quoted by Bancroft, Nat. Races, I, 460, 1882). Arguello (H. R. Ex. Doc. 76, 34th Cong., 3d sess., 117, 1857) mentions a Las Flores as a Diegueño pueblo in San Diego co., established after the secularization act of 1834, which may be the same.

Las Mulas (Span.: 'the mules'). A rancheria near the presidio of La Bahia and the mission of Espíritu Santo de Zúñiga on the lower Rio San Antonio, Tex., in 1785, at which date it had only 5 inhabitants (Bancroft, No. Mex. States, I, 659, 1886), who were probably of Karankawan affinity.

Lassik (*Las'-sik*, the name of their last chief). A people of the Athapascan family formerly occupying a portion of main Eel r., Cal., and its E. tributaries, Van Duzen, Larrabee, and Dobbin crs., together with the headwaters of Mad r. They had for neighbors toward the N. the Athapascan inhabitants of the valley of Mad r. and Redwood cr.; toward the E. the Wintun of Southfork of Trinity r.; toward the s. the Wailaki, from whom they were separated by Kekawaka cr.; toward the w. the Sinkine on Southfork of Eel r. They occupied their regular village sites along the streams only in winter. Their houses were conical in form, made of the bark of Douglas spruce. They had neither sweat lodges nor dance houses. The basketry was twined, but differed considerably from that of the Hupa in its decoration. Beside the methods employed elsewhere for securing deer and elk, the Lassik used to follow a fresh track until the animal, unable to feed or rest, was overtaken. They intermarried with the Wintun, to whom they were assimilated in mourning customs, etc. Powers (Cont. N. A. Ethnol., III, 121, 1877) gives the impression that the Lassik belong with the Wintun in language, but this is a mistake. Their dialect resembles the Hupa in its morphology and the Wailaki in its phonology. The majority of them perished during the first few years of the occupancy of their country by white people, a bounty being placed on their heads and the traffic in children for slaves being profitable and unrestrained. A few families of them are still living in the neighborhood of their former homes.   (P. E. G.)

Latcha Hoa. Noted on the West Florida map (*ca.* 1775) as a Chickasaw settlement on Latcha Hoa run, an affluent of Ahoola Ihalchubba, a w. tributary of Tombigbee r., N. E. Miss.

Late-Comedu. An unidentified Dakota division, mentioned by Gale, Upper Miss., 252, 1867.

Lathakrezla. A Nataotin village on the N. side of Babine lake, Brit. Col.
Lathakrezla.—Morice in Trans. Roy. Soc. Can. 1892, 109, 1893. Na-tal-kuz.—Dawson in Geol. Surv. Can., 26B, 1881. Ni-to-atz.—Ibid., 27B.

Laulewasikaw. See *Tenskwatawa*.

Law. See *Government*.

Lawilvan. A Kawia village in Cahuilla valley, s. Cal.; perhaps identical with Alamo Bonito, q. v.
Alamo.—Barrows, Ethno.-Bot. Coahuilla Ind., 34, 1900. La-wil-van.—Ibid. Si-vel.—Ibid.

Lawokla. A Choctaw clan of the Kushapokla phratry.—Morgan, Anc. Soc., 162, 1877.

Lawunkhannek. A village of Moravian Delawares established in 1769 on Allegheny r., above Franklin, Venango co., Pa. In 1770 the inhabitants removed to Languntennenk. It seems probable that the village contained also some Seneca.   (J. M.)
Lauanakanuck.—Day, Penn., 172, 1843. Lawanaka-nuck.—Loskiel (1794) quoted by Day, Penn., 644, 1843. Lawenakanuck.—Ibid., 102–3. Lawunah-hannek.—Loskiel (1794) quoted by Rupp West. Pa., app., 353, 1846. Lawunakhannek.—Crantz, Hist. of the Brethren, 594, 1780. Lawunkhannek.—Loskiel (1794) quoted by Rupp, op. cit., 46.

Laycayamu. A former Chumashan village near Santa Barbara, Cal.—Taylor in Cal. Farmer, Apr. 24, 1863.

League. See *Confederation, Government*.

Lean Bear. An unidentified Dakota band formerly living below L. Traverse, Minn. (Ind. Aff. Rep. 1859, 102, 1860); apparently named after the chief.

Leatherlips (native name *Shā'teiaron'-hiā'*, 'Two clouds of equal size.'—Hewitt). A Huron (Wyandot) chief of the Sandusky tribe of Ohio who, in Aug., 1795, signed the treaty of Greenville in behalf of his people. His honorable character and friendship for the whites inflamed the jealousy of Tecumseh, who ruthlessly ordered him to be killed on the plea that he was a wizard, Tecumseh's fanaticism being so overmastering that he assigned the execution of Shateiaronhia to another Huron chief named Roundhead. He was apprised of his condemnation by his brother, who was sent to him with a piece of bark on which a tomahawk was drawn as a token of his death. The execution took place near his camp on the Scioto, about 14 m. N. of Columbus, in the summer of 1810, there being present a number of white men, including a justice of the peace, who made an effort to save the life of the accused, but without success. He was tomahawked by a fellow tribesman while kneeling beside his grave, after having chanted a death song. The Wyandot Club of Columbus, Ohio, in 1888, erected a granite monument to Shateiaronhia in a park surrounded by a stone wall, including the spot where he died. See Curry in Ohio Archæol. and Hist. Quar., XII, no. 1, 1906; Drake, Life of Tecumseh, 1852; Heckewelder, Hist. Ind. Nat., 1876; Howe, Hist. Coll. Ohio, I, 611, 1898.

Leatherwood (Leatherwood's Town). A former Cherokee settlement at or near the present Leatherwood village in the N. part of Franklin co., N. E. Ga. The name was probably that of a prominent chief or mixed-blood.   (J. M.)

Ledyanoprolivskoe. Perhaps a town of the Tlingit, locality not given, numbering 200 in 1835.

Laydanoprodevskie.—Elliott, Cond. Aff. Alaska, 227, 1875 (transliterated from Veniaminoff). **Led-yanoprolivskoe.**—Veniaminoff, Zapiski, II, pt. III, 29, 1840.

Leekwinai (*Lee-kwin-ǎ-ĭ'*, 'snapping turtle'). A subclan of the Delawares (q. v.).—Morgan, Anc. Soc., 172, 1877.

Leelahs. Supposed to be a division of the Kalapooian family; not identified.—Slocum in H. R. Rep. 101, 25th Cong., 3d sess., 42, 1839.

Leeshtelosh (*Leesh-te-losh*). Probably a Kalapooian band, said to have lived near the headwaters of Willamette r., Oreg.—Hunter, Captivity, 73, 1823.

Legal status. The act of July 22, 1790, contains the earliest provision relating to intercourse with Indians. By it any offense against the person or property of a peaceable and friendly Indian was made punishable in the same manner as if the act were committed against a white inhabitant (U. S. Stat., I, 138). The act of May 19, 1796, empowered the President to arrest within the limits of any state or district an Indian guilty of theft, outrage, or murder (ibid., 472). During the next 20 years the idea that the Indian tribes were distinct nations, having their own form of government and power to conduct their social polity, took form and was distinctly stated in treaties. The Indians' right to punish intruding white settlers was stipulated in treaties made with the Cherokee, Chickasaw, Chippewa, Choctaw, Creeks, Delawares, Ottawa, Potawatomi, Shawnee, Hurons, and other tribes. The act of Mar. 3, 1817, provided that the power given to the President under the act of May 19, 1796, "should not be so construed as to affect any treaty in force between the United States and any Indian nation or to extend to any offense committed by one Indian against another within any Indian boundary." The courts decided that for the United States to assume "to exercise a general jurisdiction over Indian countries within a state is unconstitutional and of no effect." The crime of murder charged against a white man for killing another white man in the Cherokee country, within the state of Tennessee, it was decided, could not be punished in the courts of the United States (U. S. v. Bailey, McLean's C. Cls. Rep., I, 234). In the case of the Cherokee Nation v. the State of Georgia (5 Peters, 1) the court states: "It may well be doubted whether those tribes which reside within the acknowledged boundaries of the United States can with strict accuracy be denominated foreign nations. They may more correctly, perhaps, be denominated domestic dependent nations. They occupy a territory to which we assert title independent of their will, which must take effect in point of possession when their right of possession ceases; meanwhile they are in a state of pupilage. Their relation to the United States resembles that of a ward to his guardian." This confused relation—neither dependence nor independence—led to many difficulties. From time to time appeals were made by the Indian Commissioner for the extension of the laws of the land over Indian reservations. On Mar. 3, 1885, an act was passed extending the law over Indians to a limited extent (U. S. Stat. L., XXIII, 385): "The right of the Indians to the reservation ordinarily occupied by them is that of occupancy alone. They have the right to apply to their own use and benefit the entire products of the reservation, whether the result of their own labor or of natural growth, so they do not commit waste. If the lands in a state of nature are not in a condition for profitable use they may be made so; if desired for the purpose of agriculture, they may be cleared of their timber to such an extent as may be reasonable under the circumstances, and the surplus timber taken off by the Indians . . . may be sold by them. The Indians may also cut dead and fallen timber and sell the surplus not needed for their own use; they may cut growing timber for fuel and for use upon the reservation; they may open mines and quarry stone for the purpose of obtaining fuel and building material; they may cut hay for the use of the live stock, and may sell any surplus . . . They may not, however, cut growing timber, open mines, quarry stone, etc., to obtain lumber, coal, building material, etc., solely for the purpose of sale or speculation. In short, what a tenant for life may do upon lands of a remainder-man the Indians may do on their reservations (Instructions, sec. 262, 1880; U. S. v. Cook, 19 Wallace, 591; acts of Mar. 22 and 31, 1882; Rep. Sec. Interior, May 19, 1882, 9636; Reg. Ind. Dept., sec. 525, 526, 527).

By their treaty of July 31, 1855, the Chippewa of Michigan were permitted to receive the title to lands taken up under the act of Aug. 4, 1854 (U. S. Stat., x, 574) without "actual occupancy or residence," in order to dispose of them (ibid., xi, 627). An act promulgated in Mar., 1875, permitted Indians to homestead land (ibid., xviii, 240). Those Indians who had availed themselves of this act were by the act of July 4, 1884, to receive from the Government a trust patent, to the effect that the United States would hold the land for 25 years, and at the expiration of that period convey it in fee to the Indian who had made entry or to his heirs "free of all charge or incumbrance whatever" (ibid., xxiii, 961). "Indians can not preempt public lands and can not remove disability by declaring their intention to become citizens . . . Citizenship is not requisite for the ordinary purchase of public lands. . . . It may be done by a foreign alien and a fortiori by a mere denizen or domestic alien, such as the Indians'' (Opinions Atty. Gen., VII, 753).

The severalty act of Feb. 8, 1887, made the allotted Indian subject to all the laws, civil and criminal, of the state in which he resides, and also conferred upon him citizenship. The courts have decided that those who come under the provision of this act are no longer wards or subject to the restrictive control of the Commissioner of Indian Affairs or his agents.

Members of the following tribes can become citizens by treaty stipulation: Delaware, Kaskaskia, Kickapoo, Miami, Munsee, Ottawa, Peoria, Piankashaw, Sioux, Stockbridge, Wea, Winnebago living in Minnesota, and the Pueblo Indians and other sedentary tribes that come under the treaty of Guadalupe Hidalgo and the Gadsden Purchase. The status of mixed bloods, the court has decided, is determined by that of the father (Ex parte Reynold: 5 Dillon, 394).

The courts of Kansas and Washington have held that "an Indian sustaining tribal relations is as capable of entering into binding contracts as any other alien," except that said contract shall not touch his lands, annuities, or statute benefits. "The right to contract necessarily draws after it the liability to be sued; therefore upon contracts of the aforesaid character Indians can sue and be sued" (Washington Rep., I, 325). The state court has jurisdiction of the person and property of Indians, except while such Indians or property are actually situated on a reserve excluded from the jurisdiction of the state (Kansas Rep., XII, 28). See *Agency system, Civilization, Education, Governmental policy, Land tenure, Office of Indian Affairs, Reservations, Treaties.* (A. C. F.)

Legends. See *Mythology.*

Leggings. See *Clothing.*

Le Have (named from Cap de la Hève, France). A Micmac village in 1760 near the mouth of Mersey r., about Lunenburg, in Lunenburg co., Nova Scotia.
Chachippé.—Jes. Rel. (1610–13), I, 153, 1896. La Have.—Frye (1760) in Mass. Hist. Soc. Coll., 1st s., X, 115–116, 1809. La Heve.—Doc. of 1740 in N. Y. Doc. Col. Hist., X, 70, 1858. Le Have.—Present name of adjacent island. Port de la Hève.—Lescarbot (1609) quoted by Thwaites, Jes. Rel., I, 153, note, 1896.

Lehigh. A variety of coal. From Lehigh, the name of a tributary of the Delaware and a county in Pennsylvania, which represents *lechau* in the Lenape (Delaware) dialect, signifying 'fork of a river.' (A. F. C.)

Lehu. The Seed-grass clan of the Ala (Horn) phratry of the Hopi.

Le'-hü wüñ-wü.—Fewkes in Am. Anthrop., VII, 401, 1894 (*wüñ-wü*='clan').

Leimin. A Yuit Eskimo village on the Siberian coast between East cape and St Lawrence bay.—Krause in Deutsche Geog. Blätt., V, 80, map, 1882.

Leitli ('the junction'). The village of the Tanotenne situated at the confluence of Stuart and Fraser rs., Brit. Col.
Fort George.—Morice, Notes on W. Dénés, 25, 1893. Ṭeitli.—Ibid. Ṭeit'ḷi.—Morice in Trans. Roy. Soc. Can. 1892, 109, 1893.

Lejagadatcah. An unidentified band of the Miniconjou Teton Sioux.
Leja-ga-dat-cah.—Culbertson in Smithson. Rep. 1850, 142, 1851.

Lekwiltok. A large Kwakiutl tribe living between Knight and Bute inlets, Brit. Col. They were divided into five septs: Wiwekae, Hahamatses or Walitsum, Kueha, Tlaaluis, and Komenok. The last is now extinct. The towns are Husam, Tsakwalooin, Tsaiiyeuk, and Tatapowis. Total pop. 218 in 1904.
Acolta.—Poole, Queen Charlotte Ids., 289, 1872. Enclataws.—Can. Ind. Aff., 142, 1879. Euclataw.—Ibid., 92, 1876. Euclitus.—Downie in Mayne, Brit. Col., 448, 1861. Laek-que-libla. — Kane, Wand. in N. A., app., 1859. Laich-kwil-tacks. — Can. Ind. Aff., 142, 1879. Leequeeltoch.—Scouler in Jour. Ethnol. Soc. Lond., I, 233, 1848. Lékwiłdaᵉχᵘ.—Boas in Mem. Am. Mus. Nat. Hist., V, pt. 2, 318, 1902. Lē'kwiltok·.—Boas in 6th Rep. N. W. Tribes Can., 55, 1890 (Salish name). Lē'kwiltoq.—Boas in Petermanns Mitt., pt. 5, 131, 1887. Lienkwiltak.—Can. Ind. Aff. for 1901, pt. 2, 166. Liew-kwiltah.—Can. Ind. Aff. 1895, 362, 1896. Lï-kwil-tah.—Tolmie and Dawson, Vocabs. Brit. Col., 118B, 1884. Likwiltoh.—Ibid. Neaquiltough.—Brit. Col. map, 1872. Ne-cul-ta.—Kane, Wand. in N. A., app., 1859. Saich-kioie-tachs. — Can. Ind. Aff. 1883, 190, 1884. Saich-kwil-tach.—Sproat, ibid., 145, 1879. Tah-cultus.—Lord, Natur. in Brit Col., I, 155, 1866. Toungletats.—Smet, Oregon Miss., 56, 1847. Ucaltas.—Anderson quoted by Gibbs in Hist. Mag., 74, 1863. Uchulta.—Taylor in Cal. Farmer, July 19, 1862. U-cle-ta.—Mayne, Brit. Col., 74, 1862. Ucle-tah.—Ibid., 243. Ucletes.—Keane in Stanford, Compend., 541, 1878. Uctetahs.—St John, Sea of Mts., II, 16, 1877. Uculta.—Dawson in Trans. Roy. Soc. Can. for 1887, sec. II, 74. Ucultas.—Lennard and Barrett, Brit. Col., 36, 1862. Yookilta.—Tolmie and Dawson, Vocabs. Brit. Col., 118B, 1884. Yukletas.—Grant in Jour. Roy. Geog. Soc., 293, 1857. Yū'-kwilta.—Boas in Petermanns Mitt., pt. 5, 131, 1887.

Lelaka (*Lē'lacha*). An ancestor of a Nakomgilisala gens who also gave his name to the gens.—Boas in Petermanns Mitt., pt. 5, 131, 1887.

Lelek (*Lᴇlᴇ'k*). A Songish band residing at Codboro bay, s. end of Vancouver id.—Boas in 6th Rep. N. W. Tribes Can., 17, 1890.

Lelengtu. The Flute clan of the Lengya (Flute) phratry of the Hopi.
Leleñtu wiñwû.—Fewkes in 19th Rep. B. A. E., 583, 1901 (*wiñwû*='clan'). Lenbaki.—Stephen in 8th Rep. B. A. E., 18, 1891.

Lelewagyila (*Lē'lᴇwagila* 'the heaven makers': mythical name of the raven). A gens of the Tsawatenok, a Kwakiutl tribe.—Boas in Rep. Nat. Mus. 1895, 331, 1897.

Lelewayou (*Le-le-wa'-you*, 'birds' cry'). A subclan of the Delawares (q. v.).—Morgan, Anc. Soc., 172, 1877.

Lelikian. A former Nishinam village in the valley of Bear r., N. Cal.

Láylekeean.—Powers in Overland Mo., XII, 22, 1874.
Le'-li-ki-an.—Powers in Cont. N. A. Ethnol., III, 316, 1877.

Leliotu. The Tiny Ant (*sp. incog.*) clan of the Ala (Horn) phratry of the Hopi.
Le-li-o-tü wün-wü.—Fewkes in Am. Anthrop., VII, 401 1894 (*wüñ-wii*='clan').

Lema. One of the more important of the old villages of the Pomo; situated in Knight's valley, about 4 m. N. W. of Hopland, Mendocino co., Cal. (s. A. B.)
Lá-ma.—Powers in Cont. N. A. Ethnol., III, 172, 1777. **Lema.**—S. A. Barrett, inf'n, 1906.

Lemaltcha (Le-mɑl-tcha). A former Lummi village on Waldron id., Wash. (Gibbs, Clallam and Lummi, 39, 1863). The name is the same as Lilmalche, q. v.

Lemitas. Mentioned by Villa-Señor (Theatro Am., pt. 2, 412, 1748) as a wild tribe hostile to the people of New Mexico. Possibly the local name of an Apache band or of its chief.

Lenahuon. One of the tribes formerly occupying "the country from Buena Vista and Carises lakes and Kern r. to the Sierra Nevada and Coast range," Cal. (Barbour (1852) in Sen. Ex. Doc. 4, 32d Cong., spec. sess., 256, 1853). By treaty of June 10, 1851, these tribes reserved a tract between Tejon pass and Kern r., and ceded the remainder of their lands to the United States. Kroeber suggests that the name is perhaps intended for Sanahuon, Spanish orthography of Sanakhwin, a Yokuts and perhaps other Indian corruption of *San Joaquin* or a similar Spanish geographical term.
Lenahuon.—Barbour, op. cit. **Senahuow.**—Royce in 18th Rep. B. A. E., 782, 1899.

Lenape stone. A perforated tablet of shale, of the form usually classed as gorgets, found by Bernard Hansell while plowing on his father's farm half a mile E. of Doylestown, Bucks co., Pa. A large fragment of the stone was found on the surface of the ground in the spring of 1872; and a second, the smaller piece, was picked up in 1881. The length is nearly 4½ in., and the width varies from 1½ to 1¾ in The surface on both sides has been smoothed, and on one side are carved in outline the figure of an elephant or mammoth, two rude human forms, the sun, and a number of unidentified objects. On the other are outline figures of a turtle, fishes, a bird, a pipe, etc. There are two round perforations in the tablet, about a third of its length from the ends. The specimen may possibly be genuine Indian workmanship, but the carving is apparently modern and executed after the stone had been broken. For further notice consult Mercer, The Lenape Stone, or the Indian and the Mammoth, 1885. See *Gorgets, Perforated Tablets.* (c. T.)

Lengya. The Flute phratry of the Hopi, consisting of the Flute (Lelengtu), Blueflute (Shakwalengya), Drab-flute (Masilengya), and Mountain-sheep (Pangwa) clans, and probably others. They claim to have come from a region in s. Arizona called Palatkwabi and from Little Colorado r., and after their arrival in Tusayan joined the Ala (Horn) phratry, forming the Ala-Lengya group.—Fewkes in 19th Rep. B. A. E., 583, 587, 1901.
Leñya.—Fewkes, ibid.

Lengyanobi ('high place of the Flute clans'). The legendary home of the Lengya (Flute) clans of the Hopi, now a large ruin on a mesa about 30 m. N. E. of Walpi, N. E. Ariz. The village is said to have been abandoned just before the arrival of the Spaniards (1540), its inhabitants becoming amalgamated with the Hopi. The people of Lengyanobi at that time belonged to two consolidated phratries, the Ala (Horn) and the Lengya (Flute), of which the latter built the village. (J. W. F.)

Lentes. Said to have been a former pueblo of the Tigua, but more likely a village established for the benefit of Genizaros (q. v.), on the w. bank of the Rio Grande near Los Lunas, N. Mex. By 1850 the natives had become completely "Mexicanized."
Lentes.—Simpson in Rep. Sec. War, 143, 1850.
Lentis.—Calhoun in Schoolcraft, Ind. Tribes, III, 633, 1853. **Leunis.**—Schoolcraft, ibid., I, 519, 1851.
Leutis.—Ibid. **Los Lentes.**—Lane (1854), ibid., v, 689, 1855.

Lesamaiti. A former village of the Awani about one-fifth of a mile from Notomidula, in Yosemite valley, Mariposa co., Cal.
Laysamite.—Powers in Overland Mo., x, 333, 1874.
Le-sam'-ai-ti.—Powers in Cont. N. A. Ethnol., III, 365, 1877.

Leschi. A Nisqualli chief, prominent in the war which involved all the tribes of Washington and adjacent regions in 1855–58, and commonly known as the Yakima war. While Kamaiakan (q. v.) headed the Yakima and their confederates E. of the mountains, Leschi took command w. of the Cascades, particularly about Puget sd. His most notable exploit was an attack on the new town of Seattle, Jan. 29, 1856, at the head of about 1,000 warriors of several tribes. The assailants were driven off by means of a naval battery upon a vessel in the harbor. On the collapse of the outbreak Leschi fled to the Yakima, who, having already submitted, refused him shelter except as a slave. A reward was offered for his capture, and being thus outlawed, he was at last treacherously seized by two of his own men in Nov., 1856, and delivered to the civil authorities, by whom, after a long legal contest, he was condemned and hanged, Feb. 19, 1857. See Bancroft, Hist. Wash., 1890. (J. M.)

Les Noire Indians. Mentioned by Say (Long, Exped. Rocky Mts., II, lxxxiv, 1823) as a people known to the Hidatsa,

LETAIYO—LILLOOET

who applied to them the name At-te-shu-pe-sha-loh-pan-ga, which Matthews states is probably an attempt to give the Hidatsa word for Black-lodge people.

Letaiyo. The Gray-fox clan of the Kokop (Firewood) phratry of the Hopi.
Letaiyo wiñwû.—Fewkes in 19th Rep. B. A. E., 584, 1900 (*wiñwû* = 'clan'). Le-tai-yo wün-wû.—Fewkes in Am. Anthrop., VII, 403, 1894.

Leush (*Le'-ush*). A former Modoc settlement on the N. side of Tule (Rhett) lake, s. w. Oreg.—Gatschet in Cont. N. A. Ethnol., II, pt. I, xxxii, 1890.

Lewistown. A village of Shawnee and Seneca, taking its name from the Shawnee chief Captain Lewis, formerly near the site of the present Lewistown, Logan co., Ohio, on lands granted to them by treaty of Sept. 29, 1817, but sold under the provisions of the Lewistown treaty of July 20, 1831. See Howe, Hist. Coll. Oh`o, II, 102, 1896; Royce in 18th Rep. B. A. E., 686, 732, 1899. (J. M.)

Leyva. Located on various early maps apparently as a settlement of New Mexico, but in reality designed to indicate a point supposed to have been reached by Francisco Leyva Bonilla on an unauthorized expedition, about 1594–96, to the Quivira region, by whose inhabitants he and his party were killed. See Bancroft, Ariz. and N. Mex., 108, 1889; D'Anville, map Am. Sept., 1746; Squier in Am. Review, II, 520, 1848.
Leyza.—Güssefeld, Charte America, 1797 (misprint).

Lgalaiguhl-lanas (*L'gala'-iguł lā'nas*). A former subdivision of the Gitins of Skidegate, Queen Charlotte ids., Brit. Col., a family of the Eagle clan of the Haida. It has long been extinct. The name may mean 'people of the town of Lgalai.'— Swanton, Cont. Haida, 274, 1905.

Liam. A former Chumashan village in Ventura co., Cal.—Taylor in Cal. Farmer, July 24, 1863.

Liaywas. An unidentified tribe which participated in the Yakima treaty of 1855, and was placed on Yakima res., Wash. It may have been a division of the Yakima. (L. F.)
Li-ay-was.—U. S. Ind. Treat. (1855), II, 524, 1903. Siaywas.—Ind. Aff. Rep., 110, 1874.

Libantone. A former village, presumably Costanoan, connected with Dolores mission, San Francisco, Cal.—Taylor in Cal. Farmer, Oct. 18, 1861.

Lichtenau (Ger.: 'pastures of light'). A village of Moravian Delawares on the E. side of the Muskingum, 3 m. below Coshocton, Coshocton co., Ohio, established in 1776. Some time afterward it was abandoned by the Moravians on account of the hostilities of the Hurons and other warlike tribes, and reoccupied, under the name of Indaochaie, by hostile Indians, until destroyed by the Americans in 1781. See *Missions*. (J. M.)

Indaochaie.—Butterfield,Washington-IrvineCorr., 52, 1882. Lichtenau.—Loskiel, Hist. Miss. United Breth., pt. 3, 110, 1794; Heckewelder in Trans. Am. Philos. Soc., n. s., IV, 390, 1834.

Lichtenfels (Ger.: 'rocks of light'). A Moravian mission station in w. Greenland.—Crantz, Hist. Greenland, I, map, 1767.

Lick Town. A Shawnee (?) village, in 1776–82, on upper Scioto r., Ohio, probably near Circleville. The true name was probably Piqua or Chillicothe. (J. M.)
Lick Town.—Hutchins, map in Smith, Bouquet's Exped., 1766. Salt Lick Town.—Smith, ibid., 67 (not Salt Lick Town on Mahoning cr.).

Lidlipa. A former Nishinam village in the valley of Bear r., N. Cal.
Lidlepa.—Powers in Overland Mo., XII, 22, 1874. Lid'-li-pa.—Powers in Cont. N. A. Ethnol., III, 316, 1877.

Liebigstag. An Ahtena village on the left bank of Copper r., Alaska, lat. 61° 57', lon. 145° 45'; named from its chief.
Liebigstag's village.—Allen, Rep. on Alaska, 120, 1887.

Liesnoi (Russian: 'woody'). A Kaniagmiut village on Wood id., near Kodiak, Alaska.; pop. 157 in 1880, 120 in 1890.
Lesnoi. — Eleventh Census, Alaska, 75, 1893. Lesnova.—Petroff in 10th Census, Alaska, map, 1884. Tanignagmjut.—Holmberg, Ethnog. Skizz., map, 1855.

Liggigé. A village connected with Concho, or Loreto, 2 leagues N. of that mission, which was situated opposite the island of Carmen, lat. 26°, Lower California (Picolo in Stöcklein, Neue Welt-Bott, no. 72, 35, 1726). Not to be confounded with Liguí, about 14 leagues farther s.

Lightning stick. See *Bull-roarer*.

Lignite. See *Jet*.

Likatuit. A division of the Olamentke, occupying a part of Marin co., Cal. Their last great chief was Marin (q. v.), according to Powers, and they were among the Indians under San Rafael mission.
Lecatuit.—Bancroft, Nat. Races, I, 453, 1874. Likat'-u-it.—Powers in Cont. N. A. Ethnol., III, 195, 1877.

Lilibeque. A Chumashan village on one of the Santa Barbara ids., Cal., probably Santa Rosa, in 1542.
Lilibique.—Cabrillo, Narr. (1542), in Smith, Colec. Doc. Fla., 186, 1857. Lillibique.—Taylor in Cal. Farmer, Apr. 17, 1863.

Lillooet ('wild onion'). One of the 4 principal Salish tribes in the interior of British Columbia, situated on Fraser r. around the mouths of Cayoosh cr. and Bridge r., on Seton and Anderson lakes, and southward from them to Harrison lake. Pop. 978 in 1904. Bands: Anderson Lake, Bridge River, Cayoosh Creek (2), Douglas, Enias, Fountain, Kanlax, Lillooet (2), Mission, Niciat, Pemberton Meadows, and Schloss. It is sometimes divided into the Lower Lillooet, including the Douglas and Pemberton Meadows bands, and the Upper Lillooet, including all the rest. Consult Teit, Lillooet Indians, in Mem. Am. Mus. Nat. Hist., III, pt. 5, 1906. (J. R. S.)

Chin Nation.—Schoolcraft, Ind. Tribes, v, 173, 1855.
Lillooet.—Can, Ind. Aff. Rep. 1889, 115, 1890.
Lilowat.—Gibbs in Cont. N. A. Ethnol., I, 268, 1877.
Loquilt Indians.—Mayne, Brit. Col., 299, 1862.
Sclavthamuk.—Brit. Col. map, Ind. Aff., Victoria,

LILLOOET MAN.   (AM. MUS. NAT. HIST.)

1872. Stā′-tlum-ooh.—Dawson in Trans. Roy. Soc.
Can., sec. II, 5, 1891. Stetlum.—Survey map, Hydr.
Office, U. S. N., 1882. Stlat-limuh.—Mackay quoted
by Dawson in Trans. Roy. Soc. Can. for 1891, sec.

LILLOQET WOMAN.   (AM. MUS. NAT. HIST.)

II, 5. Stla′tliumH.—Boas in 5th Rep. N. W. Tribes
Can., 10, 1889 (own name). Stlā′tliumQ.—Boas in
6th Rep. N. W. Tribes Can., 80, 1890. Stlā′tlumQ.—
Boas as quoted by Dawson in Trans. Roy. Soc.
Can. for 1891, sec. II, 5.

Lillooet. A band and town of Upper Lillooet on Fraser r., where it is joined by Cayoosh cr. The Canadian Reports on Indian Affairs give two divisions of the Lillooet band, of which one numbered 57 and the other 6 in 1904.
Lillooet.—Can. Ind. Aff. Rep., pt. II, 72, 1902.
SEtL.—Teit in Mem. Am. Mus. Nat. Hist., II, 172, 1900 (native name of the village of Lillooet).

Lilmalche (*Lẹmā′tlca*). One of the two Cowichan tribes on Thetis id., off the s. E. coast of Vancouver id.; pop. 19 in 1904. Given as a band of the Penelakut (q. v.) by the Canadian Indian Office.
Lẹmā′tlca.—Boas, MS., B. A. E., 1887. Lilmalche.—
Can. Ind. Aff. for 1901, pt. II, 164. Ll-mache.—Ibid.,
1897, 362, 1898. Ll-mal-che.—Ibid., 1898, 417. Llmal-
ches.—Ibid., 1883, 190.

Lilshiknom. A branch of the Yuki who lived on the w. bank of Eel r., a short distance below the junction of Middle fork and South Eel r., N. Cal.   (A. L. K.)

Lincoln Island. An island in Penobscot r., Me., near Lincoln, 37 m. above Oldtown, occupied by about 30 Penobscot Indians.
Lincoln.—So called by the whites. Madnáguk.—
Gatschet, Penobscot MS., B. A. E., 1887 (Penob-
scot name).

Linguistic families. The linguistic diversity of the Indians is perhaps the most remarkable feature of American ethnology. While certain general features, such, for example, as incorporation, use of verb and pronoun, employment of generic particles, use of nongrammatical genders, etc., usually occur, most of the languages of the New World exhibit analogies justifying their classification, on psychic grounds at least, as a single family of speech; nevertheless, the comparison of their vocabularies leads to the recognition of the existence of a large number of linguistic families or stocks having lexically no resemblance to or connection with each other. Boas (Science, XXIII, 644, 1906) is of the opinion, however, that, considering the enormous differences in the psychological bases of morphology in American Indian languages, such psychic unity in one family of speech can hardly be predicated with confidence. Also, it may be that the Paleo-Asiatic languages of Siberia may perhaps belong with the American tongues. This linguistic diversity was perceived and commented on by some of the early Spanish historians and other writers on American subjects, such as Hervas, Barton, and Adelung; but the "founder of systematic philology relating to the North American Indians" (in the words of Powell) was Albert Gallatin, whose Synopsis of the Indian Tribes within the United States East of the Rocky Mountains and in the British and Russian Possessions in North America was published in 1836 in the Transactions and Collections of the American Antiquarian Society (Archæologia Americana, II), of Worcester, Mass. The progress of research and of linguistic cartography since Gallatin's time is sketched in Powell's epoch-marking article, "Indian linguistic families" (7th Rep. B. A. E., 1–142, 1891), with accompanying map, embodying the author's own researches and those of the experts of the Bureau. Taking vocabulary and dictionary as the factors of discrimination, Powell recognized, N. of the Mexican boundary, the following 58 "distinct linguistic families" or stocks: Adaizan (since determined to be a part of the Caddoan), Algonquian, Athapascan, Attacapan, Beothukan, Caddoan, Chimakuan, Chimarikan, Chimmesyan, Chinookan, Chitimachan, Chumashan, Coahuiltecan, Copehan, Costanoan, Eskimauan, Esselenian, Iroquoian, Kalapooian, Karankawan, Keresan, Kiowan, Kitunahan, Koluschan, Kulanapan, Kusan, Lutuamian, Mariposan, Moquelumnan, Muskhogean, Natchesan, Palaihnihan (since consolidated with Shastan), Piman, Pujunan, Quoratean, Salinan, Salishan, Sastean (Shastan), Shahaptian, Shoshonean, Siouan, Skittagetan, Takilman, Tanoan, Timuquanan, Tonikan, Tonkawan, Uchean, Waiilatpuan, Wakashan, Washoan, Weitspekan, Wishoskan, Yakonan, Yanan, Yukian, Yuman, Zuñian. This is the working list for students of American languages, and, with minor variations, will remain the authoritative document on the classification of American linguistic stocks. (See Kroeber in Am. Anthrop, VII, 570–93, 1905, where modifiations are proposed.) A revised edition of the map, containing the results of the latest investigations, appears in this Handbook.

A marked feature of the distribution of Indian linguistic families N. of Mexico is the presence or former existence in what are now the states of California and Oregon of more than one-third of the total number, while some other stocks (Algonquian, Athapascan, Siouan, Shoshonean, Eskimauan) have a very wide distribution. The Pacific coast contrasts with the Atlantic by reason of the multiplicity of its linguistic families as compared with the few on the eastern littoral. The distribution of the Eskimauan family along the whole Arctic coast from Newfoundland to Bering sea, and beyond it in a portion of Asia, is remarkable. The Uchean and the extinct Beothuk of Newfoundland are really the only small families of the Atlantic slope. The Catawba and related tribes in the Carolinas prove the earlier possession of that country by the primitive Siouan, whose migrations were generally westward. The Tuscarora and related tribes of Virginia and southward show the wanderings of the Iroquois, as do the Navaho and Apache those of the Athapascans.

In 1896 McGee (The Smithson. Inst., 1846–96, 377, 1897) estimated the number of tribes belonging to the various linguistic families as follows: Algonquian 36, Athapascan 53, Attacapan 2, Beothukan 1, Caddoan 9, Chimakuan 2, Chimarikan 2, Chimmesyan (Tsimshian) 8, Chinookan 11, Chitimachan 1, Chumashan 6, Coahuiltecan 22, Copehan 22, Costanoan 5, Eskimauan 70, Esselenian 1, Iroquoian 13, Kalapooian 8, Karankawan 1, Keresan 17, Kiowan 1, Kitunahan 4, Koluschan 12, Kulanapan 30, Kusan 4, Lutuamian 4, Mariposan 24, Moquelumnan 35, Muskhogean 9, Nahuatlan ?, Natchesan 2, Palaihnihan 8, Piman 7, Pujunan 26, Quoratean 3, Salinan 2, Salishan 64, Sastean 1, Serian 3, Shahaptian 7, Shoshonean 12, Siouan 68, Skitttagetan (Haida) 17, Takilman 1, Tanoan 14, Timuquanan 60, Tonikan 3, Tonkawan 1, Uchean 1, Waiilatpuan 2, Wakashan (Kwakiutl-Nootka) 37, Washoan 1, Weitspekan 6, Wishoskan 3, Yakonan 4, Yanan 1, Yukian 5, Yuman 9, Zuñian 1. Of this large number of tribes, some are of little importance, while others may be local divisions and not tribes in the proper sense of the term. This is true, for example, of two at least of the divisions of the Kitunahan family, and of not a few of the Algonquian "tribes." Some families, it will be seen, consist of but a single tribe: Beothukan, Chitimachan, Esselenian, Karankawan, Kiowan, Takilman, Tonkawan, Uchean, Washoan, Yanan, Zuñian; but of these a few (such as Zuñian and Kiowan) are very important. The amount of linguistic variation serving as an index of tribal division varies considerably, and in many cases, especially with the older writers, the delimitations are very imperfect. Researches now in progress will doubtless elucidate some of these points.

Besides the classification noted above, based on vocabulary, certain others are possible which take into consideration grammatical peculiarities, etc., common to several linguistic families. Thus, groups may be distinguished within the 56 families of speech, embracing two or more of them which seem to be grammatically or syntactically related, or in both these respects, while in nowise resembling each other in lexical content. From considerations of this sort Boas finds resemblances between several of the N. W. Pacific coast families. Grammatically, the Koluschan (Tlingit) and Skittagetan (Haida) and the Athapascan seem to be distantly related, and some lexical coincidences have been noted. The occurrence of pronominal gender in the Salishan and Chimakuan stocks is thought by Boas to be of great importance as suggesting relationship between these two families. The

Wakashan (Kwakiutl-Nootka), Salishan, and Chimakuan stocks all possess suffix-nouns and inflected adverbs, similarities pointing, perhaps, to a common source (Mem. Internat. Cong. Anthrop., 339–346, 1894). The languages of California have recently been carefully studied by Dixon and Kroeber (Am. Anthrop., v, 1–26, 1903; vii, 213–17, 1905; viii, no. 4, 1906), and the former has determined, as Gatschet had suspected, that the Sastean and Palaihni-han (Achomawi) constitute one stock, to which the Bureau of American Ethnology applies the name Shastan. A similar coalescence of the Costanoan and Moquelum-nan stocks is also suggested. Taking other than lexical elements into consideration, the languages of California (exclusive of the Yuman and Yanan) may be arranged in three groups: Southwestern, or Chumash type; northwestern, or Yurok type; central, or Maidu type—the last being by far the most numerous. This systematization for California rests on pronominal incorporation, syntactical cases, etc.

Morphological peculiarities, possessed in common, according to some authorities, indicate a relationship between Piman, Nahuatlan (Mexican), and Shoshonean. The Kitunahan of N. Idaho and S. E. British Columbia has some structural characteristics resembling those of the Shoshonean, particularly the method of object-noun incorporation. Gatschet, in 1891 (Karank. Inds., 1891), suggested the probability of some relationship between the Karankawan, Pakawa (Coahuilte-can), and Tonkawan. It is nearly certain also, as supposed by Brinton, that Natchez is a Muskhogean dialect. The now extinct Beothukan of Newfoundland has been suspected of having been a mixed and much distorted dialect of one or other of the great linguistic families of the region adjacent. Brinton (Amer. Race, 68, 1891) was of opinion that "the general morphology seems somewhat more akin to Eskimo than to Algonkin examples."

The amount of material extant in the languages of the various stocks, as well as the literature about them, is in nowise uniform. Some, like the Beothukan, Esselenian, and Karankawan, are utterly extinct, and but small vocabularies of them have been preserved. Of others, who still survive in limited or decreasing numbers, like the Chimakuan, Chimarikan, Chitimachan, Chumashan, Coahuiltecan, Costanoan, Kalapooian, Mariposan, Moquelumnan, Natchesan, Pujunan, Salinan, Shastan, Takilman, Washoan, Weitspekan, Yakonan, and Yukian, the vocabularies and texts collected are not very extensive or conclusive. The Algonquian, Athapascan, Eskimauan, Iroquoian, Muskhogean, Salishan, Skittagetan, Koluschan, and Siouan

families are represented by many grammars, dictionaries, and native texts, both published and in manuscript. The extent and value of these materials may be seen from the bibliographies of the late J. C. Pilling, of the Algonquian, Athapascan, Chinookan, Eskimauan, Iroquoian, Muskhogean, Salishan, Siouan, and Wakashan stocks, published as bulletins by the Bureau of American Ethnology.   (A. F. C.)

Linoklusha (*Lin-ok-lŭ′-sha*, 'crayfish'). A clan of the Kushapokla phratry of the Choctaw.—Morgan, Anc. Soc., 162, 1877.

Lintchanre ('flat sides of dogs'). A clan or division of the Thlingchadinne living N. and E. of the N. arm of Great Slave lake, in Mackenzie Ter., Canada. **Klin-tchanρe.**—Petitot, Autour du lac des Esclaves, 363, 1891. **Klin-tchonρèh.**—Ibid., 303. **Lin-tchanrè.**—Petitot in Bul. Soc. de Géog. Paris, chart, 1875. **ꞌLin-tchanρè.**—Petitot, MS. vocab., B. A. E., 1865. **L'in-tchanρè.**—Petitot, Dict. Dènè-Dindjié, xx, 1876. **Plats-côtés-de-chien du fort Raë.**—Ibid.

Lintja. A former Chumashan village near Santa Barbara, Cal. **Lintja.**—Taylor in Cal. Farmer, Apr. 24, 1863. **Luijta.**—Bancroft, Nat. Races, i, 459, 1874 (misquoted from Taylor).

Lions Creek. The local name for a former band of Salish under Fraser superintendency, Brit. Col. **Leon's Creek.**—Can. Ind. Aff. for 1878, 78. **Lion's Creek.**—Ibid., 1879, 138.

Lipajenne. A subdivision of the Lipan. **Lipajen-ne.**—Orozco y Berra, Geog., 59, 1864. **Lipanjen-né.**—Escudero, Not. Estad. de Chihuahua, 212, 1834.

Lipan (adapted from *Ipa-n'de*, apparently a personal name; *n'de*='people'). An Apache tribe, designating themselves Náizhan ('ours,' 'our kind'), which at various periods of the 18th and 19th centuries roamed from the lower Rio Grande in New Mexico and Mexico eastward through Texas to the Gulf coast, gaining a livelihood by depredations against other tribes and especially against the white settlements of Texas and Mexico. The name has probably been employed to include other Apache groups of the southern plains, such as the Mescaleros and the Kiowa Apache. The Franciscan mission of San Sabá (q. v.) was established among the Lipan in Texas in 1757, but it was soon destroyed by their enemies, the Comanche and Wichita. In 1761–62 the missions of San Lorenzo and Candelaria were also founded, but these met a like fate in 1767. In 1805 the Lipan were reported to be divided into 3 bands, numbering 300, 350, and 100 men, respectively; this apparently gave rise to their subdivision by Orozco y Berra in 1864 into the Lipa-jenne, Lipanes de Arriba, and Lipanes de Abajo. In 1839, under chief Castro, they sided with the Texans against the Comanche (Schoolcraft, Thirty Years, 642, 1851); they were always friends with their congeners, the Mescaleros, and with the Tonkawa after 1855, but were enemies of the Jicarillas and the Ute. Between 1845 and 1856 they suffered severely in the Texan wars, the design of which was the extermination of the Indians within the Texas border. Most of them were driven into Coahuila, Mexico, where they resided in the Santa Rosa mts. with Kickapoo and other refugee Indians from the United States, until the 19 survivors were taken to N. w. Chihuahua, in Oct., 1903, whence they were brought to the United States about the beginning of 1905 and placed on the Mescalero res., N. Mex., where they now (1905) number about 25 and are making more rapid progress toward civilization than their Indian neighbors. In addition there are one or two Lipan numbered with the 54 Tonkawa under the Ponca, Pawnee, and Oto agency, Oakland res., Okla., and a few with the Kiowa Apache in the same territory, making the total population about 35. The Lipan resemble the other Apache in all important characteristics. They were often known under the designation Cancy, Chanze, etc., the French form of the Caddo collective name (*Kä'ntsi*) for the eastern Apache tribes.   (F. W. H.)

Apaches Lipanes.—MS., 1791-92, in Tex. State archives. Á-tagúi.—Mooney, field notes, B. A. E., 1897 ('timber Apache': Kiowa name, used also for Mescaleros). Canceres.—Escudero, Not. Nuevo Méx., 84, 1849. Cancers.—Lewis, Trav., 195, 1809. Cances.—Sibley (1805), Hist. Sketches, 74, 1806 (Caddo name: 'deceivers'). Cancey.—Fr. Doc. of 1719 quoted by Bandelier in Arch. Inst. Papers, III, 173, 1890. Canchy.—Bienville (1700) in Margry, Déc., IV, 442, 1880. Cancy.—La Harpe (1719), ibid., VI, 277, 285, 1886. Canecis.—Jefferys, Am. Atlas, map 8, 1776. Caneeci.—Anville, map N. Am., 1752. Canees.—Schoolcraft, Ind. Tribes, V, 571, 1855. Canessy.—Iberville (1700) in Margry, Déc., IV, 374, 1880. Cannecis.—Baudry des Lozières, Voy. La., 242, 1802. Cannecy.—La Harpe (1719) in Margry, Déc., VI, 262, 1880. Cannensis.—French, Hist. Coll. La., II, 11, 1875. Cannessi.—Carte des Poss. Angloises, 1777. Cantey.—Joutel (1687) in Margry, Déc., III, 409, 1878. Chancré.—Joutel (1687) in Margry, Déc., III, 288, 1878. Chanzes.—Joutel (1687) in French, Hist. Coll. La., I, 138, 846. Concee.—Sibley, Hist. Sketches, 110, 1806. Gipanes.—Hamilton, Mex. Handbk., 48, 1883. Hu-ta'-ci.—ten Kate, Synonymie, 9, 1884 ('forest Apache': Comanche name). Húχul.—Gatschet, Tonkawe MS., B. A. E. (Tonkawa name). Ipa-nde.—Arricivita (1792) quoted by Bandelier in Arch. Inst. Papers, III, 181, 1890. Ipandi.—Ibid., 180. K'än'-dzi.—ten Kate, Synonymie, 10, 1884 (Caddo name). Kantsi'.—Gatschet, Caddo and Yatassi MS., B. A. E., 65. Kareses.—McKenney and Hall, Ind. Tribes, III, 79, 1858 (probably identical). Lanecy.—Walche, Charte von Am., 1805 (misprint). Lapan.—Niles' Register, LXXI, 119, 1846. Lapanas.—Bollaert in Jour. Ethnol. Soc. Lond., II, 276, 1850. Lapane.—Drake, Bk. Inds., vi, 1848. Lapanne.—Ibid., viii. Lee Panis.—Pike, Trav., 337, 1811. Lee Pawnees.—Pike, Exped., app., pt. 3, 29, 1810. Lepan.—Sen. Ex. Conf. Doc. 13, 29th Cong., 2d sess., 1, 1846. Le Panis.—Pike, Exped., app., pt. 3, 9, 1810. Lipaines.—Alegre, Hist. Comp. Jésus, I, 336, 1841. Lipane.—MS. in Tex. State arch., no. 155, 1792. Lipanes Llaneros.—Doc. of 1828 in Bol. Soc. Geog. Mex., 264, 1870. Lipanis.—Drake, Bk. Inds., ix, 1848. Lipanos.—Escudero, Not. Estad. de Chihuahua, 244, 1834. Lipau.—Ind. Aff. Rep., 176, 1875 (misprint). Lipaw.—Hoffman in Bul. Soc. d'Anthrop. de Paris, 3d s., VI, 206, 1883 (misprint). Lippans.—Butler and Lewis (1846) in H. R. Doc. 76, 29th Cong., 2d sess., 4, 1847 Na'-izhǎ'ñ.—Mooney, field notes, B. A. E., 1897 (own name: 'ours', 'our kind' + *dina*, 'people': cf. Kiowa Apache). Navóne.—Gatschet, Comanche MS., B. A. E., 1884 (Comanche name). Nipán.—Ibid. (Comanche pron. of Lipan) Ocanes.—Uhde, Länder, 121, 1861 (probably identical). Pawnee.—Schermerhorn (1812) in Mass. Hist. Coll., 2d s., II, 29, 1814 (mistake). Seepans.—Lane (1854) in Schoolcraft, Ind. Tribes, V, 689, 1855. Shi'íni.—Mooney, field notes, B. A. E., 1897 ('summer people' (?): former Mescalero name). Siapanes.—Uhde, Länder, 121, 1861. Sinapans.—Iberville (1699) in Margry, Déc., IV, 316, 1880. Sipan.—Latham in Trans. Philol. Soc. Lond., 102, 1856. Sypanes.—Robin Voy. Louisiane, III, 15, 1807. Tu-tsän-nde.—Mooney, field notes, B. A. E., 1897 ('great water people': Mescalero name). Úχul.—Gatschet, Tonkawe MS., B. A. E. (Tonkawa name for a spiral shell; applied to the Lipan on account of their coiled hair). Yabipais Lipan.—Garcés (1776), Diary, 404, 1900. Yavipai-Lipanes.—Garcés (1776) cited by Bandelier in Arch. Inst. Papers, III, 114, 1890.

Lipanes de Abajo (Span.: 'lower Lipans'). A former branch of the Lipan. Lipanes de Abajo.—Orozco y Berra, Geog., 59, 1864. Lipanes del Sur.—Doc. of 1828 in Bol. Soc. Geog. Mex., 504, 1869.

Lipanes de Arriba (Span.: 'upper Lipans'). A former branch of the Lipan. Lipanes de Arriba.—Orozco y Berra, Geog., 59, 1864. Lipanes del Norte.—Doc. of 1828 in Bol. Soc. Geog. Mex., 504, 1869.

Lipillanes. Mentioned as a division of the Llaneros. See *Gohlkahin, Guhlkainde, Kwahari*. Lipallanes.—Escudero, Not. de Chihuahua, 226, 1834. Lipillanes.—Orozco y Berra, Geog., 59, 1864. Lipiyanes.—Escudero, Not. de Sonora y Sinaloa, 68, 1849.

Lipook. A former Chumashan village near Purísima mission, Santa Barbara co., Cal.—Taylor in Cal. Farmer, May 4, 1860.

Lisahuato. A former Chumashan village near Purísima mission, Santa Barbara co., Cal.—Taylor in Cal. Farmer, Oct. 18, 1861.

Lisichi. A former Chumashan village in Ventura co., Cal.—Taylor in Cal. Farmer, July 24, 1863.

Lisuchu. A former Chumashan village near Santa Barbara Cal. (Taylor in Cal. Farmer, Apr. 24, 1863). Perhaps identical with the preceding.

Lithonca. A former village, presumably Costanoan, connected with San Juan Bautista mission, Cal.—Taylor in Cal. Farmer, Nov. 25, 1860.

Littefutchi. A former Upper Creek town at the head of Canoe cr., in St Clair co., Ala. It was burned by Col. Dyer, Oct. 29, 1813. Littafatchee.—Royce in 18th Rep. B. A. E., Ala. map, 1899. Littafutchee.—Flint, Ind. Wars, 175, 1833. Littefutchee.—Pickett, Hist. Ala., II, 294, 1851. Olitifar.—Juan de la Vandera (1579) in Smith, Colec. Doc. Fla., I, 18, 1857.

Little Abraham. See *Abraham*.

Little Carpenter. See *Attakullaculla*.

Little Crow (*Chetañ wakan mañi*, 'the sacred pigeon-hawk which comes walking'). A chief of the Kaposia division of the Mdewakanton Sioux, which, under his father Little Crow, as under his grandfather Little Thunder, had its headquarters at Kaposia (Kapozha), a village on the w. bank of the Mississippi, 10 or 12 m. below the mouth of Minnesota r. In 1846, while intoxicated, he was shot and wounded by his brother; this caused him to try to discourage drinking among his followers, and probably induced him the same year to ask of the Indian agent at Ft Snelling a missionary to reside at his village, as a result of which Rev. Thomas S. Williamson was sent. Although Little Crow was a signer (under the name of Ta-oya-te-duta, 'His people are red') of the treaty of Mendota, Minn., Aug. 5, 1851, by which the Dakota ceded most of their Minnesota lands to the United States, he used the treaty as a means of creating dissatisfaction and ultimately in bringing on the disastrous outbreak of 1862. In this outbreak, during which more than a thousand settlers were killed, Little Crow was the recognized leader. Subsequent to the cession of 1851 several bands, including the Kaposia, were removed to a large reservation on the upper Minnesota, where they dwelt peacefully, professing genuine friendship for the white settlers, until they rose suddenly on Aug. 18, 1862, and spreading themselves along the frontier for more than 200 m., killed white men, women, and children without mercy. Little Crow led the fierce though unsuccessful attack on Ft Ridgely, Minn., Aug. 20–22, 1862, in

LITTLE CROW THE ELDER.   (McKENNEY AND HALL)

which he was slightly wounded. After the defeat of the hostiles at Wood lake, Sept. 23, 1862, by Gen. Sibley, Little Crow with 200 or 300 followers fled to the protection of his kindred on the plains far-

ther w. He was killed by a settler named Lampson, July 3, 1863, at a place N. of Hutchinson, McLeod co., Minn. He was probably nearly 60 years of age at the time of his death. Little Crow had had

LITTLE CROW THE YOUNGER

6 wives and 22 children. Consult Minn. Hist. Soc. Coll., III, 1880; IV, 1876; Bryant and Murch, History of the Great Massacre by the Sioux Indians in 1862; Indian Affairs Report for 1863; Neill, Hist. Minn., 1858.   (C. T.)

Little Forks. A Chippewa res. formerly on Tittibawassee r., in lower Michigan, sold in 1837.

Little Munsee Town. A former Munsee village a few miles E. of Anderson, Madison co., Ind., on land sold in 1818 (Royce in 1st Rep. B. A. E., map, 1881). It may be identical with Kiktheswemud.

Little Osage Village. A former Osage village on Osage res., Okla., on the w. bank of Neosho r.—McCoy (1837) in Sen. Doc. 120, 25th Cong., 2d sess., map, 952, 1838.

Little Raven (*Hósa*, 'Young Crow'). An Arapaho chief. He was first signer, for the Southern Arapaho, of the treaty of Fort Wise, Colo., Feb. 18, 1861. At a later period he took part with the allied Arapaho and Cheyenne in the war along the Kansas border, but joined in the treaty of Medicine Lodge, Kans., in 1867, by which these tribes agreed to go on a reservation, after which treaty all his effort was consistently directed toward keeping his people at peace with the Government and leading them to civilization. Through his influence the body of the Arapaho remained at peace with the whites when their allies, the Cheyenne and Kiowa, went on the warpath in 1874–75. Little Raven died at Cantonment, Okla., in the winter of 1889, after having maintained for 20 years a reputation as the leader of the progressive element. He was succeeded by Nawat, 'Left-hand'. (J. M.)

Little Rock Band. Mentioned by Parker (Minn. Handbk., 141, 1857) as a Sisseton division. Not identified.

Little Rock Village. A Potawatomi village in N. E. Illinois in 1832 (Camp Tippecanoe treaty (1832) in U. S. Ind. Treat., 698, 1873); situated on the N. bank of Kankakee r., about the boundary of Kankakee and Will cos.

Little Thunder. A Brulé Sioux chief during the middle of the 19th century. He was present at the Grattan massacre near Ft Laramie in 1854, and assumed command when chief Singing Bear was killed; he also took part in the battle of Ash Hollow, Nebr., with Gen. Harney, in 1855, and continued chief until his death some years later. Physically Little Thunder was a giant, fully six feet six inches tall and large in proportion, and is spoken of as of superior intelligence.

Little Turtle (*Michikinikwa*). A chief of the Miami tribe, born at his village on Eel r., Ind., in 1752. His father was a Miami chief and his mother a Mahican; hence, according to the Indian rule, he was a Mahican and received no advantage from his father's rank—that is, he was not chief by descent. However, his talents having attracted the notice of his countrymen, he was made chief of the Miami while a comparatively young man. Little Turtle was the principal leader of the Indian forces that defeated Gen. Harmar on Miami r. in Oct. 1790, and Gen. St Clair, at St. Marys, Nov. 4, 1791, and he and Bluejacket were among the foremost leaders of the Indians in their conflict with Gen. Wayne's army in 1795, although he had urged the Indians to make peace with this "chief who never sleeps." After their defeat by the whites he joined in the treaty at Greenville, Ohio, Aug. 3, 1795, remarking, as he signed it, "I am the last to sign it, and I will be the last to break it." Faithful to this promise he remained passive and counseled peace on the part of his people until his death at Ft Wayne, July 14, 1812. Early in 1797, accompanied by Capt. Wells, his brother-in-law, he visited President Washington at Philadelphia, where he met Count Volney and Gen. Kosciusko, the latter presenting him with his own pair of elegantly mounted pistols. Although Tecumseh endeavored to draw him away from his peaceful relations with the whites, his efforts were in vain. Llitte Turtle's Indian name as signed to different treaties varies as follows: Greenville, Aug. 3, 1795, Meshekunnoghquoh; Ft Wayne, June 7, 1803, Meseekunnoghquoh; Vincennes, Aug. 21, 1805, Mashekakahquoh; Ft Wayne, Sept. 30, 1809, Meshekenoghqua. Consult Drake, Inds. N. Am., 1880; Brice, Hist. Fort Wayne, 1868; Appleton's Cyclop. Am. Biog., III, 1894. (C. T.)

Little Turtle's Village. A former Miami village on Eel r., Ind., about 20 m. N. w. of Ft Wayne; named after the celebrated chief, Little Turtle, who was born there in 1752 and made it his home. It was in existence as late as 1812, the year of Little Turtle's death.

LITTLE TURTLE. (FROM A PAINTING BY STUART IN 1797, SINCE DESTROYED)

Lituya. A name given by Niblack to a Tlingit division living about Lituya bay, S. E. Alaska. They are properly a part of the Huna, q. v.

Lituya.—Niblack, Coast Ind. of Alaska, chart I, 1889. Ltuiskoe.—Veniaminoff, Zapiski, II, pt. III, 29, 1840 (a town with 200 pop.). Shltuja.—Holmberg, Ethnog. Skizz., map, 1855.

Livangebra. A former rancheria, presumably Costanoan, connected with Dolores mission, San Francisco, Cal.

Livangebra.—Taylor in Cal. Farmer, Oct. 18, 1861. Livangelva.—Ibid. (mentioned as distinct, though seemingly identical). Luianeglua.—Ibid. (also mentioned as distinct).

Liwaito (Wintun: = *liwai*, 'waving'). A former village of the Patwin subfamily of the Wintun, on the site of the present town of Winters, Yolo co., Cal. The Wintun applied the name also to Putah cr. (S. A. B.)

Lewytos.—Powers in Overland Mo., XIII, 542, 1874. Liguaytoy.—Bancroft, Hist. Cal., IV, 71, 1886.

Li-wai'-to.—Powers in Cont. N. A. Ethnol., III, 218, 1877.

Liyam (*Li'-yăm*). A former Chumashan village on Santa Cruz id., Cal.—Henshaw, Buenaventura MS. vocab., B. A. E., 1884.

Llagas (Span.: 'wounds'). A former group of Cocopa rancherias on the w. side of the Rio Colorado, just below tidewater, about lat. 32°, in N. E. Lower California. Visited and so named by Fray Francisco Garcés, Sept. 17, 1771, which is given as the day of the wounds or sores of St Francis Assisi.—Garcés (1775), Diary, 188, 1900.

Llaneros (Span.: 'plainsmen'). A term indefinitely applied to the former wild tribes of the Staked plains of w. Texas and E. New Mexico, including the Kwahari Comanche (q. v.) and parts of the Jicarillas and the Mescaleros. See *Gohlkahin, Guhlkainde*.

Llano. A Papago village in s. Arizona; pop. 70 in 1858.
Del Llano.—Bailey in Ind. Aff. Rep., 208, 1858.

Lochchiocha. A former Seminole town 60 m. E. of Apalachicola, and near Okloknee, Fla.; Okoskaamathla was chief in 1823.—H. R. Ex. Doc. 74 (1823), 19th Cong., 1st sess., 26, 1826.

Locobo. A Costanoan village situated in 1819 within 10 m. of Santa Cruz mission, Cal.—Taylor in Cal. Farmer, Apr. 5, 1860.

Locust Necktown. A village in Maryland, occupied in 1792 by that band of the Nanticoke known as Wiwash, q. v.
Locust Neck.—Mt Johnson conf. (1755) in N. Y. Doc. Col. Hist., VI, 983, 1855. Locust Necktown.—Gallatin in Trans. Am. Antiq. Soc., II, 53, 1836.

Lodges. See *Earth lodge, Grass lodge, Habitations*.

Lodges without horses. A former Crow band.—Culbertson in Smithson. Rep. 1850, 144, 1851.

Lofka. A former Kaiyuhkhotana settlement on the w. bank of Yukon r., Alaska. The place probably consisted of only a single hut occupied by an Indian named Lofka, at which the earliest American travelers on the Yukon used to spend the night.
Lofka's barrabora.—Dall, Alaska, 211, 1870.

Logan. A synonym of *pokeloken*, in use in Maine, and probably a corruption of that word. (A. F. C.)

Logan, John (?) (native name *Tah-gah-jute*, lit. 'his eyelashes stick out or above,' as if looking through or over something, and so could well mean 'spying.'—Hewitt). A noted Indian chief, born at Shamokin, Pa., about 1725. His father, called by the English Shikellamy and by the Moravians Shikellemus, according to Crantz (Hist. of the Brethren, 269, 1780), was a white man, taken prisoner in Canada and reared among the Indians, and was later made chief of all or a part of the Indians residing at Shamokin. He is usually spoken of as a Cayuga chief, while others call him a Mingo, the common term in the colonial period for those Iroquois living beyond their proper boundaries. Bartram says that he was a Frenchman born in Montreal, but as a prisoner was adopted by the Oneida. The same authority further states that his son (presumably Tah-gah-jute) took the name Logan from his friend James Logan, who was secretary and for a time acting governor of Pennsylvania. He lived a number of years near Reedsville, Pa., supporting himself and family by hunting and the sale of dressed skins. Later, about 1770, he removed to the Ohio and was living at the mouth of Beaver cr. when visited by Heckewelder in 1772; and in 1774, about the time of the Dunmore war, he resided at Old Chillicothe, now Westfall, on the w. bank of Sciota r., Pickaway co., Ohio. In 1774 a number of Indians, including some of Logan's relatives, were brutally massacred at the mouth of Yellow cr. by settlers on the Ohio, in retaliation, it was claimed, for the murder of white emigrants, and for a time Michael Cresap was supposed to be the leader in this massacre. There has been much controversy as to the facts in this case. A careful study of the evidence given by Jefferson in the appendix to his Notes on Virginia, by J. J. Jacob in his Biographical Sketch of the Life of Michael Cresap, and by Brantz Mayer in his Tah-gah-jute, leads to the conclusion that the massacre of the Indians was by Greathouse and a party of white settlers, and that Cresap was not present; that Logan's sister, and possibly some other relative, were killed; that his wife was not murdered, and that he had no children. It seems evident, however, that Logan was brought in some way to believe that Cresap led the attack. For several months Logan made war on the border settlements, perpetrating fearful barbarities upon men, women, and children. In the celebrated speech attributed to him he boasts of these murders. This supposed speech was probably only a memorandum written down from his statement and afterward read before the treaty meeting at Chillicothe, at which Logan was not present. His intemperate habits, begun about the time of his removal to the Ohio, grew upon him, and after the return of peace compelled him to forbear the use of the tomahawk he became an abandoned sot. On his return from a trip to Detroit in 1780 he was killed by his nephew, apparently in a quarrel. His wife, who was a Shawnee woman, survived him, but no children resulted from their union. A monument to Logan stands in Fort Hill cemetery, Auburn, N. Y. (C. T.)

Consult Doddridge, Settlement and Indian Wars, 1821; Howe, Hist. Coll. Ohio, ii, 402, 1896; Jacob, Sketch of Cresap, 1866; Jefferson, Notes on Va., 1802, 1804; Kercheval, Hist. of the Valley of Va., 1833; Loudon, Narratives, ii, 1811; Mayer, Tah-gah-jute or Logan, 1867; Stevenson in W. Va. Hist. Mag., iii, 144, 1903.

Logstown. An important village formerly on the right bank of Ohio r., about 18 m. below Pittsburg, in Allegheny co., Pa. It was originally settled by Shawnee and Delawares prior to 1748, and in the following year was reported by Céloron to contain 40 cabins occupied by Iroquois, Shawnee, "Loups" (Delaware, Munsee, and Mahican), as well as Iroquois from Sault St Louis and Lake of Two Mountains, with some Nipissing, Abnaki, and Ottawa. Father Bonnecamps, of the same expedition, estimated the number of cabins at 80, and says "we called it Chiningué, from its vicinity to a river of that name" (Mag. Am. Hist., ii, 142, 1878); but it should not be confounded with the Shenango some distance N., on Beaver cr. Croghan in 1765 (Thwaites, Early West. Trav., i, 127, 1904) speaks of Logstown as an old settlement of the Shawnee. It was abandoned about 1750 and reoccupied by a mixed population of Mingo (chiefly Seneca), Mahican, Ottawa, and others in the English interest. About this time a new village was built with the aid of the French on a hill overlooking the old site. Logstown was an important trading rendezvous, one of Croghan's trading houses being established there; it was also the home of Half-King (Scruniyatha or Monakatuatha) in 1753–54 (although it is stated that his dwelling was situated a few miles away), and was a customary stopping place of colonial officers and emissaries, as Weiser, Gist, Croghan, Céloron, and Washington, the latter remaining here five days while on his way to Venango and Le Bœuf in 1753, and again making it a resting place while on his way to Kanawha r. in 1770. Logstown was also the scene of the treaty between the Virginia commissioners and the Indians of this section in 1752. According to the author of Western Navigation (76, 1814), and Cuming (Western Tour, 80, 1810), there was also a settlement known as Logstown on the opposite side of the Ohio. It was abandoned by the Indians in 1758, immediately after the capture of Ft Du Quesne. In addition to the authorities cited, see Darlington, Christopher Gist's Journals, 1893; Pa. Col. Rec., v, 348 et seq., 1851.　　　　(c. t.)

Chiningué.—Céloron (1749) in Mag. Am. Hist., ii, 143, 1878. Chinningé.—Thwaites, Early West. Trav., i, 24, note, 1904. Lockstown.—Narr. of Marie Le Roy and Barbara Leininger (1759) transl. in Pa. Mag. Hist. and Biog., xxix, no. 116, 412, 1905. Loggs Town.—Dinwiddie Papers (1751), i, 6, 1883.

Logg's-Town.—Hamilton (1749) in N. Y. Doc. Col. Hist., vi, 531, 1855. Loggs-town.—Bouquet (1764), Exped., 45, 1868. Logs Town.—Croghan (1748) in N. Y. Doc. Col. Hist., vii, 267, 1856. Log's Town.—French officer (1749), ibid., iv, 533, 1855. Shenango.—Thwaites, op. cit.

Lohastahni (*Lo-hās-tāh'-ni*). A former Chumashan village in Ventura co., Cal.—Henshaw, Buenaventura MS. vocab., B. A. E., 1884.

Lohim. A small Shoshonean band living on Willow cr., a s. affluent of the Columbia, in s. Oregon, and probably belonging to the Mono-Paviotso group. They have never made a treaty with the Government and are generally spoken of as renegades belonging to the Umatilla res. (Mooney). In 1870 their number was reported as 114, but the name has not appeared in recent official reports. Ross mistook them for Nez Percés.

Lo-hĭm.—Mooney in 14th Rep. B. A. E., 743, 1896. Low-him.—Ross, Fur Hunters, i, 186, 1855. Willow Creek Indians.—Mooney, op cit.

Lojos. A former Chumashan village in Ventura co., Cal.—Taylor in Cal. Farmer, July 24, 1863.

Loka ('reeds' [*phragmites*]). A Navaho clan.

Lòka.—Matthews in Jour. Am. Folk-lore, iii, 104, 1890. Lòkaɡine.—Ibid. (ɡine = 'people'). Lòka-dĭne'.—Matthews, Navaho Legends, 31, 1897 (dine = 'people').

Loko. A tribe, probably Paviotso, formerly living on or near Carson r., w. Nev.—Holeman in Ind. Aff. Rep., 152, 1852.

Loksachumpa. A former Seminole town at the head of St Johns r., Fla. Lokpoka Takoosa Hajo was chief in 1823.—H. R. Ex. Doc. 74 (1823), 19th Cong., 1st sess., 27, 1826.

Lolanko (the Sinkine name of Bull cr.). A part of the Sinkine dwelling on Bull and Salmon crs., tributaries of the s. fork of Eel r., Humboldt co., Cal.

Flonk'-o.—Powers in Cont. N. A. Ethnol., iii, 113, 1877 (so called by whites). Loloncooks.—Bancroft, Nat. Races, i, 447, 1874. Lo-lon'-kŭk.—Powers, op. cit. Loolanko.—A. L. Kroeber, inf'n, 1903 (Bull cr.).

Lolsel (*lol* 'tobacco', *sel* 'people'). The name applied to the Wintun living in and about Long valley, E. of Clear lake, Lake co., Cal. Their territory extended w. to the summit of the mountain range just E. of Clear lake and was there contiguous to Pomo territory.　　　　(s. a. b.)

Lold'-la.—Powers in Cont. N. A. Ethnol., iii, 219, 1877. Loldlas.—Powers in Overland Mo., xiii, 542, 1874. Lol'-sel.—Powers in Cont. N. A. Ethnol., iii, 219, 1877.

Lomavik. A Kuskwogmiut Eskimo village on the left bank of Kuskokwim r., Alaska; pop. 81 in 1880, 53 in 1900.

Lomavigamute.—Nelson (1879) quoted by Baker, Geog. Dict. Alaska, 269, 1902. Lomavik.—Baker, ibid. Lomawigamute.—Petroff, Rep. on Alaska, 53, 1881.

Lompoc. A former Chumashan village near Purísima mission, Santa Barbara co., Cal.—Taylor in Cal. Farmer, Oct. 18, 1861.

Lone Wolf (*Gúipä'go*). A Kiowa chief, one of the 9 signers of the treaty of Medicine Lodge, Kans., in 1867, by which the

Kiowa first agreed to be placed on a reservation. In 1872 he headed a delegation to Washington. The killing of his son by the Texans in 1873 embittered him against the whites, and in the outbreak of the following year he was the recognized leader of the hostile part of the tribe. On the surrender in the spring of 1875 he, with a number of others, was sent to military confinement at Ft Marion, Fla., where they remained 3 years. He died in 1879, shortly after his return, and was succeeded by his adopted son, of the same name, who still retains authority in the tribe. (J. M.)

LONE WOLF

Longe. An abbreviation in common use among English-speaking people of the region of the great lakes, particularly the N. shore of L. Ontario, for *maskalonge*, a variant of *maskinonge* (q. v.). The form *lunge* represents another variant, *muskelunge*. The name is applied also to the Great Lake trout (*Salvelinus namaycush*). See *Mackinaw*. (A. F. C.)

Long Island (*Ămăye'lĭ-gŭnăhi'ta*, from *ămăye'lĭ* 'island', *gŭnăhi'ta* 'long'). A former Cherokee town at the Long id. in Tennessee r., on the Tennessee-Georgia line. It was settled in 1782 by Cherokee who espoused the British cause in the Revolutionary war, and was known as one of the Chickamauga towns. It was destroyed in the fall of 1794. See Royce in 5th Rep. B. A. E., map, 1887; Mooney in 19th Rep. B. A. E., 508, 526, 1900. (J. M.)

Long Lake. A former Chippewa village on Long lake, in Bayfield co., N. Wis.—Warren (1852) in Minn. Hist. Soc. Coll., v, 191, 1885.

Long Lake. A Chippewa band on Long lake, N. of L. Superior, between Nipegon lake and Pic r., Ontario; pop. 311 in 1884, 341 in 1904.

Long Sioux. The chief of one of the Dakota bands not brought into Ft Peck agency, Mont., in 1872 (H. R. Ex. Doc. 96, 42d Cong., 3d sess., 5, 1873). It had 28 tipis. Not identified.

Long Tail. In 1854 a Shawnee chief of this name ruled a band at "Long Tail's settlement" in Johnson co., Kans.—Washington treaty (1854) in U. S. Ind. Treat., 795, 1873.

Longushharkarto (*Long-ush-har-kar'-to*, 'brush log'). A sub-clan of the Delawares (q. v.).—Morgan, Anc. Soc., 172, 1877.

Lookout Mountain Town (adapted from the Cherokee *Â'tălĭ da'ndaka'nĭhă*, 'mountains looking at each other'). A former Cherokee town at or near the present Trenton, Dade co., N. W. Ga. It was settled in 1782 by Cherokee who espoused the British cause in the Revolutionary war, and was known as one of the Chickamauga towns. It was destroyed in the fall of 1794. (J. M.)
Â'tălĭ da'ndaka'nĭhă.—Mooney, inf'n, 1906 (full Cherokee name). Danda' gănŭ'.—Mooney in 19th Rep. B. A. E., 514, 1900 ('Two looking at each other': Cherokee name). Lookout Mountain.—Doc. of 1799 quoted by Royce in 5th Rep. B. A. E., 144, 1887. Lookout Mt. Town.—Royce in 5th Rep. B. A. E., map, 1887. Ottilletaraoonohah.—Ballew (1789) in Am. State Papers, Ind. Aff., I, 56, 1832.

Loolego (*Lo-o-le-go*). A Yurok village on lower Klamath r., Cal., 2 m. above the fork with the Trinity. A fish dam was regularly built here.—A. L. Kroeber, inf'n, 1904.

Lopotatimni. A division of the Miwok formerly living in Eldorado or Sacramento co., Cal.
Lapototot.—Bancroft, Nat. Races, I, 450, 1874. Lopotalimnes.—Gallatin in Trans. Am. Ethnol. Soc., II, 123, 1848. Lopotatimnes.—Hale in U. S. Expl. Exped., VI, 630, 1846. Lopstatimnes.—Bancroft, op. cit. (misquoted from Hale). Sapototot.—Ibid.

Loquasquscit. A former Wampanoag "plantation" near Pawtucket r., Providence co. (?), R. I. It was sold in 1646.
Loquasquscit.—Deed of 1646 in R. I. Col. Rec., I, 33, 1856. Loqusquscit.—Ibid., 32. Loqusqusitt.—Ibid.

Lorenzo. A former Diegueño village N. E. of San Diego, Cal.—Hayes (1850) quoted by Bancroft, Nat. Races, I, 458, 1882.

Loreto. A village, probably of the Tubare, on the N. bank of the s. fork of Rio del Fuerte, lat. 26° 45', lon. 107° 30', s. w. Chihuahua, Mexico.

Loreto. A Varohio village and the seat of a Spanish mission, situated N. of Chinipas valley, lat. 27° 48', lon. 108° 30', N. Sinaloa, Mexico.
Nuestra Señora de Loreto de Voragios.—Orozco y Berra, Geog., 324, 1864. Sinoyeca.—Ibid. (native name).

Lorette. A Huron village situated 8 m. N. W. of Quebec, Canada. The present village, properly distinguished as Jeune

Lorette, is some miles distant from Ancienne Lorette, the old village, w. of and nearer to Quebec, which was abandoned for the present location after 1721. The inhabitants are a remnant of the Hurons (q. v.) who fled from their country on account of the Iroquois about 1650. After stopping on Orleans id. they removed in 1693 to Ancienne Lorette. In 1884 they numbered 289; in 1904, 455. See *Huron, Missions*. (J. M.)

Lorett.—German Flats conf. (1770) in N. Y. Doc. Col. Hist., VIII, 229, 1857. Loretta.—Jefferys, Fr. Dom., pt. 1, map, 1761. Lorette.—Clinton (1745) in N. Y. Doc. Col. Hist., VI, 276, 1855. Loretto.— Doc. of 1693, ibid., IX, 557, 1855. Pematnawiak.— Gatschet, Penobscot MS., B. A. E., 1887 (Penobscot name).

Los Angeles. A former rancheria, inhabited apparently by both Pima Alta and Seri, on the w. bank of Rio Horcasitas, central Sonora, Mexico. It dates from early Spanish times, but is probably not now known by this name.

Angeles.—Kino, map (1702) in Stöcklein, Neue Welt-Bott, 74, 1726. Los Angeles.—Doc. of 1730 quoted by Bancroft, No. Mex. States, I, 513, 1884.

Los Luceros (Span.: 'the morning stars'). A small settlement situated at the site of the ancient pueblo of Pioge, on the E. bank of the Rio Grande, near Plaza del Alcalde, Rio Arriba co., N. Mex. Mentioned by Gatschet in 1879 as a pueblo of the Tewa Indians, whereas it is a Mexican village, although it may have contained at that time a few Tewa from San Juan pueblo, about 3 m. s.

Los Leuceuros.—Yarrow in Ann. Rep. Wheeler Surv., app. LL, 143, 1875. Los Luceros.—Gatschet in Wheeler Surv. Rep., Archæol., VII, 417, 1879.

Lost Ten Tribes of Israel. The belief, for which no positive authority seems to exist, has long been current that in 721 B. C., Sargon, king of Assyria, the successor of Shalmaneser, carried off into captivity ten of the twelve tribes of Israel. Other deportations are attributed to Tiglath-Pileser and Shalmaneser. Not all the people were deported; nor were those who were, actually lost. Still, the assumption that they were lost has given rise to absurd theories, according to which these missing tribes have been discovered in every quarter of the globe. The most popular theories are one which identifies them with the Anglo-Saxons and another which sees their descendants in the American Indians. Father Duran in 1585 was one of the first to state explicitly that "these natives are of the ten tribes of Israel that Shalmaneser, king of the Assyrians, made prisoners and carried to Assyria." The latest variants of the theory may be met with in the present-day newspapers. Antonio de Montezinos, a Marano (secret Jew), while journeying in South America in 1641 claimed that he met savages who followed Jewish practices. This story he repeated in Holland, in 1644, to Manasseh ben Israel, who printed it in his work, Hope of Israel.

From it Thomas Thorowgood, in 1652, published Digitus Dei, in which he sought to prove that the Indians were the Jews "lost in the world for the space of near 2,000 years." From this work many subsequent writers obtained their chief arguments. This theory, however, found opponents even in the 17th century. Among these were William Wood, author of the curious New England's Prospect (1634); L'Estrange in Americans no Jews (1652); Hubbard in History of New England (ca. 1680). The identification of the American aborigines with the "lost ten tribes" was based on alleged identities in religions, practices, customs and habits, traditions, and languages. Adair's History of the American Indians, published in 1775, was based on this theory. An enthusiastic successor of Adair was Dr Elias Boudinot, whose work, A Star in the West; or, a Humble Attempt to Discover the Long Lost Ten Tribes of Israel, Preparatory to Their Return to Their Beloved City, Jerusalem, was published at Trenton, N. J., in 1816. Lord Kingsborough's magnificent Antiquities of Mexico (9 vols., 1830–48) represents a fortune spent in efforts to sustain this theory. To-day the idea crops out occasionally in pseudo-scientific works, missionary literature, etc., while the friendly interest which the Mormon church has always taken in the Indians is said to be due to this belief. Certain identities and resemblances in customs, ideas, institutions, etc., of the American Indians and the ancient Jews are pointed out by Mallery in his Israelite and Indian: A Parallel in Planes of Culture (Proc. A. A. A. S., XXXVIII, 287–331, 1889), though the address contains many misconceptions. It may be remarked that the Jews and the Indians have no physical characteristics in common, the two races belonging to entirely distinct types. See *Popular fallacies*.

In addition to the above works consult Neubauer in Jewish Quarterly Review, I, 1889; Jacobs in Jewish Encyclopedia, XII, 249–53, 1906. (A. F. C.)

Lotlemaga (*Ĺŏ'lɛmaga*, 'ghost-face woman.'—Boas). The ancestor of a gens of the Nakomgilisala, also applied to the gens itself.

Lŏ'tlemaq.—Boas in Petermanns Mitt., pt. 5, 131, 1887.

Loucheux (Fr.: 'squinters'). The Kutchin speaking the dialect of the Tukkuthkutchin. This language, which resembles more nearly the Chipewyan than the intervening Etatchogottine and Kawchogottine dialects, is spoken by the Tatlitkutchin, Vuntakutchin, Kutchakutchin, Natsitkutchin, and Trotsikkutchin (Hardisty in Smithson. Rep. 1866, 311, 1872). The term was extended by the Hudson's Bay Co. men to include all the

Kutchin, though the Tukkuthkutchin, or they and the Tatlitkutchin together, constituted the Loucheux proper.

The Loucheux of Alaska are reported by Hardisty to have been divided into three castes, Chitsah, Tangeesatsah, and Natsingh, names which seem to signify 'fair,' 'partly swarthy,' and 'swarthy,' respectively. Those of the first caste lived principally on fish, and those of the last mentioned by hunting. They occupied different districts, and marriage between two individuals of the same caste was almost prohibited. Petitot gives the names of these bands as Etchian-Kρét, 'men of the left,' Nattséïn-Kρét, 'men of the right,' and Tsendjidhaettset-Kρét, 'men of the middle.' As the children belonged to the mother's clan, but lived usually with that of the father, these people are said to have exchanged countries slowly in successive generations. The three clans or castes are now represented by the Chitsa, Tangesatsa, and Natesa. According to Strachan Jones (Smithson. Rep., op. cit., 326), this system of castes of successive rank prevailed generally among the Kutchin. For the synonymy, see *Kutchin*.

Love songs. See *Music and Musical instruments*.

Lowako ('northern (?) people'). A people mentioned in the Walam Olum record of the Delawares (Brinton, Lenape Leg., 206, 1885). Rafinesque says the name refers to the Eskimo, but Brinton says it may mean any northern people.
Lowako.—Walum Olum (1833) in Brinton, Lenape Leg., 206, 1885. Lowaniwi.—Ibid., 182. Lowanuski.—Ibid., 198. Lowushkis.—Rafinesque (1833) quoted by Brinton, ibid., 232.

Lower Chehalis. A collective term for the Salish tribes on lower Chehalis r. and affluents, as well as those about Grays harbor and the N. end of Shoalwater bay, Wash. It included the Satsop, Wenatchi, Whiskah, Humptulip, and other small tribes. According to Ford (Ind. Aff. Rep. 1857, 341, 1858) the term is properly restricted to the Grays Harbor Indians, and Gibbs confines it to those about the N. end of Shoalwater bay. See *Atsmitl*.
Artsmilsh.—Swan quoted by Mooney in 14th Rep. B. A. E., pl. lxxxviii, 1896. Salt-water band.—Simmons in Ind. Aff. Rep., 233, 1858.

Lower Chinook. Chinookan tribes of the lower Columbia r., strictly the Chinook proper and the Clatsop, who speak one language, while all the other tribes (Upper Chinook) present marked dialectic differences. Most writers include all the tribes from the mouth of the Columbia to Willamette r. under the term.
Ahei'pudin.—Gatschet, Kalapuya MS., B. A. E. (Atfalati name). Bas-Tchinouks.—Duflot de Mofras, Explor. de l'Oregon, II, 335, 1844. Lower Chinook.—Hale in U. S. Expl. Exped., VI, 215, 1846. Tχaiχ-wā'tχsh.—Gatschet, MS., B. A. E. (Clackama name).

Lower Creeks. The name formerly applied to that part of the Creek confederacy centering on the lower Chattahoochee and its tributaries, in South Carolina and Alabama, as distinguished from the Upper Creeks on the Coosa and Tallapoosa. They included Muscogee, Hitchiti, and Yuchi. In the 18th century the terms Coweta (Kawita) and Apalachucla (Apalachicola) were often used to designate the Lower Creeks. Bartram and other authors use the term Seminole as an equivalent, but the Seminole were an offshoot of the Lower Creeks and owed no allegiance to the confederacy. According to Rivers the Lower Creeks had 10 villages with 2,406 people in 1715, but by 1733 they had lost 2 of their 10 towns, according to the statement of a Kawita chief to Oglethorpe at the Savannah council. The chief did not give the names of the 2 lost towns, but the 8 remaining ones were Apalachicola, Chiaha, Hitchiti, Kasihta, Kawita, Oconee, Osotchi, and Eufaula. In 1764 (Smith, Bouquet's Exped., 1766) the Lower Creeks numbered 1,180 men, representing a total population of about 4,100. In 1813, according to Hawkins (Am. St. Papers, Ind. Aff., I, 842, 1832), they had 14 towns on Flint and Chattahoochee rs., but in the same year (ibid., 851) these had increased to 16. The Lower Creeks were frequently called Ucheesee, or Ochesee (Ochisi), from the town of that name. According to Barton they called the Upper Creeks "uncles," and by them were called "cousins." For a list of their towns, see *Creeks*.　　　　(A. S. G.)
Basses Rivières.—Gatschet, inf'n (French name for Lower Creeks). Lower Creeks.—Smith, Bouquet's Exped. 71, 1766. Maskō'ki Hatcháta.—Gatschet, Creek Migr. Leg., I, 237, 1884 (Creek name). Ochesees.—Rivers, Hist. S. C., 94, 1874. Ucheesees.—Gussefeld, Charte der 13 Ver. Staaten, 1784.

Lower Delaware Town. A former Delaware village on the extreme headwaters of Mohican r., 5 or 6 m. directly N. of the site of the city of Ashland, in Ashland co., Ohio.—Royce in 18th Rep. B. A. E., Ohio map, 1899.

Lower Kutenai. A division of the Kutenai living on Kootenai lake and r., and in the neighboring plains of Idaho and British Columbia. From the time of their earliest contact with the whites they have been called Flatbows, for what reason is not known, but they are now generally called Lower Kootenay. They numbered 172 in British Columbia in 1904, and 79 from Idaho were connected with the Flathead agency, Montana.
Akoklako.—Tolmie and Dawson, Comp. Vocabs., 124B, 1884 (corruption of *Aqkōqtlā'tlqō*). Akuchäklactas.—Wilson in Trans. Ethnol. Soc. Lond., 304, 1866 (corruption of *Aqkōqtlā'tlqō*). Aqkōqtlā'-tlqō.—Chamberlain in 8th Rep. N. W. Tribes Can., 6, 1892. Aquqenu'kqō.—Boas in 5th Rep. N. W. Tribes Can., 10, 1889. Aquqtlā'tlqō.—Boas, ibid.

Arc Plattes.—Mayne, Brit. Col., 298, 1862. **Arcs-a-plats.**—De Smet, Oreg. Miss., 112, 1847. **Arcs-Plats.**—Duflot de Mofras, Expl., II, 335, 1844. **Arcs-plattes.**—Anderson quoted by Gibbs in Hist. Mag., 80, 1863. **Flachbogen.**—Berghaus, Physik. Atlas, map 17, 1852. **Flat Bow.**—Can. Ind. Aff. for 1902, pt. 2, 74. **Flat-bows.**—Hale in U.S. Expl, Exped., VI, 204, 1846 (said to be a translation of *Åqkōqtlătl*, the Kutenai name of Kootenai r., but this is doubtful). **Indians of the Lower Kootenay.**—Chamberlain, op. cit., 6. **Kertani.**—Kingsley, Stand. Nat. Hist., VI, 140, 1883. **Lake Indians.**—Henry (1811) quoted by Maclean, Canad. Sav. Folk, 138, 1896. **Lower Kootanais.**—Mayne, Brit. Col., 298, 1862. **Lower Kootanie.**—Tolmie and Dawson, Comp. Vocabs., 124B, 1884. **Lower Kootenay.**—Boas, op. cit., 10. **Lower Kootenays.**—Chamberlain, op. cit., 6.

Lower Quarter Indians. A tribe or division in 1700, living 10 m. from Neuse r. and 40 m. from Adshusheer town, probably about the site of Raleigh, N. C.—Lawson (1714), Hist. Car., 98, 1860.

Lower Sauratown. A Cheraw village in 1760, situated on the s. bank of Dan r., N. Car., near the Virginia border.—Mooney, Siouan Tribes of the East, Bul. B. A. E., 59, 1894.

Lower Thompson Indians. The popular name for the Ntlakyapamuk living on Fraser r., between Siska and Yale, Brit. Col.

Cañon Indians.—Teit in Mem. Am. Mus. Nat. Hist., II, 168, 1900. **Lower Thompson Indians.**—Ibid. **Lower Thompsons.**—Ibid. **Utā′mqt.**—Boas, inf'n, 1906 (own name). **Utā′mqtamux.**—Teit, op. cit. ('people below' : own name).

Lowertown. A name applied at different periods to two distinct Shawnee villages in Ohio. The one commonly so called was originally on the Ohio, just below the mouth of the Scioto, until it was carried off by a flood, when it was rebuilt on the opposite side of the Scioto, about the site of Portsmouth, Scioto co. It was here in 1750–54, but before 1766 the inhabitants removed upstream to Chillicothe, in Ross co., which was frequently known as Lowertown, or Lower Shawnee Town, to distinguish it from Lick Town, 25 m. above. See *Chillicothe, Scioto.* (J. M.)

Lower Shawnee Town.—Common names used by early writers. **Lowertown.**—Common name used by early writers. **Shawnoah Basse Ville.**—Esnauts and Rapilly, map, 1777.

Lowrey, George. A cousin of Sequoya and second chief of the Eastern Cherokee under John Ross, commonly known as Major Lowrey. His native name was Agi′lï ('He is rising'), possibly a contraction of an old personal name, Agin′-agi′lï ('Rising-fawn'). He joined Ross in steadily opposing all attempts to force his people to move from their eastern lands, and later, after this had been accomplished, he was chief of council of the Eastern Cherokee at the meeting held in 1839 to fuse the eastern and western divisions into the present Cherokee Nation. See Mooney in 19th Rep. B. A. E., 115, 135, 1900.

Lowrey, John. A Cherokee chief, commonly known as Colonel Lowrey. He commanded the friendly Cherokee who helped Gen. Andrew Jackson in the war against the Creeks in 1813–14, and with Col. Gideon Morgan and 400 Cherokee surrounded and captured the town of Hillabi, Ala., Nov. 18, 1813. The two were conspicuous also in the battle of Horseshoe Bend, Mar. 27, 1814, for which they were commended. Lowrey was one of the signers of the treaties made at Washington, June 7, 1806, and Mar. 22, 1816. See Mooney in 19th Rep. B. A. E., 90, 1900.

Lowwalta. A former Seminole village, probably E. of Appalachee bay, Fla., as the map of Bartram (Travels, I, 1799) notes a Noowalta r. emptying into the bay. It was settled by Creeks from Coosa r., who followed their prophets McQueen and Francis after the war of 1813–14.—Bell in Morse, Rep. to Sec. War, 306, 1822.

Loyola. See *Etsowish Semmegee-itshin.*

Lu ('mud,' 'clay'). A former Attacapa village on L. Prien (Cyprien), in Calcasieu parish, La.

Lo.—Gatschet, Attacapa MS., B. A. E., 45, 1885. **Lu.**—Ibid.

Luchasmi. A Costanoan village situated in 1819 within 10 m. of Santa Cruz mission, Cal.—Taylor in Cal. Farmer, Apr. 5, 1860.

Luckton. A tribe, comprising 200 people, residing in 1806 on the Oregon coast s. of the Tillamook.

Luck-tons.—Orig. Jour. Lewis and Clark, VI, 117, 1905. **Lukton.**—Amer. Pioneer, 189, 1843.

Lugups. A former Chumashan village near Santa Barbara, Cal. (Taylor in Cal. Farmer, Apr. 24, 1863); perhaps the same as Luupch, q. v.

Luidneg. A former village, presumably Costanoan, connected with Dolores mission, San Francisco, Cal.—Taylor in Cal. Farmer, Oct. 18, 1861.

Luiseño. The southernmost Shoshonean division in California, which received its name from San Luis Rey, the most important Spanish mission in the territory of these people. They form one linguistic group with the Aguas Calientes, Juaneños, and Kawia. They extended along the coast from between San Onofre and Las Animas crs., far enough s. to include Aguas Hedionda, San Marcos, Escondido, and Valley Center. Inland they extended N. beyond San Jacinto r., and into Temescal cr.; but they were cut off from the San Jacinto divide by the Diegueños, Aguas Calientes, Kawia, and Serranos. The former inhabitants of San Clemente id. also are said to have been Luiseños, and the same was possibly the case with those of San Nicolas id. Their population was given in 1856 (Ind. Aff. Rep., 243) as between 2,500 and 2,800; in 1870, as 1,299; in 1885, as 1,142. Most of them were subsequently placed on small reservations included under the Mission Tule River agency, and no separate tribal count has been made. Their villages, past and present, are Ahuanga, Apeche, Bruno's Village, La Joya, Las Flores, Pala, Pauma, Pedro's Village (?), Potrero, Rincon, Saboba, San Luis Rey (mission), Santa Margarita (?), Temecula, and Wahoma. Taylor (Cal. Farmer, May 11, 1860) gives the following list of villages in the neighborhood of San Luis Rey mission, some of which may be identical with those here recorded: Cenyowpreskel, Ehutewa, Enekelkawa, Hamechuwa, Hatawa, Hepowwoo, Itaywiy, Itukemuk, Milkwanen, Mokaskel, and Mootaeyuhew.

Ghecham.—A. L. Kroeber, inf'n, 1905 (from Ghech, native name of San Luis Rey mission, and sometimes appears to be applied to themselves). **Kechi.**—Gatschet in Wheeler Surv. Rep., VII, 413, 1879. **Kechis.**—Shea, Cath. Miss., 108, 1855. **Khecham.**—Kroeber, inf'n, 1905 (alternative for Ghecham). **San Louis Indians.**—Winder in H. R. Ex. Doc. 76, 34th Cong., 3d sess., 124, 1857. **San Luisenians.**—Couts quoted by Henley in Ind. Aff. Rep. 1856, 240, 1857. **San Luiseños.**—Bancroft, Nat. Races, I, 460, 1882. **San Luisieños.**—Ibid. **San Luis Rey [tribe].**—Ind. Aff. Rep. 1871, 682, 1872.

Lukaiasta. A former village of the Kalindaruk division of the Costanoan family, connected with San Carlos mission, Cal.

Lucayasta.—Taylor in Cal. Farmer, Apr. 20, 1860.

Lukfa ('clay,' 'loam'). A former village of the Opatukla or "Eastern party" of the Choctaw, on the headwaters of a branch of Sukinatcha cr., in Kemper co., Miss.

Lookfa.—W. Florida map ca. 1775. **Lukfa.**—Halbert in Pub. Miss. Hist. Soc., VI, 424, 1902.

Lulakiksa. A Choctaw clan of the Kushapokla phratry.

Lulak.—Morgan, Anc. Soc., 162, 1877. **Lu-lak Ik'-sä.**—Ibid.

Lulanna. A Haida town referred to by Work in 1836–41. It is perhaps intended for Yaku, opposite Graham id., Queen Charlotte ids., Alaska, or it may have been that town and Kiusta considered as one. Its population was estimated by Work at 296 in 20 houses.

Lu lan na.—Work in Schoolcraft, Ind. Tribes, V, 489, 1855. **Su-lan-na.**—Kane, Wand. N. A., app., 1859 (misprint from Work).

Lululongturkwi (Hopi: 'plumed-serpent mound.'—Fewkes). A ruined pueblo, of medium size, situated across the Jeditoh valley from Kokopki, in the Hopi country, N. E. Arizona. It was possibly one of a group of pueblos built and occupied by the Kawaika people. See Hough in Rep. Nat. Mus. 1901, 336, pl. 82, 1903.

Lululongtuqui.—Hough, ibid., pl. 82. **Lululongturqui.**—Ibid., 336.

Lummi. A Salish tribe on and inland from Bellingham bay, N. W. Wash. They are said to have lived formerly on part of a group of islands E. of Vancouver id., to which they still occasionally resorted in 1863. According to Gibbs their language is almost unintelligible to the Nooksak, their northern neighbors. Boas

classes it with the Songish dialect. The Lummi are now under the jurisdiction of the Tulalip school superintendent, Washington, and numbered 412 in 1905. Their former villages were Hutatchl, Lemaltcha, Stashum, and Tomwhiksen. The Klalakamish, of Orcas id., were a former band.

Há-lum-mi.—Gibbs, Clallam and Lummi, vi, 1863 (name given them by some other (Salish?) tribes). **Hookluhmic.**—Schoolcraft, Ind. Tribes, I, 521, 1851. **Lummas.**—Fitzhugh (1856) in H. R. Ex. Doc. 37, 34th Cong., 3d sess., 75, 1857. **Lummi.**—Gibbs in Pac. R. R. Rep., I, 433, 1855. **Lummie.**—Stevens (1856) in H. R. Ex. Doc. 37, 34th Cong., 3d sess., 46, 1857. **Lummi-neuk-sack.**—Shaw in Ind. Aff. Rep. 1859, 398, 1860 (two tribal names connected through error). **Nooh-lum-mi.**—Tolmie (1844) in Pac. R. R. Rep., I, 434, 1855. **Nooklulumic.**—Lane (1849) in Sen. Ex. Doc. 52, 31st Cong., 1st sess., 173, 1850. **Nooklulumu.**—Lane in Ind. Aff. Rep., 162, 1850. **Nooklummie.**—Bauer in Am. Quar. Reg., III, 389, 1849. **Nookluolamic.**—Thornton (1849) in Schoolcraft, Ind. Tribes, VI, 701, 1857. **Noot-hum.**—Starling in Ind. Aff. Rep., 170, 1852. **Noot-hum-mic.**—Ibid., 171. **Nugh-lemmy.**—Mallet in Ind. Aff. Rep., 198, 1877. **Nuh-lum-mi.**—Gibbs in Cont. N. A. Ethnol., I, 180, 1877 (proposed as a collective name for Samish, Lummi, and Nuksak). **Nūkhlésh.**—Gibbs, Clallam and Lummi, vi, 1863 (so called by Skagit). **Nūkh'-lum-mi.**—Ibid (own name). **Qtlumi.**—Boas in 5th Rep. N. W. Tribes Can., 10, 1889.

Lunge. See *Longe, Maskinonge.*

Lunikashinga ('thunder-being people'). A Kansa gens.

Ledan unikacinga.—Dorsey in 15th Rep. B. A. E., 232, 1897 ('gray hawk people'). **Lo-ne'-kä-she-gä.**—Morgan, Anc. Soc., 156, 1877. **Loo nika-shing-ga.**—Stubbs, Kaw MS. vocab., B. A. E., 25, 1877. **Lu.**—Dorsey in Am. Natur., 671, 1885 ('thunder'). **Lu nikacinga.**—Dorsey in 15th Rep. B. A. E., 232, 1897. **Thunder.**—Morgan, Anc. Soc., 156, 1877.

Lupies. Mentioned in connection with some mythical as well as existent tribes of the plains in the 17th century (Vetancurt, 1693, Teatro Am., III, 303, repr. 1871). Possibly the Pawnee Loups.

Lushapa. A former Choctaw town, evidently in Neshoba co., Miss., and possibly on Lussalaka cr., a small tributary of Kentarky cr.—Halbert in Pub. Miss. Hist. Soc., VI, 430, 1902.

Lushapa.—Romans, Florida, map, 1775. **Lusthhapa.**—West Florida map, ca. 1775.

Lutchapoga (Creek: *lútcha* 'terrapin', *póka* 'gathering place': 'terrapin pen'). A former Upper Creek town, of which Atchinaalgi was a branch or colony, probably on or near Tallapoosa r., Ala.

Lookoportay.—Ex. Doc. 425, 24th Cong., 1st sess., 279, 1836. **Loo-chau po-gau.**—Hawkins (1799), Sketch, 47, 1848. **Luchepoga.**—Tanner, map, 1827. **Lu chi paga.**—Parsons in Schoolcraft, Ind. Tribes, IV, 578, 1854. **Luchipoga.**—Campbell (1836) in H. R. Doc. 274, 25th Cong., 2d sess., 20, 1838. **Luchipogatown.**—Garrett (1837) in H. R. Doc. 452, 25th Cong., 2d sess., 58, 1838. **Lutchapóga.**—Gatschet, Creek Migr. Leg., I, 138, 1884.

Lutchopoga. A township in the Creek Nation, on middle Arkansas r., Okla.

Lutuamian Family. A linguistic family consisting of two branches, the Klamath and the Modoc (q. v.), residing in S. W. Oregon E. of the Cascade range and along the California border. Their former boundary extended from the Cascades to the headwaters of Pit and McCloud rs., thence E. to Goose lake, thence N. to lat. 44°, and thence w. to the Cascades. The more permanent settlements of the family were on the shores of Klamath lakes, Tule lake, and Lost r., the remainder of the territory which they claimed being hunting ground. In 1864 both divisions of the family entered into a treaty with the United States whereby they ceded the greater part of their lands to the Government and were placed on Klamath res. in Oregon. It was an attempt on the part of the Modoc to return to their former seat on the California frontier that brought about the Modoc war of 1872–73 (see *Kintpuash*). The climate and productions of their country were most favorable, edible roots and berries were plentiful, and the region abounded in game and fish. As a consequence the tribes were fairly sedentary and seem to have made no extensive migrations. They were not particularly warlike, though the Modoc had frequent struggles with the tribes to the s., and after the coming of the whites resisted the aggressions of the latter with persistence and fierceness.

Slavery seems to have been an institution of long standing, and the Modoc, assisted by the Klamath, made annual raids on the Indians of Pit r. for the capture of slaves, whom they either retained for themselves or bartered with the Chinook of Columbia r. The habitations were formerly of logs, covered with mud and circular in shape, a type of building which is still occasionally seen on the reservation. The women were noted as expert basket weavers. No trace of a clan or gentile system has been discovered among them. The family organization is a loose one and inheritance is in the male line. The language spoken by the two divisions of the Lutuamian family is ordinarily called Klamath, and while there are dialectic differences between the speech of the Klamath proper and the Modoc, they are so slight that they may be disregarded. The Lutuamian language is apparently entirely independent, though further study may disclose relationship with the Shahaptian. (L. F.)

Clamets.—Hale in U. S. Expl. Exped., VI, 218, 569, 1846 (alternative of Lutuami). Klamath.—Gatschet in Mag. Am. Hist., 164, 1877 (used for family). Lutnami.—Irving, Astoria, map, 1849. Lutuami.—Hale, op. cit., 199, 204. Lutuanis.—Domenech, Deserts of N. A., I, 442, 1860. Lutumani.—Latham, Opuscula, 341, 1860 (misprint). Luturim.—Gallatin in Schoolcraft, Ind. Tribes, III, 402, 1853 (misprint). Máklaks.—Gatschet in Cont. N. A. Ethnol., II, pt. I, xxxiii, 1890 (collective name for Klamath and Modoc). Sutuami.—Medill in H. R. Ex. Doc. 76, 30th Cong., 1st sess., 7, 1848 (misquoted from Hale). Tlamatl.—Hale, op. cit., 218, 569 (alternative of Lutuami).

Luupch. A former Chumashan village in Ventura co., Cal.—Taylor in Cal. Farmer, July 24, 1863. Cf. *Lugups*.

Luúptc.—Henshaw, Buenaventura MS. vocab., B. A. E., 1884.

Lynx. See *Peshkewah*.

Lytton band. One of 4 subdivisions of the Upper Thompson Indians, in the interior of British Columbia. In 1904 they numbered 463, under the Kamloops-Okanagan agency.

Lkamtci'nEmux.—Teit in Mem. Am. Mus. Nat. Hist., II, 170, 1900 ('people of Lkamtci'n [Lytton]'). Lytton band.—Ibid. NLak·a'pamux.—Ibid. (generally used for all the Ntlakyapamuk). NLak·apamux'ō'ē.—Ibid. (the Nlak·a'pamux proper).

Maak ('loon'). A gens of the Potawatomi (q. v.).—Morgan, Anc. Soc., 167, 1877. Cf. *Mong*.

Maakoath (*Maa'kōath*). A sept of the Toquart, a Nootka tribe.—Boas in 6th Rep. N. W. Tribes Can., 32, 1890.

Maam (*Ma'-am*). Apparently a gentile organization among the Pima, belonging to the Suwuki-ohimal, or Red Ants, phratral group.—Russell, Pima MS., B. A. E., 313, 1903.

Maamtagyila. A gens of the Kwakiutl, found in two septs, the Guetela and the Matilpe.

Maa'mtag·ila.—Boas in Rep. Nat. Mus. 1895, 330, 1897. Matakī'la.—Boas in Petermanns Mitt., pt. 5, 131, 1887.

Maangreet (*Mä-an'-greet*, 'big feet'). A subclan of the Delawares (q. v.).—Morgan, Anc. Soc., 172, 1877.

Maate (*Mā-ātē*). A summer village of the Koskimo on the s. side of Quatsino sd., Vancouver id.—Dawson in Trans. Roy. Soc. Can. for 1887, sec. II, 69.

Maawi. The extinct Antelope clan of the Zuñi of New Mexico.

Máawi-kwe.—Cushing in 13th Rep. B. A. E., 368, 1896 (*kwe*='people').

Macamo. A former Chumashan village on San Lucas id., Cal.; so named by Cabrillo in 1542.—Cabrillo (1542) in Smith, Colec. Doc. Fla., 181, 1857.

Macaque. See *Mocuck*.

Macariz. A former Yamasi (?) town a mile N. of St Augustine, Fla., existing in 1680 and with others destroyed by Col. Palmer in 1727.

Macarisqui.—Fairbanks, Hist. Fla., 189, 1858. Mascarasi.—Barcia, Ensayo, 240, 1723.

Maccarib. The old and original form from a cognate of which has been derived the Algonquian word *caribou*. Josselyn (N. Eng. Rar., 1672, 55, repr. 1865) wrote of "the Maccarib, Caribo, or Pohano, a kind of Deer, as big as a Stag." *Maccarib* corresponds to the Passamaquody *megalip*. See *Caribou*. (A. F. C.)

Maccoa. The name of a chief and of a small tribe living on the s. coast of South Carolina, in the vicinity of St Helena id., where they were visited by Ribault in 1562. They possibly belonged to the Cusabo group, long since extinct.

Maccoa.—Laudonnière (1562) in French, Hist. Coll. La., n. s., 205, 1869. Maccou.—Ibid., 209.

McGillivray, Alexander. A mixed-blood Creek chief who acquired considerable note during the latter half of the 18th century by his ability and the affection in which he was held by his mother's people. Capt. Marchand, in command of the French Ft Toulouse, Ala., in 1722, married a Creek woman of the strong Hutali or Wind clan, from which it was customary to select the chief. One of the children of this marriage was Sehoy, celebrated for her beauty. In 1735 Lachlan McGillivray, a Scotch youth of wealthy family, landed in Carolina, made his way to the Creek country, married Sehoy, and established his residence at Little Talasi, on the E. bank of Coosa r., above Wetumpka, Elmore co., Ala. After acquiring a fortune and rearing a family he abandoned the latter, and in 1782 returned to his native country. One of his children was Alexander, born about 1739; he was educated at Charleston under care of Farquhar McGillivray, a relative. At the age of 17 he was placed in a counting house in Savannah, but after a short time returned to his home, where his superior talents began to manifest themselves, and he was soon at the head of the Creek tribe. Later his authority extended also over the Seminole and the Chickamauga groups, enabling him, it is said, to muster 10,000 warriors. McGillivray is first heard of in his new rôle as "presiding at a grand national council at the town of Coweta, upon the Chattahoochie, where the adventurous Leclerc Milfort was introduced to him" (Pickett, Hist. Ala., 345, 1896). Through the advances made by the British authorities, the influence of Col. Tait, who was stationed on the Coosa, and the conferring on him of the title and pay of colonel, McGillivray heartily and actively espoused the British cause during the Revolution. His father had left him property on the Savannah and in other parts of Georgia, which, in retaliation for his abandonment of the cause of the colonists, was confiscated by the Georgia authorities. This action greatly embittered him against the Americans and led to a long war against the western settlers, his attacks being directed for a time against the people of E. Tennessee and Cumberland valley, whence he was successively beaten back by Gen. James Robertson. The treaty of peace in 1783 left McGillivray without cause or party. Proposals from the Spanish authorities of Florida through his business partner, Wm. Panton, another Scotch adventurer and trader, induced him to visit Pensacola in 1784, where, as their "emperor," he entered into an agreement with Spain in the name of the Creeks and the Seminoles. The United States made repeated overtures to McGillivray for peace, but he persistently refused to listen to them until invited to New York in 1790 for a personal conference with Washington. His journey from Little Talasi, through Guilford, Richmond, Fredericksburg, and Philadelphia, was like a triumphal march, and the prospective occasion for such display was a strong inducement for the shrewd chief to accept the invitation. According to Pickett (p. 406) there was, in addition to the public treaty, a secret treaty between McGillivray and Washington which provided "that after two years from date the commerce of the Creek nation should be carried on through the ports of the United States, and, in the meantime, through the present channels; that the chiefs of the Okfuskees, Tookabatchas Tallases, Cowetas, Cussetas, and the Seminole nation should be paid annually by the United States $100 each, and be furnished with handsome medals; that Alexander McGillivray should be constituted agent of the United States with the rank of brigadier-general and the pay of $1,200 per annum; that the United States should feed, clothe, and educate Creek youth at the North, not exceeding four at one time." The public treaty was signed Aug. 7, 1790, and a week later McGillivray took the oath of allegiance to the United States. Nevertheless he was not diverted from his intrigue with Spain, for shortly after taking the oath he was appointed by that power superintendent-general of the Creek nation with a salary of $2,000 a year, which was increased in 1792 to $3,500.

The versatile character of McGillivray was perhaps due in part to the fact that there flowed in his veins the blood of four different nationalities. It has been said that he possessed "the polished urbanity of the Frenchman, the duplicity of the Spaniard, the cool sagacity of the Scotchman, and the subtlety and inveterate hate of the Indian." Gen. James Robertson, who knew him well and despised the Spaniards, designated the latter "devils" and pronounced McGillivray as the biggest devil among them—"half Spaniard, half Frenchman, half Scotchman, and altogether Creek scoundrel." That Alexander McGillivray was a man of remarkable ability is evident from the consummate skill with which he maintained his control and influence over the Creeks, and from his success in keeping both the United States and Spain paying for his influence at the same time. In 1792 he was at once the superintendent-general of the Creek nation on behalf of Spain, the agent of the United States, the mercantile partner of Panton, and "emperor" of the Creek and Seminole nations. As opulence was estimated in his day and territory, he was a wealthy man, having received $100,000 for the property confiscated by the Georgia authorities, while the annual importations by him and Panton were estimated in value at £40,000 (Am. St. Papers, Ind. Aff., I, 458, 1832). Besides two or three plantations, he owned, at the time of his death, 60 negroes, 300 head of cattle, and a large stock of horses. In personal appearance McGillivray is described as having been six feet in height, sparely built, and remarkably erect; his forehead was bold and lofty; his fingers long and tapering, and he wielded a pen with the greatest rapidity; his face was handsome and indicative of thought and sagacity; unless interested in conversation he was inclined to be taciturn, but was polite and respectful. While a British colonel he dressed in the uniform of his rank; when in the Spanish service he wore the military garb of that country; and after Washington appointed him brigadier-general he sometimes donned the uniform of the American army, but never when Spaniards were present. His usual costume was a mixture of Indian and American garments. McGillivray always traveled with two servants, one a half-blood, the other a negro. Although ambitious, fond of display and power, crafty, unscrupulous in accomplishing his purpose, and treacherous in affairs of state, the charge that he was bloodthirsty and fiendish in disposition is not sustained. He had at least two wives, one of whom was a daughter of Joseph Curnell. Another wife, the mother of his son Alexander and two daughters, died shortly before or soon after her husband's death, Feb. 17, 1793, at Pensacola, Fla. He was buried with Masonic honors in the garden of William Panton, his partner.   (c. t.)

Machapunga ('bad dust'; from *matchi* 'bad', *pungo* 'dust' (Heckewelder), or perhaps 'much dust,' from *massa* 'great', in allusion to the sandy soil of the district). An Algonquian tribe formerly living in Hyde co., N. E. N. C. In 1701 they numbered only about 30 warriors, or perhaps 100 souls, and lived in a single village called Mattamuskeet. They took part in the Tuscarora war of 1711–12 and at its conclusion the remnant, together with the Coree, were settled on a tract on Mattamuskeet lake, where the two tribes occupied one village.   (j. m.)
Machapunga.—Lawson (1714), Hist. Car., 383, repr. 1860. Matchapangos.—Martin, N. C., I, 263, 1829. Matchapongos.—Ibid., 260. Matchapungos.—Ibid., 244. Matchepungo.—Letter of 1713 in N. C. Col. Rec., II, 29, 1886.

Machapunga. A village of the Powhatan confederacy in Northampton co., Va. It was nearly extinct in 1722.
Matchapunko.—Hermann, map (1670), in Rep. on Line between Va. and Md., 1873.

Machapunga. A village on Potomac r. about 1612.
Matchopongo.—Strachey (*ca.* 1612), Va., 98, 1849.

Macharienkonck. A Minisink village formerly in the bend of Delaware r., in Pike co., Pa., opposite Port Jervis.—Van der Donck (1656) quoted by Ruttenber, Tribes Hudson R., 96, 1872.

Machawa. A former Timucua town in N. w. Florida, 24 m. E. of Ayavalla fort, now Iola, on a river called Wicassa.
Machaba.—Jefferys, French Dom. Am., map, 1761. Machaha.—Ibid., map, 135. Machalla.—Roberts, Fla., 15, 1763. Machua.—French, Hist. Coll. La., 2d s., 255, note, 1875.

Machemni. A division of the Miwok who lived between Cosumnes and Mokelumne rs., in Eldorado and Amador cos., Cal.
Matchemnes.—Hale, Ethnog. and Philol., 630, 1846. Omochamne.—Bancroft, Nat. Races, I, 450, 1874. Omochumnies.—Taylor in Cal. Farmer, June 8, 1860. Omutchamne.—Bancroft, Nat. Races, I, 450, 1874. Omutchumnes.—Hale, op. cit.

Machemoodus (properly *Matche-mádosé*, 'there is a bad noise.'—Trumbull). A tract on the E. bank of Connecticut r., now included in East Haddam tp., Middlesex co., Conn., formerly the residence of a "numerous tribe," who were independent and famous for conjuring. The Indians sold the tract in 1662. For an account of the "Moodus noises" see Trumbull, Hist. Conn., II, 91, 92, 1818; Barber, Hist. Coll., 525, 1839.   (j. m.)
Machamádoset.—Doc. of 1674 cited by Trumbull, Ind. Names Conn., 18, 1881. Machamoodus.—Doc. of 1691, ibid. Mache Moodus.—Kendall, Travels, I, 100, 1809. Machmadouset.—Doc. of 1671 cited by Trumbull, op. cit. Matche Moodus.—Kendall, op. cit. Matchi Moodus.—Ibid. Matchit Moodus.—Doc. cited by Trumbull, op. cit.

Macheno. An ancient village, probably Timuquanan, in w. central Florida, lat. 29° 30′.—Bartram, Voy., I, map, 1799.

Macheto. A former village of the Awani at the foot of Indian canyon, Yosemite valley, Mariposa co., Cal.
Macháyto.—Powers in Overland Mo., x, 333, 1874. Ma-che′-to.—Powers in Cont. N. A. Ethnol., III, 365, 1877.

Machias ('bad little place,' referring to the current in Machias r.; from *matche* 'bad', *sis* the diminutive). A village of the Passamaquoddy on Machias r., Me.
Mechias.—Treaty rep. (1726) in Me. Hist. Soc. Coll., III, 390, 1853.

Machonee. An Ottawa village, commonly called "Machonee's village," from the name of the resident chief, formerly near the mouth of Au Vaseau r., which flows into L. St Clair, in lower Michigan, on land ceded to the United States by treaty of May 9, 1836. The chief, whose name is also spelled Machonce, Maconce, and Makonee, was drowned, while intoxicated, about the year 1825 (Mich. Pion. Coll., v, 464, 1884).   (j. m.)
Machonce's village.—Detroit treaty (1807) in U. S. Ind. Treat., 194, 1873 (misprint?). Machonee's village.—Detroit treaty (1807) in Am. State Papers, Ind. Aff., I, 747, 1832.

MacIntosh, Chilly. A Creek chief. After his brother William was slain by Menewa for having betrayed the Creeks by "selling the graves of their ancestors," he became the head of the minority party that acquiesced in the proposed emigration to Indian Ter. As such he frequently visited Washington to treat with officials regarding the transfer of lands and acquitted himself as a capable man of business.—Stanley, Portraits Am. Inds., 13, 1852.

MacIntosh, William. A mixed-blood Creek, son of a Scotch trader and an Indian woman. The United States, in consideration of the relinquishment by Georgia of the Mississippi territories, engaged in 1802 to extinguish the Indian titles to lands within the borders of the state as early as could be peaceably done on reasonable terms. A cession was procured in 1805 by which millions of acres of Creek lands were transferred to Georgia. The people of the state constantly clam-

WILLIAM MACINTOSH. (McKenney and Hall)

ored for the fulfilment by the Government of its compact, and the Creeks, alarmed at the prospective wholesale alienation of their ancient domain, on the motion of MacIntosh made a law in general council in 1811 forbidding the sale of any of the remaining land under penalty of death. MacIntosh, who by his talents and address had risen to be chief of the Lower Creeks, led the Creek allies of the Americans in the war of 1812 with the rank of major and took the chief part in the massacre of 200 of the hostile Creeks, who were surprised at Atasi on Nov. 29, 1813. He was prominent also in the final battle with the hostiles, Mar. 27, 1814, when, at Horseshoe Bend, Ala., nearly a thousand warriors were exterminated. A large part of the territory of

the conquered tribe was confiscated and opened to white settlement. In 1818 more lands were acquired by treaty, and in 1821 the fifth treaty was negotiated by Georgian citizens acting on behalf of the United States, with MacIntosh, who was in the pay of the whites, and a dozen other chiefs controlled by him, while 36 chiefs present refused to sign and made clear to the commissioners the irregularity of a cession arranged with a party representing only a tenth of the nation, which to be legal must have the consent of the entire nation assembled in council. After an attempt made by MacIntosh to convey more land in 1823 the law punishing with death any Creek who offered to cede more land was reenacted in 1824, when 15,000,000 acres had already been transferred and 10,000,000 acres remained in possession of the Creeks, who had so advanced in education and agriculture that they valued their lands far more highly than before. In the beginning of 1825 Georgian commissioners, working upon the avarice of MacIntosh, induced him and his followers to set their names to a treaty ceding what remained of the Creek domain. Although Secretary John C. Calhoun had declared that he would not recognize a treaty in which the chiefs of the Creek nation did not acquiesce, President Monroe laid it before the Senate, and after the accession of President Adams it was approved. The Creeks did not rise in rebellion, as was expected, but, in accordance with the tribal law already mentioned, formal sentence of death was passed on MacIntosh, and was executed on May 1, 1825, by a party of warriors sent for that purpose, who surrounded his house and shot him and a companion as they tried to escape. MacIntosh was a signer of the treaties of Washington, Nov. 4, 1805; Ft Jackson, Ala., Aug. 9, 1814; Creek Agency, Ga., Jan. 22, 1818; Indian Springs, Ga., Jan. 8, 1821, and Feb. 12, 1825.   (J. M.)

Mackinaw. (1) A sort of bateau or large flatboat formerly much used by traders and others; also called Mackinaw boat. (2) A heavy blanket, also known as Mackinaw blanket, formerly an important item of western trade. (3) A coarse straw hat. (4) A species of lake trout (*Salvelinus namaycush*), also termed Mackinac trout. The word which has assumed all these meanings is the place name Mackinac, applied to the famous trading post between L. Huron and L. Michigan. Mackinaw, representing the Canadian French Mackinac, is identical with *makinǎk*, the word for 'turtle' in Chippewa and closely related dialects of Algonquian; said also to be a reduction of Michilimackinac (q. v.), a corruption of an earlier *mitchi makinak*, signifying 'big turtle' in Chippewa. According to Dr William Jones the Chippewa of Minnesota claim the word to be a shortened form of *mishīnīma'kīnunk*, 'place of the big wounded or big lame person.' This, however, may be an instance of folk etymology. (A. F. C.)

Macocanico ('great house'). A village on the w. bank of Patuxent r., in St Marys co., Md., in 1608.
Macocanaco.—Bozman, Maryland, I, 141, 1837. Maco comaco.—Tooker, Algonq. Series, VIII, 49, 1901 (misquoting Smith). Mococanico.—Smith (1629), Virginia, I, map, repr. 1819.

Macock gourd. See *Maycock*.

Macocks (perhaps from *mahcawq*, 'pumpkin.'—Brinton. See *Maycock*). A village located on Smith's map of 1608 (Smith, Va., I, repr. 1819) some distance N. of Chikohoki, which, according to Brinton, was near the present Wilmington, Del. This would make Macocks a Delaware village in s. E. Pennsylvania, and Brinton thinks it may have been the village of the Okahoki (q. v.), a band of the Delawares, formerly in Delaware co., Pa. (J. M.)

Macocqwer. See *Maycock*.

Macombo. A Papago village, probably in Pima co., Ariz., with 57 people in 1865.—Ind. Aff. Rep., 135, 1865.

Macousin. A Potawatomi village, named after the resident chief, on the w. bank of St Joseph r., Berrien co., s. w. Mich., in 1828.
Macousin's Village.—Royce in 18th Rep. B. A. E., Mich. map, 1899. Macousin Village.—U. S. Ind. Treat. (1828), 676, 1873.

Macoyahui. A settlement in Sonora, Mexico, formerly one of the principal villages of the Mayo. In 1900 it contained 182 Mayo in a total population of 972.

McQueen's Village. A former Seminole village on the E. side of Tampa bay, w. Fla.—Bell in Morse, Rep. to Sec. War, 306, 1822.

Macsinum. A former village, presumably Costanoan, connected with Dolores mission, San Francisco, Cal.—Taylor in Cal. Farmer, Oct. 18, 1861.

Mactati. A former Diegueño rancheria near San Diego, s. Cal.
Mactati.—Ortega (1775) quoted by Bancroft, Hist. Cal., I, 254, 1884. Magtate.—Ibid. San Miguel.—Ibid.

Madawehsoos (*Mä-dä'-weh-soos*, 'porcupine'). A gens of the Abnaki (q. v.).—Morgan, Anc. Soc., 174, 1877.

Madokawando. A Penobscot chief, born in Maine about 1630, and adopted as a son by Assaminasqua, a Kennebec chief. His tribe was at peace with the English colonists until made their enemy by depredations upon his lands, when hostilities began, and, uniting with the French, war was waged against the English settlements. In 1691 he attacked York, Me., killed 77 of the inhabitants, and laid the place in ashes. This was but one of his many raids, in which he was generally aided by the French. His death occurred in 1698. It is stated that, although a determined foe, Madokawando's treatment of prisoners was humane. The wife, or perhaps more correctly the principal wife, of the notorious Baron Castine, was a daughter of Madokawando. (C. T.)

Magaehnak. An "Indian cornfield" or settlement in 1678, 6 m. from Sudbury, Middlesex co., Mass., probably belonging to the Praying Indians of the Massachuset confederacy. Mentioned by Salisbury (1678) in N. Y. Doc. Col. Hist., XIII, 520, 1881.

Magayuteshni ('eats no geese'). A band of the Mdewakanton Sioux.
Grey-Iron.—Neill, Hist. Minn., 144, note, 1858 (trans. of Mazarota, the chief's name). Ma-ga-yu-tesh-ni. Neill in Minn. Hist. Coll., I, 263, 1872. Maġa-yute-śni.—Dorsey in 15th Rep. B. A. E., 215, 1897. Maxa-yute-cni.—Ibid. Ma-za-ro-ta.—Neill, Hist. Minn., 144, note, 1858.

Magdalena. A former Spanish mission among the Indians of Lower California; consolidated with the mission of San Ignacio Kadakaman and abandoned prior to 1740. Distinct from Santa María Magdalena in the N.—Alcedo, Dic. Geog., III, 19, 1783; Taylor in Browne's Res. Pac. Slope, app., 50, 1869.

Magemiut ('mink people'). An Eskimo tribe inhabiting the lake country of Alaska from C. Romanof almost to the Yukon. They differ from the Kuskwogmiut chiefly in dialect. They are vigorous and strong, finding in the waters of the tundra plenty of blackfish to nourish them at all seasons. In winter they kill many hair seal on the floes, on which they venture with their sleds, carrying canoes on which the sleds are transported in turn when it is necessary to take to the water. They build good houses of driftwood and the bones of whales killed by the whaling fleet, and the carcasses floating ashore have long supplied them with food. The tribe numbered 2,147 in 1890. The following are Magemiut villages: Anovok, Chalit, Chifukluk, Gilak, Igiak, Kashunuk, Kipniak, Kweakpak, Nanvogaloklak, Nunochok, Tefaknak, and Tiengak.
Ikvagmutes.—Raymond in Sen. Ex. Doc. 12, 42d Cong., 1st sess., 28, 1871. Inkaliten.—Wrangell quoted by Dall in Cont. N. A. Ethnol., I, 18, 1877. Lower Kvichpaks.—Raymond in Sen. Ex. Doc. 12, 42d Cong., 1st sess., 28, 1871. Magagmjuten.—Holmberg, Ethnog. Skizz., 5, 1885. Magamutes.—Colyer in Ind. Aff. Rep. 1869, 593, 1870. Mage-mutes.—Dall in Proc. A. A. A. S., 267, 1869. Magimut.—Wrangell quoted by Dall in Cont. N. A. Ethnol., I, 18, 1877. Magimüten.—Wrangell, Ethnog. Nachr., 122, 1889. Magmiüt.—Worman quoted by Dall in Cont. N. A. Ethnol., I, 18, 1877. Magmjuten.—Holmberg, Ethnog. Skizz., 5, 1855. Magmutes.—Elliott, Cond. Aff. Alaska, 291, 1874. Magmutis.—Latham in Jour. Ethnol. Soc. Lond., 183, 1848. Mayimeuten.—Richardson, Arct. Exped., 370, 1851 (from Wrangell). Nunivak people.—Worman quoted by Dall in Cont. N. A. Ethnol., I, 18, 1877.

Magic. There are authentic accounts from various observers in many parts of

the New World, from the earliest historical period to the present time, that the
Indians practised so-called magic arts, or
sorcery. The earlier writers marveled
at these arts, and evidently wished their
readers to marvel. They often attributed
the power of the Indians to Satan. Father
Acosta, in the 16th century, spoke in awe
of the Mexican magicians flying through
the air, assuming any form they pleased
and having telepathic knowledge of
events occurring at distant places, and
the same may be said in a general way
of the Eskimo. The Rev. Peter Jones
wrote in the first decade of the 19th century: "I have sometimes been inclined

NAVAHO ARROW-SWALLOWER. (MATTHEWS)

to think that, if witchcraft still exists in
the world, it is to be found among the
aborigines of America." His personal
experience was among the Chippewa.
The Nipissing were called Jongleurs by
the French on account of the expertness in magic of their medicine men.
Some writers of the present day marvel
as much as did their predecessors; but
instead of attributing the phenomena to
Satan, seek the cause in spirits or something equally occult. The feats of Indian
magicians, as a rule, may be easily explained as sleight-of-hand tricks, and their

prophecy and telepathy as the results of
collusion. Their tricks are deceptions,
very ingenious when it is considered how
rude their tools and appliances are, but
not to be compared with the acts of civilized conjurers who make claim to no
superhuman aid.

Distinct from such tricks of illusion and
deceit, there is evidence that the Indians
were and still are versed in hypnotism,
or, better, "suggestion." Carver (1776-
78) speaks of it among the Sioux, and
J. E. Fletcher observed it among the
Menominee about the middle of the last
century. Mooney describes and pictures
the condition among modern Indians
(see *Ghost dance*).

Sleight-of-hand was not only much employed in the treatment of disease, but was
used on many other occasions. A very
common trick among Indian charlatans
was to pretend to suck foreign bodies, such
as stones, out of the persons of their patients. Records of this are found among
many tribes, from the lowest in culture to
the highest, even among the Aztecs. Of
course such trickery was not without some
therapeutic efficacy, for it, like many
other proceedings of the shamans, was
designed to cure disease by influence on
the imagination. A Hidatsa residing in
Dakota in 1865 was known by the name
Cherry-in-the-mouth because he had a
trick of producing from his mouth, at any
season, what seemed to be fresh wild cherries. He had found some way of preserving cherries, perhaps in whisky, and it was
easy for him to hide them in his mouth
before intending to play the trick; but
many of the Indians considered it wonderful magic.

The most astonishing tricks of the Indians were displayed in their fire ceremonies and in handling hot substances,
accounts of which performances pertain
to various tribes. It is said that Chippewa sorcerers could handle with impunity red-hot stones and burning brands,
and could bathe the hands in boiling water
or syrup; such magicians were called "fire-
dealers" and "fire-handlers." There
are authentic accounts from various parts
of the world of fire-dancers and fire-walks
among barbarous races, and extraordinary
fire acts are performed also among widely
separated Indian tribes. Among the Arikara of what is now North Dakota, in the
autumn of 1865, when a large fire in the
center of the medicine lodge had died
down until it became a bed of glowing
embers, and the light in the lodge was dim,
the performers ran with apparently bare
feet among the hot coals and threw these
around in the lodge with their bare hands,
causing the spectators to flee. Among
the Navaho performers, naked except for
breechcloth and moccasins, and having

their bodies daubed with a white infusorial clay, run at high speed around a fire, holding in their hands great fagots of flaming cedar bark which they apply to the bare backs of those in front of them and to their own persons. Their wild race around the fire is continued until the fagots are nearly all consumed, but they are never injured by the flame. This immunity may be accounted for by supposing that the cedar bark does not make a very hot fire, and that the clay coating protects the body. Menominee shamans are said to handle fire, as also are the female sorcerers of Honduras.

Indians know well how to handle venomous serpents with impunity. If they can not avoid being bitten, as they usually can, they seem to be able to avert the fatal consequences of the bite. The wonderful acts performed in the Snake dance (q. v.) of the Hopi have often been described.

A trick of Navaho dancers, in the ceremony of the Mountain chant, is to pretend to thrust an arrow far down the throat. In this feat an arrow with a telescopic shaft is used; the point is held between the teeth; the hollow part of the handle, covered with plumes, is forced down toward the lips, and thus the arrow appears to be swallowed. There is an account of an arrow of similar construction used early in the 18th century by Indians of Canada who pretended a man was wounded by it and healed instantly. The Navaho also pretend to swallow sticks, which their neighbors of the pueblo of Zuñi actually do in sacred rites, occasionally rupturing the esophagus in the ordeal of forcing a stick into the stomach. Special societies which practise magic, having for their chief object rain making and the cure of disease, exist among the southwestern tribes. Swallowing sticks, arrows, etc., eating and walking on fire, and trampling on cactus are performed by members of the same fraternity.

Magicians are usually men; but among the aborigines of the Mosquito coast in Central America they are often women, who are called *sukias*, and are said to exercise great power. According to Hewitt Iroquois women are reported traditionally to have been magicians.

A trick of the juggler among many tribes of the N. was to cause himself to be bound hand and foot and then, without visible assistance or effort on his part, to release himself from the bonds. Civilized conjurers who perform a similar trick are hidden in a cabinet and claim supernatural aid; but some Indian jugglers performed this feat under observation. It was common for Indian magicians to pretend they could bring rain, but the trick consisted simply of keeping

up ceremonies until rain fell, the last ceremony being the one credited with success. Catlin describes this among the Mandan in 1832, and the practice is still common among the Pueblo tribes of the arid region. The rain maker was a special functionary among the Menominee.

To cause a large plant to grow to maturity in a few moments and out of season is another Indian trick. The Navaho plant the root stalk of a yucca in the ground in the middle of winter and apparently cause it to grow, blossom, and bear fruit in a few moments. This is done by the use of artificial flowers and fruit carried under the blankets of the performers; the dimness of the firelight and the motion of the surrounding dancers hide from the spectators the operations of the shaman when he exchanges one artificial object for another. In this way the Hopi grow beans, and the Zuñi corn, the latter using a large cooking pot to cover the growing plant. See *Dramatic representation, Medicine and Medicine-men, Orenda*.

Consult the works of H. H. Bancroft, Carver, Catlin, Fewkes, Fletcher, Hoffman, Peter Jones, Lummis, Matthews, Mooney, M. C. Stevenson, and others, in the Bibliography.　　　　(w. m.)

Magnus. A woman chief of the Narraganset, sister of Ninigret, one of the six sachems of their country in 1675 (Drake, Abor. Races, 248, 1880). She was killed by the English after her capture in a swamp fight near Warwick, R. I., in 1676. She was also known as Matantuck, of which Magnus is probably a corruption, and as Quaiapen, Old Queen, etc. Her husband was a son of Canonicus. (a. f. c.)

Magtok. A former Aleut village on Agattu id., Alaska, one of the Near id. group of the Aleutians, now uninhabited.

Maguaga. A Huron village on Maguaga cr., Mich., 14 m. s. w. of Detroit, on a tract reserved for the use of the Indians by act of Feb. 28, 1809, and ceded to the United States by treaty of St Marys, O., Sept. 20, 1818.

Magaugo.—Drake, Bk. Inds., v, 125, 1848. Maguaga.—Brown, W. Gaz., 164, 1817. Maguago.—Drake, Ind. Chron., 196, 1836. Maguagua.—Royce in 18th Rep. B.A.E., Mich. map, 1899. Maguawgo.—Doc. of 1809 in Am. St. Pap., Ind. Aff., I, 796, 1832. Maugaugon.—Miami Rapids treaty (1819) in U. S. Ind. Treaties, 201, 1873. Menquagon.—Wyandot petition (1812) in Am. State Papers, op. cit., 795. Monguagon.—Howe, Hist.Coll., 262, 1851.

Maguhleloo ('caribou'). A gens of the Abnaki, q. v.

Magalibô.—J. D. Prince, inf'n, 1905 (modern St Francis Abnaki form). Mä-gŭh-le-loo'.—Morgan, Anc. Soc., 174, 1877.

Maguiaqui. A division of the Varohio, in s. Sonora, Mexico, on the w. bank of Rio Mayo, N. of Alamos, lat. 27° 25′, lon. 109° 20′. They occupied a village of the same name, and some of them lived with the Chinipas at San Andrés Chinipas.—Orozco y Berra, Geog., 58, 324, 1864.

Maguina. A pueblo in w. Chihuahua, Mexico, probably between lat. 28° and 29°. As it is on the border land of the Nevome and Tarahumare and not far from the main habitat of the Tepehuane, it doubtless contains or contained a mixed population. The village has therefore been assigned by various writers to one or another of those tribes. Orozco y Berra's map includes the village in Nevome country.

San Juan B[autista]. Maguina.—Orozco y Berra, Geog., 324, 1864.

Magunkaquog (originally *Magwonkko-muk,* 'place of the gift,' or 'granted place' (Eliot), possibly afterward changed by the Indians to the present form, meaning 'place of great trees.'—Trumbull). A village of Christian Indians in Nipmuc territory, at Hopkinton, Middlesex co., Mass., in 1674. On the name, see Trumbull and Tooker, cited below. Cf. *Mangunckakuck.*

Magoncog.—Livingston (1678) in N. Y. Doc. Col. Hist., XIII, 528, 1881. Magwonkkomuk.—Eliot (1669) quoted by Tooker, Algonq. Ser., x, 26, 1901. Maguncog.—Rawson (1678) in N. Y. Doc. Col. Hist., XIII, 521, 1881. Magunkahquog.—Trumbull, Ind. Names Conn., 18, 1881. Magunkakook.—Tooker, Algonq. Ser., x, 27, 1901. Magunkaquog.—Gookin (1674) in Mass. Hist. Soc. Coll., 1st s., I, 188, 1806. Magunkoag.—Gookin (1677) in Trans. Am. Antiq. Soc., II, 443, 1836. Magunkog.—Ibid., 470. Majunkaquog.—Eliot quoted by Tooker, Algonq. Ser., x, 25, 1901. Makunkokoag.—Gookin (1677) in Trans. Am. Antiq. Soc., II, 435, 1836. Mogkunkakauke.—Tooker, op. cit., 27. Moogunkawg.—Stone (1767) in Mass. Hist. Soc. Coll., 1st s., x, 82, 1809.

Magwa (*Ma-gwä',* 'loon'). A gens of the Shawnee (q. v.).—Morgan, Anc. Soc., 168, 1877.

Maha ('caterpillar'). Given by Bourke (Jour. Am. Folk-lore, II, 181, 1889) as a clan of the Mohave, q. v.

Mahackemo. The principal chief of a small band on Norwalk r., s. w. Conn., which sold lands in 1640 and 1641. See *Norwalk.*

Mahackemo.—De Forest, Inds. of Conn., 177, 1851. Mahackeno.—De Forest as quoted by Ruttenber, Tribes Hudson R., 82, 1872.

Mahahal. A former Chumashan village on San Cayetano ranch, Ventura co., Cal.—Henshaw, Buenaventura MS. vocab., B. A. E., 1884.

Mahala mats. A California name of *Ceanothus prostratus,* also known as squaw's carpet. *Mahala,* more often *mohale,* is often used as synonymous with "squaw" in California by the whites. If not from Spanish *mujer,* 'woman,' it is from Yokuts *muk'ela,* having the same meaning. (A. F. C. A. L. K.)

Maharolukti (*Mä-har-o-luk'-ti,* 'brave'). A subclan of the Delawares (q. v.).—Morgan, Anc. Soc., 172, 1877.

Mahaskahod. A hunting village of the Manahoac in 1608, on Rappahannock r., Va., at the limit of the Powhatan confederacy, probably near Fredericksburg.

Mahaskahod.—Smith (1629), Va., I, map, repr. 1819. Mohaskahod.—Simons in Smith, ibid., 186.

Mahcoah. The principal village of the

Toquart (q.v.) on Village passage, Barclay sd., w. coast of Vancouver id.—Can. Ind. Aff., 263, 1902.

Mahewala. A village formerly on the lower Mississippi, destroyed about the close of 1681 or early in 1682; perhaps a settlement of the Tangibao, q. v.

Mahehoualaima.—La Salle (1682) in Margry, Déc., II, 198, 1877. Maheouala.—Ibid., 190. Maheoula.—La Métairie (1682) quoted by French, Hist. Coll. La., II, 23, 1875.

Mahican ('wolf'). An Algonquian tribe that occupied both banks of upper Hudson r., in New York, extending N. almost to L. Champlain. To the Dutch they were known as River Indians, while the French grouped them and the closely connected Munsee and Delawares under the name of Loups ('wolves'). The same tribes were called Akochakaneñ ('stammerers') by the Iroquois. On the w. bank they joined the Munsee at Catskill cr., and on the E. bank they joined the Wappinger near Poughkeepsie. They extended E. into Massachusetts and held the upper part of Housatonic valley. Their council fire was at Schodac, on an island near Albany, and it is probable that they had 40 villages within their territory. The name, in a variety of forms, has been applied to all the Indians from Hudson r. to Narragansett bay, but in practical use has been limited to two bodies, one on lower Connecticut r., Conn., known dialectically as Mohegan (q. v.), the other, on Hudson r., known as Mahican. They were engaged in a war with the Mohawk, their nearest neighbors on the w., when the Dutch appeared on the scene, which lasted until 1673. In 1664 the inroads of the Mohawk compelled them to remove their council fire from Schodac to Westenhuck, the modern Stockbridge, Mass. As the settlements crowded upon them the Mahican sold their territory piecemeal, and about 1730 a large body of them emigrated to Susquehanna r. and settled near Wyoming, Pa., in the vicinity of the Delawares and Munsee, with whom they afterward removed to the Ohio region, finally losing their identity. A previous emigration had formed the main body of the mixed tribe of the Scaticook. As early as 1721 a band of Mahican found their way to Indiana, where they had a village on Kankakee r. In 1736 those living in Housatonic valley were gathered into a mission at Stockbridge, Mass., where they maintained a separate existence under the name of Stockbridge Indians. These are the only Mahican who have preserved their identity. In 1756 a large body of Mahican and Wappinger removed from the Hudson to the E. branch of the Susquehanna, settling, with the Nanticoke and others, under Iroquois protection at Chenango, Chugnut, and Owego, in Broome and Tioga cos., N.Y. They probably later found their way to their kindred in the W. A few Mahican remained about their ancient homes on the Hudson for some years after the Revolution, but finally disappeared unnoticed. If any remain they are included among the Stockbridge.

According to Ruttenber the Mahican confederacy comprised at least 5 divisions or subtribes—the Mahican proper, Wiekagjoc, Mechkentowoon, Wawyachtonoc, and Westenhuck (Stockbridges). It is impossible to estimate their population, as the different bands were always confounded or included with neighboring tribes, of whom they afterward became an integral part.

According to Ruttenber's account the government of the Mahican was a democracy, but his statement that the office of chief sachem was hereditary by the lineage of the wife of the sachem, which appears to be correct, does not indicate a real democracy. His statement in regard to the duties of the sachem and other officers is as follows: "The sachem was assisted by counselors, and also by one hero, one owl, and one runner; the rest of the nation were called young men or warriors. The sachem, or more properly king, remained at all times with his tribe and consulted their welfare; he had charge of the *mnoti*, or bag of peace, which contained the belts and strings used to establish peace and friendship with different nations, and concluded all treaties on behalf of his people. The counselors were elected, and were called chiefs. Their business was to consult with their sachem in promoting the peace and happiness of their people. The title of hero was gotten only by courage and prudence in war. When a war-alliance was asked, or cause for war existed with another tribe, the sachem and the counselors consulted, and if they concluded to take up the hatchet, the matter was put in the hands of the heroes for execution. When peace was proposed, the heroes put the negotiations in the hands of the sachem and counselors. The office of owl was also one of merit. He must have a strong memory, and must be a good speaker. His business was to sit beside his sachem, and proclaim his orders to the people with a loud voice; and also to get up every morning as soon as daylight and arouse the people, and order them to their daily duties. The business of runner was to carry messages, and to convene councils."

The Mahican were generally well built. As fighting men they were perfidious, accomplishing their designs by treachery, using stratagem to deceive their enemies, and making their most hazardous attacks under cover of darkness. The women

ornamented themselves more than the men. "All wear around the waist a girdle made of the fin of the whale or of sewant." The men originally wore a breechcloth made of skins, but after the Dutch came those who could obtain it wore "between their legs a lap of duffels cloth half an ell broad and nine quarters long," which they girded around their waists and drew up in a fold "with a flap of each end hanging down in front and rear." In addition to this they had mantles of feathers, and at a later period decked themselves with "plaid duffels cloth" in the form of a sash, which was worn over the right shoulder, drawn in a knot around the body, with the ends extending down below the knees. When the young men wished to look especially attractive they wore "a band about their heads, manufactured and braided, of scarlet deer hair, interwoven with soft shining red hair." According to Van der Donck, the women wore a cloth around their bodies fastened by a girdle which extended below the knees, but next to the body, under this coat, they used a dressed deerskin coat, girt around the waist. The lower body of this skirt they ornamented with strips tastefully decorated with wampum which was frequently worth from 100 to 300 guilders ($40 to $120). They bound their hair behind in a club, about a hand long, in the form of a beaver's tail, over which they drew a square wampum-ornamented cap; and when they desired to be fine they drew around the forehead a band also ornamented with wampum, which was fastened behind in a knot. Around their necks they hung various ornaments; they also wore bracelets, curiously wrought and interwoven with wampum. Polygamy was practised to some extent, though mostly by chiefs. Maidens were allowed to signify their desire to enter matrimonial life, upon which a marriage would be formally arranged; widows and widowers were left to their own inclinations. In addition to the usual manifestations of grief at the death of a relative or friend, they cut off their hair and burned it on the grave. Their dead, according to Ruttenber, were usually interred in a sitting posture. It was usual to place by the side of the body a pot, kettle, platter, spoon, and provisions; wood was then placed around the body, and the whole was covered with earth and stones, outside of which pickets were erected, so that the tomb resembled a little house. Their houses were of the communal sort and differed usually only in length; they were formed by long, slender, hickory saplings set in the ground in a straight line in two rows. The poles were then bent toward each other in the form of an arch and secured together, giving the appearance of a garden arbor; the sides and roof were then lathed with split poles, and over this bark was lapped and fastened by withes to the lathing. A smoke-hole was left in the roof, and a single doorway was provided. These houses rarely exceeded 20 ft in width, but they were sometimes 180 ft long. Their so-called castles were strong, firm structures, and were situated usually on a steep, high, flat-topped hill, near a stream. The top of the hill was inclosed with a strong stockade, having large logs for a foundation, on both sides of which oak posts, forming a palisade, were set in the ground, the upper ends being crossed and joined together. Inside the walls of such inclosures they not infrequently had 20 or 30 houses. Besides their strongholds they had villages and towns which were inclosed or stockaded and which usually had woodland on one side and corn land on the other. Their religious beliefs were substantially the same as those of the New England Indians.

Barton gives the Mahican 3 clans: Muchquauh (bear), Mechchaooh (wolf), Toonpaooh (turtle). According to Morgan they had originally the same clans as the Delawares and Munsee—the Wolf, Turtle, and Turkey; but these ultimately developed into phratries, subdivided into clans as follows: The Tooksetuk (wolf) phratry into the Nehjao (wolf), Makwa (bear), Ndeyao (dog), and Wapakwe (opossum) clans; the Tonebao (turtle) phratry into the Gakpomute (little turtle), ——— (mud turtle), Tonebao (great turtle), and Wesawmaun (yellow eel) clans; ———, the Turkey phratry into the Naahmao (turkey), Gahko (crane), and ——— (chicken) clans.

The villages of the Mahican, so far as their names have been recorded, were Aepjin, Kaunaumeek (Stockbridge), Maringoman's Castle, Monemius, Potic, Scaticook (3 villages in Dutchess and Rensselaer cos., N. Y., and Litchfield co., Conn.), Schodac, Wiatiac, Wiltmeet, Winooskeek, and Wyantenuc.

(J. M. C. T.)

Agotsaganes.—Clark quoted by Brinton, Lenape Leg., 255, 1885 ('stutterers,' 'those who speak a strange tongue': Mohawk name). Agotsagenens.—Jogues (ca. 1640) quoted by Shea, Miss. Val., 165, 1852. Agozhagàuta.—Ettwein (1848) quoted by Brinton, op. cit., 14. Akochakaneñ'.—Hewitt, inf'n, 1906 (Iroquois name). Aquatsagané.—Esnauts and Rapilly, map, 1777. Aquatzagane.—Schoolcraft, Ind. Tribes, III, 532, 1853. Atsayongky.—De Laet (1633) in N. Y. Hist. Soc. Coll., 2d s., I, 315, 1841. Canoe Indians.—Gale, Upper Miss., 169, 1867 (so called by whites). Hikanagi.—Gatschet, Shawnee MS., B. A. E. (Shawnee name). Loo's.—Coffen (1754) in N. Y. Doc. Col. Hist., VI, 836, 1855. Loups.—French doc. of 1665, ibid., IX, 38, 1855. Machicans.—Hendricksen (1616), ibid., I, 14, 1856. Machingans.—Jefferys, French Doms., pt. 1, 136, 1761. Mahakanders.—Markham (1691) in N. Y. Doc. Col. Hist., III, 809, 1853. Mahakans.—Hazard, Coll. Am. State Papers, I, 520, 1792.

Mahckanders.—Dongan (1687) in N. Y. Doc. Col. Hist., III, 439, 1853 (misprint). Mahegan.—Vaillant (1688), ibid., 521. Maheingans.—Iberville (1699) in Margry, Déc., IV, 342, 1880. Mahekanders.—Livingston (1687) in N. Y. Doc. Col. Hist., III, 481, 1853. Mahhekaneew.—Vater, Mith., pt. 3, sec. 3, 268, 1816. Mahicanders.—Doc. of 1646 in N. Y. Doc. Col. Hist., I, 184, 1856. Mahicanni.—Barton, New Views, xxxi, 1797. Mahicans.—Map ca. 1614 in N. Y. Doc. Col. Hist., I, 1856. Mahiccanni.—Heckewelder quoted by Thompson, Long. Id., I, 76, 1843. Mahiccans.—Barton, New Views, xxxix, 1797. Mahiccon.—Thomson (ca. 1785) quoted by Barton, ibid., xxxii. Mahicon.—Barton, ibid., xi, 1798. Mahigan.—Vaillant (1688) in N. Y. Doc. Col. Hist., III, 522, 1853. Mahiganathicoit.—Champlain (1619) Voy., II, 142, 1830. Mahiganaticois.—Champlain (1627), Œuvres, V, pt. 2, 135, 1870. Mahigan-Aticois.—Ibid., 209. Mahigane.—La Salle (1681) in Margry, Déc., II, 148, 1877. Mahiggins.—Clobery (1633) in N. Y. Doc. Col. Hist., I, 78, 1856. Mahik'.—Hewitt, inf'n, 1886 (Tuscarora name). Mahikan.—Doc. of 1644 in N. Y. Doc. Col. Hist., I, 151, 1856. Mahikanders.—Doc. of 1651, ibid., 542. Mahikkanders.—Romer (1700), ibid., IV, 799, 1854. Mahillendras.—Dongan (1688), ibid., III, 533, 1853 (misprint?). Mahinganak.—Jes. Rel. for 1646, 3, 1858. Mahinganiois.—Jes. Rel. for 1652, 26, 1858. Mahingans.—Jes. Rel. for 1646, 3, 1858. Mahingaus.—Richardson, Arct. Exped., II, 39, 1851 (misprint). Mahycander.—Doc. of 1660 in N. Y. Doc. Col. Hist., XIII, 165, 1881. Maicanders.—Doc. (ca. 1643), ibid., I, 196, 1856. Maikans.—Wassenaar (ca. 1626) quoted by Ruttenber, Tribes Hudson R., 58, 1872. Maikens.—Wassenaar (1632) quoted by Ruttenber, ibid. Makicander.—Nicolls (1678) in N. Y. Doc. Col. Hist., XIII, 516, 1881. Makihander.—Boudinot, Star in the West, 99, 1816. Makimanes.—Map of 1616 in N. Y. Doc. Col. Hist., I, 1856. Makingans.—Jefferys, French Doms., pt. I, 11, 1761. Malukander.—Glen (1699) in N. Y. Doc. Col. Hist., IV, 558, 1854 (misprint). Manhikani.—De Laet (1633) quoted by Vater, Mith., pt. 3, sec. 3, 390, 1816. Manhikans.—Vater, ibid. Manhingans.—Ruttenber, Tribes Hudson R., 57, 1872. Manikans.—De Laet (ca. 1633) quoted by Jones, Ind. Bull., 6, 1867. Mankikani.—De Laet quoted by Barton, New Views, xxxi, 1797. Mauraigans.—Bacqueville de la Potherie, III, 126, 1753. Mauraygans.—Writer of 1691 in N. Y. Doc. Col. Hist., IX, 513, 1855. Mayekanders.—De Vries (1655) quoted by Ruttenber, Tribes Hudson R., 105, 1872. Mayganathicoise.—Champlain (ca. 1619) in Shea, Miss. Val., 165, 1852. Maykanders.—Doc. of 1650 in N. Y. Doc. Col. Hist., I, 412, 1856. Mehihammers.—New York conf. (1753), ibid., VI, 782, 1855. Mhíkana.—Gatschet, Shawnee MS., B. A. E., 1880 (Shawnee form). Miheconders.—Canajoharie conf. (1759) in N. Y. Doc. Col. Hist., VII, 393, 1856. Mihicanders.—Ft Johnson conf. (1756), ibid., 50. Moheakanneews.—Morse, Mod. Geog., I, 54, 1814. Moheakenunks.—Clark, Onondaga, I, 18, 1849. Moheakounuck.—Doc. of 1774 quoted by Ruttenber, Tribes Hudson R., 269, 1872. Moheakunnuks.—Morse, Rep. to Sec. War., 76, 1822. Mohecan.—Dawson in Drake, Bk. Inds., V, 77, 1848. Moheckons.—Peters (1761) in Mass. Hist. Soc. Coll., 4th s., IX, 440, 1871. Moheconnock.—Doc. of 1791 quoted by Schoolcraft, Ind. Tribes, V, 668, 1855. Mo-heegan.—Stiles (1756) quoted by Brinton, Lenape Leg., 35, 1885. Mohekin.—Letter of 1771 quoted by Ruttenber, Tribes Hudson R., 194, 1872. Mo-he-kun-e-uk.—Morgan, Anc. Soc., 113, 1877. Mo-he'-kun-ne-uk.—Morgan, Consang. and Affin., 289, 1870. Mohekunnuks.—Morgan, League Iroq., 45, 1851. Mohekunuh.—Belknap and Morse in Mass. Hist. Soc. Coll., 1st s., V, 12, 1816. Mohicander.—Johnson (ca. 1756) quoted by Ruttenber, Tribes Hudson R., 231, 1872. Mohicands.—Lovelace (1669) in N. Y. Doc. Col. Hist., XIII, 439, 1881. Mohicanrs.—Doc. of 1676, ibid., XIV, 718, 1883. Mohicans.—Michaelius (1628), ibid., II, 769, 1858. Mohiccons.—Hutchins (1768) quoted by Jefferson, Notes, 142, 1825. Mohickan.—Doc. of 1755 quoted by Rupp, Northampton Co., 88, 1845. Mohickanders.—Johnson (1756) in N. Y. Doc. Col. Hist., VII, 136, 1856. Mohicken.—Croghan (1760) in Mass. Hist. Soc. Coll., 4th s., IX, 378, 1871. Mohickons.—Weiser (1748) quoted by Rupp, West. Penn., app., 16, 1846. Mohigon.—Yong (1634) in Mass. Hist. Soc.

Coll., 4th s., IX, 129, 1871. **Mohikan.**—Bouquet (1761), ibid., 431. **Mohikander.**—Ft Johnson conf. (1756) in N. Y. Doc. Col. Hist., VII, 152, 1856. **Mohikonders.**—Johnson (1756), ibid., 118. **Mohikons.**—Hutchins map in Smith, Bouquet's Exped., 1766. **Mohingans.**—McKenney and Hall, Ind. Tribes, III, 79, 1854. **Mohingaus.**—Ibid. **Mohocanders.**—Salisbury (1678) in N. Y. Doc. Col. Hist., XIII, 520, 1881. **Mohogans.**—Owaneco's Rep. (1700), ibid., IV, 614, 1854. **Mohokanders.**—Deed quoted by Ruttenber, Tribes Hudson R., 88, 1872. **Mohuccons.**—Boudinot, Star in the West, 127, 1816. **Mohuccories.**—I b i d. **Morahicanders.**—Louwrensen (1658) in N. Y. Doc. Col. Hist., XIII, 90, 1881. **Moraigane.**—La Salle (1681) in Margry, Déc., II, 148, 1877. **Moraiguns.**—Doc. of 1759 in N. Y. Doc. Col. Hist., X, 982, 1858. **Moraingans.**—Vaudreuil (1757), ibid., 579. **Morargans.**—Vaudreuil (1760), ibid., 1091. **Mourigan.**—Boudinot, Star in the West, 99, 1816. **Muckhekanies.**—Ibid., 127. **Muhekannew.**—Vater, Mith., pt. 3, sec. 3, 391, 1816. **Muhheakunneuw.**—Holmes (1804) in Mass. Hist. Soc. Coll., 1st s., IX, 100, 1804. **Muhheakunnuk.**—Ibid. **Muhheconnuck.**—Pickering (1791) in Am. State Pap., Ind. Aff., I, 169, 1832. **Muhheeckanew.**—Ruttenber, Tribes Hudson R., 41, 1872. **Muh-hee-kun-eew.**—Stockbridge letter, H. R. Misc. Doc. 69, 32d Cong., 1st sess., I, 1852. **Muhhekaneew.**—Edwards (1788) in Mass. Hist. Soc. Coll., 2d s., X, 84, 1823. **Muhhekaneok.**—Ibid. (pl. of Muhhekaneew). **Muhhekanew.**—E d w a r d s (1801) quoted by Kendall, Trav., II, 305, 1809. **Muhhekaniew.**—Schoolcraft quoted by Ruttenber, Tribes Hudson R., 51, 1872. **Muhhekanneuk.**—Boyd, Ind. Local Names, 27, 1885. **Muhhekanok.**—Hopkins quoted by Ruttenber, Tribes Hudson R., 320, 1872. **Muhhekenow.**—Clinton quoted by Schoolcraft, Trav., 29, 1821. **Muhhekunneau.**—Daggett (1821) in Mass. Hist. Soc. Coll., 2d s., IX, xli, 1822. **Muhhekunneyuk.**—Holmes (1804), ibid., 1st s., IX, 100, 1804 (plural). **Muhkekaneew.**—Drake, Bk. Inds., II, 87, 1848. **Mukickans.**—Weiser (1748) quoted by Schoolcraft, Ind. Tribes, IV, 605, 1854. **Mukkekaneaw.**—Boudinot, Star in the West, 99, 1816. **Nhíkana.**—Gatschet, Shawnee MS., B. A. E., 1880 (Shawnee name). **Orunges.**—Chauvignerie (1736) quoted by Schoolcraft, Ind. Tribes, III, 554, 1853. **Ouiagies.**—McKenney and Hall, Ind. Tribes, III, 79, 1854. **Ourages.**—Macauley, N. Y., II, 162, 1829. **Ouragies.**—Colden (1727), Five Nations, 95, 1747. **Poh-he-gan.**—Stiles in Mass. Hist. Soc. Coll., 1st s., IX, 76, 1804. **River Indians.**—Early Dutch name. **Tumewand.**—Rafinesque, Am. Nations, I, 138, 1836. **Uragees.**—Colden (1727), Five Nations, 102, 1747.

Mahktosis. The principal village of the Ahousaht (q. v.), on Matilda cr., Clayoquot sd., w. coast of Vancouver id.—Can. Ind. Aff., 264, 1902.

Mahoa. Probably the same as Maxua, the chief of the Maamtagyila, a Kwakiutl gens, but applied by Galiano (Relacion, 103, 1802), in the Spanish form Majoa, to his village or to the gens itself.

Mahohivas (*Máhohivás*, 'red shield'). A warrior society of the Cheyenne (q. v.); also sometimes known as Hotóa-nútqiu, 'Buffalo-bull warriors.' (J. M.)
Red Shield.—Dorsey in Field Columb. Mus. Pub., no. 99, 15, 1905.

Mahoning ('at the salt-lick.'—Heckewelder). A Delaware village in 1764 on the w. bank of Mahoning r., perhaps between Warren and Youngstown, Trumbull co., Ohio. (J. M.)
Mahoning.—Hutchins' map (1764) in Smith, Bouquet's Exped., 1766. **Mahónink.**—Heckewelder in Trans. Am. Philos. Soc., n. s., IV, 365, 1834 (correct form). **Mahony Town.**—Ibid., 390.

Mahow. A Chumashan village placed by Taylor at José Carrillo's rancho, Ventura co., Cal. Perhaps the site was the Las

Posas rancho, as stated by Ventura Indians in 1884.
Ma-hau.—Henshaw, Buenaventura MS. vocab., B. A. E., 1884 (name from Indian in 1884). **Mahow.**—Taylor in Cal. Farmer, May 4, 1860 (name from 1856).

Mahoyum (*Má-ho-yum*, 'red tipi'). The name of a special heraldic tipi belonging to the Cheyenne, erroneously given by Clark (Cheyenne MS.) as the name of a band. (J. M.)
Miayŭma.—Clark quoted by Mooney in 14th Rep. B. A. E., 1026, 1896.

Mahsolamo. Given as the name of a body of Salish on the s. side of Chemanis lake, near the E. coast of Vancouver id.—Brit. Col. map, Ind. Aff., Victoria, 1872.

Mahtoiowa ('the bear that whirls, 'Whirling Bear'). A Brulé Teton Sioux chief. While the Brulés, Oglala, and Miniconjou Sioux were camped near Ft Laramie, Wyo., in 1854, having come to receive the annual presents from the Government, an ox belonging to some Mormon emigrants was killed by the Indians. According to the most reliable information, obtained by Grinnell from Wm. Rowland, who was at Ft Laramie during the trouble, the commandant demanded the surrender of the offender, and Mahtoiowa, in response, pointed out the tipi of the guilty Indian, informing Lieut. Grattan that he might arrest him; but Grattan insisted that Mahtoiowa should bring the man out and deliver him. When the chief declined to do so, Grattan ordered his men to fire a howitzer at the lodge in the middle of the village. A shell killed an Indian, and 17 of the 18 soldiers were at once shot down with arrows, the single survivor escaping by the aid of an Indian friend. The Sioux besieged Ft Laramie until it was relieved. Mahtoiowa was killed in an action before the fort, and the war, which was the beginning of Sioux hostilities, was carried on by Little Thunder.

Mahusquechikoken. A former village, under Iroquois rule, situated on Allegheny r., Pa., about 20 m. above Venango, and inhabited chiefly by Seneca and Munsee Delawares; it was destroyed by Brodhead in 1779. This village, together with Buckaloon and Connewango, formed a settlement 8 m. in length along Allegheny r., the 3 villages together containing about 35 large houses (Brodhead (1779) in Jour. Mil. Exped. of Maj. Gen. Sullivan, 308, 1887). (J. N. B. H.)

Maicoba. A settlement of the Nevome and the seat of a mission established in 1676; situated on or near the upper Rio Yaqui, in E. Sonora, Mexico. In 1678 the population numbered 153. The town now consists of a mixed population of whites, Pima, Yaqui, and a few Mayo, numbering in all 199 in 1900.

Maicoba.—Orozco y Berra, Geog., 351, 1864. **S. Francisco Borja Maicoba.**—Zapata (1678) in Doc. Hist. Mex., 4th s., III, 345, 1857.

Maidu ('man', 'Indian'). A tribe formerly dwelling in Sacramento valley and the adjacent Sierra Nevada in California. This single tribe constitutes the entire Pujunan linguistic family of Powell, all the divisions of which called themselves Maidu, and distinguished themselves one from another by their local names only. The Maidu proper, comprising the divisions N. of Bear r. valley, were formerly considered a different stock from the Nishinam, who are now recognized as the southern branch of the family. The names of the Maidu villages and of the inhabitants were usually local place names. It

OLD MAIDU MAN. (UNIVERSITY OF CALIFORNIA)

may be doubted if, in the following list of the divisional and village names, the former have a greater value than the latter or were in fact anything more than the larger villages with perhaps outlying settlements of a more or less temporary character. Divisions: Cohes, Cushna, Hoitda, Honkut, Kiski, Konkau, Kulomum, Molma, Nimsewi, Pakamali, Tsaktomo, Tsamak, Tsulumsewi, Tummeli, Ustoma, Willi, Yumagatok, and Yunu. Villages: Bamom, Bauka, Bayu, Benkomkomi, Botoko, Eskini, Hembem, Hoako, Hoholto, Hokomo, Hopnomkoyo, Indak, Kalkalya, Kotasi, Kulaiapto, Kulkumish, Michopdo, Mimal, Molma, Nakankoyo, Oidoingkoyo, Okpam, Ola, Ololopa, Onchoma, Opok, Otaki, Paki,

Panpakan, Pitsokut, Pulakatu, Sekumne, Sesum, Silongkoyo, Siwim Pakan, Sunusi, Tadoiko, Taikus, Taisida, Tasikoyo, Tchikimisi, Tishum, Tomcha, Totoma, Tsam Bahenom, Tsekankan, Tsuka, Wokodot, Yalisumni, Yamako, Yauko, Yiikulme, Yodok, Yotammoto, Yumam, and Yupu. Consult Dixon in Bul. Am. Mus. Nat. Hist., XVII, pt. 3, 1905. See *Pujunan Family.*

Mai'-deh.—Powers in Cont. N. A. Ethnol., III, 282, 1877. **Mai'-du.**—Ibid. **Meidoos.**—Powers in Overland Mo., XII, 21, 1874. **Midu.**—Merriam in Science, n. s., XIX, 914, June 15, 1904 (pron. Mi-doo). **Wawáh.**—Powers, Inds. West Nevada, 14, 1876 ('strangers': Paiute name for all Sacramento r. tribes).

Mailam-ateuna ('those of the lowermost'). A Zuñi phratry consisting of the Takya (Toad) and Chitola (Rattlesnake) clans. (F. H. C.)

Maitheshkizh ('Coyote pass,' referring to the pueblo of Jemez). A Navaho clan, descended from a captive Jemez girl and now affiliated with the Tsedzhinkini. **Maiɸeckíj.**—Matthews in Jour. Am. Folk-lore, III, 104, 1890. **Maiɸeckíjni.**—Ibid. **Maidĕskï'z.**—Matthews, Navaho Legends, 30, 1897. **Maidĕskï'zni.**—Ibid.

Maitho ('Coyote spring'). A Navaho clan. **Maiɔò'.**—Matthews in Jour. Am. Folk-lore, III, 103, 1890. **Maiɔò'ḏine.**—Ibid. **Maitó'.**—Matthews, Navaho Legends, 30, 1897. **Maito'dine'.**—Ibid.

Maize (from the Arawak *marise*, changed to *maysi* and *mahiz* in the Antilles). This giant cereal, known in the United States and Canada as 'Indian corn,' or simply 'corn,' and to botanists as *Zea mays* Linn., was the great food plant of those American Indians who sought the aid of cultivation in obtaining food. It is now generally supposed to have been derived from native grasses— the *Euchlœna mexicana* of s. Mexico and *E. luxurians* of Guatemala, the latter approximating most nearly the cultivated corn. These are the only known species of North American endogens from which the numerous varieties now in use could have been developed. Harshberger says linguistic evidence shows that maize was introduced into the United States from the tribes of Mexico and from the Carib of the West Indies, but the time of this introduction can only be conjectured. That it was long before the appearance of Europeans, however, is evident, not only from its early and widespread cultivation by tribes of the area now embraced in the United States, but from the fact that indications of its cultivation are found in mounds and in the ancient pueblo ruins and cliff dwellings, while corroborative evidence is found in the fact that several varieties of maize had already been developed at the time of discovery, four being mentioned as in use among the Indians of Virginia (Beverley, Hist. Virginia, 125–128, 1722). Jacques Cartier, the first European to enter the St

Lawrence, observed large fields of growing maize at Hochelaga (now Montreal) in 1534, and Champlain in 1604 found it in cultivation at almost every point visited from Nova Scotia to upper Ottawa r. The supplies of maize obtained from the Indians by the New England and Virginia colonists are well known. Hennepin, Marquette, Joliet, La Salle, and other early French explorers of the Mississippi valley found all the tribes they visited, from the Minnesota r. to the Gulf, and even into Texas, cultivating maize; and the same was true of the tribes between N. w. Mexico and the plains of Kansas when visited by Coronado in 1540–42. Even the Mandan and Arikara on the upper Missouri had their maize patches when first seen by the whites. How far northward on the Pacific slope the cultivation of maize had extended at the time of the discovery is not known. Evidence that it or anything else was cultivated in California w. of the Rio Colorado valley is still lacking. Brinton (Am. Race, 50, 1891) expresses the opinion that maize "was cultivated both north and south to the geographical extent of its productive culture." Such at least appears to have been true in regard to its extent northward on the Atlantic slope, except in the region of the upper Mississippi and the Red r. of the North.

The ease with which maize can be cultivated and conserved, and its bountiful yield, caused its rapid extension among the Indians after it first came into use. With the exception of better tillage the method of cultivation is much the same to-day among civilized men as among the natives. Thomas Hariot, who visited Virginia in 1586, says the Indians put four grains in a hill "with care that they touch not one another." The extent to which the cereal was cultivated in prehistoric times by the Indians may be inferred from these facts and from the observations of early explorers. It seems evident from the history of the expeditions of De Soto and Coronado (1540–42) that the Indians of the Gulf states and of the Pueblo region relied chiefly on maize for food. It is also probable that a moiety of the food supply of the Indians of Virginia and the Carolinas, and of the Iroquois and Huron tribes, was from the cultivation of corn. Du Pratz says the Indians "from the sea [Gulf] as far as the Illinois" make maize their principal subsistence. The amount of corn of the Iroquois destroyed by Denonville in 1687 has been estimated at more than a million bushels (Charlevoix, Hist. Nouv. France, II, 355, 1744), but this estimate is probably excessive. According to Tonti (French, Hist. Coll. La., I, 70, 1846), who took part in the expedition, the army was engaged

seven days in cutting up the corn of four villages. Thaumer de la Source (Shea, Early Voy. Miss., 81, 1861) says, "the Tounicas [Tonika] live entirely on Indian corn." Gen. Wayne, writing in 1794 of the Indian settlements, asserts that "the margins of these beautiful rivers, the Miamis of the Lake and the Au Glaize, appear like one continued village for a number of miles, both above and below this place, Grand Glaize, nor have I ever before beheld such immense fields of corn in any part of America from Canada to Florida" (Manypenny, Ind. Wards, 84, 1880). From the Indians are derived ash-cake, hoe-cake, succotash, samp, hominy, the hominy mortar, etc., and even the cribs elevated on posts are patterned after those of the Indians of the Southern states. Corn was used in various ways by the natives in their ceremonies, and among some tribes the time of planting, ripening, and harvesting was made the occasion for festivities. See *Agriculture, Food.*

Consult Carr, Mounds of the Mississippi Historically Considered, 1883; Cushing, Zuñi Breadstuffs; Harshberger, Maize: a Botanical and Economic Study, 1893; Payne, Hist. New World, I, 1892; Stickney in Parkman Club Pub., no. 13, 1897; Thomas in 12th Rep. B. A. E., 614–622, 1894.　　　　　　　　　　　　(C. T.)

Majalayghua. A former Chumashan village near Los Prietos, adjacent to Santa Barbara, Cal.
Inajalayehua.—Bancroft, Nat. Races, I, 459, 1874 (misquoted from Taylor). Majalayghua.—Taylor in Cal. Farmer, Apr. 24, 1863.

Makache ('owl'). An Oto gens.
Ma-ka'-tce.—Dorsey in 15th Rep. B. A. E., 240, 1897. Mä'-kotch.—Morgan, Anc. Soc., 156, 1877.

Makah ('cape people'). The southernmost tribe of the Wakashan stock, the only one within the United States. They belong to the Nootka branch. According to Swan the Makah claimed the territory between Flattery rocks, 15 m. s., and Hoko r., 15 m. E. of C. Flattery, Wash., also Tatoosh id., near the cape. Their winter towns were Baada, Neah, Ozette, Tzues, and Waatch; their summer villages, Ahchawat, Kiddekubbut, and Tatooche. Gibbs (MS., B. A. E.) mentions another, called Kehsidatsoos. They now have two reservations, Makah and Ozette, Wash., on which, in 1905, there were respectively 399 and 36, a total of 435 for the tribe. In 1806 they were estimated by Lewis and Clark to number 2,000. By treaty of Neah bay, Wash., Jan. 31, 1855, the Makah ceded all their lands at the mouth of the Strait of Juan de Fuca except the immediate area including C. Flattery. This reservation was enlarged by Executive order of Oct. 26, 1872, superseded by Executive order of Jan. 2, 1873, and in turn revoked by Executive order of Oct. 12 of the same year, by which the Makah res. was definitely defined. The Ozette res. was established by order of Apr. 12, 1893.

Ba-qa-ŏ.—McCaw, Puyallup MS. vocab., B. A. E., 1885 (Puyallup name). **Cape Flattery.**—Lane in Ind. Aff. Rep., 162, 1850. **Classet.**—Farnham, Trav., II, 310, 1843 (Nootka name: 'outsiders'). **Clatset.**—Dunn, Hist. Oregon, 231, 1844. **Clossets.**—Starling in Ind. Aff. Rep., 171, 1852. **Flattery.**—Ibid., 170. **Klaizarts.**—Armstrong, Oregon, 136, 1857. **Kla-iz-zarts.**—Jewitt, Narr., 75, 1849. **Klasset.**—Swan in Smithson. Cont., XVI, 1, 1870. **Kwenēt-che-chat.**—Ibid. (own name: 'cape people'). **Kwe-nēt-sat'h.**—Ibid. (Salish name). **Macau.**—Lane in Ind. Aff. Rep., 162, 1850. **Ma-caw.**—Starling in Ind. Aff. Rep., 170, 1852. **Maccaws.**—Hanna in Ind. Aff. Rep. 1857, 337, 1858. **Mackahs.**—Taylor in Cal. Farmer, Aug. 1, 1862. **Makahs.**—Gibbs, Clallam and Lummi, v, 1863. **Makans.**—Stevens in Ind. Aff. Rep., 448, 1854. **Makas.**—Simmons in Ind. Aff. Rep., 335, 1857. **Makaw.**—Lane in Sen. Ex. Doc. 52, 31st Cong., 1st sess., 173, 1850. **Makha.**—U. S. Ind. Treat. (1855), 461, 1873. **Mak-kah.**—Swan in Smithson. Cont., XVI, 1, 1870. **Mi-caws.**—Jones (1853) in H. R. Ex. Doc. 76, 34th Cong., 3d sess., 7, 1857. **Quenait chechat.**—Swan, inf'n, Feb. 1886. **Que-nait'-sath.**—Swan, N.W. Coast, 211, 1857. **Quinechart.**—Orig. Jour. Lewis and Clark (1806), VI, 70, 1905. **Quin-na-chart.**—Ibid., IV, 169, 1905. **Quinnechant.**—Lewis and Clark, Exped., II, 120, 1814. **Quinnechart.**—Ibid., 474. **Tatouche.**—Nicolet, Oregon, 143, 1846. **Tla'asath.**—Boas in 6th Rep. N. W. Tribes Can., 31, 1890 ('outside people': Nootka name). **Yacaws.**—Schoolcraft, Ind. Tribes, VI, 689, 1857.

Makak. An Ikogmiut Eskimo village on the right bank of the Yukon below Anvik, Alaska; pop. 121 in 1880, 50 in 1890.

Akka.—Baker, Geog. Dict. Alaska, 226, 1902. **Makagamute.**—Raymond in Sen. Ex. Doc. 12, 42d Cong., 1st sess., 25, 1871. **Makag'mūt.**—Dall in Cont. N. A. Ethnol., I, 17, 1877. **Makeymut.**—Nelson in 18th Rep. B. A. E., map, 1899. **Makeymute.**—Petroff, Rep. on Alaska, 57, 1881. **Makki.**—Zagoskin in Nouv. Ann. Voy., 5th s., XXI, map, 1850. **Manki.**—Raymond, op. cit., 31 (so called by whites).

Makak. See *Mocuck.*

Makan ('medicine'). A Ponca gens, in two subgentes: Real Ponka and Gray Ponka.

Maχaⁿ.—Dorsey in 15th Rep. B. A. E., 228, 1897. **Noñ'-ga.**—Morgan, Anc. Soc., 155, 1877. **Ḽe-sĭnde-it'ajĭ.**—Dorsey, op. cit. ('does not touch buffalo tails').

Makataimeshekiakia. See *Black Hawk.*

Makatananamaki. See *Black Thunder.*

Makatapi ('black men.'—Hewitt). A name given in the Walam Olum of the Delawares as that of a tribe encountered by them during their migrations.—Brinton, Lenape Leg., 190, 1885.

Makawichia (*Ma-ka-wi-chia'*, 'place of many doves'). A Tarahumare rancheria near Palanquo, Chihuahua, Mexico.—Lumholtz, inf'n, 1894.

Makay. An unidentified village formerly on Pamlico r., N. C., marked on the map of the Homann heirs, 1756.

Makhelchel. A name applied by Powers to the people of the vicinity of Lower lake, one of the southern arms of Clear lake, Lake co., Cal. The name was used particularly to designate the people of Lower Lake id., who were supposed by Powers (Cont. N. A. Ethnol., III, 214,

1877) to belong to the Copehan (Wintun) linguistic stock, but who have been found to belong to the Kulanapan (Pomo) stock. The people inhabiting this island called the island and the village itself Koi. (s. A. B.)

Hesley.—Powers in Cont. N. A. Ethnol., III, 214, 1877 (from *hösch'-la*, 'island', in the Makhelchel dialect; applied by the whites both to the island and its original inhabitants). **Hessler.**—Ibid. **Kelsey.**—Ibid. **Kessler.**—Ibid. **Makh'-el-chel.**—Ibid.

Makhenikashika (*Maqe-nikaci'ʏa*, 'upper world people'). A Quapaw gens; probably identical with the Wakantaenikashika.—Dorsey in 15th Rep. B. A. E., 230, 1897.

Makhpíya-lúta. See *Red Cloud.*

Makhpiyamaza ('iron cloud'). A band of the Matantonwan division of the Mdewakanton Sioux, named from its chief. It numbered 153 in 1836 and 123 in 1859, at which latter date they resided on the w. bank of the Mississippi, above the mouth of St Croix, at the site of the present Hastings, Minn.

Iron-Cloud.—Neill, Hist. Minn., 144, note, 1858. **Iron Cloud's Village.**—Royce in 18th Rep. B. A. E., Minn. map, 1899. **Marcpeeah Mahzah.**—Schoolcraft, Ind. Tribes, III, 612, 1853. **Ma-rpi-ya-ma-za.**—Neill, op. cit.

Makhpiyawichashta ('cloud man'). A village of the Mdewakanton Sioux in Minnesota in 1836, numbering 157; named from the chief.

Cloud Man's band.—Ind. Aff. Rep. 1859, 100, 1860. **Marc pee wee Chastah.**—Schoolcraft, Ind. Tribes, III, 612, 1853. **Sky-Man.**—Neill, Hist. Minn., 144, note, 1858.

Maklykaut. An Eskimo missionary station on Disko bay, w. Greenland.

Maklykout.—Crantz, Hist. Greenland, I, map, 1767.

Makokos. See *Maycock.*

Makoma. A name used, evidently owing to some confusion on the part of early writers, for the Indians who formerly lived in the vicinity of Clear lake and the mountains of Napa and Mendocino cos., Cal., but they are said by Wrangell (Ethnog. Nachr., 80, 1839) to have dwelt northward of Ft Ross in Russian r. valley. The term undoubtedly comes from Maiyákma, the name of a prominent Yukian Wappo village near Calistoga, Napa co. (s. A. B.)

Maiyákma.—S. A. Barrett, inf'n, 1906 (correct name). **Mayacmas.**—Bancroft, Nat. Races, I, 451, 1874. **Mayacomas.**—Ibid., 363. **Mipacmas.**—Ibid., 362. **Myacmas.**—Taylor in Cal. Farmer, June 22, 1860. **Myacomaps.**—Ibid., June 7, 1861.

Makomitek. An Algonquian tribe or band mentioned in 1671 as residing in the vicinity of Green bay, Wis. Tailhan identifies them with the Makoukuwe, which is doubtful.

Makamitek.—Sieur de St Lusson (1671) in N. Y. Doc. Col. Hist., IX, 803, 1855. **Makomiteks.**—Prise de Possession (1671) in Tailhan, Perrot Mém., 293, 1864.

Makoua ('bear'). A tribe or band living near the village of St Michel, in central Wisconsin, in 1673; probably a division or gens of the Foxes.

Makou.—Lapham, Inds. of Wis., 4, 1870. **Maкoua.**—Jes. Rel. (1672), LVIII, 40, 1899.

Makoukuwe. A band or gens, probably of the Foxes, found living near Green bay, Wis., in 1673.
Maкoucoué.—Jes. Rel. (1673), LVIII, 40, 1899. **Makoueoue.**—Jes. Rel. quoted by Shea in Wis. Hist. Soc. Coll., III, 131, 1857. **Makoukoué.**—MS. Jes. Rel. of 1673 quoted by Tailhan, Perrot Mém., 293, 1864. **Makoukoueks.**—Ibid.

Maktlaiath (*Mā'ktl'aiath*). A sept of the Seshart, a Nootka tribe.—Boas in 6th Rep. N. W. Tribes Can., 32, 1890.

Makushin. An Aleut village on Makushin bay, Unalaska id., Alaska. Pop. 35 in 1834, according to Veniaminoff; 49 in 1874, according to Shiesnekov; 62 in 1880; 51 in 1890.
Makooshenskoi.—Elliott, Cond. Aff. Alaska, 225, 1875. **Makooshin.**—Elliott, Our Arct. Prov., map, 1886. **Makuschinskoje.**—Holmberg, Ethnog. Skizz., map, 142, 1855. **Makushin.**—Petroff in 10th Census, Alaska, 23, 1884. **Makushinsk.**—Coxe, Russ. Discov., 163, 1787. **Makushinskoe.**—Veniaminoff, Zapiski, II, 202, 1840. **Makuski.**—Coxe, Russ. Discov., 158, 1787.

Makwa ('bear'). According to Morgan, one of the 11 clans of the Mahican. According to Barton it is one of the 3 divisions of the Mahican, corresponding to Morgan's phratries. Morgan gives the wolf, turtle, and turkey; Barton gives the wolf, turtle, and bear, and puts the bear first.   (J. M.)
Mä'-kwä.—Morgan, Anc. Soc., 174, 1877. **Muchquanh.**—Keane in Stanford, Compend., 523, 1878 (misprint). **Much-quauh.**—Barton, New Views, xxxix, 1798. **Muk-wah.**—Warren in Minn. Hist. Soc. Coll., v, 44, 1885.

Makwa ('bear'). A gens of the Chippewa, q. v.
Mä-kwä'.—Morgan, Anc. Soc., 166, 1877. **Mukkwaw.**—Tanner, Narrative, 314, 1830. **Muk-wah.**—Ramsey in Ind. Aff. Rep., 91, 1850.

Makwisuchigi ('they who go by the name of the bear'). The "royal" (ruling) gens of the Foxes.   (W. J.)
Ma-kwis-so-jik.—Morgan, Anc. Soc., 170, 1877. **Ma'kwisutcigⁱ.**—Wm. Jones, inf'n, 1906.

Malahue. A former Chumashan village in Ventura co., Cal., at the Rancho de Maligo.
Hu-ma-li-wu.—Henshaw, Buenaventura MS. vocab., B. A. E., 1884. **Malahu.**—Taylor in Cal. Farmer, July 24, 1863.

Malaka. A tribe of the Patwin division of the Copehan family that formerly lived in Lagoon valley, Solano co., Cal.
Malaccas.—Powers in Overland Mo., XIII, 542, 1874. **Ma-lak'-ka.**—Powers in Cont. N. A. Ethnol., III, 218, 1877.

Malakut (*Mā'lexaL*). A Salish tribe on Saanich inlet, s. E. end of Vancouver id., speaking the Cowichan dialect; pop. 14 in 1901, 10 in 1904.
Mal-a-hut.—Can. Ind. Aff. 1889, 270, 1890. **Malakut.**—Ibid., 1901, pt II, 164. **Mā'leqatl.**—Boas, MS., B. A. E., 1887.

Malashaganay. A name of the sheepshead or fresh-water drum (*Haplodinotus grunniens*). Through Canadian French *malashigané* or *malashigane*, from *manashigan* in the Chippewa-Nipissing dialects of the Algonquian stock, signifying 'ugly ashigan.' The *ashigan* is the black bass of American English.   (A. F. C.)

Male (*Mā'lē*). A village of the Musqueam, a Cowichan tribe, situated N. of Sea id., in the delta of Fraser r., Brit. Col. According to Hill-Tout it was claimed by the Squawmish.
Mā'lē.—Hill-Tout in Rep. Brit. A. A. S., 54, 1894. **Mā'-li.**—Ibid., 473, 1900.

Malecite. Various explanations of this name have been given. According to Chamberlain it is from their Micmac name *Malisit*, 'broken talkers'; Tanner gives the form as *Mahnesheets*, meaning 'slow tongues'; Baraga derives it through the Cree from *mayisit* or *malisit*, 'the disfigured or ugly foot'; Lacombe (Dict. Cris, 707) agrees with Baraga and gives the etymology as *mayi* or *mal*, 'deformed,' and *sit*, 'foot.' Maurault's explanation is radically different from all, as he says it is from *Maroudit* or *Malouidit*, 'those who are of Saint Malo.' Vetromile says it "comes from *malike*, which in old Abnaki and also in Delaware means witchcraft," but adds, "hence the French name Micmac is a substitute for *Mareschite*," as he writes the name. According to Chamberlain the name they apply to themselves is *Wulastuk-wiuk*, 'dwellers on the beautiful river,' or, as given by Maurault, *Ouarastegouiaks*, 'those of the river whose bed contains sparkling objects.'

The Malecite belong to the Abnaki group of the Algonquian stock. Maurault makes a distinction between the Malecite and the Etchimin, but adds that "the remnants of this tribe and the Etchimins are called at the present day Malecites." Their closest linguistic affinity is with the Passamaquoddy, the language of the two being almost identical, and is closely allied to the New England dialects, but more distant from that of the Micmac.

Although the New Brunswick coast was visited by or soon after the middle of the 16th century, and St John r. located on maps as early as 1558, making it quite probable that the people of this tribe had come in contact with the whites at that early date, the earliest recorded notice of them is in Champlain's narrative of his voyage of 1604. He found the country along the banks of the St John in the possession of Indians named "Les Etchemons," by whom his party was received with hospitality and rejoicing, and says they were the "first Christians" who had been seen by these savages, which may have been true of the particular party he met, but doubtful in the broader sense. That these were Malecite there is no reasonable doubt. "When we were seated," says Champlain, "they began to smoke, as was their custom, before making any discourse. They made us presents of game and venison. All that day and the night following they continued to sing, dance, and feast until day reappeared. They were clothed in beaver skins.''

Early in the 17th century Ft La Tour was built on St John r., which became the rallying point of the tribe, who there learned the use of firearms, and first obtained cooking vessels of metal and the tools and instruments of civilized life. The few French settlers on this river intermarried with the Indians, thus forming a close alliance, which caused them to become enemies of the New England settlers, between whom and the French there was almost constant warfare. After the English came into possession of the country there were repeated disputes between them and the Malecite in regard to lands until 1776. Afterward lands were assigned them. In 1856, according to Schoolcraft, ''the Tobique river, and the small tract at Madawaska, Meductic Point, and Kingsclear, with their small rocky islands near St John, containing 15 acres,'' constituted all the lands held or claimed by them in the country which was formerly their own. In 1884 they numbered 767, of whom 584 were in New Brunswick and the others in Quebec province. According to the report of Canadian Indian Affairs for 1904 their number was 805, of whom 103 were in Quebec province and 702 in New Brunswick.   (J. M. C. T.)

Amalecites.—Chauvignerie (1736) in N. Y. Doc. Col. Hist., IX, 1052, 1855. Amalicites.—Clinton (1749), ibid., VI, 540, 1855. Amalingans.—Shea, Cath. Miss., 144, 1855. Amalistes.—Am. Pioneer, I, 257, 1842. Amelestes.—Buchanan, N. Am. Inds., 156, 1824. Amelicks.—Smith (1785) in Schoolcraft, Ind. Tribes, III, 553, 1853. Amelingas.—Vetromile, Abnakis, 50, 1866. Amelistes.—Hutchins (1764) in Schoolcraft, Ind. Tribes, III, 553, 1853. Amelistis.—Imlay, West Terr., 293, 1797. Amenecis.—Writer of 1757 in Lettres Edifiantes, I, 698, 1838. Amilicites.—Keane in Stanford, Compend., 522, 1878. Canoemen.—Gallatin in Trans. Am. Antiq. Soc., II, 31, 1836. Echemins.—Am. Pioneer, I, 408, 1842. Estechemains.—Champlain (1603), Œuvres, II, 49, 1870. Estecheminès.—Barton (probably from De Laet, |1633), New Views, XXXVII, 1797. Estechemins.—Champlain, Œuvres, II, 8, 1870. Etchemins.—La Galissonière (1750) in N. Y. Doc. Col. Hist., X, 227, 1858. Etchemons.—Champlain (ca. 1604) in Schoolcraft, Ind. Tribes, V, 674, 1855. Etchimins.—Ibid., 22 (said to be derived from tchinem, 'men'). Etchmins.—McKenney and Hall, Ind. Tribes, III, 79, 1854. Etechemies.—Bobé (1723) in N. Y. Doc. Col. Hist., IX, 913, 1855. Etechemin.—Jes. Rel. 1611, 5, 1858. Etechemines.—Vater, Mith., pt. 3, sec. 3, 389, 1816. Etecheminii.—Du Creux map (1660), fide Vetromile, Abnakis, 21, 1866. Etecheneus.—McKenney and Hall, Ind. Tribes, III, 79, 1854. Etemânkiaks.—Maurault, Histoire des Abenakis, 5, 1866 ('those of the country of the skins for rackets'). Eteminquois.—Jes. Rel. 1611, 8, 1858. Etichimenes.—Lords of Trade (1721) in N. Y. Doc. Col. Hist., V, 592, 1855. Etschimins.—Vetromile, Abnakis, 130, 1866. Kiukuswĕskitchimi-ûk.—Chamberlain, Malesit MS., B. A. E., 1882 (='muskrat Indians'; one of the names applied to them by the Micmac, on account of their hunting the muskrat). Mahnesheet.—James in Tanner, Narrative, 333, 1830. Malacite.—French trans. in N. Y. Doc. Col. Hist., VI, 564, 1855. Malecetes.—Dawson, Inds. of Canada, 2, 1877. Maléchites.—Baraga, Eng.-Otch. Dict., 299, 1878. Malecites.—Vaudreuil (1722) in N. Y. Doc. Col. Hist., IX, 912, 1855. Málesít.—Chamberlain, Malesit MS., B. A. E., 1882. Malicetes.—McKenney and Hall, Ind. Tribes, III, 79, 1854. Malicites.—Begon (1715) in N. Y. Doc. Col. Hist., IX, 932, 1855. Malisít.—Chamberlain, Malesit MS., B. A. E., 1882 (Micmac name; pl. Malisitchik). Maneus.—Chauvignerie (1736) in N. Y. Doc. Col. Hist., IX, 1052, 1855. Marachite.—Drake, Bk. Inds., VI, 1848. Marashites.—Wood (1769) quoted by Hawkins, Missions, 361, 1845. Marechites.—Macauley, N. Y., II, 162, 1829. Mareschites.—Vetromile, Abnakis, 23, 1866 (old French name). Marisizis.—Cadillac (1692) in N. Y. Doc. Col. Hist., IX, 548, 1855. Melecites.—Schoolcraft, Ind. Tribes, V, 38, 1855. Melicite.—Chamberlain, Malesit MS., B. A. E., 1882. Melisceet.—Brinton, Lenape Legends, 11, 1885. Milicetes.—Keane in Stanford, Compend., 522, 1878. Milicite.—Schoolcraft, Ind. Tribes, V, 674, 1855. Mouskouasoaks.—Rouillard, Noms Géographiques, 11, 1906 ('water-rats': Abnaki name). 8arasteg8iaks.—Maurault, Histoire des Akenakis, 6, 1866 (includes Norridgewock in part). St. John's (tribe).—Penhallow (1726) in N. H. Hist. Soc. Coll., I, 123, 1824. St. John's river [Indians].—Gyles (1726) in Me. Hist. Soc. Coll., III, 357, 1853. Ulastĕkwi.—Gatschet, Penobscot MS., B. A. E., 1887 (Penobscot name; pl. Ulastekwiak). Wu'lastûk'-wiûk.—Chamberlain, Malesit MS., B. A. E., 1882 (='dwellers on the beautiful river'; name used by themselves. Boyd (Ind. Local Names, 1885) gives the Indian name of the river as Looshtook, 'long river').

Malemiut. An Eskimo tribe occupying the coast of Norton sd., N. of Shaktolik and the neck of Kaviak penin., Alaska. They have established permanent or summer settlements at points on Kotzebue sd., where they have become mixed with tribes of Kaviak penin. and the islands that visit their villages for barter and social enjoyment. Those of pure blood present the squat type of the Arctic Eskimo, with scant hair, broad flat noses, and high cheek bones with a thick covering of flesh. The tribe numbered 630 in 1900. Once more numerous and powerful, its villages now lie scattered among those of the Unaligmiut and Kavigmiut. Subdivisions are the Attenmiut, Inglutaligemiut, Koyugmiut, Kugaramiut, Kungugemiut, Shaktoligmiut, and Tapkachmiut. Their villages are Akchadak, Atten, Chamisso, Kongik, Koyuktolik, Kugaluk, Kviguk, Kvinkak, Kwik (2), Napaklulik, Nubviakchugaluk, Nuklit, Shaktolik, Taapkuk, Ulukuk, and Ungalik.

Mahlemoöt.—Elliott, Our Arctic Prov., 444, 1886. Mahlemutes.—Dall in Proc. Am. A. A. S., 266, 1869 (between Kotzebue sd. and Norton bay). Mahlemuts.—Dall in Proc. Cal. Acad. Sci., IV, 35, 1873. Malegmjuti.—Erman quoted by Dall in Cont. N. A. Ethnol., 17, 1877. Maleigmjuten.—Holmberg, Ethnog. Skizz., 6, 1855. Maleïmioute.—Zagoskin in Nouv. Ann. Voy., 5th s., XXI, map, 1850. Malemukes.—Whymper in Jour. Roy. Geog. Soc., 220, 1868. Malemut.—Nelson in 18th Rep. B. A. E., passim, 1899. Malemutes.—Whymper, Trav. in Alaska, 143, 318, 1868. Māliegmūt.—Holmberg quoted by Dall in Cont. N. A. Ethnol., I, 16, 1877. Malimiūt.—Wrangell quoted by Dall, ibid. Malimuten.—Wrangell, Ethnog. Nachr., 122, 1839. Malimyut.—Turner in 11th Rep. B. A. E., 178, 1894. Malmiut.—Tikhmenief quoted by Dall in Cont. N. A. Ethnol., I, 16, 1877. Mamelute.—Whymper in Trans. Ethnol. Soc. Lond., VII, 167, 1869. Tschuagmuti.—Erman quoted by Dall in Cont. N. A. Ethnol., I, 16, 1877.

Malhokshe (Mal-hok-ce). A former Chumashan village in the interior of Ventura co., Cal., at a place called Cuesta de la Mojonera.—Henshaw, Buenaventura MS. vocab., B. A. E., 1884.

Maliacones. An unidentified tribe mentioned by Cabeza de Vaca as living near the Avavares, in Texas, in 1528–34, and speaking a different tongue. Possibly they are identical with the Meracouman of Joutel and the Manico of Manzanet.
Maliacones.—Cabeza de Vaca, Rel., Smith trans., 125, 137, 1871. Malicans.—Harris, Voy. and Trav., II, 276, 1705. Maliconas.—Herrera, Hist. Gen., v, 95, 1726. Malicones.—Cabeza de Vaca (1542) quoted by Barcia, Ensayo, 13, 1723. Maticones.—Harris, Voy. and Trav., 803, 1705.

Malica. A village N. of the mouth of St Johns r., Fla., in 1564. De Bry's map locates it inland, s. of the mouth.
Malica.—Laudonnière in French, Hist. Coll. La., N. s., 331, 1869. Mallica.—Martin, N. C., I, 87, 1829.

Malico. A former Chumashan village near Somo hills, Ventura co., Cal.—Taylor in Cal. Farmer, July 24, 1863.

Malika (*Ma-li-ka*). Given by Bourke (Jour. Am. Folk-lore, II, 181, 1889) as a clan of the Mohave, q. v.

Malito (*Ma-li-'tö*). A former Chumashan village in Ventura co., Cal., in a locality called Punta del Pozito.—Henshaw, Buenaventura MS. vocab., B. A. E., 1884.

Malki. A Kawia village on the Potrero res., in Cahuilla valley, E. of Banning, s. Cal.
Mal-ki.—Barrows, Ethno.-Bot. Coahuilla Ind., 33, 1900. Potrero.—Ibid.

Mallin. A Costanoan village situated in 1819 within 10 m. of Santa Cruz mission, Cal.—Taylor in Cal. Farmer, Apr. 5, 1860.

Mallopeme. One of the tribes of w. Texas, some at least of whose people were neophytes of the mission of San José y San Miguel de Aguayo.—MS. in Texas State archives, Nov., 1790.

Malockese. Mentioned by Blue Jacket as a tribe or band at a conference held at Greenville, Ohio, in 1807. Possibly the Mequachake division of the Shawnee, although apparently distinct.—Drake, Tecumseh, 94, 1852.   (J. M.)

Malssum ('wolf'). A gens of the Abnaki, q. v.
Mals'-sŭm.—Morgan, Anc. Soc., 174, 1877. Môlsem.—J. D. Prince, inf'n, 1905 (modern St Francis Abnaki form).

Maltshokamut (*Mal-tsho'-qa-mŭt*, 'valley people': Chugachigmiut name). An unidentified division of the Knaiakhotana of Cook inlet, Alaska.—Hoffman., MS., B. A. E., 1882.

Maluksilak (*Maluksilaq*). A settlement of the Aivilirmiut Eskimo on Lyons inlet, Hudson bay, Canada.—Boas in 6th Rep. B. A. E., 476, 1886.

Malulowoni (*Mal-u-lö-wö'-ni*). A former Chumashan village in the interior of Ventura co., Cal., at a place called Cuesta Santa Rosa.—Henshaw, Buenaventura MS. vocab., B. A. E., 1884.

Malvaitac. A former village, presumably Costanoan, connected with Dolores mission, San Francisco, Cal.—Taylor in Cal. Farmer, Oct. 18, 1861.

Mamakume (*Mā'-mak·ume*). A village of the Matsqui tribe of Cowichan on the s. side of Fraser r., Brit. Col., opposite Matsqui reserve.—Boas in 64th Rep. Brit. A. A. S., 454, 1894.

Mamalelekala. A Kwakiutl tribe on Village id., Brit. Col. According to Boas they were divided into four gentes: Temtltemtlels, Wewamaskem, Walas, and Mamalelekam. Their only town is Memkumlis, which they occupy jointly with the Koeksotenok. The population was estimated at about 2,000 in 1836–41; in 1904 it numbered 111.
Mah-ma-lil-le-kulla.—Sproat in Can. Ind. Aff., 145, 1879. Mah-ma-lil-le-kullah.—Can. Ind. Aff. 1884, 189, 1885. Mahmatilleculaats.—Brit. Col. map, 1872. Mamaleilakitīsh.—Tolmie and Dawson, Vocabs. Brit. Col., 118B, 1884. Mamaleilakulla.—Ibid. Ma'malělek·ala.—Boas in 6th Rep. N. W. Tribes Can., 54, 1890. Mā'malělēqala.—Boas in Petermanns Mitt., pt. 5, 130, 1887. Mama-lil-a-cula.—Mayne, Brit. Col., 249, 1862. Ma-ma-lil-li-kulla.—Can. Ind. Aff. 1894, 279, 1895. Mā'-me-li-li-a-ka.—Dawson in Trans. Roy. Soc. Can. for 1887, sec. II, 65. Mam-il-i-li-a-ka.—Tolmie and Dawson, Vocabs. Brit. Col., 118B, 1884. Mar-ma-li-la-cal-la.—Kane, Wand. in N. Am., app., 1859.

Mamalelekam. A gens of the Mamalelekala.
Mā'lělēqala.—Boas in Petermanns Mitt., pt. 5, 130, 1887. Mā'malělēk·am.—Boas in 6th Rep. N. W. Tribes Can., 54, 1890. Ma'malēleqala.—Boas in Rep. Nat. Mus. for 1895, 330, 1897.

Mamalty. Mentioned in the narrative of Marie Le Roy and Barbara Leininger (Pa. Mag. Hist. and Biog., XXIX, 412, 1905) as a (Delaware?) village in w. Pennsylvania or E. Ohio in 1759.

Mamanahunt. A village of the Powhatan confederacy in 1608, on Chickahominy r., Charles City co., Va.—Smith (1629), Virginia, I, map, repr. 1819.

Mamanassy. A village of the Powhatan confederacy in 1608, at the junction of Pamunkey and Mattapony rs., in King and Queen co., Va.—Smith (1629), Virginia, I, map, repr. 1819.

Mamekoting. A chieftaincy of the Munsee, formerly living in Mamakating valley, w. of the Shawangunk mts. in Ulster co. (?), N. Y. It was one of the 5 Esopus tribes.—Ruttenber, Tribes Hudson R., 95, 1872.

Mameoya ('fish-eaters'). A (former?) division of the Kainah tribe of the Siksika, q. v.
Fish Eaters.—Culbertson in Smithson. Rep. for 1850, 144, 1851. Mä-me-o'-ya.—Morgan, Anc. Soc., 171, 1877. Mum-i'-o-yiks.—Hayden, Ethnog. and Philol. Mo. Val., 264, 1862.

Mamikininiwug ('lowland people'). A subdivision of the Paskwawininiwug, or Plains Cree.
Mamikiwininiwag.—Wm. Jones, inf'n, 1906. Mamikiyiniwok.—Lacombe, Dic. Langue Cris, x, 1874.

Mamorachic. A Tarahumare settlement in Chihuahua, Mexico; definite locality unknown.—Orozco y Berra, Geog., 322, 1864.

Mamtum. Given as the name of a body of Indians on Cowitchin lake, s. end of Vancouver id. (Brit. Col. map, Ind. Aff., Victoria, 1872). Perhaps the Quamichan or the Comiakin of Cowitchin valley.

Mamun-gitunai (*Mă'm⁴n gĭt⁴nă'-i*, 'Gî′tuns of Mamun r.'). The most important division of the Gituns, a family of the Eagle clan of the Haida, living at Masset, Queen Charlotte ids., Brit. Col. They derived their name from that of a small stream which falls into Masset inlet near its head, where they used to camp. A subdivision in the town of Yaku was called Ao-gitunai.—Swanton, Cont. Haida, 275, 1905.

Manabush, Manabozo. See *Nanabozo.*

Manahoac (Algonquian: 'they are very merry.'—Tooker). A confederacy or group of small tribes or bands, possibly Siouan, in N. Virginia, in 1608, occupying the country from the falls of the rivers to the mountains and from the Potomac to North Anna r. They were at war with the Powhatan and Iroquois, and in alliance with the Monacan, but spoke a language different from any of their neighbors. Among their tribes Smith mentions the Manahoac, Tanxnitania, Shackaconia, Ontponea, Tegninateo, Whonkenti, Stegaraki, and Hassinunga, and says there were others. Jefferson confounded them with the Tuscarora. Mahaskahod is the only one of their villages of which the name has been preserved. Others may have borne the names of the tribes of the confederacy. The Mahocks mentioned by Lederer in 1669 seem to be identical with them. See Mooney, Siouan Tribes of the East, 18, 1894.

Manahoac. A tribe or band of the Manahoac group. According to Jefferson they lived on Rappahannock r. in Stafford and Spottsylvania cos., Va.

Mahoc.—Lederer, Discov., 2, 1672 (possibly identical, although given as distinct). Mahocks.—Lederer (1669) as quoted by Hawks, N. C., II, 44, 1858. Managog.—Lederer, Discov., 2, 1672 (misprint). Manahoacks.—Loudon, Selec. Int. Nar., II, 235, 1808. Manahoacs.—Jefferson, Notes on Va., 134, 1794. Manahoaks.—Am. Pioneer, II, 189, 1843. Manahocks.—Simons in Smith, Va., I, 188, 1819. Manahokes.—Smith, Va., I, 74, 1819. Mannahannocks.—Kingsley, Stand. Nat. Hist., pt. 6, 151, 1883. Mannahoacks.—Strachey, Va., 37, 1849. Mannahoags.—Domenech, Deserts.N. Am., I, 442, 1860. Mannahoaks.—Strachey, Va., 104, 1849. Mannahocks.—Ibid., 41. Mannahokes.—Smith, Va., I, 120, 1819. Monahoacs.—Jefferson quoted by Bozman, Md., I, 113, 1837.

Manam. A tribe that formerly lived on the road from Coahuila to the Texas country; possibly the people elsewhere referred to as Mazames, and probably belonging to the Coahuiltecan linguistic stock.—Manzanet, MS. (1690), cited by H. E. Bolton, inf'n, 1906.

Manamoyik. A former Nauset village near Chatham, Barnstable co., Mass.

In 1685 it contained 115 Indians over 12 years of age. In 1762 the population had become reduced to fewer than 30 under the chief Quasson and were known as the Quasson tribe.   (J. M.)

Manamoiak.—Bradford (ca. 1650) in Mass. Hist. Soc. Coll., 4th s., III, 97, 1856. Manamoick.—Drake, Bk. Inds., bk. 2, 15, 1848. Manamoyck.—Winslow (1622) in Mass. Hist. Soc. Coll., 1st s., VIII, 249, 1802. Manamoyet.—Hinckley (1685), ibid., 4th s., v, 133, 1861. Manamoyik.—Bourne (1674), ibid., 1st s., I, 197, 1806. Mannamoyk.—Gookin (1674), ibid., 148. Maramoick.—Mourt (1622), ibid., 2d s., IX, 53, 1822. Monamoy.—Treat (1687), ibid., 4th s., v, 186, 1861. Monamoyik.—Drake, Bk. Inds., bk. 2, 118, 1848. Monimoy.—Rawson and Danforth (1698) in Mass. Hist. Soc. Coll., 1st s., x, 133, 1809. Monomoy.—Freeman (1685), ibid., 4th s., v, 132, 1861. Monymoyk.—Stiles (1762?), ibid., 1st s., x, 114, 1809. Quasson.—Stiles (1762), ibid.

Manamosay. See *Maninose.*

Manato (*Ma-na-to'*, 'snake'). A gens of the Shawnee (q. v.).—Morgan, Anc. Soc., 168, 1877.

Manchaug (meaning unknown). A village of Christian Indians, in 1674, in Nipmuc territory, near the present Oxford, Worcester co., Mass.

Manchage.—Gookin (1674) in Mass. Hist. Soc. Coll., 1st s., I, 189, 1806. Manchauge.—Gookin (1677) in Trans. Am. Antiq. Soc., II, 467, 1836. Mauchage.—Gookin in Mass. Hist. Soc. Coll., 3d s., II, 59, 1830 (misprint). Mauchaug.—Barber, Hist. Coll., 593, 1839 (misprint?). Mônuhchogok.—Eliot quoted by Trumbull, Ind. Names Conn., 21, 1881.

Manckatawangum. A former Iroquois town near the site of Barton, Bradford co., Pa., about 10 m. below Tioga.

Fitzgerald's Farm.—Lieutenant Beatty's Journal (1779) in Jour. Mil. Exped. Maj. Gen. Sullivan, 25, 1887. Mackatowando.—Campfield (1779), ibid., 55. Macktowanuck.—Major Norris' Journal (1779), ibid., 230. Manckatawangum.—Note to Beatty's Journal, ibid., 25 (misprint). Mauckatawangum.—Lieutenant Jenkin's Journal (1779), ibid., 171. Mohontowonga.—Map cited, ibid., 25.

Mandan. A Siouan tribe of the northwest. The name, according to Maximilian, originally given by the Sioux is believed by Matthews to be a corruption of the Dakota *Mawatani*. Previous to 1830 they called themselves simply Numakiki, 'people' (Matthews). Maximilian says "if they wish to particularize their descent they add the name of the village whence they came originally." Hayden gives Miah'tanēs, 'people on the bank,' as the name they apply to themselves, and draws from this the inference that "they must have resided on the banks of the Missouri at a very remote period." According to Morgan (Syst. Consang. and Affin., 285), the native name of the tribe is Metootahäk, 'South villagers.' Their relations, so far as known historically and traditionally, have been most intimate with the Hidatsa; yet, judged by the linguistic test, their position must be nearer the Winnebago. Matthews appears to consider the Hidatsa and Mandan descendants from the same immediate stem. Their traditions regarding their early history are scant and almost entirely mythological. All that can be gathered from them is the indication that at some time they lived in a more easterly locality in the vicinity of a lake. This tradition, often repeated by subsequent authors, is given by Lewis and Clark, as follows: "The whole nation resided in one large village underground near a subterraneous lake; a grapevine extended its roots down to their habitation and gave them a view of the light; some of the most adventurous climbed up the vine and were delighted with the sight of the earth, which they found covered with buffalo and rich

MANDAN

with every kind of fruits; returning with the grapes they had gathered, their countrymen were so pleased with the taste of them that the whole nation resolved to leave their dull residence for the charms of the upper region; men, women, and children ascended by means of the vine; but when about half the nation had reached the surface of the earth, a corpulent woman who was clambering up the vine broke it with her weight, and closed upon herself and the rest of the nation the light of the sun. Those who were left on earth made a village below,

where we saw the nine villages; and when the Mandan die they expect to return to the original seats of their forefathers, the good reaching the ancient village by means of the lake, which the burden of the sins of the wicked will not enable them to cross." Maximilian says: "They affirm that they descended originally from the more eastern nations, near the seacoast." Their linguistic relation to the Winnebago and the fact that their movements in their historic era have been westward up the Missouri correspond with their tradition of a more easterly origin, and would seemingly locate them in the vicinity of the upper lakes. It is possible that the tradition which has long prevailed in the region of N. W. Wisconsin regarding the so-called "ground-house Indians" who once lived in that section and dwelt in circular earth lodges, partly underground, applies to the people of this tribe, although other tribes of this general region formerly lived in houses of this character. Assuming that the Mandan formerly resided in the vicinity of the upper Mississippi, it is probable that they moved down this stream for some distance before passing to the Missouri. The fact that when first encountered by the whites they relied to some extent on agriculture as a means of subsistence would seem to justify the conclusion that they were at some time in the past in a section where agriculture was practised. It is possible, as Morgan contends, that they learned agriculture from the Hidatsa, but the reverse has more often been maintained. Catlin's theory that they formerly lived in Ohio and built mounds, and moved thence to the N. W. is without any basis. The traditions regarding their migrations, as given by Maximilian, commence with their arrival at the Missouri. The point where this stream was first reached was at the mouth of White r., S. Dak. From this point they moved up the Missouri to Moreau r., where they came in contact with the Cheyenne, and where also the formation of "bands or unions" began. Thence they continued up the Missouri to Heart r., N. Dak., where they were residing at the time of the first known visit of the whites, but it is probable that trappers and traders visited them earlier.

The first recorded visit to the Mandan was that by the Sieur de la Verendrye in 1738. About 1750 they were settled near the mouth of Heart r. in 9 villages, 2 on the E. and 7 on the w. side. Remains of these villages were found by Lewis and Clark in 1804. Having suffered severely from smallpox and the attacks of the Assiniboin and Dakota, the inhabitants of the two eastern villages consolidated and moved up the Missouri to a point opposite the

Arikara. The same causes soon reduced the other villages to 5, whose inhabitants subsequently joined those in the Arikara country, forming 2 villages, which in 1776 were likewise merged. Thus the whole tribe was reduced to 2 villages, Metutahanke and Ruptari, situated about 4 m. below the mouth of Knife r., on opposite sides of the Missouri. These two villages were visited by Lewis and Clark in 1804. In 1837 they were almost destroyed by smallpox, only 31 souls out of 1,600, according to one account, being left, although other and probably more reliable accounts make the number of survivors from 125 to 145. After that time they occupied a single village. In 1845, when the Hidatsa removed from Knife r., some of the Mandan went with them, and others followed at intervals. According to Matthews, some moved up to the village at Ft Berthold as late as 1858. By treaty at the Mandan village, July 30, 1825, they entered into peaceable relations with the United States. They participated in the Ft Laramie (Wyo.) treaty of Sept. 17, 1851, by which the boundaries of the tribes of the N. W. were defined, and in the unratified treaty of Ft Berthold, Dak., July 27, 1866. By Executive order of Apr. 12, 1870, a large reservation was set apart for the Mandan, Hidatsa, and Arikara Indians in North Dakota and Montana, along Missouri and Little Missouri rs., which included the Mandan village, then situated on the left bank of the Missouri in lat. 47° 34′, lon. 101° 48′. By agreement at Ft Berthold agency, Dec. 14, 1866, the Mandan, Arikara, and Hidatsa ceded that portion of their reservation N. of lat. 48°, and E. of a N. and S. line 6 m. w. of the most westerly point of the big bend of Missouri r., s. of lat. 48°. Provision was also made for allotment in severalty of the remaining portion.

According to Maximilian the Mandan were vigorous, well made, rather above medium stature, many of them being robust, broad-shouldered, and muscular. Their noses, not so long and arched as those of the Sioux, were sometimes aquiline or slightly curved, sometimes quite straight, never broad; nor had they such high cheek bones as the Sioux. Some of the women were robust and rather tall, though usually they were short and broad-shouldered. The men paid the greatest attention to their headdress. They sometimes wore at the back of the head a long, stiff ornament made of small sticks entwined with wire, fastened to the hair and reaching down to the shoulders, which was covered with porcupine quills dyed of various colors in neat patterns. At the upper end of this ornament an eagle feather was fastened horizontally, the quill end of which was covered with red cloth and the tip ornamented with a bunch of horsehair dyed yellow. These ornaments varied and were symbolic. Tattooing was practised to a limited extent, mostly on the left breast and arm, with black parallel stripes and a few other figures.

The Mandan villages were assemblages of circular clay-covered log huts placed close together without regard to order. Anciently these were surrounded with palisades of strong posts. The huts were slightly vaulted and were provided with a sort of portico. In the center of the roof was a square opening for the exit of the smoke, over which was a circular screen made of twigs. The interior was spacious. Four strong pillars near the middle, with several crossbeams, supported the roof. The dwelling was covered outside with matting made of osiers, over which was laid hay or grass, and then a covering of earth. "The beds stand against the wall of the hut; they consist of a large square case made of parchment or skins, with a square entrance, and are large enough to hold several persons, who lie very conveniently and warm on skins and blankets." They cultivated maize, beans, gourds, and the sunflower, and manufactured earthenware, the clay being tempered with flint or granite reduced to powder by the action of fire. Polygamy was common among them. Their beliefs and ceremonies were similar to those of the Plains tribes generally. The Mandan have always been friendly to the United States, and since 1866 a number of the men have been enlisted as scouts.

In Lewis and Clark's time the Mandan were estimated to number 1,250, and in 1837 1,600 souls, but about the latter date they were reduced by smallpox to between 125 and 150. In 1850 the number given was 150; in 1852 it had apparently increased to 385; in 1871, to 450; in 1877 the number given was 420; it was 410 in 1885, and 249 in 1905.

There were, according to Morgan (Anc. Soc., 158, 1877), the following divisions, which seem to have corresponded with their villages before consolidation: (1) Horatamumake (Kharatanumanke), (2) Matonumake (Matonumanke), (3) Seepooshka (Sipushkanumanke), (4) Tanatsuka (Tanetsukanumanke), (5) Kitanemake (Khitanumanke), (6) Estapa (Histapenumanke), and (7) Meteahke.

In addition to the works cited, see Catlin (1) North American Indians, 1841, (2) O-kee-pa, 1867; Coues, Lewis and Clark Exped., 1893; Orig. Jour. Lewis and Clark, 1904–05; Dorsey (1) A Study of Siouan Cults, 11th Rep. B. A. E., 1894, (2) Siouan Sociology, 15th Rep. B. A. E., 1897; Hayden, Ethnog. and Philol. Mo. Val., 1862; McGee in 15th Rep. B. A. E., 1897; Mat-

thews, Hidatsa Inds., 1877; Will and Spinden, The Mandans, 1906.   (J. O. D.   C. T.)
Å-răch-bŏ-cŭ. — Long, Exped. Rocky Mts., II, lxxxiv, 1823 (Hidatsa name). As-a-ka-shi.—Hayden, Ethnog. and Philol. Mo. Val., 402, 1862 (Crow name). How-mox-tox-sow-es.—Henry, Blackfoot MS. vocab., 1808 (Hidatsa name). Huatanis.—Rafinesque in Marshall, Hist. Ky., I, 28, 1824. Kanit'.—Hayden, Ethnog. and Philol. Mo. Val., 357, 1862 (Arikara name). Kwowahtewug.—Tanner, Narr., 316, 1830 (Ottawa name). Les Mandals.—Maximilian, Trav., 334, 1843 (so called by the French Canadians). Madan.—Orig. Jour. Lewis and Clark (1804), I, 202, 1904. Mahna-Narra.—Maximilian, Trav., 335, 1843 ('the sulky': so called because they left the rest of their nation and went higher up Missouri r.). Mandams.—U. S. Stat., XIV, 493, 1868. Mandan.—Lewis and Clark, Discov., 6, 1806. Mandane.—Orig. Jour. Lewis and Clark (1805), I, 256, 1904. Mandanes.—Du Lac, Voy. dans les Louisianes, 262, 1805. Mandani.—Capellini, Trav., 226, 1867. Mandanne.—Gass, Voy., 80, 1810. Mandannes.—Du Lac, Voy. dans les Louisianes, 225, 1805. Mandan's.—Brackenridge, Views of La., 70, 1814. Mandaus.—Sen. Misc. Doc. 53, 45th Cong., 3d sess., 85, 1879 (misprint). Mandens.—Orig. Jour. Lewis and Clark (1804), I, 188, 1904. Mandians.—Janson, Stranger in Am., 233, 1807. Mandins.—Orig. Jour. Lewis and Clark (1804), I, 201, 1904. Mandon.—Mass. Hist. Coll., 1st s., III, 24, 1794. Mandˢ.—Orig. Jour. Lewis and Clark (1804), I, 203, 1904. Mantanes.—Verendrye (1738) in Margry, Déc., VI, 590, 1886. Manton.—Neill, Hist. Minn., 173, 1858. Maŋ-wa'-ta-niŋ. — Cook, Yankton MS. vocab., B. A. E., 184, 1882 (Yankton name). Maudaus.—Mitchell (1854) in Schoolcraft, Ind. Tribes, V, 686, 1855 (misprint). Mawadoⁿǧin.—Dorsey, Çegiha MS., B. A. E., 1880 (Omaha and Ponca name). Ma-wa'-ta-daŋ.—Riggs, Dak. Gram. and Dict., 137, 1852 (Santee name). Mawatani.—Iapi Oaye, XIII, no. 9, 33, Sept. 1884 (Yankton name). Ma-wa'-taŋna.—Riggs, Dak. Gram. and Dict., 137, 1852 (Yankton name). Maw-dân.—Sibley (1804) in Am. St. Pap., Ind. Aff., I, 710, 1832. Meandans.—Gale, Upper Miss., 182, 1867. Me-too'-ta-häk.—Morgan, Consang. and Affin., 285, 1871 (own name: sig. 'south villagers'). Métutahanke. — Matthews, Ethnog. Hidatsa, 14, 1877 (own name since 1837, after their old village). Mi-ah'-ta-nes.—Hayden, Ethnog. and Philol. Mo. Val., 426, 1862 ('people on the bank'). Mo-no'-ni-o.—Ibid., 290 (Cheyenne name). Nohar-taney.—Corliss, Lacotah MS. vocab., B. A. E., 106, 1874 (Teton name). Numakaki.—Matthews, Ethnog. Hidatsa, 14, 1877 ('men', 'people': own name prior to 1837). Numakshi.—Maximilian, Trav., 364, 1843. Numangkake.—Ibid., 335. Núweta.—Matthews, Ethnog. Hidatsa, 14, 1877 ('ourselves': used sometimes in speaking of themselves and the Hidatsa together). U-ka'-she.—Hayden, Ethnog. and Philol. Mo. Val., 402, 1862 ('earth houses': Crow name). Us-suc-carshay.—Crow MS. vocab., B. A. E. (Crow name). Wahtani.—Keane in Stanford, Compend., 520, 1878 (see Mawatani, above).

Mandhinkagaghe ('earth makers'). An Omaha gens on the Inshtasanda side of the camp circle. The subgentes given are Inewakhubeadhin, Khube, Minghasanwetazhi, Mikasi, and Ninibatan.
Earth-lodge.—Dorsey in Bul. Philos. Soc. Wash. 130, 1880. Madhinka-gaghe.—Dorsey, Omaha MS., B. A. E., 1878. Maⁿdinka-gáxe.—Dorsey in 3d Rep. B. A. E., 219, 1885. Mikasi-unikaciⁿga.—Dorsey, Omaha MS., op. cit. ('prairie-wolf people'). Moneka-goh-ha.—Long, Exped. Rocky Mts., I, 327, 1823. O-non-e'-kä-gä-hä'.—Morgan, Anc. Soc., 155, 1877 ('many seasons'). Prairie-Wolf people.—Dorsey, Omaha MS., B. A. E., 1878. Wolf People.—Dorsey in Bul. Philos. Soc. Wash., 130, 1880.

Manexit (contr. of maïaniksĭt, 'at the little meeting-house'; lit. 'at the assembling (or gathering) little wigwam.'—Gerard). A village of Christian Indians in 1674, in Nipmuc territory, near the present Thompson, Windham co.,

Conn. It was about 6 m. N. of Quantisset.   (J. M.)
Maanexit.—Gookin (1674) in Mass. Hist. Soc. Coll., 1st s., I, 190, 1806. Manänexit.—Trumbull, Ind. Names Conn., 28, 1881. Manexit.—Mass. Hist. Soc. Coll., 1st s., VI, 205, 1800. Mayaneexit.—Trumbull, op. cit. Mayanexit.—Ibid. Myanexit.—Ibid. Wanexit.—Drake, Bk. Inds., bk. 3, 88, 1848.

Mangachqua (Mang-ach-qua). A Potawatomi village on Peble (?) r., in s. Michigan, on a tract sold in 1827.—Potawatomi treaty (1827) in U. S. Ind. Treat., 675, 1873.

Mangas Coloradas (Span: 'red sleeves'). A Mimbreño Apache chief. He pledged friendship to the Americans when Gen. S. W. Kearny took possession of New Mexico in 1846. The chief stronghold of the Mimbreños at that time was at the Santa Rita copper mines, s. w. N. Mex., where they had killed the miners in 1837 to avenge a massacre committed by white trappers who invited a number of Mimbreños to a feast and murdered them to obtain the bounty of $100 offered by the state of Chihuahua for every Apache scalp. When the boundary commission made its headquarters at Santa Rita trouble arose over the taking from the Mimbreño Apache of some Mexican captives and over the murder of an Indian by a Mexican whom the Americans refused to hang on the spot. The Mimbreños retaliated by stealing some horses and mules belonging to the commission, and when the commissioners went on to survey another section of the boundary the Indians conceived that they had driven them away. In consequence of indignities received at the hands of miners at the Pinos Altos gold mines, by whom he was bound and whipped, Mangas Coloradas collected a large band of Apache and became the scourge of the white settlements for years. He formed an alliance with Cochise to resist the Californian volunteers who reoccupied the country when it was abandoned by troops at the beginning of the Civil war, and was wounded in an engagement at Apache pass, s. E. Ariz., that grew out of a misunderstanding regarding a theft of cattle. His men took him to Janos, in Chihuahua, and left him in the care of a surgeon with a warning that the town would be destroyed in case he were not cured. According to one account, soon after his recovery he was taken prisoner in Jan., 1863, by the Californians and was killed while attempting to escape, goaded, it is said, with a red-hot bayonet (Dunn, Massacres of Mts., 365, 374, 382, 1886), while Bell (New Tracks, II, 24, 1869) states that in 1862 he was induced to enter Ft McLane, N. Mex., on the plea of making a treaty and receiving presents. The soldiers imprisoned him in a hut, and at night a sentry shot him under the pretext that he feared the Indian would escape. Consult also Bancroft, Ariz. and N. Mex., 1889; Bartlett, Pers. Narr., I–II, 1854.

Mange. A Pima rancheria on the Rio Gila, s. Ariz., visited and named by Kino (after Juan Mateo Mange) about 1697.—Bernal quoted by Bancroft, Ariz. and N. Mex., 356, 1889.

Mangoraca. A village of the Powhatan confederacy in 1608, on the N. bank of the Rappahannock, in Richmond co., Va.—Smith (1629), Va., I, map, repr. 1819.

Mangunckakuck ('place of great trees.'—Trumbull). A village in 1638, occupied by conquered Pequot subject to the Mohegan. It seems to have been on Thames r. below Mohegan, New London co., Conn.—Williams (1638) in Mass. Hist. Soc. Coll., 4th s., VI, 251, 1863. Cf. *Magunkaquog.*

Manhasset (*mänähäsĕt*, 'at the small island.'—Gerard; referring to Shelter id.). A small tribe or band, belonging to the Montauk group, formerly living on Shelter id., at the E. end of Long Island, N. Y. Their chief, according to some authorities, lived at Sachem's Neck on Shelter id., but according to Tooker either at Cockles Harbor or Menantic cr. For the application of the name to Shelter id., see Tooker, Algonq., Ser., VII, 1901. (J. M.)
Manhaset.—Wood in Macauley, N. Y., II, 252, 1829. Manhasset.—N. Y. Doc. Col. Hist., II, 145, 1888. Manhassett.—Deed (1648) in Thompson, Long Id., 181, 1839. Mohansick.—Writer ca. 1650 in Drake, Bk. Inds., bk. 2, 74, 1848 (probably the Manhasset, or perhaps the Montauk). Monhauset.—Trumbull, Conn., I, 146, 1818.

Manhattan ('an island formed by the tide.'—J. D. Prince). A tribe of the Wappinger confederacy that occupied Manhattan id. and the E. bank of Hudson r. and shore of Long Island sd., in Westchester co., N. Y. Early Dutch writers applied the name also to people of neighboring Wappinger tribes. The Manhattan had their principal village, Nappeckamack, where Yonkers now stands, and their territory stretched to Bronx r. From their fort, Nipinichsen, on the N. bank of Spuyten Duyvil cr., they sallied out in two canoes to attack Hendrik Hudson when he returned down the river in 1609. Manhattan id. contained several villages which they used only for hunting and fishing. One was Sapohanikan. The island was bought from them by Peter Minuit on May 6, 1626, for 60 guilders' worth of trinkets (Martha J. Lamb, Hist. City of N. Y., I, 53, 1877). Their other lands were disposed of by later sales. See Ruttenber, Ind. Tribes Hudson R., 77, 1872; Ruttenber, Ind. Geog. Names, 1906; Prince in Am. Anthr., XI, 643, 1909. (J. M.)
Mahatons.—Boudinot, Star in the West, 127, 1816. Manathanes.—De Laet, Nov. Orbis, 72, 1633.—Manathe.—La Honton, New Voy., I, 47, 1703. Manathens.—La Salle (1681) in Margry, Déc., II, 148, 1877. Manhates.—Dutch map (1616) in N. Y. Doc. Col. Hist., I, 1856. Manhatesen.—De Rasières (1628) in Ruttenber, Tribes Hudson R., 77, 1872. Manhat-

tae.—De Laet, Nov. Orbis, 72, 1633. Manhattanese.—Schoolcraft, Ind. Tribes, II, 23, 1852. Manhattes.—Map ca. 1614 in N. Y. Doc. Col. Hist., I, 1856. Manhattons.—Boudinot, Star in the West, 127, 1816. Monatons.—Ruttenber, Tribes Hudson R., 362, 1872. Monatuns.—Schoolcraft in N. Y. Hist. Soc. Proc., 96, 1844. Rechgawawanc.—Treaty of 1643 in N. Y. Doc. Col. Hist., XIII, 14, 1881 (so called after their chief). Rechkawick.—N. Y. Doc. Col. Hist., XIII, 147, 1881. Rechkawyck.—Treaty of 1660, ibid. Reckawancks.—Ruttenber, Tribes Hudson R., 106, 1872. Reckawawanc.—Treaty (1643) quoted by Ruttenber, ibid., 110. Reckewackes.—Breeden Raedt (ca. 1635), ibid., 78. Reckgawawanc.—Doc. of 1643 quoted by Winfield, Hudson Co., 42, 1874. Reweghnoncks.—Doc. of 1663 in N. Y. Doc. Col. Hist., XIII, 303, 1881.

Manhazitanman (*Manʼhaziʼtanman*, 'village on a yellow cliff'). A former Kansa village on Kansas r., near Lawrence, Kans.—Dorsey, Kansas MS. vocab., B. A. E., 1882.

Manhazulin (*Manʼhazúlin*, 'village at the yellow bank'). A former Kansa village on Kansas r., one of those occupied before the removal to Council Grove, Kans., in 1846.—Dorsey, Kansas MS. vocab., B. A. E., 1882.

Manhazulintanman ('village where they dwelt at a yellow cliff'). One of the last villages of the Kansa, on Kansas r., Kans. Manʼhazúliⁿ taⁿʼmaⁿ.—Dorsey, Kansas MS. vocab., B. A. E., 1882. Miⁿʼqudje-iⁿʼ tsʼe.—Ibid. (='where Minkhudjein died').

Manhukdhintanwan (*Manγuχǫinʼ-tanwan*, 'dwelling place at a cliff village'). An ancient Osage village on a branch of Neosho r., Kans.—Dorsey, Osage MS. vocab., B. A. E., 1883.

Manico. A tribe mentioned by Manzanet (MS., 1690, cited by H. E. Bolton, inf'n, 1906) as living on the road from Coahuila to the Texas country. Perhaps identical with the Maliacones of Cabeza de Vaca and the Meracouman of Joutel.

Maninose. A name used in Maryland for the soft-shell clam (*Mya arenaria*), called *mananosay* in more northerly parts of the Atlantic coast. Dr L. M. Yale, of New York (inf'n, 1903), states that the local name at Lewes, Del., is *mullinose*. The word appears also as *mannynose*. The word is derived from one of the southern Algonquian dialects, Virginian or Delaware; probably the latter. The derivation seems to be from the radical *man-*, 'to gather.' (A. F. C.)

Manistee. Mentioned as if an Ottawa village in Michigan in 1836, of which Keway Gooshcum (Kewigushkum) was then chief (U. S. Ind. Treaties, 656, 1837). Kewigushkum is earlier mentioned as an Ottawa chief of L'Arbre Croche (Waganakisi), in which vicinity, on Little Traverse bay, Manistee may have been.

Maniti (*Mani-ti*, 'those who camp away from the village'). A Sisseton band; an offshoot of the Kakhmiatonwan.—Dorsey in 15th Rep. B. A. E., 217, 1897.

Manito. The mysterious and unknown potencies and powers of life and of the universe. As taken over from Algonquian into the vocabulary of the white man, it has signified spirit, good, bad, or indifferent; Indian god or devil, demon, guardian spirit, genius loci, fetish, etc. The spelling manitou indicates French influence, the earlier writers in English using manitto, manetto, manitoa, etc. Cuoq says that the Nipissing manito was formerly pronounced manitou. Some writers use manito, or good manito, for Good or Great Spirit, and evil manito for the devil. It is declared by some that the signification of such terms as Kitchi manito, Great Spirit, has been modified by missionary influence. The form manito of English literature comes from one of the E. Algonquian dialects, the Massachuset manitto, he is a god, the Narraganset (Williams, 1643) manit, god, or the Delaware manitto. The form manitou comes with French intermediation from the central dialects, the Chippewa, and Nipissing or Cree manito (Trumbull in Old and New, I, 337, 1870). The term has given rise to many place names in Canada and the United States. For a discussion of manito from the Indian point of view, consult Jones in Jour. Am. Folk-lore, XVIII, 183–190, 1905. See *Mythology, Orenda, Religion.*   (A. F. C.)

Manitsuk. An Eskimo village on the S. E. coast of Greenland, about lat. 62° 30′; pop. 8 in 1829.
Maneetsuk.—Graah, Exped. Greenland, map, 1837.

Mankato (properly *Ma-ka′-to,* 'blue earth'). A former band and village of the Mdewakanton Sioux, probably at or near the site of the present Mankato, at the mouth of Blue Earth r., Faribault co., Minn., named from a chief known as Old Mankato. A later Mdewakanton chief who bore the name Mankato, the son of Good Road, was a member of the delegation who signed the Washington treaty of June 18, 1858, in which his name appears as "Makawto (Blue Earth)," and he is referred to also in the Indian Affairs Report for 1860, in connection with his band, as under the Lower Sioux Agency, Minn. He took an active part in the Sioux outbreak of 1862, and was one of the leaders in the second attack, in Aug. 1862, on Ft Ridgely, Minn., in which, it is said, about 800 Sioux and Winnebago were engaged. He participated also in the fight at Birch Coolie, Minn., on Sept. 3 of the same year, and was killed by a cannon ball at the battle of Wood (or Battle) lake, Sept. 23.   (C. T.)
Blue Earth band.—Gale, Upper Miss., 261, 1867.
Makato's band.—Ind. Aff. Rep., 68, 1860.

Mankoke ('owl'). An Iowa gens, now extinct.
Mä′-kotch.—Morgan, Anc. Soc, 156, 1877. Mañ′-ko-ke.—Dorsey in 15th Rep. B. A. E., 239, 1897.

Mannynose. See *Maninose.*

Manomet. A village of Christian Indians in 1674 near the present Monument, Sandwich township, Barnstable co., Mass. It may have belonged to the Nauset or to the Wampanoag. In 1685 it contained 110 Indians over 12 years of age.
Manamet.—Doc. in Smith (1622), Va., II, 235, repr. 1819. Manamete.—Bradford (ca. 1650) in Mass. Hist. Soc. Coll., 4th s., III, 234, 1856. Mananiet.—Bourne (1674), ibid., 1st s., I, 198, 1806. Mannamett.—Hinckley (1685), ibid., 4th s., V, 133, 1861. Mannamit.—Bourne (1674), ibid., 1st s., I, 198, 1806. Manomet.—Winslow (1623), ibid., VIII, 252, 1802. Manumit.—Freeman (1792), ibid., I, 231, 1806. Monomete.—Doc. in Smith (1622), Va., II, 233, repr. 1819. Monument.—Freeman (1792) in Mass. Hist. Soc. Coll., 1st s., I, 231, 1806. Monumet.—Davis, ibid., VIII, 122, 1802.

Manosaht ('houses-on-spit people'). A Nootka tribe formerly dwelling at Hesquiat pt., between Nootka and Clayoquot sds., w. coast of Vancouver id. In 1883, the last time their name appears, they numbered 18.
Mānnă-wōusŭt.—Mayne, Brit. Col., 251, 1862. Manoh-ah-sahts.—Can.Ind.Aff.,52,1875. Mā′nōosath.—Boas in 6th Rep. N. W. Tribes Can., 31, 1890. Manosaht.—Sproat, Sav. Life, 308, 1868. Manosit.—Swan, MS., B. A. E. Mau-os-aht.—Can. Ind. Aff. 1883, 188, 1884.

Manos de Perro (Span.: 'dog-feet,' lit. 'dog hands'). One of the tribes formerly living near the lower Rio Grande in Texas; mentioned by Garcia (Manual, title, 1760) among those speaking the Coahuiltecan language, for which his Manual was prepared.

Manos Prietas (Span.: 'dark hands'). A former tribe of N. E. Mexico or s. Texas, probably Coahuiltecan, although farther inland than the best determined Coahuiltecan tribes. They were found in the neighborhood of the Rio Grande and in 1677 were gathered into the mission of Santa Rosa de Nadadores.
Manos Prietas.—Fernando del Bosque (1675) in Nat. Geog. Mag., XIV, 340, 1903. Manosprietas.—Orozco y Berra, Geog., 302, 1864.

Manshkaenikashika ('crawfish people'). A Quapaw gens.
Hañ′ʞa tañʞa.—Dorsey in 15th Rep. B. A. E., 230, 1897 ('large Hañ′ka'). Maⁿcka′ e′nikaci′ʞa.—Ibid.

Manso (Span.: 'mild'). A former semi-sedentary tribe on the Mexican frontier, near El Paso, Tex., who, before the coming of the Spaniards, had changed their former solid mode of building for habitations constructed of reeds and wood. Their mode of government and system of kinship were found to be the same as those of the Pueblos proper—the Tigua, Piros, and Tewa—from whom their rites and traditions clearly prove them to have come. They are divided into at least four clans—Blue, White, Yellow, and Red corn—and there are also traces of two Water clans. This system of clanship, however, is doubtful, since it bears close resemblance to that of the Tigua, with whom the Mansos have extensively intermarried.

According to Bandelier it is certain that the Mansos formerly lived on the lower Rio Grande in New Mexico, about Mesilla valley, in the vicinity of the present Las Cruces, and were settled at El Paso in 1659 by Fray Garcia de San Francisco, who founded among them the mission of Nuestra Señora de Guadalupe de los Mansos, the church edifice being dedicated in 1668. At this date the mission is reported by Vetancurt (Teatro Mex., III, 309, 1871) to have contained upward of 1,000 parishioners. About their idiom nothing is known. They have the same officers as the Pueblos, and, although reduced to a dozen families, maintain their organization and some of their rites and dances, which are very similar to those of the northern Pueblo peoples, whom the Mansos recognize as their relatives. They are now associated with the Tigua and Piros in the same town.

The term "manso" has also been applied by the Spaniards in a general sense to designate any subjugated Indians. (See Bandelier in Arch. Inst. Rep., v, 50, 1884; Arch. Inst. Papers, III, 86, 165–68, 248, 1890; IV, 348–49, 1892.)

Gorretas.—Zarate-Salmeron (*ca.* 1629) in Land of Sunshine, 183, Feb. 1900 (Span.: 'little caps'); Benavides, Memorial, 9, 1630. Gorrites.—Linschoten, Descr. de l'Amérique, map 1, 1638. Lanos.—Perea (1629) quoted by Vetancurt, Teatro Mex., III, 300, 308, 1871 (or Mansos). Maises.—Linschoten, Descr. de l'Amérique, map 1, 1638. Mansa.—Benavides, Memorial, 9, 1630. Manses.—Sanson, L'Amérique, 27, map, 1657. Mansos.—Benavides, Memorial, 9, 1630. Manxo.—Oñate (1598) in Doc. Inéd, XVI, 243, 1871 ("sus primeras palabras fueron *manxo, manxo, micos, micos,* por decir mansos y amigos"). Xptianos Manssos.—Doc. of 1684 quoted by Bandelier in Arch. Inst. Papers, III, 89, 1890 (i. e., 'Christian Mansos').

Manta (Brinton believed this to be a corruption of Monthee, the dialectic form of Munsee among the Mahican and Indians of E. New Jersey). Formerly an important division of the New Jersey Delawares, living on the E. bank of Delaware r. about Salem cr. According to Brinton they extended up the river to the vicinity of Burlington, as well as some distance inland, but early writers locate other bands in that region. Under the name of Manteses they were estimated in 1648 at 100 warriors. About the beginning of the 18th century they incorporated themselves with the Unami and Unalachtigo Delawares. They have frequently been confounded with the latter division, and Chikohoki (q. v.) has also been used as synonymous with Manta, but Brinton thinks they were a southern branch of the Munsee. (J. M.)

Frog Indians.—Proud, Pa., II, 294, 1798. Mandes.—Ibid., 295. Mantaas.—Herrman, map (1670) in Maps to Accompany the Rep. of the Comrs. on the Bndry. Line bet. Va. and Md., 1873 (refers to the river). Mantaes.—Hudde (1662) in N. Y. Doc. Col. Hist., XII, 370, 1877 ("Mantaes hoeck"). Mantaesy.—De Laet (1633) in N. Y. Hist. Soc. Coll., 2d s., I, 315, 1841. Mantas.—Doc. of 1656 in N. Y. Doc. Col. Hist., I, 598, 1856. Mantaws.—Macauley, N. Y., II, 293, 1829. Mantes.—Boudinot, Star in the West, 127, 1816. Manteses.—Evelin (*ca.* 1648) in Proud, Pa., I, 113, 1797. Mantos.—Brinton, Lenape Leg., 44, 1885. Maritises.—Sanford, U. S., cxlvi, 1819 (misprint). Salem Indians.—Proud, Pa., II, 295, 1798.

Mantouek. A tribe, possibly the Mdewakanton Sioux or its Matantonwan division, known to the French missionaries; placed by the Jesuit Relation of 1640 N. of a small lake W. of Sault Ste Marie, and by the Relation of 1658 with the Nadouechiouek (Nadowessioux, Dakota), the two having 40 towns 10 days' travel N. w. of the mission St Michael of the Potawatomi.

Mantoughquemec. A village of the Powhatan confederacy, in 1608, on Nansemond r., Nansemond co., Va.—Smith (1629), Virginia, I, map, repr. 1819.

Mantuenikashika ('those who made or adopted the grizzly bear as their mark or means of identification as a people.'—La Flesche). A Quapaw gens.
Grizzly-bear (?) gens.—Dorsey in 15th Rep. B. A. E., 229, 1897. Maⁿtu' e'nikaci'ɥa.—Ibid.

Manuelito. A Navaho chief. When Gov. Merriwether conferred with the Navaho in 1855 about putting an end to

MANUELITO

murders and robberies committed by members of this tribe, the head chief avowed that he could not command the obedience of his people, and resigned. The chiefs present at the council thereupon elected Manuelito to fill the place. The lawless element did not cease their depredations, and the obligation to surrender evil doers was no greater than it had been because the Senate neglected to confirm the treaty signed at the conference. When Col. D. G. Miles started out to punish the Navaho in 1859 he destroyed the houses and shot the horses and cattle belonging to Manuelito's band. When the Navaho finally applied themselves thoroughly to peaceful and productive pursuits, their old war chief was chosen to take command of the native police force that was organized in 1872. He died in 1893. See Dunn, Massacres of Mts., 1886; Matthews, Navaho Leg., 11, 1897.

Manufactures. See *Arts and Industries; Implements, Tools, and Utensils; Invention,* and the articles thereunder cited.

Manumaig (*Myänamäk,* 'catfish'). A gens of the Chippewa, q. v.
Cat Fish.—Morgan, Anc. Soc., 166, 1877. Man-um-aig.—Warren in Minn. Hist. Soc. Coll., v, 44, 1885. Myänamäk.—Wm. Jones, inf'n, 1906.

Many Horses. A Piegan Siksika chief, sometimes mentioned as 'Dog' and also as 'Sits in the Middle'; born about the close of the 18th century. He was noted not only for his warlike character but for the large number of horses he acquired; hence his name. According to the account given by the Indians to Grinnell (Story of the Indian, 236, 1895), he commenced to gather and to breed horses immediately after the Piegan first came into possession of them from the Kutenai (1804–06), and also made war on the Shoshoni for the purpose of taking horses from them. His herd became so extensive that they numbered more than all the others belonging to the tribe and required a large number of herders to take care of them. Many Horses was a signer of the first treaty of his tribe with the whites, on the upper Missouri, Oct. 17, 1855, which he signed as "Little Dog." He was killed in 1867 at the battle of Cypress Hill between the Piegan and the allied Crows and Hidatsa, at which time he was an old man.   (c. t.)

Manyikakhthi (*Ma-nyi'-ka-qçi',* 'coyote'). A subgens of the Michirache or Wolf gens of the Iowa.—Dorsey in 15th Rep. B. A. E., 238, 1897.

Manyinka ('earth lodge'). A Kansa gens, the 1st on the Ishtunga side of the tribal circle. Its subgentes are Manyinkatanga and Manyinkazhinga.
Earth.—Morgan, Anc. Soc., 156, 1877. Maⁿyiñka.—Dorsey in 15th Rep. B. A. E., 230, 1897. Maⁿyiñkagaxe.—Dorsey in Am. Natur., 671, 1885 ('earth-lodge makers'). Mo-e'-ka-ne-kä'-she-gä.—Morgan, Anc. Soc., 156, 1877. Moi-ka ñika-shing-ka.—Stubbs, Kansa MS. vocab., 25, 1877. Ujañge wakixe.—Dorsey, Kansa MS., B. A. E., 1882 ('road makers').

Manyinkainihkashina (*Maⁿyiñ'ka i'niy-k'ăcin'a,* 'earth people'). A social division of the Osage.—Dorsey in 15th Rep. B. A. E., 235, 1897.

Manyinkatanga (*Maⁿyinka tañga,* 'large earth'). A subgens of the Manyinka gens of the Kansa.—Dorsey in 15th Rep. B. A. E., 230, 1897.

Manyinkatuhuudje (*Maⁿyiñ'ka tu'hu iidje',* 'lower part of the blue earth'). A former Kansa village at the mouth of Big Blue r., Kans.—Dorsey, Kansa MS. vocab., B. A. E., 1882.

Manyinkazhinga (*Maⁿyiñka jiñga,* 'small earth'). A subgens of the Manyinka gens of the Kansa.—Dorsey in 15th Rep. B. A. E., 230, 1897.

Manzanita (Span.: 'little apple', but referring here to *Arctostaphyla manzanita*). A reservation of 640 acres of unpatented desert land occupied by 59 so-called Mission Indians, situated 170 m. from Mission Tule River agency, s. Cal.—Ind. Aff. Rep., 175, 1902; Kelsey, Rep., 25, 1906.

Manzano (Span.: 'apple tree'). A small New Mexican village 6 m. N. W. of the ruins of Quarai and about 25 m. E. of the Rio Grande, at which is an old apple orchard that probably dates from the mission period prior to 1676. Whether the orchard pertained to the neighboring mission of Quarai, or whether the former Tigua settlement adjacent to Manzano had an independent mission, is not known. A remnant of the Tigua now living near El Paso claim to have come from this and neighboring pueblos of the Salinas country. The aboriginal name of the pueblo near Manzano is unknown. The present white village dates from 1829. Consult Bandelier in Arch. Inst. Papers, IV, 259 et seq., 1892. See *Pueblos, Tanoan, Tigua.*
Mansano.—Abert quoted in Trans. Am. Ethnol. Soc., II, xciv, 1848. Manzana.—Pac. R. R. Rep., III, pt. 4, 98, 1856. Manzanas.—Parke, map N. Mex., 1851. Manzano.—Edwards, Campaign, map, 1847.

Maon. An unidentified tribe on upper Cumberland r., at the beginning of the 18th century; perhaps the Cherokee, or possibly the Shawnee.—Tonti (*ca.* 1700) in French, Hist. Coll. La., I, 82, 1846.

Maple sugar. In some of the Eastern states and parts of Canada the production of maple sugar and sirup is one of the thriving industries of the country. The census statistics of 1900 show that during the year 1899 there were made in the United States 11,928,770 pounds of maple sugar and 2,056,611 gallons of sirup. The total values of the sugar and sirup for 1899 were respectively $1,074,260 and $1,562,451. The production of maple sirup seems to have increased somewhat, while that of maple sugar appears to have declined. This industry is undoubtedly of American Indian origin. The earliest extended notice of maple sugar is "An Account of a sort of Sugar made of the Juice of the Maple in Canada," published in the Philosophical Transactions of the Royal Society for 1684–85, where it is stated that "the savages have practiced this art longer than any now living among them can remember." In the Philosophical Transactions for 1720–21 is printed an account of sugar-making in New England by a Mr Dudley. The Indian origin of maple sugar is indicated also by notices in Joutel; Lafiteau, who states directly that "the French make it better than the Indian women, from whom they have learned how to make it"; Bossu, who gives similar details about French sugar-making in the Illinois country; and other early writers. In various parts of the country the term "Indian sugar" (Canad. Settlers' Guide, 66, 1860) has been in use, affording further proof of the origin of the art of making maple sugar among the aborigines. Some of the Indian names of the trees from which the sap is obtained afford additional evidence, while maple sap and sugar appear in the myths and legends of the Menominee, Chippewa, and other tribes. The technique of maple-sugar making also reveals its Indian origin, not merely in the utensils employed, but also in such devices as straining through hemlock boughs, cooling on the snow, etc. For maple sugar cooled on the snow the Canadian-French dialect has a special term, *tire*, besides a large number of special words, like *sucrerie*, 'maple-sugar bush'; *toque*, 'sugar snowball'; *trempette*, 'maple-sugar sop', etc. The English vocabulary of maple-sugar terms is not so numerous. *Humbo* (q. v.), a New Hampshire term for 'maple sirup,' is said to be of Indian origin. The details of the evidence of the Indian origin of this valuable food product will be found in H. W. Henshaw, "Indian Origin of Maple Sugar," Am. Anthrop., III, 341–351, 1890, and Chamberlain, "The Maple amongst the Algonkian Tribes," ibid., IV, 39–43, 1891, and "Maple Sugar and the Indians," ibid., 381–383. See also Loskiel, Hist. Miss. United Breth., 179, 1794.   (A. F. C.)

Maqkuanani (*Ma'qkuana'ni*, 'red-tail hawk'). A subphratry or gens of the Menominee.—Hoffman in 14th Rep. B. A. E., pt. I, 42, 1896.

Maquanago. A former village, probably of the Potawatomi, near Waukesha, s. E. Wis., on lands ceded to the United States in 1833.—Royce in 18th Rep. B. A. E., Wis. map, 1899.

Maquantequat. A tribe or band at war with Maryland in 1639 (Bozman, Md., II, 164, 1837). The commission to Nicholas Hervey, from which Bozman obtained his information, does not give the locality of these Indians, but indicates that they resided in the territory of the colony. In the Archives (Proc. Council, 1636–67, 363, 1885), "Indians of Maquamticough" are mentioned; these are undoubtedly the same, but the locality has not been identified further than that it was on the Eastern shore. It is possible they were not Algonquian.

Mancantequuts.—Md. Archives, Proc. Council 1636–67, 87, 1885. Maquamticough.—Ibid., 36. Maquantequat.—Bozman, Md., II, 164, 1837.

Maquinanoa. A Chumashan village between Goleta and Pt Conception, Cal., in 1542.

Maquinanoa.—Cabrillo (1542) in Smith, Colec. Doc. Fla., 183, 1857. Maquin, Nanoa.—Taylor in Cal. Farmer, Apr. 17, 1863 (mistaken for two villages).

Maquinna. A chief of the Mooachaht, a Nootka tribe, who attained notoriety as the chief who captured the brig *Boston*, in Mar., 1803, and massacred all of her crew except the blacksmith, John Jewitt, and a sailmaker named Thompson. After being held in captivity until July, 1805, they were liberated by Capt. Hill of the brig *Lydia*, also of Boston. The story of the captivity of these two men was afterward extracted from Jewitt by Roland Alsop of Middletown, Conn., and published in America and Europe. A point near the entrance of Nootka sd. is now called Maquinna pt. See Narrative of the Adventures and Sufferings of John R. Jewitt, in various editions from 1815 to 1869.   (J. R. S.)

Maracock. See *Maypop*.

Marameg (from *Man-um-aig*, Chippewa for 'catfish.'—Verwyst). Evidently a band or division of the Chippewa, which seems to have been, at the dawn of the history of the upper lake region, in the process of disintegration. The first notice of them is that given by Dablon in the Jesuit Relation of 1670, at which time they resided on L. Superior, apparently along the E. half of the N. shore. They were then in close union with the Sauteurs, or Chippewa of Sault Ste Marie. Dablon, speaking of the Chippewa of the Sault, says: "These are united with three other nations, who are more than 550 persons, to whom they granted like rights of their native country. . . . These are the Noquets who are spread along the s. side of L. Superior, where they are the originals; and the Outchibous with the Marameg of the N. side of the same lake, which they regard as their proper country." Here the Chippewa of the N. side of the lake are distinguished from those of Sault Ste Marie to the same extent as are the Marameg and Noquet. The Chippewa settlement at the Sault, where the fishing was excellent, seems to have drawn thither the other divisions, as this gave them strength and control of the food supply. The early notices of the Marameg and Noquet appear to indicate that these two tribes became absorbed by the Chippewa and their tribal or subtribal distinction lost, but there are reasons (see *Noquet* and *Menominee*) for believing that these two peoples were identical. Tailhan, in his notes on Perrot's Mémoire, assumes without question that the two tribes were incorporated with the Chippewa of the Sault, who were distinguished by the name Pahouitigouchirini. The Marameg are mentioned under the name Malamechs in the Proces-verbal of the Prise de Possession in 1671 as present at the conference on that occasion. According to Shea they are mentioned in the MS. Jesuit Relation of 1672–73 as being near the Mascoutin, who were then on Fox r., Wis. If, as supposed, the people of this tribe are those referred to by La Chesnaye (Margry, VI, 6) under the name "Malanas ou gens de la Barbue," they must have resided in 1697, in part at least, at Shaugawaumikong (the present Bayfield, Wis.), on the s. shore of L. Superior. The attempt to identify them with the "Miamis of Maramek" mentioned in a document of 1695 (N. Y. Doc. Col. Hist., IX, 619) as residing on Maramec (Kalamazoo) r., in Michigan, is certainly erroneous.   (J. M.   C. T.)

Gens de la Barbue.—La Chesnaye (1697) in Margry, Déc., VI, 6, 1886. Malamechs.—Prise de Possession (1671), ibid., I, 97, 1875. Malanas.—La Chesnaye, op. cit. Marameg.—Jes. Rel. 1669–70, Thwaites ed., LIV, 133, 1899.

Maramoydos. A former Dieguéño rancheria near San Diego, s. Cal.—Ortega (1775) quoted by Bancroft, Hist. Cal., I, 254, 1884.

Maraton. A Chowanoc village in 1585 on the E. bank of Chowan r., in Chowan co., N. C.

Maraton.—Smith (1629), Va., I, map, repr. 1819. Mavaton.—Martin, N. C., I, 13, 1829. Waratan.—Dutch map (1621) in N. Y. Doc. Col. Hist., I, 1856.

Marble. The various forms of the carbonates of lime and magnesia, classed as marbles, were used to some extent by the Indian tribes for carvings, utensils, and ornaments. They include many varieties of ordinary marbles such as are used for building, as well as the cave forms known as stalactite, deposited as pendent masses by dripping water, and stalagmite, which is deposited by the same agency upon the floor. Travertine formed by rivers and springs is of nearly identical character. These deposits frequently present handsome translucent and banded effects. The purer, less highly colored varieties are sometimes called alabaster (see *Gypsum*), and the compact, beautifully marked forms are known as onyx. See *Mines and Quarries*.
(W. H. H.)

Maria. A Micmac settlement in Maria township, Bonaventure co., Quebec, containing 80 Indians in 1884, 93 in 1904.

Mariames. A tribe mentioned by Cabeza de Vaca as living, in 1528–34, "behind" the Quevenes, probably in the vicinity of Matagorda bay, Texas. The people subsisted mainly on roots and seem never to have enjoyed plenty except in the season of the prickly pears. They ground the bones of fish, mixed the dust with water, and used the paste as food. They are said to have killed their female infants to prevent their falling into the hands of their enemies, and also, because of their continued warfare, to avoid the temptation of marrying within their tribe. The region where the Mariames lived was within the later domain of the Karankawan tribes, which are now extinct (see Gatschet, Karankawa Inds., 46, 1891). Manzanet (1670) mentions a tribe called the Muruam, probably identical with this, and Orozco y Berra (Geog., 303, 1864) mentions the Mahuames as a former tribe of N. E. Mexico or s. Texas, which was gathered into the mission of San Juan Bautista, Coahuila, in 1699. These also may be identical.
(A. C. F.)

Mahuames.—Orozco y Berra, op. cit. (identical?). Mariames.—Cabeza de Vaca (1542), Bandelier trans., 82, 1905. Marianes.—Cabeza de Vaca, Narr., Smith trans., 58, 1851. Marians.—Harris, Voy. and Trav., I, 802, 1705. Mariarves.—Cabeza de Vaca, Narr., Smith trans., 93, 1871. Muruam.—Manzanet (1690), MS., cited by H. E. Bolton, inf'n, 1906 (identical?).

Marian. The Christian Hurons, so called by their pagan brethren on account of their frequent repetition of the name of Mary.—Shea, Cath. Miss., 183, 1855.

Maricopa. An important Yuman tribe which since early in the 19th century has lived with and below the Pima and from about lat. 35° to the mouth of Rio

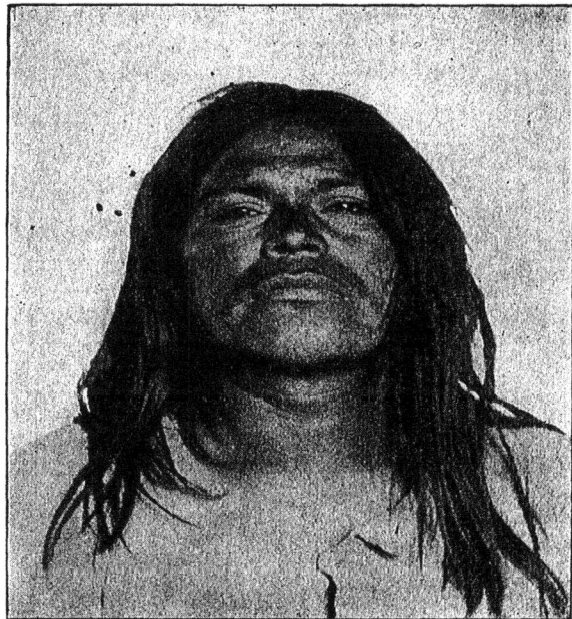

MARICOPA MAN.   (AM. MUS. NAT. HIST.)

Gila, s. Ariz. In 1775, according to Garcés, their rancherias extended about 40 m. along the Gila from about the mouth of the Hassayampa to the Aguas Calientes, although Garcés adds that "some of them are found farther down river." They call themselves *Pipatsje*, 'people,'

Maricopa being their Pima name. Emory states that they have moved gradually from the Gulf of California to their present location in juxtaposition with the Pima, Carson having found them, as late as 1826, at the mouth of the Gila. They joined the Pima, whose language they do not understand, for mutual protection

MARICOPA WOMAN.   (AM. MUS. NAT. HIST.)

against their kindred, but enemies, the Yuma, and the two have ever since lived peaceably together. In 1775 the Maricopa and the Yuma were at war, and as late as 1857 the latter, with some Mohave and Yavapai, attacked the Maricopa near Maricopa Wells, s. Ariz., but with the aid of the Pima the Maricopa routed the Yuma and their allies, 90 of the 93 Yuma warriors being killed. After this disaster the Yuma never ventured so far up the Gila. Heintzelman states, probably correctly, that the Maricopa are a branch of the Cuchan (Yuma proper), from whom they separated on the occasion of an election of chiefs (H. R. Ex. Doc. 76, 34th Cong., 1857). Like the Pima, the Maricopa are agriculturists, and in habits and customs are generally similar to them. Venegas (Hist. Cal., II, 182, 185, 192, 1759) states that about 6,000 Pima and Cocomaricopa lived on Gila r. in 1742, and that they extended also to the Salado and the Verde; they are also said to have had some rancherias on the w. side of Colorado r., in a valley 36 leagues long. Garcés estimated the population at 3,000 in 1775. There were only 350 under the Pima school superintendent, Arizona, in 1905.

By act of Feb. 28, 1859, a reservation was set apart for the Maricopa and the Pima on Gila r., Ariz.; this was enlarged by Executive order of Aug. 31, 1876; revoked and other lands set apart by Executive order of June 14, 1879; enlarged by Executive orders of May 5, 1882, and Nov. 15, 1883. No treaty was ever made with them.

The following rancherias and other settlements at different periods are judged, from their situation, to have belonged to the Maricopa tribe: Aicatum, Amoque, Aopomue, Aqui, Aquimundurech, Aritutoc, Atiahigui, Aycate, Baguiburisac, Caborh, Caborica, Cant, Choutikwuchik, Coat, Cocoigui, Cohate, Comarchdut, Cuaburidurch, Cudurimuitac, Dueztumac, Gohate, Guias, Hinama, Hiyayulge,

MARICOPA YOUNG MAN AND WOMAN

Hueso Parado (in part), Khauweshetawes, Kwatchampedau, Norchean, Noscaric, Oitac, Ojiataibues, Pipiaca, Pitaya, Rinconada, Sacaton, San Bernardino, San Geronimo, San Martin, San Rafael, Santiago, Sasabac, Shobotarcham, Sibagoida, Sibrepue, Sicoroidag, Soenadut, Stucabitic, Sudac, Sudacsasaba, Tadeo Vaqui,

Tahapit, Toa, Toaedut, Tota, Tuburch, Tuburh, Tubutavia, Tucavi, Tucsani, Tucsasic, Tuesapit, Tumac, Tuquisan, Tutomagoidag, Uparch, Upasoitac, Uitorrum, Urchaoztac, and Yayahaye. (F. W. H.)

Atchihwa'.—Gatschet, Yuma-Spr., II, 123, 1877 (Yavapai name). **A'wp-pa-pa.**—Grossman, Pima and Papago vocab., B. A. E., 1871 (Pima name). **Cocamaricopa.**—Kino (ca. 1699) in Doc. Hist. Mex., 4th s., I, 349, 1856. **Cocomarecopper.**—Pattie, Pers. Narr., 92, 1833. **Cocomari.**—Carver, Travels, map, 1778. **Cocomaricopas.**—D'Anville, map Am. Sept., 1746. **Cocomarisepas.**—Mota-Padilla, Hist. de la Conquista, 361, 1742. **Cocomiracopas.**—Hughes, Doniphan's Exped., 220–1, 1848. **Cokomaricopas.**—D'Anville, map N. A. (Bolton's ed.), 1752. **Comaniopa.**—Villa-Señor, Theatro Am., pt. 2, 405, 1748. **Comaricopas.**—Rudo Ensayo (ca. 1763), 24, 103, 1863. **Coro Marikopa.**—Eastman, map (1853) in Schoolcraft, Ind. Tribes, IV, 24–25, 1854. **Mapicopas.**—Keane in Stanford, Compend., 520, 1878. **Maracopa.**—Cooke in Emory, Recon., 561, 1848. **Marecopas.**—Simpson in Rep. Sec. War, 57, 1850. **Maricopa.**—Emory, Recon., 89, 1848. **Miracopas.**—Hughes, Doniphan's Exped., 221, 1848. **Mirocopas.**—Ibid. **Oohpáp.**—ten Kate, Reizen in N. A., 160, 1885 (Oöpáp or; Pima name for). **Oöpáp.**—Ibid. **Oopas.**—Rudo Ensayo (ca. 1763), 24, 1863. **Opas.**—Venegas, Hist. Cal., I, 297, 301, 1759. **Ozaras.**—Zarate-Salmeron (ca. 1629), Rel., in Land of Sunshine, 106, Jan. 1900 (probably identical). **Ozarrar.**—Bandelier (after Salmeron) in Arch. Inst. Papers, III, 110, 1890. **Pí-pás.**—A. Hrdlicka, inf'n, 1905 (own name). **Pipátsje.**—ten Kate, Reizen in N. A., 160, 1885 ('people': own name). **Si-ke-na.**—White, MS. Hist. Apaches, 1875, B. A. E. (Apache name for Pima, Papago, and Maricopa: 'living in sand houses,' from Apache *sai* 'sand,' *ki* 'house'; pronounced Sai'kine). **Tá'hba.**—Gatschet, Yuma-Spr., 86, 1886 (Yavapai name). **Tchihogásat.**—Ibid. (Havasupai name). **Widshi itíkapá.**—Ibid., 371, 1886 (Tonto name; also applied to Pima and Papago).

Marin. A chief of the Licatiut, apparently a band or village of the Gallinomero, about the present San Rafael, Marin co., Cal., in the early part of the 19th century. The Spanish accounts relating to him are conflicting. According to the most definite authority he was defeated and captured in battle with Spanish troops in 1815 or 1816 and carried to San Francisco, but escaped and resumed hostilities from his refuge place on the Marin ids. He was retaken in 1824, and accepting his fate, retired to San Rafael mission, where he died in 1834, or, according to other accounts, as late as 1848. The county takes its name from him. See Bancroft, Hist. Cal., II, VII, 1886–1890.

Maringoman's Castle. A palisaded village, so named after a Waoranec chief who occupied it in 1635, formerly on Murderer's cr., at Bloominggrove, Orange co., N. Y.—Ruttenber, Tribes Hudson R., 94, 1872.

Mariposan Family (adapted from Span. *mariposa*, 'butterfly,' the name of a county in California). The name applied by Powell to a linguistic stock of Indians, generally known as Yokuts, in San Joaquin valley, Cal. Their territory extended from the lower Sierra Nevada to the Coast range, and from mounts Pinos and Tehachapi to Fresno and Chowchilla rs. A separate body dwelt in the N., in a narrow strip of territory along the San Joaquin, between Tuolumne and Calaveras rs., about the site of Stockton. These were the Cholovone. The Coconoon, said to have been Mariposan, occupied an area within the limits of Moquelumnan territory.

Physically the southern members of this family, from Kaweah and Tule rs. and from Tejon, are very similar to the Yuman tribes of s. California. They are fairly tall (169 cm.) and rather shortheaded (cephalic index 82 to 83). Their superficial appearance is rather similar to that of the tribes of central California. They are not infrequently fat (Boas in Proc. A. A. A. S., XLIV, 261–9, 1896).

Their houses, especially those in the plains, were generally made of tules, and were often erected in rows, a village of the tribes about Tulare lake consisting of a row of such houses united into one. These long communal houses had an entrance and a fireplace for each family. Earth-covered sweat-houses were also built. Their implements and utensils were generally rude; the working of wood seems to have been confined to a few objects, such as bows and pipes, true wood carving not being practised. Their bows were of two types, one used for war and one for the hunt. Some of the tribes made a very crude and undecorated pottery similar to that of their Shoshonean neighbors of the mountains, which is the only occurrence of pottery in central California, and the art is probably a recent acquisition. The women were proficient basket makers, their product being predominantly of the coiled type. Shapes with a flat top and restricted opening are characteristic of this region and of the Shoshoneans immediately to the E.

The social organization of the tribes was very simple, with no trace of totemism or of any gentile system. Prohibition of marriage extended only to actually known blood relationships, entirely irrespective of groups. Chieftainship tended to be hereditary in the male line. The groups, or tribes, had more solidarity than elsewhere in California, as is shown by the occurrence of well-recognized names for the tribes. Hostilities were occasionally carried on between groups or with Shoshonean tribes, but in general the tribes were peaceful and friendly, even with their neighbors speaking alien languages. An initiation ceremony for young men consisted of a period of preparation followed by an intoxication produced by a decoction of jimson weed. A puberty ceremony for girls was not practised. The tabus and restrictions applied chiefly to childbirth and death. Death was followed by singing, dancing, and wailing. The body was buried or burned, the practice varying with the different tribes; the property of the deceased was destroyed, his house burned, and his name tabued. There was an elaborate annual mourning ceremony for the dead of the year, which took place about a large fire in which much property was consumed. This ceremony, which has been described as the Dance of the Dead, was followed by dancing of a festive character.

The Mariposan Indians were encountered by the Spaniards soon after their settlement in California, and with the other tribes of San Joaquin valley were generally known as Tulareños, etc., from the name of the lakes and of San Joaquin r., which during the Mission period bore the name Rio de los Tulares. No very considerable portion of the group seems to have come under the control of the Franciscan missionaries, but there was some intercourse and trade between the converted Indians of the coast regions and the Mariposan tribes of the interior. The Cholovone, Chukchansi, Tachi, Telamni, and other tribes were, however, at least in part, settled at San Antonio, San Juan Bautista, and other missions.

On the sudden overrunning of their country by the whites after the discovery of gold in California, the Indians of this family were either friendly or unable to make an effectual resistance. The Kaweah river tribes seem to have been the most hostile to the Americans, but no general Indian war took place in their territory, and treaties were made with all the tribes in 1851, by which they ceded the greater part of their territory (Royce in 18th Rep. B. A. E., 782, 1900). Many of the northern tribes were soon gathered on the Fresno River res., near Madera, and the southern tribes at Tejon; but the former was abandoned in 1859 and the latter in 1864. The Indians at Tejon were removed to Tule r., where, after another removal, the present Tule River res. was set apart for them in 1873 and occupied in 1876. The Indians of this reservation, mostly from Tejon and from Tule and Kaweah rs., numbered 154 in 1905. North of Tule r. the remaining Indians of this stock now live in and near their old homes; their numbers have greatly decreased and are not accurately known, while the Cholovone seem to be extinct.

About 40 tribes, each of about the numerical size of a village community, but possessing a distinct dialect, constituted the Yokuts or Mariposan family. About half of these are now extinct. These tribes, according to information furnished by Dr A. L. Kroeber, were the Cholovone, or, more correctly, Chulamni, about Stockton; the Chaushila, Chukchansi, Talinchi (properly Dalinchi), Heuchi, Toltichi, Pitkachi, Hoyima, Tumna (Dumna), and Kechayi, on San Joaquin r. and N. to Chowchilla r.; the Kassovo (Gashowu), on Dry cr.; the Choinimni, Michahai, Chukaimina, Iticha (Aiticha), Toikhichi, Wechikhit, Nutunutu, Wimilchi, Apiachi, and perhaps the Kochiyali, on Kings r.; the Tachi, Chunut, and Wowol, on Tulare lake, and the Tulamni and a tribe remembered only as Khomtinin ('southerners') on the smaller lakes to the s.; the Kawia (Gawia), Yokol or Yokod, Wikchamni, Wolasi, Telamni, and Choinok, on Kaweah r.; and the Yaudanchi, Bokninuwad, Kumachisi, Koyeti, Paleuyami, Truhohayi, and Yauelmani, on the streams from Tule r. to Kern r.

Names given as if of Yokuts tribes, but which may be place names or may refer to Shoshonean or other groups, are Carise, Caruana, Chebontes, Cheticnewash, Holeclame, Holmiuk, Lenahuon, Nonous, Sohonut, and Tatagua; also, entirely unidentifiable, Amonce, Kowsis, Nopthrinthres, Oponoche, and Ptolme.

Mariposa.—Latham in Trans. Philol. Soc. Lond., 84, 1856. **Mariposan.**—Powell in 7th Rep. B. A. E., 90, 1891. **Noaches.**—Cortez (1799) in Pac. R. R. Rep., III, pt. 3, 120, 1856. **Noche.**—Garcés (1776), Diary, 279 et seq., 1900. **Nochi.**—Font (1777), map, in Garcés, ibid. **Yocut.**—Bancroft, Native Races, I, 457, 1874. **Yo'kuts.**—Powers in Cont. N. A. Ethnol., III, 369, 1877.

Marmasece. Reported by some old Lummi as an extinct tribe on Puget sd., Wash., in about the habitat of their own people, by whom they may have been exterminated. They are also said to have killed three white men before the occupancy of the country by the Hudson's Bay Co. or the arrival of the first ships.

Mar-ma-sece.—Fitzhugh in Ind. Aff. Rep. 1857, 327, 1858.

Marracou. A town and tribe, probably Timuquanan, situated, in 1564, 40 leagues s. of the mouth of the St Johns r., Fla.— Laudonnière (1564) in French, Hist. Coll. La., n. s., 279, 1869.

Marriage. Except that marital unions depend everywhere on economic considerations, there is such diversity in the marriage customs of the natives of North America that no general description will apply beyond a single great cultural group.

The Eskimo, except those tribes of Alaska that have been led to imitate the institutions of neighboring tribes of alien stocks, have no clan organization. Accordingly the choice of a mate is barred only by specified degrees of kinship. Interest and convenience govern the selection. The youth looks for a competent housewife, the girl for a skilled hunter. There is no wedding ceremony. The man obtains the parents' consent, presents his wife with garments, and the marriage is completed. Frequently there are child betrothals, but these are not considered binding. Monogamy is prevalent, as the support of several wives is possible only for the expert hunter. Divorce is as informal as marriage; either party may leave the other on the slightest pretext, and may remarry. The husband may discard a shrewish or miserly wife, and the wife may abandon her husband if he maltreats her or fails to provide enough food. In such cases the children generally remain with the mother.

On the N. W. coast marriage between members of the same clan is strictly forbidden. The negotiations are usually carried on by the parents. The Kwakiutl purchases with his wife the rank and privileges of her family, to be surrendered later by her father to the children with interest, depending on the number of offspring. When the debt is paid the father has redeemed his daughter, and the marriage is annulled unless the husband renews his payment. Among the other tribes of the group an actual sale of the girl is rare. The Tlingit, Tsimshian, coast Salish, and Bellacoola send gifts to the girl's parents; but presents of nearly equal or even superior value are returned. Monogamy predominates. In case of separation Salish parents divide their children according to special agreement. Among the Tlingit, Haida, Tsimshian, and Heiltsuk the children always belong to the mother. If a husband expels his wife from caprice he must return her dowry; if she has been unfaithful he keeps the dowry and may demand his wedding gifts.

On the lower Pacific coast the clan system disappears. The regulations of the Indians of California vary considerably. Some tribes have real purchase of women; others ratify the marriage merely by an exchange of gifts. Polygamy is rare. Divorce is easily accomplished at the husband's wish, and where wives are bought the purchase money is refunded. Among the Hupa the husband can claim only half of his payment if he keeps the children. Wintun men seldom expel their wives, but slink away from home, leaving their families behind.

The Pueblos, representing a much higher stage of culture, show very different marriage conditions. The clan organization is developed, there is no purchase, and the marriage is arranged by the parents or independently by the young couple. The Zuñi lover, after bringing acceptable gifts, is adopted as a son by the father of his betrothed, and married life begins in her home. She is thus mistress of the situation; the children are hers, and she can order the husband from the house should occasion arise.

Of the Plains Indians some had the gentile system, while others lacked it completely. They seem to have practised polygamy more commonly, the younger sisters of a first wife being potential wives of the husband. Among the Pawnee and the Siksika the essential feature of the marriage ceremony was the presentation of gifts to the girl's parents. In case of elopement the subsequent presentation of gifts legitimized the marriage and removed the disgrace which would otherwise attach to the girl and her family (Grinnell). The men had absolute power over their wives, and separation and divorce were common. The Hidatsa, Kiowa, and Omaha had no purchase. The women had a higher social position, and the wishes of the girls were consulted. Wives could leave cruel husbands. Each consort could remarry and the children were left in the custody of their mother or their paternal grandmother. Separation was never accompanied by any ceremony.

East of the Mississippi the clan and gentile systems were most highly developed. The rules against marriage within the clan or gens were strictly enforced. Descent of name and property was in the female line among the Iroquoian, Muskhogean, and S. E. Algonquian tribes, but in the male line among the Algonquians of the N. and W. Among some tribes, such as the Creeks, female descent did not prevent the subjection of women. As a rule, however, women had clearly defined rights. Gifts took the place of purchase. Courtship was practically alike in all the Atlantic tribes of the Algonquian stock; though the young men sometimes managed the matter themselves, the parents generally arranged the match. A Delaware mother would bring some game killed by her son to the girl's relatives and receive an appropriate gift in return. If the marriage was agreed upon, presents of this kind were continued for a long time. A Delaware husband could put away his wife at pleasure, especially if she had no children, and a woman could leave her husband. The Hurons and the Iroquois had a perfect matriarchate, which limited freedom of choice. Proposals made to the girl's mother were submitted by her to the women's council, whose decision was final among the Hurons. Iroquois unions were arranged by the mothers without the consent or knowledge of the couple. Polygamy was permissible for a Huron, but forbidden to the Iroquois. Divorce was discreditable, but could easily be effected. The children went with the mother.

Monogamy is thus found to be the prevalent form of marriage throughout the continent. The economic factor is everywhere potent, but an actual purchase is not common. The marriage bond is loose, and may, with few exceptions, be dissolved by the wife as well as by the husband. The children generally stay with their mother, and always do in tribes having maternal clans. See *Adoption, Captives, Child life, Clan and Gens, Government, Kinship, Women.*

Consult Crantz, History of Greenland, 1767; Boas, Central Eskimo, 1888; Nelson, Eskimo about Bering Strait, 1899; Krause, Tlinkit-Indianer, 1885; Boas, Reps. on N. W. Tribes of Can. to Brit. A. A. S., 1889–98; Powers, Tribes of California, 1877; J. O. Dorsey, (1) Omaha Sociology, 1884; (2) Siouan Sociology, 1897; Farrand, Basis of American History, 1904; Goddard in Univ. Cal. Pub., Am. Archæol. and Ethnol., I, no. 1, 1903; Mooney, Calendar Hist. Kiowa, 1900; Grinnell, (1) Blackfoot Lodge Tales, 1892, (2) Pawnee Hero Stories, 1889; Cushing, Adventures in Zuñi, Century Mag., 1883; Powell, Wyandot Government, 1881; Morgan, League of the Iroquois, 1851; Heckewelder, Hist. Manners and Customs Indian Nations, 1876; Voth in Am. Anthrop., II, no. 2, 1900; Owen, Musquakie Folk-lore, 1904; Dixon in Bull. Am. Mus. Nat. Hist., XVII, pt. 3, 1905; Kroeber in Bull. Am. Mus. Nat. Hist., XVIII, pt. 1, 1902; Holm, Descr. New Sweden, 1834. (R. H. L.　L. F.)

Marriskintom. A village marked on Esnauts and Rapilly's map of 1777 on the E. side of lower Scioto r. in Ohio. It may have belonged to the Shawnee or to the Delawares, and is distinct from Muskingum. (J. M.)

Martha's Vineyard Indians. Martha's Vineyard id., off the s. coast of Massachusetts, was called by the Indians Nope, or Capawac. These may have been the names of tribes on the island and the smaller islands adjacent. The Indians thereon were subject to the Wampanoag and were very numerous at the period of the first settlement, but their dialect differed from those on the mainland. They seem not to have suffered by the great pestilence of 1617. In 1642 they were estimated at 1,500. The Mayhews carried on active missionary work among them and succeeded in bringing nearly all of them under church regulations and secured their friendship in King Philip's war. In 1698 they were reduced to about 1,000, in 7 villages: Nashanekammuck, Ohkonkemme, Seconchqut, Gay Head, Sanchecantacket or Edgartown, Nunnepoag, and Chaubaqueduck. In 1764 there were only 313 remaining, and about this time they began to intermarry with negroes, and the mixed race increased so that in 1807 there were about 360, of whom only about 40 were of pure blood. At that time they lived in 5 villages on or near the main island, the majority being at Gay Head. Soon thereafter they ceased to have any separate enumeration as Indians. (J. M.)
Vineyard Indians.—Alden (1797) in Mass. Hist. Soc. Coll., 1st s., V, 56, 1816.

Martinez. A small village on Torres res., under the Mission agency, s. Cal.—Ind. Aff. Rep., 170, 1904.

Martoughquaunk. A village of the Powhatan confederacy, in 1608, on Mattapony r., in Caroline co., Va.—Smith (1629), Virginia, I, map, repr. 1819.

Marychkenwikingh (from *Men'achkhawik-ink,* 'at his fenced or fortified house,' referring, no doubt, to its being the residence of the sachems.—Tooker). A village formerly on the site of Red Hook, in what is now the twelfth ward of Brooklyn, Long Island, N. Y., in Canarsee territory.
Marechhawieck.—Treaty of 1645 in N. Y. Doc. Col. Hist., XIII, 18, 1881. Marechkawick.—Doc. of 1643 quoted by Tooker, Algonq. Ser., II, 10, 1901. Marechkawieck.—Doc. of 1644 in N. Y. Doc. Col. Hist., XIV, 56, 1883. Marychkenwikingh.—Deed of 1637, ibid., 5. Merechkawick.—Doc. of 1645 cited by Tooker, op. cit. Merrakwick.—Doc. of 1648 cited by Tooker, ibid.

Marysiche. A small Opata settlement in Sonora, Mexico.—Hrdlicka in Am. Anthrop., VI, 72, 1904.

Masacauvi. A small Opata settlement in Sonora, Mexico.—Hrdlicka in Am. Anthrop., VI, 72, 1904.

Masac's Village. A former Potawatomi village on the w. bank of Tippecanoe r., in the N. E. part of Fulton co., Ind., on a reservation sold in 1836. The name is also written Mosack. (J. M.)

Masamacush. A name of Hood's salmon (*Salmo hoodii*), found in the fresh-water lakes of the Atlantic slope of Canada (Rep. U. S. Com. Fish., 1872–73, p. 159): from *masamegos* or *masamekus,* a name of the salmon-trout in the Chippewa and Cree dialects of Algonquian. The word signifies 'like a trout,' from *namekus,* 'trout,' and the prefix *mas-,* which has somewhat the force of the English suffix *-ish.* (A. F. C.)

Mascalonge. See *Maskinonge.*

Maschal. A Chumashan village given in Cabrillo's Narrative as on San Lucas id., Cal., in 1542; located on Santa Cruz id. by Taylor in 1863 and by San Buenaventura Indians in 1884.
Maschal.—Taylor in Cal. Farmer, Apr. 24, 1863. Mas-toâl.—Henshaw, Buenaventura MS. vocab., B. A. E., 1884. Maxul.—Cabrillo, Narr. (1542), in Smith, Colec. Doc. Fla., 181, 1857.

Mascoming. A Weapomeioc village, in 1585, on the north shore of Albemarle sd., in Chowan co., N. C., adjoining the territory of the Chowanoc. (J. M.)
Mascoming.—Smith (1629), Virginia, I, map, repr. 1819. Muscamunge.—Lane (1586), ibid., I, 87.

Mascoutens ('little prairie people,' from *muskuta* (Fox) or *mashcodé* (Chippewa), 'prairie'; *ens,* diminutive ending. By the Hurons they were called Assistaeronon,

'Fire people,' and by the French 'Nation du Feu.' These last names seem to have arisen from a mistranslation of the Algonquian term. In the Chippewa dialect 'fire' is *ishkote*, and might easily be substituted for *mashkodé*, 'prairie'). A term used by some early writers in a collective and indefinite sense to designate the Algonquian tribes living on the prairies of Wisconsin and Illinois; La Salle even includes some bands of Sioux under the name. The name (*Mashkótens*) is at present applied by the Potawatomi to that part of the tribe officially known as the "Prairie band" and formerly residing on the prairies of N. Illinois. The modern Foxes use the term Muskutáwa to designate themselves, the Wea, Piankashaw, Peoria, and Kaskaskia, on account of their former residence on the prairies of Illinois and Indiana. Gallatin was not inclined to consider them a distinct tribe, and Schoolcraft was of the opinion that they, together with the Kickapoo, were parts of one tribe. It is asserted by the Jesuit Allouez that the Kickapoo and Kitchigami spoke the same Algonquian dialect as the Mascoutens. Gallatin says the Sauk, Foxes, and Kickapoo "speak precisely the same language." Their close association with the Kickapoo would indicate an ethnic relation. According to an Ottawa tradition recorded by Schoolcraft there was at an early day a tribe known as Assegun (q. v.), or Bone Indians, residing in the vicinity of Michilimackinac. These, after a severe contest, were driven by the Ottawa into the southern peninsula of Michigan as far as Grand r. During this war on the eastern shore of L. Michigan the Ottawa and Chippewa, who had confederated with them, became involved in a quarrel with a people known as Mushkodainsug (or Mascoutens). From this period, according to the tradition, the Assegun and Mascoutens were confederates, and were driven still farther southward in the peninsula, after which they are lost to the tradition, except that it attributes to them the well known "garden beds" of southwestern Michigan. Although this tradition stands to a large extent alone, it is possibly not wholly unsupported. The chief items which seem to accord with it are the close relations between the Mascoutens and the Sauk, who are known to have resided at an early period in the lower Michigan peninsula, whence they passed into Wisconsin, where the two tribes were found closely associated; and the statement by Denonville (N. Y. Doc. Col. Hist., IX, 378) that Champlain, in 1612, found (heard of) the people of this tribe residing at Sakinan, or Saginaw bay. To the same locality have the Sauk been traced. Although the evidence is not entirely satisfactory, it is probable that this tribe entered Wisconsin from southern Michigan, passing around the southern end of L. Michigan.

The first mention of the Mascoutens is by Champlain, in 1616, under the name Asistaguerouön (Œuvres, IV, 58, 1870); on his map (V, 1284) he locates them, under the name Assistagueronons, beyond and S. of L. Huron, L. Michigan being unknown to him. He says the Ottawa were then at war with them. Sagard (1636) places them nine or ten days journey W. of the S. end of Georgian bay (Hist. du Canada, 194, 1866). According to the Jesuit Relation for 1640 they were then at war with the Neuters, who were allies of the Ottawa. The first actual contact of the French with the Mascoutens of which there is any record was the visit of Perrot to their village near Fox r. Wis., previous to 1669. Winsor (Cartier to Frontenac, 152) says Nicolet visited their village in 1634. That he passed up Fox r., probably to the portage, is doubtless true, but that he visited the Mascoutens is not positively known, as it is stated in the Jesuit Relation for 1646 that up to that time they had seen no European, and that the name of God had not reached them. They were visited in 1670 by Allouez and in 1673 by Marquette, both finding them in their village near the portage between Fox and Wisconsin rs., living in close relation with the Miami and the Kickapoo. After the visit by Marquette they are mentioned by Hennepin, who places them in 1680 on L. Winnebago; though Membré at the same date locates at least a part of the tribe and some of the Foxes on Milwaukee r. Marest, writing in 1712, says that a short time previous thereto they had formed a settlement on the Ohio at the mouth of the Wabash, or more likely at Old Fort Massac, whose occupants had suffered greatly from contagious disorders. In the same year the upper Mascoutens and the Kickapoo joined the Foxes against the French. In the same year the Potawatomi and other northern tribes made a combined attack on the Mascoutens and Foxes at the siege of Detroit, killing and taking prisoners together nearly a thousand of both sexes. In 1718 the Mascoutens and Kickapoo were living together in a single village on Rock r., Ill., and were estimated together at 200 men. In 1736 the Mascoutens are mentioned as numbering 60 warriors, living with the Kickapoo on Fox r., Wis., and having the wolf and deer totems. These are among the existing gentes of the Sauk and Foxes. They are last mentioned as living in Wisconsin in the list of tribes furnished to James Buchanan (Sketches N. A. Inds., I, 139) by Heckewelder, which relates to the period between 1770 and 1780. The last definite notice of them is in Dodge's list of 1779, which refers to those on the Wabash in connection with the Piankashaw and Vermilions (Kickapoo). After this the Mascoutens disappear from history, the northern group having probably been absorbed by the Sauk and Fox confederacy, and the southern group by the Kickapoo.

Notwithstanding some commendatory expressions by one or two of the early missionaries, the Mascoutens, like the Kickapoo, bore a reputation for treachery and deceit, but, like the Foxes, appear to have been warlike and restless. According to the missionaries, they worshiped the sun and thunder, but were not much given to religious rites and ceremonies, and did not honor as large a variety of minor deities as many other tribes; but such early statements regarding any tribe must be taken with allowance. Their petitions to their deities were usually accompanied by a gift of powdered tobacco.

The missions established among the Mascoutens were St Francis Xavier and St James.   (J M.   C. T.)

Asistagueronon.—Champlain (1616), Œuvres, v, 1st pt., 275, 1870. **Asistaguerouon.**—Ibid. (1616), IV, 58, 1870. **Assestagueronons.**—Schoolcraft, Ind. Tribes, IV, 206, 1854. **Assista Ectaeronnons.**—Jes. Rel. 1670, 99, 1858. **Assistaeronons.**—Jes. Rel. 1670-1 quoted by Schoolcraft, Ind. Tribes, IV, 244, 1854. **Assistagueronon.**—Sagard (1636), Hist. Can., I, 194, 1864; Champlain (1632), Œuvres, v, map, 1870. **Assistaqueronons.**—Champlain (ca. 1630) as quoted by Schoolcraft, Ind. Tribes, IV, 244, 1854. **Athistaëronnon.**—Jes. Rel. 1646, 77, 1858. **Atsistaehronons.**—Jes. Rel. 1641, 72, 1858. **Atsistagherronnons.**—Jes. Rel. 1658, 22, 1858. **Atsistahéroron.**—Champlain, Œuvres, IV, 58, note, 1870. **Atsistarhonon.**—Sagard (1632), Can., IV, Huron Dict., 1866 (Huron name). **Attistae.**—Schoolcraft, Ind. Tribes, IV, 244, 1854 (quoted from Ragueneau's map in Jes. Rel., 1639-40). **Attistaehronon.**—Jes. Rel. 1640, 35, 1858. **Attistaeronons.**—Jes. Rel. 1640 quoted by Schoolcraft, Ind. Tribes, IV, 244, 1854. **Fire Indians.**—Drake, Bk. Inds., ix, 1848. **Fire Nation.**—Schoolcraft, Ind. Tribes, IV, 206, 1854. **Gens de Feu.**—Champlain (1616), Œuvres, IV, 58, 1870. **Little Prairie Indians.**—Schoolcraft, Ind. Tribes, I, 307, 1851. **Machkoutench.**—Jes. Rel. 1670, 99, 1858. **Machkoutenck.**—Ibid., 97. **Machkouteng.**—Ibid., 100. **Macoutens.**—Vaugondy, Map of Am., 1778. **Macoutins.**—Doc. of 1668 in French, Hist. Coll. La., II, 125, 1875. **Makoüten.**—Hervas (ca. 1785) in Vater, Mith., pt. 3, sec. 3, 347, 1816. **Makoutensak.**—Jes. Rel. 1658, 21, 1858. **Makskouteng.**—Ibid., 1670, 94, 1858. **Mascautins.**—Chauvignerie (1736) in Schoolcraft, Ind. Tribes, III, 554, 1853. **Mascoaties.**—Boudinot, Star in the West, 99, 1816. **Mascontans.**—Morse, N. Am., 256, 1776. **Mascontenec.**—Browne in Beach, Ind. Miscel., 115, 1877. **Mascontens.**—Coxe, Carolana, 17, 1741. **Mascontins.**—Le Sueur (1692-3) in Minn. Hist. Soc. Coll., v, 419, 1885. **Mascontires.**—McKenney and Hall, Ind. Tribes, III, 115, 1854. **Mascordins.**—Buchanan, N. Am. Inds., I, 139, 1824. **Mascotens.**—Gale, Upper Miss., 43, 1867. **Mascotins.**—Schoolcraft, Ind. Tribes, I, 307, 1851. **Mascouetechs.**—Perrot (ca. 1721), Mémoire, 127, 1864. **Mascoutens.**—La Salle (1679) in Margry, Déc., I, 463, 1875. **Mascoutins.**—Prise de Possession (1671) in N. Y. Doc. Col. Hist., IX, 803, 1855. **Mascoutons.**—Boudinot, Star in the West, 127, 1816. **Mashkoutens.**—Baraga, Eng.-Otch. Dict., 299, 1878. **Maskoutechs.**—Bacqueville de la Potherie, Hist. Am., II, 49, 1753. **Maskouteins.**—Ibid., 98. **Maskouteins.**—Frontenac (1672) in N. Y. Doc. Col. Hist., IX, 92, 1855. **Maskoutenek.**—La Famine Council (1684), ibid., 238. **Maskoutens.**—La Salle (1682) in Margry, Déc., II, 215, 249, 258, 1877. **Mask8tens.**—

Marquette map (ca. 1678) in Shea, Miss. Val., 1852. **Maskoutins.**—Du Chesneau (1681) in N. Y. Doc. Col. Hist., IX, 161, 1855. **Maskuticks.**—McKenney and Hall, Ind. Tribes, III, 79, 1854. **Mathkoutench.**—Jes. Rel. 1671, 25, 1858. **Mauscoutens.**—Iberville (1702) in Minn. Hist. Soc. Coll., I, 341, 1872. **Meadow Indians.**—Howe, Hist. Coll., 118, 1851. **Mécontins.**—Le Sueur (ca. 1690) in Shea, Early Voy., 92, 1861. **Mecoutins.**—Neill, Hist. Minn., 154, 1858. **Messcothins.**—Boudinot, Star in the West, 127, 1816. **Miscóthins.**—Hutchins (1778) in Jefferson, Notes, 144, 1825. **Miscotins.**—Croghan (1765) in Monthly Am. Jour. Geol., 272, 1831. **Moshkos.**—Ruttenber, Tribes Hudson R., 336, 1872 (same?). **Mosquitans.**—Hough, map in Ind. Geol. Rep., 1883. **Mosquitos.**—Domenech, Deserts, I, 442, 1860. **Motarctins.**—St Cosme (1699) in Shea, Early Voy., 50, 1861. **Muscoten.**—Gale, Upper Miss., map, 1867. **Muscoutans.**—Hildreth, Pioneer Hist., 129, 1848. **Mushkodains.**—Schoolcraft, Ind. Tribes, I, 307, 1851. **Mush-ko-dains-ug.**—Ibid. (Ottawa name). **Muskantins.**—Tanner, Narrative, 315, 1830 (French name). **Musketoons.**—Writer of 1778 in Schoolcraft, Ind. Tribes, III, 561, 1853 (collective term for Wea, Piankashaw, etc.). **Muskoghe.**—Maximilian, Travels, 81, 1843 (incorrectly so called). **Muskotanje.**—Tanner, Narrative, 315, 1830 (Ottawa name). **Muskoutings.**—Rasle (ca. 1723) in Mass. Hist. Soc. Coll., 2d s., VIII, 251, 1819. **Muskulthe.**—Dalton (1783), ibid., 1st s., X, 123, 1809. **Muskutáwa.**—Gatschet, Fox MS., B. A. E., 1882. (='prairie people': Fox name, used collectively for themselves and the Wea, Piankashaw, Peoria, and Kaskaskia). **Musquetens.**—Conf. of 1766 in N. Y. Doc. Col. Hist., VII, 860, 1856. **Musquitans.**—Writer of 1812 in Schoolcraft, Ind. Tribes, III, 554, 1853. **Musquitoes.**—Knox (1792) in Am. State Papers, Ind. Aff., I, 319, 1832. **Musquitons.**—Hutchins (1778) in Schoolcraft, Ind. Tribes, VI, 714, 1857. **Nation du Feu.**—Jes. Rel. 1641, 72, 1858. **Nation of Fire.**—Jefferys, French Doms., pt. 1, 48, 1761. **Odistastagheks.**—Boudinot, Star in the West, 99, 1816.

Masewuk. A former Chumashan village near Santa Barbara, Cal.—Taylor in Cal. Farmer, May 4, 1860.

Mashawauk (Méshäwagi, 'elks', for Mëshäwisuchigi, 'they who go by the name of the elk.'—W. J.). A gens of the Sauk and Foxes. See Sauk.
Mă-shă-wă-uk'.—Morgan, Anc. Soc., 170, 1877. **Mëshäwisutoigi.**—Wm. Jones, inf'n, 1906.

Mashekakahquoh. See Little Turtle.

Mashematak (Mă-she'-mă-täk, 'big tree'). A gens of the Sauk and Foxes.—Morgan, Anc. Soc., 170, 1877. See Sauk.

Masherosqueck. A village on or near the coast of Maine in 1616, probably belonging to the Abnaki.—Smith (1616) in Mass. Hist. Soc. Coll., 3d s., VI, 107, 1837.

Mashik. An Aleut village at Port Moller, Alaska penin., Alaska; pop. 40 in 1880, 76 in 1890.
Mashik.—Petroff, Rep. on Alaska, 45, 1881. **Meshik.**—11th Census, Alaska, 164, 1893.

Mashpee (from massa-pee or missi-pi, 'great pool.'—Kendall). A former settlement on a reservation on the coast of Marshpee tp., Barnstable co., Mass. The reservation was established in 1660 for the Christian Indians of the vicinity, known as South Sea Indians, but it was afterward recruited from all s. E. Massachusetts, and even from Long Island. In 1698 they numbered about 285, and their population generally varied from 300 to 400 up to the 19th century. They intermarried with negroes and afterward with

Hessians; in 1792 the mixed-bloods formed two-thirds of the whole body, and the negro element was then increasing, while the Indians were decreasing. In 1832 the mixed race numbered 315. (J. M.)

Marshpaug.—Cotton (1674) in Mass. Hist. Soc. Coll., 1st s., I, 204, 1806. Marshpee.—Coffin (1761) in Maine Hist. Soc. Coll., IV, 271, 1856. Mashpah.—Rawson and Danforth (1698) in Mass. Hist. Soc. Coll., 1st s., X, 133, 1809. Mashpee.—Bourne (1674), ibid., I, 197, 1806. Mashpege.—Eliot (1673), ibid., X, 124, 1809. Mashpey.—Hinckley (1685), ibid., 4th s., V, 133, 1861. Masphis.—Alcedo, Dic. Geog., III, 458, 1788. Massapee.—Hawley (1762) in Mass. Hist. Soc. Coll., 1st s., X, 113–14, 1809. Old Colony Indians.—Eliot quoted by Davis (1819), ibid., 2d s., IX, xxv, 1822. Southern Indians.—Ibid. South Sea Indians.—Freeman (1802), ibid., 1st s., VIII, 127, 1802.

Masi. The Masauu (Death-god) clan of the Hopi of Arizona.
Másauwuu.—Voth, Hopi Proper Names, 93, 1905 (trans. 'skeleton'). Masi wiñwû.—Fewkes in 19th Rep. B. A. E., 584, 1900 (wiñwû='clan'). Ma-si wüñ-wû.—Fewkes in Am. Anthrop., VII, 404, 1894. Massauwu.—Dorsey and Voth, Oraibi Soyal, 13, 1901 (trans. 'skeleton').

Masiaca. A settlement of the Mayo, apparently on the Rio Mayo, under the municipality of Promontorios, in the district of Alamos, s. w. Sonora, Mexico. The total population was 364 in 1900. See Orozco y Berra, Geog., 608, 1864; Censo del Estado de Sonora, 1901.

Masikota (Masǐ'kotă, sing. Masǐ'kot, apparently from a root denoting 'shriveled,' 'drawn up'). A principal division of the Cheyenne, q. v. (J. M.)
Grasshoppers.—Dorsey in Field Columb. Mus. Pub. no. 103, 62, 1905. Mäh sǐhk' kü ta.—Grinnell, Social Org. Cheyennes, 143, 1905. Mä sǐh kuh ta.—Ibid., 136. Matsǐ'shkota.—Clark quoted by Mooney in 14th Rep. B. A. E., 1026, 1896.

Masilengya. The Drab Flute clan of the Hopi of Arizona.
Macileñya wiñwû.—Fewkes in 19th Rep. B. A. E., 583, 1901 (wiñwû='clan'). Ma-si'-len-ya wûn-wü.—Fewkes in Am. Anthrop., VII, 401, 1894.

Masipa ('coyote'). Given by Bourke (Jour. Am. Folk-lore, II, 181, 1889) as a gens of the Mohave who are said to have been originally a band of the Maricopa.

Maskasinik. A division of the Ottawa, mentioned in the Jesuit Relation for 1657–58 with the Nikikouek, the Michesaking (Missisauga), and others, as nations long known to the French in Canada. There is no other known reference to them. They may possibly be the same as the Achiligouan. (J. N. B. H.)

Maskeg. See Muskeg.

Maskegon (Mŭskīgŏk, 'they of the marshes or swamps.'—W. J.). An Algonquian tribe so closely related to the Cree that they have appropriately been called a subtribe. According to Warren the Maskegon, with the Cree and the Monsoni, form the northern division of the Chippewa group, from which they separated about eight generations before 1850. The traders knew them as Swampy Crees. From the time the Maskegon became known as a distinct tribe until they were placed on reserves by the Canadian government they were scattered over the swampy region stretching from L. Winnipeg and L. of the Woods to Hudson bay, including the basins of Nelson, Hays, and Severn rs., and extending s. to the watershed of L. Superior. They do not appear to be mentioned in the Jesuit Relations or to have been known to the early missionaries as a distinct people, though the name "Masquikoukiaks" in the Proces-verbal of the Prise de Possession of 1671 (Perrot, Mém., 293, 1864) may refer to the Maskegon. Tailhan, in his notes to Perrot, gives as doubtful equivalents "Mikikoueks ou Nikikoueks," the Otter Nation (see Amikwa), a conclusion with which Verwyst (Missionary Labors) agrees. Nevertheless their association with the "Christinos" (Cree), "Assinipouals" (Assiniboin), and "all of those inhabiting the countries of the north and near the sea" (Hudson bay), would seem to justify identifying them with the Maskegon. If so, this is their first appearance in history.

Their gentes probably differ but little from those of the Chippewa. Tanner says that the Pezhew (Besheu) or Wildcat gens is common among them. No reliable estimate can be formed of their numbers, as they have generally had no distinct official recognition. In 1889 there were 1,254 Maskegon living with Chippewa on reservations in Manitoba at Birch, Black, Fisher, Berens, and Poplar rs., Norway House, and Cross lake. The Cumberland, Shoal lake, Moose lake, Chemewawin, and Grand Rapids bands of Saskatchewan, numbering 605 in 1903, consisted of Maskegon, and they formed the majority of the Pas band, numbering 118, and part of the John Smith, James Smith, and Cumberland bands of Duck Lake agency, numbering 356. There were also some under the Manitowpah agency and many among the 1,075 Indians of St Peter's res. in Manitoba. (J. M.)

Big-Heads.—Donnelly in Can. Ind. Aff. for 1883, pt. 1, 10, 1884 (but see Têtes de Boule). Coast Crees.—Back, Arct. Land Exped., app., 194, 1836. Cree of the lowlands.—Morgan, Consang. and Affin., 287, 1871. Mashkegonhyrinis.—Bacqueville de la Potherie, Hist. Am., I, 168, 1753. Mashkegons.—Belcourt (ca. 1850) in Minn. Hist. Soc. Coll., I, 227, 1872. Mashkégous.—Petitot in Can. Rec. Sci., I, 48, 1884. Mas-ka-gau.—Kane, Wanderings of an Artist, 105, 1859. Maskego.—Writer of 1786 in Mass. Hist. Soc. Coll., 1st s., III, 24, 1794. Maskegonehirinis.—Bacqueville de la Potherie, Hist. Am., I, 177, 1753. Maskegons.—Henry, Trav., 26, 1809. Maskégous.—Petitot in Jour. Roy. Geog. Soc., 649, 1883. Maskègowuk.—Hutchins (1770) quoted by Richardson, Arct. Exped., II, 37, 1851. Maskigoes.—Schoolcraft, Ind. Tribes, II, 36, 1852. Maskigonehirinis.—Dobbs, Hudson Bay, 25, 1744. Masquikoukiaks.—Prise de Possession (1671) in Perrot, Mémoire, 293, 1864. Masquikoukioeks.—Prise de Possession (1671) in Margry, Déc., I, 97, 1875. Meskigouk.—Long, Exped. St Peter's R., II, 151, 1824. Mis-Keegoes.—Ross, Fur Hunters, II, 220, 1855. Miskogonhirinis.—Dobbs, Hudson Bay, 23, 1744. Muscagoes.—Harmon, Jour., 84, 1820. Musconogees.—Schermerhorn (1812) in Mass. Hist. Soc. Coll., 2d s., II, 11, 1814. **Muscononges.**—Pike, Exped., app. to pt. 1, 64, 1810. **Mushkeags.**—Schoolcraft, Ind. Tribes, VI, 33, 1857. **Muskagoes.**—Harmon (1801) quoted by Jones, Ojebway Inds., 166, 1861. **Mus-ka-go-wuk.**—Morgan, Consang. and Affin., 287, 1871. **Muskeegoo.**—Jones, Ojebway Inds., 178, 1861. **Muskeg.**—Hind, Red R. Exped., I, 112, 1860. **Muskeggouck.**—West, Jour., 19, 1824. **Muskegoag.**—Tanner, Narr., 315, 1830 (Ottawa name). **Muskegoe.**—Ibid., 45. **Muskegons.**—Gallatin in Trans. Am. Antiq. Soc., II, 24, 1836. **Muskego Ojibways.**—Warren (1852) in Minn. Hist. Soc. Coll., V, 378, 1885. **Muskegoo.**—Can. Ind. Aff. (common form). **Muskigos.**—Maximilian, Trav., II, 28, 1841. **Musk-keeg-oes.**—Warren (1852) in Minn. Hist. Soc. Coll., V, 45, 1885. **Mustegans.**—Hind, Labrador Penin., II, 16, 1863. **Omushke-kok.**—Belcourt (ca. 1850) in Minn. Hist. Soc. Coll., I, 227–8, 1872. **Omush-ke-goag.**—Warren (1852), ibid., V, 33, 1885. **Omushke-goes.**—Ibid., 85. **People of the Lowlands.**—Morgan, Consang. and Affin., 287, 1871. **Savannas.**—Chauvignerie (1736) in N. Y. Doc. Col. Hist., IX, 1054, 1855. **Savanois.**—Charlevoix, Nouv. Fr., I, 277, 1744. **Swampee.**—Reid in Jour. Anthrop. Inst. of G. Br., VII, 107, 1874. **Swampies.**—M'Lean, Hudson Bay, II, 19, 1849. **Swamp Indians.**—West, Jour., 19, 1824. **Swampy Creek Indians.**—Hind, Labrador Penin., I, 8, 1863 (for Swampy Cree Indians). **Swampy Crees.**—Franklin, Journ. to Polar Sea, 38, 1824. **Swampy Krees.**—Keane in Stanford, Compend., 536, 1878. **Swampys.**—Hind, Labrador Penin., I, 323, 1863. **Waub-ose.**—Warren (1852) in Minn. Hist. Soc. Coll., V, 86, 1885 ('rabbit': Chippewa name, referring to their peaceful character; applied also to the Tugwaundugahwininewug).

Maskinonge. A species of pike (*Esox estor*) found in the great lakes and the waters of the adjacent regions. The word is variously spelled maskinonge, mascalonge, muskelunge, muskellunge, etc., and abbreviated into lunge or longe. As one of the earlier forms of this word, masquinongy, and the Canadian French masquinongé and maskinongé, indicate, the terminal *e* was once sounded. The origin of the word is seen in mashkinonge or maskinonge, which in the Chippewa and Nipissing dialects of Algonquian is applied to this fish; although, as the etymology suggests, it might also be used of other species. According to Cuoq (Lex. Algonq., 194, 1886), mashkinonje is derived from *mash*, 'big,' and *kinonje*, 'fish.' This is perhaps better than the etymology of Lacombe and Baraga, which makes the first component to be *mashk* or *mask*, 'ugly.' The folk-etymological *masque allongé* of Canadian French has been absurdly perpetuated in the pseudo-Latin *mascalongus* of ichthyologists. (A. F. C.)

Masks. Throughout North America masks were worn in ceremonies, usually religious or quasi-religious, but sometimes purely social in character. Sometimes the priests alone were masked, sometimes only those who took part, and again the entire company. In all cases the mask served to intensify the idea of the actual presence of the mythic animal or supernatural person. The simplest form of mask was one prepared from the head of an animal, as the buffalo, deer, or elk. These realistic masks did not stand for the actual buffalo, deer, or elk,

but for the generic type, and the man within it was for the time endowed with or possessed of its essence or distinctive quality where the belief obtained that the mask enabled the wearer to identify himself for the time being with the supernatural being represented. A ceremony of purification took place when the mask was removed (Culin). Among the Eskimo the belief prevailed "that in early days all animated beings had a dual existence, becoming at will either like man or the animal form they now wear; if an animal wished to assume its human form the forearm, wing, or other limb was raised and pushed up the

WESTERN ESKIMO MASK.   (MURDOCH)

muzzle or beak as if it were a mask, and the creature became manlike in form and features. This idea is still held, and it is believed that many animals now possess this power. The manlike form thus appearing is called the *inua*, and is supposed to represent the thinking part of the creature, and at death becomes its shade." Many of the masks of the N. and the Pacific coast are made with double faces

KWAKIUTL COMPOUND MASK.   (BOAS)

to illustrate this belief. "This is done by having the muzzle of the animal fitted over and concealing the face of the *inua* below, the outer mask being held in place by pegs so arranged that it can be removed quickly at a certain time in the ceremony, thus symbolizing the transformation." Sometimes the head of a bird or animal towered above the face mask; for instance, one of the sand-hill crane was 30 inches long, the head and beak, with teeth projected at right angles, about 24 inches; the head was hollowed out to admit a small lamp which shone through the holes representing the eyes; below the slender neck, on the breast, was a human face. The shaman who fashioned this mask stated that once when he was alone on the tundra he saw a sand-hill crane standing and looking at him. As he approached, the feathers on the breast of the bird parted, revealing the face of the bird's *inua*. In certain cere-monies women wore masks upon the fin-ger of one hand. "The mask festival was held as a thanksgiving to the shades and powers of earth, air, and water for giving the hunters success." (Nelson in 18th Rep. B. A. E., 1899.)

In the N., on the Pacific coast, in the S. W., among some of the tribes of the plains, and among probably all the east-ern tribes, including the ancient pile dwellers of Florida, masks made of wood, basketry, pottery, or hide were carved, painted, and orna-mented with shell, bark fiber, hair, or feathers. They might be either male or fe-male. The colors used and the designs carved or painted were always sym-bolic, and varied with the mythology of the tribe. Frequently the mask was provided with an interior device by which the eyes or the mouth could be opened or closed, and sometimes the differ-ent parts of the mask

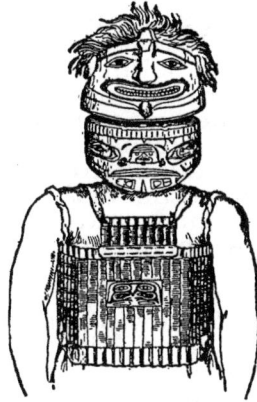

TLINGIT COMPOUND MASK.
(NIBLACK)

were so hinged as to give the wearer power to change its aspect to represent the move-ment of the myth that was being cere-monially exemplified. With the sacred masks there were prescribed methods for consecration, handling, etc.; for instance, among the Hopi they were put on or off only with the left hand. This tribe, ac-cording to Fewkes, also observed rites of bodily purification before painting the masks. Some of the latter were a simple face covering, sometimes concealing only the forehead; to others was attached a helmet, symbolically painted. The Hopi made their masks of leather, cloth, or basketry, and adorned them with ap-pendages of wood, bark, hair, woven fabrics, feathers, herbs, and bits of gourd which were taken off at the close of the ceremony and deposited in some sacred place or shrine. The mask was not al-ways worn; in one instance it was car-ried on a pole by a hidden man. Altars were formed by masks set in a row, and

sacred meal was sprinkled upon them. The mask of the plumed serpent was spoken of as "quiet"; it could never be used for any purpose other than to repre-sent this mythical creature; nor could it be repainted or adapted to any other pur-pose, as was sometimes done with other masks. Masks were sometimes spoken of as *kachinas*, as many of them repre-sented these ancestral and mythical be-ings, and the youth who put on such a mask was temporarily transformed into the kachina represented. Paint rubbed from a sacred mask was regarded as effi-cacious in prayer, and men sometimes invoked their masks, thanking them for services rendered. Some of the Hopi masks are very old; others are made new yearly. Certain masks belong to certain clans and are in their keeping. No child not initiated is allowed to look upon a kachina with its mask removed, and cer-tain masks must never be touched by pregnant women. Among the Hopi also a mask was placed over the face of the dead; in some instances it was a mere covering without form, in others it was made more nearly to fit the face. "A thin wad of cotton, in which is punched holes for the eyes, is laid upon the face . . . and is called a rain-cloud, or prayer to the dead to bring the rain." (Fewkes in 15th Rep. B. A. E., 1897.)

Young people sometimes indulged in festivities and made queer masks with which to disguise themselves; for ex-ample, masks of bladder or rawhide representing the head of the Thunder-bird were made by the boys of the poorer classes among some of the Siouan tribes when the thunder was first heard in the spring. Covering their heads and faces with the masks, the boys proceeded to their uncles' tents and, imitating the sound of thunder, struck the doorflaps with sticks. Then with much merriment at the expense of the boys the uncles in-vited them in and gave them presents of leggings, moccasins, or blankets. On the N. W. coast masks were occasionally made as toys for the amusement of children. But generally the mask was a serious rep-resentation of tribal beliefs, and all over the country the fundamental idea em-bodied in it seems to have been that herein described.

In addition to the authorities cited, consult Boas in Rep. Nat. Mus. for 1895; Dall in 3d Rep. B. A. E., 1884; Dorsey and Voth in Field Columb. Mus. Pub. nos. 55, 66, 1901, 1902; Matthews in Mem. Am. Mus. Nat. Hist., vi, 1902; Nelson in 18th Rep. B. A., E., 1899.　　(A. C. F.)

Mason's Ruins. A small ruined house group, so named by Lumholtz (Unknown Mex., i, 48, 1902) from a Mexican mem-ber of his expedition; situated on the end of a ridge near Rio Bavispe, N. W. Chihuahua, Mex. The walls, which stand 3 to 5 ft high, consist of felsite blocks averaging 6 by 12 in., laid in gypsiferous clay mortar and coated with white plaster. The structure is ascribed to the Opata.

Maspeth. A small Algonquian tribe or band, a branch of the Rockaway, formerly living in a village about the site of the present Maspeth, between Brooklyn and Flushing, Long Island, N. Y. The name occurs as early as 1638. Ruttenber speaks of Mespath as a considerable Canarsee village, attacked by the Dutch in 1644.   (J. M.)

Maspeth.—Thompson, Long Id., 410, 1839 (tribe). Mespacht.—Tienhoven (1650) in N. Y. Doc. Col. Hist., I, 426, 1856. Mespadt.—Ruyven (1666), ibid., II, 473, 1858. Mespaetches.—Doc. of 1638 quoted by Flint, Early Long Id., 162, 1896 ("Mespaetches Swamp"). Mespat.—Council of war (1673) in N. Y. Doc. Col. Hist., II, 591, 1858. Mespath.—Ruttenber, Tribes Hudson R., 114, 1872 (village). Mespath's Kill.—Council of 1673 in N. Y. Doc. Col. Hist., II, 661, 1858. Mespat Kil.—Ibid., 586. Mespats-kil.—Stuyvesant (1663), ibid., 448. Metsepe.—Flint, op. cit., 162 (given as Indian form).

Masque allongé, Masquinongé, Masquinongy. See *Maskinonge.*

Massachuset (*Massa-adchu-es-et*, 'at or about the great hill'; from *massa* 'great', *wadchu* 'hill or mountain', *es* 'small', *et* the locative.—Trumbull. In composition *wadchu* becomes *adchu* and adds *ash* for the plural. The name refers to the Blue Hills of Milton. Williams substitutes *euk* for *et* in forming the tribal designation, and uses the other as the local form. Cotton in 1708 translated the word 'a hill in the form of an arrowhead'). An important Algonquian tribe that occupied the country about Massachusetts bay in E. Massachusetts, the territory claimed extending along the coast from Plymouth northward to Salem and possibly to the Merrimac, including the entire basin of Neponset and Charles rs. The group should perhaps be described as a confederacy rather than as a tribe, as it appears to have included several minor bodies. Johnson described the group as formerly having "three kingdoms or sagamoreships having under them seven dukedoms or petty sagamores." They seem to have held an important place among the tribes of S. New England prior to the coming of the whites, their strength being estimated as high as 3,000 warriors, although it is more likely that the total population did not exceed that number. Capt. John Smith (1614) mentions 11 of their villages on the coast and says they had more than 20. In consequence of war with the Tarratine and the pestilence of 1617 in which they suffered more than any other tribe, the English colonists who arrived a few years later found them reduced to a mere remnant and most of the villages mentioned by Smith depopulated. In 1631 they numbered only about 500, and 2 years later were still further reduced by smallpox, which carried off their chief, Chickatabot. Soon thereafter they were gathered, with other converts, into the villages of the "Praying Indians," chiefly at Natick, Nonantum, and Ponkapog, and ceased to have a separate tribal existence. As they played no important rôle in the struggles between the settlers and natives, the chief interest that attaches to them is the fact that they owned and occupied the site of Boston and its suburbs and the immediately surrounding territory when the whites first settled there. In 1621, when Standish and his crew from Plymouth visited this region, they found the Indians but few, unsettled, and fearful, moving from place to place to avoid the attacks of their enemies the Tarratine.

Although the Algonquian Indians of Massachusetts, Connecticut, and Rhode Island, taken as a whole, formed a somewhat homogeneous group, yet there were linguistic differences which seem to justify De Forest (Indians Conn., 1853) in doubting Gookin's statement that the languages were so much alike that the people of the different tribes could easily understand one another. The Massachuset were more closely allied to the Narraganset than to any other of the surrounding tribes whose languages are known, the people of the two being able to understand each other without difficulty. For their customs, beliefs, etc., see *Algonquian Family.*

Following are the villages of the Massachuset Indians so far as known, some of them being more or less conjectural: Conohasset, Cowate, Magaehnak, Massachuset, Mishawum, Mystic (Middlesex co.), Nahapassumkeck, Nasnocomacack, Natick, Naumkeag (Essex co.), Neponset, Nonantum, Patuxet, Pequimmit, Pocapawmet, Punkapog, Sagoquas, Saugus, Seccasaw, Titicut, Topeent, Totant, Totheet, Wessagusset, Winnisimmet, and Wonasquam.   (J. M.   C. T.)

Macachusetts.—Writer *ca.* 1690 in Mass. Hist. Soc. Coll., 3d s., I, 212, 1825. Macetuchets.—Underhill (1640), ibid., 4th s., VII, 180, 1865. Macetusetes.—Underhill (1639), ibid., 178. Mantachusets.—Writer *ca.* 1648 in Proud, Pa., I, 115, 1797. Masathulets.—Higgeson (1630) in Mass. Hist. Soc. Coll., 1st s., I, 123, 1806. Masetusets.—Underhill (1647), ibid., 4th s., VII, 181, 1865. Masichewsetts.—Hooke (1637), ibid., 195. Massachewset.—Smith (1616), ibid., 3d s., VI, 119, 1837. Massachisans.—Gorges (1658) in Me. Hist. Soc. Coll., II, 62, 1847. Massachuselts.—Dee in Smith (1629), Virginia, II, 263, repr. 1819 (misprint). Massachusets.—Smith (1616) in Mass. Hist. Soc. Coll., 3d s., VI, 119, 1837. Massachuseuks.—Mourt (1622), ibid., 1st s., VIII, 241, 1802. Massachusiack.—Josselyn (1675), ibid., 3d s., III, 343, 1833. Massachussets.—Dermer (1620), ibid., 4th s., III, 97, 1856. Massachusuks.—Morton, New Eng. Memorial, 305, 1855. Massadzosek.—Jesuit Rel., III, index, 1858. Massajosets.—Maurault, Abenakis, III, 1866. Massathusets.—Allyn (1666) in Mass. Hist. Soc. Coll., 3d , X, 63, 1849. Massatuchets.—Doc. of 1636, ibid., III, 129, 1833. Massatusitts.—Records (1662) in R. I. Col. Rec., I, 473, 1856. **Massechuset.**—Brewster (1635) in Mass. Hist. Soc. Coll., 4th s., III, 338, 1856. **Massetusets.**—Cleeve (1646), ibid., VII, 371, 1865. **Masstachusit.**—Dermer (1619) in Drake, Bk. Inds., bk. 2, 20, 1848. **Matachuses.**—Tinker (1639) in Mass Hist. Soc. Coll., 4th s., VII, 220, 1865. **Matachusets.**—Doc. of 1665 in R. I. Col. Rec., II, 128, 1857. **Matathusetts.**—Weare (1690) in N. H. Hist. Soc. Coll., I, 138, 1824. **Mathatusets.**—Clark (1652) in Mass. Hist. Soc. Coll., 4th s., II, 22, 1854. **Mathatusitts.**—Records (1662) in R. I. Col. Rec., I, 468, 1856. **Mathesusetes.**—Godfrey (1647) in Mass. Hist. Soc. Coll., 4th s., VII, 378, 1865. **Mattachucetts.**—Robinson (1632), ibid., 94, note. **Mattachusetts.**—Downing (1630), ibid., VI, 37, 1863. **Mattachussetts.**—Pelham (1648), ibid., VII, 140, 1865. **Mattaousets.**—Whitfield (1651), ibid., 3d s., IV, 118, 1834. **Mattahusets.**—Weare (1690) in N. H. Hist. Soc. Coll., I, 138, 1824. **Mattatusetts.**—Nowell (1645) in R. I. Col. Rec., I, 133, 1856. **Messachusetts.**—Maverick (1666) in Mass. Hist. Soc. Coll., 4th s., VII, 312, 1865. **Messachusiack.**—Gorges patent (ca. 1623), ibid., 3d s., VI, 75, 1837. **Messathuset.**—Shurt (1638), ibid., 4th s., VI, 571–2, 1863. **Messthusett.**—Ibid. **Passonagesit.**—Morton (ca. 1625) in Drake, Bk. Inds., bk. 2, 43, 1848 (mentioned as the village over which Chickatabot was sachem).

Massachuset. One of the villages of the tribe of the same name in 1614, according to Capt. John Smith; probably the chief settlement of the tribe, which then held their territory about Massachusetts bay, Mass. In 1617 that portion of the coast extending northward into Maine was ravaged by a pestilence, so that the tribe was almost extinct before the arrival of the Puritans in 1620.

Massachuset.—Smith (1629), Hist. Va., II, 183, repr. 1819.

Massapequa ('great pond,' from massa, 'great,' and peag or pequa, 'pond.' It occurs frequently in dialectic forms in New England and on Long Island). An Algonquian tribe formerly on the s. coast of Long Island, N. Y., about Seaford and Babylon, extending from Ft Neck E. to Islip. Their chief village, which was probably of the same name as the tribe, appears to have been at Ft Neck. "Under constant fear of attack from their more warlike neighbors, the Indians at each end of the island had built at Ft Neck and at Ft Pond, or Konkhongauk, a place of refuge capable of holding 500 men" (Flint, Early Long Island, 1896). The stronghold of the Massapequa was destroyed in 1653 by Capt. Underhill in the only great Indian battle fought on Long Island. The women and children took refuge on Squaw id. during the battle. Until lately the remains of a quadrangular structure, its sides 90 feet in length, marked the place where the fort stood. Tackapousha, the Massapequa sachem, was a thorn in the flesh of the settlers in his vicinity, it being impossible to satisfy his demands. The records show that both the English and the Dutch were obliged to pay tribute to him time and again. He was one of the most turbulent characters known to the aboriginal history of Long Island. (J. M. C. T.)

Marospino.—Doc. of 1644 in N. Y. Doc. Col. Hist., XIV, 56, 1883. **Marossepinck.**—Deed of 1639, ibid., 15. **Marsapeag.**—Doc. of 1669, ibid., 621. **Marsapeague.**—Wood in Macauley, N. Y., II, 252, 1829. **Marsapege.**—Doc. of 1657 in N. Y. Doc. Col. Hist., XIV, 416, 1883. **Marsapequas.**—Ruttenber, Tribes Hudson R., 73, 1872. **Marsepain.**—Doc. of 1655 in N. Y. Doc. Col. Hist., XIII, 58, 1881. **Marsepeack.**—Stuyvesant (1660), ibid., XIV, 460, 1883. **Marsepeagues.**—Note, ibid., XIII, 341, 1881. **Marsepeague.**—Doc. of 1675, ibid., XIV, 705, 1883. **Marsepeqau.**—Ruttenber, Tribes Hudson R., 155, 1872 (misprint?). **Marsepin.**—Stuyvesant (1660) in N. Y. Doc. Col. Hist., XIV, 474, 1883. **Marsepinck.**—Doc. of 1656, ibid., 369. **Marsepingh.**—Treaty of 1660, ibid., XIII, 147, 1881. **Marsepyn.**—Doc. of 1660, ibid., 184. **Marsey.**—Addam (1653) in Drake, Bk. Inds., bk. 2, 79, 1848 (same?). **Masapequa.**—Thompson, Long Island, 68, 1839. **Masepeage.**—Deed of 1643 in N. Y. Doc. Col. Hist., XIV, 530, 1883. **Mashapeag.**—Doc. of 1683, ibid., 774. **Masha-Peage.**—Andros (1675), ibid., 706. **Mashpeage.**—Doc. of 1675, ibid., 696. **Massapeags.**—Macauley, N. Y., II, 164, 1829. **Massapege.**—Deed (1657) in Ruttenber, Tribes Hudson R., 344, 1872. **Massapequa.**—Thompson, Long Island, 67, 1839. **Massepeake.**—Doc. of 1675 in N. Y. Doc. Col. Hist., XIV, 705, 1883. **Mersapeage.**—Doc. of 1657, ibid., 416. **Mersapege.**—Treaty of 1656 in Ruttenber, Tribes Hudson R., 125, 1872.

Massassauga. A western species of rattlesnake (*Sistrurus catenatus*). This reptile is more properly termed Mississauga and derives its appellation from the place and ethnic name Missisauga (Chamberlain, Lang. of Mississagas, 59, 1892), from the Chippewa *misi*, 'great,' and *sãg* or *sauk*, 'river mouth.' (A. F. C.)

Massassoit ('great chief'; proper name, Woosamequin [Wasamegin, Osamekin, etc.], 'Yellow Feather'). A principal chief of the Wampanoag of the region about Bristol, R. I., who was introduced by Samoset to the Puritans at Plymouth in 1621. He was preeminently the friend of the English. Drake (Aborig. Races, 81, 1880) says of him: "He was a chief renowned more in peace than war, and was, as long as he lived, a friend to the English, notwithstanding they committed repeated usurpations upon his lands and liberties." He had met other English voyagers before the advent of the Puritans. While ill in 1623 he was well treated by the English. In 1632 he had a brief dispute with the Narraganset under Canonicus, and in 1649 he sold the site of Duxbury to the English. His death took place in 1662. Of his sons, one, Metacomet, became famous as King Philip (q. v.), the leading spirit in a long struggle against the English. (A. F. C.)

Massawoteck. A village of the Powhatan confederacy, in 1608, on the N. bank of Rappahannock r., King George co., Va. (J. M.)

Massawoteck.—Smith (1629), Virginia, I, map, repr. 1819. **Massawteck.**—Simons, ibid., I, 185.

Masset. A Haida town on the E. side of Masset inlet, near its mouth, Queen Charlotte ids., Brit. Col. Its name in the Masset dialect is Ataiwas (ᵍatᵍē′was, 'white slope', which in the Skidegate dialect appears as Gatgai′xiwas). According to the inhabitants the sea formerly came in over the ground now occupied by houses, but the latter were then situated on higher ground just back of the present site. At that time, too, there was an independent town around a hill called Edjao (⁸I′djao), which stands at the eastern end. Until lately the band holding possession was the Skidaokao. According to John Work's estimate, made between 1836 and 1841, there were 160 houses and 2,473 people at Masset, but this enumeration must have included all the neighboring towns, and probably numbered the smokehouses. The number of houses, enumerated by old people, in the two towns, Masset proper and Edjao (27 and 6 respectively) would indicate a total population of about 528, 432 in the former and 96 in the latter. Adding to these figures the estimated numbers in the two neighboring towns of Yan and Kayung, the grand total would be 1,056, or less than half of Work's figure. It is probable, however, that the population had decreased between Work's time and that which the old men now recall. According to the Canadian Report of Indian Affairs for 1904 there were 356 people at Masset; these include the remnant of all the families that lived once between Chawagis r. and Hippa id. A few people have moved to the neighboring town of Kayung. A mission of the Anglican Church is maintained at Masset, the oldest on the Queen Charlotte ids., and all the Indians are nominal Christians.

(J. R. S.)

⁸Atē′was.—Swanton, Cont. Haida, 281, 1905 (native name). G·at′aiwa′s.—Boas, Twelfth Report N. W. Tribes Canada, 23, 1898. Gatgaxiwas.—Ibid. (Skidegate dialect). Maasets.—Scouler (1846) in Jour. Ethnol. Soc. Lond., I, 233, 1848. Masseets.—Scouler in Jour. Roy. Geog. Soc., XI, 219, 1841. Massets.—Dunn, Hist. Oregon, 281, 1844. Massett.—Can. Ind. Aff. 1904, pt. 2, 69, 1905. Massetta.—Schoolcraft, Ind. Tribes, V, 489, 1855 (after Work, 1836–41). Massettes.—Scouler in Jour. Roy. Geog. Soc., XI, 219, 1841. Māss hāde.—Krause, Tlinkit Indianer, 304, 1885. Mossette.—Kane, Wand. in N. Am., app., 1859 (after Work, 1836–41). Ut-te-was.—Dawson, Q. Charlotte Ids., 183, 1880.

Massi. A former town on the E. bank of Tallapoosa r., Ala. (Bartram, Voy, I, map, 1799). Not identified, but probably Creek.

Massikwayo. The Chicken-hawk clan of the Pakab (Reed) phratry of the Hopi.
Mas-si′ kwa′-yo.—Stephen in 8th Rep. B. A. E., 39, 1891.

Massinacac. A tribe of the Monacan confederacy, formerly living in Cumberland and Buckingham cos., Va. Strachey speaks of their village as the farthest town of the Monacan.
Massinacack.—Smith (1629), Virginia, I, map, repr. 1819. Massinacacs.—Jefferson, Notes, 179, 1801. Massinnacacks.—Strachey (1612), Va., 102, 1849.

Massomuck. An Indian location in 1700, mentioned as if near the Wabaquasset country, in s. Massachusetts (Doc. of 1700 in N. Y. Doc. Col. Hist., IV, 615, 1854). Probably identical with Ma-

shamoquet (Massamugget, Mashamugget, Mashamugket, Machi-mucket, Moshamoquett), given by Trumbull (Ind. Names Conn., 25, 1881) as the name of a tract and a small tributary of Quinebaug r. at Pomfret, N. E. Conn., and rendered by him 'at the great fishing place.'

Mastohpatakiks (*Ma-stoh′-pa-ta-kĭks*, 'raven bearers'). A society of the Ikunuhkahtsi, or All Comrades, in the Piegan tribe of the Siksika.—Grinnell, Blackfoot Lodge Tales, 221, 1892.

Masut. A former northern Pomo village on Forsythe cr., one of the headwaters of Russian r., about 3 m. N. W. of the present Calpella, Mendocino co., Cal. (S. A. B.)
Masu-ta-kaya.—Gibbs (1851) in Schoolcraft, Ind. Tribes, III, 112, 1853. Ma-su-ta-kéa.—Ibid.

Mata. A former rancheria, probably of the Soba, N. of Caborca, which is on the Rio de la Asuncion, between Quitobac and Aribaiba, N. W. Sonora, Mexico. The place was visited by Anza and Font in 1776.
Santa Maíta.—Hardy, Travels, 422, 1829 (same?). S. Juan de Mata.—Anza and Font (1776) quoted by Bancroft, Ariz. and N. M., 393, 1889.

Matachic. A Tarahumare settlement on the headwaters of the Rio Yaqui, lat. 28° 45′, lon. 107° 30′, w. Chihuahua, Mexico.—Orozco y Berra, Geog., 323, 1864.

Mataguay. A former Diegueño rancheria on upper San Luis Rey r., San Diego co., Cal.; later on Agua Caliente No. 1 res., occupied by Warner's ranch. By decision of the U. S. Supreme Court the Indians were dispossessed of their lands, and by act of May 27, 1902, an additional tract was purchased at Pala, and the Mataguay people, who numbered 11 in 1903, were removed thereto in that year.
Mataguay.—Jackson and Kinney, Rep. Miss. Ind., 24, 1883. Matahuay.—Hayes (1850) cited by Bancroft, Nat. Rac., I, 458, 1882. Matajuiai.—H. R. Ex. Doc. 76, 34 Cong., 3d sess., 133, 1857. Mootaeyuhew.—Taylor in Cal. Farmer, May 11, 1860.

Mataitaikeok (*Ma-tái-tai-ke-ók*, 'many eagles'). A former Cree band, named from their chief, who was known to the French as Le Sonnant. In 1856 they roamed and hunted in the country along the "Montagnes des Bois," and traded with the fur companies on Red r. of the North and on the Missouri near the mouth of the Yellowstone. They numbered about 300 lodges.—Hayden, Ethnog. and Philol. Mo. Val., 237, 1862.

Matamo. A Diegueño rancheria near San Diego, s. Cal.; probably the same as Matmork la Puerta, represented in the treaty of 1852 at Santa Isabel.
Matamó.—Ortega (1775) cited by Bancroft, Hist. Cal. I, 253, 1884. Matmork la Puerta.—H. R. Ex. Doc. 76, 34th Cong., 3d sess., 132, 1857.

Matanakons. Mentioned by De Laet about 1633 (N. Y. Hist. Soc. Coll., 2d s., I, 303, 1841) as a Delaware tribe formerly in New Jersey. The name may have some connection with Manta (q. v.) or with Matiniconk, the Indian name of an island in Delaware r. Cf. *Matinecoc.* (J. M.)

Matantonwan (said to mean 'village of the great lake which empties into a small one,' and therefore probably from *mdo-te,* 'the outlet of a lake'). One of the two early primary divisions of the Mdewakanton Sioux (Neill, Hist. Minn., 144, 1858). They seem to have been a distinct tribe when visited by Perrot in 1689. They are mentioned as residing at the mouth of Minnesota r. in 1685. To this division belonged in 1858 the Khemnichan, Kapozha, Maghayuteshni, Makhpiyamaza, Kheyataotonwe, and Tintaotonwe bands. All these are now on Santee res., Nebr. **Mah-tah-ton.**—Lewis and Clark, Discov., 34, 1806. **Mantantans.**—Perrot (1689), quoted by Neill, Hist. Minn., 144, 1858. **Mantantons.**—La Harpe quoted by Neill, Hist. Minn., 170, 1858. **Mantanton Scioux.**—Le Sueur (1700) quoted by Neill, ibid., 166. **Mantantous.**—Prise de Possession (1689) in Margry, Déc., V, 34, 1883. **Mantautous.**—Perrot, Mém., 304, 1864 (misprint). **Matabantowaher.**—Balbi, Atlas Ethnog., 55, 1826. **Mententons.**—Pénicaut (1700) in Minn. Hist. Soc. Coll., II, pt. 2, 6, 1864. **Mentonton.**—Pénicaut (1700) in Margry, Déc., V, 414, 1883.

Matantuck. See *Magnus.*

Matanza (Span.: 'massacre'). A name frequently appearing on early Spanish maps, and on maps derived therefrom, apparently as settlements, but in reality to mark the locality or supposed locality where a massacre had taken place. A Matanza appears on maps of the Quivira region, in which Francisco Leyva Bonilla and his companions were killed by the natives about 1594–96; and another on the E. coast of Florida, below St Augustine, where the Huguenot colonists were massacred by the Spaniards in 1565.

Matapan (probably from the Nahuatl *matlalli, atl,* and *pan,* which suggests 'in the blue water.'—Buelna). A subdivision of the Tehueco that inhabited a village of the same name on the lower Rio Fuerte, in N. W. Sinaloa, Mex.—Orozco y Berra, Geog., 58, 1864.

Matape. A Eudeve settlement, which evidently contained also some Coguinachi Opata, in lat. 29°, lon. 110°, central Sonora, Mexico. Identified by Bandelier with the Vacapa or Vacupa of Marcos de Niça (1539). The mission of San José de Matape was established there in 1629; it had 482 inhabitants in 1678 and but 35 in 1730. According to Davila (Sonora Histórico, 317, 1894) it was a Coguinachi pueblo. Not to be confounded with Bacapa, a Papago settlement. **Bacapa.**—Coues, Garcés Diary, II, 481, 1900. **Matapa.**—Bandelier in Arch. Inst. Papers, V, 123, 1890. **Matape.**—Sonora Materiales (1730) quoted by Bancroft, No. Mex. States, I, 513, 1884. **San José de Matape.**—Zapata (1678) in Doc. Hist. Mex., 4th s., III, 353, 1857. **S. José Matape.**—Bancroft, No. Mex. States, I, 246, 1884. **Vacapa.**—Marcos de Niça (1539) in Ternaux-Compans. Voy., IX, 259, 1838. **Vacupa.**—Niça (1539) in Hakluyt, Voy., III, 439, 1600.

Matapeake. Mentioned as a tribe that once occupied Kent id., Queen Anne co., Md. (Davis, Daystar of American Freedom, 45, 1855). They lived at one time near Indian Spring, and at another on Matapax Neck.

Matarango. A tribe living w. of Darwin, S. E. Cal.; probably an offshoot of the Panamint, as they speak a similar language. (H. W. H.)

Matatoba. A tribe or band of the Dakota, probably the Mantantonwan division of the Mdewakanton. **Matatoba.**—Pachot (1722) in Margry, Déc., VI, 518, 1886. **Sioux of the Prairies.**—Ibid. (distinct from the Teton).

Mataughquamend. A village on the N. bank of the Potomac, in 1608, in Charles co., Md., probably near Mattawoman cr.—Smith (1629), Virginia, I, map, repr. 1819.

Matawachkarini ('people of the shallows.'—Hewitt). A small tribe or band living in 1640 on middle Ottawa r., but found in 1672 in the vicinity of the S. end of Hudson bay, near the Monsoni. They were doubtless one of the bands, known to the French as Algonkin, which were broken and dispersed by the Iroquois invasion about 1660. See *Mattawan.* **Madaouaskairini.**—Champlain, Œuvres, III, 302, 1870. **Mataouachkariniens.**—Jes. Rel. 1643, 61, 1858. **Mataoûakirinouek.**—Ibid., 1672, 54, 1858. **Mataouchkairini.**—Ibid, III, index, 1858. **Mataouchkairinik.**—Ibid., 1658, 22, 1858. **Mataouchkairiniouek.**—Ibid., 1646, 34, 1858. **Mataouchkairiniwek.**—Ibid., 1646, 145, 1858. **Mataouchkairini.**—Ibid., 1640, 34, 1858. **Matawachkaïrini.**—Ibid., III, index, 1858. **Matawachwarini.** — Ibid. **Matou-ouescarini.** — Champlain (1613), Œuvres, III, 302, 1870.

Matawoma. A former village, probably of the Delawares, on Juniata r., Mifflin co., Pa., near the present McVeytown.—Royce in 18th Rep. B. A. E., Pa. map, 1899.

Matchasaung. A former Iroquois village on the left bank of the E. branch of Susquehanna r., about 13 m. above Wyoming, Pa.—Doc. Hist. N. Y., II, 715, 1851.

Matchcoat. During the era of trade with the Indians almost throughout the Algonquian seaboard certain garments supplied in traffic were called by the English "matchcoats," a corruption of a name belonging to one of the cloaks or mantles of the natives. The Algonquian word from which it was derived is represented by Chippewa *matshigoté,* Delaware *wachgotey,* 'petticoat.' (A. F. C.)

Matchcouchtin. A Nanticoke village in 1707, probably in Pennsylvania.—Evans (1707) in Day, Penn., 301, 1843.

Matcheattochousie. A Nanticoke village in 1707, probably in Pennsylvania.—Evans (1707) in Day, Penn., 391, 1843.

Matchebenashshewish ('ill-looking bird,' or 'ill-natured bird.'—Hewitt). A Potawatomi village, called after a chief of this name, formerly on Kalamazoo r., probably in Jackson co., Mich. The reservation was sold in 1827. The name is also written Matchebenarhshewish. (J. M.)

Matchedash. A name formerly used to designate those Missisauga living at Matchedash bay, Ontario.
Matchedach.—Chauvignerie (1736) in N. Y. Doc. Col. Hist., IX, 1056, 1855. **Matchedash.**—Henry, Travels, 35, 179, 1809. **Matchitashk.**—Ibid. **Matechitache.**—Memoir of 1718 in N. Y. Doc. Col. Hist., IX, 889, 1855.

Matchinkoa. A village containing 600 families of Illinois, Miami, and others, situated 30 leagues from Ft Crevecœur, near Peoria, Ill., in 1682 (La Salle in Margry, Déc., II, 201, 1877). The word may be connected with Chinko (q. v.).

Matchopick ('bad bay or inlet.'—Hewitt). A village of the Powhatan confederacy, in 1608, on the N. bank of the Rappahannock, in Richmond co., Va. Cf. *Matchotic.*
Machopeake.—Purchas, Pilgrimes, IV, 1716, 1625–26. **Matchopeak.**—Simons in Smith (1629), Virginia, I, 185, repr. 1819. **Matchopick.**—Smith, ibid., map.

Matchotic ('bad inlet.'—Hewitt). A group of tribes of the Powhatan confederacy occupying the country between Potomac and Rappahannock rs. down to about the middle of Richmond co., Va., comprising the Tauxenent, Potomac, Cuttatawomen, Pissasec, and Onawmanient. They numbered perhaps 400 warriors in 1608, but 60 years later, according to Jefferson, had become reduced to 60 warriors. See *Appomattoc.* (J. M.)
Appamatox.—Jefferson, Notes, table, 138, 1801. **Appamatriox.**—Herrman, map (1670) in Rep. on Line between Va. and Md., 1873. **Matchoatickes.**—Archives Md., Proc. Council, 1636–67, 281, 1885. **Matchotics.**—Jefferson, op. cit. **Matox.**—Ibid.

Matchotic. A former village on the s. bank of Potomac r. in Northumberland co., Va., a short distance below Nominy inlet.
Mattschotick.—Herrman, map (1670) in Rep. on Line between Va. and Md.

Matchotic. A former village on Machodoc cr., King George co., Va.
Upper Matchodic.—Jefferson, Notes, 138, 1801. **Upper Mattschotick.**—Herrman, map (1670) in Rep. on Line between Va. and Md.

Matchut. A village of the Powhatan confederacy, in 1608, on Pamunkey r., New Kent co., Va.
Matchot.—Smith (1629), Virginia, II, 15, repr. 1819. **Matchut.**—Ibid., I, map.

Mategarele (*mategá* 'juniper', *relé* 'below': 'below the junipers'). A Tarahumare rancheria near Palanquo, Chihuahua, Mexico.—Lumholtz, inf'n, 1894.

Mathews, Mary. See *Bosomworth, Mary.*

Mathiaca. A Timuquanan tribe and village on the w. side of upper St Johns r., Fla., in the 16th century.
Mathiaca.—De Bry, Brev. Nar., II, map, 1521. **Mathiaqua.**—Laudonnière (1565) quoted by Shipp, De Soto and Fla., 525, 1881. **Matthiaqua.**—Fairbanks, Hist. Fla., 105, 1871.

Mathomauk. A village of the Powhatan confederacy, in 1608, on the w. bank of James r., in Isle of Wight co., Va.—Smith (1629) Virginia, I, map, repr. 1819.

Mathue. A tribe that traded in 1652 with Indians on Patuxent r., Md. There is no means of determining its location

(Bozman, Maryland, II, 467, 1837). Possibly the Mantua, Monthees, or Munsees, or perhaps the Manta division of the Delawares. (J. M.)

Mathwa (*M'-ath-wa*, 'owl'). A gens of the Shawnee (q. v.).—Morgan, Anc. Soc., 168, 1877.

Matiliha. A large Chumashan village, said by Indians to have been on Buenaventura r., Ventura co., Cal. A village of this name is mentioned in mission archives as having been situated near Santa Inés mission.
Ma'-ti-la-ha.—Henshaw, Buenaventura MS. vocab., B. A. E., 1884. **Matiliha.**—Taylor in Cal. Farmer, Oct. 18, 1861. **Matilija.**—Ibid., July 24, 1863.

Matilpe ('head of the Maamtagyila'). A Kwakiutl sept which has recently branched off from the rest of the true Kwakiutl. The gentes are Maamtagyila, Gyeksem, and Haailakyemae. The principal winter village is Etsekin. Pop. 55 in 1904.
Mah-tee-oetp.—Can. Ind. Aff., 189, 1884. **Mahtilpi.**—Ibid., pt. 2, 166, 1901. **Mahtulth-pe.**—Sproat in Can. Ind. Aff., 145, 1879. **Mar-til-par.**—Kane, Wand. in N. Am., app., 1859. **Matelpa.**—Tolmie and Dawson, Comp. Vocabs. Brit. Col., 118B, 1884. **Mateltphpahs.**—Brit. Col. map, Victoria, 1872. **Mā-tilhpī.**—Dawson in Trans. Roy. Soc. Can. for 1887, sec. II, 65. **Mā'tilpē.**—Boas in 6th Rep. N. W. Tribes Can., 54, 1890. **Mā'tilpis.**—Boas in Petermanns Mitt., pt. 5, 130, 1887. **Mat-ul-pai.**—Tolmie and Dawson, Comp. Vocabs. Brit. Col., 118B, 1884. **Mur til par.**—Schoolcraft, Ind. Tribes, V, 488, 1855.

Matinecoc. An Algonquian tribe which formerly inhabited the N. w. coast of Long Island, N. Y., from Newtown, Queens co., to Smithtown, Suffolk co. They had villages at Flushing, Glen Cove, Cold Spring, Huntington, and Cow Harbor, but even before the intrusion of the whites they had become greatly reduced, probably through wars with the Iroquois, to whom they paid tribute. In 1650 Secretary Van Tienhoven reported but 50 families left of this once important tribe. Ruttenber includes them in his Montauk group, which is about equivalent to Metoac (q. v.); but the interrelationship of the tribes in the western part of Long Island has not been definitely determined. (J. M. C. T.)
Mantinacooks.—Macauley, N. Y., II, 164–65, 1829. **Mantinecooks.**—Clark, Onondaga, I, 18, 1849. **Mantinicooks.**—Macauley, N. Y., II, 292, 1829. **Martinne houck.**—Van Tienhoven (1650) in N. Y. Doc. Col. Hist., I, 366, 1856. **Matinecoc.**—Wood in Macauley, Long Id., II, 253, 1829. **Matinecocke.**—Terry (1670) in N. Y. Doc. Col. Hist., XIV, 639, 1883. **Matinecogh.**—Doc. of 1656, ibid., 369. **Matinecongh.**—Ibid. **Matinicock.**—Doc. of 1666, ibid., 589. **Matiniconck.**—Nicolls (1669), ibid., 621. **Matinnekonck.**—Doc. of 1644, ibid., 56. **Matinnicock.**—Nicolls (1666), ibid., 587. **Matninicongh.**—Nicolls (1664), ibid., 557. **Mattinacock.**—Houldsworth (1663), ibid., 530. **Mattinnekonck.**—Van Tienhoven (1655), ibid., 314.

Matironn. One of the Diegueño rancherias represented in the treaty of 1852 at Santa Isabel, s. Cal.—H. R. Ex. Doc. 76, 34th Cong., 3d sess., 133, 1857.

Matlaten (*Mat-la-ten*). A summer village of the Wiweakam between Bute and Loughborough inlets, Brit. Col.; pop. 125

in 1885.—Boas in Bull. Am. Geog. Soc., 230, 1887.

Matoaks. See *Pocahontas*.

Matomkin. A village of the Powhatan confederacy, still existing in 1722, about Metomkin inlet in Accomack co., Va. Not long before this time it had much decreased in population owing to an epidemic of smallpox.

Matampken.—Herrman map (1670) in Maps to Accompany the Rep. of the Comr's on the B'nd'ry Bet. Va. and Md., 1873 (Great and Little Matampken marked). **Matomkin.**—Beverley, Virginia, 199, 1722.

Matonumanke ('bear'). A Mandan band.

Bear.—Morgan, Anc. Soc., 158, 1877. **Mato-Mihte.**—Maximilian, Trav., 335, 1843. **Mä-to'-no-mäke.**—Morgan, op. cit. **Mato-Numangkake.**—Maximilian, op. cit. **Ma-to' nu-mañ'-ke.**—Dorsey in 15th Rep. B. A. E., 241, 1897.

Matora. An unidentified tribe placed by Marquette (Shea, Discov. Miss. Val., 268, 1852), on his map of 1673, w. of the Mississippi, about the w. border of Arkansas.

Matsaki ('salt city,' because the Zuñi Goddess of Salt is said to have made a white lake there). A ruined pueblo of the Zuñi near the N. W. base of Thunder mt., 3 m. E. of Zuñi pueblo, Valencia co., N. Mex. It was the Maçaque of Castañeda's narrative of Coronado's expedition in 1540–42, hence formed one of the Seven Cities of Cibola. It was occupied until the beginning of the Pueblo revolt of Aug., 1680, when it was permanently abandoned, the inhabitants fleeing with the other Zuñi to the summit of the adjacent Thunder mtn., there remaining for several years. During the mission period Matsaki was a visita of Halona. See Mindeleff in 8th Rep. B. A. E., 86, 1891, and the writers cited below. (F. W. H.)

Maçaque.—Castañeda (1596) in 14th Rep. B. A. E., 517, 1896. **Maçaqui.**—Bandelier in Mag. West. Hist., 669, Sept. 1886. **Macaqui.**—Oñate (1598) in Doc. Inéd., XVI, 133, 1871. **Macaquia.**—Bandelier in Arch. Inst. Papers, IV, 337, 1892 (misquoting Oñate, op. cit.). **Masaguia.**—De l'Isle, Atlas Nouveau, map 60, 1733. **Masaquia.**—De l'Isle, Carte Mexique et Floride, 1703. **Masiki.**—Peet in Am. Antiq., XVII, 352, 1895. **Ma-tsa-ki.**—Cushing in Century Mag., 38, 1888 (Zuñi name). **Mát-sa-kí.**—Cushing in Millstone, IX, 55, Apr. 1884 (Zuñi name). **Matsúki.**—ten Kate, Reizen in N. A., 290, 1885 (misquoting early Spanish form). **Matza-ki.**—Bandelier in Mag. West. Hist., 669, Sept. 1886. **Ma-tza Ki.**—Bandelier in Arch. Inst. Papers, III, 133, 1890. **Mâ-tza-qui.**—Bandelier in Revue d'Ethnographie, 201, 1886. **Matzaqui.**—Ibid., 208. **Mazaquia.**—Vetancurt (1693), Teatro Mex., III, 320, 1871. **Mazquía.**—Bancroft, Ariz. and N. Mex., 173, 1889 (misquoting Vetancurt). **Mazuqui.**—Bandelier quoted by Cushing in Millstone, IX, 55, Apr. 1884. **Mozaqui.**—Cushing in Compte-rendu Internat. Cong. Am., VII, 156, 1890. **Muzaque.**—Castañeda (1596) in Ternaux-Compans, Voy., IX, 163, 1888. **Muzaqui.**—Cushing in Compte-rendu Internat. Cong. Am., VII, 156, 1890 (misquoting Castañeda). **Salt City.**—Cushing, Zuñi Folk Tales, I, 32, 1901.

Matsnikth (*Măts-nĭk'ç'*). A former village of the Siuslaw on Siuslaw r., Oreg.—Dorsey in Jour. Am. Folk-lore, III, 230, 1890.

Matsqui (*Mă'çqui*). A Cowichan tribe on Fraser r. and Sumass lake, Brit. Col. Their villages are Mamakume and Kokoaeuk. Pop. 44 in 1904.

Mā'çqui.—Boas in 64th Rep. Brit. A. A. S., 454, 1894. **Maisqui.**—Brit. Col. map, Ind. Aff., Victoria, 1872. **Mamskey.**—Custer quoted by Gatschet, notes, B. A. E. **Matsqui.**—Can. Ind. Aff. for 1901, pt. II, 158.

Mattabesec (from *massa-sepuēs-et*, 'at a [relatively] great rivulet or brook.'—Trumbull). An important Algonquian tribe of Connecticut, formerly occupying both banks of Connecticut r. from Wethersfield to Middletown or to the coast and extending westward indefinitely. The Wongunk, Pyquaug, and Montowese Indians were a part of this tribe. According to Ruttenber they were a part of the Wappinger, and perhaps occupied the original territory from which colonies went out to overrun the country as far as Hudson r. The same author says their jurisdiction extended over all s. w. Connecticut, including the Mahackemo, Uncowa, Paugusset, Quinnipiac, Montowese, Sukiaug, and Tunxis. (J. M.)

Matabesec.—Kendall, Trav., I, 92, 1809. **Matabezeke.**—Doc. of 1646 cited by Trumbull, Ind. Names Conn., 26, 1881. **Matebeseck.**—Writer (ca. 1642) in Mass. Hist. Soc. Coll., 3d s., III, 161, 1833. **Matowepesack.**—Uncas deed (1665) cited by Trumbull, Ind. Names Conn., 26, 1881. **Mattabeeset.**—Stiles (1761) in Mass. Hist. Soc. Coll., 1st s., X, 105, 1809. **Mattabeseck.**—Record (1646) quoted by Trumbull, Conn., I, 510, 1818. **Mattabesett.**—Ind. deed (1673) cited by Trumbull, Ind. Names Conn., 26, 1881. **Mattabesicke.**—Haynes (1643) in Mass. Hist. Soc. Coll., 4th s., VI, 355, 1863. **Mattapeaset.**—Doc. of 1657 cited by Trumbull, Ind. Names Conn., 26, 1881. **Mattebeseck.**—Hoyt, Antiq. Res., 54, 1824. **Sequeen.**—Doc. of 1633 in N. Y. Doc. Col. Hist., II, 140, 1858 (title of chief). **Sequins.**—De Laet (1640) in N. Y. Hist. Soc. Coll., 2d s., I, 295, 1841. **Seqvins.**—Dutch map (1616) in N. Y. Doc. Col. Hist., I, 1856.

Mattabesec. The principal village of the Mattabesec, the residence of Sowheag, their head chief. It occupied the site of Middletown, Conn.

Mattabesett.—Field, Middlesex Co., 34, 1819.

Mattacock. A village of the Powhatan confederacy, in 1608, on the N. bank of York r., in Gloucester co., Va.—Smith (1629), Virginia, I, map, repr. 1819.

Mattacunt. A village of the Powhatan confederacy, in 1608, on the s. side of Potomac r., in King George co., Va.—Smith (1629), Virginia, I, map, repr. 1819.

Mattakeset. A village in E. Massachusetts, about the site of Yarmouth, Barnstable co. It is said to have been subject to the Wampanoag, but was in Nauset territory. It is mentioned in 1621, and in 1685 was still in existence, with a population of 70 Indians exceeding 12 years of age. (J. M.)

Matakees.—Gookin (1674) in Mass. Hist. Soc. Coll., 1st s., I, 148, 1806. **Matakeeset.**—Arnold and Morton (1683), ibid., 4th s., V, 86, 1861. **Matakeesit.**—Barber, Hist. Coll., 517, 1839. **Mattacheese.**—Mass. Hist. Soc. Coll., 1st s., III, 15, 1794. **Mattacheeset.**—Ibid. **Mattacheest.**—Ibid. **Mattachiest.**—Mourt (1622) quoted by Drake, Bk. Inds., bk. 2, 16, 1848. **Mattachist.**—Dee in Smith (1629), Virginia, II, 233, repr. 1819. **Mattakeese.**—Hinckley (1685) in Mass. Hist. Soc. Coll., 4th s., v, 133, 1861. **Mattakeeset.**—Humphreys (1815), ibid., 2d s., iv, 92, 1816. **Mattakesit.**—Rawson and Danforth (1698), ibid., 1st s., x, 129–34, 1809.

Mattakeset. A former village situated about the site of Duxbury, Plymouth co., Mass. It was probably subject to the Wampanoag. In 1685 it had 40 inhabitants exceeding 12 years of age. (J. M.)
Namatakeeset.—Hinckley (1685) in Mass. Hist. Soc. Coll., 4th s., v, 133, 1861.

Mattamuskeet. A village of the Machapunga, the only one belonging to the tribe in 1700–01, and containing then, according to Lawson, 30 warriors. Probably situated on the lake of the same name in Hyde co., N. C.
Marimiskeet.—Lawson (1714), Hist. Car., 383, repr. 1860. **Masammaskete.**—Col. Rec. N. C. (1713), II, 32, 1886. **Matamaskite.**—Ibid., 29. **Matamuskeet.**—Ibid., 31. **Mattamuskeets.**—Ibid., 45. **Mattecumska.**—Col. Rec. N. C. (1713), II, 2, 1886. **Mattemusket.**—Ibid., 168.

Mattanock. A village of the Powhatan confederacy, in 1608, on the w. side of Nansemond r., near its mouth, in Nansemond co., Va.—Smith (1629), Virginia, I, map, repr. 1819.

Mattapanient (probably of the same meaning as Mattapony, q. v.). An Algonquian tribe or band that formerly lived on Patuxent r., Md., probably in St Marys co. Their principal village, of the same name, may have been at Mattapony cr. A Catholic mission was established there in 1636. In 1651 they, with others, were removed to a tract on Wicomico r. They were possibly but a band or division of the Conoy (q. v.), and are to be distinguished from the Mattapony of Virginia, sometimes written Mattapanient. (J. M.)
Matapaman.—Map, ca. 1640 or 1650, in Maps to Accompany the Rept. of the Comr's on the Bnd'y bet. Va. and Md., 1873. **Matpanient.**—Bozman, Md., I, 141, 1837. **Mattapament.**—Strachey (ca. 1612), Virginia, 39, 1849. **Mattapanians.**—Bozman, Md., II, 421, 1837. **Mattapanient.**—Smith (1629), Virginia, I, 118, repr. 1819. **Mattapany.**—Herrman, Map (1670), in Maps to Accompany the Rept. of the Comr's on the Bnd'y bet. Va. and Md., 1873. **Mattpament.**—Smith (1629), Virginia, I, map, repr. 1819. **Metapawnien.**—White (1639), Relatio Itineris, 63, 1874.

Mattapoiset (a form of Mattabesec, q. v.). A village, in 1622, near the present Mattapoisett, Plymouth co., Mass.
Mataopoisett.—Deed of 1664 in Drake, Bk. Inds., bk., 3, 14, 1848. **Mattapoiset.**—Watts (1734) in Mass. Hist. Soc. Coll., 2d s., x, 31, 1823. **Mattapuist.**—Harris, Voy. and Trav., I, 856, 1705. **Mattapuyst.**—Mourt (1622) in Mass. Hist. Soc. Coll., 1st s., VIII, 258, 1802.

Mattapony. The proper form of this name, both in Virginia and Maryland, appears to be Mattapanient, although both that and Mattapament occur on Capt. John Smith's map and in his text, the latter being probably a misprint. Heckewelder's attempted interpretation of 'bad bread', or 'no bread at all', based on the theory that it contains the word *pona*, 'pone', 'bread', is evidently without value. The Mattapony is a small tribe

of the Powhatan confederacy (q. v.) living in 1608, according to Smith, on Mattapony r., Va., and having 30 men, or a total of perhaps a little more than 100. On Smith's map the town "Mattapanient" appears to be located in the upper part of the present James City co., near the mouth of Chickahominy r. In 1781, according to Jefferson (Notes on Va., 1825), they still numbered 15 or 20, largely of negro blood, on a small reservation on the river of their name. These figures, however, are probably too low, as the name is still preserved by about 45 persons of mixed blood on a small state reservation on the s. side of Mattapony r., in King William co. These survivors are closely related to the Pamunkey, whose reservation is only 10 m. distant. See *Mattapanient*. (J. M.)
Mattapament.—Smith, Hist. Va. (1624), Arber ed., 347, 1884. **Mattapanient.**—Ibid., map. **Mattapomens.**—Boudinot, Star in the West, 127, 1816. **Mattapoments.**—Macauley, N, Y., II, 168, 1829. **Mattaponies.**—Jefferson (1781), Notes, 130, 1825.

Mattawamkeag ('a bar of gravel divides the river in two.'—Vetromile). A principal Penobscot village formerly on Penobscot r., about Mattawamkeag point, Penobscot co., Me.
Madawamkee. — Gyles (1736) in Drake, Trag. Wild., 78, 1841. **Mattawamkeag.**—Godfrey in Me. Hist. Soc. Coll., VII, 4, 1876. **Mattawankeag.**—Vetromile, Abnakis, 52–53, 1866. **Metta8akik.**—Maurault, Abenakis, v, 1866. **Montawanekeag.**—Conf. (1786) in Me. Hist. Soc. Coll., VII, 10, 1876.

Mattawan ('river of shallows.'—Hewitt). A popular name for the Algonquian Indians living on Mattawan r., a branch of upper Ottawa r., Ontario. They are probably a part of the Nipissing or of the Temiscaming, q. v. Cf. *Matawachkarini*. (J. M.)
Mataoüiriou.—Jes. Rel. 1672, 46, 1858. **Mataovan.**—La Hontan (1703), New Voy., map, 1735. **Matawáng.**—Wm. Jones, inf'n, 1905 (correct form). **Matawin**—McLean, Hudson Bay, I, 87, 1849.

Mattawottis. A former Diegueño rancheria under the mission of San Miguel de la Frontera, N. Lower California.—Taylor in Cal. Farmer, May 18, 1860.

Mattinacook. A band of the Penobscot who, in 1876, occupied Mattinacook id. in Penobscot r., near Lincoln, Penobscot co., Me.
Mattanawcook. — Me. Hist. Soc. Coll., VII, 103, note, 1876.

Mattituck (*Matuh'tugk*, 'place without wood', or 'badly wooded.'—Trumbull). A Corchaug village, about 1640, on the site of the present Mattituck, Suffolk co., Long Island, N. Y. (J. M.)
Mattatovan.—Trumbull, Ind. Names Conn., 27, 1881 (early form). **Mattatuck.** — Records (1649) in Thompson, Long Id., I, 378, 1843. **Mattetuck.**—Thompson, ibid., 392.

Mattole (*Wishosk* name). An Athapascan tribe whose principal settlements were along Bear and Mattole rs., Cal. They resisted the white race more vigorously than the natives of this region generally did and suffered practical extermination in return. They were gathered on a reservation near C. Mendocino for a time, and some of them were afterward taken to Hupa Valley res. A few still live in their old territory. They differ somewhat from their Athapascan neighbors in language and culture; they burn the dead; the men tattoo a distinctive mark on the forehead, but in other respects they are similar to the Hupa. (P. E. G.)

Matole.—Bancroft, Nat. Races, III, 643, 1874. Mattóal.—Powers in Cont. N. A. Ethnol., III, 107, 1877. Mattole.—Ind. Aff. Rep. 1864, 119, 1865. Tul'bush.—Powers, op. cit., 124 ('foreigners': Wailaki name).

Mattowacca. A name of the hickory shad (*Clupea mediocris*), found from Newfoundland to Florida; probably from one of the southeastern dialects of the Algonquian stock. (A. F. C.)

Matyata (or *Mák'yana*, contracted from *Mák'yanawin*, 'country of the salt lake.'—Cushing). Described by Fray Marcos de Niza in 1539, under the name Marata, as a province s. E. of Cibola (Hakluyt, Voy., III, 440), although Coronado, in the following year, asserted that "the kingdom of Marata is not to be found, neither have the Indians any knowledge thereof." Bandelier and Cushing identify Marata with Matyata, or Makyata, "the name given by the Zuñi to a cluster of now ruined pueblos which they declare to have been occupied by a branch of their own people. After long dissensions and even warfare with the inhabitants of the Zuñi basin, those of Matyata were compelled to submit, and to join the former in their settlements. The group of ruins called Matyata or Makyata lies s. E. of Zuñi on the trail leading to Acoma; and the condition of the ruins (described by Alvarado in 1540) shows that their abandonment is more recent than that of other ancient pueblos in that region." According to Cushing descendants of the former inhabitants of Matyata are to-day residents of Zuñi. Consult Bandelier in Arch. Inst. Papers, III, 120, 1890; v, 174, 1890; and for Alvarado's description of these supposed ruins see Winship in 14th Rep. B. A. E., 1896. See *Kyama-kyakwe, Kyatsutuma, Pikyaaiwan.*

Ar-che-o-tek-o-pa.—Fewkes in Jour. Am. Eth. and Arch., I, 100, 1891. Ma'-k'ya-na.—Cushing, inf'n, 1891 (or Ma'-k'ya-na-win: 'country of the salt lake'). Ma-kya-ta.—Cushing quoted by Bandelier in Arch. Inst. Papers, III, 120, 1890 (Ma-tya-ta, or). Marata.—Marcos de Niza (1539) in Hakluyt, Voy., III, 440, 1600. Marta.—Mota-Padilla, Hist. de la Conquista, 169, 1742 (Marata, or). Ma-tya-ta.—Cushing quoted by Bandelier, op. cit. (or Ma-kya-ta). Ma-tyâta.—Bandelier in Revue d'Ethnographie, 206, 1886.

Maugna. A former Gabrieleño rancheria in Los Angeles co., Cal., at a locality later called Rancho Felis.—Ried (1852) quoted by Taylor in Cal. Farmer, June 8, 1860.

Maukekose (probably for *Ma'kons,* 'bear cub,' or 'little bear.'—W. J.). A former Potawatomi village, commonly known as Mau-ke-kose's village, from the name of

its chief, near the head of Wolf cr., in Marshall co., Ind., on a reservation sold under the provisions of the treaty of Dec. 10, 1834. The name is also written Muckkose and Muck-Rose. (J. M.)

Mauls. See *Hammers.*

Maumee Towns. A common name for a group of villages formerly at the head of Maumee r., near Ft Wayne, Allen co., Ind. When destroyed by the whites in 1790 there were 7 villages, all within a few miles of each other, on the Maumee or its branches. Two of these were Miami, three Delaware, and two Shawnee. Omee was the principal one, and together they contained about 225 houses. See *Kekionga.*

Maumee towns.—So called from their situation on Maumee r. Omee towns.—Harmar (1790) in Rupp, West. Pa., app., 225, 1846 (commonly so called; Omee is the French Au Mi, contracted from Au Miami; Omee is given by Harmar as the name of the principal village, on the site of Kekionga, while he puts "Kegaiogue" on the opposite bank of St Joseph r.).

Maushantuxet ('at or in the little place of much wood,' or 'smaller wooded tract of land,' in contradistinction to Mashantucket, or Mashantackuck, the name of a tract on the w. side of Thames r., in Montville.—Trumbull). A Pequot settlement in 1762, at the site of the present Ledyard, New London co., Conn.

Mashantucket.—Early records quoted by Trumbull, Ind. Names Conn., 26, 1881 (an occasional form). Maushantuxet.—Stiles (1761) in Mass. Hist. Soc. Coll., 1st s., X, 102, 1809. Musshuntucksett.—Stiles quoted by Trumbull, op. cit.

Maushapogue (probably 'great pond,' from *massa,* 'great', *pog* or *peag,* 'pond'; or *massa-pe-auk,* 'great-water land'; cf. *Mashpee* and *Massapequa*). A village, probably belonging to the Narraganset, in Providence co., R. I., in 1637.

Mashapauge.—Williams (1661) in R. I. Col. Rec., I, 18, 1856. Mashapawog.—Doc. of 1640, ibid., 28. Maushapogue.—Deed of 1637, ibid., 18.

Mauthæpi (Wood Cree: *mathipi,* 'bad water.'—Gerard). A Montagnais tribe in 1863 on the reservation at Manicouagan, on St Lawrence r., Quebec.—Hind, Lab. Penin., II, 124, 1863.

Mawakhota ('skin smeared with whitish earth'). A band of the Two-kettle Sioux.

Ma-waḣota.—Dorsey in 15th Rep. B. A. E., 220, 1897. Ma-waqota.—Ibid.

Mawsootoh (*Maw-soo-toh'*, 'bringing along'). A subclan of the Delawares (q. v.).—Morgan, Anc. Soc., 172, 1877.

Mayaca. A Timucuan district and village, about 1565, on the E. coast of N. Florida. De Bry locates it E. of upper St Johns r.; Bartram, E. of L. George.

Macoiya.—Fairbanks, Hist. Fla., 139, 1871. Macoya.—Barcia, Ensayo, 129, 1723. Maquarqua.—Shipp, De Soto and Fla., 517, 1881. Masarquam.—Barcia, Ensayo, 51, 1723. Mayaca.—Fontaneda (1575), Memoir, Smith trans., 21, 1854. Mayaco.—Bartram, Voy., I, map, 1799. Mayarca.—De Bry, Brev. Nar., II, map, 1591. Mayarqua.—Laudonnière (1564), L'Hist. Notable, 108, 1853.

Mayajuaca. A former Timuquanan village on the E. coast of Florida, N. of the Ais country.

Mayaguaci.—Fontaneda (1575) in Doc. Inéd., v, 544, 1866. **Mayajuaca**.—Fontaneda in Ternaux-Compans, Voy., xx, 26, 1841. **Nayajuaca**.—Ibid., 35.

Mayara. A Timucuan chief, said to have been "rich in gold and silver," and also the name of his town on lower St Johns r., Fla., in the 16th century.

Maiera.—De Bry, Brev. Nar., II, map, 1591. **Mayara.**—Laudonnière (1564) in French, Hist. Coll. La., 242, 1869. **Mayrra**.—Laudonnière, Hist. Notable, 88, 1853.

Maycock. A sort of squash or pumpkin. According to Schele de Vere (Americanisms, 60, 1871) it is still found in Virginia. Trumbull (Sci. Pap. Asa Gray, I, 336, 1889) cites as early forms *macocks* (Smith, 1606–08), *macock* gourd (Strachey, 1610), *macokos* (Strachey), and *macocqwer* (L'Ecluse, 1591–1605). Beverley (Hist. Va., 124, 1705) identifies the *maycock* with the squash of New England. Smith (Arber ed., 359, 1884) describes *macocks* as "a fruit like unto a muske mellon, butt lesse and worse." The word is derived from a form of *mahawk*, 'gourd', in the Virginian dialect of Algonquian, cognate with the Delaware *machgachk*, 'pumpkin.' See *Macocks*. (A. F. C.)

Mayes, Joel Bryan. A prominent mixed-blood of the Cherokee tribe and twice principal chief of the nation. He was born Oct. 2, 1833, in the old Cherokee Nation, near the present Cartersville, Ga. His father, Samuel Mayes, was a white man from Tennessee, while his mother, Nancy Adair, was of mixed blood, the daughter of Walter Adair, a leading tribal officer, and granddaughter of John, one of the Adair brothers, traders among the Cherokee before the Revolution. The boy removed with the rest of his tribe in 1838 to Indian Ter., where he afterward was graduated from the male seminary at Tahlequah, and after a short experience at teaching school, engaged in stockraising until the outbreak of the Civil war in 1861, when he enlisted as a private in the First Confederate Indian Brigade, coming out at the close of the war as quartermaster. He returned to his home on Grand r. and resumed his former occupation, but was soon after made successively clerk of the district court, circuit judge (for two terms of 10 years in all), associate justice, and chief justice of the Cherokee supreme court. In 1887 he was elected principal chief of the Cherokee Nation, succeeding D. W. Bushyhead, and was reelected in 1891, but died in office at Tahlequah, Dec. 14 of that year, being succeeded by Col. C. J. Harris. Chief Mayes was of fine physique, kindly disposition, and engaging personality. He was three times married, his last wife having been Miss Mary Vann, of a family distinguished in Cherokee history. (J. M.)

Mayeye. A former Tonkawan tribe which, in the first half of the 18th century, lived near San Xavier r., Tex., apparently either modern San Gabriel or Little r. Joutel in 1687 (Margry, Déc., III, 288, 1878) heard of the Meghey N. of Colorado r., somewhere near where the Spaniards later actually found the Mayeye. Rivera (Diario, leg. 2062, 1736) in 1727 met them at springs called Puentezitas, 15 leagues w. of the junction of the two arms of the Brazos and 35 leagues from the Colorado. In 1738 they were mentioned with the Deadoses (q. v.) of the same locality (Orobio y Basterra, letter of Apr. 26, Archivo General, MS.). About 1744 Fray Mariano Francisco de los Dolores visited a ranchería of Mayeyes, Yojuanes, Deadoses, Bidais, and others near San Xavier r. (Arricivita, Chronica, pt. 2, 322, 1792). In 1740 it had been planned to take this and the Sana (Zana) tribes to San Antonio (Descripción, 1740, Mem. Nueva España, xxviii, 203, MS.), where a few of the Sanas and Ervipiames had already been gathered. As a result of the efforts of Father Dolores, 4 chiefs of the "Yojuanes, Deadoses, Maieyes, and Rancheria Grande" went to San Antonio to ask for a mission (Despatch of the Viceroy, Mar. 26, 1751, Lamar Papers, MS.), and about 1747 the San Xavier group of missions was founded for them. When the site was abandoned, "notwithstanding the tenacity with which the Mayeyes especially had always clung to the district of San Xavier," some of them were moved to the Guadalupe, where an abortive attempt was made to reestablish them (Arricivita, op. cit., 337). Some of the Mayeye who had been baptized at San Xavier entered San Antonio de Valero mission at San Antonio, and were living there as late as 1769 (MS. Burial records). The Mayeye and their relations were bitter enemies of the Apache, and in the middle of the 18th century, when the Comanche forced the Apache southward, the Mayeye and other Tonkawans were apparently pushed to the S. E., where they mingled with the Karankawan tribes. In 1772 Mezières (Informe, July 4, 1772, MS.) said the Mayeye wandered with the Tonkawa and Yojuane between the Trinity and the Brazos; and in the same year Bonilla, quoting Mezières, associated them with the same tribes, all of whom, though in alliance with the Wichita and their congeners, were despised by the latter as vagabonds. Such has been the usual attitude of other tribes toward the Tonkawa ever since. While Bucareli existed on the Trinity, from 1774 to 1779, the Mayeye visited it. In 1778 Mezières (Carta, Mar. 18, MS.) reported 20 families of Coco and Mayeye apostates opposite Culebra id., in the

Karankawa country. In 1779 the Spanish government feared an alliance of Mayeye, Coco, Karankawa, and Arkokisa (Croix to Cabello, Dec. 4, MS.). The Mayeye were included in the census of 1790, and were in the jurisdiction of Nacogdoches. Sibley, in 1805, says the "Mayes" were then living on San Gabriel cr., near the mouth of the Guadalupe, on St Bernard bay, Tex., and numbered about 200 men; they were hostile to the Spaniards, but professed friendship for the French; they were surrounded by tribes speaking languages different from their own and were adept in the sign language. The last trace of the tribe was found by Gatschet in 1884 (Karankawa Inds., 36, 1891), when he met an old Indian who had known this people in his early days on the Texas coast, and who stated that they spoke a dialect of the Tonkawa.

(A. C. F.   H. E. B.)

Macheyes.—Mezières (1772) quoted by Bonilla in Tex. Hist. Ass'n Quar., VIII, 66, 1905. **Maghai.**—Joutel (1687) in French, Hist. Coll. La., I, 137, 1846. **Maheyes.**—Mezières (1772), op. cit. **Maieces.**—Orobio y Basterra (1738), op. cit. **Maieyes.**—Span. Doc., Mar. 6, 1768, in Bexar archives. **Malleyes.**—Rivera, Diario, leg. 2602, 1736. **Mayeces.**—Barrios, Informe, MS., 1771. **Mayees.**—Brackenridge, Views La., 87, 1814. **Mayes.**—Sibley, Hist. Sketches, 72, 1806. **Mayeyes.**—Census of 1790 quoted by Gatschet, Karankawa Inds., 35, 1891. **Meghay.**—Joutel cited by Shea, note in Charlevoix, New France, IV, 78, 1870. **Meghey.**—Joutel (1687) in Margry, Déc., III, 288, 1878. **Meghty.**—Joutel (1687) in French, Hist. Coll. La., I, 152, 1846. **Meihites.**—Barcia, Ensayo, 271, 1723. **Méye.**—Gatschet, op. cit., 36, 1891 (Tonkawa name). **Miyi.**—Ibid. **Muleyes.**—Morfi, Mem. Hist. Tex., ca. 1782.

Mayi. An important Pomo village on upper Clear lake, Cal.—A. L. Kroeber, Univ. Cal. MS., 1903.

Mayndeshkish ('Coyote pass'). An Apache clan or band at San Carlos agency and Ft Apache, Ariz., in 1881 (Bourke in Jour. Am. Folk-lore, III, 112, 1890). The corresponding clan of the Navaho is Maltheshkizh.

Mayne Island. The local name for a body of Sanetch on the s. e. coast of Vancouver id.; pop. 28 in 1904.—Can. Ind. Aff. for 1902 and 1904.

Mayo ('terminus', because the Mayo r. was the dividing line between them and their enemies.—Ribas). One of the principal tribes of the Cahita group of the Piman stock, residing on the Rio Mayo, Sinaloa, Mexico. Their language differs only dialectically from that of the Yaqui and the Tehueco. The first notice of the tribe is probably that in the "Se-

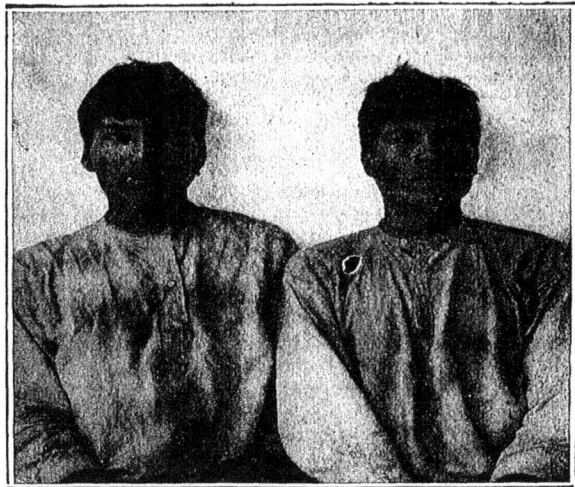

MAYO MEN.   (AM. MUS. NAT. HIST.)

gunda Relacion Anonima" of the journey of Nuño de Guzman, about 1530 (in Icazbalceta, Coleccion de Documentos, II, 300, 1866), where it is stated that after passing over the Rio de Tamachola (Fuerte) and traveling 30 leagues (northward) they came to a river called Mayo on which lived a people of the same name. Ribas (p. 237) declares that in his day it was the most populous of all the tribes of Sinaloa, estimating their number at 30,000, some 8,000 or 10,000 of whom were warriors. He did not consider them so

MAYO GIRLS.   (AM. MUS. NAT. HIST.)

warlike as the surrounding tribes, but in their customs, dwellings, and other respects the Mayo resembled them. Hardy (Travels in Mexico, 424, 1829) states that at the time of his visit there were 10 towns on the Rio Mayo, with an estimated population of 10,000. According to Davila (Sonora, 315, 1894) their industries were reduced to the cultivation of the soil, the raising of sheep and domestic birds, and the manufacture of woolen shawls. He says the Mayo pueblos are larger than those of the Yaqui, but the number of people of the latter is now greater than that of the former. The

Mayo settlements, so far as known, are Baca, Batacosa, Camoa, Conicari, Cuirimpo, Echojoa, Huatabampo, Macoyahui, Masiaca, Navojoa, San Pedro, Santa Cruz de Mayo, Tepahue, Tesia, and Toro. See *Cahita*. (F. W. H.)

Mago.—ten Kate in Bull. Soc. d'Anthrop. de Paris, 375, 1883 (misprint). **Maya.**—Ribas, Hist. Triumphos, 237, 1645. **Mayo.**—Rel. Anonima (1530), op. cit.

Maypop. The fruit of the passion-flower (*Passiflora incarnata*). Capt. John Smith (Va., 123, repr. 1819) and Strachey (Trav. Va., 72) speak of this fruit as *maracock* and state that the Indians cultivated it before the coming of the whites. Trumbull (Sci. Pap. Asa Gray, 342, 1889) considers that *maracock* is the Brazilian Tupi *mburucuia*, related to the Carib *merécoya* (Breton, 1665), the fruit of a vine, the name and the thing having both come from South America. *Maypop* would thus ultimately represent, through *maracock*, this Tupi loan-word. (A. F. C.)

Maysonec. A village of the Powhatan confederacy, in 1608, on the N. bank of the Chickahominy, in New Kent co., Va.— Smith (1629), Va., I, map, repr. 1819.

Mazakutemani ('shoots the gun [iron] as he walks'). A chief of the Sisseton Sioux, born at Lac-qui-Parle, Minn., in 1806; died near Sisseton, S. Dak., in 1887. In his early manhood he followed strictly the customs of his tribe; in 1850 he was a member of the Sisseton and Wahpeton delegation to Washington, and a signer of the Traverse des Sioux treaty of July 23, 1851. About 1855 he became a convert to Christianity and thenceforward was an ardent supporter of the missionary work of Rev. Stephen R. Riggs. It was in the spring of 1857, when the massacre at Spirit Lake, Iowa, by Inkpaduta's band occurred, that Mazakutemani particularly manifested his friendship for the whites by following the murderous band and rescuing Miss Gardner, the only surviving white captive. Again, in 1862, on receiving word of the Sioux outbreak, he employed every effort to stay the massacre and to rescue the white captives, going boldly into the hostile camps and using his oratorical powers to accomplish his purpose. The final escape of the captives from death on this occasion was due largely to Mazakutemani's efforts and his cooperation with Gen. Sibley. He was the chief speaker for the Sisseton in their tribal deliberations as well as in their treaty negotiations with the United States commissioners. In addition to the treaty of Traverse des Sioux he signed the treaties of Washington, June 19, 1858; Sisseton agency, Dak., Sept. 20, 1872, and Lac Traverse agency, Dak., May 2, 1873. Consult S. R. Riggs (1) in Minn. Hist. Soc. Coll., III, 82, 90, 1880; (2) Mary and I, 141, 1880; Heard, Hist. Sioux War, 156, 1863; Robinson in Monthly S. Dakotan, III, 208, 1900. (C. T.)

Mazapes. A former tribe of N. E. Mexico or S. Texas, probably Coahuiltecan, drawn from Nuevo Leon and gathered into the mission of San Antonio Galindo Moctezuma, in Coahuila. Cf. *Mahuames*.

Mazames.—Archivo General, XXXI, fol. 208, quoted by Orozco y Berra, Geog., 306, 1864 (probably identical). **Mazapes.**—Orozco y Berra, ibid., 302.

Mazapeta ('iron fire'). A chief of a village of 627 Yankton and Sisseton Sioux on Big Stone lake, Minn., in 1836. He was probably chief of the Yankton in the village, while The Grail was chief of the Sisseton.

Mahzahpatah.—Schoolcraft, Ind. Tribes, III, 612, 1853.

Mazpegnaka ('piece of metal in the hair'). A band of the Sans Arcs Sioux.—Dorsey in 15th Rep. B. A. E., 219, 1897.

Mdeiyedan (French: '*Lac qui parle*,' 'Speaking lake'). A band of the Wahpeton Sioux whose habitat was around Lac qui Parle, Minn. In 1836 (Schoolcraft, Ind. Tribes, III, 612, 1853) the band numbered 530 under Little Chief.

Lac qui Parle band.—Ind. Aff. Rep. 1859, 102, 1860. **Lacquiparle Indians.**—Sibley (1852) in Sen. Ex. Doc. 29, pt. 2, 32d Cong., 2d sess., 9, 1853. **Upper Wahpaton.**—Sibley (1873) in Minn. Hist. Soc. Coll., III, 250, 1880.

Mdewakanton ('mystery lake village,' from *mde* 'lake', *wakan* 'sacred mystery', *otonwe* 'village'). One of the subtribes composing the Santee division of the Dakota, the other 3 being the Sisseton, Wahpeton, and Wahpekute. A. L. Riggs contends that the Mdewakanton are the only Dakota entitled to the name Isanyati ('Santee'), given them from their old home on Mille Lac, Minn., called by them Isantamde, 'knife lake.' In every respect this tribe appears to be most intimately related to the Wahpeton. Wahpekute, and Sisseton. It is possible that the Mdewakanton formed the original stem from which the other 3 subtribes were developed. It is probable that the Nadowessioux mentioned by early missionaries and explorers were in most cases the people of this tribe and the tribes associated with them then living in the region of Mille Lac and the headwaters of the Mississippi. Dr Williamson, who spent years among these Indians, fixes the home of this tribe (who by tradition had once lived on Lake of the Woods and N. of the great lakes and had migrated toward the S. w.) at Mille Lac, the source of Rum r., which is apparently the ancient location of the Issati of Hennepin. This identifies the Issati with the Mdewakanton and sustains the conclusion of Riggs. After the Mdewakanton came to the Mississippi they appear to have scattered themselves along that river in several villages extending from Sauk Rap-. ids to the mouth of Wisconsin r. and up the Minnesota 35 m. According to Neill (Minn. Hist. Coll., I, 262, 1872) this splitting into bands was due to the influence of French traders. This author asserts that the people of this division were still residing at Mille Lac at the time Le Sueur built his post near the mouth of Blue Earth r. in 1700, and that their change of location to the region of lower Minnesota r. was due to the establishment of trading posts in that section. This would indicate a later removal to that locality than Williamson supposed. Rev. G. H. Pond, as quoted by Neill, says: "When to this we add the fact that traders taught them to plant corn, which actually took the place of wild rice, nothing was wanting to bring the Mdewakantons south to the Minnesota r. Accordingly tradition tells us that this division of the Dakotas no sooner became acquainted with traders, and the advantage of the trade, than they erected their teepees around the log hut of the white man and hunted in the direction of the Minnesota r., returning in the 'rice-gathering moon' (September) to the rice swamps nearest their friends." In Le Sueur's list of the eastern Dakota tribes the name Issati is dropped and that of Mdewakanton, under the form Mendeouacantons, is used, evidently for the first time. The whites came into more intimate relation with this tribe than with any other of the Dakota group, but the history—which is not of general interest except in so far as it relates to the outbreak of 1862, in which some of them took an active part— is chiefly that of the different bands and not of the tribe as a whole. After their defeat by the United States, they and the Winnebago were removed to Crow Creek res., Dakota Ter. Subsequently the Mdewakanton and Wahpekute were transferred to the Santee res. in Nebraska. Ultimately lands were assigned them in severalty, the reservation was abolished, and the Indians became citizens of the United States. In general customs and beliefs they resemble the other divisions of the eastern Sioux. (See *Dakota.*)

The tribe joined in the following treaties with the United States: Prairie du Chien, Wis., July 15, 1830, by which they and other eastern Sioux tribes ceded a strip 20 m. wide from the Mississippi to Des Moines r., Ia. Convention at St Peters, Minn., Nov. 30, 1836, with the upper Mdewakanton, agreeing on certain stipulations regarding the treaty of July 15, 1830. Treaty of Washington, Sept. 29, 1837, by which they ceded to the United States all their interest in lands E. of the Mississippi. Treaty of Mendota, Minn., Aug. 5, 1851, by which they ceded all

their lands in Iowa and Minnesota, retaining as a reservation a tract 10 m. wide on each side of Minnesota r. Treaty of Washington, June 19, 1858, by which they sold that part of their reservation N. of Minnesota r., retaining the portion s. of the river, which they agreed to take in severalty. By act of Mar. 3, 1863, the President was authorized to set apart for them a reserve beyond the limits of any state and remove them thereto, their reserve in Minnesota to be sold for their benefit. The new reserve was established by Executive order, July 1, 1863, on Crow cr., S. Dak. See *Reservations.*

Lewis and Clark (1804) estimated them at 300 fighting men or 1,200 souls; Long in 1822 (Exped. St Peter's R., 380, 1824) estimated the various bands as follows:

MDEWAKANTON

Keoxa (Kiyuksa), 400; Eanbosandata (Khemnichan), 100; Kapozha, 300; Oanoska (Ohanhanska), 200; Tetankatano (Tintaotonwe), 150; Taoapa, 300; Weakaote (Khemnichan), 50. According to the Census of 1890 there were 869 Mdewakanton and Wahpekute on Santee reservation, Nebr., and 292 at Flandreau, S. Dak. The report for 1905 mentions as not under an agent 150 at Birch Cooley and 779 elsewhere in Minnesota. The recognized divisions are as follows: (1) Kiyuksa, (2) Ohanhanska, (3) Tacanhpisapa, (4) Anoginajin, (5) Tintaotonwe, and (6) Oyateshicha, belonging to the Wakpaatonwedan division, which seems to have constituted the whole tribe in early times, and (7) Khemnichan, (8) Kapozha, (9) Magayuteshni, (10) Mahpiyamaza, (11) Mahpiyawichasta, (12) Kheyataotonwe, and (13) Taoapa, constituting the Matantonwan division, which early French writers spoke of as a powerful tribe associated with but not a part of the Mdewakanton. The following subdivisions have not been identified: Town band Indians, Mankato, Nasiampaa, Star band, and Upper Medawakanton.

See Dorsey, Siouan Sociology, 15th Rep. B. A. E., 1897; Long, Exped. St Peter's R., 1824; Ind. Aff. Rep., 1847; Ramsey in Minn. Hist. Coll., I, 1872; Neill, Hist. Minn., 1858. (J. O. D. C. T.)

Gens de Lac.—Pike, Exped., 93, 1810. **Gens De Lai.**—Schermerhorn (1812) in Mass. Hist. Soc. Coll., 2d s., II, 40, 1814 (misprint). **Gens du Lac.**—Long, Exped. St. Peter's R., I, 380, 1824. **Mad-a-wakan-toan.**—Sweetser (1853) in Sen. Ex. Doc. 61, 33d Cong., 1st sess., 2, 1854. **Madawakanton.**—Manypenny in H. R. Rep. 138, 33d Cong., 1st sess., 10, 1854. **Manchokatous.**—Prise de Possession (1689) in Margry, Déc., v, 34, 1883. **Mandawakantons.**—Ind. Aff. Rep., 853, 1847. **Mandawakanton Sioux.**—Ibid. **Mandeouacantons.**—Le Sueur (1700) in Margry, Déc., VI, 81, 1886. **Mawtawbauntowahs.**—Carver, Trav., 60, 1778. **Mdawakontons.**—Minn. Hist. Soc. Coll., III, 86, 1880. **Mdawakontonwans.**—Ibid., 84. **M'day-wah-kaun-twan Dakotas.**—Ramsey, ibid., I, 45. 1872. **M'day-wah-kauntwaun Sioux.**—Sibley, ibid., 47. **M'daywakantons.**—Ibid., III, 250, 1880. **M'daywawkawntwawns.**—Neill, Hist. Minn., 144, note, 1858. **Mdeiyedan.**—Ashley, letter to Dorsey, Jan. 1886. **Mde-wahantonwan.**—Schoolcraft, Ind. Tribes, I, 248, 1851. **M'dewakanton.**—Nicollet, Rep. on Upper Miss. R., map, 1843. **Mde-wa-kan-ton-wan.**—Neill, Hist. Minn., 144, note, 1858. **Mdewakantonwan.**—Riggs, Dakota Gram. and Dict., vii, 1852. **M'de-wakan-towwans.**—Ramsey in Ind. Aff. Rep. 1849, 78, 1850. **M'dewakant'wan.**—Ibid. **Md-Wakans.**—Peet in Am. Antiq., VIII, 304, 1886. **Mdwakantonwans.**—Riggs in Minn. Hist. Soc. Coll., III, 126, 1880. **Medaquakantoan.**—Ramsey (1853) in Sen. Ex. Doc. 61, 33d Cong., 1st sess., 324, 1854. **Medawah-Kanton.**—Maximilian, Trav., 507, 1843. **Med-a-wakan-toan.**—Sweetser in Sen. Ex. Doc. 61, 33d Cong., 1st sess., 2, 1854. **Medawakantons.**—Ind. Aff. Rep., 494, 1839. **Med-a-wa-kanton Sioux.**—Ind. Aff. Rep., 495, 1838. **Medawakantwan.**—Parker, Minn. Handbk., 140, 1857. **Me-da-we-con-tong.**—U. S. Ind. Treat., 368, 1826. **Medaykantoans.**—Ramsey in Sen. Ex. Doc. 61, 33d Cong., 1st sess., 337, 1854. **Med-ay-wah-kawn-t'waron.**—Ramsey in Ind. Aff. Rep. 1849, 78, 1850. **Medaywakanstoan.**—Ind. Aff. Rep., 18, 1851. **Med-ay-wa-kan-toan.**—U. S. Stat., x, 56, 1853. **Medaywokant'wans.**—Pike quoted by Neill, Hist. Minn., 288, 1858. **Me-de-wah-kan-toan.**—Sweetser in Sen. Ex. Doc. 61, 33d Cong., 1st sess., 321, 1854. **Medewakantoans.**—Sweetser in Sen. Ex. Doc. 29, 32d Cong., 2d sess., 14, 1853. **Medewakantons.**—Neill in Minn. Hist. Soc. Coll., I, 260, 1872. **Mede-wakan-t'wans.**—Ramsey in Ind. Aff. Rep. 1849, 72, 1850. **Mediwanktons.**—Keane in Stanford, Compend., 521, 1878. **Medwakantonwan.**—Minn. Hist. Soc. Coll., III, 190, 1880. **Menchokatonx.**—Perrot (1689) quoted by Neill, Hist. Minn., 144, 1858. **Menchokatouches.**—Perrot (1689) in Minn. Hist. Soc. Coll., II, pt. 2, 31, note, 1864. **Mencouacantons.**—Relation of Pénicaut (1700) in Minn. Hist. Soc. Coll., III, 6, 1880. **Mendawahkanton.**—Prescott (1847) in Schoolcraft, Ind. Tribes, II, 168, 1852. **Men-da-wa-kan-ton.**—Prescott, ibid., 170. **Mendeouacanton.**—Le Sueur (1700) in Margry, Déc., VI, 86, 1886. **Mendeouacantous.**—La Harpe (1700) in Shea, Early Voy., 104, 1861. **Mendewacantongs.**—Schoolcraft, Trav., 307, 1821. **Mende Wahkan toan.**—Long, Exped. St Peter's R., I, 378, 1824. **Mende-Wakan-Toann.**—Maximilian, Trav., 149, 1843. **Mendouca-ton.**—La Harpe (1700) in French, Hist. Coll. La., III, 27, 1851. **Menduwakanton.**—Huebschmann in Schoolcraft, Ind. Tribes, VI, 707, 1857. **Menowa Kautong.**—Boudinot, Star in the West, 127, 1816. **Menowa Kontong.**—

Farnham, Trav., 32, 1843. **Midewakantonwans.**—Domenech, Deserts N. Am., II, 26, 1860. **Min'-da-wâr'-oâr-ton.**—Lewis and Clark, Discov., 30, 1806. **Minokantongs.**—Schoolcraft, Trav., 308, 1821. **Minowakanton.**—Lewis and Clark, Exped., I, 145, 1814. **Minowa Kantong.**—Brown, West. Gaz., 208, 1817. **Minoway-Kantong.**—Schermerhorn (1812) in Mass. Hist. Soc. Coll., 2d s., II, 40, 1814. **Minoway Kautong.**—Ibid. (misprint). **Minow Kantong.**—Schoolcraft, Trav., 286, 1821. **Mundaywahkanton.**—McKenney and Hall, Ind. Tribes, I, 303, 1854. **Munday Wawkantons.**—Snelling, Tales of N. W., 231, 1830. **O-man-ee.**—Schoolcraft, Ind. Tribes, II, 141, 1852. **O-maum-ee.**—Warren in Minn. Hist. Soc. Coll., v, 162, 1885. **People of the Lake.**—Lewis and Clark, Exped., 145, 1814. **Siou Mendeouacanton.**—Le Sueur (1700) in Margry, Déc., VI, 80, 1886. **Sioux Mindawarcarton.**—Lewis and Clark, Discov., 28, 1806. **Sioux of the River.**—Seymour, Sketches of Minn., 133, 850. **Siouxs of the Lakes.**—U. S. Ind. Treaties (1815), 869, 1873. **Win-de-wer-rean-toon.**—Arrowsmith, map. N. Am. (1795), 1814.

Meamskinisht ('porcupine-foot grove'). A Tsimshian mission village founded in 1889 and settled by the Kitksan. In 1897 the population was about 50 —Dorsey in Am. Antiq., XIX, 280, 1897

Measurements. Among civilized people, previous to the introduction of the metric system, linear measurements were derived mostly, if not exclusively, from the human body, and although in later centuries these measurements became standardized, it is not long since they were all determined directly from the human frame. It is still common, even for white men, in the absence of a graduated rule, to compute the inch by the transverse dimension of the terminal joint of the thumb, and for women to estimate a yard by stretching cloth from the nose to the tips of the fingers—the arm being extended and thrown strongly backward—or to estimate an eighth of a yard by the length of the middle finger. The use of the span as a standard of lineal measure is also still quite common. Within the last 30 years it has been a custom for traders to sell cloth to Indians by the natural yard or by the brace, and although this measure on a trader of small stature might be much less than 3 feet, the Indians preferred it to the yardstick. Below is given a list of what may be called natural measures which are known to have been employed by Indians. Some of the larger measures have been in general use among many tribes, while some of the smaller ones have been used by the Navaho and Pueblo shamans in making sacrificial and other sacred objects and in executing their dry-paintings. Some are also employed by Pueblo women in making and decorating their pottery.

Linear measures.—1. One finger width: the greatest width of the terminal joint of the little finger in the palmar aspect. 2. Two finger widths: the greatest width of the terminal joints of the first and second fingers held closely together, taken in the palmar aspect. 3. Three finger widths: the greatest width of the terminal joints of the first, second, and third fingers, taken as above. 4. Four finger widths: the width of the terminal joints of all four fingers of one hand, taken under the same conditions. 5. The joint: the length of a single digital phalanx, usually the middle phalanx of the little finger. 6. The palm: the width of the open palm, including the adducted thumb. 7. The finger stretch: from the tip of the first to the tip of the fourth finger, both fingers being extended. 8. The span: the same as our span, i. e., from the tip of the thumb to the tip of the index finger, both stretched as far apart as possible. 9. The great span: from the tip of the thumb to the tip of the little finger, all the digits being extended, while the thumb and little finger are strongly adducted. 10. The cubit: from the point of the elbow to the tip of the extended middle finger, the arm being bent. 11. The short cubit: from the point of the elbow to the tip of the extended little finger. 12. The natural yard: from the middle of the chest to the end of the middle finger, the arm being outstretched laterally at right angles with the body; this on a tall Indian equals 3 feet or more; among some tribes the measure is taken from the mouth to the tip of the middle finger. 13. The natural fathom, or brace: measured laterally on the outstretched arms, across the chest, from the tip of one middle finger to the tip of the other; this is twice the natural yard, or about 6 feet. The stature of white men usually equals or exceeds this measure, while among Indians the contrary is the rule—the arm of the Indian being usually proportionally longer than the arm of the white. This standard was commonly adopted by Indian traders of the N. in former days. They called it "brace," a word taken from the old French. There seems to be no evidence that the foot was ever employed by the Indians as a standard of linear measure, as it was among the European races; but the pace was employed in determining distances on the surface of the earth.

Circular measures.—1. The grasp: an approximate circle formed by the thumb and index finger of one hand. 2. The finger circle: the fingers of both hands held so as to inclose a nearly circular space, the tips of the index fingers and the tips of the thumbs just touching. 3. The contracted finger circle: like the finger circle but diminished by making the first and second joints of one index finger overlap those of the other. 4. The arm circle: the arms held in front as if embracing the trunk of a tree, the tips of the middle fingers just meeting.

Scales and weights were not known on the western continent previous to the discovery. There is no record of standards of dry or liquid measure, but it is probable that vessels of uniform size may have been used as such. See *Exchange*, and the references thereunder.   (w. m.)

Mecadacut. An Indian village on the coast of Maine, between Penobscot and Kennebec rs., in Abnaki territory, in 1616.

Macadacut.—Smith (1629), Virginia, II, 183, repr. 1819. Mecadacut.—Smith (1616) in Mass. Hist. Soc. Coll., 3d s., III, 22, 1833. Mecaddacut.—Smith (1629), Virginia, II, 192, repr. 1819.

Mecastria. Mentioned by Oñate (Doc. Inéd., XVI, 114, 1871) as a pueblo of the Jemez in New Mexico in 1598. It can not be identified with the present native name of any of the ruined settlements in the vicinity of Jemez. In another list by Oñate (ibid., 102), Quiamera and Fía are mentioned. A comparison of the lists shows the names to be greatly confused, the *mera* (of Quiamera) and *fía* making a contorted form of "Mecastría."

Mechemeton. A division of the Sisseton Sioux, perhaps the Miakechakesa.

Machemeton.—Carte des Poss. Angl., 1777. Mechemeton.—De l' Isle, map (1703) in Neill, Hist. Minn., 164, 1858. Mechemiton.—Anville, map of N. Am., 1752.

Mechgachkamic. A former village, perhaps belonging to the Unami Delawares, probably near Hackensack, N. J.

Mechgachkamic.—Doc. of 1649 in N. Y. Doc. Col. Hist., XIII, 25, 1881. Mochgeychkonk.—Doc. of 1655, ibid., 48 (identical?).

Mechkentowoon. A tribe of the Mahican confederacy formerly living, according to Ruttenber, on the w. bank of Hudson r. above Catskill cr., N. Y. De Laet and early maps place them lower down the stream.   (j. m.)

Machkentiwomi.—De Laet, Nov. Orb., 72, 1633. Mechkentiwoom.—Map ca. 1614 in N. Y. Doc. Col. Hist., I, 1856. Mechkentowoon.—Wassenaar (ca. 1630) in Ruttenber, Tribes Hudson R., 71, 1872. Wechkentowoons.—Ruttenber, ibid., 86 (misprint).

Mecopen. An Algonquian village, in 1585, s. of Albemarle sd., near the mouth of Roanoke r., N. C.

Mecopen.—Smith (1629), Virginia, I, map, repr. 1819. Moquopen.—Dutch map (1621) in N. Y. Doc. Col. Hist., I, 1856.

Medals. From time immemorial loyalty has been rewarded by the conferring of land and titles of nobility, by the personal thanks of the sovereign, the presentation of medals, and the bestowal of knightly orders the insignia of which were hung on the breast of the recipient. With the Indian chief it was the same. At first he was supplied with copies of his own weapons, and then with the white man's implements of war when he had become accustomed to their use. Brass tomahawks especially were presented to the Indians. Tecumseh carried such a tomahawk in his belt when he was killed at the battle of the Thames, in Canada, and his chief warrior, John Naudee, removed it and the silver belt buckle from the body. There were also presented to the Indian chiefs silver hat-bands, chased and engraved with the royal arms; silver gorgets to be worn suspended from the neck and having the royal arms and emblems of peace engraved upon them; and silver belt buckles, many of which exceeded 3 in. in diameter. The potency of the medal was soon appreciated as a means of retaining the Indian's allegiance, in which it played a most important part. While gratifying the vanity of the recipient, it appealed to him as an emblem of fealty or of chieftainship, and in time had a place in the legends of the tribe.

The earlier medals issued for presentation to the Indians of North America have become extremely rare from various causes, chief among which was the change of government under which the Indian may have been living, as each government was extremely zealous in searching out all medals conferred by a previous one and substituting medals of its own. Another cause has been that within recent years Indians took their medals to the nearest silversmith to have them converted into gorgets and amulets. After the Revolution the United States replaced the English medals with its own, which led to the establishment of a regular series of Indian peace medals. Many of the medals presented to the North American Indians were not dated, and in many instances were struck for other purposes.

SPANISH MEDALS.—Early Spanish missionaries also presented medals to the Indians; these are often found in graves

CATHOLIC MEDAL FROM A MOUND IN ALEXANDER CO., ILL.

in those portions of the United States once occupied by the Spanish. Several of these medals were found at the old Cayuga mission in New York, established in 1657 for the Huron refugees among the Iroquois and discontinued 30 years later. "The medals are of a religious character, and are supposed to have been given, in recognition of religious zeal or

other service, by the early Catholic missionaries" (Betts, p. 32). One of these medals is as follows:

1682. Obverse, the Virgin Mary, standing on a crescent and clouds, surrounded by a rayed glory, in field *1682;* legend, *Nuestra Señora de Guadalupe Ora Pro Nobis, Mexico.* Reverse, bust of San Francisco de Assisi in dress of a monk, a halo above; legend, *Francisco Ora Pro Nobis.* Brass and silver; size, 1⅜ by 1¼ in.

In 1864 there was found at Prairie du Chien, Wis., in an Indian grave, a silver medal, now in possession of the Wisconsin Historical Society, "supposed to have been given to Huisconsin, a Sauk and Fox chief" (Betts, p. 239). This was one of the regular "service medals" awarded by Spain to members of her army.

Obverse, bust of king to left; legend, *Carolus III Rey de España e de las Indias.* Reverse, within a cactus wreath, *Por Merito.* Silver; size, 2¼ in., with loop.

FRENCH CANADIAN MEDALS.—The earliest record of peace medals in connection with the Canadian Indians is found in Canada Correspondence General, vol. IV, in which mention is made of "a Caughnawaga chief, November 27, 1670, who holds preciously a medal presented to him by the king." Leroux (p. 14) includes a medal caused to be struck by Cardinal Richelieu in 1631 for presentation to Canadian Indians. A large medal was issued in France in commemoration of the reigning family; this example proved so acceptable to the Indians that a series of six, varying slightly in design and in size from 1³⁄₁₆ to 3¹⁄₁₆ in., was issued for presentation to them. Very few of the originals are now known to exist, but many restrikes have been made from the dies in the Musée Monetaire at Paris.

1693. Obverse, head of the king to right, laureated; legend, *Ludovicus Magnus Rex Christianissimus.* Reverse, four busts in field; legend. *Felicitas Domus Augustæ. Seren Dolph, Lud. D, Burg. Phid D. Card. D. Bitur. M.D.C.X.C.III.*

After the death of the Dolphin, in 1712, the reverse type was changed, two figures replacing the four busts of Louis, the Dauphin, and his two sons. Of this medal only restrikes are now known.

171-. Obverse, bust of king to right; legend, *Ludovicus XIIII, D. G. FR. NAV. REX.* Reverse, two Roman warriors; legend, *HONOR ET VIRTUS.* Silver; bronze, size, 2¼ in.

In the succeeding reign a smaller medal of similar design was issued, bearing on the obverse the head of the king to the right, draped and laureated; legend, *Louis XV Rex Christianissimus.* A copy of this medal has been found with the legend erased and *George III* stamped in its place (McLachlan, p. 9). Silver; bronze; size, 2 in.

The General De Levi medal of 1658, and that of the first Intendant-General of Canada, Jean Varin, of 1683, though included by Leroux (p. 15) among the peace medals, are excluded by Betts and other writers. Leroux (p. 17) figures the French Oswego medal of 1758 as belonging to the peace medal series. "As medals were freely distributed about this time, some of them may have been placed in Indian hands" (Beauchamp, p. 64).

1758. Obverse, head of king to left, nude and hair flowing; legend, *Ludovicus XV Orbis Imperator;* in exergue, *1758.* Reverse, in field four forts; legend, *Wesel, Oswego, Port Mahon;* in exergue, *Expung. Sti. Davidis Arce et Solo Equata.* Silver; brass; size, 1¼ in.

BRITISH MEDALS.—The earliest medals presented to American Indians by the English colonists are those known as the Pamunkey series. By Act 38, Laws of Virginia, in the 14th year of King Charles II, March, 1661 (see Hening's Statutes, II, 185), there were caused to be made, possibly in the colony, "silver and plated plaques to be worn by the Indians when visiting the English settlements." They were plain on the reverse, in order to permit the engraving of the names of the chiefs of the Indian towns.

1670. Obverse, bust of king to right; legend in outer circle, *Charles II, King of England, Scotland, France, Ireland and Virginia;* the center of the shield a slightly convex disk bearing the legend, the royal arms, and in one corner a tobacco plant. Encircled by ribbon of the Garter, below the disk in an oval surface, is the inscription: *The Queen of Pamaunkee;* above the disk a crown. Reverse, plain, with 5 rings attached for suspension. Silver; copper; oval; size, 4 by 6 in.

1670. Obverse, same as last; legend, *Ye King of ——.* Reverse, a tobacco plant; legend, *Piomock.* Silver; copper; oval; size, 4 by 6 in.

In a proposal made by Robert Hunter, captain-general, etc., to the chief of the Five Nations, at Albany, Aug. 16, 1710, during the reign of Queen Anne, it is recorded: "Your brothers who have been in England and have seen the great Queen and her court, have no doubt informed you how vain and groundless the French boasting has been all along. Her Majesty has sent you as pledges of her protection a medal for each nation, with her royal effigies on one side and the last gained battle on the other. She has sent you her picture, in silver, twenty to each nation, to be given to the chief warriors, to be worn about their necks, as a token that they should always be in readiness to fight under her banner against the common enemy." This was probably the silver medal struck in 1709 in commemoration of the battle and capture of Tournay by the British.

1710. Obverse, bust of Queen Anne to left, hair bound in pearls, lovelock on the right shoulder; in gown, and mantle on the right shoulder, legend, *ANNA D. G. MAG. BRI. ET HIB. REG.;* below, *J. C.* [John Crocker]. Reverse, Pallas seated, to right, resting her left hand upon a Gorgian shield and holding in her right hand a spear, murally crowned, near her a pile of

arms and flags, a town in the distance; legend, *Turnace Expurgato;* in exergue, *M.D.C.C.IX.* Gold; silver; size, 1¹⁰⁄₁₆ in.

A series of six medals was issued during the reigns of George I and George II, of similar design, in brass and copper; sizes, 1½ to 1⅞ in. "The medals were not dated, and it is known that the later Georges used the same design" (Beauchamp, p. 27).

1714. Obverse, bust of king to right, laureated, with flowing hair, in armor, draped; legend, *George King of Great Britain.* Reverse, an Indian at right drawing his bow on a deer, standing at left on a hill, sun above, to right above tree one star, to left above Indian three stars. Brass; size, 1⅜ in., with loop for suspension.

1753. Obverse, bust of king to left, laureated; legend, *Georgius II, D. G. MAG. BRI. FRA. ET HIB. REX. F. D.* Reverse, the royal arms, within the Garter, surmounted by a crown and a lion; upon ribbon, below, *DIEU ET MON DROIT.* Silver; cast and chased; size, 1⅞ in., with loop and ring.

The last was one of 30 medals brought from England in 1753 by Sir Danvers Osborne, governor of New York, for presentation to friendly Indians of the Six Nations. The medals were provided with broad scarlet ribbons (Hist. Mag., Sept. 1865, p. 85; Betts, p. 177).

In July, 1721, the governor of Pennsylvania presented to the Seneca chief, Ghosont, a gold coronation medal of George I, charging him "to deliver this piece into the hands of the first man or greatest chief of the Five Nations, whom you call Kannygoodt, to be laid up and kept as a token of friendship between them" (Hawkins, II, 426).

1721. Obverse, bust of king to right, laureated, hair long, and in scale armor, lion's head on breast and mantle; legend, *Georgius. D. G. MAG. BRI. FR. ET HIB. REX.;* on truncation, *E. Hannibal,* Reverse, the king seated, to right, beneath a canopy of state, is being crowned by Britannia, who rests her hand upon a shield; in exergue, *INAUGURAT* ²⁰⁄₂₅, *Oct. MDCCXIIII.*

The following medal seems to have been a trader's token or store card, possibly given to the Indians to gain their good will:

1757. Obverse, a trader buying skins from an Indian; legend, *The Red Man Came to Elton Daily.* Reverse, a deer lying beneath a tree; legend, *Skins bought at Eltons;* in exergue, *1757* (Am. Jour. Numismat., VII, 90). Copper, size, 1⅜ in.

The first Indian peace medal manufactured in America is thought to have been the following. It was presented by The Friendly Association for the Regaining and Preserving Peace With the Indians by Pacific Means, a society composed largely of Quakers. The dies were engraved by Edward Duffield, a watch and clock maker of Philadelphia, and the medals were struck by Joseph Richardson, a member of the society. Many restrikes have been issued.

1757. Obverse, bust of the king to right, hair long and laureated; legend, *Georgius II Dei Gratia.*

Reverse, Indian and white man seated, a council fire between them; white man offers calumet and Indian extends hand for it; above Indian a rayed sun, back of white man a tree; legend, *Let us Look to the Most High who Blessed our Fathers with Peace;* in exergue, *1757.* Silver; copper; pewter; size, 1¾ in.

INDIAN PEACE MEDAL OF 1757

On the capture of Montreal by Sir Jeffrey Amherst, Sept. 8, 1760, an interesting series of medals, known as the conquest medals, was issued. McLachlan says they "were evidently made in America, and presented to the Iroquois and Onondagas, and other chiefs who assisted in the campaign." To each of the 23 chiefs, though they did but little fighting, was presented a medal by Sir William Johnson, who, in his diary, under date of July 21, 1761, says: "I then delivered the medals sent me by the General for those who went with us to Canada last year, being twenty-three in number." Beauchamp (p. 61) says: "In 1761 Johnson had similar medals for the Oneidas, but none of them have been found."

1760. Obverse, view of a town, with bastions, on a river front, five church spires, island in river; in foreground, to left, a bastion with flag of St George; in exergue, in an incused oval, *D. C. F.;* this side is cast and chased. Reverse, in field engraved, *Montreal*, remainder plain for insertion of name and tribe of the recipient. Silver; size, $1\frac{13}{14}$ in. Pewter; size, $1\frac{7}{8}$ in.

Beauchamp (p. 66) says: "Two medals, relating to the capture of Montreal and conquest of Canada, seem more likely to have been given by Johnson to the Indians in 1761. As the two medals have Indian symbols, and one Amherst's name, and that of Montreal, they seem to suit every way Johnson's lavish distribution of medals at Otsego, when sent by his leader."

1761. Obverse, a laureated nude figure, typifying the St Lawrence, to right, reclining, right arm resting on the prow of a galley, paddle in left hand, a beaver climbing up his left leg; in background a standard inscribed *Amherst* within a wreath of laurel, surmounted by a lion. In exergue, a shield with fleur-de-lis; above, a tomahawk, bow, and quiver; legend, *Conquest of Canada.* Reverse, a female figure, to right, seated beneath a pine tree; an eagle with extended wings standing on a rock; before the female a shield of France, with club and tomahawk; legend, *Montreal Taken, MDCCLX;* in exergue, *Soc. Promoting Arts and Commerce.* Silver; size, $1\frac{1}{3}$ in.

1761. Obverse, head of King George, to right, nude, with flowing hair, laureated; legend, *George II. King.* Reverse, female figure seated beneath a pine tree, to left, weeping, typical of Canada; behind her a beaver climbing up a bank; legend, *Canada Subdued;* in exergue, *MDCCLX.;* below, *S. P. A. C.* Silver; bronze; size, $1\frac{1}{3}$ in.

To commemorate the marriage of George III and Queen Charlotte a small special medal was struck, in 1761, for general distribution to insure the allegiance of the savages in the newly acquired province (McLachlan, p. 13).

1761. Obverse, bust of king and queen facing each other; above, a curtain with cords and tassels falling midway between the heads. Reverse, the royal arms, with ribbon of the Garter, and motto on ribbon below, *Dieu et Mon Droit.* Silver; size, $1\frac{1}{4}$ in., pierced for suspension.

The following series of medals is supposed to have been struck for presentation to Indian chiefs in Canada at the close of the French and Indian wars. There were five in the series, differing in size and varying slightly in design; they were formed of two shells joined together; one of lead and others of pewter, with tracings of gilding, have been found.

1762. Obverse, youthful bust of king, to right, in armor, wearing ribbon of the Garter, hair in double curl over ear; legend, *Dei Gratia.* Reverse, the royal arms encircled by the ribbon of the Garter, surmounted by a crown, supported by the lion and the unicorn; legend, *Honi Soit qui Mal y Pense;* on a ribbon below the motto, *Dieu et Mon Droit.* Silver; size, $1\frac{1}{2}$ by $3\frac{1}{8}$ in.

In 1763 Pontiac rebelled against British rule, and the Government entered into treaty with the remaining friendly chiefs. A council was held at Niagara in 1764, at which time the series of three medals known as the "Pontiac conspiracy medals" was presented to the chiefs and and principal warriors.

1764. Obverse, bust of king, to left, in armor and in very high relief, long hair tied with ribbon, laureated; legend, *Georgius III. D. A. M. BRI. FRA. ET HIB. REX. F. D.* Reverse, an officer and an Indian seated on a rustic bench in foreground; on the banks of a river, to right, three houses on a rocky point; at junction of river with ocean, two ships under full sail. The Indian holds in his left hand a calumet, with his right grasps the hand of the officer; at left of Indian, in the background, a tree, at right a mountain range; legend, *Happy While United;* in exergue, *1764.* In field, stamped in two small incused circles, *D. C. F.* and *N York.* Silver; size, $3\frac{3}{16}$ by $3\frac{1}{8}$ in.; loop, a calumet and an eagle's wing.

In 1765 a treaty was made with the British and Pontiac, and his chiefs were presented by Sir William Johnson, at Oswego, with the medals known as "the lion and wolf medals." A large number of these were distributed, and two reverse dies have been found. The design represents the expulsion of France from Canada (see Parkman, Pontiac Conspiracy, chap. xxxi; Betts, p. 238; Leroux, p. 156; McLachlan, p. 13).

1765. Obverse, bust of king to right, in armor, wearing the ribbon of the Garter; legend, *Georgius III Dei Gratia.* Reverse, to left, the British lion reposing under a tree; to right, a snarling wolf; behind lion, a church and two houses; behind wolf, trees and bushes. Silver; size, $2\frac{3}{8}$ in.

A large body of Indians assembled in general council at Montreal, Aug. 17, 1778, representing the Sioux, Sauk, Foxes, Menominee, Winnebago, Ottawa, Potawatomi, and Chippewa. It is generally supposed that at this time the presentation of the medals took place, in consideration of the assistance rendered the British in the campaigns of Kentucky and Illinois and during the War of the Revolution. Gen. Haldimand, commander in chief of the British forces in Canada, also gave a certificate with each medal (see Hoffman in 14th Rep. B. A. E., 1896; Betts, p. 284–286).

1778. Obverse, bust of king to right, wearing ribbon of the Garter. Reverse, the royal arms, surrounded by ribbon of the Garter and motto, surmounted by a crown, supported by the lion and the unicorn; at bottom ribbon, with motto, *Dieu et Mon Droit;* shield of pretense crowned. Silver; size, 2⅜ in., with loop for suspension.

The following medals were presented, until about the time of the war of 1812, to Indian chiefs for meritorious service, and continued in use possibly until replaced by those of 1814 (Leroux, p. 157):

1775. Obverse, bust of the king, to left, with hair curled, wearing ribbon of the Garter; legend, *Georgius III Dei Gratia.* Reverse, the royal arms with supporters; surmounted by crown and ribbon of the Garter; below, ribbon with motto, *Dieu et Mon Droit.* Silver; size, 2¼ in., with loop for suspension.

1794. Obverse, bust of king to right, in armor, wearing ribbon of the Garter, hair long, cloak over shoulders; two laurel branches from bottom of medal to height of shoulders of bust; legend, *Georgius III Dei Gratia;* in exergue, *1794.* Reverse, on plain field, the royal arms with supporters, surmounted by helmet and crest, encircled by ribbon of the Garter, and below ribbon and motto. Silver; size, 1¼ in.

At the close of the war of 1812, the Government, desirous of marking its appreciation of the services rendered by its Indian allies, besides making other presents and grants of land, caused the following medal, in three sizes, to be struck in silver for presentation to the chiefs and principal warriors (Leroux, p. 158):

1814. Obverse, bust with older head of king to right, laureated, draped in an ermine mantle, secured in front with a large bow of ribbon, wearing the collar and jewel of St George; legend, *Georgius III Dei Gratia Britanniarum Rex F. D.;* under bust, *T. Wyon, Jun. S.* Reverse, the royal arms of Great Britain with shield of pretense of Hanover, surmounted by a crown and crested helmet, all encircled by ribbon of the Garter and supporters, below a ribbon with motto, *Dieu et Mon Droit;* above ribbon, a rose, thistle, and shamrock; behind helmet on both sides, a display of acanthus leaves; in exergue, *1814.* Silver; size, 2⅜ to 4½ in.

The following medal, in three sizes, was struck in 1840 for participants in the early treaties of the Queen's reign. It is possible that it may have been presented also to the Indians of Lower Canada who took no part in the abortive uprising of 1837 (McLachlan, p. 36; Leroux, p. 161):

1840. Obverse, bust of Queen, to right, crowned; legend, *Victoria Dei Gratia Britanniarum Regina*

F. D.; under neck *W. Wyon, R. A.* Reverse, arms of Great Britain, surmounted by crown and crested helmet, encircled by ribbon of the Garter, supported by the lion and the unicorn; below, ribbon with motto, *Dieu et Mon Droit,* the rose and thistle; in exergue, *1840.* Silver; sizes, 2⅜ to 4⁹⁄₁₆ in.

The medal known as the Ashburton treaty medal was given through Lord Ashburton, in 1842, to the Micmac and other eastern Indians for services as guards and hunters, and assistance in laying out the boundary between the United States and Canada.

1842. Obverse, bust of queen in an inner dentilated circle, garland of roses around psyche knot; under bust, *B. Wyon;* no legend. Reverse, arms of Great Britain in an inner circle, surmounted by a crowned and crested helmet, encircled by the ribbon of the Garter; legend, *Victoria Dei Gratia Britanniarum Regina Fid. Def.* Ribbon in lower field backed by the rose and thistle (Betts, p. 159). Silver; size, 2⁹⁄₁₆ in.

In 1848 the Peninsular War medal was issued, to be given to any officer, noncommissioned officer, or soldier who had participated in any battle or siege from 1793 to 1814. In general orders, dated Horse Guards, June 1, 1847, were included the battles of Chateaugay, Oct. 26, 1813, and of Chrystlers Farm, Nov. 11, 1813, covering the invasion of Canada by the American army in 1813. "The medal was also conferred upon the Indians, the name of the battles engraved on clasps, and the name of the recipient on the edge of the medal, with title of warrior" (Leroux, p. 177).

1848. Obverse, bust of the queen to right, crowned; legend, *Victoria Regina;* below bust, *1848,* and *W. Wyon, R. A.* Reverse, figure of the queen in royal robes, standing on a dais, crowning with a wreath of laurel the Duke of Wellington, who is kneeling before her; by side of dais a crouching lion; in exergue, *1703–1814.* Silver; size, 2¼ in., with loop for suspension.

The Prince of Wales on his visit to Canada in 1860 was received by Indians in full ceremonial dress. Each chief was presented with a large silver medal, while the warriors received smaller medals. This medal is known as the Prince of Wales medal.

1860. Obverse, head of queen to right, undraped and crowned; legend, *Victoria D. G. Regina F. D.* In lower right-hand field, the three feathers and motto; lower left-hand field, *1860.* Reverse, the royal arms surmounted by a helmet, crown, and lion, with ribbon of the Garter, and on the ribbon below, *Dieu et Mon Droit;* at back, roses, shamrock, and thistle; in exergue, *1860.* Silver; size, 2 in., with loop for suspension.

In 1860, when the Government had acquired the lands of the Hudson's Bay Company's territory and after the extinction of the Indian land titles, the following medal was presented to the Indians under Treaty No. 1. In the Report of the Commissioners it is stated: "In addition each Indian received a dress, a flag, and a medal as marks of distinction." These medals at first were not struck for this occasion.

1860. Obverse, head of the queen to right, crowned; legend, *Victoria Regina;* under bust, *J. S.* and *B. Wyon, S C.* Reverse, two branches of oak, center field plain for the engraving of name and tribe of recipient. Silver; size, 3$\frac{3}{16}$ in.

The very large Confederation medal of 1867, with an extra rim soldered on it, was used in 1872 for Treaty No. 2. It was presented to the Indians subsequent to the acquisition of the Hudson's Bay Company's territory, at which time the Indian titles were extinguished. "Twenty-five were prepared, but found so cumbersome no more were used" (Leroux, p. 219).

1872. Obverse, bust of queen to right, within an inner circle having milled edge ground, with veil and necklace; legend, *Dominion of Canada;* below, *Chiefs Medal, 1872;* below bust, *S. Wyon.* Reverse, in inner circle Britannia seated with lion and four female figures, representing the four original provinces of the Canadian confederation; legend, *Juvenatus et Patrius Vigor Canada Instaurata, 1867;* in outer circle, *Indians of the North West Territories.* Silver; bronze; size, 3$\frac{3}{4}$ in.

The following medal was struck especially to replace the large and inartistic medal last described, and was intended for presentation at future treaties:

1873. Obverse, head of queen to right, crowned with veil and necklace, draped; legend, *Victoria D. G. Britt. REG. F. D.;* below bust, *J. S. Wyon.* Reverse, a general officer in full uniform, to right, grasping the hand of an Indian chief who wears a feather headdress and leggings; pipe of peace at feet of figures; in background, at back of Indian, several wigwams; back of officer, a half sun above horizon; legend, *Indian Treaty No. ——,* on lower edge, *187-.* Silver; size, 3 in., with loop for suspension.

A series of three medals was struck by the Hudson's Bay Company for presentation to the Indians of the great Northwest for faithful services. These were engraved by G. H. Kuchler of the Birmingham mint, 1790 to 1805.

1793. Obverse, bust of king to left, long hair and draped; legend, *Georgius III D. G. Britanniarum Rex Fidei. Def.;* under bust, *G. H. K.* Reverse, arms of the Hudson's Bay Company; argent, a cross gules, four beavers proper, to the left, surmounted by a helmet and crest, a fox supported by two stags; motto on ribbon, *Pro Pelle Cutem* (Leroux, p. 59). Silver; sizes, 1$\frac{13}{16}$ by 3 in.

MEDALS OF THE UNITED STATES.—The earliest known Indian medal struck within the United States is that of 1780, as follows:

1780. Obverse, arms of Virginia; legend, *Rebellion to Tyrants is Obedience to God.* Reverse, an officer and an Indian seated under a tree, the In-dian holding a calumet in his hand; in the background, a sea on which are three ships; in the middle-ground, a rocky point and a house; legend, *Happy While United.* Silver; pewter; size, 2$\frac{7}{8}$ in.; loop, a calumet and an eagle's wing.

The pewter medal presented by the Government to the Indians represented at the Ft Harmar treaty in Ohio, in 1789, bears on the obverse the bust of Washington with full face, and on the reverse the clasped hands and crossed calumet and tomahawk, with the date 1789, and legend, *Friendship, the Pipe of Peace.* The tribes present at the treaty were the Ottawa, Delawares, Hurons, Sauk, Potawatomi, and Chippewa.

Of the early United States medals possibly the most interesting is that known as the Red Jacket medal, presented to this celebrated Seneca by Washington at Philadelphia in 1792. This was one of several similar medals, one of which is dated 1793. Of it Loubat says: "The medals were made at the United States Mint when Dr Rittenhouse was director, 1792–1795." See *Red Jacket.*

1792. Obverse, Washington in uniform, bareheaded, facing to the right, presenting a pipe to an Indian chief, who is smoking it; the Indian is standing, and has a large medal suspended from his neck. On the left is a pine tree, at its foot a toma-

THE "RED JACKET" MEDAL, DATED 1793

hawk; in the background, a farmer plowing; in exergue, *George Washington President 1792*—all engraved. Reverse, arms and crest of the United States on the breast of the eagle, in the right talon of which is an olive branch, in the left a sheaf of arrows, in its beak a ribbon with the motto *E Pluribus Unum;* above, a glory breaking through the clouds and surrounded by 13 stars. Size, 6$\frac{3}{4}$ by 4$\frac{3}{4}$ in.

In the Greenville treaty of 1795, between the United States and representatives of the Hurons, Delawares, Ottawa, Chippewa, Potawatomi, Sauk, and other tribes, a part of the function, as usual, involved the presentation of peace medals. The medal in this case was a facsimile of the oval Red Jacket medal, in silver, engraved and chased, with a change in the date to 1795. Size, 4 by 6 in. As there were many signers, a considerable number of these medals must have been distributed.

During the second administration of Washington, in 1796, there was issued a series of four medals, in silver and bronze, called "the Season medals," which Snow-

den (p. 95) states were Indian peace medals. These are as follows:

1796. No. 1. Obverse, a shepherd with staff in left hand, and a cow, two sheep, and a lamb in foreground; in background, a hill, tree, and farmhouse with open door, in which two persons are seen; on base, *C. H. Kuchler, F.;* in exergue, *U. S. A.* Reverse, legend in five parallel lines, *Second Presidency of George Washington MDCCXCVI,* within a wreath of olive branches; in bow, the letter *K.* Size, 1⅞ in.
No. 2. Obverse, interior of a room; in background, a woman; in foreground, a woman spinning, at left a child guarding a cradle, on right an open fireplace; on base, *C. H. K. F.;* in exergue, *U. S. A.* Reverse, same as No. 1.
No. 3. Obverse, in foreground, farmer sowing; in background, a farmhouse and a man plowing; on base, *Kuchler;* in exergue, *U. S. A.* Reverse, same as No. 1.
No. 4. Obverse, bust of Washington in uniform, to left, in a wreath of laurel; legend, *In War Enemies.* Reverse, bust of Franklin, to left, in wreath of laurel; legend, *In Peace Friends.* Tin; size, ⅞ in.

"Of the medals taken along and of which use was made by the explorers [Lewis and Clark] there were three sizes, or grades, one, the largest and preferred one, 'a medal with the likeness of the President of the United States'; the second, 'a medal representing some domestic animals'; the third, 'medals with the impression of a farmer sowing grain'. I have found in 'The Northwest Coast,' by James G. Swan, a cut of a medal of the third class, but I have seen no representation of the second class. The third class medal was made of pewter. These medals were given to chiefs only" (Wheeler, Trail of Lewis and Clark, 139–140).

THE JEFFERSON MEDAL OF 1801

The following were struck especially for presentation to Indian chiefs, and had their inception, Apr. 20, 1786, when Representative McKean moved "that the Board of the Treasury ascertain the number and value of the medals received by the Commission appointed to treat with the Indians, from the said Indians, and have an equal number with the arms of the United States, made in silver and returned to the chiefs, from whom they were received." The result was the final adoption of a series of medals, each bearing on the obverse the bust of a President, and on the reverse a symbol of peace. This series began with the administration of President Jefferson. The John Adams medal was made many years after his administration, and though not so considered at first, it is now regarded as included in the series. At the time of the first issue, however, a die was made for the obverse of the Adams medal. The reverse used was that of the smaller Jefferson medal; a few were struck in soft metal, which are now exceedingly rare.

Obverse, bust of president to right, clothed, hair in curls and cue; legend, *John Adams, Pres. U. S. A.;* on truncation, *Leonard.* Reverse, two hands clasped, on cuff of one three stripes and as many buttons with displayed eagle; the other wrist has a bracelet with spread-eagle; legend, *Peace and Friendship,* and crossed calumet and tomahawk.

The medal of Adams now used is practically the same, except the arrangement of the face, and the legend, *John Adams, President of the United States;* in exergue, *A. D. 1797;* in truncation, *Furst.* Reverse, the same as last. Bronze; size, 2 in.

The Jefferson medal is as follows:

Obverse, bust of president to right; legend, *Th. Jefferson, President of the U. S. A. D. 1801.* Reverse, same as last. Silver and bronze; sizes, 4 in., 2⅞ in., 2 in.

The medals that followed were the same in design, metal, and size, with the names of the respective Presidents, until the administration of Millard Fillmore, in 1850, when the reverse was entirely changed, as follows:

An Indian in war dress and a pioneer in foreground, the latter leaning on a plow; to right a hill, in center background a river and a sailing boat; to left two cows beyond a farmhouse; American flag back of the figures; legend, *Labor, Virtue, Honor;* in exergue, *J. Wilson, F.* Silver and bronze; size, 3 in.

During the next two administrations this type was retained, but in 1862, during the administration of Abraham Lincoln, another change in the reverse was made:

In field, an Indian plowing, children playing at ball, a hill and a log cabin and a church; a river with boats and ships in background; in an outer circle, following curve of medal, an Indian scalping another; below, an Indian woman weeping, a quiver of arrows with bow and calumet. Silver and bronze; size, 2⅞ in.

The reverse was again changed during the administration of Andrew Johnson, as follows:

Figure of America clasping the hand of an Indian in war dress, before a monument surmounted by a bust of George Washington; at feet of Indian are the attributes of savage life; at feet of America those of civilization. Silver and bronze; size, 2⅜ in.

The medal issued during the administration of President Grant was entirely different:

Obverse, bust of president within a wreath of laurel; legend, *United States of America, Liberty, Justice and Equality;* below, *Let us have peace,* a calumet and a branch of laurel. Reverse, a globe resting on implements of industry with the Bible above and rays behind it; legend, *On earth peace, good will toward men.*

In 1877, during the administration of President Hayes, change was made to an oval medal:

Obverse, bust of president to right, nude; legend, *Rutherford B. Hayes, President of the United States, 1877.* Reverse, figure of a pioneer with ax in left hand and pointing with right to a cabin in right background, before which a woman is seated with a child in her lap; in middle background, a man plowing, a mountain beyond, figure of an Indian in full war dress facing pioneer, to right a tree, above in rays *Peace;* in exergue, crossed calumet and tomahawk within wreath. Silver; bronze; size, 2⅜ by 3¼ in.

No change was made in size or type until the administration of Benjamin Harrison, when the old round form of medal was resumed:

Obverse, bust of president to right, draped; legend, *Benjamin Harrison, President of the United States, 1889.* Reverse, two hands clasped, crossed calumet and tomahawk; legend, *Peace and Friendship.* Sizes, 3 in., 2¼ in., 2 in.

This medal was continued to the administration of President Roosevelt.

The issuance of peace medals was not confined to the governments, as the various fur companies also presented to Indian chiefs medals of various kinds and in various metals, as, for example, the medals of the Hudson's Bay Company from 1790 to 1805, above described. The Chouteau Fur Company, of St Louis, caused to be given by its agents in the N. W. the following:

Obverse, bust of Pierre Chouteau, to left, clothed; legend, *Pierre Chouteau, Jr., & Co., Upper Missouri Outfit.* Reverse, in field, crossed tomahawk and calumet, and clasped hands; legend, *Peace and Friendship, 1843.* Silver; size, 3⅜ in.

Consult Beauchamp, Metallic Ornaments of the New York Indians, 1903; Betts, American Colonial History Illustrated by Contemporaneous Medals, 1894; Carr, Dress and Ornaments of Certain American Indians, 1897; Carter, Medals of the British Army, 1861; Catalogue du Musée Monetaire, 1833; Clark, Onondaga, 1849; Fisher, American Medals of the Revolution, in Mass. Hist. Soc. Coll., 3d s., VI; Halsey, Old New York Frontier, 1901; Hawkins, Medallic Illustrations of British History; Hayden, Silver and Copper Medals, in Proc. Wyo. Hist. and Geol. Soc., II, pt. 2, 1886; Irwin, War Medals, 1899; Leroux, Medaillier du Canada, 1888; McLachlan in Canadian Antiq. and Numismat. Jour., 3d s., II, 1899; Wheeler, Trail of Lewis and Clark, 1900; Miner, History of Wyoming Valley, 1845; O'Callaghan, Documentary History of the State of New York, 1856–87; Penhallow, History of the Wars of New England, 1824; Pinkerton, Medallic History of England, 1790; Snowden, Medals of Washington in the U. S. Mint, 1861.

(P. E. B.)

Medfield. In 1677 there was a settlement of Christian Indians (perhaps Nipmuc) at this place, in Norfolk co., Mass.—Gookin (1677) in Drake, Bk. Inds., bk. 2, 115, 1848.

Medicine and Medicine-men. Medicine is an agent or influence employed to prevent, alleviate, or cure some pathological condition or its symptoms. The scope of such agents among the Indians was extensive, ranging, as among other primitive peoples, from magic, prayer, force of suggestion, and a multitude of symbolic and empirical means, to actual and more rationally used remedies. Where the Indians are in contact with whites the old methods of combating physical ills are slowly giving way to the curative agencies of civilization. The white man in turn has adopted from the Indians a number of valuable medicinal plants, such as cinchona, jalapa, hydrastis, etc.

In general the tribes show many similarities in regard to medicine, but the actual agents employed differ with the tribes and localities, as well as with individual healers. Magic, prayers, songs, exhortation, suggestion, ceremonies, fetishes, and certain specifics and mechanical processes are employed only by the medicine-men or medicine-women; other specific remedies or procedures are proprietary, generally among a few old women in the tribe; while many vegetal remedies and simple manipulations are of common knowledge in a given locality.

The employment of magic consists in opposing a supposed malign influence, such as that of a sorcerer, spirits of the dead, mythic animals, etc., by the supernatural power of the healer's fetishes and other means. Prayers are addressed to benevolent deities and spirits, invoking their aid. Healing songs, consisting of prayers or exhortations, are sung. Harangues are directed to evil spirits supposed to cause the sickness, and often are accentuated by noises to frighten such spirits away. Suggestion is exercised in many ways directly and indirectly. Curative ceremonies usually combine all or most of the agencies mentioned. Some of them, such as Matthews describes among the Navaho, are very elaborate, prolonged, and costly. The fetishes used are peculiarly shaped stones or wooden objects, lightning-riven wood, feathers, claws, hair, figurines of mythic animals, representations of the sun, of lightning, etc., and are supposed to embody a mysterious power capable of preventing disease or of counteracting its effects. Mechanical means of curing consist of rubbing, pressure with the hands or feet, or with a sash or cord (as in labor or in painful affections of the chest), bonesetting, cutting, cauterizing, scarifying, cupping (by sucking), blood-letting, poulticing, clysmata, sweat bath, sucking of snake poison or abscesses, counter irritation, tooth pulling, bandaging, etc. Dieting and total abstinence from food were forms of treatment in vogue in various localities. Vegetal medicines were, and in some tribes still are, numerous. Some of these are employed by reason of a real or fancied resemblance to the part affected, or as fetishes, because of a supposed mythical antagonism to the cause of the sickness. Thus, a plant with a worm-like stem may be given as a vermifuge; one that has many hair-like processes is used among the Hopi to cure baldness. Among the Apache the sacred tule pollen known as *ha-dn-tin* is given or applied because of its supposed supernatural beneficial effect. Other plants are employed as remedies simply for traditional reasons, without any formulated opinion as to their modes of action. Finally, all the tribes are familiar with and employ cathartics and emetics; in some cases also diaphoretics, diuretics, cough medicines, etc. Every tribe has also knowledge of some of the poisonous plants in its neighborhood and their antidotes.

The parts of plants used as medicines are most often roots, occasionally twigs, leaves, or bark, but rarely flowers or seeds. They are used either fresh or dry, and most commonly in the form of a decoction. Of this a considerable quantity, as much as a cupful, is administered at a time, usually in the morning. Only exceptionally is the dose repeated. Generally only a single plant is used, but among some Indians as many as four plants are combined in a single medicine; some of the Opata mix indiscriminately a large number of substances. The proprietary medicines are sold at a high price. Some of these plants, so far as they are known, possess real medicinal value, but many are quite useless for the purpose for which they are prescribed. There is a prevalent belief that the Indians are acquainted with valuable specifics for venereal diseases, snake bites, etc., but how far this belief may be true has not yet been shown.

Animal and mineral substances are also occasionally used as remedies. Among Southwestern tribes the bite of a snake is often treated by applying to the wound a portion of the ventral surface of the body of the same snake. The Papago use crickets as medicine; the Tarahumare, lizards; the Apache, spiders' eggs. Among the Navaho and others red ocher combined with fat is used externally to prevent sunburn. The red, barren clay from beneath a campfire is used by White Mountain Apache women to induce sterility; the Hopi blow charcoal, ashes, or other products of fire on an inflamed surface to counteract the supposed fire which causes the ailment. Antiseptics are unknown, but some of the cleansing agents or healing powders employed probably serve as such, though undesignedly on the part of the Indians.

The exact manner of therapeutic action is as absolutely unknown to the Indian as it is to the ignorant white man. Among some tribes the term for medicine signifies "mystery," but among others a distinction is made between thaumaturgic practices and actual medicines. Occasionally the term "medicine" is extended to a higher class of greatly prized fetishes that are supposed to be imbued with mysterious protective power over an individual or even over a tribe (see *Orenda*). Such objects form the principal contents of the so-called medicine-bags.

In many localities there was prepared on special occasions a tribal "medicine." The Iroquois used such a remedy for healing wounds, and the Hopi still prepare one on the occasion of their Snake dance. Among the tribes who prepare *tiswin*, or *tesvino*, particularly the Apache, parts of a number of bitter, aromatic, and even poisonous plants, especially a species of datura, are added to the liquid to make it "stronger"; these are termed medicines.

The causation and the nature of disease being to the Indian in large part mysteries, he assigned them to supernatural agencies. In general, every illness that could not plainly be connected with a visible influence was regarded as the effect of an introduction into the body, by malevolent or offended supernatural beings or through sorcery practised by an enemy, of noxious objects capable of producing and continuing pain or other symptoms, or of absorbing the patient's vitality. These beliefs, and the more rational ones concerning many minor indispositions and injuries, led to the development of separate forms of treatment, and varieties of healers.

In every Indian tribe there were, and in some tribes still are, a number of men, and perhaps also a number of women, who were regarded as the possessors of supernatural powers that enabled them to recognize, antagonize, or cure disease; and there were others who were better acquainted with actual remedies than the average. These two classes were the "physicians." They were oftentimes distinguished in designation and differed in influence over the people as well as in responsibilities. Among the Dakota one was called *wakan witshasha*, 'mystery man', the other *pejihuta witshasha*, 'grass-root man'; among the Navaho one is *khathali*, 'singer', 'chanter', the other *izëëlini*, 'maker of medicines'; among the Apache one is *taiyin*, 'wonderful,' the other simply *izé*, 'medicine.'

The mystery man, or thaumaturgist, was believed to have obtained from the deities, usually through dreams, but sometimes before birth, powers of recognizing and removing the mysterious causes of disease. He was "given" appropriate songs or prayers, and became possessed of one or more powerful fetishes. He announced or exhibited these attributes, and after convincing his tribesmen that he possessed the proper requirements, was accepted as a healer. In some tribes he was called to treat all diseases, in others his functions were specialized, and his treatment was regarded as efficacious in only a certain line of affections. He was feared as well as respected. In numerous instances the medicine-man combined the functions of a shaman or priest with those of a healer, and thus exercised a great influence among his people. All priests were believed to possess some healing powers. Among most of the populous tribes the medicine-men of this class were associated in guilds or societies, and on special occasions performed great healing or "life (vitality) giving" ceremonies, which abounded in songs, prayers, ritual, and drama, and extended over a period of a few hours to nine days.

The ordinary procedure of the medicine-man was about as follows: He inquired into the symptoms, dreams, and transgressions of tabus of the patient, whom he examined, and then pronounced his opinion as to the nature (generally mythical) of the ailment. He then prayed, exhorted, or sang, the last, perhaps, to the accompaniment of a rattle; made passes with his hand, sometimes moistened with saliva, over the part affected; and finally placed his mouth over the most painful spot and sucked hard to extract the immediate principle of the illness. This result he apparently accomplished, often by means of sleight-of-hand, producing the offending cause in the shape of a thorn, pebble, hair, or other object, which was then thrown away or destroyed; finally he administered a mysterious powder or other tangible "medicine," and perhaps left also a protective fetish. There were many variations of this method, according to the requirements of the case, and the medicine-man never failed to exercise as much mental influence as possible over his patient. For these services the healer was usually well compensated. If the case would not yield to the simpler treatment,

a healing ceremony might be resorted to. If all means failed, particularly in the case of internal diseases or of adolescents or younger adults, the medicine-man often suggested a witch or wizard as the cause, and the designation of some one as the culprit frequently placed his life in jeopardy. If the medicine-man lost several patients in succession, he himself might be suspected either of having been deprived of his supernatural power or of having become a sorcerer, the penalty for which was usually death.

These shaman healers as a rule were shrewd and experienced men; some were sincere, noble characters, worthy of respect; others were charlatans to a greater or less degree. They are still to be found among the less civilized tribes, but are diminishing in number and losing their influence. Medicine-women of this class were found among the Apache and some other tribes.

The most accomplished of the medicine-men practised also a primitive surgery, and aided, by external manipulation and otherwise, in difficult labor. The highest surgical achievement, undoubtedly practised in part at least as a curative method, was trephining. This operation was of common occurrence and is still practised in Peru, where it reached its highest development among American tribes. Trephining was also known in quite recent times among the Tarahumare of Chihuahua, but has never been found north of Mexico.

The other class of medicine men and women corresponds closely to the herbalists and the old-fashioned rural midwives among white people. The women predominated. They formed no societies, were not so highly respected or so much feared as those of the other class, were not so well compensated, and had less responsibility. In general they used much more common sense in their practice, were acquainted with the beneficial effects of sweating, poulticing, moxa, scarification, various manipulations, and numerous vegetal remedies, such as purgatives, emetics, etc. Some of these medicine-women were frequently summoned in cases of childbirth, and sometimes were of material assistance.

Besides these two chief classes of healers there existed among some tribes large medicine societies, composed principally of patients cured of serious ailments. This was particularly the case among the Pueblos. At Zuñi there still exist several such societies, whose members include the greater part of the tribe and whose organization and functions are complex. The ordinary members are not actual healers, but are believed to be more competent to assist in the particular line of diseases which are the specialty of their society and therefore may be called by the actual medicine-men for assistance. They participate also in the ceremonies of their own society. See *Anatomy, Artificial Head Deformation, Health and Disease, Physiology.*

For writings on the subject consult Hrdlicka, Physiological and Medical Observations, Bull. 34, B. A. E., 1908 (in press). (A. H.)

Medilding ('place of boats'). A Hupa village, the most important of the southern division of this people, on the E. side of Trinity r., Cal., 2 m. from the s. end of Hupa valley. (P. E. G.)
Ipupukhmam.—Goddard, inf'n, 1903 (Karok name). Kahtetl.—Gibbs, MS., B. A. E., 1852 (Yurok name). Ka-la-tih.—Meyer, Nach dem Sacramento, 282, 1855. Ka-tah-te.—McKee (1851) in Sen. Ex. Doc. 4, 32d Cong., spec. sess., 194, 1853. Matilden.—Spalding in Ind. Aff. Rep., 82, 1870. Matilton.—Goddard, Life and Culture of the Hupa, 12, 1903. Medildiñ.—Ibid. Mi-til'-ti.—Powers in Cont. N. A. Ethnol., III, 73, 1877. Olleppauh'l-kah-teht'l.—Gibbs in Schoolcraft, Ind. Tribes, III, 139, 1853.

Medoctec. A former Malecite village on St John r., New Brunswick, about 10 m. below the present Woodstock. In 1721 the name occurs as that of an Abnaki tribe. (J. M.)
Madocteg.—St Maurice (1760) in N. Y. Doc. Col. Hist., X, 1064, 1858. Medocktack.—Gyles (1736) in Drake, Trag. Wild., 78, 1841. Medoctec.—Writer of 1723 in Me. Hist. Soc. Coll., VII, 5, 1876. Medocteck.—Memoir of 1724 in N. Y. Doc. Col. Hist., IX, 940, 1855. Medoctek.—Vaudreuil (1721), ibid., 904. Medoctet.—Beauharnois (1745), ibid., X, 13, 1858. Médoethek.—Iberville (1701), ibid., IX, 733, 1855 (the river). Medoktek.—Shea, Cath. Miss., 143, 1855. Medostec.—Lotter, map, ca. 1770.

Medvednaia (Russ.: 'bearish', from *medved*, 'bear'). A Yukonikhotana settlement on the s. side of Yukon r., Alaska; pop. 15 in 1880.—Petroff in 10th Census, Alaska, 12, 1884.

Meecombe. An Abnaki village on lower Penobscot r., Me., in 1602–09.—Purchas (1625) in Me. Hist. Soc. Coll., V, 156, 1857.

Meeshawn. A former Nauset village near Truro, Barnstable co., Mass. In 1698 it contained about 50 inhabitants.
Meeshawn.—Bourne (1674) in Mass. Hist. Soc. Coll., 1st s., I, 196, 1806. Meshawn.—Freeman, ibid., 1st s., VIII, 160, 1802.

Meetkeni. A former Tolowa village on the s. fork of Smith r., Cal.
Mê'-ĕt-ke'-ni.—Dorsey, Smith River MS. vocab., B. A. E., 1884 (Khaamotene name). Mê'-rxĕt-ke.—Dorsey, Chetco MS. vocab., B. A. E., 1884 (Chetco name).

Meggeckessou. Mentioned as if a Delaware village in 1659. The editor of the New York Colonial Documents locates it at Trenton Falls, N. J., on Delaware r.
Mecheckesiouw.—Hudde (1662) in N. Y. Doc. Col. Hist., XII, 370, 1877. Meggeckesjouw.—Beeckman (1663), ibid., 446. Meggeckessou.—Beeckman (1659), ibid., 255.

Mehashunga (*Me-hä-shun'-gä*, 'duck'). A Kansa gens.—Morgan, Anc. Soc., 156, 1877.

Meherrin. An Iroquoian tribe formerly residing on the river of the same name on the Virginia-North Carolina border. Jefferson confounded them with the Tutelo. According to official colonial documents they were a remnant of the Conestoga or Susquehanna of upper Maryland, dispersed by the Iroquois about 1675, but this also is incorrect, as they are found noted under the name "Menheyricks" in the census of Virginia Indians in 1669, at which time they numbered 50 bowmen, or approximately 180 souls (Neill, Virginia, Carolorum, 326, 1886). It is possible that the influx of refugee Conestoga a few years later may have so overwhelmed the remnant of the original tribe as to give rise to the impression that they were all of Conestoga blood. They were commonly regarded as under the jurisdiction of Virginia, although their territory was claimed also by Carolina. They were closely cognate with the Nottoway, q. v. (J. M.)
Maharim.—Newnam (1722) in Humphreys, Acct., 140, 1730. Maherin.—Doc. of 1705 in N. C. Col. Rec., I, 615, 1886. Maherine.—Doc. of 1703, ibid., 570. Mahering.—Boundary Com'rs (1728), ibid., II, 748. Maherrin.—Council of 1726, ibid., 640. Maherring.—Lawson (1710), Hist. Car., 383, 1860. Maherron.—Council of 1726 in N. C. Col. Rec., II, 640, 1886. Meherine.—Council of 1724, ibid., 525. Meherins.—Doc. of 1712, ibid., I, 891. Meheron.—Doc. of 1721, ibid., II, 426. Meherries.—Schoolcraft, Ind. Tribes, V, 36, 1855. Meherrin.—Council of 1726 in N. C. Col. Rec., II, 643, 1886. Meherring.—Doc. of 1715, ibid., 204. Meherrins.—Pollock (1712), ibid., I, 884. Meherron.—Hyde (1711), ibid., 751. Menchærink.—Lederer (German, 1670) in Hawks, N. C., II, 52, 1858. Menderink.—Ogilby map (1671), ibid. (misprint after Lederer's map). Mendoerink.—Lederer, map (1670), ibid. (German form misprinted). Mendwrink.—Lederer (1670), Discov., map, repr. 1902. Menherring.—Doc. of 1722 in N. C. Col. Rec., II, 475, 1886. Menheyricks.—Census of 1669 quoted by Neill, Va. Carolorum, 326, 1886. Meterries.—Keane in Stanford, Compend., 522, 1878 (misprint).

Mehkoa ('squirrel'). A gens of the Abnaki, q. v.
Meh-ko-ă'.—Morgan, Anc. Soc., 174, 1877. Mi'kowa.—J. D. Prince, inf'n, 1905 (modern St Francis Abnaki form).

Meipontsky. A former tribe of piedmont Virginia, probably of Siouan stock, incorporated about 1700 with the Christanna Indians. See Mooney, Siouan Tribes of the East, Bull. B. A. E., 1894.
Meipontsky.—Albany conf. (1722) in N. Y. Doc. Col. Hist., V, 673, 1855. Meipoutsky.—Byrd, Hist. Div. Line, II, 257, 1866.

Mejia. A hacienda 5 leagues below Isleta, N. Mex., on the Rio Grande, in 1692. At this date it probably contained a few Piros, or perhaps some Tigua from Isleta.—Vargas (1692) quoted by Davis, Span. Conq. N. Mex., 351, 1869; Bancroft, Ariz. and N. Mex., 200, 1889.

Mekadewagamitigweyawininiwak (*Mä'kadäwägami'tigweyä-wininiwüg*, 'people of the black water river.'—W. J.). A Chippewa band formerly living on Black r., S. E. Mich.

Black-River band.—Washington treaty (1836) in U. S. Ind. Treat., 227, 1873. **Mä'kadäwägami'tigwĕyä-wininiwạg.**—Wm. Jones, inf'n, 1906. **Mekadewaga-mitigweya-wininiwak.**—Gatschet, Ojibwa MS., B. A. E., 1882. **Wakazoo.**—Smith in Ind. Aff. Rep., 53, 1851.

Mekewe. A former Chumashan village near Santa Inés, Santa Barbara co., Cal.—Taylor in Cal. Farmer, May 4, 1860.

Mekichuntun (*Mĕ'-ki-tcŭn'-tŭn*). A former village of the Chastacosta on Rogue r., Oreg.—Dorsey in Jour. Am. Folk-lore, III, 234, 1890 (given as a gens).

Mekumtk (*Me'-kŭmtk*, 'long tree moss'). A former Alsea village, the highest on the N. side of Alsea r., Oreg.—Dorsey in Jour. Am. Folk-lore, III, 230, 1890.

Melejo. A Diegueño rancheria near San Diego, s. Cal.; probably identical with "Mileotonac, San Felipe," which was represented in the treaty of Santa Isabel in 1852.
Melejó.—Ortega (1775) quoted by Bancroft, Nat. Races, I, 253, 1884. **Mielo-to-nac, San Felipe.**—H. R. Ex. Doc. 76, 34th Cong., 3d sess. 132, 1857.

Meletecunk. Given as the name of a Delaware tribe formerly on the coast of New Jersey. Proud in 1798 applies this name to Metedeconk r. in Ocean co.
Meletecunk.—Macauley, N. Y., II, 293, 1829. **Moeroahkongy.**—De Laet (*ca.* 1633) in N. Y. Hist. Soc. Coll., 2d s., I, 315, 1841.

Melona. A Timucuan village on the s. bank of lower St Johns r., Fla., in the 16th century.—De Bry, Brev. Nar., II, map, 1591.

Melozikakat. A Yukonikhotana village of 30 inhabitants, on Melozikakat r., a N. affluent of the Yukon, Alaska.—Petroff in 10th Census, Alaska, 12, 1884.

Melukitz. A Kusan village or tribe on the N. side of Coos bay, coast of Oregon. Probably the village most often referred to by writers.—Milhau, Coos bay MS. vocab., B. A. E.; also MS. letter to Gibbs, B. A. E.

Melungeon. See *Croatan Indians*.

Memkumlis ('islands in front'). A village of the Mamalelekala and Koeksotenok, on Village ids., at the mouth of Knight inlet, Brit. Col.; pop. 215 in 1885.
Mēm-koom-līsh.—Dawson in Trans. Roy. Soc. Can. for 1887, sec. II, 65. **Mĕmkumlis.**—Boas in Bull. Am. Geog. Soc., 227, 1887.

Memoggyins (*Mĕ'mogg'ins*, 'having salmon traps'). A gens of the Koeksotenok, a Kwakiutl tribe.—Boas in Rep. Nat. Mus. for 1895, 330.

Memramcook (same as *amlamkook*, 'variegated'). Mentioned by Rand (First Reading Book in Micmac, 81, 1875) as one of the 7 districts of the Micmac country.
Memruncook.—Alcedo, Dic. Geog., III, 147, 1788.

Menapucunt. A village of the Powhatan confederacy, in 1608, on Pamunkey r., King William co., Va.—Smith (1629), Virginia, I, map, repr. 1819.

Menaskunt. A village of the Powhatan confederacy, in 1608, on the N. bank of Rappahannock r., Richmond co., Va.—

Smith (1629), Virginia, I, map, repr. 1819.

Menatonon. A chief, in 1585–86, of the Chowanoc (q. v.), an Algonquian tribe formerly living in N. E. North Carolina, but now extinct. He was prominent during the time that Ralph Layne was in charge of the party sent out by Sir Walter Raleigh to establish a colony, and was one of the chiefs from whom Layne obtained most of his information regarding the country visited, Menatonon being made a prisoner a few days for the purpose. This knowledge of the new country is included in the report sent to Raleigh. According to Layne (Hakluyt, Voy., III, 312, 1810), Menatonon was lame, but for a savage was very grave and wise, and well acquainted not only with his own territory but with the surrounding regions and their productions. It is probable that he died soon after Layne's visit, as John White, who was in the country two years later, mentions his wife and child as belonging to Croatan, but says nothing of him. (c. t.)

Menawzhetaunaung. An Ottawa village, about 1818, on an island in the Lake of the Woods, on the s. boundary of Manitoba, Canada. (J. M.)
Me-nau-zhe-tau-naung.—Tanner, Narr., 202, 1830. **Me-nau-zhe-taw-naun.**—Ibid., 198. **Me-naw-zhe-tau-naung.**—Ibid., 236.

Menchú. Apparently a former Cochimi rancheria in Lower California, not far from Concho bay, on the gulf coast.—Doc. Hist. Mex. 4th s., v, 66, 1857.

Mendica. A tribe, met by Cabeza de Vaca during the earlier part of his stay in Texas (1527–34), that lived "in the rear," i. e., inland. Nothing further is known of it. The country mentioned was probably occupied by Karankawan tribes, which are now extinct. See Cabeza de Vaca, Smith trans., 84, 1851; Gatschet, Karankawa Inds., 46, 1891. (A. C. F.)

Menemesseg. A rendezvous of Nipmuc, Narraganset, and other hostile Indians in 1676, during King Philip's war, near New Braintree, Worcester co., Mass.
Meminimisset.—Fiske (1775) in Mass. Hist. Soc. Coll., 1st s., I, 258, 1806. **Menemesseg.**—Mass. Hist. Soc. Coll., 1st s., VI, 205, 1800. **Menumesse.**—Gookin (1677) in Trans. Am. Antiq. Soc., II, 487, 1836. **Miminimisset.**—Hutchinson in Mass. Hist. Soc. Coll., 1st s., I, 259, 1806. **Mominimisset.**—Whitney in Barber, Hist. Coll., 559, 1839.

Menenquen. An unidentified tribe or band represented at the mission of San Antonio de Valero, Texas, between 1740 and 1750. They allied in their gentile state with the Caguas (Cavas?) and Sijames, who were related to the Emets and Sanas. There is some indication that they were from the middle or lower Guadalupe country. Some words of their language are preserved (Manzanet, 1690, in Texas Hist. Ass'n Quar., II, 309, 1899;

MS. Baptismal records of Mission Valero, partidas 564, 571, 869). See *Meracouman*.
(H. E. B.)

Menanque.—Baptismal records cited, partida 869. **Menanquen.**—Ibid., 571. **Menaquen.**—Ibid., 577. **Merguan.**—Ibid., 448 (identical?). **Merhuan.**—Ibid., 455 (identical?).

Menesouhatoba. A Dakota tribe or division, probably the Mdewakanton.

Menesouhatoba.—Pachot (1722) in Margry, Déc., VI, 518, 1886. **Sicioux des Lacs.**—Ibid.

Menewa ('great warrior'). A half-breed Creek, second chief of the Lower Creek towns on Tallapoosa r., Ala.; born about 1765. He was noted for trickery and daring in early life, when he was known as Hothlepoya ('crazy war hunter') and annually crossed the Cumberland to rob the white settlers in Tennessee of their horses. A murder committed in his neighborhood was charged to his band, and the people of Georgia burned one of their towns in revenge. It was suspected that MacIntosh had instigated the murder for the very purpose of stirring up trouble between the whites and his rival. When Tecumseh came to form a league against the white people, Menewa, foreseeing that MacIntosh with American aid and support would attack him in any event, readily joined in the conspiracy. He began the Creek war and was the war chief of his people, the head chief of the tribe being a medicine-man. Relying on a prophecy of the latter, Menewa made a wrong disposition of his men at the battle of the Horseshoe Bend, Gen. Jackson quickly discerning the vulnerable point in the Indian defenses. Menewa slew the false prophet with his own hand before dashing at the head of his warriors from the breastworks, already breached by the American cannon, into the midst of the Tennesseans, who were advancing to the assault. Of 900 warriors 830 were killed, and all the survivors, save one, were wounded. Menewa, left for dead on the field, revived in the night and, with other survivors, reached the hidden camp in the swamps where the women and children were waiting. The men on their recovery made their submission individually. Menewa's village was destroyed and his wealth in horses and cattle, peltry, and trade goods had disappeared. After his wounds were healed he reassumed authority over the remnant of his band and was in later years the leader of the party in the Creek Nation which opposed further cession of land to the whites and made resistance to their encroachments. MacIntosh counseled acquiescence in the proposal to deport the whole tribe beyond the Mississippi, and when for this he was condemned as a traitor, Menewa was reluctantly persuaded to execute the death sentence.

In 1826 he went with a delegation to Washington to protest against the treaty by which MacIntosh and his confederates, representing about one-tenth of the nation, had at Indian Spring, Jan. 8, 1821, presumed to cede to the United States the fertile Creek country. He proposed, in ceding the Creek country to the Government for white settlement, to reserve some of the land to be allotted in severalty to such of the nation as chose to remain on their native soil rather than to emigrate to a strange region. Through his advocacy the Government was induced to parcel some of the land among the Creeks who were desirous and capable of subsisting by agriculture, to be held in fee simple after a probationary term of five years. An arbitrary method of allotment deprived Menewa of his own farm and, as the one that he drew was undesirable, he sold it and bought other land in Alabama. When some of the Creeks became involved in the Seminole war of 1836, he led his braves against the hostiles. In consideration of his services he obtained permission to remain in his native land, but nevertheless was transported with his people beyond the Mississippi.
(F. H.)

Mengakonkia. A division of the Miami, living in 1682 in central Illinois with the Piankashaw and others.

Mangakekias.—Shea in Wis. Hist. Soc. Coll., III, 134, 1857. **Mangakekis.**—Bacqueville de la Potherie, II, 261, 1753. **Mangakokis.**—Ibid., 335. **Mangakonkia.**—Jes. Rel. 1674, LVIII, 40, 1899. **Megancockia.**—La Salle (1682) in Margry, Déc., II, 201, 1877.

Menhaden. A fish of the herring family (*Alosa menhaden*), known also as bonyfish, mossbunker, hardhead, pauhagen, etc., found in the Atlantic coast waters from Maine to Maryland. The name is derived from the Narraganset dialect of Algonquian. Roger Williams (1643) calls *munnawhatteaug* a "fish like a herring," the word being really plural and signifying, according to Trumbull (Natick Dict., 69, 1903), 'they manure.' The reference is to the Indian custom of using these fish as manure for cornfields, which practice the aborigines of New England transmitted to the European colonists. *Menhaden* is thus a corruption of the Narraganset term for this fish, *munnawhat*, 'the fertilizer.' See *Pogy*. (A. F. C.)

Meniolagomoka. A former Delaware or Munsee village on Aquanshicola cr., Carbon co., Pa. In 1754 the inhabitants, or part of them, joined the Moravian converts at New Gnadenhuetten in the same county. (J. M.)

Meniolagamika.—Heckewelder in Trans. Am. Philos. Soc., n. s., IV, 359, 1834. **Meniolagomekah.**—Loskiel, Hist. Miss. United Breth., pt. 2, 26, 1794.

Menitegow (prob. for *Minĭ tĭgunk*, 'on the island in the river.'—W. J.). A former Chippewa village on the E. bank of Saginaw r., in lower Michigan.—Saginaw treaty (1820) in U. S. Ind. Treat., 142, 1873.

Menominee (*meno*, by change from *mino*, 'good', 'beneficent'; *min*, a 'grain', 'seed', the Chippewa name of the wild rice.—Hewitt. Full name *Menominiwok inini-wok*, the latter term signifying 'they are men'). An Algonquian tribe, the members of which, according to Dr William Jones, claim to understand Sauk, Fox, and Kickapoo far more easily than they do Chippewa, Ottawa, and Potawatomi, hence it is possible that their linguistic relation is near to the former group of Algonquians. Grignon (Wis. Hist. Soc.

AMISKQUEW—MENOMINEE MAN.   (MCKENNEY AND HALL)

Coll., III, 265, 1857) speaks of the Noquet as a part of the Menominee, and states that "the earliest locality of the Menominee, at the first visits of the whites, was at Bay de Noque and Menominee r., and those at Bay de Noque were called by the early French Des Noques or Des Noquia." (See *Noquet*.) The Jesuit Relation for 1671 includes the Menominee among the tribes driven from their country—that is, "the lands of the south next to Michilimackinac," which is the locality where the Noquet lived when they first became known to the French. It is generally believed that the Noquet, who disappeared from history at a comparatively early date, were closely related to the Chippewa and were incorporated into their tribes; nevertheless, the name Menominee must have been

adopted after the latter reached their historic seat; it is possible they were previously known as Noquet. Charlevoix (Jour. Voy., II, 61, 1761) says: "I have been assured that they had the same original and nearly the same languages with the Noquet and the Indians at the Falls."

The people of this tribe, so far as known, were first encountered by the whites when Nicolet visited them, probably in 1634, at the mouth of Menominee r., Wis.-Mich. In 1671, and henceforward until about 1852, their home was on or in the vicinity of Menominee r., not far from where they were found by Nicolet, their settlements extending at times to Fox r. They have generally been at peace with the whites. A succinct account of them, as well as a full description of their manners, customs, arts, and beliefs, by Dr W. J. Hoffman, appears in the 14th Rep. Bureau of Ethnology, 1896. In their treaty with the United States, Feb. 8, 1831, they claimed as their possession the land from the mouth of Green bay to the mouth of Milwaukee r., and on the west side of the bay from the height of land between it and L. Superior to the headwaters of Menominee and Fox rs., which claim was granted. They now reside on a reservation near the head of Wolf r., Wis.

Major Pike described the men of the tribe as "straight and well made, about the middle size; their complexions generally fair for savages, their teeth good, their eyes large and rather languishing; they have a mild but independent expression of countenance that charms at first sight." Although comparatively indolent, they are described as generally honest, theft being less common than among many other tribes. Drunkenness was their most serious fault, but even this did not prevail to the same extent as among some other Indians. Their beliefs and rituals are substantially the same as those of the Chippewa. They have usually been peaceful in character, seldom coming in contact with the Sioux, but bitter enemies of the neighboring Algonquian tribes. They formerly disposed of their dead by inclosing the bodies in long pieces of birchbark, or in slats of wood, and burying them in shallow graves. In order to protect the body from wild beasts, three logs were placed over the grave, two directly on the grave, and the third on these, all being secured by stakes driven on each side. Tree burial was occasionally practised.

The Menominee—as their name indicates—subsisted in part on wild rice (*Zizania aquatica*); in fact it is spoken of by early writers as their chief vegetal food. Although making such constant use of it from the earliest notices we have of them, and aware that it could be readily grown by sowing in proper ground, Jenks (19th Rep. B. A. E., 1021, 1901), who gives a full account of the Menominee method of gathering, preserving, and using the wild rice, states that they absolutely refuse to sow it—evidently owing to their common unwillingness to "wound their mother, the earth."

Chauvignerie gives their principal totems as the Large-tailed Bear, the Stag, and the Kilou (a sort of eagle). Neill (Hist. Minn., 1858) classes the Menominee, evidently on French authority, as Folles Avoines of the Chat and Orignal or Wild Moose and Elk. Hoffman gives the modern totems as follows:

I. The Owa′sse wi′dishi′anun, or Bear phratry, consisting of the following totems and subphratries: Owa′sse (Bear), Miqkä′no (Mud-turtle), Kitä′mi (Porcupine), with the Namä′nu (Beaver) and O′sass (Muskrat).

II. The Kině′uᵛ wi′dishi′anun, or Eagle phratry, consisting of the following totems: Pinäsh′iu (Bald Eagle), Kaka′k (Crow), Inä′qtěk (Raven), Ma′qkuana′ni (Red-tail Hawk), Hinanä′shiuᵛ (Golden Eagle), Pe′niki′konau (Fish-hawk).

III. The Otä′tshia wi′dishi′anun, or Crane phratry, consisting of the following totems: Otä′tshia (Crane), Shakshak′eu (Great Heron), Os′se ("Old Squaw" Duck), O′kawa′siku (Coot).

IV. The Moqwai′o wi′dishi′anun, or Wolf phratry, consisting of the following totems: Moqwai′o (Wolf), "Hana" [änä′m] (Dog), Apaq′ssos (Deer).

V. The Mons wi′dishi′anun, or Moose phratry, with the following totems: Mōⁿs (Moose), Oma′skos (Elk), Wabä′shiu (Marten), Wū′tshik (Fisher).

The earlier statements of Menominee population are unreliable. Most of the estimates in the nineteenth century vary from 1,300 to 2,500, but those probably most conservative range from 1,600 to 1,900. Their present population is about 1,600, of whom 1,370 are under the Green Bay school superintendency, Wis. Their villages (missions) were St Francis and St Michael.

The Menominee have entered into the following treaties with the United States: (1) Treaty of peace at St Louis, Mo., Mar. 30, 1817; (2) Treaty of Prairie du Chien, Wis., Aug. 19, 1825, with the Menominee and other Indians, fixing boundary lines between the several tribes; (3) Treaty of Butte des Morts, Wis., Aug. 11, 1827, defining boundary lines between the Menominee, Chippewa, and Winnebago; (4) Treaty of Washington, Feb. 8, 1831, defining boundary lines and ceding lands to the United States, a portion of the latter to be for the use of certain New York Indians; (5) Treaty of Washington, Feb. 17, 1831, modifying the treaty of Feb. 8, 1831, in regard to the lands ceded for the use of the New York Indians; (6) Treaty of Washington, Oct. 27, 1832, in which certain modifications are made in regard to the lands ceded for the use of the New York Indians (Stockbridges and Munsee), and to certain boundary lines; (7) Articles of agreement made at Cedar Point, Wis., Sept. 3, 1836, ceding certain lands to the United States; (8) Treaty of Lake Pow-aw-hay-kon-nay, Oct. 18, 1848, ceding all their lands in Wisconsin, the United States to give them certain lands which had been ceded by the Chippewa; (9) Treaty at the Falls of Wolf r., May 12, 1854, by which they ceded the reserve set apart by treaty of Oct. 18, 1848, and were assigned a reserve on Wolf r., Wis.; (10) Treaty of Keshena, Wis., Feb. 11, 1856, ceding two townships of their reserve for the use of the Stockbridges and the Munsee.　　　　(J. M.　C. T.)

Addle-Heads.—Jefferys, French Dom., pt. I, 48, 1761 (given as the meaning of Folles Avoines). **Falsavins.**—Doc. of 1764 in N. Y. Doc. Col. Hist., VII, 641, 1856. **Felles avoins.**—Lords of Trade (1721), ibid., V, 622, 1855. **Folleavoine.**—Vaudreuil (1720) in Margry, Déc., VI, 511, 1886. **Folle Avoines.**—Memoir of 1718 in N. Y. Doc. Col. Hist., IX, 889, 1855. **Folles Avoines.**—Cadillac (1695) in Margry, Déc., V, 121, 1883. **Fols Avoin.**—Pike, Expedition, 13, 1810. **Fols Avoines.**—Brown, West. Gaz., 265, 1817. **Folsavoins.**—Johnson (1763) in N. Y. Doc. Col. Hist., VII, 583, 1856. **Fols-avoise.**—Schermerhorn (1812) in Mass. Hist. Soc. Coll., 2d s., II, 10, 1814. **Folsovoins.**—Harrison (1814) in Drake, Tecumseh, 162, 1852. **Fulawin.**—Dalton (1783) in Mass. Hist. Soc. Coll., 1st s., X, 123, 1809. **Fulsowines.**—Edwards, Hist. Ill., 39, 1870. **Les Fols.**—Featherstonhaugh, Canoe Voyage, I, 174, 1847. **Les Fols.**—Ann. de la Prop. de la Foi, IV, 537, 1830. **Macomilé.**—La Chesnaye (1697) in Margry, Déc., VI, 6, 1886 (misprint?). **Mahnomoneeg.**—Tanner, Narrative, 315, 1830 (Ottawa name). **Mahnomonie.**—James in Tanner, ibid., 326. **Malhoming.**—Bacqueville de la Potherie, Hist. Am., II, 90, 1753. **Malhominis.**—Ibid. **Malhomins.**—Ibid., IV, 206, 1753. **Malhominy.**—Cadillac (1695) in Margry, Déc., V, 121, 1883. **Malhommes.**—Jefferys, French Dom., pt. I, 48, 1761. **Malhommis.**—Perrot (ca. 1720), Memoirs, 127, 1864. **Malomenis.**—Frontenac (1682) in N. Y. Doc. Col. Hist., IX, 182, 1855. **Malomimis.**—Lahontan, New Voy., I, 231, 1703. **Malomines.**—Bellin, map, 1755. **Malominese.**—Blue Jacket (1807) in Drake, Tecumseh, 94, 1852. **Malominis.**—Lahontan, New Voy., I, 104, 1703. **Malouin.**—Sagard (1636), Hist. Can., II, 424, 1864. **Malouminek.**—Jes. Rel. 1658, 21, 1858. **Maloumines.**—Warren (1852) in Minn. Hist. Soc. Coll., V, 33, 1885 (French form). **Manōmanee.**—Kane, Wanderings of an Artist, 29, 1859. **Manomines.**—Henry, Travels, 107, 1809. **Manominik.**—Gatschet, Ojibwa MS., B. A. E., 1882 (Chippewa name). **Maroumine.**—Jes. Rel. 1640, 35, 1858. **Mathomonis.**—Bacqueville de la Potherie, Hist. Am., II, 71, 1753. **Mathominis.**—Ibid., 81. **Melhominys.**—Croghan (1759) in Proud, Pa., II, 296, 1798. **Melomelinoia.**—La Salle (1680) in Margry, Déc., II, 201, 1877 (in central Illinois; apparently identical). **Melominees.**—Perkins and Peck, Annals of the West, 713, 1850. **Memonomier.**—Vater, Mith., pt. 3, sec. 3, 406, 1816. **Menamenies.**—Rupp, West. Pa., 346, 1846. **Mennominies.**—Goldthwait (1766) in Mass. Hist. Soc. Coll., 1st s., X, 121, 1809. **Menomenes.**—Pike (1806) in Schoolcraft, Ind. Tribes, III, 562, 1853. **Me-nó-me-ne-uk′.**—Morgan, Consang. and Affin., 288, 1871. **Menomenies.**—Brown, West. Gaz., 265, 1817. **Menominees.**—Treaty of 1825 in U. S. Ind.

Treaties, 376, 1837. **Menominies.**—Treaty of 1826, ibid., 155. **Menominny.**—Featherstonhaugh, Canoe Voyage, II, 25, 1847. **Menomoee.**—Gale, Upper Miss., map, 1867. **Menomonees.**—Edwards (1788) in Mass. Hist. Soc. Coll., 2d s., x, 86, 1823. **Menomonei.**—McKenney in Ind. Aff. Rep., 90, 1825. **Menomones.**—Long, Exped. St Peters R., I, 171, 1824. **Menomonies.**—Boudinot, Star in the West, 100, 1816. **Menomonys.**—Lapham, Inds. of Wis., map, 1870. **Menonomees.**—La Pointe treaty (1842) in Minn. Hist. Soc. Coll., v, 494, 1885. **Menonomies.**—Howe, Hist. Coll., 436, 1851. **Meynomenys.**—Johnson (1763) in N. Y. Doc. Col. Hist., VII, 583, 1856. **Meynomineys.**—Johnson (1764), ibid., 648. **Mineamies.**—Trader (1778) in Schoolcraft, Ind. Tribes, III, 560, 1853. **Miniamis.**—Keane in Stanford, Compend., 522, 1878. **Minominees.**—Jones, Ojebway Inds., 39, 1861. **Minominies.**—Warren (1852) in Minn. Hist. Soc. Coll., v, 33, 1885. **Minomonees.**—Edwards (1788) in Mass. Hist. Soc. Coll., 1st s., IX, 92, 1804. **Minoniones.**—Boudinot, Star in the West, 107, 1816. **Minoomenee.**—Jones, Ojebway Inds., 178, 1861. **Monis.**—Perrin du Lac, Voy. Deux Louisianes, 232, 1805 (probably identical; mentioned with Puans [Winnebago] and Oyoa [Iowa]). **Monomeni.**—Gatschet, Fox MS., B. A. E., 1882 (Fox name; pl. Monomenihak). **Monomins.**—Henry, Travels, 107, 1809. **Monomonees.**—Schoolcraft, Ind. Tribes, v, 145, 1855. **Monomunies.**—Lindsay (1749) in N. Y. Doc. Col. Hist., vI, 538, 1855. **Moon-calves.**—Jefferys, French Dom., pt. I, 48, 1861 (given as the meaning of Folles Avoines). **Mynomamies.**—Imlay, West. Ter., 292, 1797. **Mynomanies.**—Hutchins (1778) in Schoolcraft, Ind. Tribes, vI, 714, 1857. **Mynonamies.**—Croghan (1765) in Monthly Am. Jour. Geol., 272, 1831. **Nation de la folle avoine.**—Jes. Rel. 1671, 25, 1858. **Nation of the Wild-Oats.**—Marquette (ca. 1673), Discov., 319, 1698. **Omanomineu.**—Kelton, Ft Mackinac, 149, 1884 (own name, pronounced O-man-o-me-na-oo). **Omanomini.**—Ibid. (Chippewa name). **O-mun-o-min-eeg.**—Warren (1852) in Minn. Hist. Soc. Coll., v, 33, 1885. **Oumalominis.**—Prise de Possession (1671) in Margry, Déc., I, 97, 1876. **Oumalouminek.**—Jes. Rel. 1670, 94, 1858. **Oumaloumines.**—Jes. Rel. 1671, 25, 1858. **Oumalouminetz.**—Jes. Rel. 1670, 100, 1858. **Oumaominiecs.**—Du Chesneau (1681) in N. Y. Doc. Col. Hist., IX, 161, 1855. **Ounabonims.**—Prise de Possession (1671) ibid., 803 (misprint). **Rice Indians.**—Franchère, Narr., 145, 1854. **Walhominies.**—McKenney and Hall, Ind. Tribes, III, 79, 1854 (misprint). **White Indians.**—Long, Exped. St Peters R., I, 175, 1824. **Wild Rice.**—Document of 1701 in N. Y. Doc. Col. Hist., IX, 722, 1855. **Wild Rice Eaters.**—Lapham, Inds. Wis., 15, 1870 (given as the meaning of Menominee). **Wild Rice Men.**—Schoolcraft, Ind. Tribes, v, 145, 1855.

Menominee. A Potawatomi village, taking its name from the resident chief, formerly situated on the N. side of Twin lakes, near the site of Plymouth, Marshall co., Ind., on a reservation sold in 1836. The name is also written Menomonee.

(J. M.)

Menoquet (possibly for *Mino'kwat*, 'good ice,' or *Mina'kwŭt*, 'banked cloud,' or *Mena'kwatwⁱ*, 'fair weather.'—W. J.). A Potawatomi village, commonly called "Menoquet's village" from the name of a chief, formerly situated near the present Monoquet, Kosciusko co., Ind., on a reservation sold in 1836. The name is spelled also Menoequet, Menoga (Indiana Geol. Rep., map, 1883), Minoquet, and Monoquet.

Menoquet's Village. A Chippewa village, so called after its chief, formerly on Cass r., lower Michigan, on a reservation sold in 1837.

Menostamenton. An unidentified division of the Sioux.
Manostamenton.—Jefferys, Am. Atlas, map 5, 1776. **Menostamenton.**—De l'Isle, map of La., in Neill, Hist. Minn., 164, 1858.

Mento. A name used by French writers of the 17th and 18th centuries to designate a people in the vicinity of Arkansas r. and the southern plains. Marquette heard of them during his descent of the Mississippi in 1673, and located them on his map as w. of that river; Douay (1687) placed them near Red r. of Louisiana; Tonti (1690) states that they were in the vicinity of the Quapaw, and De l'Isle's map (1703) puts them on middle Arkansas r. La Harpe (1719) says they were 7 days' journey s. w. of the Osage. Beaurain about that time visited the people and gives the names of the 9 "nations" which, he says, formed one continuous village lying in a beautiful situation, the houses joining one another from E. to w. on the border of a s. w. branch of Arkansas r. The "nations" mentioned include the Tonkawa, Wichita, Comanche, Adai, Caddo, Waco, etc. The Mento were enemies of the Spaniards and the Apache tribes.   (A. C. F.)
Manton.—Iberville (1702) in Margry, Déc., IV, 599, 1886. **Manⁿ-ʠu-we.**—Dorsey, Kansa MS., B. A. E., 1882 (Kansa name). **Matora.**—Marquette, map (1673) in Shea, Discov., 268, 1852. **Matoua.**—Shea, ibid. **Mauton.**—Tonti (ca. 1690) in French, Hist. Coll. La., I, 83, 1846. **Mento.**—La Harpe (1719) in Margry, Déc., vI, 315, 1886. **Mentons.**—Jefferys, Am. Atlas, map 5, 1776. **Mentous.**—Hennepin, New Discov., pt. II, 43, 1698. **Mintou.**—Coxe, Carolana, 11, map, 1741.

Mentokakat. A Koyukukhotana village on the left bank of the Yukon, Alaska, 20 m. above the mouth of Melozi r.; pop. 46 in 1844; 20 in 1880.
Mentokakat.—Petroff in 10th Census, Alaska, 12, 1884. **Minkhotliatno.**—Zagoskin quoted by Petroff, ibid., 37. **Montekakat.**—U. S. Land Off. map of Alaska, 1898.

Menunkatuc (prob. from *munonqutteau*, 'that which fertilizes or manures land,' hence 'menhaden country.'—Trumbull). A village, under a sachem squaw, formerly at Guilford, New Haven co., Conn., on a tract sold in 1639.   (J. M.)
Manuncatuck.—Doc. of 1641 cited by Trumbull, Ind. Names Conn., 29, 1881. **Menuncatuk.**—Drake, Ind. Chron., 157, 1836. **Menunkatuck.**—Ruggles in Mass. Hist. Soc. Coll., 1st s., IV, 182, 1795. **Menunketuck.**—Trumbull, op. cit. **Menunquatucke.**—Ibid. **Monunkatuck.**—Ibid. **Munnucketucke.**—Ibid. **Mununketucke.**—Ibid.

Meochkonck. A former Minisink village probably situated about upper Delaware r. in s. E. New York.—Van der Donck (1656) quoted by Ruttenber, Tribes Hudson R., 96, 1872.

Mepayaya. A tribe mentioned in the manuscript relation of Francisco de Jesus María, in 1691, in his list of the Texias (i. e., the group of customary allies, including the Hasinai), as s. w. of the Nabedache country of Texas. This may be the Payaya tribe, who were in the vicinity of San Antonio. (H. E. B.)

Mequachake ('red earth.'—Hewitt). One of the 5 general divisions of the Shawnee, whose villages on the headwaters of Mad r., Logan co., Ohio, were destroyed by United States troops in 1791. See *Spitotha*. (J. M.)

Machachac.—Drake, Tecumseh, 50, 1852. **Machichac.**—Ibid., 71. **Mackacheck.**—Howe, Hist. Coll., 150, 1851. **Mackacheek.**—Royce in 18th Rep. B. A. E., Ohio map, 1899. **Magueck.**—Alcedo, Dic. Geog., III, 22, 1788 (probably identical). **Makostrake.**—McKenney and Hall, Ind. Tribes, III, 111, 1854. **Maquichees.**—Stone, Life of Brant, II, 43, 1864. **Menekut'thégi.**—Gatschet, Shawnee MS., 1879. **Mequachake.**—Johnston (1819) in Brinton, Lenape Leg., 29, 1885.

Meracouman. A tribe or village mentioned by Joutel as being on or near the route taken when going with La Salle in 1687 from Ft St Louis on Matagorda bay to Maligne (Colorado) r., Tex. If the list of so-called tribes given by the Ebahamo Indians and recorded by Joutel followed the geographic order of his line of march, the Meracouman must have dwelt near the Colorado r. of Texas. Joutel remarks that when the Indians approached or bathed in the current of the river, the horses always fled. Gatschet states that the custom of the Karankawa Indians of anointing their skin with shark's oil caused horses and cattle to run from the disagreeable odor to the distance of two or three miles. As Karankawan tribes are said to have dwelt in the vicinity of Colorado r., it is possible that the Meracouman may have belonged to that stock (see Gatschet, Karankawa Inds., 1891). Perhaps they are the Maliacones of Cabeza de Vaca or the Manico of Manzanet. In 1739 there were neophytes of the Merguan, or Merhuan, tribe at San Antonio de Valero mission (Baptismal records, partidas 448, 455, MS., cited by H. E. Bolton, inf'n, 1906). They were with others who appear to have come from near Guadalupe r., and they may be identical with the Meracouman, as well as with the Menenquen (q. v.). (A. C. F. H. E. B.)

Meracouman.—Joutel (1687) in French, Hist. Coll. La., I, 137, 1846. **Meraquaman.**—Joutel (1687) in Margry, Déc., III, 288, 1878. **Muracumanes.**—Barcia, Ensayo, 271, 1723.

Merced (Span.: 'grace', 'mercy'). A group of Cajuenche rancherias, situated, in 1775, in N. E. Lower California, w. of the Rio Colorado, and 4 leagues s. w. of Santa Olalla, a Yuma rancheria. These settlements contained about 300 natives when visited by Father Garcés in 1775 and were provided with abundant corn, melons, calabashes, and beans, but with little wheat. See Garcés, Diary (1775), 172–173, 1900.

Merced. A Pima rancheria, visited by Father Kino in 1700, and placed on maps of Kino (1701) and Venegas (1759) N. E. of San Rafael, in what is now s. Arizona.

La Merced.—Venegas, Hist. Cal., I, 300, map, 1759. **Merced.**—Kino map (1701) in Bancroft, Ariz. and N. Mex., 360, 1889.

Merced. Mentioned as a tribe apparently inhabiting the Merced r. region, California. Probably Moquelumnan.

Mercedes.—Barbour et al. (1851) in Sen. Ex. Doc. 4, 32d Cong., spec. sess., 60, 1853.

Mer, Gens de la (French: 'people of the sea,' or Gens de la Mer du Nord, 'people of the sea of the north'). A collective term applied by the early Jesuits to the Algonquian tribes about Hudson bay, Canada. (J. M.)

Gens de la Mer du Nord.—Jes. Rel. 1670, 79, 1858. **Gens de Mer.**—Ibid., 1643, 3, 1858.

Merip. A Yurok village on Klamath r., Cal., about 10 m. below the mouth of the Trinity. (A. L. K.)

Merkitsok. An Eskimo winter habitation near Bute bay, s. w. Greenland.—Crantz, Hist. Greenland, I, 8, 1767.

Merric. A small Algonquian tribe or division formerly inhabiting the s. coast of Queens co., Long Island, N. Y., from Rockaway to South Oyster bay. Their name survives in the hamlet of Merricks, which is on the site of their principal village. (J. M.)

Marricoke.—Doc. of 1675 in N. Y. Doc. Col. Hist., XIV, 705, 1883. **Meracock.**—Treaty of 1656 in Ruttenber, Tribes of Hudson River, 125, 1872. **Mericock.**—Doc. of 1657 in N. Y. Doc. Col. Hist., XIV, 416, 1883. **Mericoke.**—Thompson, Long Id., 344, 1839. **Merikoke.**—Wood in Macauley, N. Y., II, 252, 1829. **Meroke.**—Thompson, Long Id., 67, 1839. **Merriack.**—Deed of 1643 in N. Y. Doc. Col. Hist., XIV, 530, 1883. **Merric.**—Thompson, Long Id., 67, 1839. **Merricocke.**—Doc. of 1675 in N. Y. Doc. Col. Hist., XIV, 705, 1883.

Mershom. A former Chumashan village at Cañada de los Sauces, w. of San Buenaventura, Ventura co., Cal.

Mer-cöm.—Henshaw, Buenaventura MS. vocab., B. A. E., 1884 (c=sh).

Mesa Chiquita (Span.: 'small mesa' or table-land). A Diegueño village in w. San Diego co., Cal.—Jackson and Kinney, Rep. Miss. Inds., 24, 1883.

Mesa del Nayarit. A pueblo of the Cora in the Sierra de Nayarit, on the upper waters of the Rio de Jesus María, in the N. part of the Territory of Tepic, lat. 23° 25', Mexico.—Lumholtz, Unknown Mex., I, 500, 1902.

Mesa Grande (Span.: 'large mesa' or table-land). A small Diegueño village in w. San Diego co., Cal., with 103 inhabitants in 1880. The name is now applied to a reservation of 120 acres of patented, largely desert land, 75 m. from Mission Tule River agency. See Jackson and Kinney, Rep. Mission Inds., 24, 1883; Ind. Aff. Rep., 175, 1902.

Mescal (Aztec: *mexcalli*, '*metl* [maguey] liquor'). The fleshy leaf bases and trunk of various species of agave. It was roasted in pit ovens and became a sweet and nutritious food among the

Indians of the states on both sides of the Mexican boundary. Mescal pits are usually circular depressions in the ground, 6 to 20 ft in circumference, sloping evenly to the center, a foot to 3 ft in depth, and lined with coarse gravel. A fire was built in the pit, raked out after the stones had become hot, and the mescal plants put in and covered with grass. After two days' steaming the pile was opened and the mescal was ready for consumption.

The product must not be confounded with the distilled spirit known in Mexico under the same name, nor with the *peyote* cactus. Mescal is a valuable food resource among the Apache (a division of whom, the Mescaleros, is named from their custom of eating mescal), as well as among the Mohave, Yuma, Ute, Paiute, and practically every tribe of the region producing the agave. An extensive commerce in this sweet was carried on with outlying tribes, as the Hopi and other Pueblos. So far as known mescal was not fermented by the Indians to produce an intoxicating drink before the coming of the Spaniards. The food value of mescal is regarded as of such importance that the entire population of Presidio del Norte (El Paso), on the failure of their crops half a century ago, subsisted for six months on roasted agave (Bartlett, Pers. Narr., ii, 291, 1854). See *Peyote*. (w. h.)

Mescaleros (Span.: 'mescal people,' from their custom of eating mescal). An Apache tribe which formed a part of the Faraones and Vaqueros of different periods of the Spanish history of the S. W. Their principal range was between the Rio Grande and the Pecos in New Mexico, but it extended also into the Staked plains and southward into Coahuila, Mexico. They were never regarded as so warlike as the Apache of Arizona, otherwise they were generally similar. Mooney (field notes, B. A. E., 1897) records the following divisions: Nataina, Tuetinini, Tsihlinainde, Guhlkainde, and Tahuunde. These bands intermarry, and each had its chief and subchief. The Guhlkainde are apparently identical with the "Cuelcajenne" of Orozco y Berra and others, who classed them as a division of the Llaneros; the "Natages" are probably the same as the Nataina rather than the Lipan or the Kiowa Apache, while the Tsihlinainde seem to be identifiable with the "Chilpaines." In addition Orozco y Berra gives the Lipillanes as a Llanero division.

The Mescaleros are now on a reservation of 474,240 acres in s. New Mexico, set apart for them in 1873. Population 460 in 1905, including about a score of Lipan, q. v. (F. W. H.)

Ahuátcha.—Gatschet, Yuma-Spr., i, 413, 1883 (Mohave name). Apaches des 7 Rivières.—Baudry des Lozières, Voy. Louisiane, map, 1802 (named from Seven rivers in s. E. N. Mex.). Apaches Llaneros.—Bonnycastle, Span. Am., 68, 1819. Apaches Mescaleros.—Ibid. Apaches of Seven Rivers.—Jefferys, Am. Atlas, map 5 (1763), 1776. Apachos Mescaleros.—Morse, Am. Univ. Geog., i, 685, 1819. Chï-shë'.—Hodge, field notes, B. A. E., 1895 (Keresan name). Ebikuita.—Gatschet, Creek Migr. Leg., i, 28, 1884 (here given as a synonym of Cherokee). Escequatas.—Neighbors in H. R. Doc. 100, 29th Cong., 2d sess., 5, 1847. Ésikwíta.—Mooney in 17th Rep. B. A. E., 245, 1898 (Kiowa name). Es-ree-que-tees.—Butler and Lewis in H. R. Doc. 76, 29th Cong., 2d sess., 6, 1847. És-sẹ-kwĭt'-ta.—ten Kate, Synonymie, 9, 1884 (Comanche name: trans., 'gray buttocks', but really signifying 'gray dung'). Essekwítta.—ten Kate, Reizen in N. Am., 376, 1885. Esse-qua-ties.—Butler and Lewis in H. R. Doc. 76, 29th Cong., 2d sess., 7, 1847. Euquatops.—Schoolcraft (after Neighbors), Ind. Tribes, i, 518, 1851 (probably misprint of Esequatops=Esikwita). Ho-tashĭn.—Mooney, field notes, B. A. E., 1897 (Comanche name: apparently a corrupted Mescalero word). Ĭnátahĭn.—Ibid. ('mescal people': Lipan name). Mamakans Apaches.—Warden, Account U. S. A., iii, 562, 1819 (probably identical). Mascaleros.—Schoolcraft, Ind. Tribes, v, 207, 1855. Masceleros.—Ibid. Mescaleres.—Robin, Voy. à la Louisiane, iii, 15, 1807. Mescalero Apaches.—Bell in Jour. Ethnol. Soc. Lond., i, 240, 1869. Mescaleros.—Tex. State Arch., doc. 503, 1791. Mescalers.—Ind. Aff. Rep., 218, 1861. Mescallaros.—Haines, Am. Indian, 134, 1888. Mescalos.—Taylor in Cal. Farmer, Apr. 17, 1863. Mescaloro Apaches.—Meriwether in Sen. Ex. Doc. 69, 34th Cong., 1st sess., 15, 1856. Mescaluros.—Box, Advent., 320, 1869. Mescateras.—Ind. Aff. Rep., 439, 1853 (misprint). Mescolero.—Ind. Aff. Rep. 1857, 288, 1858. Mezcaleros.—Gregg, Comm. Prairies, i, 290, 1844. Miscaleros.—Morgan in N. Am. Rev., 58, 1870. Moscalara.—Parker, Unexplored Texas, 221, 1856. Mu-ca-la-moes.—Butler and Lewis in H. R. Doc. 76, 29th Cong., 2d sess., 7, 1847. Musaleros.—Ind. Aff. Rep., 257, 1853. Mus-ca-lar-oes.—Butler and Lewis in H. R. Doc. 76, 29th Cong., 2d sess., 6, 1847. Muscaleros.—Schoolcraft, Ind. Tribes, v, 203, 1855. Muscallaros.—Pattie, Pers. Narr., 117, 1833. Mus-ka-le-ras.—Schoolcraft, Ind. Tribes, i, 518, 1851. Mus-ka-leros.—Ind. Aff. Rep. 1849, 28, 1850. Mus-keleras.—Neighbors in H. R. Doc. 100, 29th Cong., 2d sess., 5, 1847. Muskeleros.—Ind. Aff. Rep., 574, 1848. Nashkáli dinne.—Gatschet, notes, 1886 (Navaho name). Nátahë'.—Mooney, field notes, B. A. E., 1897 ('mescal people': Lipan name). Nátahĭ'n.—Ibid. (Jicarilla name). Na-ta'-në.—Hodge, field notes, B. A. E., 1895 (Picuris name). Ndátahë'.—Mooney, field notes, B. A. E., 1897 (Lipan name). Pa-ha-sa-be'.—ten Kate, Synonymie, 8, 1884 (Tesuque name). Sacramantenos.—Hamilton, Mex. Handbk., 48, 1883. Sacramento Apaches.—Parke, Map New Mex., 1851 (doubtless identical although located as distinct). Saline Apaches.—Vargas (1692) quoted by Davis, Span. Conq. N. Mex., 864, 1869. Sejen-né.—Escudero, Not. Estad. de Chihuahua, 212, 1834 (native name). Táshi.—ten Kate, Reizen in N. Am., 376, 1885. Tiχitíwa hupónun.—Gatschet, notes, 1885 (Isleta name). Tsi'-se'.—Hodge, field notes, B. A. E., 1895 (San Ildefonso Tewa name, cf. *Chï-shë'*, above).

Mescales. A former tribe or tribes in n. e. Mexico and s. Texas. The one oftenest referred to lived not far from the junction of the Salado with the Rio Grande, and Mescales are mentioned at the neighboring mission of San Juan Bautista, founded in 1699. These spoke a Coahuiltecan dialect. De Leon, in 1689, mentions them in connection with the Hapes, Jumenes, and Xiabu. (H. E. B.)

Mescale.—De Leon (1689) in Tex. Hist. Ass'n Quar., viii, 205, 1905. Mescate.—Manzanet, ibid,

Meseekunnoghquoh. See *Little Turtle*.

Mesheka (*Me-she'-kă*, 'mud turtle'). A gens of the Chippewa, q. v.—Morgan, Anc. Soc., 166, 1877.

Meshekenoghqua. See *Little Turtle*.

Mesheketeno. A Potawatomi village which took its name from the resident chief, situated on Kankakee r., a short distance above the present Kankakee, N. E. Illinois, in 1833.—Camp Tippecanoe treaty (1834) in U. S. Ind. Treaties, 698, 1873.

Meshekunnoghquoh. See *Little Turtle*.

Meshingomesia. A former Miami village, commonly called after a chief of this name, situated on a reservation on the N. E. side of Mississinewa r., in Liberty tp., Wabash co., Ind. The reserve was originally established for Meshingomesia's father, Metosinia, or Matosinia, in 1838, and its inhabitants were known as Meshingomesia's band. In 1872 the land was divided among the surviving occupants and patented to them, being the last land held as an Indian reservation in Indiana. (J. M.)

Me-shing-go-me-sia.—Royce in 1st Rep. B. A. E., 262, 1881. Me-shing-go-me-zia.—Treaty of 1840 in U. S. Ind. Treat., 510, 1873. Me-shin-gi-me-yia.—Hough, map in Indiana Geol. Rep., 1883. Shingle-masy.—Common local form.

Meshkemau. An Ottawa village, commonly called "Meshkemau's village," from the name of its chief, formerly existing on Maumee bay, Lucas co., Ohio, on land sold in 1833. The name is also written Meskemau and Mishkemau.

Meshtshe (*Mĕc'-tcĕ*, 'village at the mouth of a small creek'). A former Mishikhwut-metunne village on upper Coquille r., Oreg.—Dorsey in Jour. Am. Folk-lore, III, 232, 1890.

Mesitas (Span.: 'little mesas' or table-lands). An ancient settlement of the Tepecano, the ruins of which are situated E. of the Rio de Bolaños, about 3 m. s. E. of Mezquitic, in Jalisco, Mexico.—Hrdlicka in Am. Anthrop., v, 389, 409, 1903.

Meskwadare (for *Mĭskwādäsⁱ*, 'small water-turtle.'—W. J.). A gens of the Chippewa, q. v.

Me-skwä-da'-re.—Morgan, Anc. Soc., 166, 1877. Miskwädäsⁱ.—Wm. Jones, inf'n, 1906.

Mesquawbuck ('red rock place.'—Hewitt). A former Potawatomi village, commonly known as "Mesquawbuck's village," from a chief of this name, near the present Oswego, Kosciusko co., Ind., on a reservation sold in 1836. The name is spelled also Mesquabuck and Musquabuck. (J. M.)

Mesquite (adapted from Aztec for *Prosopis juliflora*). A village of the central Papago, probably in Pima co., s. Ariz.; said to have 500 inhabitants in 1863 and 70 families in 1865.

Mesquit.—Poston in Ind. Aff. Rep. 1863, 385, 1864. Mesquite.—Browne, Apache Country, 291, 1869. Misquito.—Bailey in Ind. Aff. Rep., 208, 1858. Mus-quito.—Ibid., 135, 1865. Raiz del Mesquite.—Orozco y Berra, Geog., 348, 1864 (sig. 'Mesquite root' probably identical).

Mesquites. A tribe represented in the 18th century at the San Antonio missions, Texas. They are mentioned as early as 1716, by Espinosa, who met one Indian of this tribe w. of Arroyo Hondo (Diario, 1716, MS.); he also met others near the Brazos with the Tonkawan Indians of Ranchería Grande. In 1727 Rivera mentions them at San Antonio with the Payayas and Aguastayas (Diario, leg. 1994, 1736). There are proofs that in their gentile state they intermarried with the Ervipiames and Muruames (Baptismal Rec. of Valero, partidas 194, 418), and also with the Payayas (ibid., partida 90). The first baptism of one of this tribe recorded at San Antonio de Valero is dated Nov. 8, 1720. In 1734 one person at a residencia in San Antonio acted as interpreter for Xarame, Payaya, Siaguan, Aguastaya, and Mesquite witnesses (Residencia de Bustillos y Zevallos, Béxar archives, 1730–36); but too much must not be inferred from this circumstance. In 1768 Solis reported Mesquites at San José mission, with Pampopas, Aguastallas, Pastias, and Xarames (Diario, Mem. Nueva España, XXVII, 270), and in 1793 Revillagigedo implied that this tribe constituted a part of the few neophytes still at this mission (Carta, Dic., 27, 1793). A tribe called Mesquites lived in 1757 across the Rio Grande at Villa de Santander. These were divided into 4 bands, consisting of 150 families (Tiendo de Cuervo, Revista, Archivo General, MS.). (H. E. B.)

Mesquita.—Baptismal records cited above, partida 310. Mesquites.—Solis (1767) quoted by H. E. Bolton, inf'n, 1906. Mesquittes.—Residencia, cited above, 1734. Mezquites.—Rivera, Diario, leg. 1994, 1736.

Messiah legends. See *Ghost dance*.

Mestethltun (*Mĕs-tĕçl'-tûn*). A former village of the Tolowa, on the coast near Crescent, Cal.—Dorsey in Jour. Am. Folk-lore, III, 236, 1890.

Mestizo. See *Métis, Mixed-bloods*.

Meta. A Yurok village on Klamath r., Cal., 4 or 5 m. above Klamath bluffs.

Mē'h-teh.—Gibbs in Schoolcraft, Ind. Tribes, III, 138, 1853. Meta.—A. L. Kroeber, inf'n, 1905. Mí-ta.—Powers in Cont. N. A. Ethnol., III, 44, 1877.

Metacom, Metacomet. See *King Philip*.

Metal-work. Before the arrival of the whites, the tribes N. of Mexico had made considerable progress in the arts of metallurgy, dealing almost exclusively with copper (q. v.). The other metals utilized were gold, silver, iron, and galena (lead ore). Galena was known only in the form of ore, and the same is true of iron (hematite, pyrites, etc.), except where chance bits of meteoric iron came into the hands of the native artisan. Copper alone was mined (see *Mines and Quarries*).

The four metals, copper, gold, silver, and iron (meteoric), were shaped mainly by cold-hammering and grinding, but heat no doubt was employed to facilitate the hammering processes and in annealing. It is believed that copper was sometimes swedged, or in sheet form pressed into molds. But the remarkable repoussé figures representing elaborately costumed

REPOUSSÉ FIGURE IN SHEET-COPPER, FROM A GEORGIA MOUND. (THOMAS)

and winged personages in sheet metal, found in mounds in Georgia (Thomas), and other more highly conventionalized figures from Florida mounds (Moore), give evidence of a degree of skill seemingly out of keeping with what is known of the general accomplishments of the northern tribes. Cushing, however, has demonstrated that repoussé work of like char-

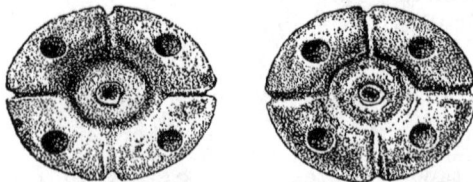

COPPER EAR ORNAMENT, WITH COPY BY WILLOUGHBY, USING ONLY STONE TOOLS; 1-2. (WILLOUGHBY)

acter can be accomplished by simple methods—the employment of pressure with a bone or an antler point, the sheet being placed upon a yielding surface, as of buckskin; but some of this work, especially the Georgia specimens, shows a degree of precision in execution apparently beyond the reach of the methods thus suggested.

Examples of overlaying or plating with thin sheets of copper, found by Moore in the mounds of Florida and Alabama, and by Putnam, Moorehead, Mills, and others in the mounds of Ohio, are hardly less remarkable; but that these are well within the range of workmen of intelligence employing only stone tools has been amply proved by Willoughby. The thin sheets of copper are readily produced by hammering with stone tools with the aid of annealing processes and the skilful use of rivets (Moore). It can hardly be doubted that copper, gold, and silver were sometimes melted by aboriginal metal-workers N. of Mexico, and that

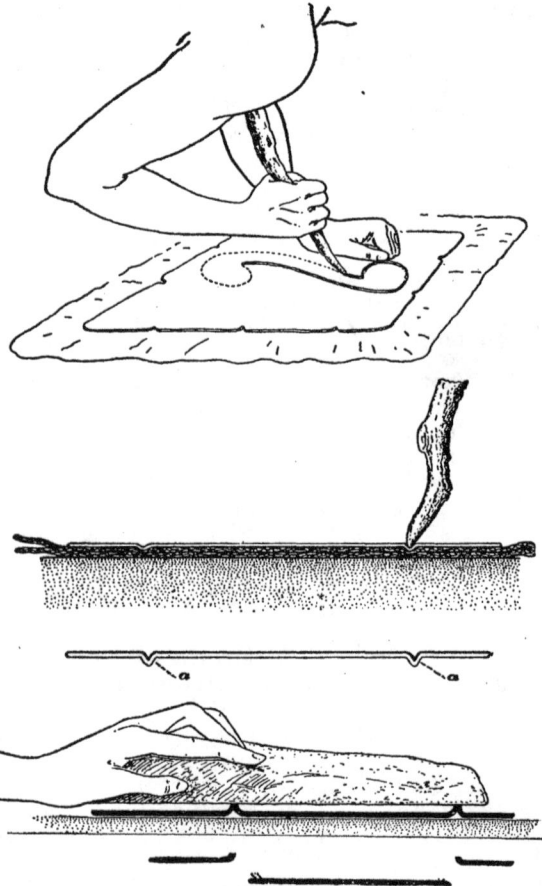

METHOD OF INDENTING AND CUTTING COPPER PLATES. (CUSHING)

bits of native copper were freed from the matrix of rock by this means. There seems to be no satisfactory record, however, of casting the forms of objects even in the rough, and there is no proof that ores of any kind were reduced by means of heat. It is a remarkable fact that up to the present time no prehistoric crucible, mold, pattern, or metal-working tool of any kind whatsoever has been identified. No metal-worker's shop or furnace has been located, although caches of implements and of the blank forms of implements more or less worked have been found in various places, suggesting manufacture in numbers by specialists in the art. The use of artificial alloys was unknown, the specimens of gold-silver and gold-copper alloys obtained in Florida being of exotic origin. Stories of the hardening of copper by these or other American tribes, otherwise than by mere hammering, are all without a shadow of foundation. A few of the tribes, notably the Navaho and some of the Pueblos of Arizona and New Mexico, and the Haida, Tlingit, and others in the far Northwest, are skilful metal-workers, although the art as practised by the Navaho and described by Matthews, while primitive in character, was adopted from the Spaniards. The Haida, Tlingit, and other tribes of British Columbia and Alaska have probably retained the aboriginal methods in part at least. Niblack (Rep. Nat. Mus. 1888, p. 320) speaks of this work as follows: "The tools with which the Indian artisan works out the surprisingly well-finished metal ornaments and implements of this region are few in number. For bracelet making the silversmith has a hammer, several cold chisels, and an etching tool which is merely a sharpened steel point or edge. Improvised iron anvils replace the stone implements of this kind doubtlessly used in former days. Copper is beaten into the required shapes. Steel tools now used are very deftly tempered and sharpened by the native artisan, who retains the primitive form of his implement or tool, and merely substitutes the steel for the former stone blade or head. The ingenuity which the Indians show in adapting iron and steel to their own uses is but one of the many evidences of their cleverness and intelligence." See *Copper, Gold, Iron, Silver.*

The working of metals by primitive methods are treated more or less fully in the following works: Cushing in Am. Anthrop., VII, 1894; Foster, Prehist. Races, 1878; Fowke, Archæol. Hist. Ohio, 1902; Holmes in Am. Anthrop., III, 1901; Hoy in Trans. Wis. Acad. Sci., IV, 1878; McGuire in Am. Anthrop., V, no. 1, 1903; Matthews in 2d Rep. B. A. E., 1883; Moore (1) in Am. Anthrop., V, no. 1, 1903, (2) in Jour. Acad. Nat. Sci. Phila., 1894–1903; Moorehead in Am. Anthrop., V, no. 1, 1903; Niblack in Rep. Nat. Mus. 1888, 1890; Packard in Smithson. Rep. 1892, 1893; Putnam in Ann. Reps. Peabody Mus.; Schoolcraft, Ind. Tribes, I–VI, 1851–57; Squier and Davis, Ancient Monuments, 1848; Thomas in 12th Rep. B. A. E., 1894; Willoughby in Am. Anthrop., V, no. 1, 1903. 　　　　　　(W. H. H.)

Metamapo. A Calusa village on the s. w. coast of Florida, about 1570.—Fontaneda Memoir (*ca.* 1575), Smith trans., 19, 1854.

Metate (Aztec: *metlatl*). The name commonly given to the somewhat flat stones on which maize, acorns, seeds, chile, and other foods are ground by crushing and rubbing with a hand-stone called a muller, or mano (Spanish 'hand'). With tribes depending largely on such materials for food, mealing stones of one kind or another are an important factor in their domestic economy. The metates of middle America are often elaborate in shape, many of them being carved to represent animal forms, the upper surface, or back, serving for the grinding plate. In New Mexico and Arizona the slabs, although carefully shaped, are usually without legs or other projections; often they are trough-shaped, and

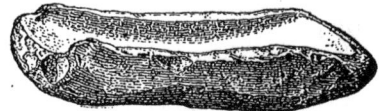

METATE USED BY UINTA UTES (1-8)

the muller used is an oblong flattish stone of subrectangular outline. The modern Pueblo Indians combine two or more of the mealing plates in a group bedded side by side in clay and separated and surrounded by stone slabs, adobe, or boards to retain

OBLONG MULLER; NEW MEXICO (1-5)

the meal. The surfaces of the metates, as well as of the mullers, are of different textures, grading from coarse lava to fine sandstone, and corn crushed on the coarser stone is passed to the others in succession for further refinement until the product is almost as fine as wheat flour. The processes for pulverizing and for pulping are practically the same, the grain or other substance being treated dry in one case and

SET OF GRADED METATES; HOPI (MINDELEFF)

moist in the other. The Mexican type of metate does not extend northward much beyond the limits of the Pueblo region, although similar flattish stones were and are used for grinding in many parts of the country. The typical grinding plate grades through many intermediate forms into the typical mortar, and the mano or muller similarly passes from the typical flattish form into the discoidal and cylindrical pestle. Many of these hand-stones serve equally well for rubbing, rolling, and pounding. See *Mortars, Mullers, Notched plates, Pestles.*

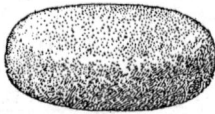

DISCOIDAL MULLER; CALIFORNIA (1-3)　　PESTLE-MULLER; ILLINOIS (1-4)

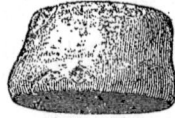

Consult Cushing in Millstone, IX, X, 1884–1885; Fewkes (1) in 17th Rep. B. A. E., 1898, (2) 22d Rep. B. A. E., 1903; Mindeleff in 8th Rep. B. A. E., 1891; James Stevenson in 2d Rep. B. A. E., 1883; M. C. Stevenson in 23d Rep. B. A. E., 1904. (W. H. H.)

Metate ruin. A prehistoric pueblo ruin in the Petrified Forest, across the wash from the "petrified bridge," near the Navaho-Apache co. boundary, Arizona; locally so called on account of the numerous stone milling troughs, or metates, set on edge in circular or linear form and scattered over the surface. The builders of the pueblo are unknown. The pottery, gray-brown and black in color, is coarse in texture and decorated with rude incision and by indented coiling.—Hough in Rep. Nat. Mus. 1901, 318, 1903.

Metates. A former Opata pueblo at the E. base of the Sierra de Teras, about 12 m. w. of Baseraca, E. Sonora, Mexico. Possibly identical with Teras, Guepacomatzi, or Toapara, which pueblos are mentioned in early documents as being in that vicinity.—Bandélier in Arch. Inst. Papers, IV, 524 et seq., 1892.

Metea (prob. for *Metawä*, 'he sulks.'—W. J.). A Potawatomi chief, distinguished in his tribe as a warrior and an orator. When the Potawatomi were subsidized by the British at the beginning of the War of 1812 he was one of the leaders of the party that massacred the families of the garrison and citizens of Chicago as they were retreating to Detroit. He led the band that harassed the troops who marched in the fall of 1812 to the relief of Ft Wayne and was shot in the arm by Gen. W. H. Harrison. At a council held at Chicago in 1821 he impressed the whites by his eloquence and reasoning powers, and also when the treaty of the Wabash was concluded in 1826. He advocated the education of Indian youth and sent several from his tribe to the Choctaw academy in Kentucky. He died in a drunken debauch at Ft Wayne, in 1827, after having conducted difficult negotiations with dignity and skill in a conference with commissioners of the Government.—McKenney and Hall, Ind. Tribes, 59–64, 1858. See *Muskwawasepeotan.*

Meteahke. A Mandan band.
High Village.—Morgan, Anc. Soc., 158, 1877. Me-te-ah'-ke.—Ibid.

Metewemesick ('place of black earth'). A former Nipmuc (?) settlement on Quinebaug r., near Sturbridge, Mass.—Roger Williams (1643) quoted by Tooker, Algonquian Series, VIII, 33, 1901.

Methow (*Met'-how*). A Salishan tribe of E. Washington, formerly living about Methow r. and Chelan lake, now chiefly gathered on the Colville res. Their number is not officially reported.
Battle-le-mule-emauch.—Ross, Adventures, 290, 1847. Lahtohs.—Van Valkenburgh in Ind. Aff. Rep., 235, 1865 (perhaps a misprint for Methows). Meat-who.—Ross, op. cit. Meshons.—Mooney in 14th Rep. B. A. E., 734, 1896. Met-cow-we.—Orig. Jour. Lewis and Clark, IV, 321, 1905. Metcoowwee.—Lewis and Clark, Exped., II, 252, 1814. Meteow-wee.—Ibid., II, 318, 1817. Methau.—Ind. Aff. Rep., 253, 1877. Methews.—H. R. Doc. 102, 43d Cong., 1st sess., 1, 1874. Methoms.—Shanks, et al. (1873), ibid., 4. Methow.—Ind. Aff. Rep., 302, 1877. Mitaui.—Mooney in 14th Rep. B. A. E., pl. lxxxviii, 1896. Mithouies.—Winans in Ind. Aff. Rep., 23, 1870.

Methy. The burbot (*Lota maculosa*), the *loche* of the Canadian French, a fish common in the waters of N. W. Canada. The word is taken from the name of this fish in the Wood Cree dialect of Algonquian, the Cree proper term being *mihyey*, according to Lacombe. L. Methy in Athabasca is named from this fish; also a lake in Labrador. (A. F. C.)

Meti. A former rancheria of gentile (probably Diegueño) Indians near San Diego, S. Cal.—Ortega (1775) quoted by Bancroft, Hist. Cal., I, 253, 1884.

Métis ('mixed,' from French *métis*, a derivative of Latin *miscere*, 'to mix'), or *metif.* A term used by the French-speaking population of the N. W. to designate persons of mixed white and Indian blood. Among the Spanish-speaking population of the S. W. the word *mestizo*, of the same derivation, is used, but is applied more especially to those of half-white and half-Indian blood. The term *mustee*, a corruption of *mestizo*, was formerly in use in the Gulf states. In the W. the term "half-breed" is loosely applied to all persons of mixed white and Indian blood, without regard to the proportion of each. See *Mixed-bloods.* (J. M.)

Maitiffs.—Brevel *fide* Sibley (1805) in Am. State Papers, Ind. Aff., I, 730, 1832. Mestigos.—Williams, Vt., I, 494, 1809 (misprint). Mestizo.—Correct Spanish form; feminine *mestiza*. Métis.—Correct French form. Mustees.—Report of 1741 in Carroll, Hist. Coll. S. C., II, 353, 1836. Mustees.—Bermuda Royal Gazette, July 13, 1875, *fide* Jour. Anthrop. Inst., V, 491, 1876 (used in Bermuda for descendants of Indian slaves brought from the U. S.). Wissâkodé-winini.—Baraga, Otchipwe-Eng. Dict., 421, 1880 (Chippewa name: 'half-burnt wood man'; from *wissâkode*, 'burnt trees,' referring to their mixed light and dark complexion; pl. *Wissâkodéwinini-wog*. He gives *aiabitâwisid* as the literal word for 'half-breed').

Metlakatla. A Tsimshian town 15 m. s. of Port Simpson, Brit. Col. Anciently there were many towns in this neighborhood, and while the mission station of the Church of England (established in 1857 at a Tsimshian village of the same name) was conducted by Rev. Wm. Duncan, Metlakatla was a flourishing place. Trouble arising over the conduct of his work, Duncan moved in 1887 to Port Chester, or New Metlakatla, on Annette id., Alaska, and most of the Indians followed him. The old town, which contained 198 inhabitants in 1906, is now the site of an Indian school of the Church of England. New Metlakatla, including whites and Indians, numbered 823 in 1890 and 465 in 1900. See *Missions*. (J. R. S.)

Metlah Catlah.—Horetzky, Canada on Pac., 148, 1874. Metlahcatlah.—Tolmie and Dawson, Vocabs. Brit. Col., map, 1884. Metlahkatlah.—Heming in Can. Pacific R. R. Rep. Prog., iii, 1877. Metlakahtla.—Whymper, Alaska, 59, 1869. Metlakatla.—Can. Ind. Aff., pt. ii, 68, 1902. Metla-katla.—Dawson, Queen Charlotte Ids., 123B, 1880.

Metoac (*meteaŭ-hok*, the periwinkle, from the columella of which beads were made.—Gerard). A collective term embracing the Indians of Long Island, N. Y., who seem to have been divided into the following tribes, subtribes, or bands: Canarsee, Corchaug, Manhasset, Massapequa, Matinecoc, Merric, Montauk, Nesaquake, Patchoag, Rockaway, Secatoag, Setauket, and Shinnecock. There were besides these some minor bands or villages which have received special designations. They were closely connected linguistically and politically, and were probably derived from the same immediate ethnic stem. Ruttenber classes them as branches of the Mahican. The Montauk, who formed the leading tribe in the eastern part of the island, are often confounded with the Metoac, and in some instances the Canarsee of the western part have also been confounded with them. The eastern tribes were at one time subject to the Pequot and afterward to the Narraganset, while the Iroquois claimed dominion over the western tribes. They were numerous at the first settlement of the island, but rapidly wasted away from epidemics and wars with other Indians and with the Dutch, disposing of their lands piece by piece to the whites. About 1788 a large part of the survivors joined the Brotherton Indians in Oneida co., N. Y. The rest, represented chiefly by the Montauk and Shinnecock, have dwindled to perhaps a dozen individuals of mixed blood. The Indians of Long Island were a seafaring people, mild in temperament, diligent in the pursuits determined by their environment, skilled in the management of the canoe, seine, and spear, and dexterous in the making of seawan or wampum (Flint). The chieftaincies were hereditary by lineal descent, including females when there was no male representative.

The Metoac villages were Canarsee, Cotsjewaminck, Cutchogue (Corchaug), Jameco, Keskaechquerem (?), Marychkenwikingh, Maspeth (Canarsee), Mattituck (Corchaug), Merric, Mirrachtauhacky, Mochgonnekonck, Montauk, Nachaquatuck, Nesaquake, Ouheywichkingh, Patchoag, Rechquaakie, Setauket, Sichteyhacky, Wawepex (Matinecock). (J. M.)

La Porcelaine.—Vaudreuil (1724) in N. Y. Doc. Col. Hist., ix, 937, 1855. Long Island Indians.—Common early English name. Malowwacks.—Hall, N. W. States, 34, 1849 (misprint form and wrongly located). Matauwakes.—Thompson, Long Id., 53, 1839. Matowacks.—Patent of 1664 in N. Y. Doc. Col. Hist., ii, 296, 1858 ("Matowacks or Long Island"). Mattouwacky.—De Laet (*ca.* 1633) in N. Y. Hist. Soc. Coll., 2d s., i, 296, 1841. Mattowax.—Shea, Cath. Miss., 16, 1855. Matuwacks.—Yates and Moulton in Ruttenber, Tribes Hudson R., 75, 1872. Mertowacks.—Boudinot, Star in the West, 127, 1816. Metoacs.—Schoolcraft in N. Y. Hist. Soc. Proc., ii, 85, 1844. Metouwacks.—Winfield, Hudson Co., 9, 1874. Metowacks.—Brodhead in Ruttenber, Tribes Hudson R., 75, 1872. Milowacks.—Boudinot, Star in the West, 127, 1816 (misprint). Sewan-akies.—Schoolcraft, Ind. Tribes, vi, 147, 1857 ('Shell land bands,' from *sewan*, 'the wampum shell,' and *aukie*, 'land').

Metocaum. A village, probably of the Chowanoc, situated on Chowan r., in the present Bertie co., N. C., in 1585.

Metackwem.—Lane (1586) in Hakluyt, Voy., iii, 312, 1810. Metocaum.—Smith (1629), Va., i, map, repr. 1819. Metocunent.—Dutch map (1621) in N. Y. Doc. Col. Hist., i, 1856.

Metouscepriniouek (prob. for *Mĕʹtusäneniwŭgi*, lit. 'men who walk with bare [feet]'; it is not the idiom for that phrase, however, but a term referring to people in general.—W. J.). A term apparently applied by Bacqueville de la Potherie (Hist. Am., ii, 103, 1753) to the Foxes, Illinois, Kickapoo, Miami, etc., collectively.

Metsmetskop ('low, miserable, stinking'). A name applied by Natchez of the upper class to those of the lowest social grade. This was composed principally of people of the same blood but also included some small alien tribes. Cf. *Stinkards*. (J. R. S.)

Miche-Miche-Quipy.—Du Pratz, Hist. La., ii, 393, 1758. Miché Michéquipi.—Bossu (1751), Travels La., 65, 1771 (sig. 'stinking fellow'). Puants.—Ibid., 394 (applied also to the Winnebago). Stincards.—Latham, Essays, 408, 1860. Stinkards.—Pénicaut (1704) in French, Hist. Coll. La., n. s., 94, 1869.

Metstoasath (*Mɛtstō'asath*). A sept of the Toquart, a Nootka tribe.—Boas in 6th Rep. N. W. Tribes of Canada, 31, 1890.

Metukatoak. A Kaviagmiut village at Port Clarence, Alaska.—Eleventh Census, Alaska, 102, 1893.

Metutahanke ('lower village'). One of two Mandan villages in 1804; situated on Missouri r., about 4 m. below Knife r., N. Dak. It was almost exterminated by smallpox in 1837.

Matoolonha.—Thwaites, Orig. Jour. Lewis and Clark, vii, index, 1905. Matootonha.—Lewis and Clark, Exped., i, 120, 1814. Ma-too-ton'-ka.—Lewis and Clark, Discov., 24, 1806. Métutahanke.—Matthews, Ethnog. and Philol. Hidatsa, 14, 1877. Mih-tutta-hang-kusch.—Maximilian as quoted by Matthews, op. cit. Mih-Tutta-Hang-Kush.—Maximilian, Trav., 335, 1843. **Mitutahankish.**—Matthews, Ethnog. and Philol. Hidatsa, 14, 1877. **Mitutahaṅkuc.**—Dorsey in Am. Natur., 829, Oct. 1882.

Mexam. See *Mriksah*.

Meyascosic. A village of the Powhatan confederacy, in 1608, on the N. side of James r., in Charles City co., Va.—Smith (1629), Va., I, map, repr. 1819.

Meyemma. Mentioned by Gibbs (Schoolcraft, Ind. Tribes, III, 139, 1853) as a Hupa village in Hupa valley, Cal., in 1851. Not identified. The name is perhaps of Yurok origin.

Meyo. The Lizard clan of the pueblo of Laguna, N. Mex. Although Laguna was not founded until 1699, the origin of the clan is unknown to the natives. It forms a phratry with the Skurshka (Water-snake), Sqowi (Rattlesnake), and Hatsi (Earth) clans, which came from Sia, Oraibi (probably), and Jemez, respectively. (F. W. H.)
Méyo-hánoᶜʰ.—Hodge in Am. Anthrop., IX, 351, 1896 (*hánoᶜʰ*='people').

Mezquital (Span: 'mesquite grove'). A former pueblo of the Tepehuane on the upper waters of Rio de San Pedro, s. Durango, Mexico, and the seat of a Spanish mission. It is now a Mexican town.
S. Francisco del Mezquital.—Orozco y Berra, Geog., 318, 1864.

Mgezewa (for *Me'gezi*, 'bald eagle'). A gens of the Potawatomi, q. v.
Mégezi.—Wm. Jones, inf'n, 1906. **M'-ge-ze'-wä.**—Morgan, Anc. Soc., 167, 1877.

Miacomit. A village formerly on Nantucket id., off the s coast of Massachusetts.—Writer of 1807 in Mass. Hist. Soc. Coll., 2d s., III, 26, 1846.

Miahwahpitsiks (*Mi-ah-wah'-pĭt-sĭks*, 'seldom lonesome'). A division of the Piegan tribe of the Siksika.
Mi-ah-wah'-pĭt-sĭks.—Grinnell, Blackfoot Lodge Tales, 209, 1892. **Seldom Lonesome.**—Ibid., 225.

Miakechakesa. One of the two divisions of the Sisseton Sioux. Their habitat in 1824 was the region of Blue Earth and Cottonwood rs., Minn., extending westward to the Coteau des Prairies. Unlike the Kahra, they had no fixed villages, no mud or bark cabins. They hunted on Blue Earth r. in winter, and during the summer pursued the buffalo as far as Missouri r. They numbered about 1,000.
Lower Sissetons.—Minn. Hist. Soc. Coll., III, 250, 1880. **Mi-ah-kee-jack-sah.**—Lewis and Clark, Discov., 34, 1806. **Mia Kechakesa.**—Long, Exped. St Peter's R., I, 378, 1824. **South Sussetons.**—Ind. Aff. Rep., 495, 1839.

Miami (?Chippewa: *Omaumeg*, 'people who live on the peninsula'). An Algonquian tribe, usually designated by early English writers as Twightwees (*twanh twanh*, the cry of a crane.—Hewitt), from their own name, the earliest recorded notice of which is from information furnished in 1658 by Gabriel Druillettes (Jes. Rel. 1658, 21, 1858), who called them the Oumamik, then living 60 leagues from

St Michel, the first village of the Potawatomi mentioned by him; it was therefore at or about the mouth of Green bay, Wis. Tailhan (Perrot, Mémoire) says that they withdrew into the Mississippi valley, 60 leagues from the bay, and were established there from 1657 to 1676, although Bacqueville de la Potherie asserts that, with the Mascoutens, the Kickapoo, and part of the Illinois, they came to settle at that place about 1667. The first time the French came into actual contact with the Miami was when Perrot visited them about 1668. His second visit was in 1670, when they were living at the headwaters of Fox r., Wis. In 1671 a part at least of the tribe were living with the Mascoutens in a palisaded

LUM-KI-KUM—MIAMI

village in this locality (Jes. Rel. 1671, 45, 1858). Soon after this the Miami parted from the Mascoutens and formed new settlements at the s. end of L. Michigan and on Kalamazoo r., Mich. The settlements at the s. end of the lake were at Chicago and on St Joseph r., where missions were established late in the 17th century, although the former is mentioned as a Wea village at the time of Marquette's visit, and Wea were found there in 1701 by De Courtemarche. It is likely that these Wea were the Miami mentioned by Allouez and others as being united with the Mascoutens in Wisconsin. The chief village of the Miami on St Joseph r. was, according to Zenobius (Le Clercq, II, 133), about 15 leagues inland, in lat. 41°. The extent of territory occupied by this tribe a few years later compels the conclusion that the Miami in Wisconsin, when the whites first heard of them, formed but a part of the tribe, and that other bodies were already in N. E. Illinois and N. Indiana. As the Miami and their allies were found later on the Wabash in Indiana and in N. W. Ohio, in which latter territory they gave their name to three rivers, it would seem that they had moved S. E. from the localities where first known within historic times. Little Turtle, their famous chief, said: "My fathers kindled the first fire at Detroit; thence they extended their lines to the headwaters of the Scioto; thence to its mouth; thence down the Ohio to the mouth of the Wabash, and thence to Chicago over L. Michigan." When Vincennes was sent by Gov. Vaudreville in 1705 on a mission to the Miami they were found occupying principally the territory N. W. of the upper Wabash. There was a Miami village at Detroit in 1703, but their chief settlement was still on St Joseph r. In 1711 the Miami and the Wea had three villages on the St Joseph, Maumee, and Wabash. Kekionga, at the head of the Maumee, became the chief seat of the Miami proper, while Ouiatenon, on the Wabash, was the headquarters of the Wea branch. By the encroachments of the Potawatomi, Kickapoo, and other northern tribes the Miami were driven from St Joseph r. and the country N. W. of the Wabash. They sent out colonies to the E. and formed settlements on Miami r. in Ohio, and perhaps as far E. as the Scioto. This country they held until the peace of 1763, when they retired to Indiana, and the abandoned country was occupied by the Shawnee. They took a prominent part in all the Indian wars in Ohio valley until the close of the war of 1812. Soon afterward they began to sell their lands, and by 1827 had disposed of most of their holdings in Indiana and had agreed to remove to Kansas, whence they went later to Indian Ter., where the remnant still resides. In all treaty negotiations they were considered as original owners of the Wabash country and all of W. Ohio, while the other tribes in that region were regarded as tenants or intruders on their lands. A considerable part of the tribe, commonly known as Meshingomesia's band, continued to reside on a reservation in Wabash co., Ind., until 1872, when the land was divided among the survivors, then numbering about 300.

The Miami men were described in 1718 as "of medium height, well built, heads rather round than oblong, countenances agreeable rather than sedate or morose, swift on foot, and excessively fond of racing." The women were generally well clad in deerskins, while the men used scarcely any covering and were tattooed all over the body. They were hard-working, and raised a species of maize unlike that of the Indians of Detroit, described as "white, of the same size as the other, the skin much finer, and the meal much whiter." According to the early French explorers the Miami were distinguished for polite manners, mild, affable, and sedate character, and their respect for and perfect obedience to their chiefs, who had greater authority than those of other Algonquian and N. W. tribes. They usually spoke slowly. They were land travelers rather than canoemen. According to Hennepin, when they saw a herd of buffalo they gathered in great numbers and set fire to the grass about the animals, leaving open a passage where they posted themselves with their bows and arrows; the buffalo, seeking to escape the fire, were compelled to pass the Indians, who killed large numbers of them. The women spun thread of buffalo hair, with which they made bags to carry the meat, toasted or sometimes dried in the sun. Their cabins were covered with rush mats. According to Perrot, the village which he visited was situated on a hill and surrounded by a palisade. On the other hand, Zenobius says that La Salle, who visited the villages on St Joseph r., taught them how to defend themselves with palisades, and even made them erect a kind of fort with intrenchments. Infidelity of the wife, as among many other Indians, was punished by clipping the nose. According to early explorers, they worshiped the sun and thunder, but did not honor a host of minor deities, like the Huron and the Ottawa. Three forms of burial appear to have been practised by the division of the tribe living about Ft Wayne: (1) The ordinary ground burial in a shallow grave prepared to receive the body in a recumbent position. (2) Surface burial in a hollow log; these have been found in heavy forests; sometimes a tree was split and the halves hollowed out to receive the body, when it was either closed with withes or fastened to the ground with crossed stakes; sometimes a hollow tree was used, the ends being closed. (3) Surface burial wherein the body was covered with a small pen of logs, laid as in a log cabin, the courses meeting at the top in a single log.

The French authors commonly divided the Miami into six bands: Piankashaw, Wea, Atchatchakangouen, Kilatika, Mengakonkia, and Pepicokia. Of these the first two have come to be recognized as distinct tribes; the other names are no longer known. The Pepicokia, mentioned in 1796 with the Wea and Piankashaw, may have been absorbed by the latter. Several treaties were made with a band known as Eel Rivers, formerly living near Thorntown, Boone co., Ind., but they afterward joined the main body on the Wabash.

According to Morgan (Anc. Soc., 168, 1877) the Miami have 10 gentes: (1) Mowhawa (wolf), (2) Mongwa (loon), (3) Kendawa (eagle), (4) Ahpakosea (buzzard), (5) Kanozawa (Kanwasowau, panther), (6) Pilawa (turkey), (7) Ahseponna (raccoon), (8) Monnato (snow), (9) Kulswa (sun), (10) Water. Chauvignerie, in 1737, said that the Miami had two principal totems—the elk and crane—while some of them had the bear. The French writers call the Atchatchakangouen (Crane) the leading division. At a great conference on the Maumee in Ohio in 1793 the Miami signed with the turtle totem. None of these totems occurs in Morgan's list.

It is impossible to give a satisfactory estimate of the numbers of the Miami at any one time, on account of confusion with the Wea and Piankashaw, who probably never exceeded 1,500. An estimate in 1764 gives them 1,750; another in the following year places their number at 1,250. In 1825 the population of the Miami, Eel Rivers, and Wea was given as 1,400, of whom 327 were Wea. Since their removal to the W. they have rapidly decreased. Only 57 Miami were officially known in Indian Ter. in 1885, while the Wea and Piankashaw were confederated with the remnant of the Illinois under the name of Peoria, the whole body numbering but 149; these increased to 191 in 1903. The total number of Miami in 1905 in Indian Ter. was 124; in Indiana, in 1900, there were 243; the latter, however, are greatly mixed with white blood. Including individuals scattered among other tribes, the whole number is probably 400.

The Miami joined in or made treaties with the United States as follows: (1) Greenville, O., with Gen. Anthony Wayne, Aug. 3, 1795, defining the boundary between the United States and tribes w. of Ohio r. and ceding certain tracts of land; (2) Ft Wayne, Ind., June 7, 1803, with various tribes, defining boundaries and ceding certain lands; (3) Grouseland, Ind., Aug., 21, 1805, ceding certain lands in Indiana and defining boundaries; (4) Ft Wayne, Ind., Sept. 30, 1809, in which the Miami, Eel River tribes, and Delawares ceded certain lands in Indiana, and the relations between the Delawares and Miami regarding certain territory are defined; (5) Treaty of peace at Greenville, O., July 22, 1814, between the United States, the Wyandot, Delawares, Shawnee, Seneca, and the Miami, including the Eel River and Wea tribes; (6) Peace treaty of Spring Wells, Mich., Sept. 8, 1815, by the Miami and other tribes; (7)

St Mary's, O., Oct. 6, 1818, by which the Miami ceded certain lands in Indiana; (8) Treaty of the Wabash, Ind., Oct. 23, 1826, by which the Miami ceded all their lands in Indiana, N. and w. of Wabash and Miami rs.; (9) Wyandot village, Ind., Feb. 11, 1828, by which the Eel River Miami ceded all claim to the reservation at their village on Sugar Tree cr., Ind.; (10) Forks of Wabash, Ind., Oct. 23, 1834, by which the Miami ceded several tracts in Indiana; (11) Forks of the Wabash, Ind., Nov. 6, 1838, by which the Miami ceded most of their remaining lands in Indiana, and the United States agreed to furnish them a reservation w. of the Mississippi; (12) Forks of the Wabash, Ind., Nov. 28, 1840, by which the Miami ceded their remaining lands in Indiana and agreed to remove to the country assigned them w. of the Mississippi; (13) Washington, June 5, 1854, by which they ceded a tract assigned by amended treaty of Nov. 28, 1840, excepting 70,000 a. retained as a reserve; (14) Washington, Feb. 23, 1867, with Seneca and others, in which it is stipulated that the Miami may become confederated with the Peoria and others if they so desire.

Among the Miami villages were Chicago, Chippekawkay, Choppatee's village, Kekionga, Kenapacomaqua, Kokomo, Kowasikka, Little Turtle's village, Meshingomesia, Missinquimeschan (Piankashaw, Mississinewa, Neconga (?), Osage, Papakeecha, Piankashaw (Piankashaw), Pickawillanee, White Raccoon's village, Seek's village, St Francis Xavier (mission, with others), Thorntown (Eel River Miami). (J. M. C. T.)

Allianies.—Beckwith in Indiana Geol. Rep., 43, 1883 (misprint). Maiama.—Janson, Stranger in Am., 192, 1807. M'amiwis.—Rafinesque, Am. Nations, I, 157, 1836. Maumee.—Washington (1790) in Am. St. Papers, Ind. Aff., I, 143, 1832. Maumes.—Schoolcraft, Ind. Tribes, v, 89, 1855. Maumies.—Warren (1852) in Minn. Hist. Soc. Coll., v, 33, 1885. Mawmee.—Imlay, West Ter., 364, 1797. Me-ä-me-ä-ga.—Morgan, Consang. and Affin., 287, 1871. Meames.—La Barre (1683) in N. Y. Doc. Col. Hist., IX, 202, 1855. Meamis.—Ibid. Memilounioue.—Jes. Rel. 1672, LVIII, 40, 1899. Memis.—Le Barre (1683), op. cit., 208. Mencamis.—Boudinot, Star in the West, 127, 1816 (misprint). Metousceprinioueks.—Bacqueville de la Potherie, Hist. Am., II, 103, 1753 ('Walkers', 'well on their feet'; so called because they traveled much on foot, and not in canoes). Miamee.—Jones, Ojebway Inds., 178, 1861. Miames.—Lewis and Clark, Travels, 12, 1806. Miami.—Gatschet, Potawatomi MS., B. A. E., 1878 (Potawatomi name; plural, Miamik). Miamiha.—Coxe, Carolana, 49, 1741. Miamioüek.—Jes. Rel. 1670, 90, 1858. Miamis.—Du Chesneau (1681) in N. Y. Doc. Col. Hist., IX, 153, 1855. Mineamies.—Trader of 1778 in Schoolcraft, Ind. Tribes, III, 561, 1853. Miramis.—De Bougainville (1757) in N. Y. Doc. Col. Hist., X, 608, 1858 (misprint). Miyamis.—Jefferys, French Doms., pt. 1, map, 1761. Myamicks.—Lamberville (1686) in N. Y. Doc. Col. Hist., III, 489, 1853. Myamis.—Membré (ca. 1680) in Shea, Miss. Val., 152, 1852. Naked Indians.—Doc. of 1728 in Min. of Prov. Coun. of Pa., III, 312, 1840. Nation . . . de la Grüe.—Bacqueville de la Potherie, Hist. Am., IV, 55, 1753. Omameeg.—Warren (1852) in Schoolcraft,

Ind. Tribes, v, 39, 1855 (Chippewa name). **O-maum-eeg.**—Warren (1852) in Minn. Hist. Soc. Coll., v, 33, 1885 (Chippewa name). **Omianicks.**—Lamberville (1686) in N. Y. Doc. Col. Hist., III, 489, 1853. **Omie.**—Writer of 1786 in Mass. Hist. Soc. Coll., 1st s., III, 26, 1794. **Ouimiamies.**—N. Y. Doc. Col. Hist., III, 489, note, 1853. **Oumamens.**—Neill in Minn. Hist. Soc. Coll., v, 413, 1885. **Oumami.**—Jes. Rel. 1670, 94, 1858. **Oumamik.**—Ibid., 1658, 21, 1858. **Oumanies.**—Lahontan, New Voy., I, map, 1735. **Oumeami.**—La Famine council (1684) in N. Y. Doc. Col. Hist., IX, 238, 1855. **Oumiamies.**—Bechefer (1682), ibid., 170. **Pkíwi-léni.**—Gatschet, Shawnee MS., B. A. E., 1879 (Shawnee name; plural, Pkíwi-lénigi, 'dust or ashes people'). **Quitways.**—Doc. of 1747 in N. Y. Doc. Col. Hist., VI, 391, 1855 (=Twightwees? They do not appear to have been the Quatoghees or Hurons, as thought by the editor). **Qwikties.**—Colden (1727), Hist. Five Nations, 69, 1747 (misprint for Twiktwies). **Sänshkiá-a-rúnû.**—Gatschet, Wyandot MS., B. A. E., 1881 (Huron name, meaning 'people dressing finely, fantastically', i. e., 'dandy people'). **Tawatawas.**—Brinton, Lenape Legends, 146, 1885 (from the Algonquian *tawa*, 'naked'; hence Twightwees). **Tawatawee.**—Doc. of 1759, ibid., 232. **Tawixtawes.**—Goldman in West. Reserve Hist. Soc., Tract no. 6, 1, July 1871. **Tawixti.**—Güssefeld, map, 1797 (used for Pickawillanee village, *q. v.* According to Harris, Tour, 137, 1805, the name occurs on Hutchins' map, *ca.* 1764. It is another form of Twightwee). **Tawixtwi.**—La Tour, map, 1784 (used for Pickawillanee village, *q. v.*). **Tewicktowes.**—Harrison (1814) in Drake, Tecumseh, 159, 1852. **Titwa.**—Doc. (*ca.* 1700) in Min. of Prov. Coun. of Pa., I, 411, 1838. **Tooweehtoowees.**—Edwards (1751) in Mass. Hist. Soc. Coll., 1st s., X, 147, 1809. **Tuihtuihronoons.**—Colden (1727), Five Nations, 61, 1747 (Iroquois name). **Twechtweys.**—Doc. of 1728 in Min. of Prov. Coun. of Pa., III, 312, 1840. **Tweeghtwees.**—Albany conf. (1754) in N. Y. Doc. Col. Hist., VI, 873, 1855. **Twghtwees.**—Domenech, Deserts, I, 444, 1860. **Twichtwees.**—Loskiel (1794) in Ruttenber, Tribes Hudson R., 336, 1872. **Twichtwichs.**—Dongan (1687) in N. Y. Doc. Col. Hist., III, 439, 1853. **Twichtwicks.**—Livingston (1687), ibid., III, 443, 1853. **Twichtwighs.**—Schuyler (1702), ibid., IV, 979, 1854. **Twichwiches.**—Bleeker (1701), ibid., 918. **Twicktwicks.**—Albany conf. (1726), ibid., v, 791, 1855. **Twicktwigs.**—Doc. of 1688, ibid., III, 565, 1853. **Twictwees.**—Crepy, map, *ca.* 1755. **Twictwicts.**—Bellomont (1701) in N. Y. Doc. Col. Hist., IV, 834, 1854. **Twight.**—Lattré, map, 1784 (error for Twightwees; the 'Miamis' are also given as distinct). **Twightees.**—Hamilton (1750) in N. Y. Doc. Col. Hist., VI, 593, 1855. **Twighteeys.**—Johnson (1753), ibid., 779. **Twighties.**—Johnson (1763), ibid., VII, 572, 1856. **Twightwees.**—Weiser (1748) in Rupp, West. Pa., app., 14, 1846. **Twightwicks.**—Jamison (1697) in N. Y. Doc. Col. Hist., IV, 294, 1854. **Twightwies.**—Lahontan (1703) in Drake, Bk. Inds., bk. 5, 6, 1848. **Twightwighs.**—Doc. of 1687 in N. Y. Doc. Col. Hist., III, 431, 1853. **Twightwis Roanu.**—Dobbs, Hudson Bay, 27, 1744. **Twigtees.**—Martin, N. C., II, 62, 1829. **Twigthtwees.**—Dwight and Partridge in Mass. Hist. Soc. Coll., 1st s., v, 121, 1816. **Twig-Twee.**—Lindesay (1751) in N. Y. Doc. Col. Hist., VI, 706, 1855. **Twigtwees.**—Weiser (1748) in Rupp, West. Pa., app., 15, 1846. **Twigtwicks.**—Cornbury (1708) in N. Y. Doc. Col. Hist., v, 65, 1855. **Twigtwies.**—Lindesay (1749), ibid., VI, 538, 1855. **Twigtwig.**—Cortland (1687), ibid., III, 434, 1853. **Twiswicks.**—Dongan (1687), ibid., 476. **Twitchwees.**—Hamilton (1749), ibid., VI, 531, 1855. **Twithuays.**—Conf. of 1793 in Am. State Pap., Ind. Aff., I, 477, 1832. **Ḷwĭtwĭhenon'.**—Hewitt, Onondaga MS., B. A. E., 1888 (Onondaga name). **Utamis.**—Barcia, Ensayo, 289, 1723 (misprint from Lahontan). **Wa-yä-tä-no'-ke.**—Morgan, Consang. and Affin., 287, 1871. **Wemiamik.**—Squier in Beach, Ind. Miscel., 34, 1877 (='Beaver children').

Miami River. A Seminole settlement, with 63 inhabitants in 1880, about 10 m. N. of the site of Ft Dallas, not far from Biscayne bay, on Little Miami r., Dade co., Fla.—MacCauley in 5th Rep. B. A. E., 478, 1887.

Miantonomo. A noted chief of the Narraganset, nephew of Canonicus. In 1632 he visited Boston and was received by the governor. He was more than once suspected of disloyalty to the English, but managed to clear himself when summoned to Boston in 1636. He helped the English against the Pequot the next year and warred against the Mohegan. In 1638 he signed the tripartite agreement between the English of Connecticut, the Narraganset, and the Mohegan. He is said to have been impressed by the preaching of Roger Williams in 1643. During the years 1640–42 he was suspected of treachery to the English, but again made satisfactory explanations. In 1643 war broke out between the Mohegan and the Narraganset, and in a battle in which the latter were defeated Miantonomo was taken prisoner. He was delivered to the English at Hartford, was tried at Boston in September, 1643, by the Court of Commissioners of the United Colonies of New England, who, after referring the matter to the convocation of the clergy, which condemned him, sentenced him to death at the hands of Uncas. This sentence was barbarously executed by Wawequa, the brother of Uncas, in the presence of the latter. For this disgraceful proceeding the English authorities were to blame, as otherwise Uncas would never have taken his prisoner's life. De Forest (Hist. Inds. of Conn., 198, 1852) takes a rather high view of the character of Miantonomo, whom he characterizes as "respected and loved by everyone who was not fearful of his power." Theological bias against Roger Williams and his Indian friends played some part in the matter of his treatment by the commissioners. He was buried where he fell, and the spot, on which a monument was erected in 1841, has since been known as Sachem's Plains. Miantonomo is praised in Durfee's poem, "What cheer." Nanantenoo was a son of Miantonomo.   (A. F. C.)

Miawkinaiyiks ('big topknots'). A division of the Piegan tribe of the Siksika. **Big Topknots.**—Grinnell, Blackfoot Lodge Tales, 209, 1892. **Mi-aw'-kin-ai-yiks.**—Ibid., 225.

Mica. This durable and showy mineral was in very general use by the Indian tribes E. of the great plains, the translucent variety known as muscovite being most highly prized. It was mined at many points in the Appalachian highland, from Georgia to St Lawrence r. (see *Mines and Quarries*). It occurs also in South Dakota, but it is not probable that the mound-building tribes obtained it from this source. From the Eastern highland it passed, by trade or otherwise, to remote parts: to Florida in the s. and to the upper Mississippi valley in the N. W. The crystals were often of large size, measuring 2 ft or more in diameter. The sheets into which they were readily divided were much prized for mirrors, and were also cut into a great variety of shapes for personal ornaments, and possibly also for ceremonial use. Sheets of mica were used also for burial with the dead and as sacrificial offerings. Squier and Davis give an account of the discovery of 14 human skeletons that were carefully covered with mica plates, estimated at 15 or 20 bushels, some of the plates being from 8 to 10 in. long and from 4 to 5 in. wide, and all from ½ to 1 in. in thickness. Atwater describes the discovery of many thick sheets, one of which measured 36 in. long by 18 in. wide. With a skeleton in the Grave Creek mound, near Wheeling, W. Va., 150 disks of sheet mica, measuring from 1½ to 2 in. in diameter and having each 1 or 2 perforations, were found. From the Turner mounds in Hamilton co., Ohio, several ornamental figures of sheet mica were obtained; one of them is a grotesque human figure, others are animal forms, including a serpent (Putnam). Mica occurs on many sacrificial altars of the mound-builders, who no doubt regarded it as of special significance.

Consult Atwater, Antiq. of Ohio, 1820; Putnam in Peabody Mus. Reps.; Rau in Smithson. Rep. 1872, 1873; Squier and Davis in Smithson. Cont., I, 1848; Moorehead in The Antiquarian, I, 1897.

(W. H. H.)

Micacuopsiba. An unidentified Dakota division formerly roaming on the upper St Peter's (Minnesota) r., Minn., in 1804.
Cut bank.—Orig. Jour. Lewis and Clark, I, 133, 1904. Mi ca cu op si ba.—Ibid.

Michacondibi (*mitcha* 'large', *indibe* or *gindibe* 'head': 'big head' (Baraga), possibly referring to the Têtes de Boule). An Algonquian (?) tribe or band, probably a part of the Cree or of the Maskegon, formerly on a river of the same name (Albany r.?) entering the s. end of Hudson bay from the s. w. Lahontan placed them about the head waters of Ottawa r.
Machakandibi.—Lahontan, New Voy., I, 231, 1703. Machandibi.—Lahontan (1703), New Voy., map, 1735. Machantiby.—La Chesnaye (1697) in Margry, Déc., VI, 6, 1886. Michacondibis.—Bacqueville de la Potherie, Hist. Am., II, 49, 1753.

Michahai. A Yokuts (Mariposan) tribe near Squaw valley, in the Kings r. drainage, s. central Cal.
Michaha.—Wessells (1853) in H. R. Ex. Doc. 76, 34th Cong., 3d sess., 31, 1857. Michahai.—A. L. Kroeber, inf'n, 1906.

Michibousa. Mentioned by Tonti (French, Hist. Coll. La., I, 82, 1846) in connection with and apparently as one of the tribes of the Illinois confederacy in 1681. The name is perhaps an erroneous designation for some well-known tribe or band.

Michigamea (Algonquian: 'great water,' from *michi* 'great,' 'much,' *guma* 'water'. Baraga gives the correct form of 'Michigan' as *Mishigamaw*, 'the big lake', while Dr Wm. Jones says that the Chippewa of the N. shore of L. Superior refer to L. Michigan by the name *Mishawĭgŭma*, 'big, wide, or expansive waste,' on account of the few or no islands). A tribe of the Illinois confederacy, first visited by Marquette when he descended the Mississippi in 1673. Their village was situated at that time on the w. side of the Mississippi and near a lake bearing the same name as the tribe, probably Big lake, between the St Francis and Mississippi rs., Ark. This tribe was the most southerly of the confederacy, and its extreme southern situation has led some authors to the conclusion that the people were not Algonquian, but this is an evident error. It must have been shortly previous to the time that the first knowledge of the tribes of this general region was obtained that a group or division of the Illinois confederacy, including the Cahokia, Tamaroa, and possibly the Michigamea, pushed southward to escape the attacks of the Sioux and the Foxes. It is therefore probable that at this period the Michigamea moved on into s. Illinois, and thence passed over into s. E. Missouri. The intimate relation of the ancient remains of these two sections would seem to confirm this opinion. About the end of the 17th century they were driven out by the Quapaw or Chickasaw, crossing over into Illinois and joining the Kaskaskia. According to Chauvignerie their totem was the crane. He attributed to them 250 warriors, which is evidently an exaggeration, as he estimated the whole Illinois confederacy at only 508 warriors. It is probable that the Michigamea were only a remnant at the time they joined the Kaskaskia. They were never prominent in Indian affairs. In 1803 Gen. W. H. Harrison supposed that there was but one man of the tribe left alive, but as late as 1818 the names of 3 Michigamea appear as signers of a treaty with the Illinois.

(J. M. C. T.)

Machégamea.—Joutel (1687) in Margry, Déc., III, 465, 1878. Machigama.—French, Hist. Coll. La., I, 82, 1846. Machigamea.—Joutel (1687), op. cit., 460. Matchagamia.—Coxe, Carolana, 11, 1741. Matsigamea.—Hennepin, New Discov., 169, 1698. Medsigamea.—Iberville (1702) in Margry, Déc., IV, 601, 1880. Meosigamia.—Neill, Minn., 173, 1858. Mesigameas.—Proces Verbal (1682) in French, Hist. Coll. La., II, 25, 1875. Metchagamis.—Lattré, map, 1784. Metchigamea.—Marquette, map (1673) in Shea, Miss. Val., 268, 1852. Metchis.—Writer in Smith, Bouquet's Exped., 65, 1766. Metehigamis.—La Tour, map, 1782 (misprint). Métésigamias.—Le Sueur (ca. 1700) in Shea, Early Voy., 92, 1861. Metsigameas.—Proces Verbal (1682) in French, Hist. Coll. La., II, 21, 1875. Michiagamias.—

Shea, Rel. M. Miss., 36, 1861. **Michigamea.**—Marquette (*ca.* 1673), Discov., 344, 1698. **Michigamias.**—Boudinot, Star in the West, 127, 1816. **Michigamis.**—Kingsley, Stand. Nat. Hist., pt. 6, 151, 1883. **Michigania.**—Nourse (1820) in Schoolcraft, Ind. Tribes, II, 588, 1852. **Michiganians.**—Harrison (1814) in Drake, Tecumseh, 160, 1852. **Michigans.**—Sanford, U. S., clii, 1819. **Michigourras.**—Martin, La., I, 262, 1827. **Mitchigamas.**—Hutchins (1778) in Schoolcraft, Ind. Tribes, VI, 714, 1857. **Mitchigamea.**—Marquette (*ca.* 1673), Discov., 346, 1698. **Mitchigamias.**—Jefferys, Fr. Doms., pt. 1, 165, 1761.

Michikinikwa. See *Little Turtle.*

Michilimackinac (*Mĭshĭnĭmaʻkĭnung,* 'place of the big wounded person,' or 'place of the big lame person.'—W. J.). A name applied at various times to Mackinac id. in Mackinac co., Mich.; to the village on this island; to the village and fort at Pt St Ignace on the opposite mainland, and at an early period to a considerable extent of territory in the upper part of the lower peninsula of Michigan. It is derived from the name of a supposed extinct Algonquian tribe, the Mishinimaki or Mishinimakinagog.

According to Indian tradition and the Jesuit Relations, the Mishinimaki formerly had their headquarters at Mackinac id. and occupied all the adjacent territory in Michigan. They are said to have been at one time numerous and to have had 30 villages, but in retaliation for an invasion of the Mohawk country they were destroyed by the Iroquois. This must have occurred previous to the occupancy of the country by the Chippewa on their first appearance in this region. A few were still there in 1671, but in Charlevoix's time (1744) none of them remained. When the Chippewa appeared in this section they made Michilimackinac id. one of their chief centers, and it retained its importance for a long period. In 1761 their village was said to contain 100 warriors. In 1827 the Catholic part of the inhabitants, to the number of 150, separated from the others and formed a new village near the old one. When the Hurons were driven w. by the Iroquois they settled on Mackinac id., where they built a village some time after 1650. Soon thereafter they removed to the Noquet ids. in Green bay, but returned about 1670 and settled in a new village on the adjacent mainland, where the Jesuits had just established the mission of St Ignace. After this the Hurons settled near the mission; the fugitive Ottawa also settled in a village on the island where Nouvel established the mission of St Francis Borgia among them in 1677, and when the Hurons removed to Detroit, about 1702, the Ottawa and Chippewa continued to live at Michilimackinac. (J. M. C. T.)

Machilimachinack.—Watts (1763) in Mass. Hist. Soc. Coll., 4th s., IX, 483, 1871. **Machillimakina.**—Bouquet (1760), ibid., 345. **Mackanaw.**—Drake, Bk. Inds., bk. 5, 134, 1848. **Mackelimakanac.**—Campbell (1760) in Mass. Hist. Soc. Coll., 4th s., IX, 358,

1871. **Mackilemackinac.**—Ibid., 383. **Mackinac.**—Jefferson (1808) in Am. St. Pap., Ind. Aff., I, 746, 1832. **Mackinaw.**—Hall, N. W. States, 131, 1849. **Mackinang.**—Baraga, Eng.-Otch. Dict., 165, 1878 (Chippewa form, abbreviated). **Massillimacinac.**—Map of 1755 in Howe, Hist. Coll., 35, 1851. **Mesh e ne mah ke noong.**—Jones, Ojebway Inds., 45, 1861 (Chippewa name). **Mesilimakinac.**—Hennepin, New Discov., map, 1698. **Michelimakina.**—Writer of 1756 in N. Y. Doc. Col. Hist., X, 482, 1858. **Michellimakinac.**—Campbell (1761) in Mass. Hist. Soc. Coll., 4th s., IX, 417, 1871. **Michihimaquinac.**—Homann Heirs Map U. S., 1784 (misprint). **Michilemackinah.**—Campbell (1761) in Mass. Hist. Soc. Coll., 4th s., IX, 426, 1871. **Michilimackinac.**—Johnson (1763) in N. Y. Doc. Col. Hist., VII, 533, 1856. **Michilimacquina.**—Doc. of 1691, ibid., IX, 511, 1855. **Michilimakenac.**—Albany conf. (1726), ibid., V, 791, 1855. **Michilimakina.**—Vaudreuil (1710), ibid., IX, 843, 1855. **Michilimakinac.**—Du Chesneau (1681), ibid., 153. **Michilimakinais.**—Jefferys, French Doms., pt. 1, 19–20, 1761 (tribe). **Michilimakinong.**—Marquette (*ca.* 1673) in Kelton, Annals Ft Mackinac, 121, 1884. **Michilimaquina.**—Denonville (1686) in N. Y. Doc. Col. Hist., III, 461, 1853. **Michilimicanack.**—Bradstreet (*ca.* 1765), ibid., VII, 690, 1856. **Michilimickinac.**—Peters (1760) in Mass. Hist. Soc. Coll., 4th s., IX, 319, 1871. **Michillemackinack.**—Amherst (1760), ibid., 348. **Michillemakinack.**—Malartic (1758) in N. Y. Doc. Col. Hist., X, 853, 1858. **Michillimacinac.**—Johnstown conf. (1774), ibid., VIII, 506, 1857. **Michillimackinacks.**—Lords of Trade (1721), ibid., V, 622, 1855 (used as synonymous with Ottawas). **Michillimakenac.**—Bouquet (1761) in Mass. Hist. Soc. Coll., 4th s., IX, 392, 1871. **Michillimakinak.**—Cadillac (1703) in Minn. Hist. Soc. Coll., V, 407, 1885. **Michillimaquina.**—Denonville (1687) in N. Y. Doc. Col. Hist., IX, 336, 1855. **Michillmiackinock.**—Domenech, Deserts, II, 452, 1860. **Michi Mackina.**—Brown, West. Gaz., 161, 1817 (Indian form). **Michimmakina.**—M'Lean, Hudson Bay, I, 51, 1849. **Michinimackinac.**—Henry, Travels, 107, 1809 (Chippewa form). **Michlimakinak.**—Montreal conf. (1700) in N. Y. Doc. Col. Hist., IX, 709, 1855. **Micilimaquinay.**—Joutel (*ca.* 1690) in Kelton, Annals Ft Mackinac, 121, 1884. **Mĭcinimaʻkinunk.**—Wm. Jones, inf'n., 1905 (proper form). **Mikinac.**—La Chesnaye (1697) in Margry, Déc., VI, 6, 1886 (same?; mentioned with Ojibwas, Ottawa Sinagos, etc., as then at Shaugawaumikong on L. Superior). **Miscelemackena.**—Croghan (1764) in N. Y. Doc. Col. Hist., VII, 603, 1856. **Misclimakinack.**—Colden (1727), ibid., III, 489, note, 1853. **Mishinimaki.**—Kelton, Annals Ft Mackinac, 9, 10, 1884 (tribe). **Mishinimakina.**—Ibid., 151 (correct Indian name). **Mishinimakinago.**—Baraga, Otchipwe-Eng. Dict., 248, 1880 (Chippewa name of the mythic(?) tribe, whence comes Michilimackinac; the plural takes *g*). **Mishini-makinak.**—Kelton, Annals Ft Mackinac, 135, 1884. **Mishinimakinang.**—Baraga, Eng.-Otch. Dict., 165, 1878 (Chippewa form). **Mishinimákinank.**—Gatschet, Ojibwa MS., B. A. E. 1882. **Misilimakenak.**—Burnet (1723) in N. Y. Doc. Col. Hist., V, 684, 1855. **Misillimakinac.**—Vaudreuil conf. (1703), ibid., IX, 751, 1855. **Mislimakinac.**—Memoir of 1687, ibid., 319. **Misselemachinack.**—Croghan (1760) in Mass. Hist. Soc. Coll., 4th s., IX, 377, 1871. **Misselemakinach.**—Ibid. **Misselemaknach.**—Ibid., 372. **Missilikinac.**—Hennepin, New Discov., 308, 1698. **Missilimachinac.**—Hennepin (1683) in Harris, Voy. and Trav., II, 918, 1705. **Missilimakinak.**—De la Barre (1687) in Minn. Hist. Soc. Coll., V, 418, 1885. **Missilimakenak.**—Colden (*ca.* 1723) in N. Y. Doc. Col. Hist., V, 687, 1855. **Missilimakinac.**—Jes. Rel. 1671, 37, 1858. **Missilimakinak.**—Cadillac (1694) in N. Y. Doc. Col. Hist., IX, 587, 1855. **Missilimaquina.**—Denonville (1687), ibid., III, 466, 1853. **Missilinaokinak.**—Hennepin, New Discov., 316, 1698. **Missilinianac.**—Mt Johnson conf. (1755) in N. Y. Doc. Col. Hist., VI, 975, 1855. **Missillimackinac.**—Johnson (1763), ibid., VII, 573, 1856. **Missillimakina.**—Denonville (1686), ibid., IX, 287, 1855. **Missilmakina.**—Denonville (1687), ibid., 325. **Mitchinimackenucks.**—Lindsey (1749), ibid., VI, 538, 1855 (here intended for the Ottawa). **Monsiemakenack.**—Albany conf. (1723), ibid., V, 693, 1855. **St. Francis**

Borgia.—Shea, Cath. Miss., 370, 1855 (Ottawa mission on Mackinaw id. in 1677). **Teijaondoraghi.**—Albany conf. (1726) in N. Y. Doc. Col. Hist., v, 791, 1855 (Iroquois name).

Michipicoten (*Mishibigwadunk*, 'place of bold promontories,' or 'region of big places.'—W. J.). The designation of the Algonquian Indians living on Michipicoten r., Ontario, N. of L. Superior, and extending into Ruperts Land. In Canada they are officially classed as "Michipicoten and Big Heads," consisting of two bands belonging to different tribes. The smaller band consists of Chippewa and are settled on a reservation known as Gros Cap, on the w. side of the river, near its mouth; the other band belongs to the Maskegon and resides mainly near the Hudson's Bay Co.'s post on Brunswick lake, on the N. side of the dividing ridge. The two bands together numbered 283 in 1884, and 358 in 1906. See *Têtes de Boule.* (J. M.)

Michirache. An Iowa phratry. Its gentes are Shuntanthka, Shuntanthewe, Shuntankhoche, and Manyikakhthi.
Me-je′-rä-ja.—Morgan, Anc. Soc., 156, 1877. **Mintcí-ratce.**—Dorsey, Tciwere MS. vocab., B. A. E., 1879. **Mi-tcí′-ra-tce.**—Dorsey in 15th Rep. B. A. E., 238, 1897. **Wolf.**—Morgan, op. cit.

Michiyu (*Mitc-hi-yu*). A former Chumashan village between Pt Conception and Santa Barbara, Cal., at the place now called San Onofre.—Henshaw, Buenaventura MS. vocab., B. A. E., 1884.

Michopdo. A former Maidu village near Chico, at the edge of the foothills, about 5 m. s. of the junction of Little and Big Butte crs., in Butte co., Cal.; pop. 90 in 1850. (R. B. D.)
Ma-chuck-nas.—Johnston (1850) in Sen. Ex. Doc. 4, 32d Cong., spec. sess., 45, 1853. **Ma-chuo-na.**—Day (1850), ibid., 39. **Michoapdos.**—Powers in Overland Mo., xii, 420, 1874. **Mich-ōp′-do.**—Powers in Cont. N. A. Ethnol., iii, 282, 1877. **Michopdo.**—Dixon in Bull. Am. Mus. Nat. Hist., xvii, pl. xxxviii, 1905. **Mitshopda.**—Curtin, MS. vocab., B. A. E., 1885. **Wachuknas.**—Schoolcraft, Ind. Tribes, vi, 710, 1857.

Mickkesawbee. A former Potawatomi village at the site of the present Coldwater, Mich., on a reservation sold in 1827.
Mickesawbe.—Treaty of 1827 in U. S. Ind. Treat., 675, 1873. **Mick-ke-saw-be.**—Chicago treaty (1821), ibid., 152.

Micksucksealton. Said by Lewis and Clark to be a tribe of the Tushepaw (q. v.) living on Clarke r. above the falls, and numbering 300, in 25 lodges, in 1805.
Micksicksealtom.—Clark and Voorhis (1805) in Orig. Jour. Lewis and Clark, vi, 114, 1905. **Micksuck-seal-tom.**—Lewis and Clark, Exped., i, map, 1814. **Micksucksealton.**—Ibid., ii, 475, 1814. **Miksuksealton.**—Drake, Bk. Inds., ix, 1848.

Micmac (*Migmak*, 'allies'; *Nigmak*, 'our allies.'—Hewitt). The French called them *Souriquois.* An important Algonquian tribe that occupied Nova Scotia, Cape Breton and Prince Edward ids., the N. part of New Brunswick, and probably points in s. and w. Newfoundland. While their neighbors the Abnaki have close linguistic relations with the Algon-

quian tribes of the great lakes, the Micmac seem to have almost as distant a relation to the group as the Algonquians of the plains (W. Jones). If Schoolcraft's supposition be correct, the Micmac must have been among the first Indians of the N. E. coast encountered by Europeans, as he thinks they were visited by Sebastian Cabot in 1497, and that the 3 natives he took to England were of this tribe. Kohl believes that those captured by Cortereal in 1501 and taken to Europe were Micmac. Most of the early voyagers to this region speak of the great numbers of Indians on the N. coast of Nova Scotia and New Brunswick, and of their fierce and warlike character. They early became friends of the French, a friendship which was lasting and which the English—after the treaty of Utrecht in 1713, by which Acadia was ceded to them—found impossible to have transferred to themselves for nearly half a century. Their hostility to the English prevented for a long time any serious attempts at establishing British settlements on the N. coasts of Nova Scotia and New Brunswick, for although a treaty of peace was concluded with them in 1760, it was not until 1779 that disputes and difficulties with the Micmac ceased. In the early wars on the New England frontier the Cape Sable Micmac were especially noted.

The missionary Biard, who, in his Relation of 1616, gives a somewhat full account of the habits and characteristics of the Micmac and adjacent tribes, speaks in perhaps rather too favorable terms of them. He says: "You could not distinguish the young men from the girls, except in their way of wearing their belts. For the women are girdled both above and below the stomach and are less nude than the men. . . . Their clothes are trimmed with leather lace, which the women curry on the side that is not hairy. They often curry both sides of elk skin, like our buff skin, then variegate it very prettily with paint put on in a lace pattern, and make gowns of it; from the same leather they make their shoes and strings. The men do not wear trousers . . . they wear only a cloth to cover their nakedness." Their dwellings were usually the ordinary conical wigwams covered with bark, skins, or matting. Biard says that "in summer the shape of their houses is changed; for they are broad and long that they may have more air." There is an evident attempt to show their summer bowers in the map of Jacomo di Gastaldi, made about 1550, given in vol. iii of some of the editions of Ramusio. Their government was similar to that of the New England Indians; polygamy was not common, though practised to some extent by the chiefs; they were expert canoemen, and drew much of their subsistence from the waters. Cultivation of the soil was very limited, if practised at all by them, when first encountered by the whites. Biard says they did not till the soil in his day.

According to Rand (Micmac First Reading Book, 1875), they divided their country, which they called Megumage, into 7 districts, the head-chief living in the Cape Breton district. The other six were Pictou, Memramcook, Restigouche, Eskegawaage, Shubenacadie, and Annapolis. The first three of these formed a group known as Siguniktawak; the other three another group known as Kespoogwit. In 1760 the Micmac bands or villages were given as Le Have, Miramichi, Tabogimkik, Pohomoosh, Gediak (Shediac), Pictou, Kashpugowitk (Kespoogwit), Chignecto, Isle of St Johns, Nalkitgoniash, Cape Breton, Minas, Chigabennakadik (Shubenacadie), Keshpugowitk (Kespoogwit, duplicated), and Rishebouctou (Richibucto). The Gaspesians are a band of Micmac differing somewhat in dialect from the rest of the tribe.

In 1611 Biard estimated the Micmac at 3,000 to 3,500. In 1760 they were reported at nearly 3,000, but had been lately much wasted by sickness. In 1766 they were again estimated at 3,500; in 1880 they were officially reported at 3,892, and in 1884 at 4,037. Of these, 2,197 were in Nova Scotia, 933 in New Brunswick, 615 in Quebec, and 292 on Prince Edward id. In 1904, according to the Report of Canadian Indian Affairs, they numbered 3,861, of whom 579 were in Quebec province, 992 in New Brunswick, 1,998 in Nova Scotia, and 292 on Prince Edward id. The number in Newfoundland is not known.

The Micmac villages are as follows: Antigonishe (?), Beaubassin (mission), Boat Harbor, Chignecto, Eskusone, Indian Village, Isle of St Johns, Kespoogwit, Kigicapigiak, Le Have, Maria, Minas, Miramichi, Nalkitgoniash, Nipigiguit, Pictou, Pohomoosh, Restigouche, Richibucto, Rocky Point, Shediac, Shubenacadie, and Tabogimkik. (J. M.　C. T.)

Acadean.—Latham in Trans. Philol. Soc. Lond., 59, 1856 (misprint). Acadian Indians.—Jefferys, French Doms., pt. 1, 66, 1761 (Dawson in Hind, Lab. Penin., II, 44, 1863, says Acadia is a Micmac word used in composition to denote the local abundance of objects referred to). Bark Indians.—Buchanan, N. Am. Inds., 156, 1824. Kinckemoeks.—Rasle (1724) in Mass. Hist. Soc. Coll., 2d s., VIII, 248, 1819 (misreading of MS. or misprint). Matu-ĕs′-wi skitchi-nú-ûk.—Chamberlain, Malesit MS., B. A. E., 1882 (Malecite name, meaning 'porcupine Indians'; so called on account of their using porcupine quills in ornamentation). Mechimacks.—Boudinot, Star in the West, 127, 1816. Megum.—Rand, Micmac First Reading Book, 81, 1875 (a Micmac so calls himself). Megŭmawaach.—Rand, Eng.-Micmac Dict., 169, 1888. Michmacs.—Trader in Smith, Bouquet's Exped., 69, 1766. Mickemac.—Lahontan (1703) quoted by Richard-

son, Arctic Exped., II, 38, 1851. Mickmacks.—Longueuil (1726) in N. Y. Doc. Col. Hist., IX, 956, 1855. Mickmaks.—Quotation in Drake, Bk. Inds., bk. 3, 137, 1848. Micmacks.—Longueuil (1726) in N. Y. Doc. Col. Hist., IX, 956, 1855. Micmaks.—Begon (1725), ibid., 943. Mic Macs.—Potter in Me. Hist. Soc. Coll., IV, 192, 1856. Micmacs.—Doc. of 1696 in N. Y. Doc. Col. Hist., IX, 643, 1855. Miggaamacks.—Rouillard, Noms Géographiques, 63, 1906. Mikemak.—Lahontan, New Voy., I, 223, 1703 (given also by Gatschet, Penobscot MS., 1887, as their Penobscot name, 'Mĭkĕmak'; singular, Mĭkĕma). Mikmacs.—Vaudreuil (1757) in N. Y. Doc.Col. Hist., X, 658, 1858. Mikmak.—Cocquard (1757), ibid., 529. Mukmacks.—Buchanan, N. Am. Inds., I, 139, 1824. Shannok.—Gatschet in Proc. Am. Philos. Soc., 409, 1885. Shanung.—Gatschet, quoting Latham, ibid. Shawnuk.—Gatschet, ibid. Shŏnăck.—Lloyd, quoting Payton, in Jour. Anthrop. Inst., IV, 29, 1875 ('bad Indians': Beothuk name). Soricoi.—DuCreux map of Canada (1660) cited by Vetromile, Abnakis, 21, 1866 (Latin form). Sorriquois.—Vetromile in Me. Hist. Soc. Coll., VI, 210, 1859. Souricois.—Champlain (1603), Œuvres, II, 58, 1870. Sourikois.—Jes. Rel. 1652, 26, 1858. Sourikwosiorum.—De Laet (1633) quoted by Tanner, Narr., 329, 1830. Souriquois.—Jes. Rel. 1611, 8, 1858. Souriquosii.—De Laet (1633) quoted by Barton, New Views, XXXV, 1798. Sourriquois.—Vetromile in Me. Hist. Soc.Coll., VI, 208, 1859. Suriquois.—Lords of Trade (1721) in N. Y. Doc. Col. Hist., V, 592, 1855.

Micoma. A Chumashan village between Goleta and Pt Conception, Cal., in 1542.—Cabrillo, Narr. (1542) in Smith, Colec. Doc. Fla., 183, 1857.

Miconope. See *Mikanopy*.

Middle Creeks. A term used by some English writers to designate the Creeks on lower Tallapoosa r., Ala., Spanish and French writers sometimes using the name Talipuce, or Talepuse. (A. S. G.)

Middle-settlement Indians. The Cherokee formerly living in upper Georgia and w. North Carolina, as distinguished from those in South Carolina and Tennessee.—Imlay, W. Ter., 363, 1797.

Middle Town. A former Seneca village, 3 m. above the site of Chemung, N. Y., destroyed by Sullivan in 1779.—Jones (1780) in N. Y. Doc. Col. Hist., VIII, 785, 1857.

Miduuski. An Ahtena village on the E. bank of Copper r., Alaska, below the mouth of Tonsina cr.

Miemissouks. Given as the name of a tribe somewhere between Bellingham bay and Fraser r., in Washington or British Columbia. Probably Salishan, otherwise unidentifiable.

Mie-mis-souks.—Starling in Ind. Aff. Rep., 170, 1852. Misonk.—Ibid., 171.

Mienikashika ('those who became human beings by means of the sun'). A Quapaw gens.

Mi e′nikaci′ʞa.—Dorsey in 15th Rep. B. A. E., 229, 1897. Sun gens.—Ibid.

Migichihiliniou (*Migiziwininiwŭg*, 'people of the Eagle clan'; or perhaps *Migisiwininiwŭg*, 'people with wampum', or 'people with the cowrie shells.'—W. J.). Given by Dobbs as the name of a band of (Algonquian?) Indians residing on the "Lake of Eagles," between L. Winnipeg and Lake of the Woods—probably Eagle lake, some distance N. E. of Lake of the Woods. He thinks they were related to the Assiniboin, "because of the great affinity of their language." As this statement is in contradiction to his subsequent assertion, known from other evidence to be correct, that the Assiniboin dwelt w. of L. Winnipeg, it may be inferred that these "Eagle-men" belong to the Chippewa, who have among their gentes one named *Omegeeze*, "Bald Eagle." (J. M.   C. T.)

Eagle ey'd Indians.—Dobbs, Hudson Bay, 24, 1744. **Eagle Eyed Indians.**—Ibid., map. **Migichihilinious.**—Ibid., 24.

Miguihui. A Chumashan village, one of the two popularly known as Dos Pueblos, in Santa Barbara co., Cal.; also a village in Ventura co.

Migiu.—Henshaw, Buenaventura MS. vocab., B. A. E., 1884. **Miguigui.**—Taylor in Cal. Farmer, July 24, 1863 (Ventura co). **Miguihui.**—Ibid., Apr. 24, 1863.

Mihtukmechakick. A name, signifying 'tree eaters,' which, according to Roger Williams' Key (Mass. Hist. Soc. Coll., 1st s., III, 209, 1794), referred to "a people so called (living between three or four hundred m. w. into the land) from their eating *mih-tuck-quash,* 'trees.' They are men-eaters; they set no corn, but live on the bark of chestnut and walnut and other fine trees. They dry and eat this bark with the fat of beasts and sometimes of men. This people are the terrour of the neighboring natives." The name Adirondack (q. v.), applied by the Iroquois to certain Algonquian tribes of Canada, signifies 'they eat trees'. (J. M.   C. T.)

Miitsr. The Humming-bird clan of San Felipe pueblo, N. Mex., of which there were only one or two survivors in 1895.

Míitsr-hano.—Hodge in Am. Anthrop., IX, 351, 1896 (*háno*='people').

Mikakhenikashika ('those who made or adopted the stars as their mark or means of identity as a people.'—La Flesche). A Quapaw gens.

Mika′q′e ni′kaci′ʞa.—Dorsey in 15th Rep. B. A. E., 229, 1897. **Star gens.**—Ibid.

Mikanopy ('head chief'). A Seminole chief. On May 9, 1832, a treaty was signed purporting to cede the country of the Seminole to the United States in exchange for lands w. of the Mississippi. The Seminole had already relinquished their desirable lands near the coast and retired to the pine barrens and swamps of the interior. Mikanopy, the hereditary chief, who possessed large herds of cattle and horses and a hundred negro slaves, stood by young Osceola and the majority of the tribe in the determination to remain. Neither of them signed the agreement to emigrate given on behalf of the tribe by certain pretended chiefs on Apr. 23, 1835. In the summer of that year the Indians made preparations to resist if the Government attempted to remove them. When the agent notified them on Dec. 1 to deliver their horses

and cattle and assemble for the long journey they sent their women and children into the interior, while the warriors were seen going about in armed parties. The white people had contemned the Seminole as a degenerate tribe, enervated through long contact with the whites. Although Mikanopy, who was advanced in years, was the direct successor of King Payne, the chief who united the tribe, the agent said he would no longer recognize him as a chief when he absented himself from the council where the treaty was signed. When the whites saw that the Seminole intended to fight, they abandoned their plantations on the border, which the Indians sacked and burned. Troops were

MIKANOPY.   (McKENNEY AND HALL)

then ordered to the Seminole country, and a seven-years' war began. In the massacre of Dade's command, Dec. 28, 1836, it is said that Mikanopy shot the commander with his own hand. He took no further active part in the hostilities. He was short and gross in person, indolent, and self-indulgent in his habits, having none of the qualities of a leader.—McKenney and Hall, Ind. Tribes, II, 271, 1858.

Mikasi ('coyote and wolf people'). A subgens of the Mandhinkagaghe gens of the Omaha.

Miʞasi.—Dorsey in 15th Rep. B. A. E., 228, 1897.

Mikasuki. A former Seminole town in Leon co., Fla., on the w. shore of Miccosukee lake, on or near the site of the present Miccosukee. The name has been applied also to the inhabitants as a division of the Seminole. They spoke the Hitchiti dialect, and, as appears from the title of B. Smith's vocabulary of their language, were partly or wholly emigrants from the Sawokli towns on lower Chattahoochee r., Ala. The former town appears to have been one of the 'red' or 'bloody' towns, for at the beginning of the Seminole troubles of 1817 its inhabitants stood at the head of the hostile element and figured conspicuously as "Red Sticks," or "Batons Rouges," having painted high poles, the color denoting war and blood. At this time they had 300 houses, which were burned by Gen. Jackson. There were then several villages near the lake, known also as Mikasuki towns, which were occupied almost wholly by negroes. In the Seminole war of 1835–42 the people of this town became noted for their courage, dash, and audacity.   (A. S. G.   C. T.)

Bâton Rouge.—Drake, Abor. Races of N. Am., bk. 4, 404, 1880. Mackasookos.—U. S. Ind. Treat. (1797), 69, 1837. Mecosukee.—Hitchcock (1836) in Drake, Bk. Inds., bk. 4, 93, 1848. Mekasousky.—Pénière in Morse, Rep. to Sec. War, 311, 1822. Micasukee.—Knox (1791) in Am. State Papers, Ind. Aff., I, 127, 1832. Micasukeys.—Morse, Rep. to Sec. War, 364, 1822. Micasukies.—Jesup (1837) in H. R. Doc. 78, 25th Cong., 2d sess., 81, 1838. Micasukys.—Galt (1837) in H. R. Doc. 78, 25th Cong, 2d sess., 104, 1838. Miccasooky.—Hawkins (1813) in Am. State Papers, Ind. Aff., I, 852, 1832. Miccosaukie.—Schoolcraft, Ind. Tribes, II, 335, 1852. Mic-co sooc-e.—Hawkins (1799), Sketch, 25, 1848. Mickasauky.—Drake, Bk. Inds, bk. 4, 125, 1848. Micka Sukees.—Duval (1849) in Senate Ex. Doc. 49, 31st Cong., 1st sess., 144, 1850. Mickasukians.—Belton (1836) in Drake, Bk. Ind., bk. 4, 77, 1848. Mikasaukies.—Ibid., ix. Mikasuki.—Gatschet, Creek Migr. Leg., I, 76, 1884. Mikasuky.—Drake, Ind. Chron., 200, 1836. Mikkesoeke.—ten Kate, Reizen in N. A., 462, 1885 (Mikasaukies, or). Red-stick.—Pénière in Morse, Rep. to Sec. War, 311, 1822.

Mikaunikashinga ('raccoon people'). A subgens of the Ibache gens of the Kansa. Coon.—Stubbs, Kaw MS. vocab., B. A. E., 25, 1877. Me-kä'.—Morgan, Anc. Soc., 156, 1877. Mika nika-shing-ga.—Stubbs, op. cit. Mika qla jiñga.—Dorsey in 15th Rep. B. A. E., 231, 1897 (' small lean raccoon'). Mika unikaciⁿga.—Ibid. Raccoon.—Morgan, op. cit.

Mikechuse. A former hostile tribe living N. and E. of San Joaquin r., Cal., among the foothills of the Sierra Nevada on the headwaters of Tuolumne, Merced, and Mariposa rs. Probably Moquelumnan. See Barbour, et al. (1851) in Sen. Ex. Doc. 4, 32d Cong., spec. sess., 61, 1853.

Mikinakwadshiwininiwak (*Mĭ'kĭnă'kĭwadshĭwĭnĭnĭwŭg*, 'people of the Turtle mtn.'—W. J.). A Chippewa band living in the Turtle mtn. region, North Dakota, adjoining the Canadian line. In 1905 they were under the jurisdiction of the Fort Totten School, and numbered 211 full-bloods and 1,996 mixed-bloods. Mi'kinā'kiwadciwininiwag.—Wm. Jones, inf'n, 1906 (correct form). Mikinakwadshi-wininiwak.—Gatschet, Ojibwa MS., B. A. E., 1882. Montagnèse.—De Smet, Missions, 109, 1844. Turtle Mountain Chippewa.—Common name.

Mikissioua (*Mĕgĕsĭwĭsowᵃ*, 'he goes by the name of the bald eagle.'—W. J.). A gens of both the Sauk and the Foxes, q. v. Cf. *Pamissouk.* Megesiwisōwᵃ.—Wm. Jones, inf'n, 1906 (correct form). Miкissioua.—Jes. Rel. 1672–73, LVIII, 40, 1899. Mikissoua.—Lapham, Inds. Wis., 15, 1870.

Miko. See *Mingo.*

Mikonoh (*Mĭ'kĭnă'k,* 'snapping turtle'). A gens of the Chippewa, q. v. Mi'kina'k.—Wm. Jones, inf'n, 1906. Mik-o-noh'.—Morgan, Anc. Soc., 166, 1877.

Mikonotunne ('people among the white-clover roots'). A former Tututni village on the N. side of Rogue r., Oreg., 14 m. from its mouth. Parrish (Ind. Aff. Rep. 1854, 496, 1855) stated that the village was about 7 m. above the Tututni and that the inhabitants claimed about 12 m. of Rogue r., extending as far as the territory of the Chastacosta. In 1854 they were connected with Pt Orford agency and numbered 124; in 1884 J. O. Dorsey found the survivors on Siletz res., Oreg., numbering 41 persons. Macanoota.—Ind. Aff. Rep. 1864, 505, 1865. Maca-nootna.—Newcomb, ibid., 162, 1861. Macanooto-onys.—Taylor in Cal. Farmer, June 8, 1860. Macanotens.—Palmer in Ind Aff. Rep. 1856, 219, 1857. Mac-en-noot-e-ways.—Ind. Aff. Rep., 470, 1865. Mac-en-oot-en-ays.—Victor in Overland Monthly, VII, 347, 1871. Mac-en-o-tin.—Kautz, MS. Toutouten census, B. A. E., 1855. Mackan-ootenay's Town.—Harper's Mag., XIII, 525, 1856. Mackanotin.—Parrish in Ind. Aff. Rep. 1854, 496, 1855. Mack-en-oot-en-ay.—Huntington in Ind. Aff. Rep. 1867, 62, 1868. Mac-not-na.—Dorsey, Siletz Agency MS. census roll, 1884. Mac-o-no-tin.—Kautz, MS. Toutouten census, B. A. E., 1855. Mak-in-o-ten.—Gibbs, MS., B. A. E. Maknooten-nay.—Everette, Tutu MS. vocab., B. A. E., 1883. Mak-nu'-těne'.—Ibid. (='people by the land along the river'). Maquelnoteer.—Taylor in Cal. Farmer, June 8, 1860. Maquelnoten.—Schoolcraft, Ind. Tribes, VI, 702, 1857. Mec-a-no-to-ny.—Abbott, MS. Coquille census, B. A. E., 1858. Me-ka-nē-ten.—Schumacher in Bull. U. S. Geog. and Geol. Surv., III, 31, 1877. Mĭ'-ko-no' ʇûnně'.—Dorsey in Jour. Am. Folk-lore, III, 233, 1890 (Tututni name). Mĭ'-kwun-nu' ʇûnně'.—Ibid. (Naltunetunne name).

Mikulitsh (*Mĭ-ku-lĭtc'*). A former village of the Kuitsh at the mouth of Winchester bay, Oreg.—Dorsey in Jour. Am. Folk-lore, III, 231, 1890.

Milakitekwa. Classed by Gibbs as a band of Okinagan, though more nearly connected with the Colville, formerly residing on the W. fork of Okinakane r., Wash. Mil-a-ket-kun.—Stevens in Ind. Aff. Rep., 445, 1854. Milakitekwa.—Gibbs in Pac. R. R. Rep., I, 412, 1855.

Milijaes. A former tribe of N. E. Mexico or S. Texas, probably Coahuiltecan, gathered into the mission of San Bernardo de la Candela.—Orozco y Berra, Geog., 302, 1864.

Military Societies. Although the various tribes were in a state of chronic warfare one with another, little is known of their system of military organization, with the exception, perhaps, of those of the Plains and the Pueblo regions. There is abundant evidence, however, that the military code was as carefully developed as the social system among most of the tribes N. of Mexico. The exceptions were the Eskimo and the thinly scattered bands of the extreme N., the California tribes, and the various bands W. of the Rocky mts. commonly grouped as Paiute. East of the Mississippi, where the clan system was dominant, the chief military functions of leadership, declaration, and perhaps conclusion of war, seem to have been hereditary in certain clans, as the Bear clan of the Mohawk and Chippewa, and the Wolf or Munsee division of the Delawares. It is probable that if their history were known it would be found that most of the distinguished Indian leaders in the colonial and other early Indian wars were actually the chiefs of the war clans or military societies of their respective tribes. If we can trust the Huguenot narratives, the ancient tribes of N. Florida and the adjacent region had a military system and marching order almost as exact as that of a modern civilized nation, the various grades of rank being distinguished by specific titles. Something similar seems to have prevailed among the Creeks, where, besides war and peace clans, there were war and peace towns, the war or "red" towns being the assembly points for all war ceremonies, including the war dance, scalp dance, and torture of prisoners. The "Red Stick" band of the Seminole, noted in the Florida wars as the most hostile portion of the tribe, seem to have constituted in themselves a war society. Among the confederated Sauk and Foxes, according to McKenney and Hall, nearly all the men of the two tribes were organized into two war societies which contested against each other in all races or friendly athletic games and were distinguished by different cut of hair, costume, and dances. With the more peaceful and sedentary Pueblo tribes, as the Zuñi and Hopi, military matters were regulated by a priesthood, as the "Priesthood of the Bow" of the Zuñi, which formed a close corporation with initiation rites and secret ceremonies.

Throughout the plains from N. to S. there existed a military organization so similar among the various tribes as to suggest a common origin, although with patriotic pride each tribe claimed it as its own. Maximilian was inclined to ascribe its origin to the Crows, perhaps on the ground of their well-known ceremonial temperament, but it is probably much older than their traditional separation from the Hidatsa. In each tribe the organization consisted of from 4 to 12 societies of varying rank and prominence, ranging from boys or untried warriors up to old men who had earned retirement by long years of service on the warpath and thenceforth confined themselves to the supervision of the tribal ceremonies. The name of each society had reference to some mystic animal protector or to some costume, duty, or peculiarity connected with the membership. Thus, among the Kiowa there were 6 warrior societies, known respectively as Rabbits, Young Mountain Sheep, Horse Caps, Black Legs, Skunkberry People (alias Crazy Horses), and Chief Dogs. The Rabbit society consisted of boys of about 10 to 12 years of age, who were trained in their future duties by certain old men, and who had a dance in which the step was intended to imitate the jumping motion of a rabbit. The next four societies named were all of about equal rank, varying only according to the merit or reputation of the officers at any particular time; but the K'oitseñko or 'Chief Dogs' were limited to 10 picked and tried warriors of surpassing courage, each of whom, at his investiture with the sacred sash of the order, took a solemn obligation never, while wearing it, to turn his face from the enemy in battle except at the urgent appeal of the whole war party. It was the duty of the leader, who wore a black sash passing around his neck and hanging down to the ground, to dismount and anchor himself in the front of the charge by driving his lance through the end of the sash into the earth, there to exhort the warriors without moving from his station unless, should the battle be lost, they released him by pulling out the lance. Should they forget or be prevented in the hurry of flight, he must die at his post. In consequence of the great danger thus involved, the K'oitseñ scarf was worn only when it was the deliberate intention to fight a pitched and decisive battle.

Each society had its own dance, songs, ceremonial costume, and insignia, besides special tabus and obligations. The ceremonial dance of one society in each tribe was usually characterized by some species of clown play, most frequently taking the form of speech and action the reverse of what the spectators were expecting. The organization among the Arapaho, Cheyenne, Sioux, and other tribes was essentially the same as among the Kiowa. At all tribal assemblies, ceremonial hunts, and on great war expeditions, the various societies took charge of the routine details and acted both as performers and as police. Among the Cheyenne the Hotámitäneo, or Dog Men society ("Dog Soldiers"), acquired such prominence in the frontier wars by virtue of superior number and the bravery of their leadership that the name has frequently been used by writers to designate the whole organization.

Consult Clark, Ind. Sign Lang., article "Soldier" and tribal articles, 1885; Cushing in 2d Rep. B. A. E., 1883; De Bry, Brev. Narr., 1591; G. A. Dorsey in Field Columb. Mus. Pub., Anthrop. ser., IX, no. 1, 1905; J. O. Dorsey in Am. Nat., XIX, no. 7, 1885; Gatschet, Creek Migr. Leg., I, II, 1884–88; Grinnell, Blackfoot Lodge Tales, 1892; Maximilian, Travels, 1843; Mooney (1) in 14th Rep. B. A. E., 1896; (2) in 17th Rep. B. A. E., 1898. (J. M.)

Milkwanen. A Luiseño village formerly in the neighborhood of San Luis Rey mission, s. Cal.—Taylor in Cal. Farmer, May 11, 1860.

Milky Wash ruin. A prehistoric pueblo ruin extending ¾ of a mile along the edge of Milky hollow, about 9 m. E. of the Petrified Forest, Apache co., Ariz. Much of the ruin has disappeared over the bluff. The houses were small and rudely constructed; the pottery is coarse and undecorated, and red, gray, and black in color; stone implements show excellent workmanship. A feature of the ruin is its stove-like fire altars. See Hough in Rep. Nat. Mus. 1901, 319–20, 1903.
Milky Hollow Ruin.—Hough, ibid., pl. 53.

Milluch. The Chehalis name of a village on the s. side of Grays harbor, Wash.—Gibbs, MS. no. 248, B. A. E.

Milly. The handsome young daughter of Hillis Hadjo (q. v.), a Seminole chief. When, in Dec. 1817, a party of Seminole captured an American named McKrimmon and carried him to Mikasuki, Hillis Hadjo, who resided in that town, ordered him to be burnt to death. The stake was set, McKrimmon with his head shaved was bound to it, and wood was piled about him. When the Indians finished their dance and were about to kindle the fire, Milly rushed to her father and upon her knees begged that he would spare the prisoner's life; but it was not until she evinced a determination to perish with him that her plea was granted. McKrimmon was subsequently sold to the Spaniards and thus obtained his liberty. After Hillis Hadjo's death, Milly, who with her father's family was captured by American troops, received an offer of marriage from McKrimmon, but refused to accept it until she was satisfied that the offer was prompted by motives other than his obligation to her for saving his life. See McKenney and Hall, Ind. Tribes, III, 193, 1838; Drake, Inds., 403, 1880.

Milpais. A Papago village with 250 inhabitants in 1869 (Browne, Apache Country, 291, 1869). Probably intended for *Malpais* (Span.: 'bad land', locally referring specifically to spread-out lava), or for *Milpas* ('cultivated patches').

Milpillas. Two Tepehuane pueblos, one known as Milpillas Grandes (Span. 'great little-cultivated-patches'), the other as Milpillas Chiquitas, both situated in s. w. Durango, Mexico. The inhabitants of both villages are now much mixed with whites and Aztecs.
Milpillas.—Orozco y Berra, Geog., 281, 1864. Santa María Milpillas.—Ibid., 319.

Milwaukee ('fine land', from *milo* or *mino* 'good', *aki* 'land.'—Baraga.. Cf. Kelton, cited below). A former village with a mixed population of Mascoutens, Foxes, and Potawatomi, situated on Milwaukee r., Wis., at or near the site of the present Milwaukee, in 1699. See St Cosme, cited below, and Warren, Hist. Ojibways, 32, 1885. Cf. *Miskouakimina.*
Meliwarik.—St Cosme (1699) in Shea, Early Voy., 50, 1861. Melleki.—Old map (ca. 1699), followed in map in Lapham, Inds. Wis., 1870. Melleoki.—Shea, Early Voy., 50, 1861 (early map form). Melloki.—Ibid. Melwarck.—St Cosme (1699) quoted by Latham, op. cit., 5. Melwarik.—Ibid. Milwaukie.—Dick (1827) in H. R. Doc. 66, 33 Cong., 2d sess., 15, 1855 (refers to tribe). Minewagi.—Kelton, Annals Ft Mackinac, 175, 1895 (given as correct aboriginal form, meaning 'there is a good point,' or 'there is a point where huckleberries grow').

Mimal. A former Maidu village on the w. bank of Feather r., just below Yuba city, Sutter co., Cal. (R. B. D.)
Mimai.—Dixon in Bull. Am. Mus. Nat. Hist., XVII, pl. xxxviii, 1905 (misprint). Mimal.—Bancroft, Nat. Races, I, 450, 1882. Wí-ma.—Powers in Cont. N. A. Ethnol., III, 282, 1877.

Mimbreños (Span.: 'people of the willows'). A branch of the Apache who took their popular name from the Mimbres mts., s. w. N. Mex., but who roamed over the country from the E. side of the Rio Grande in N. Mex. to San Francisco r. in Arizona, a favorite haunt being near Lake Guzman, w. of El Paso, in Chihuahua. Between 1854 and 1869 their number was estimated at 400 to 750, under Mangas Coloradas (q. v.). In habits they were similar to the other Apache, gaining a livelihood by raiding settlements in New Mexico, Arizona, and Mexico. They made peace with the Mexicans from time to time and before 1870 were supplied with rations by the military post at Janos, Chihuahua. They were sometimes called Coppermine Apache on account of their occupancy of the territory in which the Santa Rita mines in s. w. N. Mex. are situated. In 1875 a part of them joined the Mescaleros and a part were under the Hot Springs (Chiricahua) agency, N. Mex. They are now divided between the Mescalero res., N. Mex., and Ft Apache agency, Ariz., but their number is not separately reported. (F. W. H.)
Apaches Mimbreños.—Humboldt, Atlas Nouv. Esp., carte 1, 1811. Coppermine Apaches.—Bartlett, Pers. Narr., I, 323, 1854. Iccujen-ne.—Orozco y Berra, Geog., 59, 1864. Mangus Colorado's band.—Ind. Aff. Rep., 206, 1858 (=Mangas Coloradas' band). Membrenos.—Mill, Hist. Mex., 185, 1824. Miembre Apaches.—Ind. Aff. Rep., 175, 1875. Miembrenos.—Ind. Aff. Rep., 380, 1854. Miembres.—Davis, Span. Conq. N. Mex., 52, 1869. Mienbre.—Ind. Aff. Rep., 246, 1877. Mimbrenas.—Browne, Apache Country, 290, 1869. Mimbreno.—Bonny-

castle, Spanish Am., 68, 1819. **Mimbrereños.**—Barreiro, Ojeada sobre Nuevo-México, app., 3, 1832. **Mimbres.**—Anza (1769) in Doc. Hist. Mex., 4th s., II, 114, 1856 **Mimbres Apaches.**—Cremony, Life among Apaches, 33, 1868. **Mimvre.**—Ind. Aff. Rep. 1859, 336, 1860. **Yecujen-né.**—Escudero, Not. Estad. de Chihuahua, 212, 1834 (own name).

Mina. The extinct Salt clans of Sia and San Felipe pueblos, N. Mex.
Mína-háno.—Hodge in Am. Anthrop., IX, 352, 1896 (*háno*='people').

Minas. A Micmac village or band in Nova Scotia in 1760.—Frye (1760) in Mass. Hist. Soc. Coll., 1st s., x, 115, 1809.

Minatti. A village, probably Seminole, formerly at the source of Peace cr., w. central Florida, probably in the present Polk co. (H. R. Doc. 78, 25th Cong., 2d sess., map, 768–9, 1838). The name evidently bears no relation to the present Manatee in Manatee co.

Minemaung. A Potawatomi village, called after a chief of this name, near the present Grantpark, Kankakee co., N. E. Illinois, on land ceded in 1832.—Camp Tippecanoe treaty (1832) in U. S. Ind. Treaties, 698, 1873.

Mines and Quarries. The term mining is usually applied to operations connected with the procuring of metals from the earth, while the term quarrying is applied to the procuring of stone. The former term sometimes refers also to the obtaining of minerals occurring in minute quantities, as turquoise, or of substances, as clay, salt, and ocher, not usually removed in solid or bulky bodies, especially where deep excavations or tunneling are required. Gold, silver, and copper were used by many of the more progressive American tribes before the discovery; but copper was the only metal extensively used N. of Mexico. The smelting of ores was probably imperfectly understood, even by the most advanced tribes, and iron, except in meteoric form or in the ore, was unknown. Their most important mines of copper (q. v.) with which we are acquainted were in N. Michigan penin. and on Isle Royale in L. Superior. Here the native metal occurs in masses and bits distributed in more or less compact bodies of eruptive rock. The mining operations consisted in removing the superficial earth and débris and in breaking up the rock with stone sledges and by the application of heat, thus freeing the masses of metal, some of which were of large size. One specimen, partially removed from its bed by the aborigines and then abandoned, weighed nearly 3 tons. "It was 16½ feet below the surface, and under it were poles, as if it had been entirely detached, but it had not been much displaced" (Winchell in Pop. Sci. Monthly, Sept. 1881). Another very large mass encountered in the shaft of the Minnesota mine on Ontonagon r., Mich., which had been partially

removed by the native miners, is referred to by MacLean: "The excavation [ancient] reached a depth of 26 ft., which was filled up with clay and a matted mass of moldering vegetable matter. At a depth of 18 ft., among a mass of leaves, sticks, and water, Mr Knapp discovered a detached mass of copper weighing 6 tons. This mass had been raised about 5 ft. along the foot of the lode on timbers by means of wedges and was left upon a cobwork of logs. These logs were from 6 to 8 in. in diameter, the ends of which plainly showed the marks of a cutting tool. The upper surface and edges of the mass of copper were beaten and pounded smooth, showing that the irregular protruding pieces had been broken off. Near it were found other masses. On the walls of the shaft were marks of fire. Besides charcoal there was found a stone sledge weighing 36 pounds and a copper maul weighing 25 pounds. Stone mauls, ashes, and charcoal have been found in all these mines" (MacLean, Mound Builders, 76–77, 1904). The excavations were generally not deep, being merely pits, but tunneling was occasionally resorted to (Gillman). In McCargole's cove, on Isle Royale, nearly a square mile of the surface has been worked over, the pits connecting with one another over a large part of the area. Countless broken and unbroken stone sledges, mostly roundish bowlders of hard stone brought from the lake shore many miles away, are scattered over the surface and mixed with the débris. As indicated by the presence of rough grooves and notches, these implements were generally hafted for use. A remnant of a withe handle was preserved in one instance, and a wooden shovel, a wooden basin, a wooden ladder, and a piece of knotted rawhide string are among the relics obtained from the ancient pits by modern miners.

In glacial times extensive surfaces of the copper-bearing rocks were swept by the under surfaces of the great ice sheets, and thus many masses and bits of the metal, more or less scarred and battered, were carried southward over Michigan, Wisconsin, and Minnesota, and even farther s. These masses, deposited with the rocky débris of moraines, were collected and utilized by the natives. The masses of copper, when obtained, were probably in the main carried away to distant settlements to be worked into implements, utensils, and ornaments. The distribution of the product was very wide, extending over the entire country E. of the great plains. Cinnabar, ocher, salt, alum, and clay were mined in many sections of the country, Indians sometimes going long distances in quest of these materials. Coal was and is obtained from exposures in the bluffs, by the Hopi Indians, and there is historical testimony that it was thus procured for pottery-burning in former times. Iron oxides were extensively mined by some tribes, as is illustrated in an iron mine recently opened in Franklin co., Mo., where deep, sinuous galleries had been excavated in the ore body for the purpose of obtaining the red and yellow oxides for paint (Holmes).

SECTION OF PAINT MINE IN A BED OF IRON ORE; MISSOURI. DEPTH OF EXCAVATIONS ABOUT 20 FT. (HOLMES)

The quarrying of stone for the manufacture of implements, utensils, and ornaments was one of the great industries of the native tribes. Ancient excavations, surrounded by the débris of implement-making, are of common occurrence in the United States. Flint (q. v.) and other varieties of stone sufficiently brittle to be shaped by the fracture processes were especially sought, but soapstone, mica, and turquoise were also quarried. The flinty rocks include chert (usually called flint), novaculite, quartz, quartzite, jasper, argillite, rhyolite, and obsidian (q. v.). The best known flint quarries are those on Flint Ridge, Licking co., Ohio; at Mill Creek, Union co., Ill., and in the vicinity of Hot Springs, Ark. Many others have been located, and doubtless still others remain undiscovered in the forests and mountains.

At Flint Ridge extensive beds of richly colored flint of excellent quality occur, forming the summit of the flattish ridge. The ancient pittings cover hundreds of acres, and in numerous cases are still open to a depth of from 10 to 20 ft. About the pits are ridges and heaps of débris and many shop sites where the implement forms were roughed out, and masses of fractured flint and flakage, as well as countless hammerstones used in the shaping operations (see *Stone-work*). The flint body was first uncovered, probably with the aid of stone, antler, and wooden tools, and then broken up with heavy stone hammers, aided by the application of heat. Similar quarries occur in Coshocton co., as well as in other parts

of Ohio, and in West Virginia, Indiana, Kentucky, and Tennessee. The quarries in Arkansas are perhaps even more extensive than those in Ohio, the stone in the best known examples being a fine-grained variety of chert known as novaculite (q. v.), which occurs in beds of great thickness and undetermined extent. The phenomena of the quarries correspond closely with those of Flint Ridge (Holmes). Similar quarries of chert are found at many points in Missouri and Indian Territory (Holmes). The great group of quarries found in the vicinity of Mill Creek, Ill., presents superficial indications corresponding closely with those of the Ohio and Arkansas quarries, but the stone obtained was a gray flint, which occurs in the form of nodular and lenticular masses, mostly of irregular outline. These concretions were well suited to the manufacture of the large flaked implements—spades, hoes, knives, and spearheads—found distributed over a vast area in the middle Mississippi valley. The original pittings, excavated in the compact deposits of calcareous clay and sand in which the nodules are embedded, often reached a depth of 25 ft or more. A rude stone pick was used in excavating, and stone as well as antler hammers were employed in the flaking work (Phillips). See *Flint*. Quarries of quartzite (q. v.) occur in Wyoming (Dorsey); of argillite (q. v.) in Bucks co., Pa. (Mercer); of jasper (q. v.) in the same county (Mercer); and of rhyolite (q. v.) in Adams co. (Holmes). Differing in type from the preceding are the extensive quarries on Piney branch of Rock cr., in the suburbs of Washington, D. C. Here quartzite bowlders were quarried from the Cretaceous bluffs for the manufacture of flaked implements (Holmes). See *Quartzite*.

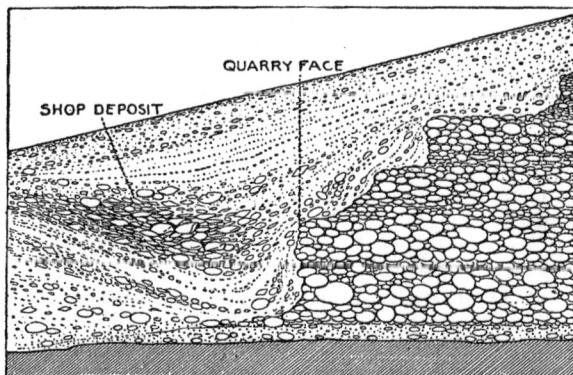

SECTION OF FILLED-UP BOWLDER QUARRY; D. C. HEIGHT OF QUARRY FACE ABOUT 10 FT. (HOLMES)

Steatite (q. v.), called also soapstone, was quarried at many points along the Atlantic slope of the Appalachian highland from Georgia to New York, also in the New England states, and in the far West, especially in California. This stone was easily carved, and, because it is not

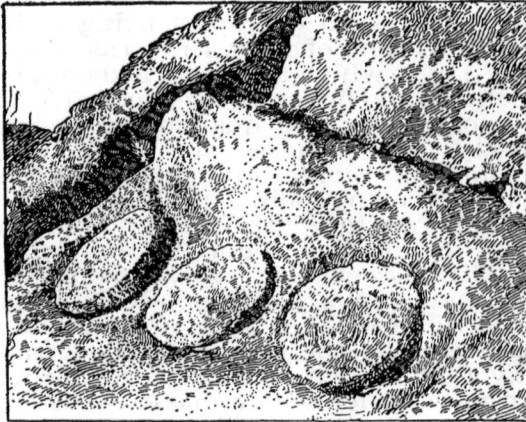

WALL OF SOAPSTONE QUARRY SHOWING STUMPS LEFT IN REMOVING LUMPS OF THE ROCK; CALIFORNIA. (HOLMES)

readily fractured by heat, was much used by the Indians for cooking vessels and for tobacco pipes. The masses of this rock were uncovered, and lumps large enough to be shaped into pots were cut out with the aid of well-sharpened picks and chisels of stone (Holmes, McGuire, Schumacher, Reynolds, Angell).

Mica (q. v.) was quarried in many places in Virginia and North Carolina, the pittings being numerous and large. The sheets of this material were used by the natives for mirrors and for the manufacture of ornaments. Building stone was required in great quantities in the building of pueblos and cliff-dwellings in the arid region, but surface rock was so readily available that deep quarrying was not necessary. Catlinite (q. v.), a red-clay stone, was extensively quarried for the manufacture of tobacco pipes and ornaments. The quarries are situated in Pipestone co., Minn., and are still worked to some extent by the neighboring Siouan tribes. The industry is not regarded as a very ancient one, although the manu-

CATLINITE (PIPESTONE) QUARRY WORKED BY SIOUX INDIANS. THE LEDGE OF PIPESTONE APPEARS NEAR BASE OF WALL. (BENNETT)

factured articles are widely distributed (Catlin, Holmes).

Turquoise (q. v.) is found in several of the Western states, but so far as known was mined extensively at only two points, Los Cerrillos, near Santa Fé, N. Mex. (Blake, Silliman), and at Turquoise mtn., Cochise co., Ariz. These mines were operated by the natives before the arrival of the Spanish, as is indicated by the pittings and rude stone mining tools found associated with them. The mines were operated also by the Spaniards, and in more recent years in a desultory way by the present inhabitants of the region. The mines at Los Cerrillos seem to have been extensively worked by the aborigines. Blake, who examined the site about 1855, says: "On reaching the locality I was struck with astonishment at the extent of the excavation. It is an immense pit with precipitous sides of angular rock, projecting in crags, which sustain a growth of pines and shrubs in the fissures. On one side the rocks tower into a precipice and overhang so as to form a cave; at another place the side is low and formed of the broken rocks which were removed. From the top of the cliff the excavation appears to be 200 ft in depth and 300 or more in width. The bottom is funnel-shaped and formed by the sloping banks of the débris of fragments of the sides. On this débris, at the bottom of the pit, pine trees over a hundred years old are now growing, and the bank of refuse rock is similarly covered with trees. This great excavation is made in the solid rocks, and tens of thousands of tons of rock have been broken out. This is not the only opening; there are several pits in the vicinity more limited in extent, some of them being apparently much more recent" (Blake in Am. Jour. Sci., 2d s., xxv, 227, 1858). Silliman (Eng. and Min. Jour., xxxii, 169, 1881) speaks of finding in these mines "numerous stone hammers, some to be held in the hand and others swung as sledges, fashioned with wedge-shaped edges and a groove for a handle. A hammer weighing over 20 pounds was found while I was at the Cerrillos, to which the withe was still attached, with its oak handle; the same scrub-oak which is found growing abundantly on the hillsides, now quite well preserved after at least two centuries of entombment in this perfectly dry rock. The stone used for these hammers is the hard and tough hornblende andesite, or propylite, which forms the Cerro de Oro and other Cerrillos hills. With these rude tools, and without iron and steel, using fire in place of explosives, these patient old workers managed to break down and remove the incredible masses of these tufaceous rocks which form the mounds already described."

Among the various works which may be consulted on the native copper mines are: Foster and Whitney in H. R. Ex. Doc. 69, 31st Cong., 1st sess., 1850; Gillman in Smithson. Rep. 1873, 1874; Holmes in Am. Anthrop., n. s., III, 1901; McLean, Mound Builders, 1879; Packard in Am. Antiq., XV, no. 2, 1893; Whittlesey in Smithson. Cont., XIII, 1862; Winchell in Pop. Sci. Mo., Sept. 1881. Quarries of brittle varieties of stone are described by Dorsey in Pub. 51, Field Columbian Mus., 1900; Smith (Fowke) in Nat. Mus. Rep. 1884, 1885; Holmes (1) in Bull. 21, B. A. E., 1894, (2) in 15th Rep. B. A. E., 1897; Mercer (1) in Am. Anthrop., VII, 1894, (2) in Proc. A. A. A. S., XLII, 1894, (3) in Proc. Am. Philos. Soc., XXXIV, 396, 1895; Phillips in Am. Anthrop., n. s., II, 37, 1900. Soapstone quarries are described by Angell in Am. Nat., XII, 1878; Holmes in 15th Rep. B. A. E., 1897; McGuire in Trans. Anthrop. Soc. Wash., II, 1883; Schumacher in 11th Rep. Peabody Mus., 1878. Pipestone quarries by Catlin, N. Am. Inds., I, 1866; Holmes in Proc. A. A. A. S., XLI, 1892. Turquoise by Blake (1) in Am. Jour. Sci., 2d s., XXV, 1858, (2) in Am. Antiq., XXI, 1899; Kunz, Gems and Precious Stones, 1890; Silliman in Eng. and Min. Jour., XXXII, 1881. (W. H. H.)

Minesetperi ('those who defecate under the bank.'—H. L. Scott). A division of the Crows, more commonly known as River Crows, who separated from the Mountain Crows about 1859 and settled on Missouri r.
Mine-set-peri.—Culbertson in Smithson. Rep. 1850, 144, 1851. Mĭnĕsupĕ′rik.—Col. H. L. Scott, inf'n, 1906 (proper form, with meaning above given). Minneh-sup-pay-deh.—Anon. MS. Crow vocab., B. A. E. River Crows.—Pease in Ind. Aff. Rep. 1871, 420, 1872. Sap-suckers.—Culbertson, op. cit.

Mingan (*Ma′ingŭn*, 'wolf'). A Montagnais (Algonquian) village near the mouth of Mingan r., on the N. shore of the Gulf of St Lawrence, Quebec. It is the general rendezvous for all the Indians for several hundred miles around. The name occurs in the grant of the seigniory in 1661, and a mission was probably established there soon after (Hind, Lab. Penin., I, 43–44, 1863). The village numbered 178 inhabitants in 1884, and 241 in 1906.
(J. M.)
Ma′īngą̆n.—Wm. Jones, inf'n, 1906.

Minghasanwetazhi (*Minxa-san-wet'ajĭ*, 'touches not swans'). A subgens of the Mandinkagaghe gens of the Omaha.—Dorsey in 15th Rep. B. A. E., 228, 1897.

Minghaska (*Minxa′ska*, 'swan'). A gentile subdivision of the Osage.—Dorsey in 15th Rep. B. A. E., 234, 1897.

Minghaskainihkashina (*Minxa′ ska i′niɥk'ăcin′a*, 'swan people'). A subgens of the Minkin gens of the Osage.—Dorsey in 15th Rep. B. A. E., 233, 1897.

Mingko. The 'Royal' clan of the Ishpanee phratry of the Chickasaw, so called because it was the chief or ruling clan.
Ming-ko—Morgan, Anc. Soc., 163, 1877. Míngo.—Gatschet, Creek Migr. Leg., I, 96, 1884.

Mingo. The Choctaw and Chickasaw equivalent of the Muskogee *miko*, 'chief', both words being of frequent use by historians and travelers in the Gulf states during the colonial period. (A. F. C.)

Mingo (Algonquian: *Mingwe*, 'stealthy, treacherous'). A name applied in various forms by the Delawares and affiliated tribes to the Iroquois and cognate tribes, and more particularly used during the late colonial period by the Americans to designate a detached band of Iroquois who had left the villages of the main body before 1750 and formed new settlements in Pennsylvania, on upper Ohio r., in the neighborhood of the Shawnee, Delawares, and neighboring tribes. From that period their relations were more intimate with the western tribes than with the Iroquois, and they were frequently hostile to the whites while the parent body was at peace. They gradually moved down the Ohio, and just previous to the Revolution were living in the vicinity of Steubenville, Ohio. In 1766 their settlement, known as Mingo town, contained 60 families, and was the only Indian settlement on the Ohio from Pittsburg to Louisville (Hutchins, Descrip., 1778). From the Ohio they crossed over to the headwaters of Scioto and Sandusky rs., where they began to be known as the Senecas of Sandusky, either because the majority were Seneca or because all the western Iroquois were supposed to be Seneca. They were called Seneca in their first relations with the Government, and that name thus became their official designation, generally with a descriptive addition to indicate their habitat. About 1800 they were joined by a part of the Cayuga, who had sold their lands in New York. In Ohio one part formed a connection with the Shawnee at Lewistown, while the rest had their village on Sandusky r. The mixed band at Lewistown became known as the Mixed Senecas and Shawnees, to distinguish them from the others, who were still called Senecas of Sandusky. In 1831 both bands sold their lands in Ohio and removed to a tract in Kansas, on Neosho r., whence they removed in 1867 to Indian Territory, where they now are, the two bands being united and having no connection with the Shawnee. In 1831 the Sandusky band numbered 251, but by 1885 the entire body had become reduced to 239. In 1905 they numbered 366.

On Herman's map of 1670 is a notice of a tribe called the Black Mincquas living beyond the mountains on the large Black Mincqua r., probably the Ohio r. Formerly, by means of a branch of this river which approached a branch of the Susquehanna above the Conestoga fort (probably the Juniata r.), "those Black Mincquas came over and as far as Delaware to trade, but the Sassquahana and Sinnicus Indians [Conestoga and Seneca] went over and destroyed that very great Nation." This statement and the location make it probable that the Black Mincquas were the Erie, q. v. (J. M.)

Five Nations of the Sciota Plains.—Bouquet (1764), quoted by Rupp, W. Penn., app., 144, 1846. Mineoes.—Cowley (1775) in Arch. of Md., 94, 1892 (misprint). Mingo.—See *Iroquois*. Neosho-Senecas.—Schoolcraft, Ind. Tribes, IV, 591, 1854. Sandusky Senecas.—Lang and Taylor, Rep., 26, 1843. Senecas of Ohio.—Ft Stanwix treaty (1768) in N. Y. Doc. Col. Hist., VIII, 111, 1857. Senecas of Sandusky.—Seneca Agency treaty (1832) in U. S. Ind. Treaties, 559, 1837. Senecas of Sandusky and Stony creek.—Greenville treaty (1814) in Am. St. Papers, Ind. Aff., I, 826, 1832. Senecas of the Glaize.—Maumee council (1793), ibid., 357. Six Nations living at Sandusky.—Greenville treaty (1795) quoted by Harris, Tour, 250, 1805.

Miniconjou ('those who plant beside the stream'). A division of the Teton Sioux. Their closest affinity is with the Oglala, Brulé, and Hunkpapa Teton. As the whites did not come into actual contact with the Teton tribes until recent times, there is no evidence as to their antiquity as distinct organizations. The first mention of the Miniconjou, unless under some unidentified name, is by Lewis and Clark (1804). These authors (Expedition, I, 61, 1814) speak of them as "Tetons Minnakenozzo, a nation inhabiting both sides of the Missouri above the Cheyenne r., and containing about 250 men." This indicates a population of perhaps 800, probably much below their actual number. Their history since they became known to the whites consists, like that of the other Sioux, of little else than war with and raids upon other tribes and depredations on the whites. They are frequently alluded to in official and other reports as among the most

unruly and troublesome of the Teton tribes. Hayden says: "This band, though peaceable when ruled by good chiefs, has always been very wild and independent, seldom visiting the trading posts, either on the Platte or on the Missouri, and having no intercourse with white men except with a few traders during the winter season." They were estimated in 1850 by Culbertson (Smithson. Rep. for 1850, 142) at 270 lodges, or between 2,100 and 2,200 people. At this time, and until brought upon reservations, they roamed over the Black hills and headwaters of Cheyenne r., being usually found from Cherry cr. on the Cheyenne to Grand r. Gen. Warren (1856) estimated them at 200 lodges and 1,600 souls. The Ind. Aff. Rep. for 1863 gives 1,280 as the population. They are now located with other Sioux bands on Cheyenne River res., S. Dak., but are not separately enumerated.

The divisions given by Lewis and Clark are as follows: (1) Minnakineazzo (Miniconjou), (2) Wanneewackataonelar, (3) Tarcoehparh. Culbertson (Smithson. Rep. 1850, 142, 1851), mentions four: (1) River that Flies, (2) Those that Eat no Dogs, (3) Shell-earring band, (4) Lejagadatcah. Swift (1884), from information received from Indian sources, gives the following divisions (15th Rep. B. A. E., 220, 1897): (1) Unkcheyuta, (2) Glaglahecha, (3) Shungkayuteshni (Those that Eat no Dogs), (4) Nighetanka, (5) Wakpokinyan, (6) Inyanhaoin (Shell-earring band), (7) Shikshichela, (8) Waglezaoin, (9) Wannawegha (probably the Wanneewackataonelar).

The Miniconjou were participants in the peace treaty of Ft Sully, S. Dak., Oct. 10, 1865, and in the treaty of Ft Laramie, Wyo., Apr. 29, 1868, by which they and other Sioux tribes were pledged to cease hostilities and the United States agreed to set apart for them a reservation.

(J. O. D. C. T.)

Mee-ne-cow-e-gee.—Catlin, N. Am. Inds., I, 211, 1844. Memacanjo.—Clark quoted by Coues, Lewis and Clark Exped., I, 101, note, 1893 (trans. 'make fence on the river'). Men-i-cou-zha.—Hoffman in H. R. Doc. 36, 33d Cong., 2d sess., 3, 1855. Minecogue.—Ind. Aff. Rep., 285, 1854. Minecosias.—Sage, Scenes in Rocky Mts., 58, 1846. Minecougan.—Vaughan in H. R. Doc. 36, 33d Cong., 2d sess., 6, 1855. Mi-ne-kaŋ'-zús.—Hayden, Ethnog. and Philol. Mo. Val., 374, 1862. Mini-con-gsha.—Culbertson in Smithson. Rep. 1850, 142, 1851. Mini-Conjou.—Smithson. Misc. Coll., XIV, art. 5, 6, 1878. Minioughas.—Hoffman in H. R. Doc. 36, 33d Cong., 2d sess., 4, 1855. Minicoujons.—Winship in H. R. Rep. 63, 33d Cong., 2d sess., 5, 1855. Mini-kan-jous.—Warren (1855), Neb. and Ariz., 48, 1875. Minikan oju.—Cleveland, letter to J. O. Dorsey, 1884. Minikanyes.—Warren, Dacota Country, 16, 1855. Minikaŋye wožupi.—Riggs, Dakota Gram. and Dict., xvi, 1852 (trans. 'those who plant by the water'). Min-i-kaŋ'-žu.—Hayden, Ethnog. and Philol. Mo. Val., 376, 1862. Minikiniad-za.—Brackenridge, Views of La., 78, 1814. Minikomjoos.—Smet, Letters, 37, note, 1843. Minikonga.—Schoolcraft, Ind. Tribes, 5, 494, 1855.

Minikongshas.—Keane in Stanford, Compend., 522, 1878. **Minikooju.**—Dorsey in 15th Rep. B. A. E., 220, 1897 (own name). **Minnake-nozzo.**—Coyner, Lost Trappers, 70, 1847. **Min-na-kine-az-zo.**—Lewis and Clark, Discov., 34, 1806. **Minnecarguis.**—Ind. Aff. Rep. 1856, 68, 1857. **Minnecaushas.**—Ind. Aff. Rep., 301, 1854. **Minnecogoux.**—Ind. Aff. Rep. 1859, 120, 1860. **Minnecojous.**—Corliss, Lacotah MS. vocab., B. A. E., 107, 1874. **Minnecongew.**—Boller, Among Inds. in Far W., 29, 1868. **Minnecongou.**—Gale, Upper Miss., 226, 1867. **Minneconjon.**—U. S. Ind. Treat. (1866), 890, 1873. **Minneconjos.**—Sen. Ex. Doc. 94, 34th Cong., 1st sess., 11, 1856. **Minneconjoux.**—Stanley in Poole, Among the Sioux, app., 232, 1881. **Minnecoujos.**—Harney in Sen. Ex. Doc. 94, 34th Cong., 1st sess., 1, 1856. **Minnecoujou.**—Brackett in Smithson. Rep. for 1876, 466. **Minne Coujoux Sioux.**—Ind. Aff. Rep. 1855, 79, 1856. **Minne-Cousha.**—Bordeau in H. R. Rep. 63, 33d Cong., 2d sess., 13, 1855. **Minnecowzues.**—Ind. Aff. Rep., 295, 1854. **Min-ne-kaŋ'-zu.**—Hayden, Ethnog. and Philol. Mo. Val., 371, 1862. **Minnekonjo.**—Ind. Aff. Rep., 247, 1877. **Minnicongew.**—Parkman, Oregon Trail, 126, 1883. **Minnikan-jous.**—Warren (1855), Neb. and Ariz., 48, 1875. **Minnikanye Wozhipu.**—Burton, City of Sts., 119, 1861 (trans. 'those who plant by the water'). **Monecoshe Sioux.**—Ind. Aff. Rep. 1864, 228, 1865. **Teton-Menna-Kanozo.**—Lewis and Clark, Exped., I, map, 1814. **Té-ton-min-na-kine-az'-zo.**—Lewis and Clark, Discov., 30, 1806. **Tetons Mennakenozzo.**—Long, Exped. St Peter's R., I, 381, 1824. **Tetons Minnakenozzo.**—Lewis and Clark, Exped., I, 61, 1814. **Tetons Minnakineazzo.**—Lewis, Trav., 171, 1809. **Tetons Minnekincazzo.**—Farnham, Trav., 32, 1843. **Winnakenozzo.**—Ramsey in Ind. Aff. Rep., 87, 1850 (misprint).

Mininihkashina (*Mini'niɥ k'ācina*, 'sun people'). A subgens of the Minkin gens of the Osage.—Dorsey in 15th Rep. B. A. E., 233, 1897.

Minisha ('red water'). An Oglala band under Eagle-that-Sails, in 1862. Cf. *Itazipcho*.
Min-i-sha'.—Hayden, Ethnog. and Philol. Mo. Val., 376, 1862. **Red water band.**—Culbertson in Smithson. Rep. 1850, 142, 1851.

Minishinakato. A band of the Assiniboin.
Gens du Lac.—Hayden, Ethnog. and Philol. Mo. Val., 387, 1862. **Min'-i-shi-nak'-a-to.**—Ibid.

Minisink ('the place of the Minsi.'—Heckewelder). The leading division of the Munsee (q. v.), with whom they are often confounded. They lived on the headwaters of Delaware r., in the s. w. part of Ulster and Orange cos., N. Y., and the adjacent parts of New Jersey and Pennsylvania. Their principal village, which bore the same name, was the council place of the Munsee, and seems to have been in Sussex co., N. J., near the point where the state line crosses Delaware r. They are said to have had three villages in 1663. The Munsee who moved w. with the Delawares were mainly of this division. (J. M.)
Manessings.—Kregier (1663) in N. Y. Doc. Col. Hist., XIII, 339, 1881. **Manissing.**—Ibid., 325. **Mannissing.**—Ibid. **Menesikns.**—Croghan (1759) in Proud, Pa., II, 297, 1798. **Menessinghs.**—Doc. of 1663 in N. Y. Doc. Col. Hist., XIII, 276, 1881. **Menisink.**—Doc. of 1755 in Rupp, Northampton, etc., Cos., 88, 1845. **Menissinck.**—Doc. of 1663 in N. Y. Doc. Col. Hist., XIII, 289, 1881. **Menissing.**—Beeckman (1660), ibid., XII, 315, 1877. **Menissinges.**—Conference of 1660, ibid., XIII, 167, 1881. **Menissins.**—Beeckman (1663), ibid., XII, 438, 1877. **Mennisink.**—Doc. (1756) in Rupp, Northampton, etc., Cos., 106, 1845. **Mennissinck.**—Schuyler

(1694) in N. Y. Doc. Col. Hist., IV, 99, 1854. **Minisincks.**—Swartwout (1662), ibid., XIII, 229, 1881. **Minising.**—Mandrillon, Spectateur Américain, map, 1785. **Minisinks.**—Boudinot, Star in the West, 127, 1816. **Minissens.**—La Salle (1681) in Margry, Déc., II, 148, 1877 (probably intended for Munsee). **Minissingh.**—Beeckman (1660) in N. Y. Doc. Col. Hist., XII, 306, 1877. **Minissinks.**—Beeckman (1663), ibid., 438. **Minisuk.**—McKenney and Hall, Ind. Tribes, III, 80, 1858. **Minnessinck.**—Van der Donck (1656) in Ruttenber, Tribes Hudson R., 96, 1872. **Minnisink.**—Canajoharie conf. (1759) in N. Y. Doc. Col. Hist., VII, 382, 1856 (location). **Minnissincks.**—Schuyler (1694), ibid., IV, 99, 1854. **Minnissinke.**—New York conf. (1681), ibid., XIII, 551, 1881. **Minusing.**—Proud, Pa., II, 320, 1798. **Monnesick.**—Addam (1653) in Drake, Bk. Inds., bk. 2, 79, 1848.

Miniskuyakichun ('wears salt'). A band of the Brulé Teton Sioux.
Miniskuya kiçuŋ.—Dorsey (after Cleveland) in 15th Rep. B. A. E., 219, 1897. **Miniskuya-kitc'uⁿ.**—Ibid.

Minkekhanye (*Minqe' qan'-ye*, 'big raccoon'). A subgens of the Ruche, the Pigeon gens of the Iowa.—Dorsey in 15th Rep. B. A. E., 239, 1897.

Minkeyine (*Minke' yin'-e*, 'young raccoon'). A subgens of the Ruche, the Pigeon gens of the Iowa.—Dorsey in 15th Rep. B. A. E., 239, 1897.

Minkin (*Min k'in*, 'sun-carrier'). The 3d gens on the Tsishu side of the Osage tribal circle; also the 8th Kansa gens.—Dorsey in 15th Rep. B. A. E., 231, 233, 1897.

Minnehaha. The heroine in Henry Wadsworth Longfellow's *Song of Hiawatha*. Her father, home, and nationality are given in the lines—

> At the doorway of his wigwam
> Sat the Ancient Arrow-maker,
> In the land of the Dacotahs,
> Making arrow heads of jasper,
> Arrow heads of chalcedony.
> At his side, in all her beauty,
> Sat the lovely Minnehaha,
> Sat his daughter, Laughing Water.

Minnehaha of the song is the poet's own creation. Some of the elements of her creation, such as nationality and name, were suggested from a book called *Life and Legends of the Sioux*, by Mrs Mary Eastman (N. Y., 1849). The book contains some observations on life of the Sioux, together with a miscellaneous assortment of sentiment and romance. The scene of the events related in the narratives is on the Mississippi with the center in and around Ft Snelling. This lay on the borderland between the Sioux and the Chippewa, who at the time were constantly at war with each other. So when the Algonkin hero is told by his grandmother that the time has come for him to marry, and he replies and makes known his selection in the words that—

> In the land of the Dacotahs
> Lives the Arrow-maker's daughter,

we have the following dialogue which may be taken as an embodiment of the underlying motive in the poet's mind in the creation of his Minnehaha:

> Bring not to my lodge a stranger
> From the land of the Dacotahs!
> Very fierce are the Dacotahs,
> Often is there war between us,
> There are feuds yet unforgotten,
> Wounds that ache and still may open!
>
> For that reason, if no other,
> Would I wed the fair Dacotah,
> That our tribes might be united,
> That old feuds might be forgotten,
> And old wounds be healed forever!

The name Minnehaha is first met with in Mrs Eastman's book. In the introduction of that work she makes the statement that between Ft Snelling and the Falls of St Anthony "are the Little Falls 40 ft. in height on a stream that empties into the Mississippi. The Indians call them Minnehaha, or 'Laughing Waters.'" This is plainly the source of the heroine's name. The word Minnehaha is taken from the Teton dialect of the Dakota language. It is a compound, the first part of which is *mini* and means water. *Mini* occupies initial place in composition, as, *minito* blue water, *minisapa* black water, *miniyaya* water-cask. The rendering of Minnehaha as 'Laughing Water' is explained as follows: The verb to laugh is *iḣa* (ḣ=German *ch*); to laugh at, *iḣaḣa;* and the noun laughter is *ḣaḣa.* Hence, Minnehaha is literally 'water laughter.' The more reasonable definition of Minnehaha is to be sought from such a source as that given in the Dakota-English Dictionary of Stephen Return Riggs, according to whom *ḣaḣa* as a noun in compounds denotes 'cascade,' 'cataract'; hence *mini-ḣaḣa* would signify 'waterfall.' (w. j.)

Minnepata ('falling water'). A division of the Hidatsa.

Minipătă.—Matthews, inf'n, 1885. **Min-ne-pä'-ta.**—Morgan, Anc. Soc., 159, 1877. **Water.**—Ibid.

Minnetarees of Knife River. An unidentified Hidatsa division, mentioned by Lewis and Clark (Exped., I, 330, 1814). Possibly the Amahami.

Mipshuntik (*Mi'-p'căn-tik*). A former Yaquina village on the N. side of Yaquina r., on the site of Toledo, Benton co., Oreg.—Dorsey in Jour. Am. Folk-lore, III, 229, 1890.

Miqkano ('mud-turtle'). A subphratry or gens of the Menominee.—Hoffman in 14th Rep. B. A. E., pt. I, 42, 1896.

Miramichi. A former Micmac village on the right bank of Miramichi r., New Brunswick, where it flows into the Gulf of St Lawrence. The French had a mission there in the 17th century, and in 1760 there was a Micmac village or band of that name. (J. M.)

Merimichi.—Frye (1760) in Mass. Hist. Soc. Coll., 1st s., X, 115, 1809. **Merrimichi.**—Mass. Hist. Soc. Coll., 1st s., III, 100, 1794. **Miramichi.**—Beauharnois (1745) in N. Y. Doc. Col. Hist., X, 5, 1858.

Mirimichy.—Stiles (1761) in Mass. Hist. Soc. Coll., 1st s., X, 116, 1809. **Mizamichis.**—Shea, Miss. Val., 86, 1852 (misprint).

Miscanaka. The site of San Buenaventura mission, Cal. (Taylor in Cal. Farmer, July 24, 1863). Said by Indians in 1884 to be the name of a former Chumahsan village at the site of the present schoolhouse in that town. (H. W. H.)

Miscanaka.—Taylor, op. cit. **Mitc-ka'-na-kau.**—Henshaw, Buenaventura MS. vocab., B. A. E., 1884 (*tc=ch*).

Miseekwigweelis. A division of the Skagit tribe, now on Swinomish res., Wash. They participated with other tribes in the treaty of Pt Elliott, Wash., Jan. 22, 1855, by which they ceded lands to the United States and agreed to settle on a reservation.

Bes-he-kwe-guelts.—Mallet in Ind. Aff. Rep., 198, 1877. **Mee-see-qua-guilch.**—U. S. Ind. Treat. (1855), 378, 1873. **Miseekwigweelis.**—Gibbs in Cont. N. A. Ethnol., I, 180, 1877. **Mis-kai-whu.**—Gibbs in Pac. R. R. Rep., I, 436, 1855.

Misesopano. A Chumashan village w. of Pueblo de las Canoas (San Buenaventura), Ventura co., Cal.; in 1542; placed by Taylor on the Rafael Gonzales farm.

Misesopano.—Cabrillo (1542) in Smith, Colec. Doc. Fla., 181, 1857. **Mississipone.**—Taylor in Cal. Farmer, Apr. 17, 1863. **Pona.**—Ibid.

Mishawum (probably from *mishawumut*, 'a great spring'—S. D. in Mass. Hist. Soc. Coll., 2d s., X, 174, 1823; Jones (Ind. Bul., 1867) translates it 'large peninsula'). A Massachuset village formerly at Charlestown, near Boston, Mass. It was commonly known as Sagamore John's town, from the name of a resident chief. The English settled there in 1628. (J. M.)

Misham.—Drake, Ind. Chron., 155, 1836. **Mishawum.**—Pemberton in Mass. Hist. Soc. Coll. 1st s., III, 241, 1794. **Sagamore John's Town.**—Early English writers.

Mishcup. One of the New England names of the porgy (*Sparus argyrops*). Roger Williams (1643) gives *mishcuppaŭog*, the plural form, as the word for bream in the Narraganset dialect of Algonquian. *Mishcup*, the singular, is derived from *mishe*, 'great', and *kuppi*, 'close together,' referring to the scales of the fish. From *mischcuppaŭog* have been derived *scuppaug* and *scup;* also *porgy* or *paugee*. (A. F. C.)

Mishikhwutmetunne ('people who dwell on the stream called Mishi'). An Athapascan tribe formerly occupying villages on upper Coquille r., Oreg. In 1861 they numbered 55 men, 75 women, and 95 children (Ind. Aff. Rep., 162, 1861). In 1884 the survivors were on Siletz res. Dorsey (Jour. Am. Folk-lore, III, 232, 1890) in that year obtained the following list of their villages (which he calls gentes) as they formerly existed on Coquille r. from the Kusan country to the head of the stream, although not necessarily at one period: Chockrelatan, Chuntshataatunne, Duldulthawaiame, Enitunne, Il-sethlthawaiame, Katomemetunne, Khinukhtunne, Khweshtunne, Kimestunne, Kthukhwestunne, Kthunataachuntunne, Meshtshe, Nakhituntunne, Nakhochatunne, Natarghiliitunne, Natsushltatunne, Nilestunne, Ṛghoyinestunne, Sathlrekhtun, Sekhushtuntunne, Sunsunnestunne, Sushltakhotthatunne, Thlkwantiyatunne, Thltsharghiliitunne, Thltsusmetunne, Thlulchikhwutmetunne, Timethltunne, Tkhlunkhastunne, Tsatarghekhetunne, Tthinatlitunne, Tulwutmetunne, Tuskhlustunne, and Tustatunkhuushi.

Coquell.—Ind. Aff. Rep., 263, 1884. **Coquill.**—Newcomb in Ind. Aff. Rep., 162, 1861. **Coquilla.**—Ibid., 221. **Coquille.**—Abbott, MS. Coquille vocab., B. A. E., 1858. **De-d'á téné.**—Everette, Tutu MS. vocab., B. A. E., 1883 (='people by the northern water'). **Ithalé téni.**—Gatschet, Umpqua MS. vocab., B. A. E., 1877 (Umpqua name). **Kiguel.**—Robertson, Oregon, 129, 1846. **Kukwil'.**—Dorsey, Alsea MS. vocab., B. A. E., 1884 (Alsea name). **Ku-kwil' ɋunně.**—Dorsey, Chetco MS. vocab., B. A. E., 1884 (Chetco name). **Ku-kwil'-tûn ɋunně.**—Dorsey, Naltûnne-tûnně MS. vocab., B. A. E., 1884 (Naltunne name). **Mi-ci'-kqwŭt-me' tûnně.**—Dorsey in Jour. Am. Folk-lore, III, 232, 1890. **Mi-cí-qwŭt.**—Dorsey, Chastacosta MS. vocab., B. A. E., 1884. **Upper Coquille.**—Dorsey in Am. Antiq., VII, 41, 1885.

Mishikinakwa. See *Little Turtle.*

Mishongnovi (*Mi-shong'-no-vi*, from *mishóniniptuovi*, 'at the place of the other which remains erect,' referring to two irregular sandstone pillars, one of which has fallen. A. M. Stephen). A pueblo of the Hopi in N. E. Arizona, on the Middle mesa of Tusayan. The original pueblo, which stood w. of the present Mishongnovi and formed one of the villages of the ancient province of Tusayan, was abandoned about 1680 and the present town built. Mishongnovi was a visita of the mission of Shongopovi during the mission period (1629–80) and bore the name of San Buenaventura. Pop. 221 in 1870; 241 in 1877; 289 in 1882; 242 in 1891. See Mindeleff in 8th Rep. B. A. E., 26, 66–70, 1891; Fewkes in 17th Rep. B. A. E., 582, 1898; Dorsey and Voth in Field Columb. Mus. Pub. no. 66, 1902. (F. W. H.)

Buenaventura.—Vargas (1692) quoted by Davis, Span. Conq. N. Mex., 368, 1869. **Macanabi.**—Senex, map, 1710. **Maconabi.**—De l'Isle, Carte Mex. et Floride, 1703. **Majananí.**—Oñate (1598) in Doc. Inéd., XVI, 207, 1871. **Manzana.**—Schoolcraft, Ind. Tribes, I, 519, 1851. **Masagnebe.**—Garcés (1776), Diary, 1900 (Yavapai form). **Masagneve.**—Garcés (1775-6) quoted by Bancroft, Ariz. and N. Mex., 137, 1889. **Masanais.**—Arrowsmith, map N. A., 1795, ed. 1814. **Masaqueve.**—Garcés (1775 6) quoted by Bancroft, Ariz. and N. Mex., 395, 1889 (Yavapai form). **Ma-shong'-ni-vi.**—Powell, 4th Rep. B. A. E., xl, 1886. **Mashóniniptuovi.**—Stephen in 8th Rep. B. A. E., 26, 1891. **Mas-sang-na-vay.**—Irvine in Ind. Aff. Rep., 160, 1877. **Mausand.**—Calhoun quoted by Donaldson, Moqui Pueblo Inds., 14, 1893. **Meeshom-o-neer.**—French, Hist. Coll. La., II, 175, note, 1875. **Me-shong-a-na-we.**—Crothers in Ind. Aff. Rep., 324, 1872. **Meshongnavi.**—Mason quoted by Donaldson, Moqui Pueblo Inds., 14, 1893. **Me-shung-a-na-we.**—Palmer in Ind. Aff. Rep., 133, 1870. **Me-shung-ne-vi.**—Shipley in Ind. Aff. Rep., 310, 1891. **Michonguave.**—Moffet in Overland Monthly, 243, Sept. 1889. **Micongnivi.**—Ind Aff. Rep., lxxx, 1886. **Mi-coñ'-în-o-vi.**—Fewkes in Am. Anthrop., V, 225, 1892. **Mi-con-o-vi.**—Ibid, 13. **Mi-shan-qu-na-vi.**—Ward (1861) quoted by Donaldson, Moqui PuebloInds.,14,1893. **Mi-shong-i-niv.**—Powell, ibid. (misquoted). **Mi-shong'-i-ni-vi.**—Powell in Scribner's Mag., 196, 202, Dec. 1875. **Mi-shong-in-ovi.**—Stephen quoted by Donaldson, Moqui Pueblo Inds., 14, 1893. **Mishongnavi.**—Donaldson, ibid., 4. **Mishongop-avi.**—Bandelier in Arch. Inst. Papers, III, 135, 1890. **Mi-shon-na-vi.**—Donaldson, Moqui Pueblo Inds., pl. p. 62, 1893. **Monsonabi.**—Vargas (1692) quoted by Davis, Span. Conq. N. Mex., 367, 1869. **Monsonavi.**—Davis, El Gringo, 115, 1857. **Mooshahneh.**—Ives, Colorado R., 124, 1861. **Mooshanave.**—Taylor in Cal. Farmer, Apr. 10, 1863. **Moo-sha-neh.**—Ives, Colorado R., map, 1861. **Mooshongae nayvee.**—Eastman, map in Schoolcraft, Ind. Tribes, IV, 24–25, 1854. **Mooshongeenayvee.**—Eastman misquoted by Donaldson, Moqui Pueblo Inds., 14, 1893. **Moosong'-na-ve.**—Jackson quoted by Barber in Am. Nat., 730, Dec. 1877. **Mosanais.**—Humboldt, Atlas Nouv.-Espagne, carte 1, 1811. **Mosanis.**—Pike, Expeditions, 3d map, 1810. **Mosasnabi.**—Morfi (1782) quoted by Bandelier in Arch. Inst. Papers, III, 135, 1890. **Mosasnave.**—Escudero, Not. de Chihuahua, 231, 1834. **Moshanganabi.**—Taylor in Cal. Farmer, June 19, 1863. **Moshóngnavé.**—ten Kate, Reizen in N. A., 245, 1885. **Mossonganabi.**—Dominguez and Escalante (1776) in Doc. Hist. Mex., 2d s., I, 548, 1854. **Moszasnavi.**—Cortez (1799) quoted in Pac. R. R. Rep., pt. 3, 121, 1856. **Mowshaï-i-nà.**—Domenech, Deserts N. A., I, 185, 1860. **Moxainabe.**—Vetancurt (1693), TeatroMex., III, 321, 1871. **Moxainabi.**—Vetancurt misquoted by Bancroft, Ariz. and N. Mex., 173, 1889. **Moxainavi.**—Bancroft, ibid., 349. **Moxionavi.**—Vargas (1692) quoted, ibid., 201. **Moxonaui.**—Alcedo, Dic. Geog., III, 260, 1788. **Moxonavi.**—Villa-Señor, Theatro Am., pt. 2, 425, 1748. **Mú-shài-è-nòw-à.**—Pac. R. R. Rep., III, pt. 3, 13, 1856 (Zuñi name). **Mú-shài-ì-nà.**—Ibid. (own name). **Musháñganevi.**—Gatschet in Mag. Am. Hist., 206, 1882. **Mushangene-vi.**—Loew in Pop. Sci. Monthly, V, 352, 1874. **Mu-shang-newy.**—Bourke, Moquis of Ariz., 90, 1884. **Mushanguewy.**—Bourke misquoted by Donaldson, Moqui Pueblo Inds., 14, 1893. **Mushá-ni.**—Barber in Am. Nat., 730, 1877. **Mushaugnevy.**—Bourke in Proc. Am. Antiq. Soc., I, 244, 1881. **S. Buen. de Mossaquavi.**—Vargas (1692) quoted by Bancroft, Ariz. and N. Mex., 201, 1889. **Tse-itso-kĭt'.**—Stephen, MS., B. A. E., 1887 (Navaho name: 'Great rocky dune'). **Tset-so-kít.**—Eaton in Schoolcraft, Ind. Tribes, IV, 220, 1854 (Navaho name).

Mishpapsna (*Mic-páp'-snâ*). A former Chumashan village at the arroyo near Carpinteria, Santa Barbara co., Cal.—Henshaw, Buenaventura MS. vocab., B. A. E., 1884.

Mishtapalwa (*Mic-ta-pal'-wa*). A former Chumashan village at La Matanza, near San Buenaventura, Ventura co., Cal.—Henshaw, Buenaventura MS. vocab., B. A. E., 1984.

Mishtapawa (*Mic-ta-pä-wă*). One of the former Chumashan villages near Santa Inés mission, Santa Barbara co., Cal.—Henshaw, Santa Inez MS. vocab., B. A. E., 1884.

Mishtawayawininiwak. The Chippewa name for that part of the tribe living in Canada.

Mictawayáng.—Wm. Jones, inf'n, 1905 (c=sh). **Mishtawaya-wininiwak.**—A. S. Gatschet, Ojibwa MS., B. A. E., 1882 (wininiwak='people').

Mishumash (*Mic-hu'-mac*, native name of Santa Cruz id. and the islanders). A village of the Santa Cruz islanders of California, who belonged to the Chumashan family.—Henshaw, Buenaventura MS. vocab., B. A. E., 1884.

Misinagua. A Chumashan village w. of Pueblo de las Canoas (San Buenaventura), Ventura co., Cal., in 1542. Placed by Taylor near San Marcos.
Misinagua.—Cabrillo (1542) in Smith, Colec. Doc. Fla., 181, 1857. Misinajua.—Taylor in Cal. Farmer, Apr. 17, 1863.

Misisagaikaniwininiwak (*Mĭshĭsagaï-ganĭwĭnĭnĭwăg*, 'people of the big lake.'—W. J.). A Chippewa band, taking its popular name from its residence on Mille Lac, E. Minn. They were included among the "Chippewa of the Mississippi" in the treaty of Washington, Feb. 22, 1855, by which a reserve was assigned to them in Crow Wing co., Minn. There are now (1905) 1,249 Mille Lac Chippewa under the White Earth agency in the same state. See *Sagawamick*.
Mille Lac band.—Treaty of 1863 in U. S. Ind. Treat., 215, 1873. Mishĭsāgaïganiwininiwăg.—Wm. Jones, inf'n, 1906. Misisagaikani-wininiwak.—Gatschet, Ojibwa MS., B. A. E., 1882.

Misketoiitok (*Mis-ke-toi'-i-tok*). A former Hupa village on or near Trinity r., Cal.—Powers in Cont. N. A. Ethnol., III, 73, 1877.

Miskouaha. One of the 4 divisions of the Nipissing at the Lake of the Two Mountains, Quebec, in 1736. Their totem was blood, for which reason they were also called Gens du Sang.
Gens du Sang.—Chauvignerie (1736) in N. Y. Doc. Col. Hist., IX, 1053, 1855. Mikouachakhi.—Jes. Rel. 1643, 38, 1858 (same?). Miskouaha.—Chauvignerie, op. cit. Miskuakes.—Chauvignerie as quoted by Schoolcraft, Ind. Tribes, III, 554, 1853.

Miskouakimina (prob. for *Meskwăkiwi-năwᵉ*, 'red-earth town,' i. e., 'Fox town.'—W. J.). Marked on La Tour's map of 1784 as if a Fox village near the site of Milwaukee, Wis., on the w. shore of L. Michigan. The Sauk are marked on the same map as in the adjacent region.

Miskut. A former Hupa village on the E. bank of Trinity r., Cal., about ¾ m. below Takimilding.   (P. E. G.)
Agaraits.—Gibbs in Schoolcraft, Ind. Tribes, III, 139, 1853. A-gar-it-is.—McKee in Sen. Ex. Doc. 4, 32d Cong., spec. sess., 194, 1853. Eh-grertsh.—Gibbs, MS., B. A. E., 1852. Hergerits.—Goddard, inf'n, 1903 (Yurok name). Miscolts.—Keane in Stanford, Compend., 522, 1878. Miscott.—Ind. Aff. Rep., 82, 1870. Mis'-kut.—Powers in Cont. N. A. Ethnol., III, 73, 1877. Miskût.—Goddard, Life and Culture of the Hupa, 13, 1903. O-gährit-tis.—Meyer, Nach dem Sacramento, 282, 1855.

Miskwagamiwisagaigan ('red - water lake', from *miskwa* 'red', *gami* 'fluid, water', *saga-igan* 'lake'). A Chippewa band living about Red lake and Red Lake r., N. Minn., and numbering 1,353 under the Leech Lake agency in 1905. By treaty at the Old crossing of Red Lake r., Minn., Apr. 12, 1864, this band and the Pembina ceded all their lands in Minnesota.
Chippewa of Red Lake.—Ind. Aff. Rep. 1905, 516, 1906 (official name). Chippeways of Red Lake.—Lewis, Travels, 178, 1809. Miskú-Gami-Saga-igan-anishinábeg.—Gatschet, op. cit. ('Red fluid lake

Indians'). Miskwa-gamiwi-saga-igan.—Gatschet, Ojibwa MS., B. A. E., 1882. Miskwāgamiwisāgu i·gan.—Wm. Jones, inf'n, 1905. Mĭskwă-kă̆ Mĕ̆wĕ̆ Să̆gă̆gă̆n Wĕ̆nĕ̆nĕ̆wăk.—Long, Exped. St Peter's R., II, 153, 1824.

Mismatuk (*Mĭs-ma'-tuk*). A former Chumashan village in the mountains near Santa Barbara, Cal., in a locality now called Arroyo Burro.—Henshaw, Santa Barbara MS. vocab., B. A. E., 1884.

Mispu (*Mĭs'-pu*). A former Chumashan village near the light-house at Santa Barbara, Cal., in a locality now called El Castillo Viejo.—Henshaw, Buenaventura MS. vocab., B. A. E., 1884.

Misshawa (*Mĭshäwä*, 'elk'). A gens of the Potawatomi, q. v.
Micäwä.—Wm. Jones, inf'n, 1905 (c=sh). Mis-shă'-wä.—Morgan, Anc. Soc., 167, 1877.

Missiassik (on the etymology of the name, see McAleer, Study in the Etymology of Missisquoi, 1906). An Algonquian tribe or body of Indians belonging to the Abnaki group, formerly living on Missisquoi r. in N. Vermont. Whether they formed a distinct tribe or a detached portion of some known Aknaki tribe is uncertain. If the latter, which seems probable, as the name "Wanderers" was sometimes applied to them, it is possible they were related to the Sokoki or to the Pequawket. They had a large village at the mouth of Missisquoi r., in Franklin co., on L. Champlain, but abandoned it about 1730 on account of the ravages of an epidemic, and removed to St Francis, Quebec. They subsequently sold their claims in Vermont to the "Seven Nations of Canada." Chauvignerie in 1736 gives 180 as the number of their warriors, indicating a population of 800. They seem to have been on peaceable terms with the Iroquois.
          (J. M.   C. T.)
Masiassuck.—Douglass, Summary, I, 185, 1755. Massassuk.—La Tour, map, 1784. Messiasics.—Boudinot, Star in the West, 127, 1816 (possibly the Missisauga). Michiskoui.—Chauvignerie (1736) in Schoolcraft, Ind. Tribes, III, 553, 1853. Misiskoui.—Beauharnois (1744) in N. Y. Doc. Col. Hist., IX, 1110, 1855 (village). Missiassik.—Vater, Mith., pt. 3, sec. 3, 390, 1816. Missiscoui.—De Bougainville (1757) in N. Y. Doc. Col. Hist., X, 607, 1858. Missiskouy.—Doc. of 1746, ibid., 32. Wanderers.—Chauvignerie, op. cit. (given as synonymous with Michiskoui).

Missinquimeschan. A former Piankashaw (?) village near the site of Washington, Daviess co., Ind.—Hough, map in Ind. Geol. Rep., 1883. Cf. *Meshingomesia*.

Mission. One of the three bodies of Seaton Lake Lillooet on the w. side of Seaton lake, under the Williams Lake agency, Brit. Col.; pop. 73 in 1906.—Can. Ind. Aff., pt. II, 77, 1906.

Mission (Burrard Inlet). The name given by the Canadian Dept. of Indian Affairs to one of six divisions of Squawmish under the Fraser River agency, Brit. Col.; pop. 213 in 1906.

Mission Indians of California. The first settlements in California were not made until more than a century after the earliest colonization of the peninsula of

VICTORIANO, MISSION INDIAN (LUISEÑO), CALIFORNIA

Lower California. The mission of San Diego, founded in 1769, was the first permanent white settlement within the limits of the present state; it was followed by 20 other Franciscan missions, founded at intervals until the year 1823 in the region between San Diego and San Francisco bay and just N. of the latter. With very few exceptions the Indians of this territory were brought under the influence of the missionaries with comparatively little difficulty, and more by persuasion than by the use of force. There is scarcely a record of any resistance or rebellion on the part of the natives resulting in the loss of life of even a single Spaniard at any of the missions except at San Diego, where there occurred an insignificant outbreak a few years after the foundation.

The influence of the missions was probably greater temporally than spiritually. The Indians were taught and compelled to work at agricultural pursuits and to some extent even at trades. Discipline, while not severe, was rigid; refusal to work was met by deprivation of food, and absence from church or tardiness there, by corporal punishments and confinement. Consequently the Indians, while often displaying much personal affection for the missionaries themselves, were always inclined to be recalcitrant

toward the system, which amounted to little else than beneficent servitude. There were many attempts at escape from the missions. Generally these were fruitless, both on account of the presence of a few soldiers at each mission and through the aid given these by other Indians more under the fathers' influence. The Indians at each mission lived at and about it, often in houses of native type and construction, but were dependent for most of their food directly on the authorities. They consisted of the tribes of the region in which the mission was founded and of more distant tribes, generally from the interior. In some cases these were easily induced to settle at the mission and to subject themselves to its discipline and routine, the neophytes afterward acting as agents to bring in their wilder brethren.

The number of Indians at each mission varied from a few hundred to two or three thousand. There were thus in many cases settlements of considerable size; they possessed large herds of cattle and sheep and controlled many square miles of land. Theoretically this wealth was all the property of the Indians, held in trust for them by the Franciscan fathers. In 1834 the Mexican government, against the protests of the missionaries, secularized the missions. By this step the property of the missions was divided among the Indians, and they were freed from the restraint and

WIFE OF VICTORIANO, MISSION INDIAN (LUISEÑO), CALIFORNIA

authority of their former masters. In a very few years, as might have been expected and as was predicted by the fathers, the Indians had been either deprived of their lands and property or had squandered them, and were living in a hopeless condition. Their numbers decreased rapidly, so that to-day in the region between San Francisco and Santa Barbara there are probably fewer than 50 Indians. In s. California the decrease has been less rapid, and there are still about 3,000 of what are known as Mission Indians; these are, however, all of Shoshonean or Yuman stock. The decrease of population began even during the mission period, and it is probable that the deaths exceeded the births at the missions from the first, though during the earlier years the population was maintained or even increased by accessions from unconverted tribes. At the time of secularization, in 1834, the population of many missions was less than a decade earlier. The total number of baptisms during the 65 years of mission activity was about 90,000, and the population in the territory subject to mission influence may be estimated as having been at any one time from 35,000 to 45,000. At this proportion the population of the entire state, before settlement by the whites, would have been at least 100,000, and was probably much greater. See *California, Indians of,* with accompanying map, also *Missions; Population.* (A. L. K.)

Mission Valley. The local name of a band of Salish of Fraser superintendency, Brit. Col.—Can. Ind. Aff. 1878, 79, 1879.

Missions. From the very discovery of America the spiritual welfare of the native tribes was a subject of concern to the various colonizing nations, particularly Spain and France, with whom the Christianization and civilization of the Indians were made a regular part of the governmental scheme, and the missionary was frequently the pioneer explorer and diplomatic ambassador. In the English colonization, on the other hand, the work was usually left to the zeal of the individual philanthropist or of voluntary organizations.

First in chronologic order, historic importance, number of establishments, and population come the Catholic missions, conducted in the earlier period chiefly by Jesuits among the French and by Franciscans among the Spanish colonies. The earliest mission establishments within the present United States were those begun by the Spanish Franciscan Fathers, Padilla, Juan de la Cruz, and Descalona of the Coronado expedition, among the Quivira (Wichita), Pecos, and Tigua in 1542. Three years later the work was begun among the Texas tribes by Father Olmos. A century thereafter the first Protestant missions (Congregational) were founded by Mayhew and Eliot in Massachusetts. From that period the work

was carried on both N. and S. until almost every denomination was represented, including Orthodox Russian in Alaska and the Mormons in Utah.

THE SOUTHERN STATES.—All of this region, and even as far N. as Virginia, was loosely designated as Florida in the earlier period, and was entirely within the sphere of Spanish influence until about the end of the seventeenth century. The beginning of definite mission work in the Gulf territory was made in 1544 when the *Catholic* Franciscan Father Andrés de Olmos, a veteran in the Mexican field, struck northward into the Texas wilderness, and after getting about him a considerable body of converts led them back into Tamaulipas, where, under the name of Olives, they were organized into a regular mission town. In 1549 the Dominican Father Luis Cancer with several companions attempted a beginning on the w. coast of Florida, but was murdered by the Indians almost as soon as his feet touched the land. In 1565 St Augustine (San Agustin) was founded and the work of Christianizing the natives was actively taken up, first by the Jesuits, but later, probably in 1573, by the Franciscans, who continued with it to the end. Within twenty years they had established a chain of flourishing missions along the coast from St Augustine to St Helena, in South Carolina, besides several others on the w. Florida coast. In 1597 a portion of the Guale tribe (possibly the Yamasi) on the lower Georgia coast, under the leadership of a rival claimant for the chieftainship, attacked the neighboring missions and killed several of the missionaries before the friendly Indians could gather to the rescue. In consequence of this blow the work languished for several years, when it was taken up with greater zeal than before and the field extended to the interior tribes. By the year 1615 there were 20 missions, with about 40 Franciscan workers, established in Florida and the dependent coast region. The most noted of these missionaries is Father Francisco Pareja, author of a grammar and several devotional works in the Timucua language, the first books ever printed in any Indian language of the United States and the basis for the establishment of the Timucuan linguistic family. In the year 1655 the Christian Indian population of N. Florida and the Georgia coast was estimated at 26,000. The most successful result was obtained among the Timucua in the neighborhood of St Augustine and the Apalachee around the bay of that name. In 1687 the Yamasi attacked and destroyed the mission of Santa Catalina on the Georgia coast, and to escape pursuit fled to the English colony of Carolina. The traveler Dickenson has left a pleasant picture of the prosperous condition of the mission towns and their Indian population as he found them in 1699, which contrasts strongly with the barbarous condition of the heathen tribes farther s., among whom he had been a prisoner.

The English colony of Carolina had been founded in 1663, with a charter which was soon after extended southward to lat. 29°, thus including almost the whole area of Spanish occupancy and mission labor. The steadily-growing hostility between the two nations culminated in the winter of 1703–4, when Gov. Moore, of Carolina, with a small force of white men and a thousand or more well-armed warriors of Creek, Catawba, and other savage allies invaded the Apalachee country, destroyed one mission town after another, with their churches, fields, and orange groves, killed hundreds of their people, and carried away 1,400 prisoners to be sold as slaves. Anticipating the danger, the Apalachee had applied to the governor at St Augustine for guns with which to defend themselves, but had been refused, in accordance with the Spanish rule which forbade the issuing of firearms to Indians. The result was the destruction of the tribe and the reversion of the country to a wilderness condition, as Bartram found it 70 years later. In 1706 a second expedition visited a similar fate upon the Timucua, and the ruin of the Florida missions was complete. Some effort was made a few years later by an Apalachee chief to gather the remnant of his people into a new mission settlement near Pensacola, but with only temporary result.

In the meantime the French had effected lodgment at Biloxi, Miss. (1699), Mobile, New Orleans, and along the Mississippi, and the work of evangelizing the wild tribes was taken up at once by secular priests from the Seminary of Foreign Missions in Quebec. Stations were established among the Tunica, Natchez, and Choctaw of Mississippi, the Taensa, Huma, and Ceni (Caddo) of Louisiana, but with slight result. Among the Natchez particularly, whose elaborately organized native ritual included human sacrifice, not a single convert rewarded several years of labor. In 1725 several Jesuits arrived at New Orleans and took up their work in what was already an abandoned field, extending their effort to the Alibamu, in the present state of Alabama. On Sunday, Nov. 28, 1729, the Natchez war began with the massacre of the French garrison while at prayer, the first victim being the Jesuit Du Poisson, the priest at the altar. The "Louisiana Mission," as it was called, had never flourished, and the events and after consequences of this war demoralized it until it came to an end with the expulsion of the Jesuits by royal decree in 1764.

The advance of the French along the Mississippi and the Gulf coast aroused the Spanish authorities to the importance of Texas, and shortly after the failure of La Salle's expedition 8 Spanish presidio missions were established in that territory. Each station was in charge of two or three Franciscan missionaries, with several families of civilized Indians from Mexico, a full equipment of stock and implements for farmers, and a small guard of soldiers. Plans were drawn for the colonization of the Indians around the missions, their instruction in religion, farming, and simple trades and home life, and in the Spanish language. Through a variety of misfortunes the first attempt proved a failure and the work was abandoned until 1717 (or earlier, according to La Harpe), when it was resumed—still under the Franciscans—among the various subtribes of the Caddo, Tonkawa, Carrizos, and others. The most important center was at San Antonio, where there was a group of 4 missions, including San Antonio de Padua, the famous Alamo. The mission of San Sabá was established among the Lipan in 1757, but was destroyed soon after by the hostile Comanche. A more successful foundation was begun in 1791 among the now extinct Karankawa. At their highest estate, probably about the year 1760, the Indian population attached to the various Texas missions numbered about 15,000. In this year Father Bartolomé Garcia published a religious manual for the use of the converts at San Antonio mission, which remains almost the only linguistic monument of the Coahuiltecan stock. The missions continued to flourish until 1812, when they were suppressed by the Spanish Government and the Indians scattered, some rejoining the wild tribes, while others were absorbed into the Mexican population.

In 1735 the *Moravians* under Spangenberg started a school among the Yamacraw Creeks a few miles above Savannah, Ga., which continued until 1739, when, on refusal of the Moravians to take up arms against the Spaniards, they were forced to leave the colony. This seems to be the only attempt at mission work in either Georgia or South Carolina from the withdrawal of the Spaniards until the Moravian establishment at Spring Place, Ga., in 1801.

The great Cherokee tribe held the mountain region of both Carolinas, Georgia, Alabama, and Tennessee, and for our purpose their territory may be treated as a whole. Dismissing as doubtful Bristock's account, quoted by Shea, of a Cherokee mission in 1643, the earliest missionary work among them appears to have been that of the mysterious Christian Priber, supposed, though not proven, to have been a French *Jesuit*, who established his headquarters among them at Tellico, E. Tenn., in 1736, and proceeded to organize them into a regular civilized form of government. After 5 years of successful progress he was seized by the South Carolina authorities, who regarded him as a French political emissary, and died while in prison. In 1801 the *Moravians* Steiner and Byhan began the Cherokee mission of Spring Place, N. W. Ga., and in 1821 the same denomination established another at Oothcaloga, in the same vicinity. Both of these existed until the missions were broken up by the State of Georgia in 1843. In 1804 Rev. Gideon Blackburn, for the *Presbyterians*, established a Cherokee mission school in E. Tennessee, which did good work for several years until compelled to suspend for lack of funds. In 1817 the American Board of Commissioners for Foreign Missions, under joint *Congregational* and *Presbyterian* management, established its first station in the tribe at Brainerd, not far from the present Chattanooga, Tenn., followed within a few years by several others, all of which were in flourishing condition when broken up in the Removal controversy in 1834. Among the most noted of these missionaries was Rev. S. A. Worcester, one of the principals in the founding of the 'Cherokee Phœnix' in 1828, the author of a large number of religious and other translations into Cherokee and the steadfast friend of the Indians in the controversy with the State of Georgia. He ministered to the tribe from his ordination in 1825 until his death in 1859, first in the old nation and afterward at Dwight, Ark., and Park Hill, near Tahlequah, Ind. T. Of an earlier period was Rev. Daniel S. Buttrick, 1817–47, who, however, never mastered the language sufficiently to preach without an interpreter. A native convert of the same period, David Brown, completed a manuscript translation of the New Testament into the new Cherokee syllabary in 1825.

In 1820 the American Board, through Rev. Mr Chapman, established Dwight mission for the Arkansas Cherokee, on Illinois cr., about 5 m. above its junction with the Arkansas, near the present Dardanelle, Ark. Under Rev. Cephas Washburn it grew to be perhaps the most important mission station in the S. W. until the removal of the tribe to Indian Ter., about 1839. From this station some attention also was given to the Osage. Of these missions of the American Board, Morse says officially in 1822: "They have been models, according to which other societies have since made their establishments." As was then customary, they were largely aided by Government appropriation. On the consolidation of the whole Cherokee nation in Indian Ter. the missionaries followed, and new stations were established which, with some interruptions, remained in operation until the outbreak of the Civil war.

In 1820 a *Baptist* mission was established at Valleytown, near the present Murphy, w. N. Car., in charge of Rev. Thomas Posey, and in 1821 another of the same denomination at Coosawatee, Ga. A few years later the Valleytown mission was placed in charge of Rev. Evan Jones, who continued with it until the removal of the tribe to the W. He edited for some time a journal called the 'Cherokee Messenger,' in the native language and syllabary, and also made a translation of the New Testament. The mission work was resumed in the new country and continued with a large measure of success down to the modern period. Among the prominent native workers may be named Rev. Jesse Bushyhead.

After many years of neglect the Muskhogean tribes again came in for attention. In 1818 the *Congregational-Presbyterian* American Board, through Rev. Cyrus Kingsbury, established the first station among the Choctaw at Eliot, on Yalabusha r. in N. Miss. Three years later it was placed in charge of Rev. Cyrus Byington, the noted Choctaw philologist, who continued in the work there and in the Indian Ter., for nearly half a century, until his death in 1868. The Eliot mission in its time was one of the most important in the southern country. In 1820 a second Choctaw mission, called Mayhew, was begun, and became the residence of Rev. Alfred Wright, also known for his linguistic work. On the removal of the tribe to Indian Ter., about 1830, it became necessary to abandon these stations and establish others in the new country beyond the Mississippi. Among the most noted was Wheelock, organized by Rev. Alfred Wright in 1832. Others were Stockbridge, Bennington, Mt Pleasant, and Spencer Academy. The American Board also extended its effort to the immigrant Creeks, establishing in their nation, under the supervision of Rev. R. M. Loughridge, Kowetah (Kawita) mission in 1843, and Tullahassee shortly after, with Oak Ridge, among the removed Seminole, a few years later. Most of these continued until the outbreak of the Civil war, and were reorganized after the war was over. The school at Cornwall, Conn., was also conducted as an auxiliary to the mission work of the earlier period (see *New England*). Among the Presbyterian workers who have rendered distinguished service to Muskhogean philology in the way of religious, educational, and dictionary translation may be noted the names of Byington, Williams, Alfred and Allen Wright, for the Choctaw, with Fleming, Loughridge, Ramsay, Winslett, Mrs Robertson, and the Perrymans (Indian) for the Creeks.

The *Baptists* began work in the Indian Ter. about 1832, and three years later had 4 missionaries at as many stations among the Choctaw, all salaried as teachers by the United States, "so that these stations were all sustained without cost to the funds which benevolence provided for many purposes" (McCoy). In 1839 they were in charge of Revs. Smedley, Potts, Hatch, and Dr Allen, respectively. Missions were established about the same time among the Creeks, the most noted laborers in the latter field being Rev. H. F. Buckner, from 1849 until his death in 1882, compiler of a Muskogee grammar and other works in the language, with Rev. John Davis and Rev. James Perryman, native ministers who had received their education at the Union (Presbyterian) mission among the Osage (see *Interior States*). As auxiliary to the work of this denomination, for the special purpose of training native workers, the American Baptist Board in 1819 established at Great Crossings, in Kentucky, a higher school, known as the Choctaw Academy, sometimes as Johnson's Academy. Although intended for promising youth of every tribe, its pupils came chiefly from the Choctaw and the Creeks until its discontinuance about 1843, in consequence of the Indian preference for home schools.

Work was begun by the *Methodists* among the Creeks in Indian Ter. about 1835, but was shortly afterward discontinued in consequence of difficulties with the tribe, and was not resumed until some years later.

MIDDLE ATLANTIC STATES. The earliest mission establishment within this territory was that founded by a company of 8 Spanish *Jesuits* and lay brothers with a number of educated Indian boys, under Father Juan Bautista Segura, at "Axacan," in Virginia, in 1570. The exact location is uncertain, but it seems to have been on or near the lower James or Pamunkey r. It was of brief existence. Hardly had the bark chapel been erected when the party was attacked by the Indians, led by a treacherous native interpreter, and the entire company massacred, with the exception of a single boy. The massacre was avenged by Menendez two years later, but the mission effort was not renewed.

The next undertaking was that of the English Jesuits who accompanied the Maryland colony in 1633. The work was chiefly among the Conoy and Patuxent of Maryland, with incidental attention to the Virginia tribes. Several stations were established and their work, with the exception of a short period of warfare in 1639, was very successful, the principal chiefs being numbered among the converts, until the proscription of the Catholic religion by the Cromwell party in 1649. The leader of the Maryland mission was Father Andrew White, author of the oft-quoted "Relatio" and of a grammar and dictionary of the Piscataway (?) language.

The New York mission began in 1642, among the Mohawk, with the ministration of the heroic Jesuit captive, Father Isaac Jogues, who met a cruel death at the hands of the same savages 4 years later. During a temporary peace between the French and the Iroquois in 1653 a regular post and mission church were built at Onondaga, the capital of the confederacy, by permission of the league. The Oneida, Cayuga, and Seneca invited and received missionaries. Much of their welcome was undoubtedly due to the presence in the Iroquois villages of large numbers of incorporated Christian captives from the destroyed Huron nation. The truce lasted but a short time, however, and before the summer of 1658 the missionaries had withdrawn and the war was again on. In 1666 peace was renewed and within a short time missions were again founded among all the tribes. In 1669 a few Christian Iroquois, sojourning at the Huron mission of Lorette, near Quebec, Canada, withdrew and formed a new mission settlement near Montreal, at a place on the St Lawrence known as La Prairie, or under its mission name, St François Xavier des Prés, the precursor of the later St François Xavier du Sault and the modern Caughnawaga. The new town soon became the rallying point for all the Christian Iroquois, who removed to it in large numbers from all the tribes of the confederacy, particularly from the Mohawk towns. There also gathered the Huron and other Christian captives from among the Iroquois, as also many converts from all the various eastern Algonquian tribes in the French alliance. To this period belongs the noted Jesuit scholar, Etienne de Carheil, who, arriving in 1666, devoted the remaining 60 years of his life to work among the Cayuga, Hurons, and Ottawa, mastering all three languages, and leaving behind him a manuscript dictionary of Huron radices in Latin and French.

In 1668 also a considerable body of Christian Cayuga and other Iroquois, together with some adopted Hurons, crossed Lake Ontario from New York and settled on the N. shore in the neighborhood of Quinté bay. At their request *Sulpician* priests were sent to minister to them, but within a few years the immigrant Indians had either returned to their original country or scattered among the other Canadian missions. In 1676 the Catholic Iroquois mission town of The Mountain was founded by the Sulpician fathers on the island of Montreal, with a well-organized industrial school in charge of the Congregation sisters. In consequence of these removals from the Iroquois country and the breaking out of a new war with the Five Tribes in 1687, the Jesuit missions in New York were brought to a close. In the seven years' war that followed, Christian Iroquois of the missions and heathen Iroquois of the Five Nations fought against each other as allies of French or English, respectively. The Mountain was abandoned in 1704, and the mission transferred to a new site at the Sault au Recollet, N. of Montreal. In 1720 this was again removed to the Lake of Two Mountains (Oka, or Canasadaga) on the same island of Montreal, where the Iroquois were joined by the Nipissing and Algonkin, of the former Sulpician mission town of Isle aux Tourtes. Among the noted workers identified with it, all of the scholarly Sulpician order, may be named Revs. Déperét, Güen, Mathevet, 1746–81; De Terlaye, 1754–77; Guichart, Dufresne, and Jean Andre Cuoq, 1843–90. Several of these gave attention also to the Algonkin connected with the same mission, and to the Iroquois of St Regis and other stations. All of them were fluent masters of the Iroquois language, and have left important contributions to philology, particularly Cuoq, whose "Étudos philologiques" and Iroquois dictionary remain our standard authorities.

All effort among the villages of the confederacy was finally abandoned, in consequence of the mutual hostility of France and England. In 1748 the Sulpician Father François Picquet founded the new mission settlement of Presentation on the St Lawrence at Oswegatchie, the present Ogdensburg, N. Y., which within three years had a prosperous population of nearly 400 families, drawn chiefly from the Onondaga and Cayuga tribes. About 1756 the still existing mission town of St Francis Regis (St Regis), on the S. side of the St Lawrence where the Canada-New York boundary intersects it, was founded under Jesuit auspices by Iroquois emigrants from Caughnawaga mission. The Oswegatchie settlement declined after the Revolution until its abandonment in 1807. Caughnawaga, St Regis, and Lake of Two Mountains still exist as Catholic Iroquois mis-

sion towns, the two first named being the largest Indian settlements N. of Mexico.

About the year 1755 the first mission in w. Pennsylvania was established among the Delawares at Sawcunk, on Beaver r., by the *Jesuit* Virot, but was soon discontinued, probably on account of the breaking out of the French and Indian war.

Philology owes much to the labor of these missionaries, particularly to the earlier Jesuit, Jacques Bruyas, and the later secular priest, Father Joseph Marcoux (St Regis and Caughnawaga, 1813, until his death in 1855), whose monumental Iroquois grammar and dictionary is the fruit of forty years' residence with the tribe. Of Father Bruyas, connected with the Sault Ste Louis (Caughnawaga) and other Iroquois missions from 1667 until his death in 1712, during a part of which period he was superior of all the Canadian missions, it was said that he was a master of the Mohawk language, speaking it as fluently as his native French, his dictionary of Mohawk root words being still a standard. Father Antoine Rinfret, 1796–1814, has left a body of more than 2,000 quarto pages of manuscript sermons in the Mohawk language; while Rev. Nicolas Burtin, of Caughnawaga (1855–   ), is an even more voluminous author.

The *Lutheran* minister, John Campanius Holm (commonly known as Campanius), chaplain of the Swedish colony in Delaware in 1643–48, gave much attention to missionary work among the neighboring Indians and translated a catechism into the Delaware language. This seems to have been the only missionary work in the Atlantic states by that denomination.

Under the encouragement of the English colonial government the *Episcopalians*, constituting the established Church of England, undertook work among the Iroquois tribes of New York as early as the beginning of the 18th century. In 1700 a Dutch Calvinist minister at Schenectady, Rev. Bernardus Freeman, who had already given sufficient attention to the Mohawk to acquire the language, was employed to prepare some Gospel and ritual translations, which formed the basis of the first booklet in the language, published in Boston in 1707. In 1712 the English Society for the Propagation of the Gospel sent out Rev. William Andrews, who, with the assistance of a Dutch interpreter, Lawrence Claesse, and of Rev. Bernardus Freeman, translated and published a great part of the liturgy and some parts of the Bible 3 years later. The work grew and extended to other tribes of the Iroquois confederacy, being especially fostered at a later period by Sir William Johnson, superintendent for Indian affairs, who had published at his own expense, in 1769, a new edition of the Episcopalian liturgy in the Mohawk language, the joint work of several missionaries, principal of whom was Rev. Henry Barclay. From this time until 1777 the principal worker in the tribe was Rev. John Stuart, who translated the New Testament into Iroquois. On the removal of the Mohawk and others of the Iroquois to Canada, in consequence of the Revolutionary war, a new edition was prepared by Daniel Claus, official interpreter, and published under the auspices of the Canadian provincial government. In 1787 a new translation of the Book of Common Prayer, prepared by the noted chief, Joseph Brant (see *Theyandanega*), who had been a pupil of Wheelock's school, in Connecticut, was published at the expense of the English Government. In 1816 another edition appeared, prepared by the Rev. Eleazer Williams, a mixed-blood Caughnawaga, sometimes claimed as the "Lost Dauphin." Mr Williams labored chiefly among the Oneida in New York. He was succeeded, about 1821, by Solomon Davis, who followed the tribe in the emigration to Wisconsin. The latter was the author of several religious books in the Oneida dialect, including another edition of the Book of Common Prayer, published in 1837. In 1822 the Society for the Propagation of the Gospel, already noted, definitely transferred its operations to the Iroquois res., on Grand r., Ontario, where it still continues, its principal establishment being the Mohawk Institute, near Brantford. For this later period the most distinguished name is that of Rev. Abraham Nelles, chief missionary to the Six Nations of Canada for more than 50 years, almost up to his death in 1884. He was also the author of a translation of the Common Prayer, in which he was aided by an educated native, Aaron Hill. (See also *Canada, East.*)

Of less historic importance was the Munsee mission of Crossweeksung, near the present Freehold, N. J., conducted by Rev. David Brainerd for the Society for the Propagation of the Gospel, in 1746–47.

In Virginia a school for the education of Indians was established in connection with William and Mary College, Williamsburg, about 1697, chiefly through the effort of Mr Robert Boyle, and some Indians were still under instruction there as late as 1760. Some earlier plans to the same end had been frustrated by the outbreak of the Indian war of 1622 (Stith). Under Gov. Spotswood a school was established among the Saponi about 1712, but had only a brief existence. Both of these may be considered as under *Episcopalian* auspices.

In 1766, the *Congregational* minister Rev. Samuel Kirkland began among the Oneida of New York the work which he conducted with success for a period of nearly 40 years. The Stockbridge and Brotherton missions in New York and Wisconsin by the same denomination are properly a continuation of New England history, and are so treated in this article. To a later period belongs the Congregational mission among the Seneca of New York, maintained by Rev. Asher Wright from his first appointment in 1831 until his death in 1875. A fluent master of Seneca, he was the author of a number of religious and educational works in the language, besides for some years publishing a journal of miscellany in the same dialect.

The *Friends*, or *Quakers*, in Pennsylvania and New Jersey, from their first coming among the Indians, had uniformly cultivated kindly relations with them, and had taken every opportunity to enforce the teachings of Christianity by word and example, but seem not to have engaged in any regular mission work or established any mission schools in either of these colonies.

As early as 1791 the noted Seneca chief, Cornplanter, impressed by the efforts of the Quakers to bring about a friendly feeling between the two races, requested the Philadelphia yearly meeting to take charge of three boys of his tribe for education, one of them being his own son. In 1796 the meeting began regular work among the Iroquois in New York by establishing three workers among the Oneida and the Tuscarora. These teachers gave first attention to the building of a mill and a blacksmith shop, the introduction of farm tools, and the instruction of the Indians in their use. The women were instructed in household duties, including spinning and weaving. A school was also commenced, and the work progressed until 1799, when, in consequence of the suspicions of the Indians as to the ultimate purpose, the Quakers withdrew, leaving all their working plant behind. In 1798, on invitation of the Seneca, they established a similar working mission on the Allegany res., and later at Cattaraugus and Tunesassah, with the good result that in a few years most of the bark cabins had given place to log houses, and drunkenness was almost unknown. They remained undisturbed through the war of 1812, at one time forestalling a smallpox epidemic by the vaccination of about 1,000 Indians, but were soon afterward called on to champion the cause of their wards against the efforts at removal to the W. In the meantime the New York meeting, about 1807, had started schools among the

Stockbridge and Brotherton tribes from New England, then living in the Oneida country. Owing to the drinking habits of the Indians, but little result was accomplished. The removal of the Oneida and Stockbridges, about 1822, and the subsequent disturbed condition of the tribes brought about, first, the curtailment of the work, and afterward its abandonment, about 1843.

In 1740 the *Moravian* missionary, Christian Rauch, began a mission among the Mahican at Shecomeco, near the present Pine Plains, Dutchess co., N. Y., which attained a considerable measure of success until the hostility of the colonial government, instigated by the jealousy of those who had traded on the vices of the Indians, compelled its abandonment about 5 years later. During its continuance the work had been extended, in 1742, to the Scaticook, a mixed band of Mahican and remnant tribes settled just across the line, about the present Kent, Conn. Here a flourishing church was soon built up, with every prospect of a prosperous future, when the blow came. Some of the converts followed their teachers to the W.; the rest, left without help, relapsed into barbarism. The Shecomeco colony removed to Pennsylvania, where, after a brief stay at Bethlehem, the Moravian central station, a new mission, including both Mahican and Delawares, was established in 1746 at Gnadenhuetten, on Mahoning r., near its junction with the Lehigh. A chief agent in the arrangements was the noted philanthropist, Count Zinzendorf. Gnadenhuetten grew rapidly, soon having a Christian Indian congregation of 500. Missions were founded at Shamokin and other villages in E. Pennsylvania, which were attended also by Shawnee and Nanticoke, besides one in charge of Rev. David Zeisberger among the Onondaga, in New York. The missionaries, as a rule, if not always, served without salary and supported themselves by their own labors. All went well until the beginning of the French and Indian war, when, on Nov. 24, 1755, Gnadenhuetten was attacked by the hostile savages, the missionaries and their families massacred, and the mission destroyed. The converts were scattered, but after some period of wandering were again gathered into a new mission at Nain, near Bethlehem, Pa. On the breaking out of Pontiac's war in 1763 an order was issued by the Pennsylvania government for the conveyance of the converts to Philadelphia. This was accordingly done, and they were detained there under guard, but attended by their missionary, Bernhard Grube, until the close of the war, suffering every hardship and in constant danger of massacre by the excited borderers.

On the conclusion of peace they established themselves on the Susquehanna at a new town, which was named Friedenshuetten, near the Delaware village of Wyalusing. In 1770 they again removed to Friedensstadt, on Beaver cr., in w. Pennsylvania, under charge of Zeisberger, and two years later made another removal to the Muskingum r., in Ohio, by permission of the western Delawares. By the labor of the missionaries, David Zeisberger, Bishop John Ettwein, Johannes Roth, and the noted John Heckewelder, who accompanied them to the W., the villages of Schoenbrunn and Gnadenhuetten were established in the midst of the wild tribes within the present limits of Tuscarawas co., the first-named being occupied chiefly by Delawares, the other by Mahican. The Freidensstadt settlement was now abandoned. In 1776 a third village, Lichtenau (afterward Salem), was founded, and the Moravian work reached its highest point of prosperity, the whole convert population including about 500 souls. Then came the Revolution, by which the missions were utterly demoralized until the culminating tragedy of Gnadenhuetten, Mar. 8, 1782, when nearly 100 Christian Indians, after having been bound together in pairs, were barbarously massacred by a party of Virginia borderers. Once more the missionaries, Zeisberger and Heckewelder, gathered their scattered flock, and after another period of wandering, settled in 1787 at New Salem, at the mouth of Huron r., L. Erie, N. Ohio. A part of them settled, by invitation of the British Government, at Fairfield, or Moraviantown, on Thames r., Ontario, in 1790, under the leadership of Rev. Christian Dencke, while the rest were reestablished in 1798 on lands granted by the United States at their former towns on the Muskingum. Here Zeisberger died in 1808, after more than 60 years of faithful ministry without salary. He is known to philologists as the author of a grammar and dictionary of the Onondaga, besides several smaller works in the Delaware language.

The mission, by this time known as Goshen, was much disturbed by the War of 1812, and the subsequent settlement of the country by the whites so far demoralized it that in 1823 those then in charge brought it to a close, a small part of the Indians removing to the W., constituting the present Munsee Christians in Kansas, while the remainder joined their brethren in Ontario, Canada. The latter, whose own settlement also had been broken up by the events of the same war, had been gathered a few years before into a new town called New Fairfield, by Rev. Mr Dencke, already mentioned, who had also done work among the Chippewa. Dencke died in retirement in 1839, after more than 40 years of missionary service, leaving as his monument a manuscript dictionary of the Delaware language and minor printed works, including one in Chippewa. The Moravian mission at New Fairfield was kept up for a number of years after his death, but was at last discontinued, and both the "Moravians" and the "Munsees" of the Thames are now credited officially either to the Methodist or to the Episcopal (Anglican) church (see *Canada, East*).

The Munsee who had removed with the Delawares to Kansas were followed a few years later by Moravian workers from Canada, who, before 1840, had a successful mission among them, which continued until the diminishing band ceased to be of importance. Among the workers of this later period may be named Rev. Abraham Luckenbach, "the last of the Moravian Lenapists," who ministered to his flock during a 6 years' sojourn in Indiana, and later in Canada, from 1800 to his death in 1854, and was the author of several religious works in the language. Dencke, founder of the Thames r. colony, was also the author of a considerable manuscript religious work in the language and probably also of a grammar and dictionary.

Another Moravian missionary, Rev. John C. Pyrlæus, labored among the Mohawk from 1744 to 1751, and has left several manuscript grammatic and devotional works in that and the cognate dialects, as also in Mahican and Delaware. For several years he acted as instructor in languages to the candidates for the mission service. Rev. Johannes Roth, who accompanied the removal to Ohio in 1772, before that time had devoted a number of years to the work in Pennsylvania, and is the author of a unique and important religious treatise in the Unami dialect of the Delaware.

A remarkable testimony to the value of the simple life consistently followed by the Moravians is afforded in the age attained by many of their missionaries in spite of all the privations of the wilderness, and almost without impairment of their mental faculties, viz: Pyrlæus, 72 years; Heckewelder, 80; Ettwein, 82; Zeisberger, 87, and Grube, 92.

NEW ENGLAND.—The earliest New England mission was attempted by the French *Jesuit* Father Peter Biard among the Abnaki on Mt Desert id., Maine, in 1613, in connection with a French post, but both were destroyed by an English fleet almost before the buildings were completed. In the next 70 years other Jesuits, chief among whom was Father Gabriel Druillettes (1646–57), spent much

time in the Abnaki villages and drew off so many converts to the Algonkin mission of Sillery (see *Canada, East*) as to make it practically an Abnaki mission. In 1683 the mission of St Francis de Sales (q. v.) was founded at the Falls of the Chaudière, Quebec, and two years later Sillery was finally abandoned for the new site. Among those gathered at St Francis were many refugees from the southern New England tribes, driven out by King Philip's war, the Pennacook and southern Abnaki being especially numerous. In 1700 the mission was removed to its present location, and during the colonial period continued to be recruited by refugees from the New England tribes. About 1685 missions were established among the Penobscot and the Passamaquoddy, and in 1695 the celebrated Jesuit Father Sebastian Râle (Rasle, Rasles) began at the Abnaki mission at Norridgewock on the Kennebec (the present Indian Old Point, Me.) the work which is so inseparably connected with his name. He was not, however, the founder of the mission, as the church was already built and nearly the whole tribe Christian. In 1705 the church and village were burned by the New Englanders, but rebuilt by the Indians. In 1713 a small band removed to the St Lawrence and settled at Bécancour, Quebec, where their descendants still remain. In 1722 the mission was again attacked and pillaged by a force of more than 200 men, but the alarm was given in time and the village was found deserted. As a part of the plunder the raiders carried off the manuscript Abnaki dictionary to which Râle had devoted nearly 30 years of study, and which ranks as one of the great monuments of our aboriginal languages. On Aug. 23, 1724, a third attack was made by the New England men, with a party of Mohawk allies, and the congregation scattered after a defense in which seven chiefs fell, the missionary was killed, scalped, and hacked to pieces, and the church plundered and burned. Râle was then 66 years of age. His dictionary, preserved at Harvard University, was published in 1833, and in the same year a monument was erected on the spot where he met his death. The mission site remained desolate, a large part of the Indians joining their kindred at St Francis. The minor stations on the Penobscot and St John continued for a time, but steadily declined under the constant colonial warfare. In 1759 the Canadian Abnaki mission of St Francis, then a large and flourishing village, was attacked by a New England force under Col. Rogers and destroyed, 200 Indians being killed. It was afterward rebuilt, the present site being best known as Pierreville, Quebec. The Abnaki missions in Maine were restored after the Revolution and are still continued by Jesuit priests among the Penobscot and the Passamaquoddy.

Among other names distinguished in the Abnaki mission the first place must be given to the Jesuits Aubéry and Lesueur. Father Aubéry, after 10 years' work among the Indians of Nova Scotia, went in 1709 to St Francis, where he remained until his death in 1755. He acquired a fluent use of the language, in which he wrote much. Most of his manuscripts were destroyed in the burning of the mission in 1759, but many are still preserved in the mission archives, including an Abnaki dictionary of nearly 600 pages. Father Lesueur labored first at Sillery and then at Bécancour from 1715, with a few interruptions, until 1753, leaving as his monument a manuscript 'Dictionnaire de Racines' (Abnaki) of 900 pages, now also preserved in the mission archives. To the later period belong Rev. Ciquard, who ministered from 1792 to 1815 on the Penobscot, the St John, and at St Francis; Father Romagné, with the Penobscot and the Passamaquoddy from 1804 to 1825; Rev. Demilier, a Franciscan, who labored with marked success to the same tribes from 1833 to 1843, and the Jesuit Father Eugène Vetromile in the same field from about 1855 to about 1880. Each one of these has made some contribution to the literature of the language, the last-named being also the author of a history of the Abnaki and of two volumes of travels in Europe and the Orient.

The beginning of *Protestant* work among the Indians of s. New England may fairly be credited to Roger Williams, who, on being driven from his home and ministry in Massachusetts for his advocacy of religious toleration in 1635, took refuge among the Wampanoag and Narraganset, among whom he speedily acquired such influence that he was able to hold them from alliance with the hostiles in the Pequot war. In 1643 Thomas Mayhew, jr (*Congregational*), son of the grantee of Marthas Vineyard, Mass., having learned the language of the tribe on the island, began among them the work which was continued in the same family for four generations, with such success that throughout the terror of King Philip's war in 1675–76 the Christian Indians on the island remained quiet and friendly, although outnumbering the whites by 10 to 1. Thomas Mayhew, the younger, was lost at sea in 1657, while on a missionary voyage to England. The work was then taken up by his father, of the same name, and the native convert Hiacoomes. It was continued from about 1673 by John Mayhew, son of the first-named, until his death in 1689, and then by Experience Mayhew, grandson of Thomas the elder, nearly to the time of his death in 1758. Each one of these learned and worked in the Indian language, in which Thomas, jr, and Experience prepared some small devotional works. The last of the name was assisted also for years by Rev. Josiah Torrey, in charge of a white congregation on the island. In 1720 the Indians of Marthas Vineyard numbered about 800 of an estimated 1,500 on the first settlement in 1642. They had several churches and schools, so that most of those old enough could read in either their own or the English language. The last native preacher to use the Indian language was Zachariah Howwoswe (or Hossweit), who died in 1821.

As far back as 1651 a building had been authorized at Harvard College for the accommodation of Indian pupils, but only one Indian (Caleb Cheeshateaumuck) is on record as having finished the course, and he died soon afterward of consumption.

The most noted mission work of this section, however, was that begun by the noted Rev. John Eliot (Congregational) among a remnant of the Massachuset tribe at Nonantum, now Newton, near Boston, Mass., in the fall of 1646. He was then about 42 years of age and had prepared himself for the task by three years of study of the language. The work was extended to other villages, and the reports of his and Mayhew's success led to the formation in 1649 of the English "Corporation for the Propagation of the Gospel among the Indians in New England" for the furtherance of the mission. As early as 1644 the Massachusetts government had made provision looking to the instruction of the neighboring tribes in Christianity, Eliot himself being the pioneer. In 1650 a community of Christian Indians, under a regular form of government, was established at Natick, 18 m. s. w. of Boston, and became the headquarters of the mission work. In 1674 the "Praying Indians," directly under the care of Eliot and his coadjutor, Samuel Danforth, in the Massachusetts Bay jurisdiction, numbered 14 principal villages with a total population exceeding 1,000, among the Massachuset, Pawtucket, Nipmuc, and other tribes of E. Massachusetts, each village being organized on a religious and industrial basis. The Christian Indians of Plymouth colony, in s. E. Massachusetts, including also Nantucket, Marthas Vineyard, etc., under Revs. John Cotton and Richard Bourne, were estimated at nearly 2,500 more. Most of the converts however were drawn from broken and subject tribes. The powerful Wampanoag, Narraganset, and Mohegan rejected all missionary advances, and King Philip scornfully told Eliot that he cared no more for his gospel than for a button upon his coat. Most of Eliot's work fell to the ground with the breaking out of King Philip's war in the following year. The colonists refused to believe in the friendship of the converts, and made such threats against them that many of the Indians joined the hostiles and afterward fled with them to Canada and New York. The "praying towns" were broken up, and the Indians who remained were gathered up and held as prisoners on an island in Boston harbor until the return of peace, suffering much hardship in the meantime, so that the close of the war found the two races so embittered against each other that for some time it was impossible to accomplish successful results. Of the 14 praying towns in 1674 there were left only 4 in 1684. Eliot remained at his post until his death in 1690, in his 86th year, leaving behind him as his most permanent monument his great translation of the Bible into the Natick (Massachuset) language, besides a grammar and several minor works in the language (see *Bible translations, Eliot Bible*). Daniel Gookin, whose father had been official Indian superintendent, was Eliot's coadjutor in the later mission period. Eight years after Eliot's death the Indian church at Natick had but 10 members, and in 1716 it became extinct, as did the language itself a generation later.

Among Eliot's co-workers or successsors in the same region the best known were Samuel Danforth, sr, from 1650 until his death in 1674; Rev. John Cotton, who preached to the Indians of both Natick and Plymouth from 1669 to 1697, being "eminently skilled in the Indian language"; his son, Josiah Cotton, who continued his father's work in the Plymouth jurisdiction for nearly 40 years; Samuel Treat, who worked among the Nauset Indians of the Cape Cod region from 1675 until his death in 1717, and translated the Confession of Faith into the language; Grindal Rawson, about 1687 to his death in 1715, the translator of 'Spiritual Milk'; and Samuel Danforth the younger, who labored in E. Massachusetts from 1698 to his death in 1727, and was the author of several religious tracts in the native language. These and others were commissioned and salaried by the society organized in 1649.

About 1651 Rev. Abraham Pierson, under the auspices of the same society, began preaching to the Quinnipiac Indians about Branford, w. Connecticut, and continued until his removal about 1669, when the work was undertaken by a successor,

but with little result to either, the Indians showing "a perverse contempt," notwithstanding presents made to encourage their attendance at the services. A few years later Rev. James Fitch was commissioned to work among the Mohegan, and succeeded in gathering a small congregation, but found his efforts strongly opposed by Uncas and the other chiefs. The mission probably came to an end with King Philip's war. Efforts were continued at intervals among the tribal remnants of s. New England during the next century, partly through the society founded in 1649 and partly by colonial appropriation, but with little encouraging result, in consequence of the rapid decrease and demoralization of the Indians, the only notable convert being Samson Occom (q. v.). The English society withdrew support about 1760. A last attempt was made among the Mohegan by Miss Sarah L. Huntington in 1827, and continued for several years, chiefly by aid of governmental appropriation (De Forest).

In 1734 a Congregationalist mission was begun among the Mahican in western Massachusetts by Rev. John Sergeant, under the auspices of the Society for the Propagation of the Gospel in Foreign Parts. By hard study and constant association he was soon able to preach to them in their own language, into which he translated several simple devotional works. In 1736 the converts were gathered into a regular mission town, which was named Stockbridge, from which central point the work was extended into Connecticut and New York, and even as far as the Delaware r. In 1743 Rev. David Brainerd, who had been working also among the Mahican at the village of Kaunaumeek, across the New York line, brought his congregation to consolidate with that of Stockbridge. Mr Sergeant died in 1749, and after a succession of briefer pastorates the work was taken up, in 1775, by his son, Rev. John Sergeant, jr, who continued with it until the end of his life. The westward advance of white settlement and the demoralizing influence of two wars accomplished the same result here as elsewhere, and in 1785 the diminishing Stockbridge tribe removed to New Stockbridge, N. Y., on lands given by the Oneida. Their leader in this removal was the educated Indian minister Samson Occom. Mr Sergeant himself followed in the next year. The mission was at that time supported by the joint effort of American and Scotch societies, including the corporation of Harvard College. In 1795 the settlement consisted of about 60 families, mostly improvident, unacquainted with the English language, and "in their dress and manners uncivilized" (Aborigines Com., 1844). Besides preaching to them in their own language, Mr Sergeant prepared for their use several small religious works in the native tongue.   In 1821, with their chief, Solomon Aupaumut, they removed again (their missionary being unable to accompany them on account of old age), this time to the neighborhood of Green Bay, Wis., where about 520 "Stockbridge and Munsee," of mixed blood, still keep the name. Among the later missionaries the most distinguished is Rev. Jeremiah Slingerland, an educated member of the tribe, who served, from 1849, for more than 30 years. Merged with them are all who remain of the Brotherton band of New York, made up from tribal remnants of Connecticut, Rhode Island, and Long Island—Mohegan, Pequot, Narraganset, and Montauk—gathered into a settlement also in the Oneida country by the same Occom in 1786. These in 1795 were reported as numbering about 39 families, all Christian, and fairly civilized. Among the names connected with the Stockbridge mission is that of Rev. Jonathan Edwards, jr, author of a short treatise on the Mahican ("Muhhekaneew") language (1788), and of John Quinney and Capt. Hendrick Aupaumut, native assistants and translators under the elder Sergeant. For the Scaticook mission see *Moravians— New York*.

In addition to the regular mission establishments some educational work for the Indians was carried on in accord with a declared purpose at Harvard College, Cambridge, Mass., as already noted; at Moore's charity school for Indians, founded by Rev. Eleazer Wheelock at Lebanon, Conn., in 1754, and transferred in 1769 to Hanover, N. H., under the name of Dartmouth College, and the Foreign Mission School at Cornwall, Conn., by the American Board of Commissioners for Foreign Missions, beginning in 1817. The net result was small. (See *Education*.)

THE INTERIOR STATES.—The whole interior region of the United States, stretching from the English seaboard colonies to the main divide of the Rocky mts., was included under the French rule in the two provinces of Canada and Louisiana, and with one or two exceptions the mission work was in charge of French *Jesuits* from the first occupancy up into the American period. The very first mission worker, however, within this great region was the heroic Spanish Franciscan, Father Juan de Padilla, who gave up his life for souls on the Kansas prairies, as narrated elsewhere, nearly as early as 1542 (see *New Mexico, Arizona, and California*). The first mission west of the Huron country was established in 1660, probably on Keweenaw bay, Mich., by the veteran Huron missionary, the Jesuit René Menard, in response to repeated requests of visiting Chippewa and Ottawa.   In the next year, while attempting to reach a colony of fugitive Hurons who had called him from Green Bay, he was lost in the forest and is believed to have been murdered by the Indians.   In 1665 Father Claude Allouez established the mission of Sainct Esprit on the s. shore of L. Superior, at La Pointe Chegoimegon (Shaugwaumikong), now Bayfield, Wis.   Besides working here among the Ottawa and Huron refugees from the older missions destroyed by the Iroquois, he visited all the other tribes of the upper lake region from the Miami and the Illinois to the Sioux. Within the next few years other missions were established at Sault Ste Marie (Sainte Marie), Mackinaw (St Ignace), Green Bay (St François Xavier), and among the Foxes (St Marc) and Mascoutens (St Jacques), the two last named being about the southern Wisconsin line.   Among other workers of this period were Dablon, Druillettes, and the noted discoverer, Marquette.   The mission of St Joseph on the river of that name, near the present South Bend, Ind., was established by Allouez among the Potawatomi in 1688.   It continued, with interruptions, until the removal of the tribe to the W. in 1839–41, when the missionaries accompanied the Indians and reestablished the work in the new field.   To this later period, in Indiana, belong the names of Fathers Rézé, Badin, Desseille, and Petit.   The mission at Lapointe was abandoned in 1671 on account of the hostility of the Sioux, but most of the others continued, with some interruptions, down to the temporary expulsion of the Jesuits in 1764.   A mission begun among the Sioux in 1728 was brought to a close soon after in consequence of the war with the Foxes.

The first regular mission among the Illinois (Immaculate Conception) was founded by Marquette in 1674 near the present Rockfort, Ill., where at that time 8 confederate tribes were camped in a great village of 350 communal houses.   It was known later as the Kaskaskia mission. Other missions were established also among the Peoria, on Peoria lake and at Cahokia, opposite St Louis, with such result that by 1725 the entire Illinois nation was civilized and Christian. Besides Marquette, the most prominent of the Illinois missionaries were Râle, noted elsewhere in connection with the Abnaki mission, and Father James Gravier, who arrived in 1693 and died 12 years later of wounds received from hostile Indians, leaving as his monument the great manuscript Peoria dictionary of 22,000 words.   Despite apparent success, the final result in Illinois was the same as elsewhere. The Natchez and Chickasaw wars interrupted the mission work for some years, and gave opportunity for invasion by hostile northern tribes. The dissipations consequent upon the proximity of garrison posts completed the demoralization, and by 1750 the former powerful Illinois nation was reduced to some 1,000 souls, with apparently but one mission. The Indiana missions at St Joseph (Potawatomi and Miami), Vincennes (? Piankashaw), and on the Wabash (Miami) continued to flourish until the decree of expulsion, when the mission property was confiscated by the French government, although the Jesuits generally chose to remain as secular priests until their death. Their successors continued to minister to Indians as well as to whites until the disruption and removal of the tribes to the W., between 1820 and 1840, when the work was taken up in their new homes by missionaries already on the ground. The majority of the Indians of Michigan and Wisconsin remained in their old homes at missions in those states, kept in existence either as regular establishments or as visiting stations served by secular priests. The most distinguished of these later missionaries was the noted author and philologist, Bishop Frederick Baraga, of the imperial house of Hapsburg, who, after having voluntarily forfeited his estates to devote his life to the Indians, came to America in 1830, and for 36 years thereafter until his death labored with success, first among the Ottawa at Arbre Croche in lower Michigan, and afterward at St Joseph, Green Bay, Lapointe, and other stations along the upper lakes, more particularly at the Chippewa village of L'Anse, on Keweenaw bay, which he converted into a prosperous Christian settlement. Even when past 60 years of age, this scion of Austrian nobility slept upon the ground and sometimes walked 40 m. a day on snowshoes to minister to his Indians. Besides numerous devotional works in Ottawa and Chippewa, as well as other volumes in German and Slavonic, he is the author of the great Grammar and Dictionary of the Chippewa Language, which after half a century still remains the standard authority, having passed through three editions.

In 1818 was begun, near Pembina, on Red r., just inside the U. S. boundary, the Chippewa mission, afterward known as Assumption, which became the central station for work among the Chippewa of Minnesota and the Mandan and others of the upper Missouri. The most noted name in this connection is that of Rev. G. A. Belcourt, author of a dictionary of the Chippewa language, second in im-portance only to that of Baraga. In 1837 Father Augustin Ravoux established a mission among the Santee Sioux at Faribault's trading post in E. Minnesota, learning the language and ministering to the eastern bands for a number of years. In 1843 (or 1844) he published a devotional work in that dialect, which has passed through two editions. The first regular mission station among the Menominee of Wisconsin was established in 1844, and among the Winnebago, then at Long Prairie, Minn., in 1850. For 20 years earlier missionary work had been done among them, notably by Father Samuel Mazzuchelli, whose Winnebago Prayer Book, published in 1833, is mentioned by Pilling as "the first publication, so far as I know, of a text in any of the dialects in the Siouan family." In the farther W. work was carried on among all of the immigrant, and the principal of the native, tribes, the chief laborers again being the Jesuits, whose order had been restored to full privilege in 1814. As the whole country was now explored and organized on a permanent governmental basis, and the Indian day was rapidly waning, these later missions have not the same historic interest that attaches to those of the colonial period, and may be passed over with briefer notice. Chief among them were the Potawatomi missions of St Stanislaus and St Mary, in Kansas, founded in 1836 by the Belgian Jesuits Von Quickenborne, Hoecken, Peter J. de Smet, and others, working together, and the Osage mission of St Francis Hieronymo, founded about 1847 by Fathers Shoenmaker and Bax. The girls of these two mission schools were in charge respectively of the Sisters of the Sacred Heart and the Sisters of Loretto. Temporary missions were also established in 1836 and 1847 respectively among the Kickapoo and the Miami.

The remote Flatheads in the mountains at the head of Missouri r. had heard of Christianity and had been taught the rudimentary doctrines by some adopted Caughnawaga Indians, and in 1831 they sent a delegation all the long and dangerous way to St Louis to ask of Indian Superintendent Clark that missionaries be sent among them. To do this was not possible at the time, but with persevering desire other delegations were sent on the same errand, some of the envoys dying on the road and others being murdered by the Sioux, until the request met response. In 1834 the *Methodist* missionary, Jason Lee, with several assistants, accompanied a trading expedition across the mountains, but, changing his original purpose, passed by without visiting the Flatheads and established himself in the vicinity of the trading post of Ft Vancouver, nearly opposite the mouth of the Willamette, in Washington. Another embassy from the Flatheads, in 1839, was successful, and in the next year the noted Belgian Jesuit, Peter John de Smet, priest, explorer, and author, was on the ground, 1,600 Indians of the confederated tribes being gathered to await his coming. In 1841 he founded the mission of St Mary on Bitter-root r., w. Mont., making it a starting point for other missions farther to the w., to be noted elsewhere. On account of the hostility of the Blackfeet the mission was abandoned in 1850, to be succeeded by that of St Ignatius on Flathead lake, within the present Flathead reservation, which still exists in successful operation, practically all of the confederated tribes of the reservation having been Christian for half a century. The principal co-workers in the Flathead mission were the Jesuits Canestrelli, Giorda, Mengarini, Point, and Ravalli. The first three of these have made important contributions to philology, chief among which are the Salish Grammar of Mengarini, 1861, and the Kalispel Dictionary, 1877, of Giorda, of whom it is said that he preached in six Indian languages.

Next in chronologic order in the central region, after the Catholics, come the *Moravians.* Their work among the Delawares and associated tribes in Ohio, and later in Ontario and Kansas, was a continuation of that begun among the same people in New York and Pennsylvania as early as 1740, and has been already noted.

After them came the *Friends,* or, as more commonly known, the Quakers. In all their missionary effort they seem to have given first place to the practical things of civilization, holding the doctrinal teaching somewhat in reserve until the Indians had learned from experience to value the advice of the teacher. In accord also with the Quaker principle, their method was essentially democratic, strict regard being given to the wishes of the Indians as expressed through their chiefs, their opinions being frequently invited, with a view to educating them to a point of self-government. In 1804 the Maryland yearly meeting, after long councils with the Indians, established an industrial farm on upper Wabash r. in Indiana, where several families from the neighboring Miami, Shawnee, and others soon gathered for instruction in farming. For several years it flourished with increasing usefulness, until forced to discontinue by an opposition led by the Shawnee prophet (see *Tenskwatawa*). The work was transferred to the main Shawnee settlement at Wapakoneta, Ohio, where, in 1812, a saw mill and grist mill were built, tools distributed, and a farm colony was

successfully inaugurated. The war compelled a suspension until 1815, when work was resumed. In 1822 a boarding school was opened, and both farm and school continued, with some interruptions, until the final removal of the tribe to the W. in 1832–33. The teachers followed, and by 1837 the Shawnee mission was reestablished on the reservation in Kansas, about 9 m. w. from the present Kansas City. It was represented as flourishing in 1843, being then perhaps the most important among the immigrant tribes, but suffered the inevitable result on the later removal of the Shawnee to the present Oklahoma. The work was conducted under the joint auspices of the Indiana, Ohio, and Maryland yearly meetings, aided in the earlier years by liberal contributions from members of the society in England and Ireland. The most noted of the teachers were Isaac Harvey and his son, Henry Harvey, whose work covers the period from 1819 to 1842. During the period of the "peace policy" administration of Indian affairs, for a term of about a dozen years beginning in 1870, considerable work was done by laborers of the same denomination among the Caddo, Kiowa, Cheyenne, and other tribes of Oklahoma, but without any regular mission or school establishment. The best known of these workers was Thomas C. Battey, author of 'A Quaker among the Indians,' who conducted a camp school among the Kiowa in 1873.

The *Presbyterians,* who now stand second in the number of their mission establishments in the United States, began their labors in the Central states about the same time as the Friends, with a mission farm among the Wyandot on Sandusky r. in Ohio, in charge of Rev. Joseph Badger. It continued until 1810, when it was abandoned in consequence of the opposition of the traders and the conservative party led by the Shawnee prophet. Morse's report on the condition of the tribes in 1822 makes no mention of any Presbyterian mission work at that time excepting among the Cherokee (see *Southern States*). A few years later the Rev. Isaac Van Tassel, under authority from the American Board, was in charge of a mission among the Ottawa, at Maumee, Ohio. He compiled an elementary reading book, printed in 1829, the first publication in the Ottawa language.

In 1827, under the auspices of the American Board of Commissioners for Foreign Missions, a *Congregational* mission was begun among the Chippewa on Mackinaw id., upper Michigan, by Rev. J. D. Stevens and wife, who with others afterward extended their labors into N. Wisconsin, and later were transferred to the

Sioux mission. In 1829 Rev. Frederick Ayer joined the Mackinaw station, and, after two years' study of the language, opened among the Chippewa at Sandy Lake, Minn., in 1831, what is said to have been the first school in Minnesota. He is the author of a small text-book in the language. Other stations were established soon after among the same tribe, at Lapointe, Wis., Pokegama lake, and Leech lake, Minn., but seem to have been discontinued about 1845. The Mackinaw mission had already been abandoned. Rev. Peter Dougherty, under the direct auspices of the Presbyterian mission board, labored among the Chippewa and the Ottawa at Grand Traverse bay, lower Michigan, in 1843–47+ and is the author of several text-books and small religious works in the language of the former tribe.

In 1834 two volunteer workers, Mr Samuel W. Pond and his brother Gideon, took up their residence in a village of the Santee Sioux on L. Calhoun, near the present St Paul, Minn. They afterward became regularly ordained missionaries under the American Board, continuing in the work for 18 years. In the same year Rev. Thomas S. Williamson, "the father of the Dakota mission," made a reconnoissance of the field for the same Board, and on his favorable report two mission stations were established in 1835—one at L. Harriet, near St Paul, under Rev. J. D. Stevens, formerly of the Mackinaw mission, the other under Williamson himself at Lac-qui-parle, high up on Minnesota r. With Mr Williamson then or later were his wife, his daughter, and his two sons, all of whom became efficient partners in the work. In 1837 Rev. Stephen R. Riggs, with his wife, Mary, and his son, Alfred L.—all known in mission annals—joined the station at Lac-qui-parle. In the next 10 or 12 years, as the good will of the Indians was gradually won and the working force increased, other stations were established, all among the Santee Sioux in Minnesota. Among these was the one started by Rev. John F. Aiton, in 1848, at Redwing, where Revs. Francis Denton and Daniel Gavan, for the Evangelical Missionary Society of Lucerne, had established the "Swiss mission" in 1837, these two missionaries now combining forces with the American workers. In 1852, in consequence of a cession of Indian land, the eastern station, then at Kaposia, was removed by Williamson to Yellow Medicine on the upper Minnesota, and two years later, in consequence of the burning of the Lac-qui-parle station, that mission also was removed to Hazelwood, in the same neighborhood.

The work continued with varying success until interrupted by the Sioux outbreak in the summer of 1862, when the missions were abandoned and the missionaries sought safety within the older settlements. Throughout the troubles the Christian Sioux generally remained friendly and did good service in behalf of the endangered settlers. As a result of the outbreak the Santee Sioux were removed to Niobrara, N. E. Nebr., where they now reside. The missionaries followed, and in 1866 the "Niobrara mission" was organized, the work being extended to other neighboring bands of Sioux, and the principal workers being Revs. John P. Williamson and Alfred L. Riggs, sons of the earlier missionaries. Nearly all the earlier Presbyterian work among the Sioux, as among the Cherokee, was conducted through the American Board of Commissioners for Foreign Missions.

To the Congregational missionaries we owe most of our knowledge of the Sioux language, their work being almost entirely in the Santee or eastern dialect. Stevens, the Pond brothers, all of the Williamsons, and Stephen and Alfred Riggs have all made important contributions, ranging from school text-books and small devotional works up to dictionaries, besides adapting the Roman alphabet to the peculiarities of the language with such success that the Sioux have become a literary people, the majority of the men being able to read and write in their own language. It is impossible to estimate the effect this acquisition has had in stimulating the self-respect and ambition of the tribe. Among the most important of these philologic productions are Riggs' Grammar and Dictionary of the Dakota Language, published by the Smithsonian Institution in 1852, with a later revision by Dorsey, and Riggs and Williamson's Dakota Bible, published in 1880, being then, in Pilling's opinion, with two exceptions, the only complete Bible translation in any Indian language since Eliot's Bible in 1663. In much of the earlier linguistic work the missionaries had the efficient cooperation of Joseph Renville, an educated half-blood. As an adjunct to the educational work, a monthly journal was conducted for about 2 years by Rev. G. H. Pond, chiefly in the native language, under the title of 'The Dakota Friend,' while its modern successor, 'Iapi Oaye' ('The Word Carrier'), has been conducted under the auspices of the Niobrara mission since 1871.

In 1821 two *Presbyterian* missions were established among the Osage by the United Foreign Missionary Society. One of these, Harmony, was near the junction of the Marais des Cygnes with the Osage r., not far from the present Rich Hill,

Mo.; the other, Union, was on the w. bank of Neosho r., about midway between the present Muskogee and Ft Gibson, Okla. Both were established upon an extensive scale, with boarding schools and a full corps of workers; but in consequence of differences with the agent and an opposition instigated by the traders, the Osage field was abandoned after about 15 years of discouraging effort (McCoy). One of these workers, Rev. William B. Montgomery, compiled an Osage reading book, published in 1834. Among others connected with the mission were the Revs. Chapman, Pixley, Newton, Sprague, Palmer, Vaill, Belcher, and Requa. The missions conducted by the same denomination among the removed Southern tribes in Oklahoma are noted in connection with the Southern states.

In 1834 two Presbyterian workers, Rev. John Dunbar and Mr Samuel Allis, began work among the Pawnee of Nebraska under the auspices of the American Board, and later were joined by Dr Satterlee. After some time spent in getting acquainted with the people and the language, a permanent station was selected on Plum cr., a small tributary of Loup r., in 1838, by consent of the Pawnee, who in the meantime had also acknowledged the authority of the Government. Circumstances delayed the work until 1844, when a considerable mission and a Government station were begun, and a number of families from the different bands took up their residence adjacent thereto. In consequence, however, of the repeated destructive inroads of the Sioux, the ancient enemies of the Pawnee, the mission effort was abandoned in 1847 and the tribe returned to its former wild life.

About the year 1835 work was begun by the Presbyterian Board of Foreign Missions among the Iowa and Sauk, then residing on Missouri r. in E. Nebraska. Attention was given also to some others of the removed tribes, and about 10 years later a mission was established among the Omaha and the Oto at Bellevue, near the present Omaha, Nebr., where, in 1850, Rev. Edward McKenney compiled a small Omaha primer, the first publication in that language. Both missions continued down to the modern period, despite the shifting fortunes of the tribes. Other prominent workers were Rev. Samuel Irvin, who gave 30 years of his life, beginning in 1837, to the first tribes named; and Rev. William Hamilton, who, beginning also in 1837, with the same tribes, was transferred to the Bellevue mission in 1853, rounding out a long life with a record of half a century spent in the service. Working in collaboration these two produced several religious and linguistic works in the Iowa language, published by the Mission press from 1843 to 1850, besides a collection of Omaha hymns and some manuscript translations by Mr Hamilton alone at a later period.

The pioneer *Methodist* mission work in the central region appears to have been inaugurated by a volunteer negro minister, Rev. Mr Stewart, who in 1816 began preaching among the Wyandot, about Sandusky, in Ohio, and continued with such success that 3 years later a regular mission was established under Rev. James B. Finley. This is the only work by that denomination noted in Morse's Report of 1822. In 1835, with liberal aid from the Government, as was then customary, the Southern branch established a mission about 12 m. from the present Kansas City, in Kansas, among the immigrant Shawnee. In 1839 it was in charge of Rev. Thomas Johnson, and 3 years later was reported in flourishing condition, with boarding school and industrial farm. In 1855 both this mission and another, established by the Northern branch, were in operation. Smaller missions were established between 1835 and 1840 among the Kickapoo (Rev. Berryman in charge in 1839), Kansa (Rev. W. Johnson in charge in 1839), Delawares, Potawatomi, and united Peoria and Kaskaskia, all but the last-named being in Kansas. A small volume in the Shawnee language and another in the Kansa were prepared and printed for their use by Mr Lykins, of the Shawnee Baptist mission. The work just outlined, with some work among the immigrant Southern tribes (see *Southern States*), seems to be the sum of Methodist mission labors outside of the Chippewa territory until a recent period. In 1837 a mission was started by Rev. Alfred Brunson among the Santee Sioux at Kaposia, or Little Crow's village, a few miles below the present St Paul, Minn., which existed until 1841, when, on the demand of the Indians, it was discontinued.

In 1823 the Wesleyan Methodist Society of England began work among the Chippewa and related bands in Ontario (see *Canada, East*), and some 20 years later the American Methodists began work in the same tribe along the s. shore of L. Superior in upper Michigan. In 1843 Rev. J. H. Pitezel took charge of the work, with headquarters at Sault Ste Marie as the principal station. Another station was established at Keweenaw pt. about the same time by Rev. John Clark. Others were established later at Sandy lake and Mille Lac, Minn., also among the Chippewa, and all of these were in successful operation in 1852.

The earliest *Baptist* worker in the central region was Rev. Isaac McCoy, afterward for nearly 30 years the general agent in the Indian mission work of that denomination. In 1818 he began preaching among the Wea in Indiana, and in 1820 organized at Ft Wayne, Ind., a small school for the children of the neighboring tribes, then in the lowest state of demoralization from wars, removals, drunkenness, and the increasing pressure of a hostile white population. His earliest associate was Mr Johnston Lykins, then a boy of 19, but later distinguished as a voluminous translator and author of a system of Indian orthography. Two years later this school was discontinued, and by treaty arrangement with the Government, which assumed a large part of the expense, two regular missions were established, viz: Carey (1822) for the Potawatomi, on St Joseph r. near the present South Bend, Ind., and Thomas (1823) among the Ottawa, on Grand r., Mich. Mr Lykins took charge among the Ottawa, to whom he was soon able to preach in their own language, while Mr McCoy continued with the Potawatomi. In consequence of the inauguration of the Government plan for the removal of the Indians to the W., both missions were abolished in 1830, the work being resumed among the Indians in their new homes in Kansas. A small mission established among the Chippewa at Sault Ste Marie, Mich., under Rev. A. Bingham about 1824, continued a successful existence in charge of its founder for about 25 years.

In 1831, while the removal of the Indians was still in progress, the Shawnee Mission was established under Mr Lykins about 10 m. s. w. from the present Kansas City, among the Shawnee. In the fall of 1833 Rev. Jotham Meeker, one of the former assistants in the E., arrived with a printing press and types, with which it was proposed to print for distribution among the various neighboring tribes educational and devotional works in their own languages according to a new phonetic system devised by Mr Meeker. The work of translating and printing was actively taken up, the first issue being a Delaware primer in 1834, believed to be the first book printed in Kansas. Within the next few years small volumes by various missionary workers were printed in the Shawnee, Delaware, Potawatomi, Ottawa, Wea, Kansa, Osage, Iowa, Oto, Creek, and Choctaw languages, besides a small journal in the Shawnee language. Not alone the Baptists, but also Methodists and Presbyterians working in the same field, availed themselves of the services of the Shawnee mission press. In the meantime other missions were established among the Delawares (Mr Ira D. Blanchard, 1833), Oto (Rev. Moses Merrill, 1833), Iowa

(1834?), Ottawa (Rev. Jotham Meeker, 1837), and Potawatomi (Mr Robert Simerwell, 1837), besides stations among the removed southern tribes of Indian Ter. (See Southern States.) All of these first-named were within what is now Kansas excepting the Oto mission known as Bellevue, which was at the mouth of Platte r., near the present Omaha, Nebr. At this station Mr Merrill, who had previously worked among the Chippewa, made such study of the language that within 3 years he was able to preach to the Indians without an interpreter, besides compiling a book of hymns and one or two other small works in Oto. He died in 1840. The various missions remained in successful operation until about 1855, when, in consequence of the disturbed condition of affairs in Kansas, they were discontinued. All of the tribes have since been removed to Indian Ter.

The Episcopalians appear to have done no work in the interior until about 1830, when they had a station in the vicinity of Sault Ste Marie, Mich., among the Chippewa. In 1852 a mission was established among the Chippewa of Gull lake, Minn., by Rev. J. L. Breck, and in 1856 at Leech lake by the same worker. In 1860, through the efforts of Bishop H. B. Whipple, a mission was established among the Santee Sioux at the lower Sioux agency, Redwood, Minn., in charge of Rev. Samuel D. Hinman. The work was interrupted by the outbreak of 1862, but on the final transfer of the Indians to Niobrara, Nebr., in 1866, was resumed by Mr Hinman, who had kept in close touch with them during the period of disturbance. A large mission house, known as St Mary's, was erected, which later became the central station for the work of this denomination among the Sioux and neighboring tribes. In 1870 St Paul's mission was established at the Yankton Sioux agency, S. Dak., by Rev. Joseph W. Cook, and in 1872 work was begun at the Lower Brulé Sioux agency, S. Dak., by Rev. W. J. Cleveland, and extended later to the Upper Brulé and Oglala Sioux of Rosebud and Pine Ridge agencies, S. Dak. In the meantime Rev. J. Owen Dorsey had begun to labor among the Ponca, also in South Dakota, in 1871. The work is still being actively carried on in the same field. All of the Sioux missionaries named have rendered valuable service to philology in the preparation of hymnals, prayer books, etc., in the native language, together with a small mission journal 'Anpao' ('The Daybreak'), issued for a number of years in the Yankton Sioux dialect. The ethnologic researches of Mr Dorsey place him in the front rank of investigators, chief among his many contributions being his great monograph upon the Dhegiha (Omaha and Ponca) language, published under direction of the Bureau of American Ethnology, in whose service he spent the last years of his life. In connection with the Episcopal mission may be noted the lace-making industry for Indian women instituted by Miss Sibyl Carter, chiefly among the Chippewa.

In 1847 the *Lutherans*, under the auspices of the Evangelical Lutheran Missionary Society of Dresden, Germany, began work among the Chippewa in lower Michigan, principally in the present Saginaw and Gratiot cos. The first mission school was opened in that year at Frankenmuth, on Cass r., by Rev. A. Craemer. In 1847 he was joined by Rev. Edward Baierlein, who, a year or two later, established a second station at Bethany, on Pine r., in Gratiot co. Here Mr Baierlein compiled a small volume of reading lessons and Scripture stories, published in 1852. In the next year he was recalled and we hear no more of the mission, which was probably discontinued soon after.

In 1846 the first *Mormon* emigrants crossed the plains from Illinois and, after a long and toilsome journey, settled at Great Salt lake, Utah, where they have since transformed the desert into a garden and built up a religious commonwealth which now exercises a dominant influence over large portions of the Mountain states. Their religious tradition regards the Indians as the descendants of the so-called Lost Ten Tribes of Israel (q. v.), and while no statistics are available it is known that their unsalaried missionaries from the first have given special attention to the Indian tribes, with the result that many among the Ute, Shoshoni, Paiute, and others at least nominally belong to that denomination. In 1905–6 their missionary effort was extended to the Cheyenne and other tribes of Oklahoma.

One of the most recent mission enterprises undertaken in the middle W. is that of the *Mennonites*, a small but influential denomination of German origin, professing the principles of peace and nonresistance common to the Moravians and the Quakers. After a short preliminary sojourn in 1877, regular work was begun among the Arapaho at Darlington, Okla., by Rev. Samuel D. Haury in 1880, the enterprise being aided by the active cooperation of the Government and local Indian agent. In 1883 another station was opened at Cantonment, about 70 m. N. W., among the Cheyenne, by Mr Haury, while Rev. H. R. Voth took charge of the work at Darlington and continued with it until transferred to a new field of duty in Arizona about 10 **years later.** Two other stations were

afterward established among the same tribes, and provision was made for the industrial training of Indian boys in schools and private homes in Kansas. In 1890 the Cantonment mission received an important accession in the arrival of Rev. Rudolph Petter and wife from Switzerland, who at once devoted themselves to a systematic study of the Cheyenne language in the tipi camps. The schools at both principal stations were in flourishing condition until the withdrawal of Government aid compelled their discontinuance in 1902. The Cantonment mission is still kept up, the Cheyenne work being in charge of Mr Petter and his wife, assisted by Miss Bertha Kinsinger, while Rev. John A. Funk ministers to the Arapaho. There is also a small station among the Cheyenne at Hammon, in charge of Rev. H. J. Kliewer, and another among the Northern Cheyenne at Busby, Mont., in charge of Rev. and Mrs Gustav Linscheid since its establishment in 1904. To Mr Petter we are indebted for our principal knowledge of the Cheyenne language, into which he has translated some parts of the Bible, a number of hymns, and the 'Pilgrim's Progress,' besides being the author of a reading book and an extended manuscript grammar and dictionary.

THE COLUMBIA REGION.—Through the influence of Catholic Caughnawaga and of some of the employés of the Hudson's Bay Co., many individuals among the tribes of the Columbia r., particularly Flatheads and Nez Percés, had adopted the principles and ceremonials of the Christian religion as early as 1820, leading later to the request for missionaries, as already noted. The first mission of the Columbia region was established in 1834 by a party under Rev. Jason Lee, for the *Methodists*, on the E. side of the Willamette at French Prairie, about the present Oregon City, Oreg. In 1840 it was removed to Chemeketa, 10 m. farther up the river. Other stations were established later at The Dalles of the Columbia, Oreg., by Revs. Lee and Perkins, in 1838; near Pt Adams, at the mouth of the Columbia, Oreg., by Rev. J. H. Frost, in 1841; and at Ft Nisqually on Puget sd., Wash., by Rev. J. P. Richmond in 1842. The tribes most directly concerned at the four stations, respectively, were the Kalapuya, Wasco, Clatsop, and Nisqualli, all in process of swift decline. For various reasons no success attended the project. The children in the schools sickened and died; one missionary after another resigned and went home; and Lee, as superintendent in charge, so far neglected his duties that in 1844 he was deposed and the church board, after investigation, ordered the discontinuance

of the work, which had already cost a
quarter of a million dollars. The Dalles
station was bought by the Presbyterians,
who now entered the same field (see Bancroft, Hist. Oreg., I, 1886).

In the fall of 1836 the *Presbyterians*,
under the leadership of Rev. Marcus
Whitman, established their first mission
in the Columbia region at Waiilatpu, now
Whitman, on Wallawalla r., s. E. Wash.,
in territory claimed by the Cayuse tribe.
The site had been selected by an advance
agent, Rev. Samuel Parker, a few months
earlier. Rev. H. H. Spalding, of the same
party, about the same time, established a
mission among the Nez Percés at Lapwai,
on Clearwater r., a few miles above the
present Lewiston, Idaho. Early in 1839
a second station was begun among the
Nez Percés at Kamiah, higher up the
Clearwater, but was discontinued in 1841.
Revs. E. Walker and C. C. Eells established themselves at Chemakane, N. E.
Wash., on a lower branch of Spokane r.,
among the Spokan.

The Spokane, whose chief had been educated among the whites, proved friendly,
but from the very beginning the Cayuse
and a considerable portion of the Nez
Percés maintained an insulting and hostile attitude, the Cayuse particularly
claiming that the missionaries were intruders upon their lands and were in
league with the immigrants to dispossess
the Indians entirely. In consequence the
Kamiah station was soon abandoned. At
Waiilatpu, the main station, Whitman
was more than once in danger of personal
assault, the irritation of the Indians constantly growing as the flood of immigrants
increased. In consequence of the continued opposition of the Cayuse and the Nez
Percés, the mission board in 1842 ordered
the abandonment of all the stations but
Chemakane. Whitman then crossed the
mountains to New York to intercede for
his mission, with some degree of success,
returning the next year to find his wife a
refugee at one of the lower settlements, in
consequence of the burning of a part of
the mission property by the Cayuse, who
were restrained from open war only by
the attitude of the Government agent
and the Hudson's Bay Co.'s officers.
In the summer of 1847 the Cayuse and
neighboring tribes were wasted by an
epidemic of measles and fever communicated by passing immigrant trains, all of
which made Waiilatpu a stopping point.
Two hundred of the Cayuse died within
a few weeks, while of the Nez Percés the
principal chief and 60 of his men fell victims. A rumor spread among the Cayuse
that Whitman had brought back the disease poison from the E. and unloosed it for
their destruction. The danger became so
imminent that, actuated partly also by

the opposition of the mission board, he
decided to abandon Waiilatpu and remove
to the former Methodist station at The
Dalles, which he had already bought for
his own denomination. At the same time
he began negotiations with the Catholics
for their purchase of Waiilatpu. Before
the removal could be made, however, the
blow fell. On Nov. 29, 1849, the Cayuse
attacked Waiilatpu mission, killed Dr and
Mrs Whitman and 7 others and plundered
the mission property. Within a few
days thereafter, before the Indians dispersed to their camps, 4 others of the mission force were killed, making 13 murdered, besides 2 children who died of
neglect, or 15 persons in all. The rest,
chiefly women, were carried off as prisoners and subjected to abuse until rescued
by the effort of the Hudson's Bay Co.,
a month later. The Catholic Father
Brouillet, who was on his way from below to confer with Whitman about the
sale of the mission property, was one of
the first to learn of the massacre, and
hastening forward was allowed to bury
the dead and then found opportunity to
send warning to the Lapwai mission in
time for Spalding and his party to make
their escape, some of them being shel-
tered by friendly Nez Percés, although
the mission buildings were plundered by
the hostiles. The Spokan chief, Garry,
remained faithful and gave the people at
Chemakane mission a bodyguard for their
protection until the danger was past. As
a result of the Indian war which followed
the Presbyterian missions in the Columbia region were abandoned. During the
brief period that the station at Kamiah
had continued, the missionary Rev. Asa
Smith had "reduced the Nez Percé dialect to grammatical rules." In 1839 the
Lapwai mission received a small printing
outfit with which Spalding and his assistants printed small primers, hymns, and
portions of scripture in the language of
the tribe by the aid of native interpreters.
A Spokane primer of 1842, the joint work
of Walker and Eells, is said to have been
the third book printed in the Columbia
r. region.

As we have seen, the first Christian
teaching among the tribes of the Columbia region had come from the *Catholic*
employees of the Hudson's Bay Co.,
through whose efforts many of the Nez
Percés, Flatheads, and others had voluntarily adopted the Christian forms as early
as 1820, and some years later sent delegates to St Louis to make requests for
missionaries, to which the Methodists
were first to respond. In 1838 Fathers
Francis Blanchet and Modeste Demers
arrived at Ft Vancouver, Wash., on the
Columbia, from Montreal, to minister particularly to the French employees of the

Hudson's Bay Co., having visited the various tribes farther up along the river en route. In the next year St Francis Xavier mission was established by Blanchet on the Cowlitz, in w. Washington, and St Paul mission at the French settlement on the lower Willamet, at Champoeg, Oreg., while Father J. B. Bolduc, afterward the pioneer missionary on Vancouver id., began preaching to the tribes on Puget sd. In 1841 the Jesuit de Smet had founded the mission of St Mary among the Flatheads in w. Montana (see *Interior States*), while a companion Jesuit, Father Nicholas Point, established the Sacred Heart mission among the Cœur d'Alênes in Idaho.

In 1844 de Smet brought out from Europe a number of Jesuits and several sisters of the order of Notre Dame. Regular schools were started and the tribes on both sides of the river as far up as the present Canadian boundary were included within the scope of the work. In the meantime Blanchet had been made archbishop of the Columbia territory and had brought out from Quebec 21 additional recruits—Jesuits, secular priests, and sisters—with which reinforcements 6 other missions were founded in rapid succession, viz: St Ignatius, St Francis Borgia, and St Francis Regis, in Washington, among the Upper Pend d'Oreilles, Lower Pend d'Oreilles, and Colvilles, respectively, with 3 others across the line in British Columbia. Of these the first-named was the principal station, in charge of the Jesuit Fathers De Vos and Accolti. In the summer of 1847 Father N. C. Pandosy and 3 others, the first Oblate fathers in this region, established a mission at Ahtanam among the Yakima in e. Washington; Father Pascal Ricard, Oblate, founded St Joseph on the Sound near the present Olympia; and in October of the same year, after some negotiation for the purchase of the Presbyterian establishment under Whitman at Waiilatpu, Father John Brouillet arrived to start a mission among the Cayuse. Hardly had he reached the nearest camp, however, when the news came of the terrible Whitman massacre, and Brouillet was just in time to bury the dead and send warning to the outlying stations, as already detailed. The project of a mission among the Cayuse was in consequence abandoned. In the next year the secular Fathers Rousseau and Mesplée founded a station among the Wasco, at The Dalles of Columbia r., Oreg. Work was attempted among the degenerate Chinook in 1851, but with little result. Father E. C. Chirouse, best known for his later successful work at Tulalip school, began his labors among the tribes of Puget sd. and the lower

Columbia about the same period. With the exception of the Wasco and Chinook, these missions, or their successors, are still in existence, numbering among their adherents the majority of the Christian Indians of Washington and s. Idaho. At the Tulalip school 'The Youth's Companion,' a small journal in the Indian language, set up and printed by the Indian boys, was begun in 1881 and conducted for some years. Father Louis Saintonge, for some years with the Yakima and Tulalip missions, is the author of several important linguistic contributions to the Chinook jargon and the Yakima language. Father Pandosy also is the author of a brief 'Grammar and Dictionary' of the Yakima.

NEW MEXICO AND ARIZONA.—As all of this region was colonized from Spain, the entire mission work until a very recent period was conducted by the *Catholics* and through priests of the Franciscan order. The earliest exploration of the territory w. of the Rio Grande was made by the Franciscan friar, Marcos de Niza, in 1539, and it was through his representations that the famous exploration of Coronado was undertaken a year later. Five Franciscans accompanied the army, and on the return of the expedition in 1542 three of these volunteered to remain behind for the conversion of the savages. Fray Luis de Escalona, or Descalona, chose Cicuye (Pecos) for his labors. Fray Juan de Padilla, with a few companions and a herd of sheep and mules, pushed on to distant Quivira, somewhere on the plains of Kansas. Fray Juan de la Cruz stayed at Tiguex, Coronado's winter quarters, properly Puaray on the Rio Grande, near the present Bernalillo, N. Mex. On arriving at Pecos Fray Luis sent back the message that while the tribe was friendly the medicine-men were hostile and would probably cause his death. So it apparently proved, for nothing more was ever heard of his fate or of that of Fray Juan de la Cruz at Tiguex. Of Fray Juan de Padilla it was learned years afterward that he had been killed by the Quivira people for attempting to carry his ministrations to another tribe with which they were at war.

In 1580 three other Franciscans, Rodriguez, Santa María, and Lopez, crossed the Rio Grande with a small escort and attempted to establish a mission at the same town of Tiguex, by that time known as Puaray, but were killed by the Indians within a few months of their arrival.

In 1598 Juan de Oñate with a strong party of 100 men, besides women and children, and 7,000 cattle, entered the country from Mexico and within a few months had received the submission of all the Pueblo tribes as far as the remote Hopi of Arizona, organizing a regular colonization and governmental administration and dividing the region into 7 mission districts in charge of a force of Franciscan friars. In 1617 the Pueblo missions counted 11 churches, with 14,000 "converts." In 1621 there were more than 16,000 converts, served by 27 priests in charge of Father Alonso Benavides, whose *Memorial* is our principal source of information for this period. Another distinguished name of this epoch is that of Father Geronimo de Zarate Salmeron, missionary, philologist, and historian. In 1630 there were some 50 priests serving more than 60,000 Christianized Indians in 90 pueblos, with 25 principal mission centers and churches. To this period belong the mission ruins at Abó and Tabira, or "Gran Quivira" (one of which may be the San Isidro of the lost Jumano tribe), which were abandoned in consequence of Apache invasions about 1675. The entire Pueblo population today numbers barely 10,000 souls in 25 villages.

About this time we begin to observe the first signs of revolt, due partly to the exactions of the Spanish military authorities, but more, apparently, to the attachment of the Indians, particularly the medicine-men, to their own native ceremonies and religion. About the year 1650 the wild tribes, known collectively as Apache, began the series of destructive raids which continued down almost to the present century. Increasing friction between the missionaries and the military administration prevented any united effort to meet the emergency. Missionaries were killed in outlying districts and several pueblos were wiped out by the wild tribes, until in 1675, after the murder of several missionaries and civilians and the execution or other punishment of the principals concerned, the Pueblo chiefs, led by Popé (q. v.) of San Juan, sent to the governor a message declaring that they would kill all the Spaniards and flee to the mountains before they would permit their medicine-men to be harmed. Conditions rapidly grew worse, until it was evident that a general conspiracy was on foot and an appeal was sent to Mexico by the governor for reinforcements. Before help could arrive, however, the storm broke, on August 10, 1680, the historic Pueblo revolt, organized and led by Popé.

Says Bancroft (Hist. Ariz. and N. Mex., 1889): "It was the plan of the New Mexicans to utterly exterminate the Spaniards; and in the massacre none were spared— neither soldier, priest, or settler, personal friend or foe, young or old, man or woman—except that a few beautiful women and girls were kept as captives."

Those in the S. were warned in time to escape, but those in the N., E., and W. perished to the number of over 400 persons, including 21 missionaries (see list, ibid., p. 179). Santa Fé itself, with a Spanish population of 1,000, after a battle lasting all day, was besieged nearly a week by 3,000 Indians, who were finally driven off by Gov. Otermin in a desperate sortie in which the Indians lost 350 killed. The result was the entire evacuation of New Mexico by the Spaniards until its reconquest by Vargas in 1692–94, when most of the missions were reestablished. The Pueblo spirit was not crushed, however, and in the summer of 1696 there was another outbreak by five tribes, resulting in the death of five missionaries, besides other Spaniards. The rising was soon subdued, except among the Hopi, who deferred submission until 1700, but only one of their seven or eight towns, Awatobi, would consent to receive missionaries again. For the favor thus shown to Christians the other Hopi combined forces and utterly destroyed Awatobi and killed many of its people before the close of the year. The Hopi did not again become a mission tribe, but in 1742 more than 440 Tigua, who had fled to the Hopi at the time of the great revolt, were brought back and distributed among the missions of the Rio Grande until they could be resettled in a new town of their own. (See *Sandia*.)

In 1733 Father Mirabal established a mission among the wild Jicarilla, on Trampas r., a few leagues from Taos, N. Mex. In 1746 and 1749 attempts were made to gather a part of the Navaho into 2 new missions established in the neighborhood of Laguna, but the undertaking was a failure. In the latter year the number of Christian Indians in New Mexico, including the vicinity of El Paso, was reported to be about 13,000. By this time the territory had been organized as a bishopric, and with the increase of the Spanish population the relative importance of the mission work declined. In 1780–81 an epidemic of smallpox carried off so many of the Christian Indians that by order of the governor the survivors were the next year concentrated into 20 missions, the other stations being discontinued. As the Indians assimilated with the Spanish population the missions gradually took on the character of ordinary church establishments, the Franciscans being superseded by secular priests. The majority of the Pueblo Indians of to-day, excepting those of Hopi and Zuñi, are at least nominal Christians.

In the more recent historic period work has also been conducted at several pueblos by various Protestant denominations. In 1854 a *Baptist* minister, Rev. Samuel

Gorman, began a mission at Laguna, N. Mex., which was kept up for several years. In 1894 Rev. C. P. Coe, of the same denomination, began a similar work for the Hopi of Arizona. The *Mennonites*, represented by Rev. H. R. Voth, had begun a year earlier at Oraibi a successful work among the Hopi, which is still carried on, being now in charge of Revs. Jacob Epp and John B. Frey.

About the year 1876 the *Presbyterians*, through Rev. John Menaul, established a mission at Laguna, the undertaking being afterward extended to Jemez and Zuñi, N. Mex., besides an industrial school opened at Albuquerque in 1881. By means of a printing press operated at Laguna, with the aid of Indian pupils, several small devotional and reading books have been published by Menaul and Bercovitz, connected with the mission, which still continues.

With the exception of those among the Hopi, before the great revolt, the only missions in Arizona before the transfer of the territory to the United States were two in number, viz.: San Xavier del Bac and San Miguel de Guevavi, established under *Jesuit* auspices on the upper waters of Santa Cruz r., among a subtribe of the Pima, about 1732.

The Pima missions were a northern extension of the Jesuit mission foundation of northern Sonora, Mexico. The noted German Jesuit explorer, Father Eusebio Kino (properly Kühne), made several missionary expeditions into s. Arizona between 1692 and his death in 1710, but so far as known no regular stations were established until long after his death, the first priests in charge in 1732 being two other Germans, Father Felipe Segesser, at Bac, and Father Juan Grashoffer, at Guevavi. Besides the main establishment, several other Indian villages were designated as 'visitas,' or visiting stations. The Pima mission never flourished. In 1750 the tribes revolted and the missions were plundered, most of the missionaries escaping, and by the time peace was restored the contest had begun against the Jesuits, which resulted in the expulsion of the order from Spanish territory in 1767. Their place was at once filled by the Franciscans, but the work languished and steadily declined under the attacks from the wild tribes. About the year 1780 Guevavi was abandoned in consequence of Apache raids, and Tumacacori, in the same general region, was made mission headquarters. The work came to an end by decree of the revolutionary government in 1828, shortly after the transfer of authority from Spain to Mexico.

CALIFORNIA.—As in other parts of Spanish America, the *Catholics* were the sole

mission workers in California until within a very recent period. The most noted of all the Spanish missions were the Franciscan missions of California, whose story is so closely interwoven with the history and romance of the Pacific coast, and whose ruins still stand as the most picturesque landmarks of the region. Their story has been told so often that we need not here go into details. The first one was established in 1769 at San Diego, near the s. boundary, by Father Junípero Serra (to whose memory a monument was erected at Monterey in 1891), who advanced slowly along the coast and passed the work on to his successors, until in 1828 there was a chain of 21 prosperous missions extending northward to beyond San Francisco bay. The full list, in the order of their establishment, with the names of the founders or superiors in charge of the California mission district at the time, is as follows: 1, San Diego de Alcalá (Serra, 1769); 2, San Carlos Borromeo de Monterey, alias Carmel (Serra, 1770); 3, San Antonio de Pádua (Serra, 1771, July); 4, San Gabriel Arcangel (Serra, 1771, Sept.); 5, San Luis Obispo de Tolosa (Serra, 1772); 6, San Francisco de Asis, alias Dolores (Serra, 1776, Oct.); 7, San Juan Capistrano (Serra, 1776, Nov.); 8, Santa Clara (Serra, 1777); 9, San Buenaventura (Serra, 1782); 10, Santa Barbara (Palou, 1786); 11, La Purísima Concepcion (Palou, 1787); 12, Santa Cruz (Palou, 1791, Sept.); 13, Nuestra Señora de la Soledad (Palou, 1791, Oct.); 14, San José (Lasuen, 1797, June 11); 15, San Juan Bautista (Lasuen, 1797, June 24); 16, San Miguel (Lasuen, 1797, July); 17, San Fernando Rey (Lasuen, 1797, Sept.); 18, San Luis Rey de Francia (Peyri, 1798); 19, Santa Inés (Tapis, 1804); 20, San Rafael (Payeras, 1817); 21, San Francisco Solano, alias San Solano or Sonoma (Sonoma, 1823); 22, La Purísima Concepcion, on lower Colorado r. (Garcés, 1780); 23, San Pedro y San Pablo de Bicuñer, on lower Colorado r., possibly in Lower California (Garcés, 1780).

Among the many devoted workers connected with the California missions during the 65 years of their existence the most prominent, after Serra, are Fathers Crespi, Palou, and Peyri, the last-named being the founder, and for a number of years the superior, of San Luis Rey, which shared with San Diego the honor of being the largest and most important of the series. In 1810 the neophyte population of San Diego was 1,611, while that of San Luis Rey was 1,519.

The mission buildings, constructed entirely by Indian labor under supervision of the fathers, were imposing structures of brick and stone, some of which even in their roofless condition have defied the decay of 70 years.   Around each mission, except in the extreme N., were groves of palms, bananas, oranges, olives, and figs, together with extensive vineyards, while more than 400,000 cattle ranged the pastures.   Workshops, schoolrooms, storerooms, chapels, dormitories, and hospitals were all provided for, and in addition to religious instruction and ordinary school studies, weaving, pottery-making, carpentry, and every other most useful trade and occupation were taught to the neophytes, besides the violin and other instruments to those who displayed aptitude in music.   There were fixed hours for prayers and work, with three hours of rest at noon, and dancing and other amusements after supper and the angelus, which was one hour before sunset.   The diet consisted of an abundance of fresh beef, mutton, wheat and corn bread, and beans, from their own herds and plantations.   From the sale of the surplus were bought clothing, tobacco, and trinkets for the Indians, and the necessary church supplies.   At seasonable intervals there were outing excursions to allow the neophytes to visit their wilder relatives in the hills.   The missionaries taught by practical example at the plow, the brick-kiln, and in the vineyard.   Duflot de Mofras, who made an official tour of the missions on behalf of the French government shortly before their utter ruin, says: "Necessity makes the missionaries industrious.   One is struck with astonishment at seeing that with such small resources, generally without any European workmen, and with the aid of savage populations whose intelligence was of the lowest order and who were often hostile, besides the vast agricultural culture, they have been able to execute such extensive works of architecture and mechanical structures, such as mills, machinery, and workshops, besides bridges, roads, and canals for irrigation.   The construction of almost all these missions required that timber, often cut upon steep mountains, should be brought 25 to 30 miles, and that the Indians should be taught how to make lime, cut stone, and mould bricks. This fact can not be mistaken—it was not merely by proselytism that the old missionaries succeeded in attracting the Indians.   In the work of their conversion, if religion was the end, material comfort was the means.   The missionaries had re-solved the great problem of making labor attractive."

The Indians themselves, of many tribes and dialects, were for the most part unwarlike and tractable, but without native energy, and probably, in their original condition, lower in the scale of civilization and morality than any others within the limits of the United States.   Infanti-

cide prevailed to such a degree that even the most earnest efforts of the missionaries were unable to stamp it out, the fact showing how little the new teaching really affected the deeper instinct of the savage.   Although there were frequent raids by the wild tribes, there was little serious opposition to mission discipline, which was supported when necessary by military assistance from the nearest garrison.   Despite regular life, abundance of food, and proper clothing according to the season, the Indian withered away under the restrictions of civilization supplemented by epidemic diseases introduced by the military garrisons or the seal hunters along the coast.   The death rate was so enormous in spite of apparent material advancement that it is probable that the former factor alone would have brought about the extinction of the missions within a few generations.

But all this prosperity at last excited the cupidity of the recently established revolutionary government of Mexico, and in 1833–34 decrees were passed to "secularize" the missions and to expel the missionaries, who, as Spaniards, were hated by the revolutionists.   The mission funds and vast herds were confiscated, the lands were distributed to eager political adventurers, and minor vandals completed the work of destruction by taking even the tiles from the roofs and digging up the vines and fruit trees in the gardens.   Some abortive provision was made for the Indians, of which in their helplessness they were unable to avail themselves, and in a few years, left without their protectors, they had again scattered to the mountains and swamps or sunk into the lowest degradation in the new mining towns.   In 1834, when the blow came, the California missions had 30,650 Indians, with   424,000   cattle,   62,500 horses and mules; 321,900 sheep, goats, and hogs; and produced 122,500 bushels of wheat and corn.   In 1842 there remained only 4,450 Indians, 28,220 cattle, and the rest in proportion.   To-day, according to official report, there remain of the old Mission Indians only 2,855, whose condition is a subject of constant serious concern to philanthropists.

Two other California missions have a briefer history.   In 1780 the military commander of the Sonora district determined to establish among the warlike Yuma two garrison posts with colony and mission attachments, despite the protests of the missionaries concerned, who foresaw that the combination would be disastrous to their own part of the work. Two sites were selected, however, in the fall of the year on the w. bank of the Colorado—the one, La Purísima Concepcion, occupying the site of old Ft Yuma, the other, San Pedro y Pablo de Bicuñer, being 8 or 10 m. lower down, possibly just across the present Mexican border. Purísima mission was placed in charge of Father Francisco Garcés, the explorer, with Father Juan Barreneche as his assistant, while the other was given over to Fathers Diaz and Moreno. The event was as predicted. Within a year the Yuma were roused to hostility by the methods and broken promises of the military commander. In July, 1781, both settlements were attacked almost simultaneously, the buildings plundered and burned, the commander and every man of the small garrison killed after a desperate resistance, the four missionaries and nearly all the men of the colonies also butchered, and the women and several others carried off as captives. A subsequent expedition rescued the captives and buried the dead, but the Yuma remained unsubdued and the colony undertaking was not renewed. (See *California, Indians of; Mission Indians of California*.)

ALASKA.—Alaska was discovered by the Russians in 1741 and remained a possession of Russia until transferred to the United States in 1867. In 1794 regular missionary work was begun among the Aleut on Kodiak id. by monks of the *Greek Catholic* (Russian orthodox) church, under the Archimandrite Joassaf, with marked success among the islanders, but with smaller result among the more warlike tribes of the mainland. Within a few years the savage Aleut were transformed to civilized Christians, many of whom were able to read, write, and speak the Russian language. Among the pioneer workers were Fathers Juvenal, murdered in 1796 by the Eskimo for his opposition to polygamy, and the distinguished John Veniaminof, 1823 to about 1840, the historian and philologist of the Alaskan tribes, and author of a number of religious and educational works in the Aleut and Tlingit languages, including an Aleut grammar and a brief dictionary. Fathers Jacob Netzvietoff and Elias Tishnoff also have made several translations into the Aleut language. About the time of the transfer to the United States the Christian natives numbered 12,000, served by 27 priests and deacons, with several schools, including a seminary at Sitka. Chapels had been established in every important settlement from Prince William id. to the outermost of the Aleutian ids., a distance of 1,800 m., besides other stations on the Yukon, Kuskokwim, and Nushagak rs., and regular churches at Sitka, Killisnoo, and Juneau. In 1902 the Greek church had 18 ministers at work in Alaska. (See *Russian influence*.)

The first Protestant missions after the transfer to the United States were begun by the *Presbyterians* in 1877, under the supervision of Rev. Sheldon Jackson and Mrs A. R. McFarland, with headquarters at Ft Wrangell, where a school had already been organized by some Christian Indians from the Methodist station at Ft Simpson, Brit. Col. Within the next 18 years some 15 stations had been established among the Indians of the s. coast and islands, besides two among the Eskimo, at Pt Barrow and on St Lawrence id. Among the earliest workers, besides those already named, were Rev. J. G. Brady, Rev. E. S. Willard, and Mr Walter Stiles. The principal schools were at Sitka (1878) and Juneau (1886). At Pt Barrow a herd of imported reindeer added to the means of subsistence. The majority of these missions are still in successful operation.

The next upon the ground were the *Catholics*, who made their first establishment at Wrangell in 1878, following with others at Sitka, Juneau, and Skagway. In 1886–87 they entered the Yukon region, with missions at Nulato on the Yukon, St Ignatius on the Kuskokwim, St Mary's (Akularak), St Michael, Nome, Kusilvak id., Nelson id., Holy Cross (Koserefsky), and others, the largest schools being those at Koserefsky and Nulato. With the exception of Nulato all were in Eskimo territory. In 1903 the work was in charge of 12 Jesuits and lay brothers, assisted by 11 sisters of St Anne. The Innuit grammar and dictionary of Father Francis Barnum (1901) ranks as one of the most important contributions to Eskimo philology.

In 1884 the *Moravians*, pioneer workers among the eastern Eskimo, sent a commission to look over the ground in Alaska, and as a result a mission was established at Kevinak among the Eskimo of Kuskokwim r. in the next year by Revs. W. H. Weinland and J. H. Kilbuck, with their wives. In the same year other stations were established at Kolmakof, on the upper Kuskokwim, for Eskimo and Indians together, and farther s., at Carmel, on Nushagak r. In 1903 there were 5 mission stations in Eskimo territory, in charge of 13 white workers, having 21 native assistants, with Rev. Adolf Stecker as superintendent. The reindeer herd numbered nearly 400.

In 1886 the *Episcopalians* began work with a school at St Michael, on the coast (Eskimo), which was removed next year to Anvik, on the Yukon, in charge of Rev. and Mrs Octavius Parker and Rev. J. H. Chapman. In 1890 a mission school was started at Pt Hope (Eskimo), under Dr J. B. Driggs, and about the same time another among the Tanana Indians in the middle Yukon valley, by Rev. and Mrs T. H. Canham. In 1903 the Episcopalians in Alaska, white and native, counted 13 churches, a boarding school, and 7 day schools, with a total working force of 31.

The *Baptists* also began work in 1886 on Kodiak id., under Mr W. E. Roscoe. In 1893 a large orphanage was erected on Wood id., opposite Kodiak, by the Woman's Home Mission Society, its sphere of influence now including a great part of the Alaska peninsula westward from Mt St Elias.

The *Methodists*, beginning also in 1886, have now several stations in s. E. Alaska, together with the flourishing Jesse Lee Industrial Home, under the auspices of the Methodist Woman's Home Mission Society, on Unalaska id.

In 1887 the *Swedish Evangelical* Union of Sweden, through Revs. Axel Karlson and Adolf Lydell, respectively, established stations at Unalaklik on Bering sea (Eskimo) and at Yakutat, on the s. coast among the Tlingit. In 1900, in consequence of an epidemic, an orphanage was founded on Golofnin bay. The civilizing and Christianizing influence of the Swedish mission is manifest over a large area.

In 1887 the Kansas Yearly Meeting of *Friends* began work on Douglas id., near Juneau, through Messrs E. W. Weesner and W. H. Bangham, chiefly for the white population. In 1892 a school was opened among the Kake Indians of Kuiu and Kupreanof ids., under the auspices of the Oregon meeting, and in 1897 another mission, under the auspices of the California meeting, was established among the Eskimo in Kotzebue sd. Here also is now a large reindeer herd.

In 1890 the *Congregationalists*, under auspices of the American Missionary Association, established the Eskimo mission school of Wales, at C. Prince of Wales, on Bering str., under Messrs W. T. Lopp and H. R. Thornton, the latter of whom was afterward assassinated by some rebellious pupils. In 1902 the school was in prosperous condition, with more than a hundred pupils and a herd of about 1,200 reindeer.

In 1900 the *Lutherans*, under the auspices of the Norwegian Evangelical Church, established an orphanage at the Teller reindeer station, Port Clarence, Bering str., under Rev. T. L. Brevig, assisted by Mr A. Hovick, the missionaries having charge also of the Government reindeer herds at the place. It was at Teller station that Rev. Sheldon Jackson, in 1892, inaugurated the experiment of introducing Siberian reindeer to supplement the rapidly diminishing food supply of the natives, as the whale had been practically exterminated from the Alaska coast. The experiment has proved a complete success, the original imported herd of 53 animals having increased to more than 15,000, with promise of solving the problem of subsistence for the Eskimo as effectually as was done by the sheep introduced by the old Franciscans among the Pueblos and through them the Navaho.

For METLAKATLA, see *Canada, West*.

PRESENT CONDITIONS.—It may be said that at present practically every tribe officially recognized within the United States is under the missionary influence of some religious denomination, workers of several denominations frequently laboring in the same tribe. The complete withdrawal of Government aid to denominational schools some years ago for a time seriously crippled the work and obliged some of the smaller bodies to abandon the mission field entirely. The larger religious bodies have met the difficulty by special provision, notably in the case of the Catholics, by means of aid afforded by the Preservation Society, the Marquette League, and by the liberality of Mother Katharine Drexel, founder of the Order of the Blessed Sacrament, for Indian and Negro mission work. The Catholic work is organized under supervision of the Bureau of Catholic Indian Missions, established in 1874, with headquarters at Washington. The report for 1904 shows a total of 178 Indian churches and chapels served by 152 priests; 71 boarding and 26 day schools, with 109 teaching priests, 384 sisters, and 138 other religious or secular teachers and school assistants. The principal orders engaged are the Jesuits, Franciscans, and Benedictines, and the sisters of the orders of St Francis, St Anne, St Benedict, St Joseph, Mercy, and Blessed Sacrament.

Of the other leading denominations engaged in Indian mission work within the United States proper, according to the official Report of the Board of Indian Commissioners for 1903, the *Presbyterians* come first, with 101 churches, 69 ordained missionaries and a proportionate force of other workers, and 32 schools. Next the *Methodists*, with 40 ordained missionaries, but with only one school; *Episcopalians*, 14 missions, 28 ordained missionaries, and 17 schools; *Baptists*, 14 missions, 15 ordained missionaries, and 4 schools—exclusive of the Southern Baptists, not reported; *Congregationalists* (American Missionary Association), 10 missions, 12 ordained missionaries, and 5 schools; *Friends*, 10 missions, 15 ordained missionaries, and 1 school; *Mennonites*, 5 missions, 6 ordained missionaries, but no school; *Moravians*, 3 missions, 3 ordained missionaries, and no school. Statistics for any other denominations, including the *Mormons*, are not given. The missionary work of each denomination reported is in charge of a central organization.

CANADA, EAST; NEWFOUNDLAND, ETC.—
Canada, being originally a French possession, the mission work for a century and a half was almost entirely with the *Catholics*. Port Royal, now Annapolis, Nova Scotia, was founded in 1605, and the resident priest, Father Flèche, divided his attention between the French settlers and the neighboring Micmac. In 1611 the Jesuits, Fathers Peter Biard and Enemond Masse, arrived from France, but finding work among the Micmac made difficult by the opposition of the governor, they went to the Abnaki, among whom they established a mission on Mt Desert id., Maine, in 1613. The mission was destroyed in its very beginning by the English Captain Argall (see *New England*). In 1619 work was resumed among the Micmac and the Malecite of Nova Scotia, New Brunswick, and lower Quebec under the Récollet Franciscans and continued for at least half a century. The most distinguished of these Récollets was Father Chrestien Le Clercq, who, while stationed at the Micmac mission of Gaspé, at the mouth of the St Lawrence, from 1655 to about 1665, mastered the language and devised for it a system of hieroglyphic writing which is still in use in the tribe. Another of the same order is said to have been the first to compile a dictionary of a Canadian language, but the work is now lost. The eastern missions continued, under varying auspices and fortunes, until the taking of Louisburg, Nova Scotia, by the English in 1745, when all the missionaries in Nova Scotia and New Brunswick were either deported or compelled to seek other refuge. In their absence the Abbé Maillard, of Nova Scotia, ministered for some years to the Micmac and the Malecite, at first in secret and then openly after the peace of 1760. To him we owe a Micmac grammar and a treatise on the customs of the Indians. It was not until within the last century, when international and sectarian jealousies had largely passed away, that the work was resumed, continuing without interruption to the present time.

Work was begun in 1615 by the Récollets among the roving Montagnais and Algonkin of the Saguenay, Ottawa, and lower St Lawrence region. The pioneers were Fathers Dolbeau, Jamet, and Du Plessis, together with Father Le Caron in the Huron field. In 1636 Dolbeau had extended his ministrations to the outlying bands of the remote Eskimo of Labrador. The principal missions were established at Tadousac (Montagnais), the great trading resort at the mouth of the Saguenay; Gaspé (Montagnais and Micmac) and Three Rivers (Montagnais and Algonkin), all in Quebec province; Miscou, N. B., for the Micmac, and on Georgian bay for the Hurons. In 1625 the Récollets called the Jesuits to their aid, and a few years later withdrew entirely, leaving the work to be continued by the latter order. In 1637 the Jesuit mission of St Joseph was founded by Le Jeune at Sillery, near Quebec, and soon became the most important colony of the christianized Montagnais and Algonkin. In 1646, at the request of the Abnaki, Father Gabriel Druillettes was sent to that tribe. In consequence of the later New England wars, large numbers of the Abnaki and other more southerly tribes took refuge in the Canadian missions (see *New England*).

In 1641 Fathers Charles Raymbault and Isaac Jogues, among the Ottawa bands on the headwaters of the river of that name, accompanied a party to the far W. and discovered the great L. Superior, planting a cross and preaching in the camps about the present Sault Ste Marie, Mich. In the next year a regular mission was established among the Nipissing, on the N. shore of the lake of the same name. Other missions followed, continuing until the dispersion of the Algonkin tribes by the Iroquois in 1650. Most of the fugitives fled westward, roving along the shores of L. Superior without missionary attention until visited by the Jesuit Allouez in 1667. Other names connected with this early Algonkin mission were those of Pijart, Garreau, and the pioneer explorer René Ménard. In 1657 the first Sulpicians arrived at Quebec from France, and soon afterward began work among the neighboring tribes, but with principal attention to the Iroquois colonies on both shores of L. Ontario, at Quinté and Oswegatchie (see *New York*). To this period belongs the wonderful canoe voyage of discovery by the two Sulpicians, Galinée and Dollier de Casson, in 1669–70, from Montreal up through the great lakes to Mackinaw, where they were welcomed by the Jesuits Dablon and Marquette, and then home, by way of French r., Nipissing, and the Ottawa. No less important was the discovery of an overland route from the St Lawrence to Hudson bay in 1671–72 by the Sieur St Simon, accompanied by the Jesuit Charles Albanel. Ascending the Saguenay from Tadousac they crossed the divide, and after 10 months of toilsome travel finally reached the bay near the mouth of Rupert r., where Albanel, the first missionary to penetrate this remote region, spent some time preaching and baptizing among the wandering Maskegon along the shore. In 1720 a number of the christianized Iroquois, with fragments of the Algonkin bands, after years of shifting about, were gathered into a new mission settlement at Oka, or Lake of the Two Mountains (Lac des Deux Montagnes), also known under its Iroquois name of Canasadaga, on the N. bank of the St Lawrence, above the island of Montreal. It still exists as one of the principal Indian settlements.

Among the earlier missionaries in this region who have made important contributions to Algonquian philology may be noted: Father Louis André, Jesuit, who spent more than 40 years with the Montagnais and the Algonkin, from 1669, leaving behind him a manuscript dictionary of the Algonkin, besides a great body of other material; Father Antonio Silvy, Jesuit, of the same period, author of a manuscript Montagnais dictionary; Father Pierre Laure, Jesuit, with the Montagnais, 1720–38, author of a manuscript Montagnais grammar and dictionary, and other works; Father Jean Mathevet, Sulpician, at Oka, 1746 to 1781, the author of an Abnaki dictionary; Father Vincent Guichart, ministering to Algonkin and Iroquois at Oka from 1754 until his death in 1793, master of both languages and author of a manuscript Algonkin grammar; the Abbé Thavenet, Sulpician, at Oka, from about 1793 to 1815, author of an Algonkin grammar and dictionary and other miscellany, still in manuscript; Father J. B. La Brosse, Jesuit, with the Montagnais and Malecite, 1754 to his death in 1782, author of a number of religious and teaching works in the Montagnais language. Among the most distinguished laborers within the last century in the Montagnais, Algonkin, and Maskegon territories, stretching from the St Lawrence to Hudson bay, may be named Fathers Durocher (1829–73), Garin (1845–57), Laverlochère (1845–51), Lebret (1861–69), Guéguen (1864–88+), and Prévost (1873–88+), all of the Oblate order, and each the author of some important contribution to American philology. Rev. Charles Guay has given attention to the language among the Micmac of New Brunswick. In recent years the most prominent name is that of Father J. A. Cuoq, Sulpician, already noted, missionary at Oka for more than half a century, beginning in 1847, master of the Mohawk and Algonkin languages, and author of a dictionary of each, besides numerous other important linguistic works.

According to the official Canadian Indian Report for 1906 the Catholic Indians of the five eastern provinces numbered 18,064, including all those of Prince Edward id., Nova Scotia, and New Brunswick, nearly all those of Quebec, and two-fifths of the Christian Indians of Ontario. Every settlement of importance had a church, school, or visiting priest, the standard for industry being fair, for temperance good, and for honesty and general morality exceptionally high.

The noted Huron missions hold a place by themselves. The beginning was made by the Récollet, Joseph le Caron, who accompanied Champlain on his visit to the Huron country in 1615. The tribe at that time occupied the shores of Georgian bay, Ontario, and with other incorporated bands may have numbered 10,000 souls or more (some estimates are much higher), in from 15 to 30 towns or villages, several of which were strongly palisaded. They were probably then of strength equal to that of their hereditary enemies and final destroyers, the Iroquois of New York. In more or less close alliance with the Hurons were the cognate Tionontati and Neutrals, farther to the s. and s. w., in the peninsula between L. Erie and L. Huron. Le Caron spent the winter with the Hurons and Tionontati, established the mission of St Gabriel, made a brief dictionary of the language, and returned to the French settlements in the spring. The work was continued for some years by other Récollets, Gabriel Sagard, author of a Huron dictionary and a history of the Récollet missions, and Nicholas Viel, who was murdered by an Indian about 1624. In 1625 the Jesuits arrived in Canada to assist the Récollets, and the next year the heroic Jean de Brébeuf and another Jesuit, with Father Joseph Dallion, Récollet, reached St Gabriel. The Neutrals also were now visited, but without successful result. The work was brought to a temporary close by the English occupancy of Canada in 1629.

In 1634, after the restoration of French control, the work was resumed, this time by the Jesuits alone, with Brébeuf as superior, assisted then or later by Fathers Daniel, Garnier, Jogues, and others of less note. The mission church of Immaculate Conception was built in 1637 at Ossossani, one of the principal towns; St Joseph was established at Teananstayae, the capital, in the next year; the principal war chief of the tribe was baptized, and Christianity began to take root, in spite of the suspicions engendered by two wasting epidemic visitations, for which the missionaries were held responsible and solemnly condemned to death, until the current of opposition was turned by Brébeuf's courageous bearing. In 1639 there were 4 established missions with 13 priests working in the Huron country and visiting in the neighboring tribes. St Marys, on Wye r., had been made the general headquarters. A visitation of smallpox again spread terror through the tribe and for a time rendered the position of the missionaries unsafe. In consequence of these successive epidemics within a few years several towns had been depopulated and the tribe so much weakened as to leave it an easy prey for the invading Iroquois, whose inroads now became more constant and serious than before.

In 1641 the Iroquois invaded the Huron country in force, killed many, and carried off many others to captivity. In 1648, after a temporary truce, they resumed the war of extermination, with perhaps 2,000 warriors well armed with guns obtained from the Dutch, while the Hurons had only bows. On July 4 Teananstayae, or St Joseph, on the site of the present Barrie, was attacked and destroyed, the missionary, Father Anthony Daniel, killed with several hundred of his flock, and about 700 others were carried off as captives. The whole country was ravaged throughout the fall and winter, and one town after another destroyed or abandoned. On Mar. 16, 1649, a thousand warriors attacked St Ignatius town and massacred practically the whole population, after which they proceeded at once to the neighboring town of St Louis, where the burning and massacre were repeated, and two missionaries, Brébeuf and Father Gabriel Lalemant, killed after hours of the most horrible tortures. An attack on St Marys, where Father Ragueneau was stationed, was repulsed, after which the Iroquois retired.

This was the deathblow to the Huron nation. Fifteen towns were abandoned and the people scattered in every direction. Two whole town populations submitted to the conquerors and removed in a body to the Seneca country. Others fled to the Tionontati, who were now in turn invaded by the Iroquois and compelled, by burning and massacre, with the killing of Fathers Garnier and Chabanel, to abandon their country and flee with the rest. Others took refuge on the islands of L. Huron. Some joined the Neutrals, who soon after met the same fate.

For the next 50 years the history of the confederated Huron and Tionontati remnants is a mere record of flight from pursuing enemies—the Iroquois in the E. and the Sioux in the W. A considerable body which sought the protection of the French, after several removals was finally settled by Father M. J. Chaumonot in 1693 at (New) Lorette, near Quebec, where their descendants still reside (see *Hurons; Lorette*). To Chaumonot we owe a standard grammar and dictionary of the Huron language, only the first of which is yet published. In the meantime, in 1656–57, two-thirds of this band had bodily removed to the Iroquois country to escape destruction.

The other fugitives, composed largely or principally of Tionontati, fled successively to Manitoulin id. in L. Huron; Mackinaw; the Noquet ids. in Green bay, Wis.; westward to the Mississippi; back to Green bay, where they were visited by the Jesuit Menard in 1660; to Chegoimegon, near the present Bayfield, Wis., on the shore of L. Superior, where the Jesuit Allouez ministered to them for several years; back, in 1670, to Mackinaw, whence another party joined the Iroquois, and finally down to Detroit, Mich., when that post was founded in 1702. In 1751 a part of these, under Father de la Richard, settled at Sandusky, Ohio. From this period the Wyandot, as they now began to be called, took their place as the leading tribe of the Ohio region and the privileged lighters of the confederate council fire. Their last Jesuit missionary, Father Peter Potier, died in 1781, after which they were served by occasional visiting priests and later by the Presbyterians and the Methodists, until about the period of their removal to Kansas in 1842 (see *Interior States*).

The work of the *Episcopalians* (Anglican Church) among the Iroquois of New York, beginning about 1700 and continuing in Canada after the removal of a large part of the confederacy from the United States, has already been noted (see *Middle Atlantic—New York*). In 1763 Rev. Thomas Wood of Nova Scotia, having become acquainted with the Abbé Maillard and obtained the use of his Micmac manuscript, applied himself to the study of the language, dividing his ministrations thenceforth between the Indians and the whites until his death in 1778. He preached in the native tongue, in which he produced several religious translations. This seems to have been the only work recorded for this denomination in this part of the Dominion, and in the official Canadian Indian Report for 1906 no Indians are enumerated under this heading in the provinces of Nova Scotia, New Brunswick, or Prince Edward id. In Quebec province the same report gives this denomination 119 Indians, including 60 Abnaki at St Francis and 48 Montagnais at Lake St John.

In Ontario province, besides the work already noted among the Iroquois, active and successful missionary effort has been carried on by the Episcopalians among the various Chippewa bands and others since about 1830. One of the principal stations is that at Garden River, opposite Sault Ste Marie, begun in 1835 by Rev. Mr McMurray, who was succeeded a few years later by Rev. F. A. O'Meara, afterward stationed on Manitoulin id., and later at Port Hope on L. Ontario. Besides building up a flourishing school, Mr O'Meara found time to translate into the native language the Book of Common Prayer, considerable portions of both the Old and the New Testament, and a volume of hymns, the last in cooperation with the Rev. Peter Jacobs. He died about 1870. Of the more recent period the most noted worker is Rev. E. F. Wilson, who began his labors under the auspices of the Church Mission Society in 1868. To his efforts the Indians owe the Shingwauk and Wawanosh homes at Sault Ste Marie, Ontario, where some 60 or 80 children are cared for, educated, and taught the rudiments of trades and simple industries. A school journal, set up and printed by the Indian boys, has also been conducted at intervals, under various titles, for nearly 30 years. Mr Wilson is the author of a number of Indian writings, of which the most important is probably a 'Manual of the Ojibway Language,' for the use of mission workers.

In 1835 a mission was established also on Thames r., among the Munsee, a remnant of those Delaware refugees from the United States who for so many years had been the object of Moravian care (see *Middle Atlantic States*). One of the pioneer workers, Rev. Mr Flood, translated the church liturgy into the language of the tribe.

Of 17,498 Christian Indians officially reported in 1906 in Ontario province, 5,253, or not quite one-third, are credited to the *Episcopal* or Anglican church, including—Iroquois in various bands, 3,073; "Chippewas of the Thames," 593; "Ojibbewas of L. Superior," 554; "Chippewas and Saulteaux of Treaty No. 3" (Manitoba border), 709; "Munsees of the Thames" (originally Moravian converts from the United States; see *Middle Atlantic States*), 154; "Ojibbewas and Ottawas of Manitoulin and Cockburn ids.," 169; Potawatomi of Walpole id., 79; and one or two smaller groups.

The work among the Eskimo of the Labrador coast—officially a part of Newfoundland—is conducted by the *Moravians*. In 1752 a reconnoitering missionary party landed near the present Hopedale, but was attacked by the natives, who killed Brother J. C. Ehrhardt and 5 sailors, whereupon the survivors returned home and the attempt for a time was abandoned. One or two other exploring trips were made for the same purpose, and in 1769 permission to establish missions on the Labrador coast was formally asked by the Moravians and granted by the British government. In 1771 the first mission was begun at Nain, apparently by Brother Jens Haven. It is now the chief settlement on the Labrador coast. In 1776 Okak was established by Brother Paul Layritz, followed by Hopedale in 1782, and Hebron in 1830. To these have more recently been added Zoar and Ramah. The efforts of the missionaries have been most successful, the wandering Eskimo having been gathered into permanent settlements, in each of which are a church, store, mission residence, and workshops, with dwelling houses on the model of the native iglu. Besides receiving religious instruction, the natives are taught the simple mechanical arts, but to guard against their innate improvidence, the missionaries have found it necessary to introduce the communal system, by taking charge of all food supplies to distribute at their own discretion. All the missions are still in flourishing operation, having now under their influence about 1,200 of the estimated 1,500 Eskimo along a coast of about 500 m. in length. The total number of mission workers is about 30 (see Hind, Labrador Peninsula.)

To these Moravian workers we owe a voluminous body of Eskimo literature—grammars, dictionaries, scriptural translations, hymns, and miscellaneous publications. Among the prominent names are those of Bourquin, about 1880, author of a grammar and a Bible history; Burghardt, gospel translations, 1813; Erdmann, missionary from 1834 to 1872, a dictionary and other works; Freitag, a manuscript grammar, 1839; and Kohlmeister, St John's Gospel, 1810. The majority of these Moravian publications were issued anonymously.

In 1820 the *Wesleyan Methodists*, through Rev. Alvin Torry, began work among the immigrant Iroquois of the Ontario reservations, which was carried on with notable success for a long term of years by Rev. William Case. In 1823 Mr Case extended his labors to the Missisauga, a band of the Chippewa N. of L. Ontario. The most important immediate result was the conversion of Peter Jones (Kahkewakuonaby), a half-breed, who was afterward ordained, and became the principal missionary among his people and the more remote Chippewa bands until his death in 1856. He is known as the author of a collection of hymns in his native language and also a small 'History of the Ojebway Indians.' Another noted missionary convert of this period was Shawundais, or John Sunday. Another native worker of a somewhat later period was Rev. Henry Steinhauer, Chippewa, afterward known as a missionary to the Cree. Still another pioneer laborer in the same region was Rev. James Evans, afterward also missionary to the Cree and inventor of a Cree syllabary. Contemporary with the transfer of Evans and Steinhauer to the Cree in 1840, Rev. George Barnley was sent to establish a mission at Moose Factory, James bay, which, however, was soon after abandoned. Beginning in 1851 Rev. G. M. McDougall established Methodist mission stations among the Chippewa along the N. shore of L. Superior, at Garden River and elsewhere, but afterward transferred his operations also to Cree territory. In 1861–62 Rev. Thomas Hurlburt, already a veteran worker, and considered the most competent Chippewa linguist in the Methodist mission, conducted a monthly journal, 'Petaubun,' in the language, at the Sarnia station.

According to the official Canadian Indian Report for 1906, the *Methodist* Indians of E. Canada numbered 4,557 in Ontario and 505 in Quebec, a total of 5,062, none being reported for the other eastern provinces. Those in Ontario included nearly all of the "Chippewas of the Thames," "Mississaugas," and "Iroquois and Algonquins of Watha," all of the 348 "Moravians of the Thames," and a considerable percentage of the "Six Nations" on Grand r. Those in Quebec province are chiefly Iroquois of the Oka, St Regis, and Caughnawaga settlements.

Of other denominations, the same official report enumerates 1,020 *Baptists* in Ontario, almost entirely among the Six Nations on Grand r., with 99 *Congregationalists*, 17 *Presbyterians*, and a total of 370 of all other denominations not previously noted. In the other eastern provinces—Quebec, New Brunswick, Nova Scotia, and Prince Edward id.—there is no representation.

The work of Rev. Silas T. Rand among the Micmac of Nova Scotia stands in a class by itself. Educated in a Baptist seminary, he became a minister, but afterward left that denomination to become an independent worker. His attention having been drawn to the neglected condition of the Indians, he began the study of the Micmac language, and in 1849 succeeded in organizing a missionary society for their special instruction. Under its auspices until its dissolution in 1865, and from that time until his death in 1889, he gave his whole effort to the teaching of the Micmac and to the study of their language and traditions. He is the author of a Micmac dictionary and of a collection of tribal myths as well as of numerous minor works, religious and miscellaneous.

CANADA, CENTRAL (Manitoba, Assiniboia, Saskatchewan, Alberta, s. Keewatin).—In the great plains region stretching from Hudson bay southwestward to the Rocky mts., the former battle ground of Cree, Assiniboin, and Blackfeet, the *Catholics* were again the pioneers, antedating all others by a full century. According to Bryce, "the first heralds of the cross" within this area were the French Jesuits accompanying Verendrye, who in the years 1731–1742 explored the whole territory from Mackinaw to the upper Missouri and the Saskatchewan, establishing trading posts and making alliances with the Indian tribes for the French government. Among these missionaries the principal were Fathers Nicholas Gonnor, who had labored among the Sioux as early as 1727; Charles Mesaiger, and Jean Aulneau, killed by the same tribe in 1736. No attempt was made during this period to form permanent mission settlements.

Then follows a long hiatus until after the establishment of the Red River colony in the early part of the 19th century by Lord Selkirk, who in 1818 brought out from eastern Canada Fathers Sévère Dumoulin and Joseph Provencher, to minister both to the colonists and to the Indian and mixed-blood population of the Winnipeg country. In 1822 Father Provencher was made bishop, with jurisdiction over all of Ruperts land and the Northwest territories, and carried on the work of systematic mission organization throughout the whole vast region until his death in 1853, when the noted Oblate missionary, Father Alexandre Taché, who had come out in 1845, succeeded to the dignity, in which he continued for many years.

The Catholic work in this central region has been carried on chiefly by the Oblates, assisted by the Gray Nuns. The first permanent mission was St Boniface, established at the site of the present Winnipeg by Provencher and Dumoulin in 1816. St Paul mission on the Assiniboin later became the headquarters of the noted Father George Belcourt, who gave most of his attention to the Saulteux (Chippewa of Saskatchewan region), and who from 1831 to 1849 covered in his work a territory stretching over a thousand miles from E. to W. For his services in preventing a serious uprising in 1833 he was pensioned both by the Government and by the Hudson's Bay Co. He is the author of a grammatic treatise and of a manuscript dictionary of the Saulteur (Chippewa) language, as well as of some minor Indian writings.

In the Cree field the most distinguished names are those of Fathers Albert Lacombe (1848–90), Alexandre Taché (1845–90), Jean B. Thibault (*ca.* 1855–70), Valentin Végréville (1852–90), and Émile Petitot (1862–82), all of the Oblate order, and each, besides his religious work, the author of important contributions to philology. To Father Lacombe, who founded two missions among the Cree of the upper North Saskatchewan and spent also much time with the Blackfeet, we owe, besides several religious and text-book translations, a manuscript Blackfoot dictionary and a monumental grammar and dictionary of the Cree language. Father Végréville labored among Cree, Assiniboin, and the remote northern Chipewyan, founded five missions, and composed a manuscript grammar, dictionary, and monograph of the Cree language. Father Petitot's earlier work among the Cree has been overshadowed by his later great work among the remote Athapascans and Eskimo, which will be noted hereafter. Among the Blackfeet the most prominent name is that of Father Émile Legal, Oblate (1881–90), author of several linguistic and ethnologic studies of the tribe, all in manuscript.

Episcopalian work in the central region may properly be said to have begun with the arrival of Rev. John West, who was sent out by the Church Missionary Society of England in 1820 as chaplain to the Hudson's Bay Co's establishment of Ft Garry (Winnipeg), on Red r. In the three years of his ministrations, besides giving attention to the white residents, he made missionary journeys among the Cree and others for a distance of 500 m. to the w. He was followed by Rev. David Jones in 1823, by Rev. Wm. Cochrane in 1825, Rev. A. Cowley in 1841, and Rev. R. James in 1846, by whom, together, the tribes farther to the N. were visited and brought within mission influence. In 1840 a Cree mission at The Pas, on the lower Saskatchewan, was organized by Henry Budd, a native convert, and in 1846 other stations were established among the same tribe at Lac la Ronge and Lac la Crosse, by James Settee and James Beardy respectively, also native converts. In 1838 a large bequest for Indian missions within Rupert's Land, as the territory was then known, had been made by Mr James Leith, an officer of the Hudson's Bay Co., and generously increased soon after by the company itself. With the assistance and the active effort of four missionary societies of the church, the work grew so that in 1849 the territory was erected into a bishopric, and on the transfer of jurisdiction from the Hudson's Bay Co., to the Canadian government in 1870 there were 15 Episcopal missionaries laboring at the various stations in the regions stretching from Hudson bay to the upper Saskatchewan, the most important being those at York Factory (Keewatin), Cumberland, and Carlton (Saskatchewan).

Among the most noted of those in the Cree country may be mentioned in chronologic order, Rev. Archdeacon James Hunter and his wife (1844–55), joint or separate authors of a number of translations, including the Book of Common Prayer, hymns, gospel extracts, etc., and a valuable treatise on the Cree language; Bishop John Horden (1851–90), of Moose Factory, York Factory, and Ft Churchill stations, self-taught printer and binder, master of the language, and author of a number of gospels, prayer, and hymn translations; Bishop William Bompas (1865–90), best known for his work among the more northern Athapascan tribes; Rev. W. W. Kirkby (1852–79), author of a Cree 'Manual of Prayer and Praise,' but also best known for his Athapascan work; Rev. John Mackay, author of several religious translations and of a manuscript grammar; and Rev. E. A. Watkins, author of a standard dictionary. Among the Blackfeet, Rev. J. W. Tims, who began his work in 1883, is a recognized authority on the language, of which he has published a grammar and dictionary and a gospel translation.

Methodist (Wesleyan) effort in the Cree and adjacent territories began in 1840. In that year Rev. James Evans and his Indian assistant, Rev. Henry Steinhauer, both already noted in connection with previous work in Ontario, were selected for the western mission, and set out together for Norway House, a Hudson's Bay Co's post at the N. end of L. Winnipeg. Evans went on without stop to his destination, but Steinhauer halted at Lac la Pluie (now Rainy Lake) to act as interpreter to Rev. William Mason, who had just reached that spot, having been sent out under the same auspices, the Wesleyan Missionary Society of England, by arrangement with the Canadian body. The joint control continued until 1855, when the Canadian Methodists assumed full charge. Mr Evans had been appointed superintendent of Methodist work for the whole region, and after establishing Rossville mission, near Norway House, as his central station, spent the next six years until his health failed, in traversing the long distances, founding several missions, mastering the Cree language, and devising for it a syllabary, which has ever since been in successful use for all literary purposes in the tribe. His first printing in the syllabary was done upon a press of his own making, with types cast from the sheet-lead lining of tea boxes and cut into final shape with a jackknife. In this primitive fashion he printed many copies of the syllabary for distribution among the wandering bands, besides hymn collections and scripture translations. "By means of this syllabary a clever Indian can memorize in an hour or two all the characters, and in two or three days read the Bible or any other book in his own language" (MacLean). In later years, the credit for this invention was unsuccessfully claimed by some for Rev. William Mason. Rossville for years continued to be the principal and most prosperous of all the Methodist missions in the central region.

Rev. William Mason remained at Rainy Lake until that station was temporarily discontinued in 1844; he was then sent to Rossville (Norway House), where he was stationed until 1854, when the mission was abandoned by the Wesleyans. He then attached himself to the Episcopal church, with which he had formerly been connected, and was ordained in the same year, laboring thereafter at York Factory on Hudson bay until his final return to England in 1870, with the exception of 4 years spent in that country supervising the publication of his great Bible translation in the Cree language, printed in 1861. This, with several other Scripture and hymn translations, excepting a Gospel of St John, was issued under the auspices of the Episcopal Church Missionary Society. In his earlier linguistic (Methodist) work he was aided by Rev. Mr Steinhauer and John Sinclair, a half-breed, but in all his later work, especially in the Bible translation, he had the constant assistance of his wife, the educated half-breed daughter of a Hudson's Bay Co. officer. Rev. Mr Steinhauer, after some years with Mr Mason, joined Mr Evans at Norway House as teacher and interpreter. He afterward filled stations at Oxford House (Jackson bay), York Factory, Lac la Biche, White Fish Lake, Victoria, and other remote points, for a term of more than 40 years, making a record as "one of the most devoted and successful of our native Indian missionaries" (Young). Among later Methodist workers with the Cree may be mentioned Rev. John McDougall, one of the founders of Victoria station, Alberta, in 1862, and Rev. Ervin Glass, about 1880, author of several primary instruction books and charts in the syllabary.

At the same time (1840) that Evans and Mason were sent to the Cree, Rev. Robert T. Rundle was sent, by the same authority, to make acquaintance with the more remote Blackfeet and Assiniboin ("Stonies") of the upper Saskatchewan region. Visiting stations were selected where frequent services were conducted by Rundle, by Rev. Thomas Woolsey, who came out in 1855, and by others, but no regular mission was established until

begun by Rev. George M. McDougall at Edmonton, Alberta, in 1871. In 1873 he founded another mission on Bow r., Alberta, among the Stonies (western Assiniboin), and continued to divide attention between the two tribes until his accidental death 2 years later. Other stations were established later at Ft MacLeod and Morley, in the same territory. The most distinguished worker of this denomination among the Blackfeet is Rev. John MacLean (1880–89), author of a manuscript grammar and dictionary of the language, several minor linguistic papers, 'The Indians: Their Manners and Customs' (1889), and 'Canadian Savage Folk' (1896).

Presbyterian mission work was inaugurated in 1865 by the Rev. James Nisbet, among the Cree, at Prince Albert mission on the Saskatchewan. No data are at hand as to the work of the denomination in this region, but it is credited in the official report with nearly a thousand Indian communicants, chiefly among the Sioux and the Assiniboin, many of the latter being immigrants from the United States.

According to the Canadian Indian Report for 1906, the Indians of Manitoba, Saskatchewan, Alberta, and the Northwest Territories, classified under treaties 1, 2, 3, 4, 5, 6, and 7, designated as Chippewa, Cree, Saulteaux, Sioux, Assiniboin, Blackfeet, Bloods, Piegan, Sarcee, Stonies, and Chipewyan, are credited as follows: Catholic, 5,633; Anglican (Episcopal), 4,789; Methodist, 3,199; Presbyterian, 1,073; Baptist, 83; all other denominations, 80; pagan, 5,324. Some 3,308 remote northern Cree, under Treaty No. 8, and 165 non-treaty Indians are not included in the estimate.

CANADA, BRITISH COLUMBIA (including Vancouver id. and Metlakatla).—The earliest missionary entrance into British Columbia was made by the *Catholics* in 1839. In 1838 the secular priests Demers and Blanchet (afterward archbishop) had arrived at Fort Vancouver, Washington, as already noted (see *Columbia Region*), to minister to the employees of the Hudson's Bay Co. In the next year an Indian mission was organized at Cowlitz, with visiting stations along the shores of Puget sd., and Father Demers made a tour of the upper Columbia as far as the Okinagan in British Columbia, preaching, baptizing, and giving instruction by means of a pictograph device of Father Blanchet's invention, known as the "Catholic ladder." Copies of this "ladder" were carried by visiting Indians to the more remote tribes and prepared the way for later effort. A second journey over the same route was made by Father Demers in the next year, and in 1841 he preached for the first time to a great gathering of the tribes on lower Fraser r. In the following year, 1842, by arrangement with the local Hudson's Bay Co. officers, he accompanied the annual supply caravan on its return from Ft Vancouver, on the Columbia, to the remote northern posts. On this trip, ascending the Columbia and passing over to the Fraser, he visited successively the Okinagan, Kamloops, Shuswap, and Takulli or Carriers, before arriving at their destination at Ft St James on Stuart lake. Return was made in the following spring, and on descending the Fraser he found that the Shuswap had already erected a chapel.

In the meantime de Smet and the Jesuits had arrived (see *Columbia Region* and *Interior States—Flatheads*) in the Columbia region, and between 1841 and 1844 had established a chain of missions throughout the territory, including three in British Columbia, among the Kutenai, Shuswap, and Okinagan. De Smet himself extended his visitations to the headwaters of the Athabasca, while in 1845–47 Father John Nobili, laboring among the upper tribes, penetrated to the Babines on the lake of that name. The most remote point visited was among the Carriers, at Stuart Lake. In 1843 the first Hudson Bay post had been established on Vancouver id. at Camosun, now Victoria, and the beginning of missionary work among the Songish and the Cowichan was made by the secular priest, Father John Bolduc, already well known among the Sound tribes, who had for this reason been brought over by the officers in charge to assist in winning the good will of their Indian neighbors.

Owing to difficulty of communication and pressing need in other fields, it was found necessary to abandon the British Columbia missions, except for an occasional visiting priest, until the work was regularly taken up by the Oblates about 1860. Before 1865 they had regular establishments at New Westminster, St Marys, and Okinagan, besides others on Vancouver id., and in that year founded St Joseph mission near Williams lake, on the upper Fraser, under Rev. J. M. McGuckin, first missionary to the Tsilkotin tribe. Within the next few years he extended his ministrations to the remoter Sekani and Skeena. In 1873 the Stuart Lake mission was established by Fathers Lejacq and Blanchet, and in 1885 was placed in charge of Father A. G. Morice, Oblate, the distinguished ethnologist and author, who had already mastered the Tsilkotin language in three years' labor in the tribe. Aside from his missionary labor proper, which still continues, he is perhaps best known as the inventor of the Déné syllabary, by means of which nearly all the Canadian Indians of the great Athapascan stock are now able to read and write in their own language. His other works include a Tsilkotin dictionary, a Carrier grammar, numerous religious and miscellaneous translations, an Indian journal, scientific papers, 'Notes on the Western Dénés' (1893), and a 'History of the Northern Interior of British Columbia' (1904). Father J. M. Le Jeune, of the same order, stationed among the Thompson River and Shuswap Indians since 1880, is also noted as the inventor of a successful shorthand system, by means of which those and other cognate tribes are now able to read in their own languages. He is also the author of a number of religious and text books in the same languages and editor of a weekly Indian journal, the 'Kamloops Wawa,' all of which are printed on a copying press in his own stenographic characters. Another distinguished veteran of the same order is Bishop Paul Durieu, since 1854 until his recent death, laboring successively among the tribes of Washington, Vancouver id. (Ft Rupert, in Kwakiutl territory), and Fraser r.

Episcopal work began in 1857 with the remarkable and successful missionary enterprise undertaken by Mr William Duncan among the Tsimshian at Metlakatla, first in British Columbia and later in Alaska. The Tsimshian at that time were among the fiercest and most degraded savages of the N. W. coast, slavery, human sacrifice, and cannibalism being features of their tribal system, to which they were rapidly adding all the vices introduced by the most depraved white men from the coasting vessels. Moved by reports of their miserable condition Mr Duncan voluntarily resigned a remunerative position in England to offer himself as a worker in their behalf under the auspices of the London Church Missionary Society. He arrived at Ft Simpson, N. coast of British Columbia, in Oct. 1857, and after some months spent in learning the language and making acquaintance with the tribe, then numbering 2,300, opened his first school in June, 1858. By courage and devotion through danger and difficulty he built up a civilized Christian body, which in 1860 he colonized to the number of about 340 in a regular town established at Metlakatla, an abandoned village site 16 m. s. of Ft Simpson. By systematic improvement of every industrial opportunity for years the town had grown to a prosperous, self-supporting community of 1,000 persons, when, by reason of difficulties with the local bishop, upheld by the colonial government, Mr Duncan and his Indians were compelled, in 1887, to abandon their town and improvements and seek asylum under United States protection in Alaska, where they formed a new settlement, known as New Metlakatla, on Annette id., 60 m. N. of their former home. The island, which is about 40 m. long by 3 m. wide, has been reserved by Congress for their use, and the work of improvement and education is now progressing as before the removal, the present population being about 500.

The first Episcopal bishop for British Columbia and Vancouver id. was appointed in 1859. In 1861 the Rev. John B. Good, sent out also by the London society, arrived at Esquimalt, near Victoria, Vancouver id., to preach alike to whites and Indians. At a later period his work was transferred to the Indians of Thompson and lower Fraser rs., with headquarters at St Paul's mission, Lytton. He has translated a large part of the liturgy into the Thompson River (Ntlakyapamuk) language, besides being the author of a grammatic sketch and other papers. In 1865 Kincolith mission was established among the Niska branch of the Tsimshian, on Nass r., by Rev. R. A. Doolan, and some years later another one higher up on the same stream. Kitwingach station, on Skeena r., was established about the same time. In 1871 Rev. Charles M. Tate took up his residence with the Nanaimo on Vancouver id., laboring afterward with the Tsimshian, Bellabella, and Fraser r. tribes. In 1876 Rev. W. H. Collison began work among the Haida at Masset, on the N. end of the Queen Charlotte ids., and in 1878 Rev. A. J. Hall arrived among the Kwakiutl at Ft Rupert, Vancouver id. Other stations in the meantime had been established throughout the s. part of the province, chiefly under the auspices of the London Church Missionary Society.

The first *Methodist* (Wesleyan) work for the Indians of British Columbia was begun in 1863 at Nanaimo, Vancouver id., by Rev. Thomas Crosby, who at once applied himself to the study of the language with such success that he was soon able to preach in it. In 1874 he transferred his labor to the Tsimshian at Port Simpson, on the border of Alaska, who had already been predisposed to Christianity by the work at Metlakatla and by visiting Indians from the S. Other stations were established on Nass r. (1877) and at Kitamat in the Bellabella tribe. Statistics show that the Methodist work has been particularly successful along the N. W. coast and in portions of Vancouver.

There is no record of *Presbyterian* mission work, but some 400 Indians are officially credited to that denomination along the w. coast of Vancouver id.

According to the Canadian Indian Report for 1906 the Christian Indians of British Columbia are classified as follows: Catholic, 11,270; Episcopal (Anglican), 4,364; Methodist, 3,285; Presbyterian, 427; all other, 147.

CANADA, NORTHWEST (Athabasca, Mackenzie, Yukon, North Keewatin, Franklin).—The earliest missionaries of the great Canadian Northwest, of which Mackenzie r. is the central artery, were the *Catholic* priests of the Oblate order. The pioneer may have been a Father Grollier, mentioned as the "first martyr of apostleship" in the Mackenzie district and buried at Ft Good Hope, almost under the Arctic circle. In 1846 Father Alexandre Taché, afterward the distinguished archbishop of Red River, arrived at Lac Ile à la Crosse, a Cree station, at the head of Churchill r., Athabasca, and a few months later crossed over the divide to the Chipewyan tribe on Athabasca r. Here he established St Raphael mission, and for the next 7 years, with the exception of a visit to Europe, divided his time between the two tribes. In 1847 or 1848 Father Henry Faraud, afterward vicar of the Mackenzie district, arrived among the Chipewyan of Great Slave lake, with whom and their congeners he continued for 18 years. To him we owe a Bible abridgment in the Chipewyan language. In 1852 arrived Father Valentin Végréville, for more than 40 years missionary to Cree, Assiniboin, and Chipewyan, all of which languages he spoke fluently; founder of the Chipewyan mission of St Peter, on Caribou lake, Athabasca, besides several others farther s.; and author of a manuscript grammar and dictionary of the Cree language, another of the Chipewyan language, and other ethnologic and religious papers in manuscript. In 1867 Father Laurent Legoff arrived at Caribou Lake mission, where he was still stationed in 1892. He is best known as the author of a grammar of the Montagnais, or Chipewyan language, published in 1889.

By far the most noted of all the Oblate missionaries of the great Northwest is Father Émile Petitot, acknowledged by competent Canadian authority as "our greatest scientific writer on the Indians and Eskimos" (MacLean). In 20 years of labor, beginning in 1862, he covered the whole territory from Winnipeg to the Arctic ocean, frequently making journeys of six weeks' length on snowshoes. He was the first missionary to visit Great Bear lake (1866), and the first missionary to the Eskimo of the N. W., having visited them in 1865 at the mouth of the Anderson, in 1868 at the mouth of the Mackenzie, and twice later at the mouth of Peel r. In 1870 he crossed over into Alaska, and in 1878, compelled by illness, he returned to the S., making the journey of some

1,200 m. to Athabasca lake on foot, and thence by canoe and portages to Winnipeg. Besides writing some papers relating to the Cree, he is the author of numerous ethnological and philosophical works, dealing with the Chipewyan, Slavé, Hare, Dog-rib, Kutchin, and Eskimo tribes and territory, chief among which are his Dènè-Dindjié dictionary (1876) and his 'Traditions Indiennes' (1886).

Throughout the Mackenzie region the Catholics have now established regular missions or visiting stations at every principal gathering point, among the most important being a mission at Ft Providence, beyond Great Slave lake, and a school, orphanage, and hospital conducted since 1875 by the Sisters of Charity at Ft Chipewyan on Athabasca lake.

Episcopal effort in the Canadian Northwest dates from 1858, in which year Archdeacon James Hunter, already mentioned in connection with the Cree mission, made a reconnoitering visit to Mackenzie r., as a result of which Rev. W. W. Kirkby, then on parish duty on Red r., was next year appointed to that field and at once took up his headquarters at the remote post of Ft Simpson, at the junction of Liard and Mackenzie rs., 62° N., where, with the assistance of the Hudson's Bay Co's officers, he built a church and school. In 1862, after several years' study of the language, he descended the Mackenzie nearly to its mouth and crossed over the divide to the Yukon, just within the limits of Alaska, preaching to the Kutchin and making some study of the language, after which he returned to Ft Simpson. In 1869 he was appointed to the station at York Factory, on Hudson bay, where he remained until his retirement in 1878, after 26 years of efficient service in Manitoba and the Northwest. He is the author of a number of religious translations in the Chipewyan and Slavé languages.

The work begun on the Yukon by Kirkby was given over to Rev. (Archdeacon) Robert McDonald, who established his headquarters at St Matthew's mission on Peel r., Mackenzie district, "one mile within the Arctic circle." Here he devoted himself with remarkable industry and success to a study of the language of the Takudh Kutchin, into which he has translated, besides several minor works, the Book of Common Prayer (1885), a small collection of Hymns (1889), and the complete Bible in 1898, all according to a syllabic system of his own device, by means of which the Indians were enabled to read in a few weeks. In 1865 Rev. Wm. C. Bompas, afterward bishop of Athabasca and later of Mackenzie r., arrived from England. In the next 25 years he labored among the Chipewyan, Dog-ribs, Beavers, Slavé, and Ta-

kudh tribes of the remote Northwest, and gave some attention also to the distant Eskimo. He is the author of a primer in each of these languages, as well as in Cree and Eskimo, together with a number of gospel and other religious translations. Another notable name is that of Rev. Alfred Garrioch, who began work in the Beaver tribe on Peace r., Athabasca, in 1876, after a year's preliminary study at Ft Simpson. He is the founder of Unjaga mission at Ft Vermilion, and author of several devotional works and of a considerable vocabulary in the Beaver language. To a somewhat later period belong Rev. W. D. Reeve and Rev. Spendlove, in the Slave lake region. Among the principal stations are Ft Chipewyan on Athabasca lake, Ft Simpson on the middle Mackenzie, and Fts Macpherson and Lapierre in the neighborhood of the Mackenzie's mouth. Work has also been done among the Eskimo of Hudson bay, chiefly by Rev. Edmund Peck, who has devised a syllabary for the language, in which he has published several devotional translations, beginning in 1878. The greater portion of the Episcopal work in the Canadian Northwest has been under the auspices of the Church Missionary Society of London.

GREENLAND.—Greenland was first colonized from Iceland in 985 by Scandinavians, who became Christian about A. D. 1000. The aboriginal inhabitants were the Eskimo, with whom in the succeeding centuries the colonists had frequent hostile encounters, but there is no record of any attempt at missionary work. Some time shortly before the year 1500 the colony became extinct, there being considerable evidence that it was finally overwhelmed by the Eskimo savages. In 1721 the Norse *Lutheran* minister, Rev. Hans Egede, under the auspices of the government of Denmark, landed with his family and a few other companions upon the s. end of the island, in the belief that some descendants of the lost colony might yet be in existence. Finding no white inhabitants, he turned his attention to the evangelization of the native Eskimo, and thus became the founder both of the Greenland mission and of the modern Greenland settlement. A mission station which was named Godthaab was established on Baal r. on the w. coast, about 64° N., and became the center of operations, while Egede was made bishop and superintendent of missions. After some years of hardship and discouragement the home government was about to withdraw its support, and it seemed as if the mission would have to be abandoned, when, in 1733, the *Moravians* volunteered their aid. In the spring of that year three Moravian missionaries, Christian David, and Matthew and Christian Stach, arrived from Denmark to cooperate with Egede, with such good result that the principal work finally passed over to that denomination, by which it has since been continued. Egede in 1736 returned to Denmark to establish at Copenhagen a special training seminary for the work. He died in 1758, leaving the succession in office to his son, Rev. Paul Egede. The elder Egede was the author of a 'Description of Greenland,' which has been translated into several languages, besides several scriptural works in Eskimo. His son, Paul, accompanied his father on the first trip in 1721, learned the language, and in 1734 began the missionary work which he continued to his death in 1789, having been made bishop 10 years earlier. He is the author of a standard Danish-Latin-Eskimo grammar and dictionary, besides a number of religious works in the language and a journal of the Greenland missions from 1721 to within a year of his death. Still another of the same family, Rev. Peter Egede, nephew of the first missionary, was the author of a translation of Psalms.

With the settlement of the country from Denmark and the organization of regular parishes the Lutheran missions took on new life, special attention being given to the more northern regions. Godthaab remained the principal station, and several others were established, of which the most important to-day are Nugsoak on Disko bay, w. coast, and Angmagsalik, about 66° N., on the E. coast, the northernmost inhabited spot in that direction. The friendly cooperation between the two denominations seems never to have been interrupted, the ministers in many cases sharing their labors and results in common.

The Moravian work prospered. New Herrnhut, the first and most northerly mission, was established in 1733; Lichtenfels was founded 80 m. farther s. in 1758; 300 m. farther s. Lichtenau was founded in 1774; then came Frederiksdal in 1824, Umanak in 1861, and Igdlorpait in 1864. In 1881 the mission force numbered 19 and the native membership 1,545. Since 1801 the whole Eskimo population properly resident within the Moravian mission area has been Christian, but others have since moved in from the outlying territory. The work of civilization is nearly as complete for the whole E. coast.

As the result of the literary labors of nearly two centuries of missionary students, together with a few educated natives, the Eskimo literature of Greenland is exceptionally voluminous, covering the whole range of linguistics, Bible translations, hymn books, and other religious works, school text-books, stories, and miscellanies, besides a journal published at the Godthaab station from 1861 to 1885. With so much material it is possible only to mention the names of the principal workers in this field. For details the reader is referred to Pilling's 'Bibliography of the Eskimo Language.' In the Lutheran mission the most prominent names are Egede, father and son, Fabricius (1768–73); Janssen (period of 1850); Kjer (period of 1820); the Kleinschmidts, father and son (1793–1840); Kragh (1818–28); Steenholdt (period of 1850); Sternberg (1840–53); Thorhallesen (1776–89); Wandall (1834–40), and Wolf (1803–11). In the Moravian list are found Beck (died 1777); Beyer (period of 1750); Brodersen (period of 1790); Konigseer (period of 1780); Muller (period of 1840); together with Cranz, author of the 'History of Greenland and the Moravian Mission,' first published in 1765.

In the four centuries of American history there is no more inspiring chapter of heroism, self-sacrifice, and devotion to high ideals than that afforded by the Indian missions. Some of the missionaries were of noble blood and had renounced titles and estates to engage in the work; most of them were of finished scholarship and refined habit, and nearly all were of such exceptional ability as to have commanded attention in any community and to have possessed themselves of wealth and reputation, had they so chosen; yet they deliberately faced poverty and sufferings, exile and oblivion, ingratitude, torture, and death itself in the hope that some portion of a darkened world might be made better through their effort. To the student who knows what infinite forms of cruelty, brutishness, and filthiness belonged to savagery, from Florida to Alaska, it is beyond question that, in spite of sectarian limitations and the shortcomings of individuals, the missionaries have fought a good fight. Where they have failed to accomplish large results the reason lies in the irrepressible selfishness of the white man or in the innate incompetence and unworthiness of the people for whom they labored.

Consult: Aborigines Committee, Conduct of Friends, 1844; Bancroft, Histories, Alaska, British Columbia, California, Oregon, Washington, etc., 1886–90; Barnum, Innuit Language, 1901; Bressani, Relation, 1653, repr. 1852; Brinton, Lenape, 1885; California, Missions of, U. S. Sup. Ct., 1859; Bryce, Hudson's Bay Co., 1900; Catholic Bureau of Indian Missions, Reports; Clark, Indian Sign Language, 1885; Coues, On the Trail of a Spanish Pioneer, 1900; Cranz, History of the Brethren, 1780; DeForest, Indians of Connecticut,

1851; Duflot de Mofras, Expl. de l'Oregon, 1844; Dunbar, Pawnee Indians, 1880; Eells, Ten Years, 1886; Engelhardt, Franciscans, 1897; Fletcher, Indian Education and Civilization, 1888; Gookin, Christian Indians, Archæologia Americana, 1836; Harris, Early Missions, 1893; Harvey, Shawnee Indians, 1855; Heckewelder, United Brethren, 1820; Hind, Labrador, 1863; Howe, Hist. Coll. Ohio, II, 1896; Jackson (1) Alaska, 1880, (2) Facts About Alaska, 1903; Jesuit Relations, Thwaites ed., 1896–1901; Jones, Ojebway Inds., 1861; Krehbiel, Mennonites, 1898; Loskiel, United Brethren, 1794; Lossing, Moravian Missions, American Hist. Record, 1872; MacLean, Canadian Savage Folk, 1896; McCoy, Baptist Indian Missions, 1840; McDougall, George Millard McDougall the Pioneer, 1888; Minnesota Hist. Soc. Coll., I, 1872; Mooney, Myths of Cherokee, 1900; Morice, Northern British Columbia, 1904; Morse, Report, 1822; Palfrey, New England, I, 1866; Parkman, (1) Jesuits, 1867, (2) Pioneers, 1883; Pilling, Indian Bibliographies (Bulletins of Bur. Am. Eth.), 1887–91; Pitezel, Lights and Shades, 1857; Riggs, Tah-koo Wahkan, 1869; Rink, Tales and Traditions of Eskimo, 1875; Ronan, Flathead Indians, 1890; Ryerson, Hudson's Bay, 1855; Shea, Catholic Missions, 1855; de Smet, Oregon Missions, 1847; Stefánsson in Am. Anthrop., VIII, 1906; Sutherland, Summer in Prairie Land, 1881; Thompson, Moravian Missions, 1890; Tucker, Rainbow in the North, 1851; Wellcome, Metlakahtla, 1887; Whipple, Lights and Shadows, 1899. (J. M.)

Missisauga (Chippewa: *misi*, 'large,' *ság* or *sauk*, 'outlet (of a river or bay)' = 'large outlet,' referring to the mouth of Missisauga r.—Hewitt). Although this Algonquian tribe is a division or subtribe of the Chippewa, having originally formed an integral part of the latter, it has long been generally treated as distinct. When first encountered by the French, in 1634, the Missisauga lived about the mouth of the river of the same name, along the N. shore of L. Huron, and on the adjacent Manitoulin id. Although so closely allied to the Chippewa, they do not appear to have been disposed to follow that tribe in its progress westward, as there is no evidence that they were ever found in early times so far W. as Sault Ste Marie, but appear to have clung to their old haunts about L. Huron and Georgian bay. Early in the 18th century, influenced by a desire to trade with the whites, they began to drift toward the S. E. into the region formerly occupied by the Hurons, between L. Huron and L. Erie. Although they had destroyed a village of the Iroquois near Ft Frontenac about 1705, they tried in 1708 to gain a passage through the country of the latter, to trade their peltries with the English. At this time a part or band was settled on L. St Clair. About 1720 the French established a station at the w. end of L. Ontario for the purpose of stimulating trade with the Missisauga. Near the close of the first half of the century (1746–50), having joined the Iroquois in the war against the French, the Missisauga were compelled by the latter, who were aided by the Ottawa, to abandon their country, a portion at least settling near the Seneca E. of L. Erie. Others, however, appear to have remained in the vicinity of their early home, as a delegate from a Missisauga town "on the north side of L. Ontario" came to the conference at Mt Johnson, N. Y., in June, 1755. As it is also stated that they "belong to the Chippewyse confederacy, which chiefly dwell about the L. Missilianac," it is probable that "north side of L. Ontario" refers to the shores of L. Huron. Being friendly with the Iroquois at this time, they were allowed to occupy a number of places in the country from which the Hurons had been driven. This is inferred in part from Chauvignerie's report of 1736, which locates parts of the tribe at different points on Missisauga r., Maniskoulin (Manitoulin?) id., L. St Clair, Kente, Toronto r., Matchitaen, and the w. end of L. Ontario. The land on which the Iroquois are now settled at Grand r., Ontario, was bought from them. For the purpose of sealing their alliance with the Iroquois they were admitted as the seventh tribe of the Iroquois league in 1746, at which date they were described as living in five villages near Detroit. It is therefore probable that those who went to live with the Seneca first came to the vicinity of Detroit and moved thence to w. New York. The alliance with the Iroquois lasted only until the outbreak of the French and Indian war a few years later.

According to Jones (Hist. Ojebways), as soon as a Missisauga died he was laid out on the ground, arrayed in his best clothes, and wrapped in skins or blankets. A grave about 3 ft deep was dug and the corpse interred with the head toward the w. By his side were placed his hunting and war implements. The grave was then covered, and above it poles or sticks were placed lengthwise to the height of about 2 ft, over which birch-bark or mats were thrown to keep out the rain. Immediately after the decease of an Indian, the near relatives went into mourning by blackening their faces with charcoal and putting on the most ragged and filthy clothing they possessed. A year was the usual time of mourning for a husband, wife, father or mother.

As the Missisauga are so frequently confounded with the Chippewa and other neighboring tribes who are closely connected, it is difficult to make a separate estimate of their numbers. In 1736 they were reported to number 1,300, about 250 being on Manitoulin id. and Missisauga r., and the rest in the peninsula of Ontario; in 1778 they were estimated at 1,250, living chiefly on the N. side of L. Erie, and in 1884 the number was given as 744. The population was officially reported in 1906 as 810, of whom 185 were at Mud Lake, 87 at Rice Lake, 35 at Scugog, 240 at Alnwick, and 263 at New Credit, Ontario. The New Credit settlement forms a township by itself and the Indian inhabitants have often won prizes against white competitors at the agricultural fairs. The New Credit Indians (who left the Old Credit settlement in 1847) are the most advanced of the Missisauga and represent one of the most successful attempts of any American Indian group to assimilate the culture of the whites. The Alnwick res. dates from 1830, Mud Lake from 1829, Scugog from 1842. Beldom, Chibaouinani, and Grape Island were former settlements. See *Credit Indians, Matchedash, Sandy Hill.*

Consult Chamberlain (1) Language of the Mississagas of Skūgog, 1892, and bibliography therein; (2) Notes on the History, Customs and Beliefs of the Mississagua Indians, Jour. Am. Folk-lore, I, 150, 1888.   (J. M.   C. T.)

Achsisaghecks.—Colden (1727) note in N. Y. Doc. Col. Hist., IV, 737, 1854. **Achsissaghecs.**—Colden in Schoolcraft, Ind. Tribes, III, 517, 1853. **Aghsiesagichrone.**—Doc. of 1723 in N. Y. Doc. Col. Hist., V, 695, 1855. **Aoechisacronon.**—Jes. Rel. 1649, 27, 1858 (Huron name). **Assisagh.**—Livingston (1701) in N. Y. Doc. Col. Hist., IV, 899, 1854. **Assisagigroone.**—Livingston (1700), ibid., 737, 1854. **Awechisaehronon.**—Jes. Rel., III, index, 1858. **Ishisagek Roanu.**—Dobbs, Hudson Bay, 27, 1744 (Iroquois name). **Mase-sau-gee.**—Jones, Ojebway Inds., 164, 1861 (proper form). **Massasagues.**—Macauley, N. Y., II, 249, 1829. **Massasagas.**—Morgan, League Iroq., 91, 1851. **Massasoiga.**—Chapin (1792) in Am. State Papers, Ind. Aff., I, 242, 1832. **Massesagues.**—Niles (ca. 1761) in Mass. Hist. Soc. Coll., 4th s., V, 541, 1861. **Massinagues.**—Boudinot, Star in the West, 127, 1816. **Mesasagah.**—Lindesay (1751) in N. Y. Doc. Col. Hist., VI, 706, 1855. **Messagnes.**—Drake, Ind. Chron., 180, 1836. **Messagues.**—Shirley (1755) in N. Y. Doc. Col. Hist., VI, 1027, 1855. **Messasagas.**—Ft Johnson conf. (1757), ibid., VII, 259, 1856. **Messasagies.**—Perkins and Peck, Annals of the West, 423, 1850. **Messasagoes.**—Procter (1791) in Am. State Papers, Ind. Aff., I, 158, 1832. **Messasagues.**—Writer of 1756 in Mass. Hist. Soc. Coll., 1st s., VII, 123, 1801. **Messasaugues.**—Lincoln (1793), ibid., 3d s., V, 156, 1836. **Messassagas.**—Albany conf. (1746) in N. Y. Doc. Col. Hist., VI, 322, 1855. **Messassagnes.**—Drake, Bk. Inds., IX, 1848. **Messassagues.**—Homann Heirs map, 1756. **Messesagas.**—Lindesay (1751) in N. Y. Doc. Col. Hist., VI, 729, 1855. **Messesagnes.**—Drake, Bk. Inds., bk. 5, 4, 1848. **Messesago.**—Procter (1791) in Am. State Papers, Ind. Aff., I, 163, 1832. **Messesagues.**—Colden (1727), Five Nations, app., 175, 1747. **Messessagues.**—Carver, Travels, map, 1778. **Messessaques.**—Goldthwait (1766) in Mass. Hist. Soc. Coll., 1st s., X, 122, 1809. **Messinagues.**—Boudinot, Star in the West, 107, 1816. **Messissagas.**—Ibid., 100. **Messisages.**—Albany conf. (1746) in N. Y. Doc. Col. Hist., VI, 321, 1855. **Messisagues.**—Vater, Mith., pt. 3, sec. 3, 406, 1816. **Messisaugas.**—Edwards (1788) in Mass. Hist. Soc. Coll., 1st s., IX, 92, 1804. **Messisaugers.**—Barton, New Views, xxxiii, 1798. **Messissagas.**—Albany conf. (1746) in N. Y. Doc. Col. Hist., IV, 322, 1855. **Messissauga.**—Petition of 1837 in Jones, Ojebway Inds., 265, 1861. **Messissauger.**—Adelung and Vater, Mithridates, III, pt. 3, 343, 1816. **Michesaking.**—Jes. Rel. 1658, 22, 1858. **Michisagnek.**—Ibid., 1648, 62, 1858. **Misisaga's.**—Johnson (1763) in N. Y. Doc. Col. Hist., VII, 526, 1856. **Misisagey.**—Claus (1777), ibid., VIII, 719, 1857. **Misitagues.**—Lahontan, New Voy., I, map, 1735. **Missada.**—Dobbs, Hudson Bay, 31, 1744. **Missages.**—German Flats conf. (1770) in N. Y. Doc. Col. Hist., VIII, 229, 1857. **Missasagas.**—Lindesay (1749), ibid., VI, 538, 1855. **Missasago.**—Harris, Tour, 205, 1805. **Missasagué.**—Durant (1721) in N. Y. Doc. Col. Hist., V, 589, 1855. **Missasago.**—Rupp, West Pa., 280, 1846. **Missassugas.**—Johnson (1764) in N. Y. Doc. Col. Hist., VII, 661, 1856. **Missaugees.**—Trader (1778) in Schoolcraft, Ind. Tribes, III, 560, 1853. **Missequeks.**—Clinton (1745) in N. Y. Doc. Col. Hist., VI, 281, 1855. **Missesagas.**—Ft Johnson conf. (1757), ibid., VII, 259, 1856. **Missesagues.**—Procter (1791) in Am. State Papers, Ind. Aff., I, 163, 1832. **Missesagues.**—Doc. of 1747 in N. Y. Doc. Col. Hist., VI, 391, 1855. **Missesaques.**—Clinton (1749), ibid., 484. **Missiagos.**—Johnson (1760), ibid., VII, 434, 1856. **Missinasagues.**—Boudinot, Star in the West, 127, 1816. **Missiosagaes.**—Quotation in Ruttenber, Tribes Hudson R., 29, 1872. **Missiquecks.**—Clinton (1745) in N. Y. Doc. Col. Hist., VI, 276, 1855. **Missisagaes.**—Mt Johnson conf. (1755), ibid., 975. **Missisages.**—Coxe, Carolana, map, 1741. **Missisagis.**—Doc. of 1764 in N. Y. Doc. Col. Hist., VII, 641, 1856. **Missisagos.**—Canajoharie conf. (1759), ibid., 384. **Missisagues.**—Lahontan, New Voy., I, 230, 1703. **Missisaguez.**—Bacqueville de la Potherie, Hist. Am., IV, 224, 1753. **Missisaguys.**—Charlevoix, Voy., II, 40, 1761. **Missisak.**—Jes. Rel. 1672, 33, 1858. **Missisakis.**—Bacqueville de la Potherie, Hist. Am., II, 48, 1753. **Missisaque.**—Clinton (1749) in N. Y. Doc. Col. Hist., VI, 484, 1855. **Missisaquees.**—Colden (1751), ibid., 742. **Missisaugas.**—Jones, Ojebway Inds., 208, 1861. **Missisaugas.**—Carver, Travels, 171, 1778. **Mississaga.**—Mt Johnson conf. (1755) in N. Y. Doc. Col. Hist., VI, 976, 1855. **Mississagets.**—Aigremont (1708), ibid., IX, 819, 1855. **Mississageyes.**—Mt Johnson conf. (1755), ibid., VI, 983, 1855. **Mississagez.**—Bacqueville de la Potherie, Hist. Am., IV, 245, 1753. **Mississagis.**—Schoolcraft, Ind. Tribes, V, 143, 1855. **Mississaguas.**—Official form in Can. Ind. Aff. **Mississague.**—Jes. Rel. 1670, 79, 1858. **Mississaguras.**—Beauchamp in Am. Antiq., IV, 329, 1882. **Mississakis.**—Du Chesneau (1681) in Margry, Déc., II, 267, 1877. **Mississaugas.**—Clinton (1749) in N. Y. Doc. Col. Hist., VI, 486, 1855. **Mississaugers.**—Macauley, N. Y., II, 250, 1829. **Mississauges.**—Carver, Travels, 19, 1778. **Mississaugies.**—Keane in Stanford, Compend., 522, 1878. **Mississaugues.**—Chauvignerie (1736) in Schoolcraft, Ind. Tribes, III, 555, 1853. **Mississguas.**—Macdonald in Can. Ind. Aff. 1883, xiii, 1884 (misprint). **Missitagues.**—Lahontan, New Voy., I, 215, 1703. **Mussisakies.**—McKenney and Hall, Ind. Tribes, III, 79, 1854. **Nation de Bois.**—Sagard (1636), Can., I, 190, 1866. **Naywaunaukau-raunuh.**—Macauley, N. Y., II, 180, 1829 (the name here seems to refer to the Missisauga). **Nua'ka'hn.**—Gatschet, Tuscarora MS., 1885 (Tuscarora name). **Oumisagai.**—Jes. Rel. 1640, 34, 1858. **Poils leué.**—Sagard (1636), Can., I, 192, 1866. **Sisaghroana.**—Post (1758) in Proud, Pa., II, app., 113, 1798 (same?). **Sissisaguez.**—Jefferys, French Dom., pt. I, 17, 1761. **Tisagechroann.**—Weiser (1748) in Rupp, West Pa., app., 16, 1846. **Twakanhahors.**—Macauley, N. Y., II, 250, 1829. **Wisagechroanu.**—Weiser (1748) in Schoolcraft, Ind. Tribes, IV, 605, 1854. **Zisagechroann.**—Weiser (1748) in Rupp, West Pa., app., 22, 1846. **Zisagechrohne.**—Zeisberger MS. (German, 1750) in Conover, Kan. and Geneva MS., B. A. E.

Mississauga. See *Massassauga.*

Mississinewa. A former important Miami village on the E side of the river of the same name, at its junction with the

Wabash, in Miami co., Ind. It was burned by the Americans in 1812, but was rebuilt. The reservation was sold in 1834.   (J M.)

Massasinaway.—Stickney (1812) in Am. State Papers, Ind. Aff., I, 810, 1832. Mississinaway.—Harrison (1814) in Drake, Tecumseh, 159, 1856. Mississinewa.—Mississinewa treaty (1826) in U. S. Ind. Treat., 496, 1873. Mississinewa Town.—Royce in 18th Rep. B. A. E., Indiana map, 1899.

Mississippi tablet. See *Notched plates*.

Missogkonnog. Probably a former village or band of the Nipmuc in central Massachusetts. In 1671 the colony of Plymouth raised a force against the " Missogkonnog Indians."—Eliot (1671) in Mass. Hist. Soc. Coll., 1st s., VI, 201, 1800.

Missouri ('great muddy,' referring to Missouri r.). A tribe of the Chiwere group of the Siouan family. Their name for themselves is Niútachi. According to Gale the early form of the word Missouri is Algonquian, of the Illinois dialect. The most closely allied tribes are the Iowa and the Oto. According to tradition, after having parted from the Winnebago at Green bay, the Iowa, Missouri, and Oto moved westward to Iowa r., where the Iowa stopped. The rest continued westward, reaching the Missouri at the mouth of Grand r. Here, on account of some dispute, the Oto withdrew and moved farther up Missouri r. Marquette's autograph map of 1673, which is perhaps the earliest authentic notice of the tribe, locates the 8emess8rit on Missouri r., apparently as far N. as the Platte. Joutel (1687) appears to have been the first writer to use the name Missouri in this form. It is stated that Tonti met the tribe a day and half's journey from the village of the Tamaroa, which was on the Mississippi, 6 leagues below Illinois r. About the beginning of the 18th century the French found them on the left bank of the Missouri, near the mouth of Grand r., and built a fort on an island near them. They continued to dwell in this locality until about 1800. According to Bourgmont (Margry, Déc., VI, 393, 1886) their village in 1723 was 30 leagues below Kansas r. and 60 leagues below the principal Kansa village. About 1798 they were conquered and dispersed by the Sauk and Fox tribes and their allies. Five or six lodges joined the Osage, two or three took refuge with the Kansa, and some amalgamated with the Oto, but they soon recovered, as in 1805 Lewis and Clark found them in villages s. of Platte r., having abandoned their settlements on Grand r. some time previously on account of smallpox. They were visited again by an epidemic in 1823. Although their number was estimated in 1702 at 200 families and in 1805 by Lewis and Clark at 300 souls, in 1829, when they were found with the Oto, they numbered

only 80. Having been unfortunate in a war with the Osage, part of them joined the Iowa, and the others went to the Oto previous to the migration of the latter to Big Platte r. In 1842 their village stood on the s. bank of Platte r., Nebr. They accompanied the Oto when that tribe removed in 1882 to Indian Territory. There were only 40 individuals of the tribe remaining in 1885. They are now officially classed with the Oto, together numbering 368 in 1905 under the Oto school superintendent in Oklahoma. The gentes, as given by Dorsey (15th Rep. B. A. E., 240,

GEORGE BATES—MISSOURI

1897), were Tunanpin (Black bear), Hotachi (Elk), and Cheghita (Eagle) or Wakanta (Thunder-bird).

The Missouri joined in the following treaties with the United States: (1) Peace treaty of June 24, 1817; (2) Ft Atkinson, Ia., Sept. 26, 1825, regulating trade and relations with the United States; (3) Prairie du Chien, Wis., July 15, 1830, ceding lands in Iowa and Missouri; (4) Oto village, Nebr., Sept. 21, 1833, ceding certain lands; (5) Bellevue, upper Missouri r., Oct. 15, 1836, ceding certain lands; (6) Washington, Mar. 15, 1854, ceding lands, with certain reservation; (7) Nebraska City, Nebr., Dec. 9, 1854, changing boundary of reservation.

Morgan (Beach, Ind. Miscel., 220, 1877) used the term Missouri Indians to in-

clude the Ponca, Omaha, Kansa, Quapaw, Iowa, Oto, and Missouri. These are the Southern tribes of Hale (Am. Antiq., v, 112, 1883), and the Dhegiha and Chiwere groups of J. O. Dorsey. (J. O. D. C. T.)
Emissourita.—Tonti (1684) in Margry, Déc., I, 595, 1876. **Massorites.**—Coxe, Carolana, 16, 1741. **Massorittes.**—Bacqueville de la Potherie, Hist. Am., II, map, 1753. **Massourites.**—Hennepin, New Discov., map, 1698. **Messorites.**—Ibid., 150. **Messouris.**—Coxe, Carolana, 19, 1741. **Misouris.**—Imlay, W. Ter. N. Am., 294, 1797. **Missiouris.**—Harris, Voy. and Trav., II, map, 1705. **Missoori.**—Jefferys, Am. Atlas, map, 1776. **Missounta.**—French, Hist. Col. La., I, 82, 1846. **Missouria.**—Irving, Ind. Sk., I, 96, 1835. **Missourians.**—Jefferys, Fr. Dom. Am., pt. I, 139, 1761. **Missouriens.**—Gass, Voy., 27, 1810. **Missouries.**—Lewis, Trav., 13, 1809. **Missouris.**—Joutel (1687) in Margry, Déc., III, 432, 1878. **Missourita.**—Margry, Déc., I, 611, 1876. **Missourite.**—Jefferys, Fr. Dom. Am., pt. I, 137, 1761. **Missoury.**—La Harpe (1720) in Margry, Déc., VI, 293, 1886. **Missourys.**—Jefferys, Am. Atlas, map, 5, 1776. **Missuri.**—D'Anville, Amér. Septen. map, 1756. **Missurier.**—Güssefeld, Charte von Nord America, 1797. **Missuris.**—Jefferys, Fr. Dom. Am., pt. I, map, 134, 1761. **Missurys.**—Croghan (1759) quoted by Rupp, W. Pa., 146, note, 1846. **Misuris.**—Barcia, Ensayo, 298, 1723. **Musscovi.**—Morse, N. Am., map, 1776 (misprint). **Ne-o-ge-he.**—Long Exped. Rocky Mts., I, 339, 1823. **Neojehe.**—Gallatin in Trans. Am. Antiq. Soc., II, 127, 1836. **Ne-o-ta-cha.**—Long, Exped. Rocky Mts., I, 339, 1823. **Ne-u-cha-ta.**—Hamilton in Trans. Neb. Hist. Soc., I, 48, 1885. **Ne-u-tach.**—Ibid., 47. **Neu-ta-che.**—Maximilian, Trav., 507, 1843 (trans., 'those that arrive at the mouth'). **New'-dar-cha.**—Lewis and Clark, Discov., 15. 1806. **Ne-yu-ta-ca.**—Hamilton in Trans. Neb. Hist. Soc., I, 47, 1885. **Nicúdje.**—Dorsey, Kansa MS. vocab., B. A. E., 1882 (Kansa name). **Ni-u'-t'a-tci.**—Dorsey in 15th Rep. B. A. E., 240, 1897 (own name, tc=ch). **Ni-út'-ati'.**—Dorsey, Çegiha MS. Dict., B. A. E., 1878 (Omaha and Ponca name). **Ouemessourit.**—Gale, Upper Miss., 209, 1867 (transliterated from Marquette). **8emess8rit.**—Marquette, map (1673) in Shea, Discov., 268, 1852. **Ou-missouri.**—Thevenot quoted by Shea, Discov., 268, 1852. **Waçuqǫa.**—Dorsey, inf'n, 1883 (Osage name.) **Wa-ju'-qdǫa.**—Dorsey, Kwapa MS. vocab., B. A. E., 1891 (Quapaw name). **Wemessouret.**—Marquette transliterated by Shea, Discov., 268, 1852.

Mistassin (from *mista-assini*, 'a great stone,' referring to a huge isolated rock in L. Mistassini, which the Indians regarded with veneration). An Algonquian tribe that lived on L. Mistassini, Quebec. They were divided by early writers into the Great and the Little Mistassin, the former living near the lake, the latter farther s. in the mountains. They first became known to the French about 1640, but were not visited by missionaries until some years later. They were attacked by the Iroquois in 1665, and in 1672 their country was formally taken possession of by the French with their consent. Although spoken of by Hind in 1863 as roving in bands with Montagnais and Nascapee over the interior of Labrador, it appears that in 1858 a portion of the tribe was on the lower St Lawrence.

Very little has been recorded in regard to their habits or characteristics. It is recorded that when attacked by the Iroquois in 1665 they had a wooden fort, which they defended successfully and with great bravery. Their only myth

mentioned is that in regard to the great rock in the lake, which they believed to be a manito. (J. M. C. T.)
Matassins.—Charlevoix (1721), Journal, I, letter xi, 276, 1761. **Mattassins.**—Barton, New Views, app., 12, 1798. **Misiassins (Petits).**—La Tour, map, 1779 (misprint; the Grands Mistassins are correctly named). **Misstassins.**—Report of 1858 in Hind, Lab. Penin., I, 12, 1863. **Mistapnis.**—McKenney and Hall, Ind. Tribes, III, 81, 1854. **Mistasiniouek.**—Jes. Rel. 1643, 38, 1858. **Mistasirenois.**—Memoir of 1706 in N. Y. Doc. Col. Hist., IX, 791, 1855. **Mistasirinins.**—Jes. Rel. 1672, 55, 1858. **Mistassini.**—Hind, Lab. Penin., I, 8, 1863. **Mistassinni.**—Ibid., 272. **Mistassins.**—Bellin, map, 1755 (Grands and Petits Mistassins). **Mistassirinins.**—Jes. Rel. 1672, 44, 1858. **Mistissinnys.**—Walch, map, 1805. **Mitchitamou.**—Jes. Rel. 1640, 34, 1858. **Müstassins.**—Jes. Rel. 1676–7, LX, 244, 1900.

Mistaughchewaugh. A former Chumashan village at San Marcos, 25 m. from Santa Barbara, Cal.—Father Timeno (1856) quoted by Taylor in Cal. Farmer, May 4, 1860.

Misun (*Mĭ'-sŭn*). A former Kuitsh village on lower Umpqua r., Oreg.—Dorsey in Jour. Am. Folk-lore, III, 231, 1890.

Mitaldejama. A former village, presumably Costanoan, connected with San Juan Bautista mission Cal.—Engelhardt, Franciscans in Cal., 398, 1897.

Mitcheroka ('knife'). A division of the Hidatsa.
Ma-etsi-daka.—Matthews, inf'n, 1885 (='small knives'). **Mit-che-ro'-ka.**—Morgan, Anc. Soc., 159, 1877.

Mithlausmintthai (*Mĭ-çlä'-us-mĭn-t'çai'*). A former Siuslaw village on Siuslaw r., Oreg.—Dorsey in Jour. Am. Folk-lore, III, 230, 1890.

Mitiling. See *Kalopaling*.

Mitline. A former village, presumably Costanoan, connected with Dolores mission, San Francisco, Cal.
Matalans.—Humboldt, Kingdom of New Spain, II, 345, 1811. **Mitliné.**—Taylor in Cal. Farmer, Oct. 18, 1861.

Mitlmetlelch (*Mĭ'tlmetle'ltc*). A Squawmish village community on Passage id., Howe sd., Brit. Col.—Hill-Tout in Rep. Brit. A. A. S., 474, 1900.

Mitomkai Pomo. A name, usually rendered Mtom'-kai (from *mato* 'big', *kai* 'valley'), applied to the inhabitants of Willits or Little Lake valley, Mendocino co., Cal. In the form Tomki it has been used by the whites to designate a creek E. of the range of mountains bordering Little Lake valley on the E. Most of the Mitomkai Pomo, locally known as Little Lakes, are now on Round Valley res., numbering, with the "Redwoods," 114 in 1905. (s. A. B.)
Betumki.—McKee (1851) in Sen. Ex. Doc. 4, 32d Cong., spec. sess., 146, 1853. **Bitomkhai.**—A. L. Kroeber, Univ. Cal. MS., 1903 (Upper Clear Lake form of name). **Little Lakes.**—Official form in Indian Affairs Reports. **Mi-toam' Kai Pó-mo.**—Powers in Cont. N. A. Ethnol., III, 155, 1877.

Mitrofania. A Kaniagmiut Eskimo village on Mitrofania id., s. of Chignik bay, Alaska; pop. 22 in 1880, 49 in 1890.—Petroff in 10th Census, Alaska, 28, 1884.

Mitsukwic. A former Nisqualli village "at the salmon trap on Squalli [Nisqualli] r.," Washington.—Gibbs, MS. No. 248, B. A. E.

Mittaubscut. A village of about 20 houses in 1676, situated on Pawtuxet r., 7 or 8 m. above its mouth, in Providence or Kent co., R. I. It probably belonged to the Narraganset, but its chief disputed their claim.—Williams (1676) in Mass. Hist. Soc. Coll., 3d s., I, 71, 1825.

Mittsulstik (*Mĭt-ts'ŭl'-stĭk*). A former Yaquina village on the N. side of Yaquina r., Oreg., at the site of the present Newport.—Dorsey in Jour. Am. Folk-lore, III, 229, 1890.

Mitutia. A village of the Cholovone, a division of the Yokuts, situated E. of lower San Joaquin r., Cal.—Pinart, Cholovone MS., B. A. E., 1880.

Miwok ('man'). One of the two divisions of the Moquelumnan family in central California, the other being the Olamentke. With a small exception in the W., the Miwok occupied territory bounded on the N. by Cosumnes r., on the E. by the ridge of the Sierra Nevada, on the s. by Fresno cr., and on the w. by San Joaquin r. The exception on the w. is a narrow strip of land on the E. bank of the San Joaquin, occupied by Yokuts Indians, beginning at the Tuolumne and extending northward to a point not far from the place where the San Joaquin bends to the w. The Miwok are said by Powers to be the largest "nation" in California, and a man of any of their tribes or settlements may travel from the Cosumnes to the Fresno and make himself understood without difficulty, so uniform is their language. See *Moquelumnan*. (J. C.)

Meewa.—Powers in Overland Monthly, X, 323, 1873. Meewie.—Ibid. Meewoc.—Ibid. Mewahs.—Ind. Aff. Rep. 1856, 244, 1857. Miook.—Kingsley, Standard Nat. Hist., VI, 175, 1885. Mi'-wa.—Powers in Cont. N. A. Ethnol., III, 347, 1877. Mi'-wi.—Ibid. Mi'-wok.—Ibid. Muwa.—Merriam in Science, N. S., XIX, 914, June 17, 1904.

Mixam, Mixanno. See *Mriksah*.

Mixed-bloods. To gauge accurately the amount of Indian blood in the veins of the white population of the American continent and to determine to what extent the surviving aborigines have in them the blood of their conquerors and supplanters is impossible in the absence of scientific data. But there is reason to believe that intermixture has been much more common than is generally assumed. The Eskimo of Greenland and the Danish traders and colonists have intermarried from the first, so that in the territory immediately under European supervision hardly any pure natives remain. The marriages (of Danish fathers and Eskimo mothers) have been very fertile and the children are in many respects an improvement on the aboriginal stock, in the matter of personal beauty in particular. According to Packard (Beach, Ind. Miscel., 69, 1877) the last full-blood Eskimo on Belle Isle str., Labrador, was in 1859 the wife of an Englishman at Salmon bay. The Labrador intermixture has been largely with fishermen from Newfoundland of English descent.

Some of the Algonquian tribes of Canada mingled considerably with the Europeans during the French period, both in the E. and toward the interior. In recent years certain French-Canadian writers have unsuccessfully sought to minimize this intermixture. In the Illinois-Missouri region these alliances were favored by the missionaries from the beginning of the 18th century. As early as 1693 a member of the La Salle expedition married the daughter of the chief of the Kaskaskia. Few French families in that part of the country are free from Indian blood. The establishment of trading posts at Detroit, Mackinaw, Duluth, etc., aided the fusion of races. The spread of the activities of the Hudson's Bay Company gave rise in the Canadian Northwest to a population of mixed-bloods of considerable historic importance, the offspring of Indian mothers and Scotch, French, and English fathers. Manitoba, at the time of its admission into the dominion, had some 10,000 mixed-bloods, one of whom, John Norquay, afterward became premier of the Provincial government. Some of the employees of the fur companies who had taken Indian wives saw their descendants flourish in Montreal and other urban centers. The tribes that have furnished the most mixed-bloods are the Cree and Chippewa, and next the Sioux, of N. W. Canada; the Chippewa, Ottawa, and related tribes of the great lakes; and about Green bay, the Menominee. Toward the Mississippi and beyond it were a few Dakota and Blackfoot mixed-bloods. Harvard (Rep. Smithson. Inst., 1879) estimated the total number in 1879 at 40,000. Of these about 22,000 were in United States territory and 18,000 in Canada. Of 15,000 persons of Canadian-French descent in Michigan few were probably free from Indian blood. Some of the French mixed-bloods wandered as far as the Pacific, establishing settlements of their own kind beyond the Rocky mts. The first wife of the noted ethnologist Schoolcraft was the daughter of an Irish gentleman by a Chippewa mother, another of whose daughters married an Episcopal clergyman, and a third a French-Canadian lumberer. Although some of the English colonies endeavored to promote the intermarriage of the two races, the only notable case in Virginia is that of Pocahontas (q. v.) and John Rolfe. The Athapascan and other tribes of the extreme N. W. have intermixed but little with the whites, though there are Russian mixed-bloods in Alaska. In British Columbia and the adjoining parts of the United States are to be found some mixed-bloods, the result of intermarriage of French traders and employees with native women. Some intermixture of captive white blood exists among the Apache, Comanche, Kiowa, and other raiding tribes along the Mexican and Texas border, the children seeming to inherit superior industry. The Pueblos, with the notable exception of the Lagunas, have not at all favored intermarriage with Europeans. The modern Siouan tribes have intermarried to some extent with white Americans, as some of them did in early days with the French of Canada. The Five Civilized Tribes of Oklahoma—Cherokee, Choctaw, Chickasaw, Creeks, and Seminole—have a large element of white blood, some through so-called squaw-men, some dating back to British and French traders before the Revolution. In the Cherokee Nation especially nearly all the leading men for a century have been more of white than of Indian blood, the noted John Ross himself being only one-eighth Indian. Mooney (19th Rep. B. A. E., 83, 1900) considers that much of the advance in civilization made by the Cherokee has been "due to the intermarriage among them of white men, chiefly traders of the ante-Revolutionary period, with a few Americans from the back settlements." Most of this white blood was of good Irish, Scotch, American, and German stock. Under the former laws of the Cherokee Nation anyone who could prove the smallest proportion of Cherokee blood was rated as Cherokee, including many of one-sixteenth, one-thirty-second, or less of Indian blood. In 1905 the Cherokee Nation numbered 36,782 citizens. Of these, about 7,000 were adopted whites, negroes, and Indians of other tribes, while of the rest probably not one-fourth are of even approximately pure Indian blood. Some of the smaller tribes removed from the E., as the Wyandot (Hurons) and Kaskaskia, have not now a single full-blood, and in some tribes, notably the Cherokee and Osage, the jealousies from this cause have led to the formation of rival full-blood and mixed-blood factions. During the Spanish domination in the s. E. Atlantic region intermixture perhaps took place, but not much; in Texas, however, intermarriage of whites and Indians was common. The peoples of Iroquoian stock have a large admixture of white blood, French and English,

both from captives taken during the wars of the 17th and 18th centuries and by the process of adoption, much favored by them. Such intermixture contains more of the combination of white mother and Indian father than is generally the case. Some English-Iroquois intermixture is still in process in Ontario. The Iroquois of St Regis, Caughnawaga, and other agencies can hardly boast an Indian of pure blood. According to the Almanach Iroquois for 1900, the blood of Eunice Williams, captured at Deerfield, Mass., in 1704, and adopted and married within the tribe, flows in the veins of 125 descendants at Caughnawaga; Silas Rice, captured at Marlboro, Mass., in 1703, has 1,350 descendants; Jacob Hill and John Stacey, captured near Albany in 1755, have, respectively, 1,100 and 400 descendants. Similar cases are found among the New York Iroquois. Dr Boas (Pop. Sci. Mo., XLV, 1894) has made an anthropometric study of the mixed-bloods, covering a large amount of data, especially concerning the Sioux and the eastern Chippewa. The total numbers investigated were 647 men and 408 women. As compared with the Indian, the mixed-blood, so far as investigations have shown, is taller, men exhibiting greater divergence than women.

A large proportion of negro blood exists in many tribes, particularly in those formerly residing in the Gulf states, and among the remnants scattered along the Atlantic coast from Massachusetts southward. The Five Civilized Tribes of Oklahoma, having been slaveholders and surrounded by Southern influences, generally sided with the South in the Civil war. On being again received into friendly relations with the Government they were compelled by treaty to free their slaves and admit them to equal Indian citizenship. In 1905 there were 20,619 of these adopted negro citizens in these five tribes, besides all degrees of admixture in such proportions that the census takers are frequently unable to discriminate. The Cherokee as a body have refused to intermarry with their negro citizens, but among the Creeks and the Seminole intermarriage has been very great. The Pamunkey, Chickahominy, Marshpee, Narraganset, and Gay Head remnants have much negro blood, and conversely there is no doubt that many of the broken coast tribes have been completely absorbed into the negro race. See *Croatan Indians, Métis, Popular fallacies.*   (A. F. C.   J. M.)

Mixed Senecas and Shawnees. The former official designation of the mixed band of Mingo (Seneca) and Shawnee who removed from Lewistown, Ohio, to the W. about 1833 (see *Mingo*). By treaty of 1867 the union was dissolved, the Seneca joining the band known as "Seneca of Sandusky," and the Shawnee becoming a distinct body under the name of "Eastern Shawnee." Both tribes were assigned reservations in the present Oklahoma, where they still reside, numbering 101 and 366 respectively in 1905. (J. M.)

Mixed Shoshones. Mixed bands of Bannock and Tukuarika.—U. S. Stat., XVIII, 158, 1875.

M'ketashshekakah (*Ma'katawĭmĕshĭkä-'käᵃ*, 'big black chest,' referring to the pigeonhawk.—W. J.) The Thunder gens of the Potawatomi, Sauk, and Foxes, q. v.
Ma'katawimeshikakaᵃ.—Wm. Jones, inf'n. 1906. M'-ke-tash'-she-kä-kah'.—Morgan, Anc. Soc., 167, 1877.

M'ko (*Ma'kwa*, 'bear'). A gens of the Potawatomi, q. v.
Ma''kwa.—Wm. Jones, inf'n, 1906. M'-ko'.—Morgan, Anc. Soc., 167, 1877.

M'kwa (*Ma'kwa*, 'bear'). A gens of the Shawnee, q. v.
Ma''kwa.—Wm. Jones, inf'n, 1906. M'-kwa'.—Morgan, Anc. Soc., 168, 1877.

Moache. A division of the Ute, formerly roaming over s. Colorado and N. New Mexico. In 1871 they were reported to number 645; in 1903 the combined Capote, Moache, and Wiminuche on Southern Ute res. numbered 955. The name "Taos Utes" was formerly applied to those Ute who temporarily encamped in considerable numbers about Taos pueblo, N. Mex. As these were doubtless largely Moache, their synonyms are included here, although the Capote, Tabeguache, and Wiminuche were evidently also a part of them. See *Ute*.

The Moache joined with other Ute bands in the treaty of Washington, Mar. 2, 1868, affirming the treaty of Oct. 7, 1863, with the Tabeguache and defining the boundaries of their reservation.
Maquache Utes.—Taylor in Sen. Ex. Doc. 4, 40th Cong., spec. sess., 10, 1867. Maquahache.—Dole in Ind Aff. Rep. 1864, 18, 1865. Maquoche Utahs.—Davis, ibid., 135, 1866. Menaches.—Graves, ibid., 386, 1854. Moguachis.—Villa-Señor, Theatro Am., pt. 2, 413, 1748. Mohuache.—Merriwether in Ind. Aff. Rep. 1855, 186, 1856. Mohuache Utahs.—Meriwether in Sen. Ex. Doc. 69, 34th Cong., 1st sess., 15, 1856. Mohuache Utes.—Bancroft, Ariz. and N. Mex., 665, 1889. Mohuhaches.—Bell, New Tracks in N. Am., I, 108, 1869. Moquaches.—Archuleta in Ind. Aff. Rep., 142, 1866. Mouuache Utes.—Colyer, ibid., 1871, 191, 1872. Muache.—Ute treaty (1868) in U. S. Ind. Treaties, Kappler ed., II, 990, 1904. Muahuaches.—Carson in Ind. Aff. Rep. 1859, 342, 1860. Muares.—Orozco y Berra, Geog., 59, 1864 (probably identical, although given as part of Faraon Apache). Taos.—Wilson (1849) in Cal. Mess. and Corresp., 185, 1850. Taos Indians.—Cummings in Ind. Aff. Rep., 160, 1866 (identified with Moache). Taos Yutas.—Farnham, Trav. Californias, 371, 1844. Tao Yutas.—Farnham misquoted by Bancroft, Nat. Races, I, 465, 1882. Tash-Yuta.—Burton, City of Saints, 578, 1861.

Moah (*Máhwäwᵃ*, 'wolf'). A gens of the Potawatomi, q. v.
Máhwäwᵃ.—Wm. Jones, inf'n, 1906. Mo-äh'.—Morgan, Anc. Soc., 167, 1877.

Moanahonga ('great walker'). An Iowa warrior, known to the whites as Big Neck, and called also by his people Winaugusconey ('Man not afraid to travel'), because he was wont to take long trips alone, relying on his own prowess and prodigious strength. While he was of lowly birth he was exceedingly ambitious and contended for the honors and dignity for which his courage and address fitted him, but which his fellow tribesmen were loth to accord, wherefore he built a lodge apart from the rest and collected about him a band of admirers over whom he exercised the authority of chief. Gen. Clark induced him and Mahaskah to go to Washington in 1824 and there sign a treaty that purported to convey to the United States for an annual payment of $500 for 10 years the title of all the lands of the Iowa lying within the borders of Missouri. He did not understand the treaty, and after white settlers had taken possession of a considerable part of the Indian lands he set out in 1829 to visit St Louis for the purpose of making complaint to Gen. Clark. A party of whites encountered his company of 60 men, made them all intoxicated, and decamped with their horses, blankets, and provisions. When they recovered from their stupor one of them shot a hog to satisfy their hunger. This provoked the anger of the settlers, 60 of whom rode up and commanded the Indians to leave the country. Moanahonga then withdrew his camp about 15 m. beyond the state boundary, as he supposed. When the white party followed him he went out to meet them with his pipe in his mouth in sign of peace. As he extended his hand in greeting the borderers fired, killing his brother at his side, and an infant. The Indians flew to their arms and, inspired anew by the call for vengeance of Moanahonga's sister, who was shot in the second volley, they drove the whites from the field, although these exceeded their fighting men two to one. The man who shot his sister Moanahonga burned at the stake. The U. S. troops were ordered out, and obtaining hostages from the Iowa returned to their barracks. Moanahonga and several others of his band were arrested and tried on a charge of murder, but were acquitted. He cultivated friendly relations with the whites after this, but always went with blackened face in sign of mourning, because, as he said, he had sold the bones of his ancestors. About 5 years afterward he fell in combat with a Sioux chief. See McKenney and Hall, Ind. Tribes, I, 177–183, 1858.

Moapariats (*Mo-a-pa-ri'-ats*, 'mosquito creek people'). A band of Paiute formerly living in or near Moapa valley,

s. e. Nev., and numbering 64 in 1873.—
Powell in Ind. Aff. Rep. 1873, 50, 1874.

Mobile (meaning doubtful). A Muskhogean tribe whose early home was probably Mauvila, or Mavilla, supposed to
have been at or near Choctaw Bluff on
Alabama r., Clark co., Ala., where De
Soto, in 1540, met with fierce opposition
on the part of the natives and engaged in
the most obstinate contest of the expedition. The town was then under the control of Tascalusa (q. v.) probably an Alibamu chief. If, as is probable, the Mobilian tribe took part in this contest, they
must later have moved farther s., as they
were found on Mobile bay when the
French began to plant a colony at that
point about the year 1700. Wishing protection from their enemies, they obtained
permission from the French, about 1708,
to settle near Ft Louis, where space was
allotted them and the Tohome for this
purpose. Little is known of the history
of the tribe. In 1708 a large body of
Alibamu, Cherokee, Abihka, and Catawba warriors descended Mobile r. for
the purpose of attacking the French and
their Indian allies, but for some unknown
reason contented themselves with destroying a few huts of the Mobilians.
The latter, who were always friendly to
the French, appear to have been christianized soon after the French settled
there. In 1741 Coxe wrote that the chief
city of the once great province of Tasca-
luza, "Mouvilla, which the English call
Maubela, and the French Mobile, is yet
in being, tho' far short of its former
grandeur." At this date the Mobilians
and Tohome together numbered 350 families. Mention is made in the Mobile
church registers of individual members
of the tribe as late as 1761, after which
they are lost to history as a tribe. For
subsistence they relied almost wholly on
agriculture. Clay images of men and
women and also of animals, supposed to
be objects of worship by this people, were
found by the French.

The so-called Mobilian trade language
was a corrupted Choctaw jargon used for
the purposes of intertribal communication among all the tribes from Florida
to Louisiana, extending northward on the
Mississippi to about the junction of the
Ohio. It was also known as the Chickasaw trade language. (A. S. G. C. T.)

Mobile.—Ranjel quoted by Halbert in Trans. Ala.
Hist. Soc., III, 68, 1899. Manilla.—Harris, Voy. and
Trav., I, 808, 1705 (misprint). Maouila.—La Salle
(ca. 1682) in Margry, Déc., II, 197, 1877. Maubela.—
Coxe, Carolana, 25, 1741. Maubila.—French, Hist.
Coll. La., II, 247, 1875. Maubile.—Ibid., III, 192,
1851. Maubileans.—Ibid., 170. Maubilians.—Charlevoix, Nouv. France, II, 273, 1761. Mauvila.—Garcilasso de la Vega (1540), Fla., 146, 1723. Mauvil-
ians.—French, Hist. Coll. La., III, 192, 1852. Mauvil-
iens.—Charlevoix, Nouv. France, II, 308, 1761.
Mavila.—Biedma (1544) in French, Hist. Coll. La.,
II, 102, 1850. Mavilians.—Schoolcraft, Ind. Tribes,

II, 34, 1852. Mavilla.—Gentleman of Elvas (1557)
in French, Hist. Coll. La., II, 156, 1850. Mobeluns.—
Boudinot, Star in the West, 127, 1816 (or Mouville).
Mobilas.—Barcia, Ensayo, 313, 1723. Mobile.—Pé-
nicaut (1699) in French, Hist. Coll. La., n. s., I,
43, 1869. Mobileans.—La Harpe, ibid., III, 20, 34,
1851. Mobilians.—Jefferys, French Dom. Am., I,
165, 1761. Mobiliens.—Pénicaut (1702) in Margry,
Déc., V, 425, 1883. Mouvill.—Le Page du Pratz,
Hist. La., Eng. ed., 309, 1774. Mouvilla.—Coxe,
Carolana, 24, 1741. Mouville.—Boudinot, Star in the
West, 127, 1816 (or Mobeluns). Movila.—Barcia,
Ensayo, 335, 1723. Movill.—Barton, New Views,
lxix, 1798. Mowill.—Jefferys, French Dom. Am.,
I, 162, 1761.

Mocama ('on the coast'). A former
Timucua district and dialect, probably
about the present St Augustine, Fla.
Mocama.—Pareja (ca. 1614) quoted by Gatschet in
Am. Philos. Soc. Proc., XVI, 627, 1877. Moscama.—
Brinton, Floridian Penin., 135, 1859.

Moccasin. The soft skin shoe of the
North American Indians and its imitations on the part of the whites. The word,
spelled formerly also *moccason*, is derived
from one of the eastern Algonquian dialects: Powhatan (Strachey, 1612), *mock-
asin, mawhcasun;* Massachuset (Eliot, ante
1660), *mohkisson, mohkussin;* Narraganset
(Williams, 1643), *mocussin;* Micmac,
m'cusun; Chippewa, *makisin.* It came into
English through Powhatan in all probability, as well as through Massachuset.
The latter dialect has also *mokus* or *mokis,*
of which the longer word seems to be a
derivative. Hewitt suggests that it is
cognate with *makak,* 'small case or box'
(see *Mocuck*). After the moccasin have
been named moccasin-fish (Maryland
sunfish), moccasin-flower or moccasin-
plant (lady's-slipper, known also as Indian's shoe), moccasin-snake or water-
moccasin (*Ancistrodon piscivorus*), the upland moccasin (*A. atrofuscus*). In some
parts of the South the term 'moccasined'
is in colloquial use in the sense of intoxicated. (A. F. C.)

With the exception of the sandal-
wearing Indians living in the states along
the Mexican boundary, moccasins were
almost universally worn. The tribes of
s. e. Texas were known to the southern
Plains Indians as "Barefoot Indians,"
because they generally went without foot-
covering, only occasionally wearing sandals. The Pacific coast Indians also as
a rule went barefoot, and among most
tribes women did not customarily wear
moccasins. There are two general types
of moccasins—those with a rawhide sole
sewed to a leather upper, and those with
sole and upper consisting of one piece of
soft leather with a seam at the instep and
heel. The former belongs to the Eastern
or timber tribes, the latter to the Western
or plains Indians. The Eskimo have soled
footwear. The chief causes influencing
this distribution are the presence or absence of animals furnishing thick rawhide,
the character of trails and travel, and tribal
usages. The boot or legging moccasin,

worn from Alaska to Arizona and New Mexico, is still commonly a part of the woman's costume, and among most of the Pueblos the legging portion is a white-tanned deerskin to which the moccasin is attached, the skin being wrapped neatly and methodically around the calf of the leg and secured by means of a cord. Differences in cut, color, decoration, toe-piece, inset-tongue, vamp, heel-fringe, ankle-flaps, etc., show tribal and environmental characters and afford means of identification. Among the Plains tribes the decoration of moccasins presents a wide range of symbolism, and since this part of the costume has been less modified by contact with whites than other garments, it affords valuable material for the study of symbolic art.

The materials used in making moccasins are tanned skins of the larger mammals, rawhide for soles, and sinew for sewing. Dyes, pigments, quills, beads, cloth, buttons, and fur are applied to the moccasin as decoration. Many tribes make moccasins to be specially worn in ceremonies, and a number of tribes also employ their footwear in a guessing game known as the "moccasin game."

Great ingenuity was often displayed in cutting moccasins from a single piece of dressed hide, the most complicated pattern being found among the Klamath. The northern Athapascan pattern has a T-shaped seam at the toe and heel, while in the Nez Percé type the seam is along one side of the foot from the great toe to the heel. In the moccasin of the Plains Indians the upper is in one piece and is sewed to a rawhide sole. Consult Dixon in Bull. Am. Mus. Nat. Hist., XVII, pt. 3, 1905; Gerard in Am. Anthrop., IX, no. 1, 1907; Goddard in Univ. of Cal. Pub., Am. Archæol. and Ethnol., I, 1903; Kroeber in Bull. Am. Mus. Nat. Hist., XVIII, pt. 1, 1904; Mason (1) in Smithson. Rep. 1886, pt. 1, 205–238, 1889, (2) in Rep. Nat. Mus. 1894, 239–593, 1896; Morgan, League Iroquois, II, 1904; Shufeldt in Proc. Nat. Mus. 1888, 59–66, 1889; Stephen in Proc. Nat. Mus. 1888, 131–136, 1889; Willoughby in Am. Anthrop., IX, no. 1, 1907; Wissler in Trans. 13th Internat. Cong. Am., 1905. (W. H.)

Mochgonnekonck. A village on Long Island, N. Y., in 1643, probably near the present Manhasset.—Doc. of 1643 in N. Y. Doc. Col. Hist., XIV, 60, 1883.

Mochicaui (*mochic* 'tortoise', *cahui* 'hill': 'hill of the tortoise,' in allusion to the shape of a hill in the vicinity of the settlement.—Buelna). The principal settlement of the Zuaque, who speak or spoke the Tehueco and Vacoregue dialects of Cahita; situated on the E. bank of Rio Fuerte, about lat. 26° 10′, N. w. Sinaloa, Mexico. The settlement is now civilized.

Mochicahuy.—Orozco y Berra, Geog., 332, 1864. Mochicaui.—Ribas (1645) in Bancroft, Nat. Races, I, 608, 1882. Mochicohuy.—Ibid., map. Motschicahuz.—Kino, map (1702) in Stöcklein, Neue Welt-Bott, 1726.

Mochilagua. An Opata pueblo visited by Coronado in 1540; situated in the valley of the Rio Sonora, N. w. Mexico, doubtless in the vicinity of Arizpe. Possibly identical with one of the villages later known by another name.

Mochila.—Castañeda (*ca.* 1565) in Ternaux-Compans, Voy., IX, 158, 1838 (misprint). Mochilagua.—Castañeda in 14th Rep. B. A. E., 515, 1896.

Mocho (*El Mocho*, Span.: 'the cropped, shorn, mutilated', so called because he had lost an ear in a fight). An Apache, celebrated in manuscript narratives pertaining to Texas in the 18th century. He was captured by the Tonkawa, but because of his eloquence and prowess was elevated to the chiefship of that tribe on the death of its leader during an epidemic in 1777 or 1778. With the Spaniards El Mocho had a bad reputation. When he became chief the governor connived to get rid of him, to effect which Mezières bribed his rivals to allure him to the highway leading to Natchitoches, under the promise of presents when he should arrive there, and murder him, but this plot failed, and Mezières and the governor were obliged to conciliate him. Finally, in 1784, at the instigation of the government, he was killed. (H. E. B.)

Mochopa. An Opata pueblo of Sonora, Mexico, and the seat of a Spanish mission founded between 1678 and 1730, at which latter date the population had become reduced to 24. It was abandoned between 1764 and 1800, owing to Apache depredations.

Machopo.—Davila, Sonora Histórico, 317, 1894. Mochop.—Hamilton, Mexican Handbook, 47, 1883. Mochopa.—Orozco y Berra, Geog., 343, 1864. S. Ignacio Mochopa.—Sonora materiales (1730) quoted by Bancroft, No. Mex. States, I, 514, 1884.

Mocock. See *Mocuck.*

Moctobi. A small tribe formerly residing in s. Mississippi. They are mentioned by Iberville, in 1699, as living at that time on Pascagoula r., near the Gulf coast, associated with the Biloxi and Paskagula, each tribe having its own village (Margry, Déc., IV, 195, 1880). Sauvole, who was at Ft Biloxi in 1699–1700, speaks of the "villages of the Pascoboulas, Biloxi, and Moctobi, which together contain not more than 20 cabins." Nothing is known respecting their language, nor has anything more been ascertained in regard to their history, but from their intimate relations with the Biloxi it is probable they belonged to the same (Siouan) linguistic stock. The name Moctobi appears to have disappeared from Indian memory and tradition, as repeated inquiry among the Choctaw and Caddo has failed to elicit any knowledge of such a tribe. What seems to be a justifiable supposition, in the absence of further knowledge, is that the three or four small bands were the remnants of a larger tribe or of tribes which, while making their way southward, had been reduced by war, pestilence, or other calamity, and had been compelled to consolidate and take refuge under the Choctaw. Consult Mooney, Siouan Tribes of the East, Bull. B. A. E., 1894. See *Capinans*.

Moctobi.—Sauvole (1700) in Margry, Déc., IV, 451, 1880. **Moctoby.**—Iberville (1699), ibid., 195. **Moelobites.**—Gayarré, La., 66, 1851. **Mouloubis.**—Iberville (1699) in French, Hist. Coll. La., II, 99, 1875.

Mocuck. Defined by Bartlett (Dict. of Americanisms, 399, 1877) as "a term applied to the box of birch bark in which sugar is kept by the Chippewa Indians." In the forms *makak, mocock, mocuck, mowkowk, mukuk*, the word is known to the literature of the settlement of Canada and the W. in the early years of the 19th century, and is now in use among the English-speaking people of the maple-sugar region about the great lakes, and among the Canadian French as *macaque*. A trader in Minnesota in 1820 (cited by Jenks in 19th Rep. B. A. E., 1103, 1900) speaks of "a mocock of sugar, weighing about 40 pounds." The word is derived from *mă'kaʿk*, which in the Chippewa and closely related Algonquian dialects signifies a bag, box, or other like receptacle of birch-bark.   (A. F. C.)

Modoc (from *Móatokni*, 'southerners'). A Lutuamian tribe, forming the southern division of that stock, in s. w. Oregon. The Modoc language is practically the same as the Klamath, the dialectic differences being extremely slight. This linguistic identity would indicate that the local separation of the two tribes must have been comparatively recent and has never been complete. The former habitat of the Modoc included Little Klamath lake, Modoc lake, Tule lake, Lost River valley, and Clear lake, and extended at times as far E. as Goose lake. The most important bands of the tribe were at Little Klamath lake, Tule lake, and in the valley of Lost r. Frequent conflicts with white immigrants, in which both sides were guilty of many atrocities, have given the tribe an unfortunate reputation. In 1864 the Modoc joined the Klamath in ceding their territory to the United States and removed to Klamath res. They seem never to have been contented, however, and made persistent efforts to return and occupy their former lands on Lost r. and its vicinity. In 1870 a prominent chief named Kintpuash (q. v.), commonly known to history as Captain Jack, led the more turbulent portion of the tribe back to the California border and obstinately refused to return to the reservation. The first attempt to bring back the runaways by force brought on the Modoc war of 1872–73. After some

struggles Kintpuash and his band retreated to the lava-beds on the California frontier, and from Jan. to Apr., 1873,

CHIKCHIKAM LUPATKUELATKO ("SCAR-FACED CHARLEY")—MODOC

successfully resisted the attempts of the troops to dislodge them. The progress of the war had been slow until April of

WINEMA (TOBY RIDDLE)—MODOC

that year, when two of the peace commissioners, who had been sent to treat with the renegades, were treacherously assassinated. In this act Kintpuash played the chief part. The campaign was then pushed with vigor, the Modoc were finally dispersed and captured, and Kintpuash and 5 other leaders were hanged at Ft Klamath in Oct., 1873. The tribe was then divided, a part being sent to Indian Ter. and placed on the Quapaw res., where they had diminished to 56 by 1905. The remainder are on Klamath res., where they are apparently thriving, and numbered 223 in 1905.

The following were the Modoc settlements so far as known: Agawesh, Chakawech, Kalelk, Kawa, Keshlakchuish, Keuchishkeni, Kumbatuash, Leush, Nakoshkeni, Nushaltkagakni, Pashka, Plaikni, Shapashkeni, Sputuishkeni, Stuikishkeni, Waisha, Wachamshwash, Welwashkeni, Wukakeni, Yaneks, and Yulalona. (L. F.)

Aígspaluma.—Gatschet in Cont. N. A. Ethnol., II, pt. I, xxxiii, 1890 (Sahaptin name for all Indians on Klamath res. and vicinity). La-la-cas.—Meacham, Wigwam and War-path, 291, 1875 (original name). Lutmáwi.—Gatschet, op. cit., xxxiv (name given by a part of the Pit River Indians). Lutuam.—Gatschet in Mag. Am. Hist., I, 165, 1877. Lutuami.—Curtin, Ilmawi MS. vocab., B. A. E., 1889 (Ilmawi name). Madoc.—Ind. Aff. Rep. 1867, 71, 1868. Man'-ʠa.—Dorsey, Kwapa MS. vocab., B. A. E., 1891 (Quapaw name). Moadoc.—Ind. Aff. Rep. 1864, 11, 1865. Moahtockna.—Taylor in Cal. Farmer, June 22, 1860. Móatakish.—Gatschet in Cont. N. A. Ethnol., II, pt. II, 216, 1890 (variation of Mō'dokish). Móatokgĭsh.—Ibid. Móatokni.—Ibid. (own name). Modanks.—Wright (1853) in H. R. Ex. Doc. 76, 34th Cong., 3d sess., 28, 1857. Modoc.—Palmer in Ind. Aff. Rep., 471, 1854. Mo-docks.—Ibid., 470. Modoes.—Taylor in Cal. Farmer, June 22, 1860 (misprint). Modok.—Powers in Cont. N. A. Ethnol., III, 252, 1877. Mō'dokish.—Gatschet in Cont. N. A. Ethnol., II, pt. II, 216, 1890. Mō'dokni.—Ibid. (own name). Modook.—Ind. Aff. Rep., 221, 1861. Mówatak.—Gatschet in Cont. N. A. Ethnol., II, pt. I, xxxiv, 1890 (Sahaptin name). Mû'atokni.—Ibid., pt. 2, 216. Plaíkni.—Ibid., pt. 1, xxxv (collective for Modoc, Klamath, and Snakes on Sprague r.). Pχánai.—Ibid. (Yreka Shasta name). Saidoka.—Ibid. (Shoshoni name).

Moenkapi ('place of the running water'). A small settlement about 40 m. N. W. of Oraibi, N. E. Ariz., occupied during the farming season by the Hopi. The present village, which consists of two irregular rows of one-story houses, was built over the remains of an older settlement—apparently the Rancheria de los Gandules seen by Oñate in 1604. Moenkapi is said to have been founded within the memory of some of the Mormon pioneers at the neighboring town of Tuba City, named after an old Oraibi chief. It was the headquarters of a large milling enterprise of the Mormons a number of years ago. (F. W. H.)

Concabe.—Garcés (1775–76) quoted by Bancroft, Ariz. and N. Mex., 137, 395, 1889. Moencapi.—Coues, Garcés Diary, 393, 1900. Moen-kopi.—Mindeleff in 8th Rep. B. A. E., 14, 1891. Moqui concave.—Ibid. Moyencopi.—Bourke, Moquis of Arizona, 229, 1884. Muabe.—Ibid. Müenkapi.—Voth, Trad. of the Hopi, 22, 1905 (correct Hopi form). Munqui-concabe.—Garcés (1776), Diary, 393, 1900. Muqui concabe.—Ibid., 394–395 (Yavapai form). Rancheria de los Gandules.—Oñate (1604) in Doc. Inéd., XVI, 276, 1871 (apparently identical).

Mogg. An Abnaki chief. He had long been sachem of the Norridgewock and had been converted to Christianity by Père Râle when the English settlers in Maine, in order to make good their title to territory which the Abnaki declared they had not parted with, began a series of attacks in 1722. Col. Westbrook in the first expedition found the village deserted and burned it. In 1724 the English surprised the Indians. The killing of Râle and many of the Indians, the desecration of the church, etc., left a blot on the honor of the colonists (Drake, Bk. Inds., 312, 1880). In the fight fell Mogg and other noted warriors. Whittier's poem "Mogg Megone" recounts the story. See *Missions*. (A. F. C.)

Mogollon (from the mesa and mountains of the same name in New Mexico and Arizona, which in turn were named in honor of Juan Ignacio Flores Mogollon, governor of New Mexico in 1712–15). A subdivision of the Apache that formerly ranged over the Mogollon mesa and mts. in W. New Mexico and E. Arizona (Ind. Aff. Rep., 380, 1854). They were associated with the Mimbreños at the Southern Apache agency, N. Mex., in 1868, and at Hot Springs agency in 1875, and are now under the Ft Apache and San Carlos res., Ariz. They are no longer officially recognized as Mogollones, and their number is not separately reported. (F. W. H.)

Be-ga'-kŏl-kizjn.—ten Kate, Synonymie, 5, 1884. Mogall.—Ind. Aff. Rep. 1867, 12, 1868. Mogallones.—Browne, Apache Country, 290, 1869. Mogogones.—Ind. Aff. Rep., 380, 1854. Mogoll.—Ibid., 1867, 193, 1868. Mogollon.—Ibid., 1857, 289, 1858. Mogollone.—Ibid., 1858, 206. Mogoyones.—Ibid., 1856, 181, 1857.

Mohanet. An Indian settlement of the colony of Pennsylvania, on the E. branch of the Susquehanna, probably Iroquois.—Alcedo, Dic. Geog., III, 225, 1788.

Moharala (*Mo-har-ä'-lä*, 'big bird'). A subdivision or clan of the Delawares.—Morgan, Anc. Soc., 172, 1877.

Mohave (from *hamok* 'three', *avi* 'mountain'). The most populous and warlike of the Yuman tribes. Since known to history they appear to have lived on both sides of the Rio Colorado, though chiefly on the E. side, between the Needles (whence their name is derived) and the entrance to Black canyon. Ives, in 1857, found only a few scattered families in Cottonwood valley, the bulk of their number being below Hardyville. In recent times a body of Chemehuevi have held the river between them and their kinsmen the Yuma. The Mohave are strong, athletic, and well developed, their women attractive; in fact, Ives characterized them as fine a people physically as any he had ever seen. They are famed for the artistic painting of their bodies. Tattooing was universal, but

confined to small areas on the skin.
According to Kroeber (Am. Anthrop., IV,
284, 1902) their art in recent times consists chiefly of crude painted decorations

MOHAVE MAN. (AM. MUS. NAT. HIST.)

on their pottery. Though a river tribe,
the Mohave made no canoes, but when
necessary had recourse to rafts, or balsas,
made of bundles of reeds. They had no
large settlements, their dwellings being
scattered. These were four-sided and
low, with four supporting posts at the
center. The walls, which were only 2
or 3 ft high, and the almost flat roof were
formed of brush covered with sand.
Their granaries were upright cylindrical
structures with flat roofs. The Mohave hunted but little, their chief reliance for food being on the cultivated
products of the soil, as corn, pumpkins,
melons, beans, and a small amount of
wheat, to which they added mesquite
beans, mescrew, piñon nuts, and fish to
a limited extent. They did not practise
irrigation, but relied on the inundation
of the bottom lands to supply the needed
moisture, hence when there was no over-
flow their crops failed. Articles of skin
and bone were very little used, materials
such as the inner bark of the willow,
vegetable fiber, etc., taking their place.
Pottery was manufactured. Baskets were
in common use, but were obtained from
other tribes.

According to Kroeber, "there is no full
gentile system, but something closely akin
to it, which may be called either an in-
cipient or a decadent clan system. Certain men, and all their ancestors and

descendants in the male line, have only
one name for all their female relatives.
Thus, if the female name hereditary in
my family be Maha, my father's sister,
my own sisters, my daughters (no matter
how great their number), and my son's
daughters, will all be called Maha. There
are about twenty such women's names,
or virtual gentes, among the Mohave.
None of these names seems to have any
signification. But according to the myths
of the tribe, certain numbers of men
originally had, or were given, such names
as Sun, Moon, Tobacco, Fire, Cloud, Coyote, Deer, Wind, Beaver, Owl, and others,
which correspond exactly to totemic clan
names; then these men were instructed
by Mastamho, the chief mythological
being, to call all their daughters and
female descendants in the male line by
certain names, corresponding to these
clan names. Thus the male ancestors of
all the women who at present bear the
name Hipa, are believed to have been
originally named Coyote. It is also said
that all those with one name formerly
lived in one area, and were all considered
related. This, however, is not the case
now, nor does it seem to have been so
within recent historic times." Bourke
(Jour. Am. Folk-lore, II, 181, 1889) has
recorded some of these names, called by
him gentes, and the totemic name to
which each corresponds, as follows: Hualga (Moon), O-cha (Rain-cloud), Ma-ha
(Caterpillar), Nol-cha (Sun), Hipa (Coy-

MOHAVE WOMAN. (AM. MUS. NAT. HIST.)

ote), Va-had-ha (Tobacco), Shul-ya
(Beaver), Kot-ta (Mescal or Tobacco),
Ti-hil-ya (Mescal), Vi-ma-ga (a green
plant, not identified), Ku-mad-ha (Oca-

tilla or Iron Cactus), Ma-li-ka (unknown), Mus (Mesquite), Ma-si-pa (Coyote).

The tribal organization was loose, though, as a whole, the Mohave remained quite distinct from other tribes. The chieftainship was hereditary in the male line. Their dead were cremated. The population of the tribe in 1775–76 was conservatively estimated by Garcés (Diary, 443, 1900) at 3,000, and by Leroux, about 1834 (Whipple, Pac. R. R. Rep., III, 1856), to be 4,000; but the latter is probably an overestimate. Their number in 1905 was officially given as 1,589, of whom 508 were under the Colorado River school superintendent, 856 under the Ft Mohave

MOHAVE FAMILY GROUP

school superintendent, 50 under the San Carlos agency, and about 175 at Camp McDowell, on the Rio Verde. Those at the latter two points, however, are apparently Yavapai, commonly known as Apache Mohave.

No treaty was made with the Mohave respecting their original territory, the United States assuming title thereto. By act of Mar. 3, 1865, supplemented by Executive orders of Nov. 22, 1873, Nov. 16, 1874, and May 15, 1876, the present Colorado River res., Ariz., occupied by Mohave, Chemehuevi, and Kawia, was established.

Pasion, San Pedro, and Santa Isabel have been mentioned as rancherias of the Mohave.   (H. W. H.   F. W. H.)

Amacabos.—Zarate-Salmeron (ca. 1629), Relacion, in Land of Sunshine, 105, Jan. 1900. Amacava.—Ibid., 48, Dec. 1899. A-mac-há-vès.—Whipple in Pac. R. R. Rep., III, pt. 3, 16, map, 1856. Amaguaguas.—Duflot de Mofras, Voyages, I, 338, 1844. Amahuayas.—Taylor in Cal. Farmer, Mar. 21, 1862. Amajabas.—Bancroft, Ariz. and N. Mex., 545, 1889. Amajavas.—Bancroft, Hist. Cal., II, 332, 1885. A-moc-há-ve.—Whipple in Pac. R. R. Rep., III, pt. 3, 102, 1856 (own name). Amóhah.—Zeitschrift f. Ethnologie, 378, 1877 (after 18th century source). Amojaves.—Cremony, Life Among the Apaches, 148, 1868. Amoχami.—Hoffman in Bull. Essex Inst., XVII, 33, 1885. Amoχawi.—Ibid. Amu-chaba.—Smith (1827) in Zeitschr. f. Ethnologie, 378, 1877. Dil-zhay'.—White, Apache Names of Ind. Tribes, MS., B. A. E., 1, n. d. ('Red soil with red ants': Apache name). Hamockhaves.—Ind Aff. Rep. 1857, 302, 1858. Hamoekhávé.—ten Kate, Reizen in N. A., 130, 1885. Hamokába.—Corbusier, MS. vocab., B. A. E., 1885. Hamokavi.—Thomas, Yuma MS. vocab., B. A. E., 1868. Hamoke-avi.—Ibid. Hamukahava.—Ibid. Har-dil-zhay.—White, Apache Names of Ind. Tribes. MS., B. A. E., 1, n. d. ('Red soil with red ants': Apache name). Hatilshé.—White in Zeitschr. f. Ethnologie, 370, 1877 (Apache name for Mohave, Yuma, and Tonto). Húkwats.—Ibid. ('weavers': Ute and Paiute name). I-at.—Simpson, Exped. Great Basin, 474, 1859 ('elegant fellows': Paiute name). Jamajabas.—Font, MS. Diary, 56, Dec. 7, 1775 (or Soyopas). Jamajabs.—Garcés (1775–76), Diary, passim, 1900. Jamajas.—Kern in Schoolcraft, Ind. Tribes, IV, 38, 1854. Jamalas.—Hinton, Handbook to Arizona, 28, 1878. Mac-há-vès.—Whipple in Pac. R. R. Rep., III, pt. 3, 16, map, 1856. Mac-há-vìs.—Ibid., pt. 1, 110. Macjave.—Froebel, Seven Years' Travels, 511, 1859. Ma há os.—Whipple, Exped. from San Diego, 17, 1851. Majabos.—Soc. Geogr. Mex., 504, 1869. Majave.—Tolmie and Dawson, Comp. Vocabs., 128, 1884. Mohahve.—Brenchley, Journ. to Great Salt Lake, II, 441, 1841. Mohave.—Ibid. Mohavi.—Bartlett, Pers. Narr., II, 178, 1854. Mohawa.—Pattie, Pers. Narr., 93, 1833. Mohawe.—Möllhausen, Journ. to Pacific, I, 46, 1858. Mojaoes.—Bourke, Moquis of Ariz., 118, 1884. Mojaris.—Ind. Aff. Rep., 109, 1866. Mojaur.—Ibid., 94. Mojave.—Brenchley, Journ. to Great Salt Lake, II, 441, 1841. Mokhabas.—Corbusier in Am. Antiq., VIII, 276, 1886 (Mohaves, or). Molxaves.—Burton (1856) in H. R. Ex. Doc. 76, 34th Cong., 3d sess., 116, 1857. Moyave.—Haines, Am. Indian, 153, 1888. Nāks'-ăt.—ten Kate, Synonymie, 4, 1884 (Pima and Papago name). Soyopas.—Font, MS. Diary, 56, Dec. 7, 1775 (Jamajabas, or). Tamajabs.—Schoolcraft, Ind. Tribes, III, 298, 1853 (misprint of Garcés' 'Jamajabs'). Tamasabes.—Taylor in Cal. Farmer, May 11, 1860 (misprint from Garcés). Tamasabs.—Forbes, Hist. Cal., 162, 1839. Tzi-na-ma-a.—Bourke in Jour. Am. Folk-Lore, II, 185, 1889 (own name "before they came to the Colorado river"). Wah muk a-hah'-ve.—Ewing in Great Divide, 204, Dec. 1892 (trans.' dwelling near the water'). Wamak-a'va.—Cushing, inf'n (Havasupai name). Wibu'-ka pa.—Gatschet, inf'n (Yavapai name). Wili idahapá.—White in Zeitschr. f. Ethnol., 371, 1877 (Tulkepaya name). Yamágas.—Mayer, Mexico, II, 38, 1853. Yamajab.—Garcés (1776) misquoted by Bancroft, Ariz. and N. Mex., 395, 1889. Yamaya.—Pike, Expeditions, 3d map, 1810.

Mohawk (cognate with the Narraganset *Mohowaůuck*, 'they eat (animate) things,' hence 'man-eaters'). The most easterly tribe of the Iroquois confederation. They called themselves Kaniengehaga, 'people of the place of the flint.'

In the federal council and in other intertribal assemblies the Mohawk sit with the tribal phratry, which is formally called the "Three Elder Brothers" and of which the other members are the Seneca and the Onondaga. Like the Oneida, the Mohawk have only 3 clans, namely, the **Bear**, the **Wolf**, and the **Turtle**. The tribe is represented in the federal council by 9 chiefs of the rank of *roianer* (see *Chiefs*), being 3 from every clan. These chiefships were known by specific names, which were conferred with the office. These official titles are Tekarihoken, Haienhwatha, and Satekarihwate, of the first group; Orenrehkowa, Deionhehkon, and Sharenhowanen, of the second group; and Dehennakarine, Rastawenserontha, and Shoskoharowanen, of the third group. The first two groups or clans formed an intratribal phratry, while the last, or Bear clan group, was the other phratry. The people at all times assembled by phratries, and each phratry occupied a side of the council fire opposite that occupied by the other phratry. The second title in the foregoing list has been Anglicized into Hiawatha (q. v.).

From the Jesuit Relation for 1660 it is learned that the Mohawk, during a period of 60 years, had been many times both at the top and the bottom of the ladder of success; that, being insolent and warlike, they had attacked the Abnaki and their congeners at the E., the Conestoga at the S., the Hurons at the W. and N., and the Algonquian tribes at the N.; that at the close of the 16th century the Algonkin had so reduced them that there appeared to be none left, but that the remainder increased so rapidly that in a few years they in turn had overthrown the Algonkin. This success did not last long. The Conestoga waged war against them so vigorously for 10 years that for the second time the Mohawk were overthrown so completely that they appeared to be extinct. About this time (?1614) the Dutch arrived in their country, and, being attracted by their beaver skins, they furnished the Mohawk and their congeners with firearms, in order that the pelts might be obtained in greater abundance. The purpose of the Dutch was admirably served, but the possession of firearms by the Mohawk and their confederates rendered it easy for them to conquer their adversaries, whom they routed and filled with terror not alone by the deadly effect but even by the mere sound of these weapons, which hitherto had been unknown. Thenceforth the Mohawk and their confederates became formidable adversaries and were victorious most everywhere, so that by 1660 the conquests of the Iroquois confederates, although they were not numerous, extended over nearly 500 leagues of territory. The Mohawk at that time numbered not more than 500 warriors and dwelt in 4 or 5 wretched villages.

The accounts of Mohawk migrations **previous** to the historical period are largely conjectural. Some writers do not clearly differentiate between the Mohawk and the Huron tribes at the N. and W. and from their own confederates as a whole. Besides fragmentary and untrustworthy traditions little that is definite is known regarding the migratory movements of the Mohawk.

In 1603, Champlain, while at Tadousac, heard of the Mohawk and their country. On July 30, 1609, he encountered on the lake to which he gave his own name a party of nearly 200 Iroquois warriors, under 3 chiefs. In a skirmish in which he shot two of the chiefs dead and wounded the third, he defeated this party, which was most probably largely Mohawk. Dismayed by the firearms of the Frenchman, whom they now met for the first time, the Indians fled. The Iroquois of this party wore arrow-proof armor and had both stone and iron hatchets, the latter having been obtained in trade. The fact that in Capt. Hendricksen's report to the States General, Aug. 18, 1616, he says that he had "bought from the inhabitants, the Minquaes [Conestoga], 3 persons, being people belonging to this company," who were "employed in the service of the Mohawks and Machicans," giving, he says, for them, in exchange, "kettles, beads, and merchandise," shows how extensively the inland trade was carried on between the Dutch and the Mohawk. The latter were at war with the Mohegan and other New England tribes with only intermittent periods of peace. In 1623 a Mohegan fort stood opposite Castle id. in the Hudson and was "built against their enemies, the Maquaes, a powerful people." In 1626 the Dutch commander of Ft Orange (Albany), and 6 of his men, joined the Mohegan in an expedition to invade the Mohawk country. They were met a league from the fort by a party of Mohawk armed only with bows and arrows, and were defeated, the Dutch commander and 3 of his men being killed, and of whom one, probably the commander, was cooked and eaten by the Mohawk. This intermittent warfare continued until the Mohegan were finally forced to withdraw from the upper waters of the Hudson. They did not however relinquish their territorial rights to their native adversaries, and so in 1630 they began to sell their lands to the Dutch. The deed to the Manor of Rensselaerwyck, which extended W. of the river two days' journey, and was mainly on the E. side of the river, was dated in the year named. In 1637 Kilian Van Rensselaer bought more land on the E. side. Subsequently the Mohegan became the friends and allies of the Mohawk, their former adversaries.

In 1641 Ahatsistari, a noted Huron chief, with only 50 companions, attacked and defeated 300 Iroquois, largely Mohawk, taking some prisoners. In the preceding summer he had attacked on L. Ontario a number of large canoes manned by Iroquois, probably chiefly Mohawk, and defeated them, after sinking several canoes and killing a number of their crews. In 1642, 11 Huron canoes were attacked on Ottawa r. by Mohawk and Oneida warriors about 100 m. above Montreal. In the same year the Mohawk captured Father Isaac Jogues, two French companions, and some Huron allies. They took the Frenchmen to their villages, where they caused them to undergo the most cruel tortures. Jogues, by the aid of the Dutch, escaped in the following year; but in 1646 he went to the Mohawk to attempt to convert them and to confirm the peace which had been made with them. On May 16, 1646, Father Jogues went to the Mohawk as an envoy and returned to Three Rivers in July in good health. In September he again started for the Mohawk country to establish a mission there; but, owing to the prevalence of an epidemic among the Mohawk, and to the failure of their crops, they accused Father Jogues of "having concealed certain charms in a small coffer, which he had left with his host as a pledge of his return," which caused them thus to be afflicted. So upon his arrival in their village for the third time, he and his companion, a young Frenchman, were seized, stripped, and threatened with death. Father Jogues had been adopted by the Wolf clan of the Mohawk, hence this clan, with that of the Turtle, which with the Wolf formed a phratry or brotherhood, tried to save the lives of the Frenchmen. But the Bear clan, which formed a phratry by itself, and being only cousins to the others, of one of which Father Jogues was a member, had determined on his death as a sorcerer. On Oct. 17, 1646, the unfortunates were told that they would be killed, but not burned, the next day. On the evening of the 18th Father Jogues was invited to a supper in a Bear lodge. Having accepted the invitation, he went there, and while entering the lodge a man concealed behind the door struck him down with an ax. He was beheaded, his head elevated on the palisade, and his body thrown into the river. The next morning Jogues' companion suffered a similar fate. Father Jogues left an account of a Mohawk sacrifice to the god Aireskoi (i. e., *Aregwĕns′ gwă*′, 'the Master or God of War'). While speaking of the cruelties exercised by the Mohawk toward their prisoners, and specifically toward 3 women, he said: "One of them (a thing not hitherto done)

was burned all over her body, and afterwards thrown into a huge pyre." And that "at every burn which they caused, by applying lighted torches to her body, an old man, in a loud voice, exclaimed, 'Daimon, Aireskoi, we offer thee this victim, whom we burn for thee, that thou mayest be filled with her flesh and render us ever anew victorious over our enemies.' Her body was cut up, sent to the various villages, and devoured." Megapolensis (1644), a contemporary of Father Jogues, says that when the Mohawk were unfortunate in war they would kill, cut up, and roast a bear, and then make an offering of it to this war god with the accompanying prayer: "Oh, great and mighty Aireskuoni, we know that we have offended against thee, inasmuch as we have not killed and eaten our captive enemies—forgive us this. We promise that we will kill and eat all the captives we shall hereafter take as certainly as we have killed and now eat this bear." He adds: "Finally, they roast their prisoners dead before a slow fire for some days and then eat them up. The common people eat the arms, buttocks, and trunk, but the chiefs eat the head and the heart."

The Jesuit Relation for 1646 says that, properly speaking, the French had at that time peace with only the Mohawk, who were their near neighbors and who gave them the most trouble, and that the Mohegan (Mahingans or Mahinganak), who had had firm alliances with the Algonkin allies of the French, were then already conquered by the Mohawk, with whom they formed a defensive and offensive alliance; that during this year some Sokoki (Assok8ekik) murdered some Algonkin, whereupon the latter determined, under a misapprehension, to massacre some Mohawk, who were then among them and the French. But, fortunately, it was discovered from the testimony of two wounded persons, who had escaped, that the murderers spoke a language quite different from that of the Iroquois tongues, and suspicion was at once removed from the Mohawk, who then hunted freely in the immediate vicinity of the Algonkin N. of the St Lawrence, where these hitherto implacable enemies frequently met on the best of terms. At this time the Mohawk refused Sokoki ambassadors a new compact to wage war on the Algonkin.

The introduction of firearms by the Dutch among the Mohawk, who were among the first of their region to procure them, marked an important era in their history, for it enabled them and the cognate Iroquois tribes to subjugate the Delawares and Munsee, and thus to begin a career of conquest that carried their war parties to the Mississippi and to the shores of Hudson bay. The Mohawk villages were in the valley of Mohawk r., N. Y., from the vicinity of Schenectady nearly to Utica, and their territory extended N. to the St Lawrence and s. to the watershed of Schoharie cr. and the E. branch of the Susquehanna. On the E. their territories adjoined those of the Mahican, who held Hudson r. From their position on the E. frontier of the Iroquois confederation the Mohawk were among the most prominent of the Iroquoian tribes in the early Indian wars and in official negotiations with the colonies, so that their name was frequently used by the tribes of New England and by the whites as a synonym for the confederation. Owing to their position they also suffered much more than their confederates in some of the Indian and French wars. Their 7 villages of 1644 were reduced to 5 in 1677. At the beginning of the Revolution the Mohawk took the side of the British, and at its conclusion the larger portion of them, under Brant and Johnson, removed to Canada, where they have since resided on lands granted to them by the British government. In 1777 the Oneida expelled the remainder of the tribe and burned their villages.

In 1650 the Mohawk had an estimated population of 5,000, which was probably more than their actual number; for 10 years later they were estimated at only 2,500. Thenceforward they underwent a rapid decline, caused by their wars with the Mahican, Conestoga, and other tribes, and with the French, and also by the removal of a large part of the tribe to Caughnawaga and other mission villages. The later estimates of their population have been: 1,500 in 1677 (an alleged decrease of 3,500 in 27 years), 400 in 1736 (an alleged decrease of 1,100 in 36 years), 500 in 1741, 800 in 1765, 500 in 1778, 1,500 in 1783, and about 1,200 in 1851. These estimates are evidently little better than vague guesses. In 1884 they were on three reservations in Ontario: 965 at the Bay of Quinté near the E. end of L. Ontario, the settlement at Gibson, and the reserve of the Six Nations on Grand r. Besides these there are a few individuals scattered among the different Iroquois tribes in the United States. In 1906 the Bay of Quinté settlement contained 1,320; there were 140 (including "Algonquins") at Watha, the former Gibson band which was removed earlier from Oka; and the Six Nations included an indeterminate number.

The Mohawk participated in the following treaties with the United States: Ft Stanwix, N. Y., Oct. 22, 1784, being a treaty of peace between the United States and the Six Nations and defining their boundaries; supplemented by treaty of Ft Harmar, O., Jan. 9, 1789. Konondaigua (Canandaigua), N. Y., Nov. 11, 1794, establishing peace relations with the Six Nations and agreeing to certain reservations and boundaries. Albany, N. Y., Mar. 29, 1797, by which the United States sanctioned the cession by the Mohawk to New York of all their lands therein.

The following were Mohawk villages: Canajoharie, Canastigaone, Canienga, Caughnawaga, Chuchtononeda, Kanagaro Kowogoconnughariegugharie, Nowadaga, Ohnowalagantles, Ohsarakas, Onekagoncka, Onoalagona, Osguage, Osquake, Saratoga, Schaunactada (Schenectady), Schoharie, Teatontaloga, and Tewanondadon. (J. N. B. H.)

Agnechronons.—Jes. Rel. for 1652, 35, 1858. **Agnée.**—Jes. Rel. for 1642, 83, 1858. **Agneehronon.**—Jes. Rel. for 1640, 35, 1858. **Agneronons.**—Jes. Rel. for 1643, 63, 1858. **Agnic.**—Homann Heirs' map, 1756 (misprint). **Agniehronnons.**—Jes. Rel. for 1664, 34, 1858. **Agniehroron.**—Jes. Rel. for 1637, 119, 1858. **Agnierhonon.**—Jes. Rel. for 1639, 70, 1858. **Agnieronnons.**—Jes. Rel. for 1656, 2, 1858. **Agnieronons.**—Dollier and Gallinée (1669) in Margry, Déc., I, 141, 1875. **Agnierrhonons.**—Jes. Rel. for 1635, 34, 1858. **Agniers.**—Hennepin, New Discov.,101, 1698. **Agniez.**—Frontenac (1673) in Margry, Déc., I, 213, 1875. **Agnizez.**—Vaillant (1688) in N. Y. Doc. Col. Hist., III, 527, 1853. **Aguierhonon.**—Sagard (1632), Hist. Can., IV, 1866 (Huron name) **Amóhak.**—Gatschet, Penobscot MS., B. A. E., 1887 (Penobscot name). **A'muhak.**—Gatschet, Caughnawaga MS., B. A. E., 1882 (Caughnawaga name). **Anaguas.**—Le Beau, Avantures, II, 2, 1738. **Aniáka-háka.**—Gatschet, Caughnawaga MS., B. A. E., 1882 (Caughnawaga name). **Anié.**—Bacqueville de la Potherie, Hist. de l'Am. Sept., III, 27, 1753. **Aniez.**—De l'Isle, map (1718), quoted in N. Y. Doc. Col. Hist., V, 577, 1855. **Anniegué.**—Jes. Rel. for 1665, 21, 1858. **Anniehronnons.**—Jes. Rel. for 1653, 5, 1858. **Anniengehronnons.**—Jes. Rel. for 1657, 58, 1858. **Anniehronnons.**—Ibid., 36. **Annieronnons.**—Ibid., 15. **Annieronons.**—Jes. Rel. for 1656, 11, 1858. **Annierronons.**—Jes. Rel. for 1646, 3, 1858. **Anniés.**—Tracy (1667) in N. Y. Doc. Col. Hist., III, 152, 1853. **Anniez.**—Frontenac (1673) in Margry, Déc., I, 203, 1875. **Aquieeronons.**—Jes. Rel. for 1641, 37, 1858. **Aquiers.**—Charlevoix, Jour., I, 270, 1761 (misprint). **Auniers.**—Chauvignerie (1736), quoted by Schoolcraft, Ind. Tribes, III, 555, 1853. **Aunies.**—McKenney and Hall, Ind. Tribes, III, 80, 1854. **Canaoneuska.**—Montreal conf. (1756) in N. Y. Doc. Col. Hist., X, 500, 1858. **Caniengas.**—Hale quoted in Minn. Hist. Soc. Coll., v, 42, 1885. **Canniungaes.**—N. Y. Doc. Col. Hist., IX, 262, note, 1855. **Canungas.**—Mallery in Proc. A. A. S., XXVI, 352, 1877. **Cauneeyenkees.**—Edwards (1751) in Mass. Hist. Soc. Coll., 1st s., X, 143, 1809. **Cayingahaugas.**—Macauley, N. Y., II, 174, 1829. **Conninggahaughgaugh.**—Ibid., 185. **Da-gä-e-ó-gä.**—Morgan, League Iroq., 97, 1851 (name used in the Iroquois councils). **Gagnieguez.**—Hennepin, New Discov., 92, 1698. **Ganeagaonhoh.**—Mallery in Proc. A. A. A. S., XXVI, 352, 1877. **Gä-ne-ä'-ga-o-no'.**—Morgan, League Iroq., 523, 1851 (Seneca name). **Gä-ne-ga-hä'-gä.**—Ibid., 523 (Mohawk form). **Ganiegueronons.**—Courcelles (1670) in Margry, Déc., I, 178, 1875. **Gani-inge-hága.**—Pyrlæus (ca. 1750) quoted by Gatschet in Am. Antiq., IV, 75, 1882. **Ganingehage.**—Barclay (1769) quoted by Shea, Cath. Miss., 208, 1855. **Ganniag8ari.**—Bruyas quoted in Hist. Mag., II, 153, 1858. **Ganniagwari.**—Shea, note in Charlevoix, New Fr., II, 145, 1872. **Ganniegéhaga.**—Bruyas quoted by Shea, Cath. Miss., 208, 1855. **Ganniégeronon.**—Ibid. **Ganniegez.**—Hennepin, New Discov., 28, 1698. **Ganniegué.**—Shea, Cath. Miss., 258, 1855. **Ganniekez.**—Hennepin (1683) quoted by Le Beau, Avantures, II, 2, 1738. **Ganningehage.**—Barclay (1769) quoted in Hist.

Mag., II, 153, 1858. **Guagenigronnons.**—Doc. of 1706 in N.Y. Doc. Col. Hist., IX, 786, 1855. **Hatiniéye-runu.**—Gatschet, Tuscarora MS., B. A. E., 1883 (Tuscarora name). **Ignerhonons.**—Champlain, Œuv., III, 220, 1870. **Ignierhonons.**—Sagard (1636), Can., I, 170, 1866. **Iroquois d'enbas.**—Jes. Rel. for 1656, 7, 1858 (French name). **Iroquois inferieurs.**—Jes. Rel. for 1656, 2, 1858. **Kajingahaga.**—Megapolensis (1644) quoted in Hist. Mag., II, 153, 1858. **Kanáwa.**—Gatschet, Shawnee MS., B. A. E., 1879 (Shawnee name, from Kanawági). **Kaníeke-háka.**—Gatschet, Tuscarora MS., B. A. E. ('flint tribe': Tuscarora name). **Kaniénge-ono[n].**—Gatschet, Seneca MS., B. A. E. (Seneca name). **Kayingehaga.**—Ruttenber, Tribes Hudson R., 35, 1872. **Kwĕdĕch'.**—Rand, Micmac Dict., 172, 1888, (Micmac name). **Maaquas.**—Jogues (1643) in N. Y. Doc. Col. Hist., XIII, 577, 1881. **Mackwaes.**—De Laet (1625) in N. Y. Hist. Soc. Coll., 2d s., I, 299, 1841. **Mackwasii.**—De Laet, Nov. Orb., 73, 1633. **Mackwes.**—De Laet (1633) quoted in Jones, Ind. Bull., 6, 1867. **Macqs.**—Maryland treaty (1682) in N. Y. Doc. Col. Hist., III, 323, 1853. **Macquaas.**—Doc. of 1660, ibid., XIII, 183, 1881. **Macquaaus.**—Penhallow (1726) in N. H. Hist. Soc. Coll., I, 41, 1824. **Macquas.**—Rawson (1678) in N. Y. Doc. Col. Hist., XIII, 521, 1881. **Macquaus.**—Penhallow (1726) in N. H. Hist. Soc. Coll., I, 41, 1824. **Macques.**—Rawson (1678) in N. Y. Doc. Col. Hist., XIII, 522, 1881. **Macquess.**—Maryland treaty (1682), ibid., III, 326, 1853. **Macquis.**—Ibid., 325. **Macquiss.**—Ibid., 321. **Maechibaeys.**—Michaelius (1628), ibid., II, 769, 1858. **Mahacks.**—Schuyler (1699), ibid., IV, 563, 1854. **Mahacqs.**—Meadows (1698), ibid., 395. **Mahakas.**—Megapolensis (1644) in N. Y. Hist. Soc. Coll., 2d s., III, pt. 1, 153, 1857. **Mahakes.**—Andros (1680) in Me. Hist. Soc. Coll., V, 42, 1857. **Mahakinbaas.**—Hazard in Am. State Pap., I, 520, 1792. **Mahakinbas.**—Megapolensis (1644) in N. Y. Hist. Soc. Coll., 2d s., III, pt. 1, 153, 1857. **Mahakobaas.**—Ibid. **Mahaks.**—Wharton (1673) quoted in Hist. Mag., 2d s., I, 300, 1867. **Mahakuaas.**—Hist. Mag., 1st s., II, 153, 1858. **Mahakuase.**—Megapolensis (1644) quoted in N. Y. Doc. Col. Hist., I, 496, 1856. **Mahakuasse.**—Megapolensis (1644) quoted by Vater, Mith., pt. 3, sec. 3, 330, 1816. **Mahakwa.**—Shea, Cath. Miss., 208, 1855 **Mahaukes.**—Doc. of 1666 in N. Y. Doc. Col. Hist., III, 118, 1853. **Mahogs.**—Church (1716) quoted by Drake, Ind. Wars, 115, 1825. **Makquás.**—Denonville (1687) in N. Y. Doc. Col. Hist., III, 518, 1853. **Makwaes.**—Wassenaar (1632) quoted by Ruttenber, Tribes Hudson R., 58, 1872. **Maqaise.**—Bleeker (1701) in N. Y. Doc. Col. Hist., IV, 919, 1854. **Maqas.**—Doc. of 1676, ibid., XIII, 500, 1881. **Maquaas.**—Map of 1614, ibid., I, 1856. **Maquaes.**—Doc. of 1651, ibid., XIII, 28, 1881. **Maquaese.**—Bellomont (1698), ibid., IV, 347, 1854. **Maquais.**—Nicolls (1616), ibid., III, 117, 1853. **Maquaise.**—Bleeker (1701), ibid., IV, 920, 1854. **Maquas.**—De Laet (1625) quoted by Ruttenber, Tribes Hudson R., 34, 1872 **Maquasas.**—Doc. of 1655 in N. Y. Doc. Col. Hist., XII, 98, 1877. **Maquase.**—Doc. of 1678, ibid., XIII, 528, 1881. **Maquases.**—Lovelace (1669), ibid., XIII, 439, 1881. **Maquash.**—Romer (1700), ibid., IV, 800, 1854. **Maquass.**—Talcott (1678), ibid., XIII, 517, 1881. **Maquasse.**—Doc. of 1687, ibid., III, 432, 1853. **Maquees.**—Bradstreet (1680) in Mass. Hist. Soc. Coll., 3d s., VIII, 334, 1843. **Maques.**—Clobery (1633) in N. Y. Doc. Col. Hist., I, 78, 1856. **Maquese.**—Livingston (1710), ibid., V, 227, 1855. **Maqueses.**—Gardner (1662), ibid., XIII, 227, 1881. **Maquess.**—Harmetsen (1687), ibid., III, 437, 1853. **Maquesyes.**—Lovelace (1669), ibid., XIII, 439, 1881. **Maquez.**—Graham (1698), ibid., IV, 430, 1854. **Maquis.**—Davis (ca. 1691) in Mass. Hist. Soc. Coll., 3d s., I, 108, 1825. **Maquoas.**—Doc. of 1697 in N. Y. Doc. Col. Hist., V, 75, 1855. **Maquois.**—Jes. Rel. for 1647, 34, 1858 (Dutch form). **Mauguawogs.**—Mallery in Proc. A. A. S., XXVI, 352, 1877. **Mauhauks.**—Doc. of 1666 in N. Y. Doc. Col. Hist., III, 118, 1853. **Maukquogges.**—Warner (1644) in R. I. Col. Rec., I, 140, 1856. **Mauquaoys.**—Eliot (1680) in Mass. Hist. Soc. Coll., 1st s., III, 180, 1794. **Mauquas.**—Salisbury (1678) in N. Y. Doc. Col. Hist., XIII, 519, 1881. **Mauquauogs.**—Williams (ca. 1638) in Mass. Hist. Soc. Coll., 4th s., VI, 238, 1863. **Mauquaw.**—Williams (1648), ibid., 3d s., IX, 272, 1846. **Mau-**

quawogs.—Williams (1637), ibid., 4th s., VI, 201, 1863. **Mauquawos.**—Williams(1650), ibid., 284. **Mauques.**—Andros (1675) in N. Y. Doc. Col. Hist., XII, 520, 1877. **Mawhakes.**—Rec. of 1644 quoted by Drake, Bk. Inds., bk. 2, 90, 1848. **Mawhauogs.**—Williams (1637) in Mass. Hist. Soc. Coll., 4th s., VI, 207, 1863. **Mawhawkes.**—Haynes (1648) in Mass. Hist. Soc. Coll., 4th s., VI, 358, 1863. **Mawques.**—Hubbard (1680), ibid., 2d s., VI, 629, 1815. **Meguak.**—Gatschet, Penobscot MS., 1887 (Penobscot name). **Megual.**—Ibid. **Megue.**—Ibid. **Megwe.**—Ibid. **Mequa.**—Vetromile in Me. Hist. Soc. Coll., VI, 215, 1859 (Abnaki name). **Moacks.**—Vaillant (1688) in N. Y. Doc. Col. Hist., III, 528, 1853. **Moak.**—Doc. of 1746, ibid., X, 54, 1858. **Moawk.**—Doc. of 1758, ibid., 679. **Mockways.**—Wadsworth (1694) in Mass. Hist. Soc. Coll., 4th s., I, 102, 1852. **Mocquages.**—Sanford, (1657), ibid., 2d s., VII, 81, 1818. **Mocquayes.**—Sanford (1657) in R. I. Col. Rec., I, 362, 1856. **Mohaakx.**—Clarkson (1694) in N. Y. Doc. Col. Hist., IV, 93, 1854. **Mohacks.**—Colve (1673), ibid., XIII, 478, 1881. **Mohacqs.**—Meadows (1698), ibid., IV, 393, 1854. **Mohacques.**—Doc. of 1698, ibid., 337. **Mohacs**—Miller (1696), ibid., 188. **Mohaes.**—Pouchot, map (1758), ibid., X, 694, 1858. **Mohaggs.**—Livingston (1691), ibid., III, 781, 1853. **Mohags.**—Livingstone (1702), ibid., IV, 988, 1854. **Mohaks.**—Wessells (1692), ibid., III, 817, 1853. **Mohaq[o].**—Doc. of 1695, ibid., IV, 120, 1854. **Mohaqs.**—Wessells (1693), ibid., 59. **Mohaques.**—Winthrop (1666), ibid., III, 137, 1854. **Mohaucks.**—Mason (1684) in N. H. Hist. Soc. Coll., II, 200, 1827. **Mohaugs.**—Quanapaug (1675) in Mass. Hist. Soc. Coll., 1st s., VI, 206, 1800. **Mohaukes.**—Doc. of 1666 in N. Y. Doc. Col. Hist., III, 118, 1853. **Mohauks.**—Gardener (1660) in Mass. Hist. Soc. Coll., 3d s., III, 154, 1833. **Mohawcks.**—Owaneco's rep. (1700) in N. Y. Doc. Col. Hist., IV, 614, 1854. **Mohawkes.**—Doc. ca. 1642 in Mass. Hist. Soc. Coll., 3d s., III, 162, 1833. **Mohawks.**—Hendricksen (1616) in N. Y. Doc. Col, Hist., I, 14, 1856. **Mohawques.**—Schuyler (1691), ibid., III, 801, 1853. **Mohaws.**—Conf. of 1774 in Rupp, W. Penn., app., 223, 1846. **Mohegs.**—Dongan (1688) in N. Y. Doc. Col. Hist., III, 521, 1853. **Mohoakk.**—Schnectady treaty (1672), ibid., XIII, 464, 1881. **Mohoakx.**—Ibid., 465. **Mohocks.**—Vincent (1638) in Mass. Hist. Soc. Coll., 3d s., VI, 29, 1837. **Mohocs.**—Boudinot, Star in the West, 127, 1816. **Mohoges.**—Schuyler (1694) in N. Y. Doc. Col. Hist., IV, 82, 1854. **Mohoggs.**—Livingston (1711), ibid., V, 272, 1855. **Mohogs.**—Hogkins(1685) in N. H. Hist. Soc. Coll., I, 221, 1824. **Mohokes.**—Gardner (1662) in N. Y. Doc. Col. Hist., XIII, 226, 1881. **Mohoks.**—Ibid., 225. **Mohoukes.**—Harmetsen (1687), ibid., III, 436, 1853. **Mohowaugsuck.**—Williams (1643) in Mass. Hist. Soc. Coll., 1st s., III, 209, 1794. **Mohowawogs.**—Williams (ca. 1638), ibid., 4th s, VI, 239, 1863. **Mohowks.**—Burnet (1720) in N. Y. Doc. Col. Hist., V, 578, 1855. **Mohox.**—Vaillant (1688), ibid., III, 527, 1853. **Mohucks.**—Doc. of 1676 quoted by Drake, Ind. Chron., 88, 1836. **Mokaus.**—Alcedo, Dic. Geog., IV, 604, 1788. **Mokawkes.**—Doc. ca. 1684 in N. H. Hist. Soc. Coll., I, 220, 1824. **Moohags.**—Church (1716) quoted by Drake, Ind. Wars, 50, 1825. **Moquaes.**—Wessells (1698) in N. Y. Doc. Col. Hist., IV, 372, 1854. **Moquakues.**—Gardener (1660) in Mass. Hist. Soc. Coll., 3d s., III, 154, 1833. **Moquas.**—Andros (1678) in N. Y. Doc. Col. Hist., III, 271, 1853. **Moquase.**—Talcott (1678), ibid., XIII, 517, 1881. **Moquauks.**—Winthrop (1645) in Mass. Hist. Soc. Coll., 2d s., VI, 460, 1816. **Moquawes.**—Hubbard (1680), ibid., V, 33. **Moqui.**—Doc. of 1690, ibid., 3d s., I, 210, 1825. **Mosquaugsett.**—Baily (1669) in R. I. Col. Rec., II, 274, 1857. **Mouhaks.**—Gardner (1652) in Mass. Hist. Soc. Coll., 4th s., VII, 62, 1865. **Mowaks.**—Treaty of 1644, ibid., III, 430, 1856. **Mowakes.**—Winthrop (1637), ibid., 358. **Mowaks.**—Bradford (ca. 1650), ibid., 431. **Mowhakes.**—Ibid., 361. **Mowhaks.**—Bradford (1640), ibid., VI, 159, 1863. **Mowhakues.**—Gardener (1660), ibid., 3d s., III, 152, 1833. **Mowhaugs.**—Williams (1637), ibid., IX, 301, 1846. **Mowhauks.**—Mason (1643), ibid., 4th s., VII, 411, 1865. **Mowhauogs.**—Williams (1637), ibid., 3d s., IX, 300, 1846. **Mowhawkes.**—Haynes (1643), ibid., I, 230, 1825. **Mowhawks.**—Clinton (1743) in N. Y. Doc. Col. Hist., VI, 250, 1855. **Mowhoake.**—Patrick (1637) in Mass. Hist. Soc. Coll., 4th s., VII, 323, 1865. **Mowhoks.**—Gardner (1662) in N. Y.

Doc. Col. Hist., XIII, 225, 1881. **Mowquakes.**—Gardener (1660) in Mass. Hist. Soc. Coll., 3d s., III, 152, 1833. **Oyanders.**—Shea, Cath. Miss., 214, 1855 (probably a Dutch form of Agniers). **Sankhicani.**—Heckewelder quoted by Gallatin in Trans. Am. Antiq. Soc., II, 46, 1836 (Delaware name: 'flint users'). **Teakawreahogeh.**—Macauley, N. Y., II, 174, 1829. **Tehawrehogeh.**—Ibid., 185. **Tehur-lehogugh.**—Ibid. **Tekau-terigtego-nes.**—Ibid., 174. **Tgarihóge.**—Pyrlæus MS. (ca. 1750) quoted in Am. Antiq., IV, 75, 1882. **Yanieye-róno.**—Gatschet, Wyandot MS., B. A. E., 1881 (Huron name: 'bear people').

Mohawk. One of the Lakmiut bands of the Kalapooian stock, on Mohawk r., an E. tributary of the Willamette, just N. of Eugene City, Oreg.—U. S. Ind. Treat. (1855), 19, 1873; Sanders in Ind. Aff. Rep. 1863, 88, 1864.

Mohegan (from *maïngan*, 'wolf.'—Trumbull). An Algonquian tribe whose chief seat appears originally to have been on Thames r., Conn., in the N. part of New London co. They claimed as their proper country all the territory watered by the Thames and its branches N. to within 8 or 10 m. of the Massachusetts line, and by conquest a considerable area extending N. and E. into Massachusetts and Rhode Island, occupied by the Wabaquasset and Nipmuc. On the w. their dominion extended along the coast to East r., near Guilford, Conn. After the destruction of the Pequot in 1637 the Mohegan laid claim to their country and that of the western Nehantic in the s. part of New London co. The tribes w. of them on Connecticut r., whom they sometimes claimed as subjects, were generally hostile to them, as were also the Narraganset on their E. border.

The Mohegan seem to have been the eastern branch of that group of closely connected tribes that spread from the vicinity of Narragansett bay to the farther side of the Hudson (see *Mahican*), but since known to the whites the eastern and western bodies have had no political connection. At the first settlement of New England the Mohegan and Pequot formed but one tribe, under the rule of Sassacus, afterward known as the Pequot chief. Uncas, a subordinate chief connected by marriage with the family of Sassacus, rebelled against him and assumed a distinct authority as the leader of a small band on the Thames, near Norwich, who were afterward known in history as Mohegan. On the fall of Sassacus in 1637 the greater part of the survivors of his tribe fell under the dominion of the Mohegan chief, who thus obtained control of the territory of the two tribes with all their tributary bands. As the English favored his pretensions he also set up a claim to extensive adjoining territories in the possession of rival chiefs. He strengthened his position by an alliance with the English against all other tribes, and after the destruction of the Indian power in s.

New England, by the death of King Philip in 1676, the Mohegan were the only important tribe remaining s. of the Abnaki. As the white settlements extended the Mohegan sold most of their lands and confined themselves to a reservation on Thames r., in New London co., Conn. Their village, also called Mohegan, was on the site of the present town of that name on the w. bank of the river. Their ancient village seems to have been farther up, about the mouth of the Yantic. Besides the village at Mohegan, the villages of Groton and Stonington, occupied mainly by the remnant of the Pequot, were considered to belong to the Mohegan. They rapidly dwindled away when surrounded by the whites. Many joined the Scaticook, but in 1788 a still larger number, under the leadership of Occom, joined the Brotherton Indians in New York, where they formed the majority of the new settlement. The rest of the tribe continue to reside in the vicinity of Mohegan or Norwich, Conn., but are now reduced to about 100 individuals of mixed blood, only one of whom, an old woman, retained the language in 1904. They still keep up a September festival, which appears to be a survival of the Green Corn dance of the Eastern tribes. For interesting notes on this remnant, see Prince and Speck in Am. Anthrop., 1903 and 1904.

In 1643 the Mohegan were estimated to number from 2,000 to 2,500, but this included the Pequot living with them, and probably other subordinate tribes. In 1705 they numbered 750, and in 1774 were reported at 206. Soon after they lost a considerable number by removal to New York, and in 1804 only 84 were left, who were reduced to 69 five years later. They were reported to number 300 in 1825, and about 350 in 1832, but the increased numbers are probably due to the enumeration of negroes and mixed-bloods living with them, together with recruits from the Narraganset and others in the vicinity. The Mohegan villages were Groton, Mohegan, Showtucket, and Wabaquasset. For further information and synonyms, see *Mahican*. (J. M.)

Manheken.—Brewster (1651) in Mass. Hist. Soc. Coll., 4th s., VII, 71, 1865. **Manhigan-euck.**—Tooker, Algonq. Ser., V, 23, 1901 (English form of tribal name). **Mawchiggin.**—Johnson (1654) in Mass. Hist. Soc. Coll., 2d s., VII, 47, 1818. **Mawhickon.**—Easton treaty (1757) in N. Y. Doc. Col. Hist., VII, 294, 1856. **Mawhiggins.**—Johnson (1654) in Mass. Hist. Soc. Coll., 2d s., IV, 28, 1816. **Mogekin.**—Hopkins (1646), ibid., 4th s., VI, 334, 1863. **Mogian-eucks.**—Williams (1637), ibid., 210. **Mohagin.**—Adams (1738), ibid., I, 35, 1852 (Connecticut village). **Moheag.**—Mather (ca. 1640) in Drake, Bk. Inds., bk. 2, 86, 1848. **Moheagan.**—Horsmanden (1744) in N. Y. Doc. Col. Hist., VI, 256, 1855. **Moheaganders.**—Trumbull, Conn., I, 350, 1818. **Moheages.**—Mason (ca. 1670) in Mass. Hist. Soc. Coll., 2d s., VIII, 146, 1819. **Moheagues.**—Peters (ca. 1644) in Drake, Bk.

Inds., bk. 2, 69, 1848. **Moheegins.**—Patrick (1637) in Mass. Hist. Soc. Coll., 4th s., VII, 325, 1865. **Moheegs.**—Wainwright (1735) in Me. Hist. Soc. Coll., IV, 123, 1856. **Moheek.**—Fitch (1674) in Mass. Hist. Soc. Coll., 1st s., I, 208, 1806 (village in Connecticut). **Moheganicks.**—Pynchon (1645), ibid., 4th s., VI, 374, 1863. **Mohegans.**—Haynes (1643), ibid., 357 (used by Hubbard in 1680 for the New York tribe). **Mohegen.**—Coddington (1640), ibid., 318 (Connecticut village). **Moheges.**—Stiles (*ca.* 1770), ibid., 1st s., X, 101, 1809. **Mohegin.**—Leete (1659), ibid., 4th s., VII, 543, 1865. **Mohegs.**—Hyde (1760) in Drake, Bk. Inds., bk. 2, 66, 1848. **Moheken.**—Brewster (1656) in Mass. Hist. Soc. Coll., 4th s., VII, 76, 1865. **Mohigan.**—Mass. Records (1642) in Drake, Bk. Inds., bk. 2, 63, 1848. **Mohiganeucks.**—Williams (1637) in Mass. Hist. Soc. Coll., 3d s., I, 163, 1825. **Mohiganie.**—Williams (1637), ibid., 4th s., VI, 207, 1863. **Mohigens.**—Vincent (1638), ibid., 3d s., I, 35, 1837 (used by Harris in 1805 for the New York tribe). **Mohiggans.**—N. Y. Hist. Soc. Coll., 2d s., I, 72, 1841. **Mohiggen.**—Cushman (1622) in Mass. Hist. Soc. Coll., 4th s., III, 122, 1856 (Connecticut, or; may mean Monhegan id.). **Mohiggeners.**—Underhill (1638), ibid., 3d s., VI, 15, 1837. **Mohighens.**—Vincent (1638), ibid., 39. **Mohigin.**—Stephens (1675), ibid., X, 117, 1849 (Connecticut village). **Mohigoners.**—Higginson (1637), ibid., 4th s., VII, 396, 1865. **Mohogin.**—Writer of 1676 quoted by Drake, Ind. Chron., 116, 1836. **Monahegan.**—Winthrop (1638) quoted by Drake, Bk. Inds., bk. 2, 87, 1848. **Monahiganeucks.**—Williams (1637) in Mass. Hist. Soc. Coll., 4th s., VI, 215, 1863. **Monahiganick.**—Ibid., 215 (Connecticut village). **Monahiggan.**—Williams (1638) quoted by Trumbull, Ind. Names Conn., 31, 1881 (Connecticut village). **Monahigganie.**—Williams (1638) in Mass. Hist. Soc. Coll., 4th s., VI, 231, 1863. **Monahiggannick.**—Williams (1639), ibid., 260. **Monahiggens.**—Williams (1638), ibid., 3d s., I, 167, 1825. **Monahiggon.**—Williams (1637), ibid., 4th s., VI, 215, 1863. **Monahigon.**—Williams (1638), ibid., 224. **Monhagin.**—Adams (1738), ibid., I, 35, 1852. **Monheagan.**—Mason (1648), ibid., VII, 416, 1865. **Monheags.**—Ibid., 413. **Monhegans.**—Williams (1670), ibid., 1st s., I, 277, 1806. **Monhege.**—Mason (1643), ibid., 4th s., VII, 411, 1865. **Monhegen.**—Treaty (1645), ibid., III, 437, 1856. **Monhiggin.**—Williams (1637), ibid., VI, 220, 1863. **Monhiggons.**—Williams (1675), ibid., 302. **Monhiggs.**—Bradford (*ca.* 1650), ibid., III, 361, 1856. **Monohegens.**—Eliot (1650), ibid., 3d s., IV, 139, 1834. **Morahtkans.**—Opdyck (1640) in N. Y. Doc. Col. Hist., II, 141, 1858. **Morhicans.**—Map of 1616, ibid., I, 1856. **Mowheganneak.**—Mason (1648) in Mass. Hist. Soc. Coll., 4th s., VII, 413, 1865. **Muhhekaneuk.**—Trumbull, Ind. Names Conn., 31, 1881 (English form of tribal name). **Munhegan.**—Pynchon (1643) in Mass. Hist. Soc. Coll., 4th s., VI, 373, 1863. **Munhicke.**—Brewster (1636), ibid., VII, 67, 1865 (Connecticut village). **Nanhegans.**—Sanford (1657) in R. I. Col. Rec., I, 362, 1856. **River Heads.**—Am. Pioneer, II, 191, 1843 (misprint, probably for "River Inds"). **River Indians.**—See under this title. **Sea-side People.**—Morgan, Consang. and Affin., 289, 1871. **Unkus Indians.**—Salisbury (1678) in N. Y. Doc. Col. Hist., XIII, 526, 1881. **Upland Indians.**—Church (1716) in Drake Ind. Wars, 67, 1825. **Vpland Indianes.**—Brewster (1656) in Mass. Hist. Soc. Coll., 4th s., VII, 75, 1865.

Mohemencho. A tribe of the Monacan confederacy, formerly living on the upper waters of James r., Va. Jefferson locates them in Powhatan co., on the s. side of the river, a few miles above Richmond, but Strachey seems to place them higher up, in the mountains. (J. M.)

Mohemenchoes.—Jefferson, Notes, 179, 1801. **Mohemenehoes.**—Macauley, N. Y., II, 178, 1829 (misprint). **Mohemonsoes.**—Boudinot, Star in the West, 127, 1816. **Mowhemcho.**—Smith, Va., I, map, 1819. **Mowhemenchouch.**—Pots, ibid., 196. **Mowhemenchuges.**—Strachey (*ca.* 1612), Va., 102, 1849. **Mowhemenchughes.**—Smith, op. cit., 134. **Mowhemincke.**—Strachey (*ca.* 1612), Va., 131, 1849.

Moheton. An unclassified tribe living in 1671 in the mountains of s. w. Virginia, or the adjacent part of West Virginia, on the upper waters of a river flowing N. w.—perhaps New r. They had removed a short time previously from the headwaters of the Roanoke, in the mountains farther to the E. They were friends and neighbors of the Tutelo, and were possibly a cognate tribe, or they may have been Shawnee. (J. M.)

Mohetan.—Batts (1671) in N. Y. Doc. Col. Hist., III, 197, 1853 (cf. Bushnell in Am. Anthrop., IX, no. 1, 1907). **Mohetons.**—Ibid., 196.

Mohickon John's Town. A village, probably occupied by a band of Mahican under a chief known as Mohickon John, formerly on the upper waters of Mohican r., probably on Jerome fork, in the present Ashland co., Ohio. It is probably the Mohicken Village mentioned by Croghan in 1760. (J. M.)

Mohican Johnstown.—Howe, Hist. Coll. Ohio, II, 832, 1896. **Mohicken Village.**—Croghan (1760) in Mass. Hist. Soc. Coll., 4th s., IX, 378, 1871. **Mohickon John's Town.**—Hutchins map in Smith, Bouquet's Exped., 1766. **Ville de Jean.**—La Tour, map, 1784 ("Mohickon ou Ville de Jean").

Mohock. From the reputation of the Mohawk, an Iroquoian people of central New York and parts of Canada, their name was used by the colonists in the sense of 'fierce fellow,' then 'ruffian,' or 'tough' in modern parlance. The word was specially applied to one of the many bands of ruffians who infested the streets of London at the beginning of the 18th century. As it appears in English literature it is spelled Mohock. Gay, the poet and dramatist (1688–1732), asks—

Who has not heard the Scowrer's midnight fame?
Who has not trembled at the Mohock's name?

(A. F. C.)

Mohominge. A village of the Powhatan confederacy near the falls of James r., at Richmond, Va., about 1610 (Strachey, *ca.* 1612, Va., 25, 1849). It is not marked on Capt. John Smith's map.

Mohongo (or Myhangah). The wife of Kihegashugah, an Osage chief. These two, with four other members of the tribe, sailed from New Orleans in 1827, and on July 27 arrived at Havre, France, under the care of David Delaunay, a Frenchman who had lived 25 years in St Louis, and who is said to have been a colonel in the service of the United States. The Indians later went to Paris, and, as at Havre, were the objects of marked attention, being showered with gifts, entertained by people of prominence, and received at court by Charles X. The desire of Kihegashugah to visit France was inspired by a journey to that country by his grandfather in the time of Louis XIV. Kihegashugah and two others of the party died of smallpox on shipboard while returning to America. It is said that the expense of their return was borne by Lafayette.   Landing at Norfolk, Va., the survivors of the party proceeded to Washington, where the accompanying portrait of Mohongo, from Kenney and Hall, was painted.   See Six Indiens rouges de la tribu Osages (with portraits), 1827; Histoire de la tribu Osages, par P. V., 1827; McKenney and Hall, Ind. Tribes, I, 29, 1858; Fletcher in Am. Anthrop., II, 395, 1900.

MOHONGO   (McKENNEY AND HALL)

Mohonk Indian Conferences.   A series of annual meetings of friends of the Indians intended to facilitate intelligent discussion and conscientious agitation for desirable reforms.   In these conferences a novel and effective way of forming and disseminating sound public opinion has been devised and for a score of years successfully employed, and through their instrumentality public speakers and those who write for the press have been kept in touch with the experts who know the facts.   The Mohonk conferences, in their inception and their maintenance, are the idea and the work of Albert K. Smiley, member of the U. S. Board of Indian Commissioners, formerly professor of natural science at Haverford College, later in charge of the Friends' Boarding School at Providence, R. I.   Having purchased the picturesque hotel overlooking beautiful L. Mohonk, in the Catskill range, w. of lower Hudson r., N. Y., Mr Smiley made it a resort for people of education, high principle, and philanthropic interests.   Led by the wish to promote reform in the management of Indian affairs, he conceived the idea of inviting each year,

as his personal guests for the greater part of a week in October, the people who knew most about Indian life, education, and .mission work, and the relations of the Government to the Indians.   Besides these experts in Indian affairs, were invited from 100 to 250 other people, leaders in shaping public opinion, such as editors of the secular and religious press, writers for reviews, clergymen of all denominations, presidents of universities and colleges, leading men and women teaching in public schools, lawyers and judges, Senators and Representatives in Congress, members of the Cabinet and heads of Departments, expert ethnologists, and, preeminently, such workers from the field as Indian agents of character and intelligence, teachers of Indian schools, army officers with a personal knowledge of Indians, and philanthropic people who had studied the Indians on the reservations.   These meetings Mr Smiley, as a member of the Board of Indian Commissioners, called "Conferences with the Board," and until 1902 a member of the Board presided—Gen. Clinton B. Fisk, from 1883 until his death in 1890; Dr Merrill E. Gates, former president of Amherst College, chairman (now secretary) of the Board, from 1890 to 1902; in 1903, Hon. John D. Long, ex-Secretary of the Navy, and in 1904, Hon. Charles J. Bonaparte, present Secretary of the Navy.   The proceedings of the conference for the first 20 years were printed as an appendix in the Annual Reports of the Board of Indian Commissioners.

During the four days of the meeting, in the mornings a three or four hours' session and in the evenings two to three hours have been given to addresses, papers, reports, and the freest discussion, in which the widest differences of opinion have been welcomed and carefully considered and discussed.   Sympathetic attention to views the most divergent has resulted in such conservatively sound utterances in the annual Mohonk platform as have generally commanded the support of the great body of the best friends of the Indians.   In the afternoon, in drives and walks about the lake and through the forest, congenial groups of interested friends often continued the discussions of the morning sessions, shaped resolutions, and devised plans for aiding reform.

At its first meeting in 1883 the conference reported in favor of larger appropriations for Indian education and more school buildings; the extension of laws relating to crime, marriage, and inheritance so as to cover Indians on reservations then "lawless"; more of religious education for Indians; the gradual withdrawal of rations from the able-bodied

Indians because rations pauperized them; the inexpediency of leasing Indian grazing lands, and the need of greater care in selecting men of character as Indian agents. Still more progressive policies have been advocated in subsequent years. The conference early declared for land in severalty, with inalienable homesteads for Indian families; for educating Indians industrially as well as intellectually for citizenship, to be conferred as rapidly as practicable; and for uniform insistance upon monogamy, the sacredness of marriage, and the preservation at each agency of family records of marriages and relationships. The abolition of the system of appointing Indian agents as a reward for partisan service with little regard to fitness, was urgently advocated. The advantages of the "outing system," by which Indian children of school age were placed in carefully chosen homes of white people, to attend school with white children, and learn to work on white men's farms, were discussed and demonstrated. The breaking up of the tribal system in Indian Territory was advocated several years before the Commission to the Five Civilized Tribes (q. v.) was appointed; and the conference has advocated the division of the great tribal trust funds into individual holdings, each Indian to have control of his own share of that money as soon as he shows himself able to begin to use it wisely. The development of native Indian industries, wherever practicable, has been intelligently favored. Sympathetic appreciation of all that is fine, artistically suggestive, and worthy of development in the nature, institutions, and arts of the Indian, has been marked and constant. (M. E. G.)

Mohotlath (*Mō-hotl'ath*). A sept of the Opitchesaht, a Nootka tribe.—Boas in 6th Rep. N. W. Tribes Canada, 32, 1890.

Moicaqui. A former rancheria, probably of the Nevome, in Sonora, Mexico, visited by Father Kino in 1694.—Doc. Hist. Mex., 4th s., I, 253, 1856.

Moingwena. The name (the etymology of which is doubtful) of a small tribe of the Illinois confederacy, closely affiliated with the Peoria. The name was applied also to the village in which they resided. The first recorded notice of the tribe is by Marquette in the account of his descent of the Mississippi with Joliet in 1673, when he found them residing in the vicinity of the Peoria village on the w. side of the Mississippi near the mouth of a river supposed to have been the Des Moines. Franquelin's map of 1688 gives the name of the river as "Moingana," and marks the Indian village of "Moingoana" on it. When Marquette returned from the S. in 1674, he passed up Illinois r. and found the Peoria in the vicinity of

L. Peoria, the tribe having removed hither after his descent the previous year. He does not mention the Moingwena in this connection, but from the fact that Gravier found them with the Peoria in this locality in 1700, it is presumed that they migrated thither with the latter tribe. As no mention is made of them after this time they probably were incorporated with the Peoria, thus losing their tribal distinction. (J. M. C. T.)

Moeng8ena.—Joliet, maps in Coues, Pike's Exped., I, 13, 1895. Moingoana.—La Salle (1681) in Margry, Déc., II, 134, 1877. Moingona.—Pénicaut (1700), ibid., V, 411, 1883. Moingwenas.—Shea, Cath. Miss., 404, 1855. Moins.—Nuttall, Journal, 251, 1821. Mouingoueña.—Gravier (1701) in Jes. Rel., LXV, 101, 1900.

Moiseyu (*Móïséyu*, a word of uncertain origin, sometimes rendered as a Cheyenne name meaning 'many flies' or 'flint people', but probably of foreign derivation). An Algonquian tribe which, according to the tradition of the Cheyenne, adjoined them on the N. E. in their old home in Minnesota, and started with them on their westward migration about the year 1700, but turned back before reaching the Missouri r. It is said that some of their descendants are still with the Cheyenne. They are possibly identical with the Monsoni. (J. M.)

Arrow Men.—Dorsey in Field Columb. Mus. Pub. 103, pl. xix, 1905. Mo wĭs sĭ yū.—Grinnell, Social Org. Cheyennes, 136, 1905.

Moisie. A summer village of Montagnais and Nascapee at the mouth of Moisie r., on the N. shore of the Gulf of St Lawrence, Quebec (Hind, Lab. Penin., I, 290, 1863). In 1906 the Montagnais and Nascapee at Moisie and Seven Islands numbered 376.

Moiya. Given by Gibbs (Schoolcraft, Ind. Tribes, III, 112, 1853) as the name of a Pomo village in the vicinity of Hopland, Mendocino co., Cal.

Mojualuna. A former Taos village in the mountains above the present Taos pueblo, N. Mex.

Mojual-ua.—Bandelier in Arch. Inst. Papers, IV, 32, 1892. Mojua-lu-na.—Ibid.

Mokaich. The Mountain Lion clan of the Keresan pueblos of Laguna, Sia, San Felipe, and Cochiti, N. Mex. The Mountain Lion clan of Laguna went to that village from the Rio Grande, dwelling first at Mt Taylor, or Mt San Mateo. With the Hapai (Oak) clan it formed a phratry, but it is probably now extinct. The clans of this name at Sia and San Felipe are quite extinct. (F. W. H.)

Móhkach-hánuch.—Hodge in Am. Anthrop., IX, 351, 1896 (Cochiti name; hánuch = 'people'). Mókaich-háno.—Ibid. (Sia and San Felipe form). Mókaiqoh-hánoch.—Ibid. (Laguna form). Mo'-kaitc.—Stevenson in 11th Rep. B. A. E., 19, 1894 (Sia form; tc=ch). Mo-katsh.—Bandelier in Arch. Inst. Papers, III, 293, 1890. Mokatsh hanutsh.—Bandelier, Delight Makers, 464, 1890 (hanutsh = 'people').

Mokaskel. A former Luiseño village in the neighborhood of San Luis Rey mission, s. Cal.—Taylor in Cal. Farmer, May 11, 1860.

Mokelumne. A division of the Miwok in the country between Cosumne and Mokelumne rs., in Eldorado, Amador, and Sacramento cos., Cal. See *Moquelumnan Family.*
Locklomnee.—Bancroft, Nat. Races, I, 450, 1874. **Mokelemnès.**—Duflot de Mofras, Expl., II, 383, 1844. **Mo-kel-um-ne.**—Frémont, Geog. Memoir, 16, 1848. **Moquelumnes.**—Bancroft, Hist. Cal., IV, 73, 1886. **Mukeemnes.**—Bancroft, Nat. Races, I, 450, 1874. **Mukelemnes.**—Ibid. **Muthelemnes.**—Hale in U. S. Expl. Exped., VI, 630, 1846. **Socklumnes.**—Bancroft, Nat. Races, I, 450, 1874 (identical?).

Mokete. A village of the Powhatan confederacy, in 1608, on Warrasqueoc cr., Isle of Wight co., Va.—Smith (1629), Va., I, map, repr. 1819.

Mokohoko (*Mokohoko*[a], 'he who floats visible near the surface of the water'). A chief of the band of Sauk that took the lead in supporting Black Hawk (q. v.) in the Black Hawk war. He was of the Sturgeon clan, the ruling clan of the Sauk, and was a bitter enemy of Keokuk (q. v.). The band still retains its identity. It refused to leave Kansas when the rest of the tribe went to Indian Ter., and had to be removed thither by the military. It is now known as the Black Hawk band, and its members are the most conservative of all the Sauk. (w. J.)

Mokumiks ('red round robes'). A band of the Piegan division of the Siksika.
Mo-kŭm'-iks.—Grinnell, Blackfoot Lodge Tales, 210, 1892. **Red Round Robes.**—Ibid., 225.

Molala. A Waiilatpuan tribe forming the western division of that family. Little is known of their history. When first met with they resided in the Cascade range between Mts Hood and Scott and on the w. slope, in Washington and Oregon. The Cayuse have a tradition that the Molala formerly dwelt with them s. of Columbia r. and became separated and driven westward in their wars with hostile tribes. Their dialect, while related, is quite distinct from that of the Cayuse, and the separation probably took place in remote times. The name Molala is derived from that of a creek in Willamette valley, Oreg., s. of Oregon City. A band of these Indians drove out the original inhabitants and occupied their land. Subsequently the name was extended to all the bands. The present status of the tribe is not certain. In 1849 it was estimated to number 100; in 1877 Gatschet found several families living on the Grande Ronde res., Oreg., and in 1881 there were said to be about 20 individuals living in the mountains w. of Klamath lake. Those on the Grande Ronde res. are not officially enumerated, but are regarded as absorbed by the other tribes with whom they live. With regard to the rest nothing is known. It is probable, however, that there are a few scattered survivors. The Molala joined with other bands of

Willamette valley in the treaty of Dayton, Oreg., Jan. 22, 1855, and by treaty at the same place, Dec. 21, 1855, they ceded their lands and agreed to remove to a reservation. Chakankni, Chimbuiha, and Mukanti are said to have been Molala bands or settlements. (L. F.)
Amole'lish.—Gatschet, Calapooya MS., B. A. E., 31, 1877 (Calapooya name). **Kúikni.**—Gatschet in Cont. N. A. Ethnol., II, pt. 2, 157, 1890 (Klamath name). **Láti-u.**—Gatschet, Molala MS., B. A. E. (own name). **La'tiwĕ.**—Ibid. **Malala.**—Sen. Ex. Doc. 48, 34th Cong., 3d sess., 10, 1857. **Molala.**—Treaty of 1854 in U. S. Stat., X, 675, 1854. **Molalallas.**—Treaty of Dayton (1855) in U. S. Stat., XII, 981, 1863. **Molale.**—Gatschet, Umpqua MS. vocab., B. A. E., 1877. **Molalla.**—Hedges in H. R. Ex. Doc. 37, 34th Cong., 3d sess., 130, 1857. **Molallah.**—White, Ten Years in Oregon, 266, 1850. **Molallalas.**—Ind. Aff. Rep. 1856, 267, 1857. **Molallales.**—Hedges in H. R. Ex. Doc. 37, 34th Cong., 3d sess., 130, 1857. **Molalle.**—Armstrong, Oregon, 114, 1857. **Molallie.**—McClane in Ind. Aff. Rep., 269, 1889. **Mo-lay-less.**—Lyman in Oregon Hist. Soc. Quar., I, 323, 1900. **Moleaaleys.**—Meek in H. R. Ex. Doc. 76, 30th Cong., 1st sess., 10, 1848. **Molealleg.**—Lane in Schoolcraft, Ind. Tribes, III, 632, 1853. **Mole Alley.**—Lane in Sen. Ex. Doc. 52, 31st Cong., 1st sess., 171, 1850. **Moleallies.**—Browne (1857) in H. R. Ex. Doc. 38, 35th Cong., 1st sess., 7, 1858. **Molel.**—Treaty of Dayton (1855) in U. S. Stat., XII, 981, 1863. **Molele.**—Hale in U. S. Expl. Exped., VI, 214, 1846. **Molelie.**—McClane in Ind. Aff. Rep., 203, 1888. **Molell.**—Hedges in H. R. Ex. Doc. 37, 34th Cong., 3d sess., 130, 1857. **Mollallas.**—White in Ind. Aff. Rep., 203, 1844. **Moolal-le.**—Ex. Doc. 39, 32d Cong., 1st sess., 2, 1852. **Moolalles.**—Schoolcraft, Ind. Tribes, III, 200, map, 1853. **Mooleilis.**—Tolmie and Dawson, Comp. Vocabs., 11, 1884. **Morlal-les.**—Lea in Ind. Aff. Rep., 8, 1851. **Straight Mólale.**—Gatschet in Cont. N. A. Ethnol., II, pt. 2, 157, 1890 (name for those on Grande Ronde res.) **Wrole Alley.**—Lane in Ind. Aff. Rep., 160, 1850. **Ya'-ide'sta.**—Gatschet, Umpqua MS. vocab., B. A. E., 1877 (Umpqua name).

Molma. A Maidu village near Auburn, Placer co., Cal.—Dixon in Bull. Am. Mus. Nat. Hist., XVII, pl. xxxviii, 1905.

Momi (*Mo'mi*, 'a people who eat no small birds which have been killed by larger ones'). A subgens of the Missouri gens Cheghita, formerly a distinct people.—Dorsey in 15th Rep. B. A. E., 240, 1897.

Momobi (*Mo'-mo-bi*, a species of lizard). A clan of the Lizard (Earth or Sand) phratry of the Hopi.—Stephen in 8th Rep. B. A. E., 39, 1891.

Monacan (possibly from an Algonquian word signifying a digging stick or spade). A tribe and confederacy of Virginia in the 17th century. The confederacy occupied the upper waters of James r. above the falls at Richmond. Their chief village was Rasawek. They were allies of the Manahoac and enemies of the Powhatan, and spoke a language different from that of either. They were finally incorporated with other remnants under the names of Saponi and Tutelo (q. v.). The confederacy was composed of the Monacan proper, Massinacac, Mohemencho, Monahassano, Monasiccapano, and some other tribes.

The Monacan proper had a chief settlement, known to the whites as Monacantown, on James r. about 20 m. above the falls at Richmond. In 1669 they still had 30 bowmen, or perhaps about 100 souls. Thirty years later, the Indian population having died out or emigrated, a Huguenot colony took possession of the site. Consult Mooney, Siouan Tribes of the East, Bull. B. A. E., 1894. (J. M.)

Manacans.—Smith, Va., I, 136, 1819. Manachees.— Neill, Va. Carolorum, 325, 1886. Manakan.—Doc. of 1701 in Va. Hist. Coll., n. s., v, 42, 1886. Manakins.—Stith (1747) quoted by Burk, Va., I, 128, 1804. Manikin.—Doc. of 1700 in Va. Hist. Coll., op. cit., 48. Mannacans.—Strachey (ca. 1612), Va., 41, 1849. Mannachin.—Doc. of 1701 in Va. Hist. Coll., op. cit., 45. Mannakin.—Lawson (1714), Hist. Carolina, 187, 1860. Manskin.—Herrman, map (1670) in Rep. Bound. Com., 1873 (erroneously located on Pamunkey r.). Manyoan.—Doc. of 1700 in Va. Hist. Coll., op. cit., 51. Monacans.— Smith, Va., I, 116, 1819. Monachans.—Yong (1634) in Mass. Hist. Soc. Coll., 4th s., IX, 112, 1871. Monakins.—Lederer, Discov., 9, 1672. Monanacah Rahowacah.—Archer (1607) in Smith, Works, Arber ed., xlvi, 1884. Monanacans.—Ibid., 1. Monocans.—Strachey, op. cit., 27.

Monack. See *Moonack*.

Monahassano (a name of uncertain etymology, but most probably connected with *Yesán*, the name which the Tutelo applied to themselves). A tribe of the Monacan confederacy, formerly living on the s. side of James r., near the mountains, in Bedford and Buckingham cos., Va. Lederer describes them as tall and warlike, and says their totem was three arrows. In 1671 they were 25 m. from the Saponi, on Staunton r. They seem to have been next in importance to the Monacan in the confederacy. See *Tutelo*. Consult Mooney, Siouan Tribes of the East, Bull. B. A. E., 1894. (J. M.)

Flanakaskies.—Batts (1671) quoted by Fernow, Ohio Val., 221, 1890 (misprint). Hanahaskies.— Batts (1671) in N. Y. Doc. Col. Hist., III, 197, 1853. Hanohaskies.—Batts, ibid., 194. Monahasanugh.— Smith (ca. 1629), Va., I, map, 1819. Monahassanoes.—Jefferson, Notes, 134, 1794. Monahassanughes.—Strachey (ca. 1612), Va., 102, 1849. Nahyssans.—Lederer, Discov., 9, 1672. Nobissan.—Ibid., map (misprint). Yesah.—Hale in Proc. Am. Philos. Soc., XXI, 11, 1883-4 (own name; see *Tutelo*). Yesán.—Hale, MS., B. A. E., 1877. Yesang.— Hale in Proc. Am. Philos. Soc., op. cit.

Monakatuatha. See *Half King*.

Monanauk. A village, possibly Conoy, on the Potomac in 1608, about Breton bay, or Clements branch, St. Marys co., Md.

Monashackotoog. A tribe which, with the Wunnashowatuckoog, lived w. of Boston, Mass., in 1637. They were friends of the Pequot and enemies of the Narraganset.—Williams (1637) in Mass. Hist. Soc. Coll., 4th s., VI, 194, 1863.

Monasiccapano. A tribe of the Monacan confederacy, formerly living in Louisa and Fluvanna cos., Va., between the James and the headwaters of the Pamunkey. The derivation of the name is unknown, but it may have some connection with Saponi. See Mooney, Siouan Tribes of the East, Bull. B. A. E., 1894. (J. M.)

Massicapanoes.—Macauley, N. Y., II, 178, 1829. Monasiccapanoes.—Jefferson, Notes, 134, 1794. Monasiceapanoes.—Boudinot, Star in the West, 127,

1816. Monasickapanoughs.—Smith (ca. 1629), Va., I, 134, 1819. Monasukapanough.—Ibid., map.

Monax. See *Moonack*.

Moncachtape ('killer of pain and fatigue'). A Yazoo Indian, noted chiefly on account of his real or supposed travels and his knowledge of various Indian languages. Le Page du Pratz, during his residence in Louisiana about the middle of the 18th century, met Moncachtape and obtained from him an account of his wanderings, according to which (DuPratz, Hist. La., III, 89–128, 1758), after the loss of his wife and children, he had devoted much of his time to traveling. One of his journeys was to the N. E., in which he passed up the Ohio, visited the Shawnee and Iroquois, and wintered among the Abnaki; thence he went up the St Lawrence and returned to his home by way of the Mississippi. His second trip was to the N. W. coast by the route subsequently traveled by Lewis and Clark. He mentions the Tamaroa, Kansa, and Amikwa, and although he alludes to numerous tribes seen during his passage down Columbia r., he mentions no tribal names. He finally reached the Pacific coast, where, in addition to Indians, he met with bearded white men, who "came from sun-setting, in search of a yellow stinking wood which dyes a fine yellow color." With other Indians he ambushed and killed 11 of these strangers, 2 of whom bore firearms. These whites are described as small, but having large heads and long hair in the middle of the crown and wrapped in a great many folds of stuff, while their clothes were soft and of several colors. This story, so far as it relates to the western trip, is very doubtful on its face, and the names of tribes which it gives extend only as far as DuPratz' own knowledge of them; yet Quatrefages (Human Species, 205, 1895) accepts the story as credible, and that Moncachtape understood a number of languages is clearly proven. See also Clarke, Pion. Days in Oreg., 1905. (C. T.)

Monemius. A village of the Mahican tribe, known as Monemius' Castle from the name of the resident chief, situated in the 17th century on Haver id., in Hudson r., near Cohoes falls, Albany co., N. Y. (J. M.)

Moeneminos Castle.—Deed of 1630 in N. Y. Doc. Col. Hist., XIV, 1, 1883. Moeneminnes Castle.—Patent of 1630, ibid., I, 44, 1856. Monemiu's castle.— Ruttenber, Tribes Hudson R., 85, 1872.

Mong (*Mang*, 'loon'). A gens of the Chippewa (q. v.). Cf. *Maak*.

Mahng.—Tanner, Narrative, 314, 1830. Māng.— Wm. Jones, inf'n, 1906. Mänk.—Gatschet, Ojibwa MS., B. A. E., 1882. Mong.—Warren (1852) in Minn. Hist. Soc. Coll., v, 44, 1885.

Mongwa (*Mon-gwä′*, 'loon'). A gens of the Miami (q. v.).—Morgan, Anc. Soc., 168, 1877.

Monk's Mound. See *Cahokia Mound.*

Monnato (*Mon-nă'-to,* 'snow'). A gens of the Miami (q. v.).—Morgan, Anc. Soc., 168, 1877.

Mono. A general term applied to the Shoshonean tribes of s. E. California by their neighbors on the w. The origin and meaning of the name are obscure, its identity with the Spanish *mono,* 'monkey,' and its similarity, at least in certain dialects, to the Yokuts word for 'fly' (*monai,* etc.), are probably only coincidences. For subdivisions, see *Mono-Paviotso.*

Honachees.—Bunnell quoted by Powers in Cont. N. A. Ethnol., III, 350, 1877. Manaché.—Purcell in Ind. Aff. Rep., 87, 1870. Moan'-au-zi.—Powers in Cont. N. A. Ethnol., III, 320, 1877 (Nishinam name). Monache.—Belknap in Ind. Aff. Rep., 17, 1876 ("the usual form of the name as heard among the southern Yokuts; cf. the Maidu (Nishinam) name, preceding"—A. L. K.). Mona'-chi.—Powers in Cont. N. A. Ethnol., III, 350, 1877. Monas.—Johnston in Sen. Ex. Doc. 61, 32d Cong., 1st sess., 22, 1852. Monoes.—Johnston in Ind. Aff. Rep., 251, 1851. Mono Pi-Utes.—Campbell in Ind. Aff. Rep., 119, 1866. Monos.—Taylor in Cal. Farmer, May 8, 1863. Noo-tah-ah.—Wessels (1853) in H. R. Ex. Doc. 76, 34th Cong., 3d sess., 31, 1857. Nutaa.—A. L. Kroeber, inf'n, 1905 (Chukchansi name; denotes that they are E. or upstream). Nŭt'-ha.—Powers in Cont. N. A. Ethnol., III, 396, 1877.

Mono–Paviotso. One of the three great dialectic groups into which the Shoshoneans of the great plateau are distinguished. It includes the Mono of s. E. California, the Paviotso, or "Paiute," of w. Nevada, and the "Snakes" and Saidyuka of E. Oregon. Part of the Bannock may be related to these, but the eastern Bannock have affinities with the Ute.

The bands which seem to have formed the social unit of these people were each under one chief, and several of these are said to have been united into confederacies, such as the "Paviotso confederacy," but it is doubtful whether the relations existing between the constituent parts should properly be so termed.

The bands or divisions mentioned within the area occupied by this group are the following: Agaivanuna, Genega's band, Hadsapoke's band, Holkoma, Hoonebooey, Intimbich, Itsaatiaga, Kaidatoiabie, Kaivanungavidukw, Koeats, Kokoheba, Kosipatuwiwagaiyu, Kotsava, Koyuhow, Kuhpattikutteh, Kuyuidika, Laidukatuwiwait, Lohim, Loko, Nahaego, Nim, Nogaie, Odukeo's band, Olanche, Oualuck's band, Pagantso, Pagwiho, Pamitoy, Pavuwiwuyuai, Petenegowat, Petodseka, Piattuiabbe, Poatsituhtikuteh, Poskesa, San Joaquins' band, Sawagativa, Shobarboobeer, Sunananahogwa, Temoksee, Togwingani, Tohaktivi, Toiwait, Tonawitsowa, Tonoyiet's band, Toquimas, To Repe's band, Tosarke's band, Tsapakah, Tubianwapu, Tupustikutteh, Tuziyammos, Wahi's band, Wahtatkin, Walpapi, Warartika, Watsequeorda's band, Winnemucca's band, Woksachi, Yahuskin, and Yammostuwiwagaiya.

Numaltachi, given as a village on Tuolomne r., Cal., may in reality be another band.

From figures given in the report of the Indian office for 1903 it would appear that the total number in this division is in the neighborhood of 5,400.

Monongahela. A variety of whisky. Says Bartlett (Dict. of Americanisms, 401, 1877): "A river of Pennsylvania, so called, gave its name to the rye whisky of which large quantities were produced in its neighborhood, and indeed to American whisky in general, as distinguished from Usquebaugh and Inishowen, the Scotch and Irish sorts." The name is of Algonquian origin, but its etymology is uncertain.   (A. F. C.)

Monsoni (*Mongsoaeythinyuwok,* 'moose people.'—Franklin). An Algonquian tribe in British America, often classed as a part of the Cree, to whom they are closely related, although they seem to be almost as closely related to the northern Chippewa. The first notice of them is in the Jesuit Relation for 1671. In that of 1672 they are located on the shore of James bay, about the mouth of Moose r., which, according to Richardson, received its name from them. They are referred to under the name Aumonssoniks in the Proces verbal of the Prise de possession (1671), but were not represented at the ceremony, though Charlevoix asserts the contrary. Although Dobbs (1744) speaks of them as the Moose River Indians, he locates a village or band on the w. bank of Rainy r., near Rainy lake, and others on the N. shore of this lake. Some confusion has arisen in regard to the habitat and linguistic connection of the tribe from the fact that the geographic designation "Mosonee" is frequently used to include all that portion of Keewatin and adjacent territory stretching along Hudson bay from Moose r. northward to Nelson r., a region occupied chiefly by the Maskegon. The usual and most permanent home of the Monsoni, however, has been the region of Moose r. According to Chauvignerie their totem was the moose. There is no separate enumeration of them in the recent Canadian official reports. See *Mousonee.*   (J. M. C. T.)

Aumonssoniks.—Prise de possession (1671) in Perrot, Mém., 293, 1864. Aumossomiks.—Verwyst, Missionary Labors, 232, 1886. Aumoussonnites.—Prise de possession (1671) in Margry, Déc., I, 97, 1875. Crees of Moose Factory.—Franklin, Journ. to Polar Sea, I, 96, 1824. Gens de marais.—Bacqueville de la Potherie, Hist. Am. Sept., I, 174, 1753. Mongsoa Eithynyook.—Gallatin in Trans. Am. Antiq. Soc., II, 24, 1836. Mongsoa-eythinyoowuc.—Franklin, Journ. to Polar Sea, I, 96, 1824. Monsaunis.—Bacqueville de la Potherie, Hist. Am. Sept., I, 174, 1753. Monsonics.—Keane in Stanford, Compend., 523, 1878. Monsonies.—Franklin, Journ. to Polar Sea, 56, 1824. Monsonis.—Chauvignerie (1736) in N. Y. Doc. Col. Hist., IX, 1054, 1855. Monsounic.—Jes. Rel. 1671, 30, 1858. Monzoni.—Lahontan, New Voy., I, 231, 1703. Moose-deer Indians.—Franklin,

Journ. to Polar Sea, I, 96, 1824. **Moose Indians.**—Horden, Bk. of Common Prayer in Language of Moose Indians, title-page, 1859. **Moose River Indians.**—Dobbs, Hudson Bay, 13, 1744. **Morisons.**—Chauvignerie (1736) quoted by Schoolcraft, Ind. Tribes, III, 556, 1853 (misprint). **Mousonis.**—McKenney and Hall, Ind. Tribes, III, 80, 1858. **Nation of the Marshes.**—Dobbs, Hudson Bay, 24, 1744. **Ou-Monssonis.**—Tailhan, note to Perrot, Mém., 293, 1864. **Wamussonewug.**—Tanner, Narr., 316, 1830 (Ottawa name).

Monswidishianun (*Mōⁿs wiˊdishiˊanum*). The Moose phratry of the Menominee, also a subphratry or gens thereof.—Hoffman in 14th Rep. B. A. E., pt. 1, 42, 1896.

Montagnais (French 'mountaineers', from the mountainous character of their country). A group of closely related Algonquian tribes in Canada, extending from about St Maurice r. almost to the Atlantic, and from the St Lawrence to the watershed of Hudson bay. The tribes of the group speak several well-marked dialects. They are the Astouregamigoukh, Attikiriniouetch, Bersiamite, Chisedec, Escoumains, Espamichkon, Kakouchaki, Mauthæpi, Miskouaha, Mouchaouaouastiirinioek, Nascapee, Nekoubaniste, Otaguottouemin, Oukesestigouek, Oumamiwek, Papinachois, Tadousac, and Weperigweia. Their linguistic relation appears to be closer with the Cree of Athabasca lake, or Ayabaskawininiwug, than with any other branch of the Algonquian family. Champlain met them at the mouth of the Saguenay in 1603, where they and other Indians were celebrating with bloody rites the capture of Iroquois prisoners. Six years later he united with them the Hurons and Algonkin in an expedition against the Iroquois. In the first Jesuit Relation, written by Biard (1611–16), they are spoken of as friends of the French. From that time their name has a place in Canadian history, though they exerted no decided influence on the settlement and growth of the colony. The first missionary work among them was begun in 1615, and missions were subsequently established on the upper Saguenay and at L. St John. These were continued, though with occasional and long interruptions, until 1776. The Montagnais fought the Micmac, and often the Eskimo, but their chief and inveterate foes were the Iroquois, who drove them for a time from the banks of the St Lawrence and from their strongholds about the upper Saguenay, compelling them to seek safety at more distant points. After peace was established between the French and the Iroquois they returned to their usual haunts. Lack of proper food, epidemics, and contact with civilization are reducing their numbers. Turner (11th Rep. B. A. E., 1894) says they roam over the areas s. of Hamilton inlet as far as the Gulf of St Lawrence. Their western limits are imperfectly known. They trade at all the stations along the accessible coast, many of them at Rigolet and Northwest r. Sagard, in 1632, described them as Indians of the lowest type in Canada. Though they have occasionally fought with bravery, they are comparatively timid. They have always been more less nomadic and, although accepting the teachings of the missionaries, seem incapable of resigning the freedom of the forest for life in villages, nor can they be induced to cultivate the soil as a means of support. Mr Chisholm describes them as honest, hospitable, and benevolent, but very superstitious. Those who were induced to settle on the lower St Lawrence appear to be subject to sickness, which is thinning their numbers. All who have not been brought directly under religious influence are licentious. Conjuring was much practised by their medicine-men. Some of the early missionaries speak highly of their religious susceptibility. They bury their dead in the earth, digging a hole 3 ft deep and occasionally lining it with wood. The corpse is usually laid on its side, though it is sometimes placed in a sitting position. Above the grave is built a little birch-bark hut and through a window the relatives thrust bits of tobacco, venison, and other morsels. No reliable estimate can be given of their former numbers, but it is known that they have greatly decreased from sickness and starvation consequent on the destruction of game. In 1812 they were supposed to number about 1,500; in 1857 they were estimated at 1,100, and in 1884 they were officially reported at 1,395, living at Betsiamits, (Bersimis), Escoumains, Godbout, Grand Romaine, Lake St John, and Mingan, in Quebec. In 1906 they, together with the Nascapee, numbered, according to the Canadian official report, 2,183, distributed as follows: Bersimis, 499; Escoumains, 43; Natashquan, 76; Godbout, 40; Grand Romaine, 176; Lake St John, 551; Mingan, 241; St Augustine, 181; Seven Islands and Moisie, 376. Consult Chamberlain in Ann. Archæol. Rep. Ontario 1905, 122, 1906.

The bands and villages of the Montagnais are: Appeelatat, Assuapmushan, Attikamegue, Bonne Espérance, Chicoutimi, Esquimaux Point, Godbout, Ile Percée (mission), Itamameou (mission), Islets de Jeremie (mission), Kapiminakouetiik, Mauthæpi, Mingan, Moisie, Mushkoniatawee, Musquarro, Nabisippi, Natashquan, Pashasheebo, Piekouagami, Romaine, and St Augustine. (J. M. C. T.)

Algonkin Inférieures.—Hind, Lab. Penin., II, 10, 1863. **Algonquins Inférieurs.**—Jes. Rel., III, index, 1858. **Bergbewohner.**—Walch, map of Am., 1805 (German: 'Mountaineers'). **Chauhaguéronon.**—Sagard (1632), Hist. Can., IV, 1866 (Huron name). **Chauoironon.**—Ibid. **Kebiks.**—Schoolcraft Ind.

Tribes, v, 40, 1855 (on account of their warning cry of "Kebik!" when approaching in canoes the rapids of the St Lawrence near Quebec). **Lower Algonkins.**—Jefferys, Fr. Doms., pt. 1, 46, 1761. **Montagnais.**—Jes. Rel. 1611, 8, 1858. **Montagnaits.**—Jes. Rel. 1633, 3, 1858. **Montagnards.**—Jes. Rel. 1632, 5, 1858. **Montagnars.**—Champlain (1609), Œuvres, III, 194, 1870. **Montagnés.**—Champlain (1603), ibid., II, 9, 1870. **Montagnets.**—Jes. Rel. 1611, 15, 1858. **Montagnez.**—Champlain (1603), Œuvres, II, 8, 1870. **Montagnois.**—Lahontan, New Voy., I, 207, 1703. **Montagrets.**—Me. Hist. Soc. Coll., I, 288, 1865 (misprint). **Montagues.**—McKenney and Hall, Ind. Tribes, III, 81, 1854 (misprint). **Montaignairs.**—Champlain (1615), Œuvres, IV, 22, 1870. **Montaigners.**—Champlain (1618), ibid., 113, 1870. **Montaignes.**—Champlain (1603), ibid., II, 49, 1870. **Montaignets.**—Ibid. (1609), v, pt. 1, 144. **Montainiers.**—Schoolcraft, Ind. Tribes, v, 40, 1855. **Montanaro.**—Hervas (ca. 1785) quoted by Vater, Mith., pt. 3, sec. 3, 347, 1816. **Montaniak.**—Gatschet, Penobscot MS., 1887 (Penobscot name). **Mountaineers.**—Mass. Hist. Soc. Coll., 1st s., VI, 16, 1800. **Mountain Indians.**—Kingsley, Stand. Nat. Hist., pt. 6, 149, 1885. **Mountaneers.**—Lahontan, New Voy., I, 230, 1703. **Mountanees.**—Vater, Mith., pt. 3, sec. 3, 344, 1816. **Neconbavistes.**—Lattré, map, 1784 (misprint). **Ne-e-no-il-no.**—Hind, Lab. Penin., II, 10, 1863 ('perfect people', one of the names used by themselves). **Nehiroirini.**—Kingsley, Stand. Nat. Hist., pt. 6, 149, 1885. **Nekoubanistes.**—Bellin, map, 1755. **Neloubanistes.**—Esnauts and Rapilly, map, 1777 (misprint). **Sheshatapoosh.**—Gallatin in Trans. Am. Ethnol. Soc., II, ciii, 1848. **Sheshatapooshshoish.**—Mass. Hist. Soc. Coll., 1st s., VI, 16, 1800. **Shoudămŭnk.**—Peyton quoted by Lloyd in Jour. Anthrop. Inst., IV, 29, 1875 ('good Indians': Beothuk name). **Skatapushoish.**—Keane in Stanford, Compend., 536, 1878. **Sketapushoish.**—Mass. Hist. Soc. Coll., 1st s., VI, 16, 1800. **Tshe-tsi-uetin-euerno.**—Hind, Lab. Penin., II, 101, 863 ('people of the north-northeast': name used by themselves). **Uskwawgomees.**—Tanner, Narr., 316, 1830. **Ussagĕne'wi.**—Gatschet, Penobscot MS., 1887 ('people of the outlet' [Hewitt]: Penobscot name). **Ussaghenick.**—Vetromile, Abnakis, 50, 1866 (Etchimin name).

Montagnais. An Athapascan group, comprising the Chipewyan, Athabasca, Etheneldeli, and Tatsanottine tribes, which, though now living on the plains and in the valleys of British North America, migrated from the Rocky mts.—Petitot, Dict. Dènè-Dindjié, xx, 1876. For synonymy, see *Chipewyan*.

Montagnard. An ethnic and geographic Athapascan group comprising the Tsattine, Sarsi, Sekani, and Nahane tribes living in the Rocky mts. of British North America. The name was also formerly applied to the eastern Algonquian people now known as Montagnais.
Montagnardes.—Kingsley, Stand. Nat. Hist., pt. 6, 143, 1885. **Montagnards.** — Petitot, Dict. Dènè-Dindjié, xx, 1876. **Mountaineers.**—Morgan in N. Am. Rev., 58, 1870.

Montauk (meaning uncertain). A term that has been used in different senses, sometimes limited to the particular band or tribe known by this name, but in a broader sense including most of the tribes of Long Island, excepting those about the w. end. It is occasionally used incorrectly as equivalent to Metoac, q. v.

The Indians of Long Island were closely related to the Indians of Massachusetts and Connecticut. Tooker (Cockenoe-de-Long Island, 1896) says that the dialect of the Montauk was more nearly related to the Natick of Massachusetts than was the Narraganset.

The Montauk, in the limited sense, formerly occupied Easthampton tp., Suffolk co., at the E. end of Long Island, and controlled all the other tribes of the island, except those near the w. end. That these so-called tribes were but parts of one group or tribe, or the loosely connected elements of what had been an organized body, seems apparent. Ruttenber, speaking of the Montauk in the limited sense, says: "This chieftaincy was acknowledged both by the Indians and the Europeans as the ruling family of the island. They were indeed the head of the tribe of Montauk, the other divisions named being simply clans

DAVID PHARAOH, "LAST KING OF THE MONTAUK"

or groups, as in the case of other tribes. . . . Wyandance, their sachem, was also the grand sachem of Paumanacke, or Sewanhackey, as the island was called. Nearly all the deeds for lands were confirmed by him. His younger brothers, Nowedonah and Poygratasuck [Poggatacut], were respectively sachems of the Shinecock and the Manhasset." The Rockaway and Cannarsee at the w. end were probably not included. It is doubtful whether he is correct in including the west-end Indians in the confederacy. The principal Montauk village, which probably bore the name of the tribe, was about Ft Pond, near Montauk pt. The Pequot made them and their subordinates tributary, and on the destruction of that tribe in 1637, the Narraganset began a series of attacks which finally, about 1659, forced the Montauk, who had lost the greater part of their number by pestilence, to retire for protection to the whites at Easthampton. Since 1641 they had been tributary to New England. When first known they were numerous, and even after the pestilence of 1658–59, were estimated at about 500. Then began a rapid decline, and a century later only 162 remained, most of whom joined the Brotherton Indians of New York, about 1788, so that in 1829 only about 30 were left on Long Island, and 40 years later these had dwindled to half a dozen individuals, who, with a few Shinnecock, were the last representatives of the Long Island tribes. They preserved a form of tribal organization into the 19th century and retained their hereditary chiefs until the death of their last "king," David Pharaoh, about 1875. A few mixed-bloods are still officially recognized by the state of New York as constituting a tribe under Wyandanch Pharaoh, son of David.　　　　　　　　　　(J. M.)

Mantacut.—Gardener (1660) in Mass. Hist. Soc. Coll., 3d s., III, 154, 1833. **Mantaoke.**—Deed of 1657 in Thompson, Long Id., 344, 1839. **Mantauket.**—Gardener (1660) in Mass. Hist. Soc. Coll., 3d s., III, 156, 1833. **Meantacut.**—Ibid., 153. **Meantaukett.**—Doc. of 1671 in N. Y. Doc. Col. Hist., XIV, 648, 1883. **Meanticut.**—Gardener (1660) as quoted by Drake, Bk. Inds., bk. 2, 63, 1848. **Melotaukes.**—Boudinot, Star in the West, 127, 1816 (misprint). **Menataukett.**—Lovelace (1671) in N. Y. Doc. Col. Hist., XIV, 652, 1883. **Mentakett.**—Deed (1661) in Thompson, Long Id., I, 299, 1843 (place). **Mentoake.**—Deed of 1657, ibid., 344, 1839. **Meontaskett.**—Baily (1669) in R. I. Col. Rec., II, 276, 1857. **Meontawket.**—Clarke (1669), ibid., 285. **Meuntacut.**—Indian deed of 1648 cited by W. W. Tooker, inf'n, 1906. **Mirrachtauhacky.**—Doc. of 1645 in N. Y. Doc. Col. Hist., XIV, 60, 1883 (said by Tooker, Algong. Ser., II, 15, 1901, to be a Dutch form of Montauk). **Montacut.**—James (ca. 1654) in Mass. Hist. Soc. Coll., 4th s., VII, 482, 1865. **Montake.**—Doc. of 1657 in N. Y. Doc. Col. Hist., XIV, 416, 1883. **Montaks.**—Vater, Mith., pt. 3, sec. 3, 339, 1816. **Montank.**—Smithson. Miscel. Coll., XIV, art. 6, 25, 1878 (misprint). **Montauckett.**—Doc. of 1675 in N. Y. Doc. Col. Hist., XIV, 700, 1883. **Montaug.**—Latham in Trans. Philol. Soc. Lond., 59, 1856. **Montauk.**—Deed of 1666 in Thompson, Long Id., I, 312, 1843. **Montaukett.**—Deed (ca. 1655), ibid., 183, 1839. **Montaukut.**—Doc. of 1675 in N. Y. Doc. Col. Hist., XIV, 699, 1883. **Montauque.**—Doc. of 1669, ibid., 618. **Montoake.** — Doc. of 1657, ibid., 416. **Montocks.**—Tryon (1774), ibid., VIII, 451, 1857. **Montok.**—Johnson (1777), ibid., 714. **Montuoks.**—Devotion (ca. 1761) in Mass. Hist. Soc. Coll., 1st s., X, 106, 1809. **Mountacutt.**—Deed of 1648 in Thompson, Long Id., I, 294, 1843. **Muntake.**—Doc. of 1677 in N. Y. Doc. Col. Hist., XIV, 729, 1883. **Muntauckett.**—Doc. of 1675, ibid., 696. **Muntaukett.**—Doc. of 1668, ibid., 606.

Monterey Indians. The Costanoan Indians of Monterey co., Cal., numbering more than 100 in 1856. A vocabulary taken by Taylor (Cal. Farmer, Apr. 20, 1860) at that time is Rumsen. There are probably also remnants of the Esselen and other divisions of the Mutsun in the region of Monterey.

Montezuma, Carlos. An educated full-blood Apache, known among his people in childhood as Wasajah ('Beckoning'), born about 1866 in the neighborhood of the Four Peaks of the Mazatzal mts., present s. E. Arizona. In Oct., 1871, he was taken captive, with 16 or 18 other children including his two sisters, in a midnight raid by the Pima on his band, during the absence of the men on a mission of peace, while encamped in the Superstition mts., 40 or 50 m. w. of Globe. In this raid 30 or more of the Apache were killed. The captives were taken by the Pima to their rancherias on the Gila, whence, after a week's detention, Wasajah was taken to Adamsville, below Florence, and sold to Mr C. Gentile, a native of Italy, who was then prospecting in Arizona. Some months after the raid Wasajah's mother, who had escaped, was informed by an Indian runner that her boy had been seen at Camp Date Creek. Determined to recover her child, she applied to the agent for permission to leave the reservation, and being refused departed without leave. Her body was found later in a rugged pass in the mountains, where she had been shot by a native scout. Wasajah was taken by Mr. Gentile to Chicago and was called by him Carlos Montezuma—Carlos, from his own name, Montezuma, from the so-called Casa Montezuma (q. v.), near the Pima villages. He entered the public schools of Chicago in 1872, remaining until 1875, from which time until 1884 his education was continued in the public schools of Galesburg, Ill., Brooklyn, N. Y., and Urbana, Ill., and in the University of Illinois at the last-named place. In 1884 he entered the Chicago Medical School, from which he was graduated in 1889, receiving in the same year an appointment as physician in the U. S. Indian School at Stevenson, N. Dak. From 1890 until 1896 Dr Montezuma has served as physician successively at the Western Shoshone agency in Nevada, the Colville agency in Washington, and at the Carlisle Indian School. In the latter year he resigned from the service of the Indian department and settled in Chicago, where he is now engaged in the practice of his profession, in teaching in the College of Physicians and Surgeons and in the Post-graduate Medical School, and in arousing interest in his people through his writings.

Montezuma Castle. A prehistoric cliff-dwelling on the right bank of Beaver cr., a tributary of Rio Verde, 3 m. from old Camp Verde, central Arizona; popularly so-called because supposed to have been once occupied by the Aztecs, whereas there is no ground whatever for the belief that any Southwestern pueblo or cliff-village is of Mexican origin. The building is constructed in a natural recess in the side of a limestone cliff, the base of which is 348 ft from the edge of the stream and about 40 ft above it. The building, which is accessible only by means of ladders, consists of 5 stories, and in the same cliff are several cave-dwellings. The foundation of Montezuma Castle rests on cedar timbers laid longitudinally on flat stones on the ledge. The front wall is about 2 ft thick at the bottom and 13 in. at the top, and leans slightly toward the cliff. The first story consists of two small living rooms and a storeroom. The second floor, access to which is gained through a small opening in the ceiling of the first story, is more extensive, consisting of 4 apartments, bounded behind by the most massive wall of masonry in the entire structure, and resting on a ledge even with the floor of the second story. It is 28 ft in height, rising to the fifth story, around the front of which it forms a battlement 4½ ft high. It leans slightly toward the cliff, and is strongly but not symmetrically curved inward. The chord of the arc described by the top of the wall measures 43 ft, and the greatest distance from chord to circumference 8 ft. The third floor comprises the most extensive tier of rooms in the structure, extending across the entire alcove in the cliff in which the house is built. There are 8 of these rooms, in addition to 2 porches. The fourth floor consists of 3 rooms, neatly constructed, through the ceiling of one of which access is gained to the fifth or uppermost floor, which consists of a long porch or gallery having a battlement in front and an elevated backward extension on the right, with 2 rooms filling the corresponding space on the left. These 2 rooms are roofed by the rocky arch of the cliff, and are loftier than the lower chambers. Montezuma Castle, or Casa Montezuma, shows evidence of long occupancy in prehistoric times. Some of the rooms are smoothly plastered and smoke-blackened; the plas-

MONTEZUMA CASTLE. (MEARNS)

tering bears finger-marks and impressions of the thumb and hand. The rooms are ceiled with willows laid horizontally across rafters of ash and black alder; upon this is a thick layer of reeds placed transversely, and the whole plastered on top with mortar, forming a floor to the chamber above. The ends of the rafters exhibit hacking with stone implements. The building, which threatened to collapse, was repaired by the Arizona Antiquarian Association about 1895, and in 1906 it was declared a national monument by proclamation of the President of the United States. Its origin is unknown. See Mearns in Pop. Sci. Month., Oct. 1890 (from whose description the above details are extracted); Hewett in Am. Anthrop., VI, 637, 1904; Land of Sunshine, Los Angeles, X, 44, 1898.

Montezuma Well. A large depression in the form of a "tank" or well in the summit of a low mesa on Beaver cr., about 9 m. N. of old Camp Verde, Ariz., in which are the well-preserved remains of several cliff-dwellings.

Montochtana ('a corner in the back part of the hut'). A Knaiakhotana clan of Cook inlet, Alaska. — Richardson, Arct. Exped., I, 407, 1851.

Montour. About 1665 a French nobleman named Montour settled in Canada, where, by an Indian woman, probably a Huron, he became the father of a son and two daughters. This son of Montour grew up among those Indians, who were at that time in alliance with the French. In 1685, while in the French service, he was wounded in a fight with two Mohawk warriors on L. Champlain. Subsequently he deserted the French cause to live with the "upper nations" of Indians. Through him, in 1708, Lord Cornbury succeeded in persuading 12 of these western tribes, including the Miami and the Hurons, to trade at Albany. For this work, in alienating the upper nations from the French trade and cause, he was killed in 1709 by order of the Marquis de Vaudreuil, governor of Canada, who boasted that, had Montour been taken alive, he would have had him hanged. One of the two daughters of the French nobleman, while living on the Susquehanna and the Ohio, became a noted interpreter and friend of the English, and was known as Madam Montour. Her sister appears to have married a Miami Indian.

Authorities regarding the Montours are not always consistent and are sometimes not reconcilable as to statements of material facts. Madam Montour appears to have been born in Canada previous to the year 1684. When about 10 years of age she was captured by some Iroquois warriors and adopted, probably by the Seneca, for at maturity she married a Seneca named Roland Montour, by whom she had 4, if not 5, children, namely, Andrew, Henry, Robert, Lewis, and Margaret, the last becoming the wife of Katarioniecha, who lived in the neighborhood of Shamokin, Pa. Roland had a brother called "Stuttering John" and a sister variously known as Catherine, Kate, Catrina, and Catreen. After the death of Roland, Madam Montour married the noted Oneida chief named Carondowanen, or "Big Tree," who later took the name Robert Hunter in honor of the royal governor of the province of New York. About 1729 her husband, Robert, was killed in battle with the Catawba, against whom he was waging war. Madam Montour first appeared as an official interpreter at a conference at Albany in August, 1711, between the delegates of the Five Nations and Gov. Hunter of New York. This was probably the occasion on which her husband adopted the name Robert Hunter. The wanton murder of her brother Andrew by Vaudreuil was bitterly resented by Madam Montour, and she employed her great influence among the Indians with such telling effect against the interests of the French that the French governor sought to persuade her to remove to Canada by the offer of great compensation and valuable emoluments. His efforts were unsuccessful. Finally, in 1719, he sent her sister to attempt to prevail on her to forsake the people of her adoption and the English cause, whereupon the Commissioners of Indian Affairs, learning of the overtures of the French governor, appreciating the value of her services to the province, and fearing the effect of her possible disaffection, invited her to Albany. It was then discovered that for a year she had not received her stipulated pay, so it was agreed by the commission-

ers that she should thereafter receive a "man's pay," and she was satisfied. Madam Montour acted also as interpreter in 1727 in Philadelphia at a conference between Lieut. Gov. Gordon and his council on the one hand and the several chiefs and delegates of the Six Nations, the "Conestogas, Gangawese, and the Susquehanna Indians," on the other. It is claimed that Madam Montour was a lady in manner and education, was very attractive in mind and body, and that at times she was entertained by ladies of the best society of Philadelphia; but as her sister was married to a Miami warrior, and she herself was twice married to Indians of the Five Nations, it is probable that her refinement and education were not so marked as claimed, and that the ladies of Philadelphia treated her only with considerate kindness, and nothing more. Nevertheless, from the testimony of those who saw and knew her, but contrary to the statement of Lord Cornbury, who knew her brother, it seems almost certain that she was a French-Canadian without any admixture of Indian blood in her veins, and that for some unaccountable reason she preferred the life and dress of her adopted people.

Whatever Roland's attitude was toward the proprietary government, that of his wife was always uniformly friendly, and after her second marriage it was even more cordial. Such was the loyalty of the family of Madam Montour that at least two of her sons, Henry and Andrew, received large grants of "donation lands" from the government; that of the former lay on the Chillisquaque, and that of the latter on the Loyalsock, where Montoursville, Pa., is now situated.

Witham Marshe refers to Madam Montour as the "celebrated Mrs Montour, a French lady," who, having "lived so long among the Six Nations, is become almost an Indian." Referring to her visits to Philadelphia, he says, "being a white woman," she was there "very much caressed by the gentlewomen of that city, with whom she used to stay for some time." Marshe, who visited her house, saw two of her daughters, who were the wives of war chiefs, and a lad 5 years old, the son of one of the daughters, who was "one of the finest featured and limbed children mine eyes ever saw, . . . his cheeks were ruddy, mixed with a delicate white, had eyes and hair of an hazel colour." In 1734 Madam Montour resided at the village of Ostonwackin, on the Susquehanna, at the mouth of Loyalsock cr., on the site of the present Montoursville, Lycoming co., Pa. It was sometimes called Frenchtown. In 1737 Conrad Weiser, while on his way to Onondaga, lodged here with Madam

Montour, who, he states, was "a French woman by birth, of a good family, but now in mode of life a complete Indian." In 1744, at the great treaty of Lancaster between the Six Nations and the provinces of Virginia, Maryland, and Pennsylvania, Madam Montour was present with two of her daughters, on which occasion she related to Marshe the story of her life. He represented her as genteel, of polished address, and as having been attractive in her prime; he also learned that her two sons-in-law and her only son were then absent, at war with the Catawba. In 1745 Madam Montour was living on an island in the Susquehanna, at Shamokin, having left Ostonwackin permanently. Prior to 1754 she became blind, but she was still vigorous enough to make a horseback trip from Logstown, on the Ohio, to Venango, a distance of 60 m., in two days, her son Andrew, on foot, leading the horse all the way.

When Count Zinzendorf visited Shamokin in 1742 he was welcomed by Madam Montour and her son Andrew. Seeing the Count and hearing that he came to preach the gospel, the truths of which she had almost forgotten, she burst into tears. It was learned that she believed that Bethlehem, the birthplace of Christ, was situated in France, and that it was Englishmen who crucified him—a silly perversion of the truth that originated with French religious teachers.

In view of the fact that there is no record of a governor of Canada named Montour, the belief that she was the daughter of such a personage seems groundless, notwithstanding her own statement to this effect to Marshe. Equally doubtful is the assertion that she was alive during the American Revolution, a statement possibly arising from the fact that she was confounded with her reputed granddaughter, Catherine of Catherine's Town, situated near the head of Seneca lake and destroyed by Sullivan's army in 1779. Being more than 60 years of age in 1744, it is not probable that she could have been an active participant in the Wyoming massacre, 34 years later, and there is no authentic evidence connecting Madam Montour with the shedding of blood, white or Indian.

ESTHER MONTOUR, justly infamous as the "fiend of Wyoming," a daughter of French Margaret, hence a granddaughter of Madam Montour and a sister of French Catherine and Mary, and the wife of Eghohowin, a ruling chief of the Munsee, was living in 1772 at Sheshequin, 6 m. below Tioga Point; but in this year she removed 6 m. above, to a place where she founded a new settlement, later known as Queen Esther's Town, which was destroyed by Col. Hartley in 1778. Thence she removed, probably to Chemung. It is known that there were Montours at the battle of Wyoming, for "Stuttering John" and Roland admitted it some years afterward. John and Catrina were always relentless enemies of the English colonies. That John, Roland, Esther, and Catherine and Mary were half-breeds is quite probable. But Esther's bloody work at Wyoming, July 3, 1778, has made her name execrated wherever known. Toward the end of June of the year named the Tory Colonel, John Butler, with about 400 British and Tories and about 700 Indians, chiefly Seneca, under Sagaiengwaraton, descended the Susquehanna on his way to attack the settlements in Wyoming valley, Pa. To defend the valley against this force there were 40 or 50 men under Capt. Detrick Hewitt, and the militia—about 400 men and boys, the residue of the three companies that had been enlisted in the Continental army. Col. Zebulon Butler, happening to be in the valley, took command of the little army, aided by Maj. Garret, Col. Dennison, and Lieut. Col. Dorrance.

The 400 undisciplined militia were soon outflanked and broken in the ensuing battle. After the enemy had gained the rear, an officer said to Hewitt: "See! the enemy has gained the rear in force. Shall we retreat?" "I'll be d——d if I do," was Hewitt's reply, and, like the other officers killed in action, he fell at the head of his men. The battle was lost. Then followed a most dreadful slaughter of the brave but overpowered soldiers of Wyoming. Without mercy and with the most fearful tortures, they were ruthlessly butchered, chiefly in the flight, and after having surrendered themselves prisoners of war. Placed around a huge rock and held by stout Indians, 16 men were killed one by one by the knife or tomahawk in the hands of "Queen Esther." In a similar circle 9 others were killed in the same brutal manner. From these two circles alone only one, a strong man named Hammond, escaped by almost superhuman effort. This slaughter, which made 150 widows and 600 orphans in the valley, gave Esther her bloody title.

CATHERINE MONTOUR, a noted character in the colonial history of Pennsylvania, and who gave the name of Catherine's Town to Sheoquaga, was another daughter of French Margaret, hence a granddaughter of Madam Montour. She became the wife of Telelemut, a noted Seneca chief, named Thomas Hudson by the English, by whom she had a son named Amochol ('Canoe'), or Andrew, and two daughters. The statement that

Catherine was an educated and refined woman and was admitted into good society in Philadelphia is, under the circumstances, most improbable. On Sept. 3, 1779, Sullivan's army destroyed Catherine's Town. Catherine, with several friends, lived in 1791 "over the lake not far from Niagara." Her son Amochol joined the Moravian church and was living at New Salem, or Petquotting, in 1788. John and Roland Montour were her brothers, the latter being the son-in-law of Sagaiengwaraton, a leading Seneca chief. Both Roland and John were famous war chiefs in the border warfare against the English colonies.

MARY MONTOUR, a sister of Catherine, Esther, and Andrew, was the wife of John Cook, another noted Seneca chief named Kanaghragait, sometimes also called "White Mingo," who lived on the Allegheny and the Ohio, and died in 1790 at Ft Wayne. From Zeisberger's Diary (II, 149, 1885) the curious information is obtained that Mary was a "Mohawk Indian woman," and that Mohawk was "her mother tongue." It is also stated that when a child Mary was baptized in Philadelphia by a Catholic priest. In 1791, on the removal of the Moravian mission from New Salem to Canada, among the new converts who accompanied the congregation was Mary, "a sister of the former Andrew Montour," and "a living polyglot of the tongues of the West, speaking the English, French, Mohawk, Wyandot [Huron], Ottawa, Chippewa, Shawnese, and Delaware languages."

ANDREW MONTOUR, whose Indian name was Sáttelihu, the son of Madam Montour by her first husband, was for many years in the employ of the proprietary government of Pennsylvania as an assistant interpreter. In 1745 he accompanied Weiser and Shikellimy, the viceroy of the Six Nations on the Susquehanna, on a mission to Onondaga, the federal capital of the confederation. In 1748 Andrew was presented to the council of the proprietary government by Weiser as a person especially qualified to act as an interpreter or messenger. At this time he was prominent among the Delawares. Hitherto Weiser and Andrew were held asunder by jealousy, because of Andrew's efforts to secure the position of interpreter for Virginia in her negotiations with the Six Nations. But Weiser now needed Andrew to secure to the proprietary government the alliance of the Ohio Indians, and so sunk all personal differences. In introducing him to the council Weiser stated that he had employed Andrew frequently on matters of great moment and importance, and that he had found him "faithful, knowing, and prudent." At

this time Andrew was fully remunerated for what he had already done for Weiser. Deputies from the Miami were expected at Philadelphia, but instead they went to Lancaster. Andrew Montour was the interpreter for the western Indians and Weiser for the Six Nations. Scaroyady, a noted Oneida chief, living on the Ohio, and exercising for the Six Nations jurisdiction over the western tribes similar to that exercised by Shikellimy over those in Pennsylvania, was to have been the speaker on this occasion, but he was incapacitated by a fall, and so Andrew was chosen speaker for the western Indians. He enjoyed remarkable influence and power over the Ohio tribes, and by his work at the various conferences of the colonies with them came into enviable prominence in the province. His growing power and influence, about 1750, attained such weight that the management of Indian affairs by Pennsylvania was seriously embarrassed. In 1752 Gov. Hamilton commissioned him to go and reside on Cumberland cr., over the Blue hills, on unpurchased lands, to prevent others from settling or trading there. In the following year the French authorities set a price of $500 on his head. In 1755 he was still on his grant, living 10 m. N. W. of Carlisle, Pa., and was captain, later major, of a company of Indians in the English service. In 1762 he was the King's interpreter to the united nations. Andrew served as an interpreter for the Delawares at Shamokin, where Conrad Weiser held a conference with the several tribes in that region for the purpose of bringing about peace between the southern confederation of Indians and the Six Nations and their allies. He also served as interpreter to the governor of Virginia at several important treaties. After receiving his grants from the government he was regarded as a man of great wealth, but in his public acts he found other means of swelling his fortune. Consult Bliss, Zeisberger's Diary, I-II, 1885; Darlington, Gist's Journals, 1893; Freeze in Pa. Mag., III, 1879; Marshe in Mass. Hist. Soc. Coll., 1st s., VII, 1801; N. Y. Doc. Col. Hist., v, 65, 1855; Walton, Conrad Weiser, 1900.   (J. N. B. H.)

Montowese ('little god,' diminutive from *manito*, 'spirit.'—Trumbull). Applied by Ruttenber (Tribes Hudson R., 82, 1872), to Indians on Connecticut r. s. w. of Middletown, Middlesex co., Conn., though De Forest (Hist. Inds. Conn., 55, 1853), his authority, does not give the name as that of a tribe, but says: "Southwest of the principal seat of the Wangunks [Middletown] a large extent of country was held by a son of Sowheag [chief of the Mattabesec, q. v.] named Montowese." This area probably lay partly in

Middlesex, but chiefly in New Haven co. This chief, in 1638, sold a tract N. of the site of New Haven comprising a large portion of that county. As his father was chief of the Mattabesec, his band probably belonged to that tribe. (J. M. C. T.)

Mantoweeze.—Davenport (1660) in Mass. Hist. Soc. Coll., 4th s., VII, 518, 1865.

Monts Pelés. A tribe, called from the nature of their country the Nation des Monts Pelés ('nation of the bare mountains'), living in the N. E. part of Quebec province in 1661. Hind (Lab. Penin., II, 1863) thinks they may have been a part of the Nascapee.

Mont-Pelés.—Keane in Stanford, Compend., 523, 1878. **Nation des Monts pelez.**—Jes. Rel. 1661, 29, 1858.

Mooachaht ('deer people'). A tribe on the N. side of Nootka sd., Vancouver id. This is the tribe to which the term Nootka was applied by the discoverers of Vancouver id. Pop. 153 in 1906. Their principal village is Yuquot. The noted Maquinna (q. v.) was chief of this tribe in 1803.

Bo-wat-chat.—Swan in Smithson. Cont., XVI, 56, 1870. **Bowatshat.**—Swan, MS., B. A. E. **Moachet.**—Mayne, Brit. Col., 251, 1862. **Mō'atcath.**—Boas in 6th Rep. N. W. Tribes Can., 31, 1890. **Mooach-aht.**—Can. Ind. Aff., 188, 1883. **Mooacht-aht.**—Ibid., 357, 1897. **Moo-cha-ahts.**—Ibid., 52, 1875. **Moouchaht.**—Sproat, Sav. Life, 308, 1868. **Mouchatha.**—Swan, MS., B. A. E. **Mowaches.**—Armstrong, Oregon, 136, 1857. **Mo-watch-its.**—Jewitt, Narr., 36, 1849. **Mowatshat.**—Swan, MS., B. A. E. **Mowitchat.**—Swan in Smithson. Cont., XVI, 56, 1870. **Nootka.**—Schedule of Reserves, Can. Ind. Aff., Suppl. to Ann. Rep., 82, 1902.

Moodyville Saw Mills. The local name for a body of Salish of Fraser River agency, Brit. Col.; pop. 86 in 1889.

Moodyville Saw Mills.—Can. Ind. Aff. Rep. 1889, 268, 1890. **Moonyville Saw Mills.**—Can. Ind. Aff. Rep. 1886, 229, 1887.

Mooharmowikarnu (*Moo-har-mo-wi-kar'-nu*). A subdivision of the Delawares (q. v.).—Morgan, Anc. Soc., 172, 1877.

Mookwungwahoki (*Moo-kwung-wa-ho'-ki*). A subdivision of the Delawares (q. v.).—Morgan, Anc. Soc., 172, 1877.

Moonack. A Maryland-Virginia name of the ground-hog (*Arctomys monax*); also, by transference, the name of a mythic animal feared by many Southern negroes. The word occurs very early. Glover, in his account of Virginia (Philos. Trans. Roy. Soc., XI, 630, 1676), speaks of *monacks*. John Burroughs (Winter Sunshine, 25, 1876), says: "In Virginia they call woodchucks '*moonacks*.'" Lewis and Clark (Orig. Jour., II, IV, 1905) use the forms *moonax* and *moonox*. It is probable that the *monax* in the scientific name of this animal is a Linnean latinization of its aboriginal appellation. The Virginian *moonack*, or *monack*, is cognate with the Delaware *monachgeu* (German form), the Passamaquoddy *monimquess*, the Micmac *munumkwech*, etc. The word signifies 'the digger,' from the Algonquian radical

muna, or *mona*, 'to dig'; seen also in the Chippewa *monaike*, 'he scratches up'; in Cree, *monahikew*. The Sauk, Fox, and Kickapoo language has *monanäᶜa*, 'little digger', for woodchuck, according to Dr William Jones. (A. F. C.)

Moonhartarne (*Moon-har-tar-ne*, 'digging'). A subdivision of the Delawares (q. v.).—Morgan, Anc. Soc., 172, 1877.

Moors. See *Croatan Indians*.

Moose. The common name of a species of large deer (*Cervus alces*) found in Maine and parts of Canada and formerly over most of N. E. North America. An identical term for this animal occurs in many Algonquian dialects: Virginian, *moos;* Narraganset and Massachuset, *moos;* Delaware, *mos;* Passamaquoddy, *mus;* Abnaki, *moñz;* Chippewa, *moⁿs;* Cree, *monswa*. All these words signify 'he strips or eats off,' in reference to the animal's habit of eating the young bark and twigs of trees. The word came into English from one of the New England dialects. Derivative words and expressions are: Moose bird (Canada jay); moose call, moose horn, or moose trumpet (a bark trumpet used to imitate notes of this animal); moose elm (slippery elm); moose fly (a large brown fly common in Maine); moosewood (applied variously to the striped maple, *Acer pennsylvanica*); the leatherwood (*Dirca palustris*), and the hobblebush (*Viburnum lantanoides*); moose yard (the home and browsing-place of the moose in winter). (A. F. C.)

Moosehead Lake Indians. The common name of a band of Penobscot living on Moosehead lake, Me.—Vetromile, Abnakis, 22, 1866.

Moosemise. A name current in parts of New England, Vermont in particular, for the false wintergreen (*Pyrola americana*). The name seems to have been transferred from another plant, since in Chippewa and Nipissing *moⁿsomish*, signifying 'moose shrub,' designates the hobblebush (*Viburnum lantanoides*), called in Canadian French bois d'orignal. The word, which is written *moosemize* also, is derived from some Algonquian dialect of the Chippewa group or a closely related one of the E. (A. F. C.)

Mooshkaooze ('heron'). A gens of the Chippewa, q. v.

Moosh-kä-oo-ze'.—Morgan, Anc. Soc., 166, 1877. **Moshka·u·sig.**—Wm. Jones, inf'n, 1906.

Mooskwasuh ('muskrat'). A gens of the Abnaki, q. v.

Moos-kwä-suh'.—Morgan, Anc. Soc., 174, 1877. **Moskwas.**—J. D. Prince, inf'n, 1905 (modern St Francis Abnaki form).

Mootaeyuhew. A Luiseño village formerly in the neighborhood of San Luis Rey mission, s. Cal.—Taylor in Cal. Farmer, May 11, 1860.

Moqtavhaitaniu (*Moqta'vhitä'niu*, 'black men,' i. e. Ute; sing. *Moqta'vhaitä'n*).

A band of the Cheyenne, possibly of mixed Ute descent.　　　　(J. M.)

Mōhk ta hwá tan in.—Grinnell, Social Org. Cheyennes, 136, 1905 (misprint *in* 1or *iu*). **Ute.**—Dorsey in Field Columb. Mus. Pub. no. 103, 62, 1905.

Moquats (*Mo'-quats*). A band of Paiute formerly living near Kingston mt., S. E. Cal.—Powell in Ind. Aff. Rep. 1873, 51, 1874.

Moquelumnan Family (adapted from Moquelumne, a corruption of the Miwok *Wakalumitoh*, the name of a river in Calaveras co., Cal.). A linguistic family, established by Powell (7th Rep. B. A. E., 92, 1891), consisting of three divisions, the Miwok, the so-called Olamentke, and the Northern or Lake County Moquelumnan. The territory originally occupied was in three sections, one lying between Cosumnes and Fresno rs.; another in Marin, Sonoma, and Napa cos., the territory extending along the coast from the Golden Gate to Salmon cr., N. of Bodega bay and E. as far as the vicinity of Sonoma; and the third a comparatively small area in the S. end of Lake co., extending from Mt St Helena northward to the E. extremity of Clear lake (see Kroeber in Am. Anthrop., VIII, no. 4, 1906). The Miwok division, which constituted the great body of the family, was described as late as 1876 as the largest Indian group of California, both in population and in extent of territory.

Their houses were very rude, those of the Miwok having been simply frameworks of poles and brush, which in winter were covered with earth. In the mountains cone-shaped summer lodges of puncheons were made. Acorns, which formed their principal food, were gathered in large quantities when the harvest was abundant and stored for winter use in granaries raised above the ground. It has been asserted that the Miwok ate every variety of living creature indigenous to their territory except the skunk. They were especially fond of jackrabbits, the skins of which were rudely woven into robes. From lack of cedar they purchased bows and sometimes arrows from the mountain Indians, the medium of barter being shell money.

With the Miwok, chiefship was hereditary when the successor was of commanding influence, but this was seldom the case. As with most of the tribes of California, marriage among the Miwok tribes was practically by purchase, but in return for the presents given by the groom the father of the bride gave the new couple various substantial articles, and gifts of food were often continued by the parents for years after the marriage. The father, in old age, was ill treated, however, being little else than a slave to his daughter and her husband. When twins were born one of the children was killed. Shamanistic

rites were performed by both men and women, and scarification and suction were the principal remedial agents. California balm of gilead (*Picea grandis*), and plasters of hot ashes and moist earth were also used in certain cases. Payment for treatment was made by the patient, and in case of non-recovery the life of the practitioner was demanded. The acorn dance, as well as a number of other ceremonies, principally for feasting or amusement, were formerly celebrated by the Miwok. They had no puberty dance, nor did they hold a dance for the dead, but an annual mourning and sometimes a special mourning were observed. All the possessions of the dead were burned with them, their names were never afterward mentioned, and those who bore the same name changed it for others. Formerly widows generally covered their faces with pitch and the younger women singed their hair short as signs of widowhood. Cremation generally prevailed among the Miwok tribes, but was never universal.

Comparatively few of the natives of the Miwok division of this stock survive, and these are scattered in the mountains, so that no accurate census has been taken. Six individuals of the so-called Olamentke division lived on Tomales bay in 1888.

The Moquelumnan tribes or rancherias that have been recognized are as follows:

Miwok.—Awani, Chowchilla, Chumidok, Chumtiya, Chumuch, Chumwit, Hittoya, Howeches, Koni, Lopotatimni, Machemni, Mokelumne, Newichumni, Nuchu, Olowitok, Pohonichi, Sakaiakumne, Servushamne, Talatui, Tamuleko, Tumidok, Tumun, Walakumni, and Yuloni.

Olamentke.—Bolinas, Chokuyem, Guimen, Jukiusme, Likatuit, Nicassias, Numpali, Olumpali, Sonoma, Tamal, Tulares, Tumalehnias, Utchium.

Tribes or rancherias not classified are: Apangasi, Aplache, Chupumni, Cosumni, Cotoplanemis, Hokokwito, Keeches, Kumaini, Lapapu, Lesamaiti, Macheto, Merced, Mikechuses, Nelcelchumnee, Noketrotra, Notomidula, Numaltachi(?), Nutrecho, Okechumne, Pahkanu, Petaluma, Potawackati, Potoyanti, Sakaya, Seantre, Siyante, Succaah, Suscols, Threse, Tiposies, Wahaka, and Wiskala.

(H. W. H.　A. L. K.)

=**Meewoc.**—Powers in Overland Month., 322, Apr. 1873 (general account of family with allusions to language); Gatschet in Mag. Am. Hist., 159, 1877 (gives habitat and bands of family); Gatschet in Beach, Ind. Miscel., 433, 1877. =**Mí-wok.**—Powers in Cont. N. A. Ethnol., III, 346, 1877 (nearly as above). =**Moquelumnan.**—Powell in 7th Rep. B. A. E., 92, 1891. >**Moquelumne.**—Latham in Trans. Philol. Soc. Lond., 81, 1856 (includes Hale's Talatui, Tuolumne from Schoolcraft, Mumaltachi, Mullateco, Apangasi, Lapappu, Siyante or Typoxi, Hawhaw's band of Aplaches, San Rafael vocabulary, Tshokoyem vocabulary, Cocouyem and Yonkiousme Paternosters, Olamentke of Kostromitonov, Paternosters for Mission de Santa Clara and the Vallee de los Tulares of Mofras, Paternoster of the Langue Guiloco de la Mission de San Francisco); Latham, Opuscula, 347, 1860; Latham, Elem. Comp. Philol., 414, 1862 (same as above). >**Mutsun.**— Powell in Cont. N. A. Ethnol., III, 535, 1877 (vocabs. of Mi'-wok, Tuolumne, Costano, Tcho-ko-yem, Mūtsūn, Santa Clara, Santa Cruz, Chumte'-ya, Kawéya, San Raphael Mission, Talatui, Olamentke); Gatschet in Mag. Am. Hist., 157, 1877 (gives habitat and members of family); Gatschet in Beach, Ind. Miscel., 430, 1877. ×**Runsiens.**—Keane in Stanford, Compend., Cent. and So. Am., app., 476, 1878 (includes Olhones, Eslenes, Santa Cruz, San Miguel, Lopillamillos, Mipacmacs, Kulanapos, Yolos, Suisunes, Talluches, Chowclas, Waches, Talches, Poowells). <**Tcho-ko-yem.**—Gibbs in Schoolcraft, Ind. Tribes, III, 421, 1853 (mentioned as a band and dialect).

Moquino (said to have been named from a Mexican family that occupied the site). Formerly a small pueblo inhabited during the summer season by the Laguna Indians, but now entirely Mexicanized. Situated on Paguate r., Valencia co., N. Mex., about 9 m. N. of Laguna.
Mogino.—Powell in Am. Nat., XIV, 604, Aug. 1880. **Moguino.**—Loew (1875) in Wheeler Survey Rep., VII, 345, 1879. **Moquino.**—Emory, Recon., 133, 1848.

Moquoso. A former tribe and village in w. Florida. The map of De Bry (1591) places it w. of the headwaters of St Johns r.; according to the Gentleman of Elvas it lay 2 leagues from the gulf and 2 days' journey from Bahia de Espíritu Santo, which is thought to be Tampa bay.
Mocoço.—Barcia, Ensayo, 48, 1723. **Mocosa.**—Mercator map (1569) cited in Maine Hist. Soc. Coll., 2d s., I, 392, 1869. **Mocoso.**—Drake, Tragedies, 15, 1841. **Mocosson.**—De Bry, Brev. Narr., II, map, 1591. **Mogoso.**—Fontaneda (1575) in Ternaux-Compans, Voy., xx, 24, 1841. **Mogozo.**—Ibid., 21. **Moquoso.**—Laudonnière (1564) in French, Hist. Coll. La., n. s., 243, 1869. **Mucoço.**—Garcilasso de la Vega, Fla., 28, 1723.

Moqwaio ('wolf'). A phratry and also a subphratry or gens of the Menominee.
Má'hwawᵃ.—Wm. Jones, inf'n, 1906. **Moqwaio.**—Hoffman in 14th Rep. B. A. E., pt. 1, 42, 1896.

Mora. A rancheria near the presidio of La Bahía and the mission of Espíritu Santo de Zúñiga on the lower Rio San Antonio, Tex., in 1785, at which date it had 26 inhabitants (Bancroft, No. Mexican States, I, 659, 1886). The people were probably of Karankawan affinity.

Moratiggon. The village where Samoset lived in 1621. It was distant "one day from Plymouth by water with great wind, and five days by land." Probably in s. Maine, in Abnaki or Pennacook territory.
Moratiggon.—Harris, Voy. and Trav., I, 853, 1705. **Morattiggon.**—Mourt (1621) in Mass. Hist. Soc. Coll., 1st s., VIII, 226, 1802.

Moratoc. A tribe described in 1586 as living 160 m. up Roanoke r., perhaps near the s. Virginia line. A map of that period places their village on the N. side of the river, which then bore their name. They are said to have been an important tribe which refused to hold intercourse with the English.
Moratico.—Simons in Smith (1629), Va., I, 176, repr. 1819. **Moratocks.**—Lane (1586), ibid., 87. **Moratoks.**—Ibid. **Moratuck.**—Smith (1629), ibid., map.

Moraughtacund. A tribe of the Powhatan confederacy, formerly living on the N. bank of the Rappahannock, in Lancaster and Richmond cos., Va. In 1608 they numbered about 300. Their principal village, of the same name, was near the mouth of Moratico r. in Richmond co. (J. M.)
Moranghtaouna.—Smith (1629), Va., I, map, repr. 1819 (the village; evidently a misprint for Moraughtacund). **Morattico.**—Purchas, Pilgrimes, IV, 1713, 1626. **Moraughtacud.**—Ibid., 1715. **Moraughtacunds.**—Strachey (ca. 1612), Va., 37, 1849.

Moravians. Mahican, Munsee, and Delawares who followed the teachings of the Moravian brethren and were by them gathered into villages apart from their tribes. The majority were Munsee. In 1740 the Moravian missionaries began their work at the Mahican village of Shekomeko in New York. Meeting with many obstacles there, they removed with their converts in 1746 to Pennsylvania, where they built the new mission village of Friedenshuetten on the Susquehanna. Here they were more successful and were largely recruited from the Munsee and Delawares, almost all of the former tribe not absorbed by the Delawares finally joining them. They made another settlement at Wyalusing, but on the advance of the white population removed to Beaver r. in w. Pennsylvania, where they built the village of Friedensstadt. They remained here about a year, and in 1773 removed to Muskingum r. in Ohio, in the neighborhood of the others of their tribes, and occupied the three villages of Gnadenhuetten, Salem, and Schoenbrunn. In 1781, during the border troubles of the Revolution, the Hurons removed them to the region of the Sandusky and Scioto, in N. Ohio, either to prevent their giving information to the colonists or to protect them from the hostility of the frontiersmen. The next spring a party of about 140 were allowed to return to their abandoned villages to gather their corn, when they were treacherously attacked by a party of border ruffians and the greater part massacred in the most coldblooded manner, after which their villages were burned. The remaining Moravians moved to Canada in 1791, under the leadership of Zeisberger, and built the village of Fairfield on Thames r. This village was burned by the Americans in the War of 1812, in consequence of which the Indians removed and rebuilt on the opposite side of the river, in Orford tp., Kent co., Ontario. The number in 1884 was 275, but had increased to 348 in 1906. There were until recently a few in Franklin co., Kans. See *Missions.* (J. M. C. T.)
Big Beavers.—Rupp, W. Pa., 47, 1846 ("Christian Indians or Big Beavers," because of their residence about 1770 on (Big) Beaver cr. in w. Pa.). **Christian Indians.**—Schoolcraft, Ind. Tribes, V, 495, 1855 (frequently used as synonymous with

Munsee, but properly refers only to those of the tribe under Moravian teachers). **Moravins.**—Can. Ind. Aff., pt. 2, 65, 1906 (misprint).

Morbah (*Mor-bäh*). The Parrot clan of the Pecos people of N. Mex.—Hewett in Am. Anthrop., VI., 439, 1904.

Morbanas. A former tribe, probably Coahuiltecan, met in 1693 on the road from Coahuila to mission San Francisco, Texas.—Salinas (1693) in Dictamen Fiscal, Nov. 30, 1716, MS. cited by H. E. Bolton, inf'n, 1906.

Morongo. A reservation of 38,600 acres of fair land, unpatented, in Riverside co., s. Cal., occupied by 286 Mission Indians under Mission Tule River agency.—Ind. Aff. Rep., 175, 1902; ibid., 192, 1905; Kelsey, Rep., 32, 1906.

Mortars. Utensils employed by Indian tribes for the trituration of food and other substances. The Southwestern or Mexican type of grinding stone is known as a metate, and its operation consists in placing the substance to be treated, dry or moist, on the sloping upper surface of the slab and crushing and rubbing it with a flattish hand-stone until it is reduced to the required consistency or degree of fineness (see *Metates, Mullers*). This form of the utensil passes with many variations in size and shape into the typical mortar, a more or less deep receptacle in which the substance is pulverized if dry, or reduced to pulp if moist, by crushing with a pestle, which may be cylindrical, discoidal, globular, or bell-shaped. Mortars are made of stone, wood, bone (whale vertebræ), or improvised of rawhide or other substances depending on the region and the materials nearest at hand. The more primitive stone forms are bowlders or other suitable pieces hollowed out on the upper surface sufficiently to hold the material to be reduced, while the more highly specialized forms are tastefully shaped and carefully finished, the stone in some cases, as in s. California, being obtained by quarrying from the rock in place. California furnishes the greatest variety of these utensils.

GLOBULAR STONE MORTARS FROM AURIFEROUS GRAVELS, CALIFORNIA. (HOLMES)

In one district globular concretions were used: a segment of the shell was broken away and the softer interior removed, thus affording a deep symmetrical receptacle. In other localities cylindrical forms were worked out of lava or sandstone. In others still, the under surface was conical, so as to be conveniently set in the ground.

ALASKAN MORTAR WITH SCULPTURED ORNAMENT; 1-12.

Ordinary mortars when in use are usually set in the ground to give them greater stability. The remarkable and handsome sandstone vessels and soapstone pots of s. California are not here classed as mortars. Occasionally the smaller mortars were embellished with

YOKUTS WOMEN GRINDING SEED.   (SANTA FE RAILROAD)

SIMPLE FORMS OF STONE MORTARS.   *a* CALIFORNIA (1-8);
b, RHODE ISLAND (1-8)

engraved lines or sculptured to represent animal forms. Alaskan mortars, especially those of the Haida, are superior in this respect. An artistic mortar of this class, illustrated by Niblack, was used for pulverizing tobacco, and this is a type in very general use among the Northwestern tribes at the present time.

Perhaps the most remarkable mortars are those occurring frequently in the acorn-producing districts of the Pacific slope, where exposures of massive rock in place have worked in them groups of mortars, the conical receptacles numbering, in several observed cases, nearly a hundred. Some of the Western tribes set a conical basket, after removing its bottom, within the rim of the mortar bowl to serve as a hopper for retaining the meal.

GROUP OF MORTARS IN GRANITE SURFACE, CALIFORNIA (HOLMES)

Primitive forms of this utensil are the rawhide mortars used by the Plains tribes for pounding pemmican, the piece of rawhide being forced into a depression in the ground, forming a basin. Again, the hide was placed beneath the stone or wooden mortar to catch the particles that fell over. The rough basket-like receptacle of sticks

STONE MORTAR WITH BASKET HOPPER; CALIFORNIA

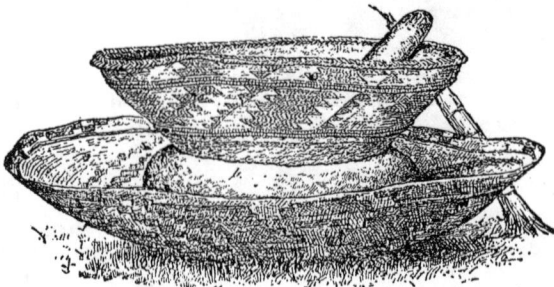

set in the ground by the Yuman tribes of lower Colorado r. is probably the rudest known form of this utensil. In

HUPA MORTAR WITH BASKET HOPPERS. (MASON)

size stone mortars vary from that of the tiny paint cup found among the toilet articles of the warrior to the substantial basin holding several gallons. The larger ones, especially those excavated in rock masses, were probably often used for "stone-boiling." (See Food.)

SMALL PAINT MORTAR, HUPA; 1-7 (MASON)

The substances pulverized in mortars were the various minerals used for paint, potsherds and shells for tempering clay, etc., medicinal and ceremonial substances of many kinds, including tobacco, and a wide range of food products, as maize, seeds, nuts, berries, roots, bark, dried meats, fish, grasshoppers, etc. A noteworthy group of paint mortars or plates, the use of which has heretofore been regarded as problematical, are described under the heading Notched plates. The wooden mortar was usually made of a short section of a log, hollowed out at one end and in some cases sharpened at the other for setting in the ground; but the receptacles were sometimes made in the side of a log or were cut out as individual utensils in basin or trough shape. The wooden mortar was in much more general use in districts where suitable stone was not available, as in Florida, in portions of the Mississippi valley, and on lower Colorado r. Among the remarkable

WOODEN MORTAR, COCOPA

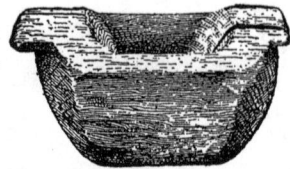

WOODEN MORTAR, CHIPPEWA; 1-16. (HOFFMAN)

archeologic finds made by Cushing at Key Marco, Fla., are a number of small cup-like mortars with mallet-shaped pestles, handsomely formed and carefully finished.

ANCIENT WOODEN MORTAR, FLORIDA; 1-4. (CUSHING)

WOODEN MORTAR, IROQUOIS (LAFITAU)

Speaking of the Indians of Carolina, Lawson says: "The savage men never beat their corn to make bread, but that is the women's work, especially the girls, of whom you shall see four beating with long great pestles in a narrow wooden mortar; and everyone keeps her stroke so exactly that 'tis worthy of admiration."

Mortars are referred to by numerous writers, including Abbott (1) in Surveys West of 100th Merid., VII, 1879, (2) Prim. Indus., 1881; Cushing in Proc. Am. Philos. Soc., XXXV, 153, 1896; Fowke, Archæol. Hist. Ohio, 1902; Hoffman in 14th Rep. B. A. E., 1896; Holmes in Nat. Mus. Rep. 1902, 1903; Jones, Antiq. So. Inds., 1873; Lawson (1701), Hist. Car., repr. 1860; MacCauley in 5th Rep. B. A. E., 1887; Meredith in Moorehead's Prehist. Impls., 1900; Morgan, League of Iroquois, 1904; Niblack in Rep. Nat. Mus. 1888, 1890; Nordenskiöld, Cliff Dwellers of the Mesa Verde, 1893; Powers in Cont. N. A. Ethnol., III, 1877; Rau in Smithson. Cont., XXII, 1876; Schoolcraft, Ind. Tribes, I, 1851; Thruston, Antiq. of Tenn., 1897; Yates in Moorehead's Prehist. Impls., 1900.　　　(W. H. H.)

Mortuary customs. Yarrow (1st Rep. B. A. E., 1881) classifies Indian modes of burial as follows:

(1) Inhumation, (2) Embalmment, (3) Deposition in urns, (4) Surface burial, (5) Cremation, (6) Aerial sepulture, (7) Aquatic burial. As the second relates to the preparation of the body, and the third, fourth, sixth, and seventh refer chiefly to the receptacles or the place of deposit, the disposal of the dead by the Indians may be classed under the heads *Burial* and *Cremation*.

The usual mode of burial among North American Indians has been by inhumation, or interment in pits, graves, or holes in the ground, in stone cists, in mounds, beneath or in cabins, wigwams, houses, or lodges, or in caves. As illustrations it may be stated that the Mohawk formerly made a large round hole in which the body was placed in a squatting posture, after which it was covered with timber and earth. Some of the Carolina tribes first placed the corpse in a cane hurdle and deposited it in an outhouse for a day; then it was taken out and wrapped in rush or cane matting, placed in a reed coffin, and deposited in a grave. Remains of this kind of wrapping have been found in some of the southern mounds, and in one case in a rock shelter. The bottom of the grave was sometimes covered with bark, on which the body was laid, and logs or slabs placed over it to prevent the earth from falling on the remains. An ancient form of burial in Tennessee, s. Illinois, at points on Delaware r., and among ancient pueblo dwellers in N. New Mexico, was in box-shape cists of rough stone slabs. Sepulchers of this kind have been found in mounds and cemeteries. In some instances they were placed in the same general direction, but in excavations made by the Bureau of American Ethnology it was found that these cists, as well as the uninclosed bodies in mounds, were gen-erally placed without regard to uniformity of direction. When uniformity did occur, it was generally an indication of

STONE GRAVE, SHOWING ORDINARY CONSTRUCTION

a comparatively modern interment. The Creeks and the Seminole of Florida generally buried in a circular pit about 4 ft deep; the corpse, with a blanket or cloth wrapped about it, being placed in a sitting posture, the legs bent under and tied together. The sitting position in ancient burials has often been erroneously inferred from the bones occurring in a heap. It appears to have been a custom in the N. W., as well as in the E. and S. E., to remove the flesh by previous burial or otherwise, and then to bundle the bones and bury them, sometimes in communal pits. It was usual in grave burials to place the body in a horizontal position on its back, although the custom of placing on the side, often with the knees drawn up, was also practised; burial face downward,

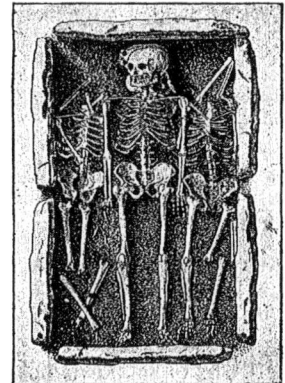

STONE GRAVE, TOP VIEW; ILLINOIS. (THOMAS)

STONE GRAVE WITH OFFSET ARCH; IOWA. (THOMAS)

ARCHED STONE GRAVE; OHIO. (THOMAS)

however, was rare. In addition to those mentioned, modes of burials in mounds varied. Sometimes a single body and sometimes several were placed in a wooden vault of upright timbers or of logs laid horizontally to form a pen. Dome-shaped stone vaults occur over a single sitting skeleton.

BURIAL UNDER HEAP OF STONES; HUDSON BAY ESKIMO. (TURNER)

Not infrequently the body was laid on the ground, slightly covered with earth, and over this a layer of plastic clay was spread on which was built a fire, forming an earthen shield over the corpse before additional earth was added. Caverns, fissures in rocks, rock shelters, etc., were frequently used as depositories for the dead. According to Yarrow, a cave near the House mts., Utah, in which the Gosiute Indians were in the habit of depositing their dead, was quite filled with human remains in 1872.

Embalmment and mummification were practised to a limited extent; the former chiefly in Virginia, the Carolinas, and

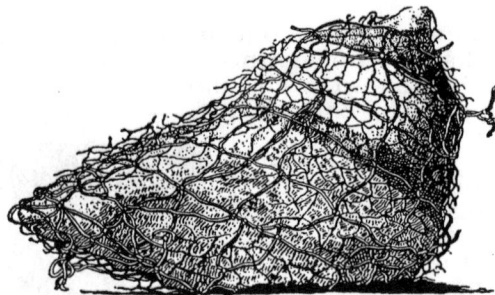

MUMMY FROM AN ALASKAN CAVE. (DALL)

Florida, and the latter in Alaska. Of the modes of disposing of the dead, included by Yarrow under "aerial sepulture," the following are examples: Burial in lodges, observed among the Sioux; these appear to have been exceptional and were merely an abandonment of the dead during an epidemic; a few cases of burial in lodges, however, have been observed in Alabama. Burial beneath the floor of the house and then at once burning the house were practised to some extent in E. Arkansas. Scaffold and tree burial was practised in Wisconsin, Minnesota, the Dakotas, Montana,

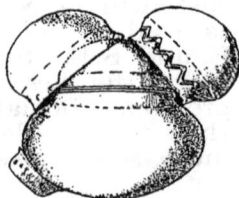

URN BURIAL ALABAMA MOUND; 1-22. (MOORE)

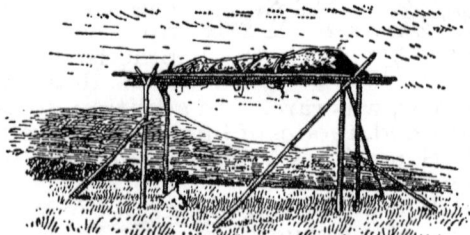

DAKOTA SCAFFOLD BURIAL. (YARROW)

etc., by the Chippewa, Sioux, Siksika, Mandan, Grosventres, Arapaho, and other Indians. The burial mounds of Wisconsin indicate this mode of disposing of the dead in former times, as the skeletons were buried after the removal of the flesh, and the bones frequently indicate long exposure to the air. The Eskimo of

the w. coast of Alaska sometimes placed the dead on a platform 2 or 3 ft above ground and built over it a double roofing, or tent, of driftwood. It was also the custom among the Indians of the Lake

DAKOTA TREE BURIAL. (YARROW)

region to have at certain periods what may be termed communal burials, in which the bodies or skeletons of a district were removed from their temporary

DAKOTA SCAFFOLD BURIAL. (YARROW)

burial places and deposited with much ceremony in a single large pit (see Brebeuf in Jes. Rel. for 1636, 128–139, 1858).

On the N. W. coast, N. of Columbia r., the dead were usually placed in little cabin-shaped mortuary houses, or box-shaped wooden receptacles raised on posts, on the ground, or occasionally in trees, and sometimes in caves, though cremation, except of

BURIAL HOUSES, NORTHWEST COAST TRIBES.   (YARROW)

the shamans, was formerly common in this section. The bodies of shamans were placed in small rectangular houses built up of poles; the bones of children were sometimes suspended in baskets. Another method of disposing of the dead is that known as canoe burial, the bodies being deposited in canoes which were placed on posts or in the forks of trees. This

CANOE BURIAL, CHINOOK.   (SWAN)

method was practised by the Clallam, Twana, and other tribes of the N.W. coast. Cremation was formerly practised by a number of tribes of the Pacific slope. The ancient inhabitants of s. Arizona practised cremation in addition to house burial, the ashes of the cremated dead being placed in urns; but among the modern Pueblos, especially those most affected by Spanish missionaries, burials are made in cemeteries in the villages.

The ceremonies attending and following burial were various. The use of fire was common, and it was also a very general custom to place food, articles especially prized by or of interest to the dead, and sometimes articles having a symbolic signification, in or near the grave. Scarifying the body, cutting the hair, and blackening the face by the mourners were common customs, as, in some tribes, were feasts and dancing at a death or funeral. As a rule the bereaved relatives observed some kind of mourning for a certain period, as cutting the hair, discarding ornaments and neglecting the personal appearance, carrying a bundle representing the husband (among the Chippewa, etc.), or the bones of the dead husband (among some northern Athapascan tribes), and wailing night and morning in solitary places. It was a custom among some tribes to change the name of the family of the deceased, and to drop the name of the dead in whatever connection.

Consult Bancroft, Native Races, 1874; Dixon in Bull. Am. Mus. Nat. Hist., XVII, pt. III, 1905; Farrand, Basis of Am. Hist., 1904; Holm, Descr. New Sweden, 1834; Jesuit Relations, Thwaites ed., I–LXXII, 1896–1901; Kroeber in Bull. Am. Mus. Nat. Hist., XVIII, pt. I, 1902; Owen, Musquakie Folk-lore, 1904; and the various reports of the B. A. E., especially the 1st Report, containing Yarrow's Mortuary Costoms of the N. A. Indians, and authorities therein cited. See *Mourning, Religion, Urn Burial.*   (C. T.)

Morzhovoi (Russian: 'walrus'). An Aleut village at the end of Alaska penin., Alaska, formerly at the head of Morzhovoi bay, now on the N. shore, on Traders cove, which opens into Isanotski bay. Pop. 45 in 1833 (according to Veniaminof), 68 in 1890.

Morshevoi.—Petroff in 10th Census, Alaska, 19, 1884. **Morshewskoje.**—Holmberg, Ethnog. Skizz., map, 142, 1855. **Morzaivskoi.**—Elliott, Cond. Aff. Alaska, 225, 1875. **Morzhevskoe.**—Veniaminof, Zapiski, II, 203, 1840. **Morzovoi.**—Post route map, 1903. **New Morzhovoi.**—Baker, Geog. Dict. Alaska, 1902. **Old Morzhovoi.**—Ibid. **Protasso.**—Petroff in 10th Census, Alaska, map, 1884 (strictly the name of the Greek church here). **Protassof.**—Ibid., 23. **Protassov.**—Petroff, Rep. on Alaska, 25, 1881.

Mosaic. An art carried to high perfection among the more cultured aborigines of Mexico, where superb work was done, several examples of which enrich European museums. The art was but little in vogue N. of Mexico. Hopi women of to-day wear pendants made of small square or oblong wooden tablets upon which rude turquoise mosaics are set in black piñon gum. These are very inferior, however, to specimens recovered from ancient ruins in the Gila and Little Colorado valleys in Arizona, and in Chaco canyon, N. Mex., which consist of gorgets, ear pendants, and other objects, some of which are well preserved while others are represented only by the foundation form surrounded by clusters of settings loosened by decay of the matrix. Turquoise was the favorite material, but bits of shell and various bright-colored stones were also employed. The foundation form was of shell, wood, bone, and jet and other stone, and the matrix of gum or asphaltum. Although the work is neatly executed, the forms are simple and the designs not elaborate. One of the best examples, from the Little Colorado drainage in Arizona, is a pendant rudely representing a frog, the foundation of which is a bivalve shell, the matrix of pitch, and the settings of turquoise are arranged in lines conforming neatly to the shape of the creature, a bit of red jasper being set in the center of the back (Fewkes). Unfortunately the head of the frog has disintegrated. Among the specimens of inlaying obtained by the Hyde Expedition of the American Museum of Natural History, from Pueblo Bonito ruin, N. Mex., are a jet or lignite frog with turquoise eyes and neckband, a scraper-like implement of deer bone with encircling ornamental bands in turquoise and jet, and a small bird of hematite tastefully set with turquoise and shell (Pepper).

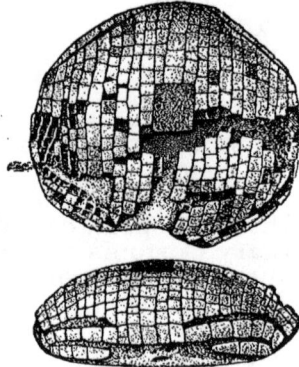

ANCIENT MOSAIC FROG, ARIZONA; 1-2. (FEWKES)

The ancient graves of s. California have yielded a number of specimens of rude mosaic work in which bits of abalone

INCRUSTED OBJECTS FROM PUEBLO BONITO, NEW MEXICO; 1-4. (PEPPER)

shell are set in asphaltum as incrustations for handles of knives and for other objects (Abbott). Inlaying in other sections of the country consists chiefly of the insertion of bits of shell, bone, or stone separately in rows or in simple figures in the margins of utensils, implements, masks, etc. (Niblack, Rust).

Consult Abbott in Surv. West of 100th Merid., VII, 1879; Fewkes (1) in Am. Anthrop., IX, no. 11, 1896, (2) in Smithson. Rep. 1896, 1898, (3) in 22d Rep. B. A. E., 1903; Nelson in 18th Rep. B. A. E., 1899; Niblack in Rep. U. S. Nat. Mus. 1888, 1890; Pepper in Am. Anthrop., n. s., VII, no. 2, 1905; Rust in Am. Anthrop., n. s., VIII, no. 4, 1906. (W. H. H.)

Moshaich. The native name of the extinct Buffalo clans of Acoma and Sia pueblos, N. Mex.

Moshaich-hanoqᶜʰ.—Hodge in Am. Anthrop., IX, 349, 1896 (Acoma form; hánoqᶜʰ=‘people’). Mushä'oh-háno.—Ibid. (Sia form).

Moshoquen. A village or band apparently on or near the s. coast of Maine in 1616, and probably connected with the Abnaki confederacy. Mentioned by Smith (1616) in Mass. Hist. Soc. Coll., 3d s., VI, 107, 1837. (J. M.)

Moshulitubbee. See *Mushalatubbee.*

Mosilian. A division of the New Jersey Delawares formerly on the E. bank of

Delaware r. about the present Trenton. In 1648 they were estimated at 200.

Masselans.—Sanford, U. S., cxlvi, 1819. Mosilian.— Evelin (1648) in Proud, Pa., I, 113, 1797.

Mosookees. Mentioned only by McKenney and Hall (Ind. Tribes, III, 82, 1854) in a list of tribes; unidentified, but possibly the Muskwaki (Foxes), or the Maskoki or Muskogee (Creeks).

Mosopelea. A problematic tribe, first noted on Marquette's map, where ''Monsoupelea,'' or ''Monsouperea,'' is marked as an Indian ·village on the E. bank of the Mississippi some distance below the mouth of the Ohio. In 1682 La Salle found a Mosopelea chief with 5 cabins of his people living with the Taensa, by whom they had been adopted after the destruction of their former village by some unknown enemy.

Mansoleas.—Barcia, Ensayo, 261, 1723. Mansopela.—Douay in Shea, Discovery, 222, 224 (note), 268, 1852. Mansopelea.—Hennepin, Cont. of New Discov., 48a, 1698. Mausalea.—McKenney and Hall, Ind. Tribes, III, 81, 1858 (possibly identical). Medchipouria.—Iberville (1702) in Margry, Déc., IV, 601, 1880 (same?). Monsopela.—Coxe, Carolana, map, 1741. Mons8pelea.—Marquette's map in Shea, Discov., 1852. Monsoupelea.—Thevenot, ibid., 268. Mosopelea.—Allouez (1680) in Margry, Déc., II, 95, 1877. Mosopelleas.—Tonti (1683), ibid., I, 610, 1876. Mosopolca.—Hennepin, Cont. of New Discov., 310, 1698. Mosopolea.—LaSalle (1682) in Margry, Déc., II, 237, 1877.

Mosquito Indians. A tribe named from its habitat on Mosquito lagoon, E. coast of Florida, N. of C. Cañaveral and behind the sand bar that forms the coast line. During the Seminole war of 1835–42 they became notorious for their ferocity. The Timucua remnant settled in this region in 1706, and the Mosquito Indians may have been their descendants or a mixture of them and Seminole. See Bartram, Travels, 142, note, 1791; Roberts, Florida, 23, 1763; J. F. D. Smyth, Tour, II, 21, 1784.

Moss-bag. Some of the Athapascan and Cree Indians of extreme N. w. Canada never use cradles for their infants, but employ instead a ''moss-bag,'' made of leather or skin, lined in winter with hare skins. A layer of moss is put in, and upon this is placed the babe, naked and properly secured. ''This machine,'' says Bernard Ross (Smithson. Rep. 1866, 304), ''is an excellent adjunct to the rearing of children up to a certain age, and has become almost, if not universally, adopted in the families of the Hudson's Bay Company's employees.'' Consult also Milton and Cheadle, N. W. Passage, 3d ed., 85, 1865. (A. F. C.)

Motahtosiks (*Mo-tah'-tos-iks*, ‘many medicines’). A band of the Siksika.—Grinnell, Blackfoot Lodge Tales, 208, 1892.

Motahtosiks. A band of the Piegan.

Conjurers.—Morgan, Anc. Soc., 171, 1877. Many Medicines.—Grinnell, Blackfoot Lodge Tales, 225, 1892. Mo-tah'-tos-iks.—Ibid., 209. Mo-tä'-to-sis.— Morgan, Anc. Soc. 171, 1878. Mo-ta'-tōts.—Hayden, Ethnog. and Philol. Mo. Val., 264, 1862.

Mota's Village. A former Potawatomi village, so called from the chief, just N. of Tippecanoe r., near Atwood, Kosciusko co., Ind. The reservation was sold in 1834.

Motepori. A village of the Opata in 1726, on the Rio Sonora, lat. 30°, N. central Sonora, Mexico (Bandelier in Arch. Inst. Papers, III, 71, 1890). The place is now civilized.

Motsai (possibly from *pä-motsan*, 'a loop in a stream'). A Comanche division, nearly exterminated in a battle with the Mexicans about 1845.

Moochas.—Hazen in Sen. Ex. Doc. 18, 40th Cong., 3d sess., 17, 1869. **Motsai'.**—Mooney in 14th Rep. B. A. E., 1045, 1896. **Mŭt-shă.**—Butcher and Lyendecker, Comanche MS. vocab., B. A. E., 1867 (trans., 'big noses').

Motwainaiks ('all chiefs'). A band of the Piegan division of the Siksika.

All Chiefs.—Grinnell, Blackfoot Lodge Tales, 225, 1892. **Mo-twai'-naiks.**—Ibid., 209.

Mouanast. A village of the Powhatan confederacy in 1608, situated on the N. bank of Rappahannock r., in King George co., Va.—Smith (1629), Va., I, map, repr. 1819.

Mouchaouaouastiirinioek. A Montagnais tribe of Canada in the 17th century.—Jes. Rel. 1643, 38, 1858.

Mouisa. An unidentified tribe or village which according to Douay was found by Tonti in 1682 on or near the lower Mississippi. Cf. *Mosopelea*.

Mouisa.—Le Clercq, First Estab. of the Faith, II, 277, 1882; Shea, Discov. Miss., 226, 1852. **Mousas.**—Barcia, Ensayo, 261, 1723.

Mounds and Mound-builders. The term mounds has been used in America in two different senses as regards the scope intended. By a number of writers it has been applied in a broad sense to include not only the tumuli proper but also various other kinds of ancient monuments. In the more limited sense it refers only to the tumuli, or true mounds, whether of earth or stone. Following the usual custom the term is here used in the broader sense, and hence includes the true mounds, inclosures, walls, embankments, refuse heaps, and other fixed structures.

Although the tumuli are of various forms they may be classed, with few exceptions, as conical tumuli, elongate or wall-like mounds, pyramidal, and effigy or imitative mounds. The conical tumuli are artificial hillocks, not mere accumulations of débris. The form, except where worn down by the plow, is usually that of a low, broad, round-topped cone varying in size from a scarcely perceptible swell in the ground to elevations of 80 or even 100 ft, and from 6 to 300 ft in diameter. Most of the burial mounds are of this type. The elongate or wall-like mounds are earthworks having the appearance of walls, usually from 150 to 300 ft in length, though some are only 50 ft, while others extend to 900 ft. They seem to be confined exclusively to the effigy-mound region.

The typical form of the pyramidal mounds is a truncated quadrangular pyramid; some, however, are circular and a few are irregularly pentagonal, but are distinguished by the flat top. Some have terraces extending outward from one or two sides, and others a ramp or roadway leading up to the level surface. The sharp outlines showing the true form have been more or less obliterated in most instances.

PLATFORM MOUND, MISSOURI; 150 FT. LONG, 25 FT. HIGH. (THOMAS)

The so-called effigy mounds are those representing animal forms, and with a few notable exceptions are confined to Wisconsin and the immediately adjoining

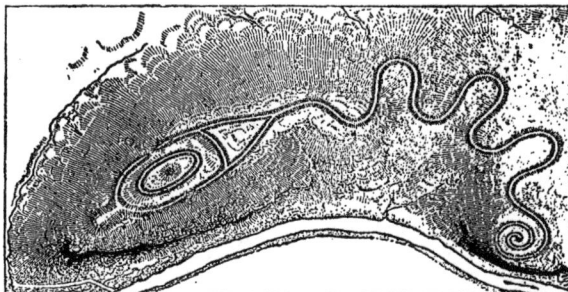

SERPENT MOUND, OHIO.   LENGTH OF WORK, 500 FT.   (HOLMES)

states. The exceptions are two in Ohio, including the noted Serpent mound, and two bird mounds in Georgia. They vary in length from 50 to 500 ft, and in height from a few inches to 4 or 5 ft.

The conical mounds are sometimes composed of earth and stones intermingled, and in a few cases are wholly of stones;

CONICAL MOUNDS, MISSISSIPPI; HEIGHT 30 FT. (THOMAS)

they are also, as a rule, depositories of the dead, but burials also occur in the pyramidal mounds, although the flat-topped structures were usually the sites for buildings, as temples, council houses, and chiefs' dwellings. Burials were rarely made in the wall-like or the effigy mounds. As a rule no special order prevailed in the arrangement of mounds in groups, but some exceptions occur, as, in the effigy-mound region, the small conical mounds are sometimes arranged in regular lines, somewhat evenly spaced and occasionally connected by low embankments; and in Calhoun co., Ill., and N. E. Minnesota they were frequently built in rows. Although a few mounds have been observed on the Pacific slope, N. of Mexico, they are limited chiefly to the Mississippi basin and the Gulf states, the areas of greatest abundance being along the banks of the Mississippi from La Crosse, Wis., to Natchez, Miss., the central and s. sections of Ohio and the adjoining portion of Indiana, and s. Wisconsin. The E. side of Florida is well dotted with shell-heaps.

Inclosures include some of the most important and interesting monuments of the United States. In form they are circular, square, oblong, octagonal, or irregular. Those which approach regularity in figure are either circular, square, or octagonal, and with few exceptions are found in Ohio and the adjoining portions of Indiana,

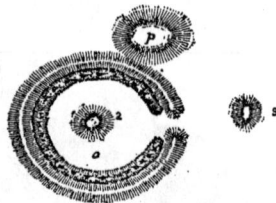

MOUND WITH MOAT AND ENCIRCLING WALL, WEST VIRGINIA; DIAM. 100 FT. (THOMAS)

Kentucky, and West Virginia. These works vary in size from an area of less than an acre to that of more

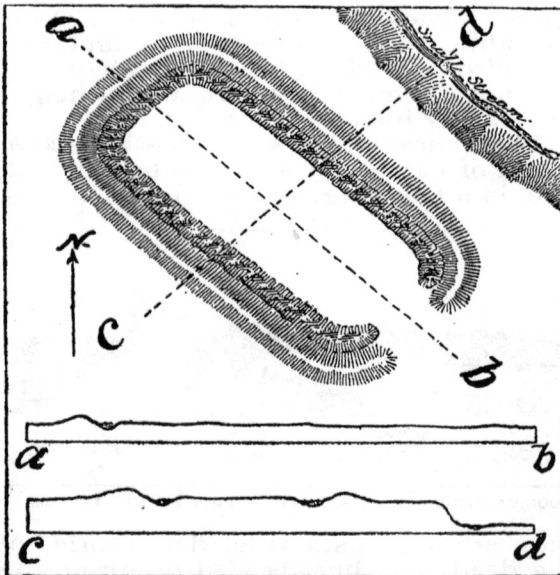

OBLONG INCLOSURE WITH MOAT; WEST VIRGINIA; LENGTH 287 FT. (THOMAS)

than 100 acres. Some are exceedingly interesting because of the near approach they make to true geometrical figures. The diameters of the circle in one or two

instances vary less than 10 ft in 1,000 ft, and the corners of the square in one or two other examples vary less than one degree from 90°.

In S. E. Missouri and in one or two other sections the inclosures have scattered through them small earthen circles marking the sites of circular dwellings. There are indications that some at least of the Ohio inclosures contained similar circles which were obliterated by cultivation.

Another important class of ancient monuments are the refuse or shell heaps found along tidewater and at a few points on the banks of inland streams and lakes, and the mound-like heaps which cover the ruined pueblo dwellings of the S. W. Many hundreds of the mounds and many of the refuse heaps have been opened and their contents examined. Although one or two artifacts, especially certain copper plates with stamped figures, have been discovered which are difficult to account for, the contents otherwise present nothing inconsistent with the conclusion that they are the works of the Indians who inhabited these regions prior to the advent of the whites. It has been contended that many of the artifacts found in the mounds indicate a higher degree of culture than that reached by the later Indians of the mound area. After excluding those derived from the whites or otherwise introduced, this is found to be a mistake, as it appears from the evidence that the historic Indians could and did make articles similar in type and equal in finish to those of the mounds. Some of the articles found show contact with Europeans, and hence indicate that the mounds in which they were discovered are comparatively modern. Notwithstanding these facts and many others tending to the same conclusion, it was maintained by the majority of writers on American archeology, until very recently, that the builders of the mounds of the Mississippi basin and the Gulf states were a specific people of higher culture than the Indians found inhabiting this region; that they were overrun by incoming Indian hordes and finally became extinct, leaving the monuments as the only evidence of their former existence. Other writers suppose that they were Mexicans (Aztec) who were driven s. into Mexico, while others concluded that they were driven into the Gulf states and were the ancestors of the tribes inhabiting that section. The more careful exploration of the mounds in recent years, and the more thorough study of the data bearing on the subject, have shown these opinions to be erroneous. The articles found in the mounds and the character of the various monuments indicate a culture stage much the same as that of the more advanced tribes found inhabiting this region at the advent of the whites. Moreover, European articles found in mounds, and the statements by early chroniclers, as those of De Soto's expedition, prove beyond question that some of these structures were erected by the Indians in post-Columbian times. The conclusion, reached chiefly through the investigations of the Bureau of American Ethnology, and now generally accepted, is that the mound builders were the ancestors of the Indians found inhabiting the same region by the first European explorers. The dearth of mounds east of the Allegheny mts., N. of Tennessee and North Carolina, seems to mark the mountain range along this stretch as a prehistoric boundary line. This would seem to indicate that the mound builders did not enter their territory from the Atlantic coast N. of North Carolina. The few ancient structures in New York are now conceded to be Iroquoian, but the particular tribes or groups to which the other mounds are attributable can not always be stated with certainty. It is known that some of the tribes inhabiting the Gulf states when De Soto passed through their territory in 1540-41, as the Yuchi, Creeks, Chickasaw, and Natchez, were still using and probably constructing mounds, and that the Quapaw of Arkansas were also using them. There is likewise documentary evidence that the "Texas" tribe still used mounds at the end of the 17th century, when a chief's house is described as being built on one (Bolton, inf'n, 1906). There is also sufficient evidence to justify the conclusion that the Cherokee and Shawnee were mound builders. No definite conclusion as to what Indians built the Ohio works has yet been reached, though it is believed that they were in part due to the Cherokee who once inhabited eastern Ohio. According to Miss Fletcher, the Winnebago build miniature mounds in the lodge during certain ceremonies.

The period during which mound building N. of Mexico lasted can not be determined with certainty. That many of the mounds were built a century or two before the appearance of the whites

BIRDSEYE VIEW OF CAHOKIA MOUND, ILLINOIS.   GREATEST LENGTH, ABOUT 1,000 FT.

is known from the fact that when first observed they were covered with a heavy forest growth. Nothing, however, has been found in them to indicate great antiquity, and the present tendency among archeologists is to assign them to the period subsequent to the beginning of the Christian era.

For the literature of the mounds consult the bibliography under *Archeology;* see also Thomas, (1) Catalogue Prehist. Works E. of Rocky Mts., Bull. B. A. E., 1891, (2) in 12th Rep. B. A. E., 1894, and authorities therein cited. See also *Antiquity, Archeology, Cahokia Mound, Elephant Mound, Etowah Mound, Fort Ancient, Fortifications, Grave Creek Mound, Newark Works, Popular fallacies, Serpent Mound, Shell-heaps.* (C. T.)

Mountain Crows. A name applied to the Crows who hunted and roamed in the mountains away from upper Missouri r. They separated from the River Crows about 1859.

Essapookoon.—Henry, MS. vocab., B. A. E., 1808 (Sihasapa name). **Mountain Crows.**—Pease in Ind. Aff. Rep. 1871, 420, 1872. S k o i s ' c h i n t.— G i o r d a , Kalispelm Dict., pt. 2, 81, 1879 (Kalispelm name).

Mountain Lake. Officially mentioned as a body of 800 Indians under the Eastern Oregon (Dalles) agency in 1861. The name dropped out of use after 1862, and they have not been identified. See Ind. Aff. Rep., 220, 1861; Taylor in Cal. Farmer, June 12, 1863.

Mountain Snakes. A name used by Ross (Fur Hunters, I, 250, 1855) for some of the northern Shoshoni; otherwise unidentified.

Mount Pleasant. A former Yuchi town in s. E. Georgia, on Savannah r., probably in Screven co., near the mouth of Brier cr.

Mourning. Mourning customs vary in different tribes, but there are certain modes of expressing sorrow that are common to all parts of the country, and indeed to all parts of the world, as wailing, discarding personal ornaments, wearing disordered garments, putting clay on the head and sometimes on the joints of the arms and legs, and the sacrifice of property. Other practices are widespread, as shedding one's blood by gashing the arms or legs, cutting off joints of the fingers, unbraiding the hair, cutting off locks and throwing them on the dead or into the grave, and blackening the face or body. These signs of mourning are generally made immediately at the death, and are renewed at the burial and again when the mourning feast takes place.

In some tribes it is customary when anyone dies for a priest or other respected person to stand outside the dwelling in which the deceased lies and, with hand uplifted, proclaim in a loud voice to the spirits of the kindred that their kinsman has started on his way to join them; meanwhile swift runners speed through the tribe, spreading the news of the death among the living.

More or less ceremony usually attends the preparation of the body for burial. Among the Hopi wailing takes place during the washing of the body. In some tribes the characteristic tribal moccasin must be put on the feet of the dead by a member of a certain clan, in order that the kindred may be safely reached. In others the face must be ceremonially painted for the journey and the best clothing put on, so that the dead may go forth properly attired and honored. Personal belongings are placed with the corpse. On the N. W. coast, after the body has been arrayed it is propped up at the rear of the house and surrounded by the property, and the relatives and mourners pass by the remains in token of respect. The conventional sign of mourning among the Salish, according to Hill-Tout, is the severing of the hair of the surviving relatives, who dispose of it in various ways according to the tribe—by burning it to prevent its falling into the hands of a sorcerer; by burying it where vegetation is dense, thus insuring long life and strength; by putting it away for final burial at their own death; by casting it into running water, and by fastening it to the branches on the eastern side of a red-fir tree. Among the Hopi wailing is confined to the day of the death and to anniversaries of that event. When a number die from an epidemic a date is officially fixed for the mourning anniversary, and this is kept even when it intercepts a festival or other rite. Professional mourners are employed among the Zuñi, Hopi, Mohave, and neighboring tribes. The observance of the anniversary of a death is common. Among some tribes it is observed with great ceremony; in all cases the guests are served with food, and gifts are made to them in honor of the dead. There are differences observed in mourning for a man or a woman and for an adult or a child. Among the Dakota the widow passed around the circle of the tribe, each circuit standing for a promise to remain single during a year. The general sign of widowhood is loosening the hair and cutting it short in a line with the ears. It was the wife's duty to light a fire for four nights on her husband's grave and watch that it did not die out before dawn. She had to wail at sunrise and sunset, eat little, and remain more or less secluded. The length of her seclusion varied in different tribes from a few weeks or months to two years. At the expiration of the period relatives of her former husband brought her gifts and bade her return to her former pleasures. She was then free to marry again. In some tribes wives, slaves, or horses and dogs were formerly slain at the death of a man, for it was the general belief that relations of all kinds which were maintained on earth would continue in the dwelling place of spirits.

It was usual for the tribe to abstain from festivities when a death occurred in the community. The various societies omitted their meetings, and general silence was observed. In some tribes all the people wailed at sunrise and sunset. Where these general observances of sorrow were the custom, the mourners were visited by the leading men a few days after death, when the pipe was offered, and after smoking, the family of the deceased gave a feast, a signal for the tribe to resume its wonted pleasures.

The black paint that was put upon men, women, and children of some tribes as a sign of mourning might not be washed off, but must be worn until it disappeared by some other means. The announcement of the mourning feast was generally made in a formal way at the close of the burial ceremony. Among most of the Plains tribes black paint was a sign of victory and mourners refrained entirely from paint or other adornment.

The customs of mourning seem to have a twofold aspect—one relating to the spirit of the deceased, the other to the surviving relatives and friends. This dual character is clearly revealed in a custom that obtained among the Omaha and cognate tribes: On the death of a man or a woman who was respected in the community, the young men, friends of the deceased, met at a short distance from the lodge of the dead and made two incisions in their left arms so as to leave a loop of skin. Through this loop was passed a small willow twig, with leaves left on one end; then, with their blood dripping upon the willow leaves, holding a willow stem in each hand, they walked in single file to the lodge, and, standing abreast in a long line, they sang there the tribal song to the dead, beating the willow stems together to the rhythm of the song. At the sound of the music, a near relative came forth from the lodge and, beginning at one end of the line, pulled out the blood-stained twigs from the left arm of each singer, and laid a hand on his head in token of thanks for the sympathy shown. The song continued until the last twig was thrown to the ground. The music of the song was in strange contrast to the bloody spectacle. It was a blithe major melody with no words, but only breathing vocables to float the voice. According to the Indian explanation the song was addressed to the spirit, bidding it go gladly on its way; the blood shed was the tribute of sorrow—grief for the loss of a friend and sympathy for the mourners. The same idea underlies the Omaha custom of ceasing the loud wail at the close of the burial ceremonies lest the sound make it harder for the spirit who must go to leave behind its earthly kindred. See *Mortuary customs.* (A. C. F.)

Mous (*Mo*ⁿ*s*, 'moose'). A gens of the Chippewa, q. v.

Mōns.—Gatschet, Chippewa MS., B. A. E., 1882. **Mo**ⁿ**s.**—Wm. Jones, inf'n, 1906. **Moons.**—Tanner, Narrative, 314, 1830. **Mous.**—Warren (1852) in Minn. Hist. Soc. Coll., v, 45, 1885.

Mousonee (*Mo*ⁿ*sone*, 'moose'). A phratry of the Chippewa (q. v.). The Mous (Moose) gens is one of its leading gentes, as is also the Waubishashe (Marten). Warren calls the phratry the Waubishashe group. (J. M.)

Gens de Orignal.—Dobbs, Hudson Bay, 33, 1744 (same?). **Monsone.**—Warren in Minn. Hist. Soc. Coll., v, 44, 1885 (misprint?). **Mōⁿsonē.**—Wm. Jones, inf'n, 1906. **Monsoni.**—Dobbs, Hudson Bay, 33, 1744 (same?). **Mosonique.**—Ibid. (same?) **Mous-o-neeg.**—Warren in Minn. Hist. Soc. Coll., v, 50, 1885..

Movas. A former Nevome pueblo and the seat of the mission of Santa María, founded in 1622; situated on one of the s. tributaries of the Rio Yaqui, lat. 28° 10′, lon. 109° 10′, Sonora, Mexico; pop. 308 in 1678, and 90 in 1730. Its inhabitants, known as Mova, or Moba, from the name of their settlement, probably spoke a dialect differing slightly from Nevome proper. (F. W. H.)

Concepcion Mobas.—Sonora Materiales (1730) quoted by Bancroft, No. Mex. States, I, 514, 1884. **Mobas.**—Zapata (1678) in Doc. Hist. Mex., 4th s., III, 361, 1857. **Movas.**—Rudo Ensayo (*ca.* 1762), 124, 1863. **Santa María Mobas.**—Zapata, op. cit., 360.

Movwiats (*Mo-vwi'-ats*). A Paiute band formerly living in s. E. Nevada; pop. 57 in 1873.

Mo-vwi'-ats.—Powell in Ind. Aff. Rep. 1873, 50, 1874.—**Mowi'ats.**—Gatschet in Wheeler Surv. Rep., VII, 410, 1879.

Mowhawa (*Mahwäw*ᵃ, 'wolf.') A gens of the Miami, q. v.

Ma″hwäwᵃ**.**—Wm. Jones, inf'n, 1906. **Mo-wha'-wä.**—Morgan, Anc. Soc., 168, 1877.

Mowhawissouk (*Ma'hwäwisowŭg*, 'they go by the name of the wolf.'—W. J.). A gens of the Sauk and Foxes. See *Sauk.*

Ma'hwäwisōwạg.—Wm. Jones, inf'n, 1906. **Mo-whă-wis'-so-uk.**—Morgan, Anc. Soc., 170, 1877.

Mowkowk. See *Mocuck.*

Moxus. A chief of the Abnaki, called also Agamagus, the first signer of the treaty of 1699, and seemingly the successor of Madokawando (Drake, Inds. of N. Am.,

294, 1880). He signed also the treaty with Gov. Dudley in 1702, but a year afterward unsuccessfully besieged the English fort at Casco, Me. He treated with the English in 1713, and again in 1717. It was he who in 1689 captured Pemaquid from the English. (A. F. C.)

Moyawance. A tribe living in 1608 on the N. bank of the Potomac, about Prince George co., Md. Their principal village, of the same name, was about Broad cr. They numbered about 400, but their name drops from history at an early date. They were probably a division of the later Conoy.

Moyaoncs.—Smith (1629), Va., II, 86, repr. 1819. **Moyaonees.**—Bozman, Md., I, 119, 1837. **Moyaones.**—Simons in Smith (1629), Va., I, 177, repr. 1819. **Moyaons.**—Ibid., map. **Moyawance.**—Ibid., 118. **Moyoones.**—Strachey (*ca.* 1612), Va., 38, 1849. **Moyowahcos.**—Macauley, N. Y., II, 168, 1829. **Moyowance.**—Bozman, Md., I, 139, 1837.

Moytoy. A Cherokee chief of Tellico, Tenn., who became the so-called "emperor" of the seven chief Cherokee towns. Sir Alexander Cuming, desirous of enlisting the Cherokee in the British interest, decided to place in control a chief of his own selection. Moytoy was chosen, the Indians were induced to accept him, giving him the title of emperor; and, to carry out the program, all the Indians, including their new sovereign, pledged themselves on bended knees to be the faithful subjects of King George. On the next day, April 4, 1730, "the crown was brought from Great Tennessee, which, with five eagle-tails and four scalps of their enemies, Moytoy presented to Sir Alexander, empowering him to lay the same at His Majesty's feet." Nevertheless, Moytoy afterward became a bitter enemy of the whites, several of whom he killed without provocation at Sitico, Tenn. See Mooney in 19th Rep. B. A. E., pt. 1, 1900.

Mozeemlek. A problematic people who, according to Lahontan, dwelt somewhere in the region of w. Dakota or Wyoming, in 1700. They wore beards, were clothed like the whites, had copper axes, and lived on a river which emptied into a large salt lake.

Moseem-lek.—Vaugondy, map, 1778. **Mozamleeks.**—Featherstonhaugh, Canoe Voy., I, 280, 1847. **Mozeemleck.**—Lahontan, New Voy., I, 125, 1703. **Mozeemlek.**—Ibid., 119. **Mozeenlek.**—Barcia, Ensayo, 297, 1723. **Mozemleks.**—Harris, Voy. and Trav., II, 920, 1705.

Mriksah. The eldest son of Canonicus, the celebrated Narraganset chief; known also as Mexam, Mixam, Mixanno, and Meika. After the death of his father in 1647 he was made chief sachem of the tribe. He married a sister of Ninigret, who was the noted Quaiapen, called also Old Queen, Sunk Squaw, and Magnus (q. v.). Mriksah was one of the sachems to whom the English commissioners at Boston sent interrogations regarding their connection with the Dutch of New York. He was in close relations with Ninigret in his movements. (c. t.)

Msepase (*Mĕshĭpĕshĭ*, 'big lynx.'— W. J.). A gens of the Shawnee, q. v.
Meshipeshi.—Wm. Jones, inf'n, 1906. M′-se′-pa-se.—Morgan, Anc. Soc., 168, 1877. Panther.—Ibid.

Muanbissek. Mentioned in a letter sent by the Abnaki to the governor of New England in 1721 as one of the divisions of their tribe. Not identified.

Muayu. The Yaudanchi name of a village site on Tule r., Cal.; also known as Chesheshim. It is not the name of a tribe, as stated by Powers.
Chesheshim.—A. L. Kroeber, inf'n, 1903. Maiai′-u.—Powers in Cont. N. A. Ethnol., iii, 370, 1877. Muayu.—A. L. Kroeber, inf'n, 1906.

Muchalat. A Nootka tribe on Muchalat arm of Nootka sd., w. coast of Vancouver id.; pop. 62 in 1906. Their principal village is Cheshish.
Match-clats.—Mayne, Brit. Col., 251, 1862. Matchitl-aht.—Can. Ind. Aff. 1884, 186, 1885. Michalits.—Armstrong, Oregon, 136, 1857. Mich-la-its.—Jewitt, Narr., 36, 1849. Mö′tclath.—Boas in 6th Rep. N. W. Tribes Can., 31, 1890. Muchalaht.—Brit. Col. map, 1872. Muchlaht.—Sproat, Sav. Life, 308, 1868.

Muckawis. A name of the whippoorwill. Wordsworth has the "melancholy *muckawis*" in his poem The Excursion. Carver (Travels, 468, 1778) writes, "the whipperwill, or, as it is termed by the Indians, the *muckawiss*." This onomatopœic word is probably of Algonquian origin. It occurs as *múckkowheesce* in Stiles' Pequot vocabulary of 1762 (Trumbull, Natick Dict., Bull. 25, B. A. E., 1903). (a. f. c.)

Muertos (Span.: El Pueblo de los Muertos, 'the village of the dead'). A group of prehistoric ruined pueblos 9 m. s. e. of Tempe, in the Salt River valley, Ariz.— Cushing in Compte-rendu Internat. Cong. Am., vii, 162, 1892.
Los Muertans.—Cushing, ibid., 168 (referring to the former inhabitants).

Mugg. An Arosaguntacook chief in the latter half of the 17th century, conspicuous in the war beginning in 1675, into which he was drawn by the ill-treatment he received from the English. With about 100 warriors he made an assault, Oct. 12, 1676, on Black Point, now Scarboro, Me., where the settlers had gathered for protection. While the officer in charge of the garrison was parleying with Mugg, the whites managed to escape, only a few of the officers' servants falling into the hands of the Indians when the fort was captured; these were kindly treated. Mugg became embittered toward the English when on coming in behalf of his own and other Indians to treat for peace he was seized and taken a prisoner to Boston, although soon released. He was killed at Black Point, May, 16, 1677, the place he captured the preceding year. (c. t.)

Mugu. A former populous Chumashan village, stated by Indians to have been on the seacoast near Pt Mugu, Ventura co., Cal., and placed by Taylor on Guadalasca ranch, near the point.
Mugu.—Cabrillo, Narr. (1542) in Smith, Colec. Doc. Fla., 181, 1857; Taylor in Cal. Farmer, July 24, 1863. Mu-wú.—Henshaw, Buenaventura MS. vocab., B. A. E., 1884.

Mugulasha. A former tribe, related to the Choctaw, living on the w. bank of the Mississippi, 64 leagues from the sea, in a village with the Bayogoula, whose language they spoke. They are said variously to have been the tribe called Quinipissa by La Salle and Tonti, and encountered by them some distance lower down the river, or to have received the remnants of that tribe reduced by disease. At all events their chief was chief over the Quinipissa when La Salle and Tonti encountered them. In January or February, 1700, the Bayogoula attacked the Mugulasha and killed nearly all of them. The name has a generic signification, 'opposite people'—*Imuklasha* in Choctaw—and was applied to other tribes, as Muklassa among the Creeks and West Imongolasha on Chickasawhay r., and it is sometimes difficult to distinguish the various bodies one from another. Among the Choctaw it usually refers to people of the opposite phratry from that to which the speaker belongs. See *Imongalasha*, *Muklassa*. (a. s. g. j. r. s.)
Moglushah town.—H. R. Doc. 15, 27th Cong., 2d sess., 5, 1841. Mogolushas.—Ind. Aff. Rep., 877, 1847. Mogoulachas.—Sauvole (1699) in Margry, Déc., iv, 453, 455, 1880. Mongontatchas.—McKenney and Hall, Ind. Tribes, iii, 81, 1858. Mongoulacha.—La Harpe (1723) in French, Hist. Coll. La., iii, 17, 1851. Mongoulatches.—Drake, Bk. Inds., ix, 1848. Mougolaches.—Coxe, Carolana, 7, 1741. Mougoulachas.—Iberville (1699) in Margry, Déc., iv, 113, 119, 124, 1880.

Mugwump. Norton (Political Americanisms, 74, 1890) defines this word as "an Independent Republican; one who sets himself up to be better than his fellows; a Pharisee." Since then the term has come to mean an Independent, who, feeling he can no longer support the policy of his party, leaves it temporarily or joins the opposite party as a protest. The term was applied to the Independent Republicans who bolted the nomination of Blaine in 1884, and it at once gained popular favor. The earlier history of the term is doubtful, though it seems to have been for some time previous in local use in parts of New England to designate a person who makes great pretensions but whose character, ability, or resources are not equal to them. The word is derived from the Massachuset dialect of Algonquian, being, as Trumbull pointed out, the word *mukquomp*, by which Eliot in his translation of the Bible (Gen., xxxvi, 40–43; Matt. vi, 21, etc.) renders such terms as duke, lord, chief, captain, leader, great man. The components of the word are *moqki* 'great', *-omp* 'man.' In newspaper and political writings *mug-*

wump has given rise to mugwumpery, mugwumpian, mugwumpism. (A. F. C.)

Muhhowekaken (*Muh-ho-we-kä'-ken*, 'old shin'). A subdivision of the Delawares (q. v.).—Morgan, Anc. Soc., 172, 1877.

Muhkarmhukse (*Muh-karm-huk-se*, 'red face'). A subdivision of the Delawares (q. v.).—Morgan, Anc. Soc., 172, 1877.

Muhkrentharne (*Muh-krent-har'-ne*, 'root digger'). A subdivision of the Delawares (q. v.).—Morgan, Anc. Soc., 172, 1877.

Muingpe. A former village, presumably Costanoan, connected with Dolores mission, San Francisco, Cal.—Taylor in Cal. Farmer, Oct. 18, 1861.

Muinyawu. The Porcupine clan of the Hopi, q. v.
Mü-i-nyan wüñ-wü.—Fewkes in Am. Anthrop., VII, 405. 1894. **Muiyawu wiñwû.**—Fewkes in 19th Rep. B. A. E., 584, 1900. **Müñ-ya'u-wu.**—Stephen in 8th Rep. B. A. E., 39, 1891.

Muiva. A Sobaipuri rancheria in 1697, about which date it was visited by Father Kino. Situated on the Rio San Pedro, probably near the mouth of Arivaipa cr., s. Ariz.
Muihibay.—De l'Isle, map Am., 1703. **Muiva.**—Kino (1697) in Doc. Hist. Mex., 4th s., I, 280, 1856.

Mukanti. A band or village of the Molala formerly on the w. slope of the Cascade mts., Oreg. It is not definitely located.   (A. S. G.)

Mukchiath. A sept of the Toquart, a Nootka tribe.—Boas in 6th Rep. N. W. Tribes Canada, 32, 1890.

Mukh (*mŭkh*, 'beaver'). A gens of the Potawatomi (q. v.).
Ami'k.—Wm. Jones, inf'n, 1906 (Chippewa form). **Muk.**—Morgan, Anc. Soc., 167, 1877.—**Mŭkh.**—J. P. Dunn, inf'n, 1907 (Potawatomi form).

Muklasalgi (*Muχlásalgi*, 'people of Muklassa town'). An extinct Creek clan.—Gatschet, Creek Migr. Leg., I, 156, 1884.

Muklassa. Formerly a small Upper Creek town, a mile below Sawanogi and on the same side of Tallapoosa r., in Montgomery co., Ala. Its inhabitants were of the Alibamu tribe or division. Cf. *Mugulasha.*
Amooklasah Town.—Adair, Am. Ind., 277, 1775. **Mackalassy.**—Robin, Voy., II, map, 1807. **Moadassa.**—Bartram, Trav., I, map, 1799. **Mocalasa.**—Alcedo, Dic. Geog., III, 220, 1788. **Mooklausa.**—Pickett, Hist. Ala., II, 267, 1851. **Mooklausan.**—Hawkins (1813) in Am. State Pap., Ind. Aff., I, 854, 1832 (misprint). **Mook-lau-sau.**—Hawkins (1799), Sketch, 35, 1848. **Mucclasse.**—Bartram, Travels, 446, 1791. **Muckeleses.**—Swan (1791) in Schoolcraft, Ind. Tribes, V, 262, 1855.

Mukugnuk. A former Aleut village on Agattu id., Alaska, one of the Near id. group of the Aleutians, now uninhabited.

Mukuk. See *Mocuck.*

Mulamchapa ('long pond by the trees'). A former Nishinam village in the valley of Bear r., N. of Sacramento, Cal.
Moolamchapa.—Powers in Overland Mo., XII, 22, 1874.—Mu-lam'-cha-pa.—Powers in Cont. N. A. Ethnol., III, 316, 1877.

Mulatos. One of the tribes of w. Texas, some of whose people were baptized at the mission of San José y San Miguel de Aguayo in 1784–85, together with people of other tribes called Gincape, Salaphueme, and Tanaicapeme (MS. Baptismal records, 1784–85, partidos 901–926). (H. E. B.)

Mulatto Girls' Town. A former Seminole town s. of Cuscowilla lake, probably in Alachua co., N. Fla.—Bell in Morse, Rep. to Sec. War, 307, 1822.

Mulchatna. A settlement of 180 Eskimo on Mulchatna r., a branch of Nushagak r., Alaska.
Malchatna. — Petroff, Rep. on Alaska, 48, 1881. **Molchatna.**—Petroff in 10th Census, Alaska, 17, 1884. **Mulchatna.**—Baker, Geog. Dict. Alaska, 1902.

Mullers. Flattish stones employed by the native tribes for crushing and pulverizing food substances on a metate (q. v.) or other flat surface; sometimes called *mano*, the Spanish for 'hand.' They were in very general use, especially among the agricultural tribes, and in both form and use grade imperceptibly into the pestle. They may be merely natural bowlders of shape suited to the purpose, or they may have been modified by use into artificial form or designedly shaped by pecking and grinding according to the fancy of the owner. In the Pueblo country mullers are usually oblong slabs of lava or other suitable stone, flat on the undersurface and slightly convex in outline and superior surface, and of a size to be conveniently held in the hand. In some sections, as in the Pacific states and in the Mississippi valley, they are frequently flattish or cheese-shaped cylinders or disks, smooth on the underside and somewhat roughened above. They are sometimes pitted on one or both surfaces, indicating a secondary use, perhaps for cracking nuts. Others show battering, as if subjected to rough usage as hammers. The term muller is properly applied only to grinders having a flat undersurface and shaped to be held under the hand; the pestle has a flat or rounded undersurface and is shaped to be held in the hand in an upright position. See *Metates, Mortars, Pestles,* and consult the authorities thereunder cited.   (W. H. H.)

Mullinose. See *Maninose.*

Mulluk. A former Kusan village or tribe on the N. side of the mouth of Coquille r., on the coast of Oregon. It was on the site of the present town of Randolph.   (L. F.)
Coquille.—Abbott, MS. Coquille Census, B. A. E., 1858. **Delmash.**—Huntington in Ind. Aff. Rep. 1867, 62, 1868. **Delwashes.**—Ind. Aff. Rep., 470, 1865. **Lower Coquille.**—Dorsey, Mûllŭk MS. vocab., B. A. E., 1884. **Mûl'lŭk.**—Ibid. (native name). **Ntûl-mûc'-ci.**—Dorsey, Tutu MS. vocab., B. A. E., 1884 (so called by Tututni, etc.). **Tal-hush-to-ny.**—Abbott, MS. Coquille Census, B. A. E., 1858.

Mulshintik (*Mul'-cin-tik*). A former Yaquina village on the s. side of Yaquina r., Oreg.—Dorsey in Jour. Am. Folklore, III, 229, 1890.

Multnomah (*Nĕ′maᴌnōmax*, 'down river'). A Chinookan tribe or division formerly living on the upper end of Sauvies id., Multnomah co., Oreg. In 1806 they were estimated at 800, but by 1835, according to Parker, they were extinct as a tribe. The term is also used in a broader sense to include all the tribes living on or near lower Willamette r., Oreg. See Lewis and Clark, Exped., II, 472, 1814.
Maltnabah.—Franchère, Narr., 111, 1854. **Mathlanobes.**—Stuart in Nouv. Ann. Voy., x, 115, 1821. **Mathlanobs.**—Morse, Rep. to Sec. War, 368, 1822. **Moltnomas.**—Ross, Advent., 87, 1849. **Mulknomans.**—Orig. Jour. Lewis and Clark (1805), III, 198, 1905. **Multinoma.**—Palmer, Jour. of Trav., 87, 1847. **Mult-no-mah.**—Orig. Jour. Lewis and Clark (1806), IV, 219, 1905. **Multnomia.**—Bond in H. R. Rep. 830, 27th Cong., 2d sess., 63, 1842. **Nĕ′maᴌnōmax.**—Boas, inf'n, 1905.

Mumitupio (*Mum-i′-tup-i-o*, 'fish people'). The Blackfoot name of an unidentified tribe.—Hayden, Ethnog. and Philol. Mo. Val., 264, 1862.

Mummachog. See *Mummychog*.

Mummapacune. A tribe of the Powhatan confederacy, which, according to Strachey, lived on York r., Va., about 1612, and numbered about 350. Mentioned as distinct from the Mattapony in the same neighborhood.—Strachey (*ca.* 1616), Va., 62, 1849.

Mummychog. The barred killifish (*Fundulus pisculentus*); also spelled *mummachog*. This word, in use in certain regions of the N. Atlantic coast of the United States, is corrupted from *moamitteaúg* in the Narraganset dialect of Algonquian, which Roger Williams (1643) defined as "a little sort of fish, half as big as sprats, plentiful in winter." According to Trumbull (Natick Dict., 298, 1903) the fish originally designated by this name was the smelt, whence the name was transferred to the killifish. The Narraganset word, a plural, signifies 'they go gathered together.' The word is sometimes abbreviated to *mummy*. (A. F. C.)

Mumtrak. A Kuskwogmiut Eskimo village on Good News bay, Alaska. Pop. 162 in 1880, and the same in 1890.
Mumtrahamiut.—Eleventh Census, Alaska, 99, 1893. **Mumtrahamut.**—Nelson in 18th Rep. B.A.E., map, 1889. **Mumtrahamute.**—Petroff in 10th Census, Alaska, 17, 1884. **Mumtrekhlagamute.**—Petroff, Rep. on Alaska, 53, 1881. **Mumtrelega.**—Baker, Geog. Dict. Alaska, 96, 1902.

Mumtrelek ('smoke-house'). A Kuskwogmiut Eskimo village on the w. bank of lower Kuskokwim r., Alaska. Pop. 41 (and of the station 29) in 1880, 33 in 1890.
Mumtrekhlagamiut. — Eleventh Census, Alaska, 104, 1893.

Munceytown. A Munsee village in Ontario, N. w. of Brantford, on or near Thames r.
Añ′ti-häⁿ.—J. N. B. Hewitt, inf'n, 1887 (Tuscarora name). **Munceytown.**—Common name.

Munchinye (*Mŭⁿ-tcĭ′-nye*, 'short black bear'). A subgens of the Tunanpin gens

of the Iowa.—Dorsey in 15th Rep. B. A. E., 238, 1897.

Mundua (*Mondawä*, 'one that keeps calling or sounding [through the night]': a word used for the whippoorwill by the Chippewa about Rat portage, Lake of the the Woods.—W. J.). A tribe, or supposed tribe, which the Chippewa claim to have exterminated at an early period, with the exception of a remnant incorporated into their tribe and whose descendants constitute the Wabezhaze or Marten gens. The statements in regard to them, if identified with the Mantouek of the Jesuit writers, are at variance, and may relate to two different groups. The Mantoue of the Jesuit Relation of 1640 are located apparently on the upper peninsula of Michigan, not far w. of Sault Ste Marie, a little N. of the Noquet. In the Relation of 1658 they appear to be placed farther w. and associated with the Sioux. In the Relation of 1671 apparently the same people appear to be situated under the name Nantoue, near Fox r. and in the vicinity of the Miami band, which once resided in this region with or near the Mascoutens. In the tradition given by Warren the scene of the conflict between the Chippewa and this people is indefinite, but the period assigned appears to antedate the entrance of the people into Wisconsin, and thus Schoolcraft interprets it. The tradition, notwithstanding Warren's assertion that it can be considered history, is so exaggerated and indefinite as to date and locality as to render doubtful the propriety of identifying the Mundua of the tradition with the Mantouek of the Jesuit writers. Moreover, Warren's tradition in regard to the Marten gens can not be reconciled with the tradition regarding the Mundua and with what is stated by the Jesuit Relations in regard to the Mantouek. It has been suggested that Amikwa, Noquet, and Mundua or Mantouek, respectively Beaver, Bear, and Whippoorwill gentes, are all names for one and the same people. See *Amikwa, Noquet*. (J. M. C. T.)
Mantoue.—Jes. Rel. 1640, 34, 1858. **Mantouecks.**—Bacqueville de la Potherie, Hist. Am., II, 81, 1753. **Mantouek.**—Jes. Rel. 1658, 21, 1858. **Mantoueouec.**—Map of 1671 (?) in Wis. Hist. Soc. Coll., III, 131, 1856. **Meendua.**—Ramsay in Ind. Aff. Rep., 83, 1850. **Mun-dua.**—Warren (1852) in Minn. Hist Soc. Coll., v, 50, 1885. **Mundwa.**—Schoolcraft, Ind. Tribes, v, 39, 1855. **Nantoüe′.**—Jes. Rel. 1671, 42, 1858.

Munnawhatteaug. See *Menhaden*.

Munominikasheenhug ('rice-makers'). A Chippewa division living on St Croix r., Wis. They had villages at upper St Croix, Yellow, and Rice lakes, and on Snake r., and others named Namakagon and Pokegama. They were incorporated with the Betonukeengainubejig. (J. M.)
Foille avoine Chippeways.—Schoolcraft, Trav., 321, 1821. **Fols Avoin Sauteaux.**—Pike, Trav., 130, 1811.

Fols-avoin-Sauters.—Schermerhorn (1812) in Mass. Hist. Soc. Coll., 2d s., II, 12, 1814. **Fols-avoise.**—Ibid., 13. **la Fallorine.**—Lewis and Clark, Discov., 28, 1806 (misprint). **La Follovoine.**—Ibid., 30. **Manōminikäciyag.**—Wm. Jones, inf'n, 1905 (proper form). **Mun-o-min-ik-a-sheenh-ug.**—Warren (1852) in Minn. Hist. Soc. Coll., V, 38, 1885. **Mun o-min-ik-a-she-ug.**—Ramsey in Ind. Aff. Rep., 86, 1850. **Rice Makers.**—Ibid. **St Croix Indians.**—Warren (1852) in Minn. Hist. Soc. Coll., V, 335, 1885.

Munsee (*Min-asin-ink*, 'at the place where stones are gathered together.'—Hewitt). One of the three principal divisions of the Delawares, the others being the Unami and Unalachtigo, from whom their dialect differed so much that they have frequently been regarded as a distinct tribe. According to Morgan they have the same three gentes as the Delawares proper, viz, Wolf (*Tookseat*), Turtle (*Pokekooungo*), and Turkey (*Pullaook*). Brinton says these were totemic designations for the three geographic divisions of the Delawares and had no reference to gentes (see *Delaware*). However this may be, the Wolf has commonly been regarded as the totem of the Munsee, who have frequently been called the Wolf tribe of the Delawares.

The Munsee originally occupied the headwaters of Delaware r. in New York, New Jersey, and Pennsylvania, extending s. to Lehigh r., and also held the w. bank of the Hudson from the Catskill mts. nearly to the New Jersey line. They had the Mahican and Wappinger on the N. and E., and the Delawares on the s. and s. E., and were regarded as the protecting barrier between the latter tribe and the Iroquois. Their council village was Minisink, probably in Sussex co., N. J. According to Ruttenber they were divided into the Minisink, Waoranec, Warranawonkong, Mamekoting, Wawarsink, and Catskill. The Minisink formed the principal division of the Munsee, and the two names have often been confounded. The bands along the Hudson were prominent in the early history of New York, but as white settlements increased most of them joined their relatives on the Delaware. In 1756 those remaining in New York were placed upon lands in Schoharie co. and were incorporated with the Mohawk. By a fraudulent treaty, known as the "Walking Purchase," the main body of the Munsee was forced to remove from the Delaware about the year 1740, and settled at Wyalusing on the Susquehanna on lands assigned them by the Iroquois. Soon after this they removed to Allegheny r., Pa., where some of them had settled as early as 1724. The Moravian missionaries had already begun their work among them (see *Missions; Moravians*), and a considerable number under their teaching drew off from the tribe and became a separate organization. The others moved w. with the Delawares into Indiana, where most of them were incorporated with that tribe, while others joined the Chippewa, Shawnee, and other tribes, so that the Munsee practically ceased to exist as an organized body. Many removed to Canada and settled near their relatives, the Moravian Indians.

On account of the connection of the Munsee with other tribes, it is impossible to estimate their numbers at any period. In 1765 those on the Susquehanna were about 750. In 1843 those in the United States were chiefly with the Delawares in Kansas, and numbered about 200, while others were with the Shawnee and Stockbridges, besides those in Canada. In 1885 the only Munsee officially recognized in the United States were living with a band of Chippewa in Franklin co., Kans., both together numbering only 72. The two bands were united in 1859, and others are incorporated with the Cherokee in Indian Ter., having joined them about 1868. These Munsee were more commonly known in recent years as "Christians." In Canada the band of Munsee settled with the Chippewa on Thames r., in Caradoc tp., Middlesex co., Ontario, numbered 119 in 1886, while the Moravians, who are mainly Munsee, living near them in Oxford township, Kent co., numbered 275 in 1884. According to the Canadian Ind. Aff. Rep. for 1906, the Moravians of the Thames numbered 348 persons, and the "Munsees of the Thames" numbered 118. There are also a few with the Stockbridges at Green Bay agency, Wis.

The Munsee have been parties to the following treaties with the United States: Treaty of Fort Industry, O., July 4, 1805, with the Ottawa, Wyandot, and other tribes. Appendix to the Menominee treaty with the United States at Green Bay, Wis., Oct. 27, 1832, by the Stockbridges, Munsee, Brothertons, and others. Treaty of Stockbridge, Wis., Sept. 3, 1839, by Stockbridges and Munsee. Treaty of Stockbridge, Wis., Feb. 5, 1856, amending treaty of Sept. 3, 1839. Treaty at Sac and Fox agency, Kans., July 16, 1859, in connection with certain Chippewa. (J. M.)

Humenthí.—Gatschet, Shawnee MS., B. A. E. 1882 (Shawnee name; pl. Humonthígi, from *mĕnethí*, 'island'). **Mantuas.**—Authority of 1840 quoted by Jones, Ojebway Inds., 121, 1861. **Mincees.**—Winfield, Hudson Co., 8, 1874. **Minci.**—Morgan, League Iroq., map, 1851. **Minissi.**—Barton, New Views, app., 2, 1798. **Minseys.**—Heckewelder in Trans. Am. Philos. Soc., n. s., IV, 368, 1834. **Minsimini.**—Walam Olum (1833) in Brinton Lenape Leg., 214, 1885. **Minsis.**—Stuyvesant (1660) quoted by Ruttenber, Tribes Hudson R., 140, 1872. **Moncey.**—Writer of 1842 in Day, Penn., 640, 1843. **Monsays.**—Croghan (1765) in Monthly Am. Jour. Geol., 271, 1831. **Monsees.**—Barton, New Views, xxvii, 1797. **Monseys.**—Ft Johnson Conference (1756) in N. Y.

Doc. Col. Hist., VII, 178, 1856. **Monsi.**—Vater, Mith., pt. 3, sec. 3, 367, 1816. **Monsies.**—German Flats Conference (1770) in N. Y. Doc. Col. Hist., VIII, 243, 1857. **Monsys.**—Loskiel, Hist. Mission United Breth., pt. 3, 119, 1794. **Monthees.**—Aupaumut (1791) in Brinton, Lenape Leg., 45, 1885. **Montheys.**—Brinton, Lenape Leg., 36, 1885. **Munceys.**—Schoolcraft, Ind. Tribes, V, 495, 1855. **Muncies.**—Writer of 1782 in Butterfield, Washington-Irvine Corr., 377, 1882. **Muncy.**—Rupp, West. Pa., 178, 1846. **Munsays.**—Hutchins (1778) in Schoolcraft, Ind. Tribes, VI, 714, 1857. **Munsees.**—Trader (1778) in Schoolcraft, Ind. Tribes, III, 561, 1853. **Mun-see-wuk.**—Morgan, Consang. and Affin., 289, 1871. **Munses.**—Croghan (1765) in Rupp, West Pa., app., 173, 1846. **Munsey.**—Easton Conference (1757) in N. Y. Doc. Col. Hist., VII, 285, 1856. **Munseyis.**—Vater., Mith., pt. 3, sec. 3, 367, 1816. **Munsi.**—Barton, New Views, X, 1798. **Munsies.**—Croghan (1768) in Rupp, West. Pa., app., 181, 1846. **Munsy.**—Smith, Boquet Exped., 89, 1766. **Nunseys.**—Delaware treaty (1765) in N. Y. Doc. Col. Hist., VII, 741, 1856 (misprint). **Ptuksit.**—Brinton, Lenape Leg., 39, 1885 ('Round foot', referring to the Wolf; the totemic designation of the Munsee). **Took'-seat.**—Morgan, Anc. Soc., 172, 1878 ('Wolf', one of the three Delaware gentes; according to Brinton these divisions are *not* gentes). **Wemintheew.**—Aupaumut (1791) in Brinton, Lenape Leg., 20, 1885 (Mahican name). **Wolf tribe of the Delawares.**—The Munsee have frequently been so called.

Muoc. A Chumashan village on one of the Santa Barbara ids., Cal., probably Santa Rosa, in 1542.
Muoc.—Cabrillo, Narr. (1542) in Smith, Colec. Doc. Fla., 186, 1857. **Muoe.**—Taylor in Cal. Farmer, Apr. 17, 1863.

Mupu. A populous Chumashan village stated by Indians to have been at Santa Paula, Ventura co., Cal. Mupu arroyo drains into the Saticoy. See Taylor in Cal. Farmer, July 24, 1863. (H. W. H.)

Murek. A Yurok village on Klamath r., Cal., 12 or 13 m. below the mouth of the Trinity.
Moor-i-ohs.—McKee in Sen. Ex. Doc. 4, 32d Cong., spec. sess., 194, 1853. **Moo-ris.**—Ibid., 162. **Morai-uh.**—Gibbs in Schoolcraft, Ind. Tribes, III, 138, 1853. **Morias.**—McKee in Sen. Ex. Doc. 4, 32d Cong., spec. sess., 193, 1853. **Mo-ri-ohs.**—Ibid., 161. **Mrh.**—Powers in Overland Monthly, VIII, 530, 1872. **Murek.**—A. L. Kroeber, inf'n, 1905. **Mur-iohs.**—Meyer, Nach dem Sacramento, 282, 1855.

Muruam. A former Texas tribe, numerous members of which were baptized during the first half of the 18th century at the San Antonio missions. One individual by this name was baptized in 1707 at Mission San Francisco Solano, on the Rio Grande. At San Antonio their baptism was first recorded under "Baptisms of the Hyerbipiamos" (Ervipiames) with those of the Ervipiames destined for Mission San Xavier de Náxera, called the "Hyerbipiamo suburb" (1721–26). The records show that in their gentile state the Muruam intermarried with these Ervipiames, who were Tonkawan, and who came from Ranchería Grande (q. v.). This points to the conclusion that the Muruam were Tonkawan. A difficulty is raised, however, by the fact that at the Ervipiame suburb were also numerous Ticmamares, some of which tribe had been baptized at San Francisco Solano mission and were apparently natives of that region (Records

of Mission San Antonio de Valero, MS.). After 1726 the Muruam neophytes were incorporated under Mission Valero (ibid.). Their name is most frequently found in the baptismal books of this mission before the year 1730, but members of the tribe were still living there as late as 1775. Compare *Mariames*, who may have been identical. (H. E. B.)
Moroame.—Baptismal Records, op. cit. **Moruames.**—Ibid. **Muruam.**—Ibid. **Muruami.**—Ibid.

Murzibusi. The Bean clan of the Yoki (Rain) phratry of the Hopi. See *Patki*.
Mu'r-zi-bu-si.—Stephen in 8th Rep. B. A. E., 39, 1891.

Mus ('mesquite'). Given by Bourke (Jour. Am. Folk-lore, II, 181, 1889) as a clan (properly gens) of the Mohave, q. v.

Musalakun. A name, originally that of a captain or chief of one of the villages in the vicinity of Cloverdale, Cal., applied to all the Pomo living along Russian r. from Preston southward to the vicinity of Geyserville. (S. A. B.)
Maj-su-ta-ki-as.—McKee (1851) in Sen. Ex. Doc. 4, 32d Cong., spec. sess., 144, 1853. **Masalla Magoons.**—Bancroft, Nat. Races, I, 449, 1874. **Mi-sal'-la Magun'.**—Powers in Cont. N. A. Ethnol., III, 183, 1877. **Mu-sal-la-kūn'.**—Ibid.

Muscongus. A village on the coast of Maine in 1616, probably belonging to the Abnaki. It seems to have been near Muscongus id., in Lincoln co.
Muskoncus.—Smith (1624) in Me. Hist. Soc. Coll., V, 155, 1857. **Nusconcus.**—Smith (1616) in Mass. Hist. Soc. Coll., 3d s., VI, 107, 1837. **Nuscoucus.**—Smith (1629), Va., II, 183, repr. 1819. **Nuskoncus.**—Ibid., 173. **Nuskoucus.**—Ibid., 192.

Muscupiabit ('piñon place'). Mentioned by Rev. J. Cavalleria (Hist. San Bernardino Val., 39, 1902) as a village (probably Serrano) at a place now called Muscupiabe, near San Bernardino, s. Cal.

Musgrove, Mary. See *Bosomworth*.

Mushalatubbee. A Choctaw chief, born in the last half of the 18th century. He was present at Washington, D. C., in Dec., 1824, as one of the Choctaw delegation, where he met and became acquainted with Lafayette on his last visit to the United States. He led his warriors against the Creeks in connection with Jackson in 1812. He signed as leading chief the treaty of Choctaw Trading House, Miss., Oct. 24, 1816; of Treaty Ground, Miss., Oct. 18, 1820; of Washington, D. C., Jan. 20, 1825; and of Dancing Rabbit Creek, Miss., Sept. 27, 1830. He died of smallpox at the agency in Arkansas, Sept. 30, 1838. His name was later applied to a district in Indian Ter.

Mushkoniatawee. A Montagnais village on the s. coast of Labrador.—Stearns, Labrador, 271, 1884.

Music and Musical instruments. Indian music is coextensive with tribal life, for every public ceremony, as well as each important act in the career of an individual, has its accompaniment of song. The music of each ceremony has its peculiar rhythm, so also have the classes of songs which pertain to individual acts: fasting and prayer, setting of traps, hunting, courtship, playing of games, facing and defying death. An Indian can determine at once the class of a strange song by the rhythm of the music, but not by that of the drumbeat, for the latter is not infrequently played in time differing from that of the song. In structure the Indian song follows the outline of the form which obtains in our own music—a short, melodic phrase built on related tones which we denominate chord lines, repeated with more or less variation, grouped into clauses, and correlated into periods. The compass of songs varies from 1 to 3 octaves.

Some songs have no words, but the absence of the latter does not impair the definite meaning; vocables are used, and when once set to a melody they are never changed. Occasionally both words and vocables are employed in the same song. Plural singing is generally in unison on the plains and elsewhere, the women using a high, reedy, falsetto tone an octave above the male singers. Among the Cherokee and other Southern tribes, however, "round" singing was common. Men and women having clear resonant voices and good musical intonation compose the choirs which lead the singing in ceremonies, and are paid for their services. Frequently two or three hundred persons join in a choral, and the carrying of the melody in octaves by soprano, tenor, and bass voices, produces harmonic effects.

Songs are the property of clans, societies, and individuals. Clans and societies have special officers to insure the exact transmission and rendition of their songs, which members alone have the right to sing, and a penalty is exacted from the member who makes a mistake in singing. The privilege to sing individual songs must sometimes be purchased from the owner. Women composed and sang the lullaby and the spinning and grinding songs. Among the Pueblos men joined in singing the latter and beat time on the floor as the women worked at the metates. Other songs composed by women were those sung to encourage the warrior as he went forth from the camp, and those sung to send to him, by the will of the singers, strength and power to endure the hardships of the battle.

On the N. Pacific coast, and among other tribes as well, musical contests were held, when singers from one tribe or band would contend with those from another tribe or band as to which could remember the greatest number or accurately repeat a new song after hearing it given for the first time. Among all the tribes

accurate singing was considered a desirable accomplishment.

Among the Baffinland Eskimo grudges are settled by the opponents meeting by appointment and singing sarcastic songs at each other. The one who creates the most laughter is regarded as the victor. The Danish writers call these controversial songs "nith songs."

In ceremonial songs, which are formal appeals to the supernatural, accuracy in rendering is essential, as otherwise "the path would not be straight"; the appeals could not reach their proper destination and evil consequences would follow. Consequently, when an error in singing occurs, the singers stop at once, and either the song or the whole ceremony is begun again; or, as in some tribes, a rite of contrition is performed, after which the ceremony may proceed. Official prompters keep strict watch during a ceremony in order to forestall such accidents.

MUSICIANS, PEYOTE CEREMONY; KIOWA

The steps of ceremonial dancers follow the rhythm of the drum, which frequently differs from the rhythm of the song. The drum may be beaten in 2/4 time and the song be in 3/4 time, or the beat be in 5/8 time against a melody in 3/4, or the song may be sung to a rapid *tremolo* beating of the drum. The beat governs the bodily movements; the song voices the emotion of the appeal. The native belief which regards breath as the symbol of life is in part extended to song; the invisible voice is supposed to be able to reach the invisible power that permeates nature and animates all natural forms. The Indian sings with all his force, being intent on expressing the fervor of his emotion and having no conception of an objective presentation of music. The straining of the voice injures its tone quality, stress sharpens a note, sentiment flattens it, and continued *portemento* blurs the outline of the melody, which is often further confused by voice pulsations, making a rhythm within a rhythm, another complication being added when the drum is beaten to a measure different from that

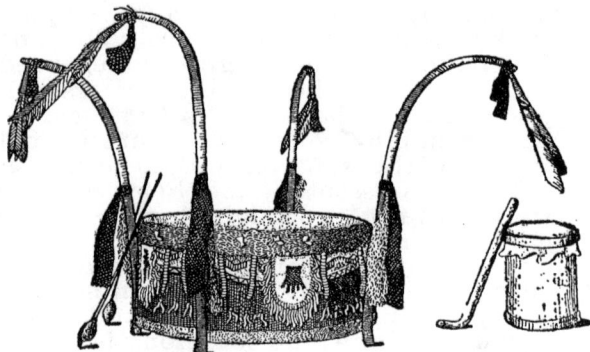

CHIPPEWA DRUMS. (JENKS)

of the song; so that one may hear three rhythms, two of them contesting, sometimes with syncopation, yet resulting in a well - built whole. It has always been difficult for a listener of another race to catch an Indian song, as the melody is often "hidden by overpowering noise." When, however, this difficulty has been overcome, these untrammeled expressions of emotions present a rich field in which to observe the growth of musical form and the beginning of musical thinking. They form an important chapter in the development of music. Apart from this historic value, these songs

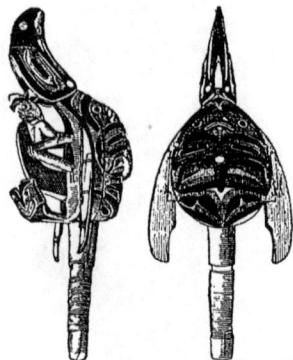

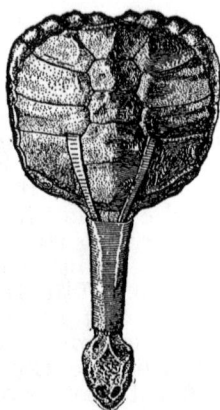

KWAKIUTL RATTLES; 1-8. (BOAS)

TURTLE-SHELL RATTLE;
IROQUOIS (1-8)

HUPA RATTLE; 1-3
(MASON)

offer to the composer a wealth of melodic and rhythmic movements, and that peculiar inspiration which heretofore has been obtained solely from the folk songs of Europe.

Musical Instruments.—Drums vary in size and structure, and certain ceremonies have their peculiar type. On the N. W. coast a plank or box serves as a drum. Whistles of bone, wood, or pottery, some producing two or more tones, are employed in some ceremonies; they symbolize the cry of birds or animals, or the voices of spirits. Pandean pipes, which occur in South America, were unknown in the northern continent until recent times. In the S. W., notched sticks are rasped together or on gourds, bones, or baskets, to accentuate

GOURD RATTLE; HOPI;
1-6. (STEVENSON)

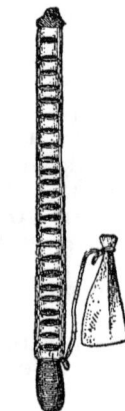

NOTCHED STICK
AND DEER
SCAPULA USED
FOR RATTLE;
HOPI; 1-12.
(STEVENSON)

KWAKIUTL
WHISTLE;
1-8. (BOAS)

OMAHA FLUTE.
(J. O. DORSEY)

rhythm. The flageolet is widely distributed and is played by young men during courtship; it also accompanies the songs of certain Pueblo ceremonies. Rattles (q. v.) were universal. The intoning of rituals, incantations, and speeches can hardly be regarded as of musical character. The musical bow is used by the Maidu of California and by the Tepehuane, Cora, and Huichol tribes of the Piman stock in Mexico. Among the Maidu this bow plays an important part in religion and much sorcery is connected with it.

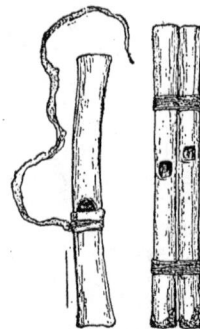

BONE WHISTLES; HUPA;
1-5. (POWERS)

For further information consult Baker, Ueber die Musik des Nordamerikanischen Wilden, 1882; Boas (1) in 6th Rep. B. A. E., 1888, (2) in Rep. Nat.

Mus. 1895; Brown in Am. Anthrop., VIII, no. 4, 1906; Cringan, Iroquois Folk-songs, Archæol. Rep. Provin. Mus., Toronto, 1902; Curtis, Songs of Ancient America, 1905; Cushing in Millstone, x, Jan. 1885; Dixon in Bull. Am. Mus. Nat. Hist., XVII, pt. 3, 1905; Farrand, Basis of American History, 1904; Fillmore in Am. Anthrop., n. s., I, 1899; Fletcher (1) in Pub. Peabody Mus., I, no. v, (2) Indian Story and Song, 1900; Hoffman in 7th Rep. B. A. E., 1891; Hough in Am. Anthrop., XI, no. 5, 1897; Hrdlicka, ibid., n. s., VII, no. 3, 1905, and VIII, no. 1, 1906; Lumholtz, Unknown Mexico, I, 475, 1902; Matthews, (1) Navaho Legends, 1897, (2) Night Chant, Memoirs Am. Mus. Nat. Hist., Anthrop. ser., v, 1902; Mooney in 14th Rep. B. A. E., 1896; Sammelbände der Internationalen Musikgesellschaft; Stumpf in Vierteljahrsschrift für Musikwissenschaft; Voth in Field Columb. Mus. Pub., Anthrop. ser., III, VI, 1901, 1903; Wallaschek, Primitive Music, 1893; Willoughby in Am. Anthrop., n. s., IX, no. 1, 1907. (A. C. F.)

Muskeg (Chippewa, *mŭskig*; Kickapoo, *maskyägⁱ*, 'grassy bog.'—W. J.). Low, wet land; a quagmire, marsh, swamp, the equivalent of *savane* in Canadian French. A word much used in parts of Ontario, the Canadian Northwest, and the adjoining regions of the United States; spelled also *maskeg*. In the N. W. *muskeg* is the usual form. (A. F. C.)

Muskelunge. See *Maskinonge*.

Muskhogean Family. An important linguistic stock, comprising the Creeks, Choctaw, Chickasaw, Seminole, and other tribes. The name is an adjectival form of *Muskogee*, properly *Măskóki* (pl. Maskokalgi or Muscogulgee). Its derivation has been attributed to an Algonquian term signifying 'swamp' or 'open marshy land' (see *Muskeg*), but this is almost certainly incorrect. The Muskhogean tribes were confined chiefly to the Gulf states E. of the Mississippi, occupying almost all of Mississippi and Alabama, and parts of Tennessee, Georgia, Florida, and South Carolina. According to a tradition held in common by most of their tribes, they had reached their historic seats from some starting point w. of the Mississippi, usually placed, when localized at all, somewhere on the upper Red r. The greater part of the tribes of the stock are now on reservations in Oklahoma.

Through one or another of its tribes the stock early came into notice. Panfilo de Narvaez met the Apalachee of w. Florida in 1528, and in 1540–41 De Soto passed E. and w. through the whole extent of the Muskhogean territory. Mission effort was begun among them by the Spanish Franciscans at a very early period, with such success that before the year 1700, besides several missions in lower Georgia, the whole Apalachee tribe, an important single body, was civilized and Christianized, and settled in 7 large and well-built towns (see *Missions.*) The establishment of the French at Mobile, Biloxi, and other points about 1699–1705 brought them into contact with the Choctaw and other western branches of the stock. The powerful Creek confederacy had its most intimate contact with the English of Carolina and Georgia, although a French fort was long established in the territory of the Alibamu. The Chickasaw also were allies of the English, while the Choctaw were uncertain friends of the French. The devotion of the Apalachee to the Spaniards resulted in the destruction of the former as a people at the hands of the English and their Indian allies in the first years of the 18th century. The tide of white settlement, both English and French, gradually pressed the Muskhogean tribes back from the shores of the Atlantic and the Gulf, some bands recrossing to the w. of the Mississippi as early as 1765. The terrible Creek war in 1813–14 and the long drawn-out Seminole war 20 years later closed the struggle to maintain themselves in their old territories, and before the year 1840 the last of the Muskhogean tribes had been removed to their present location in Oklahoma, with the exception of a few hundred Seminole in Florida, a larger number of Choctaw in Mississippi, Alabama, and Louisiana, and a small forgotten Creek remnant in E. Texas. (See the several tribal articles.)

There existed between the tribes marked dissimilarities as to both physical and cultural characteristics. For instance, the Choctaw were rather thickset and heavy, while those farther E., as the Creeks, were taller but well-knit. All the tribes were agricultural and sedentary, occupying villages of substantially built houses. The towns near the tribal frontiers were usually palisaded, while those more remote from invasion were left unprotected. All were brave, but the Choctaw claimed to fight only in self-defense, while the Creeks, and more particularly the Chickasaw, were aggressive. The Creeks were properly a confederacy, with the Muskogee as the dominant partner, and including also in later years the alien Yuchi, the Natchez, and a part of the Shawnee. The Choctaw also formed a loose confederacy, including among others several broken tribes of alien stock.

In their government the Muskhogean tribes appear to have made progress corresponding to their somewhat advanced culture in other respects. In the Creek government, which is better known than that of the other tribes of the family, the unit of the political as well as of the social structure was the clan, as in many Indian tribes, marriage being forbidden within the clan, and the children belonged to the clan of the mother. Each town had its independent government, its council being a miniature of that of the confederacy; the town and its outlying settlements, if it had any, thus represented an autonomy such as is usually implied by the term "tribe." Every considerable town was provided with a "public square," formed of 4 buildings of equal size facing the cardinal points, and each divided into 3 apartments. The structure on the E. side was allotted to the chief councilors, probably of the administrative side of the government; that on the s. side belonged to the warrior chiefs; that on the N. to the inferior chiefs, while that on the w. was used for the paraphernalia belonging to the ceremony of the black drink, war physic, etc. The general policy of the confederacy was guided by a council, composed of representatives from each town, who met annually, or as occasion required, at a time and place fixed by the chief, or head *mico*. The confederacy itself was a political organization founded on blood relationship, real or fictitious; its chief object was mutual defense, and the power wielded by its council was purely advisory. The liberty within the bond that held the organization together was shown by the fact that parts of the confederacy, and even separate towns, might and actually did engage in war without reference to the wishes of the confederacy. The towns, especially those of the Creeks, were divided into two classes, the White or Peace towns, whose function pertained to the civil government, and the Red or War towns, whose officers assumed management of military affairs.

The square in the center of the town was devoted to the transaction of all public business and to public ceremonies. In it was situated the sweat house, the uses of which were more religious than medicinal in character; and here was the chunkey yard, devoted to the game from which it takes its popular name, and to the *busk* (q. v.), or so-called Green-corn dance. Such games, though not strictly of religious significance, were affairs of public interest, and were attended by rites and ceremonies of a religious nature. In these squares strangers who had no relatives in the town—i. e., who possessed no clan rights—were permitted to encamp as the guests of the town.

The settlement of disputes and the punishment of crimes were left primarily to the members of the clans concerned; secondly, to the council of the town or tribe involved. The *busk* was an important institution among the Muskhogean people, and had its analogue among most, if not all, other American tribes; it was chiefly in the nature of an offering of first fruits, and its celebration, which occupied several days, was an occasion for dancing and ceremony; new fire was kindled by a priest, and from it were made all the fires in the town; all offenses, save that of murder, were forgiven at this festival, and a new year began. Artificial deformation of the head seems to have been practised to some extent by all the tribes, but prevailed as a general custom among the Choctaw, who for this reason were sometimes called "Flatheads."

The Muskhogean population at the time of first contact with Europeans has been estimated at 50,000. By the census of 1890 the number of pure-bloods belonging to the family in Indian Ter. was as follows: Choctaw, 9,996; Chickasaw, 3,464; Creek, 9,291; Seminole, 2,539; besides perhaps 1,000 more in Florida, Mississippi, Louisiana, and Texas. In 1905 their numbers were: Choctaw by blood, 17,160; by intermarriage, 1,467; freedmen, 5,254; in Mississippi, 1,235. Chickasaw by blood, 5,474; by intermarriage, 598; freedmen, 4,695. Creeks by blood, 10,185; freedmen, 5,738. Seminole by blood, 2,099; freedmen, 950; in Florida (1900), 358.

The recognized languages of the stock, so far as known, each with dialectic variants, are as follows:

1. Muskogee (including almost half of the Creek confederacy, and its offshoot, the Seminole).

2. Hitchiti (including a large part of the Lower Creeks, the Mikasuki band of the Seminole, and perhaps the ancient Apalachee tribe).

3. Koasati (including the Alibamu, Wetumpka, and Koasati towns of the Creek confederacy).

4. Choctaw (including the Choctaw, Chickasaw, and the following small tribes: Acolapissa, Bayogoula, Chakchiuma, Chatot, Chula, Huma, Ibitoupa, Mobile, Mugalasha, Naniba, Ofogoula, Tangipahoa, Taposa, and Tohome).

To the above the Natchez (q. v.) should probably be added as a fifth division, though it differs more from the other dialects than any of these differ from one another. The ancient Yamasi of the Georgia-South Carolina coast may have constituted a separate group, or may have been a dialect of the Hitchiti. The Yamacraw were renegades from the Lower Creek towns and in the main were probably Hitchiti. (H. W. H. J. M.)

>Chahtahs.—Prichard, Phys. Hist. Mankind, v, 403, 1847 (or, Choktahs or Flatheads). =Chahta-Muskoki.—Trumbull in Johnson's Cyclopædia, II, 1156, 1877. >Chahtas.—Gallatin in Trans. Am.

Antiq. Soc., II, 100, 306, 1836. =**Chata-Muskoki.**—Hale in Am. Antiq., 108, Apr. 1883. >**Choctah.**—Latham, Nat. Hist. Man, 337, 1850 (includes Choctahs, Muscogulges, Muskohges); Latham in Trans. Philol. Soc. Lond., 103, 1856; Latham, Opuscula, 366, 1860. >**Chocta-Muskhog.**—Gallatin in Trans. Am. Ethnol. Soc., II, pt. 1, xcix, 77, 1848. >**Choctaw Muskhogee.**—Gallatin in Trans. Am. Antiq. Soc., II, 119, 1836. >**Coshattas.**—Latham, Nat. Hist. Man, 349, 1850 (not classified). >**Flat-heads.**—Prichard, Phys. Hist. Mankind, v, 403, 1847. >**Humas.**—Latham, Nat. Hist. Man, 341, 1850 (E. of Mississippi above New Orleans). =**Maskoki.**—Gatschet, Creek Migr. Leg., I, 50, 1884. >**Mobilian.**—Bancroft, Hist. U. S., 249, 1840. >**Muscogee.**—Keane in Stanford, Compend., app., 460, 1878. >**Muskhogee.**—Gallatin in Trans. Am. Antiq. Soc., II, 94, 1836. **Muskhogies.**—Berghaus (1845), Physik. Atlas, map 17, 1848. >**Tschahtas.**—Ibid.; ibid., 1852.

Muskingum ('moose eye or face.'—Hewitt). A Delaware (?) village marked on old maps as on the w. bank of Muskingum r., Ohio.
Muskingom.—La Tour, map, 1779. **Muskingum.**—Güssefeld, map, 1784. **Muskingun.**—Alcedo, Dic. Geog., III, 274, 1788. **Muskinkum.**—Esnauts and Rapilly, map, 1777.

Muskwawasepeotan ('the town of the old redwood creek'). A Potawatomi village formerly near Cedarville, Allen co., N. E. Ind., on land sold in 1828, and commonly known as Metea's Village from the name of its chief. (J. M.)
Metea's Village.—Mississinewa treaty (1826) in U. S. Ind. Treat., 670, 1873. **Muskwawasepeotan.**—Long cited by McKenney and Hall, Ind. Tribes, II, 61, 1849.

Muskwoikakenut (*Mus-kwoi-ká-ke-nut*, 'He shoots bears with arrows'). A Cree band, so called after its chief, living in 1856 in the vicinity of Ft de Prairie, Northwest Ter., Canada.—Hayden, Ethnog. and Philol. Mo. Val., 237, 1862.

Muskwoikauepawit (*Mus-kwoi-káu-e-pá-wit*, 'Standing bear'). A Cree band, so called after its chief, living in 1856 about Ft de Prairie, Northwest Ter., Canada.—Hayden, Ethnog. and Philol. Mo. Val., 237, 1862.

Musme (*Mûs-mĕ'*). A former village of the Chastacosta on Rogue r., Oreg.—Dorsey in Jour. Am. Folk-lore, III, 234, 1890.

Muspa. A Calusa village on the s. w. coast of Florida about 1570 (Fontaneda), probably about the mouth of Caloosahatchee r. The people of Muspa were among the last of the Calusa to retain their name and territory. C. Romano is marked on old English maps as Punta de Muspa and the coast strip extending thence northward to the entrance of Caloosahatchee r. is marked on some Spanish maps as La Muspa (B. Smith). The Muspa Indians, according to Brinton (Flor. Penin., 114, 1859), occupied the shore and islands of Boca Grande, the main entrance of Charlotte harbor, until toward the close of the 18th century, when they were driven to the keys by the Seminole; but according to Douglas (Am. Antiq., VII, 281, 1885) they were still in the vicinity of Pine id., in Charlotte harbor, as late as 1835. There is even reason to believe that they took part in some of the raiding in the Seminole war as late as 1840. (J. M.)
Muspa.—Fontaneda (*ca.* 1575), Memoir, Smith trans., 19, 1854.

Musquarro. A former Montagnais rendezvous and mission station on the N. shore of the Gulf of St Lawrence, opposite Anticosti id. The Indians deserted it in recent years for Romaine.
Mashquaro.—McLean, Hudson Bay, II, 53, 1849. **Maskouaro.**—Hind, Lab. Penin., II, 180, 1863. **Masquarro.**—Ibid., 26. **Musquahanos.**—Can. Ind. Aff. 1880, 313, 1881 (applied to the band there; misprint?). **Musquarro.**—Hind, Lab. Penin., II, 133, 1863.

Musquash. A name for the muskrat (*Fiber zibethicus*), used in Canada and N. and w. parts of the United States. In early writings on Virginia the forms *mussascus* and *musquassus* (Capt. John Smith, 1616), *muscassus* (Hakluyt, 1609), and others, occur. Cognate words in other Algonquian dialects are the Abnaki *muskwessu*, and the Chippewa *miskwasi*, signifying 'it is red,' which was therefore the original signification of the Virginian name whereof Smith's word is a corruption, and referred to the reddish color of the animal. See *Mooskwasuh*. (A. F. C.)

Musqueam. A Cowichan tribe occupying the N. part of the Fraser delta, Brit. Col.; pop. 98 in 1906. Male is their village.
Miskwiam.—Tolmie and Dawson, Vocabs., Brit. Col., 119B, 1884. **Misqueam.**—Can. Ind. Aff. for 1880, 316, 1881. **Musqueam.**—Ibid., 1901, pt. II, 158. **Musqueeam.**—Ibid., 1877, LI. **Musqueom.**—Ibid., 1902, 72. **QmE' okoyim.**—Boas in 64th Rep. Brit. A. A. S., 454, 1894. **Qmuskī'Em.**—Hill-Tout in Ethnol. Surv. Can., 54, 1902.

Mussauco. A former village, probably near Hartford, Conn. Its chief, Arrhamamet, was conquered by Uncas, the Mohegan chief, about 1654.—Trumbull, Conn., I, 129, 1818.

Mussundummo ('water snake.'—Tanner, Narr., 314, 1830). Given as one of the totems among the Ottawa and Chippewa. It may be an Ottawa totem, as it is not mentioned by Morgan or Warren.

Mustak. A former village of the Kalindaruk division of the Costanoan family, connected with San Carlos mission, Cal.
Mustac.—Taylor in Cal. Farmer, Apr. 20, 1860.

Mustoo. A name given by Dawson to a supposed town on Hippa id., Queen Charlotte ids., Brit. Col., but in reality the word is a corruption of Nastó, the Haida name for Hippa id., on which there were several towns. See *Atanus*, *Gatga-inans*, *Sulu-stins*. (J. R. S.)

Muswasipi (cognate with Chippewa *Moswa-sibĭ*, 'moose river.'—W. J.). The name of one of the divisions of the Upeshipow, an Algonquian tribe of Labrador, living in 1770 on Moose r., Ruperts Land, Brit. Am.—Richardson, Arctic Exped., II, 38, 1851.

Mutchut. A village of the Powhatan confederacy, situated in 1608 on the N. bank of Mattapony r., in King and Queen co., Va.—Smith (1629), Va., I, map, repr. 1819.

Mutistul. An important Yukian Wappo village in Knight's valley, Sonoma co., Cal. (S. A. B.)
Mutistals.—Stearns in Am. Naturalist, XVI, 208, 1882. Mu-tistul. — Gibbs in Schoolcraft, Ind. Tribes, III, 110, 1853.

Mutsiks (*Mŭt'-siks*, 'braves'). A society of the Ikunuhkahtsi, or All Comrades, in the Piegan tribe; it consists of tried warriors.—Grinnell, Blackfoot Lodge Tales, 221, 1892.

Mutsun. A Costanoan village near San Juan Bautista mission, San Benito co., Cal. The name was used for a group and dialect of the Costanoan family. The Mutsun dialect being better known than others allied to it, owing to a grammar and a phrasebook written by Arroyo de la Cuesta in 1815 (Shea, Lib. Am. Ling., I, II, 1861), the name came to be used for the linguistic family of which it formed part and which was held to extend northward beyond the Golden Gate and southward beyond Monterey, and from the sea to the crest of the sierras. Gatschet and Powell used it in this sense in 1877. Subsequently Powell divided the Mutsun family, establishing the Moquelumnan family (q. v.) E. of San Joaquin r. and the Costanoan family (q. v.) w. thereof.
Motssum.—Engelhardt, Franciscans in Cal., 398, 1897. Mutseen.—Taylor in Cal. Farmer, Nov 23, 1860. Mutsunes.—Ibid., Feb. 22. Mutzun.—Simeon, Dict. Nahuatl, xviii, 1885. Mutzunes.—Taylor in Cal. Farmer, Apr. 20, 1860. Nuthesum.—Ibid.

Muttamussinsack. A village of the Powhatan confederacy in 1608, on the N. bank of the Rappahannock, in Caroline co., Va.—Smith (1629), Va., I, map, repr. 1819.

Mututicachi. A former pueblo, apparently of the Teguima division of the Opata, on the upper Rio Sonora, Sonora, Mexico. It is said to have been abandoned on the establishment of the mission of Suamca in 1730. According to the Rudo Ensayo (ca. 1762) it was a Pima settlement, but this is doubtless an error. The present hamlet of Mututicachi contained 27 persons in 1900.
Motuticatzi.—Rudo Ensayo (ca. 1762), 160, 1863. Mututicachi.—Bandelier in Arch. Inst. Papers, IV, 483, 1892.

Muutzizti (from Cora *muuti*, 'head'). A subdivision of the Cora proper, inhabiting the central part of the Nayarit mts., Jalisco, Mexico.
Muutzicat.—Ortega, Vocab. en Lengua Castellana y Cora, 1732, 7, 1888 (sing. form). Muutzizti.—Orozco y Berra, Geog., 59, 1864.

Muvinabore. Mentioned by Pimentel (Lenguas, II, 347, 1865) as a division of the Comanche, but no such division is recognized in the tribe.

Muyi (*Mŭ'yi*). The Mole clan of the Hopi of Arizona.—Voth, Traditions of the Hopi, 37, 40, 1906.

Mwawa (*Ma'ʿhwäwᵃ*, 'wolf'). A gens of the Shawnee, q. v.
Maʿhwäwᵃ.—Wm. Jones, inf'n, 1906. M'-wa-wä.—Morgan, Anc. Soc., 168, 1877.

Myeengun (*Maˑiˑngŭn*, 'wolf'). A gens of the Chippewa, q. v.
Mah-een-gun.—Warren (1852) in Minn. Hist. Soc. Coll., V, 44, 1885. Ma'-ingan.—Gatschet, Ojibwa MS., B. A. E., 1882. Maˑiˑngan.—Wm. Jones, inf'n, 1906. My-een'-gun.—Morgan, Anc. Soc., 166, 1877.

Myghtuckpassu. A village of the Powhatan confederacy in 1608, on the s. bank of Mattapony r., King William co., Va.—Smith (1629), Va., I, map, repr. 1819.

Myhangah. See *Mohongo*.

Mystic (from *missi-tuk*, 'great tidal river.'—Trumbull). The name of at least two former villages in New England, one on the river of the same name at Medford, Middlesex co., Mass., which was occupied in 1649 and was in the Massachuset country. The other was a Pequot village on the w. side of Mystic r., not far from the present Mystic, New London co., Conn. It was burned by the English in 1637. (J. M.)
Mestecke.—Brewster (1657) in Mass. Hist. Soc. Coll., 4th s., VII, 82, 1865. Mestick.—Eliot (1649), ibid., 3d s., IV, 88, 1834. Mistick.—Dudley (ca. 1630), ibid., 1st s., VIII, 39, 1802. Mystick.—Pike (1698) in N. H. Hist. Soc. Coll., III, 49, 1870.

Mythology. The mythology of the North American Indians embraces the vast and complex body of their opinions regarding the genesis, the functions, the history, and the destiny not only of themselves but also of every subjective and of every objective phenomenon, principle, or thing of their past or present environment which in any marked manner had affected their welfare.

Among savage tribal men a myth is primarily and essentially an account of the genesis, the functions, the history, and the destiny of a humanized fictitious male or female personage or being who is a personification of some body, principle, or phenomenon of nature, or of a faculty or function of the mind, and who performs his or her functions by imputed inherent *orenda* (q. v.), or magic power, and by whose being and activities the inchoate reasoning of such men sought to explain the existence and the operations of the bodies and the principles of nature. Such a being or personage might and did personify a rock, a tree, a river, a plant, the earth, the night, the storm, the summer, the winter, a star, a dream, a thought, an action or a series of actions, or the ancient or prototype of an animal or a bird. Later, such a being, always humanized in form and mind, may, by his assumed absolute and mysterious control of the thing or phenomenon personified, become a hero or a god to men, through his relations with them—relations which are in fact the action and interaction of men with the things of their environments. A mythology is composed of a body of such myths and fragments thereof. But of course no myth that has come down to the present time is simple. Myths and parts of myths have necessarily been employed to define and explain other myths or other and new phenomena, and the way from the first to the last is long and often broken. Vestigial myths, myths whose meaning or symbolism has from any cause whatsoever become obscured or entirely lost, constitute a great part of folklore, and such myths are also called folktales.

A study of the lexic derivation of the terms "myth" and "mythology" will not lead to a satisfactory definition and interpretation of what is denoted by either term, for the genesis of the things so named was not understood when they received these appellations. In its broadest sense, *mythos* in Greek denoted whatever was uttered by the mouth of man—a saying, a legend, a story of something as understood by the narrator, a word. But in Attic Greek it denoted also any prehistoric story of the Greeks, and these were chiefly stories of gods and heroes, which were, though this fact was unknown to the Greeks themselves, phenomena of nature. And when the term received this specific meaning it fell into discredit, because the origin and true character of myths not being understood, these prehistoric stories by the advance in knowledge came into disrepute among the Greeks themselves, and after the rise of Christianity they were condemned as the wicked fables of a false religion. Hence, in popular usage, and quite apart from the study of mythology, the term "myth" denotes what is in fact nonexistent—a nothing with a name, a story without a basis of fact—"a nonentity of which an entity is affirmed, a nothing which is said to be something." Besides *mythos* in Greek, *logos*, signifying 'word,' was employed originally with approximately the same meaning in ordinary speech at the time of Homer, who sometimes used them interchangeably. But, strictly speaking, there was a difference from the beginning which, by the need for precision in diction, finally led to a wide divergence in the signification of the two terms. *Logos*, derived from *legein*, 'to gather,' was seldom used by Homer to denote 'a saying, a speaking, or a signification,' but to denote usually 'a gathering,' or, strictly, 'a telling, casting up or counting.' In time this term came to mean not only the inward constitution but the outward form of thought, and finally to denote exact thinking or reason—not only the reason in man, but the reason in the universe—the Divine Logos, the Volition of God, the Son of God, God Himself. It is so employed in the opening lines of the

first chapter of the Gospel of St John. Such is a brief outline of the uses of the two terms which in their primal signification formed the term "mythology," from which but little can be gathered as to what constitutes a myth.

Up to a certain point there is substantial agreement among students in the use of the term myth. But this means but little. To the question, What is the nature and origin of a myth? wholly different replies, perplexing in number, are given, and for this reason the study of mythology, of a definite body of myths, has not yet become a science. By careful study of adequate materials a clue to the meaning and significance of myths may be found in the apprehension—vague in the beginning, increasingly definite as the study progresses—that all these things, these tales, these gods, although so diverse, arise from one simple though common basis or motive.

Every body, element, or phenomenon of nature, whether subjective or objective, has its myth or story to account for its origin, history, and manner of action. Portions of these myths, especially those concerning the most striking objects of an environment, are woven together by some master mind into a cycle of myths, and a myth of the beginnings, a genesis, or creation, story is thus developed. The horns and the cloven feet of the deer, the stripes of the chipmunk's back, the tail of the beaver, the flat nose of the otter, the rattles of the snake, the tides of rivers, the earthquake, the meteor, the aurora borealis; in short, every phenomenon that fixed the attention required and received an explanation which, being conventional, satisfied the commonsense of the community, and which later, owing to its imputation of apparently impossible attributes to fictitious personages to account for the operations of nature, became, by the growing knowledge of man, a myth.

A myth is of interest from three viewpoints, namely, (1) as a literary product embodying a wondrous story of things and personages; (2) for the character of the matter it contains as expressive of human thought and the interpretation of human experience, and (3) for the purpose of comparison with the myths of alien or of cognate peoples and for the data it contains relating to the customs, arts, and archeology of the people among whom it exists.

With the available data, it is as yet impossible to define with satisfactory clearness all the objective realities of the personal agencies or men-beings of the American Indian myths. In Indian thought these personages are constantly associated in function, and sometimes they exercise derivative powers or are joined in mysterious kinship groups, always combining the symbolism of personified objective phenomena with imputed life, mind, and volition, and with the exercise of attributed *orenda*, or magic power, of diverse function and potency. Moreover, the size and the muscular power of the objective reality personified have little, if any, relation to the strength of the *orenda* exercised by the man-being.

To explain in part the multiform phenomena of different and successive environments, the philosophic ancestors of the Indians of to-day subconsciously imputed mind and immortal life to every object and phenomenon in nature, and to nearly every faculty and affection of the human mind and body. Concomitantly with this endowment of lifeless things with life and mind was the additional endowment with *orenda*, which differed in strength and function with the individual. These dogmas underlie the mythology and religion of all the Indians, as they supplied to the latter's inchoate reasoning satisfactory explanations of the phenomena of nature—life and death, dreams and disease, floral and faunal growth and reproduction, light and darkness, cold and heat, winter and summer, rain and snow, frost and ice, wind and storm. The term "animism" has been applied by some to this doctrine of the possession of immortal life and mind by lifeless and mindless things, but with an insufficient definition of the objective for which it stands. The uses and definitions of this term are now so numerous and contradictory that the critical student can not afford to employ it without an exact objective definition. Primarily, animism, or the imputation of life to lifeless things, was selected to express what was considered the sole essential characteristic basis of the complex institutions called mythology and religion. But if the ascription of life to lifeless things is animism, then it becomes of fundamental importance to know exactly what kind of life is thus ascribed. If there is one difference between things which should be carefully distinguished, it is that between the alleged ghosts of dead human beings and those other alleged spiritual beings which never have been real human beings—the animal and the primal spirits. Does animism denote the ascription of only one or of all these three classes of spirits? Definite explanation is here lacking. So, as a key to the satisfactory interpretation of what constitutes mythology and religion, animism as heretofore defined has failed to meet the criticism of such scholars as Spencer, Max Müller, and Brinton, and so has fallen into that long category of equivocal words of which

fetishism, shamanism, solarism, ancestor-worship, personification, and totemism are other members. Every one of these terms, as commonly employed, denotes some important phase or element in religion or mythology which, variously defined by different students, does not, however, form the characteristic basis of mythology and religion.

The great apostle of ancestor-worship, Lippert, makes animism a mere subdivision of the worship of ancestral spirits, or ghosts. But Gruppe, adding to the confusion of ideas, makes animism synonymous with fetishism, and describes a fetish as the tenement of a disembodied human spirit or ghost, and erroneously holds that fetishism is the result of a widely prevalent belief in the power of the human ghost to take possession of any object whatsoever, to leave its ordinary dwelling, the remains of the human body, to enter some other object, such as the sky, the sun, the moon, the earth, a star, or what not. Even the chief gods of Greece, Rome, and India are by some regarded as fetishes developed through the exaltation of ancestral ghosts to this state. Their cult is regarded as a development of fetishism, which is an outgrowth of animism, which is, in turn, a development of ancestor-worship. To add to this array of conflicting definitions, Max Müller declares that fetishism is really the "very last stage in the downward course of religion." Gruppe further holds that when a sky fetish or a star fetish becomes a totem, then the idea of "sons of heaven," or "children of the sun," is developed in the human mind, and so, according to this doctrine, every religion, ancient and modern, may be explained by animism, fetishism, and totemism. Moved by this array of conflicting definitions, Max Müller declares that, to secure clear thinking and sober reasoning, these three terms should be entirely discarded, or, if used, then let animism be defined as a belief in and worship of ancestral spirits, whence arises in the mind the simplest and most primitive ideas of immortality; let fetishism be defined as a worship of chance objects having miraculous powers; and, finally, let totemism be defined as the custom of choosing some emblem as the family or tribal mark to which worship is paid and which is regarded as the human or superhuman ancestor. Müller has failed to grasp the facts clearly, for no one of these excludes the others.

Stahl (1737), adopting and developing into modern scientific form the classical theory of the identity of life and soul, employed the term "animism" to designate this doctrine.

Tylor (1871), adopting the term "animism" from Stahl, defines it as "the belief in spiritual beings," and as "the deep-lying doctrine of spiritual beings, which embodies the very essence of spiritualistic as opposed to materialistic philosophy"; and, finally, he says, "animism is, in fact, the groundwork of the philosophy of religion, from that of savages up to that of civilized men." He further makes the belief in spiritual beings "the minimum definition of religion." Hence, with Tylor, animism is broadly synonymous with religion.

But, strict definition shows that a belief in spiritual beings, as such, did not, does not, and can not form the sole material out of which primitive thought has developed its gods and deities. To this extent, therefore, animism does not furnish the key to an accurate and valid explanation of mythology and religion.

Brinton (1896) denies that there is any special religious activity taking the form of what Tylor calls "animism," and declares that the belief that inanimate objects possess souls or spirits is common to all religions and many philosophies, and that it is not a trait characteristic of primitive faiths, but merely a secondary phenomenon of the religious sentiment. Further, he insists that "the acceptance of the doctrine of 'animism' as a sufficient explanation of early cults has led to the neglect, in English-speaking lands, of their profounder analysis."

So far as is definitely known, no support is found in the mythologies of North America for the doctrine of ancestor-worship. This doctrine seeks to show that savage men had evolved real gods from the shades of their own dead chiefs and great men. It is more than doubtful that such a thing has ever been done by man. Competent data and trained experience with the Indians of North America show that the dominant ideas of early savage thought precluded such a thing. One of the most fundamental and characteristic beliefs of savage thought is the utter helplessness of man unaided by the magic power of some favoring being against the bodies and elements of his environment. The deities, the masters and controllers—the gods of later times—differed greatly in strength of body and in the potency of the magic power exercised by them, in knowledge and in astuteness of mind; but each in his own sphere and jurisdiction was generally supreme and incomprehensible. Human shades, or ghosts, did not or could not attain to these godlike gifts. To change, transform, create by metamorphosis, or to govern, some body or element in nature, is at once the prerogative and the function of a master—a controller—humanly speaking, a god.

The attribution of power to do things magically, that is, to perform a function in a mysterious and incomprehensible manner, was the fundamental postulate of savage mind to account for the ability of the gods, the fictitious personages of its mythology, to perform the acts which are in fact the operations of the forces of nature. To define one such man-being or personage, the explanation, to be satisfactory, must be more than the mere statement of the imputation of life, mind, and the human form and attributes to an objective thing. There must also be stated the fact of the concomitant possession along with these of *orenda*, or magic power, differing from individual to individual in efficacy, function, and scope of action.

While linguistics may greatly aid in comprehending myths, it is nevertheless not always safe for determining the substance of the thought, the concept; and the student must eschew the habit of giving only an etymology rather than a definition of the things having the names of the mythic persons, which may be the subject of investigation. Etymology may aid, but without corroborative testimony it may mislead.

Many are the causes which bring about the decline and disintegration of a myth or a cycle of myths of a definite people. The migration or violent disruption of the people, the attrition or the superposition of diverse alien cultures, or the change or reformation of the religion of the people based on a recasting of opinions and like causes, all tend to the decline and dismemberment and the final loss of a myth or a mythology.

All tribes of common blood and speech are bound together by a common mythology and by a religion founded on the teachings of that mythology. These doctrines deal with a vast body of all kinds of knowledge, arts, institutions, and customs. It is the creed of such a people that all their knowledge and wisdom, all their rites and ceremonies, and all that they possess and all that they are socially and politically, have come to them through direct revelation from their gods, through the beneficence of the rulers of the bodies and elements of their environment.

The social and political bonds of every known tribe are founded essentially on real or fictitious blood kinship, and the religious bonds that hold a people to its gods are founded on faith in the truth of the teachings of their myths. No stronger bonds than these are known to savage men. The disruption of these, by whatever cause, results in the destruction of the people.

The constant struggle of man with his physical environment to secure welfare was a warfare against elements ever definitely and vividly personified and humanized by him, thus unconsciously making his surroundings quite unreal, though felt to be real; and his struggle with his environment was a ceaseless strife with animals and plants and trees in like manner ever mythically personified and humanized by him; and, finally, his tireless struggle with other men for supremacy and welfare was therefore typical, not only fundamentally and practically, but also mythically and ideally; and so this never-ceasing struggle was an abiding, all-pervading, all-transforming theme of his thoughts, and an ever-impending, ever-absorbing business of his life, suffered and impelled by his ceaseless yearning for welfare.

An environment would have been regarded by savage men very differently from what it would be by the cultured mind of to-day. To the former the bodies and elements composing it were regarded as beings, indeed as man-beings, and the operations of nature were ascribed to the action of the diverse magic powers, or *orendas*, exercised by these beings rather than to the forces of nature; so that the action and interaction of the bodies and elemental principles of nature were regarded as the result of the working of numberless beings through their *orendas*. Among most known tribes in North America the earth is regarded as a humanized being in person and form, every particle of whose body is living substance and potent with the quickening power of life, which is bestowed on all who feed upon her. They that feed upon her are the plants and the trees, who are indeed beings living and having a being because they receive life substance from the earth, hence they are like the primal beings endowed with mind and volition, to whom prayer (q. v.) may be offered, since they rule and dispose in their several jurisdictions unless they are overcome by some more powerful *orenda*. Now, a prayer is psychologically the expression of the fact that the petitioner in need is unable to secure what is required for the welfare, or in distress to prevent what will result in the ill-fare, of himself or his kind. The substance of the prayer merely tells in what direction or in what respect this inability exists. In turn, the animals and men live on the products of the trees and plants, by which means they renew life and gain the quickening power of life, indirectly from the earth-mother, and thus by a metaphor they are said to have come up out of the earth. As the giver of life, the earth is regarded affectionately and is called Mother, but as the taker of life and the devourer of their dead bodies, she is regarded as wicked and a cannibal.

In the science of opinions mythology is found to be a fruitful field in which to gather data regarding the origin and growth of human concepts relating to man and the world around him. A study of the birth and evolution of the concepts of the human mind indicates clearly that the beginnings of conventional forms and ideas and their variations along the lines of their development are almost never quite so simple, or rather quite so direct, as they may seem—are seldom, even in the beginning, the direct product of the environmental resource and exigency acting together so immediately and so exclusively of mental agency as students are apt to assume. As a rule they are rather the product of these things—these factors and conditions of environment acting very indirectly and sometimes very subtly and complexly—through the condition of mind wrought by long-continued life and experience therein, or, again, acting through the state of mind borne over from one environment to another. It is the part of wisdom to be more cautious in deriving ideas and concepts, arts, or even technic forms of a people too instantly, too directly, from the environing natural objects or elements they may simulate or resemble. The motive, if not for the choice, at least for the persistency, of a given mode of a concept in relation to any objective factor is always a psychic reason, not a mere first-hand influence of environment or of accident in the popular sense of this term. This disposition of the "mere accident" or "chance" hypothesis of origins dispels many perplexities in the formation of exact judgment concerning comparative data, in the identifications of cognate forms and concepts among widely separated peoples; for instance, in the drawing of sound inferences particularly regarding their common or generic, specific or exceptional, origin and growth, as shown by the data in question.

As it is evident that independent processes and diverse factors combined can not be alike in every particular in widely separated parts of the world, there is found a means for determining, through minute differences in similarity, rather than through general similarities alone, howsoever striking they may appear, whether such forms are related, whether or not they have a common genesis whence they have inherited aught in common. Hence caution makes it incumbent on students to beware of the alluring fallacy lurking in the frequently repeated epigram that "human nature is everywhere the same." The nature of men differs widely from differences of origin, from differences of history, from differences of education, and from differences of environment. Hence, to produce the same human nature everywhere, these factors must everywhere be the same. The environments of no two peoples are ever precisely the same, and so the two differ in their character, in their activities, and in their beliefs.

To the primitive inchoate thought of the North American Indian all the bodies and elements of his subjective and objective environment were humanized beings—man-beings, or beings that were persons, that were man in form and attributes and endowed with immortal life (not souls in the modern acceptation of this term), with omniscience, and with potent magic power in their several jurisdictions. These beings were formed in the image of man, because man was the highest type of being known to himself and because of his subjective method of thought, which imputed to outside things, objective realities, his own form and attributes. He could conceive of nature in no other way. They sometimes, however, had the power of instant change or transmigration into any desired object through the exercise of peculiar magic power.

The world of the savage was indeed of small extent, being confined by his boundless ignorance to the countries bordering on his own, a little, if any, beyond his horizon. Beyond this, he knew nothing of the world, nothing of its extent or structure. This fact is important and easily verified, and this knowledge aids in fully appreciating the teachings of the philosophy of savage men. Around and through this limited region traveled the sun, the moon, the stars, the winds, the meteors and the fire dragons of the night, and the fitful auroral cherubim of the north. All these were to him man-beings. All trees and plants—the sturdy oak, the tall pine, and the wild parsnip—were such beings rooted to the earth by the mighty spell of some potent wizard, and so, unlike the deer, they do not ordinarily travel from place to place. In like manner, hills and mountains and the waters of the earth may sometimes be thus spellbound by the potency of some enchantment. Earthquakes are sometimes caused by mountains which, held in pitiless thralldom by the *orenda* of some mighty sorcerer, struggle in agony to be freed. And even the least of these are reputed to be potent in the exercise of magic power. But rivers run and rills and brooks leap and bound over the land, yet even these in the ripeness of time may be gripped to silence by the mighty magic power of the god of winter.

Among all peoples in all times and in all planes of culture there were persons whose opinions were orthodox, and there were also persons whose opinions were heterodox, and were therefore a constant protest against the common opinions, the commonsense of the community; these were the agnostics of the ages, the prophets of change and reformation.

Every ethnic body of myths of the North American Indians forms a circumstantial narration of the origin of the world of the myth-makers and of all things and creatures therein. From these narratives it is learned that a world, earlier than the present, situated usually above the visible sky, existed from the beginning of time, in which dwelt the first or prototypal personages who, having the form and the attributes of man, are herein called man-beings. Each of these man-beings possessed a magic power peculiar to himself or herself, by which he or she was later enabled to perform his or her functions after the metamorphosis of all things. The life and manner of living of the Indians to-day is patterned after that of these man-beings in their first estate. They were the prototypes of the things which are now on this earth.

This elder world is introduced in a state of peace and harmony. In the ripeness of time, unrest and discord arose among these first beings, because the minds of all, except a very small number, becoming abnormal, were changed, and the former state of tranquillity was soon succeeded by a complete metamorphosis of all things and beings, or was followed by commotion, collision, and strife. The transformed things, the prototypes, were banished from the sky-land to this world, whereupon it acquired its present appearance and became peopled by all that is upon it—man, animals, trees, and plants, who formerly were man-beings. In some cosmologies man is brought upon the scene later and in a peculiar manner. Each man-being became transformed into what his or her attributes required, what his primal and unchangeable nature demanded, and then he or she became in body what he had been, in a disguised body, before the transformation. But those man-beings whose minds did not change by becoming abnormal, remained there in the skyland—separate, peculiar, and immortal. Indeed they are but shadowy figures passing into the shoreless sea of oblivion.

Among the tribes of North American Indians there is a striking similarity in their cycles of genesis myths, in that they treat of several regions or worlds. Sometimes around and above the mid-world, the habitat of the myth, are placed a group of worlds—one at the east, one at the south, one at the west, one at the north, one above, and one below—which, with the midworld, number seven in all. Even each of the principal colors is assigned to its appropriate world (see *Color symbolism*). Hence, to the primitive mind, the cosmos (if the term be allowed here) was a universe of man-beings whose activities constituted the operations of nature. To it nothing was what it is to scientific thought. Indeed, it was a world wholly artificial and fanciful. It was the product of the fancy of savage and inchoate thinking, of the commonsense of savage thought.

So far as is definitely known, the various systems of mythology in North America differ much in detail one from another, superficially giving them the aspect of fundamental difference of origin and growth; but a careful study of them discloses the fact that they accord with all great bodies of mythology in a principle which underlies all, namely, the principle of change, transmigration, or metamorphosis of things, through the exercise of *orenda*, or magic power, from one state, condition, or form, to another. By this means things have become what they now are. Strictly, then, creation of something from nothing has no place in them. In these mythologies, purporting to be philosophies, of course, no knowledge of the real changes which have affected the environing world is to be sought; but it is equally true that in them are embedded, like rare fossils and precious gems, many most important facts regarding the history of the human mind.

For a definite people in a definite plane of culture, the myths and the concomitant beliefs resting on them, of their neighbors, are not usually true, since the personages and the events narrated in them have an aspect and an expression quite different from their own, although they may in the last analysis express fundamentally identical things—may in fact spring from identical motives.

Among the Iroquois and the eastern Algonquian tribes, the Thunder people, human in form and mind and usually four in number, are most important and staunch friends of man. But in the Lake region, the N. W. coast to Alaska, and in the northern drainage of the Mississippi and Missouri valleys, this conception is replaced by that of the Thunderbird.

Among the Algonquian and the Iroquoian tribes the myths regarding the so-called fire-dragon are at once striking and important. Now, the fire-dragon is in fact the personification of the meteor. Flying through the air among the stars, the larger meteors appear against some midnight sky like fiery reptiles sheathed in lambent flames. It is believed of them that they fly from one lake or deep river to another, in the bottom of which they are bound by enchantment to dwell, for should they be permitted to remain on the land they would set the world on fire. The Iroquois applied their name for the fire-dragon, 'light-thrower,' to the lion when first seen, thus indicating their conception of the fierceness of the fire-dragon. The Ottawa and Chippewa *missibizi*, or *missibizhu*, literally 'great lynx,' is their name for this mythic being. The horned serpent does not belong here, but the misnamed tigers of the Peoria and other Algonquian tribes do. Among the Iroquois it was the deeds of the fire-dragon that hastened the occasion for the metamorphosis of the primal beings.

As early as 1868 Brinton called attention to the curious circumstance that in the mythology of those Eskimo who had had no contact with European travelers, there were no changes or transformations of the world affecting the aspect and character of the earth. In this statement he is followed by Boas (1904), who also claims that the animal myth proper did not belong originally to Eskimo mythology, although there are now in this mythology some animal myths and weird tales and accounts regarding monsters and vampire ghosts and the thaumaturgic deeds of shamans and wizards. This is in strong contrast with the content of the mythologies of the Indian tribes that have been studied.

In its general aspects the mythology of the North American Indians has been instructively and profitably discussed by several American anthropologists, who have greatly advanced the study and knowledge of the subject. Among these are Powell, Brinton, Boas, Curtin, Fletcher, Matthews, Cushing, Fewkes, and Dixon.

Powell treated the subject from the philosophic and evolutional point of view, and sought to establish successive stages in the development of the mythologic thought or concept, making them imputation, personification, and reification; and the product he divided into four stages from the character of the dominant gods in each, namely, (1) *hecastotheism*, wherein everything has life, personality, volition, and design, and the wondrous attributes of man; (2) *zoötheism*, wherein life is not attributed indiscriminately to lifeless things, the attributes of man are imputed to the animals and no line of demarcation is drawn between man and beast, and all facts and phenomena of nature are explained in the mythic history of these zoömorphic gods; (3) *physitheism*, wherein a wide difference is recognized between man and the animals, the powers and phenomena of nature are personified, and the gods are anthropomorphic; and (4) *psychotheism*, wherein mental attributes and moral and social characteristics with which are associated the powers of nature are personified and deified, and there arise gods of war, of love, of revelry, plenty, and fortune. This last stage, by processes of mental integration, passes into monotheism on the one hand and into pantheism on the other. It is found that these four stages are not thus successive, but that they may and do overlap, and that it is best perhaps to call them phases rather than stages of growth, in that they may exist side by side.

Brinton learnedly calls attention to the distinctively native American character of the large body of myths and tales rehearsed among the American aborigines. His studies include also much etymological analysis of mythic and legendary names, which is unfortunately largely inaccurate, analysis being apparently made to accord with a preconceived idea of what it should disclose. This vitiates a large part of his otherwise excellent identifications of the objective realities of the agents found in the mythology. He also treats in his instructive style the various cults of the demiurge, or the culture-hero or hero-god; but it must be borne in mind that here the so-called hero-god is not solely or even chiefly such in character. In discussing the hero-myths of the N. W. Pacific coast tribes, Boas points out the fact that the culture-hero of that area was not always prompted by altruistic motives in "giving the world its present shape and man his arts." The hero is credited with failures as well as with successes, and in character is an "egotist pure and simple." On the other hand, Boas finds in the life and character of the Algonquian Nanabozho (q. v.) altruistic motives dominant. This tendency to displace the egotistic motives of the primitive transformer with preeminently altruistic ones is strongly marked in the character of the Iroquoian Tharonhiawagon (q. v.), a parallel if not a cognate conception with that of the Alonquian Nanabozho. As showing a transitional stage on the way to altruism, Boas states that the transformer among the Kwakiutl brings about the changes for the benefit of a friend and not for himself. While there are some Algonquian myths in which Nanabozho appears as a trickster and teller of falsehoods, among the Iroquois the trickster and buffoon has been developed alongside that of the demiurge, and is sometimes reputed to be the brother of Death. The mink,

the wolverene, tne bluejay, the raven and the coyote are represented as tricksters in the myths of many of the tribes of the Pacific slope and the N. W. coast.

Matthews, in "The Night Chant, a Ceremony of the Navaho" (Mem. Am. Mus. Nat. Hist., v, 1902), introduces an interesting account of the striking symbolism and mythic philosophy of this remarkable people.

Miss Fletcher, in her many excellent and instructive writings on the customs and symbolism of the Indians whom she has studied, has placed the study of mythology on a scientific basis. In her "Hako: A Pawnee Ceremony" (22d Rep. B. A. E., 1903), Miss Fletcher treats in masterful manner this interesting series of rites, which, with marked sympathy and the skill of ripe experience, she analyzes and interprets in such wise that the delicately veiled symbolism and mythic conceptions are clearly brought to view.

In the Zuñi record of the genesis of the worlds, as recorded by Cushing (13th Rep. B. A. E., 1896), Awonawilona, the Maker and Container of all, alone and unperplexed awaiting fate, existed before the beginning of time in the darkness which knew no beginning. Then he conceived within himself, and projecting his thinking into the void of night, around him evolved fogs of increase—mists potent with growth. Then, in like manner, the Allcontainer took upon himself the form and person of the Sun, the Father of men, who thus came to be, and by whose light and brightening the cloud mists became thickened into water, and thus was made the world-holding sea. Then from "his substance of flesh outdrawn from the surface of his person," he made the seed of two worlds, fecundating therewith the sea. By the heat of his rays there was formed thereon green scums, which increasing apace became "The Four-fold Containing Mother-earth" and the "All-covering Father-sky." Then from the consorting together of these twain on the great world-waters, terrestrial life was generated, and therefrom sprang all beings of earth—men and the creatures, from the "Four-fold womb of the World." Then the Earth-mother repulsed the Skyfather, and growing heavy sank into the embrace of the waters of the sea, and thus she separated from the Sky-father, leaving him in the embrace of the waters above. Moreover, the Earth-mother and the Sky-father, like all surpassing beings, were changeable, metamorphic, even like smoke in the wind, were "transmutable at thought, manifesting themselves in any form at will, as dancers may by mask-making." Then from the nethermost of the four caves (wombs) of the world, the seed of men and the creatures took form and grew; even as within eggs in warm places worms quickly form and appear, and, growing, soon burst their shells and emerge, as may happen, birds, tadpoles, or serpents; so men and all creatures grew manifoldly and multiplied in many kinds. Thus did the lowermost world cave become over-filled with living things, full of unfinished creatures, crawling like reptiles one over another in black darkness, thickly crowd-ing together and treading one on another, one spitting on another and doing other in-decency, in such manner that the murmur-ings and the lamentations became loud, and many amidst the growing confusion sought to escape, growing wiser and more manlike. Then Poshaiyankya, the fore-most and wisest of men, arising from the nethermost sea, came among men and the living things, and, pitying them, obtained egress from that first world cave through such a dark and narrow path that some seeing somewhat, crowding after, could not follow him, so eager mightily did they strive one with another. Alone then did Poshaiyankya come from one cave to another into this world, then, island-like, lying amidst the world waters, vast, wet, and unstable. He sought and found the Sun-father and besought him to deliver the men and the creatures from that neth-ermost world.

Speaking of the Maidu myths, Dixon (Bull. Am. Mus. Nat. Hist., XVII, pt. 3, 1905) says that from present knowledge of them, the facts of most interest are the large measure of system and sequence found in the mythology of the stock; the prominence given to the "creation episode" and to the events connected with it; the strongly contrasted charac-ters of the "Creator" and the Coyote; the apparent absence of a myth of migra-tion, and the diversity shown within the stock; that "beginning with the cre-ation, a rather systematic chain of events leads up to the appearance of the ances-tors of the present Indians, with whose coming the mythic cycle came to a close. This mythic era seems to fall into a number of periods, with each of which a group or set of myths has to deal." During the first era occurs the coming of Kōdōyanpĕ (Earth-namer) and Coyote, the "discovery" of this world by them,

and the preparation of it for the "first people"; next, the "creation" of the first people and the making and plant-ing of the germs of human beings, the Indians (in the form of small wooden figures), who were to follow; third, the long period in which the first people were engaged in violence and conflict, and were finally transformed into the various ani-mals in the present world. During this period Earth - maker (or Earth-namer) sought to destroy Coyote, whose evil ways and desires antagonized his own. In this struggle Earth-namer was assisted by the Conqueror, who destroyed many monsters and evil beings who later would have endangered the life of men who should come on the scene. In the final period comes the last struggle, wherein Earth-maker strives in vain with Coyote, his defeat and flight to the East synchronously with the coming of the human race, the Indians, who sprang up from the places where the original pairs had long before been buried as small wooden figures. Dixon further says: "Nor is the creation here merely an epi-sode—a re-creation after a deluge brought on by one cause or another—as it is in some mythologies. Here the creation is a real beginning; beyond it, behind it, there is nothing. In the beginning was only the great sea, calm and unlimited, to which, down from the clear sky, the Creator came, or on which he and Coyote were floating in a canoe. Of the origin or previous place of abode of either Crea-tor or Coyote, the Maidu knew nothing." But Dixon adds that the Achomawi, northern neighbors of the Maidu, push this history much farther back, saying that at first there were but the shoreless sea and the clear sky; that a tiny cloud appeared in the sky, which, gradually increasing in size, finally attained large proportions, then condensed until it be-came the Silver-Gray Fox, the Creator; that immediately there arose a fog which in turn condensed until it became Coyote. See *Calumet, Fetish, Orenda, Religion.*

The bibliography of the mythology of the Indians N. of Mexico is very exten-sive. For an excellent summary of the literature of the subject, consult Cham-berlain in Jour. Am. Folk-lore, XVIII, 111, 1905, and the continuous Record of Ameri-can Folk-lore published in the same magazine.　　　　　　　　(J. N. B. H.)

O

www.ingramcontent.com/pod-product-compliance
Lightning Source LLC
Chambersburg PA
CBHW061758260326
41914CB00006B/1160